Business Law with UCC Applications

Paul A. Sukys
PROFESSOR OF LAW AND APPLIED PHILOSOPHY
NORTH CENTRAL STATE COLLEGE | MANSFIELD, OHIO

Gordon W. Brown
PROFESSOR EMERITUS
NORTH SHORE COMMUNITY COLLEGE | DANVERS, MASSACHUSETTS

14e

Mc
Graw
Hill
Education

BUSINESS LAW WITH UCC APPLICATIONS, FOURTEENTH EDITION

Published by McGraw-Hill Education, 2 Penn Plaza, New York, NY 10121. Copyright © 2017 by McGraw-Hill Education. All rights reserved. Printed in the United States of America. Previous editions © 2013, 2009, and 2006. No part of this publication may be reproduced or distributed in any form or by any means, or stored in a database or retrieval system, without the prior written consent of McGraw-Hill Education, including, but not limited to, in any network or other electronic storage or transmission, or broadcast for distance learning.

Some ancillaries, including electronic and print components, may not be available to customers outside the United States.

This book is printed on acid-free paper.

1 2 3 4 5 6 7 8 9 0 DOW/DOW 1 0 9 8 7 6

ISBN   978-0-07-773373-5
MHID   0-07-773373-8

Senior Vice President, Products & Markets: *Kurt L. Strand*
Vice President, General Manager, Products & Markets: *Marty Lange*
Vice President, Content Design & Delivery: *Kimberly Meriwether David*
Managing Director: *Tim Vertovec*
Senior Brand Manager: *Kathleen Klehr*
Director, Product Development: *Rose Koos*
Product Developer: *Jaroslaw Szymanski*
Director, Digital Content: *Patricia Plumb*
Director, Content Design & Delivery: *Linda Avenarius*
Program Manager: *Faye M. Herrig*
Content Project Managers: *Jane Mohr, Angela Norris, and Karen Jozefowicz*
Buyer: *Susan K. Culbertson*
Design: *Studio Montage, St. Louis, MO.*
Content Licensing Specialist: *Lorraine Buczek*
Cover Image: *Getty Images*
Compositor: *Aptara®, Inc.*
Printer: *R. R. Donnelley*

All credits appearing on page or at the end of the book are considered to be an extension of the copyright page.

Library of Congress Cataloging-in-Publication Data

Sukys, Paul, author.
   Business law / Paul A. Sukys, professor of law and applied philosophy, North Central State College, Mansfield, Ohio; Gordon W. Brown, professor emeritus, North Shore Community College, Danvers, Massachusetts.—Fourteenth edition.
      pages cm
   ISBN 978-0-07-773373-5 (alk. paper)—ISBN 0-07-773373-8 (alk. paper)
   1. Commercial law—United States. I. Brown, Gordon W., 1928- author. II. Title.
KF889.85.B76 2017
346.7307—dc23
                                                          2015030915

The Internet addresses listed in the text were accurate at the time of publication. The inclusion of a website does not indicate an endorsement by the authors or McGraw-Hill Education, and McGraw-Hill Education does not guarantee the accuracy of the information presented at these sites.

This book is dedicated with much love and many thanks to my wife, Susan. As I've learned during our life together—as a team—the possibilities are limitless.

Also to Jennifer, Ashley, and Megan, all three of whom have grown up to be excellent educators in their own right. They have made me very proud.

Paul Sukys

About the Authors

Paul A. Sukys is a professor of law and applied philosophy at North Central State College in Mansfield, Ohio. He is coauthor of *Business and Personal Law* and *Civil Litigation,* a textbook for paralegals. He is also the author of *Lifting the Scientific Veil: Science Appreciation for the Nonscientist,* which explores the relationships among science and other disciplines, focusing on the relationships that exist among science, philosophy, and the law. He has a PhD in applied philosophy and art history from The Union Institute and University in Cincinnati. Dr. Sukys received his law degree from Cleveland State University. He is a member of the Ohio Bar.

Gordon W. Brown, Professor Emeritus, North Shore Community College, Danvers, Massachusetts, where he has taught for 30 years, is the author of *Legal Terminology* and *Administration of Wills, Trusts, and Estates* and the coauthor, with Dr. Paul A. Sukys, of *Understanding Business and Personal Law.* Mr. Brown received his law degree from Suffolk University and practiced law in Beverly, Massachusetts, while teaching full time at North Shore Community College. He is a member of the Massachusetts and federal Bars.

Preface

The fourteenth edition of *Business Law with UCC Applications* now includes SmartBook. This first and only adaptive reading experience is designed to transform the way students read. Proven to help students improve grades and study more efficiently, SmartBook contains the same content within the print book, but actively tailors that content to the needs of the individual.

This edition updates many significant areas of the law. As in previous editions, a great deal of care has been taken to present legal concepts in the most coherent and accessible way and to provide up-to-date coverage of both business and general law topics that are essential to today's students. All of the chapters for this edition have been updated, and we have continued to enhance our coverage of these important topics.

Some topics that have been added to the new edition include:

- The evolving relationship between the Religious Freedom Restoration Act and contract law.
- New developments related to the Collective Science Court Proposal.
- Changes in the Dodd–Frank Wall Street Reform and Consumer Protection Act.
- The fate of the Defense of Marriage Act.
- Developments related to Stand-Your-Ground Laws in various states.
- The use of subterranean rights as they relate to fracking contracts.
- The implementation of a Revised Children's Online Privacy Protection Rule.

More details follow in the "Important Changes in the Fourteenth Edition of *Business Law with UCC Applications*" section.

The popular format of previous editions has been preserved, with learning objectives identified in the margin where that material appears in the text. Each chapter begins with an outline followed by the Opening Case, with numbered questions and Chapter Objectives. Titles have been given to every example. Major headings and chapter summaries continue to be numbered, following the chapter outline. The popular case illustrations, presenting either hypothetical or actual situations based on well-founded court decisions, have been retained and updated. Our Quick Quiz feature appears in each chapter and allows students to test their knowledge of the chapter topics while they actively study the text. A new Classic Cases feature has been included in many chapters in this edition, giving both the instructor and the students an opportunity to explore topics related to the content of the chapter in a provocative and stimulating way.

We also have retained case studies pertaining to each of the nine parts of the book, which summarize an actual litigated case, present a lengthy extract from the justice's or the judge's decision, and provide follow-up questions that are pertinent to the cases and are appropriate as a review of the legal concepts involved. The new Case Study for Part 8 is *Obergefell, et al., v. Hodges,* the recent case in which the U.S. Supreme Court declared state statutes and state constitutional provisions outlawing same sex marriages as unconstitutional. Activities at the end of each chapter, including Key Terms, Questions for Review and Discussion, and Cases for Analysis, help students self-check their understanding of the terms and concepts presented in the chapter. We also have continued to include the Question of Ethics element at various strategic points throughout the text. The U.S. Constitution appears in Appendix A. Included in Appendix B are four articles of the Uniform Commercial Code. Marginal references within the chapters tie these specific documents to the content. The fourteenth edition of *Business Law* thus offers a comprehensive package of materials to meet both instructors' and students' needs.

Important Changes in the Fourteenth Edition of *Business Law with UCC Applications*

Chapter 1 Ethics, Social Responsibility, and the Law

- Chapter 1 begins with a new Opening Case, *Verizon v. Federal Communications Commission*, which focuses on the *Open Internet Order (OIO)*, an order that changes how the FCC will police the activities of internet service providers (ISPs) such as Verizon, Time-Warner, Comcast, and so on. The order is ostensibly designed to protect "net neutrality" by outlawing discrimination.

- A new look at market value ethics and neoliberalism, including an innovative take on both ideological positions as explained by Michael Sandel, in *What Money Can't Buy: The Moral Limits of the Market*.

- A creative look at the relationships among John Locke, Thomas Hobbes, and the core rights outlined in the Declaration of Independence.

- A novel examination of political ethics as explained by reference to a political/ governmental ethical dyad, that includes the ethic of benevolence and the ethic of responsibility.

- A note on the ethical and legal ramifications of the drug use epidemic in the world of professional sports.

- A note on Ohio's attempt to return a level of dignity to politics by making the telling of lies in political campaigns a crime.

Chapter 2 Sources of the Law

- Chapter 2 begins with a new Opening Case, entitled *Roman Catholic Archdiocese of Washington D.C., et al. v. Kathleen Sebelius, Secretary of the United States Department of Health and Human Services, et al.*, which focuses on the mandate (commandment) issued by the Department of Health and Human Services (HHS) that requires employers to provide insurance that covers a variety of contraceptive services.

- A new take on the development of the Constitution and the Bill of Rights, (Re-Engineering the Constitution) that focuses the Constitution's general structural orientation toward insulating the leadership of the new republic from the influence of the people.

- A new Classic Cases Feature that focuses on the writing of James Madison's *Memorial and Remonstrance* in reaction to Patrick Henry's Tax Assessment Bill.

- A new look at the law (or, perhaps, more accurately the legal ecosystem) as a complex adaptive system (CAS), specifically focusing on the law as a complex adaptive system and its effects on the Affordable Care Act and the Bill of Rights.

Chapter 3 The Judicial Process and Cyber-procedure

- Chapter 3 begins with two new Opening Cases, entitled *CLS Bank International v. Alice Corporation Pty. Ltd.* and *State Street Bank v. Signature Financial Group*, in which the court reveals the complexity of patent law as interpreted by the Court of Appeals for the Federal Circuit.

- A discussion about whether the Federal Circuit's decisions have lately become too narrow and too formalistic.
- A renewed discussion of the Classic Case of *Diamond v. Chakrabarty,* the landmark case in which the United States Supreme Court decided that it was possible to patent a life-form.
- A discussion of cyber-discovery and the newly established Discovery Protocols Pilot Project.

Chapter 4 Alternative Dispute Resolution

- Chapter 4 begins with a new Opening Case, entitled, *Mt. Holyoke Homes, LP, et al. v. Jeffer Mangels Butler and Mitchell,* which discusses some of the problems with ADR, in general, and arbitration, in particular.
- A new Question of Ethics box feature that discusses the ethical pitfalls of unconscionable arbitration clauses as shown in the case of *Chavarria v. Ralphs Grocery Company.*
- An update on the collective science court (CSC) that would act as a forum for disputes involving scientific and technological controversies.
- A renewed discussion of the Classic Case of *Daubert v. Merrell Dow Pharmaceuticals, Inc.,* the landmark case in which the United States Supreme Court established a five-stage test for determining the scientific accuracy of expert testimony.
- A look at the Advanced Science and Technology Adjudication Resources (ASTAR) in Washington D.C. which was established by Congress as a scientific and technological educational resource center for judges.

Chapter 5 Criminal Law and Cybercrimes

- Chapter 5 begins with a new Opening Case, a Supreme Court case, entitled *Woodward v. Alabama,* in which the death penalty is discussed at length.
- A new look at *Gregg v. Georgia* and *Furman v. Georgia,* two cases that established the parameters for the death penalty.
- A renewed discussion of the Classic Case of *Wickard v. Filburn,* in which the Supreme Court extended the power of Congress under the Commerce Clause.
- A new Question of Ethics box feature that discusses the ethical pitfalls of the Paramilitary nature of the modern urban police department.
- A new examination of *posse comitatus* and insurrection.
- An update on the passage of multiple state Stand-Your-Ground Laws.

Chapter 6 Tort Law and Cybertorts

- Chapter 6 begins with an examination of the now famous (infamous?) McDonald's coffee case, that is, the case of *Stella Liebeck v. McDonald's Restaurants, P.T.S., Inc. and McDonald's International, Inc.* The Opening Case features and corrects the many misconceptions surrounding this case.
- A new examination of the concept of the temporary public figure in defamation cases as seen in the case of *Duckett v. the City and County of San Francisco, et al.*
- A renewed discussion of the Classic Case of *Overseas Tankship (UK) Ltd. v. Morts Dock and Engineering Co. Ltd.,* one of several landmark cases involving proximate cause in negligence.

- An updated examination of the "bring your own device" or BYOD tactic as contrasted with its sister tactic of "company-owned, personally enabled devices" or COPEs.

Chapter 7 The Essentials of Contract Law

- Chapter 7 begins with a new Opening Case, entitled, *Mt. Holyoke Homes, LP, et al. v. Jeffer Mangels Butler and Mitchell,* which discusses some essential elements of a written contract.
- A renewed discussion of the historical and cultural development of the law merchant.
- A renewed discussion of the characteristics the law merchant.
- A new discussion of the statute of frauds in the Classic Case of *Tubelite Co., Inc. v. Original Sign Studio.*

Chapter 8 Offer, Acceptance, and Mutual Assent

- Chapter 8 begins with a new Opening Case, entitled, *Sharp v. Andisman,* which discusses the nature of acceptance.
- A new discussion of the Classic Case of *Lefkowitz v. Great Minneapolis Surplus Store,* which discusses the nature of contractual offers and invitations to trade.

Chapter 9 Consideration and Cyber-payments

- Chapter 9 begins with a new Opening Case, entitled, *Lightbody v. Rust,* which explores what happens when the amount of consideration is not known at the time that a contract is made.
- A renewed discussion of the Classic Case of *Hamer v. Sidway,* which explores the true nature of detriment in consideration.
- A new discussion of the EU Data Protection Directive, the EU E-Privacy Directive, and the Commerce Department's Safe Harbor Principles.

Chapter 10 Capacity and Legality: The Final Elements

- Chapter 10 begins with a new Opening Case, entitled *Sidco Paper Company v. Aaron,* which looks at the nature of restrictive employment agreements.
- A new discussion of the Classic Case of *R.R. v. M.H. and Another* that discusses surrogate parenting contracts.

Chapter 11 Written Contracts and Cyber-Commerce

- Chapter 11 begins with the new Opening Case of *Perez Bar & Grill v. Schneider* that looks at what happens when a party to a lease contract fails to "get it in writing."
- A new discussion of the elements that must be included in a contract for the sale or lease of residential real estate.

- A new discussion of the elements that must be included in a real property construction project contract.
- A new discussion of the meaning of the term "workmanlike conduct" as it appears in real property contracts.
- A new discussion of the Classic Case of *Holland Furnace Co. v. Trumbull Sav. & Loan Co.*, that looks at the question of fixtures in real property contracts.

Chapter 12 Third Parties, Discharge, and Remedies

- Chapter 12 starts with a new Opening Case, *Fed. Home Loan Mtge. Corp. v. Schwartzwald,* which looks at some of the confusion that results from the multiple assignment of real property contracts.
- A new discussion of the Classic Case of *State Farm Mutual Automobile Ins. Co. v. Campbell,* that looks at the question of damages as a remedy in a breach of contract case.

Chapter 13 Sales Contracts: Formation, Title, and Risk of Loss

- Chapter 13 starts with the new Opening Case of *Conopco, Inc. v. McCreadie and Ernst & Young*, that looks at the differences between service contracts and sale of goods contracts.
- A new discussion of the mixed, blended, or hybrid contract.
- A new discussion of the Classic Case of *XCEL Mold & Machine v. DeVault Indus.* that examines the straightforward usefulness and applicability of the Uniform Commercial Code.

Chapter 14 Sales Contracts Rights, Duties, Breach, and Warranties

- Chapter 14 starts with a new Opening Case, entitled *Christine Seney v. Rent-A-Center, Inc.,* which looks at the differences between lease contracts and sale of goods contracts.
- A new discussion of the Classic Case of *Ninth Street East, Ltd. v. Harrison,* that examines what happens when a shipment of goods never arrives at its destination.
- A new discussion of the commercial docket pilot project in the Ohio courts that provides a legal forum limited to commercial lawsuits that are handled by judges and mediators who receive special education sessions devoted exclusively to commercial law.
- A new Question of Ethics box feature that discusses the ethical ramifications of the proposed science court as compared and contrasted to the commercial docket pilot project.

Chapter 15 Product Liability and Consumer Protection

- Chapter 15 starts with a new Opening Case, *Federal Trade Commission v. Kristy Ross and Innovating Marketing, Inc.,* which examines the FTC standard for determining whether a defendant has committed consumer fraud.

- A new discussion of the Classic Case of *Huff v. White Motor Co.* that examines the difference between dangerous and unsafe products.
- A new Question of Ethics box feature that discusses the ethical ramifications of selling both unsafe and dangerous products.
- A new discussion of the Revised Children's Online Privacy Protection Rule.
- A new discussion of the "Reclaim Your Name Program."

Chapter 16 The Nature of Negotiable Instruments

- Chapter 16 starts with a new Opening Case, *Trump Plaza, v. Haas and Meridian Bank,* which looks at the differences between personal checks and money orders.
- A new discussion of the Classic Case of *Getty Petroleum Corp. v. American Express Travel Related Services, Co., Inc.* that explores the nature of the relationships between a merchant and a credit card company

Chapter 17 Holders in Due Course, Defenses, and Liabilities

- Chapter 17 starts with a new Opening Case, *Any Kinds Checks Cashed, Inc. v. Talcott, et al.,* which takes a look at the true nature of a holder in due course.
- A new discussion of the Classic Case of *Maine Family Federal Credit Union v. Sun Life Assurance Company of Canada* that explains how in . . . cases involving holders in due course, the "pure heart, empty head" standard of "honesty in fact" has been supplemented by the "reasonable commercial standards (and) fair dealing" standard.

Chapter 18 Bank–Depositor Relationships and Cyber-Banking

- Chapter 18 starts with a new Opening Case, *Dorothy Woods v. MONY Legacy Life Insurance Company*, which examines the UCC's regulations on banks, forgeries, and the depositors' duties.
- A new discussion of the Classic Case of *Matin v. Chase Manhattan Bank*, 10 A.S. 3d 447 that studies the clever ways that banks attempt to dodge their duties to their customers.

Chapter 19 Insurance

- Chapter 19 begins with a new Opening Case, *Granger, et al. v. Auto Owners, Insurance,* which, oddly for a chapter on insurance, examines a case based on racial discrimination.
- A new discussion on the double-sided mirror of risk assessment and peril management.
- A new update on the Affordable Care Act.
- A new discussion of umbrella policies.
- A new discussion of the Classic Case of *Aviation Charters Inc. v. Avemco Insurance Company* that emphasizes the importance of the language that is used in a contract, but especially insurance contracts.

Chapter 20 Mortgages, Security Interests, and the 21st-Century Financial Crisis

- Chapter 20 begins with a new Opening Case, *National City Bank v. Gumm, et al.*, which examines the very tricky question of who has preference when a mortgagee defaults, the party that executes first or the one that files first?

- A creative new look at the relationships between the short term solutions to the 21st-Century Financial Crisis and possible long term solutions to that same 21st-Century Crisis (including a philosophical solution, an economic-political solution, and a quantifiable, applied, practical solution).

- Additional coverage of the Fannie and Freddie Takeover.

- New coverage of the Federal Housing Finance Agency (FHFA).

- New coverage of the Home Affordable Refinance Program (HARP).

Chapter 21 Bankruptcy Law: In Theory, in History, and in Practice

- Chapter 21 begins with a new Opening Case, *Hanover National Bank of New York v. Max Moyses,* which examines the constitutionality of federal bankruptcy laws.

- New coverage of the historical development of bankruptcy law in the United States.

- New coverage of the states' control of bankruptcy.

Chapter 22 Agency Law

- Chapter 22 begins with a new Opening Case, *Doe v. Liberatore,* which explores the nature of agency, the nature of vicarious liability in tort law and criminal law, and the defenses associated with vicarious liability as they are related to this case and to similar cases.

- A new Classic Case, *Peggy Lee Penley, Appellant, v. C.L. Westbrook, Jr. Appellee*, which examines the difference between clergy malpractice and professional negligence.

- New coverage of the defense of charitable immunity.

Chapter 23 Employment Law

- Chapter 23 begins with a new Opening Case, *Garcetti, et al. v. Ceballos*, which explores the nature of the First Amendment rights of government employees.

- Additional coverage of the details included in employment contracts.

- Additional, more in-depth coverage of retaliation and constructive discharge.

- Additional, more in-depth coverage of the development of federal Civil Rights legislation.

- A new Classic Case, *Griggs v. Duke Power Co.*, which examines the disparate impact doctrine.

- Additional, more in-depth coverage of the whistleblower acts.

- New coverage of the anti-retaliation safeguards.

Chapter 24 Labor Law

- Chapter 24 begins with a new Opening Case, *Northwestern University, Employer v. College Athletes Players Association, Petitioner*, which involves the unionization of college athletes.
- A new Question of Ethics box feature that discusses the ethical ramifications of having a double standard in relation to free speech that penalizes public employees by limiting (eliminating?) their first amendment rights.
- Additional, more in-depth coverage and exploration of how the law defines the terms "employee" and labor "organization."

Chapter 25 The Business Entity: An Introduction

- Chapter 25 begins with a new Opening Case, *PNC Bank v. Michael Farinacci,* which involves a study of the differences between the Uniform Partnership Act (UPA) and the Revised Uniform Partnership Act (RUPA).
- New coverage of national economic reform movements.
- Additional, more in-depth coverage of traditional business entities, including sole proprietorships, general partnerships, limited partnerships, limited liability partnerships, private corporations, public (or state owned) corporations, quasi-public corporations, limited liability corporations, joint ventures, and franchises.
- New coverage of unorthodox business entities, including failure-proof public corporations, public–private corporate analogs, cross-owned corporations, public bodies corporations, social corporations, cooperative corporations, cooperative corporations with wage earning employees, and cooperatives with non-employee owners.

Chapter 26 The Corporate Entity

- Chapter 26 begins with a new Opening Case, *William Stewart d/b/a Stewart Coal Co. v. R. A. Eberts Company Inc., et al.,* which involves a close examination of the corporate law doctrine of piercing the corporate veil.
- New coverage of crisis management and the corporate entity.
- New coverage of capitalism and the corporate entity.
- Additional coverage of certain key corporate legal principles, including the free transfer of ownership, central management principles, and the nature of corporate personhood.
- A new Question of Ethics box feature that focuses on the debate between Justice Antonin Scalia and Judge Richard Posner on whether judges should use textualism or pragmatism in their interpretation of statutory and constitutional law.
- Additional coverage of piercing the corporate veil, including a new look at the alter ego doctrine, the instrumentality test, and the three step test.

Chapter 27 Managing the Corporate Entity

- Chapter 27 begins with a new Opening Case, *Aronson v. Lewis,* which involves the creation of the *demand futility* doctrine in corporate law.
- More in-depth coverage of independent director control of the corporate board of directors.
- Additional, more in-depth coverage of managerial control of the corporate board of directors.

- New coverage of stakeholder control of the corporate board of directors.
- A new Question of Ethics box feature that discusses the ethical ramifications of the Sarbanes–Oxley Act (SarbOx).
- Additional, more in-depth coverage of derivative lawsuits, including the addition of the demand futility doctrine.
- Additional, more in-depth coverage of the insider trading rule.

Chapter 28 Government Regulation of the Corporate Entity

- Chapter 28 begins with a new Opening Case, *Egan v. TradingScreen,* which involves the use of a textualist approach to statutory interpretation from the bench.
- Additional, more in-depth coverage of the historical development of federal power under the commerce clause especially as it relates to the corporation.
- Additional coverage of residual state power over commerce and corporate law.
- Additional, more in-depth coverage of the Model Business Corporation Act.
- Additional, more in-depth coverage of state common law in relation to corporations.
- New coverage of stakeholder corporate law in Delaware.
- New coverage of swap transactions.
- New coverage of changes in the Dodd–Frank Act.
- New coverage of the quick-look standard in antitrust law.

Chapter 29 Personal Property and Bailments

- Chapter 29 begins with a new Opening Case, *Berglund v. Roosevelt University Energy Corporation,* which looks at the issue of bailments on college campuses.
- A new discussion of the Classic Case of *American Ambassador Casualty Co. v. City of Chicago* as it relates to the principles of bailments.

Chapter 30 Real Property and Landlord and Tenant Law

- Chapter 30 begins with a new Opening Case, *Wellington Resource Group, LLC. v. Beck Energy Corporation,* which looks at the very nature of gas and oil contracts. Are they real property contracts or something else?
- A report on the use of subterranean rights as they relate to fracking contracts.
- An update on the dormant minerals statutes now in use in relation to fracking contracts.
- Additional coverage of the fee simple determinable.
- A new discussion of the Classic Case of *Kelo v. City of New London* as it relates to the doctrine of eminent domain.

Chapter 31 Wills, Trusts, and Advanced Directives

- Chapter 31 begins with a new Opening Case, *Windsor v. United States,* which examines the Defense of Marriage Act and its relationship to same sex marriages entered in other jurisdictions.

- A new discussion of civil unions and registered domestic relationships in relation to estate planning.

- A new discussion of the Classic Case *Gonzales, Attorney General v. Oregon* as it relates to physician assisted suicide.

- The new Case Study for Part 8 is *Obergefell, et al., v. Hodges,* the recent case in which the U.S. Supreme Court declared state statutes and state constitutional provisions outlawing same sex marriages as unconstitutional.

Chapter 32 Professional Liability

- Chapter 32 begins with a new Opening Case, *Delollis v. Friedberg,* which examines the concept of near-privity, as it relates to the accountant-client relationship.

- New coverage of type one accounting arrangements.

- New coverage of type two accounting arrangements.

- New coverage of the Cardoza Standard of Actual Privity.

- A new discussion of the Classic Case of *Ultramares Corp. v. Touche* as it relates to the creation of an indeterminate class of persons in accountant-client relationships.

- An update on accounting liability theories, including: actual privity (also the Cardoza Standard; near-privity (also the Actually Named Third-Party Standard); near-privity plus (also the Specifically Foreseen Third-Party Standard); near-privity plus-2 (also the Reasonably Foreseeable Third-Party Standard); and the platonic stabilizing standard (also called the Balancing Standard).

- A new discussion of the Classic Case of *State of Florida, et al. v. U.S. Department of Health and Human Services* as it relates to the question of whether it is ethically appropriate to bring an *illegal lawsuit* to stop an *unconstitutional statute* from going into effect.

Chapter 33 Science, Technology, and Law in the 21st Century

- Chapter 33 begins with a new Opening Case that examines the first lawsuit filed in an American court involving the Ebola crisis.

- New coverage of the Constitution and Science, including a more in-depth examination of the Commerce Clause, the necessary and Proper Clause, and the Taxation Clause.

- New coverage of the Constitution and Science, including additional coverage of the supremacy clause and the treaty clause.

- New coverage of the Patent Court Pilot Program in the federal court system.

- New coverage of existing residual state regulatory power over science.

- New coverage of science and common law.

- New coverage of the historical development of those federal programs that support science and technology.

- A new discussion of the Classic Case of *Sherely v. Sebelius* that involves a clash between the Dickey-Wicker (DW) budget amendment which forbids research that directly destroys a human embryo and the *Chevron Doctrine* which says that, when a Congressional rule is truly ambiguous, a court must acquiesce to an agency's interpretation of that rule.

- New more in-depth coverage of nongovernmental international organizations (NIOs), especially including a look at transnational organizations (*transnats*), including terrorist groups, drug cartels, slave traders, and pirates.

- New coverage of the World Health Organization and the Ebola Crisis.
- A new Question of Ethics box feature that discusses the ethical ramifications of the World Health Organization's possible use of experimental treatments on the most severely affected Ebola patients.
- A new discussion of the Classic Case of *Diamond v. Chakrabarty* that considered the question of whether it is possible to patent a life-form. (The court decided yes—it is possible to patent a life-form.)
- A new discussion (several new discussions, in fact) of the Classic Case involving the attempt by the J. Craig Venter Institute to patent a self-replicating completely synthetic life.

Chapter 34 International Law and the New World Order

- Chapter 34 begins with a new Opening Case that examines the relationships (political, economic, and military) that exist between the United States (a.k.a. "the beautiful country") and China ("the central country") in the 21st century.
- New coverage of the process of predictive political history.
- New coverage of the political theories of realism, liberalism, neoliberalism, and neoconservativism.
- New coverage of the Russian Invasion of Crimea.
- New coverage of the various sets of global initial conditions, including the economic initial conditions, the cultural initial conditions, the ideological initial conditions, and hybrid initial conditions.
- New coverage of the China Cycle.
- New coverage of variables, uncertainty, and unexpected events on the international scene.
- A new discussion of the Classic Case of the United States, Bin Laden, and the Just War Theory.
- A new discussion of the Authorization for the Use of Military Force of 2015 (AUMF).

Acknowledgments

We are grateful to the following individuals for their review feedback. We appreciate their ideas and suggestions.

Joan Alexander
Nassau Community College

Bonnie S. Bolinger
Ivy Tech Community College

Dennis Bromley
Salt Lake Community College

Myra Bruegger
Southeastern Community College

H. Stanley Carson
Eastern Maine Community College

Gregory L. Dalton
Genesee Community College

Nancy K. Dempsey
Cape Cod Community College

Pamela S. Evers
University of North Carolina Wilmington

John M. Golden
Slippery Rock University

Warren C. Hodges
Forsyth Technical Community College

Norman Hollingsworth
Langston University

Walter E. Lippincott
Naugatuck Valley Community College

Benjamin Neil
Towson University

Beth Snodgrass
Mountain Empire Community College

Deborah Vinecour
SUNY Rockland Community College

We extend special thanks to the following individuals who were involved with content creation.

Brad Cox
Midlands Technical College

Brian Elzweig
Texas A&M University

Brian Gravely
National American University

Cheryl Harwick

Vonda Laughlin
King University

Jeff Penley
Catawba Valley Community College

Damon Scott
Atlanta Technical College

Joseph Zavaletta
Issachar Law Group—Boise, Idaho

We also extend special thanks to Jennifer A. Chiocco for her excellent photograph of Dr. Sukys on the About the Authors page.

A Guided Tour

Business Law with UCC Applications, 14/e, is full of useful chapter features to make studying productive and hassle-free. The following pages show the kind of engaging, helpful pedagogical features that complement the accessible, easy-to-understand approach to teaching business law.

Chapter Outline

Each chapter features an outline that allows students to recognize the organization of the chapter at a glance. For reinforcement, the outline's numbering system is used throughout the body of the chapter and is repeated in the end-of-chapter Summary.

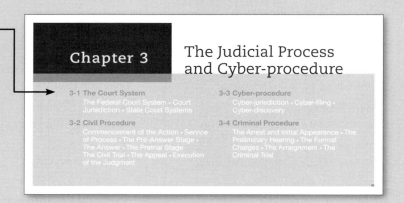

Chapter 3

The Judicial Process and Cyber-procedure

3-1 The Court System
The Federal Court System • Court Jurisdiction • State Court Systems

3-2 Civil Procedure
Commencement of the Action • Service of Process • The Pre-Answer Stage • The Answer • The Pretrial Stage • The Civil Trial • The Appeal • Execution of the Judgment

3-3 Cyber-procedure
Cyber-jurisdiction • Cyber-filing • Cyber-discovery

3-4 Criminal Procedure
The Arrest and Initial Appearance • The Preliminary Hearing • The Formal Charges • The Arraignment • The Criminal Trial

---

THE OPENING CASE *Round 1*
Frankenstein in the Federal Circuit

In theory the courts, especially the federal courts, are supposed make things as simple and straightforward as possible, at least within the limits of the law. Unfortunately, that is not always how it works. Case in point—the handling of patent law in the Court of Appeals for the Federal Circuit. Patent law may seem complex and tricky, but at its heart it has one unbreakable axiom. Three things cannot be patented: laws of nature (the laws of thermodynamics or $E = mc^2$, for instance), natural processes (river currents, earthquakes, or tornadoes), and abstract ideas (mathematical algorithms). This axiom made patent law rather straightforward until, in *State Street Bank v. Signature Financial Group*, the Court of Appeals for the Federal Circuit, which is supposed to specialize in patent law, decided that a business method, which until then had always been considered an abstract idea, could be patented. At that point, many heretofore unpatentable processes, software in particular, became patentable. The case confused a lot of people, but it should not have confused the Federal Circuit, which had created the ruling in the first place. As luck (and bad luck at that) would have it, the ruling had turned into the court's own personal Frankenstein. In a recent case, the Federal Circuit has revealed just how confusing patent law can be. The case, *CLS Bank International v. Alice Corporation*, involves four patented computer programs that reduce the risk involved in an exchange payment

agreement. Alice claims that, in using the programs, CLS violated its patent. For its part, CLS argues that the programs are unpatentable abstract ideas. The district court agreed with CLS and granted a summary judgment motion in its favor; however, when the case reached the Federal Circuit, two judges disagreed and reversed the decision. The case was so controversial that it was eventually heard in an *en banc* session of all the judges in Federal Circuit. Now remember that the courts are supposed to make things as simple and straightforward as possible. In this case, that did not happen. The court appeared to overturn *State Street Bank v. Signature Financial Group; however,* it is not as simple as that because of the 10 judges who heard the case, 7 of them felt compelled to write their own opinions. Even then the case was not quite over because the U.S. Supreme Court agreed make an attempt to unravel the Federal Circuit's Frankenstein. [See: *CLS Bank International v. Alice Corporation Pty. Ltd.,* No. 2011-130, United States Court of Appeals for the Federal Circuit (May 10, 2013); *State Street Bank v. Signature Financial Group,* 149 F.3d 1368 (Fed. Cir. Jul. 23, 1998).]

Opening Case Questions

1. What is the role of the Court of Appeals for the Federal Circuit? Explain.

The Opening Case

A brief case opens each chapter and introduces the chapter concepts, followed by numbered questions addressing legal issues in the case. Every opening case is re-examined throughout the chapter. Those scenarios that become opening cases are chosen carefully to bring a broad spectrum of illustrations to the text. Some of these are hypotheticals, created specifically for the material in the chapters. Others are drawn from today's headlines and are not yet in the courts. Still others are classic cases that have been used in law courses for decades and thus represent the best illustrations of key points in the law.

Learning Objectives

Succinct, crisply written learning objectives follow the opening case at the beginning of each chapter. The numbered objectives describe what the students can expect to learn as a result of completing the chapter. Each objective is identified by a symbol in the margin where the material appears in the text.

LO Learning Objectives

1. Explain the fundamental nature of the American courts.
2. Determine when a case can be brought in federal court.
3. Recognize those cases that can be heard by the U.S. Supreme Court.
4. Identify the structure of most state court systems.
5. Define civil litigation.
6. List the most common discovery techniques.
7. Detail the nature of an appeal.
8. Determine the extent of cyber-jurisdiction.
9. Explain the nature of electronically stored information (ESI).
10. Describe the steps in a criminal prosecution.

New Classic Cases A new Classic Cases feature has been included in many chapters in this edition, giving both the instructor and the students an opportunity to explore topics related to the content of the chapter in a provocative and stimulating way.

CLASSIC CASE Healthy, Wealthy, and Wise?

Literature instructors are fond of saying that a poem, a play, a novel, or a short story is considered good, sometimes even great, if it has stood the "test of time." The same is true of many legal cases. Such is the situation with the long-standing case of *Hamer v. Sidway*, a lawsuit that most law students and paralegals encounter (or should encounter) at some time in their academic careers. *Hamer and Sidway* begins at a golden wedding anniversary celebration. At the party, Uncle William promised his nephew and namesake, William, the Younger, that if he, the nephew, would give up a long list of vices that included smoking and swearing, until his 21st birthday, he, the uncle, would pay his nephew, William, $5,000. The challenge was made in front of a room full of family members and close friends, and William, the Younger, agreed to the arrangement. Following this and in compliance with the agreement, William embarked on an extensive period of abstinence that lasted several years. Soon after his 21st birthday, William wrote to his uncle telling him of his accomplishments and asking for the $5,000 due to him under the payment. The executor refused to pay and William brought this lawsuit. William argued that he had performed as promised and was, therefore, entitled to the money. The executor recognized that William had, indeed, refrained from smoking and swearing, but argued that, in contract law, both sides must suffer a detriment for consideration to be valid and for a contract to exist. In this case, the executor said, young William had not suffered a detriment. In fact, the opposite was true. He was much healthier than he would have been, absent the promise, and he had, therefore, benefited greatly from giving up his bad habits for such an extended period of time. In the absence of consideration, no contract ever existed and, as a result, the estate did not owe young William a single cent. The court disagreed with this analysis. The court noted that, when William gave up something that he had a legal right to do, he had suffered a detriment sufficient to provide the consideration needed to make the agreement into a *bona fide* contract. To prove its point the court referred to a standard treatise on contract law and noted that, con-

---

A QUESTION OF ETHICS

Federal Supremacy, Discrimination, and a Lesson in Ethics

A quick review of the case in Example 2-2 will remind us that Arizona passed a statute that empowered the local police to demand identification papers from anyone suspected of being in the country illegally. In response, the federal government sued the state of Arizona in an attempt to block the administration of the law arguing that federal law trumped state law in this situation because the Constitution gave the power to control immigration to the national government alone. Recall that the federal government could have argued that the law was discriminatory because it had a disparate impact on people of a particular color and a certain national origin. The question we pose here is not the relatively easy one of whether the Arizona statute is unethical. Rather, the question we ask is whether it is ethical for the Justice Department to use the relatively safe argument of federal supremacy while ignoring the far greater legal and moral transgression of deliberate, unapologetic, legislative discrimination?

A Question of Ethics boxes challenge students' understanding of previously discussed chapter examples by asking questions specifically relating to ethical dilemmas.

About the Law boxes provide additional clarification of chapter concepts.

About the Law

The American Arbitration Association booklet *National Rules for the Resolution of Employment Disputes* includes rules on both mediation and arbitration.

Some states require arbitration prior to trial in certain cases. Required arbitration is called mandatory arbitration. Some litigants have challenged government-imposed mandatory arbitration as an unconstitutional deprivation of their right to a trial by jury and equal protection under the law. Most states faced with this question have disagreed with these arguments as long as the arbitration requirement does not replace the jury trial and as long as the motives for requiring arbitration are reasonable.

An arbitration hearing can be planned and executed by the parties themselves. Generally, this step means that the parties set the ground rules for choosing the arbitrator or arbitrators, for conducting discovery, for presenting evidence, for determining the outcome, and for enforcing the reward. In addition, details such as setting the time and the place of the hearing, filling vacancies on the arbitration panel, recording the proceedings, handling objections, granting time extensions, and so on, must also be agreed upon. Because of the intricacies of such a process, many individuals who select arbitration prefer to use professional arbitration organizations such as the American Arbitration Association to handle the details of their arbitration proceeding.

Like most forms of ADR, arbitration is not without its difficulties. One shortcoming is

---

According to one system of legal thought, morality and the law are united in a common bond based on their intrinsic nature. This system of thought, which is generally known as natural law, sees law as originating from some objective, superior force that stands outside the everyday experience of most people. That superior force is generally God, but can be referred to by a variety of other titles such as Aristotle's eternal changeless primary being, Hegel's Absolute, the Being of Eckhart Tolle, or the Kami of Shintoism. Thus, according to natural law, there exists an unbreakable link joining morality to the law in a fundamental way. This link exists because law must, in its most basic form, be moral. Otherwise, it is not lawful. A law with an immoral purpose is not a law at all. Instead it is an anomaly that does not fit into our concept of either law or the legal process. It is, of course, one thing to say that laws must be firmly grounded in morality and quite another to argue that legality and morality are always the same thing. There are, in fact, some laws that have no moral content whatsoever. Thus, a city ordinance that establishes a midnight

LO2

Did You Know?

The Koran states that the equality of all humanity serves as the basic foundation for all human rights.

Did You Know? boxes are interesting factoids directly linked to the chapter concept being discussed.

EXAMPLE 2-1: Constitutional Law in the United Kingdom

Unlike the United States Constitution, the British Constitution has never been reduced to a single document. Instead, the principles that make up the British Constitution are found in many documents including the *Magna Carta*, an endless series of court cases, and a complex mix of statutory laws. There are problems with this fragmented approach. First, the amalgam of legal precedents that makes up the British constitution plays right into the problems associated with the Uncertainty Principle. This occurs because it is difficult to know what precedent will be called upon to support or to attack a particular legal position. Second, the absence of a written fail-safe system, like that found in the U.S. Constitution, opens the door to power abuse in the British system. On the other hand, following the dictates of

Examples are titled and numbered throughout each chapter and use short vignettes to explain how concepts can be applied in real-life situations.

Quick Quiz boxes follow each numbered section and give students the chance to test themselves with three true/false questions. Answers are provided at the end of each chapter.

when the chief executive makes an appointment that is nullified by the legislature. [See Chase, p. 19; Robert Skidelsky, "Keynes's Economics: Uncertainty," *Keynes: The Return of the Master* (New York: Public Affairs, 2010), pp. 83–85.] Moreover, the legal scholar Richard Posner tells us that this inclination toward uncertainty, especially as it relates to economics, is exacerbated by the fact that some people act in unpredictable ways on a regular basis, while others react to what their neighbors have done. What is true in economics is equally true in the law. [See: Richard Posner, *A Failure of Capitalism* (Cambridge; Harvard University Press, 2009), pp. 83–84.]

quick quiz 2-1

1. The law consists of rules of conduct established by the government to maintain harmony, stability, and justice within a society. — true | false
2. Often justice must be sacrificed for harmony and stability, but the opposite is never true. — true | false
3. Legislators and judges bring their own personal prejudices and biases into the process. — true | false

Questions for Review and Discussion provide a means for students and the instructor to reexamine and discuss the key points of law. All objectives listed at the beginning of each chapter are also reviewed.

Questions for Review and Discussion

1. What is the fundamental nature of the American court system?
2. Under what circumstances might a federal court have jurisdiction to hear a case?
3. Under what circumstances might the U.S. Supreme Court hear a case?
4. What is the structure of a typical state court systems?
5. What is civil litigation?
6. What are the most common discovery techniques?
7. What is involved in an appeal?
8. How is cyber-jurisdiction determined?
9. What is electronically stored information?
10. What are the steps in a criminal prosecution?

Summary

2.1 The law consists of rules of conduct established by the government to maintain harmony, stability, and justice within a society. Ideally, the primary objectives of the law are to promote harmony, stability, and justice. In everyday life, the balance is not easy to maintain. The law or, more properly, the entire legal framework consists of a series of dualities that must be resolved somehow.

2.2 A constitution is the basic law of a nation or state. The United States Constitution provides the organization of the national government. Each state also has a constitution that determines the sta'___ ___ structure. The body of law that forms its interpretation is known as constitu

2.3 The laws passed by a legislat statutes. At the federal level, these ai by Congress and signed by the pres level, statutes are enacted by state leg must be arranged, cataloged, and ind erence by compiling state and feder many different statutes are passed

The Uniform Law Commission (ULC) was founded to write these uniform laws.

2.4 Courts make law through common law, the interpretation of statutes, and judicial review. Common law is the body of previously recorded legal decisions made by the courts in specific cases. Statutory interpretation is the process by which the courts analyze those aspects of a statute that are unclear or ambiguous or that were not anticipated at the time that the legislature passed the statute, and judicial review is the process by which the courts determine the constitutionality of var___ _____ _____ _____ _____ or

Key Terms

administrative law, 47	constitutional law, 35	ter
Articles of Confederation, 35	cyber-commerce, 44	i as
binding precedent, 46	devolution, 41	ns,
code, 42	Federal Register, 48	een
Code of Federal Regulations (CFR), 48	judicial review, 47	ivi-___
common law, 45	law, 31	lict
constitution, 35	persuasive precedent, 48	ing

Summary Numbered to match the outline at the beginning of the chapter and the main heads within each chapter, the Summary provides an encapsulated review of the chapter's content.

Key Terms Each key term is printed in boldface and defined when introduced in the text. A list of key terms and the page number of first usage appears at the end of each chapter. A glossary of the key terms is provided at the back of the text.

Cases for Analysis have been updated extensively for the 14th edition and chosen for their relevance, ease of understanding, and interesting fact patterns. Many are abridgements of actual court decisions; some are taken from current news stories; and still others are hypothetical situations written to emphasize legal issues and concepts presented in the text.

Cases for Analysis

1. In San Diego in August 2009, the police stopped a car driven by David Leon Riley because the license plates on the vehicle were outdated. The police officers then discovered that Riley's driver's license had been suspended. The officers then conducted a search of Riley's car without a warrant. The officers found and seized two handguns. Further investigation connected the two handguns to a recent shooting incident. The officers also found Riley's smartphone and then, again without a warrant, searched the data that they found stored on the smartphone. The data found on the phone provided further evidence pointing to Riley's participation in gang-related activities. In addition Amendment of the United States Constitution apply to the case? When the Fourth Amendment was enacted in the 18th century, no one even dreamed of a "smartphone"? Should the Constitution be amended to include modern technological advances like smartphones? Explain. [See: *David Leon Riley v. California* (no. 13-132) United States Supreme Court (April 29, 2014).]

2. In 2012, the North Carolina Constitution was amended to include a provision that placed a ban on gay marriages in the state. The new constitutional amendment was challenged in federal court when a group of ministers representing the United

The **Case Study** at the end of each of the nine parts begins with a summary of the facts of the case, is followed by an excerpt from the court's opinion, and concludes with a series of questions.

Part 1 Case Study

Schuette, Attorney General of Michigan v. Coalition to Defend Affirmative Action and Immigration Rights and Fight for Equality By Any Means Necessary (BAMN)
United States Supreme Court
No. 12-682 (Argued October 15, 2013—Decided April 22, 2014)
572 U.S. _____ (2014)

Summary

The facts in this case are relatively straightforward. The State of Michigan, like many states, has struggled with the question of whether to continue to use race as an element in the admissions procedure at its state colleges, universities, and graduate programs. In *Gratz v. Bollinger*, 539 U.S. 244 (2003), the Supreme Court had invalidated the admissions procedures for the University of Michigan because the process had allowed the explicit consideration of a candidate's race. In response, the university revamped the admissions process in a way that was designed to satisfy the Court's objections. However, the process still involved a narrowly defined race-related element. The new plan sparked a widespread quarrel across Michigan over whether to use race as a part of the selection criteria. The controversy led to an amendment proposal that went on the ballot in 2006. The amendment (generally referred to as Proposal 2) forbid the state and state subdivisions such as cities, counties, school districts, public colleges, and public universities from using race-oriented standards in many activities and decisions. The amendment included a specific prohibition barring race-centered criteria in the admissions procedures at state colleges and universities. The amendment (now referred to as Section 26) became law based on a 4 percent margin (52 percent for and 48 percent against). Two lawsuits challenged the amendment's constitutionality almost immediately. The District Court granted a summary judgment motion that, in effect, upheld the constitutionality of Section 26. On appeal the Sixth Circuit reversed the trial court. An *en banc* session of the Sixth Circuit Court supported the earlier decision by the original three-judge panel. In doing so the court relied upon *Washington v. Seattle School District, No. 1, 458 U.S. 457 (1982)*. The Michigan case then

Four appendices provide critical material for the students: The Constitution of the United States (Appendix A), Articles 1, 2, 2a, and 3 of the Uniform Commercial Code (Appendix B), the United Nations Convention for the International Sale of Goods (Appendix C), and two final documents, Patrick Henry's Tax Assessment Bill and James Madison's "Memorial and Remonstrance" (Appendix D). Marginal references throughout the text refer students to the page of the appendix where the original source of the law being discussed can be found.

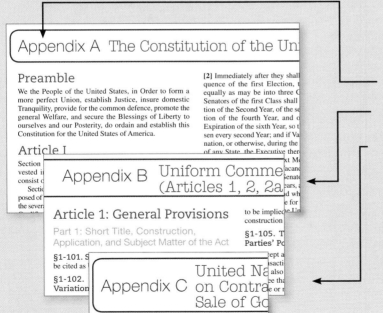

Appendix A The Constitution of the Un...

Preamble

We the People of the United States, in Order to form a more perfect Union, establish Justice, insure domestic Tranquility, provide for the common defence, promote the general Welfare, and secure the Blessings of Liberty to ourselves and our Posterity, do ordain and establish this Constitution for the United States of America.

Article I

Section...
vested i...
consist...
Sectio...
posed of...
the sever...

[2] Immediately after they shall...
quence of the first Election,...
equally as may be into three C...
Senators of the first Class shall...
tion of the Second Year, of the se...
tion of the fourth Year, and o...
Expiration of the sixth Year, so t...
sen every second Year; and if Va...
nation, or otherwise, during the...
of any State, the Executive ther...

Appendix B Uniform Comme... (Articles 1, 2, 2a...

Article 1: General Provisions

Part 1: Short Title, Construction, Application, and Subject Matter of the Act

§1-101. S... be cited as...

§1-102. Variation...

§1-105. T... Parties' Po...

Appendix C United Na... on Contra... Sale of Go...

THE STATES PARTI...
BEARING IN MIND t...
tions adopted by the six...

Appendix D Patrick Henry... and James M... and Remonst...

McGraw-Hill *Connect*®

 McGraw-Hill *Connect* is an online assignment and assessment solution that connects students with the tools and resources they'll need to achieve success.

McGraw-Hill *Connect* helps prepare students for their future by enabling faster learning, more efficient studying, and higher retention of knowledge.

McGraw-Hill *Connect* features

Connect offers a number of powerful tools and features to make managing assignments easier, so faculty can spend more time teaching. With *Connect,* students can engage with their coursework anytime and anywhere, making the learning process more accessible and efficient. *Connect* offers you the features described below.

SMARTBOOK™

Proven to help students improve grades and study more efficiently, SmartBook contains the same content within the print book, but actively tailors that content to the needs of the individual. SmartBook's adaptive technology provides precise, personalized instruction on what the student should do next, guiding the student to master and remember key concepts, targeting gaps in knowledge and offering customized feedback, driving the student toward comprehension and retention of the subject matter. Available on smartphones and tablets, SmartBook puts learning at the student's fingertips—anywhere, anytime.

Simple assignment management With *Connect,* creating assignments is easier than ever, so you can spend more time teaching and less time managing. The assignment management function enables you to:

- Create and deliver assignments easily with selectable end-of-chapter questions quiz and test bank items.
- Streamline lesson planning, student progress reporting, and assignment grading to make classroom management more efficient than ever.
- Go digital with SmartBook and online submission and grading of student assignments.

Smart grading When it comes to studying, time is precious. *Connect* helps students learn more efficiently by providing feedback and practice material when they need it, where they need it. When it comes to teaching, your time also is precious. The grading function enables you to:

- Have assignments scored automatically, giving students immediate feedback on their work and side-by-side comparisons with correct answers.

- Access and review each response; manually change grades or leave comments for students to review.
- Reinforce classroom concepts with practice tests and instant quizzes.

Instructor library   The *Connect* Instructor Library is your repository for additional resources to improve student engagement in and out of class. You can select and use any asset that enhances your lecture. The *Connect* Instructor Library includes:

- *eBook*
- *Test Bank*
- *Instructors Manual*
- *PowerPoint files*
- *Videos*
- *Business Law Newsletter archives*
- *Access to interactive study tools*

Tegrity Campus: Lectures 24/7

Tegrity Campus is a service that makes your classes available 24/7 by automatically capturing every lecture in a searchable format for students to review when they study and com-

plete assignments. With a simple one-click start-and-stop process, you capture all computer screens and corresponding audio. Students can replay any part of your class and can search for a word or phrase and be taken to the exact place in your lecture that they need to review.

To learn more about Tegrity watch a Two minute Flash demo at **http://tegritycampus. mhhe.com.**

Assurance of Learning Ready

Many educational institutions today are focused on the notion of *assurance of learning,* an important element of some accreditation standards. *Business Law with UCC Applications,* 14e is designed specifically to support your assurance of learning initiatives with a simple, yet powerful solution.

Each test bank question for *Business Law with UCC Applications* maps to a specific chapter learning outcome/objective listed in the text. You can use our test bank software, EZ Test and EZ Test Online, or in *Connect* to easily query for learning outcomes/objectives that directly relate to the learning objectives for your course. You can then use the reporting features of EZ Test to aggregate student results in similar fashion, making the collection and presentation of assurance of learning data simple and easy.

AACSB Statement

The McGraw-Hill Companies is a proud corporate member of AACSB International. The AACSB leaves content coverage and assessment within the purview of individual schools, the mission of the school, and the faculty. While *Business Law,* 14th edition and the teaching package make no claim of any specific AACSB qualification or evaluation, we have within *Business Law with UCC Applications,* 14th edition labeled selected test bank and quiz questions according to the eight general knowledge and skills areas.

Contents in Brief

Contents

Part Three
Sales and Consumer Protection   307

Part Four
Negotiable Instruments and Banking   379

Part Five

Part Six

Part Seven

Part Eight
Property Law 707

Part Nine
The Legal Environment 785

McGraw-Hill Connect®
Learn Without Limits

Connect is a teaching and learning platform that is proven to deliver better results for students and instructors.

Connect empowers students by continually adapting to deliver precisely what they need, when they need it, and how they need it, so your class time is more engaging and effective.

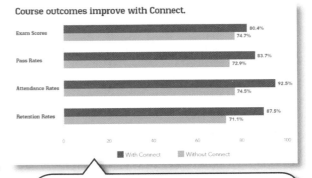

Course outcomes improve with Connect.

	With Connect	Without Connect
Exam Scores	80.4%	74.7%
Pass Rates	83.7%	72.9%
Attendance Rates	92.5%	74.5%
Retention Rates	87.5%	71.1%

> Using **Connect** improves passing rates by **10.8%** and retention by **16.4%**.

> 88% of instructors who use **Connect** require it; instructor satisfaction **increases** by 38% when **Connect** is required.

Analytics

Connect Insight®

Connect Insight is Connect's new one-of-a-kind visual analytics dashboard—now available for both instructors and students—that provides at-a-glance information regarding student performance, which is immediately actionable. By presenting assignment, assessment, and topical performance results together with a time metric that is easily visible for aggregate or individual results, Connect Insight gives the user the ability to take a just-in-time approach to teaching and learning, which was never before available. Connect Insight presents data that empowers students and helps instructors improve class performance in a way that is efficient and effective.

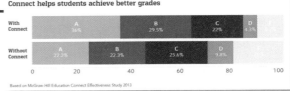

Connect helps students achieve better grades

	A	B	C	D
With Connect	36%	29.5%	22%	4.3%
Without Connect	22.2%	22.3%	25.6%	9.8%

Based on McGraw-Hill Education Connect Effectiveness Study 2013

> Students can view their results for any **Connect** course.

Mobile

Connect's new, intuitive mobile interface gives students and instructors flexible and convenient, anytime–anywhere access to all components of the Connect platform.

Adaptive

THE FIRST AND ONLY **ADAPTIVE READING EXPERIENCE** DESIGNED TO TRANSFORM THE WAY STUDENTS READ

> More students earn **A's** and **B's** when they use McGraw-Hill Education **Adaptive** products.

SmartBook®

Proven to help students improve grades and study more efficiently, SmartBook contains the same content within the print book, but actively tailors that content to the needs of the individual. SmartBook's adaptive technology provides precise, personalized instruction on what the student should do next, guiding the student to master and remember key concepts, targeting gaps in knowledge and offering customized feedback, and driving the student toward comprehension and retention of the subject matter. Available on smartphones and tablets, SmartBook puts learning at the student's fingertips—anywhere, anytime.

> Over **4 billion questions** have been answered, making McGraw-Hill Education products more intelligent, reliable, and precise.

www.learnsmartadvantage.com

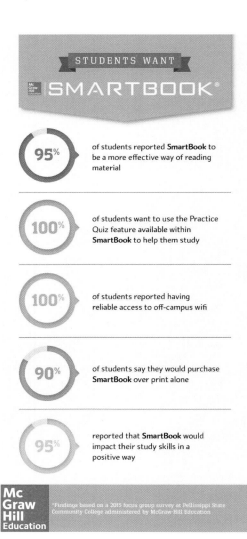

STUDENTS WANT SMARTBOOK®

95% of students reported **SmartBook** to be a more effective way of reading material

100% of students want to use the Practice Quiz feature available within **SmartBook** to help them study

100% of students reported having reliable access to off-campus wifi

90% of students say they would purchase **SmartBook** over print alone

95% reported that **SmartBook** would impact their study skills in a positive way

McGraw Hill Education

*Findings based on a 2015 focus group survey at Pellissippi State Community College administered by McGraw-Hill Education

Business Law
with UCC
Applications

Part One

Ethics, Law, and the Judicial System

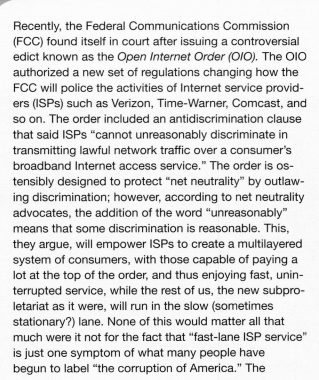

THE OPENING CASE *Round 1*
Net Neutrality, Skyboxes, and the Corruption of America

Recently, the Federal Communications Commission (FCC) found itself in court after issuing a controversial edict known as the *Open Internet Order (OIO)*. The OIO authorized a new set of regulations changing how the FCC will police the activities of Internet service providers (ISPs) such as Verizon, Time-Warner, Comcast, and so on. The order included an antidiscrimination clause that said ISPs "cannot unreasonably discriminate in transmitting lawful network traffic over a consumer's broadband Internet access service." The order is ostensibly designed to protect "net neutrality" by outlawing discrimination; however, according to net neutrality advocates, the addition of the word "unreasonably" means that some discrimination is reasonable. This, they argue, will empower ISPs to create a multilayered system of consumers, with those capable of paying a lot at the top of the order, and thus enjoying fast, uninterrupted service, while the rest of us, the new subproletariat as it were, will run in the slow (sometimes stationary?) lane. None of this would matter all that much were it not for the fact that "fast-lane ISP service" is just one symptom of what many people have begun to label "the corruption of America." The

corruption of America is rooted in an ethical system, sometimes referred to as neoliberalism, that uses quantification as the primary tool for determining value. Now using the market to evaluate goods and services that are bought and sold in the marketplace makes perfect sense; however, using market values (read *money* here) to measure activities outside the market can be risky for two reasons. First, the use of money to measure the value of activities that are, in essence, basically democratic experiences (like paying someone to wait in line for you in a public place or using the implied promise of an endowment to secure your child's enrollment in a college) is simply unfair. Second, the use of money to measure the value of communal experiences (like a day at the ballpark) corrupts that experience in subtle and often unrecognizable ways. Although both of these results are undesirable, the corruption problem is the more insidious of the two. In his book, *What Money Can't Buy,* Harvard professor Michael Sandel makes this point when he talks about the skybox transformation of the traditional American ballpark. A day at the ballpark was once an enriching community experience during which people from all walks of life rubbed shoulders and cheered on the home team. Now, with the advent of very expensive, super exclusive skyboxes, the privileged few sit among themselves in the heavens, while the rest of us, the new subproletarians as it were, sit below in the "cheap seats" commiserating among ourselves. The corruption of society is not what the FCC intends, nor may it come to pass simply because of those regulations. That, however, is not the point. The point is that the quantification of things such as "line waiting" and a day at the ballpark may ultimately replace more traditional ethical systems that, while more complicated and less clear, are, ultimately much fairer and certainly much less harmful to our identity as a legal and ethical community. [See *Verizon v. Federal Communications Commission* (No. 11-1355), United States Court of Appeals for the District of Columbia Circuit (2014); Michael Sandel, *What Money Can't Buy: The Moral Limits of the Market* (New York: Farrar, Straus, and Giroux, 2012).]

Opening Case Questions

1. Is the quantification of nonmonetary experiences fair to those of us who cannot afford to pay for the privilege of "being first in line"? Why or why not?

2. The right to pursue happiness promised in the Declaration of Independence does not guarantee the success of that pursuit. Should those of us who succeed be encouraged to enjoy that success by sitting in a skybox? Explain.

3. Is the Federal Communications Commission justified in imposing the antidiscrimination rule on ISPs? Explain.

4. How can the FCC and those opposed to the FCC's antidiscrimination rule both claim to support net neutrality? Explain.

5. Does market morality differ significantly from any other ethical system? Why or why not?

 Learning Objectives

1. Define law and morality.
2. Distinguish among natural law, positive law, negative rights.
3. Explain market value ethics.
4. Describe social contract ethics.
5. Outline the steps in applying utilitarianism.
6. Define rational ethics.
7. Explain the dyadic nature of ethics in government
8. Outline the arguments supporting social responsibility.
9. Explore the need for law in our society.
10. Clarify how the law and ethics can sometimes benefit from anarchy.

1-1 Defining the Law, Morality, and Ethics

Often people will disagree about the most trivial of matters—whether pumpkin pie tastes best with or without whipped cream, whether London or Paris offers the best theater, and whether baseball or football is the national pastime (it's baseball, by the way). Despite this, some subjects that provoke disagreement are of great importance—whether the death penalty should be outlawed or used more frequently, whether the U.S. military should engage in preemptive war, and whether the Internet should remain a neutral arena. It would be best were we to employ a commonly understood universally accepted ethical standard by which to measure these key issues. There is little disagreement on this basic premise. Nevertheless, once we cross that threshold, disagreement becomes the norm rather than the exception. Socrates, speaking through Plato, suggested centuries ago that we begin a study of ethics by understanding human nature. With that simple axiom in mind we begin our study of ethics.

First, however, we must define a few key terms. Most legal textbooks and many treatises on ethics begin by defining these disciplines. This tradition stands in marked contrast to most other studies. Few physics textbooks pause to tell the reader what physics is. Fewer history books devote space to explaining the term *history,* and almost no math texts begin by defining *math;* however, that is as it should be. These disciplines and others like them are fixed in our minds as implacable fields of study. In history, for example, the fact that Russia annexed Crimea in 2014 is not in dispute; nor is the fact that Pope Francis named both Pope John XXIII and Pope John Paul II as saints. Nor is our understanding that such events are historical facts. The same is true of the second law of thermodynamics in physics and the multiplication tables in mathematics. These facts are not debatable, except in the most esoteric way. [See: Jeffrie G. Murphy and Jules L. Coleman, *The Philosophy of Law* (Boulder, CO: Westview Press, 1990), p. 6; and John C. Calhoun, "A Disquisition on Government," in *Philosophy in America,* eds. Paul Russell Anderson and Max Harold Fisch (New York: Appleton-Century Crofts, Inc., 1939), pp. 356–357.]

The Law and Morality

This is not the case with morality and the law. People *will* argue about both, and when they do so, it is often in a most uncivil manner. They will dispute whether the law is a form of civil management or a way to dictate individual behavior, whether it ought to be created by a national government or a regional state system, and whether it should change regularly or stay the same indefinitely. They will even argue about whether the rules made by the government demand absolute, unquestioned obedience or simply ask for occasional recognition as optional guiding principles. As noted earlier, people will also argue about moral issues. This is why we pause at the beginning of *Business Law* to define the law and morality and to distinguish between ethics and morals, concepts that many of us usually do not think about on a daily basis.

The law consists of rules of conduct established by the government of a society to maintain harmony, stability, and justice. It accomplishes these objectives by defining the legal rights and duties of the people. The law also provides a way to protect the people by enforcing these rights and duties through the courts, the executive branch, and the legislature. The law is therefore a means of civil management. Certainly, the law usually cannot stop a person from doing wrong; however, the law can punish an individual who chooses to do that wrong, whatever it might be. The law then draws the line between conduct that is permissible and that which is not allowed, so people, at the very least, know that they can be punished if they choose to disobey the law.

EXAMPLE 1-1: The Government's Case Against Jack Bauer

Once upon a time, in a mythical version of post 9/11 America, a government agent named Jack Bauer worked for a federal law enforcement agency known as the Counter Terrorist Unit (CTU). In this mythical America, as depicted on the long-running and highly successful TV show *24*, Bauer pretty much did whatever he had to do to protect American interests and save American lives, up to and including torture. Neither Bauer nor CTU escape accountability, however, and in season seven of *24*, Bauer is subpoenaed to testify before a Senate oversight committee. When asked by the chairman of the committee whether he tortured a terrorist, Bauer admits that he did (saving the lives of 45 people, 10 of whom were children). The chairman then observes that Bauer clearly believes that the ends justify the means and that he cares nothing about the law. In response Bauer (well, OK, Kiefer Sutherland) makes an interesting observation. He says that he adapted to a situation in order to carry out his mission, which was to save the lives of those innocent civilians; however, when considering the question of whether he broke the law, Bauer does not duck, shift, or dodge responsibility. Instead he says, "In answer to your question, am I above the law, no sir, I am more than willing to be judged by the people." As noted earlier, Bauer clearly understands that the law draws a line between conduct that is permissible and that which is not. So Bauer, as an admitted lawbreaker, knows that he can be punished for choosing to break that law and accepts that responsibility. This is what is meant when we say that the law usually cannot stop a person from doing wrong; however, the law can punish an individual who chooses to do that wrong, whatever it might be, even torture.

In contrast, morals are values that govern a society's attitude toward right and wrong and toward good and evil. As a result, we should see morality as more fundamental than law. Therefore, morality ought to serve as a guide for those bodies within our society, such as the courts, the executive branch, the legislature, and the administrative agencies, that make, interpret, and enforce the law. Most of the time, these law-making, law-interpreting, and law-enforcing bodies will follow the belief that morality and legality ought to match up with each other. Indeed, there are even those philosophers of law who argue that morality is a necessary element of the law. They would say that you cannot have a philosophically valid law that is not grounded in morality.

Values and Ethics

So far we have defined **law** as a set of rules created by the government to establish a means of civil management that directs people to do what is right and avoid what is wrong. The purpose served by the law includes the creation of harmony, stability, and justice. The assumption is that if these purposes are met, right will be served and wrong defeated. Moreover, we have also defined **morals** as those fundamental values that tell us the difference between right and wrong in the first place. What we have not explained, however, is where those values come from. This is the job of ethics. Ethics is the attempt to develop a means of determining what these values ought to be and for formulating and applying rules that enforce those values.

Natural Law

According to one system of legal thought, morality and the law are united in a common bond based on their intrinsic nature. This system of thought, which is generally known as natural law, sees law as originating from some objective, superior force that stands outside the everyday experience of most people. That superior force is generally God, but can be referred to by a variety of other titles such as Aristotle's eternal changeless primary being, Hegel's Absolute, the Being of Eckhart Tolle, or the Kami of Shintoism. Thus, according to natural law, there exists an unbreakable link joining morality to the law in a fundamental way. This link exists because a law must, in its most basic form, be moral. Otherwise, it is not lawful. A law with an immoral purpose is not a law at all. Instead it is an anomaly that does not fit into our concept of either law or the legal process. It is, of course, one thing to say that laws must be firmly grounded in morality and quite another to argue that legality and morality are always the same thing. There are, in fact, some laws that have no moral content whatsoever. Thus, a city ordinance that establishes a midnight

Did You Know?

The Koran states that the equality of all humanity serves as the basic foundation for all human rights.

curfew for minors (those under 18 years of age) has no intrinsic moral substance, though such a law is not immoral on its face either (although most teenagers would almost certainly disagree). The natural law theorist, however, would say that such a law, if not moral in and of itself, is, at the very least, morally neutral and, therefore, has integrity as a law. Moreover, in a larger sense, a law that says minors must be safe at home after midnight, while not intrinsically moral, contributes to the orderly and stable functioning of society and is, therefore, moral because of its purpose and effect.

Positive Law

Natural law is sometimes confused with positive law because both depend on an outside force for their understanding of law, morality, and human rights. The difference is that positive law says that the law comes from social institutions rather than from God or some other outside force. **Positive law**, then, is a legal theory that says the law originates from an outside source that has emerged from within society. The process works something like this: The people of a society discover their rights as they live and work together. This discovery leads to commonly held rights that are described in a series of documents, such as the Magna Carta and the Bill of Rights. Exactly why people discover rather than invent universal rights is not clear. One argument says that rights are intuitively understood to exist within the human character. So, when people write documents such as the Bill of Rights, they include certain human rights such as the right to be treated fairly under the law. [See: Alan Dershowitz, *Rights from Wrongs: A Secular Theory of the Origin of Rights* (New York: Perseus Books Group, 2004), pp. 39–42.]

Some people say that human decency will ultimately triumph over human cruelty, giving rise to a just and moral society that will eventually abolish the worst sins of humanity. This brand of positive law is sometimes called the *Law of Peoples*. Not everyone agrees with this position, but such agreement is not necessary, so long as principles of decency and social justice can be found in certain universal documents such as the Bill of Rights in the United States Constitution or the United Nations Universal Declaration of Human Rights, Despite the differences between positive law and natural law, they hold one idea in common, namely, the belief that human values apply to all people at all times. [See: John Rawls, *The Law of Peoples* (Cambridge, MA: Harvard University Press, 1999), pp. 6–7.]

Negative Rights

One final minority position on human rights deserves our attention. That opinion argues that "rights" are a human invention designed to help people escape moral law. Thus, the right to privacy is actually a way to hide the truth from the public at large; the right to bear arms is the right to harm, perhaps even kill; the right to free speech is the right to lie and get away with it; and the right to private property is the right to exploit, plunder, and pollute that property. This theory of negative rights, as it is sometimes called, admits that the rights themselves do not create the escape from responsibility that they permit. Rather, these so-called rights give people an escape clause when they are caught doing something shameful. Thus, when people are caught with stolen goods or other contraband, they often claim that their privacy was invaded. Similarly, when media people are sued for libel, they frequently defend their actions by claiming the protection of a free press. Finally, when slumlords fail to repair dilapidated apartment buildings, they claim the right to private property. [See: Slavoj Zizek, *The Fragile Absolute* (London and New York: Verso, 2000), pp. 101–102.]

Did You Know?

The Greek word "ethos," which forms the root of the English word "ethics," means "character."

Ethical Decision Making

People make ethical decisions every day; however, how they make those decisions is not always clear. Some people say that they do not think about ethics but instead act instinctively when faced with a moral problem. Others say that they just do what they "believe" is

THE OPENING CASE *Round 2*
Net Neutrality, Skyboxes, and the Corruption of America

A quick review of the opening case at the beginning of this chapter will demonstrate the problems highlighted by the negative rights theory. For example, the rules promulgated by the FCC have been criticized by members of the Net community as an affront to their right to freedom of the press and freedom of speech. They say that, once the ISPs are permitted to give fast-lane service to those with the resources to pay for that right, they will then restrict or even eliminate access to the Internet by the smaller, financially challenged firms. Those firms will then be silenced (well nearly silenced) as they are exiled to the slow lane. On the other hand, the ISPs argue that, as the government adds additional regulations to their way of doing business, the more complicated and less profitable their businesses become, thus violating their rights and taking their property without due process of law. Finally, the end users of the Internet claim that their right of access will be limited or even eliminated by the regulations that would end up restricting their access to unconventional, nonconformist, radical, and even revolutionary views. (With the FCC's new regulations and without net neutrality, neither Copernicus nor Galileo, Darwin nor Huxley, Einstein nor Bohr, Pollack nor Dali, Disney nor Spielberg, Velikovsky nor Wegener would have been heard under the FCC's new discriminatory antidiscriminatory, pay if you can, rich folks only Internet, or so the argument goes.) Proponents of negative rights theory would look at all three groups and say each group is doing their best to escape moral law. Members of the

Net community demand a right of access, which means, "I want access to the Net without paying my fair share." The ISPs demand the right to be free from government oversight, which means, "I do not want anyone checking up on me because I want to do whatever I please, and I am afraid that your regulators just might catch me doing something immoral or illegal." Finally, the end users who claim that their right of access to unconventional, nonconformist, radical, and revolutionary views will be limited are really saying, "I want the to access whatever I want on the Net because I just might want to check up on my neighbor, buy tickets to a big game from a scalper, or look at pornography without anyone knowing." From this perspective, negative rights theory may just deserve a second look. Think about it.

right. Still others say that they follow the rules they learned in school, in their place of worship, or in their family setting. Some professions, businesses, and organizations develop guidelines, usually called rules of conduct or canons of professional responsibility. Such rules generally describe certain levels of behavior. Some behaviors are encouraged; others are discouraged. Punishments are often included in these guidelines.

Although such rules are admirable, they are often so long and complex that they end up covering pages of text that require an in-depth study just to understand the basics. A case in point involves the Ohio Rules of Professional Conduct for attorneys. The code consists of eight different subsections, each of which includes from 4 to 18 rules. Each rule is then followed by a series of official comments that review, explain, and clarify each of the rules and any amendments that have been made to those rules. In all, the Ohio Rules cover 207 pages of text. Moreover, and more to the point, such rules are aimed at professional conduct alone and often do not even address general moral conduct. Sometimes such codes even go so far as to excuse or ignore immoral conduct. For instance, Official Comment 2 following Rule 8.4 of the Ohio Rules covering the misconduct of an attorney, states that "matters of personal morality, such as adultery and comparable offenses . . . have no specific connection to fitness for the practice of law." Perhaps, most telling, is the fact that these rules frequently supply "loopholes" that permit people to escape culpability even when such culpability is obvious. Again, Official Comment 4 following Ohio Rule 8.4 states that "(a) lawyer may refuse to comply with an obligation imposed by law upon a good faith belief that no valid obligation exists." We can legitimately question the effectiveness of an obligation that can be avoided simply by manufacturing a "good faith belief that no valid obligation exists." The negative rights advocate would observe that the attorney is really saying, "I know what is ethically and legally correct here, but I'd rather do it my own way." Clearly, all of us need some other moral guide.

quick quiz 1-1

1. Natural law theory holds that there is no link between morality and law.	true | false
2. Law has nothing to do with civil management.	true | false
3. Ethical decisions are made in a variety of ways.	true | false

1-2 Ethical Theories

Throughout the history of philosophy, many scholars have offered techniques for determining those values that ought to guide all ethical decisions. Although these theories differ in their particulars, they all have one thing in common: Each theory is based on the assumption that people want to live ethical lives. If this were not the case, there would be no need to fashion these theories in the first place. Nevertheless, despite this common assumption, the theories differ greatly in their individual approaches to the problem of determining the nature of the values that underline ethical decision making. Our job here is to see that some of these theories work rather well, while others are less effective than we would prefer.

Market Value Ethics

Market value ethics uses quantification as the primary tool for determining value and, therefore, for determining whether an action is right or wrong. Having a market to gauge the price of goods, real estate, investment opportunities, and services is one thing; however, doing the same thing to the unquantifiable aspects of our lives is something else entirely. We have begun to quantify everything—art, education, human rights. Generally, most experts, economists, philosophers, theologians, politicians, and historians alike, refer to this concept as *neoliberalism*. **Neoliberalism** is defined by Jeff Faux, the founder and former president of the Economic Policy Institute and editor of *American Prospect*. Faux explains neoliberalism in his book, *The Global Class War*, in the following way:

> Neoliberalism is a vision of society in which competition for wealth is the only recognized value and virtually all social decisions are left to unregulated markets…. It is a world in which, in the words of a title to a 1996 book by Robert Kuttner, "everything [is] for sale."

Paul Treanor, the Dutch political philosopher and economist and author of *Neoliberalism: Origins, Theory, Definition*, says essentially the same thing when he writes, "Neoliberalism is not simply economic structure, it is a philosophy. This is most visible in attitudes to society, the individual, and employment. Neoliberals tend to see the world in terms of market metaphors." [See: Jeff Faux, *The Global Class War: How America's Bipartisan*

Elite Lost Our Future and What It Will Take to Win It Back (New York: Wiley, 2006), p. 5; Paul Treanor, *Neoliberalism: Origins, Theory, Definition*, http://www.web.inter.nl.net/users/Paul.Treanor/neoliberalism.html, 9 (accessed April 1, 2009).]

Neoliberalism as the New Ethical Relativism

All of this may seem quite harmless on the surface. After all what difference does it make if we rate both an automobile and an appendectomy with a monetary yardstick? The two must be rated somehow. Why not just use the market and let it go at that? In his book *What Money Can't Buy: The Moral Limits of Markets*, the noted philosopher and political scientist Michael Sandel argues that it makes a whole lot of difference. Without saying so directly, Sandel reveals that market value ethics, or neoliberalism if you will, is the new **ethical relativism**. Ethical relativism says that right and wrong have no intrinsic value but instead are determined by circumstance, situation, or even personal preference. Such a system results in a floating morality in which what is ethical for one person is not ethical for another, and so on. This attitude hides the fact that, as a society, we have already decided what is right and what is wrong and those two things are measured by the market valuation process.

Market Values and Injustice
Sandel warns that our tendency to evaluate everything based on money creates two insidious results. First, it promotes injustice, and second, it corrupts all other values. Injustice is clear enough. If we quantify everything, then those with more quantifiable assets win and those with fewer quantifiable assets lose and, as a result, the gap between these classes widens. (Note: This is classic Marxism, but it has also been picked up by Thomas Barnett in *The Pentagon's New Map*; Robert Kaplan in *Warrior Politics*; and Louis Bromfield in *A New Pattern for a Tired World*.) If the guy with the loot can buy a place at the front of the line at a ball game, he can also buy a place at the front of the line when a cure for cancer is found or when an antidote for a biological weapon is being distributed after a terror attack like 9/11. Most of us, if asked square on, would say that it is not fair for the rich to get first dibs on a cure for cancer, but, if we were the ones with the money, when that cure came out, we would jump to the front of the line arguing, probably with a straight face, "Hey, I earned the money. I can spend it any way I want. Too bad for the rest of you."

Market Values and Corruption
Worse than the injustice that emerges from market-based ethics is the corruption that results from an evaluation process based on money and money alone. How do we value parenthood when we can hire (buy?) a nanny to watch over our children? How do we value education when we can enroll in an online business law course and pay our roommate, who earned an "A" in the course last semester, to take our tests and write our papers? How do we value a gift when the gift is in the form of cash or, perhaps even more subtly, in the form of a "gift" card? How do we value an apology if the apology is written by someone else in a preprinted greetings card purchased off the rack at the local bookstore? Unfortunately, this slow process of corruption is muddied by several obstacles, and so we rarely see it in its true light. Like the frog that boils to death as it sits in water that is slowly heated, we do not notice the corrupting influence of the market. The first obstacle is the overwhelming power of the marketplace. Even when the market falters, fumbles, fails, and falls, most people still continue to place their faith in that marketplace and are willing to accept even the most severe consequences as long as they believe, whether it is true or not, that they can profit from the market's power. Everyone, it seems, believes that one day they will win the lottery.

The second reason is that the market, our main tool for measuring moral value, has no moral compass of its own. Monetary value by its very nature is based on buying and selling. I buy something if I have a need for that object or that service. Some things are valued because they are, in fact, needs—food, clothing, shelter, health care. What about the

THE OPENING CASE *Round 3*
Net Neutrality, Skyboxes, and the Corruption of America

Let's reconsider this last statement in light of the opening case at the beginning of this chapter. Recall that the new regulations proposed by the FCC have been condemned by members of the Net community as an offense to their right to freedom of press and freedom of speech. What gives value to those rights? The answer seems to be the market. The argument goes like this: Once the ISPs are empowered to give top-level service to some and not others, they will reward those with the money to pay and penalize those who cannot. This seems unjust, but only if you judge it from a nonmarket perspective. If the process is judged by the market itself, then freedom of speech and freedom of the press are measured by the market evaluation process. Let's recall that the ability to buy and sell determines value. Naturally, value is attached to those things we all require, medicine, a home, food and so on; however, does this valuation process relate to a basic human right, like freedom of speech? Free speech has no inherent monetary worth. So what gives it value? The market's only answer to this question is money. Money gives the press and free speech value. So if you can afford free speech, then you get it. If you cannot—too bad. That, in simple terms, is the morality of the marketplace.

rest? What about gourmet food, designer clothing, second homes in Florida, and elective cosmetic surgery? They have no intrinsic value. What makes them good? Is it morally correct to stock up on gourmet food, while your cousin lives on food stamps? Is it ethically proper to purchase that second home while your parents cannot afford a decent nursing home? The market's only approach to this issue reads like a day at the bank. Can you afford it? Can you get credit? Do you have collateral? Is your credit history up to it? The market is amoral, and if you can afford something or have the credit to purchase it—so be it. In this way, the market evaluation process degrades our basic human sensibilities while we, like the frog in the boiling water, do not even notice. [See: Michael Sandel, *What Money Can't Buy: The Moral Limits of the Market* (New York: Farrar, Straus, and Giroux, 2012).]

Social Contract Ethics

Clearly then the neoliberal, market value approach to making moral judgments is dangerous to our well-being. If you still do not believe it, just ask the frog. In contrast to the market-based evaluation process we have several alternatives: social contract ethics, utilitarianism, and rational ethics. **Social contract ethics** holds that right and wrong are measured by the obligations imposed on each individual by an implied agreement among all the people within a particular social system. Although social contract ethics has existed in one form or another for centuries, the English philosopher Thomas Hobbes is generally credited with formulating the modern version of the theory in his book *Leviathan* (1651). At the most fundamental level, Hobbes says that human beings have two core rights that cannot be sacrificed, traded, or relinquished in any way. Those two rights are (1) the right to live and (2) the right to live in peace and security. In order to protect those two rights, people enter a social contract under which they agree to limit all other "rights" and to establish a central governing authority whose job it is to protect those rights by establishing an orderly, safe, and secure governmental system. Hobbes prefers a monarchy because a monarchy provides not only the type of safe and secure system that he is looking for, but also the continuity guaranteed by a clear line of succession, something which oligarchies and dictatorships lack. [See: Thomas Hobbes, *Leviathan* (New York: Simon and Schuster, 1962); George Mace, *Locke, Hobbes, and the Federalist Papers: An Essay on the Genesis of the American Political Heritage* (Carbondale: Southern Illinois University Press, 1979).]

Shortcomings of Social Contract Ethics Naturally, for the social contract to work, most people must adhere to its rules, and those who do not must be punished. If this were not the case, then the social contract would disintegrate, and the society would return to a "state of nature" in which people must fend for themselves. The existence of the social contract permits people to live together in peace and harmony, but it does not permit anyone, not even the leader, to violate the core rights of life and security. Should a leader consistently violate core rights, then the people have a duty to demand that such oppressive and dangerous behavior end. For example, should a leader begin to arrest individuals indiscriminately, the people would have the duty to seek an end to that behavior, and if such behavior continued the people would have both

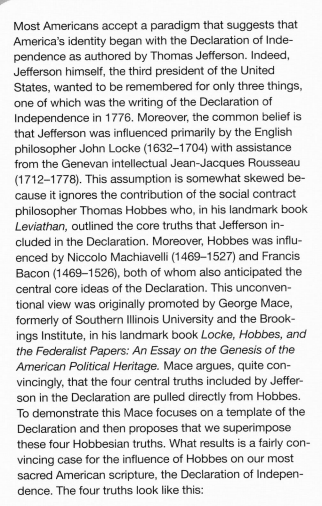

CLASSIC CASE   The Declaration of Independence

Most Americans accept a paradigm that suggests that America's identity began with the Declaration of Independence as authored by Thomas Jefferson. Indeed, Jefferson himself, the third president of the United States, wanted to be remembered for only three things, one of which was the writing of the Declaration of Independence in 1776. Moreover, the common belief is that Jefferson was influenced primarily by the English philosopher John Locke (1632–1704) with assistance from the Genevan intellectual Jean-Jacques Rousseau (1712–1778). This assumption is somewhat skewed because it ignores the contribution of the social contract philosopher Thomas Hobbes who, in his landmark book *Leviathan,* outlined the core truths that Jefferson included in the Declaration. Moreover, Hobbes was influenced by Niccolo Machiavelli (1469–1527) and Francis Bacon (1469–1526), both of whom also anticipated the central core ideas of the Declaration. This unconventional view was originally promoted by George Mace, formerly of Southern Illinois University and the Brookings Institute, in his landmark book *Locke, Hobbes, and the Federalist Papers: An Essay on the Genesis of the American Political Heritage.* Mace argues, quite convincingly, that the four central truths included by Jefferson in the Declaration are pulled directly from Hobbes. To demonstrate this Mace focuses on a template of the Declaration and then proposes that we superimpose these four Hobbesian truths. What results is a fairly convincing case for the influence of Hobbes on our most sacred American scripture, the Declaration of Independence. The four truths look like this:

1. Human beings in their natural state have a common human nature.

2. Human beings need a social contract to protect themselves from one another.

3. Social contracts must protect certain essential core rights.

4. Failing social contracts can be abolished.

The pertinent section of the Declaration looks like this:

> We hold these truths to be self-evident, that all men are created equal, that they are endowed by their Creator with certain unalienable Rights, that among these are Life, Liberty and the pursuit of Happiness. That to secure these rights, Governments are instituted among Men, deriving their just powers from the consent of the governed, That whenever any Form of Government becomes destructive of these ends, it is the Right of the People to alter or to abolish it, and to institute new Government, laying its foundation on such principles and organizing its powers in such form, as to them shall seem most likely to effect their Safety and Happiness.

What do you think? Point out where in the opening section of the Declaration we find the four central truths supported by the Machiavelli–Bacon–Hobbes triad. The same triad also influenced James Madison in the writing of the Bill of Rights. See the Classic Case feature in Chapter Two, "The Sources of the Law," for more details on this unusual interpretation of American scripture. [See: George Mace, *Locke, Hobbes, and the Federalist Papers: An Essay on the Genesis of the American Political Heritage* (Carbondale: Southern Illinois University Press, 1979).]

a right and a duty to alter or abolish that governmental system and replace it with another, more protective system.

Another problem is that social contract ethics is descriptive rather than prescriptive. A **descriptive theory** simply describes the values at work within a social system, rather than explaining how the values originated in the first place. In contrast, a **prescriptive theory** explains how to come up with the values that permit a society to run smoothly. Of course, not everyone believes that social contract ethics is descriptive only. Some ethical theorists argue that social contract ethics is a prescriptive ethics because it places a value on the obligation to protect life and security. Thus, the people benefit by knowing that others, including the sovereign himself or herself, will not violate those core rights. Social contract ethics, therefore, concentrates on each individual's obligation to everyone else and on the belief that, as long as these obligations are met, social stability will be preserved.

Utilitarianism

Utilitarianism is an ethical theory that says that the morality of an action is determined by its ultimate effects. The more good that results, the more ethical is the action. Conversely, the more bad that results, the less ethical is the action. Unlike market value ethics, which uses the amoral market as a way to determine value, and social contract ethics, which admits the social contract is inherently unstable, utilitarianism seeks only one permanent goal: the greatest good for the greatest number. Determining the greatest good for the greatest number, however, is not as simple as it sounds. For one thing, we must resist the temptation to transform the greatest good for the greatest number principle into the "greatest good for me" principle. One way to avoid mistakes that can result from an improper application of utilitarianism is to follow these steps:

1. The action to be evaluated should be stated in unemotional, general terms. For example, "stealing another person's property" is emotional language; "confiscating property for one's own use" is somewhat less emotional.
2. Every person or class of people that will be affected by the action must be identified.
3. Good and bad consequences in relation to those people affected must be considered.
4. All alternatives to the action stated in step 1 must be considered.
5. Once step 4 has been carried out, a conclusion must be reached. Whichever alternative creates the greatest good for the greatest number of people affected by the action is the one that ought to be taken.

Shortcomings of Utilitarianism
Despite its systematic approach to ethical questions, utilitarianism often fails to produce consistent moral judgments. This failure results from a tendency to confuse utilitarianism with **utility thinking**. Like its cousin neoliberalism, utility thinking fails because it relies on market values to make moral judgments. This tendency corrupts the essential elements of utilitarianism. If neoliberal utility thinking is used rather than pure utilitarianism then the concept of the "greatest good" becomes defined in terms of the market (good = more money; greatest good = the most money) and the element of the greatest number becomes the greatest number of those who receive a monetary benefit from the activity being scrutinized (greatest number = the greatest amount of money for the greatest number of people affected by the activity under scrutiny). Recall that one of the most serious of negative effects of neoliberal thought is the corruption of those nonmarket activities that are treated as if they were market activities. One such nonmarket activity is sports. Example 1-2 provides a vivid contemporary example of this corruption in action.

EXAMPLE 1-2: Drugs and Sports: A 21st Century Prisoner's Dilemma

Theoretically, taking drugs in competitive sports should be a thing of the past. Yet it persists. The question then is why? Why does such clearly unethical behavior continue almost unabated? The answer may be that the behavior is not as clearly unethical to many athletes as it is to the public at large. To athletes the situation looks like this. The athletes, say cyclists in the Tour de France, know that they should not use performance-enhancing drugs. They know that the sensible course of action is to avoid drugs. Yet each athlete knows that all the other athletes will take drugs and so, each athlete either takes drugs or loses. In theory, random testing should stop this practice, but it does not. The other alternative would be to test everyone in a universal testing process. Yet this almost never happens. Why not? Enter, Berno Buechel and his associates at the University of Hamburg who have used a mathematical process called game theory to solve the riddle. The solution according to Buechel lays in the "x" factor, in this case, the fans and the sponsors. The fans and the sponsors want to watch clean athletes, but they also want to watch a good contest. Universal testing would give them clean athletes but an unexciting contest. Random testing gives them an exciting contest and the illusion of clean athletes and that seems to be enough. But is this strategy ethical? If we apply utilitarianism to this dilemma, we seem to get a clear answer. The greatest good for the greatest number (athletes, governing bodies, fans, and sponsors) is to offer random testing that produces the rare wrongdoer, and creates the illusion of a level playing field and a fair sport. Random testing gives the impression of regulation and the fans keep their imaginary pure sport. The sponsors continue to pour money into the sport and most of the players continue to play, sometimes to win, and to often earn corporate endorsements. The greatest good for the greatest number has been achieved. Or has it? [See: "Doping in Sport: Athlete's Dilemma," *The Economist*, July 20, 2013, p. 71; "Sport: Testing times," *The Economist*, July 20, 2013, p. 12.]

Let's look at Example 1-2, "Drugs and Sports: A 21st Century Prisoner's Dilemma," a bit more closely. The greatest good for the greatest number appears to have been achieved. Random testing appears to work. The fans have their sport and their "champions." The sponsors have great advertising and marketing exposure, and the athletes continue to play, sometimes to win, and often to grab lucrative corporate sponsorships; however, something is wrong. The result simply does not feel right. Moreover, it should not feel right because the example misapplies utilitarianism. This misapplication lies at two levels: (1) The definition of "the greatest good," and (2) the concept of "the greatest number." Both have been seriously distorted by the neoliberal need to quantify everything including nonmarket activities.

First, in Example 1-2, utility thinking defines the greatest good in terms of financial and commercial success—sponsorships, award money, advertising dollars, endorsements, and so on. If we reject neoliberal thought and instead focus on pure utilitarianism, we would choose a nonmarket-related "good," such as the promotion of truth or the preservation of justice. With a new focus on truth and justice we get a different result. The random testing is both untruthful and unjust and, therefore, wrong. Second, if we define the "greatest number" in terms of the entire society, we also get a different result. The greatest good for all society cannot be measured in the amount of money earned by the athletes, spent by the fans, or invested by the sponsors. On the contrary, the greatest good lies within an unquantifiable arena, that is, in the arena of truth and justice for all members of our social structure. To promote honesty and justice in one area can affect all other areas of the social structure, leading to a truthful and just society for the true greatest number, that is, the entire social system.

Rational Ethics

Rational ethics replaces the value-laden approach of market value ethics, the prescriptive approach of social contract theory, and the result-oriented standard of utilitarianism with a system that is arguably objective, logical, and relatively consistent. Although forms of rational ethics were known in pre-Enlightenment times, the German philosopher Immanuel Kant is customarily recognized as having constructed the theory in several books including especially *Groundwork of the Metaphysics of Morals* (1785). **Rational ethics** is a philosophical theory that says ethical values can be determined by a proper application of human reason. The theory assumes, and rightfully so, that, because all human beings are rational, all human beings ought to have the same ethical values. Therefore, rational ethics ought to establish universal rules of behavior that apply to all people at all times. For this reason, rational ethics is often referred to as *objective ethics*.

As rational beings, people think for themselves and, in doing so, recognize their own self-worth as individuals. Along with self-worth comes a belief in certain rights. These rights include the right to life and the right to security. Rational beings recognize that they do not want to be killed or endangered. Thus, each individual has a duty to refrain from violating the rights of all other human beings. As rational beings, people also realize that it is logical to establish rules that support the continued existence of society. A rule that destroys a society that tries to follow it would be an illogical rule. Consider the following rule: "Kill people who annoy you." A person who adheres to rational ethics would instantly recognize that such a rule is both illogical and immoral. If everyone in a society were to adopt such a rule, that society would collapse because everyone annoys someone at some time.

Shortcomings of Rational Ethics Even though rational ethics appears to be almost foolproof on the surface, it is not without its difficulties. One difficulty lies within what are referred to as penumbra rights. **Penumbra rights** are those that are found in those indeterminate or indistinct shadow areas associated with more uniformly accepted rights, such as the right to a safe and secure life. Thus, while it is clear that people have an unalienable right to a secure life, it is not quite as clear that they, therefore, have the right to arm themselves. The right to bear arms, then, is one those penumbra rights that is found within the shadow of the right to a secure life. Similarly, while it is clear that security is a core right, it is not as clear that security includes a secure reputation that is free from defamatory attacks orchestrated by other people in the media. Such penumbra rights must be interpreted by experts, most of which are found in the court system operating as judges, mediators, and magistrates. Another difficulty with rational ethics is that it does not always consider the shadowy nuances of everyday life. Rational ethics demands a clean and orderly universe wherein words, beliefs, and actions are the same for everyone. That does not always happen, as the accompanying example illustrates.

EXAMPLE **1-3:** Lies and Politics: One State's Solution

The Ohio General Assembly, in an admirable if somewhat quixotic attempt to return a level of dignity to politics, made lying in political campaigns a crime. More specifically, Ohio Revised Code Section 3517.22 made it a criminal offense to "[p]ost, publish, circulate, distribute, or otherwise disseminate a false statement concerning a candidate, either knowing the same to be false or with reckless disregard for whether it was false or not, if the statement is designed to promote the election, nomination, or defeat of the candidate." The law was challenged by Susan B. Anthony List (SBAL), an advocacy group that wanted to erect a billboard that identified a state representative as having voted for federally funded abortions. The representative complained to the Ohio Elections Commission arguing that, since he had never voted for federally funded abortions, the billboard would be broadcasting a lie. In reaction, the billboard company decided that it would simply not erect the troublesome sign. The SBLA believed that its right to freedom of speech had been violated, and the representative believed that his right to a safe and secure reputation had also been violated. It is at this point that rational ethics has a problem. *Rational ethics* clearly declares that it is logical to establish rules that support the continued existence of society. That much is clear; however, in this case, we have conflicting rules. On the one hand, a rule that says people must have free speech in a political debate is quite logical, while on the other hand, a rule that demands that people always tell the truth in political campaigns is also quite logical. The problem is that, in this case, as in many others, the *truth* of the matter is not clear. Under the act, insurers cannot use federal money to pay for abortions directly and so the representative is correct. He did not vote for federally funded abortions; however, the act does support the use of federal dollars to pay for abortion-inclusive insurance coverage. So the advocacy group is also correct because, through an accounting strategy, federal money indirectly enables abortions. The difficulty with the precise and logical nature of rational ethics is that real life is not always that precise and logical. [See: *Susan B. Anthony List, et al., Petitioners v. Steven Driehaus, et al.*, (No. 13-193) United States Court of Appeal for the Sixth Circuit (2013).]

Notwithstanding the logical structure of rational ethics, many people are uneasy with some of its apparently incomplete parameters. As we saw in the example, one of the really difficult elements of rational ethics is that its practitioners simply assume that all concepts, terms, and ideas will have universal meaning. Thus, when Kant, for example, says that we must always tell the truth, he assumes that all things have a universally recognized meaning that is unquestionable. While such a belief works much of the time, it still falls quite short of being a consistently normative principle. If that were not the case, then we would not have the problem outlined in *Susan B. Anthony List v. Driehaus.*

quick quiz 1-2

1. Utilitarianism focuses on the consequences of an action.   true | false

2. Rational ethics is a form of ethical relativism.   true | false

3. Utilitarianism and rational ethics always reach the same moral conclusion.   true | false

1-3 Ethics and the Government

If you have concluded that determining an ethical value system is difficult, then you have clearly been reading quite closely, and you have an unobstructed view of the problems associated with ethical decision making. Unfortunately, once we apply the same process to the government, matters become even more opaque. To see this, let's start with a few basics. The government runs the nation and, on the international scene, nations run the world. This simple reality emerges because nations possess territory, raise money through taxation, police their borders, protect their people, and if necessary, use force in a legiti-mate and responsible way. The government of a nation has two objectives that simultane-ously justify its power and enable the proper exercise of that power. Those two objectives are (1) to protect its own existence, and (2) to protect the lives, health, and well-being of its own citizens. Both of these responsibilities must be carried out in an ethical way. While this sounds like a simple and straightforward mandate, it is not. Government actions re-quire a dyadic sense of responsibility that is often quite confusing to those officials who must act accordingly.

A Governmental and Ethical Dyad

Most people assume, and with good reason, that a single level of morality governs the behavior of both civilians and leaders. In an essay titled, "Politics as a Vocation," Max Weber suggests that this view is flawed. Weber argues, instead, that a **dyad** or a two-level system of morality exists, represented by the **ethic of ultimate ends** for individuals and an **ethic of responsibility** for national leaders. The ethic of ultimate ends must be practiced by individuals because individuals can never completely foresee "the ultimate ends" of their actions. Therefore, individuals must obey absolute moral precepts, such as "turn the other cheek" despite the fact that the ultimate consequences of those actions are unclear or uncomfortable. From this perspective, we can see why the ethic of ultimate ends is also often referred to as the ethic of benevolence.

On the other hand, the ethic of responsibility demands that the moral actor, in this case a national leader, must consider his or her responsibilities to those people who depend on that leader for safety and security. So, for example, if a neighboring nation is belligerent, aggressive, or determined to fight ancient cultural, religious, and ethnic wars, the leaders of the first nation cannot ignore that threat, as much as they might want to. In short, they are not permitted to "turn the other cheek" because to do so would endanger the innocent people they have the duty to protect. Unfortunately, many national leaders fail to see this distinction. The leaders of the United States have been especially guilty of this shortsight-edness. [See: Max Weber, "Politics as a Vocation," in *The Great Political Theories: From the French Revolution to Modern Times,* eds. Michael Curtis (New York: Harper, 2008), pp. 426–436).]

Shortcomings of the Ethical Dyad

The primary shortcoming of the ethical dyad is not the ethic itself, but the difficulty that leaders have executing one level of that ethic—the ethic of responsibility. Moreover, this is not a minor error. In a study titled *A New Pattern for a Tired World,* the essayist Louis Bromfield develops an argument that echoes the approach suggested by Weber. In doing so, Bromfield focuses on the United States, maintaining that American leaders have mis-handled their basic responsibilities by focusing on what Bromfield calls "world responsi-bility" rather than national responsibility. What results, ironically enough, is a pattern of irresponsibility. American leaders try to help other nations as they might try to reform the poor in their local neighborhood, by giving every homeless person a handout but helping none of them get a job. In international terms Bromfield says this means momentarily res-cuing failing nations by transferring billions into their treasuries, but never dealing with the actual cause of the problem. This level of ineptitude on the part of the Americans may be understandable since the United States was ill prepared for world leadership when it assumed that role in 1918. Understandable, however, is not the same as defensible. Bromfield argues that to be truly responsible, leaders must adopt a far-reaching vision that measures what is best for the nation's citizens in terms of what is best for the economic stability of the world. Ironically, this requires disengagement from the world and a focus on the economic and civic health of the United States.

Bromfield argues that the United States, Europe, Russia, China, Japan, and India must develop economic alliances with those nations closest to them, geographically and culturally. Economic alliances are crucial to global stability because, when people are fed, clothed, housed, and healthy, they do not resort to violence. Bromfield's economic alliances would look like this: The United States would join with Canada, Mexico, and other nations in the Western Hemisphere; Russia, China, and Japan would unite; the European nations would join with one another; and India would join with Pakistan (and probably with Australia and New Zealand). Once these alliances were economically healthy, they would trade with the other members in their own bloc, until they institute a network of trust. The four major economic blocs would then form trade agreements among themselves and later with smaller nations, offering help only to those nations that request assistance. This would be an effective exercise in the ethic of responsibility, first in relation to their people, and, second, in relation to the rest of the world. Bromfield goes so far as to predict a unified world economy in the far future, as long as national leaders act responsibly. He does not use the word *globalization*, but he might was well have. [See: Louis Bromfield, *A New Pattern for a Tired World* (New York: Harper, 1954).]

EXAMPLE 1-4: The Ethical Dyad in Action: Russia and China

On the surface, the 2014 energy agreement between Russia and China looks like an ordinary contract, bargained for by two sides with much to gain from dealing with one another peacefully. Moreover, and more to the point here, the deal validates Weber's ethic of responsibility and Bromfield's new global pattern. The contract is between two major global powers, Russia and China. Russia has natural gas to sell and needs a new customer willing to pay more than lowest market value. China needs the gas. On another level, this is the beginning of an alliance that may very well be the first step in Bromfield's new global pattern. Both nations have acted according to the second half of Weber's ethical dyad—the ethic of responsibility. The ethic of responsibility demands that national leaders, in this case Vladimir Putin of Russia and Xi Jinping of China, focus, first and foremost, on the duty to protect their own people. Both Putin and Xi have done just that. At the time of this contract, the Russian economy was rushing toward a recession and Putin's aggressive attitude toward the Ukraine threatened to damage Russia's relationship with its biggest customer, the European Union. Russia needed a new customer. China filled the bill. China, on the other a hand, needed to diversify its energy imports. Its consumption of energy had grown exponentially over the previous two decades, forcing it to make deals with nations that were dangerously unfriendly, unstable, and undeveloped. China needed Russia's natural gas. Thus, to fulfill the ethic of responsibility, the two nations agreed to deal with one another. Especially significant is that the agreement between Russia and China reflects the type of agreement that Bromfield supports in his book, *A New Pattern for a Tired World*, as the next step in global development. According to Bromfield, economic alliances, such as the one recounted here, are vital to international security because, when people are no longer hungry, homeless, and unemployed, they do not seek revolution. Moreover, Bromfield suggests that one such alliance should involve Russian, China, and Japan. It would seem that Russia and China, at least at the moment, agree. [See: Jane Perlez, "Russia and China Finally Complete 30-Year Gas Deal," *The New York Times*, May 22, 2014, pp. A-1, A-10; Clifford Krauss and Keith Bradsher, "China's Global Search for Energy: As Its Consumption Rises, A Nation Dominates Markets," *The New York Times*, May 22, 2014, pp. B-1, B-8.]

The Threat of the Global Skybox

Despite the Russian and Chinese fulfillment of Bromfield and Weber's predictions, something is wrong with the ethical dyad or at least Bromfield's contribution to it. Bromfield suggests that international decision making be based on economic motivations. His position would reduce most (all?) international decisions to market-based, value-driven decisions, aimed at preserving international peace through trade and through commerce—period. There is certainly much logic to the notion that many international problems can be solved by creating economic alliances; however, there may also be a small but significant flaw in Bromfield's thinking. The success of Bromfield's plan depends upon the benevolence of the rich nations; however, the basic rule of Weber's ethical dyad is that leaders must not think benevolently but must, instead, think in terms of national responsibility. The danger is that, as the gap between the rich and poor nations grows, the rich may no longer feel it is in their national best interests to invite the poor nations to Bromfield's rich regional alliances; therefore, the gap between the rich and poor may soon become impassable. Thus, the Bromfield alliances may not lead to the global cooperation he envisions but, instead, to the global equivalent of a dual class system—the rich law-abiding nations and the lawless proletarian rogues. None of this would be all that troublesome to those of us in the skyboxes were it not for Bromfield's other premise—that people who are hungry, homeless, sick, and poor have nothing to lose by using violence. Even this would not be all that troubling were it not for the fact that, in the modern, wireless world of global interconnectedness, asymmetrical warfare makes even the richest nation vulnerable to attack from agents of cyber terror, chemical and biological warfare, and nuclear weapons.

quick quiz 1-3

1. Weber supports the idea of a dyadic or two-level system of morality in government.	true	false
2. The main shortcoming of the ethical dyad is that leaders cannot execute the ethic of responsibility.	true	false
3. Bromfield suggests that the major powers develop military alliances.	true	false

1-4 Social Responsibility in the Corporate Sector

Corporations carry a great deal of influence over the economy, the community, and the people. There are those who say that a corporation has no social responsibility beyond making a profit for its shareholders. This is, in fact, the traditional view of corporate responsibility. It is a view that has remained so ingrained in our system that, until recently, it was the only view built into statutory and common law. Recently, however, voices have been raised arguing that corporations have a high degree of social responsibility to those people affected by their decisions.

The Traditional Corporate Culture

Although all businesses affect the economy and the community, the greatest force in the American industrial state is the corporation, in general, and the multinational corporation, in particular. The reality of corporate power is revealed by the fact that philosophers on both ends of the political spectrum can point to the corporation as a guiding force in modern civilization. For instance, in his treatise, *Individualism Old and New,* the *pragmatic* American philosopher, John Dewey, notes, "The United States has steadily moved from an earlier pioneer individualism to a condition of corporate dominance." Similarly, the *theoretical* philosopher Herbert Marcuse once remarked that no one, not even the former enemies of capitalism, can escape the influence of corporate power. In fact, Marcuse goes so far as to say that in the modern global marketplace, "the socialist and communist systems are linked with capitalism." [See: John Dewey, *Individualism: Old and New* (New York: Capricorn Books, 1962); Herbert Marcuse, *Five Lectures: Psychoanalysis, Politics, and Utopia,* trans. Jeremy J. Shapiro and Shierry M. Weber (Boston: Beacon Press, 1970).]

One reason that corporations have such power is that they are legal persons, created under the authority of federal and state statutes. This status as a "legal person" gives the corporation certain rights and abilities that other business entities do not always have. For instance, as legal persons they are accorded certain constitutional rights, such as the right not to be deprived of property without due process of law. They can also own property in their own name and have lawsuits filed to protect them or vindicate their rights. There are, of course, many types of corporations. Our focus will be on those corporations that are privately run to make a profit for their owners, who are referred to as shareholders. The traditional view says that privately owned corporations are created solely to make a profit for their shareholders. Consequently, the foremost job of any manager is to maximize those profits. In fact, under the traditional rule of shareholder dominance, the managers of a corporation could be held liable in a court of law for making decisions that do not guarantee that the shareholders would receive a maximum return on their investment.

As defined previously, the type of thinking promoted by the court in Example 1-5 is referred to as utility thinking or cost–benefit thinking. Using utility thinking, a corporate manager simply looks at the action he or she is about to take and asks whether the benefit to the shareholders will outweigh the cost to the corporation. If the shareholders' benefits offset corporate costs, then the action is taken. If not, the action is abandoned. Proponents of this position justify cost–benefit thinking in three ways. First, the profits to the shareholders must always come first. Second, it would be unfair to divert funds that belong to the shareholders to activities that do not directly benefit the shareholders. Third, a corporation's managers are accountable to the shareholders and to no one else. The problem with utility thinking is that it often results in actions that are clearly unethical and potentially illegal.

EXAMPLE 1-5: Corporate Culture and Utility Thinking

When Lynn Cummings discovered that the managers of a corporation in which she owned stock had made a decision that had caused shareholders to lose money in a merger plan, she sued, seeking a reversal of the merger or a suitable payment from the managers that would make up for her losses. Basically, Cummings second-guessed the way that the managers had made their decision, arguing that they had not properly researched the merger and had not placed the shareholders' profits first. The managers argued that they had made their decision based on the long-term benefits of the merger to everyone involved, including the local community and the economy of the nation and state. The court sided with Cummings, noting that the job of the managers was to look out for the shareholders' profits, not the long-term benefits to the community or the economy.

EXAMPLE 1-6: Maximum Corporate Irresponsibility

The managers of Taylor-Beechaum Pharmaceuticals, Inc., received a report that the corporation's latest weight-loss drug, biomiocin, was having unpredicted side effects that caused problems for several people. The managers of Taylor-Beechaum ordered the accounting department to determine how much it would cost to recall all the biomiocin now on the market, suspend manufacturing, and conduct more tests on the drug's safety. The accountants reported that it would be more cost effective to simply leave the drug on the market and pay off anyone who might be injured and who might bring a lawsuit against Taylor-Beechaum. Keeping the drug on the shelves would allow the corporation to continue to pay dividends to the shareholders. In contrast, if the drug were taken off of the market, the payment of dividends would be suspended pending the outcome of the new testing program. Consequently, the corporate managers decided to leave biomiocin on the shelves. This decision not only violated virtually every ethical standard that we've studied thus far (except ethical relativism) but also evaded the corporation's social responsibility to consumers, to the government, to the shareholders, and to the public at large.

Reasons for Social Responsibility

The fact that corporate officers and directors have made such irresponsible decisions should not be surprising. Nor should it be surprising that, until recently, the law supported such decisions. The idea that a corporation is a legal person did not spring full grown into the law when the first corporations were formed. In fact, it took jurists quite some time to see that corporations were neither partnerships nor miniature democratic states but instead vehicles for making a profit. Once jurists recognized the unique position that corporations hold within the hierarchy of business associations, however, they easily granted certain privileges to corporate entities. Despite this, as the jurists entered the modern age, they began to see that there were a number of reasons that corporations, like Taylor-Beechaum in Example 1-6, should accept social responsibility for their actions. Some of these reasons are built on the legal advantages granted to corporations. Others are based on the idea that many corporations are powerful forces in their communities. Still others focus on the self-interest of the corporation. Whatever the case, these arguments are being voiced more loudly and with more conviction with each passing fiscal year.

Legal Advantages Granted to the Corporation
The first argument supporting corporate social responsibility is based on the premise that corporations are granted certain rights as a result of the incorporation process. For example, the corporate form offers limited liability to those who share in its ownership. This means that the personal assets of the corporate owners cannot be taken if the corporation defaults on a contract or commits a tort or a crime. In addition, under provisions of most incorporation statutes, a corporation is considered an artificially created person. This means that, under provisions of the U.S. Constitution and those of most state constitutions, a corporation, like a natural person, cannot be deprived of life, liberty, or property without due process of law. This also means that a corporation can own property in its own name and bring a lawsuit to vindicate its rights. Because corporations have all these rights, they owe an obligation to the public and to the community at large to act responsibly. In practical terms, this means that the decisions of corporate managers must not be narrowly focused on the profits of the shareholders.

As part of a downsizing campaign, the Andrean-Harrison Corporation was about to close operations in Tulsa. The company owned an office building and a small laboratory on the outskirts of Tulsa that are adjacent to 30 acres of undeveloped land. The corporation had a chance to sell the land at a price that would have made a profit for the shareholders of the company. Rather than take advantage of this offer, Andrean-Harrison decided to donate the land to the city. The fact that the corporation was a legal person meant that it owned the land and could donate it to the city. Corporate officials acted responsibly in this case, taking advantage of the corporation's right to own land in its own name.

The Impact of Corporate Decision Making A second reason for demanding social responsibility from corporations is that corporate decision making clearly has an impact on more people than just the shareholders and the managers. Those who support corporate social responsibility often argue that many corporate decisions, such as whether to open or close a factory, will affect everyone in the local community. Those affected by such decisions include suppliers, consumers, employees, support businesses, and community members. Consequently, the argument goes, all of these groups should be taken into consideration when corporate managers make decisions. Some individuals who support this form of extreme corporate social responsibility would like to see representatives from the employees' union, from consumer protection groups, from environmental protection groups, and from the local chamber of commerce on every corporation's board of directors. Others, however, argue that because corporate decisions affect more individuals and groups than just the shareholders and managers, those decisions should be made by an impartial group of corporate outsiders. Often the corporate outsiders named are governmental officials.

When the directors of Igar International Corporation were working on plans to diversify their operation, they considered opening a chemical plant in Santa Ana. Before making the decision, they sent a team of experts to Santa Ana to investigate the possibility of establishing an operation just within the city limits. Although the city officials promised Igar a tax abatement and agreed to donate several acres of land to the corporation, citizens' groups were against the plant because of environmental and health concerns. The corporation could have simply found a more receptive or, perhaps, a less vocal city in which to locate; however, instead of simply discarding their consideration of Santa Ana, they worked with the citizens' groups to meet their concerns. Ultimately the two sides agreed on modifications to the project and moved forward. The willingness of the company to discuss the proposed changes in its operation reflected an understanding of the corporation's social responsibility based on the fact that corporate decisions have a far-ranging impact.

Enlightened Corporate Self-Interest Finally, there are those who argue, rather convincingly, that accepting social responsibility is actually in the long-term best interests of the corporation. This argument, which is generally referred to as enlightened self-interest, is based on the notion that socially responsible corporations benefit by creating goodwill for themselves, thus motivating consumers to purchase their products, investors to buy their stock, and lawmakers to grant them further legal advantages. In addition, the corporation benefits because the community at large gains from such decisions. If the community at large is healthy, the argument goes, then the corporation that relies on that community will be healthy also.

EXAMPLE 1-9: Failed Negotiations Lead to Problems

The president of Pilder and Wesselkamper International, Inc., decided to suspend negotiations with union representatives when he learned that they were about to demand a salary increase that he believed was untenable given the corporation's financial health, or lack thereof. The union threatened to file a complaint with the National Labor Relations Board, charging that the president and his staff were not cooperating with the collective bargaining process. The union also indicated that it was considering publishing an advertisement in *The New York Times* denouncing the president's decision and eventually would authorize a strike. The president continued to resist further negotiations and simply shut down operations. Eventually, the company filed for bankruptcy and dissolved its operation. Neither of the parties involved in this case opted to pursue a course of enlightened self-interest, which resulted in the worst possible conclusion for all those involved.

Efforts to Promote Social Responsibility

As noted previously, the traditional view of a corporation says that its primary role is to make a profit for its shareholders. This means that corporate managers are obligated to make decisions that maximize those profits. Moreover, under the traditional role of corporate managers, those managers could be sued for making a decision that hurt the corporation's profits and thereby reduced or eliminated dividends; however, recent amendments to many corporate statutes have been designed to encourage corporate managers to make broader-based decisions. Thus, some statutes now permit managers to consider factors beyond profit in making corporate decisions. These factors include the economic well-being of the nation, the state, and the local community; the interests of employees, consumers, and suppliers; and the betterment of the environment, the economy, and the overall social structure. These statutes generally hold managers immune from shareholder lawsuits, which claim that the managers did not put the shareholders' profits first.

EXAMPLE 1-10: Corporate Trade-Offs Mean Corporate Survival

The directors of Chindi-Mowry Enterprises, Inc., were under fire because of a takeover bid against Chindi-Mowry engineered by an alien corporation known as Rixensart Industries. To stave off the assault, the directors invited a friendly bid from Sandoff, Inc., a firm that promised not to dismantle Chindi-Mowry after the deal was entered. The final amount of the offer from Sandoff was less than that offered by Rixensart, and so those shareholders who sold their stock received less on the sale to Sandoff than they would have received had the directors endorsed the Rixensart plan; however, in making their decision, the directors were persuaded that the deal offered by Sandoff would save jobs, help the community, boost the national and state economy, and eventually result in a long-term gain for the corporation and for those shareholders who remained with the company.

quick quiz 1-4

1. Cost–benefit thinking will always result in ethical decisions.   true | false

2. Corporations are not allowed to own property.   true | false

3. Some statutes allow corporate managers to consider factors   true | false
   beyond shareholder profits in making business decisions.

1-5 The Relationship between Law and Ethics

Thus far, we have seen that ethics and morals can be distinguished from one another. We have defined values, examined the causes of unethical conduct, and determined how to develop an ethical lifestyle. Some people determine an ethical lifestyle as simply doing what is legal. Such a course of action may often result in ethical conduct; however, that is not always the case. Even when most people know that a particular type of conduct is illegal, that does not prevent some people from engaging in that conduct. For example, everyone knows that killing is illegal. Yet that knowledge does not stop the national murder rate from remaining disturbingly high. Similarly, everyone knows that child abuse, spousal abuse, and elder abuse are immoral, but that consensus has not eliminated the problem of abuse from our society.

The Need for Law in Our Society

The law is needed because, though people know better, they do not always follow ethical principles. As noted previously, the law consists of rules of conduct established by the government of a society to maintain harmony, stability, and justice in that society. It does so by defining the legal rights and duties of the people. It also provides a way to protect the people by enforcing these rights and duties through the courts and the legislature. Ethical principles can tell us what is right, but they cannot stop us from doing that which is wrong. The law also cannot stop us from doing wrong; however, the law can punish us if we choose to do wrong. The law draws the line between permissible and impermissible conduct, so that people, at the very least, are punished if they hurt or cheat one another or threaten society as a whole.

Of course the law also has other functions. For instance, the law serves as the ultimate rule maker, providing a sense of stability and harmony when order breaks down in any other area of society, from our schools and universities to the family itself. This is why each state has established a system of juvenile courts and a network of domestic relations courts to handle such disputes when they arise. The law also promotes economic growth by granting tax abatements, by rezoning certain urban areas for the establishment of stores and businesses, and by exercising the power of *eminent domain* to confiscate privately owned land for community purposes. In addition, the law guards property rights by enforcing contracts and other similar agreements and providing a forum for tort victims and their families. The law also protects the environment by regulating those industries that might overdevelop the land and those that dump waste materials and other pollutants on to the land and into the waterways. Finally, as noted, the law is responsible for advancing social justice and guaranteeing personal freedom by granting all people due process and equal protection and providing a system by which legitimate grievances can be resolved in an orderly and timely fashion.

Ethical and Legal Anarchy

Is the law perfect? Does the law always succeed in its goals and objectives? Certainly not. As is true of all institutions, the law is flawed. It is filled with loopholes, foolishness, red tape, and, at times, absolute idiocy, much of which is unintentional and most of which could be avoided if people just take the time to think coolly and rationally. For example, it makes very little sense for Congress to pass legislation to punish flag burners when it is quite clear that the Supreme Court will declare that legislation unconstitutional. Or, in a similar vein, it makes no sense for Congress to pass unfunded mandates that force the state governments to raise money to perform tasks that the federal government should have taken care of in the first place. Yet this type of thing happens all of the time. Nevertheless, having an imperfect but functioning legal system *is always preferable* to the alternative—anarchy.

THE OPENING CASE *Round 4, The Final Round*
Net Neutrality, Skyboxes, and the Corruption of America

Let's look at this chapter's opening case one more time. Recall that the problem in the opening case involved an order from the FCC that empowers ISPs to create a multilayered system of consumers, with those capable of paying a lot at the top of the order, and thus enjoying fast, uninterrupted service, while the rest of us, the new subproletariat as it were, will run in the slow lane. One argument used by those who oppose the FCC's proposed order states that, using market values to measure activities outside the market is unfair because those with the money always have a clear and unbeatable advantage over the rest of us. On the other hand, those who favor market value measurement claim there is no better way to place a value on unmeasurable things (sports, art, philosophy, hugs, days at the beach, friendship, forgiveness, remembering someone's birthday), and so market values might as well be used to simplify things. But is this true? Is there no better way? Kropotkin believes so. He contends that non-money-driven social units have a better chance of survival than money-driven units because the non-moneyed units promote justice. In contrast, money-driven societies will always sidestep or marginalize justice; however, marginalizing justice, Kropotkin says, lasts only so long and then the victims of that injustice will rise in revolution, the goal of which will be to abolish that unjust system. (If all of this sounds familiar you might want to look at "The Classic Case" in this chapter and read the Declaration of Independence one more time.) Such flashes of anarchy are filled with peril because at such moments people risk their lives and their livelihoods. In fact, the entire society may be at risk (the American Revolution comes to mind here). If a society that suffers through that period of anarchy learns from the experience, that society may (will?) create a new social system that demands justice. In such a system, a different central value, referred to as *appretiare,* will replace market-driven money-oriented values. Appretiare (which has the same root as *appreciate*) is based on a single commandment, "Do to others as you would have it done to you in like case." Under a system based upon *appretiare,* self-worth comes not from material wealth but from the respect that others have for those individuals who do their job and do it well. If you think that no such societies exist—you are wrong. You are sitting in the middle of one right now—academia—where students compete for letters (A and B) or numbers (4.0 and 3.5, and so on) with no intrinsic monetary value, where teachers vie for titles of honor (assistant professor, associate professor) often with no corresponding salary increase, and where researchers scramble to have articles published in journals that pay them zero! What are they all looking for? Simple—they are competing for the respect that comes from others who believe that they have done their job and done it well. Think about it. [See: P. Eltzbacher, "Kropotkin's Teachings," *The Great Anarchists: Ideas and Teachings of Seven Major Thinkers* (Dover, New York, 1908), pp. 144–71); Michael Sandel, *What Money Can't Buy: The Moral Limits of the Market* (New York: Farrar, Straus, and Giroux, 2012).]

Or is it? Is having an imperfect but functioning legal system always preferable to the alternative—anarchy? Not everyone thinks that way. In fact, the Russian intellectual Peter Kropotkin has a different take on the entire situation. Kropotkin believes that, in a utopian society, ethics and the law would always coincide. Kropotkin, along with Jean Jacques Rousseau, argues that society is dysfunctional because it ignores the fact that human nature is not competitive, as Hobbes and Madison contest, but is, instead, cooperative. They also believe that a little anarchy now and again is useful, despite the horrors that often result in such a state, but only when what emerges from that period of anarchy is a system blessed by legal and ethical harmony. To explain this further, Kropotkin introduces two human forces: (1) energy and (2) justice. Energy is found in a society that manages to redirect the collective human will toward the welfare of the entire species, instead of toward individual or corporate survival measured only by monetary gain. Justice is present when all people are treated equally based on some intangible quality that has nothing to do with money. As we have seen repeatedly in our examination of the ethical theories, the difficult task is finding that intangible measuring stick.

Of course, Kropotkin's ethical and legal system based on **appretiare** is not without cost, and so sometimes operating an imperfect but functioning legal system is preferable to anarchy. Nor is Kropotkin's system without practical difficulties. His socioeconomic theory suffers from an inadequate, or at least unsatisfying, explanation of the mechanism by which the human race promotes cooperation over competition and establishes appretiare. Unlike Aldous Huxley who, in *Brave New World*, provides the reader with a genetically grounded and behavioral-based process for reprograming human nature, Kropotkin assumes that humans will, on their own, rediscover their inherent tendency to cooperate with and to respect one another finding it preferable to both anarchy and the market-based system. Given the fact that Kropotkin and others like him (Rousseau comes to mind) lack a practical venue, we will now turn to a more pragmatic, hands-on approach to the topic, the American legal system: what it is and how it came to be. For this we now turn to Chapter 2, "Sources of the Law." [See: P. Eltzbacher, "Kropotkin's Teachings," *The Great Anarchists: Ideas and Teachings of Seven Major Thinkers* (Dover, New York, 1908,) pp. 144–71; Aldous Huxley, *Brave New World and Brave New World Revisited* (New York: Harper and Brothers, 1960.)]

quick quiz 1-5

1. The law cannot stop us from doing wrong, but it can punish us if we choose to do wrong.	true | false
2. In a perfect society, ethics and law would always coincide.	true | false
3. The law and the legal system need not be founded on ethical considerations.	true | false

Summary

1.1 The law consists of rules of conduct established by the government of a society to maintain harmony, stability, and justice. Morals involve the values that govern a society's attitude toward right and wrong. Ethics, in contrast, attempts to develop a means for determining what those values ought to be and for formulating and applying rules in line with those values.

1.2 Market value ethics uses quantification as the primary tool for determining value and, therefore, for determining whether an action is right or wrong. Having a market to gauge the price of goods, real estate, investment opportunities, and services is one thing; however, doing the same thing to the unquantifiable aspects of our lives is something else entirely. Generally, most experts—economists, philosophers, theologians, politicians, and historians alike—refer to this concept as *neoliberalism*. Sandel warns that our tendency to evaluate everything based on money creates two insidious results. First, it promotes injustice, and second, it corrupts all other values.

1.3 The government of a nation-state has two objectives that simultaneously justify its power and enable the proper exercise of that power. Those two objectives are (1) to protect its own existence and (2) to protect the lives, health, safety, and well-being of its own citizens. To meet those two objectives, national leaders must recognize the conflict that emerges from within a *dyad* or two-level system of morality: (a) the exercise of individual morality, represented by the ethic of ultimate ends, and (b) the exercise of national morality, represented by the ethic of responsibility.

1.4 Corporations owe society a level of responsibility because the government has granted certain legal advantages to corporations. Another reason for expecting socially responsible decisions from corporate executives is that corporations have a great deal of power in the economic structure, and with power comes responsibility. Finally, corporations should act responsibly because it is in their own best interest to do so.

1.5 In a perfect society, ethics and the law would always coincide. Our society is not perfect and is not likely to become so in the foreseeable future. Therefore, our society needs the law and the legal system to give it structure, harmony, predictability, and justice.

Key Terms

Questions for Review and Discussion

1. What is the difference between law and morality?
2. What are the differences among positive law, natural law, and negative rights?
3. What are market value ethics?
4. What is social contract ethics?
5. What are the steps in applying utilitarianism?
6. What is rational ethics?
7. What is the dual nature of ethics in government?
8. What are the arguments supporting social responsibility?
9. Why is law needed in our society?
10. How can the law and ethics sometimes benefit from anarchy?

Cases for Analysis

1. One of the latest fads among many young people (and a few not so young people) involves the use of something referred to as the "e-cigarette." E-cigarettes are not "real" cigarettes because they do not burn tobacco and thus do not release tar and other toxic chemicals, or so the argument goes. The device operates on a battery that vaporizes nicotine and permits the "smoker" to breathe

in the nicotine-laced vapor, just as if it were smoke from a "real" cigarette. In reaction to all of this, the Food and Drug Administration (FDA) is set to enter the e-cigarette market with regulations that will forbid sales to minors, require photo identification for all sales, eliminate vending machine sales (except in facilities limited to adults), list ingredients, and include health-related warnings on all labels. Using the negative rights theory, defend the FDA's new rules. Using utilitarianism, construct an argument that opposes the new rules. Now use rational ethics to construct an argument that goes even further by opposing the manufacture and sale of all e-cigarettes. Explain each argument and determine which of the three positions you prefer. Explain that preference. [See: "Wise Controls on E-Cigarettes," *The New York Times*, April 26, 2014, p. A-18.]

2. Once upon a time in the far distant past, Las Vegas (and her little sister Reno) monopolized the use of gambling casinos in the United States. Later Atlantic City followed suit (pun intended). Now the trend has spread across the nation. Many states and uncounted cities have attempted to deal with severe economic difficulties by legalizing gambling at licensed casinos. New York state alone now has 14 casinos. The establishment of these urban casinos is supposed to create new jobs both in the construction of the casinos and in the hiring of employees to manage the activities at these 24-hour establishments. In addition, casinos need suppliers for their in-house restaurants, health clubs, gift shops, pools, bars, and coffee shops. Jobs are also created by the support facilities that spring up around the new casinos, including hotels, restaurants, parking garages, dry cleaners, valet services, and so on. While all of this may sound great, some people believe that the establishment of casinos contributes to crime and leads to an increase in the number of people addicted to gambling. Using the negative rights theory create an argument that opposes the establishment of more urban casinos. Using utilitarianism, construct an argument that supports the urban casino trend. Explain each argument and determine which of the two positions you prefer. Explain that preference. [See: "Casinos in the Exurbs," *The New York Times*, April 26, 2014, p. A-18.]

3. Market-based evaluation processes have been part of college and university life since the beginning of higher education. Most of this market-based evaluation has been controlled by the institutions themselves, by professional accrediting organizations, and by regional accrediting bodies such as the Higher Education Commission of the North Central Association of Colleges and Schools. Over the decades this type of evaluation has been palatable because the "data," if it can be called that, collected during evaluation processes (self-studies, site visits, and so on) conducted in-house was used to make changes that reflect issues related to daily activities in classrooms and labs, as well as governance, finance, operations, the physical plant, and so on. Now, however, the federal government has threatened to get into the act by evaluating all such institutions including small liberal arts colleges, big state universities, community colleges, online institutions, business colleges, university hospitals, and so on and issuing ratings based on such things as graduation rates, affordability, accessibility, graduate performance, enrollment, academic awards, alumni contributions, number of buildings, faculty credentials and publications, staff turnover, and so on. Moreover, the government also intends to penalize schools with low ratings by diminishing or even eliminating federal aid, thus, in effect, issuing a death sentence to these institutions. Using utilitarianism create two lines of argument, one that supports the federal government's plan and one that attacks it. Be careful not to confuse utilitarianism with utility thinking in this process. [See: Haley Sweetland Edwards, "Should U.S. Colleges Be Graded by the Government?" *Time,* April 28, 2014, pp. 33–35.]

4. Many times political leaders must make tough decisions in international politics—whether to conduct a preventative war, whether to use drones to bomb terrorist training grounds, whether to issue sanctions against aggressive nations that annex parts of independent nations, whether to order the Seventh Fleet into the South China Sea as a warning to China, whether to use American ships to deter Somalian pirate raids, and so on. Sometimes, however, political leaders make small, insignificant decisions that may even seem petty. Case in point, in the spring of 2014, the United States decided that the new Iranian ambassador to the United Nations, Hamid Aboutalebi, would not be given a visa to enter the country because some 40 years ago he acted as a translator for the Iranian terrorists who invaded the U.S. Embassy in Iran and held Americans captive for over a year.

Legally, the United States cannot refuse to issue the visa, but that seemed not to matter, nor did the ambassador's long career as an Iranian diplomat who served in the EU, Australia, Italy, and Belgium as the official Iranian representative in those areas. Construct an argument that shows that this decision is not in line with the dyadic moral system devised by Max Weber for judging governmental decision making. Now explore whether such a decision can be justified using any one of the following ethical theories: negative rights theory, rational ethics, social contract ethics, or utilitarianism. [See: "Three Essential Facts about the U.S.-Iran Spat," *Time,* April 28, 2014, p. 14.]

5. The legal system in the United States has granted corporations personhood. This is significant because this status as a "legal person" gives the corporation certain powers and abilities far beyond those of mortal business entities. For instance, as legal persons they are accorded certain constitutional rights, such as the right not to be deprived of property without due process of law. They can also own property in their own name and have lawsuits filed to protect them or vindicate their rights. Now in one of the most unusual, though not unexpected twists in the law, a lawsuit has been filed on behalf of a chimpanzee that seeks a declaration from the court that such animals have human-like rights not dissimilar to the rights according corporations. The plaintiff in the case is a chimpanzee named Tommy who has been imprisoned in a small cage since his original owner's death. The suit has been brought on Tommy's behalf by the Nonhuman Rights Project (NhRP). The overall objective of the lawsuit is to alter current law, which characterizes higher cognitive animals such as chimpanzees, gorillas, dolphins, orcas, and so on, as property. The immediate goal in the case of Tommy is to have the court, at the very least, declare that such nonhuman-cognitively superior beings (NhCSBs) have the right not to be imprisoned without good reason. The case for Tommy and others like him is based on *habeas corpus,* a legal principle that says that a person cannot be held without just cause. To seek a writ of habeas corpus is to ask the court to compel the person's keeper to bring him or her to the court so that the court can determine if the imprisonment is justified. The initial hurdle is, of course, to demonstrate that a chimpanzee is a legal person—a legal person not a human being—which may turn upon the cognitive abilities of the chimpanzee. Now explore whether such an argument can be justified using any one of the following ethical theories: negative rights theory, rational ethics, social contract ethics, or utilitarianism. [See: Charles Siebert "The Rights of Man and Beast," *New York Times Magazine*, April 27, 2014, pp. 28–33, 49–50, 53.]

6. In 1985 at the very beginning of the AIDS epidemic a young family found themselves faced with a difficult decision. Their infant son was suffering from a blood disorder that would require, at least in the expert opinion of the physicians in charge of the case, the complete removal of the child's blood, followed by a transfusion with the hospital's blood products. This was a risky procedure at that point in history given the epidemic and the unpredictability of the screening process in place at the time. An alternative process suggested by the child's medically trained mother would remove half the child's blood replacing it with a saline solution. With half of the bad blood gone and the rest diluted by the saline the hope was that the child's body would produce healthy blood to replace the unhealthy blood. Despite the position of the experts, the parents chose the second option and the child was saved. Using rational ethics, defend the decision made by the parents as the correct one, despite the risks involved and the opinion of the experts in the case. [See: Brooks Haxton, "Playing the Cards," *New York Times Magazine*, April 27, 2014, p. 54.]

7. Peter Kropotkin is one of those philosophical economists who warned against the deepening gulf between the wealthy and the poor. Kropotkin characterized this trend as unjust and, like Marx, predicted social upheaval—anarchy—as the coming phase from which a new social system may emerge, one based on cooperation rather than competition. More than 50 years later, Louis Bromfield made a similar observation about the split between the haves and the have-nots. Bromfield's analysis was made at a global level and suggested that those nations with wealth form alliances designed to make them stable before helping the have-not nations. About fifty years after that, Thomas Piketty, a French economist, tackled the same problem in a book titled, *Capital in the Twenty-First Century*. Piketty was also troubled by the rising gap between those with capital

and those who earn wages and concludes that capital will always grow faster than the economy ($r > g$). Simply put this means that those who have wealth continue to accumulate more wealth, and those without wealth, remain poor. Piketty, however, offers a different solution. He proposes gradually increasing the tax rates applied to capital, the net effect of which will ultimately be to redistribute the wealth, thus reducing the growing gulf between the two groups, reestablishing both equality and injustice on a global basis, and forestalling the revolution predicted by Kropotkin. Is Piketty's

plan ethical? Before answering the question, reexamine Piketty's plan based on any one of the following ethical theories: negative rights theory, rational ethics, social contract ethics, or utilitarianism. [See: Thomas Piketty, *Capital in the Twenty-First Century* (Cambridge, MA: Harvard UP, 2014); "Capitalism and its Critics: A Modern Marx," *The Economist,* May 3, 2014, pp. 12–13; "Picketty Fever: Bigger than Marx: A Wonky Book on Inequality Becomes a Blockbuster," *The Economist,* May 3, 2014, p. 67.]

quick quiz Answers

1-1	1-2	1-3	1-4	1-5
1. F	1. T	1. T	1. F	1. T
2. F	2. F	2. T	2. F	2. T
3. T	3. T	3. T	3. T	3. F

Chapter 2 — Sources of the Law

THE OPENING CASE *Round 1*
When the Church Challenges the Commandments (of the Government)

In an attempt to deal with the nation's health care crisis, Congress passed the Affordable Care Act (ACA). Since its passage, the ACA has had many difficulties, not the least of which stems from a mandate (commandment) issued by the Department of Health and Human Services (HHS) that requires employers to provide insurance that covers a variety of contraceptive services. Immediately after the law went into effect, over one dozen lawsuits were filed against HHS challenging the mandate as an unconstitutional violation of the Free Exercise Clause of the First Amendment. One lawsuit was filed by the Archdiocese of Washington, D.C., along with a variety of other plaintiffs including Archbishop Carroll High School, the Catholic Charities of Washington, the Catholic University of America, and the Consortium of Catholic Academies. The plaintiffs' argument is based on four logical steps. First, the First Amendment guarantees that the government will not interfere in the people's right to practice their religion. Second, a central belief of Catholicism is the sanctity of life, which includes opposition to the death penalty, assisted suicide, abortion, and birth control. Third, the HHS mandate requires Catholic institutions, including universities,

hospitals, and social service organizations, to provide insurance for certain birth control—related services that the Church forbids. Fourth, therefore, the plaintiffs conclude that the HHS mandate represents an unconstitutional attempt by the government to interfere with the practice of their religion. The defense is equally straightforward, if somewhat shorter, consisting of only two steps. First, universities, hospitals, and social service organization are not religious institutions even when operated by a church or other religious institution, because they provide nonreligious services to others regardless of faith. Second, therefore, these universities, schools, hospitals, and social service organization are actually secular institutions, despite their peripheral religious contact and cannot be permitted to take federal money without, at the same time, submitting to the control of federal "commandments." The case, thus, turns on an interesting question: Are these universities, schools, hospitals, and social service organizations actually religious institutions? The test for making this determination is twofold. First, to be a religious institution, the primary mission of the organization must be to promote (evangelize?) a particular set of religious beliefs.

Second, the institution must employ and aid mostly people of that denomination. Ironically, it is now up to the government to determine if the *Catholic* Charities of Washington, the *Catholic* University of America, and the Consortium of *Catholic* Academies are "*Catholic enough*" to be protected by the First Amendment. [See: *Roman Catholic Archdiocese of Washington D.C., et al. v. Kathleen Sebelius, Secretary of the United States Department of Health and Human Services, et al.* (Civil Action No. 12-0815 (ABJ).]

Opening Case Questions

1. What is the difference between the Establishment Clause and the Free Exercise Clause of the First Amendment? Explain.

2. Which clause is in contention in this case? Explain.

3. What is the test for determining whether an institution is "religious enough" to qualify for First Amendment protection? Explain.

4. Who or what is responsible for determining if an institution is "religious enough" to qualify for First Amendment protection? Explain.

5. Should a religious institution be judged in this manner? Why or why not?

LO Learning Objectives

1. List the objectives of the law.
2. Clarify the duality of the law.
3. Outline the content of the U.S. Constitution.
4. Explain several central constitutional principles and powers.
5. Explain the role of statutory law in the legal system.
6. Defend the need to set up a system of uniform laws.
7. State the role of common law in the legal system.
8. Describe how the principle of *stare decisis* provides stability within the law.
9. Differentiate between statutory interpretation and judicial review.
10. Account for the legislature's need to establish administrative agencies.

2-1 The Purpose and Operation of the Law

As explained in Chapter 1, the **law** consists of rules of conduct established by the government to maintain harmony, stability, and justice within a society. Ideally, the primary objectives of the law should be balanced equally at all times. Unfortunately, in 'real life,' this balance is not easy to maintain. Often justice must be sacrificed for harmony and stability. Sometimes the opposite is true.

The Law as a Balancing Act

The law should be viewed as a delicate balancing act. One person's rights are enforced while another's are not. One group is allowed to act while another group is limited in what it is permitted to do. One person is allowed to go free while another is imprisoned, fined, and forced to forfeit his property. One corporation's contracts are upheld while another's are struck down. Trade-offs like this occur within the law on a regular basis. Generally, the objectives of harmony, stability, and justice are kept in mind when such decisions are made. Because the law is made by people, however, it is not perfect. Legislators, judges, and administrators bring their own limitations into the process. Still, most of them do their best to be as objective and fair as possible. The law is made even more complex because it involves a series of competing dualities.

The Dualities within the Law

What is often *not* clear is that the need to balance rights and duties within the law is not unusual. Rather, this balancing act is part of the law's fundamental nature. As Anthony Chase explains in his study, *Law and History,* the legal system is shaped by several dualities, each of which is essential to the law's success. These dualities include the balance between the spirit and the letter of the law, between legal words and their interpretation, and between abstract principles and concrete situations. This balancing act also comes into play in the application of the Uncertainty Principle to the law. [See: Anthony Chase, "Historical Jurisprudence: I. Inside/Outside," *Law and History: The Evolution of the American Legal System* (New York: The New Press, 1997), pp. 12–19.]

The Spirit and the Letter of the Law   According to Chase, one of the most obvious dualities in the law is the balance between the **spirit** and the **letter of the law.** Generally, a person who follows the spirit of the law has found its actual intent, while one who is tied to the letter of the law has missed its true meaning; however, this is not always the case. Sometimes, following the letter of the law to avoid the spirit of the law can be a good thing. Thus, a shop owner who is discouraged by the complexity and intrusiveness of the law might avoid a prohibition against the sale of alcohol on Sunday by "giving away" bottles of wine to his customers who come in the next day and "give" the shop owner cash, which just happens to be equivalent to the cost of their Sunday "gift." The shop owner has met the letter of the law by not "selling" alcohol on Sunday, but he and his customers have clearly violated the spirit of the law. Is this a good thing? We'll leave that to your imagination. [See: Chase, pp. 12–14.]

Words versus Interpretation   Chase explains that much of the confusion over the spirit of the law emerges when the law is written down. Because words are often ambiguous, the language of the law can become a hindrance rather than a help in the execution of the law. This is why it is sometimes necessary to manipulate the language in order to uncover the actual intent of the lawmakers and to apply that intent in a consistent and fair fashion. Certainly, this oddity opens the law to adjustments that are sometimes good and sometimes bad. However, to view this particular brand of duality, **words** versus **interpretation,** as either a strength or a weakness would be an error because it is neither. Instead, it is merely how the law works. [See: Chase, pp. 14–15.]

The Abstract and the Concrete   According to Chase, duality in the law is also seen in the work of judges, legislators, and administrators. In one way or another, all three are involved in the law-making process, and as a result, all three must tackle a third type of duality, that which exists between *abstract* principles and *concrete* situations. [See: Chase, p. 15.] Thus, at times, legislators must take a principle, such as the idea that the government should be fair and equitable whenever it enacts a new tax bill, and apply that abstraction to a concrete piece of legislation. Similarly, a judge must take an abstract principle, such as the notion that all physicians must act with due care in performing their duties, and apply that principle in a case in which Dr. Jones' fails to properly diagnose

THE OPENING CASE *Round 2*
When the Church Challenges the Commandments (of the Government)

Recall that in the opening case, the plaintiffs in the case included several Catholic institutions not the least of which was the Archdiocese of Washington, D.C. Recall also that the lawsuit challenged a mandate (commandment?) issued by the Department of Health and Human Services that required institutions to provide their employees with insurance packages that covered contraceptive services, which violate church doctrine. The plaintiffs argued that the mandate was an unconstitutional violation of the Free Exercise Clause of the First Amendment. The Free Exercise Clause is one of two clauses in the First Amendment that protect religious freedom. The other clause is referred to as the Establishment Clause. The first clause says that the government cannot stop a person from practicing a set of religious beliefs, and the second clause says that the government cannot establish a religion. These two abstract principles have been part of American Constitutional Law for over 200 years. So far so good. However, now the Catholic Church and the government are engaged in a battle over a mandate that says institutions must provide insurance coverage for their employees for contraceptive services, services that are forbidden by a religious employer. This concrete mandate would seem to violate the abstract principle that guarantees that religious institutions can practice religious beliefs without government interference.

Here is the catch. The government says that religious universities, schools, hospitals, and social service institutions are not really religious institutions. They are, instead, secular institutions and can, thus, be regulated by the government. This sounds good, until we add one additional element—the determination factor. The determination factor says that an institution is religious if its primary mission is to promote a particular set of religious beliefs and if it employs and aids mostly people of that denomination. Again, so far so good. However, and here is the really sticky part, the government applies the test. No matter what branch a party is entangled with in the case—executive, judiciary, or legislative—the government is going to make this determination. That's right. The government establishes whether an institution is a religious institution. This is a classic case of how a clear-cut and straightforward abstract principle—*the government cannot establish a religious institution*—becomes muddled when it becomes concrete—*but the government can establish whether an institution is a religious institution.* Think about it. [See: *Roman Catholic Archdiocese of Washington D.C., et al. v. Kathleen Sebelius, Secretary of the United States Department of Health and Human Services, et al.* (Civil Action No. 12-0815 (ABJ).]

Mr. Smith's ailment. In all such cases, it is not possible to eliminate the tension that exists between the duality of the abstract and the concrete. The only thing that can be done is for lawmakers to deal with the concrete incident without violating the abstract principle. This is not the end to the duality issue, however. In another study of the law, Gerald Turkel points out that this duality (Turkel calls is bipolarity) exists in the very nature of a lawsuit when the plaintiff and the defendant face off against one another. This bipolarity, is the essence of the adversarial system. [See: Gerald Turkel, *Law and Society: Critical Approaches* (Boston: Allyn and Bacon, 1996), p. 13.]

The Uncertainty Principle
Duality also exists in the way a decision is intended and the way it is actually executed. The two, intent and result, almost never coincide, and when they do it is generally a matter of luck, nothing more. This principle, which is generally referred to as the *uncertainty principle,* exists in physics, in politics, and in economics. John Maynard Keynes recognized the uncertainty principle in economics and made it one of the linchpins of his economic theory. Uncertainty between intentions and results in the law is very common. It occurs when legislators pass statutes that are vetoed by the chief

THE OPENING CASE *Round 3*
When the Church Challenges the Commandments (of the Government)

The opening case affirms that Congress passed and the president signed the Affordable Care Act making it the law of the land in 2010. The intended goal of the new legislative package was to extend health care insurance coverage to millions of Americans who for years had been without such protection. However, the new law unexpectedly ignited a series of protests from people who saw it as just one more way for the federal government to interfere with their private lives. This experience vividly dramatizes the Uncertainty Principle in action. The administration intended one result, affordable health care for all, and instead it received a number of unexpected protests that included, but were not limited to, dozens of lawsuits. As is typically true of the Uncertainty Principle, it was not that people were against health insurance (although some actually were) as they were against the authorities telling them that they had to obtain such insurance—or else! The law

also indirectly, but dramatically, caused some people to suffer unexpected financial loss. Since the law required employers to provide benefits for full-time employees, many employers cut back on the hours for full-time employees, effectively transforming them into part-time employees. Furthermore, as noted earlier, the law also sparked dozens of lawsuits brought by private businesses and by religious organizations. The organizations and institutions found themselves under orders issued by HHS demanding that they provide insurance coverage to their employees for certain contraceptive services that clearly violates their religious beliefs and thus, on the surface at least, seems to violate the First Amendment guarantee of religious freedom. [See: *Roman Catholic Archdiocese of Washington D.C., et al. v. Kathleen Sebelius, Secretary of the United States Department of Health and Human Services, et al.* (Civil Action No. 12-0815 (ABJ).]

executive; when a trial judge rules on a case that gets overturned by an appellate court; and when the chief executive makes an appointment that is nullified by the legislature. [See Chase, p. 19; Robert Skidelsky, "Keynes's Economics: Uncertainty," *Keynes: The Return of the Master* (New York: Public Affairs, 2010), pp. 83–85.] Moreover, the legal scholar Richard Posner tells us that this inclination toward uncertainty, especially as it relates to economics, is exacerbated by the fact that some people act in unpredictable ways on a regular basis, while others react to what their neighbors have done. What is true in economics is equally true in the law. [See: Richard Posner, *A Failure of Capitalism* (Cambridge; Harvard University Press, 2009), pp. 83–84.]

quick quiz 2-1

1. The law consists of rules of conduct established by the government to maintain harmony, stability, and justice within a society.   true | false

2. Often justice must be sacrificed for harmony and stability, but the opposite is never true.   true | false

3. Legislators and judges bring their own personal prejudices and biases into the process.   true | false

2-2 Constitutional Law

Uncertainty in the nature, purpose, and effect of the law is complicated further by the myths that surround the entire legal process. It is true that the law can be defined as rules of conduct created by the government to maintain order, stability, and justice; however, it is also true that the law is made to regulate, control, and limit the conduct of the people. In fact, the need for a strong central government that separates the people from power, and insulates the leadership from unnecessary and counterproductive contact with the people was clearly recognized by the Framers not the least of which was James Madison. The historical myth is that the Framers (under the influence of thinkers like John Locke, David Hume, and Montesquieu) wrote the Constitution to give power to the people. The truth is somewhat different from this myth. Several of the unrecognized contributors to the development of the American political system were Niccolo Machiavelli, Francis Bacon, and Thomas Hobbes. Once this reality is recognized, many of the puzzles within the Constitution, puzzles like the Electoral College, for example, become quite clear. Separating myth from reality is important in the study of constitutional law, because a **constitution** is the fundamental law of a nation. The body of law that makes up the study of the constitution is called **constitutional law**. Constitutional law is rarely found in one document, one case, or one treatise, even when the constitution itself is one document. Make no mistake, however. A constitution need not be a single document, just so long as most everyone intuitively understands its basic concepts.

EXAMPLE 2-1: Constitutional Law in the United Kingdom

Unlike the United States Constitution, the British Constitution has never been reduced to a single document. Instead, the principles that make up the British Constitution are found in many documents including the *Magna Carta,* an endless series of court cases, and a complex mix of statutory laws. There are problems with this fragmented approach. First, the amalgam of legal precedents that makes up the British constitution plays right into the problems associated with the Uncertainty Principle. This occurs because it is difficult to know what precedent will be called upon to support or to attack a particular legal position. Second, the absence of a written fail-safe system, like that found in the U.S. Constitution, opens the door to power abuse in the British system. On the other hand, following the dictates of the Uncertainty Principle, there are some unexpected but not unappreciated advantages to a less definite constitution. First, the British constitutional method avoids the ambiguities associated with the need to determine the difference between the words and the interpretation of those words. True, the British must still deal with this duality whenever statutes and cases are interpreted by the courts, but this is a minor issue when compared to U.S. constitutional battles. Finally, when interpreting the British Constitution, there is no need to distinguish between the letter of the law and the spirit of the law since, at least in relation to constitutional law, in the British system, there simply is no letter of the law. [See: Sarah Lyall, "As a New Government Goes to Work, the Constitution Offers Britain Few Guides," *The New York Times,* May 25, 2010, p. A6.]

The Articles of Confederation

The Constitution of the United States, as it exists today, is not the nation's first constitution. The first constitution was known as the **Articles of Confederation**. The Articles of Confederation were created to hold together a fragile coalition of states, each of which was determined to maintain its own independent existence. Although the Articles of Confederation fulfilled a much-needed function during the first years in the life of the United States, they contained certain weaknesses.

One of the primary weaknesses was the fact that the United States in Congress, as the national legislature was known under the Articles, could not impose taxes or tariffs. Although a common treasury was supposed to be supplied by the states in proportion to the value of the land within each state, the states retained the power to levy and collect taxes. In essence, this rule meant that the United States in Congress had to rely on the goodwill of the states to obtain money. Such revenues were rarely forthcoming. Some states paid nothing at all; others turned over a portion of what they owed but rarely by the date the payments were due. Part of this problem was caused by the fact that the states were not about to trade one dictatorial central government for another and, therefore, simply ignored the national government.

Moreover, the desire to prevent the type of tyranny that the colonies had experienced under the rule of King George and the British Parliament led the framers of the Articles to include other limitations on the national government. For instance, all delegates to the Congress were appointed by the state legislatures and served at their pleasure. Several times, the national government found itself powerless to act, because some of the legislatures did not even bother to send delegates to Congress. In addition, whereas the United States in Congress had the authority to regulate the value of any money created under its own authority or under the authority of a state, the states retained the power to issue their own currency.

Reengineering the Articles

These problems and others like them were uppermost in the minds of the delegates to the Constitutional Convention, when they gathered in Philadelphia in 1787 to *revise* the Articles of Confederation. Also on their minds was a recent rather troubling incident in Massachusetts, an incident remembered as Shays' Rebellion. The rebellion, which was actually led by a preacher named Samuel Ely and involved over two thousand angry farmers, may have been unsuccessful, but that did not diminish the impact that it had on the delegates, many of whom were nervous about a possible new revolution. [See: Walter A. MacDougal, *Freedom Just Around the Corner* (New York: Harper Collins, 2004), p 295.] Enter James Madison, whose broad-based educational background made him not unfamiliar with Machiavelli, Bacon, and Hobbes. In fact, Madison owned a copy of Hobbes' principal political work, *Leviathan*. We can, therefore, be relatively certain of the Hobbesian influence on Madison. [See: George Mace, *Locke, Hobbes, and the Federalist Papers* (Carbondale: Southern Illinois University Press, 1979), pp. 9, 123.] As for Bacon and Machiavelli, Hobbes worked directly with Bacon for a number of years and owes his scientific view of human nature to Bacon who, in turn, owed his views on human nature at least in part to Machiavelli. All three of these philosophers have at least one thing in common in relation to human nature: Humans will protect themselves, even if it means using violence against others, and, therefore, must be controlled by a strong central government. Madison did his best to provide that type of strong central government in the Constitution.

The Constitution itself displays a general structural orientation toward insulating the leadership of the new republic from the influence of the people. One case in point is the Electoral College (Article II, Section 1); others include the election of senators (Article I, Section 3); the Supremacy Clause (Article VI); and the religion clauses of the First Amendment. To many people, the Electoral College is a mystery both in operation and intent. In effect, the Electoral College acts as a buffer between the people and the election of the president. It is likely that many of the delegates to the convention would have actually preferred that Congress choose the president; however, such a move was viewed as a bit too extreme. The Electoral College was the compromise solution. The people would choose electors. The electors, not the people, would then "elect" the president. The framers assumed that the electors would always be landowning, educated men of their own class, thus providing them with a dependable buffer between the chief executive and the people. [See: Walter A. MacDougal, *Freedom Just Around the Corner* (New York: Harper Collins, 2004), p. 302.] As an extra safeguard, the state governments would choose the method for seating the electors, thus giving the state legislators the power to guarantee the election of trustworthy electors. [See: Bernard Schwartz, *Constitutional Law* (New York: McMillan Publishing Co. Inc., 1972), pp. 135–36.]

The delegates assumed that the election of senators would require the same type of safeguard that insulated the election of the president from the vagaries of the people. Under the original Constitution (Article I, Section 3) the senators were to be elected by the state legislatures, guaranteeing that senators would always be upper-class property owners, chosen by upper-class property owners. This process remained in place until the 17th Amendment in 1913. (This was the same year, interestingly enough, that the Constitution was changed to allow an income tax under the 16th Amendment.) Senators were also given the longest term of office, six years, ensuring that the real political power at the national level would remain with the landed gentry. Even so, some of the delegates, Madison in particular, did not fully trust the state legislators to be wholly in control of the electorate in their respective states. To allay his fears Madison campaigned to add a congressional veto to Article I of the Constitution that would empower Congress to invalidate any law passed by a state legislature that Congress deemed to be unsuitable. Some commentators argue, rather convincingly, that the only reason the congressional veto was, well, vetoed by the delegates in Philadelphia was that most of the southern representatives figured out that a congressional veto would likely sound the death knell for slavery soon after ratification. [See: Steven Waldman, *Founding Faith* (New York: Random House, 2008), p. 132.] This, of course, does not mean the federal government cannot "veto" state legislation. It just means that to do so, it must file a lawsuit and bring the case to court, arguing that the statute in question violates the Supremacy Clause of the Constitution (Article VI). The Supremacy Clause of the U.S. Constitution does in fact state that, "(t)his Constitution and the Laws of the United States . . . shall be the supreme Law of the Land."

EXAMPLE 2-2: Reengineering the Constitution and Vetoing Arizona Law

In an attempt to deal with the problems associated with illegal immigration, the State of Arizona passed a new statute that empowered local law enforcement officials to inspect the identification papers of anyone who might be in the country illegally. The law caused a wave of protests across the nation, mostly from people who saw the statute as racially biased. Arizona state officials argued that they had been forced to act because the federal government had done a terrible job of policing the borders and that, as a result of this neglect, there had been an unprecedented rise in violence associated with illegal border crossings. Many American citizens supported the Arizona law and encouraged their state governments to pass similar legislation. Remember that during the Constitutional Convention in Philadelphia in 1787, Madison had campaigned to add a congressional veto to Article I of the Constitution that would empower Congress to invalidate any law passed by a state legislature that Congress deemed to be unsuitable. Had Madison managed to win that contest, Congress could have simply invoked its veto power and the Arizona statute would have been void, just like that. Instead, in the real world, to eliminate the law, the federal government was forced to sue the State of Arizona in an attempt to block the administration of the law. The Justice Department, under the control of Attorney General Eric Holder, argued that federal law trumped state law in this case because the Constitution gave the power to control immigration to the national government. The Supremacy Clause of the U.S. Constitution does in fact state that, "(t)his Constitution and the Laws of the United States . . . shall be the supreme Law of the Land." Thus, it would seem that the federal government had a solid argument. Still the process would have been so much easier had Madison got his way. Right? What do you think? [See: "Immigration: Why Did Obama Sue Arizona?" *The Week*, July 23, 2010, p. 6.]

The last piece of textual evidence that demonstrates rather soundly that Madison and many of his fellow Framers sought protection from the masses is found in the First Amendment, in general, and, in particular, within the two Religion Clauses. This radical proposition, however, is best examined in relation to the structure of the Constitution. It is to that subject that we now turn.

The Structure of the United States Constitution

The Constitution of the United States is based on two fundamental principles that were supported by many of the delegates to the convention in Philadelphia. Those two principles promote, first, a separation of national powers among three distinct branches of government and, second, a checks and balances system that allows each branch to oversee the operation of the other two branches. The principle of the separation of powers set up the now familiar three branches of the national government: the executive branch, the legislative branch, and the judicial branch. The principle of checks and balances allows each branch to share in the power of the other two branches. The U.S. Constitution is divided into two parts: the articles and the amendments. The articles establish the organization of the national government. The amendments change provisions in the original articles and add ideas that the framers did not include in those articles.

U.S. Const. Articles I–VII (see pages 909–913)

The Articles The first three of the seven articles distribute the power of the government among the legislative, executive, and judicial branches. Article I establishes Congress as the legislative (statute-making) branch of the government. Article II gives executive power to the president, and Article III gives judicial power to the Supreme Court and other courts established by Congress. Article IV explains the relationships among the states and the relationship between the federal government and the states, while Article V outlines the methods for amending the Constitution. Article VI establishes the U.S. Constitution, federal laws, and treaties as the supreme law of the land. Finally, Article VII outlines how the original 13 states would go about ratifying the new Constitution. Table 2-1 outlines the content of each article in the Constitution.

Did You Know?

Roman law was first codified into The Law of the Twelve Tables in 450 BC. The Twelve Tables declared that all free citizens had certain fundamental rights.

The Bill of Rights Structurally, the Bill of Rights should have been part of the original Constitution, probably as Article V; however, from a political and a pragmatic perspective this was not advisable. Many of the delegates to the Philadelphia convention, including Madison, believed that there was no need to add a Bill of Rights to the original Constitution. The power to regulate and protect rights, if it existed at all, was the responsibility of the states, not the national government. As the Constitution was to be written, it would be clear that the federal government, especially the legislative branch, would have only those powers that are expressly listed in the document. The Constitution would not mention rights. Therefore, Congress would have no power to enforce, eliminate, or modify rights—period. Some of the delegates also argued that, if some rights were listed, it would give the impression that those were the only rights that mattered. Therefore, it would be better to leave all mention of rights out of the Constitution.

U.S. Const. Amendments I–XXVII (see pages 913–917)

These arguments were solid enough to convince New Jersey, Delaware, Connecticut, Massachusetts, Pennsylvania, and Georgia to ratify the Constitution with no Bill of Rights. However, Virginia remained unmoved, and the overwhelming fear was that if Virginia voted not to ratify then, the Constitution would die a premature death. [See: Steven Waldman, *Founding Faith* (New York: Random House, 2008), p. 136.] Still, despite the threat of defeat, Madison opposed the Bill of Rights. It was not until he saw that the Bill of Rights could be used to control political factions that he changed his mind. Madison's greatest fear was that political factions would destroy the unity of the government. To save the national government, these factions had to be brought under control, and the factions that

Table 2-1 Articles of the U.S. Constitution

Articles	Content
Article I	Establishes the legislative branch of the federal government (the Congress) Defines the duties and powers of each house Outlines how Congress must conduct its business Lists legislative powers granted to Congress Lists powers denied to Congress Lists powers denied to the states
Article II	Gives executive power and responsibilities to the president Outlines the president's term of office, qualifications, and manner of election Identifies the president as commander in chief Gives the president power to make treaties
Article III	Establishes the Supreme Court and authorizes the establishment of other federal courts Provides for trial by jury for crimes Defines treason against the United States
Article IV	Defines interstate relations Sets up the full faith and credit clause obligating each state to recognize the public acts and proceedings of other states Provides for extradition of those accused of crimes in other states
Article V	Outlines the method of amending the Constitution
Article VI	Establishes the Constitution, federal laws, and federal treaties as the supreme law of the land
Article VII	Provides for the original ratification of the Constitution

required the greatest control were those that emerged from within the church. Madison (and Jefferson too, for that matter) believed that the best way to prevent religious factions from fracturing the unity of the government was to encourage them to fight among themselves, outside of the political arena. Ultimately, this conviction became one of Madison's motives for supporting the Bill of Rights.

As a dedicated Federalist and a follower of Hobbes, Madison believed that the national government needed a free hand in determining most political questions and, therefore, could not risk contradiction from any factions, but especially factions within the church; therefore, the church had to be "handled." From a tactical point of view the church could not be eliminated. However, a message had to be sent that the church could not interfere in the political arena. The religion clause accomplished this objective by placing all religions into the same arena, giving no single religion any preference, and permitting every belief to battle on its own in the marketplace of ideas. The strategy is brilliantly conceived because it limits the power of the church without seeming to do so, in fact, while appearing to do exactly the opposite. [See: Benjamin Wiker, *Worshipping the State: How Liberalism Became Our State Religion* (Washington, D.C.: Regnery Publishing, 2013).]

The Post Bill of Rights Amendments Outside of the Bill of Rights, the Constitution has been amended only 17 times. On average this means that the Constitution is amended every 13 years; however, the amendments do not fall into neat packages that spring up every decade (plus three years). Instead, they tend to come in clusters and generally reflect some sort of flashpoint in the socioeconomic system (see Table 2-2). Thus, for

Table 2-2 Amendments to the U.S. Constitution

The Bill of Rights		Pre–Civil War Amendments	Civil War Amendments	Progressive Amendments	Depression-Era Amendments	Modern Amendments
Amendment I Freedom of religion, speech, press, assembly	*Amendment VI* Procedures allowed in criminal cases	*Amendment XI* Lawsuits against the states	*Amendment XIII* Slavery is abolished	*Amendment XVI* The income tax is established	*Amendment XX* Terms of president, vice president, senators and representatives altered	*Amendment XXII* President's terms limited to two
Amendment II The right to bear arms and set up a militia	*Amendment VII* Jury trials in common law cases guaranteed	*Amendment XII** President and vice president elected together	*Amendment XIV* Equal protection of the law, due process, citizenship	*Amendment XVII* Senators elected by direct election		*Amendment XXIII* Washington, DC gets electors
Amendment III The quartering of soldiers in homes is prohibited	*Amendment VIII* Bill of Rights guaranteed, cruel and unusual punishment prohibited		*Amendment XV*† Voting rights guaranteed	*Amendment XVIII*‡ Prohibition established	*Amendment XXI* Prohibition repealed	*Amendment XXIV* Poll taxes outlawed
Amendment IV Search and seizure by probable cause	*Amendment IX* People retain other rights			*Amendment XIX* Women given right to vote		*Amendment XXV* Disability of the president; vacancies in the vice presidency
Amendment V Grand juries, double jeopardy, self-incrimination, due process, and eminent domain	*Amendment X* Powers reserved to states					*Amendment XXVI* Vote extended to 18-year-olds
						Amendment XXVII Congress prevented from voting itself instant pay raises

*Altered somewhat by the 20th Amendment. †Voting age changed by 26th Amendment. ‡Repealed by 21st Amendment.

example, the Civil War gave birth to Amendments 13, 14, and 15, which abolished slavery, guaranteed due process and equal protection of the law, and expanded voting rights, all within a five-year span. In the second decade of the 20th century, the income tax was established, the states' election of senators was eliminated, and the vote given to women, all within seven years. Finally, the revolutionary years of the 1960s produced a widening of political inclusiveness as the District of Columbia got electors, the poll tax was eliminated, and 18-year-olds earned the right to vote. The single most important amendment outside of the Bill of Rights is the 14th Amendment, which guaranteed due process and the equal protection of the law to all people. Since its inception in 1868, the 14th Amendment has been interpreted by the courts to mean that the Bill of Rights must be enforced by the states as well as by the national government. States may expand rights but they cannot limit or eliminate them.

State Law, Supremacy, Preemption, and Devolution

Each state in the union adopts its own constitution. A state constitution establishes the state's government. It also sets down principles to guide the state government in making state laws and conducting state business. Most state constitutions are patterned after the U.S. Constitution; however, state constitutions tend to be longer and more detailed than the U.S. Constitution, because they must deal with local as well as statewide matters. A basic principle of constitutional law is that the U.S. Constitution is the supreme law of the land. This principle of constitutional supremacy means that all other laws must be in line with constitutional principles. If a law somehow conflicts with the Constitution, that law is said to be unconstitutional. If it does not conflict, it will be upheld by the court as constitutional.

U.S. Const. Article VI
(see page 913)

The Constitution also says that all federal laws that are made in line with constitutional principles are to be considered the supreme law of the land. Cases that involve such conflicts, however, are not always as clear cut as those that involve state statutes that conflict with the Constitution. **Preemption** is the process by which the courts decide that a federal statute must take precedence over a state statute. The preemption of a state statute can occur in three situations. First, Congress can be very clear about its intent and explicitly state that the federal statute preempts any state statute that covers the same issues. If that is the case, then all that remains for the courts is to determine which statutes are covered by the preemption clause. Second, state statutes can be preempted by federal statutes when they conflict with the objectives of federal legislation. Third, the courts will preempt a state statute that has entered an area of the law that is traditionally an area that the federal government handles, such as foreign affairs or banking.

Devolution occurs when the courts redefine a right and shift the obligation to enforce a right from an upper-level authority to a lower one. For instance, a court may decide that a state agency, rather than a federal one, can control what governmental employees, in the course of performing their duties, are permitted to talk or write about in relation to official policies, procedures, and programs. Such a prohibition might appear to violate the employee's constitutional right of free speech as a U.S. citizen; however, in such cases, the court has decided that the duty and the power to define and enforce that right belongs to the state rather than to the federal government. It is important to note that the devolution of a right does not destroy that right. Rather, devolution simply redistributes the authority to define the nature of that right in certain situations. [See: Isidore Silver, "Recent Supreme Court Opinions: A Devolving Constitution," *The National Law Journal,* March 12, 2007, p. 22; Robert Tannenwald, "Devolution: The New Federalism—An Overview," *New England Economic Review,* May/June 1998, pp. 1–7.]

A QUESTION OF ETHICS

Federal Supremacy, Discrimination, and a Lesson in Ethics

A quick review of the case in Example 2-2 will remind us that Arizona passed a statute that empowered the local police to demand identification papers from anyone suspected of being in the country illegally. In response, the federal government sued the state of Arizona in an attempt to block the administration of the law arguing that federal law trumped state law in this situation because the Constitution gave the power to control immigration to the national government alone. Recall that the federal government could have argued that the law was discriminatory because it had a disparate impact on people of a particular color and a certain national origin. The question we pose here is not the relatively easy one of whether the Arizona statute is unethical. Rather, the question we ask is whether it is ethical for the Justice Department to use the relatively safe argument of federal supremacy while ignoring the far greater legal and moral transgression of deliberate, unapologetic, legislative discrimination?

quick quiz 2-2

1. The present U.S. Constitution is the only constitution that the United States has ever had.	true | false
2. The principle of separation of powers was never adopted by the framers of the U.S. Constitution.	true | false
3. A basic principle of constitutional law is that state law is the supreme law of the land.	true | false

2-3 Statutory Law

Laws passed by a legislature are known as **statutes**. At the federal level, statutes are the laws made by Congress and signed by the president. At the state level, statutes are enacted by state legislatures, such as the Ohio General Assembly or the Oregon Legislative Assembly. Many statutes prohibit certain activities. Most criminal statutes are prohibitive statutes. For instance, Ohio criminal law prohibits hazing, which is defined as coercing someone into doing an act of initiation that has a substantial risk of causing mental or physical harm. Other statutes demand the performance of some action. For instance, Ohio statutory law requires all motor vehicle drivers and passengers to wear safety belts. Some statutes, such as those that create governmental holidays or name state flowers, simply declare something.

Codes and Titles

Statutes must be arranged, cataloged, and indexed for easy reference. This is done by compiling state and federal codes. A **code** is a compilation of all the statutes of a particular state or the federal government. All federal statutes, for instance, are gathered in the United States Code (USC), while all Ohio statutory law is collected in the Ohio Revised Code (ORC). In general, codes are subdivided into **titles**, which are groupings of statutes that deal with a particular area of the law. Title 17 of the Ohio Revised Code, for example, covers corporations and partnerships. Often titles are subdivided into chapters, and chapters subdivided into sections. Thus, ORC 1701.03, *Purposes of a Corporation,* can be read from right to left as the third section of the first chapter of Title 17 of the ORC.

Uniform Laws

Because many different statutes are passed each year by the 50 state legislatures, statutory law differs from state to state. This lack of consistency can cause problems when legal matters cross state boundaries. One solution to the problem of inconsistent statutory law is for all the state legislatures to adopt the same statutes. The Uniform Law Commission (ULC) which is also called the The National Conference of Commissioners on Uniform State Laws (NCCUSL) was founded to write these uniform laws. The ULC is composed of commissioners that come from every state, the District of Columbia, Puerto Rico, and the Virgin Islands. These commissioners are usually selected by the governor. Most of the commissioners serve for a term of years set by the state. Some have no set term and can be replaced by the governor at any time. The number of commissioners from each jurisdiction is established by that jurisdiction. Some jurisdictions decide to have a lot of commissioners, while others decide to send only a few. California, for example, appoints 14, while New Hampshire limits its number to 4. The states are also responsible for sending money to the ULC to support its activities. The more populated states generally pay more than the smaller states.

A QUESTION OF ETHICS

The ULC and a Lesson in Ethics

Very few people, even those commentators who are concerned with the injustice associated with the Affordable Care Act, the Religious Freedom Restoration Act, the Arizona Immigration Law, or even the First Amendment cases, discuss, or even notice the vast power that has been placed in the hands of a group of unelected legal experts who write uniform laws and then pass those laws on to state legislators, many of whom simply enact those uniform codes into law, sometimes without changing a single word. The ULC manufactures dozens of these uniform codes covering such diverse topics as tort law, corporate law, family law, and surrogate parenting law, just to name a few. Is it ethical for legislators to abdicate their responsibility for the state's legislative agenda by turning it over to these unelected, private "experts"?

The Uniform Commercial Code

The most significant development in uniform state legislation has been the Uniform Commerical Code. The **Uniform Commercial Code (UCC)** is a unified set of statutes designed to govern almost all commercial transactions. The basic principles of commercial law were not changed by the UCC provisions. By defining and clarifying often misunderstood business and legal terms, the UCC helps parties involved in commercial transactions prepare their contracts. Even the famed UCC, however, has been adjusted by various states, and not all states decide to accept the suggested amendments that come from the ULC from time to time. Some states have even eliminated some of the chapters and articles in the UCC that they have found obsolete or irrelevant or that do not fit within their established legal traditions. Louisiana, for example, which still uses the Napoleonic Code, has adopted only four of the nine articles. Nevertheless, the UCC remains one of the most successful achievements of the ULC. The Uniform Law Commission maintains a website that includes the final drafts of all uniform acts that have been approved and recommended for adoption by the state legislatures.

Cyber-Law Statutes

The advent of the information age has sparked the need for specific cyber-law statutes that address the problems associated with cyber-commerce. **Cyber-commerce** is the term

CLASSIC CASE Memorial and Remonstrance

Statutory law is a product of the legislative process that has many stages, each of which affords a chance to push the bill forward or stop it in its tracks. Despite these safeguards and precautions, sometimes a bill succeeds or fails not on its merits, which is as it should be, but under the influence, reputation, charisma, or fortune of a famous, well-liked, or feared supporter (or opponent). Such was the case in 1785 when, in the Virginia Legislature, Patrick Henry and James Madison faced each other in a classic battle of states' rights, legislative process, and religious freedom.

Concerned about a post-war decline in the moral values of the people of Virginia, Patrick Henry introduced a bill in the Virginia legislature that was designed to help solve the problem. The bill, officially known as "A Bill for Establishing a Provision for Teachers of the Christian Religion," but generally referred to as the "Tax Assessment Bill," would assess a small property tax to support religious education. The proceeds from the tax would go to a denomination chosen by the taxpayer. The funds would be used to employ ministers and teachers who would help, "correct the morals of men, restrain their vices, and preserve the peace of society."

Madison's tract, *Memorial and Remonstrance against Religious Assessment,* has been described as a great defense of religious liberty. While the tract is certainly very well crafted and while it undoubtedly contributed to defeat of the bill, it falls far short of being a great defense of religious freedom. Yet the myth of its greatness persists. Why? A dissection of the essay, paragraph by paragraph, argument by argument,

reveals its rhetorical weaknesses. This is our challenge to you. Read the Tax Assessment Bill and *Memorial and Remonstrance* (both are in Appendix D). Once you have completed reading both, make your own evaluation. Focus especially on Argument 4, which is the heart of Madison's message.

Argument 4 maintains that the most offensive consequence of the bill will be to deny religious freedom to nonbelievers. Madison finds this aspect of the bill especially reprehensible since Americans are so insistent on their own religious freedom. The problem is that the Tax Assessment Bill does none of this and here is why. (1) Taxpayers are empowered to designate where their money is to go; (2) designated denominations spend the funds as they please, just as long as it goes to the teaching of morality; (3) Quakers and Mennonists are granted an exception due to their beliefs; (4) taxpayers who belong to no sect or object to their tax money going to any religious denomination will see their money go into a general fund that will use the proceeds to support seminaries of learning.

Perhaps even more significantly, Madison's arguments never really respond to the real purpose of the bill, addressing the moral decline of the people in the aftermath of the war. That is what the bill was supposed to do. It does not persecute the church or oppress nonbelievers. The bill actually goes out of its way to be inclusive, accommodating, and compassionate to different beliefs. In fact, the bill was a model of religious tolerance for the 18th century. Think about it. [See: Steven Waldman, *Founding Faith* (New York: Random House, 2008), pp. 115–26.]

applied to all cyber-transactions. The ULC has responded to this challenge by creating several new uniform laws. For example, the Uniform Computer Information Transactions Act (UCITA) is designed to deal directly with cyber-contracts that involve the sale or licensing of digital information. Another uniform cyber-law approved by the commissioners for enactment by state legislatures is the Uniform Electronic Transactions Act (UETA). This uniform cyber-law points out those principles that should be used in every state to make certain that cyber-contracts are enforceable.

---

quick quiz 2-3

1. Laws passed by a legislature are known as amendments.   true | false

2. Once the NCCUSL adopts a uniform law, it becomes binding in   true | false
   all states.

3. Cyber-commerce is the term that is applied to all   true | false
   cyber-transactions.

2-4 Court Decisions

When most people think of the law, they think of the Constitution or of statutes passed by Congress and the state legislatures. Although these two sources are important, they are not the only two sources of law in this country. The courts also make law in the following ways:

- Common law
- Interpretation of statutes
- Judicial review

Common Law

The term *common law* comes from the attempts of early English kings to establish a body of law that all the courts in the kingdom would hold in common. At that time, judges in towns and villages had instructions to settle all disputes in as consistent a manner as possible. The judges maintained this consistency by relying on previous legal decisions whenever they faced a similar set of circumstances. In this way, they established a body of common law. As the process continued, judges began to record their decisions and share them with other judges. **Common law** is the body of previously recorded legal decisions made by the courts in specific cases. The process of relying on these previously recorded legal decisions is called *stare decisis* (let the decision stand). The previously recorded legal decisions themselves are referred to as precedents.

The legal system of the United States, except Louisiana, is rooted in the common law of England. These roots derive from the early American colonists who came from England and were governed by the English monarchy. Over time, English common law has been eroded in the United States by the passing of state statutes and court decisions that better meet the needs of today's society. Nevertheless, parts of the common law as practiced in England still exist in the laws of the United States today. Courts still apply the common law when there are no modern court decisions or statutes dealing with an issue in dispute.

Precedents, past decisions, form the basis of common law.

Today's judges make decisions in the same way as their counterparts from the Middle Ages. They rely on precedent according to the principle of *stare decisis*. A **precedent** is a model case that a court can follow when facing a similar situation.

There are two types of precedent: binding and persuasive. **Binding precedent** is precedent that a court must follow. **Persuasive precedent** is precedent that a court is free to follow or ignore. Generally, whether a precedent is binding or persuasive is determined by the court's location. For instance, decisions made by the Florida Supreme Court would be binding in all Florida state courts but persuasive in all other states' courts.

The U.S. Supreme Court has frequently emphasized the crucial role that precedent plays in the American legal system. In emphasizing the importance of precedent, the Court has outlined a series of questions that judges should ask as they contemplate whether to overturn a rule of law established in an earlier case. These questions include the following:

- Is the established rule still practical?
- Have so many people relied upon the rule that overturning it would cause difficulty and injustice?
- Is the rule still legally viable, or has it become merely a relic of an outdated and deserted legal doctrine?
- Is the rule still up to date, or has it become obsolete because of changes in society?

Only if judges can answer these questions satisfactorily should they consider overturning an established precedent.

Statutory Interpretation

A second way that court decisions make law is in the interpretation of statutes. **Statutory interpretation** is the process by which the courts analyze those aspects of a statute that are unclear or ambiguous or that were not anticipated at the time the legislature passed the statute. When legislators enact a new statute, they cannot predict how people will react to the new law. Nor can they foresee all of its future ramifications and implications. Thus, when two or more parties have a dispute that challenges the statute, they may differ as to what the legislature had in mind when it wrote the statute. Also, legislators may have purposely made the language of a statute general. The job of reacting to unforeseen circumstances and making generalities fit specific circumstances falls to the courts. As a result, a judge may be called upon to determine how a certain statute should be interpreted.

Courts are not, however, free to interpret a statute at random. A court cannot interpret a statute unless it is faced with a case involving that statute. In interpreting a statute, a court looks to a variety of sources, including the legislative history of the statute and the old statute that the new statute replaced, if any. Naturally, the court also must review any binding precedent that interprets that statute. This requirement exists because the court must still rely upon previous cases when engaged in statutory interpretation, just as it does when deciding questions of common law.

Judicial Review

A third way that courts make law is through **judicial review**, which is the process of determining the constitutionality of various legislative statutes, administrative regulations, or executive actions. In exercising the power of judicial review, a court will look at the statute, regulation, or action and compare it with the Constitution. If the two are compatible, no problem exists; however, if they are contradictory, one of the two must be declared void. Because the Constitution is the supreme law of the land, the Constitution always rules, and the statute, regulation, or action is ruled unconstitutional.

Naturally, in exercising the power of judicial review, the court also must review any binding precedent involved in the constitutional issue, because the court still must rely upon previous cases in judicial review, just as it does in common law and statutory interpretation. The lower courts in this country have the capacity to review issues of constitutionality and interpret the meaning of provisions within the U.S. Constitution; however, the ultimate authority, and therefore the final word, on such issues rests with the United States Supreme Court.

---

quick quiz 2-4

1. The process of relying on previous decisions is called *stare decisis*.   true | false

2. Common law originated in France.   true | false

3. Judicial review is another name for statutory interpretation.   true | false

---

2-5 Administrative Regulations

Neither legislators nor judges can administer to all aspects of today's society. Moreover, legislators are generalists; they are rarely experts in all areas over which they have power. Because legislators are generalists and today's problems are so complex, statutory law, created by legislators, is very limited in what it can do. To broaden the power of statutory law, legislators delegate their power to others. They do this when they create administrative agencies.

Administrative Agencies

Federal administrative agencies administer statutes enacted by Congress in specific areas, such as communication, aviation, labor relations, working conditions, and so on. Similarly, agencies have been designated by the states to supervise intrastate activities. These agencies create rules, regulate and supervise, and render decisions that have the force of law. Their decrees and decisions are known as **administrative law**.

Administrative Procedures Act

Problems sometimes occur because administrative agencies have the power to make the rules, enforce the rules, and interpret the rules. To help prevent any conflict of interest that could arise from these overlapping responsibilities, Congress passed the federal Administrative Procedures Act. Similarly, most states have adopted a uniform law known as the

Model State Administrative Procedures Act. Under these two acts, an administrative agency planning new regulations must notify the affected parties and hold hearings to allow those parties to express their views. These acts also allow the courts to review agency decisions and rulings.

The Federal Register and the Code of Federal Regulations

The **Federal Register** is a publication that produces a daily compilation of new regulations issued by federal administrative agencies. The Federal Register operates within the National Archives and Records Administration under the authority of the Office of the Federal Register. The Government Printing Office is reponsible for actually printing the document, though today it is also available online. Most of the documents included within the Federal Register are directly related to the agencies. Those subdivisions devoted to the agencies include a section on rules and regulations, one on proposed rules, and one on notices of hearings, meetings, application deadlines, and administrative orders. There is also a section devoted to presidential orders and proclamations. Once a rule is finalized, it is included in the **Code of Federal Regulations (CFR)**, which is updated each year.

The Legal Ecosystem

The law does not operate in a vacuum. The various agents within the system, the President, Congress, the courts, and the administrative agencies intersect, overlap, sometimes get unduly entangled with one another, and habitually act at cross purposes. There is, however, an emergent order to the system that is not always evident on a day-to-day basis. One effective way to understand the operation of the law is to examine it by way of analogy. It is, therefore, useful to consider the legal ecosystem in terms of a complex adaptive system.

Complex Adaptive Systems

A complex adaptive system (CAS) is a network of interacting conditions that reinforce one another while at the same time adjust to change from agents outside and inside the system. The purpose of a CAS is the survival and improvement of the system itself. Natural examples of CASs would include beehives, anthills, and the neural network of the human brain. All CASs share at least five elements. First, every CAS operates as a result of the interaction of a variety of agents (the economy, for instance, includes producers, consumers, marketers, wholesalers, retailers, shippers, investors, brokers, bankers, salespeople, and so on.) Second, in a CAS there is no central controlling agent, no single all powerful "boss" as it were. Instead, control is dispersed among various actors (think of the checks and balances system here). Third, complex adaptive systems are just that—complex. This means that multiple levels of organization work within the system. Fourth, the longer a CAS lasts, the more change it encounters and the more adept it becomes at dealing with those changes. Finally, as part of the process, a CAS can infer the direction of future events and can adjust to those changing events. [See M. Mitchell Waldrop, Complexity: The Emerging Science on the Edge of Chaos (New York: Simon and Schuster, 1992, pp. 145–147; Note: Waldrop provides six elements; we have eliminated the last, "embedded niches."]

Complex Adaptive Systems and the Affordable Care Act In addition to the ACA cases involving church related institutions are cases filed by corporations (Hobby Lobby and Conestoga Wood, in particular) that argue that the HHS mandate violates their constitutional rights and their rights under the Religious Freedom Restoration Act (RFRA). These cases can demonstrate the operation of the law as a CAS. First, the case involves multiple interacting agents, including Congress, which enacted the law; the Department of Health and Human Services, which issued the troublesome mandate; and the courts, which scrutinized the ACA, the RFRA, and the HHS. Second, as the cases have passed through the various levels of the court system, no single controlling agent acted or could have acted to put an end to the matter. Third, the conflict between two congressional laws, the ACA and the RFRA, and the quarrel between two courts, which have issued inconsistent decisions, demonstrate the complexity of the system. Fourth, the Church adapted to the HHS mandate by filing dozens of lawsuits, and the HHS reacted to those lawsuits by altering the mandate somewhat and extending the deadline. Fifth and finally, the politicians, clergy members, laypeople, and lawyers involved in the mandate and in the cases have repeatedly made it clear that the results of these cases will have far-reaching effects extending into the distant future.

Complex Adaptive Systems and the Bill of Rights The campaign for the Bill of Rights also demonstrates how the law has acted as a CAS in the past. First, the campaign for the Bill of Rights involved a variety of agents within the system: delegates to the Philadelphia convention, the state legislators, the representatives to the ratification conventions, the first members of the first Congress, and so on. Second, much of this interaction was caused by the fact that the system lacked a central controlling agent at that time. Third, as with all CASs, the campaign was an intricate and complex network of organizational levels. Thus, in this case, delegates had to negotiate with their state legislators, candidates for the ratification conventions had to interact with voters, and so on. Fourth, the campaign for the Bill of Rights also showed how complex systems adapt. Madison, in particular, had to adapt, first, when he decided to run for a convention seat; second, when he altered his position on the Bill of Rights; and ultimately, when he became the author of that document. Fifth and finally, the campaign also demonstrated that such systems can infer the direction of future events. This is why Jefferson tried to change Madison's mind and why Madison did, in fact, eventually change his mind about the issue. [See: Steven Waldman, *Founding Faith* (New York: Random House, 2008), pp. 139–42.] The Bill of Rights emerged from this CAS not because it was perfect but because it managed to please more people than it offended. Sometimes that is enough. The next chapter will focus on one agent in the CAS, the agent responsible for explaining the law—the court system.

quick quiz 2-5

1. Together, legislators and judges can administer all aspects of today's society.   true | false

2. Most legislators are specialists.   true | false

3. The decrees and decisions made by administrative agencies are known as administrative law.   true | false

Summary

2.1 The law consists of rules of conduct established by the government to maintain harmony, stability, and justice within a society. Ideally, the primary objectives of the law are to promote harmony, stability, and justice. In everyday life, the balance is not easy to maintain. The law or, more properly, the entire legal framework consists of a series of dualities that must be resolved somehow.

2.2 A constitution is the basic law of a nation or state. The United States Constitution provides the organization of the national government. Each state also has a constitution that determines the state's governmental structure. The body of law that forms a constitution and its interpretation is known as constitutional law.

2.3 The laws passed by a legislature are known as statutes. At the federal level, these are the laws made by Congress and signed by the president. At the state level, statutes are enacted by state legislatures. Statutes must be arranged, cataloged, and indexed for easy reference by compiling state and federal codes. Because many different statutes are passed each year by the 50 state legislatures, there are important differences in state statutory law throughout the nation. One solution to the problem of inconsistent statutory law is for the legislatures of all the states to adopt the same statutes.

The Uniform Law Commission (ULC) was founded to write these uniform laws.

2.4 Courts make law through common law, the interpretation of statutes, and judicial review. Common law is the body of previously recorded legal decisions made by the courts in specific cases. Statutory interpretation is the process by which the courts analyze those aspects of a statute that are unclear or ambiguous or that were not anticipated at the time that the legislature passed the statute, and judicial review is the process by which the courts determine the constitutionality of various legislative statutes, administrative regulations, or executive actions.

2.5 Federal administrative agencies administer statutes enacted by Congress in specific areas, such as commerce, communication, aviation, labor relations, and working conditions. Similar agencies have been designated by the states to supervise intrastate activities. These agencies create rules, regulate and supervise, and render decisions. To help prevent any conflict of interest that could arise from these overlapping responsibilities, Congress passed the federal Administrative Procedures Act. Similarly, most states have adopted a uniform law known as the Model State Administrative Procedures Act.

Key Terms

administrative law, 47

Articles of Confederation, 35

binding precedent, 46

code, 42

Code of Federal Regulations (CFR), 48

common law, 45

constitution, 35

constitutional law, 35

cyber-commerce, 44

devolution, 41

Federal Register, 48

judicial review, 47

law, 31

persuasive precedent, 48

precedent, 46

preemption, 41

statutes, 42

statutory interpretation, 46

titles, 42

Uniform Commercial Code (UCC), 43

Questions for Review and Discussion

1. What are the objectives of the law?
2. How does the law reflect a series of complex dualities?

3. What are the functions of the articles and the amendments of the U.S. Constitution?

4. What is the difference between the principle of preemption and the doctrine of devolution?

5. What is the role of statutory law in the legal system?

6. Why does this country need to set up a system of uniform state laws?

7. What is the role of common law in the legal system?

8. How does the principle of *stare decisis* provide stability to our legal system?

9. What is the difference between statutory interpretation and judicial review?

10. Why does the legislature need to establish administrative agencies?

Cases for Analysis

1. In San Diego in August 2009, the police stopped a car driven by David Leon Riley because the license plates on the vehicle were outdated. The police officers then discovered that Riley's driver's license had been suspended. The officers then conducted a search of Riley's car without a warrant. The officers found and seized two handguns. Further investigation connected the two handguns to a recent shooting incident. The officers also found Riley's smartphone and then, again without a warrant, searched the data that they found stored on the smartphone. The data found on the phone provided further evidence pointing to Riley's participation in gang-related activities. In addition, other data on the phone supported the belief that Riley had been involved in the shooting incident in question. Despite the warrantless nature of the searches that obtained the evidence, the court allowed the evidence to be admitted during Riley's trial. As a result, he was sentenced to 15 years to life after being convicted of attempted murder. Riley now argues that the evidence that was obtained from his smartphone was gathered by the police in violation of his Fourth Amendment right to be free from warrantless searches. The Fourth Amendment states, "The right of the people to be secure in their persons, houses, papers, and effects, against unreasonable searches and seizures, shall not be violated, and no Warrants shall issue, but upon probable cause, supported by Oath or affirmation, and particularly describing the place to be searched, and the person or thing to be seized." The appeals court upheld Riley's conviction, and the case then went to the United States Supreme Court. Since Riley's entire case involves the California police and was held in a California state court, how and why does the Fourth Amendment of the United States Constitution apply to the case? When the Fourth Amendment was enacted in the 18th century, no one even dreamed of a "smartphone." Should the Constitution be amended to include modern technological advances like smartphones? Explain. [See: *David Leon Riley v. California* (no. 13-132) United States Supreme Court (April 29, 2014).]

2. In 2012, the North Carolina Constitution was amended to include a provision that placed a ban on gay marriages in the state. The new constitutional amendment was challenged in federal court when a group of ministers representing the United Church of Christ, as one of the plaintiffs, filed a lawsuit arguing that the North Carolina amendment violated their freedom of religion as guaranteed by the First Amendment of the United States Constitution. In a novel argument, the clergy members contended that their religious beliefs required that they follow their consciences and, when requested, perform marriages for gay couples in their congregations. The constitutional amendment, by preventing this, violates their constitutional right to religious freedom. They also argue that, since the United States Supreme Court has ruled that the federal government must recognize gay marriages, the state of North Carolina must also do so. Opponents contend that the amendment was approved by the 60 percent of the voters in the state and to invalidate the amendment would dismantle the voters' clear support for traditional marriage. Similar cases involving gay marriage bans generally end with the state law being invalidated by the courts. This has been the case in Virginia, Oklahoma, Texas, Utah, and Michigan. Which clause of the First Amendment is under

scrutiny in this case? The Establishment Clause or the Free Exercise Clause? Explain. Since the case involves an amendment to the North Carolina Constitution, how and why does the First Amendment of the United States Constitution apply to the case? Should the U. S. Constitution be amended to include a protection for traditional marriage? For gay marriage? How should the court rule in this case? Explain. [See: *General Synod of the United Church of Christ, et al. v. Roy Cooper, Attorney General of North Carolina, et al.,* Case no. 3: 14-cv-00213, United States District Court, Western District, North Carolina, Charlotte Division (April 28, 2014).]

3. The Town Council of Greece in New York state had a long tradition of opening town council meetings with a prayer offered by a town chaplain. Although the town council had repeatedly invited chaplains of all faiths to participate, the prayer was generally, but not always, offered by a Christian chaplain and often, but not always, used Christian language as part of an opening ceremony that included the Pledge of Allegiance. Town meetings were not just for elected officials but also included observers and people with issues to discuss with the council. In effect then, each council meeting was an open forum rather than an assembly of lawmakers. Two citizens filed suit against the town arguing that the use of a consistently Christian prayer at the council meetings violated the First Amendment of the Constitution and its guarantee of religious freedom. The plaintiffs also indicated that the level of use of the Christian prayers injured them on a personal level. The town argues that the prayer is in line with past precedent, specifically a 1983 case, *Marsh v. Chambers.* In that case, the United States Supreme Court decided that the Nebraska legislature's practice of using a prayer to open legislative business did not violate the First Amendment. The plaintiffs point out that the town council meeting is more than a purely legislative session since observers and townspeople with local concerns participate in the gatherings. The court of appeals concurred with the plaintiffs. The court's decision turned on the nonlegislative nature of the town council meetings. The case then went to the United States Supreme Court, which agreed to hear it. Which clause of the First Amendment is under scrutiny in this case? The Establishment Clause or the Free Exercise Clause? Explain. How should the court rule in the case? Explain. [See: *Town of Greece, New York v. Galloway, et al.* (No. 12-696) United States Supreme Court (May 5, 2014); *Marsh v. Chambers,* 463 U.S. 783 (1983).]

4. Barbara Rome entered Flower Memorial Hospital to undergo a series of X-rays. When she was ready for the X-rays, she was assisted by a student radiological intern. The intern placed Rome on the X-ray table and strapped her onto the table correctly; however, the intern did not properly fasten the footboard, which was located at the foot of the table. As a result of this error, Rome fell and was hurt when the table was raised. As a consequence, Rome brought a lawsuit against Flower Memorial Hospital alleging that the ordinary negligence of the intern had caused her injury. In contrast, the hospital argued that the lawsuit involved a medical claim, as defined under the state's medical malpractice statute. Whether a case involves ordinary negligence or a medical claim would determine whether the state's two-year statute of limitations for negligence or the state's one-year statute of limitations for medical claims would apply. This case clearly involves a difference of opinion on the interpretation of a statute. What sources might the court consider when interpreting the statute in question? [See: *Rome v. Flower Memorial Hospital,* 635 N.E.2d 1239 (OH).]

5. The Heart of Atlanta Hotel brought an action against the United States seeking a judgment that would declare Title II of the Civil Rights Act of 1964 unconstitutional. Congress's power to enact the Civil Rights Act is based upon Article I, Section 8, Clause 3, which gives Congress the power to regulate commerce among the states. The Heart of Atlanta Hotel argued that the statute was an unconstitutional extension of congressional power. The hotel also contended that the unconstitutional nature of the act especially applied to establishments like itself, which are incorporated and do business in only one state. However, because at any given time, three-fourths of the hotel's registered guests came from other states, the hotel clearly had an impact on interstate commerce. Do the lower federal courts have the authority to determine the constitutionality of Title II of the Civil Rights Act? What court has

the ultimate authority to determine the constitutionality of the Civil Rights Act? Speculate on the outcome of this case. Do you think that the court should uphold the act? Explain. [See: *Heart of Atlanta Hotel v. United States,* 370 U.S. 241 (U.S. Sup. Ct.).]

quick quiz Answers

2-1	2-2	2-3	2-4	2-5
1. T	1. F	1. F	1. T	1. F
2. F	2. F	2. F	2. F	2. F
3. T	3. F	3. T	3. F	3. T

The Judicial Process and Cyber-procedure

THE OPENING CASE *Round 1*
Frankenstein in the Federal Circuit

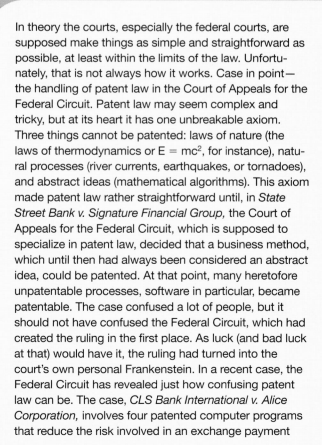

In theory the courts, especially the federal courts, are supposed make things as simple and straightforward as possible, at least within the limits of the law. Unfortunately, that is not always how it works. Case in point—the handling of patent law in the Court of Appeals for the Federal Circuit. Patent law may seem complex and tricky, but at its heart it has one unbreakable axiom. Three things cannot be patented: laws of nature (the laws of thermodynamics or $E = mc^2$, for instance), natural processes (river currents, earthquakes, or tornadoes), and abstract ideas (mathematical algorithms). This axiom made patent law rather straightforward until, in *State Street Bank v. Signature Financial Group,* the Court of Appeals for the Federal Circuit, which is supposed to specialize in patent law, decided that a business method, which until then had always been considered an abstract idea, could be patented. At that point, many heretofore unpatentable processes, software in particular, became patentable. The case confused a lot of people, but it should not have confused the Federal Circuit, which had created the ruling in the first place. As luck (and bad luck at that) would have it, the ruling had turned into the court's own personal Frankenstein. In a recent case, the Federal Circuit has revealed just how confusing patent law can be. The case, *CLS Bank International v. Alice Corporation,* involves four patented computer programs that reduce the risk involved in an exchange payment

agreement. Alice claims that, in using the programs, CLS violated its patent. For its part, CLS argues that the programs are unpatentable abstract ideas. The district court agreed with CLS and granted a summary judgment motion in its favor; however, when the case reached the Federal Circuit, two judges disagreed and reversed the decision. The case was so controversial that it was eventually heard in an *en banc* session of all the judges in Federal Circuit. Now remember that the courts are supposed to make things as simple and straightforward as possible. In this case, that did not happen. The court appeared to overturn *State Street Bank v. Signature Financial Group; however,* it is not as simple as that because of the 10 judges who heard the case, 7 of them felt compelled to write their own opinions. Even then the case was not quite over because the U.S. Supreme Court agreed make an attempt to unravel the Federal Circuit's Frankenstein. [See: *CLS Bank International v. Alice Corporation Pty. Ltd.,* No. 2011-130, United States Court of Appeals for the Federal Circuit (May 10, 2013); *State Street Bank v. Signature Financial Group,* 149 F.3d 1368 (Fed. Cir. Jul. 23, 1998).]

Opening Case Questions

1. What is the role of the Court of Appeals for the Federal Circuit? Explain.

2. What is a summary judgment motion and how is it involved in this case? Explain.

3. What is the test for determining whether an action should be dismissed in response to a summary judgment motion? Explain.

4. What does it mean when a court is said to sit *en banc* to hear a case? Explain.

5. Under what circumstances will the U.S. Supreme Court agree to review a case that it does not have to review? Explain.

LO Learning Objectives

1. Explain the fundamental nature of the American courts.
2. Determine when a case can be brought in federal court.
3. Recognize those cases that can be heard by the U.S. Supreme Court.
4. Identify the structure of most state court systems.
5. Define civil litigation.
6. List the most common discovery techniques.
7. Detail the nature of an appeal.
8. Determine the extent of cyber-jurisdiction.
9. Explain the nature of electronically stored information (ESI).
10. Describe the steps in a criminal prosecution.

3-1 The Court System

The laws of the American government are interpreted and implemented by a system of courts authorized by either the federal or state constitutions and generally established by legislative authority. **Courts** are judicial tribunals that meet in a regular place and apply the law in an attempt to settle disputes by weighing the arguments presented by advocates for each party. Each of these official bodies is a forum for the party who presents a complaint, the party who responds to the complaint, and the jury and/or judge who settles the dispute. As noted in the previous chapter, the law involves a set of competing dualities including the spirit of the law versus the letter of the law, the words of the law versus the interpretation of those words, and the abstract principles of the law versus the concrete situations to which those principles are applied. Nowhere in the law are these dualities more obvious on a daily basis than in the court system. The same is true of the uncertainly principle that is played out every time a plaintiff and defendant place their case in the hands of a judge and jury.

The Federal Court System

The federal court system is authorized by Article III of the U.S. Constitution, which states, "The Judicial Power of the United States shall be vested in one supreme court, and in such inferior courts as Congress may from time to time ordain and establish." The present federal court system includes the Supreme Court, courts of appeals, and federal district courts.

U.S. Const. Article III
(see page 912)

Court Jurisdiction

The authority of a court to hear and decide cases is called the court's **jurisdiction**. It is set by law and limited as to territory and type of case. A court of **original jurisdiction** has the authority to hear a case when it is first brought to court. Those courts that have the power to review a case for errors are courts of appellate jurisdiction. Most of the time courts with appellate jurisdiction will be empowered to determine whether the lower courts have made errors of law. This process is referred to as plenary review. Sometimes an appellate court will review the factual decisions made by the judge or the jury in lower courts. Such a review, however, only occurs when the appeals court determines that the decision made in the lower court was undeniably wrong, given the facts and evidence in the case. This determination relies on the clearly erroneous standard. Appellate courts also have the ability to determine whether the judge in the lower court has in some way misused his or her authority. This type of review is referred to as abuse of discretion.

Courts with the power to hear any type of case are said to exercise general jurisdiction. Those with the power to hear only certain types of cases have special jurisdiction. Examples of courts with special jurisdiction are probate courts and courts of claims. Courts also exercise subject matter jurisdiction and personal jurisdiction. Subject matter jurisdiction is the court's power to hear a particular type of case. Personal jurisdiction is the court's authority over the parties to a lawsuit.

Federal District Courts
Each state and territory in the United States has at least one federal district court. These courts are also known as *U.S. district courts.* The district courts are the courts of general jurisdiction in the federal system. Most federal cases begin in the federal district court. Not all cases belong there, however. The federal courts have subject matter jurisdiction over two types of cases: those involving federal law and those involving diversity.

Federal district courts have subject matter jurisdiction over cases that pertain to a federal question. A federal question could involve the U.S. Constitution, a federal statute or statutes, or a treaty. A state law issue can be included in a suit involving a federal question if the state claim is part of the same situation that created the federal question. If the federal claim is thrown out by the federal court, the state law issue usually cannot stand by itself. The people bringing the lawsuit would have to take their case to a state court.

Subject matter jurisdiction in federal court also arises in cases of diversity, even when no federal law is involved. Diversity cases include lawsuits that are (1) between citizens of different states, (2) between citizens of a state or different states and citizens of a foreign nation, and (3) between citizens of a state and a foreign government as the plaintiff. This last method of establishing jurisdiction usually applies only when a foreign government sues a citizen of a state. Congress has, however, provided an exception to this rule: Federal law now permits lawsuits in the federal courts against a foreign state when that state supports terrorism. The lawsuit must involve a request for damages arising from terrorist acts related to that support and as those acts are defined by law.

In diversity cases, and for other legal purposes, corporations are considered citizens of the state in which they are incorporated and the state where they have their principal place of business. In federal court, if even one defendant is a citizen of the same state as one of the plaintiffs, diversity cannot be established. In such a case, the law says that "diversity is not complete." Diversity cases also must involve an amount over $75,000.

Establishing subject matter jurisdiction will not be enough to get a case into federal court if the federal court does not have personal jurisdiction over a party. To establish personal jurisdiction, the court must look at the long-arm statute in the state in which the federal court is physically located. The court must then look to see if an appropriate level of contact has been made with the home state. A long-arm statute lists circumstances in which a court can exercise personal jurisdiction over an out-of-state defendant. Typically, these circumstances include the following:

- Owning real property in the state.
- Soliciting business in the state.

- Having an office or a store in the state.
- Committing a tort within the state.
- Transacting business in the state.

Some of the circumstances listed in the long-arm statute are relatively clear. Committing a tort in a state, for instance, leaves little room for misunderstanding. Other circumstances, however, such as "transacting business in the state," are not as precise. Therefore, personal jurisdiction under a state long-arm statute also requires meeting the required minimum contacts with the state. The concept of **minimum contacts** identifies the fewest number of contacts needed to allow the court to exercise jurisdiction over the out-of-state defendant. For example, let's say that a state allows the court to establish personal jurisdiction over any person who transacts business in the state. Now suppose a person buys a newspaper at an airport during a layover in the state. Does the purchase of that single newspaper constitute "transacting business" in the state?

The question turns on whether the purchase establishes a minimum contact with the state. In this case, the answer is probably "no." In general, the courts exclude contacts that are passive or that do not rise to a level that would permit the person transacting the business to reasonably foresee that he or she would come under the court's jurisdiction as a result of that transaction. It is difficult to conclude that the casual purchase of a newspaper at an airport kiosk would lead a person to foresee that he or she has voluntarily submitted to the jurisdictional power of a state. Something more would have to be involved. For instance, if the person in question specifically targeted the airport layover time to conduct negotiations with a client, and if a contract resulted from those negotiations, then the minimum contacts requirement would have been met and jurisdiction established.

Most of the time a court will determine subject matter jurisdiction before turning to the question of personal jurisdiction. Determining subject matter jurisdiction first, however, is not absolutely necessary. If the issue of personal jurisdiction is very obvious to the court, the court is free to dismiss the case before considering the question of subject matter jurisdiction. For example, this dismissal might happen if the defendant meets none of the categories in the long-arm statute or clearly does not meet the minimum contacts required by the case law of a state. In fact, if determining subject matter jurisdiction is especially difficult, the court is free to look at personal jurisdiction first, without even considering the question of subject matter jurisdiction.

EXAMPLE 3-1: The Stream of Commerce Theory

When attempting to establish personal jurisdiction over an out-of-state defendant, the plaintiff must convince the judge that the defendant had a set of "minimum contacts" with the state. Generally, the establishment of "minimum contacts" requires some kind of proactive strategy on the part of the defendant. This proactive strategy might involve opening a store, an office, a manufacturing plant, or a service center in the state; however, in some jurisdictions this is not always true. In the case of *Nicastro v. McIntyre,* for example, the Supreme Court of New Jersey established a standard called the *stream of commerce theory*. In this case, the plaintiff was injured by a product made by a British manufacturer. The plaintiff sued the manufacturer for failing to warn the ultimate user of a danger involved in the operation of the product, a metal press, and for a manufacturing defect related to the absence of an appropriate safety guard. The trial court dismissed the case because the plaintiff had failed to demonstrate the needed minimum contacts. The Supreme Court of New Jersey agreed that the plaintiff had not met the minimum contact test. Oddly, this did not stop the court from establishing personal jurisdiction over the manufacturer. To establish personal jurisdiction, the New Jersey court embraced a new theory of jurisdiction, the stream of commerce test. Under the **stream of commerce** test, the plaintiff must demonstrate that the defendant, in this case a foreign manufacturer, sent one of its products into "the stream of commerce" using a plan of national distribution that the manufacturer knew or at least reasonably should have known would in some way impact New Jersey. The New Jersey Supreme Court was satisfied that this was what had happened in the *Nicastro v. McIntyre* case. However, the New Jersey court *did limit* the stream of commerce standard to *product liability cases,* that is, cases in which the plaintiff claims to have been injured by a product manufactured or sold by the defendant. [See: *Nicastro v. McIntyre,* 2010 N.J. Lexis 19 (N.J. Feb. 2, 2010); and J. Russell Jackson "Buy Globally, Sue Locally for Products Liability," *The National Law Journal,* March 22, 2010, p. 10.]

U.S. Courts of Appeals The judges at the appellate level must be guided by the standard of review that is appropriate to each case. The standard of review tells the appellate-level judges the degree to which they must remain faithful to the decision of the lower court judge. As noted previously, the three standards of review are *plenary, clearly erroneous,* and *abuse of discretion.* Although they do not hear as many cases each year as the district courts, there are fewer U.S. courts of appeals and therefore fewer judges to hear those cases. The U.S. Courts of Appeals hear appeals from the district courts, the U.S. Tax Court, and many of the administrative agencies. At present, there are 13 U.S. courts of appeals within the federal court system (see Figure 3-1). Eleven of these appellate courts cover geographical groupings of states. For example, the Sixth Circuit Court of Appeals

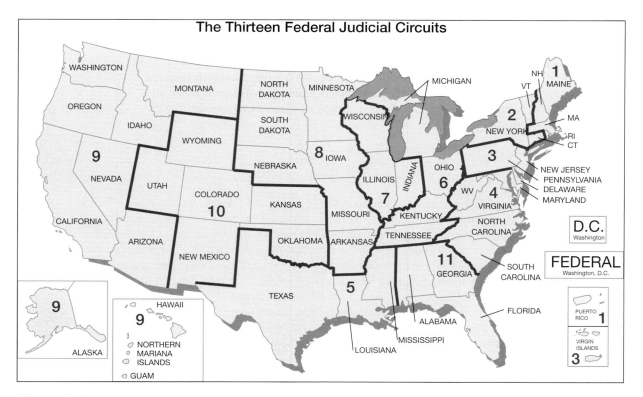

Figure 3-1   The U.S. federal court system is divided into 13 circuits, including the Washington, D.C., and federal circuits. Each circuit has several district courts.

includes Michigan, Ohio, Kentucky, and Tennessee. The Fifth Circuit includes Texas, Louisiana, and Mississippi. There is also a special appellate court for the District of Columbia called the U.S. Court of Appeals for the District of Columbia.

In addition to 12 appellate courts, organized on a geographical basis, there is a thirteenth appellate court that has special jurisdiction over certain types of cases. This court is known as the U.S. Court of Appeals for the Federal Circuit. The Federal Circuit was established by Congress primarily to streamline and unify patent law. However, the Federal Circuit was also given the power to hear appeals in cases that entail government contracts, trademark disputes, federal workers, veterans' benefits, and international trade, among others. Still, more than one-third of the appeals that end up in the Federal Circuit are patent cases that come either from the U.S. district courts or the U.S. Patent and Trademark Office. Some critics of the Federal Circuit have argued that the court's approach to patent law has become too narrow and too formalistic. [See: Marcia Cole, "Critics Target Federal Circuit," *The National Law Journal,* October 16, 2006, pp. 1, 20–21.] Others have held the opposite view. These critics contend that the standard the Federal Circuit uses to judge the patentability of abstract ideas, especially as they relate to computer software programs, has been ill advised, hopelessly vague, and virtually unusable. [See: "Difference Engine: Stalking Trolls," *The Economist Technology Quarterly,* March 8, 2014, p. 14.]

THE OPENING CASE *Round 2*
Frankenstein in the Federal Circuit

Recall that in the opening case, the plaintiff, Alice Corporation, brought suit against CLS Bank for patent infringement because CLS was using four of its patented programs without payment or permission from Alice. For its part, CLS argued that the programs were unpatentable abstract ideas. The District Court for the District of Columbia agreed with CLS and granted a summary judgment motion in its favor. In essence, the district court had declared that the four programs owned by Alice were abstract ideas that could not be patented. Or to put it more simply, no patent, no patent infringement. The case then went to the Court of Appeals for the Federal Circuit. This was the natural course of events in such a case because the Federal Circuit is supposed to be an expert forum for dealing with patent cases. In fact, 33 percent of its caseload each term involves patent law; however, when the case reached the Federal Circuit, two judges disagreed and reversed the decision, and then, when the case went to an *en banc* hearing, the court ended up reversing its own previous ruling. Even then the case was not quite over because U.S. Supreme Court agreed to make an

attempt to unravel the Federal Circuit's own personal Frankenstein. Some critics believe that the time has come for an overhaul of the Federal Circuit, perhaps following the models found in Europe and Japan. Europe, for instance, has drawn up an agreement to establish a Unified Patent Court for those 25 nations that have signed it. Similarly, Japan has already established a court of experts for such matters referred to as the Intellectual Property High Court. It might even be a good idea to resurrect the Court of Custom and Patent Appeals, which was abolished in 1982 when the Court of Appeals for the Federal Circuit was established to take its place or, at the very least, to examine whether the court might need some sort of reorganization that harkens back to the old days of the Court of Custom and Patent Appeals. Not all innovation works that well and often, after the fact, it becomes clear that older ideas really are better. [See: *CLS Bank International v. Alice Corporation Pty. Ltd.,* No. 2011-130, United States Court of Appeals for the Federal Circuit (May 10, 2013); "Difference Engine: Stalking Trolls," *The Economist Technology Quarterly,* March 8, 2014, p. 14.]

U.S. Const. Article III
(see page 912)

The United States Supreme Court

Established by the Constitution, the U.S. Supreme Court is the court of final jurisdiction in all cases appealed from the lower federal courts and in cases coming from state supreme courts. It has original jurisdiction in cases affecting ambassadors or other public ministers and consuls and in cases in which a state is a party. The Supreme Court is composed of a chief justice and eight associate justices. They are appointed by the president with the consent of the Senate and hold office during good behavior.

In many situations, a case will reach the U.S. Supreme Court only if the court agrees to issue a writ of certiorari. A **writ of certiorari** is an order from the Supreme Court to a lower court to deliver its records to the U.S. Supreme Court for review. The Court will issue a writ of certiorari if several lower courts have dealt with an issue but cannot agree on how it should be handled. If the case involves an issue that affects a large segment of society, the Court is likely to grant a writ. Finally, the Court may also hear a case if it involves a constitutional issue.

Applicable Law

When a federal court hears a case involving only federal law or the U.S. Constitution, it must follow that federal law, the Constitution, and/or any line of federal precedent that can be used to interpret the situation. Circumstances are different in diversity cases or federal law cases that also concern issues of state law. For instance, if a federal judge in Minnesota hears a diversity case between a Minnesota citizen and an Iowa citizen, would that judge use federal law, Minnesota law, or Iowa law? As a general rule, a federal court hearing a diversity case will apply the law of the state in which it is physically located.

EXAMPLE 3-2: The "Foreign-Cubed" Theory

Often, the question of what law to apply in a case is crucial to the management of a lawsuit. The law of one jurisdiction may favor the plaintiff while another may support the defendant. Often whoever wins the battle of jurisdictions also wins the battle of the law and, ultimately, the war itself. Such was the situation in the case of *Morrison v. Australian National Bank.* In that case, Morrison, the plaintiff, and the Australian National Bank, the defendant, were foreign citizens and the alleged fraud was carried out in a foreign country. Despite all of this, the case ended up in the United States District Court and eventually in the United States Supreme Court. The class action lawsuit was filed by the investors who argued that the bank had defrauded them by overvaluing the bank's mortgage portfolio. The suit was filed in federal court in the United States because much of the original data used to create the overvalued portfolio was compiled in the United States. When a foreign plaintiff files a case against a foreign defendant alleging fraud committed in a foreign country, that plaintiff has filed a "foreign-cubed" lawsuit. What makes a foreign-cubed case so complicated, besides the obvious jurisdictional problems, is the fact that often the alien plaintiffs file in the United States because their own home jurisdictions do not consider the behavior of the bank to be fraudulent. Thus, the questions of jurisdiction and choice of law become more than simply legal issues. They become ethical issues as well. Should the United States become the "world police" guarding against investment fraud anywhere on the planet, or should the American courts stay out of the dispute, thus respecting foreign traditions? [See: Tony Mauro, "A Border Battle Over Lawsuits: High Court Challenges the Use of American Courts by Foreign Plaintiffs," *The National Law Journal,* March 29, 2010, pp. 1 and 26.]

State Court Systems

The courts of each state are organized according to the provisions of the state constitution. Despite differences from state to state, such as the names for similar types of courts, there are basic similarities. For example, each state has an arrangement of inferior, or lower-level,

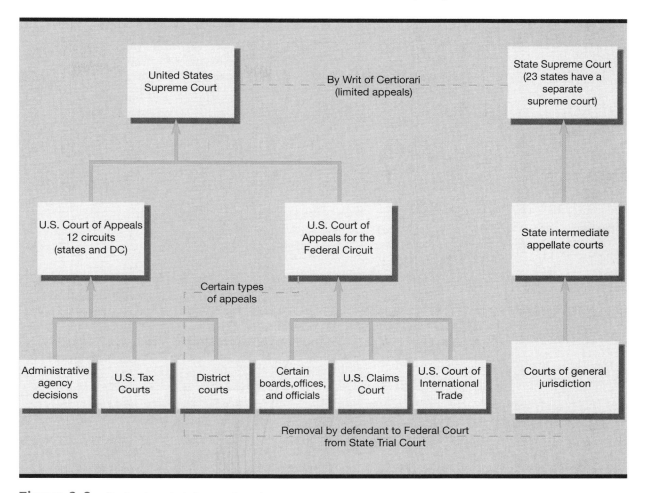

Figure 3-2 Federal and state court systems.

courts that serve as limited jurisdiction trial courts. Higher-level trial courts with broader jurisdiction are also provided. In addition, each state has appellate courts to which questions of law (not questions of fact) may be appealed. Figure 3-2 provides a general outline of the federal and the state court systems.

State Trial Courts The state trial courts, also known as general jurisdiction courts, have the power to hear any type of case. They are often called superior courts, circuit courts, or courts of common pleas. Some states, notably New York, refer to them as supreme courts. These courts are usually organized around the counties of the state, so that each county has its own trial court of general jurisdiction. Most states also have other trial courts that are lower than the general jurisdiction courts. These limited jurisdiction courts usually hear only certain types of cases. For instance, a municipal court may be empowered to hear only those cases that involve municipal ordinances, criminal cases involving crimes within the city limits, and other cases that involve monetary claims of less than $10,000. Many localities have small-claims courts that hear civil cases involving small dollar amounts, ranging from $500 to $5,000, depending on state law.

State Intermediate Appellate Courts State court systems provide for a variety of appellate court structures. Still, the purpose of the appellate courts remains the same, that is, to hear appeals on questions of law from the lower courts. Usually, appeals are heard by a three-judge panel. The panel examines the records of the lower court, reads the written arguments submitted by the attorneys, studies the law on its own, and listens to the oral arguments of the attorneys. If the panel agrees with the lower court, it will affirm the decision of that court; however, if the panel disagrees with the lower court's decision, it can set aside or modify the decision of that court.

State Supreme Courts Twenty-seven states rely on their supreme court as their only appellate court. These states have no intermediate appellate courts. The other 23 states have both intermediate appellate courts and state supreme courts. Most supreme courts consist of a panel of three to nine judges. As is true at the intermediate appellate level, the panel of judges examines the records of the lower court, reads the written arguments submitted by the attorneys, studies the law on its own, and listens to the oral arguments of the attorneys. The decisions of state supreme courts are final unless a federal issue or a constitutional right is involved.

---

quick quiz 3-1

1. Courts are judicial tribunals that meet in a regular place and apply the laws in an attempt to settle disputes fairly.	true | false
2. The authority of a court to hear and decide cases is called the court's jurisdiction.	true | false
3. A writ of certiorari is an order from the Supreme Court to a lower court to deliver its records to the U.S Supreme Court for review.	true | false

---

3-2 Civil Procedure

In a civil lawsuit, one individual, organization, or corporation brings an action against another individual, organization, or corporation. The objective of a civil suit is usually to obtain money to compensate the victim. **Civil litigation** is another name for the process of bringing a case to court to enforce a right.

Commencement of the Action

The principal parties to a lawsuit are the plaintiff and the defendant. The **plaintiff** is the person who begins the lawsuit by filing a complaint in the appropriate trial court of general jurisdiction. The **defendant** is the person against whom the lawsuit has been brought and from whom a recovery is sought.

Filing the Complaint The **complaint** sets forth the names of the parties to the lawsuit, identifying them as plaintiffs or defendants. Generally, the complaint includes the addresses of all parties. The complaint also sets forth the following:

- The facts in the case from the plaintiff's perspective.
- The alleged legal violations by the defendant.
- The injuries that the plaintiff suffered.
- The plaintiff's request for relief.

If the plaintiff wants a jury trial, this information must also be specified in the complaint. In federal court, the complaint must also include a statement of jurisdiction, which will tell the court whether the case has been brought in federal court because of a federal question or because of diversity among the plaintiffs and the defendants.

Class Action Lawsuits At times filing a complaint is pointless because the amount of recovery for one plaintiff would be so low that it would not be worth the effort, energy, and expense of a lawsuit. Sometimes, however, the extent of the harmful conduct is so pervasive and the number of plaintiffs so high that the cost of conducting the lawsuit is justified. This was the motivation that led to the creation of the class action lawsuit. A **class action** is a lawsuit in which one (or a small number) of the potential plaintiffs file a lawsuit on behalf of the entire class. The courts will permit a class action lawsuit provided that (1) it is not feasible for the members of the group to bring the action on their own; (2) the members of the group share common questions of law that can be tried together; and (3) the class action approach is far better than forcing the plaintiffs to file separate actions.

Unfortunately, class action lawsuits are easy to abuse. One of the most common abuses is forum shopping. **Forum shopping** occurs when a plaintiff searches for a jurisdiction with law that is favorable to its case, and then files the case in that jurisdiction. The defendant can do something similar by filing a motion to remove a case filed in state court to federal court. When a case features multiple plaintiffs, as in a class action lawsuit, forum shopping becomes easier because the number of possible jurisdictions increases as the number of plaintiffs from different states increases. In order to counteract abuses, Congress enacted the Class Action Fairness Act (CAFA). The act included a number of innovations designed to limit forum shopping and to counteract some of the other abuses associated with class actions. [See: Archis Parasharami and Kevin Ranlett, "The Class Action Fairness Act, Five Years Later," *The National Law Journal,* April 12, 2010, pp. 14 and 18; and Michael McNamara and Christine Henge, "'Hertz' Expands Companies Access to Federal Court," *The National Law Journal,* April 12, 2010, pp. 16–17.]

Service of Process

The complaint is presented to the appropriate court officer, usually the clerk of courts. The clerk will then see that the defendant is served with a copy of the complaint and a summons. The *summons* names the court of jurisdiction, describes the nature of the action, and demands that the defendant answer the complaint within a specified period of time, usually between 20 and 30 days, depending on the state rules of civil procedure. Giving the summons and the complaint to the defendant is called **service of process**.

The Pre-Answer Stage

As noted, once the defendant has been served, he or she has 20 to 30 days to file an answer. Usually, however, the defendant will ask for and receive an extension of that time period. The time between service and the answer is termed the *pre-answer stage.* During this stage, the defendant will take some time to examine the nature of the claim that has been filed by the plaintiff. The defendant may, as a result of this initial examination, decide to file one or more pre-answer motions. A *motion* is a request for the court to rule on a particular issue. One possible motion is a motion for dismissal of the case for failure to state a claim for which relief can be granted. Some states call this a **demurrer**. Other motions to dismiss may be based on the grounds that the court lacks subject matter jurisdiction, that the court lacks personal jurisdiction, or that the court cannot hear the case because the statute of limitations has passed.

EXAMPLE 3-3: To Demurrer or Not to Demurrer

Lauren Jensen agreed to purchase a desk for $295 from the Stephens Sisters Furniture Store. During a management change at Stephens, Jensen's order was lost, and the furniture was never delivered. Jensen never contacted Stephens but instead purchased a similar desk for $495 at another store. Five years later, Jensen decided to bring suit against Stephens for breach of contract. She wants to recover the extra $200 that she paid to the second store. Stephens' attorney realizes that the state statute of limitations for such contracts is four years. As a result, she files a motion to dismiss for failure to state a claim for which relief can be granted. Some states call this motion a demurrer. If Stephens' attorney is correct, the suit will be dismissed.

The Answer

The **answer** is the defendant's official response to the complaint. In the answer, the defendant admits or denies the allegations in the complaint. The defendant's answer can also include affirmative defenses. An **affirmative defense** is a set of circumstances that indicate the defendant should not be held liable, even if the plaintiff proves all of the facts in the complaint. One affirmative defense is *assumption of the risk.*

EXAMPLE 3-4: Assessing the Risk of a Risky Business

Carol Jennings took a cruise of the Mediterranean on the Underwood Cruise Line, a firm incorporated and doing business in the United States. While the cruise ship *Principia* was docked at a Greek island, Jennings joined a tour group. She was cautioned numerous times to remain with the tour group and not to wander off by herself because of the danger of being attacked and robbed. Nevertheless, Jennings ignored the warnings and left the tour group. While on her own, she wandered into a particularly dangerous part of the city where she was beaten and robbed. She later brought a lawsuit against the Underwood Cruise Line. In its answer to Jennings' complaint, the cruise line may wish to use the defense of assumption of the risk. Such a defense would argue that Jennings was aware of danger when she chose to abandon the tour group and wander off by herself. As a result, the cruise line might argue, she assumed the risk of being attacked and robbed.

The defendant's answer may also contain counterclaims and cross-claims. A *counterclaim* is a claim that a defendant has against a plaintiff. A *cross-claim* is a claim filed by a defendant against another defendant in the same case. At this time, a defendant may also wish to file a *third-party complaint,* which is a complaint filed by the defendant against a third party not yet named in the lawsuit.

The Pretrial Stage

After the answer has been filed, the parties must await trial. During this waiting period, cleverly dubbed the pretrial stage, several activities can be carried out, including the pretrial conference, discovery, and the filing of pretrial motions.

Pretrial Conference Some courts require cases to go to a pretrial conference after the complaint and the answer have been filed. A pretrial conference usually has

THE OPENING CASE *Round 3*
Frankenstein in the Federal Circuit

Think back to the opening case. Recall that the plaintiff, Alice Corporation, initiated a cause of action against CLS Bank for patent infringement because CLS was using four Alice patents without permission or payment. When the case arrived in the District Court of the District of Columbia, the attorneys representing CLS filed a motion for a summary judgment. A summary judgment motion asks the court for a speedy judgment for the party filing the motion. This motion is filed when there is no genuine issue as to any material fact, and the party filing the motion is entitled by law to a favorable judgment. The motion must be supported by a brief that sets forth the legal arguments supporting the claim, along with applicable supporting evidence. So in this case, CLS admits it used the programs specified, it did not ask permission, and it has made no payments just as Alice has claimed. Those are the material facts (here, "material" means of "central importance") and CLS does not deny them. In fact, when deciding the summary judgment motion, the court will examine the facts in a light that is favorable to the party that did not file the motion in question.

However, and here is the catch, despite this situation, or perhaps because of it, when the law is applied to the facts as stated, CLS contends that as a matter of law it is entitled to a favorable judgment. The "matter of law" to which CLS refers in the motion is the patentability of the Alice programs. CLS says that those programs are abstract ideas and cannot be patented and so, once again, quite simply, no patent, no patent infringement. The district court agreed and granted the CLS summary judgment motion. Once a summary judgment motion is granted, it ends the case, just as if that case had gone to trial. However, once such an order is issued, that order can appealed. That is how the case reached the Court of Appeals for the Federal Circuit, where all the fun began. So, as sometimes happens, this case will end up in the U.S. Supreme Court without ever going to trial. [See: *CLS Bank International v. Alice Corporation Pty. Ltd.,* No. 2011-130, United States Court of Appeals for the Federal Circuit (May 10, 2013); "Difference Engine: Stalking Trolls," *The Economist Technology Quarterly,* March 8, 2014, p. 14.]

two purposes. One is to discuss the possibility of settling the case without the need for a trial. Another is to decide on the details involved in bringing the case to trial. Such a conference is generally called a *case management conference.* Issues that might be discussed at a case management conference include the way that the parties will conduct discovery or the need to place a limit on the number of expert witnesses that will be called at trial.

Pretrial Motions Several motions may be filed during the pretrial stage. One motion available at this time is a motion for summary judgment. A **summary judgment motion** asks the court for an immediate judgment for the party filing the motion. This motion is filed when there is no genuine issue as to any material fact, and the party filing the motion is entitled by law to a favorable judgment. The motion cannot be filed without supporting legal arguments written out in a brief and accompanied by applicable supporting evidence.

Discovery **Discovery** is the process by which the parties to a civil action search for information that is relevant to the case. The objective is to simplify the issues and avoid unnecessary arguments and surprises in the subsequent trial. Discovery techniques and tools include the following:

LO6

Depositions are oral statements made out of court under oath by witnesses or parties to the action in response to questions from the opposing attorneys. The answers are recorded by a court stenographer and can be used for later reference.

Interrogatories are written questions that must be answered in writing under oath by the opposite party. Interrogatories cannot be given to witnesses. Only plaintiffs and defendants can be required to answer interrogatories.

Requests for real evidence ask a party to produce documents, records, accounts, correspondence, photographs, or other tangible evidence. The request may also seek permission to inspect land.

Requests for physical or mental examination ask a party to undergo a physical or a mental examination. Such requests can be made only if the physical or the mental condition of the party is in controversy; it must be a central concern to the lawsuit.

Requests for admissions are made to secure a statement from a party that a particular fact is true or that a document or set of documents is genuine. An admission eliminates the need to demonstrate the truthfulness of the fact or the genuineness of the documents at trial.

The Civil Trial

Upon completion of discovery, the pretrial conference, and any hearings held on pretrial motions, the case is ready for trial. A trial by jury is an adversarial proceeding in which the judge's role is secondary to that of the jury's. Competition between attorneys permits the jury to sort out the truth and arrive at a just solution to the dispute.

Jury Selection   Once it is decided that the case will involve a jury, the process of *voir dire* (to speak the truth) begins. In this process, the lawyers for both parties question prospective jurors to determine whether they will be allowed to sit on the jury. Prospective jurors may be rejected if they are unable to render an impartial judgment. One reason for rejecting a prospective juror is if he or she had a personal relationship with the litigant or with a witness.

Prospective jurors may also be rejected if they have a financial interest in the outcome of the trial; however, the financial interest must be a direct, substantial interest. Remote financial interests in a trial will not disqualify a juror. Thus, the fact that the outcome of a trial may result in higher insurance rates would not disqualify a juror who has an insurance policy. Another reason might be if the prospective juror has had past experience that would prevent him or her from being impartial in the present case. Thus, a juror who has had a bad experience with a psychologist, for instance, might be unable to judge impartially the actions of a psychologist who has been sued for malpractice.

In most lawsuits, *voir dire* is conducted in the open, which means that the process is generally accessible to the press and the mass media. However, in cases that have attracted a lot of public attention, the judge may order that the media's access to the *voir dire* process be limited. Often news reporters will be limited to reading abridged copies of the transcript of the *voir dire* process after the process has been completed. The names of the jurors may also be censored, along with personal data about those jurors. This limit on the access to *voir dire* usually occurs in notorious criminal trials, but it could also happen in high-profile civil lawsuits.

Prospective jurors may be selected or rejected based on their ability to render an impartial judgment.

Opening Statements   At the beginning of the trial, both attorneys have the opportunity to make an opening statement. In the *opening statement,* an attorney presents the facts in the case and explains what he or she intends to show during the trial. Attorneys are not permitted to argue their case in the opening statement. There is widespread disagreement, however, as to what constitutes "arguing the case" during the opening statement. Consequently, the degree of argument permitted during the opening statement often depends on what the judge will allow.

The Plaintiff's Case in Chief

The plaintiff's **case in chief** is the plaintiff's opportunity to present evidence that will prove his or her version of the case to the jury. The plaintiff's attorney calls witnesses and immediately subjects those witnesses to **direct examination**. Direct examination is designed to present the facts that will support the plaintiff's version of those facts. Opposing attorneys then have the chance to challenge the truthfulness of each piece of evidence presented. In this process of **cross-examination**, the witnesses answer questions of the defense attorney.

The Defendant's Case in Chief

After the plaintiff has ended the presentation of his or her case in chief, the defendant has the opportunity to present his or her case in chief. The defendant's attorney calls witnesses for direct examination, and the plaintiff's attorney has an opportunity to cross-examine the defendant's witnesses.

The Rebuttal and the Surrebuttal

Once the plaintiff and the defendant have presented their cases in chief, each attorney may present evidence to discredit the evidence presented by the opposition and reestablish the credibility of his or her own evidence. This step is called the **rebuttal**. The term **surrebuttal** is used in some states when referring to the defendant's rebuttal.

Closing Statements

After the rebuttals are completed, each attorney makes a closing statement. In this statement, the attorneys emphasize aspects of the testimony and other evidence they believe will best persuade the judge or jury.

Jury Instructions

Because juries comprise many people who are not familiar with particular aspects of the law, someone must explain the law to the jury. This is one of the duties of the judge. Although the attorneys may suggest to the judge what instructions ought to be used, the judge makes the decision. The judge's instructions explain the rules of law that the jurors are to apply to the facts in reaching their decision.

Verdict and Judgment

After receiving the judge's instructions, the members of the jury retire to a private room, where they apply the rules stated by the judge to the evidence presented by the witnesses. The jury eventually reaches a verdict. A **verdict** is a finding of fact. The verdict may be limited to the question of liability, or it can be extended to include the issue of damages. **Liability** means that the defendant is held legally responsible for his or her actions. The term **damages** refers to the money recovered by the plaintiff for the injury or loss caused by the defendant. The verdict is entered by the judge in the court records, and the case is said to be decided. According to the terms of the judgment, the defeated party either is required to pay the amount specified or do a specific thing, such as perform the terms of the contract. Court costs are usually paid by the losing party.

   In some cases, money will not be adequate to satisfy the plaintiff. In such cases, the plaintiff may seek an equitable remedy. An **equitable remedy** requires a party to do something or to refrain from doing something beyond the payment of money. One equitable remedy is **specific performance**, which would require a party to a contract to go through with the terms of the contract. Usually, specific performance is permitted only in cases involving real estate or unique, one-of-a-kind goods such as art objects or rare antiques.

Another equitable remedy is an injunction. An **injunction** stops a party from doing something. For instance, an employer may seek an injunction against a former employee to prevent that employee from using a trade secret on his or her new job if that trade secret is the property of the original employer.

A QUESTION OF ETHICS

Televised Trials: Threat or Transformation

In California, Proposition 8 was placed on the ballot in order to outlaw same sex marriages. The legality of the proposition was challenged in the federal trial court in the Northern District of California. Noting the great interest in the case and recognizing its social and political significance, the presiding judge suggested televising the trial at least within the courthouse in San Francisco where the trial was located. Later the judge, in consultation with the Chief Judge of the 9th Circuit, suggested widening the broadcast field to include all courthouses in the 9th Circuit. Those who supported the proposition opposed the plan to televise the trial and attempted to get a *writ of mandamus* to prevent the broadcast. The 9th Circuit denied the *writ,* but the United States Supreme Court reversed the decision and stopped the broadcast indefinitely. The Supreme Court stated that it suspended the broadcast to protect witnesses who might otherwise be threatened or harassed. The ethical issue here is not the morality of Proposition 8. Rather the question is whether a trial of this transformative significance should be broadcast or "gagged" as the Supreme Court ruled. Using both utilitarianism and rational ethics (See Chapter 1, "Ethics, Social Responsibility, and the Law"), analyze the decision made by the U.S. Supreme Court and decide whether the Supreme Court's decision can be defended using either theory. Explain your rationale using each theory. [See: David R. Fine, "Television Trials," *The National Law Journal,* January 25, 2010, p. 38.]

The Appeal

An **appeal** is the referral of a case to a higher court for review. For an appeal to be successful, it must be shown that some legal error occurred. For example, a party could argue that some of the evidence that was admitted should have been excluded or that evidence that was not allowed should have been allowed. A party could also argue that the judge's instructions were erroneous or were stated in an inappropriate manner. Generally, an appeal is filed by the party that lost the case in the trial court; however, it is also possible that the party that prevailed at trial may wish to file an appeal. This step is referred to as a **cross-appeal**. For instance, if the trial court upheld most of the claims made by the plaintiff but denied one or two key claims, the plaintiff may wish to file a cross-appeal. It may also be advisable to file a cross-appeal if the trial court did not award the appropriate amount in damages, if it refused to grant attorney's fees, or if it allowed money damages but refused to permit equitable relief. [See: Aaron S. Bayer, "Appellate Law: The Cross-Appeal," *The National Law Journal,* February 9, 2004, p. 13.]

Execution of the Judgment

In civil cases, if the judgment is not paid, the court will order the loser's property to be sold by the sheriff to satisfy the judgment. This order by the court is known as a **writ of execution**. Any excess from the sale must be returned to the loser. Execution of the judgment also may be issued against any income due to the loser, such as wages, salaries, or dividends. This process is known as execution against income, or garnishment, and the proceedings are known as garnishee proceedings. Checking accounts are also subject to garnishment.

quick quiz 3-2

1. In state court, a complaint must include a statement of jurisdiction.　　true | false

2. The defendants' answer must not include either counterclaims or cross-claims.　　true | false

3. *Voir dire* must always be open to the press.　　true | false

3-3 Cyber-procedure

The world of litigation has changed dramatically because of the electronic revolution. Gone are the days when litigators could wait until the last minute to conduct discovery prior to trial because they could see the limited number of paper documents sitting in a neat pile on their desks. Also gone are the days when attorney-client privilege could be protected by simply closing the office door. Electronically stored data comes in so many different formats (e-mail, texting, Facebook, LinkedIn, voice mail, spreadsheets, instant messages, databases, and so on) and is stored in so many different electronic devices (laptops, mobile phones, iPods, Kindles, GPS units, PDAs, desktop PCs, fax machines, scanners, smartphones, and so on) that litigators have to get the jump on the process from the first moment that a lawsuit is threatened. Add to that the fact that many courts now expect and some even require the electronic filing of documents, and it becomes obvious that lawyers, paralegals, and business people cannot ignore the electronic age even if they want to.

Cyber-jurisdiction

Whether courts have jurisdiction over out-of-state defendants has been complicated by the electronic age. Previously, back in the age of face-to-face, U.S. mail, and over-the-phone transactions, it was fairly obvious where a corporation or an institution had its principal place of business. Of course, exactly what was meant by "principal place of business" might be at issue, but at least everyone knew the alternative sites available. Doing business on the Internet complicates all of this. Using the Internet, sellers can solicit business on their website, negotiate and enter a contract using "the point and click method," receive payment using PayPal, and deliver goods via FedEx or UPS without leaving the comfort of their home office and without revealing where the sellers are located, how the goods were obtained, where they were stored, and how they were transported and delivered to the seller before being loaded on a FedEx or UPS truck.

Does the type of activity described earlier reach the level of minimum contacts needed to establish personal jurisdiction? Should the minimum contacts standard be replaced by the New Jersey stream of commerce standard for electronic buying and selling? **Cyber-jurisdiction,** (AKA **electronic jurisdiction** and **e-jurisdiction**) is the power of the court to hear a case based on Internet-related transactions. While this area of the law is still in its adolescence, we can, nevertheless, extract at least one general principle: Because of its complex nature, cyber-jurisdiction is a moving target. To help attorneys, paralegals, and business people hit this moving target, the courts have established a sliding scale on which several types of jurisdiction can be measured.

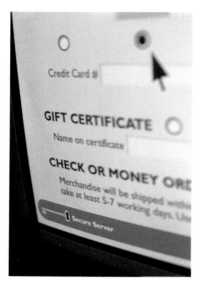

Cyber-transactions must be handled on a case-by-case basis.

On one side of the scale are business transactions that are carried out from beginning to end using the Internet. These would include operations that are run like those engineered by Amazon.com and eBay. Transactions that involve solicitation, negotiation, finalization, payment, and shipping arrangements exclusively on the Internet, establish the minimum contacts needed for the state of the buyer. Moreover, if a case involves product liability, the type of transaction described earlier would satisfy New Jersey's stream of commerce standard. Of course, it is possible for the seller to specify the state that will serve as the forum for settling any dispute that arises from the contract. Still, such stipulations can always be challenged if the matter actually gets to court.

On the other side of the sliding scale are those cases in which the defendant simply placed an inactive advertisement on the Internet. Such inactive advertisements will not usually establish jurisdiction under the minimum contacts test or the New Jersey stream of commerce test. The final type of transaction falls between the two extremes. These cases include cyber-transactions that involve more than simply placing an advertisement on the Internet. The courts have not established any single normative approach to such transactions and so the matter must be handled on a case-by-case basis.

CLASSIC CASE "It Is Alive!" Or Is It a Moving Target?

In the case of *Diamond v. Chakrabarty,* the U.S. Supreme Court decided that it was possible to patent a life-form. As is often the case in sensitive issues like this, no one was happy with the Court's decision except, perhaps, the new patent holder. Some experts felt compelled to criticize the Supreme Court for stepping outside the bounds of its authority. Others accused the Court of a thoughtless ruling that would open the door to the abusive use of biotechnology. However, one of the most interesting points was made when a commentator noted that it was strange that the Supreme Court was willing to grant a patent for a new life-form when, in a previous case, the case of *Roe v. Wade,* the court had refused to define life. Is it ethical, or even logical, for the justices of the Supreme Court to avoid the definition of life when it comes to the rights of women and then turn around and permit a megacorporation, like General Electric, to reap potential profit from the decision? (Note: The microbiologist who developed the DNA plasmid that was the subject of *Diamond v. Chakrabarty,* was employed by General Electric.) Think about it and try to come up with a rationale for each side of the issue. Once you have done this, think about the same type of sliding scale that the Federal Circuit used in the *CLS Bank International v.*

Alice Corporation in the opening case. At times it seems like abstract ideas can be patented, and at other times it seems like that type of patent is forbidden. Moreover, it does not help the situation when seven different opinions are issued by the court. This type of uncertainty in relation to technology and the law also plagues procedural law. This problem is covered at length in the section on cyber-jurisdiction. Computer technology has robbed jurisdiction of its traditional certainty. As noted earlier, while this area of the law is still in its adolescence, we can, nevertheless, extract at least one general principle: Because of its complex nature, cyber-jurisdiction is a moving target. It might be good to take a cue from this finding and generalize the rule so that it looks like this: Due to the complex nature of technology and the law, whenever the two intersect, overlap, or just pass each other at a distance, the result will be a moving target! [See: *Diamond v. Chakrabarty,* 447 U.S 303, 100 S.Ct . 204 (1980); *Roe V. Wade,* 410 U.S. 113, 93 S.Ct. 705 (1973); *CLS Bank International v. Alice Corporation Pty. Ltd.,* No. 2011-130, United States Court of Appeals for the Federal Circuit (May 10, 2013); and "Difference Engine: Stalking Trolls," *The Economist Technology Quarterly,* March 8, 2014, p. 14.]

Cyber-filing

The federal court system officially joined the 21st century when it added a provision to the Federal Rules of Civil Procedure that permits lawyers to file court documents electronically. Moreover, under Rule 5 (3) the courts can even go so far as to require that documents be filed electronically, as long as the court also accepts reasonable exceptions from those unable to comply with the new provision. Those federal courts that have adopted the new procedure have found that cyber-filing (electronic filing or e-filing) is more cost effective and efficient than paper filing. Because some of the electronic systems used to keep track of court documents are accessible on the Internet, papers are no longer lost or misplaced as often as they once were. The Internet filing network also permits people to access the papers at their own convenience. This is an important feature of the electronic system because, once a party has been served properly, that party is sent a notice whenever a new document is filed electronically with the court. This eliminates the old-fashioned and time-consuming process of filing a formal notice with each party.

Still, cyber-filing does have its disadvantages. Not every law firm is properly equipped for cyber-filing and so the courts must maintain a dual filing system to accommodate "cyber-challenged" firms. Moreover, just because a firm is electronically up to date does not guarantee that its attorneys are cyber-savvy. Consequently, many courts have been forced to provide training and ongoing assistance to these attorneys at the court's expense. Also, from the attorney's perspective, since cyber-filing process is controlled by local rules, learning one set of electronic rules is rarely enough. Instead, the attorney must learn the rules for every court in which he or she does regular business. Fortunately, however, there are consistent features in these rules from one court to the next and so a diligent and conscientious attorney can survive as long as he or she is willing to be flexible.

Cyber-discovery

The discovery process is one of the most costly and time-consuming steps in a lawsuit. As noted previously, discovery is the process by which the parties to a civil action search for information that is relevant to the case. While the goal and the philosophy behind discovery have not changed since American litigation began, the process of identifying, categorizing, evaluating, saving, and using the evidence has gone through some radical changes over the past two decades, thanks to the revolution in electronic evidence. As the use of e-evidence began to creep into the law, many attorneys were satisfied to just ignore the changes or, more frequently, to treat e-evidence as if it were just another type of paper evidence. This is no longer possible. In fact, the time is rapidly coming when attorneys who do not keep up with changes in technology may be found liable for malpractice. Once upon a time, clients hoped that their attorney would be electronically literate. Now they not only expect it, but they also demand it.

Electronically Stored Information For the sake of consistency and to prevent confusion, computerized evidence has been officially designated as **electronically stored information (ESI)**. Simply changing the name, however, does not solve the unexpected problems that have emerged because of the special nature of ESI. For example, ESI is embedded in many diverse and mysterious formats, making its retrieval difficult for most attorneys. As a result, attorneys must pay close attention to all aspects of ESI, including its preservation, storage, and communication. Attorneys who are not careful may inadvertently turn over privileged information to their opponents and not discover the error until it is too late. Fortunately, most state bar associations run continuing education seminars and annual legal conferences to help attorneys and judges keep current with these matters. The Federal Rules of Civil Procedure and most state procedural rules have also have been amended to make e-discovery more manageable.

These changes were designed to alter the behavior of attorneys so that they adjust to the peculiar characteristics of ESI. First, the rules now force attorneys to get an early start on all discovery plans or they will be unable to comply with the time limits built into the rules. Second, attorneys must now deal with the question of which electronic format will be used to request and deliver data. Third, attorneys can rest assured that the rules provide several ways to deal with those problems that arise with ESI and privilege. Fourth, attorneys can use the rules to help in the recovery of ESI that might otherwise be difficult to find. Fifth, to deal with the expenses that are involved in the identification and collection of ESI, attorneys can now refer to provisions in the rules that guarantee a fair apportionment of these expenses. Finally, attorneys can also be certain that everyone will cooperate with the new electronic discovery process, because the rules have provided severe penalties for those who ignore or disobey the new ESI discovery rules.

The Discovery Protocols Pilot Project The Judicial Conference Advisory Committee on Civil Rules (Advisory Committee), which operates under the authority of the Federal Judicial Center, has introduced an innovative set of protocols aimed at simplifying and economizing the discovery process in federal employment law cases. The protocols apply only to certain employment-related lawsuits and then only to those district courts and judges that agreed to be involved in the project. The protocols themselves are grounded on three basic beliefs: first, that the rules of discovery work best when they are adapted to certain set cases; second, that discovery is much more efficient when practitioners have no choice but to release key documents at designated times; and third, that the process works best when it starts early. Since the same types of records are used in most employment cases—employment manuals, employment contracts, disciplinary records, weekly work schedules, time cards, and so on—employment law seemed to be the perfect choice for this project. However, patent law cases also involve similar sets of documents and often benefit from being placed on a fast track regulated by uniform deadlines. As a result, patent law cases and the Court of Appeals for the Federal Circuit have also been targeted for a new pilot project, as discussed in The Opening Case Round 4. [See: Robert A. Steinberg, "Historical Origins of the Initial Discovery Protocols Pilot Project for

THE OPENING CASE *Round 4*
Frankenstein in the Federal Circuit

In Round 2 of our reconsideration of the opening case, we discussed the idea of resurrecting the Court of Custom and Patent Appeals, which was replaced by the Court of Appeals for the Federal Circuit in 1982. Now it seems that steps have been taken in that direction, or at least in a similar direction, by the Federal Judicial Center. The center has recently inaugurated a decade-long pilot project aimed at determining what improvements might be made to the way that patent law cases are handled by the Federal Circuit. The pilot project will institute an education program for training judges in the intricacies of patent law that will help them develop a

technique for effectively managing a patent law caseload. A dedicated website has been set up to assist those judges who are involved in the project. The website includes patent law publications, sample patent law rules, and case management resources that have been especially designed for patent law cases. Both the House and Senate Judiciary Committees will receive regular progress reports from the project. [See: Karen Redmond, "District Courts Selected for Patent Pilot Program," *The Third Branch News,* June 7, 2011; "The Patent Pilot Program Takes Off Around the Country," *Gibbons IP Law Alert,* October 20, 2011.]

Employment Cases," *The Ohio State Bar Association: 2013 Annual Convention* (May 10, 2013): 55–56. See also: "Pilot Program Introduces Protocols for Employment Cases," *The Third Branch News,* February 2012; *Pilot Project Regarding Initial Discovery Protocols for Employment Cases Alleging Adverse Action,* The Judicial Conference Advisory Committee on Civil Rules (November 2011).]

---

quick quiz 3-3

1. Cyber-jurisdiction is the power of the court to hear a case based on Internet-related transactions. true | false

2. The Federal Rules of Civil Procedure do not permit lawyers to file court documents electronically. true | false

3. The Federal Rules now refer to cyber-evidence as data compilations. true | false

---

3-4 Criminal Procedure

The objectives of a criminal prosecution are to protect society and to punish the wrongdoer by a fine or imprisonment. The steps in a criminal prosecution include the following:

- Arrest and initial appearance.
- Preliminary hearing.
- Formal charges.
- Arraignment.
- Trial.

The Arrest and Initial Appearance

A crime is an offense against the people. Once a law enforcement agency learns that a crime has been committed, the agency begins a criminal prosecution. The first step in a criminal prosecution is to gather evidence of the crime and identify all possible suspects. When the law enforcement agency is convinced that it has ample evidence of both the crime and the identity of the suspect, an arrest warrant is issued, and the suspect is arrested. At the time of arrest, the defendant must be informed of his or her rights. One of the principal rights of the accused is the right to be represented by counsel. This right is guaranteed by the Sixth Amendment to the Constitution. Another important right is the right to remain silent, which is protected under the Fifth Amendment, which states that a criminal defendant cannot be compelled to be a witness against him- or herself. The U.S. Supreme Court has ruled that the 14th Amendment to the Constitution requires that both the right to remain silent and the right to representation by counsel must also be protected by state governments. The defendant is then brought before a judge or a magistrate for an initial appearance, where once again the defendant is reminded of his or her rights. At this time, a preliminary hearing is also scheduled.

Defendants must be informed of their rights at the time of arrest. Two important rights are the right to representation by counsel and the right to remain silent.

The Preliminary Hearing

A **preliminary hearing** is a court procedure during which the judge decides whether probable cause exists to continue holding the defendant for the crime. The government is represented by an attorney called the **prosecutor**. In some states, this government official is called the district attorney. During the preliminary hearing, the prosecution and the defendant are permitted to make arguments and call witnesses. The case will move on to the next step if there is probable cause to hold the defendant. If not, the defendant is set free.

The Formal Charges

In the United States, formal charges against the defendant may be brought either by indictment or by information. Some states do not have a grand jury system and therefore can bring formal charges only by an information. In those states that use both, the indictment is usually used to bring formal charges for serious crimes.

A QUESTION OF ETHICS

Reading Rights: What Is Right and What Is Wrong?

Edward McDonough, assistant district attorney for the city of Middletown, has just left a session with Harold Harrison, a criminal defendant accused of armed robbery. During the session, acting under the advice of Jennifer Miller, his attorney, Harrison confessed to the crime and entered a plea bargain agreement that will place him in prison for 10 years. On his way back across the city square to his office, ADA McDonough is stopped by Sgt. Anne Wade, who confesses to him that neither she nor her partner, Sgt. Sam Newton, read Harrison his rights. McDonough knows that this admission means that the confession he just obtained is tainted and would be thrown out of court if it were challenged by Miller on behalf of Harrison. From an ethical point of view, what action should McDonough take now?

An Indictment The federal courts and many state courts bring formal charges against the defendant by issuing an indictment. An **indictment** is a set of formal charges against a defendant issued by a grand jury. A *grand jury* consists of citizens who serve as jurors for a specified period of time to review a variety of criminal cases. The objective of a grand jury review is to determine whether probable cause exists to believe that a crime has been committed and that this particular defendant may have committed the crime. Grand jury proceedings are held in secret and are directed by the prosecutor or district attorney. If the grand jury finds probable cause exists, an indictment is issued.

An Information An **information** is a set of formal charges against a defendant drawn up and issued by the prosecutor or district attorney. No grand jury is involved in this process. Nevertheless, an information does the same thing that an indictment does. If the prosecutor has found that probable cause exists to indicate that a crime has been committed and that this particular defendant committed the crime, an information is issued.

The Arraignment

The **arraignment** is a formal court proceeding, during which the defendant, after hearing the indictment or information read, pleads either guilty or not guilty. Should the defendant enter a guilty plea, a sentence may be imposed immediately. If the defendant enters a plea of not guilty, the case moves on to the trial.

The Criminal Trial

If the defendant has requested a jury trial, a jury is selected. After the jury has been seated, each side makes its opening statement. Opening statements are followed by the production of evidence by both the prosecution and the defendant. One very significant difference between a criminal trial and a civil trial is the burden of proof. In a civil trial, the plaintiff must prove his or her case by a preponderance of evidence. In contrast, in a criminal case, the prosecution must prove the defendant's guilt beyond a reasonable doubt. As is the case with civil procedure, the criminal trial is completed by the attorneys' closing statements and the judge's instructions to the jury. The jury members are then allowed to retire to deliberate and decide on a verdict. In most states, a defendant can be found guilty only by the unanimous agreement of all of the jurors. A defendant who is found not guilty is released. One who has been found guilty is sentenced by the judge.

---

quick quiz 3-4

1. The objectives of a criminal prosecution are to protect society and to punish the wrongdoer by a fine or imprisonment.   true | false

2. The steps in a criminal prosecution include the arrest and initial appearance, the preliminary hearing, the formal charges, the arraignment, and the trial.   true | false

3. A crime is an offense against a single individual.   true | false

---

Summary

3.1 Courts are judicial tribunals that meet in a regular place and apply the laws in an attempt to settle disputes fairly. The federal court system is divided into three levels: the district courts, the courts of appeals, and the U.S. Supreme Court. State systems vary in structure but often consist of several levels, including lower-level limited jurisdiction trial courts, higher-level trial courts, intermediate appellate courts, and state supreme courts.

3.2 Litigation begins when the plaintiff files a complaint with the appropriate trial court. The defendant must then be given a copy of the complaint and a summons. During the pre-answer stage, the defendant may attempt to dismiss the lawsuit by filing certain pre-answer motions. In the answer stage, the defendant will file an answer, which may contain affirmative defenses, counterclaims, and/or cross-claims. The defendant at this time may also file third-party complaints. During the pretrial stage, conferences may be held, motions may be made, and discovery conducted. The trial includes the opening statement, each side's case in chief, the opportunity for rebuttal and surrebuttal, the closing arguments, and the jury instructions. The jury then renders a verdict. Either party may appeal the case if that party believes that a legal error was made during the trial that influenced the verdict unfavorably. If a judgment is not paid, the court may issue a writ of execution.

3.3 Cyber-jurisdiction (AKA electronic jurisdiction and e-jurisdiction) is the power of the court to hear a case based on Internet-related transactions. The Federal Rules of Civil Procedure now permit federal courts to allow, and at times even require, lawyers to file court documents electronically. The Federal Rules now refer to cyber-evidence as electronically stored information (ESI). The rules also now deal with special situations involving ESI and discovery.

3.4 The steps in a criminal prosecution include the arrest and initial appearance, the preliminary

hearing, the formal charges, the arraignment, and the trial. At the time of the arrest, the defendant must be informed of his or her rights. Immediately following the arrest, the defendant is brought before a judge or a magistrate for an initial appearance, at which time the defendant is again reminded of his or her rights. A preliminary hearing is also scheduled. A preliminary hearing is a court procedure during which the judge will decide whether probable cause exists to continue to hold the defendant pending formal charges. Formal charges against the defendant may be brought either by indictment or by information. The arraignment is a formal court proceeding, during which the defendant pleads guilty or not guilty. The trial includes the opening statement, each side's case, the closing arguments, and the jury instructions. The jury then renders a verdict.

Key Terms

abuse of discretion, 56

affirmative defense, 64

answer, 64

appeal, 68

appellate jurisdiction, 56

arraignment, 75

case in chief, 67

civil litigation, 62

class action, 63

clearly erroneous standard, 56

complaint, 62

courts, 55

cross-appeal, 68

cross-examination, 67

cyber-jurisdiction, 69

damages, 67

defendant, 62

demurrer, 63

depositions, 65

direct examination, 67

discovery, 65

diversity cases, 56

electronic/e-jurisdiction, 69

electronically stored information (ESI), 71

equitable remedy, 67

federal question, 56

forum shopping, 63

general jurisdiction, 56

indictment, 74

information, 74

injunction, 68

interrogatories, 66

jurisdiction, 55

liability, 67

minimum contacts, 57

original jurisdiction, 55

personal jurisdiction, 56

plaintiff, 62

plenary review, 56

preliminary hearing, 74

prosecutor, 74

rebuttal, 67

request for admissions, 66

request for a physical or mental examination, 66

request for real evidence, 66

service of process, 63

special jurisdiction, 56

specific performance, 67

stream of commerce, 57

subject matter jurisdiction, 56

summary judgment motion, 65

surrebuttal, 67

verdict, 67

writ of certiorari, 60

writ of execution, 68

Questions for Review and Discussion

1. What is the fundamental nature of the American court system?
2. Under what circumstances might a federal court have jurisdiction to hear a case?
3. Under what circumstances might the U.S. Supreme Court hear a case?
4. What is the structure of a typical state court systems?
5. What is civil litigation?
6. What are the most common discovery techniques?
7. What is involved in an appeal?
8. How is cyber-jurisdiction determined?
9. What is electronically stored information?
10. What are the steps in a criminal prosecution?

Cases for Analysis

1. William Stevenson offered to help Rayford LeBlanc remove his truck from the mud. At first, LeBlanc refused. However, later, when the towing company that LeBlanc had called proved to be unavailable, he accepted Stevenson's offer of assistance. LeBlanc then bought a towing strap from a nearby store to help in the removal of his truck from the mud. The first two attempts at removing the truck failed. On the third attempt, while LeBlanc was still in the process of connecting the straps to his truck, Stevenson, apparently without warning, pulled his vehicle forward. This movement caught LeBlanc by surprise. His hand was still wrapped up in the strap, and therefore, as Stevenson's vehicle moved forward, LeBlanc's hand was severely injured. LeBlanc sued Stevenson for damages related to the injuries to his hand. The jury decided that Stevenson was not at fault, and LeBlanc found himself on the losing end of the lawsuit. Accordingly, he appealed the case. The appellate court threw out the jury's factual finding and awarded LeBlanc over $190,000 in damages. Stevenson hollered "foul" and asked the Supreme Court of Louisiana to hear his request to have the decision reversed. The high court accepted the case. One of the central issues involved the question of whether, and under what circumstances, an appellate court can overturn decisions of fact made by a jury. Should the supreme court uphold the appellate court's decision? What standard of review should be involved here? Explain. [See: *LeBlanc v. Stevenson*, 770 So.2d 766 (Sup. Ct. LA).]

2. On October 12, 2000, an American naval vessel, the U.S.S. *Cole*, was bombed while it was berthed in Aden Harbor in Yemen in the Middle East. The bombing, which killed 17 American sailors, was planned and executed by Al-Qaeda. Relatives of those 17 sailors brought a lawsuit in U.S. District Court against the foreign state of the Republic of Sudan, alleging that Sudan was responsible for the bombing because that government supported al-Qaeda in general and the terrorists who carried off this assault in particular. The government of the Republic of Sudan moved to dismiss the case, arguing that the court lacked subject matter jurisdiction. The argument was based on the fact that the case involved citizens of states of the United States in an attempt to sue a foreign government, something not permitted under federal law. Is the government of Sudan correct in this case? Explain. [See: *Rux v. Republic of Sudan*, 461 F.3d. 461 (4th Cir. 2006).]

3. The state of Alabama was required under the provisions of its own constitution to reapportion its electoral districts every 10 years; however, the state had failed to reapportion districts for more than half a century. Since then, the population of Alabama had grown to such an extent that severe inequalities existed among the electoral districts. The inequalities were so great in some cases that the votes of citizens in some parts of the state carried as much as 10 times the weight of the votes of citizens in other parts of the state. A suit was brought in federal court on the grounds that the

inequalities in voting power violated certain guarantees found in the U.S. Constitution. The defendants argued that the federal court should not interfere in what is essentially a state matter and that by doing so, it would upset the delicate balance between the states and the federal government. Nevertheless, the federal district court struck down the apportionment scheme as unconstitutional. Does this case belong in the U.S. Supreme Court? Explain the reasons for your response. Should the Supreme Court uphold or overturn the federal district court's decision? Explain. [See: *Reynolds v. Sims,* 377 U.S. 533 (U.S. Sup. Ct.).]

4. Speculate on which of the following cases the U.S. Supreme Court might decide to review: a case involving a dispute over whether computer software can be copyrighted; a case involving an appeal of a zoning board's decision to limit the number of adult book stores on any single city block; a case involving the constitutionality of an abortion statute; a case involving an antitrust suit based on a violation of a federal antitrust statute between the National Football League and a former seller of NFL sports gear; a libel case against a small town newspaper involving allegations of the mayor's dishonesty; a case involving the placement of a religious scene on city property; a case brought by a steel company to enjoin employees from going on strike; a case involving the distribution of anti-war flyers at a private shopping mall; and a case involving the search of a high school student's locker without her permission. In each case, give reasons for your answer.

5. Eight limited partners filed a lawsuit in the Lucas County Court of Common Pleas, alleging that the general partners in 10 different limited partnerships had engaged in an extensive pattern of self-dealing that had involved converting partnership property for their own personal use. Also named in the lawsuit was the accounting firm of Donald J. Goldstein, CPA, a resident of Florida, and Goldstein, Lewis, and Company, a professional corporation located in Florida. The plaintiffs claimed that the accountant and the accounting firm had known of the general partners' misconduct and were therefore liable to the plaintiff for that malpractice. The accountant and the accounting firm decided to end the suit as quickly as possible. Consequently, they filed a motion for dismissal.

The motion stated that the courts of Ohio lacked personal jurisdiction over them because they were from Florida. They further stated that they did not solicit business in Ohio, maintained no place of business in Ohio, had no license to act as accountants in Ohio, owned no property in Ohio, provided all services from Florida, and filed no documents with the state of Ohio. Thus, they concluded that they fell outside the power of Ohio's long-arm statute. Conversely, the plaintiffs argued that the defendants transacted business in the state of Ohio on a continuing and ongoing basis by regularly submitting financial statements to the limited partners in Ohio and by being actively involved in the decisions of the general partnership. Did the activities of the accountant and the accounting firm place them under the jurisdiction of the Ohio court, according to the state "long-arm" statute? Explain. [See: *Goldstein v. Christiansen,* 638 N.E.2d 541 (OH).]

6. The criminal defendant in this case, a man named Gideon, broke into a pool room in Florida with the objective of committing a minor crime. Because Gideon was without any means of financial support, he could not afford an attorney. He asked for but was denied representation by a court-appointed attorney. Consequently, he represented himself at trial. Ultimately, he was found guilty and sentenced to five years in prison. Gideon later challenged his conviction on the grounds that he had been deprived of his constitutional right to representation by an attorney. In opposition, Florida argued that, though all fundamental rights guaranteed by the federal government through the Bill of Rights should also be guaranteed by state governments, the right to legal representation was not such a fundamental right. In fact, the right to a court-appointed attorney arose only when the criminal defendant had been accused of a very serious crime. The U.S. Supreme Court agreed to hear the case. How should the Supreme Court rule in this case? Is the right to an attorney a fundamental right that should be guaranteed to criminal defendants by the states, regardless of the seriousness of the crime? Explain. Examine the Constitution and find the amendment that guarantees the right to representation by an attorney. Examine the Constitution and find the amendment that extends that right to defendants in state criminal actions. [See: *Gideon v. Wainwright,* 372 U.S. 355 (U.S. Sup. Ct.).]

7. Ernesto Miranda was arrested in his own home for a serious crime and held in an interrogation room. He was not informed of his right to remain silent, nor was he informed that he could be represented by an attorney. Eventually, after a two-hour interrogation conducted by two police officers, Miranda signed a statement that indicated he had voluntarily confessed to the crime of which he was accused. On the basis of the confession, Miranda was found guilty. He appealed to the Arizona Supreme Court, which affirmed the guilty verdict. Miranda asked the U.S. Supreme Court to hear his appeal. Is this the type of case that belongs in the U.S. Supreme Court? Explain the reasons for your response. Should the Supreme Court uphold or overturn the state court's conviction of Miranda? Explain the Constitution and find the amendment that guarantees the right to remain silent when arrested for a criminal action. Examine the Constitution and find the amendment that extends that right to defendants in state criminal actions. [See: *Miranda v. Arizona,* 384 U.S. 436 (U.S. Sup. Ct.).]

quick quiz Answers

3-1	3-2	3-3	3-4
1. T	1. F	1. T	1. T
2. T	2. F	2. F	2. T
3. T	3. F	3. F	3. F

Chapter 4 — Alternative Dispute Resolution

THE OPENING CASE *Round 1*
Revelation: A Referee's Reference Ruins Reward

Alternative dispute resolution (ADR) techniques, including such things as arbitration and mediation, have become very popular recently, especially in state courts. ADR techniques are preferred because they keep costs down, provide quick decisions, and produce unbiased results—maybe. Case in point: Mt. Holyoke Homes, LP (MHH) brought a malpractice lawsuit against Jeffer Mangels Butler and Mitchell, LLP (JMBM), a law firm that had represented MHH in an earlier case. The contract between MHH and JMBM called for arbitration, and the trial court decided to enforce that requirement. As often happens in these situations, the parties had some difficulty finding an unbiased arbitrator. The first arbitrator, a judge named Patricia Collins, was dismissed because she had previous dealings with the accused. The next candidate on the list, Judge Eli Chernow, was found to be acceptable to both parties, despite having been a mediator in a previous case involving the defendant. The arbitration process went sour almost immediately for MHH. The arbitrator not only decided that JMBM was not at fault, but also ordered MHH to pay $18,132.81 in back attorney's fees from the earlier action, $285,000 in legal fees in the present action, and $150,000 in court costs also in the current case. Bowed but not beaten, an MHH representative did a computer search for information about Judge Chernow and learned that he had listed one of

JMBM's partners as a reference on his vita. MHH yelled "foul" and appealed. The trial court affirmed the arbitrator's decision, but the appeals court disagreed, stating that the plaintiff was justified in feeling that the arbitrator might be biased. JMBM asked the California Supreme Court to review the case, but the court refused to do so. The appellate court, however, thought that parties who discover such information should be prepared to reveal it immediately, or lose the chance to assert it later. The moral of the story seems to be fourfold. (1) Arbitrators should be open and honest about past entanglements or risk having their decisions vacated. (That's what happened here.) (2) The arbitration parties have no duty to research the arbitrator's background on their own. (3) The real issue before the court is whether a reasonable person standing in the place of a party to the arbitration would be justified in believing that the arbitrator might be biased, not whether the arbitrator really was biased. (4) On the other hand, parties who have reason to believe that an arbitrator might be biased, but do not speak up, ask questions, or challenge the arbitrator until after the arbitrator's decision has been made, may find that the arbitrator's judgment will stand. That was not what happened here, but the court did feel it necessary to explain this caveat before closing the opinion. [See: *Mt. Holyoke Homes, LP, et al. v. Jeffer Mangels Butler and Mitchell,*

LLP, 219 Cal. App. 4th 1299 (Cal. Rptr. 3d. 567) (2013); John S. Warnlof and Leslie A. Fales, "Updates on Alternative Dispute Resolution," *Contra Costa Lawyer Online,* February 1, 2014.]

Opening Case Questions

1. What is the difference between arbitration and mediation and which one was used in this case? Explain.

2. Why would the parties in the original contract agree to the ADR clause in the first place? Explain.

3. Which of the alleged advantages to ADR seems to have been frustrated in this case? Explain.

4. What did the second arbitrator do wrong, if anything, that led to the result in the case? Explain.

5. What duty do the parties have when they uncover negative information about an arbitrator? What consequences should follow when they do not live up to that duty? Explain.

 Learning Objectives

1. Examine the shortcomings of litigation.
2. List the advantages and the disadvantages of ADR.
3. Identify the advantages of mediation.
4. Explain the nature of an arbitration hearing.
5. Outline the med-arb process.
6. Relate the role of the early neutral evaluator.
7. Describe the process of running a summary jury trial.
8. Clarify the private options available under proactive ADR.
9. Specify the governmental options available under proactive ADR.
10. Discuss the pros and cons of the collective science court proposal.

4-1 A Briefing on ADR Strategies

As we have seen at various points throughout the text, the law is often reflected in a series of dualities. These dualities include the symmetry sought between the spirit and the letter of the law, between legal words and their interpretation, and between abstract principles and concrete situations. This synchronization is also involved in the application of the uncertainty principle to legal disputes. Thus far we have focused on the dispute-solving process known as litigation. Litigation has always been part of the American legal system. Lately, however, things have begun to change. The complexity, the expense, and the time involved in litigation have discouraged many potential litigants who have decided to sidestep the regular court system in favor of pursuing more efficient, effective, and economical methods of settling their disputes. These unconventional methods are referred to as the alternative dispute resolution process, or simply as ADR. **Alternative dispute resolution (ADR)** occurs whenever people move outside the traditional adversarial system and try to solve their legal dispute by using creative settlement techniques, many of which have fact-finding, and truth as their goals rather than simply achieving a final victory. Thus, we have a fourth duality in the law: the duality that exists between the traditional litigation system and the unorthodox ADR process.

Problems with Litigation

Many people choose a dispute resolution process that sidesteps the adversarial approach of civil litigation because they believe that it is the best way to achieve justice. Part of this belief is based on the suspicion that, with an adversarial approach, victory often depends not on who is in the right but on which advocate is the better tactician. Watching hours of television dramas such as *Damages, Silk, The Good Wife, Boston Legal, L.A. Law,* and *Law and Order* has probably contributed to this extreme notion of how the law operates. Unfortunately, the best tactician is often one of the most expensive advocates available, which can mean that justice often goes to those who can afford it. For this reason, many people seek an alternative that is less costly to both sides.

Litigation can also be expensive because of the initial steps that lead to the filing of a lawsuit. For instance, before an attorney can file a medical malpractice lawsuit, he or she must obtain the client's medical records, which means paying an initial copying fee that can amount to hundreds or even thousands of dollars. The attorney must then hire an expert to evaluate the records to determine whether the information in the records indicates that the client has a viable claim. Again this expense can run into hundreds or thousands of dollars. All these expenses are encountered before the attorney even knows that a claim actually exists.

In addition to being expensive, litigation can be time consuming. The initial steps after the filing of a complaint can delay progress on a lawsuit for many months. For instance, should the defendant's motion for dismissal be granted by the court, a lengthy and time-consuming appeal process may ensue. In some cases, the appeal could even find its way to the highest court in the jurisdiction. In such a case, if the highest court reverses the lower court's dismissal of the action, the case quite literally returns to the starting line. Another time-consuming step in litigation is the process of discovery. Taking depositions, answering interrogatories, filing, and responding to requests for real evidence and handling requests for mental or physical examinations can tie up a lawsuit for months.

Moreover, some jurisdictions require litigants to submit to case management hearings and settlement hearings before they can secure a trial date. Even when a court date is secured, many court dockets, especially those in large urban areas, are backed up for months, or even years, which often means that the parties to a lawsuit must wait for long periods of time before having their day in court. Even once a trial has occurred and a decision rendered, recovery can be delayed as the parties enter a second phase of the lawsuit, the execution of the judgment phase. This process involves its own complex set of procedures, which, like the actual lawsuit, can cause expensive and time-consuming delays.

The ADR Option

ADR can, however, provide an economical and efficient alternative to litigation. Depending on the ADR technique employed, the time involved in settling a dispute can be shortened considerably and the expenses lowered significantly. Arbitration and mediation, for example, can be scheduled quickly, even before a lawsuit is filed. When scheduling either a mediation or an arbitration session, the parties need not consult the court's dockets or worry about any preliminary requirements, such as a case management conference. Moreover, even if the arbitration or mediation session does not end the dispute, it can save time by narrowing the issues or providing an evaluation of the strength of each side's case. The arbitration or mediation session may also, in some cases, provide a shortcut to discovery, thus saving time and lowering expenses.

Other ADR approaches, such as early neutral evaluation (ENE), can save money and time by providing an assessment of the issues at stake and the range of damages available, should the outcome of the case demand a remedy of some sort. Summary jury trials, private trials, and mini-trials can all be inexpensive and quick because they can be scheduled without regard to the court's docket and can be held without the expenses involved in hiring expert witnesses and providing travel and hotel accommodations for those witnesses. The cost and time involved in lengthy discovery processes can also be avoided by selecting any one of these ADR techniques.

Private proactive ADR techniques such as drafting contract clauses and entering partnering agreements can help to make litigation unnecessary from the out-set. The idea behind the proactive ADR approach is to anticipate and deal with disputes before they occur. By providing a solution to problems before those problems arise, proactive ADR eliminates the uncertainty and risk inherent within the litigation process.

ADR options provide a timely, cost-efficient method for resolving legal issues.

Shortcomings of ADR

Yet ADR is not without problems. On the contrary, some critics of the process have pointed out that the private administration of justice hampers the development of the law. Because many ADR techniques sidestep the courts, many critical social issues may never reach the judicial system, causing gaps in the evolution of case law and the progression of legislation. Another criticism of ADR involves its limited scope. Some legal conflicts, notably employment, contract, and tort cases, are especially well suited for ADR; however, other legal problems, primarily those involving constitutional law, civil rights, and criminal law, could never be brought before an ADR panel.

THE OPENING CASE *Round 2*
Revelation: A Referee's Reference Ruins Reward

Recall that in the opening case, the plaintiff, Mt. Holyoke Homes, LP (MHH), brought a malpractice lawsuit against Jeffer Mangels Butler and Mitchell, LLP (JMBM), a law firm that had represented MHH in an earlier case. The contract between MHH and JMBM called for arbitration, and the trial court decided to enforce that requirement. Now recall that one key advantage to the use of any ADR strategy is that the process is supposed to save time and money. This case not only did not save time but also ended up being outrageously expensive. The first problem emerged when the parties could not settle on an arbitrator. Recall that their first choice was rejected because she had previous dealings with the accused. The next candidate on the list was acceptable and the matter proceeded. The second problem cropped up when, after losing, MHH decided to do some post-decision Web surfing and uncovered that the arbitrator had listed one of JMBM's partners as a reference on his vita. This led to a reconsideration of the

case by the trial court, an appeal to the appellate court, and after that, a request that the California Supreme Court hear the case, a request that was refused. The third problem emerged from the arbitrator's original ruling, which found in favor of JMBM and ordered MHH to pay $285,000 in legal fees and $150,000 in the present action. Now, the arbitrator's decision was overturned, but that $435,000 bill is still floating out there somewhere and someone is going to have to pay it (or JMBM will be forced to absorb the costs). Moreover, the case continued after that ruling and more legal fees and court costs piled up and up and up. So is ADR less expensive and less time consuming? Just ask MHH and JMBM, and you'll have a fairly straightforward answer. [See: *Mt. Holyoke Homes, LP, et al. v. Jeffer Mangels Butler and Mitchell, LLP,* 219 Cal. App. 4th 1299 (Cal. Rptr. 3d. 567) (2013); John S. Warnlof and Leslie A. Fales, "Updates on Alternative Dispute Resolution," *Contra Costa Lawyer Online,* February 1, 2014.]

Other difficulties associated with ADR have also appeared in recent years. One problem is that ADR does not always save time and money the way it is supposed to. Typically, two of the advantages that supporters of ADR promote are the ideas that ADR is less expensive and less time consuming because such procedures do not get tangled up in the red tape of the court system. Unfortunately, this is not always the case. Sometimes even cases that are decided by arbitration end up in the court system. Most often this happens when one or more of the parties decide to challenge the decision of the arbitrator. When such challenges occur, there is only one place for the parties to go: to court.

Two additional advantages of ADR are that little discovery and very few motions are involved in the process, thus saving the litigants a lot of money. Although this argument sounds good in theory, it does not always play out in reality. Unfortunately, sometimes a case may actually take longer to resolve because there is no discovery or motion practice involved. Part of the delay is due to the fact that discovery and motion practice often help attorneys focus on the most crucial issues in a case. Also, discovery will sometimes reveal that it is necessary to settle a case rather than proceeding to trial. When there is no discovery or motion practice, the issues remain wide open. This gap means that attorneys must anticipate all the possible moves that their opponents might make. The lack of discovery also means that the small flaws in an argument may not be revealed, and a case that would have been settled during a conventional lawsuit might drag on in arbitration.

Admittedly, ADR is not intended as a replacement for the legal system. Rather, it is intended to provide potential litigants with a wider variety of choices when they are facing a legal dispute. As noted previously, because of the delays and the expense involved in litigation, many people would like to avoid that route altogether. Others would like to find a way to streamline the litigation process, so that, should the need for a trial finally present itself, the preliminary steps can be administered as painlessly as possible. With these facts in mind, we will proceed with an examination of ADR techniques.

quick quiz 4-1

1. Adversarial litigation has only recently become a part of the American legal system.   true | false

2. Two of the advantages that supporters of ADR promote are the ideas that ADR is less expensive and less time consuming than litigation.   true | false

3. ADR is not intended as a replacement for the legal system.   true | false

Did You Know?

When mediation is used to settle cases of sexual harassment in the workplace, 85 percent of those cases are resolved successfully without anyone having to go to court.

4-2 Responsive ADR Strategies

Numerous ADR techniques can be invoked once a dispute has arisen between parties. These include but are not limited to mediation, arbitration, med-arb, early neutral evaluation, summary jury trials, and private civil trials.

Mediation

According to the American Arbitration Association, **mediation** is "a non-binding process where a neutral third party works with the parties to reach a mutually agreeable settlement." The neutral third party is referred to as a **mediator**. Some people erroneously confuse mediation with negotiation. Negotiation is the usual way that attorneys handle disputes before they end up in litigation. Such negotiation is part, or at least should be of every dispute that might possibly lead to litigation. In fact, negotiation is something that can take place before a lawsuit is filed, after it has been filed, before trial, and even during trial. There is no specially designated neutral third party "negotiator" during negotiation as there is during mediation. The job of the mediator is to convince parties to adjust or settle their dispute. The mediator will try to persuade the parties to reach some sort of compromise but cannot decide what the parties will do. [See: American Arbitration Association, FAQ's. Retrieved June 28, 2010, from http://www.aamediation.com/FAQ.]

Like the timing of a negotiation conference, the timing of a mediation session can vary. Sometimes mediation follows the filing of a lawsuit but sometimes it occurs to prevent a lawsuit from being filed. Mediation can occur before a conflict, during a conflict, after a conflict, or when a settlement following a conflict is not being followed properly. [See: The JAMS Foundation, retrieved July 28, 2010 from http://ww.jamsdr.com.] Mediation is often more successful than litigation, because in mediation the parties remain involved in the settlement of the dispute. Unlike litigation, which is decided by a judge or jury, a mediation session is in the hands of the parties. The mediator does not decide the disagreement. Rather, he or she serves as an intermediary who attempts to understand what brought the parties into disagreement and what issues lay at the heart of the disagreement. The mediator does not act as a therapist, a judge, or an advocate. Rather, he or she acts as an impartial outsider who can suggest solutions that will please all the parties involved in the dispute. Often the mediator can cut to the center of a dispute in objective ways that are unavailable to the parties themselves.

EXAMPLE 4-1: Mediation: Practical Solutions to Practical Problems

Bruce Langton brought suit against David Winchester in small claims court after Winchester's daughter, Jackie, backed her car into Langton's truck, causing extensive damage to the front end of the vehicle. Langton wanted damages in the amount of $4,000. Langton's sister-in-law, Wendy Miller, suggested that the parties hire a mediator to try to reach a settlement. During the mediation session, the mediator saw that the real issue was the fact that Langton's truck was still damaged. Winchester's brother, who owned and operated an auto body shop, agreed to fix Langton's truck at no cost. This solution satisfied both parties. Langton had his truck fixed, and Winchester suffered no out-of-pocket expenses.

Arbitration

Arbitration is the process by which the parties invite a third party, called an arbitrator, to settle their dispute. The procedures involved in arbitration are generally more flexible than those followed in a lawsuit. The rules are either set by law or agreed to by an arbitration agreement. The hearing may be relaxed, with the arbitrator or arbitrators receiving informal testimony from the parties, or it may be rigidly controlled, with the arbitrator or arbitrators following strict rules of evidence and requiring lengthy explanations. The parties may agree in advance to be bound by the arbitrator's decision. If they do not so agree, the arbitrator's decision can be appealed in court. There is a common misconception that arbitration, and mediation for that matter, are carried out exclusively by non-lawyers. Sometimes arbitrators are lawyers and sometimes they are not. This is made clear by the American Arbitration Association, which states that arbitrators must have "senior level experience in law, business, industry or another profession." [See: American Arbitration Association, FAQ's. Retrieved June 28, 2010, from http://www.aamediation.com/FAQ.]

About the Law

The American Arbitration Association booklet *National Rules for the Resolution of Employment Disputes* includes rules on both mediation and arbitration.

Some states require arbitration prior to trial in certain cases. Required arbitration is called mandatory arbitration. Some litigants have challenged government-imposed mandatory arbitration as an unconstitutional deprivation of their right to a trial by jury and equal protection under the law. Most states faced with this question have disagreed with these arguments as long as the arbitration requirement does not replace the jury trial and as long as the motives for requiring arbitration are reasonable.

An arbitration hearing can be planned and executed by the parties themselves. Generally, this step means that the parties set the ground rules for choosing the arbitrator or arbitrators, for conducting discovery, for presenting evidence, for determining the outcome, and for enforcing the reward. In addition, details such as setting the time and the place of the hearing, filling vacancies on the arbitration panel, recording the proceedings, handling objections, granting time extensions, and so on, must also be agreed upon. Because of the intricacies of such a process, many individuals who select arbitration prefer to use professional arbitration organizations such as the American Arbitration Association to handle the details of their arbitration proceeding.

Like most forms of ADR, arbitration is not without its difficulties. One shortcoming is that an arbitration hearing is run like a trial but without the safeguards that come with the rules of civil procedure, discovery, and motion practice. This characteristic may actually extend the time involved in arbitration because attorneys and negotiators must prepare a wide variety of legal arguments, some of which might have been eliminated during motion practice. Discovery also sometimes reveals facts that lead the parties into settlement negotiations that might not otherwise take place. Moreover, the wide discretion that is usually granted to arbitrators has, in some cases, led to unreasonable decisions and unjustifiable awards. Sometimes the decision made by an arbitrator comes under the review of the courts, which may result in a reversal of the arbitration order and thus frustrate the whole object of entering arbitration in the first place. Some of these difficulties can be overcome by stipulating that an arbitration award cannot be reversed by the courts except to correct a violation of the arbitration agreement itself.

The difficulties associated with discovery can be solved by streamlining the discovery process in arbitration, without going to the extremes represented by the way that discovery

THE OPENING CASE *Round 3*
Revelation: A Referee's Reference Ruins Reward

Reconsider once again the opening case. Recall that one of the longest and most expensive delays in the process took place after the arbitrator's ruling had been made. It was at that time, after everything was supposed to be said and done, that somebody with MHH decided to research the background of the arbitrator. What was discovered made the case more time consuming and more expensive, and sent the entire process back to the beginning of the cycle. The search for that crucial piece of evidence about the arbitrator's background, while strictly speaking was not discovery, involves a fact-finding process

that should have been conducted earlier in the process. The time involved in allowing a compromised arbitrator to address the case and make a ruling, plus the expense involved (remember the $435,000) makes ordinary litigation look like a short-term, inexpensive, and fair-minded exercise in legal and judicial efficiency. [See: *Mt. Holyoke Homes, LP, et al. v. Jeffer Mangels Butler and Mitchell, LLP,* 219 Cal. App. 4th 1299 (Cal. Rptr. 3d. 567) (2013); John S. Warnlof and Leslie A. Fales, "Updates on Alternative Dispute Resolution," *Contra Costa Lawyer Online,* February 1, 2014.]

is conducted in litigation. Other problems can be solved by making sure that arbitrators follow the same rules in all hearings and insisting that they write down the reasons behind their decisions.

Med-Arb

Med-arb is an ADR process that combines mediation with arbitration. Under med-arb procedures, the parties first submit their dispute to a mediation session. If the dispute is settled via mediation, then all of the parties can leave satisfied. If, however, some matters are left undecided, the parties can move on to an arbitration hearing. During the hearing, the undecided issues would be placed before an arbitrator for final deliberation.

Early Neutral Evaluation

Early neutral evaluation (ENE) is an ADR process in which the parties permit a referee to assess their case on the basis of the facts and legal arguments alone. At the outset of an ENE process, an independent, objective referee is provided with an overview of the facts involved in the dispute and a summary of the legal arguments on which each side has built his or her case. The evaluator, after examining the facts and the law, renders an impartial assessment of the legal rights of each party and a determination of the amount of the award that should be rendered, if any. The parties can use this impartial evaluation to either settle the case or proceed to trial. Even if the ENE does not result in a final decision, it can be used to shape the issues, plan discovery, and guide any research that the attorneys must conduct as the case proceeds to trial.

Summary Jury Trials

A **summary jury trial** is a shortened version of a trial conducted in less than a day before an actual jury that then renders an advisory verdict in the case. The summary jury process offers litigants a chance to see how a jury would react to the facts of the case, as well as to the legal arguments that will be made by both sides at trial. On the day of the summary jury trial, lawyers from both sides present an abbreviated version of the case to an actual jury. The presentations are simplified, focusing on the essential facts and law. In this way, the summary jury trial eliminates much of the redundancy that occurs during a "real" trial and allows the judge and jury to focus on the essentials of the case.

As noted previously, the ultimate objective of a summary jury trial is to help both sides evaluate the effectiveness of their arguments in front of a judge and jury. This effort in turn helps the attorneys shape the issues and select the positions that are most advantageous to their case. This knowledge is enhanced by the fact that, after the trial, each side has the chance to interview the jurors to see why they reacted as they did.

The success or failure of a summary jury trial depends on several factors. First, only those cases that involve a *bona fide* dispute as to the facts or authentic questions of law should be considered for a summary jury trial. Second, advanced planning is necessary to ensure a successful summary jury trial. The judge must be consulted, issues should be settled, the facts should be composed properly, the jury instructions should be determined, and a date and time established before the trial begins.

Third, during the process, strict controls and ironclad time limits must be imposed on the parties. For instance, opening statements should last no more than 20 minutes. Both sides should have no more than 1 hour for the presentation of their case in chief and 30 minutes for their rebuttal. The closing arguments should also be limited to no more than 20 minutes. Finally, a conference should be held after the trial, during which the parties have the opportunity to discuss an immediate settlement. Such a conference should be held after the jury has been polled so that their input can be factored into the settlement discussion.

EXAMPLE 4-2: Summary Jury Trials: A Posttrial, Pretrial Settlement

When Ashley Utalizar was discharged from her job with Solarpower Industries Inc., she was certain that the dismissal had been in direct violation of an implied contract that had been created by Solarpower's employee policy manual. When she brought a lawsuit against Solarpower, both parties decided to hold a summary jury trial. After the trial was held, both sides participated in a posttrial settlement conference. The results of the jury poll indicated that, though the jury had decided in favor of Utalizar, they were unable to agree on the amount of damages that should be awarded to her. As a result, both Solarpower and Utalizar decided that it would be in their best interests to settle the case immediately. The attorneys for Solarpower agreed to the settlement because they saw that the jury was sympathetic to Utalizar, while Utalizar's attorneys agreed that they could not be certain that Utalizar would receive an adequate award if the jury were permitted to decide the amount of damages.

Because one reason for holding a summary jury trial is to determine how the judge and jury will react to the facts and the arguments, it is helpful to have observers gauge how the judge and the jurors react to the points made by both sides. The observers, who are often students recruited from local law schools and paralegal institutes, will record the reactions of the judge and the jurors during the trial. As an alternative, the entire process can be recorded, so that reactions can be observed later.

Private Civil Trials

A **private civil trial** is an ADR technique by which the parties hire a retired judge or magistrate to hear their dispute, following the same rules used in an official trial. Many states now permit the parties to a lawsuit to have their cases tried in a private civil trial rather than an official court. One advantage of a private trial is that the parties can hold the trial at a time and a place of their own choosing. In addition, the parties have the opportunity to choose their own judge. Decisions rendered by a judge in a private civil trial are just as binding as those made by judges on the official court docket. Moreover, private trial decisions can be appealed in the same way that public decisions are appealed.

Private civil trials are not postponed nor are they interrupted because the court has more pressing duties to perform. In addition, a private trial receives the undivided attention of the judge, who is not sidetracked by the need to attend to other matters such as the sentencing of criminal defendants. Intricate, lengthy civil cases are ideally suited for private civil trials because, in such cases, time is money. Consequently, the shorter the trial, the less expensive the final bill facing the client.

In recent years, some private firms have appeared that specialize in setting up private civil trials. Such firms will make most of the arrangements for the litigants. These arrangements include securing a judge, providing the place for the trial, and providing all necessary administrative support. These firms can also provide a jury for the trial. Jurors for private trials are generally selected from a pool of individuals who have recently served on a jury in an official trial; therefore, the jurors at the private civil trial are well acquainted with the trial procedures.

4-3 Proactive ADR Strategies

All of the ADR techniques discussed thus far are invoked after a dispute has arisen. Since ADR has become so popular in recent years, some business people are taking a proactive approach to the situation by agreeing in advance to submit to one of the alternative dispute resolution tools should a disagreement between the parties arise later. These proactive ADR techniques include, but are not limited to, partnering, ADR contract clauses, settlement week, negotiated rule making, post-appellate procedures, international arbitration agreements, and the collective science court proposal.

Partnering

Partnering is a process that establishes supportive relationships among the parties to a contract to head off disputes before they occur. Generally, partnering is best used when a contract involves complex interrelationships among a wide variety of different parties. Construction agreements are ideally suited to partnering arrangements, because construction contracts involve contractors and subcontractors, all of whom must perform in a cooperative manner to fulfill a contract that often takes a long period of time to complete.

Partnering attempts to deter the disorder that can arise during a dispute by drawing up certain ground rules that all the parties agree to observe. The entire process begins with a meeting held after the contract has been finalized but before the project has begun. The meeting is held at a location that is unrelated to the business of any party to the contract. In this way, the process can procede in an uninterrupted fashion.

Moreover, the meeting should be directed by an objective third party, whose job it is to help create an atmosphere of trust among the parties to the contract. The parties attempt to anticipate problems that may arise during the project as well as potential solutions to those problems. The parties agree to address all problems when they arise and to look for solutions that will mutually benefit all those involved in the project. Ultimately, the goal is to improve efficiency, ensure safety, and maximize profit by minimizing expenses, especially those that arise from cost overruns.

The parties agree to handle problems according to some ADR technique rather than by litigation. Finally, they agree to deal with one another in a fair manner within the confines of their legal relationships.

ADR Contract Clauses

An **ADR contract clause** will specify that the parties to the agreement have promised to use an alternative dispute resolution technique when a disagreement arises rather than litigating the issue. Like partnering, the drafting of ADR contract clauses is a proactive attempt to ensure that litigation will be avoided should a dispute arise. Unlike partnering, which is best suited to long-term construction contracts, ADR clauses can be included in just about any contract.

These ADR clauses can take many shapes and forms. It is possible, for instance, to insert a clause that states merely that the parties have the option of using an ADR technique. Such a clause is weak, at best, serving only to remind the parties that they do not have to sue one another to gain satisfaction. One step beyond the optional clause is a compulsory clause. This clause states that the parties are required to submit all claims that arise under the contract to an ADR technique, most often mediation or arbitration, before filing a lawsuit. The final type of clause would require the parties to submit any claim to binding arbitration. This strictest ADR clause forces the parties to abide by the decision of the arbitrator.

Regardless of the type of clause used by the parties, the language should include certain standard provisions. For instance, the clause should specify the types of disagreements that will be submitted to ADR, the ADR technique or techniques that can be used, the scope of discovery allowed, the substantive law and the procedural rules that will be followed in the proceeding, the remedies that will be authorized, the grounds for and the procedure to follow in an appeal, and the methods of enforcing an award. The failure to follow provisions specified in an ADR clause may be grounds for the court to revoke a ruling made by an arbitrator.

Such ADR clauses have several advantages. They are especially helpful when two or more parties have embarked on an extended affiliation that may involve numerous contracts, because ADR clauses clearly establish a reliable and predictable method of dealing with the disputes that will inevitably arise whenever two parties are involved in a lengthy association with each other. In addition, ADR clauses are very beneficial to those parties with the weakest position within a contractual relationship. Often, when a dispute does arise, the more powerful party will threaten litigation, secure in the knowledge that he or she can afford a lawsuit more easily than the weaker party. An ADR clause eliminates this leverage point.

Because the parties to an ADR clause agree, at least initially, to forgo the right to litigate any claims that arise among them, the courts prefer that such clauses be clear and precise. Clauses that are drafted in imprecise and ambiguous language may be invalidated by the court. If the parties intend to submit all the claims arising out of their contractual relationship to ADR, they should spell that out as precisely and completely as possible. Otherwise a party that later wishes to invoke the clause may find that the court is reluctant to support that position. When writing an ADR contract clause, it is best to use standard expressions that the court will recognize. Clauses that say the parties agree to use ADR for "any controversy or claim arising out of or relating to the agreement" will convince the court to enforce the clause for most disputes between the parties. Anything less may meet with judicial resistance.

The court will also be sensitive to any clauses, conditions, or procedures that are unconscionable. Something will be deemed unconscionable by the court if it is so outrageous that it literally "shocks the conscience of the court." Such clauses are usually engineered to produce results that are favorable to the party that has all, or at least most, of the power in the relationship and then uses that power to fashion an agreement that is almost totally in his or her favor. If the other party to the agreement must accept that agreement on a take-it-or-leave-it basis, the court is not likely to enforce it. Unconscionable clauses usually fall into one of two categories: (1) procedural unconscionability and (2) substantive unconscionability. Procedural unconscionability is generally related to the methods by which the agreement is obtained, while substantive unconscionability refers to the way that the agreement is to be carried out. The accompanying ethics case is a memorable illustration of unconscionability—perhaps even what might be called *super*-unconscionability.

A QUESTION OF ETHICS

A Blueprint for Procedural and Substantive *Super*-Unconscionability

When Zenia Chavarria applied for a job at Ralphs Grocery Company she was required to read, fill out, and sign a fairly complex employment application that included an arbitration clause. The clause included a politely worded request for a signature ("Please sign and date the employment application . . . to acknowledge you have read, understand and agree to the following statements.") that was followed later by a statement that indicated the policy would be in effect even if the employee did not sign the document. (Nice touch!) The arbitration clause did not actually disclose the procedure that would be followed. In fact, Chavarria did not receive the policy itself for three weeks. Moreover, when she finally did have the policy in hand, what she found was a document written in complicated legalese that ran for four pages of single-spaced text. In addition, the procedure set up for choosing the arbitrator was clearly devised so that the employer would inevitably get the final binding choice. Additionally, the appointment of arbitrators from the two most reputable arbitration organizations on record, the Judicial Arbitration and Mediation Service (JAMS) and the American Arbitration Association (AAA), was forbidden by the agreement. What is more, the policy required the arbitrator to divide the fees between the arbitrating parties regardless of the merits of the case. After Chavarria left her job at Ralphs she filed a lawsuit arguing that Ralphs violated various provisions of the California Labor Code and California Business and Professions Code.

As soon as Ralphs moved to apply the arbitration clause, Chavarria contended that the clause was unconscionable both (1) procedurally and (2) substantively. *Both* the district court *and* the court of appeals agreed with Chavarria. Why? Well, take a look: (1) Procedurally the clause was unconscionable because it forced employees to accept the contract on a take-it-or-leave-it basis, giving them no chance to object, modify, challenge, or argue. Moreover, if employees refused to sign, the contract was still valid. Additionally, the actual policy was not revealed to the employee for three weeks and then in a document that was long, complex, and difficult to comprehend. In addition, (2) substantively, the document was unconscionable because (a) it made sure the choice of the arbitrator was up to the employer; (b) made certain that the best arbitrators in the business (those in JAMS and AAA) would not sit as arbitrator; and (c) guaranteed that the costs were shared regardless of the outcome of the process. In short, what we have here is a memorable illustration of *super*-unconscionability. [See: *Chavarria v. Ralphs Grocery Company*, 733 F. 3d. 916 (9th Cir. 2013); John S. Warnlof and Leslie A. Fales, "Updates on Alternative Dispute Resolution," *Contra Costa Lawyer Online*, February 1, 2014.]

Settlement Week

Settlement week is a five-day period during which a court's docket is cleared of all business, except for settlement hearings. Prior to the opening of settlement week, all attorneys with cases pending before the court are asked to choose which of those cases might be best handled by a mediator. Judges are also permitted to nominate cases for mediation during settlement week. Also before the opening of settlement week, a list of volunteer mediators is compiled. Cases are then matched with mediators, and a schedule is established. Attorneys are required to be present for the mediation session.

A mediation session is then held for each case. Following each session, the mediator is required to file a report with the court, stipulating the results of the session and asking for the judge's approval. Occasionally, some cases, chiefly those that do not involve determining liability, are submitted to an arbitration panel rather than to a single mediator. In such a situation, the plaintiff chooses one of the arbitrators, the defendant chooses one, and the court names the final one. Not all cases scheduled for settlement week are actually resolved during that time; however, the technique is an effective way to lighten the court's docket and is becoming more and more popular.

Negotiated Rule Making

Negotiated rule making (reg-neg) is a process by which an agency invites the people and the organizations to be affected by a new rule to have input into the writing of that rule. A working team is established that consists of representatives of the affected groups, including the agency issuing the rule. One member of the team is an objective outsider trained in the art of facilitating such discussions. The objective of negotiated rule making, of course, is to avoid disputes before they have a chance to blossom.

All representatives have the opportunity to present their point of view in relation to the proposed rule. Discussions follow, during which all of these issues are examined. Eventually, the team is expected to formulate a rule that reflects a consensus of the representatives. This consensus does not necessarily mean that all parts of the rule are enthusiastically embraced by all of the representatives. Rather, it means that all of the parties agree that they have fashioned a rule that everyone on the rule-making team can live with. The text of the proposed rule is then submitted to the rule-making agency. The success of the process depends on the willingness of the members of the team to work in a cooperative fashion and the willingness of the agency to accept the results of the team's deliberations.

Despite its advantages, negotiated rule making cannot be used in all situations. Certain subject areas are more fitting than others. A suitable subject area for reg-neg would be one that will ultimately affect a wide range of individuals and institutions, is both complicated and controversial, and would meet with resistance if those individuals and institutions affected did not have a hand in shaping the rule. Reg-neg is also a wise course of action when the subject area affected involves nuances that fall outside the expertise of the agency representatives.

EXAMPLE 4-3: Reg-Neg: The Great Lakes Initiative

The Ohio Environmental Protection Agency (OEPA) was charged with drafting a series of rules to implement the Great Lakes Initiative. Rather than simply writing the rules and placing them before the affected parties, the OEPA decided to take a negotiated rule-making approach. Consequently, it created the Great Lakes Initiative External Advisory Group (EAG). The EAG was composed of representatives from the agency itself, from the regulated industry, and from environmental groups. The team engaged in eight months of intense negotiations. These negotiations followed a precisely planned series of steps carried out under the watchful eyes of professional facilitators. The EAG reached a firm consensus on most of the issues that arose during the negotiations. Consequently, the Joint Committee on Agency Rule Review of the Ohio General Assembly adopted a set of rules to implement the Great Lakes Initiative in a relatively harmonious atmosphere and with almost no conflict. This is an extremely successful example of reg-neg in action.

Post-Appellate Procedures

Post-appellate procedures involve taking a case that has been rejected or dismissed by a domestic court to an international organization such as the Inter-American Commission on Human Rights of the Organization of American States. In such a situation, a party that has exhausted all domestic remedies available, up to and including the United States Supreme Court, might ask such a **non-governmental organization (NGO)** to hear its case. The post-appellate case is brought against the government of the aggrieved party for allegedly failing to provide an appropriate legal remedy to redress the grievances of the victim. The claim generally involves the violation of some fundamental right, generally a due process or an equal protection right that is guaranteed by an international document such as the American Declaration of the Rights and Duties of Man or the United Nations Universal Declaration of Human Rights. The NGO then hears the case, considers the evidence, and determines whether the party's claim is justified. The NGO may demand that the government of the aggrieved party provide compensation for the injuries visited upon the victim. The NGO may also suggest actions beyond that compensation, including needed reforms in the governmental and/or judicial system to prevent such problems from occurring in the future. Whether the NGOs actually have jurisdiction over such claims is open to debate. Moreover, even if they have jurisdiction, whether their findings are actually enforceable against the government in question is problematic.

International Arbitration Agreements

An **international arbitration agreement** involves a pledge to use arbitration should the parties find themselves in disagreement as to the enforcement rights under the original contract. Generally, the agreement permits the parties to agree on a forum in which the arbitration will be held that is different from the home forum of either party. The parties also can agree to use the rules and procedures promulgated by an independent institution, such as the International Bar Association's Rules of International Commercial Arbitration.

There are several clear advantages to entering an international arbitration agreement. First, because the parties to the agreement are incorporated in different nation-states, they are free to specify whatever forum they can agree upon as the place to hold an arbitration hearing, should that become necessary. This agreement is in contrast to a litigation clause that might specify that the law of one or the other nation would apply to any legal dispute between the parties. Ultimately, such a clause can become very restrictive. The law of a particular nation-state might, for instance, specify that a dispute that arises within the borders of that nation-state would have to be tried within that nation-state. This rule can put one of the two corporations at a distinct disadvantage that may not become evident until the lawsuit has begun. Arbitration agreements can avoid this problem because the arbitration hearing can be held on neutral ground.

Second, when negotiating an arbitration agreement, the parties are also free to specify the identity of the arbitrators or leave open the option to choose the arbitrators at the time of the dispute from a large pool of potential experts. The arbitrators can thus reside in any location that satisfies all of the parties. Third, the same option is open to the parties in relation to their choice of legal representation. Rather than being limited to the forum in which the dispute is to be heard, the parties can bring in representation from any point on the globe. Fourth, using an international arbitration agreement avoids one of the most troublesome problems linked to international litigation: enforcement. Often a party that has won a favorable decree in one nation will find it challenging to execute that decree in any other nation. International arbitration eliminates this problem because the original arbitration contract will include the terms of enforcement.

Of course, as is often the case, the best laid plans of mice and CEOs often go astray. Thus, sometimes a corporation will find that the jurisdiction that it has chosen for an arbitration hearing has different ideas about whether certain arbitrators and/or attorneys will be permitted to practice within its borders. If a country decides that certain legal representatives and certain arbitrators are not welcome in its jurisdiction, then the parties may find themselves using local attorneys and/or arbitrators, something that not only defeats the objective of the international arbitration agreement but also places the validity and acceptability of the entire arbitration process at risk. This possibility also delays the process further because when an arbitrator is dismissed, the entire action usually must begin again.

Nor are these risks trivial. The danger is especially acute in Latin America, where some nation-states still apply a 19th century legal principle that says that foreign corporations doing business in a Latin American country or involved in an international legal dispute within the borders of such a country must apply the law of that country, regardless of any agreement made by the parties to the contrary. Sometimes this agreement means simply securing local legal assistance, but it can also mean that the foreign attorneys operating within that jurisdiction are subject to local law, which sometimes includes criminal penalties for not following the procedural rules of that jurisdiction. (Note: For a more detailed look at the problems associated with international arbitration agreements see Lawrence W. Newman and David Zaslowsky, "International Litigation/International Arbitration—Pitfalls for Participants," *International Litigation and Arbitration Newsletter* November 2006, pp. 3–7 retrieved from http://www.bakernet.com. The article first appeared in *The New York Law Journal,* September 29, 2006).

The Collective Science Court Proposal

A proposed **collective science court (CSC)** would act as a forum for disputes involving scientific and technological controversies. Individuals and institutions with concerns about certain scientific activities, such as genetic engineering, nuclear energy research, and so on, might ask the CSC to act as an impartial arbitrator in the evaluation of those concerns. The judges on the collective science court would be scientists who have had additional legal training and lawyers or judges who have received further education in scientific issues, thus allowing them to use their expertise in deciding scientific cases.

Supporters of the collective science court maintain that a panel of objective judges with scientific backgrounds would provide a neutral body capable of making unbiased, well-informed decisions. Moreover, the CSC would not necessarily provide the last word in any case held under its jurisdiction because an appellate stage would be part of the system. Finally, the decision-making process involved in science-related controversies would be centralized by the collective science court, thus providing a forum that many individuals could use to their advantage.

Critics of the CSC proposal argue that a panel made of objective judges with combined scientific and legal backgrounds would be almost impossible to convene, unless some sort of specialized scientific legal academy was established to turn lawyers into scientists and scientists into lawyers. Moreover, critics also point out that the CSC would represent an additional level of bureaucratic red tape. In addition, such a forum could rapidly become buried under an avalanche of claims, many of which would be a frivolous waste of the court's time. Furthermore, some critics argue that, because the issues placed before a collective science court would be highly controversial, the entire process could be plagued by political considerations that would threaten the legitimacy of the court itself.

This last group of critics also questions the basic need for a CSC. Some of these analysts point out that, in the main, scientific knowledge is a central issue in a lawsuit in only three situations: (1) when patent law is involved, especially in the evaluation of the validity of a current patent; (2) when scientific evidence must be evaluated by the judge or jury, which often happens in tort law, medical malpractice, product liability, environmental law, and cyber-law cases; and (3) when an experimental station (a supercollider, for example) or an environmentally risky factory or power plant (read nuclear power here) is planned for a particular locality.

Patent Law Cases

In relation to the first issue of *patent law,* the anti-CSC analysts argue that the Court of Appeals for the Federal Circuit is already in place to handle patent claims in an effective and efficient manner. There are merits to this outlook. The fact that the Federal Circuit is already in place and functioning would decrease the time needed to refurbish it as the new CSC. Also, the current judges have a great deal of experience managing such cases; however, as indicated in Chapter 3, the Federal Circuit has had its problems. For instance, the court's handling of a recent case has revealed its confusion over the criteria for patent approval.

Scientific Evidence

In relation to the second issue of *scientific evidence,* the anti-CSC lobby argues that the standard for evaluating scientific evidence, known as

CLASSIC CASE The Case for a Collective Science Court

The classic case of *Daubert v. Merrell Dow Pharmaceuticals, Inc.,* involved a lawsuit filed by the Dauberts against Merrell Dow in which the plaintiffs argued that Bendectin, a drug produced by Merrell Dow and taken by Mrs. Daubert for nausea during her pregnancy, had caused birth defects in their children. The case depended on the issue of causation, a traditional tort law principle that says that, to succeed in a negligence lawsuit, a plaintiff must prove that the defendant's action caused the plaintiff's injury; however, because of the scientific nature of the case, the court needed expert testimony to determine causation. The judges were faced with two competing lines of evidence. The defendant's evidence included peer-reviewed articles published in scientific journals and studies issued by the Federal Drug Administration (FDA). None of these reports or articles could find a link between Bendectin and birth defects. In response, the plaintiff's scientific experts offered a reanalysis of the accepted data. This reanalysis demonstrated that the original data had been badly misinterpreted by previous scientists. To determine which line of evidence should be followed, the court had to interpret Rule 702 of the Federal Rules of Evidence and *Frye v. United States,* a case that predated Rule 702, but that had, nevertheless, set up a standard that the federal courts had used for decades to evaluate expert testimony. Ultimately, the Supreme Court established the

following five-stage test for determining the scientific accuracy of expert testimony:

1. Is the theory or technique subject to testing under the falsifiability principle?

2. Has the theory or technique been subjected to peer review and publication?

3. What is the known potential error rate of the theory or technique?

4. What standards of control and measurement exist for the theory or technique?

5. Is the theory or technique generally accepted by the scientific community?

The court was also quite clear that the judge in the case is charged with the responsibility of being the "gatekeeper" who determines the admissibility of scientific evidence based on these standards. The court also emphasized that it is not the results that matter, but the reliability of "the principles and the methodology" used to reach those results. What do you think? Are judges, who are educated in legal reasoning techniques and standards, capable of making scientific decisions based on these five criteria? Would scientists retrained in legal reasoning do a better job at interpreting the standards? [See: *Daubert v. Merrell Dow Pharmaceuticals, Inc.,* (509 U.S. 579) (U.S.S.Ct.); *Daubert v. Merrell Dow Pharmaceuticals, Inc.,* 43 F.3d 1311 (Ninth Circuit).]

the *Daubert* Standard, is a clear and straightforward criteria that requires no special scientific training. While this argument seems legitimate at first glance, the *Daubert* Standard has been plagued with difficulties that are not always evident to the lay observer. The accompanying examination of the fallout from the *Daubert* case illustrates this point.

The *Daubert* standard seems to be straightforward enough and should have solved the problem of scientific evidence, but of course it did not. A survey conducted 10 years after the establishment of the standard and reported in an article that appeared in the *Ohio State Law Journal* revealed that 96 percent of the 400 judges covered by the study lacked a fundamental grasp of the first principle of falsifiability and the third principle of "error rate." These results indicate that a simple reinterpretation of the rules, even one reengineered very carefully by the Supreme Court, did not solve the problem of scientific evidence and may even have aggravated it. Additional efforts are under way short of the CSC that have helped deal with the issue of science in the courts. For example, the Advanced Science and Technology Adjudication Resources (ASTAR) in Washington, D.C., was established by Congress as a scientific and technological educational resource center for judges. Also, as noted in Chapter 3, the Federal Judicial Center has inaugurated a decade-long pilot project aimed at determining what improvements might be made to the way that patent law cases are handled by the Federal Circuit. It remains to be seen whether such steps will eliminate the need for the proposed CSC. [See: Joelle Anne Moreno, "Einstein on the Bench?" *Ohio State Law Journal* 64:531 (2003); "Science in the Court: NHGRI Scientists Present Latest Genomic Advances to Visiting Judges," *National Human Genome Research Institute,* June 2010; Karen Redmond, "District Courts Selected for Patent Pilot Program," *The Third Branch News,* June 7, 2011; "The Patent Pilot Program Takes Off Around the Country," *Gibbons IP Law Alert,* October 20, 2011.] In Chapter 6, the Daubert case is revisited to examine how the Federal Rules were amended to help judges deal with scientific evidence.

Scientific Construction   In relation to the third issue, the *scientific construction* of experimental stations, nuclear power plants, genetic engineering centers, supercolliders, and the like, those opposing the CSC insist that creating a science court to determine future development in a region gives too much authority to a nondemocratic institution. One vivid example of this type of struggle occurred in Minnesota. In that case, two power cooperatives, the Cooperative Power Association and the United Power Association, announced their intention to construct high-voltage power lines across Minnesota farmland. The owners of the farms involved challenged the project, arguing that the planned route of the lines would destroy their ability to use their own farmland appropriately. The governor of Minnesota called for the creation of a science court to resolve the issue. The science court would have been made of scientists, engineers, and other experts educated in the discipline and the industry involved in the dispute, thus allowing them to use their expertise in deciding the case.

The Minnesota experience seemed to confirm the fears of the anti-CSC lobby at least in two respects. First, a science court will not succeed unless it has the power to compel the parties to submit to its authority. In the Minnesota case, for instance, the co-ops saw no reason to cooperate with a voluntary court because their project had already been approved by conventional authorities. Second, a successful science court must have the power to halt work on any project that is the focus of the court's investigation. Otherwise, the court's entire process becomes an exercise in futility. On the other hand, these nondemocratic features could be overcome if the court is fashioned to ensure that all sides have the opportunity to present their views on all issues facing the court. Permitting certain parties to speak on certain issues while denying the same right to others can destroy the credibility of the court and of those involved in its creation and operation. [See: Barry Casper and Paul Wellstone, *Powerline: The First Battle of*

America's Energy War (Amherst: U of Massachusetts Press, 1981); Barry Casper and Paul Wellstone, "Science Court on Trial in Minnesota," *Science in Context* (Cambridge: MIT, 1982).]

quick quiz 4-3

1. The partnering process begins with a meeting held after a contract has been finalized but before the project has begun.   true | false

2. In negotiated rule making, a government agency creates a new set of regulations without the troublesome, time-consuming, expensive, and difficult step of getting input from its constituency, thus streamlining the process, saving money, and eliminating controversy.   true | false

3. The proposed science court would act as a forum for disputes involving scientific and technological controversies.   true | false

Summary

4.1 Litigation has always been a part of the American legal system. Lately, however, things have begun to change. The extensive backlog in many court systems and the perceived injustice of many verdicts have led many people to seek other methods to redress their grievances. These other methods are often grouped under the heading of alternative dispute resolutions (ADR). Alternative dispute resolution occurs whenever individuals attempt to resolve a disagreement by stepping outside the usual adversarial system and applying certain creative settlement techniques, many of which have fact finding and the discovery of truth as their goal.

4.2 There are many different ADR techniques that can be invoked once a dispute has arisen between parties. These include but are not limited to mediation, arbitration, med-arb, early neutral evaluation, summary jury trials, and private civil trials.

4.3 Since ADR has become so popular in recent years, some businesspeople are taking a proactive approach to the situation by agreeing in advance to submit to one of the alternative dispute resolution tools should a disagreement between the parties arise later. These proactive ADR techniques include, but are not limited to, partnering, ADR contract clauses, settlement week, negotiated rule making, international arbitration agreements, the post-appellate option, and the collective science court proposal.

Key Terms

ADR contract clause, 89

alternative dispute resolution (ADR), 81

arbitration, 85

arbitrator, 85

collective science court (CSC), 94

early neutral evaluation (ENE), 87

international arbitration agreement, 93

med-arb, 87

mediation, 84

mediator, 84

negotiated rule making (reg-neg), 92

non-governmental organization (NGO), 93

partnering, 89

post-appellate procedures, 92

private civil trial, 88

settlement week, 91

summary jury trial, 87

Questions for Review and Discussion

1. What are the shortcomings of litigation?
2. What are the advantages and disadvantages of ADR?
3. What are the advantages of mediation?
4. What is the nature of an arbitration hearing?
5. What happens during the med-arb process?
6. What is the role of an early neutral evaluator?
7. What happens in the running of a summary jury trial?
8. What are the private options available under proactive ADR?
9. What are the governmental options available under proactive ADR?
10. What are the pros and cons of the collective science court proposal?

Cases for Analysis

1. Turner Pte. Ltd. was the main contractor in the building of *Gateway,* a long-term project to be constructed in the heart of Singapore. One of Turner's subcontractors was a company called Builders Federal Ltd. (BFL). As part of the overall contract, the two companies signed an arbitration agreement, which was designated as Clause 22 in the main contract. When the two parties found themselves in the middle of several serious disputes, they invoked Clause 22 and began arbitration. Turner asked that David Gardam be appointed as the arbitrator, and BFL asked for Douglas Smith. The court appointed Smith. From the outset there was bad blood between Turner and Smith, which was revealed in a series of letters that went back and forth between the parties and Smith. At one point in the process, Turner realized that Clause 22 actually had no legal effect until each party activated it by giving their permission to proceed with arbitration. Smith denied that this was the case and ordered the arbitration process to continue. Turner objected, and Smith, who admitted that Turner had made a fairly convincing case, agreed to submit that argument to the High Court of Singapore. Nevertheless, Smith pushed the arbitration process forward. BFL was delighted, but Turner objected. Still the action went forward despite the precarious nature of Smith's position as arbitrator. Can the high court of Singapore dismiss Smith even though BFL is quite satisfied with his work as arbitrator? What grounds might be used to dismiss Smith? If Smith is dismissed, will the arbitration process continue or start over? [See: *Turner (East Asia) Pte. Ltd. v. Builders Federal (Hong Kong) Ltd.* SLR 532 SGHC 47 (Singapore High Court).]

2. Jessica Gonzales obtained an official restraining order from a Colorado court that prevented her estranged husband from approaching either her or her children any closer than 100 yards. The order, however, did not stop her husband, who kidnapped their three children. Mrs. Gonzales went to the police and asked for their help. The police did very little to help her, despite the restraining order. Early the next morning, Mr. Gonzales arrived at the police station and began shooting at police officers, who shot back and eventually killed him. After the shooting was over, the police found the bodies of the three young daughters in Mr. Gonzales' truck. Mrs. Gonzales brought suit against the police department, arguing that her due process rights had been violated when the police did not enforce the restraining order. The case went from trial court to the appellate court to the United States Supreme Court, with no result other than a dismissal of the suit. Mrs. Gonzales, with the assistance of the American Civil Liberties Union, filed a post-appellate complaint against the United States with the Inter-American Commission on Human Rights. In her complaint, Mrs. Gonzales argued that she had been deprived of due process and equal protection under the American Declaration of the Rights and Duties of Man, an agreement that the United States was legally bound to follow. Mrs. Gonzales and her attorneys hoped that the commission would issue a judgment in her favor and against the United States. What two initial questions must be answered first before this post-appellate case can begin? Explain. [See: *Jessica Ruth Gonzales v. The United States of America,* Petition No. P-1490-05, The Inter-American Commission on Human Rights of the Organization of American States.]

3. In a case involving an ADR clause, the parties to a contract disagreed as to whether the clause required them to submit a dispute over a trade secret problem to arbitration. The clause required the parties to submit "any controversy or claim arising out of the agreement" to arbitration. Strictly speaking, the trade secret controversy did not arise "out of" the agreement; however, it was clear that the trade secret dispute was related to the agreement. The trial court held that the language of the ADR clause was too narrow and that because the trade secret dispute did not arise out of the controversy, the parties were not required to send it to arbitration. Should the appellate court overrule the trial court's decision rejecting the requirement that the parties arbitrate the trade secret dispute? Explain your response. [See: *Tracer Research Corp. v. National Environmental Services, Co.,* 42 F.3d 1292 (9th Cir.).]

4. In the early 1990s, serious concerns about the dangers associated with genetic engineering arose after an incident pertaining to the use of certain genetically altered mice in experiments involving a highly infectious disease. In the wake of these concerns, the National Institute of Allergy and Infectious Diseases held a conference to discuss the level of safety that should be followed in laboratories involved in such research. Those involved in the conference included the researchers themselves, certain biosafety experts, representives from organizations involved in or planning to be involved in similar research, and governmental representatives from the Centers for Disease Control, the National Institutes of Health, and the Food and Drug Administration. Would this type of situation be appropriate for a reg-neg approach? Explain. Might a science court handle this type of situation even better than an agency's reg-neg procedure? Explain.

5. Adam Bontrager, the defendant, purchased a piece of land. Before the sale, the previous owner had been notified by the Department of Health that the current septic system on the property was not up to specs. Consequently, the Health Department ordered a systems upgrade. Once Bontrager bought the property the obligation to upgrade the system passed to him. Bontrager began the process of upgrading the system and then stopped. Bontrager argued that, since he was Amish and since his religion forbid him to use electricity, which the upgrade required, the Health Department order was a violation of his religious rights under the U.S. Constitution. Without the system upgrade, untreated sewage was flowing into a local stream causing a health hazard. As a result, the defendant was cited for a violation of the administrative code and fined accordingly. The case seems to be one for which ADR is well suited. Can the judge order arbitration or mediation in this case? Why or why not? [See: *State v. Bontrager,* 149 Ohio Misc.2d 33 (Newton Falls Municipal Court).]

6. Audrey Kemmelman, a freelance photographer, entered a work-for-hire agreement with *The Daily Montgomery Central Times* Corporation. During the negotiation stages, Kemmelman asked that an ADR clause be added to the contract that would compel the signatories to submit any claim to ADR. The clause stated that, in the event of any dispute, the signatories to the contract would first discuss the points of conflict informally. If after 30 days, no satisfactory solution had been reached, the signatories agreed to submit the problem to the American Arbitration Association, which would assist in selecting an objective moderator who would help the signatories decide on an appropriate ADR method. Which party is likely to benefit the most from the addition of the ADR clause to the contract? Explain.

quick quiz Answers

4-1	4-2	4-3
1. F	1. T	1. T
2. T	2. T	2. F
3. T	3. T	3. T

Chapter 5

Criminal Law and Cybercrimes

THE OPENING CASE *Round 1*
Mitigating and Aggravating Circumstances: Who Decides?

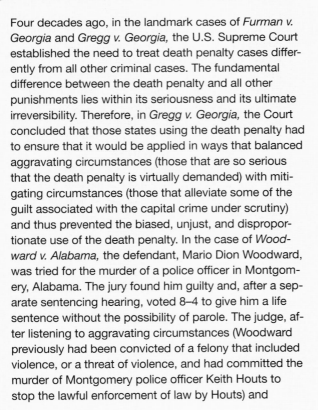

Four decades ago, in the landmark cases of *Furman v. Georgia* and *Gregg v. Georgia,* the U.S. Supreme Court established the need to treat death penalty cases differently from all other criminal cases. The fundamental difference between the death penalty and all other punishments lies within its seriousness and its ultimate irreversibility. Therefore, in *Gregg v. Georgia,* the Court concluded that those states using the death penalty had to ensure that it would be applied in ways that balanced aggravating circumstances (those that are so serious that the death penalty is virtually demanded) with mitigating circumstances (those that alleviate some of the guilt associated with the capital crime under scrutiny) and thus prevented the biased, unjust, and disproportionate use of the death penalty. In the case of *Woodward v. Alabama,* the defendant, Mario Dion Woodward, was tried for the murder of a police officer in Montgomery, Alabama. The jury found him guilty and, after a separate sentencing hearing, voted 8–4 to give him a life sentence without the possibility of parole. The judge, after listening to aggravating circumstances (Woodward previously had been convicted of a felony that included violence, or a threat of violence, and had committed the murder of Montgomery police officer Keith Houts to stop the lawful enforcement of law by Houts) and

mitigating circumstances (Woodward's beneficial relationship with his five children, ages four to nine, and his traumatic and abusive childhood) decided, instead, to sentence him to death. The Supreme Court did not grant *certiorari* in the case, but Justice Sotomayor (joined in part by Justice Breyer) submitted a dissenting opinion that argued that the Court should have granted *certiorari* because Alabama courts have a record of transforming life sentences into death sentences in a way that is more than a little disproportionate with the way that it is done in other states. In fact, Sotomayor pointed out that, of the 27 instances of sentences moving from life to death in the past 14 years, 26 are found in the Alabama criminal courts. Her conclusion? Something is rotten in the State of Alabama, and she believes that it rests on a judicial system that is held hostage by its need to satisfy the demands of the voting public. What do you think? [See: *Woodward v. Alabama,* 571 U.S.—(2013); *Gregg v. Georgia* 428 U.S. 153 (1976); and *Furman v. Georgia,* 408 U.S. 238 (1972).]

Opening Case Questions

1. Why is the death penalty different from other punishments and why does it, therefore, deserve a different set of standards? Explain.

2. What are aggravating circumstances? Explain. What are mitigating circumstances? Explain.

3. What mitigating circumstances were used by the defense to convince the jury to sentence Woodward to life instead of death? Explain.

4. Justice Sotomayor argues that the judges in Alabama are too responsive to the will of the voting public. Who or what should the judges be responsive to if not the voting public? Explain.

5. Federal judges (and justices) are appointed for life, not elected as they are in Alabama. Using the theory of human nature promoted by Hobbes and Madison, as well as the Alabama example, defend the federal appointment process.

(LO) Learning Objectives

1. Explain the purpose of criminal law.
2. Enumeate the various categories and classes of crimes.
3. Describe the nature of an act within the concept of criminal liabiliy.
4. Identify the four mental states to be found in the criminal code.
5. Explain the nature of corporate criminal liability.
6. Explain the various theories of punishment within criminal law.
7. Enumerate and explain the elements of several key crimes.
8. Define and explain the nature of cybercrimes.
9. Explain the three standards for the insanity defense in criminal law.
10. Outline the requirements of entrapment as a defense in criminal law.

5-1 Definition and Classes of Crimes

Perhaps one of the most discussed and least understood areas of the law is criminal law. Most people think they know a lot about criminal law, because they read about it frequently in the newspaper and view programs about it on television. In fact, the media spread a lot of misinformation about criminal law and procedure. This section of the chapter attempts to rectify some of these misconceptions by defining crime and explaining the various classes of crimes.

Definition of a Crime

A **crime** is an offense against the public at large. As such, a crime threatens the peace, safety, and well-being of the entire community. For this reason, crimes are punishable by the official governing body of a nation or state. Also for this reason, the state or federal government, representing the public at large, is the prosecution, that is, the one who brings the criminal action. The person accused of the crime is called the defendant. No act can be considered criminal unless it is prohibited by the law of the place where it is committed, and the law provides for the punishment of the offenders. These laws are created by the federal government and the governments of the 50 states.

The Objectives of Criminal Law
The primary objectives of criminal law are to protect the public at large, to preserve order and stability within society, to punish those who commit criminal acts, and to discourage future criminal activity. In contrast, as we shall see, tort law is concerned with private wrongs that have caused injury to an individual's physical well-being, property, business, or reputation. Because tort law involves private

wrongs rather than public ones, it focuses on the victim. Because criminal law protects the public, it seeks to eliminate crime by punishing wrongdoers and removing them from society. When a tort is committed, the victim has a cause of action against the person who has committed the tort, which may permit the victim to recover money as compensation for any injuries that he or she has suffered. In contrast, when a crime is committed the government may prosecute the accused.

A close and unbiased analysis of the objectives of tort law and those of criminal law will reveal to even the most casual observer that criminal law is more akin to the principles supported by Thomas Hobbes and James Madison, while those of tort law sound more like those upheld by John Locke. Recall that Hobbes and Madison were both concerned with protecting two core rights, the right to life and the right to a secure life. The objectives of criminal law include protecting the public at large, preserving order and stability within society, punishing those who commit criminal acts, and discouraging future criminal activity, all of which sound very much like those two core rights. In contrast, the objectives of tort law, which include the vindication of private wrongs that have caused injury to an individual's physical well-being, property, business, or reputation, are reminiscent of Locke's focus on the rights of the individual.

Prosecutions and Lawsuits

A single act can be both a crime and a tort. Thus, when a criminal battery is committed against a victim, the criminal defendant will be prosecuted for that battery in a criminal case, the results of which can include imprisonment, a fine, or both. However, the defendant can also be sued by the victim in tort law. The victim will seek damages from the defendant which can include money for hospital bills, lost wages, pain and suffering, and so on. The standard of proof required in a criminal case differs from that required in a tort case. In a criminal case the prosecutor or district attorney is required to prove that the criminal defendant is guilty of the crime *beyond a reasonable doubt*. In a tort case the plaintiff's attorney must prove that the defendant is liable for the tort *by a preponderance of the evidence*. Because criminal defendants can lose their freedom, be fined, and sometimes, in capital cases, even lose their lives, the level of proof needed for a conviction is higher than what is needed to demonstrate liability in a tort case.

Double Jeopardy

The United States Constitution protects people from being tried twice for the same crime. This principle is called the rule of double jeopardy. Double jeopardy, however, does not protect a defendant from being tried for a criminal offense and then being sued under tort law for that same wrongful act. This is what happened in the case of O.J. Simpson. After being found not guilty for the crime of murder, he was sued by his children for the wrongful death of their mother. This did not violate the rule of double jeopardy. Note that the Simpson case also illustrates the difference between the standard of proof in a criminal case and the standard in a tort case. Thus, although the prosecutors failed to prove Simpson guilty *beyond a reasonable doubt,* he was found liable for wrongful death *by a preponderance of the evidence*. It is also interesting to note that a single offense may trigger two prosecutions if the offense can be designated as two different crimes and can be tried in two different courts. Thus, it is possible, for example, for a police officer to be tried in a state court for assaulting a suspect and be tried in federal court for depriving that same suspect of his civil rights.

Victim's Rights

Under common law, criminal law did not focus on the victim. The theory was that, if the victim needed some sort of compensation for the actions of the defendant, it was up to the victim to pursue that case in tort law. This has been altered somewhat by the legislatures that have enacted statutes that create a series of victim's rights.

These rights often include notice to the victim that an offender has been arrested, the name of the criminal defendant, the defendant's eligibility for pretrial release, the telephone number of the law enforcement agency responsible for the defendant, and the date, time, and place of the defendant's release, if that occurs. Later in the legal process the victim is also generally notified of the defendant's acquittal or conviction, the defendant's incarceration, the defendant's appeal, and the defendant's release date. Victims are also permitted to provide the prosecutor with a written description of his or her injuries. In addition, in many states the victim is permitted to be present at the defendant's trial, is entitled to the return of his or her property, is empowered to give the court a victim's impact statement before sentencing and another statement when the defendant's possible release is pending. In most cases, it is the prosecutor or the district attorney who is charged by law with enforcing the rights of victims.

Criminal Law in the American System

The American legal structure consists of the federal and the state systems. Both make and enforce criminal law; however, because there are 50 states and the District of Columbia, it is actually more accurate to say that the American system is made up of 52 systems. Nevertheless, it is helpful to limit any discussion of the law to an examination of federal and state systems. We simply must remember that each state has its own code and its own procedures, which, though similar in most respects to all other states, may have its own peculiarities.

Federal Criminal Law
Another peculiarity about the American system is that the federal government has no express power in the Constitution that allows it to enact criminal law statutes or establish a national police force. Yet the federal government does enact criminal law and has set up the Federal Bureau of Investigation (FBI) as a national police force. The federal government also has a cabinet-level criminal law enforcement official called the attorney general who has the power to conduct federal criminal investigations. The existence of the federal criminal law system and the various national law enforcement agencies is made possible by the complex adaptive processes at work within the legal system itself.

Criminal Law as Adaptation
The way Congress has assumed powers never granted to it by the Framers of the Constitution demonstrates how the law is a balancing act. The process works something like this: The Framers of the Constitution intended that Congress have only those powers enumerated in Article I, Section 8, of the Constitution. Because the term "police power" is not mentioned anywhere in the Constitution, the Framers did not give that power to the federal government but instead expected the states to exercise all police power. Consequently, Congress can create criminal law statutes only in those areas over which it has jurisdiction. For instance, Congress has the power to coin money, so it can set up laws against counterfeiting. Yet, as we've seen, Congress has created criminal law statutes in areas beyond counterfeiting. If there has been no constitutional amendment explicitly handing Congress police power, how did Congress get the power to create a set of criminal law statutes and a national police force?

The answer is that Congress balanced the actual *words* of the Constitution against the need to *interpret* those words to protect the people from criminal activity. The balance occurred when Congress extended its power through a generous interpretation of the Commerce Clause. The Commerce Clause, found in Article I, Section 8, Clause 3, permits Congress to pass laws that regulate commerce "among the several States." Congress used

CLASSIC CASE The Outer Limits of Federal Jurisdiction

In the classic case of *Wickard v. Filburn,* the U.S. Supreme Court set the outer limits of the federal government's authority to create statutes that, under the Commerce Clause, regulate activities that cross state lines. The case was controversial at the time, and still is, among those commentators who favor limited federal power. This apprehension is understandable since the activities regulated in *Wickard v. Filburn* took place within the borders of a single state. The law in question was the Agriculture Adjustment Act of 1938 (AAA). The plaintiff was an Ohio farmer named Roscoe Filburn who grew winter wheat on his property every year. Filburn also produced and marketed eggs, chickens, and milk. Some of the wheat was sold at market. The rest Filburn kept for use on his own farm. He fed his chickens and cattle, baked bread, and kept some for the next planting. The AAA limited the amount of wheat that he could grow to 20.1 bushels per acre on 11.1 acres. Filburn didn't seem to care much for the limit, and so he planted on 23 acres and produced 239 bushels on the extra 11.9 acres. He was fined by the Department of Agriculture. Believing that the best defense is a good offense, Filburn sued the government, naming then Secretary of Agriculture Claude R. Wickard a defendant in the case. The issue at hand was whether the federal government could, under the authority of the Commerce Clause, regulate an activity that occurred totally within the boundaries of a single state. The case would seem to be rather straightforward. The excess wheat that Filburn produced never left Ohio. In fact, it never left his small farm. Yet Congress not only stated the amount that he could plant and harvest, but also fined him ($117.11) for planting more than he was allowed. Filburn's case climbed the ladder all the way to the Supreme Court. Then, in one fell swoop, the Court expanded the power of Congress to almost unlimited scope. The Court held:

1. The power that Congress has under the Commerce Clause of the Constitution gives it the authority not only to regulate prices but also to control every action that somehow impacts such prices.

2. This power exists whenever an activity has a "substantial economic effect on interstate commerce."

3. The only limit on this regulation is the requirement that congressional control over the activity be "rationally related" to the goal of Congress established in the act.

In this case the Court reasoned that, while the wheat grown and used by Filburn was minuscule, the overall effect, if left unchecked, could have a substantial effect on economic activity. After all, when Filburn and others like him grew wheat and used it for their own purposes, they were not buying wheat in the open market and, thus, we see an economic impact. Look back to the section on the Bill of Rights in Chapter 2, "Sources of the Law," and answer the following question: How would James Madison evaluate the wisdom and the constitutionality of giving Congress powers not literally written down in the actual words of the Constitution, much of which he actually wrote himself? Recall Madison's arguments against the Bill of Rights and you will have your answer here. After *Wickard v. Filburn* does Congress have unlimited regulatory power? Explain. [See: *Wickard v. Filburn,* 317 U.S. 111, 63 S.Ct. 82 (1941).]

this clause to regulate interstate criminal activities, which impact "commerce." Although the ultimate results were a long time coming, eventually the courts, through a series of cases, culminating in the case of *Wickard v. Filburn* (317 U.S. 111, 63 S.Ct. 82), gave their "stamp of approval" to the legislature's creative balancing act. In a sense then, Congress and the courts cooperated to give the federal government police power, a power it did not have under the Constitution. That power includes the authority to create federal criminal law.

Classes of Crimes

Under common law, crimes were dealt with in the order of their seriousness: treason, felonies, and misdemeanors. Most states now divide offenses into felonies and misdemeanors. A **felony** is a crime punishable by death or imprisonment in a federal or a state prison for a term exceeding one year. Some felonies are also punishable by fines. Some states define a felony as a crime subject to "punishment by hard labor," as an "infamous crime," or as a "crime subject to infamous punishment." Manslaughter, armed robbery, and arson are examples of felonies.

Some states also have separate categories for their most serious crimes. For instance, a state might classify premeditated murder and murder as *special felonies* or *capital felonies* if these are the only two offenses that might result in a death sentence or life imprisonment. States may also have a separate category for violent offenses. Sometimes these violent offenses are termed *aggravated felonies*. Assault with a deadly weapon might be an example of an aggravated felony.

A misdemeanor is a less serious crime, generally punishable by a prison sentence of not more than one year. Included in this category are offenses such as disorderly conduct. Some states also have a separate category for their least serious offenses. The label for these least serious offenses varies, but two of the most common are *petty offenses* and *minor misdemeanors*. Traffic violations and building code violations are usually within this classification.

Traffic violations are usually considered petty offenses or minor misdemeanors.

---

quick quiz 5-1

1. A misdemeanor is a crime punishable by death or imprisonment in a federal or a state prison for a term exceeding one year.   true | false

2. The primary objective of criminal law is to protect victims.   true | false

3. It is impossible for a single act to be both a tort and a crime.   true | false

---

5-2 Elements of a Crime

The two elements necessary to create criminal liability are a criminal act and the required state of mind. Although it is difficult to generalize about both of these concepts, certain characteristics are common to each, regardless of jurisdiction. Nevertheless, keep in mind that criminal law is largely statutory in nature. Consequently, specific statutory definitions may vary from state to state.

A Criminal Act

Under American law, a crime cannot be committed unless some act has occurred. An individual cannot be accused of a crime for merely thinking of a criminal act; however, even a small act that appears by itself to be innocent can, in the proper context, become an illegal act. For example, even something as simple as inserting a key into the ignition of a vehicle can constitute an act under the law, if the driver is intoxicated at the time. The act is such an important element to criminal liability that convictions may be avoided or overturned if defendants can show that the statute under which they were prosecuted is ambiguous in its description of the act. Often, such ambiguity will occur when the legislature passes a statute that creates a new offense, when the statute outlaws an activity that may be protected by the U.S. Constitution, or when the statute seeks to outlaw statutes or behavior that cause no imminent negative effect but may eventually lead to great public harm. For instance, the courts have frequently held statutes that outlaw a status, such as drug addiction or vagrancy, to be void for vagueness. The courts have also struck down statutes that are overbroad. The language of a criminal statute is overbroad if the courts cannot determine what specific activity the legislature intended to outlaw.

Omissions and Refusals to Act   At times, the failure to act, an omission, or the outright refusal to act may be considered criminal. Generally, however, an omission must be coupled with a legally imposed duty. An air traffic controller who sees two planes on a collision course, yet fails to warn the pilots, would be held criminally liable for this omission. This liability exists even though the controller did not act but instead failed to act.

Involuntary Movement or Behavior   Many states specifically exclude involuntary movement and behavior from their general definition of a criminal act. Convulsions, reflexes, movements during sleep or unconsciousness, or behavior during a seizure are all considered involuntary movement or behavior falling outside the limits of criminal liability. However, the mere fact that someone is unconscious during a seizure may not absolve that individual of criminal liability if that person knew that he or she might suffer the seizure, yet took no precautions to avoid harming people or property. A person who decides to drive an automobile knowing that she or he is subject to sudden, unpredictable epileptic seizures may be criminally liable if a seizure causes that person to lose control of the vehicle and kill or injure someone.

The Required State of Mind

In general, a crime cannot be committed unless the criminal act named in the statute is performed with the required state of mind. Many state criminal codes include the following four states of mind:

- Purpose
- Knowledge
- Recklessness
- Negligence

Purpose   Individuals act with **purpose** when they intend to cause the result that in fact occurs. For example, if a person were to point a loaded gun at another person with the intention of shooting that second person, and if shots are actually fired, the person with the gun would have acted with purpose. Some states choose to call this mental state *intent*. Intent or purpose should not be confused with *premeditation,* which is often an added condition in the case of aggravated or first-degree murder. Some states specifically define premeditation as an action that results from the criminal defendant's "prior calculation and design." If, in the previous example, the person with the gun had also planned to shoot the victim, and then actually carried out this plan, the shooting would have been premeditated.

Knowledge   When people act with an awareness that a particular result will probably occur, they act with **knowledge**. For instance, if the person with the gun in the preceding example took that loaded gun to a crowded shopping mall and began to fire at random, not aiming at anyone in particular, that person would be acting with the knowledge that a lot of people would be either wounded or killed. This awareness would be true even if the person with the gun were to yell, "I really don't want to shoot anyone. I hope I don't hit anybody!"

Recklessness **Recklessness** involves a perverse disregard of a known risk of negative consequences. People act recklessly when they are indifferent to a serious risk they know to exist. Two drivers who challenge each other to an illegal drag race on a public highway are acting recklessly. In other words, they have disregarded the possible serious consequences of their decision to engage in an illegal drag race.

Negligence People act with **negligence** when they fail to see the possible negative consequences of their actions. A person who cleans a hunting rifle without checking to see if it is loaded is acting with negligence, because that person has not bothered to look for any possible negative consequences that could result from those actions. Criminal negligence should not be confused with negligence in tort law. Negligence in tort law is concerned with the compensation of accident victims (see Chapter 6). In contrast, negligence in criminal law is concerned with punishing the wrongdoer and protecting the public at large.

The Matter of Motive

Motive in criminal law is the wrongdoer's reason for committing the crime. One common misconception about criminal law, which is perpetuated by television programs and films, is that motive is an element of criminal liability. Such is not the case. Establishing motive may help the prosecution persuade the jury that the accused is guilty, but proving an evil motive is not necessary for a criminal conviction.

The Matter of Corporate Liability

Criminal liability requires that the prosecutor prove that the defendant possessed a particular mental state when the criminal act was committed. Such mental states are generally stated quite clearly in the statute that creates the criminal offense. In fact, since criminal liability requires only two elements, the act and the mental state, legislators are very careful in drafting criminal law statutes to make certain that they explain both elements, stating booth with great specificity. It is not always easy for a prosecutor to prove that a defendant possessed the required mental state. Still, when the criminal defendant is an individual, at least the prosecutor knows how to proceed. The prosecutor must produce evidence, generally consisting of actions and words, that demonstrate what was in the mind of the defendant at the time that the criminal act was committed. This is hard enough with a flesh and blood defendant. Corporations, on the other hand, do not have mental states, let alone mental states that can demonstrate criminal liability. Nor do they act or speak, except through their corporate officers and employees. How, then, does a prosecutor prove criminal liability when the criminal defendant is a corporation?

Corporate Personality
The law provides a fairly complete picture of a corporate identity. The law has established that corporations are "legal people." As a corporate person, a corporation possesses an identity, a corporate self, that maintains an existence that is separate from those who formed it. The upside to this is that the corporation will exist long after its founders. The downside is that corporations are taxed directly for what they earn as part of the marketplace. The courts have also decided that corporations have just enough "personhood" to qualify for constitutional protections. Thus, under the 14th Amendment, a corporation has the right to life, liberty, and property, rights that cannot be violated by the government either at the state or the federal levels. In addition, as a legal person, a corporation can institute a lawsuit or can be the target of a lawsuit.

Corporate Liability Theories
Despite popular opinion, corporations are not modern inventions developed in the 19th century. In fact, we know that corporate-like organizations existed in the Middle Ages. At that time, however, common law judges

could not conceive of corporate liability because corporations did not possess a mind with which to form a mental state. The modern age changed all of that. Once the courts decided that a corporation was person enough to sue or be sued, it was not a huge leap to conclude that a corporation could be held criminally liable as well. One of the earliest theories on corporate criminal liability emerged from within the doctrine of *strict liability*. Strict liability was an appropriate theory at the time, because it did not require intent, something that was difficult to prove in the case of a corporation. By the beginning of the 20th century, however, the courts began to hold corporations liable for the criminal acts of their employees using the doctrine of vicarious liability, a theory which is also called *respondeat superior*. Under this approach, the courts decided that a corporation could be declared criminally responsible if one of its employees committed a crime while on the job, working for the benefit of the corporation. The doctrine has been liberalized to such an extent that today, even if a worker is expressly prohibited from doing anything outside the law, the corporation might still be declared liable for a crime committed by that worker.

EXAMPLE 5-1: The Gulf Spill Vendetta and Corporate Criminal Liability

The explosion of the Deepwater Horizon drilling rig led to a massive oil spill in the Gulf of Mexico in 2010. The destruction that followed the explosion of the rig left many people demanding that three corporations—British Petroleum, Halliburton, and Transocean—be punished for what happened to the workers on the rig, to the wildlife in the gulf, and to the lives of the people living in the area because the corporations were believed to be responsible for the explosion of the Deepwater Horizon drilling rig and the massive oil spill in the Gulf of Mexico. In response, the federal government set up a special panel to investigate the incident. More than six months after the accident, the panel reported that the problems aboard the drilling rig resulted from a substandard level of performance *common throughout the entire oil industry*. This finding could be a problem for prosecutors who, under the *respondeat superior* test, must demonstrate, first and foremost, that a corporate agent committed a crime. This may not sound difficult at first blush, but the more we consider the situation, the darker it becomes for the prosecutor. The problem plays out like this: If a crime requires intent or knowledge, then the prosecutor will have to prove, *beyond a reasonable doubt,* that the corporate agent purposely or knowingly performed the wrongful act outlined in the statute. So, for example, suppose the prosecutor wants to target one of the corporations by using an aggravated arson statute to prosecute a rig operator, who was acting as a corporate agent at the time of the explosion. Aggravated arson would require the prosecutor to demonstrate that the defendant, by fire or explosion, knowingly created a risk of serious physical harm to another person or to an occupied structure. So far, this sounds like an open and shut case. But remember the explosion was not set off by the rig operator throwing a bomb. It resulted from the day-to-day operation of the rig. If the day-to-day operation of the rig was well within industry standards (OK, substandards, but standards, nonetheless), then how can the prosecutor show that the defendant "knowingly" created a "substantial risk"? How do I knowingly create a substantial risk if I am just doing what everyone in the entire industry does as a matter of day-to-day operational conduct? The answer is that I can't, and if I can't be held responsible, neither can the corporation. Of course, the prosecutor may have a case against the agent and, therefore, the corporation, for a lesser offense, perhaps one like criminal damaging, which requires only recklessness or negligence as the appropriate state of mind. However, convictions under these lesser offenses may not satisfy those victims of the oil spill who want the prosecutor to "throw the book" at the defendants, especially the defendant corporations. [See: David M. Uhlmann, "Prosecuting Crimes Against the Earth," *The New York Times,* June 4, 2010, p. A-23.]

The Model Penal Code The Model Penal Code offers a third theory of corporate liability. Under this theory, a corporation might be held criminally liable if the directors or officers of a corporation authorize, approve, or recklessly tolerate the criminal actions of their employees. Like the doctrine of *respondeat superior,* the directors or the officers must be acting on the job when the crimes occur. On the surface, this policy looks like an effective tool for stopping corporate criminal activity; however, in practice, the Model Penal Code may simply encourage directors and officers to remain ignorant of the actions of their employees in order to develop a defense of "plausible deniability." The defense of plausible deniability allows corporate managers to "honestly" testify that they knew nothing about the criminal activity of which they, their employees, and the corporation are accused.

EXAMPLE 5-2: The Gulf Spill Vendetta and the Model Penal Code

Many people were outraged by the oil spill that resulted in the Gulf of Mexico from the explosion of British Petroleum's Deepwater Horizon drilling rig in 2010. Much of this anger was directed, in general, at British Petroleum and, in particular, at BP's CEO, Tony Hayward. In hearings held in Washington, D.C., the CEO testified that he did not directly participate in any of the decisions made in relation to that particular rig.

Under the Model Penal Code, corporate criminal liability requires the authorization, the approval, or the reckless toleration of criminal activity by the board of directors or by a managing officer who is clearly responsible for establishing corporate policy, especially in relation to the incident under investigation. If, in fact, the CEO did not know what was going on at the Deepwater Horizon drilling rig then, under the Model Penal Code, neither he nor the corporation can be held liable. By distancing himself from the decision-making process, the CEO had clearly adopted a defense of plausible deniability. In engineering this defense, he was undeniably acting in the corporation's best interests, as well as his own; however, he was not acting in the best interests of the shareholders, other employees, the community, and so on. Still, under the Model Penal Code, there was nothing wrong with his conduct. In fact, his conduct was perfectly understandable and eminently reasonable. What does that tell us about the Model Penal Code?

The Matter of Punishment

The ultimate purpose of criminal law is to protect the public. This purpose means that criminal law must outline not only the offenses that are prohibited but also the negative consequences that result when an individual has committed one of those offenses. Many legal experts disagree about what that punishment ought to be. Still, these experts have narrowed the debate to two approaches to the sentencing of convicted criminals: (1) consequences that are designed to protect the public at large and (2) those that are tailored to fit the individual offense or the individual offender.

Protecting the Public at Large Consequences that have been created to protect the public send a message not just to the convicted felon but also to all potential offenders. These techniques include deterrence, education, and retribution. Those experts who believe in *deterrence* advocate long and difficult prison sentences so that other people in society are dissuaded from committing similar offenses and thus suffering the same fate. Those who support the theory of *education* say that the criminal process should be presented in a public way so that the public will learn the difference between acceptable and unacceptable bevhavior. Finally, those who believe in *retribution* are convinced that it does society good to seek revenge against those who have disrupted the smooth running of the social system. This theory probably has the fewest supporters today. Still, some experts argue that obtaining retribution against those who seek to gratify themselves at the expense of others will prevent many potential offenders from committing similar misdeeds in the future.

Individual Offenses and Punishment

Consequences that have been created to fit a particular offense or to punish a specific offender are designed to make certain that the individual offender will no longer engage in criminal activity in the future. The techniques for promoting this approach are prevention, restraint, and rehabilitation. Those experts who believe in *prevention* support long sentences in unpleasant prisons so that criminal defendants will abandon their criminal careers. Those who support *restraint* believe that criminal defendants should be incarcerated or even executed for capital offenses to prevent them from ever committing that crime—or any crime, for that matter—ever again. Finally, those who support the theory of *rehabilitation* say that convicted defendants ought to be given the opportunity to reform their conduct, restructure their lives, and start over.

The Death Penalty

The use of the death penalty in criminal cases has been subject to a series of controls designed to limit the imposition of this punishment to those cases in which the criminal defendant truly deserves to be put to death. Generally, these limits are built into the criminal code and are applied by the court that is responsible for sentencing the convicted criminal defendant. The safeguards come in the form of aggravating and mitigating circumstances, which must be taken into consideration by the court at the time of sentencing.

Aggravating circumstances are those that involve offenses so appalling that the death penalty is clearly warranted. In most jurisdictions the list of aggravating circumstances looks like this: the assassination of the president, the vice president, the governor, or the lieutenant governor of the state; a murder for hire; a murder committed to escape detection, apprehension, trial, or punishment; a murder committed while the offender was in detention; a murder by a convicted murderer; a murder of a law enforcement officer; a murder of a witness against the offender; a murder of a child under 13 years of age; or a murder during the commission of a felony. Usually, the death penalty cannot be imposed without the presence of at least one of these aggravating circumstances.

Moreover, even if aggravating circumstances are present, the death penalty might still be avoided, if the mitigating circumstances outweigh the aggravating circumstances. Mitigating circumstances include: the victim somehow induced the offense; the offender was coerced or provoked; the offender was suffering from a mental impairment of some sort; the offender is very young; the offender has no past criminal record; the offender was not the principal actor in the offense; or the offense was subject to other factors that might be relevant to a reduced sentence. It is also extremely important for the judge who administers the death penalty to be fair and impartial and to be free from undue pressure, conflict of interest, and any other external influence.

Death Penalty Safeguards

Other safety measures are built into the judicial system that will prevent or at least minimize the dangers of which Justice Sotomayor speaks. Generally, the appellate court that reviews the application of the death penalty is required to evaluate the conduct of the sentencing judge for any hint of partiality, impropriety, or outside pressure. Also, normally the governor of a state has the power to commute the sentence of a defendant condemned to death, and final recourse to the U.S. Supreme Court is also possible. In this case, the Supreme Court did refuse to grant the *writ of certiorari,* which would seem to indicate that, although Justice Sotomayor (and Justice Breyer, in part) disagree, the remaining justices are satisfied with the system established in Alabama and with the principle of electing judges democratically.

OPENING CASE *Round 2*
Mitigating and Aggravating Circumstances: Who Decides?

Recall that in the opening case, Mario Dion Woodward was tried for the murder of a police officer in Montgomery, Alabama. Also bear in mind that the jury found him guilty and, after a separate sentencing hearing, voted 8–4 to give him a life sentence without the possibility of parole. Instead, the judge, after listening to aggravating and mitigating circumstances, sentenced him to death. One of the most interesting things about the Supreme Court's long-standing reluctance to fully support the death penalty is that, even with the long lists of aggravating and mitigating circumstances, the Court maintains that a state can still give the judge flexibility in reviewing the jury's decision. The Court's position in this matter was made clear in this case as well as in several previous cases including *Spaziano v. Florida,* 468 U.S. 447 (1984) and *Harris v. Alabama,* 513 U.S. 504 (1995). In fact, the judge's discretion is in place in four of the 32 states that still use the death penalty. This is the root of Justice Sotomayor's opposition to the Court's decision not to grant certiorari. She argues that Alabama courts have a record of transforming life sentences into death sentences in a way that is more than a little disproportionate with the way that it is

done in other states. Also, Sotomayor emphasizes that, of the 27 instances of sentences moving from life to death in the past 14 years, 26 are found in the Alabama criminal courts. Her conclusion? She believes that the judicial system in Alabama is being held hostage by its need to satisfy the demands of the voting public. This is an interesting argument. Generally, the idea behind a democracy is that the power rests in the people and the people have the chance to elect officials who will represent their views or at least the views of the majority (or plurality) who elect those officials. Is Sotomayor saying, "I've had enough democracy. Let's try something else." Or is she saying, "Democracy is OK as long as the people elected agree with me?" Or is something else going on here. Recall the discussion in Chapter 2 about James Madison's fear of the people and his campaign to build a buffer between the people and public officials. Recall also that federal judges are appointed for life precisely to ensure an independent federal judiciary. Is Sotomayor agreeing with Madison? Think about it. [See: *Woodward v. Alabama,* 571 U.S.—(2013); *Gregg v. Georgia* 428 U.S. 153 (1976); and *Furman v. Georgia,* 408 U.S. 238 (1972).]

---

quick quiz 5-2

1. The two elements needed to create criminal liability are a criminal act and the requisite state of mind.   true | false

2. Individuals act with negligence when they act with the intention to cause the result that does in fact occur.   true | false

3. Motive is an element of criminal liability.   true | false

---

5-3 Specific Crimes

Statutory definitions and classifications of crimes vary from jurisdiction to jurisdiction. Nevertheless, several generalities can be drawn to simplify an examination of specific crimes. Crimes can be classified as crimes against people, crimes against property, crimes involving business, and crimes against justice.

Crimes against People

Crimes against people include, but are certainly not limited to, first-degree murder, second-degree murder, manslaughter, battery, and assault. A more recent addition to this list involves hate speech.

First-Degree Murder Any killing of one human being by another is labeled as a homicide. Criminal homicide is either murder or manslaughter. When the unlawful killing is done with premeditation and deliberate intent, it is labeled first-degree murder, aggravated murder, or premeditated murder, depending on the jurisdiction. The definition of first-degree murder differs from state to state; however, some of the elements are consistent. In general, most states define first-degree murder to include one of the following circumstances: killing someone with premeditation (thinking about it and planning the homicide in advance with "prior calculation and design") and/or killing someone while committing a major crime, such as rape, robbery, or kidnapping. Moreover, several jurisdictions have added other circumstances to the definition of first-degree murder, including causing the death of a victim under 13 years of age; causing the death of a law enforcement officer, when the offender knows or has reasonable cause to know that the victim is a police officer; causing the death of another while the offender is escaping detention for a felony; and killing someone in a cruel way such as with torture. Some states have added most or all of these to their statutory definition of first-degree murder, while others have added a combination of these new factors. It should also be obvious that these states have included some of the aggravating circumstances related to the death sentence within the definition of first-degree murder. The inclusion of these circumstance within the core definition of first-degree murder makes the application of the death penalty more likely.

Second-Degree Murder and Manslaughter If none of the conditions for first-degree murder apply, the crime is known as second-degree murder. In many jurisdictions, the difference between first- and second-degree murder is important because first-degree murder usually carries the death penalty, whereas second-degree murder does not. In contrast to murder, manslaughter is an unlawful killing of a person without the intent to kill. A killing that results when a person is in a state of extreme fright, terror, anger, or blind rage that destroys the ability to reason is known as voluntary manslaughter. When the killing results from negligence, it is usually called involuntary manslaughter.

EXAMPLE 5-3: First Degree Murder and Voluntary Manslaughter

Brent Haywood entered a convenience store and robbed the clerk at gunpoint. As he was leaving the store, the clerk pulled a revolver from under the counter and ordered Haywood to stop. In response, Haywood fired his weapon at the clerk, who returned fire. In the exchange of gunshots, an innocent bystander, nine-year-old Teddy Newman, was shot and killed. Haywood was convicted of first-degree murder and sentenced to death by lethal injection; however, the judge, who opposed the death penalty, gave Haywood a life sentence. Teddy's father was in the courtroom when this sentence was announced. In a state of extreme rage, Teddy's father attacked and killed Haywood. Even though Teddy's father's actions were clearly intentional, they were performed in a state of extreme rage as a result of a reasonable provocation. Consequently, he was charged with voluntary manslaughter.

Battery and Assault Throughout most of English and American history, the term *battery* has been used to describe a crime in which the offender causes actual physical harm to the victim. In contrast, **assault** has generally been taken to include the threat of harm to the victim. Today, however, this simple distinction is no longer applicable because many states have created a wide variety of levels and degrees of battery and assault. Some states have even altered the actual language of the law. Ohio, for example, has eliminated the term *battery* and replaced it with the word *assault*. In Ohio, then, the term *assault* is used to describe various crimes involving the infliction of physical harm on the victim. To describe offenses that should be identified with the word *assault*, Ohio uses the terms *aggravated menacing* and *menacing*. Moreover, Ohio has added a few new offenses to the criminal code that are related to, but are not exactly the same as, assault and battery. These include stalking, hazing, and abuse. Given these subtle distinctions, it is always best to check the criminal code in your own jurisdiction before discussing assault and battery.

Has 9/11 increased hate speech focused on Muslim women?

Hate Speech In recent years, many legislative bodies have attempted to criminalize the use of certain symbols, writings, and speech intended to provoke outrage or fear on the basis of race, religion, color, or gender. These statutes and ordinances are frequently referred to as laws against *hate speech*. Such statutes are constitutional only if they are not content specific. Therefore, though it may be acceptable to draft a statute that outlaws any speech designed to rouse fear or outrage, regardless of the content of that speech, it would be impermissible to outlaw speech aimed at inciting outrage or fear based solely on race, religion, color, gender, or any similar category.

Crimes against Property

Crimes against property include but are not limited to: burglary; breaking and entering; trespass; aggravated arson; arson; aggravated robbery; robbery; theft, fraud, and related offenses.

Burglary, Breaking and Entering, and Trespass The crime of burglary has evolved since the Middle Ages. It was once limited to the unlawful entry into a dwelling place at night. Modern legislatures have extended the definition of **burglary** to include using force, deceit, or cunning to trespass into an occupied structure with the intent to commit a crime. A more serious form of burglary is generally referred to as **aggravated burglary**. Aggravated burglary includes everything that burglary includes but adds the use of a deadly weapon, the infliction of harm, the threat of harm, or the attempt to harm another person. A third related offense is **breaking and entering**, which generally includes using force, deceit, or cunning to trespass into an unoccupied structure with the intent to commit any theft or any felony. Breaking and entering can also involve trespassing on land with the intent to commit a felony. The last offense that is related to these three offenses is **trespass**, which involves knowingly entering land without permission to do so. Some, but not all, forms of trespass include entry onto the land with the intent to commit a misdemeanor.

Aggravated Arson and Arson Under common law rules, arson involved the burning of another person's home. Legislatures have expanded this definition so that arson now includes more than one offense. **Aggravated arson** includes using fire or explosives to create a substantial risk of physical harm to an individual or to an occupied building. Often also included in this offense is the hiring of another person to carry out the burning or the use of the explosives. A lesser offense is ordinary **arson**, which involves using fire or explosives to harm or cause a substantial risk of harm to the property of another or to do the same to another's property or to the offender's own property in order to carry out fraud. Again also included in this is hiring another to actually burn the property or use the explosives. Some states have expanded the arson statutes even further to specifically include the burning or use of explosives against government-owned buildings, government parklands, government wildlife preserves, and so on.

Aggravated Robbery and Robbery
Like many of the criminal offenses already discussed in this chapter, robbery involves more than one offense. Unlike many of the others, however, the definition of robbery has not changed much over the years. The more serious offense is generally known as aggravated robbery. **Aggravated robbery** involves attempting to commit or actually committing a theft using a deadly weapon or a dangerous ordnance or doing the same by inflicting physical harm on the victim. **Robbery** involves essentially the same elements as aggravated robbery; however, in ordinary robbery the offender possesses a deadly weapon but neither uses nor shows the weapon. Robbery can also involve attempting to commit or actually committing a theft by inflicting or attempting to inflict physical harm on another person.

Theft, Fraud, and Related Offenses
Today many jurisdictions will place theft, fraud, and a series of related offenses, such as receiving stolen goods or passing bad checks, together under a single heading. What each of these offenses has in common is the attempt to separate the rightful owner of property from that property or to somehow profit from that separation once it has taken place. **Theft**, the simplest, and arguably the oldest of these offenses is defined in many jurisdictions as knowingly taking or obtaining control over the property of another individual without that individual's consent using deceit, threats, or coercion. **Fraud** covers a wide variety of crimes today including such diverse activities as identity fraud, Medicaid fraud, worker's compensation fraud, telecommunications fraud, insurance fraud, defrauding a rental agency, and defrauding creditors. What each type of fraud has in common, however, is a deliberately engineered deception that the offender uses to obtain property or services that belong to another. The offenses that are related to theft and fraud cover a wide variety of situations including motion picture piracy, misuse of credit cards, trademark counterfeiting, receiving stolen property, and tampering with records.

Crimes Involving Business

Nonviolent in nature, business crimes are those carried out by a business or individual in the course of doing business to obtain a business-related advantage. Covering a wide range of illegal business practices, business crimes are directed against individuals, other businesses, the government, or the public. The business crimes discussed here include embezzlement, forgery, criminal simulation, passing bad checks, and defrauding creditors.

Embezzlement
In many jurisdictions, **embezzlement** is defined as wrongfully taking property or funds that have been entrusted to the care of the offender. Unlike similar offenses such as theft, robbery, and burglary, a fundamental element of embezzlement is that the embezzler had control over the property or the funds that were wrongfully taken. Thus, embezzlement often occurs in a business setting and frequently involves the employees of the victim.

Forgery, Criminal Simulation, and Passing Bad Checks
The crime of **forgery** involves the false making or changing of a writing (without proper authorization) with the intent to defraud. It is also forgery to possess or sell an altered or false writing with the intent to defraud. Some states have expressly added identity cards to their

forgery statutes to emphasize the criminal nature of forged IDs. These states generally make it a crime to create, sell, use, or possess a false ID. **Criminal simulation** is analogous to forgery because it also involves the alteration or falsification of an object or a document with intent to defraud. However, criminal simulation involves altering or falsifying art objects, antiques, photographs, films, tapes, recordings, and/or antiquities with the intent to defraud. **Passing bad checks** includes issuing or transferring a check or other negotiable instrument knowing it will be dishonored and with the intent to defraud.

Defrauding Creditors Many jurisdictions have statutes that are specifically designed to protect the rights of creditors. The statute against **defrauding creditors** is the crime of removing, hiding, destroying, giving away, or transferring any person's property with the intent to defraud creditors. Under these statutes it is also criminal to hide, misrepresent, or refuse to disclose information about the existence, amount, or location of a person's property to a fiduciary who has been appointed to administer that person's affairs or estate. The crime of defrauding creditors can be either a felony or a misdemeanor depending on the amount of the property involved in the fraud.

Racketeer Influenced and Corrupt Organizations Act To prevent a criminal invasion of legitimate businesses, Congress enacted the Racketeer Influenced and Corrupt Organizations (RICO) Act. Under provisions of this statute, conducting a legitimate business with the funds acquired from a "pattern of racketeering activities" can give rise to criminal liability. Many of the offenses that fall within the scope of "racketeering activity"—such as arson and robbery—are serious crimes. Others, however, are less sinister. For example, both mail fraud and wire fraud fall within the definition of racketeering activities. The provisions of RICO can give rise not only to criminal charges but also to civil liability. Thus, it is not uncommon for individuals to seek damages in lawsuits filed against corporations that have violated RICO.

Crimes against Justice

Crimes against justice involve offenses committed by or with the cooperation of a public servant or a public official. Such crimes include bribery, theft in office, and dereliction of duty. Others, such as intimidation, are committed against a public official or public servant. Still others, such as obstruction of justice, resisting arrest, perjury, and tampering with evidence are committed against the justice system itself.

Bribery and Theft in Office In most states, **bribery** involves offering, promising, or actually giving something of value to a public official with the goal of influencing that official in the discharge of his or her public duties. It is also bribery when the public official solicits or accepts a thing of value in exchange for that public official's influence in whatever capacity. Many states have further expanded the crime of bribery to include witnesses who are offered or given something of value in exchange for their testimony. The bribery can be committed by the person who offers the bribe and by the witness who solicits or accepts the bribe. Another offense that involves public servants is theft in office. Most jurisdictions define **theft in office** to include any theft offense in the criminal code that is committed by a public official or a party official. The theft must involve the use of that official's governmental or party power to obtain unlawful control over governmental or party property or services.

Dereliction of Duty In most states the crime of **dereliction of duty** can involve law enforcement officers and public servants. In relation to *law enforcement officers*, dereliction of duty is any activity that involves the officer's failure to carry out his or her lawful duties. These duties include, but are not limited to, serving lawful warrants; preventing the commission of a crime; controlling unruly prisoners; preventing the escape of prisoners; carrying out criminal proceedings; providing persons confined in a detention facility with food, shelter, and medical assistance; preserving sanitary conditions in detention facilities, and, in general, properly managing those detention facilities. *Public servants* are charged with carrying out those duties that are specifically related to the proper operation of their governmental office. In addition, many dereliction of duty statutes also expressly state that public servants have an affirmative duty to keep their department or agency within the budget set for it by the state legislature.

Intimidation

The crime of intimidation involves threats of harm to the person or property of a public servant, party official, or witness with the intention of coercing that individual into some violation of his or her public duty. Some jurisdictions have expanded the definition of intimidation to include threats of harm to the public servant's reputation by the publication of false information. This would seem to include not only the publication of false statements in newspapers and magazines and on television, but also the posting of such false information on the Internet via the various social media outlets, such as Facebook, LinkedIn, and so on.

Obstruction of Justice and Resisting Arrest

Most jurisdictions define obstruction of justice as any activity designed to prevent the discovery, apprehension, arrest, prosecution, conviction, or punishment of a criminal defendant. Each jurisdiction also specifies those activities that qualify as obstruction of justice. These activities include but are not necessarily limited to: hiding a criminal defendant; providing that defendant with money, transportation, weapons, disguises, and so on; warning that person of possible discovery or arrest; destroying or concealing evidence; and communicating false information to law enforcement officials about the defendant. Resisting arrest is defined as interfering in the lawful arrest of a criminal defendant. Most statutes defining this offense also penalize the resister for any harm that comes to a law enforcement officer involved in the arrest.

Perjury and Tampering with Evidence

Under the laws of most states, perjury is defined as making a false statement under oath; however, many jurisdictions also add that the false statement must be material to the proceeding. A statement is material if it can have an impact on the final disposition of the case. Interestingly enough, in most cases, the fact that the perjured testimony is inadmissible as evidence makes no difference; the false statement is still perjury. However, a person cannot be convicted of perjury by a single witness. Tampering with evidence means altering, destroying, or removing any piece of evidence with the intent to somehow lessen the probative value of that evidence. In addition, tampering with evidence includes presenting false evidence to a public official in order to somehow destroy the effectiveness of an official investigation.

A QUESTION OF ETHICS

The Progress of the Paramilitary Police Power

There is a difference between the police and the military. Right? The military is supposed to defend the entire nation from attacks conducted by other nations, or by terror groups, or perhaps even pirates on the high seas. The police, on the other hand, are supposed to serve and protect, by upholding the law and protecting citizens, typically from one another. This is the traditional distinction that for decades, perhaps even centuries, worked fairly well. Today, however, it has become increasingly difficult to tell the difference between the two, not because the military has become too "police-like," but because the police have been transformed (or perhaps have transformed themselves) into military combat teams. Three decades ago about 20 percent of our cities with populations between 20,000 and 50,000 had a SWAT (Special Weapons and Tactics) team. Since then, that percentage has escalated to 80 percent and continues to climb. In the 1980s the number of SWAT team raids ran around 3,000 per year, while today the number tops 50,000. Part of this is due to federal funding from the Department of Homeland Security ($35 billion between 2002 and 2011) and the Pentagon (aid has flowed to 17,000 police, sheriff, and state highway patrol departments); part is due to property seizure statutes under which crime-related resources can be confiscated by the police; and part is due to old-fashioned competition among law enforcement agencies as they battle to be the best of the best. The fact that crime-fighting agencies want to have up-to-date, state-of-the-art equipment is understandable, even admirable, and in many ways should be encouraged. However, a fundamental question remains: Are we correct that there is difference between the police and the military? Or have the two fighting forces become simple extensions of one another? If you were the mayor of a midsize city (population between 20,000 and 50,000) and in that role were offered a large outlay of ready cash from the Pentagon or Homeland Security to build a paramilitary SWAT team in your municipal police department, would you accept that funding? Explain the reason for your response using one of the ethical theories identified and explained in Chapter 1. [See: "Law Enforcement in the United States: Armed and Dangerous," *The Economist,* March 22, 2014, pp. 14, 16; "Paramilitary Police: Cops or Soldiers?" *The Economist,* March 22, 2014, pp. 27–28.]

The Posse Comitatus and Insurrection Acts States' increased use of paramilitary police operatives to deal with enforcement of the law brings up an interesting legal point often overlooked in these discussions. Both the letter and the spirit of the law in this country prevent the federal government from using the U.S. military to uphold the law of an individual state. Such responsibilities rest not with the federal government but with the state government, in general, and with the governor, in particular. The prohibition on the use of the military (first the Army, but later the Navy, Air Force, and Marines) was made official with the Posse Comitatus Act in 1878 in tandem with the Insurrection Act of 1807. The acts expressly forbid the use of the U.S. military to uphold the laws of any individual state. The laws do not cover the National Guard, which is controlled by the governor of each state, and the Coast Guard, which is now under the authority of the Department of Homeland Security. The precarious nature of this prohibition can be seen in the recent history of the law. In 2006, the act was amended to permit the use of the U.S. military to respond to natural disasters and terror attacks. In 2008 the amendment was withdrawn. Then in 2011 a narrow provision was added that permits the use of the military to deal with al-Qaeda and Taliban attacks in the United States. In 2012, the National Defense Authorization Act included a provision that permits the military to detain individuals for an undefined period of time even though charges have not been filed against that individual. Some commentators argue, rather convincingly, that this provision effectively repeals the Posse Comitatus Act. Others contend that the Posse Comitatus Act has already been repealed in a *de facto* manner, since, as noted above, the police have morphed into a military force without any need for legislative action.

quick quiz 5-3

1. In most states, the distinction between first- and second-degree murder is important because first-degree murder usually carries the death penalty while second-degree murder does not.   true | false

2. It is acceptable to draft a statute that outlaws speech aimed at inciting outrage or fear based solely on race, religion, color, gender, or any similar category.   true | false

3. Passing bad checks includes issuing or transferring a check or other negotiable instrument knowing it will be dishonored and with the intent to defraud.   true | false

5-4 Cybercrimes

As is true of most other crimes, statutory definitions and classifications of cybercrimes (electronic crimes and e-crimes) vary from state to state. Moreover, in the case of cybercrimes, the definitions are even more varied because there is no agreement on what constitutes a cybercrime. One approach is to state that cybercrimes involve any criminal act that includes a computer. This strategy, which is often referred to as cyber-trespass, computer trespass, or e-trespass, can solve many of the problems associated with cybercrime, if only by an indirect treatment of such crimes. Another way to classify cybercrimes is to distinguish between crimes committed with a computer and crimes committed against a computer.

Cyber-trespass

A problem arises when crimes that are already on the books are committed with a computer. As noted previously, one way to deal with this situation is to create a single generic offense called cyber-trespass, electronic trespass, or e-trespass. **Cyber-trespass** is the process of gaining access to a computer with the intent to commit a crime. In effect, in one single stroke, this strategy incorporates the rest of the criminal code into this one crime, making it an offense to use a computer to commit any other crime in the code. In a state that takes this approach, all criminal statutes, especially those pertaining to fraud, embezzlement, blackmail, and theft, become part of this one crime known as cyber-trespass.

Crimes Committed with a Computer

Another approach to dealing with cybercrime is to distinguish between using a computer to commit a crime and committing an offense against a computer. Naturally some of these crimes will overlap. Nevertheless, enough of a distinction exists between the two to make this a viable approach to the subject. Cybercrimes that focus on the use of a computer include cyber-stalking, cyber-harassment, cyber-assault, cyber-bullying, cyber-piracy, cyber-extortion, cyber-spoofing, phishing, smishing, and vishing.

Cyber-stalking *Cyber-stalking, e-stalking,* or *electronic stalking* involves targeting individuals for exploitation using computer connections. Cyber-stalkers usually target vulnerable individuals who may be searching for a genuine connection on the Internet. Minors are often targeted by cyber-stalkers. After gaining the trust of the minor or other innocent victim, the cyber-stalker arranges a meeting so that he or she can take advantage of the innocent party.

Cyber-harassment

Cyber-harassment, electronic harassment, or *e-harassment* involves using computer connections, often via e-mail or some other social media, to blanket the target with offensive sexual, racial, religious, or political comments, photographs, videos, and so on aimed at disrupting the victim's peace of mind. The psychological impact of cyber-harassment is severe, but often difficult to prove, thus making cyber-harassment an especially vicious crime.

Cyber-assault

Cyber-assault, electronic assault, or *e-assault* has several definitions depending on the jurisdiction. Cyber-assault can involve using social media to threaten to inflict immediate and severe bodily harm on the target victim. In this sense of the term, it is simply an extension of common law assault; however, cyber-assault can also mean a direct attack on a computer system with the intent to disrupt that system.

Cyber-bullying

Cyber-bullying, electronic bullying, or *e-bullying* involves intentional, aggressive, upsetting activities by a single individual or a group of individuals aimed at destroying the mental well-being of a peer. Generally, cyber-bullies use a variety of cyber-social media, including chatrooms, discussion groups, blogs, Web pages, texting, instant messaging, and so on to disrupt the life of the target. The term *cyber-bullying* is generally used to describe the cyber-activities of students against one another. In most jurisdictions it is not yet a crime.

Cyber-piracy

One of the most common, most lucrative, most covert, and most insidious of all e-crimes is cyber-piracy. Literally billions of dollars are siphoned off annually by cyber-pirates who sometimes profit directly and sometimes indirectly from their theft. *Cyber-piracy, electronic piracy, or e-piracy* occurs when website operators take intellectual property, usually in the form of feature films, e-books, television programming, audio recordings of songs, software, and carry them on their websites or sell them on the Internet without paying royalties to the legitimate copyright owners. The word is also sometimes used as an umbrella term for other cyber-crimes such as cyber-extortion, cyber-spoofing, phishing, smishing, and vishing.

Cyber-extortion, *electronic extortion,* or *e-extortion* can occur when an experienced hacker gains access to the computer records of a corporation or other institution and discovers some sort of illegal, negligent, unethical, or embarrassing conduct that might damage the reputation of the target organization. Using the computer, the hacker can then contact the organization to threaten exposure unless he or she is rewarded financially.

Cyber-spoofing

To commit *cyber-spoofing, electronic spoofing,* or *e-spoofing,* a cyber-criminal must falsely adopt the identity of another computer user or create a false identity on a website to commit fraud. A simple form of cyber-spoofing involves adopting the identity of an e-mailer to defraud the recipients of the original e-mail. Another type of cyber-spoofing involves creating phony websites or diverting users from legitimate websites to obtain credit card numbers, debit card numbers, PINs, passwords, or other confidential information to commit a wide variety of fraudulent activities.

Phishing and Spear Phishing

Phishing and spear phishing are two forms of cyber-spoofing. *Phishing* involves sending out phony e-mails that solicit buyers and, in the process, obtain credit card information, account numbers, PINs, account balances, and so on. When the e-mail has been customized to such an extent that the recipient believes the e-mail comes from a co-worker, a friend, or a relative, the offense is called *spear phishing.* [See: "Briefing Cyberwar: War in the Fifth Domain," *The Economist,* July 3, 2010, p. 26.]

Smishing and Vishing *Smishing* links SMS (short message service) texting with phishing. *Vishing* connects phishing to voice messaging. In both situations, cyber-criminals send out messages at random, sometimes targeting a particular city, profession, or exchange number, and sometimes using a particular phone list purchased or obtained illegally from an institution like a savings and loan, a credit card company, or a department store. The messages will warn the recipients that their credit card information needs to be updated, or that their account is overdrawn, prompting the victims to contact a number or to access an Internet site. The victims then provide private information such as account numbers, PINs, passwords, and so on. These confidential numbers and passwords are used to infiltrate the victim's financial records, credit card accounts, debit card records, and so on. [See: "Smishing and Vishing and Other Cyber Scams to Watch Out for this Holiday," *The FBI-Federal Bureau of Investigation,* November 2010, http:www.fbi.gov/news/stories/2010/ november/cyber_112410/cyber_112410.]

Crimes that Target Computers

Cybercrimes that target computers attempt to disable the computer itself, to disable the system that it operates, or to confiscate and use the information stored in the computer, sometimes after erasing the original data. Crimes that target computers include cyber-terrorism, identity theft, cyber-vandalism, and cyber-germ warfare.

Cyber-terrorism *Cyber-terrorism, electronic terrorism,* or *e-terrorism* involve using a computer to disrupt or destroy one of the critical elements of the nation's cyber-infrastructure, such as the power grid, the air traffic control system, water and sanitation plants, the ground transportation system, a harbor traffic-control network, a cell tower network, the nation's stock exchange, the banking system, hospital backup generator systems, or the national defense system.

Identity Theft Another cybercrime that targets computers and computer information is identity theft. In identity theft, a perpetrator uses one of the techniques noted previously to steal credit card information, PINs, financial data, access codes, passwords, or debit card information. The perpetrator then passes himself or herself off as the victim. Using this technique, the identity thief can clean out bank accounts, run up credit card debt, divert cash transfers, buy and sell stocks, enter electronic auction networks, approve or cancel shipments, make or revoke hotel and travel reservations, and disrupt the financial and the personal life of the victim.

Cyber-vandalism Sometimes expert vandals can attack a computer system so that a website is destroyed or paralyzed to the extent that legitimate business can no longer be conducted on that site. This type of attack is known as *cyber-vandalism, electronic vandalism,* or *e-vandalism.* Often cyber-vandalism is used to cripple a business as a form of revenge for real or imagined wrongs, to exercise power over a business, or to hurt the owner of a business just for "fun."

Cyber-germ Warfare When cyber-criminals use viruses to attack a computer system, they are engaged in *cyber-warfare, cyber-germ warfare,* or *electronic germ warfare.* Clearly, viruses can be used to enter computer systems for many of the crimes listed previously. Thus, a cyber-extortionist can threaten to unleash a virus into a computer system unless he or she is paid a certain amount of money. In effect, the cyber-extortionist is using the virus to extract ransom money from the business. Similarly, the cyber-terrorist or cyber-vandal can use a virus to disrupt a computer system for political or psychological reasons.

Federal Cybercrimes

Many states have enacted legislation to combat these cybercrimes and other cyber-offenses. The federal government has also attempted to deal with the issue by passing a number of anti-cybercrime statutes. The statutes of primary importance as determined by the Computer Crime and Intellectual Property Section of the United States Department of Justice include the Computer Fraud and Abuse Act (CFAA), the Electronic Communications Privacy Act (ECPA), the Communications Assistance for Law Enforcement Act (CALEA), the Economic Espionage Act (EEA), the National Stolen Property Act (NSPA), the Identity Theft and Assumption Deterrence Act (ITADA).

The Computer Fraud and Abuse Act (CFAA) Congress first specifically addressed the subject of cybercrime over two decades ago when, as a part of a comprehensive crime control statute, it passed the Computer Fraud and Abuse Act (CFAA). Currently, this act outlaws the following activities: obtaining national security information, compromising the confidentiality of a computer, trespassing in a government computer, accessing a computer to defraud, damaging a computer, damaging computer information, trafficking in passwords, and threatening to damage a computer.

The Electronic Communications Privacy Act (ECPA) Originally the Federal Wiretap Act was designed to cover only wire and oral communications. The Electronic Communications Privacy Act (ECPA) amended the original wiretap act to cover communication by computer. The purpose of the amendment was to protect the privacy of electronic communication in the same way that wire and oral communication are protected. To do this, the act prohibits the intentional interception of electronic communication.

The Communications Assistance for Law Enforcement Act (CALEA) The ECPA was later amended to help law enforcement officials keep pace with modern advances in electronic communication. The Communications Assistance for Law Enforcement Act (CALEA) amended the earlier law by requiring communication companies to update their electronic equipment in order to make certain that such law enforcement officers could carry out their surveillance duties properly.

The Economic Espionage Act (EEA) The Economic Espionage Act (EEA) is designed to protect trade secrets. A trade secret is a plan, process, or device that is used in a business and is known only to those employees who need to know the secret to carry out their work. Examples of trade secrets include customer lists, chemical formulas, manufacturing processes, marketing techniques, pricing methods, and food or beverage recipes (think Coca-Cola). The EEA outlaws the downloading of trade secrets.

The National Stolen Property Act (NSPA) Under the National Stolen Property Act (NSPA), it is a federal crime to use interstate or foreign commerce to transport personal property, currency, or securities that an individual is aware were stolen, were secured by fraud, or were taken by some other illegal method including an unauthorized electronic transfer.

The Identity Theft and Assumption Deterrence Act (ITADA) The Identity Theft and Assumption Deterrence Act (ITADA), which was amended by the Identity Theft Penalty Enhancement Act, outlaws the unauthorized transfer, possession, or use of a means of identifying another person to violate federal law. The amendment adds a new crime, called *aggravated identity theft* to the original statute. The section on aggravated identity theft makes it clear that identity theft is much worse when it involves certain very serious felonies, including terrorism.

The CAN SPAM Act   Spam is the nickname for all of those pop-up advertisements that appear on computer screens while users are tapped into the Internet. The CAN SPAM Act is designed to deal with this problem, as well as the problem of unsolicited commercial e-mail.

Stop Online Piracy Act (SOPA)   As noted above, cyber-piracy occurs when website operators take some form of electronic intellectual property and carry or sell it on their websites without paying royalties. One stumbling block in dealing with cyber-piracy is that it is routinely carried out by website owners that operate far outside the jurisdiction of the United States. In an indirect attack on these offshore sites, the House of Representatives recently engineered a bill referred to as the Stop Online Piracy Act, or SOPA, for short. SOPA was designed to circuitously attack cyber-pirates by penalizing American websites that carry the pirated works and service the cyber-pirates with payment processors and and advertisements. The bill would also entice Internet service providers (ISPs) to impede traffic to cyber-pirate sites using special filtering techniques. Any American entities that refused to cooperate would be vulnerable to litigation filed by the copyright owners for infringement. The Senate version was referred to as PIPA, the Protect Intellectual Property Act. The bill caused such outrage from prominent websites such as Wikipedia and Google that the House and the Senate both postponed further consideration of their respective bills pending further investigation. [See: "Online Piracy: Stopping SOPA," *The Economist,* January 21, 2012, p. 33; Don Reisinger, "SOPA Halted in House," *CNET Interactive,* January 20, 2012.]

The Global Cyber-crisis

The U.S. government, U.S. corporations, and the U.S. military have become increasingly aware of both the power and the vulnerability of the Internet. National and global computer networks tie together a wide variety of systems that are used to make the global infrastructure more manageable, more efficient, and more affordable than ever before. Moreover, given the chance, very few of us would return to the days of manually controlled banking, line-of-sight air traffic control, in-person stock market trading, three-channel television, landline rotary phones, and manually operated passenger rail service. Nevertheless, with efficiency and convenience comes a trade-off. That trade-off is vulnerability. The computer network is susceptible to collapse. A solar storm, a shift in the earth's magnetic field, a volcanic eruption, poorly written software, an incorrect file number, or inadequately maintained hardware can disrupt even the best computer system. Human operators can enter an outdated password, an inaccurate code, or the wrong person's PIN. Most of these errors are predictable and can be handled with a minimal amount of inconvenience. Other problems, those that are deliberate and knowingly target a computer system, are less easily solved.

For example, an enemy nation, a drug cartel, a crime syndicate, a gang of cyber-pirates, or a team of terrorists can, with a minimal amount of effort, send an e-mail with an attached PDF file that, when opened, will install a deadly software program in a computer system. The software might command the system to shut down, delete data, or, perhaps worse, transfer control of the system to the attacker. Generally, when this type of terror attack occurs, no one knows what happened until the damage is done. Thus, without warning, the nation's air traffic control system might be shut down, a city's water supply might be contaminated, a hospital's blood bank could lose refrigeration, or a banking system might be wiped clean of all transactions. Constructing a plan for dealing with a deliberate computer attack is difficult at best. Nevertheless, steps must be taken to deal with such attacks. [See: "Briefing Cyberwar: War in the Fifth Domain," *The Economist,* July 3, 2010, p. 25.]

Cyber-Strategies and Cyber-Solutions   One step might be to split up data and send it along a series of different routes so that, if one data stream is compromised, the others continue on their way unimpeded. This strategy is effective most of the time; however, even this tactic does not always work. One weakness in the submerged fiber-optic cable system, along which many data streams travel, is a network of bottlenecks, sites at which these streams intersect and fall under the control of a limited number of domain-name servers, making them tempting targets for cyber-criminals and cyber-terrorists. These bottlenecks appear in the Middle East, in South East Asia, and along the Eastern seaboard of the United States, any one of which is a tempting target. [See: "Briefing Cyberwar: War in the Fifth Domain," p. 25.]

Cyber-Command (Cybercom) The federal government has responded to these threats in a number of ways. First, the Pentagon has established a new cyber-command center that is charged with the job of protecting the military's computer command system. This new agency, which is officially referred to as Cyber Command or Cybercom, is under the control of the National Security Agency. It has been charged not only with protecting the American cyber-system from attack, but also with developing plans to undermine the computer systems of enemy nations. One of its goals might be to protect the "chokepoints" in the submerged fiber-optic system, but also to uncover effective ways to use the system in a way that benefits the American military [See: "Briefing Cyberwar: War in the Fifth Domain," p. 25.]

Internet Crime Complaint Center (IC3) On the homefront, the federal government has taken steps to combat domestic cybercrime by establishing the Internet Crime Complaint Center (AKA IC3). The IC3 operates as a joint venture between the National White Collar Crime Center (NW3C) and the Federal Bureau of Investigation (FBI). The IC3 handles complaints involving cybercrimes such as hacking, trade secret infringement, identity theft, cyber-extortion, and Internet fraud. Individuals and businesses can file complaints with the IC3 by accessing the agency's website. The IC3 also works closely with administrative agencies as well as with local, state, and federal law enforcement agencies. [See: *Internet Crime Complaint Center,* http://www.ic3.gov.]

Domestic Strategies The battle against cyber-abuse can now be fought in the home. Using a variety of computer software programs, parents can filter e-mails, text messages, and social site contacts on the Internet to prevent their children from receiving messages that are symptomatic of cyber-bullying and similar unwanted cyber-contacts. One popular weapon in this battle is the MouseMail software package developed by Safe Communications. The MouseMail system permits a parents to have e-mails, text messages, and other cyber-contacts heading to their children to be intercepted and filtered by a rapid comparison between the content of the message and a list of improper words. Unfamiliar senders are also tagged. The tagged messages are sent to the parents first who handle them from that point on. Other similar software packages include Cyber/Bully/Alert.com and Social Shield.com. [See: Mike Snyder, "MouseMail Traps Kids' Cyberbullies," *USA Today,* January 5, 2011, p. 1A; see also *Welcome to Mouse Mail,* http://mousemail.com.]

quick quiz 5-4

1. Statutory definitions and classifications of cybercrimes have become uniform within all jurisdictions in the United States.   true | false

2. Cyber-trespass is defined as gaining access to a computer with the intent to commit a crime.   true | false

3. The federal government has passed several cybercrime statutes.   true | false

Table 5-1   Criminal Liability and Defenses

Criminal Liability	Criminal Defenses

The act:
  Criminal behavior specifically
    outlined by statute
	Defenses to the act:
	  Act as defined is "status" only
	  Act as defined is ambiguous
	  Act as defined is overbroad

The mental state:
  Mental state specifically
    outlined by statute
  Purpose
  Knowledge
  Recklessness
  Negligence
	Defenses to the mental state:
	  Insanity
	  Entrapment
	  Justifiable force
	  Mistake

5-5 Defenses to Criminal Liability

Because criminal liability lies within the elements of an act and the required mental state, a logical defense would be aimed at eliminating one or both of those elements. Most defenses attempt to do just that. The most common defenses are insanity, entrapment, justifiable force, and mistake. (See Table 5-1.)

The Insanity Defense

Although the insanity defense has been around for a long time, many people do not understand the nature of the defense. One of the key points of confusion is the difference between *competency to stand trial* and the *insanity defense* itself.

Competency to Stand Trial Criminal defendants are generally presumed to be mentally competent to stand trial; however, the issue of competency to stand trial can be raised if the court, the defense attorney, or the prosecutor suspects that the defendant is not competent. If the issue of competency is raised, the defendant will undergo psychiatric examinations to determine his or her level of competency. Generally, defendants are considered competent to stand trial if they understand the nature and the purpose of the charges against them, and if they are capable of aiding their attorneys in their defense. When defendants are found to be incompetent, they are usually given treatment to improve their competency level so that they can understand what is going on and can assist in their case.

EXAMPLE 5-4: Competency and the Ability to Assist

The question of competency to stand trial was a key factor in a case in which Harold Gunther was prosecuted for the murder of one person and the attempted murder of two others. Listening at the door of an apartment, Gunther believed he heard three co-workers plotting against him. Convinced that he was about to be attacked, Gunther entered the apartment and assaulted his three co-workers, killing one and severely injuring the other two. Gunther consistently maintained that he was the intended target of a plot to destroy him. No evidence was ever presented that such a plot existed. In contrast, expert testimony indicated that Gunther was paranoid and delusional. Consequently, his defense attorney moved for a competency hearing. Despite the expert testimony, the judge in the case found Gunther competent to stand trial. The competency ruling was based on the fact that, despite Gunther's mental problems, he was capable of understanding the charges against him and was able to assist in his defense. Under state law, these were the only qualifications needed for a competency finding by the court. Gunther met these qualifications and was found competent to stand trial.

Not Guilty by Reason of Insanity (NGRI)
American law recognizes that individuals cannot be held responsible for their actions if they do not know what they are doing. In addition, it serves no practical purpose to imprison someone who needs the care of mental health professionals. For these reasons, insanity is recognized as a valid defense to criminal conduct.

The oldest test of insanity is the **M'Naughten Rule**. Under this rule, a defendant can be found NGRI if, at the time the criminal act was committed, he or she was suffering from a mental disease that was so serious that the defendant did not know the nature of the act or did not know that act was wrong. Another test of insanity is the **irresistible impulse test**. This test holds that criminal defendants can be found NGRI if, at the time of the offense, they were stricken with a mental disease that prevented them from knowing right from wrong or that compelled them to commit the crime.

Under the **American Law Institute (ALI) test**, a person is not responsible if "as a result of mental disease or defect he lacks substantial capacity either to appreciate the criminality of his conduct or to conform his conduct to the requirements of law." The ALI test is plainly a relaxation of the usual insanity standard, as expressed in M'Naughten and the irresistible impulse test, because both of the older tests require "total" rather than "substantial" impairment. M'Naughten requires an inability to appreciate the wrongfulness of an action, and the irresistible impulse test requires a thorough loss of self-control.

It is important to understand that people found not guilty by reason of insanity do not automatically go free. Instead, they are committed to institutions and must undergo periodic psychiatric examinations. Once they are found to be sane, they may be released. Many people object to the fact that these individuals can look forward to release without serving any time in prison.

Entrapment

If a law enforcement officer induces a law-abiding citizen to commit a crime, **entrapment** may be used as a defense. The person using the defense must show that the crime would not have been committed had it not been for the inducement of the officer. The defense of entrapment is not available to a defendant who would have committed the crime even without the involvement of the officer. This factor is referred to as the propensity to commit the crime. The entrapment defense can be used in many different types of criminal cases; however, it occurs most often when the police have engineered a sting operation designed to tempt individuals who already have the propensity to commit the crime in question. Often in a sting operation, the main players are undercover law enforcement officers; however, sometimes they can be informants or reformed criminals who are used by the police to tempt individuals who are known by the police to be presently involved in a pattern of criminal activity. The fact that the police have used informants rather than undercover agents will not negate the entrapment defense, as long as all of the other elements are present.

Justifiable Force

In general, the law will not condone the use of force to solve problems. Still, special circumstances may arise that justify the use of force. Three of these situations lead to the following defenses: self-defense, defense of others, and battered spouse syndrome.

Self-Defense

Normally the law allows people to defend themselves as long as certain elements are clearly present. This action is known as self-defense. As indicated above, the defendant must first have a *bona fide* (good faith) belief that his or her life was in danger or that he or she was in danger of severe bodily harm. Words by themselves, in most states, will be insufficient to prove the authentic belief that such harm is imminent. When self-defense is used in a criminal case, the defendant must show that he or she was not the one who started the altercation. Moreover, in all cases, the person claiming self-defense must not have used more force than necessary to stop the unprovoked attack. In some states, the person claiming self-defense must retreat, if possible, before resorting to force; however, a person does not have a duty to retreat before using force if the attack occurs in his or her own home. In many states this exception has also been extended to a person's vehicle, so in those states, a person has no duty to retreat if that person is in his or her own vehicle or lawfully in a vehicle owned by a member of that person's immediate family.

Self-defense is an affirmative defense. This means that the defendant must put forth evidence that he or she has the right to that defense. This also means that the defendant must admit that he or she committed the action for which he or she has been brought to trial. Self-defense cannot be used by a defendant who has argued that he or she committed the offense by mistake ("It was an accident!") because self-defense requires the purposeful attempt to stop the assault by using force. The two defenses are, thus, incompatible with one another. Although the burden of proof to demonstrate guilt beyond a reasonable doubt still remains with the prosecution, in some states the defendant does have the burden of proving the existence of an affirmative defense. The standard of proof in self-defense, however, is not beyond a reasonable doubt. Depending upon state law, the burden of proof is either by a preponderance of the evidence or by clear and convincing evidence. Some states do not require the defendant to prove the existence of the affirmative defense of self-defense, at all. Instead, the accused is presumed to have properly defended himself or herself, unless the prosecution can successfully attack the presumption.

Some states that usually declare that the defendant has the burden of proving the existence of an affirmative defense of self-defense will remove that burden when the defendant claiming self-defense was in his home or vehicle at the time of the alleged attack. In such cases, the defendant's claim of self-defense is to be treated as a rebuttable presumption. The prosecution then has the burden or rebutting the presumption by a preponderance of the evidence. Moreover, some states also provide that, after a defendant has properly established that a claim of self-defense was legitimate and the prosecution drops all charges, the grand jury fails to indict, or the jury or judge finds the defendant not guilty, that defendant cannot be sued in tort case emerging from that same set of facts. [See: Philip D. Bogdanoff, "Criminal Law Boot Camp. Chapter 3: Self-Defense and the Castle Doctrine," *The Ohio State Bar Association,* March 18, 2014.]

Defense of Others

If a person uses force to rescue another person who is the victim of an apparent attack, most states will allow the rescuer to escape criminal liability. This exception is known as the defense of others. As in the case of self-defense, the rescuer must have a good reason to believe that the victim was in danger of severe bodily injury or even death.

Stand-Your-Ground Laws

A variation on the traditional self-defense is the stand-your-ground defense, which some states have recently added to their statutory provisions in criminal procedure. Some states have stand-your-ground provisions within their common law tradition. A stand-your-ground statute extends self-defense by eliminating any requirement to retreat, even outside one's home or vehicle. Therefore, as long as an individual is in a place that he or she has the legal right to be, then no retreat is necessary under the law. The other elements of self-defense would still apply. Some stand-your-ground laws also include a provision that permits the defendant to seek a pretrial hearing during which the judge would decide whether to grant the defendant civil and criminal immunity. Stand-your-ground laws are also called *no-duty-to-retreat* laws in some states.

EXAMPLE 5-5: Using (or Not Using) the Stand-Your-Ground Law as a Defense

George Zimmerman, a volunteer neighborhood watch patrolman, was seated in his car when he spotted what he described as a suspicious individual in the neighborhood. He called in his report and was told to stay in his car. He did not do so and, instead, began to follow the individual who turned out to be an unarmed teenager. Exactly what transpired after this is open to debate, although the facts did reveal two critical points: The teenager was unarmed, and medical evidence indicated that Zimmerman sustained injuries consistent with a beating. The bottom line, however, is that Zimmerman shot and killed the teenager. Zimmerman was charged with second-degree murder. Zimmerman's primary strategy was to raise the affirmative defense of self-defense. Florida law allowed Zimmerman to use a stand-your-ground statute as his defense. He did not do so, however, because his attorneys did not want to reveal their case at a pretrial immunity hearing. Ultimately, the jury found the defendant not guilty by applying the classic principles of self-defense. Some legal experts have pointed to this as a flaw in the statute. Others believe that it is a legitimate safeguard. What do you think? [See: *State v. Zimmerman* (2012-CF001083-A).]

Battered Spouse Syndrome   The law also protects a married individual from being abused by his or her spouse. In most cases of spouse abuse, the wife is victimized by the violent outbursts of her husband. Many communities have established shelters where abused and battered wives can seek safety and receive counseling and legal services for themselves and their children. Wives who wish to protect themselves from the continual abuse caused by their husbands may seek legal help from the courts.

One such remedy is a *protective order*. Protective orders bar the abusing spouse from maintaining any contact with the victim. Such orders are enforced by the local police. Unfortunately, protective orders are not always effective. In some very severe cases, the victimized spouse has taken the law into her own hands and killed her tormentor. The set of circumstances that leads a woman to believe that the only way that she can escape death or severe bodily injury is to use force against her tormentor is called **battered spouse syndrome**. These circumstances are also known as *battered woman* or *battered wife syndrome*. Because the spouse had good reason to believe that she was in danger of death or severe bodily injury, battered spouse syndrome is considered a form of self-defense in some courts.

Mistake

Mistake is a defense to charges of criminal liability, as long as the mistake destroys one of the elements necessary to that crime. If the mistake does not destroy an element, it is not a valid defense. To be a successful defense, the mistake must be based on a reasonable belief. It would be no defense for a defendant to say that he shot his wife because he believed she was an invader from Mars. Note also that it is not a defense for an accused to say that she did not know that this particular conduct was prohibited by law. Nor is it a defense to a gambling charge for the defendant to argue that she did not know that the gambling law applied to her. Finally, the mistake must destroy the criminal nature of the act in the mind of the accused. It would be no defense, for example, if a defendant argued that he injured an individual by mistake when he was actually trying to injure someone else.

quick quiz 5-5

1. Most defendants who are found NGRI are released immediately.   true | false

2. A person does not have to retreat to his or her own home before resorting to force to repel an attack.   true | false

3. Mistake is never a defense to a charge of criminal liability.   true | false

Summary

5.1 A crime is an offense against the public at large. As such, a crime threatens the peace, safety, and well-being of the entire community. For this reason, crimes are punishable by the official governing body of a nation or state. A felony is a crime punishable by death or imprisonment in a federal or a state prison for a term exceeding one year. Some felonies are also punishable by fines. A misdemeanor is a less serious crime that is generally punishable by a prison sentence of not more than one year.

5.2 The two elements necessary to create criminal liability are (a) an act and (b) the requisite state of mind. Generally speaking, a crime cannot be committed unless the criminal act named in the statute is performed with the requisite state of mind. Many state criminal codes include four possible states of mind: (a) purpose, (b) knowledge, (c) recklessness, and (d) negligence. Establishing motive may help investigators pinpoint the guilty party, but proving an evil motive is not necessary for a criminal conviction. Conversely, establishing the existence of a good motive will rarely absolve a defendant of criminal liability.

5.3 Crimes against people include but are not limited to first-degree murder, second-degree murder, manslaughter, battery, and assault. A more recent addition to this list involves hate speech. Crimes against property include but are not limited to burglary; breaking and entering; trespass; aggravated arson; arson; aggravated robbery; robbery; theft, fraud, and related offenses. Crimes involving business include embezzlement, forgery, criminal simulation, passing bad checks, and defrauding creditors. RICO offenses also involve business crime. Crimes against justice include bribery, theft in office, and dereliction of duty. Others, such as intimidation, are committed against a public official or public servant. Still others, such as obstruction of justice, resisting arrest, perjury, and tampering with evidence are committed against the justice system itself.

5.4 Cybercrimes include cyber-trespass, which involves any conventional crime committed with a computer. Cybercrimes that focus on the use of a computer include cyber-extortion, cyber-stalking, cyber-harassment, cyber-assault, cyber-bullying, cyber-spoofing, phishing, smishing, and vishing. Crimes that target computers include cyber-terrorism, identity theft, cyber-vandalism, and cyber-germ warfare. Federal cybercrimes include Computer Fraud and Abuse Act (CFAA), the Electronic Communications Privacy Act (ECPA), the Communications Assistance for Law Enforcement Act (CALEA), the Economic Espionage Act (EEA), the National Stolen Property Act (NSPA), the Identity Theft and Assumption Deterrence Act (ITADA).

5.5 Because criminal liability relies on the two essential elements of act and requisite mental state, a logical defense aims at eliminating one or both of those elements. Most defenses attempt to do just that. The most common defenses are insanity, entrapment, justifiable force, and mistake.

Key Terms

Questions for Review and Discussion

1. What is the purpose of criminal law?
2. What are the various categories and classes of crimes?
3. What is the nature of an act according to the meaning of criminal liability?
4. What are the four mental states that can be found in the criminal code?
5. What is motive, and how does it differ from the elements of criminal liability?
6. What are the various crimes against people?
7. What are the various theories involved in criminal punishment?
8. What are the various ways that the federal government has dealt with cybercrime?
9. What are the three standards for the insanity defense found in criminal law?
10. What are the requirements of entrapment as a defense against criminal liability?

Cases for Analysis

1. Edison High School in San Antonio, Texas, was the scene of an incident that later became national news, when a student brought a concealed weapon on the premises. Testimony later indicated the student did not intend to use the weapon but, instead, expected a payment for delivering the .38 caliber revolver. At first, he was charged with taking firearms onto school property in violation of a state statute. Later the state dropped its case, and the student was accused of breaking provisions of a federal statute known as the Gun-Free School Zone Act of 1990 (the GFSZ Act). Sensing that this was no ordinary case, but instead one of constitutional import, the student's attorney filed a motion to dismiss the charges based on the argument that the GFSZ Act was unconstitutional. The constitutional challenge was grounded on the argument that the GFSZ Act was an unlawful extension of congressional authority under the limits set down in the Commerce Clause. The District Court disagreed, and the case went to trial. After the student was convicted, his attorney filed an appeal with the Fifth Circuit Court of Appeals. The appeals court reversed the conviction. The Supreme Court then granted *certiorari*. Using your understanding of the Commerce Clause as interpreted by the Supreme Court in *Wickard v. Filburn*, should the Supreme Court agree with the appeals court or revert to the district court's original ruling? Explain. [See: *United States v. Lopez,* 514 U.S. 549, (1995).]

2. Fred Pomeroy was an assistant traffic manager for the New York Central and Hudson River Railroad Company. In that capacity, he handed out "rebates" to the American Sugar Refining Company in New

York and New Jersey and to W. H. Edgar & Son in Detroit. The goal of the rebates was to convince the sugar refiner and the sugar dealer to use the railroad for their shipments rather than some other method. The problem with this arrangement was that the shipping rates were fixed by federal law and, thus, the rebates amounted to a bribe. Pomeroy and New York Central were prosecuted under the Elkins Act and were found guilty. On an appeal that went all the way to the U.S. Supreme Court, New York Central argued that, while Pomeroy could be prosecuted under the criminal statute, the corporation could not. Can the corporation be prosecuted? What theory would you advise the court to use in this case? Explain. What will the outcome be? [See: *New York Central & Hudson River Railroad v. United States,* 212 U.S. 481 (U.S. Supreme Court).]

3. The hospitality industry in Portland, Oregon, instituted an organization that was designed to bring convention business to the city. Association members made fixed contributions to the organization, and companies in the supply business were expected to donate funds based on a percentage of their sales. Supply companies that did not contribute were boycotted by the membership. This boycott was a clear violation of the federal Sherman Antitrust Act. Both the president of Hilton Hotels Corporation and the manager of the Portland Hilton ordered the purchasing agent of the Portland Hotel to ignore the boycott and to make purchases based only on the quality of the products and service from suppliers. The purchasing agent for the Portland Hilton, however, out of personal resentment toward the sales rep of a particular supplier, enforced the boycott. After being found guilty of violating federal law, Hilton appealed, arguing that the trial court misinterpreted the law because the corporation could only be held liable if the purchasing agent committed a crime within the scope of employment with the intention that the corporation gain some benefit from that crime. In this case, it was clear that the agent had committed a crime but the acts were not within the scope of employment because he had been expressly forbidden to continue the boycott. What was the result on appeal? Explain. [See: *United States v. Hilton Hotels Corporation,* 467 F. 2d 1000 (9th Circuit).]

4. After Charles Hood was convicted of murder, he was sentenced to death in accordance with Texas law. It was later revealed, however, that the judge who presided at Hood's trial had been involved in a lengthy affair with the prosecutor in the case. Neither the judge nor the prosecutor had revealed this relationship during the trial. Moreover, after the trial, they denied the relationship until they were compelled to tell the truth under oath. The Texas Court of Criminal Appeals later agreed to a new sentencing hearing for Hood; however, the hearing was limited to questions concerning the jury instructions and, therefore, did not involve the conflict of interest problem caused by the affair. Hood filed a petition for certiorari with the United States Supreme Court. Should the U.S. Supreme Court hear the case? Explain. [See: Mark White, "Death Penalty Must Be Fair," *The National Law Journal,* March 29, 2010, p. 43.]

5. Antonio Martinez, also known as Muhammad Hussain, discussed the killing of American soldiers with an unnamed individual who, unknown to Martinez, was actually an FBI informant. The informant passed that information to FBI agents who arranged a sting operation during which Martinez helped build a phony car bomb. Martinez was arrested as he attempted to set off the phony car bomb in front of a recruiting center in suburban Baltimore. Martinez claimed that he was entrapped by the federal agents. Martinez's attorney argued that the defendant was not capable of developing the plan to make the bomb on his own. The federal attorney also argued that Martinez had clearly been making plans to attack U.S. soldiers before the informant contacted him. The federal attorney also argued that whether Martinez was capable of actually building a bomb on his own did not matter since he not only believed that he could do it but also actually tried to do it, and would have done it had the bomb not been a fake. The prosecuting attorney also had a tape of Martinez arming the bomb. The video shows that Martinez enjoyed the prospect of killing the soldiers. Was Martinez entrapped? Explain by outlining the elements of entrapment. [See: "Lawyer Argues Entrapment in Bomb Plot," *The New York Times,* December 14, 2010, p. 18.]

6. Katie Roberts was wasting away from the effects of an incurable disease. She asked her husband Frank to help her commit suicide. In response to her request, Mr. Roberts mixed poison and water and placed the mixture on a chair within her reach. She took the poison and died several hours later. Mr. Roberts admitted placing the poison within her reach but denied having the required mental state for first-degree murder because he was

responding to his wife's request and was motivated by love and mercy. Will he prevail? Explain. [See: *People v. Roberts,* 178 N.W.690 (MI).]

7. Several teenagers taped the broken legs of a chair together to create a cross, which they then ignited and placed on the lawn of an African-American family in the neighborhood. One of the teenagers, a minor, was charged with a misdemeanor under the St. Paul Bias-Motivated Crime Ordinance. The St. Paul ordinance criminalized the placing on private property of any "symbol, object, appellation, characterization or graffiti . . . which one knows or has reasonable grounds to know arouses anger, alarm, or resentment in others on the basis of race, color, creed, religion or gender." The defendant argued that the ordinance was an unconstitutional violation of the First Amendment. The city contended that the statute was constitutional because it was necessary for the preservation of a compelling state interest, namely, the right of group members who have been discriminated against in the past "to live in peace where they wish." Is the St. Paul ordinance constitutional? Explain. [See: *R.A.V. v. St. Paul,* 505 U.S. 1992 (U.S. Sup. Ct.]

8. Tomas Reese entered a fast-food restaurant before the restaurant had opened for business through an unlocked rear entrance. The door had been left unlocked by an accomplice who was an employee of the restaurant. After entering the restaurant, Reese pushed one employee against a soda machine and, while holding a gun to the neck of the manager, forced her to open the safe. Reese then locked the employees in a cooler and fled the scene with over $5,000. Has Reese committed burglary, robbery, or larceny? Explain. [See: *State v. Reese,* 113 Ohio App. 3d. 642 (OH).]

9. Cuttiford and Banks lived in the same duplex; Banks lived upstairs and Cuttiford lived downstairs. The two apartments shared a common internal stairway at the back of the duplex. A confrontation began between Banks and Cuttiford in the rear stairway of the duplex. Banks became rather violent and threatened Cuttiford and Cuttiford's wife. Cuttiford went to his apartment on the bottom floor and retrieved two guns from his bedroom. When he returned to the back door near the stairway, Banks told him, "You don't have the guts to use that, because you're going to have to use it because I'm going to kill you!" Banks then came at Cuttiford, lunging from the common stairway into the kitchen of the Cuttiford's apartment. Cuttiford then shot and killed Banks. At trial, Cuttiford argued that he shot Banks in self-defense. The trial court refused to instruct the jury that Cuttiford did not have to retreat into his own home before acting to repel an attacker. The court apparently believed the prosecution, which had argued that because Banks and Cuttiford occupied the same duplex, Cuttiford had the duty to retreat before repelling Banks's attack. Was the trial court judge correct in his instruction to the jury regarding self-defense? Explain. [See: *State v. Cuttiford,* 639 N.E.2d 472 (OH).]

10. Cowen had on many occasions operated as a paid drug informant for the FBI and the Ventura Police Department. The Ventura police asked Cowen to keep in touch with them, should he become involved in any deals. Subsequently, Cowen asked Busby to introduce him to any drug dealers he knew. Busby introduced Cowen to Mandell, who sold Cowen several samples of cocaine in anticipation of a $41,500 deal. Cowen then contacted the Ventura police. A police officer posed as Cowen's buyer, and both Busby and Mandell were arrested and eventually turned over to the federal authorities. Busby was convicted of possession of cocaine with the intent to distribute it. He appealed this conviction, claiming that he had been entrapped by Cowen. Will Busby's entrapment defense succeed on appeal? Explain. [See: *United States v. Busby,* 780 F.2d 804 (9th Cir.).]

quick quiz Answers

5-1	5-2	5-3	5-4	5-5
1. F	1. T	1. T	1. F	1. F
2. F	2. F	2. F	2. T	2. T
3. F	3. F	3. T	3. T	3. F

THE OPENING CASE *Round 1*
Battling the Hot Coffee Tort Law Myth

One of the most discussed and least understood cases in legal history is the classic case of *Liebeck v. McDonald's Restaurants,* sometimes called the "McDonald's case" and sometimes just the "coffee case." The facts in the case are fairly straightforward. Stella Liebeck, who was 79 years old at the time in 1992, purchased a cup of coffee at the drive-through window of a McDonald's restaurant in New Mexico. Her grandson, who was driving the car, parked so that she could mix cream and sugar with the coffee. While she was trying to take the top off the cup, the coffee splashed out of the cup, onto her legs and lap. As a result, she sustained third-degree burns and was in the hospital for eight days. Her injuries led to skin grafts, permanent disfigurement, and 24 months of disability. To cover her medical expenses, Liebeck asked McDonald's for $13,000 and to make up for lost earnings she requested an additional $5,000. McDonald's refused her request and, instead, proposed a settlement of $800. As evidence unfolded in the case, it was learned that the coffee served by McDonald's was normally measured at about 180 to 190 degrees Fahrenheit.

If spilled, coffee at that temperature would lead to third-degree burns in about two seconds, maybe seven if the victim were lucky. In contrast, some (but not all) other restaurants were known to serve their coffee at the much lower temperature of 140 degrees, which, Liebeck's attorneys argued, ought to be the top temperature at which coffee is served at any restaurant. Evidence also revealed that between 1982 and 1992, McDonald's restaurants had recorded more than 700 claims from people who had been scalded by McDonald's coffee, many of them with third-degree burns similar to those suffered by Liebeck. To explain their reluctance to alter this procedure, one member of McDonald's quality control management team explained that the number of injuries reported was not high enough to lead the company to make any changes. McDonald's sells billions (billions with a "b") of cups of coffee annually, so even 700 cases must seem, initially at least, to be a low number. McDonald's also explained that many customers buy the coffee at the beginning of a long trip to work and so the high start-up temperature allows the coffee to stay hot, or at least hot enough, for the entire ride. Consequently, despite those 700 claims, McDonald's hot coffee remained, well, hot, on the day that Mrs. Liebeck purchased her fateful cup. The case of *Liebeck v. McDonald's* presents several tort law concepts and issues that will be explored in this chapter. One issue involves the elements of negligence (duty, breach of duty, proximate cause, and actual harm) and another involves the measurement of damages. [See: *Stella Liebeck v. McDonald's Restaurants, P.T.S., Inc. and McDonald's International, Inc.,* 1995 WL 360309 (Bernalillo County, N.M. Dist. Ct. 1994); Kevin G. Cain, "The McDonald's Coffee Lawsuit," *Journal of Consumer & Commercial Law,* pp. 14–19.]

Opening Case Questions

1. What duty, if any, does a restaurant owe to its customers in relation to injuries that result from its service or products? Explain.

2. What elements will the plaintiff have to prove to win her negligence case? Explain.

3. What counterarguments can the defendant raise in this case? Explain.

4. How might comparative and contributory negligence be involved in this case? Explain.

5. What type or types of damages might be sought in a negligence case like this one? Explain.

LO Learning Objectives

1. Differentiate between the objectives of tort law and those of criminal law.
2. Outline the nature of *respondeat superior.*
3. Describe the element of duty.
4. Identify the principal intentional torts and outline the elements of each.
5. Explain the four elements of negligence.
6. Contrast contributory negligence, comparative negligence, and assumption of the risk.
7. Judge when the doctrine of strict liability applies.
8. Discuss the emerging trends in cybertort law.
9. Outline the various remedies available in tort law.
10. Point out some developments in tort reform.

6-1 Tort Law Defined

A **tort** is a private wrong that injures another person's physical well-being, emotional health, business, property, or reputation. The English word *tort* comes from the Latin word *tortus,* which can be translated as "twisted." A person who commits a tort and has thus engaged in "twisted" behavior is called a **tortfeasor**. The other party is alternately referred to as the injured party, the innocent party, the victim, or the plaintiff if a lawsuit has been filed. In the case of a lawsuit, the tortfeasor would be called a defendant.

Tort Law versus Criminal Law

One purpose of tort law is to compensate the injured party for his or her loss. Another objective is to protect potential victims by deterring future tortious behavior. In contrast as noted in the previous chapter, criminal law involves a public wrong, that is, a wrong that affects the entire society. When a crime is committed, the government authorities begin a legal procedure that is designed to remove the offender from society, and to punish that offender to the fullest extent allowed by the law. As noted in the last chapter, however, it is possible for a single act to be both a crime and a tort. As noted in the chapter on criminal law, the U.S. Constitution protects people from being tried twice for the same crime. This rule is known as the principle of *double jeopardy*. Double jeopardy does not protect a defendant from being sued under tort law for the consequences of an action, even if that defendant has already been tried for the same wrongdoing in a criminal court using criminal law.

Respondeat Superior

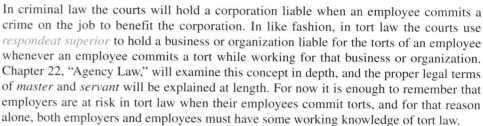

About the Law

The doctrine of *respondeat superior* is also known as vicarious liability.

In criminal law the courts will hold a corporation liable when an employee commits a crime on the job to benefit the corporation. In like fashion, in tort law the courts use *respondeat superior* to hold a business or organization liable for the torts of an employee whenever an employee commits a tort while working for that business or organization. Chapter 22, "Agency Law," will examine this concept in depth, and the proper legal terms of *master* and *servant* will be explained at length. For now it is enough to remember that employers are at risk in tort law when their employees commit torts, and for that reason alone, both employers and employees must have some working knowledge of tort law.

The Element of Duty

One approach to the law is to think of legal liability in terms of elements. This approach emphasizes that no liability can be imposed against an individual unless all the elements are present. In tort law, the first element is duty. A **duty** is an obligation placed on individuals because of the law. The second element is a violation of that duty. A duty can be violated intentionally, through negligence, or under the theory of strict liability.

Causation and Juriscience

A negligence case requires the plaintiffs to prove that the defendants caused their injuries. In negligence cases there are two kinds of causation, actual cause and proximate cause. These two types of causation will be examined at length later in the chapter; however, for now it is enough to point out that actual cause is cause "in fact" or "real" cause. Real cause exists in the physical universe and is thus subject to experiments, tests, measurements, and other forms of proof. This means that the plaintiff will often have to use scientific evidence to demonstrate how action "A" led to effect "B." Moreover, because of the scientific nature of a case, the court generally needs to hear the testimony of an expert to determine causation. This stage in a case, where science and the law intersect, is referred to as **juriscience**. Judges at all levels, but especially those in the trial courts, must determine the validity of scientific evidence. Unfortunately, because the law is an adversarial process, judges will frequently be forced to choose between two or more competing lines of scientific proof. Judges, however, are educated in the law not science, and so they need help unraveling the intricacies of scientific evidence beyond simply listening to the experts, many of whom may have hidden agendas.

EXAMPLE 6-1: Juriscience and Tort Law: Daubert v. Merrell Dow Pharmaceuticals—Revisited

The law is a balancing act that struggles to assimilate new ideas while maintaining useful and effective traditions. Sometimes this balancing act works well, and sometimes it just falls apart. A case in point is *Daubert v. Merrell Dow Pharmaceuticals, Inc.,* a U.S. Supreme Court case featured in Chapter 4, as part of our debate about the collective science court proposal. Recall that the case involves a lawsuit filed by the Dauberts against Merrell Dow in which the plaintiffs argue that Bendectin, a drug produced by Merrell Dow and taken by Mrs. Daubert for nausea during her pregnancy, had caused birth defects in their children. The case depends on the issue of causation, a traditional tort law principle that says that, to succeed in a negligence lawsuit, a plaintiff must prove that the defendant's action caused the plaintiff's injury; however, because of the scientific nature of the case, the court needed expert testimony to determine causation. This point in the case, the point at which science and the law intersect, is referred to as *juriscience.* The judges at each level, from the trial court, through the appellate court, up to the Supreme Court, and then back down to the appellate court, had to weigh the scientific evidence on causation leading from the development of the drug Bendectin to the birth defects. The judges were faced with two competing lines of evidence, one presented by the plaintiffs, the other by the defendants. The defendants' evidence included peer-reviewed articles published in scientific journals and studies issued by the U.S. Food and Drug Administration (FDA). None of these reports or articles could find a link between Bendectin and birth defects. In response, the plaintiff's scientific experts offered a reanalysis of the accepted data. This reanalysis demonstrated that the original data had been badly misinterpreted by previous scientists. To determine which line of evidence should be followed, the court had to interpret Rule 702 of the Federal Rules of Evidence and *Frye v. United States,* a case that predated Rule 702, but that had, nevertheless, set up a standard that the federal courts had used for decades to evaluate expert testimony. Ultimately, the Supreme Court decided that expert evidence did not have to be "generally accepted" as *Frye* had suggested, because some scientific discoveries may be "too particular, too new, or of too limited interest to be published." The court thus emphasized that the rules had to be interpreted liberally rather than narrowly in determining the use of expert testimony. Still, the Supreme Court concluded that such testimony did have to "rest on a reliable foundation and (be) relevant to the task at hand." Since the lower courts had used only the *Frye* standard, the case was sent back to the appeals court, which still supported Merrell Dow because the evidence produced by the plaintiffs did not demonstrate a definite causation link between Bendectin and birth defects. [See: *Daubert v. Merrell Dow Pharmaceuticals, Inc.,* (509 U.S. 579) (U.S.S.Ct.); see also *Daubert v. Merrell Dow Pharmaceuticals, Inc.,* 43 F.3d 1311 (Ninth Circuit).]

After *Daubert v. Merrell Dow,* the federal rule on expert testimony was amended somewhat to help judges make this determination. The rule states that an expert may testify on a scientific matter as long as, "(1) testimony is based upon sufficient facts or data, (2) the testimony is the product of reliable scientific principles and methods, and (3) the witness has applied the principles and methods reliably to the facts in the case." Still, even this standard is somewhat vague and ambiguous. Many questions remain unanswered. Who is to determine when testimony has reached a level of "sufficient facts or data"? What makes a scientific principle or method "reliable"? How will the judge know when a witness has applied a principle in a reliable way? Some states have tried to be more specific in the formulation of this rule. Ohio, for example, has gone so far as to say that, if an expert witness bases an opinion on a test or an experiment, that test or experiment is reliable *only* if *all* of the following apply: "(1) the theory upon which the procedure, test, or experiment is based is objectively verifiable or validly derived from widely accepted knowledge, facts, or principles; (2) the design of the procedure, test, experiment reliably implements the theory; and (3) the particular procedure, test, or experiment was conducted in a way that will yield an accurate result."

6-2 Intentional Torts

Intentional violations of duty include a vast variety of intentional torts, all of which have their own individual elements. Table 6-1 summarizes the primary intentional torts.

Assault and Battery

Under U.S. tort law, assault and battery, though often closely associated with each other, are separate torts. An **assault** occurs when the victim is placed in fear or apprehension of immediate bodily harm by a tortfeasor who has the present apparent ability to inflict that harm. No actual physical contact is needed for an assault. The essence of the tort lies in the fear or apprehension that is created in the victim.

EXAMPLE 6-2: Assault with a Deadly Dart

Terry Kline and Patrick Fisher were playing a friendly game of darts at the Wood Street Tavern one evening when they invited Fred Feeney and David Ballentine to join them. Unknown to either Kline or Feeney, Ballentine was intoxicated. After losing several games, Ballentine became enraged and tried to hit Kline by throwing several darts at him. In his intoxicated state, Ballentine's aim was poor, and he did not hit Kline. Nevertheless, Ballentine has committed an assault.

A **battery** involves an offensive or harmful, unprivileged touching. Naturally, if in Example 6-2, Ballentine had actually managed to hit Kline, he would have committed a battery; however, as the definition points out, a touching need not be harmful to be a battery. Moreover, a battery does not always require the touching of the actual person of the victim, if the tortfeasor touches something closely associated with that victim. So, if a prankster pulls a chair out from under someone before that person sits down, and the person falls to the floor, the joker has committed a battery. Or if he or she knocks a cafeteria tray out of a diner's hands, again he or she has committed a battery, despite the fact that the actual person or the victim has not been contacted.

EXAMPLE 6-3: Battery by Antibody

Lucy Pickett works as a nurse at Garner County Hospital. Because she knows that her patient, Jim Luger, is afraid of needles, she sneaked up behind him and injected him with an antibiotic that had been ordered by his primary physician. Despite her desire to help Luger, and her wish to save him from feeling unnecessary fear, Pickett has committed a battery.

Table 6-1   Intentional Torts

Tort	Definition
Assault	An assault occurs when the victim is placed in fear or apprehension of immediate bodily harm by the tortfeasor who has the present apparent ability to inflict that harm.
Battery	A battery involves an offensive or harmful, unprivileged touching.
False imprisonment	When one party prevents another party from moving about freely, the first party has committed the intentional tort of false imprisonment.
Defamation	Any false statement communicated to others that harms a person's good name or reputation may constitute the tort of defamation.
Invasion of privacy	Invasion of privacy occurs when one person unreasonably denies another person the right to be left alone.
Misuse of legal procedure	Misuse of legal procedure occurs when one person brings a legal procedure action with malice and without probable cause.
Intentional infliction of emotional distress	Intentional or reckless infliction of emotional distress occurs when an individual causes another to undergo emotional or mental suffering, even without an accompanying physical injury.
Disparagement	Disparagement involves any false statement communicated to others that somehow questions the quality of an item of property or that raises uncertainty as to who actually has legal ownership rights to the property in question.
Fraud	Fraud involves false statements or actions, or a combination thereof, that misrepresent facts so that an innocent party relies on those misrepresentations and suffers an injury or loss as a result.

False Imprisonment

When one party prevents another party from moving about freely, the first party has committed the intentional tort of **false imprisonment**. This tort is called false arrest in some states. The victim of false imprisonment need not be locked in a prison or a jail cell. All that is required is that the person's freedom of movement be restricted. For example, a physician who refuses to return a patient's clothing until a partial payment is received for a long overdue bill has committed false imprisonment.

Store owners must be very careful about detaining suspected shoplifters because such a detention could result in a false imprisonment lawsuit if not handled properly. Still, because of the growing problem of shoplifting in society today, most states have laws that allow storekeepers to detain a suspected shoplifter if they have reasonable grounds to suspect that a shoplifting incident has occurred. This protection is ordinarily referred to as the **shopkeeper's privilege**. When the privilege is created by statute, that statute is commonly called the **merchant protection statute**. Even under such laws, the storekeeper must detain the suspect in a reasonable manner and for no longer than a reasonable length of time.

Defamation and Disparagement

Intentional torts such as battery, assault, and false imprisonment involve direct physical and psychological injury to an individual. These injuries are not the only type of harm, however, that can be imposed on individuals in tort law. Sometimes the injury results from words that damage a reputation and lead to monetary loss. Two of these word-oriented torts are defamation and disparagement.

Defamation   Any false statement communicated to others that harms a person's good name or reputation may constitute the tort of **defamation**. To be defamatory, the statement must hold the victim up to ridicule, contempt, or hatred. Defamation in a temporary form, such as speech, is **slander**; in a permanent form, such as writing, it is **libel**.

People can usually bring a libel suit whenever the permanent statement is damaging to their reputation, is false, and is communicated to a third party. However, under common law, individuals can bring slander lawsuits even if they have suffered no actual loss if the false statements fall into one of the following categories:

1.   An accusation that the victim of the slanderous statements has committed a very serious crime, such as murder or rape.

2.   An accusation that the victim has a communicable disease, such as venereal disease.

3.   An accusation that the victim has engaged in improprieties in a business, trade, or profession.

4.   An accusation that an unmarried female victim has been unchaste.

Individuals may speak the truth without being sued successfully for defamation as long as it is done without spite or ill will. In addition, statements made by senators and representatives on the floor of Congress and statements made in a court of law are privileged. Privileged statements are not the proper subject of a defamation lawsuit. The idea behind creating these privileges is to promote the open debate of legislative and judicial matters.

The U.S. Supreme Court has given journalists the extra protection of the actual malice test when they write about public officials. Under the **actual malice test**, a public official must prove not only that the statement made or printed was false but also that it was made with actual malice. **Actual malice** means that the statement was made or printed either with the knowledge that it was false or with a reckless disregard for its truth or falsity. Later decisions expanded the actual malice test to cover public figures. Public figures are people like television actors, sports figures, and rock stars who seek out public fame and are readily recognizable by the public at large.

Temporary public figures are people who are placed against their will into the public view by some event beyond their control. Disaster victims, hostages, and rescuers are examples of temporary public figures. Generally, such people are held to the actual malice test as long as their notoriety lasts.

EXAMPLE 6-4: *Duckett v. the City and County of San Francisco: Temporary Public Figure?*

The plaintiff in this case, Elyse Duckett, was a veteran fire fighter with the San Francisco Fire Department. During her career, she also worked as a recruitment officer assigned to hire young women and was later appointed to integrate women and minorities into the department. This case involves the death of a passenger who was thrown from an Asiana aircraft that crashed at the San Francisco Airport. Duckett was not among the first responders because she was performing other duties that had taken her away from the station house; however, after arriving at the airport driving Aircraft Rescue Firefighting 37, she learned that a passenger had been run over by one or more of SFFD's vehicles. Later, on two occasions, Duckett was interrogated at length about the death of the passenger. Duckett informed the questioners that she and one of her colleagues had viewed a video that showed that she had not driven the vehicle that had first run over the passenger. Even so, the questioners at the first interrogation persisted in what was later described as "an aggressive, accusatory, and intimidating manner." Subsequently, a television reporter, who had tried unsuccessfully to talk to Duckett, ran a story that identified her as the driver of the vehicle that had killed the passenger. The sources for the story came from within the SFFD. The story was aired on local, national, and international news outlets. Duckett brought a lawsuit against the city and county for violations of the Firefighters Procedural Code and the California Government Code. Duckett might also pursue a defamation case against the television station that broadcast the story. In a defamation lawsuit, the television news outlet would want to label her a *temporary public figure* so that she would be forced to use the more challenging actual malice test. Under the actual malice test, Duckett would have to demonstrate not only that the story was false, broadcast, and damaging, but also that the TV station ran the story knowing it was false or ran it with a reckless disregard for its truth or falsity. [See: *Duckett v. the City and County of San Francisco, et al.* Case Number CGc-14-539201 (May 9, 2014); Dan Nakaso, "SF Firefighter . . . Alleges She Was Made a Scapegoat," *Mercury News,* May 9, 2014; Phillip Matier and Andrew Ross, "S.F. Firefighter Claims Defamation in Asiana Crash," *SF Gate,* January 28, 2014.]

Disparagement   Disparagement involves any false statement communicated to others that somehow questions the quality of property or raises uncertainty as to who has legal ownership of that property. Generally, to recover for disparagement, the plaintiff must show monetary loss. Such losses may include the loss of sales, money spent to correct the public's image of a product, or expenses spent on litigation due to the disparagement. The difference between defamation and disparagement is that in defamation, the false charge is made about the victim's reputation, whereas with disparagement, the falsehood is made about a person's property or product. The falsehood usually casts doubt on the value of the product or on the property rights of the owner.

EXAMPLE 6-5: Toys, Tots, and Tall Tales

Warren Barrington owned and operated Toys and Tots—From Two to Twelve, a toy store that specialized in educational toys for children between two and 12 years of age. Barrington and his wife, who operated the store as a partnership, did their best to market only original toys made of natural materials. Electronic toys, computers, and toys made of plastic were never sold in the store. During the National Toy and Model Association of America convention, Raymond Matthews, who owned a competitive shop, started several rumors, most of which suggested that many of the toys that were being shown by the Barringtons at the convention were not made of natural materials as advertised. He also suggested that those toys that were made of natural materials involved ideas stolen from him and that the Barringtons did not have the right to market them as they were doing at the convention. Matthews has clearly committed disparagement here. He has planted false reports about both the value of the Barrington's products and about the Barrington's property rights to the toys.

Fraudulent Misrepresentation

Another word-oriented tort is fraudulent misrepresentation. **Fraudulent misrepresentation**, or **fraud** as it is known in some states, occurs when false statements or actions, or a combination thereof, are made by one party in a way that causes another party to rely on those misrepresentations and then to suffer an injury or loss as a result. Frequently, fraud involves a business relationship and works to destroy the mutual assent that ought to exist between the parties that are involved in a contract.

To demonstrate fraud, the complaining party (also referred to as the plaintiff) must prove the existence of five elements.

1. The complaining party will have to prove that the other party made false representations (statements) about some material fact involved in the contract. A material fact is one that is very crucial to the terms of the contract. Often the courts say that a fact is material if it makes a difference to the outcome of the case. A fact that makes no difference, then, is immaterial.

2. The plaintiff must demonstrate convincingly that the other party made the representations knowing that they were false.

3. The plaintiff must show that the false representations were made with the intent that they be relied upon by the innocent party.

4. The complaining party must establish that there was a *reasonable* reliance on the false representations.

5. The plaintiff must verify that he or she actually suffered some loss by relying on those false representations after entering the contract.

Invasion of Privacy

The courts in the United States have consistently held that people have a right to privacy. Consequently, a violation of that right would involve the tort of **invasion of privacy**. The right to privacy can be violated in several ways:

1. Revelation of confidential records.
2. Intrusion.
3. Creating a false light.
4. Exploitation.

Revelation of Confidential Records   Individuals who, because of their jobs, work with confidential records containing private information must ensure that those records remain private. A failure to protect such confidential matters could result in an invasion of privacy lawsuit. Although it is not a violation of privacy for individuals to discuss confidential matters for professional reasons, it could be an invasion of privacy to discuss those same records for nonprofessional reasons. The motive of the person who releases the information does not matter. Moreover, whether there has been an invasion of privacy depends on the level of privacy expected by that person in that situation. For instance, an employee would expect privacy involving his or her employment record but not concerning the information that is printed on his or her identification badge.

Intrusion   An individual's privacy can also be violated if there is an unwarranted intrusion into the person's expectation of privacy. Such an intrusion might occur if a person's photograph is taken and then published on the front page of a local newspaper. The issue at the heart of such case is the question of whether the plaintiff had a high expectation of privacy. Recall that the expectation of privacy depends on the situation. A person walking across a college campus has a very low expectation of privacy, whereas a person who is in his or her own home has a very high expectation of privacy. Thus, the publication of a photo of a person walking across campus would *not* be actionable as an invasion of privacy, but taking a similar photo while that person was in his or her home would be.

Creating a False Light Creating a false light is closely akin to defamation because it involves the publication of information about a person that paints him or her in a way that the majority of the population would see as unfavorable. A fashion model who poses for photographs for a bathing suit catalog and finds her image printed in a sexually explicit magazine would have a cause of action for being placed in a false light.

Exploitation The courts have held that an individual holds the rights to his or her own likeness to make money. An invasion of privacy can occur when one party uses an individual's photo, likeness, or name without permission for advertising, marketing, or publicity. Some courts treat the misappropriation of a person's likeness as a separate tort, calling it an invasion of the right to publicity.

Intentional Infliction of Emotional Distress

In recent years, the courts have recognized a tort called the **intentional or reckless infliction of emotional distress**. Before these more enlightened court decisions were handed down, victims who were injured emotionally by the wrongful acts of others could not recover damages without proving some sort of bodily injury. Today, in many states, someone who intentionally or recklessly causes another individual to undergo emotional or mental suffering will be responsible, even without an accompanying physical injury. The actions complained of must be extreme and outrageous and cause severe emotional suffering.

EXAMPLE 6-6: Extreme and Outrageous Silence

Marc Christian, who gained notoriety as the live-in boyfriend of Rock Hudson, sued the estate of the late actor for the intentional infliction of emotional distress. Christian argued that he had been induced to continue having "high-risk" sexual relations with the late screen star because Hudson had remained silent and failed to inform him that he had contracted AIDS. As a result of Hudson's misrepresentations, Christian contended that he suffered extreme emotional distress when he learned that Hudson was ill. This was true, Christian argued, despite the fact that he was not HIV positive himself. Although Hudson did not attempt deliberately to transfer the virus to Christian and did not plan to cause Christian emotional distress, the inherent harmfulness of Hudson's actions could easily amount to extreme and outrageous conduct.

Misuse of Legal Procedure

The intentional tort known as the **misuse of legal procedure** occurs when one person brings a legal action with malice and without probable cause. When the misuse of the legal procedure involves the filing of a false civil lawsuit, it is called **wrongful civil proceedings**. In contrast, when the misuse involves bringing false criminal charges, it is labeled **malicious prosecution**. Some states use only the term *malicious prosecution* to refer to both forms of the tort. All of the following conditions must be present for a lawsuit based on misuse of legal procedure to succeed:

1. The defendant (the person against whom the misuse of legal procedure suit has been filed) must have brought civil or criminal charges against the plaintiff at an earlier time.
2. The earlier case must have been resolved favorably for the plaintiff.
3. The plaintiff must prove that the earlier case was brought by the defendant with malice and without probable cause.

When these conditions are present, an individual may be able to recover damages from the defendant for making the innocent party the target of a legal action without a good cause.

A related cause of action, which can easily be confused with malicious prosecution, is abuse of process. **Abuse of process** occurs when a legal procedure is used for a purpose other than that for which it is intended. It differs from malicious prosecution in that there is no requirement that the earlier case be brought without probable cause or be resolved favorably for the plaintiff. The tort can involve either a criminal or a civil case. Typically, abuse of process happens when a perfectly legal process is used as a pressure tactic to convince someone to do something he or she would not be inclined to do under ordinary circumstances.

EXAMPLE 6-7: Misuse and Abuse: Crossing the Legal Line

Janice Franklin and Karen Yalta were involved in a very difficult dissolution of their partnership. As a result of this problematic dissolution, as well as many other factors, the two young women did not like each other. Accordingly, Franklin filed a lawsuit against Yalta for defamation. The lawsuit was resolved in Yalta's favor. Yalta then sued Franklin for wrongful civil proceedings. Yalta won the case because she was able to prove that the original defamation suit against her was fabricated by Franklin, who was motivated by hatred and ill will. This suit is an example of the misuse of legal proceedings. If Franklin had filed a defamation suit to force Yalta to agree to Franklin's terms in the dissolution, she would be involved in abuse of process. This involvement would be true even if Franklin had legitimate reasons for filing the defamation suit.

quick quiz 6-2

1. Assault and battery never exist simultaneously.   true | false
2. To be defamatory, a statement need not be communicated to a third party.   true | false
3. The intentional infliction of emotional distress has yet to be recognized as a tort in any state jurisdiction.   true | false

6-3 Negligence

People and property are sometimes injured even when no one intends that the injury occur. Such an occurrence is usually labeled an accident. Although no one acted with intent, someone was injured. The victim has experienced pain and suffering, lost wages, or incurred medical or repair bills. Justice demands that the injured party be compensated. The part of tort law that is concerned with the compensation of accident victims is called **negligence**.

Elements of Negligence

The issue before the court in a negligence action is as follows: Under what circumstances can the actions of an alleged tortfeasor be labeled negligent so that the victim can be compensated? Four elements must be present to establish negligence: legal duty, breach of duty, proximate cause, and actual harm. Table 6-2 gives an overview of these four elements.

Table 6-2 The Elements of Negligence

Element	Definition
Legal duty	A determination that a legal duty exists between the parties must be made to establish liability through negligence. This is solely a question of whether the tortfeasor should have reasonably foreseen a risk of harm to the injured party.
Breach of duty	The judge or the jury must determine whether the person accused of negligence has breached the duty owed to the victim. To determine if the alleged tortfeasor has met the appropriate standard of care, the court uses the reasonable person test.
Proximate cause	For the tortfeasor to be held liable, the unreasonable conduct must be the proximate cause of the victim's injuries. Proximate cause is the legal connection between the unreasonable conduct and the resulting harm.
Actual harm	The injured party in a lawsuit for negligence must show that actual harm was suffered.

Legal Duty A determination that a legal duty exists between the parties must be made to establish liability through negligence. This issue is solely a question of whether the tortfeasor should have reasonably foreseen a risk of harm to the injured party. Often today, the element of duty is not at issue in a lawsuit; however, there are some instances, often when a novel case comes before a court, that the legal duty of the defendant may be placed at issue. The phrase "at issue" refers to a legal question that must be answered for the case to be decided.

EXAMPLE 6-8: *Booker v. Revco DS, Incorporated:* Duty, Duty, and More Duty

At age 74, Ramona Booker entered a drugstore by pushing her way through one door and then through a second. Both doors were extremely heavy, so Booker was compelled to use both hands, causing her cane to drag on the ground. As she entered the second door, the tip of her cane caught on the exposed coil of a security device, causing her to fall and injure herself. Booker brought a lawsuit against Revco, the retailer, to recover damages (read "money" here) for her injuries. The defendant filed a motion for summary judgment that was granted by the trial court but then reversed by the appellate court. In examining the question of whether the defendant was entitled to a judgment as a matter of law, the court held that there was no doubt that the defendant drugstore owed a duty to its customers to keep them safe from harm while on the premises. In making this judgment the appellate court in this case quoted an earlier appellate case that held, "[It is a] well-established rule that the possessor of premises owes a duty to an invitee to exercise ordinary or reasonable care for his or her safety and protection. This duty includes maintaining the premises in a reasonably safe condition and warning an invitee of latent or concealed defects of which the possessor has or should have knowledge." [See: *Baldauf v. Kent State Univ.* (1988), 49 Ohio App.3d 46, 47-48, 550 N.E.2d 517; *Booker v. Revco DS, Inc.*, 681 N.E.2d 499 (OH).]

Breach of Duty The judge or the jury must determine whether the person accused of negligence has breached the duty owed to the victim. A breach of duty occurs if the alleged tortfeasor has not met the appropriate standard of care. To determine if the alleged tortfeasor has met the appropriate standard of care, the court uses the reasonable person test. This test compares the actions of the tortfeasor with those of a reasonable person in a similar situation. If a reasonable person would not have done what the tortfeasor actually did, then the tortfeasor is liable. The reasonable person standard is an objective test. Circumstances may change, but the standard of care applied by a reasonable person does not. How a reasonable person would behave in one set of circumstances may not be the same in another set of circumstances.

EXAMPLE 6-9: The Case of the Unreasonable Limo Service

Luigi Tarentino hired a limousine from Highland Limo Service so that he and his wife, Maybeth, could attend their high school reunion in style. When the limousine arrived, Tarentino told the driver to take them to the Regency Hotel. Once they were on the freeway, it became clear that the driver did not know how to reach the hotel. Every time the driver took a wrong turn, Tarentino attempted to correct him. The driver continued to ignore Tarentino's instructions. Eventually, the driver, who later said he was aggravated by Tarentino's frequent interruptions, stopped the limousine and told Tarentino and his wife to walk to their reunion. He then drove off and left his passengers several miles from the hotel in the middle of an ice storm. While walking to the hotel, Tarentino slipped on a patch of ice and fell and broke his arm. Later the Tarentinos learned that the driver had a long history of similar conduct and that the limousine company had not done a proper search into the driver's work history before hiring him. The question to the jury was, "Would a reasonable person hire an employee who will be responsible for the safety of paying passengers without checking the work history of that potential employee?" The jury said no, and Highland was held liable for the injuries that befell Tarentino from this breach of duty to protect paying passengers from harm.

If the defendant in a particular case is a professional, such as a physician or an engineer, the circumstances—not the test—change. To determine whether the defendant acted reasonably, the jury would have to know how the reasonable professional would act under similar circumstances. Determining this point may require the use of expert witnesses to testify as to a reasonable professional's conduct under the circumstances.

Actual and Proximate Cause   It is not enough to simply show that the tortfeasor's actions were unreasonable. For the tortfeasor to be held liable, the unreasonable conduct must be tied to actual and proximate cause. **Actual cause**, or **cause in fact**, demonstrates that the cause (the unreasonable conduct) led to the effect (the injury to the plaintiff). The question can be viewed like a problem in physics. We look at the plaintiff's injury (the effect) and deconstruct the events that preceded it, ending with the original unreasonable behavior (the cause). Imagine a set of dominoes falling one after the other and you'll have an accurate image of this process. So, let's say that a driver is texting while driving and that inattentiveness causes him to run a red light and collide with another vehicle, injuring the other driver and totaling the other car. To find actual cause we deconstruct events from the crash and, working backwards, see that, if the driver had not been texting, then the second vehicle would not have been hit. This is called the "but for" test. Using the "but for" test, the judge tells the jury to ask themselves, "Would there have been no accident, 'but for' the unreasonable conduct of the defendant?" In this case, it is clear that the accident would not have happened "but for" the unreasonable conduct (texting while driving). This gives us actual cause.

The problem with actual cause is that there is no end to the consequences that flow from the defendant's unreasonable conduct. Thus, in the car accident mentioned above, negative effects can flow from the accident for days and weeks afterwards, events that would not have occurred "but for" the original unreasonable conduct (the texting while driving). Thus, our innocent victim may lose work, may have to pay medical bills, may have to buy new clothing, may have to cancel a dinner date, may lose the services of a baby sitter, may miss her favorite television show, might be unable to attend a Rotary luncheon, may be fined for an overdue library book because she has no car, may fail to defrost her refrigerator because she is distraught or has a broken arm, and so on. The law must place a limit on these effects. This policy is referred to as proximate cause or legal cause. The law says there must be a final effect for which we will hold the defendant liable. The test used to determine this "last effect" is referred to as the foreseeability test. In

CLASSIC CASE The Outer Limits of Causation in Negligence

The classic case of *Overseas Tankship (UK) Ltd. v. Morts Dock and Engineering Co., Ltd.,* is imbedded deep within the consciousness of all law students during their first year of law school. The case, which is customarily referred to as Wagon Mound 1 (A second Wagon Mound case, *Overseas Tankship (UK) Ltd v. Miller Steamship Co Pty Ltd* (Wagon Mound 2) [1967] 1 AC 617, also involves causation but is not examined here.), involves one of the most straightforward yet oddly complex elements in negligence—causation. The facts play out like this. A tanker ship named the Wagon Mound chartered by Overseas Tankship Ltd. was docked in Sydney and located across the harbor from Morts Dock and Engineering. Members of the crew of the Wagon Mound had carelessly let some of the bunkering oil from the ship seep into the water in the harbor. The manager of Morts had men welding on the dock at the time and so he was, understandably, just a bit apprehensive about the spilled oil. (Who wouldn't be? Right?) To allay his fears he asked the manager of Caltex Oil, which owned the dock where the Wagon Mound was berthed, whether the oil might be a danger. He was told that, since the oil was in the open and mixed with the water, it was safe. After this consultation, the welders continued to work. At some point, molten metal from the welding process flew into the water and hit some cotton rags that were also in the harbor water. When the cotton caught fire, so did the oil and the harbor, which caused extensive damage to the wharf and a ship berthed there.

Morts sued, basing the case on negligence and won at trial. Overseas appealed and the case ended up first in the New South Wales Supreme Court and ultimately in the Privy Council (the High Court) of Australia. The question before the Privy Council was not duty, nor breach of duty, nor even actual harm. Instead, it was causation. Now there is no question of actual cause here. Had the oil not been spilled carelessly, there would have been no fire. The real question then was one of proximate case. Was the original careless act of spilling the oil into the harbor the proximate cause of the damage to the wharf and the ship? The council rejected the old law, which was based on the distinction between direct and indirect causes, and substituted a new rule based on the foreseeability of harm and damage from the original careless actions of the defendants. The council ruled that the damage and the harm that results from the original careless actions of the defendants must be *reasonably foreseeable* at the time of those actions. So, if the injury (actual harm) is foreseeable, liability follows. If not, liability will not follow. In this case, the fact that the defendants had no way to reasonably know that the oil in the water could catch fire, there was no proximate (legal) cause and no liability. (If the damage complained of had been oil damage to the wharf and ship, a different result would have issued from the Privy Council.) [See: *Overseas Tankship (UK) Ltd. v Morts Dock and Engineering Co. Ltd.* [1961] UKPC 1, [1961] AC 388 [1961] All ER 404.]

determining proximate cause, the court asks whether the harm that resulted from the original unreasonable conduct was foreseeable at the time of the original action. If the effect was foreseeable at the time of the unreasonable conduct, the defendant is liable for the damages that flow from that effect. If the effect was not foreseeable, the defendant cannot be held liable for it. In this case the driver's injuries, the damage to the car, the medical bills, and the lost wages were all foreseeable. The overdue library fines, the undefrosted refrigerator, the lost babysitter, and so on, were not.

More on Proximate Cause

The Wagon Mound decision regarding causation, detailed in the Classic Case, may be straightforward, but that does not mean it is simple. On the contrary, it is actually rather complex. Still, one thing is certain: The principle of foreseeability has remained as the foundation of causation after Wagon Mound, even in the United States. This realization means that the doctrine of direct and indirect causes seems to have been discredited, if not thoroughly, then nearly so. Foreseeability itself is comprised of at least four interrelated spin-offs: (1) foreseeability and types of harm; (2) foreseeability and classes of victims; (3) foreseeability and the extent of harm; and (4) foreseeability and the nature of the victim.

The first spin-off, foreseeability and types of harm, refers to the kinds of injuries that might occur from the careless actions of the initial tortfeasor. Thus, in *Wagon Mound,* for example, when a vessel leaks oil into a harbor, oil damage to the wharf and to ships moored in the harbor is easily foreseeable. Fire damage on the surface of the water in the harbor, however, is not. The second offshoot, foreseeability and classes of victims, refers to those individuals that a tortfeasor can foresee as being within the zone of danger. Potential victims within the zone have a cause of action against the defendant; those not in the zone, have none. In **Wagon Mound,** for instance, the negligent crew members (the tortfeasors) could foresee that any dock worker or crewman who might fall into the harbor that day could be harmed by the oily water. Others in the class of foreseeable victims might be dock workers and crew men who develop long-term health problems because of prolonged exposure to the oil. In contrast, firefighters as a class would not be foreseeable when the oil was first spilled and, thus, would have no cause of action against the defendants. If the fire cannot be foreseen, then firefighters on the dock cannot be foreseen either.

The third spin-off, foreseeability and the extent of harm, encompasses a range of injuries that might flow from the original negligent act. This type of foreseeability is quite extensive and, in fact, will probably not eliminate liability. Thus, the defendants in *Wagon Mound* will be liable for all oil damage to the cargo of all ships moored to the dock, whether that cargo is gravel or the Elgin Marbles. The final corollary, foreseeability and the nature of the victim, refers to victims with unusual and undetectable conditions. The law is straightforward on this issue, stating that "the tortfeasor takes the victim as he finds him." Thus, if a victim who falls into the oily harbor suffers extra injuries because of an allergic reaction to the oil, the defendant will be liable for those injuries, as well as for the injuries that the rest of the victims, the ones with no oil allergies, might experience. Thus the tortfeasor might not foresee the weakened condition of the victim, but the law says that has no bearing on liability. This rule is commonly referred to as the "egg-shell skull principle."

Actual Harm

The injured party in a lawsuit for negligence must show that actual harm was suffered. In most cases, the harm suffered is a physical injury and is therefore visible. Harm suffered due to fright or humiliation is difficult to demonstrate. Courts often deny damages in actions for negligence unless they can see an actual physical injury. Actual harm can also come in the form of property damage.

THE OPENING CASE *Round 2*
Battling the Hot Coffee Tort Law Myth: A Complete Negligence Case

In the Opening case the plaintiff, Stella Liebeck, who was 79 years old at the time, purchased a cup of coffee at the drive-through window of a McDonald's restaurant in New Mexico. Her grandson, who was driving the car, parked so that she could mix cream and sugar into her coffee. While she was trying to take the top off the cup, the coffee splashed out of the cup, onto her legs and lap. As a result, she sustained third-degree burns and was in the hospital recovering for eight days. Her injuries led to skin grafts, permanent disfigurement, and 24 months of disability. The case of *Liebeck v. McDonald's* clearly involves the elements of negligence (duty, breach of duty and the standard of care, proximate cause, and actual harm). Analyze the facts in the case using the four elements of negligence.

(1) Does a restaurant (even a fast-food restaurant) have a duty to protect its customers from harm? (2) Did the defendants act according to the standard of care or did they breach their duty when they continued to hand customers foam containers containing coffee at a temperatures of 180 to 190 degrees Fahrenheit despite those 700 claims of coffee-related burns? (3) Is there a causal link (both actual and proximate) between the spilled hot coffee and third-degree burns? (4) Was Liebeck harmed by the spilled coffee? [See: *Stella Liebeck v. McDonald's Restaurants, P.T.S., Inc. and McDonald's International, Inc.,* 1995 WL 360309 (Bernalillo County, N.M. Dist. Ct. 1994); Kevin G. Cain, "The McDonald's Coffee Lawsuit," *Journal of Consumer & Commercial Law,* pp. 14–19.]

Defenses to Negligence

Several defenses can be used by the defendant in a negligence case. These defenses include contributory negligence, comparative negligence, and assumption of the risk.

Contributory Negligence

The defense of **contributory negligence** involves the failure of the injured party to be careful enough to ensure his or her personal safety. Contributory negligence prevents the injured party from recovering damages. In other words, if the injured party's negligence contributed to personal injury, the tortfeasor wins. **Last clear chance** is the injured party's defense to a charge of contributory negligence. Under this doctrine, a tortfeasor may be held liable if the injured party can show that the tortfeasor had the last clear chance to avoid injury.

Comparative Negligence

To soften the harsh effects of contributory negligence, many states have adopted **comparative negligence** statutes that require courts to assign damages according to the degree of fault of each party. Rather than deny all recovery, the court weighs the relative degree of wrongdoing in awarding damages. If the tortfeasor was 80 percent negligent, the injured party may be allowed to recover 80 percent of the losses suffered. Some states have adopted the "50 percent rule." Under this rule, an injured party who was found to be more than 50 percent negligent cannot recover any damages from the tortfeasor.

Assumption of the Risk

Another defense to negligence is **assumption of the risk**, which involves the voluntary exposure of the victim to a known risk. If the injured party was aware of the danger involved in a situation, and by his or her actions indicated a willingness to be exposed to the danger, then he or she has assumed that risk. An awareness of the extent of the danger is the court's primary consideration in awarding or denying damages. It is important that the victim's decision to enter the risky situation be voluntary. If he or she is forced to enter the risky situation because no other choice is available, it is not an assumption of the risk.

---

quick quiz 6-3

1. Legal duty is never at issue in any lawsuit today.   true | false

2. Proximate cause is sometimes referred to as legal cause.   true | false

3. Under the defense of comparative negligence, the plaintiff   true | false
   always loses all the damages that he or she might have been
   awarded, absent the defense.

6-4 Strict Liability

Under certain circumstances, the courts may judge a person liable for harm even though that person was not negligent and did not commit an intentional tort. This doctrine is known as **strict liability** or absolute liability. In recent years, strict liability has also been applied to product liability cases.

Grounds for Strict Liability

Under strict liability, the court will hold a tortfeasor liable for injuries to a victim even though the tortfeasor did not intend the harm and was not in any way negligent. Strict liability is generally applied when the harm results from an ultrahazardous or very dangerous activity. Such activities include using explosives and keeping wild animals. A number of dangerous activities, such as flying an airplane, operating X-ray equipment, and laying public gas lines, are not subject to liability without fault. These activities are recognized as essential to the economic health and welfare of the public.

Product Liability

Counterfeit Colgate toothpaste was recently imported from China and sold in dollar stores across the United States How does this affect Colgate's reputation?

Product liability is a legal theory that imposes liability on the manufacturer and seller of a product produced and sold in a defective condition. A product in **defective condition** is unreasonably dangerous to the user, to the consumer, or to property. Anyone who produces or sells a product in defective condition is subject to liability for the physical or emotional injury to the ultimate consumer and for any physical harm to the user's property. The courts have regularly held that liability for a defective product extends to the producer of the product, the wholesaler, and the retailer. The seller or producer must be engaged in the business of selling such products. In addition, the product manufactured or sold must be expected to reach the ultimate consumer without substantial change in the conditions under which it was originally manufactured or sold.

Product liability is not without its limits. In most states, product liability also is not available as a cause of action if the only property damaged is the defective property itself. In such a situation, the product owner must seek a remedy in sales law for breach of warranty. (Note: People who are injured by faulty products might also be able to bring a product liability lawsuit in sales law. This issue is discussed at length in Chapter 15.)

6-5 Cybertorts

Computers have provided unscrupulous individuals with new ways to commit crimes and torts. In the previous chapter, we examined several cybercrimes. In this chapter, we focus on another group of legal problems, cybertorts. We look first at the nature of cybertorts and then at the problems associated with defining, describing, and preventing cybertorts.

The Nature of Cybertorts

A **cybertort** involves the invasion, distortion, theft, falsification, misuse, destruction, or exploitation of information stored in or related to electronic devices, including but not limited to desktop PCs, laptops, mobile phones, mainframe computers, phone cameras, PDAs, and home computers that stand alone or are part of a computer network. Cybertorts rarely, if ever, involve any physical harm to a victim. Instead, the victim's reputation has been hurt because a false statement has been posted on Facebook; the victim's emotional state has been disturbed because his or her privacy has been invaded by a photograph passed from cell phone to cell phone; the victim has suffered extensive financial loss due to identity theft; or the victim has been terrified by repeated threats from cyber-bullies sending text messages in a relentless, ruthless fashion.

Cyber-defamation

Cyber-defamation is the communication of false and destructive information about an individual through the use of electronic devices. Most legal moves in cyber-defamation have been designed to limit, rather than extend liability for defamatory comments disseminated electronically. For example, when the courts were first involved in cyber-defamation, they easily extended liability for defamation from the party who posted the defamation on the Internet to the Internet Service Provider (ISP), such as America Online, that provided the vehicle for the posting. Thus, for example, it was not difficult in one case for a court in New York to decide that the Prodigy Service Company was responsible when an investment banking firm sued for defamation after false statements were posted on a **cyber-bulletin board** that was under Prodigy's control.

After the Prodigy case, however, the Communications Decency Act was enacted by Congress to protect ISPs from future defamation lawsuits for false statements posted by other individuals on the net. Despite the passage of the law, many cases have been filed attempting to hold ISPs liable for defamatory postings. Few have succeeded, but they remain a nuisance to the providers. Still, the greater nuisance, that to the innocent victims, has not been handled adequately. In one case, AOL was found not liable for defamation even though the provider had been informed of the defamatory content of a posting and still delayed its removal. Moreover, the protection granted to ISPs has gone far beyond protection for defamatory postings. The courts have found that ISPs are not liable when hackers place a virus into a system, when piracy is involved on the Net, or when an invasion of privacy takes place via a provider's link.

Cyber-disparagement

Disparagement involves false statements communicated to others that in some way casts doubt upon the ownership or the quality of an item of property or a product offered for sale. **Cyber-disparagement** involves the same activity on the Internet. The Facebook phenomenon has opened an avenue for the relatively new tort of cyber-disparagement. Businesses now solicit videos from their consumers for postings on their own websites. These businesses often go so far as to run games and contests in which clients and customers can submit homemade advertisements or videos that will be added to the website of the business. Unfortunately, this process is filled with legal risks, not the least of which is the possibility of a cyber-disparagement lawsuit. Such homemade videos typically target the product of a company's competitor. Thus, a company that posts such videos must make certain that the competitor's product is not subject to false statements and descriptions. This assurance requires an enormous effort aimed at monitoring the content of such submissions. Legal activity in this area has not been heavy as of yet, but that is because the tort is so new. As time goes on and competitors find themselves injured by such postings the activity will increase and more cyber-disparagement lawsuits will be filed.

Cyber-invasion of Privacy

A **cyber-invasion of privacy** is the unwelcome intrusion into private matters initiated or maintained by an electronic device. Because the development of computer technology is in a constant state of flux, it is not surprising that the law is still uncertain about just what constitutes a cyber-invasion of privacy. One area that has been expanded recently involves computer-related privacy in the workplace. As the result of at least one federal case, workers employed by businesses that keep a close eye on their workers' time on the Internet have no expectation of privacy, at least in relation to their Fourth Amendment rights, provided that the employer has openly informed the workers of the surveillance.

Privacy and Employees The low expectation of privacy has long been a part of the law in relation to governmental employees. Thus, it has been clear that the Fourth

Amendment right against unreasonable searches and seizures does not protect a governmental employee who knows that the government regularly monitors its employees' Internet use. The same standard now extends to employees within the private sector. How this ruling relates to the tortious invasion of privacy is problematic; however, because the standard for the invasion of privacy is based on the level of privacy expected, the fact that a worker knows that the company monitors computer use means that the expectation is low. The moral of the story is twofold: (1) Employers should routinely remind their workers that all computer use is monitored by the information technology department, and (2) workers should use computers for work-related tasks only.

When employees know that their employer monitors their Internet use, those employees have no expectation of privacy.

All of this assumes, however, that the computers being used in the workplace are owned and controlled by the employer. Unfortunately, this is not always the case. As small portable devices such as tablets, smartphones, laptops, and so on proliferate, many employers are permitting their employees to use their own devices on the job. There is a certain degree of logic to this approach, which is referred to as the "bring your own device" (BYOD) tactic. Employees are usually more familiar and more comfortable with their own devices. Moreover, permitting employees to use their own devices also cuts down on costs for the employer. Regrettably, this procedure raises legal questions in relation to privacy and property ownership. Does the employer have the right, for example, to confiscate and examine the contents of a smartphone or tablet that the employee purchased and uses for both personal and business purposes? Some employers solve the problem by having the IT department configure personal devices so that certain clearly identified functions are for business use only, while others are for personal use. The smarter approach, however, may be to sidestep the issue and distribute company-owned devices (company-owned, personally enabled devices or COPEs) that the employee is permitted to use for personal reasons, with the caveat that the personal functions on the company-owned device may be open to inspection by the employer, who does own the device. [See: Dennis Kennedy, "Does Your Firm Have a Bring-Your-Own-Device Policy?" *ABA Journal*, January 1, 2012.]

Privacy and Clients
Businesses and other organizations, such as educational institutions, health care facilities, and financial institutions, must also deal with the privacy of their customers, students, patients, and clients. Most invasions of privacy affect private records that pertain to employees who, because of their jobs, work closely with confidential files, such as educational, medical, and financial records. The failure to protect such records, whether they are on paper or in a computer, can result in an invasion of privacy lawsuit. Nevertheless, some courts have held that records that are stored in a computer require a degree of protection that is greater than the protection given to paper records because paper records can be kept hidden away or locked in a filing cabinet or a safe, whereas computer records are easy to retrieve, compile, and disseminate. Still, not every claim of a computer-related invasion of privacy automatically translates into a successful lawsuit. The law is still unsettled in several key areas, not the least of which is the question of whether ISPs are permitted to protect the privacy rights of their subscribers.

Private Privacy and Public Privacy
Most of the time, private information, or *private private information*, as it is sometimes called, includes reports on personal matters, family relationships, sexual habits, employment records, medical data, and financial records; however, the law also recognizes a fundamental difference between *private privacy* and *public privacy*. The law is familiar with private privacy concerns about matters such as health concerns, sexual preferences, family matters, and so on. However, the computer age has given rise to another privacy issue, that is, the concern over the publication of what is essentially public information, or what has been termed public-privacy matters. As noted above, many people believe that computer records deserve a higher degree of protection because, unlike paper documents, they are more readily vulnerable to hacking from remote sites.

Data Mining of Public Private Data
The process of data mining takes place when a hacker links multiple strings of data together and develops a data package that the target considers a compilation of private information, despite the public sources from which the hacker composed the package. The issue here is whether the hacker's mining of public databases to construct a private data portrait violates the target's privacy. Some commentators argue that an individual's right to privacy is invaded if, in the process of gathering the data, the hacker ignores or bypasses the target's consent to produce a data portrait that embarrasses, disturbs, ridicules, bullies, exploits, or financially harms the innocent target. To the extent that the victim is harmed, he or she ought to have a cause of action against the hacker.

EXAMPLE 6-10:   ATMs, Digital Cameras, and Data Mining

Frank Vilnius, a dedicated health enthusiast and avid cyclist, rode his recumbent bike into town each week to do his errands. One of the errands involved a stop at the ATM at the local branch of Superior Savings. Unknown to Vilnius, the ATM contained a digital camera that photographed the bank's customers when they used the machine. Vilnius suddenly found himself the target of spam, telemarketing calls, text messages, and snail mail ads, selling products for cyclists. After some investigative work of his own, Vilnius discovered that one of Superior's subsidiaries, B-A-Cyclist, was a sports equipment chain with an active Internet presence. B-A regularly tapped into Superior's data bank and used the photos and other customer data to target potential customers. Vilnius was not financially hurt by the intrusion, but he was annoyed enough to remove his savings from Superior Savings and move his business to the St. Georges Savings across town.

In the Vilnius case in Example 6-10, the various pieces of data that Superior Savings mined included Vilnius's address, phone number, e-mail address, mobile phone number, bank account balance, and his hobby as a cyclist. Arguably, all this data is public when looked at in isolation. Nevertheless, privacy rights emerge because the public pieces of data have been mined to produce a valuable public private data portrait that was exploited by Superior and its subsidiary without Vilnius's consent and in a manner that annoyed him enough to lead him to move his business to St. Georges. Unfortunately, there is still little case law on the issue of public private data portraits. Moreover, the law that does exist militates against the firm establishment of a public privacy right, despite the convincing case that can be made for its acceptance.

quick quiz 6-5

1. Cybertorts always involve information that has been invaded, distorted, stolen, falsified, or destroyed by an electronic device.   true | false

2. Most legal moves in cyber-defamation have been designed to extend liability.   true | false

3. Government employees have a high expectation of privacy in the workplace.   true | false

6-6 Remedies for Torts

When a wrongdoer has injured another person by committing a tort, the victim can usually be compensated with monetary damages. However, at times, the equitable remedy of an injunction is more appropriate.

The Right to Damages

The compensation paid to the victims of a tort is known as damages. Damages can come in several forms. Economic compensatory damages are those that are directly quantifiable. These include damages awarded for lost wages, medical expenses, and expenses incurred in the repair or replacement of property. Noneconomic compensatory damages are those that result from injuries that are intangible and, therefore, not directly quantifiable. For example, damages resulting from pain and suffering, mental anguish, and loss of companionship are considered noneconomic. An award of compensatory damages may be reduced in a state that uses comparative negligence. Thus, if compensatory damages of $1 million are awarded by the jury, but the jury also finds that the plaintiff was comparatively negligent to the tune of 40 percent, as might happen, for example, if the plaintiff was injured in a car accident while not wearing a seatbelt, then instead of $1 million, the plaintiff receives $600,000. If the tortfeasor's acts are notoriously willful and malicious, a court may also impose punitive damages. These are damages above and beyond those needed to compensate the injured party. **Punitive damages** are designed to punish the tortfeasor so that similar malicious actions are avoided by others. For this reason, they are also referred to as exemplary damages. Some courts say that another purpose of punitive damages is to comfort the victim.

The Right to an Injunction

If a tort involves a continuing problem, such as the dumping of chemical waste into a river, the injured party may ask the court for an injunction. An **injunction** is a court order preventing someone from performing a particular act. If a tort involves some permanent fixture that harms the interests of the injured party, the court may order the wrongdoer to take positive steps to alleviate the problem. Thus, the court might order a company to clean up a landfill that has become a nuisance to neighborhood homes. If the company failed to complete the cleanup, it would be in contempt of court. Contempt of court is a deliberate violation of the order of a judge that can result in a fine or in jail time for the wrongdoer.

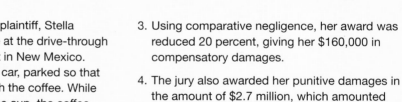

THE OPENING CASE *Round 3*
Fighting the Hot Coffee Myth: Damages

Recall in the opening case that the plaintiff, Stella Liebeck, purchased a cup of coffee at the drive-through window of a McDonald's restaurant in New Mexico. Her grandson, who was driving the car, parked so that she could mix cream and sugar with the coffee. While she was trying to take the top off the cup, the coffee splashed out of the cup, onto her legs and lap. As a result, she sustained third-degree burns and was in the hospital recovering for eight days. Her injuries led to skin grafts, permanent disfigurement, and 24 months of disability. Liebeck asked for $13,000 from McDonald's to cover her medical payments and an additional $5,000 for lost income. McDonald's proposed a settlement of $800. The damages awarded in this case, and the events that followed the awarding of damages, offer us a classic study on how the awarding of damages operates in the real world. The process worked like this:

1. As the first step in determining the damages, the jury decided that Liebeck should receive compensatory damages amounting to $200,000.

2. However, the jury also determined that Liebeck was 20 percent responsible for her own injuries.

3. Using comparative negligence, her award was reduced 20 percent, giving her $160,000 in compensatory damages.

4. The jury also awarded her punitive damages in the amount of $2.7 million, which amounted to two days' worth of McDonald's coffee revenue.

5. The judge lowered the punitive damages award to $480,000, which was three times the compensatory damages.

The total awarded to Liebeck turned out to be $640,000. After the award was finalized both Liebeck and McDonald's announced that they would appeal. However, as often happens in cases like this, there was an out-of-court settlement for an undisclosed amount. [See: *Stella Liebeck v. McDonald's Restaurants, P.T.S., Inc. and McDonald's International, Inc.,* 1995 WL 360309 (Bernalillo County, N.M. Dist. Ct. 1994); Kevin G. Cain, "The McDonald's Coffee Lawsuit," *Journal of Consumer & Commercial Law,* pp. 14–19.]

quick quiz 6-6

1. Economic and noneconomic compensatory damages are essentially the same thing.	true | false
2. Punitive damages are designed to compensate the victim of a tort.	true | false
3. An injunction is never granted by the court in any kind of tort case.	true | false

6-7 Developments in Tort Law

Tort law is in an unsettled stage of development. Much of tort law is still common law, but public dissatisfaction with the high number of tort-based lawsuits has caused some legislatures to pass statutes aimed at tort reform. Some of these moves make sense, as with the passage of wrongful death and survival statutes. The advisability of others is not quite as clear. Nevertheless, this evolutionary surge in tort law is part of the legal culture's ongoing attempt to create a balanced system. The balance this time is between the rights that victims have to be compensated for injuries caused by tortious conduct and the right that society has to be spared the heavy cost of unjustified and expensive litigation.

Survival Statutes and Wrongful Death

Under common law, if someone died from another's wrongful act, then the right to bring a lawsuit also died. This rule originated because the king would execute the wrongdoer and then take his or her property. As a result, there was no property left for the next of kin to recover in a tort suit. In the modern world, this practice makes no sense, and so the state legislatures have nullified the rule with legislation. The two statutes that deal with this problem are survival statutes and statutes that deal with wrongful death.

Survival Statutes Many state legislatures have revised common law by passing survival statues. Survival statutes allow a lawsuit to be brought even if the plaintiff, or the defendant, or both are deceased. Many states also have survival statutes that preserve the right to bring a lawsuit no matter what caused the death or deaths. Most states also allow such suits if the tort involves damage to real or personal property; however, there are some limitations placed on survival statutes. For example, suits cannot be brought for libel or slander after the death of a defamed person, because such a suit is for injury to a live person's reputation. Survival suits are brought or defended by the lawful representative of the estate of the deceased.

Wrongful Death Statutes Unlike survival statutes, **wrongful death statutes** preserve the right to bring a lawsuit only if the death is caused by the negligence or the intentional conduct of the person who caused the death. Generally, only those family members who have lost the support of the deceased have the right to bring a wrongful death suit. The definition of family members generally includes husbands, wives, children, and parents. Under wrongful death statutes, creditors, business partners, and the like have no right to bring lawsuit.

The Tort Reform Movement

Other suggestions for tort reform include the introduction of statutes of repose in product liability and medical malpractice cases, the use of comparative negligence in product liability cases, and alterations in the availability of wrongful death lawsuits.

Statutes of Repose One suggested tort reform would introduce a statute of repose into product liability lawsuits. **Statutes of repose** establish a limit in years, usually but not necessarily 15 years, beyond which an injured party could not bring a lawsuit for an injury caused by a product. The limitation would be placed on end users. An *end user* is a purchaser or a user who is not involved in the production or the assembly of the product. A statute of respose differs from a statute of limitations in that the statute of limitations begins to run when the injury occurs, while the statute of repose begins to run when the product is sold. Often such statutes carry limitations and exceptions. Thus, if the manufacturer fraudulently represented the condition of the product and that fraud led to the harm caused by the product, the statute of repose would not apply. Extremely dangerous products might also fall outside the protective zone of the statute of repose.

Statutes of respose have been suggested also as a tort reform measure in medical malpractice lawsuits. Time limits for such statutes vary from four to six years and usually begin to run when the professional services have been rendered. As is the case with statutes of repose for product liability lawsuits, the statute of respose for medical malpractice would include exceptions under which the statute would not apply. For instance, the statute would not apply if the defendant in such a lawsuit engaged in fraud in relation to the relevant facts pertaining to the professional services that form the basis of the suit.

Comparative Negligence and Product Liability Another reform that has been suggested in some states is the application of comparative negligence as an affirmative defense in some product liability cases. Under this standard, the responsibility of the manufacturer in a product liability case can be lessened by the degree to which the plaintiff's own negligence contributed to his or her injury. Some statutes even say that the manufacturer can escape liability altogether if the plaintiff's share in the responsibility exceeds 50 percent.

Wrongful Death Reform Some states have introduced a reform measure aimed at eliminating any chance of a double recovery under wrongful death statutes. Such reform provisions generally maintain that a wrongful death action cannot be instituted by family members if the deceased recovered damages from the defendant in a prior lawsuit. Thus, if during his or her lifetime, the deceased recovered damages from the defendant in a negligence action, the family cannot bring a subsequent wrongful death action based on the same facts that gave rise to the original negligence lawsuit. In essence, under such a provision, the deceased is said to have waived all rights to bring the wrongful death action when he or she recovered under the original negligence action.

Cultural Paradigms and Balance in Tort Law

There is a great deal of opposition to tort reform within the legal community, especially among attorneys who represent plaintiffs. The most fundamental complaint is that tort reform threatens the very paradigm upon which tort law is based. Fundamental to this argument is the belief that the tort law paradigm establishes a delicately balanced legal system that is threatened by the well-intentioned, but essentially clueless, supporters of tort reform.

Cultural Paradigms A **paradigm** is an unchallenged world view that establishes the rules by which everyone in a particular culture thinks, speaks, and acts. This is true whether we are dealing with a national cultural, a religious culture, a political culture, or a professional culture. The problem with tort reform is that it challenges the assumptions of the legal paradigm without offering an alternative paradigm. Instead, it offers a piecemeal, patchwork approach that borrows concepts and principles from other areas of the law and applies them in ways that are inappropriate at best. This approach to reform reveals a fundamental misunderstanding of the tort law paradigm.

Balance in Tort Law   As noted above, the delicately balanced system of tort law is threatened by legislators and reformers who mean well, but who seem unable or unwilling to understand and appreciate the intricacies and the complexities of the tort law paradigm. In his treatise, *Law's Empire,* the legal philosopher Ronald Dworkin argues that two very strong reasons exist for preserving the current tort law paradigm. Dworkin explains it this way: "Our law as a whole recognizes two principles as pertinent to the loss people should be permitted to suffer through accidents. The first is the principle of collective sympathy. It holds that the state should try to protect people from being ruined by accidents even when the accident is their own fault. The principle is most apparent in regulative safety programs of different sorts, in workmen's compensation statutes and in state-subsidized schemes of insurance for risks to property and person not adequately covered in the private insurance market. The second is the principle of apportioning the costs of an accident among the private actors in the drama that produced it. It holds that accidental loss should be bourne by the person at fault, not the innocent victim. This principle is most evidently at work in negligence law, including legislative amendments or supplements to common law of negligence." The second principle is the one that concerns us the most here. In a succinct and direct way, Dworkin has restated the fundamental rule of the tort law paradigm: People have a duty not to harm one another and when they do cause harm, whether intentionally, through carelessness, or by engaging in a dangerous activity, they pay. The principle is both logical and fair because it rehabilitates the innocent victim at the expense of the wrongdoer. It's just that simple. [See: Ronald Dworkin, *Law's Empire* (Cambridge: The Belknap Press of Harvard University, 1986) p. 269.]

---

quick quiz 6-7

1. Survival statutes allow a lawsuit to be brought even if both the plaintiff and the defendant are deceased.   true | false

2. Statutes of repose establish a limit in years beyond which an injured party could not bring a lawsuit for an injury caused by a product.   true | false

3. A paradigm is an unchallenged world view that establishes the rules by which everyone in a particular culture thinks, speaks, and acts.   true | false

---

Summary

6.1   A tort is a private wrong that injures another person's physical well-being, emotional health, property, or reputation. A person who commits a tort is called a tortfeasor. The other party is alternatively referred to as the injured party, the innocent party, or the victim. The primary purpose of tort law is to compensate the innocent party by making up for any loss suffered by that victim. The doctrine of *respondeat superior* may impose legal liability on employers and make them pay for the torts committed by their employees within the scope of the employer's business.

6.2   The principal intentional torts include assault, battery, false imprisonment, defamation, disparagement, fraudulent misrepresentation, invasion of privacy, intentional infliction of emotional distress, and malicious prosecution.

6.3   Negligence is the failure to exercise the degree of care that a reasonable person would have exercised in the same circumstances. Negligence includes four elements: duty of care, breach of duty through a failure to exercise the appropriate standard of care, proximate cause, and actual harm. Three defenses to negligence are contributory negligence, comparative negligence, and assumption of risk.

6.4 Under the doctrine of strict liability, when people engage in ultrahazardous activities, they will be liable for any harm that occurs because of that activity, regardless of intent and regardless of care.

6.5 Cybertorts involve computer data that has been invaded, distorted, falsified, misused, destroyed, or exploited financially by an electronic device. Therefore, cybertorts rarely involve any harm to a party's physical well-being. Instead, the victim's reputation has been hurt because a false statement has been placed on the Internet, the victim's emotional state has been disturbed, because his or her privacy has been invaded by a posting on Facebook, or the victim has suffered monetary harm because of identity theft.

6.6 Tort remedies include monetary damages and injunctions.

6.7 Survival statutes allow a lawsuit to be brought even if both the plaintiff and the defendant are deceased. Wrongful death statutes preserve the rights of third parties affected by the death of the deceased to bring a lawsuit. Statutes of repose establish a limit in years beyond which an injured party could not bring a lawsuit for an injury caused by a product or by medical malpractice. Another reform that has been suggested in some states is the application of comparative negligence as an affirmative defense in some product liability cases.

Key Terms

abuse of process, 142
actual cause, 144
actual malice, 138
actual malice test, 138
assault, 136
assumption of the risk, 147
battery, 136
bring-your-own-device (BYOD), 151
cause in fact, 144
company-owned, personally enabled devices (COPE), 151
comparative negligence, 147
contributory negligence, 147
cyber-bulletin board, 149
cyber-defamation, 149
cyber-disparagement, 150
cyber-invasion of privacy, 150
cybertort, 149
damages, 152

data mining, 151
defamation, 138
defective condition, 148
disparagement, 139
duty, 134
economic compensatory damages, 152
exemplary damages, 152
false imprisonment, 137
foreseeability test, 145
fraud, 139
fraudulent misrepresentation, 139
injunction, 152
intentional or reckless infliction of emotional distress, 141
invasion of privacy, 140
juriscience, 134
last clear chance, 147
legal cause, 145
libel, 138

malicious prosecution, 141
merchant protection statute, 137
misuse of legal procedure, 141
negligence, 142
noneconomic compensatory damages, 152
paradigm, 155
private information, 151
proximate cause, 145
punitive damages, 152
respondeat superior, 134
shopkeeper's privilege, 137
slander, 138
statutes of repose, 155
strict liability, 148
temporary public figures, 138
tort, 138
tortfeasor, 138
wrongful civil proceedings, 141
wrongful death statutes, 154

Questions for Review and Discussion

1. What is the difference between a tort and a crime?
2. What is *respondeat superior?*
3. What is meant by the legal term "duty"?
4. What are the principal intentional torts?

5. What are the elements of negligence?
6. What are the differences among contributory negligence, comparative negligence, and assumption of the risk?
7. When does strict liability apply?

8. What is a cybertort?
9. What remedies are available in tort law?
10. What innovations have been suggested for contemporary state tort reform?

Cases for Analysis

1. In one of the worst sea tragedies in the modern era, the South Korean Ferry Sewol capsized during what was billed as a standard trip to a vacation island. The ship, which was loaded with high school students, sank, claiming hundreds of lives. Although the accident happened in a foreign jurisdiction, consider the following allegations that surround the tragedy and try to determine if those allegations, one by one or in the aggregate, might be the basis for a negligence lawsuit against the marine company that owned and operated the vessel. Some of the allegations include: (a) the crew members were not properly trained in emergency techniques; (b) passengers were not instructed in emergency measures before the voyage began; (c) no more than a few of the 44 life rafts were in use during the emergency operation; (d) the captain was not on the bridge at the time of the incident; (e) the captain later deserted the ship while many of passengers were still on board; (f) before the incident, the captain assigned the third mate to steer the boat while he went back to his cabin; (g) the passengers were told to stay in their cabins below deck rather than to vacate the ship; (h) cargo on the ferry may not have been fastened down in the correct fashion, making the ship unstable during a sharp turn and causing the ship to capsize; and (i) the marine company that purchased the used ferry had added more rooms to the ship, making the vessel unsteady. Which of these allegations might make the strongest negligence case against the marine company? Which would make the weakest case? Explain. [See: Choe Sang-Hun, Su-Hyun Lee, and Jiha Ham, "Human Error Suspected as Hope Fades in Korean Ferry Sinking," *The New York Times,* April 17, 2014, pp. A1, A6; Choe Sang-Hun, Su-Hyun Lee, "Captain and 2 Crew Members Arrested in Sinking of Korean Ferry," *The New York Times,* April 19, 2014, pp. A-4, A-8.]

2. To supply America's energy needs, more and more crude oil is being extracted from shale and shipped to refineries. Much of this crude oil is located in the northern part of the United States, especially in the Northwest. This causes a problem since the refineries are located in the South. The pipelines that would ordinarily handle these shipments cannot manage the increased load. Consequently, much of this crude oil is being transported in tank cars on the nation's railroads. Unfortunately, many of these tank cars may not be up to the task. Evidence of the dangers involved in using these tank cars for oil shipments is mounting. For example, in 2013 the following incidents occurred: (a) a derailment in Lynchburg, Virginia, causing the loss of 25,000 gallons of oil; (b) an explosion in Casselton, North Dakota, causing the loss of 475,000 gallons; and (c) a 26-car derailment in Aliceville, Alabama, leading to the loss of 630,000 gallons. In total in 2013, 1.1 million gallons of crude oil were lost in such accidents. Government and corporate authorities know about these problems and are aware of ways to make the tank cars safer for transport. Possible improvements include: (a) the addition of head shields to absorb shock at both the front and the back of each tank car in case of a collision; (b) the addition of better-quality handles to stop those handles from opening in an crash; (c) the addition of housings to stop valves from breaking off should the car overturn; (d) the addition of pressure-relief valves; (e) and the addition of coverings that are impervious to heat to provide a barrier in case of a fire. Imagine that you are a newly hired in-house attorney for an oil company that uses the present unimproved cars for transporting crude oil from North Dakota to Houston, Texas. Considering this evidence, as legal counsel for the oil company, compose an e-mail that builds a *legal case* that will convince the CEO and the board of directors to make these improvements before the next accident occurs on a train hauling the company's crude oil. [See: Michael Scherer, "Spotlight-Crude Awakening: The Shale-Oil Boom Is Ferrying a New Danger to America's Freight Railways," *Time,* June 2, 2014, pp. 14–15.]

3. Violence at Rikers Island, a New York City prison on an island in the East River, has risen to epidemic proportions over the past five years. During the first four months in 2014 alone, a dozen prisoners suffered injuries that resulted from stab wounds and cuts, while prisoners and guards underwent treatment for broken bones, concussions, and punctured eardrums among many other similar injuries. Reports indicate that, while the population of the prison has fallen by 15 percent since 2004, the use of force by guards has risen 240 percent over that same period. Two prisoners, one who sustained extensive injuries to his neck and back and another who has back problems and a broken nose, have filed separate lawsuits naming the City of New York as defendant. Both inmates allege that their injuries resulted from beatings conducted by corrections officers at Rikers. Using your knowledge of tort law, list and explain those torts that might form the basis of these lawsuits. [See: Michael Schwirtz, "Mental Illness and Violence Rise at Vast Jail," *The New York Times,* March 19, 2014, pp. A1, A18.]

4. Patrick Clawson was described by reporter Karen Branch-Brioso in a newspaper story as a "1970s era St. Louis journalist turned private eye turned FBI informant." The story was published in the *St. Louis Post-Dispatch.* The fact that he had been characterized as an informant bothered Clawson, who saw it as damaging to his reputation. Accordingly, he brought a libel case against the *Post-Dispatch.* Recall that to be libelous, a statement must be false and "hold the victim up to ridicule, contempt, or hatred." Clawson would have preferred the term *whistleblower* rather than *informant,* because that term commands more respect. Why is the use of the term *informant* to describe Clawson not libelous? Explain. [See: *Clawson v. St. Louis Post-Dispatch,* No. 04-CV-486; see also "Media Law: Label of 'Informer' Is Found Not Defamatory," *The National Law Journal,* September 11, 2006.]

5. Curtis Ellison was riding as a passenger in his own vehicle when it was pulled over by the police for a parking violation. The vehicle had actually been targeted because the police had routinely checked the license plate through the department's database. This routine check had revealed that the owner of the vehicle had an outstanding warrant pending against him. When the police searched the van, they found two firearms hidden in the vehicle.

As a result, Ellison was charged with felonious possession of a firearm. He argued that the search had violated his Fourth Amendment rights and that his right to privacy had been infringed. The trial court agreed and dismissed the case. The case went to the appellate court. The issue before the appellate court was whether Ellison had a high expectation of privacy about the number on his license plate. Although this is a criminal case, it is still interesting to speculate on how the court would rule on the expectation of privacy in relation to a license plate. Why should the appeals court reverse the ruling by the trial court that there is a high expectation of privacy in relation to a license plate? Explain. [See: *United States v. Ellison,* No. 04-1925; see also "Criminal Practice: No Privacy Expectation on License Plate Numbers," *The National Law Journal,* September 18, 2006, p. 16.]

6. A St. Louis police officer was speeding the wrong way down a one-way street when he collided with a vehicle being driven by Ann Martin. Martin was seriously injured in the crash and brought a lawsuit against the police officer, the City of St. Louis, and the board of police commissioners. The board of commissioners is an agency of the state of Missouri. Martin passed away, and her daughter, Kimberly Hodges, took over as the plaintiff in the case. The case was settled in relation to the board and the officer but not the city. The City of St Louis argued that the officer could not be employed by both the board and the city at the same time. The city further argued that the officer's real employer was the board, so it, the city, could not be held liable under the doctrine of vicarious liability. Why should the city be held liable under the doctrine of vicarious liability? Explain. [See: *Hodges v. City of St. Louis,* No. SC87513; see also "Torts: Officer Is City Agent Even if Working for State Board," *The National Law Journal,* March 12, 2007, p. 15.]

7. At the height of the modern civil rights movement, *The New York Times* ran a full-page advertisement entitled "Heed Their Rising Voices." The advertisement detailed police efforts in Montgomery, Alabama, to suppress the nonviolent civil rights demonstrations being carried on there by thousands of college students. The police commissioner of Montgomery, L.B. Sullivan, filed a lawsuit against *The New York Times,* alleging that he had been libeled by information carried in the

advertisement, even though he was never mentioned by name. Should the Court use the actual malice test in this case to determine whether the newspaper libeled the commissioner? Explain. [See: *New York Times Co. v. Sullivan*, 376 U.S. 254 (U.S. Sup. Ct.).]

8. Five Commerce City police officers were summoned to break up a disturbance at a local party of teenagers. At the party, Ralph Crowe, who had consumed eight cups of beer and three cups of alcoholic punch, became rowdy and had to be detained by the officers. The police released Ralph after receiving the assurances of his brother Eddie that he would drive Ralph home. After leaving the party, Eddie Crowe allowed Ralph to take the wheel. Instead of going home, Ralph drove to the site of another party, where he lost control of the car and ran down six people. The police officers were sued for negligence in releasing Ralph. Did the five officers owe a duty to the six victims of Ralph's drunk-driving accident? Explain. [See: *Leake v. Cain,* 720 P.2d 152 (CO).]

9. Myers was injured when she slipped and fell on an ice patch on the front walkway of the Canton Centre Mall. The mall is owned and operated by Forest City Enterprises. Forest City had employees who were responsible for clearing the ice off of the mall walkways every morning. On this particular morning, they had cleared the ice from the walkway a short time before Myers took her tumble. Nevertheless, an ice patch had formed, and Myers did fall, sustaining injuries. Cooper, one of the employees charged with the ice-removal task, theorized that water may have been splashed up onto the sidewalk by passing cars where it froze sometime after their initial cleaning of the day. According to Cooper, "the vehicles could have splashed this back up on there . . . we're constantly

moving around the building at all times, so anything can be going on in this half of the building while you're over here doing this half coming around." Was Forest City negligent in failing to keep the sidewalk clear of ice at all times that winter? What test would be used to judge Forest City's conduct? Explain. [See: *Myers v. Forest City Enterprises, Inc.* 635 N.E.2d 1268 (OH).]

10. Michelle Wightman was driving toward a railroad crossing at which the gates were down and the lights flashing. Wightman noted a stopped train a short distance from the gate. Believing the stopped train to be the cause of the closed gate, she drove around the gate and was struck and killed by a train that suddenly appeared from behind the stopped train. The stopped train had blocked her view of the oncoming train. Both trains were owned and operated by Consolidated Rail Corporation (CRC). Wightman's mother brought a wrongful death lawsuit and a survivorship action against CRC. In response, CRC claimed that Wightman's action of driving around the gates, in violation of both state and city law regarding the operation of a motor vehicle at a railroad crossing, constituted negligence on her part. Furthermore, CRC argued that if Wightman had not crossed the tracks, she would not have been struck by the train. Therefore, her actions were the sole cause of the accident, and the railroad corporation should not be held liable for her death. The attorney for the plaintiff argued that the placement of the first train, blocking the view of the other track, contributed to the accident and that CRC should be held liable for Wightman's death. Should Wightman's own negligence be a complete bar to the plaintiff's recovery of damages in this case? Explain. [See: *Wightman v. Consolidated Railroad Corporation,* 640 N.E.2d 1160 (OH).]

quick quiz Answers

6-1	6-2	6-3	6-4	6-5	6-6	6-7
1. T	1. F	1. F	1. T	1. T	1. F	1. T
2. F	2. F	2. T	2. T	2. F	2. F	2. T
3. F	3. F	3. F	3. F	3. F	3. F	3. T

Part 1 Case Study

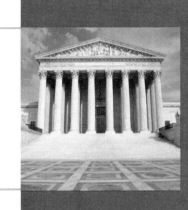

Schuette, Attorney General of Michigan v. Coalition to Defend Affirmative Action and Immigration Rights and Fight for Equality By Any Means Necessary (BAMN)
United States Supreme Court
No. 12-682 (Argued October 15, 2013—Decided April 22, 2014)
572 U.S. _____ (2014)

Summary

The facts in this case are relatively straightforward. The State of Michigan, like many states, has struggled with the question of whether to continue to use race as an element in the admissions procedure at its state colleges, universities, and graduate programs. In *Gratz v. Bollinger*, 539 U.S. 244 (2003), the Supreme Court had invalidated the admissions procedures for the University of Michigan because the process had allowed the explicit consideration of a candidate's race. In response, the university revamped the admissions process in a way that was designed to satisfy the Court's objections. However, the process still involved a narrowly defined race-related element. The new plan sparked a widespread quarrel across Michigan over whether to use race as a part of the selection criteria. The controversy led to an amendment proposal that went on the ballot in 2006. The amendment (generally referred to as Proposal 2) forbid the state and state subdivisions such as cities, counties, school districts, public colleges, and public universities from using race-oriented standards in many activities and decisions. The amendment included a specific prohibition barring race-centered criteria in the admissions procedures at state colleges and universities. The amendment (now referred to as Section 26) became law based on a 4 percent margin (52 percent for and 48 percent against). Two lawsuits challenged the amendment's constitutionality almost immediately. The District Court granted a summary judgment motion that, in effect, upheld the constitutionality of Section 26. On appeal the Sixth Circuit reversed the trial court. An *en banc* session of the Sixth Circuit Court supported the earlier decision by the original three-judge panel. In doing so the court relied upon *Washington v. Seattle School District, No. 1,* 458 U.S. 457 (1982). The Michigan case then went to the U.S. Supreme Court, which agreed to hear the case. The opinion was delivered by Justice Kennedy.

As Justice Kennedy begins his opinion, he is careful to explain that *Schuette v. BAMN* is *not* about whether it is constitutional (or even meritorious) to use race as a part of an admissions procedure for entering state-run colleges and universities. Rather the question, in general, is whether the voters of a state are permitted to amend their own state constitution (or any other legal document, for that matter) without being reversed (read "second-guessed" here) by the courts. More specifically, the issue is whether the voters can amend the state constitution by adding standards to guide the state government's decision-making processes without being overturned by the courts. Even more precisely, the question is whether the voters can alter the state constitution to eliminate racial preferences in state college and state university admissions procedures. Justice Kennedy also points out that neither the State of Michigan nor its voters should be chastised for dealing with this complex and difficult problem. In fact, the issues involved in

Schuette v. BAMN are part of a wider national dialogue that cannot be ignored. Kennedy also notes that *Schuette v. BAMN* must be judged within the context of the Sixth Circuit's decision. This is especially crucial because the decision to circumvent the voters relied upon the authority of the Supreme Court in three key cases, *Reitman v. Mulkey*, 387 U.S. 369 (1967), *Hunter v. Erickson*, 393 U.S. 385 (1969), and *Washington v. Seattle School District, No. 1*, 458 U.S. 457 (1982).

According to Kennedy, the *Seattle School District* case is the key to the Court's present analysis of *Schuette v. BAMN*. Moreover, he infers that the Supreme Court justices in the *Seattle School District* case may have gone too far in their decision. In fact, Kennedy hints that the Court may have created a misleading and ultimately damaging precedent that is badly in need of clarification. Before reaching the *Seattle School District* case and applying it to *Schuette v. BAMN*, however, Kennedy reviews two additional cases to show both the differences and the similarities among all four cases. In the first case, *Reitman v. Mulkey*, 387 U.S. 369 (1967), the Supreme Court struck down a California constitutional amendment that established a private right to discriminate in real property transactions. The amendment in question would have prevented any meddling by the government in a property owner's right to decide to whom to rent or sell. The case itself involved two situations, one a refusal to rent and one an eviction. Both the refusal to rent and the eviction were based on race. Because of the constitutional amendment, neither the displaced renters nor the evicted tenant were permitted to avail themselves of certain protections guaranteed by California statutes. In essence, then, the amendment made it impossible for the plaintiffs to get the same protection of statutory law that other people might use in a similar situation. Thus, the displaced renters and the evicted tenant were denied the equal protection of the law. The court wrote that "the effect of the state constitutional amendment was to 'significantly encourage and involve the state in private racial discrimination.'" The second case, *Hunter v. Erickson*, 393 U.S. 385 (1969), involved an Akron city ordinance prohibiting racial discrimination in housing that was overturned by the voters in a referendum that also set down a requirement that all future city ordinances touching on discrimination would be subject to voter approval via referendum. The Court ultimately stuck down this provision because it was not necessary and because it produced discriminatory results.

The *Seattle School District* case is similar to both *Reitman v. Mulkey* and *Hunter v. Erickson*. In all three cases, a government-established program is reversed by a voter initiative, which is then challenged in the courts. The government action in the *Seattle School District* case involved a busing program that was established by the school board to help eliminate a segregation process that had systematically isolated minority students in the Seattle school system. The voters passed an initiative that stopped the busing program. The *Seattle School District* case eventually found its way to the Supreme Court, which saw that case as analogous to the *Reitman v. Mulkey* and *Hunter v. Erickson*. It was clear to the Court that the Seattle school system in the 1940s and '50s had discriminated against black students by restricting their ability to transfer, while not using similar restrictions to limit the movement of white students. In a complaint filed with the Office of Civil Rights, the NAACP laid out a long list of policies and procedures that clearly perpetuated segregation in the school system. The settlement that followed included a busing plan. What is important to understand here is that, at the time of the Seattle decision, the constitutionality of using race-based criteria to correct past discrimination was never questioned. It is also important to see that the initiative that was passed by the voters specifically targeted the busing program and only the busing program. No other part of the plan was affected by that initiative. Nevertheless, the court in *Seattle School District* decided that the initiative, if allowed to stand, would perpetuate the problems that the settlement agreement was supposed to alleviate. Kennedy notes that it would have been best for the Court to stop at that point. However, the court did not stop. It persisted and that, Kennedy says, was when it got itself into trouble. The Court went too far. The case had been decided. Yet the Court continued.

The Court in *Seattle School District* seized on language in *Hunter v. Erickson* and used that language to extend its decision to hold that any state program that strongly benefits a racial minority (and which the minority in question believes to be very beneficial) must not be tampered with if the tampering changes the level of the government that is charged with handling the program in question, unless the change can be justified under a very strict review process. This ruling, Kennedy says, was a mistake. The Court's overly broad interpretation of the two previous cases actually violates equal protection, because it involves the Court in making decisions about what political policies would benefit which minority group. This is not only an ill-advised path to take, but it is also logically unsound because it assumes erroneously that all the members of a particular minority hold the same political opinions. Also, Kennedy notes that the very nature of the rule used in Seattle would require the Court to classify people based on race alone, which is "inherently suspect and carries within it the danger of perpetuating the very racial divisions the polity seeks to transcend." Moreover, adopting such a standard will encourage politically activists to define issues in terms of race, something the Court seeks to avoid. Using the specifics of *Seattle School District,* Kennedy then makes a leap to the real issue in the case. Recall that the actual question here is not whether it is constitutional to use race in an admissions process for state-run colleges and universities. Instead, the issue is whether the voters are permitted to amend their own state constitution without being ambushed and then "Monday-morning quarterbacked" by the courts. Kennedy writes that this issue has been resolved in the following way. The judicial branch of the government, he says, is not empowered to disenfranchise the voters of a state. The courts cannot stop the voters from deciding to follow one direction or another in a political dispute. When political, social, and economic policies are decided, the contest that occurs should be in the public domain in a way that encourages participation and discussion and avoids malice and mayhem. However, if malice and mayhem do enter the dispute, the courts should not provoke, promote, or prolong that malice or that mayhem. Kennedy's defense of the Court's decision follows here.

The Court's Opinion

Delivered by Justice Kennedy

This risk is inherent in adopting the *Seattle* formulation. There would be no apparent limiting standards defining what public policies should be included in what *Seattle* called policies that "inur[e] primarily to the benefit of the minority" and that "minorities . . . consider" to be "'in their interest.'" 458 U.S., at 472, 474. Those who seek to represent the interests of particular racial groups could attempt to advance those aims by demanding an equal protection ruling that any number of matters be foreclosed from voter review or participation. In a nation in which governmental policies are wide ranging, those who seek to limit voter participation might be tempted, were this Court to adopt the *Seattle* formulation, to urge that a group they choose to define by race or racial stereotypes are advantaged or disadvantaged by any number of laws or decisions. Tax policy, housing subsidies, wage regulations, and even the naming of public schools, highways, and monuments are just a few examples of what could become a list of subjects that some organizations could insist should be beyond the power of voters

to decide, or beyond the power of a legislature to decide when enacting limits on the power of local authorities or other governmental entities to address certain subjects. Racial division would be validated, not discouraged, were the *Seattle* formulation, and the reasoning of the Court of Appeals in this case, to remain in force.

Perhaps, when enacting policies as an exercise of democratic self-government, voters will determine that race-based preferences should be adopted. The constitutional validity of some of those choices regarding racial preferences is not at issue here. The holding in the instant case is simply that the courts may not disempower the voters from choosing which path to follow. In the realm of policy discussions the regular give-and-take of debate ought to be a context in which rancor or discord based on race are avoided, not invited. And if these factors are to be interjected, surely it ought not to be at the invitation or insistence of the courts.

One response to these concerns may be that objections to the larger consequences of the *Seattle* formulation need not be confronted in this case, for here race was an undoubted subject of the ballot issue. But a number of problems raised by *Seattle,* such as racial definitions, still apply. And this principal flaw in the ruling of the Court of Appeals does remain: Here there was no infliction of a specific injury of the kind at issue in *Mulkey* and *Hunter* and in the history of the Seattle schools. Here there is no precedent for extending these cases to restrict the right of Michigan voters to determine that race-based preferences granted by Michigan governmental entities should be ended.

It should also be noted that the judgment of the Court of Appeals in this case of necessity calls into question other long-settled rulings on similar state policies. The California Supreme Court has held that a California constitutional amendment prohibiting racial preferences in public contracting does not violate the rule set down by *Seattle. Coral Constr., Inc.* v. *City and County of San Francisco*, 50 Cal. 4th 315, 235 P. 3d 947 (2010). The Court of Appeals for the Ninth Circuit has held that the same amendment, which also barred racial preferences in public education, does not violate the Equal Protection Clause. *Wilson*, 122 F. 3d 692 (1997). If the Court were to affirm the essential rationale of the Court of Appeals in the instant case, those holdings would be invalidated, or at least would be put in serious question. The Court, by affirming the judgment now before it, in essence would announce a finding that the past 15 years of state public debate on this issue have been improper. And were the argument made that *Coral* might still stand because it involved racial preferences in public contracting while this case concerns racial preferences in university admissions, the implication would be 15 Cite as: 572 U.S. ____ (2014) that the constitutionality of laws forbidding racial preferences depends on the policy interest at stake, the concern that, as already explained, the voters deem it wise to avoid because of its divisive potential. The instant case presents the question involved in *Coral* and *Wilson* but not involved in *Mulkey, Hunter,* and *Seattle*. That question is not how to address or prevent injury caused on account of race but whether voters may determine whether a policy of race-based preferences should be continued.

By approving Proposal 2 and thereby adding §26 to their State Constitution, the Michigan voters exercised their privilege to enact laws as a basic exercise of their democratic power. In the federal system States "respond, through the enactment of positive law, to the initiative of those who seek a voice in shaping the destiny of their own times." *Bond*, 564 U.S., at—(slip op., at 9). Michigan voters used the initiative system to bypass public officials who were deemed not responsive to the concerns of majority of the voters with respect to a policy of granting race-based preferences that raises difficult and delicate issues.

The freedom secured by the Constitution consists, in one of its essential dimensions, of the right of the individual not to be injured by the unlawful exercise of governmental power. The mandate for segregated schools, *Brown* v. *Board of Education*, 347 U.S. 483 (1954); a wrongful invasion of the home, *Silverman* v. *United States*, 365 U.S. 505 (1961); or punishing a protester whose views offend others, *Texas* v. *Johnson*, 491 U.S. 397 (1989); and scores of other examples teach that individual liberty has constitutional protection, and that liberty's full extent and meaning may remain yet to be discovered and affirmed. Yet freedom does not stop with individual rights. Our constitutional system embraces, too, the right of citizens to debate so they can learn and decide and then, through the political process, act in concert to try to shape the course 16 SCHUETTE *v.* BAMN of their own times and the course of a nation that must strive always to make freedom ever greater and more secure. Here Michigan voters acted in concert and statewide to seek consensus and adopt a policy on a difficult subject against a historical background of race in America that has been a source of tragedy and persisting injustice. That history demands that we continue to learn, to listen, and to remain open to new approaches if we are to aspire always to a constitutional order in which all persons are treated with fairness and equal dignity. Were the Court to rule that the question addressed by Michigan voters is too sensitive or complex to be within the grasp of the electorate; or that the policies at issue remain too delicate to be resolved save by university officials or faculties, acting at some remove from immediate public scrutiny and control; or that these matters are so arcane that the electorate's power must be limited because the people cannot prudently exercise that power even after a full debate, that holding would be an unprecedented restriction on the exercise of a fundamental right held not just by one person but by all in common. It is the right to speak and debate and learn and then, as a matter of political will, to act through a lawful electoral process.

The respondents in this case insist that a difficult question of public policy must be taken from the reach of the voters, and thus removed from the realm of public discussion, dialogue, and debate in an election campaign. Quite in addition to the serious First Amendment implications of that position with respect to any particular election, it is inconsistent with the underlying premises of a responsible, functioning democracy. One of those premises is that a democracy has the capacity—and the duty—to learn from its past mistakes; to discover and confront persisting biases; and by respectful, rationale deliberation to rise above those flaws and injustices. That process is impeded, not advanced, by court decrees based on the proposition 17 Cite as: 572 U.S. ____ (2014) that the public cannot have the requisite repose to discuss certain issues. It is demeaning to the democratic process to presume that the voters are not capable of deciding an issue of this sensitivity on decent and rational grounds. The process of public discourse and political debate should not be foreclosed even if there is a risk that during a public campaign there will be those, on both sides, who seek to use racial division and discord to their own political advantage. An informed public can, and must, rise above this. The idea of democracy is that it can, and must, mature. Freedom embraces the right, indeed the duty, to engage in a rational, civic discourse in order to determine how best to form a consensus to shape the destiny of the Nation and its people. These First Amendment dynamics would be disserved if this Court were to say that the question here at issue is beyond the capacity of the voters to debate and then to determine.

These precepts are not inconsistent with the well-established principle that when hurt or injury is inflicted on racial minorities by the encouragement or command of laws or other state action, the Constitution requires redress by the courts. Cf. *Johnson* v. *California,* 543 U.S. 499, 511–512 (2005) ("[S]earching judicial review . . . is necessary to guard against invidious discrimination"); *Edmonson* v. *Leesville Concrete Co.,*

500 U.S. 614, 619 (1991) ("Racial discrimination" is "invidious in all contexts"). As already noted, those were the circumstances that the Court found present in *Mulkey, Hunter,* and *Seattle.* But those circumstances are not present here.

For reasons already discussed, *Mulkey, Hunter,* and *Seattle* are not precedents that stand for the conclusion that Michigan's voters must be disempowered from acting. Those cases were ones in which the political restriction in question was designed to be used, or was likely to be used, to encourage infliction of injury by reason of race. What is at stake here is not whether injury will be inflicted but 18 SCHUETTE *v.* BAMN whether government can be instructed not to follow a course that entails, first, the definition of racial categories and, second, the grant of favored status to persons in some racial categories and not others. The electorate's instruction to governmental entities not to embark upon the course of race-defined and race-based preferences was adopted, we must assume, because the voters deemed a preference system to be unwise, on account of what voters may deem its latent potential to become itself a source of the very resentments and hostilities based on race that this Nation seeks to put behind it. Whether those adverse results would follow is, and should be, the subject of debate. Voters might likewise consider, after debate and reflection, that programs designed to increase diversity—consistent with the Constitution—are a necessary part of progress to transcend the stigma of past racism.

This case is not about how the debate about racial preferences should be resolved. It is about who may resolve it. There is no authority in the Constitution of the United States or in this Court's precedents for the Judiciary to set aside Michigan laws that commit this policy determination to the voters. See *Sailors* v. *Board of Ed. of County of Kent,* 387 U.S. 105, 109 (1967) ("Save and unless the state, county, or municipal government runs afoul of federally protected right, it has vast leeway in the management of its internal affairs"). Deliberative debate on sensitive issues such as racial preferences all too often may shade into rancor. But that does not justify removing certain court-determined issues from the voters' reach. Democracy does not presume that some subjects are either too divisive or too profound for public debate.

The judgment of the Court of Appeals for the Sixth Circuit is reversed.

It is so ordered.

KENNEDY, J., announced the judgment of the Court and delivered an opinion, in which ROBERTS, C. J., and ALITO, J., joined. ROBERTS, C. J., filed a concurring opinion. SCALIA, J., filed an opinion concurring in the judgment, in which THOMAS, J., joined. BREYER, J., filed an opinion concurring in the judgment. SOTOMAYOR, J., filed a dissenting opinion, in which GINSBURG, J., joined. KAGAN, J., took no part in the consideration or decision of the case.

Questions for Analysis

1. It should be clear that *stare decisis* is at the central core of Justice Kennedy's opinion in *Schuette v. BAMN.* What previous case or cases does Justice Kennedy criticize here and why does he criticize it (or them)? Explain.

2. What is the negative rights theory of ethics? Now, think about the initiatives and/or constitutional amendments proposed in the cases discussed above, including *Reitman v. Mulkey, Hunter v. Erickson, Washington v. Seattle School District, Schuette v. BAMN* and explain how each of those initiatives are textbook examples of the problems related to negative rights.

3. *Schuette v. BAMN* involves a summary judgment that is first granted by the District Court and then overturned by the Court of Appeals. What is a summary judgment motion? Name one other case in Part 1 in which a summary judgment motion played a key role. What was the outcome in that case? Explain.

4. *Schuette v. BAMN* also involves an *en banc* session of the Sixth Circuit Court of Appeals. What is an *en banc* session? Name one other case in Part 1 in which an Appellate Court held an *en banc* session. What was the outcome in that case? Explain.

5. Generally, the idea behind a democracy is that the power rests in the people and the people have the chance to vote. That seems to be a key principle at work in Justice Kennedy's opinion in *Schuette v. BAMN.* In an earlier case in Part 1, *Woodward v. Alabama,* Justice Sotomayor complained about judges who were overly responsive to the voters. How can these two opposing views be reconciled on the Supreme Court? Explain.

6. When James Madison helped engineer the U.S. Constitution, he pushed for the addition of a congressional veto that would empower Congress to overturn and eliminate any state law that was unsatisfactory. Given the proliferation of such cases listed and examined in *Schuette v. BAMN,* do you now think that perhaps Madison was correct? Explain.

7. In writing the Constitution, James Madison also added as many buffers as possible in order to marginalize the power of the people and insulate the government from the whims and impulses of those people. Does this case and the others cited therein demonstrate that Madison was correct? Why or why not? Explain.

8. Madison's greatest fear was that political factions would destroy the unity of the government. Yet, in this case, Kennedy is quite clear that the people should be encouraged to participate in open debates about governmental policy. Is Justice Kennedy urging the type of factionalism that Madison so feared? Why or why not? Explain.

9. A complex adaptive system (CAS) is a network of interacting conditions that reinforce one another, while at the same time adjusting to change from agents outside and inside the system. In what ways does Justice Kennedy's opinion in *Schuette v. BAMN* reinforce the idea that the law works like a complex adaptive system? Explain.

10. Despite Justice Kennedy's reluctance to talk about the race-related criteria in this case, the case itself clearly revolves around that moral issue. Recall Max Weber's ethical dyad that distinguishes between the "ethic of ultimate ends" for individuals and an "ethic of responsibility" for national leaders. Has Kennedy fallen into the trap of singular morality or does his opinion reflect an understanding of Weber's dyad? Explain.

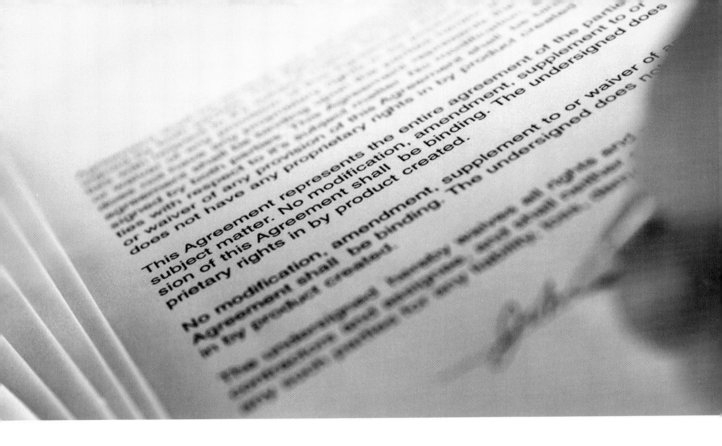

Part Two
Contract Law

The Essentials of Contract Law

THE OPENING CASE *Round 1*
Vulcans Never Lie, Although at Times They Exaggerate

Janke Construction Company, a general contractor, was in a bidding war with several other contractors trying to obtain a contract for the construction of the marine component of a larger project that would provide a cooling system for The University of Wisconsin in Milwaukee. The bidding information packet specified that the pipe for the marine subproject had to be approved by the American Water Works Association (AWWA) as either AWWA C300 or AWWA C301 level pipe or pipe that was "equal to" those specifications. Jerry Janke, vice president of Janke Construction, talked to a representative from the Vulcan Materials Company about the piping requirements for the job. The price that was quoted by the Vulcan rep came in $40,000 less than the price quoted by Interpace, Vulcan's main competitor. No mention had been made about the exact specifications for the pipe to be used on the job. The evening before the bid was to be placed at the State Office Building in Madison, Jerry and James Janke met with Alex Barry, the general manager of Vulcan, and Peter Fox, a Vulcan sales rep. The next day, at the State Office Building, they met again with Barry who, after a quick phone call to his home office, reassured the Janke brothers that his company would supply the pipe needed for the job. With this reassurance in hand, the Jankes submitted their bid. After the Jankes won the bidding contest, they asked for and received a written quotation from Vulcan. That was when they learned that the pipe that Vulcan was going to use on the project was AWWA C302, which did not meet project specifications. The state refused to use AWWA C302 because it was not steel and, therefore, would not withstand the internal pressure of the cooling systems operation. After several meetings, it became obvious that state and university officials were not going to budge on the pipe specifications. The job was on a tight schedule and when the Jankes found that Vulcan could not supply either AWWA C300 or AWWA C301 in time to meet project deadlines, they turned to Interpace, which supplied the pipe but at a price that was $39,992.40 more than they would have paid to Vulcan. The Jankes sued Vulcan, asking for that $39,992.40 plus reimbursement for the expenses involved in the extra meetings with state officials caused by Vulcan's inability to supply the right materials. Vulcan argued that it had not breached the contract because the contract did not exist until the bid had been accepted by the state and Vulcan's written quotation was turned over to the Jankes and the Jankes signed a letter of intent. So, since there was no contract, there could be no breach of contract. The court had to agree. Besides, Vulcan argued, the contract should have been in writing from the start to satisfy the requirements of Statute of Frauds. That, however, was not the end!

More was to come. [See: *Janke Construction, Co. v. Vulcan Materials, Co.* 386 F. Supp. 687 (1974), affirmed 527 F.2d 772 (1976) United States District Court, Western Division of Wisconsin.]

Opening Case Questions

1. What are the four elements of a contract? Which element seems to be missing in this case? Explain.

2. Was Vulcan correct when it argued that the contract should have been in writing? Explain.

3. What counterarguments can the Janke Construction Company raise in this case? Explain.

4. Should Janke Construction be compensated for the extra money spent on the new pipe order from Interpace? Explain.

5. Should Janke Construction be compensated for the money spent on the numerous and ultimately pointless meetings with the state officials? Explain.

LO Learning Objectives

1. Define contract.
2. Explain the origin of the law merchant.
3. Discuss the relationship between common law and the law merchant.
4. Identify the four elements of a contract.
5. Explain the objectives of contract law.
6. Explain the place of the UCC in contract law.
7. Distinguish contracts from other agreements.
8. Explain the role of privity and agency in contract law.
9. List the contracts that must be in writing to be enforceable.
10. List the characteristics of a contract.

7-1 The History of Contract Law

A **contract** is an agreement between two or more competent parties based on mutual promises and an exchange of things of value, to do or refrain from doing some particular thing that is neither illegal nor impossible. The agreement results in an obligation or a duty that can be enforced in a court of law. Most people understand the basic nature of a contract as a process of give and take. There are rules, however, that govern how those agreements are made, how they are carried out, how they end, and how disputes are resolved when someone yells, "foul." Before delving into these basic principles, however, we will pause for a moment to consider how these rules originated.

Mercantile Law, Ancient Rome, Capitalism, and the Church

The history of contract law is intertwined with the parallel development of Western **mercantile law**, often referred to alternately as the **law merchant** and *lex mercatoria*. The law merchant outlines the laws and the procedures followed by merchants in commercial transactions. As Harold J. Berman explains in his landmark study, *Law and Revolution: The Formation of the Western Legal Tradition,* mercantile law originated among the merchants themselves who needed a formalized way to deal with one another when disputes arose. According to Berman, the law merchant saw a sudden and unprecedented burst of development between the 11th and the 13th centuries in Western Europe, both on the continent and across the channel in England. This is not to say that there was no commercial law before the 11th century. Between the fall of Rome and the rise of the mercantile city-states of the late Middle Ages, which is to say during the second half of the first millennium, commercial transactions were limited to seasonal festivals, small town marketplaces, and coastal cities. The law that governed these transactions emerged from rules within the ancient traditions of the Justinian Code of the old Roman Empire. All of this began to change with a series of agricultural innovations and a sudden European population explosion. [See: Harold J. Berman, *Law and Revolution: The Formation of the Western Legal Tradition,* (Cambridge: Harvard University Press, 1983), pp. 333–41.]

Agriculture, Technology, and Population

Ancient Roman law was adequate at the time because commerce itself was limited during that era. The population of Europe barely topped 20 million at the end of the first millennium, and most people lived out their lives in the small villages and manors that dotted the countryside. Several irresistible complex adaptive systems (CASs) changed all of that in the 11th century. The technological complex adaptive system led to developments in agriculture (including a number of important inventions such as a new type of horse collar, a heavy plow, horseshoes, fish farming, three-field crop rotation, the overshot waterwheel, and the wind-powered post mill) that led to crop surpluses that could be sold for a profit; changes in manor law freed many peasants who turned to selling as a livelihood; and Europe saw an unprecedented population explosion. The technological CAS overlapped and intersected with the economic CAS to empower a new group of professional sellers who developed their own system of laws (itself a new CAS) over a relatively short time. That CAS came to be called *mercantile law* or the *law merchant.* [See: Berman, pp. 333–41; see also Rodney Stark, *The Victory of Reason: How Christianity Led to Freedom, Capitalism, and Western Science* (New York: Random House, 2005), pp. 38–44.] In his book, *The Victory of Reason,* Rodney Stark notes that, despite popular views to the contrary, an enormous amount of progress occurred during the Middle Ages, including the inventions listed above. [See: Stark, pp. 38–44.]

Development of the Law Merchant

Mercantile law is also closely associated with the development of capitalism. **Capitalism** is a complex adaptive system of overlapping economic agents that operates on the basis of competition and a free market that responds to the movement of supply and demand. Contrary to the thesis proposed by Max Weber in *The Protestant Ethic: The Spirit of Capitalism,* European capitalism did not begin with the Protestant Reformation in the 16th century, but in the 11th and 12th centuries, some 400 years before Martin Luther nailed his famous 95 theses on the cathedral door in Wittenberg. Moreover, one of the driving forces behind the growth of capitalism was the Roman Catholic Church. The medieval Church had the ability to redirect capitalism as it did because, as a system, the Roman Catholic Church lacked two essential elements of a pure CAS. The medieval Church had (1) a strong central controlling agent and (2) a concentration, rather than a dispersal, of power among various actors. Much of this power was illusory, but the illusion, supported by its moral authority (inspired by the persuasive power of eternity), was more than enough within that culture. Thus, the Church helped provide a rational and moral foundation for the principles and procedures that guided the activities of merchants in their communities, in their courts, and in the making of their contracts. The Church, which is directed by a central powerful leader, refused to condemn commercial activity. Instead, it monitored how those activities were carried out. In short, the Church encouraged this new class of sellers to establish guilds that followed the law of the Church, a legal tradition that is generally referred to as **canon law**. The Church also insisted that these emerging businessmen never engage in deceit or dishonesty and always follow a good-faith approach to contract development. As long as they followed these basic precepts, the Church reassured the members of the new and expanding class of professional sellers that there was nothing inherently wrong with their chosen profession. [See: Berman, pp. 336–41; and Stark, p. xi. See also Henri Sée, *Modern Capitalism: Its Origin and Evolutions,* trans. Homer B. Vanderblue and Georges F. Doriot (New York: Adelphi Co. 1928), pp. 7–13; Max Weber, *The Protestant Ethic: The Spirit of Capitalism* (Mineola, NY: Dover, 2003).]

A QUESTION OF ETHICS

Contract law, whether it evolved through the law merchant, the common law, or a combination of both, operates as a complex adaptive system (CAS). Each CAS emerges from a network of interacting conditions that reinforce one another while, at the same time, adjusting to change from agents outside and inside the system. Complex adaptive systems, however, do not operate within a vacuum. On the contrary, they are an integral part of a vast sea of overlapping complex systems that interact and sometimes compete with one another. The legal system, the political system, the economic system, as well as internal subsystems such the military, academia, the stock exchange, and so on are all examples of CASs (see Chapter 2 for more about CASs). Underlying all of these processes is the distribution of global wealth that both empowers the CASs and serves as a motive to ignite forward movement. However, the distribution of wealth is not itself a CAS; rather it serves as the outcome of competing and cooperative CASs. At times, the competing CASs may ignite a flash point that causes their paths to swerve in another direction. On June 28, 1914, for example, the assassination of the Archduke Ferdinand served as a flash point that caused a swerve in a series of overlapping CASs (politics, the law, the economies of Europe, the military, and so on) that ultimately led to a global conflict and an economic shift that, for a while, at least, led to a lessening of this inequality. The distribution of wealth cannot be understood absent an understanding the interaction of two tightly interwoven CASs—the political system and the legal system. It is the interaction of these two CASs that widens or closes the inequality gap that always characterizes the flow of wealth distribution, along with the *elan vital* of Henri Bergson (*power* is a better word, but the word "power" is loaded with negative subtexts that militate against its use) that permits and, at times, forces those with wealth to hold on to it, multiply their share, or redistribute it among the economically deprived segments of the system. That is the heart of the ethical question put forward here. Two recent books have proposed similar explanations for the unequal distribution of global wealth. In his book *Capital in the Twenty-First Century,* Thomas Piketty proposes that the unequal distribution of global wealth is empowered by the tendency of socioeconomic forces to diverge because (1) those with wealth, the 1 percent, have the power to use their capital to create more capital, and (2) the annual rate of return on capital (dividends, rents, profits, interest, and so on) climbs faster than the growth rate of the economy itself (the $r > g$ factor). Similarly, Daron Acemoglu and James Robinson in *Why Nations Fail* contend that those in power positions at the national and international level will always use their power to organize society in ways that increase their own wealth. In contrast, as noted above, during the Middle Ages, the economic activity of the 1 percent was directed by the Catholic Church. The ethical question then becomes: Should the Church, or perhaps religion in general, be given a stronger voice in the political and economic arena to help redirect and perhaps even equalize the distribution of wealth? Be careful as you consider this issue. Remember this is a question of ethics not a question of pragmatism or practicality! [See: Daron Acemoglu and James Robinson, *Why Nations Fail* (New York: Crown, 2012); Thomas Piketty, *Capital in the Twenty-First Century* (Cambridge: Harvard University Press, 2014).]

The Characteristics of the Law Merchant

With the Roman Catholic Church supplying political and social support, with canon law providing a moral framework, and with practicality guiding their activities over a 300-year period, this new class of businessmen developed a body of effective commercial law. Berman tells us that this new system was distinguished by six characteristics: involvement, neutrality, universality, mutuality, integration, and evolution.

Involvement and Law Merchant

Involvement requires that those affected by the law participate in its making and its execution. According to Berman, from the outset merchants were involved in the establishment and the operation of the courts that adjudicated disputes involving contracts and other commercial disagreements such as those that might question the authenticity of negotiable instruments. Involvement meant that, as a system, the law merchant, like the Roman Catholic Church, had (1) a strong central controlling agent and (2) a concentration, rather than a dispersal, of power among various actors. This allowed the law merchant to direct, at least to a certain degree, the other characteristics of neutrality, universality, mutuality, integration, and evolution. Specifically, the courts held in European markets and fairs were run by businessmen who were elected to act as judges. The courts established by the guilds were run by the elected guild leaders who often handpicked guild members to assist in deciding certain disputes. Some territories also developed staple courts that dealt with cases involving the primary product or "staple" of a certain town or village. The courts in the Italian city-states such as Milan also elected merchants to hear disputes involving contract and other commercial transactions. Many of the coastal cities created their own local courts, sometimes referred to as admiralty courts, to handle commercial disputes involving goods carried as cargo by the ships that docked at those ports. [See: Berman, pp. 346–48.]

Neutrality of the Law Merchant

The law merchant was made up of a fairly neutral system of laws and procedures. *Neutrality* characterizes any system of laws that is consistently applied in the same evenhanded way, no matter who the antagonists might be. The law was developed in the festivals, marketplaces, and coastal cities of Europe by practical men who saw the value of recording their procedures and principles in writing, so that commercial activities, financial transactions, and dispute settlements could be carried out in a customary, predictable, and evenhanded way. The legal treatises and codebooks that resulted covered the making of negotiable instruments, the execution of contracts, and the procedures used in the mercantile courts. The actual process of writing these things down was authorized and supported by the ruling classes, especially those in the merchant cities of Genoa, Milan, and Pisa, and by the birth of a class of professional notaries, whose job it was to write down contracts and draft negotiable instruments, which, by virtue of this process, were lawful, valid, and enforceable. [See: Berman, pp. 341, 355.]

Universality and the Law Merchant

Universal laws are those that apply to everyone regardless of their social status or their place of origin. The universal applicability of the law merchant was made necessary by the global nature of trade in the late Middle Ages. The city-states of Europe hosted international fairs and the coastal cities became permanent centers for international trade. Towns and coastal cities began to adhere to the law merchant rather than their local laws, which tended to be prejudiced against foreigners. In *Law and Revolution,* Berman tells us that, as the influence of the central government began to grow, some rulers agreed to incorporate the law merchant into their national documents, such as the *Magna Carta* in 1215, which contains a clause that specifically grants safe passage to foreign merchants in England. Other rulers, notably those in Italy, entered formal agreements that guaranteed that the law merchant would be used in settling any contract disagreements that might involve their people. [See: Berman, pp. 342–44.] Weber agrees with Berman that a successful capitalist system depends upon the establishment of a legal system with formal rules that emerge from a rational process. [See: Weber, p. 25.] Moreover, Henri Sée concurs that the international character of trade gave birth to modern capitalism [See: Henri Sée, pp. 25, 29–30.]

Mutuality and the Law Merchant

The concept of *mutuality* or *reciprocity* in the law merchant is the notion that commercial arrangements always involve a process of evenhanded cooperation between the parties. Mutuality in the law merchant emerged organically from within the commercial culture, which had at its foundation a belief in reciprocity. Moreover, Berman tells us that the principle of reciprocity insisted on mutuality at two levels. First, parties to any commercial transaction were expressly forbidden to cheat, lie, or trick one another. Second, all commercial transactions had to be fair to each party. This principle outlawed contracts that involved outrageous prices and those that took advantage of a party's weakened position. [See: Berman, pp. 344–46.] Of course, Weber reminds us that there is a practical foundation for the principle of reciprocity as there are for all such virtues. Honesty, he reports, has its value, if only because it will earn good credit for trustworthy merchants. [See: Weber, p. 52.] Does the utilitarian nature of reciprocity make it wrong? No. However, it does make the pursuit of reciprocity a bit less romantic.

Integration of the Law Merchant with Common Law

The characteristic of *integration* permits a system to assimilate its major elements into a common core of cooperative working parts all of which contribute to the survival of the whole. The integration of mercantile law into the diverse legal traditions in Europe was especially difficult in England where a strong common law tradition had developed during the late Middle Ages. As noted in Chapter 2, "Sources of the Law," common law was established in England as a way to bring all English law together into a single, consistent, comprehensive system. This program put the law merchant and the merchants who administered that law on a collision course with common law and with common law lawyers and judges. Although such collisions did occur from time to time, ultimately the law merchant was integrated into common law and the two evolved together. The first merchant courts in England were established in the 11th century as part of every royal charter that legalized a local fair. These **fair courts** (also known as **pie powder courts** because of the dusty feet, or *pie poudre,* of the merchants who took part in the proceedings) were empowered to hear cases involving commercial disputes, and since the juries were inevitably made up of merchants, the law merchant was used to adjudicate the cases. The fair courts lost their power with the creation of staple courts under the Ordinance of the Staple of 1353. **Staple courts** heard cases that involved certain set commodities. They were run by mayors who were forced to learn and apply mercantile law. This worked well for about two centuries. Then in the 16th century the staple courts were taken over by the judges of the King's Court and common law dominated that court. [See: E. Allan Farnsworth and John Honnold, *Commercial Law: Cases and Materials* (Mineola, NY: The Foundation Press, 1976), pp. 3–4; Berman, pp. 348–50.]

Evolution of the Law Merchant and Common Law

Finally, the *evolution* of a system permits it to adjust, change, and move forward often at the expense of competing but less pliable systems. The evolution of law merchant and common law required that the two work in tandem to deal with their chief competitor, the admiralty courts, by using both arbitration and eventually the statutory law system. **Admiralty courts** were tribunals set up in seaport towns to handle disputes involving maritime law, shipping contracts, contests over docking rights, collisions at sea, and the like. When the common law judges took over the staple courts, the merchants took their cases to the admiralty courts to ensure that the law merchant would be used to settle their disputes. This tactic became ineffective when the common law courts were given jurisdiction over most commercial cases throughout England, including those that had been handled by the admiralty courts. The merchants fought back by establishing their own arbitration groups to avoid common law altogether. The common law courts finally began to see the wisdom of incorporating common law with the law merchant, and this integration practice became more accepted by the beginning of the 18th century and the two systems finally began to evolve together. When Lord Mansfield became the chief justice, this evolutionary program kicked into high gear, and for more than three decades the chief justice worked to combine the law merchant and common law. His work continued for the next century. Then late in the 19th century, Parliament passed the Bills of Exchange Act and the Sale of Goods Act, both of which codified common law principles, which by that time had been successfully integrated with most law merchant principles. When the National Conference of Commissioners (now known as the Uniform Law Commission) was established in 1892 in the United States, it developed two model laws, the Uniform Negotiable Instruments Act, which followed the Bills of Exchange Act and the Uniform Sales Act, which was patterned after the Sale of Goods Act. [See: Farnsworth and Honnold, pp. 4–5.] Despite the initial power struggle between common law and the law merchant, the two traditions were merged, with the principles of the law merchant dominating the law governing commercial transactions. Some of these principles are charted in Table 7-1. [See: Berman, pp. 348–350, and Sée, pp. 20–24.]

The Restatement of the Law of Contracts

This telling of the story is, at best, incomplete, and at worst, terribly flawed. Elements and players are missing. The law is, after all, a complex adaptive system that is constantly changing by design and by chance, sometimes by both, under the influence of various agents within the system. A case in point is the development of the Restatements of the Law written by the American Law Institute, an organization founded in 1923, consisting of lawyers, judges, and law professors, and funded, at that time, by the Rockefeller Foundation and the Carnegie Corporation, among other similar philanthropic institutions. The Restatements (there are many in various areas of the law such as contracts, torts, agency, property, and so on) are just what they say they are, restatements of the common law made in clear, precise, everyday prose and organized in a straightforward, easy-to-understand fashion. The Restatements, which are often updated and revised (the Restatement of the Law of Contracts, for example, is in its third edition) are not binding, but they are persuasive. They are also so adaptive that they sometimes do more than restate the law. Sometimes they create the law as the lawyers, judges, and law professors struggle to compromise on the actual meaning, intent, and objectives of the common law.

One such struggle gave support and acceptance to the concept of *promissory estoppel* in contract law. Under one of the early drafts of the original writing of the first Restatement of the Law of Contracts, the concept of consideration was grounded in bargained-for-exchange, which downplayed the benefit-detriment interpretation of consideration. This narrowly defined interpretation of consideration left no room for a situation in which, before a contract exists, a promise is made, relied on, and then broken. Under this interpretation of the law, an injured party, the one who believed in and relied on the broken promise, had no legal recourse. Later the concept of *promissory estoppel* was added to the Restatement to deal with such issues. *Promissory estoppel* restricts a party from denying that a promise was made under certain conditions, even though consideration has not been exchanged to bind an agreement. To be effective, *promissory estoppel* requires that the party making the promise know, or be presumed to know, that the other party will rely on that promise and, as a result, take action that depends on the promise being fulfilled. The party relying on the promise must actually take that action and suffer a financial loss as a result.

Table 7-1 Law Merchant Principles in Modern Law

CONTRACT LAW

The division between a law that focuses only on goods and one that centers on real property

The development of the rights of a good faith purchaser in goods

The transfer of ownership of goods based on the transfer of documents

The development of the concept of warranties of fitness and warranties of merchantability

NEGOTIABLE INSTRUMENTS

The development of negotiable bills of exchange and promissory notes

BUSINESS ORGANIZATIONS

The invention of limited joint stock companies and the "company under a collective name" — forefathers of the modern corporation

The development of joint property ownership in partnerships

The development of survivorship rights among partners in a partnership

SECURED TRANSACTIONS

The invention of the chattel mortgage

CREDIT AND BANKING

The development of credit institutions at the great monasteries in Europe

The banking and lending operations of the Teutonic Knights and the Templars lead to modern banking procedures

INSURANCE CONTRACTS

The development of maritime insurance

The appearance of "private" insurance in the Middle Ages

The development of insurance companies in the 17th century

INTERNATIONAL LAW

The increased international trade leads to the need to develop international agreements

INTELLECTUAL PROPERTY

The creation of patents and trademarks

Sources: Table adapted from information in Harold J. Berman, *Law and Revolution: The Formation of the Western Legal Tradition,* (Cambridge: Harvard University Press, 1983), pp. 349–50 and Henri Sée, *Modern Capitalism: Its Origin and Evolution* (New York: Adelphi Company, 1928), pp. 20–24.

In reaching this doctrine, the lawyers, judges, law professors who wrote the first restatement accepted the principles of justice and fairness in protecting the party receiving the promise from otherwise unrecoverable losses. [See: Charles E. Clark, "The Restatement of the Law of Contracts," *Yale Law Journal* 42, no. 5 (March 1933), pp. 643–67; Joel M. Ngugi, "Promissory Estoppel: The Life Story of an Ideal Legal Transplant," *University of Richmond Law Review* 41, no. 2 (January 2007).]

THE OPENING CASE *Round 2*

Vulcans Never Lie, Although at Times They Do *Restate* Things

Recall that in the opening case, Janke Construction was about to bid on a contract that required either AWWA C300 or AWWA C301 level pipe or pipe that was "equal to" those specifications. Jerry Janke, vice president of Janke Construction, talked to a Vulcan sales rep who quoted a price that was $40,000 less than the competitors' price. No mention had been made about the exact pipe specifications. The evening before the bids were to be filed, Jerry and James Janke met with Alex Barry, the general manager of Vulcan, and Peter Fox, a Vulcan sales rep. The next day, Barry reassured them that Vulcan would supply the pipe needed for the job. With this reassurance in hand, the Jankes submitted their bid. After the Jankes won the bid, they received a written quotation from Vulcan that indicated Vulcan would use AWWA C302 pipe, which did not meet project specifications. As a result, Janke Construction had to turn to another supplier, Interpace, to get the correct pipe for $39, 992.40 more than Vulcan's price. The Jankes sued Vulcan, asking for that $39,992.40, plus reimbursement expenses involved in the meetings with state officials caused by Vulcan's inability to supply the right materials. Vulcan argued that it had not breached the contract because the contract did not exist until the bid had been accepted by the state and the written quotation was turned over to the Jankes and the Jankes had signed a letter of intent. Since there is no contract, there can be no breach of contract. The court had to agree. However, fortunately for the Jankes, the court did not stop there. Instead, it reached into the Restatement of the Law of Contracts and used *promissory estoppel* to support Janke Construction's claim for reimbursement. This situation is, in fact, a textbook example (pun intended) of *promissory estoppel.* Take a good look. *Promissory estoppel* in this case restricts Vulcan from denying that its reps made a promise to the Jankes to deliver pipe that could be used on the project. The Vulcan reps clearly knew that the Janke brothers would rely on that promise and, as a result, would enter a bid using their price. Moreover, the Jankes actually did rely on Vulcan's promise and submitted the bid. When Vulcan could not deliver the correct pipe, the Janke brothers had to turn to Interpace, which cost them an extra $39,992.40. A textbook example of *promissory estoppel* if there ever was one. [See: *Janke Construction, Co. v. Vulcan Materials, Co.* 386 F. Supp. 687 (1974), affirmed 527 F.2d 772 (1976) United States District Court, Western Division of Wisconsin.]

quick quiz 7-1

1. A valid contract results in an obligation that can be enforced in a court of law.   true | false

2. Mercantile law, the law merchant, and *lex mercatoria* are all different names for the same area of law.   true | false

3. The six characteristics of the law merchant are neutrality, universality, mutuality, involvement, integration, and evolution.   true | false

7-2 The Multidimensional Nature of Contract Law

Contract law forms the basis of all other law in the corporate capitalist setting. Without contract law there could be no buying and selling, no transfer of property rights, no properly planned and executed deliveries, no hiring of agents, no partnership agreements, no stock transfers, and so on. Like many other areas of the law, contract law is based on safeguarding people's rights. We saw this in criminal law and in tort law, and we see it now in contract law. The difference is that in criminal law and tort law, most of the time, human rights are inherent within the social setting. In other words, people have rights just because they are a part of our social structure. In contract law, people adopt new rights and duties as part of their contractual relationships, which are entered voluntarily. For this reason among a few others, contract law is a multidimensional area of the law, laying out not only what our rights and duties are, but also whether we have actually undertaken those duties and been given those rights. To explore this in more detail, we will first look at the elements of a contract and then at several additional multidimensional aspects of contract law, including the objectives of contract law, remedies in contract law, contracts and the UCC, contracts and other agreements, contracts and agency law, and contracts that must be written.

The Elements of a Contract

In order for a contract to be legally binding on all parties, four elements must be present. If even one of these elements is missing, there is no contract. This does not mean that there is no agreement. It simply means that there is no contract and no contractual relationship that can be vindicated in a court of law. The four elements are mutual assent, consideration, capacity, and legality. (Note: Before reading about these elements you might want to study Table 7-2.)

Mutual Assent   A valid *offer* requires that the *offeror* make a definite expression of the desire to enter a contract in terms that are clear and unambiguous and that are

Table 7-2 The Four Elements of a Contract	
Element	**Explanation**
Mutual Assent	Once the offer has been properly made by the offeror and accepted properly by the offeree, then mutual assent exists between them. Often the courts will say that mutual assent exists when there has been a meeting of the minds among the parties to the agreement. Those situations that might destroy assent include: fraud (both active and passive), misrepresentation, mistake, duress, and undue influence.
Consideration	Consideration is the thing of value promised to the other party in exchange for something else of value promised by the other party. Each side in a contract must give up something, their legal detriment, and must gain something, their legal benefit. The courts are generally not concerned with the adequacy of consideration.
Capacity	The third contractual element is capacity, that is, the legal ability to make a contract. All the parties to a contract are legally permitted to assume that the other parties possess capacity. This assumption, however, is a rebuttable presumption, which means that any of the parties can attack or rebut that presumption. Many, perhaps most, capacity questions involve minors. Capacity also appears as a question in cases involving some sort of mental impairment.
Legality	The final element of a binding contract is legality. Clearly, any contract to commit a crime or a tort would be illegal and, therefore, void. Some contracts are also made illegal by statutory law. These include usurious contracts, gambling contracts, unlicensed agreements, unconscionable agreements, and some Sunday agreements. There are also some contracts that have been made illegal by the courts based on the doctrine of public policy.

THE OPENING CASE *Round 3*
Vulcans Never Lie, But Sometimes They Do Not Tell You Everything

Recall that in the opening case, Janke Construction was about to bid on a contract that required either AWWA C300 or AWWA C301 level pipe or pipe that was "equal to" those specifications. After the Jankes won the bid, they received a written quotation from Vulcan that indicated that Vulcan would use pipe that failed to meet specifications. As a result, the Jankes were forced to purchase the correct pipe from another supplier for $39,992.40 more than Vulcan's price. The Jankes sued asking for that $39,992.40, plus reimbursement for the expenses involved in all the extra meetings with state officials caused by Vulcan's inability to supply the right materials. Although, as we have seen, the court used *promissory estoppel* to support Janke Construction's case against Vulcan, it will be instructive to see why mutual assent did not exist here despite all of the conversations that took place among the principals. Recall that a valid *offer* requires that the *offeror* make a definite expression of the desire to enter a contract in terms that are clear and unambiguous and that are communicated to the *offeree*. Given this starting point, it will be helpful to determine who the offeree is and who the offeror is in this case. Testimony in the case about how business is done among contractors and subcontractors in a bidding war came from Jerry Lapish, a marine contractor with extensive experience in these matters. According to Lapish,

when a quotation comes from a subcontractor, the contractor has the duty to see if the quote meets the specifications. This would imply that, if the quote does not meet specifications, the contractor can reject it. Other testimony also indicated that the contract does not exist until the bid is won by the contractor and the state project engineers have approved the materials. The contractor then signs a letter of intent to purchase the material from the subcontractor. It would, therefore, appear that the subcontractor is in the position of the offeror. The subcontractor in effect makes the offer when it sends a description of the material to be used in the construction project and asks for a signed letter of intent from the contractor. At that point, the contractor is free to reject a non-conforming quote from the subcontractor. The letter of intent, then, is, in effect, the acceptance of the terms of the offer submitted by the subcontractor. Therefore, in this case, the offeror is Vulcan, the subcontractor, and the offeree is Janke Construction, the contractor. Janke's refusal to sign the letter of intent amounted to a refusal to accept. The conclusion must be that, since there is no acceptance of the offer, there is no mutual assent and no contract. [See: *Janke Construction, Co. v. Vulcan Materials, Co.* 386 F. Supp. 687 (1974), affirmed 527 F.2d 772 (1976) United States District Court, Western Division of Wisconsin.]

communicated to the *offeree*. An *acceptance* occurs when, without changing the essential terms of the offer, the offeree communicates an acceptance to the offeror. Once the offer has been properly made by the offeror and accepted properly by the offeree, then *mutual assent* exists between them. Often the courts will say that mutual assent exists when there has been a *meeting of the minds* among the parties to the agreement. If mutual assent has been destroyed, the relationship that results is said to be defective. Those situations that might destroy assent include: *fraud* (both active and passive*), misrepresentation, mistake, duress,* and *undue influence.*

Consideration
Consideration is the thing of value promised to the other party in exchange for something else of value promised by the other party. Each side in a contract must give up something, their legal detriment, and must gain something, their legal benefit. The courts are generally not concerned with the adequacy of consideration. This means that the courts avoid determining "how much" consideration is enough consideration. That

determination is up to the parties to the contract. However, if the consideration is *uncon-scionable* (ridiculously out of line with the nature of the contract), the court might intervene. The parties can settle value-related disputes on their own through a process of *accord and satisfaction.* Some things that might at first appear to be consideration are not consideration. These things include: *past consideration, pre-existing duties, illusory promises,* and *future gifts.* On the other hand, those situations involving *promissory estoppel* will not eliminate a party's responsibility to compensate an innocent party, even in the absence of real consideration.

Capacity   The third contractual element is *capacity,* that is, the legal ability to make a contract. All the parties to a contract are legally permitted to assume that the other parties possess capacity. This assumption, however, is a *rebuttable presumption,* which means that any one of the parties to the contract can attack or rebut that presumption. Many, perhaps most, capacity questions involve minors. The law permits a minor to rescind his or her contracts. This means that minors actually have "extra-capacity," that is, the capacity to enter and the capacity to leave a contract. There are limits to this privilege, however. Minors must provide the reasonable value for *necessaries,* that is, materials that are needed for the minor's health, safety, and welfare that are not provided by a parent or a guardian. Minors must also abide by certain contracts required by law, such as insurance contracts, contracts for educational loans, agency contracts, valid marriage contracts, enlistment contracts, contracts concerning child support, and those for pregnancy care, among others. Capacity also appears as a question in cases involving a party with a mental impairment. Some mental impairments result from physical injuries; others are genetic; some are health-related illnesses; and others are psychological in nature. Whatever the source of the difficulty, a person's mental impairment may also eliminate contractual capacity, but only if the party claiming the impairment can demonstrate that the impairment was so severe at the time the contract was made that he or she could not understand the nature, the purpose, or the effect of the agreement. If that is the case, then the contract will be voidable by the party lacking capacity. In contrast, if a person has been declared incompetent by a court, then that person's contracts are absolutely void.

Legality   The final element of a binding contract is *legality.* Parties cannot be permitted to enforce a contract that involves something that the law says cannot be done. Clearly, any contract to commit a crime or a tort would be illegal and, therefore, void. Some contracts are also made illegal by statutory law. These include usurious contracts, gambling contracts, unlicensed agreements, unconscionable agreements, and some Sunday agreements. There are also some contracts that have been made illegal by the courts based on the doctrine of *public policy.* These include agreements to obstruct justice, agreements interfering with public safety, agreements to defraud creditors, agreements to escape liability (AKA exculpatory clauses), agreements in restraint of trade, and agreements to suppress competition. In some states, several of these contracts, agreements to obstruct justice, for instance, are also made illegal by statutory law.

The Objectives of Contract Law

In general the law is designed to promote harmony, stability, and justice. All the subdivisions within the law are charged with these same goals. Criminal law does this by defining criminal behavior with great specificity and then by providing a set of procedures that are followed fairly and consistently in order to make certain that those who threaten harmony, stability, and justice no longer walk among us. Tort law does the same thing by providing a system of compensation for the innocent victims of deliberate and accidental torts. Contract law is much more complicated and multidimensional than other areas of the law because it

THE OPENING CASE *Round 4*
Vulcans Never Lie. Still, on Occasion, They Do Not Keep Their Promises

Recall that in the opening case, after the Janke brothers won the bid for a marine project at the University of Wisconsin, they learned that their subcontractor, Vulcan, could not supply the correct pipe for the project. A series of meetings followed. The meetings took place in Milwaukee and Madison, requiring travel and hotel expenses for the Janke brothers. At these meetings the Janke brothers were required to obtain specifications and shop drawings from Vulcan using the AWWA C302 pipe to determine if the C302 pipe could be substituted for AWWA C300 or AWWA C301. After seeing these drawings, the state engineers decided AWWA C302 would not work, and Janke Construction had to draw up yet another set of plans and shop drawings and attend more meetings. At this point, Janke purchased the proper pipe from Interpace for a price that was $39,992.40 more than it would have paid to Vulcan. The Jankes sued, asking for that $39,992.40 back, plus reimbursement for all the expenses involved in those extra meetings with state officials. As we have seen, the court used *promissory estoppel* to support the claims made by the Jankes. The court ordered Vulcan to pay Janke $39,992.40. This payment fulfills the real objective of contract law. The courts are quite clear that the objective of contract law is rehabilitation. This means that the courts will place an innocent party, Janke in this case,

back into just as good a position as it would have been had the defendant, Vulcan, done what it was supposed to do in the first place. Janke will be in that position once it has that $39,992.40 back in its bank account. These damages are called actual or compensatory damages. Sometimes victims are entitled to damages for indirect losses. *Incidental damages* are those that are paid by the breaching party to make up for any expenses paid by the victim to prevent any additional loss. The Jankes asked for incidental damages to reimburse them for those meetings in Madison and Milwaukee. The court, however, decided not to honor that request because those losses did not result from Janke's reliance on Vulcan's false promises (remember Janke won based on *promissory estoppel*) but on Janke's desire to get the State of Wisconsin to use the substandard pipe. Presumably, once the Jankes learned that Vulcan could not supply the proper pipe, they were free to go right to another supplier. The fact that they did not do that immediately but decided, instead, to try to convince the state to use Vulcan's substandard (and cheaper) pipe was their decision, and so they pay the hotel and travel expenses that result from that decision. [See: *Janke Construction, Co. v. Vulcan Materials, Co.* 386 F. Supp. 687 (1974), affirmed 527 F.2d 772 (1976) United States District Court, Western Division of Wisconsin.]

must not only provide the mechanism for punishment or compensation but also explain why that mechanism is used and not some other simpler and more effective method.

Rehabilitation in Contract Law
The underlying objective of contract law is to determine whether the parties to the contract entered the agreement freely. If the court determines that the parties willingly entered the agreement, then the contract is valid. Then, if the court finds that one of the parties breached the contract, that party will have to **rehabilitate** the innocent party by compensating that party for any loss that results from the breach. Usually the courts will not force a party to go through with the terms of a contract, even when a breach has been proven. This is especially true of service contracts. However, the courts will compel the breaching party to rehabilitate the innocent party for any loss that resulted from the breach. The courts say that the objective of this rehabilitation is to place the innocent party in as good a position as he or she would have been had the contract been performed.

The Payment of Damages
In contract law the victims are compensated by the payment of money damages to make up for their losses. Generally, these damages are equal to the real financial loss suffered by the innocent victim. These damages are called *actual* or *compensatory damages*. Sometimes victims are entitled to damages for indirect

losses. *Incidental damages* are those that are paid by the breaching party to make up for any expenses paid by the victim to prevent any additional loss. *Consequential damages* are indirect damages that result because of special circumstances that exist with a particular contract. **Punitive damages** are designed to punish the wrongdoer for his or her outrageous conduct. As a general rule, the courts do not award punitive damages in contract cases. Such damages are generally more appropriate in tort law cases. Nevertheless, there are exceptions to this rule. For instance, in cases of fraud, a court may approve punitive damages, because a party who commits fraud has attempted to undermine the entire contract system, something the court will not abide.

Recovery Limits and Equitable Relief

There are built-in limits to the measure of the damages awarded in a contract case. For example, the innocent party cannot take advantage of the breach by deliberately raising the amount of damages that the other party must pay. This principle is called the duty to mitigate the damages or just the *duty to mitigate*. Also, there is an exception to the rule that says that the courts cannot force a party to go through with a contract. The court may force a party to perform the terms of an agreement if the contract involves land or some other unique item, such as an original work of art or a family heirloom. This is an equitable remedy called *specific performance. Equitable remedies* are those that are imposed by the courts when the payment of money would not compensate for the loss suffered by the innocent party. Another equitable remedy is injunction. In contract law, an *injunction* is a court order issued by a court directing a party to refrain from some activity that represents a breach of contract. Injunctions can be temporary or permanent. A temporary injunction is issued as a way to delay further activity until the court can decide whether to make the injunction permanent. A party who disobeys an injunction does so under threat of a contempt of court.

Multidimensional Principles of Contract Law

Stacked on top of the elements of a contract, the objectives of contract law, and the remedies offered in contract law are a series of additional aspects that must be examined to set the stage before entering a more detailed study of contract law. We have referred to these additional areas of the law as the multidimensional principles of contract law. These multidimensional principles include contracts and the Uniform Commercial Code, contracts and other agreements, contracts and privity, contracts and agency law, and contracts and the Statute of Frauds.

Contracts and the Uniform Commercial Code

The Uniform Commercial Code (UCC) is a model set of laws designed to govern almost all commercial transactions. The UCC is organized in the following way: sale of goods contracts (Article 2); commercial paper (Article 3); bank deposits and collections (Article 4); letters of credit (Article 5); bulk transfers (Article 6); warehouse receipts, bills of lading, and other documents of title (Article 7); investment securities (Article 8); secured transactions, sales of accounts, contract rights and chattel paper (Article 9); effective date and repealer (Article 10); and transition provisions (Article 11). All other types of contracts, such as employment contracts and real property (land) contracts, are covered by common law and by special statutes dedicated to some aspect of those contracts. Thus, employment contracts will be affected by labor law and minimum wage statutes; real property contracts will be covered by zoning laws and property tax laws; while both employment and real property contracts will be affected by civil rights legislation.

Contracts and Other Agreements

All contracts are agreements, but not all agreements are contracts. An agreement may or may not be legally enforceable. To be enforceable, an agreement must conform to the law of contracts. This means at the very least that to be a legally recognized contract, an agreement must possess the four elements of a

CLASSIC CASE Common Law, the UCC, or Something Else?

The classic case of *Tubelite Co., Inc. v. Original Sign Studio* concerns two (or is it, three?) agreements between Tubelite, the seller, and Original Sign Studio, the buyer. The first agreement was an application for credit, in which Original Sign agreed to pay for all materials shipped by Tubelite and to remit an 18 percent finance charge for overdue payments. In the second agreement, Tubelite agreed to be Original Sign's exclusive supplier. The terms of the contract were reduced to writing in a letter written by an agent of Original Sign but never signed by anyone from Tubelite. The agreement stated that Tubelite would supply Original Sign with all the material that it requested, but that it would bill Original Sign only for the materials that the sign company actually used and then, in exchange for being Original Sign's exclusive supplier, it would charge a discounted rate of somewhere between 10 and 25 percent. Tubelite also agreed to install shelving at Original Sign's warehouse for proper storing of the materials (the third contract?). Tubelite shipped the materials that Original Sign requested and installed the shelving as per the (third?) agreement. Tubelite billed Original Sign for all the material it shipped, not just the material used. Moreover, the bill that Tubelite sent to Original Sign ignored the discounts promised under agreement number two. Original Sign ignored the bill as written by Tubelite and, instead, paid only for the materials it had used at a 25 percent discount rate. Tubelite insisted that, under agreement one, Original Sign still owed money for the unused portion of the material. In addition, since that payment was now late, Tubelite tacked on its 18 percent penalty (remember the "finance charge"). Original Sign argued that agreement number two, the discount agreement, superseded agreement number one, the credit application. Tubelite argued

that agreement number one, the credit application, was still in effect because agreement number two was never signed by anyone from Tubelite. Therefore, the agreement failed to meet Statute of Frauds requirements (the statute that tells us what contracts must be written) and was unenforceable. Because of the various types of contacts involved here, it is not even clear what law applies. One of these contracts is for credit. One is for the actual shipment of construction materials. One is a service agreement for the construction of the shelves. So do we have a financial contract for credit? A sale of goods contract for the materials? Or a service contract for the shelves? What law applies here? Common law, the Uniform Commercial Code (UCC), construction law, or banking law? Despite the intricate paths that seem to double back upon one another here, the appellate court saw through the maze and declared without hesitation that all three agreements, the one for credit, the one for the actual shipment of construction materials, and the one for the construction of new shelving, concern goods and, therefore, fall within Article 2 of the Uniform Commercial Code. Perhaps for posterity, the appellate court felt compelled to make certain that everyone understood this because the court writes, "Goods are 'all things (including specially manufactured goods) which are movable at the time of identification to the contract for sale other than the money in which the price is to be paid, investment securities, and things in action.' R.C. 1302.01(A)(8). Here Tubelite seeks to recover payment for signage materials that it sold to Original Sign Studio. As these materials are 'movable' the Ohio Uniform Commercial Code applies to the transactions at issue." [See: *Tubelite Co., Inc. v. Original Sign Studio* 176 Ohio App.3d 241 (Tenth District).]

contract: mutual assent, consideration, capacity, and legality. The courts have never been inclined to enforce social agreements such as dates, dinner engagements, and so on. Many states have extended this concept to agreements to marry and agreements to live together without the benefit of a marriage contract.

Contracts and Privity

The general rule of contract law is that the parties must stand in privity to one another. **Privity** means that all parties must have a legally recognized interest in the subject of the contract if they are to be bound by it. Parties who do not have such an interest in the subject matter of the contract may not be bound by it. Their right to bring a lawsuit in the event of a breach of contract would also be in question. Despite the privity rule, it is possible for two or more parties to provide benefits to a third party under the terms of a contract. However, the law still makes a distinction between third parties who are *intended beneficiaries* and third parties who are *incidental beneficiaries*. For example, in a life insurance contract, the parties who are named as those who will receive payment on the death of the insured would be intended beneficiaries. Given a breach of that contract, those intended beneficiaries would have a cause of action against the defaulting life insurance company. Moreover, an exception to the general rule of privity exists in cases involving warranties and product liability.

UCC 1-201(11) and (21) (see pages 919 and 920)

Contracts and Agency Law

An *agent* is a party who has been hired or appointed by a *principal* to perform some sort of work, usually of a business nature, for the principal. Agents owe several levels of duty to the principal. For example, the agent must obey the instructions of the principal, must be loyal to the principal, must exercise due care in doing work for the principal, must perform the work for the principal personally, must account for all money and property that is entrusted to his or her care by the principal, and must communicate all relevant agency information to the principal. The agent has all of these duties because, in effect, when the agent acts the principal acts. Agents can, therefore, bind the principal to a contract, even if the principal is not present. If the agent creates a contract for the principal and there is a breach of contract suit filed by the third party, the principal will be the initial target of that lawsuit. If the principal loses the lawsuit, and the fault lies with the agent, the agent will be liable to the principal for the losses he or she incurred because of that lawsuit.

Contracts and the Statute of Frauds

The *Statute of Frauds* is a law that outlines those contracts that must be in writing to be enforceable in court. The original Statute of Frauds was passed by Parliament in 1677 and was officially named the Act for the Prevention of Frauds and Perjuries. The statute was part of colonial law in New England and was, thus, assimilated into American law by the states after the Revolution. It is still part of the statutory law covering contracts in every state and in the District of Columbia. Six types of contracts must be in writing to be enforceable. These six include (1) contracts that cannot be completed within one year; (2) contracts involving land; (3) contracts in consideration of marriage; (4) contracts made by executors to pay a debt of the estate out of his or her own finances; (5) a promise to pay the debt of another; and (6) contracts for the sale of goods valued at $500 or more. If the statute of frauds demands a written contract and, for some reason, the parties never reduce that contract to writing, the contract remains valid but is unenforceable, which means that the court will probably dismiss the action.

Exceptions to the Statutory Rule

Several interesting exceptions apply to the rules imposed by the Statute of Frauds in relation to sale of goods contracts. The statute says that a contract for the sale of goods valued at $500 or more must be in writing unless the contract is for specially manufactured goods. The writing also becomes unnecessary with a sale of goods contract if the goods have already been shipped and accepted or a payment has been received and accepted. Also, if one of the parties reduces the contract to writing and sends that writing to the other party, that unsigned paper will be sufficient as a writing under the statute unless the receiving party objects in writing within 10 days. Finally, in a court action if the party that has invoked the Statute of Frauds to escape enforcement has also admitted under oath that the contract exists, no writing is needed.

Rules of Interpretation

Despite the careful precision with which the Statute of Frauds was written, whenever contracts are reduced to writing, someone is going to disagree on what was meant by the written terms. To deal with this problem, the courts have

THE OPENING CASE *Round 5*
Vulcans Never Lie, Although at Times They Do Not Write Things Down

Recall that in the opening case, Janke Construction was about to bid on a contract that required either AWWA C300 or AWWA C301 level pipe. Jerry Janke, vice president of Janke Construction, talked to a representative from the Vulcan Materials Company who quoted a price for the pipe that was $40,000 less than the price quoted by Vulcan's competitors. No mention had been made about the exact specifications for the pipe to be used on the job. However, promise after promise seems to have been made by representatives of Vulcan. The evening before the bid was to be submitted, Alex Barry, the general manager of Vulcan, and Peter Fox, a Vulcan sales representative, met with Jerry and James Janke in their hotel room in Madison. The next day, Barry met with them at the State Office Building and reassured the Jankes that his company would supply the pipe needed for the job. With this reassurance in hand, the Jankes submitted their bid. After the Jankes won the bid, they asked for and received a written quotation from Vulcan that indicated that Vulcan would use AWWA C302 pipe, which did not meet project specifications. However, Vulcan seemed to promise Janke that the AWWA C302 pipe would work just as well as both AWWA C300 and AWWA C301. A series of meetings followed. Vulcan worked with Janke to supply specifications and shop drawings using the AWWA C302 pipe to show that the C302 pipe could be substituted for AWWA C300 or AWA C301. After seeing these drawings, the state engineers still would not accept the AWWA C302 pipe, and Janke Construction had to draw up another set of plans and shop drawings. At this point, Janke purchased the proper pipe from Interpace

for a price that was $39,992.40 more than the company would have paid to Vulcan. The Jankes sued Vulcan, asking for that $39,992.40 back, plus reimbursement for all the expenses involved in the extra meetings with state officials. Vulcan argued that it had not breached the contract because the contract did not exist until the bid had been accepted by the state and the Jankes signed a letter of intent. So, since there was no contract, there could be no breach of contract. The court had to agree. Eventually, as we have seen, the court ruled that, based on *promissory estoppel,* Vulcan would have to compensate Janke for that $39,992.40. Vulcan then argued that the agreement could not be enforced by the court because it was not in writing as required by the Statute of Frauds. Can the Statute of Frauds be raised once the court has decided that the agreement is based not on contract law but on *promissory estoppel?* The court decided that this as not a tenable argument. The court concluded that, once it has been decided that a contract never existed and that the defendant is liable to the plaintiff based on *promissory estoppel,* it is no longer credible for the defense to say, "Yeah, sure, but the agreement was not in writing." If there is no contract, and liability is based on a legal doctrine outside contract law, such as *promissory estoppel,* then, as any self-respecting Vulcan would know, it is not logical to argue that the contract (which does not exist) was supposed to be in writing. End of speech. [See: *Janke Construction, Co. v. Vulcan Materials, Co.* 386 F. Supp. 687 (1974), affirmed 527 F.2d 772 (1976) United States District Court, Western Division of Wisconsin.]

developed rules of construction to guide judges as they interpret the written word. The first rule is the *standard construction rule,* which tells judges that their primary objective in the interpretation of a written contract is to uncover the goals that the parties had when they entered the contract in the first place. As a corollary of that rule, the courts must also interpret any ambiguous clause against the party who actually wrote the contract. The goal of this rule is to encourage those parties who actually put pen to paper (or fingers to keyboard) to be as clear and straightforward as humanly possible. Otherwise, if a question of interpretation comes up later, they risk having the judge rule against them. A different problem arises when some of the terms are not just vague or ambiguous, but are actually missing from the contract. Terms such as the subject matter, the quantity, and the price to be paid are essential to a binding contractual relationship. On the other hand, at least under the UCC, it is not always necessary to have all of the terms just as long as the judge has enough information to determine a "reasonably certain basis for giving an appropriate remedy." [See: UCC 2-204 (3).]

---

quick quiz 7-2

1. The four elements are mutual assent, consideration, capacity, and legality.   true | false

2. The courts says that the objective of rehabilitation is to place the innocent party in as good a position as he or she would have been had the contract been performed.   true | false

3. All contracts must be in writing to be enforced in a court of law.   true | false

---

7-3 Contractual Characteristics

Contractual characteristics fall into five categories: valid, void, voidable, and unenforceable; unilateral and bilateral; express and implied; informal and formal; and executory and executed. Any given contract can be classifiable in all five ways. Thus, for example, a single contract could be said to be valid, bilateral, express, formal, and executed, or any other acceptable combination of characteristics.

Valid, Void, Voidable, and Unenforceable Contracts

A **valid contract** is one that is legally binding and fully enforceable by the court. In contrast, a **void contract** is one that has no legal effect whatsoever. For example, a contract to perform an illegal act would be void. A **voidable contract** is one that may be avoided or canceled by one of the parties. Contracts made by minors or induced by fraud or misrepresentation are examples of voidable contracts. An **unenforceable contract** is one that, because of some rule of law, cannot be upheld by a court of law. An unenforceable contract may have all the elements of a complete contract and still be unenforceable.

Unilateral and Bilateral Contracts

A **unilateral contract** is an agreement in which one party makes a promise to do something in return for an act of some sort. The classic example of a unilateral contract is a reward contract. A person who promises to pay $5 to the finder of a lost driver's license does not expect a promise in return. Rather, the person expects the return of the lost license. When the license is returned, the contract arises and the promisor owes the finder $5.

In contrast, a **bilateral contract** is one in which both parties make promises. Bilateral contracts come into existence at the moment the two promises are made. A **breach of contract** occurs when one of the two parties fails to keep the promise. When there is a breach of contract, the injured party has the right to ask a court of law to somehow remedy the situation. (Breach of contract and remedies are discussed in detail in Chapter 12.)

Express and Implied Contracts

A contract can be either express or implied. An **express contract** requires some sort of written or spoken expression indicating a desire to enter the contractual relationship. An **implied contract** is created by the actions or gestures of the parties involved in the transaction.

Express Contracts When contracting parties accept mutual obligations, either through oral discussion or written communication, they have created an express contract. Oral negotiations in many cases will be reduced to writing, but this is not always necessary.

A written contract does not have to be a long, formal preprinted agreement. Although such lengthy, preprinted forms are common in some businesses, other, less formal written documents are frequently used to show that a contract exists. For example, a written contract may take the form of a letter, sales slip and receipt, notation, or memorandum. A written contract may be typed, printed, keystroked, scrawled, or written in beautiful penmanship. In some situations, state laws require certain types of contracts to be in writing. (See Chapter 11.)

A QUESTION OF ETHICS

Suppose you posted a reward notice that read, "Reward: $50 for the return of my lost college class ring." Suppose further that someone who did not know of the reward offer found your ring and returned it. Legally you would not have to pay the reward money to the person who found your ring because he or she did not know about your offer. However, would it be ethical not to pay the reward to the finder? Explain.

When a contract is placed in writing, it is essential that the content be as clear and unambiguous as possible. When faced with a dispute over an ambiguous clause, the court may be compelled to look at factual evidence to determine the actual intent of the parties. This review may mean that a case that could have been dismissed early will have to go to trial so that the court can make a factual determination of intent by looking at evidence beyond the terms in the writing.

When the law does not require a written agreement, an *oral contract* resulting from the spoken words of the parties will be enough. Parties to such an agreement, however, should anticipate the difficulty of proving the contractual relationship, should disputes arise later. Nevertheless, expressing every agreement in writing, in anticipation of a future need of proof, is impractical in the fast-paced modern world of business.

Implied Contracts One who knowingly accepts benefits from another person may be obligated for their payment, even though no express agreement has been made. An agreement of this type can be either implied-in-fact or implied-in-law. A contract implied by the direct or indirect acts of the parties is known as an **implied-in-fact contract**. Pumping gas into a car at a self-service gas station is an example of an implied-in-fact contract. Because the parties to a contract enter that contract by an exercise of free will, the court follows the **objective concept rule** in interpreting the acts and gestures of a party. Under this rule, the meaning of one's actions is determined by the impression those actions would make upon any reasonable person who might have witnessed them, not by a party's self-serving claim of what was meant or intended by the actions.

About the Law

The law that declares which contracts must be in writing is called the Statute of Frauds. In its original form when it was passed by Parliament in 1677, it was known as the Act for the Prevention of Fraud and Perjuries.

EXAMPLE 7-1: Implied-in-Fact Deals: Can Inaction Create a Contract?

Herbert Ward watched workers employed by the Rice Lawn and Garden Greenhouse as they chemically treated his front lawn. In fact, Ward had no contract with Rice and had not ordered any chemical treatments of his property. The treatment should have been performed on another house at 750 Maple Street, instead of at Ward's, which had an address of 570 Maple St. Ward never stopped the work crew, even though he knew that a mistake had been made. Rice would be within its rights to believe that the work was being done with Ward's consent. In assessing damages for the cost of the improvement, the court would apply the objective concept rule. A reasonable person who might have watched Rice treat the front lawn would conclude that Ward had freely consented to the work.

An **implied-in-law contract** is imposed by a court when someone is unjustly enriched. It is used when a contract cannot be enforced or there is no actual written, oral, or implied-in-fact agreement. Applying reasons of justice and fairness, a court may obligate one who has unfairly benefited at the innocent expense of another. An implied-in-law contract is also called a **quasi-contract**.

EXAMPLE 7-2: Implied-in-Law Deals: Can Injustice Be Prevented?

Karl Rapp was found unconscious in his hotel room by Jan Stevens, the third-floor maid. She immediately called 911 and then notified Ken Kramer, the hotel manager. Kramer arranged to have Rapp placed in a hospital for emergency treatment. When Rapp regained consciousness, he refused to pay for the treatment, claiming that he was not aware of what was going on and had not agreed to what had been done to him. The case illustrates a quasi-contractual situation, wherein it would be unfair to allow the injured person to benefit at the expense of the hospital. In any suit that might arise over this expense, a court would require Rapp to pay the fair value of the services rendered.

The quasi-contract concept cannot apply, however, to obtain payment for an act that a party simply feels should be done. The concept also cannot be applied when one party bestows a benefit on another unnecessarily or through misconduct or negligence. A quasi-contract is not a contract in the true sense of the word, because it is created by the court. It does not result from the mutual assent of the parties, as do express or implied-in-fact contracts.

Informal and Formal Contracts

The law sometimes requires that contracts follow formalities prescribed by statute or common law. These are called formal contracts. All others are classified as informal.

Informal Contracts   Any oral or written contract that is not under seal or is not a contract of record is considered an **informal contract**. An informal contract is also known as a *simple contract*. An informal contract generally has no requirements as to language, form, or construction. It comprises obligations entered into by parties whose promises are expressed in the simplest and usually most ordinary, nonlegal language.

Formal Contracts   Under common law principles, a **formal contract** differs from other types of contracts in that it has to be (1) written; (2) signed, witnessed, and placed

UCC 2-203 (see page 925)

under the seal of the parties; and (3) delivered. A *seal* is a mark or an impression placed on a written contract indicating that the instrument was executed and accepted in a formal manner. The UCC removed the requirement for a seal in sale-of-goods contracts. Some states, however, still require the use of the seal in agreements related to the sale and transfer of real property.

Today, a person's seal may be any mark or sign placed after the signature intended to be the signer's seal. In states still requiring the seal or formal contract, it is sufficient to write the word *seal* after the signature.

EXAMPLE 7-3: Formal Contracts: Is a Seal Still Needed?

Audrey Kimmel signed an agreement with Corey Baumberger to buy seven acres of farmland owned by Baumberger just outside Bellville. Later that day, Baumberger found another interested buyer who was willing to pay seven times as much as Kimmel had offered for the land. Kimmel had signed the sales agreement without including any representation of the seal. In any state that required such formality in all real property contracts, Kimmel would now be helpless in attempting to enforce the original contract that she had made with Baumberger.

Contracts of Record A special type of formal contract is known as a **contract of record**. Often, such a contract is confirmed by the court with an accompanying judgment issued in favor of one of the parties. The judgment is recorded, giving the successful litigant the right to demand satisfaction of the judgment. A contract of record is not a contract in the true sense of the word, because it is court created. Although it does not have all of the elements of a valid contract, it is enforced for public policy reasons.

EXAMPLE 7-4: Contracts of Record: When Can Litigants Demand Their Money?

Mortimer Byrne installed a new roof on Alexander Harper's house in Lakeside for the agreed-upon price of $7,500. Harper paid Byrne $4,000 so that he could secure materials. After the job was completed, Byrne sent Harper a bill for $3,500. Harper sent Byrne a check for $2,500, on which was written "in full payment of all money owed." These words were in very fine print and not seen by Byrne. Byrne sued Harper in the small claims division of the Ottawa County Court of Common Pleas for the amount still owed. The court ruled in favor of Byrne and entered a judgment against Harper for the money owed. Entry of the judgment created a contract of record, which was enforceable against Harper.

Executory and Executed Contracts

A contract that has not yet been fully performed by the parties is called an **executory contract**. Such a contract may be completely executory, in which case nothing has been done, or it may be partly executory, in which case the contract is partially complete. When a contract's terms have been completely and satisfactorily carried out by both parties, it is an **executed contract**. Such contracts are no longer active agreements and are valuable only if a dispute about the agreement occurs.

quick quiz 7-3

1. A void contract is one that can be avoided by one or more of the parties.   true | false

2. A formal contract is also known as a simple contract.   true | false

3. A contract that has not yet been fully performed by the parties is called an executory contract.   true | false

Summary

7.1 With the Roman law providing a model, with the Roman Catholic Church supplying political and social support, with canon law supplying a moral framework, and with practicality guiding their activities over a 300-year period, the merchants of the late Middle Ages developed a body of active law that was characterized by neutrality, universality, mutuality, involvement, integration, and evolution. The law merchant was developed by the merchants themselves. The law merchant also successfully integrated itself into other legal tradition such as English common law. Many of its provisions still exist in today's court decisions and statutes.

7.2 Contract law is a multidimensional area of the law, laying out not only what our rights and duties are, but also whether we have actually undertaken those duties and been given those rights. To explore this in more detail, we looked at the elements of a contract and at several additional multidimensional aspects of contract law including the objectives of contract law, remedies in contract law, contracts and the UCC, contracts and other agreements, contracts and agency law, and contracts that must be written.

7.3 Contractual characteristics fall into five categories. These categories are valid, void, voidable, or unenforceable; unilateral or bilateral; express or implied; informal or formal; and executory or executed.

Key Terms

admiralty court, 173

bilateral contract, 185

breach of contract, 185

canon law, 171

capitalism, 170

contract, 169

contract of record, 188

executed contract, 188

executory contract, 188

express contract, 186

fair court, 173

formal contract, 187

implied contract, 186

implied-in-fact contract, 186

implied-in-law contract, 187

informal contract, 187

law merchant, 169

mercantile law, 169

objective concept rule, 186

pie powder court, 173

privity, 182

punitive damages, 181

quasi-contract, 187

rehabilitate, 180

staple court, 173

unenforceable contract, 185

unilateral contract, 185

valid contract, 185

void contract, 185

voidable contract, 185

Questions for Review and Discussion

1. What is a contract?
2. How did the law merchant develop?
3. How did the law merchant merge with common law?
4. What are the four elements of a contract?
5. What is the objective of contract law?
6. What is the role of the UCC in contract law?
7. How do contracts differ from other agreements?
8. What are the roles of privity and agency in contract law?
9. What contracts must be in writing to be enforceable?
10. What are the characteristics of a contract?

Cases for Analysis

1. The Borg–Warner Protective Services Corporation and Burns International Security Services contracted to provide security for the Cleveland Institute of Art (CIA). Robert Adelman was struck by an object thrown by a CIA student from the roof of one of the institute's buildings. Adelman sued both the CIA and the security corporations. The security corporations moved for summary judgment, arguing that they had contracted with CIA to protect the faculty and the students and that they therefore had no duty to protect pedestrians outside the buildings. Adelman argued that the contract specifically obligated the security corporations to control the activities of CIA students within the institute's buildings. The disputed clause read that the security corporations agreed "to control the movement and activities of students within the buildings at all hours." The trial court granted the summary judgment motion, and Adelman appealed. Should the appellate court reverse the decision of the lower court? Explain. If the case goes to trial, how will the court determine the meaning of the ambiguous clause? Explain. [See: *Adelman v. Timman,* 690 N.E.2d 1332 (OH).]

2. One of Stewart's clients gave him a check for $185.48. The check had been drawn up by the client's corporate employer and properly endorsed by the client. Nevertheless, the bank refused to cash the check for Stewart, even though there was enough money in the account to cover the $185.48. Could Stewart sue the bank for not cashing the check as he requested? Explain. [See: *J.E.B. Stewart v. Citizens and Southern National Bank,* 225 S.E.2d 761 (GA).]

3. Anderson, a farmer, orally agreed to buy a used tractor from the Copeland Equipment Company for $475. Copeland delivered the tractor to Anderson, who used it for 11 days. During this period, Anderson could not borrow enough funds to cover the purchase price. Anderson therefore returned the tractor to Copeland. Both parties agreed that their sales contract was canceled when the tractor was returned. However, Copeland later claimed that under the doctrine of quasi-contract, Anderson was required to pay for the 11-days' use of the tractor. Do you agree with Copeland? Explain your answer. [See: *Anderson v. Copeland,* 378 P.2d 1006 (OK).]

4. B.L. Nelson & Associates, Inc., entered into a contract with the city of Argyle to design and construct a sanitary sewer collection and treatment facility for the city. The city attempted to get out of the contract by citing certain provisions of the state constitution. These provisions made it illegal for the city to enter a contract for services if it did not have the money to pay for these services. Because the city did not have the funds to pay Nelson, it argued that the contract was illegal and therefore void. Was the city correct? Explain. [See: *B.L. Nelson & Associates, Inc. v. City of Argyle,* 535 S.W.2d 906 (TX).]

5. Peters entered into a contract to purchase Dowling's business. The following terms were agreed to: (a) Peters would take over all of Dowling's executory contracts, (b) Peters would purchase Dowling's tools at an agreed-to price, (c) Peters would accept full responsibility for all warranties made by Dowling on previous contracts, and (d) Dowling would remain as a consultant to the new firm for a period of five years. Analyze each part of this contract and classify each term according to whether it is executed or executory. [See: *Wagstaff v. Peters,* 453 P.2d 120 (KS).]

6. The Roman Catholic Church was not always as supportive of capitalism as it eventually became. In fact, both Henri Sée in a study titled *Modern*

Capitalism and Harold Berman in his book *Law and Revolution* refer to the work of the French historian Henri Pirenne, who wrote extensively about the development of capitalism in Europe in the Middle Ages. According to Berman, Pirenne points out that the Church often took a decidedly anti-capitalist position, especially in relation to such things as moneylending and placing an unfair value on goods. On the other hand, Sée points out that, when circumstances were right in certain areas of Europe, notably the Low Countries of Holland and Zeeland, the Church was willing to support those emerging businessmen who worked diligently to create an authentic form of modern capitalism that included moneylending. Even Max Weber does not deny that certain theologians in the medieval Church managed to support the growth of capitalism. (Specifically, he refers to Anthony of Florence and Bernhard of Siena, although, to be fair, Weber does hide this reference in a lengthy footnote at the back of his book.) The question before us is this: What religious values would operate to oppose capitalism? What is it about the very nature of religious doctrine that places it in opposition to making a profit? On the other hand, what arguments can overcome this religious opposition to making a profit? Explain all your answers. [See: Harold J. Berman, *Law and Revolution: The Formation of the Western Legal Tradition,* (Cambridge: Harvard University Press, 1983); Henri Sée, *Modern Capitalism: Its Origin and Evolutions,* trans. Homer B. Vanderblue and Georges F. Doriot (New York: Adelphi Co. 1928); Max Weber, *The Protestant Ethic: The Spirit of Capitalism* (Mineola, NY: Dover, 2003).]

7. Mers was a sales rep for Dispatch Printing. His trainer at Dispatch assured him that, as long as he was a fairly good worker, he would have continued employment. Mers did better than this, earning numerous commendations and awards for having an exemplary sales record. Unfortunately, he was arrested for a felony and shortly thereafter was suspended from Dispatch. The director of the Dispatch Employee-Labor Relations Department told Mers that he would be reinstated when he received "a clean bill of health, a clean slate." Mers was also told that he would be reinstated with back pay. Mers' felony case went to trial and the result was a hung jury. Mers had not looked for another job during this time, and so when the prosecutor announced that the case would no longer be pursued, he went back to Dispatch with his "clean slate." At that point he was told that he could not have his job back. Mers looked for work for three years before finding another job. Mers sued Dispatch using *promissory estoppel* as one of his theories of recovery. Does Mers have a good promissory estoppel case here? Explain. [See: *Mers v. Dispatch Printing Company,* 39 Ohio App.3d 99 (1988).]

8. Janis O'Brien watched snowplow drivers employed by Shawn and Doug's Emergency Services as they plowed her driveway (which was 100 yards long up a steep grade from her home at 109 South Oberlin Road). O'Brien had no contract with Shawn and Doug's and had not ordered any snow removal that winter. The treatment should have been performed on a house at 109 Wayne Street, which was one street north of South Oberlin. O'Brien never stopped the plows, even though she knew that a mistake had been made. In April, when a $379 bill came for the plowing (it was a really, really bad winter) O'Brien refused to pay because she had no contract with Shawn and Doug's. She was, by the way, correct on this point. Does Shawn and Doug's have any contract law theory to work with, should it decide to take O'Brien to small claims court in Mayville County? Explain.

quick quiz Answers

7-1	7-2	7-3
1. T	1. T	1. F
2. T	2. T	2. F
3. T	3. F	3. T

Chapter 8

Offer, Acceptance, and Mutual Assent

THE OPENING CASE Round 1
The More Things Change the More They Stay the Same

Textbook explanations of offer, acceptance, and mutual assent are generally pretty straightforward. The offeror makes an offer, the offeree accepts, creating a "meeting of the minds," and mutual assent emerges. If only that happened in real life things would be so much easier. Case in point is the lawsuit known as *Sharp v. Andisman.* The Sharps put their house up for sale and Andisman and Blakeley made an offer to purchase the house for $1.2 million, well sort of—that is part of the problem. The offer was dated November 2. For personal reasons, Blakely's name was not on the offer, although he had indicated (and everyone seems to have believed) that he intended to pay cash. In contrast, Andisman's name was on the offer, but evidence indicates that she never signed it. A purchase agreement was then drawn up and signed by the Sharps on November 7. Later, despite Blakely's promise to pay cash, an addendum was drawn up stating that the agreement was contingent on Andisman getting a loan. This document was labeled Addendum A and signed by Andisman. On November 22 Andisman's loan was preapproved. Unfortunately, after further examination of her application, the mortgage broker withdrew the preapproval. Still, this withdrawal seems to have occurred simply because the application was incomplete. The missing information was never forthcoming. Instead, a new addendum was added to the offer. This happened

in May, the original closing date having long since faded into the past. This new addendum (designated Addendum C) removed the loan contingency, made Blakely party to the agreement, and changed the closing date to June 28. Both Andisman and Blakeley signed Addendum C and faxed it to the Sharps. The new closing date came and went, again with no action from the buyers. Eventually, the sellers gave up and filed suit on September 25. In their defense, Andisman and Blakely argued that the offer was never valid because (1) neither of them signed the offer in November, (2) acceptance was made contingent on a loan that was not approved, and (3) since "time was of the essence" in this agreement and they did not close on January 15, as noted in the offer, the agreement ended automatically by operation of law on that date. The trial court found for the Sharps and awarded them $575,000 for their losses plus over $29,000 in special damages. Andisman and Blakely appealed. Should the appellate court reverse the decision of the trial court? [See: *Sharp v. Andisman,* Nos. 24999, 25005 (2010-Ohio-4452).]

Opening Case Questions

1. Who is the offeror and who is the offeree in this case? Explain.

2. Was "time of the essence" in this case as the defendants argue? Why or why not? Explain.

3. What is a condition precedent? How does it differ from a condition concurrent and a condition subsequent? Explain.

4. Is the loan approval a condition precedent, a condition concurrent, or a condition subsequent in this case? Explain.

5. Should the fact that neither defendant signed the original offer end the case at that point? Explain.

LO Learning Objectives

1. Define mutual assent.
2. Identify the elements of an offer.
3. Explain the UCC's concept of offer in contract law.
4. Explain the nature of acceptance.
5. Define the mirror image rule.
6. Explain the process of revocation.
7. Identify those statutes that affect mutual assent in cyberspace.
8. Explain the elements of fraud and misrepresentation.
9. Identify the effects of mistake on mutual assent.
10. Describe duress and undue influence.

8-1 Mutual Assent and the Offer

Contractual relationships are, to a large extent, unique relationships that people enter voluntarily. Nevertheless, once a party has agreed to the terms of a contract, he or she has assumed a set of duties that are just as binding as those that are imposed automatically by law. This is why the courts and the legislatures have been very careful about spelling out the details involved in forming a contract. Many of these rules have evolved as part of the law merchant and common law. Others have been adopted by the legislature in response to social and economic changes such as the cyberspace revolution. Whatever the case, the objective of the law is to provide a proper balance between the duties of each party and their rights, both of which emerge in the contract-making process. To understand how this works we will first examine the nature of mutual assent and the method for creating that assent through the process of offer and acceptance.

The Nature of Mutual Assent

A **contract** is an agreement between two or more competent parties based on mutual promises and an exchange of things of value, to do or refrain from doing some particular thing that is neither illegal nor impossible. The agreement results in a set of duties that can be enforced in a court of law. The power of the courts to enforce these duties comes from the fact that both parties have agreed to accept those duties. This is **mutual assent**. It is the first of the four elements of a valid contract. The courts are fond of saying that mutual assent emerges when the parties to the contract have a "meeting of the minds." In other words, both parties know what the terms of the agreement are and both willingly agree to be bound by those terms. Mutual assent can be reached quickly as in buying a Kindle on Amazon.com, or it may result from a long and involved series of negotiations as in the purchase of a house. Whatever the case, the assent that emerges comes from a communication of an open offer by an offeror that is authentically accepted by the offeree. The twin keys to mutual assent then are an "open offer" and "authentically accepted." Remember those key terms.

Requirements of an Offer

An **offer** is a proposal freely made by one party to another indicating a willingness to enter a contract. The person who makes the offer is the **offeror** and the person to whom it is made is the **offeree**. If certain requirements are met, the court concludes that the parties intended to make and accept an offer. In the case of an open offer, the courts have established three elements that must exist: (1) serious intent; (2) clear and reasonably definite terms; and (3) communication to the offeree. We now turn to a discussion of these requirements.

Serious Intent An offeror's offer is invalid if that offeror makes the alleged offer as a joke, during an emotional outburst of rage or anger, or under circumstances that convey a lack of seriousness. The offeror's words and actions must give the offeree assurance that a binding agreement is intended. This is what makes an offer an open offer, that is, it is open to acceptance by the offeree. Serious intent will be present within the actions and the words of the offeror. (see Table 8-1)

Clear and Reasonably Definite Terms The communicated terms of an offer must be sufficiently clear to remove all doubt about the contractual intentions of the offeror. No valid offer will exist when terms are indefinite, inadequate, vague, contradictory, or confusing. To determine whether the terms in the alleged offer are clear and definite enough, ask whether the terms are so clear that, if there were a breach, the court would know how to assess a remedy. If the answer is yes, the terms are probably definite enough. If the answer is no, then some critical term in the alleged offer is missing or too obscure to create a contract.

The Statute of Frauds As noted in Chapter 7, the *Statute of Frauds* outlines those contracts that must be in writing to be enforceable in court. This requirement makes the Statute of Frauds a very effective legal tool for determining intent. In fact, one of the major goals of the Statute of Frauds is to provide detailed information about the terms of an agreement. Moreover, as we have seen, the first rule of contract interpretation is the

Table 8-1 Requirements of an Offer

Requirement	Explanation
Serious intent	The offeror's words must give the offeree assurance that a binding agreement is intended.
Clarity and reasonably definite terms	The terms of an offer must be sufficiently clear to remove any doubt about the contractual intentions of the offeror. Most courts require reasonable rather than absolute definiteness.
Communication to the offeree	The proposed offer must be communicated to the offeree by whatever means are convenient and desirable. The communication of the offer can be express or implied. Public offers are made through the media but are intended for one party whose identity or address is unknown. Invitations to trade are not offers.

THE OPENING CASE *Round 2*
The More Serious Things Are at the Start, the More Serious They Become in Time

In the opening case, we learned that the Sharps put their house up for sale and that Andisman and Blakeley made an offer to purchase the house for $1.2 million. The offer was written and dated November 2. However, for personal reasons involving a pending divorce, Blakely, who had promised to pay cash for this $1.2 million home, was not listed on the offer as one of the buyers. Andisman's name was on the offer, but evidence indicates that she never signed it. A purchase agreement was then put together and signed by the Sharps on November 7. Later, despite Blakely's promise to pay cash, an addendum was drawn up stating that the agreement was contingent on Andisman getting a loan. This document was labeled Addendum A and was later signed by Andisman. In June, long after the closing date had passed, a new addendum was added to the agreement. This new addendum (designated Addendum C) removed the loan contingency, made Blakely a party to the agreement, and changed the closing date to June 28. Both Andisman and Blakeley signed Addendum C and faxed it to the Sharps. The closing date came and went, with no action from the buyers. Eventually, the sellers gave up and filed suit on September 25. The trial court found for the Sharps and awarded them $575,000 to cover their losses plus over $29,000 in special damages. Andisman and Blakeley appealed. Both Andisman and Blakeley argued that the trial judge was wrong in deciding the case for the Sharps because (1) Andisman had never signed the agreement and (2) Blakeley's name was not listed on either the offer or the agreement. The appellate court disagreed. The appellate court noted that the Restatement of the Law of Contracts allows the court to look at a series of documents to verify the terms of the agreement, even without explicit statements that the new documents are to be incorporated into the original documents. In this case, Andisman had signed Addendum A and Blakeley had signed Addendum C, both of which did contain explicit language that incorporated them into the original documents. This was enough for the court to establish the conclusion that both Andisman and Blakeley had what amounted to serious intent to be bound by the offer and the agreement. [See: *Sharp v. Andisman,* Nos. 24999, 25005 (2010-Ohio-4452).]

standard construction rule, which tells judges that their primary objective in the interpretation of a written contract is to uncover the goals that the parties had when they entered the contract. To accomplish this goal, the writing must be intelligible, but it need not follow any preset format. Nor does the written contract have to be one single continuous document. The parties' goals and, therefore, their intent, can be determined by looking at a series of written documents as long as the court can identify a continuous connection among those separate documents. Thus, intent can be found by examining letters, memos, documents, invoices, packing slips, and purchase orders that have been mailed, privately delivered, faxed, or sent electronically between the parties. It certainly helps when the parties explicitly add labels such as "Addendum C." However, the Restatement of the Law of Contracts also states that the "(e)xplicit incorporation (of the other documents) by reference is not necessary" (Section 132).

Degree of Definiteness In general, an offer should include points similar to those covered in a newspaper story—who, what, when, where, and how much—if it is to be clear, definite, and certain. This requirement means that the offer should identify (1) the parties involved in the contract, (2) the goods or services that will be the subject matter of the contract, (3) the price the offeror is willing to pay or receive, and (4) the time required for the performance of the contract. Most courts require reasonable rather than absolute definiteness. Offers will be upheld as long as the language is reasonably definite enough to enable the court to establish what the parties intended the terms to be so that, should there be a breach, a remedy can be set.

Time for Performance

When the time for performance is not stated in the offer or in the final contract, then the contract must be performed within a reasonable time. A **reasonable time** is the time that may fairly, properly, and conveniently be required to do the task that is to be done, considering attending circumstances. Whether a task is performed within a reasonable time is a question of fact to be decided by the jury in a jury trial or the judge in a nonjury trial. When the time for performance is stated in the contract but there is nothing to indicate that time is of particular importance, the court will usually allow additional time to perform. When the time for performance is stated in the contract and there is something special about the contract that indicates time is essential, the time for performance will be strictly enforced. Similarly, when the phrase **time is of the essence** is included among the terms of a written contract, the time period will be enforced. The key words "time is of the essence" are the "magic words" that make it clear that time of performance is of the highest importance to the parties. Some contracts use a "best efforts" clause to avoid committing parties to a date but instead committing them to do their best to perform by a certain date.

Offers and the UCC

The UCC permits offers to omit certain information. It states that "even though one or more terms are left open, a contract for sale does not fail for indefiniteness if the parties have intended to make a contract and there is a reasonably certain

THE OPENING CASE *Round 3*
The More Time You Have, the Longer the Job Takes

In the opening case, we learned that the Sharps put their house up for sale and that Andisman and Blakely made an offer to purchase that house for $1.2 million. The offer was written and dated November 2. However, for personal reasons involving a pending divorce, Blakely, who had promised to pay cash for this $1.2 million home, was not listed on the offer as one of the buyers. Andisman's name was on the offer, but evidence indicates that she never signed it. A purchase agreement was then put together and signed by the Sharps on November 7. Later, despite Blakely's promise to pay cash, an addendum was drawn up stating that the agreement was contingent on Andisman getting a loan. This document was labeled Addendum A and was later signed by Andisman. Addendum A also included a closing date of January 15. In June, long after the closing date had passed, a new addendum was added to the agreement. This new addendum (designated Addendum C) removed the loan contingency, made Blakely party to the agreement, and changed the closing date to June 28. Both Andisman and Blakeley signed Addendum C and faxed it to the

Sharps. The closing date came and went, with no action from the buyers. Eventually, the sellers gave up and filed suit on September 25. The trial court found for the Sharps and awarded them $575,000 to cover their losses plus over $29,000 in special damages. Andisman and Blakeley argued on appeal that the trial court judge was wrong because the closing date of January 15 meant that "time was of the essence" and, since that closing date was not met, the contract had ended automatically as a matter of law at that time. The appellate court disagreed. First, not one of the written documents in the negotiation process, not the offer, not the agreement, not Addendum A, not one of them used the phrase "time is of the essence." Second, nothing that Andisman and Blakeley did, said, or wrote after January 15 indicated that they treated January 15 as a necessary deadline in the negotiation process. Finally, in May, Addendum C was drawn up adding a new closing date of June 28, indicating that January 15 was not "of the essence" as Andisman and Blakeley were now claiming. [See: *Sharp v. Andisman*, Nos. 24999, 25005 (2010-Ohio-4452).]

basis for giving an appropriate remedy." Under this section of the UCC, cost-plus contracts, output contracts, requirement contracts, and current market price contracts are enforceable even though they are not complete in certain matters. A **cost-plus contract** does not include a final price; rather, the contract price is determined by the cost of labor and materials, plus an agreed-to percentage or dollar markup. A **requirements contract** is an agreement in which one party agrees to buy all of the goods it needs from the second party. The terms of a requirements contract must be carefully worded. If the agreement allows the buyer to purchase only those goods that the buyer desires or wishes, the agreement is unenforceable, because it is illusory in that the buyer is not really obligated to do anything. An **output contract** is an agreement in which one party consents to sell to a second party all of the goods that party makes in a given period of time. Finally, a **current market price contract** is one in which prices are determined by reference to the market price of the goods as of a specified date.

UCC 2-204 (3) (see page 925)

Communication to the Offeree To be valid an offer must be freely communicated to the offeree. The offeror's intent may be communicated by whatever means are convenient and desirable. For example, the offer may be communicated orally, by mail, by fax, by e-mail, by text, or by any other capable means. It may be implied. The proposing party's acts and conduct in many cases are successful in communicating the intention to make an offer to another party that witnesses them. When acts and conduct are sufficient to convey an offeror's intentions, an implied offer results.

Public Offers At times, an offer must be communicated to a party whose name, identity, or address is unknown. In such cases, the public offer is made. A **public offer** is one that is made through the public media but is intended for only one person whose identity or address is unknown to the offeror. A classic example of a public offer is an advertisement in a lost-and-found notice on an electronic bulletin board. Although it is a public offer, it is legally no different from other types of offers.

Invitations to Trade By contrast, invitations to trade are not offers. An **invitation to trade** is an announcement published to reach many persons for the purpose of creating interest and attracting responses. Newspaper and magazine advertisements, radio and television commercials, store window displays, price tags on merchandise, for rent signs, and prices in catalogs fall within this definition. In the case of an invitation to trade, no binding agreement develops until a responding party makes an offer that the advertiser accepts. Probably one of the most common invitations to trade is the listing price for real property. A **list price** for real property is the price that the seller asks initially when the property is placed on the market. The price is an invitation to the buyer to make an offer. Traditionally, there is little expectation that the buyer will actually make an offer based on that price. The expectation is that the buyer will make an offer at a price under the list price, which the seller will then respond to with a counteroffer. Counteroffers are discussed below.

In very rare circumstances, advertisements may be held to be offers. However, such advertisements would have to contain very particular promises, use phrases like "first-come, first-served," or limit the number of items to be sold. Because the number of people who can buy the product is very limited, the advertisement becomes an offer.

Auctions An **auction** is a sale that is open to the public, during which potential buyers compete for the right to purchase certain items by placing higher and higher bids until the highest bid is reached and the auctioneer accepts on behalf of the seller. Many people have the mistaken belief that in an auction the original property owner, that is, the seller, is the offeror and that the bidder is the offeree. These roles are true only if the auction has been expressly labeled as an **auction without reserve**. If the auction has not been so designated, it is considered an **auction with reserve**, which means that the bidders are the offerors and the seller is the offeree. Consequently, the seller can stop the bidding at any time that he or she wants, up to the time that the auctioneer declares a winner, generally by striking the podium with the gavel. A seller can also control the bidding somewhat if he or she establishes the lowest acceptable bid. In such a case, should the auctioneer *not* hear a bid that meets the least possible bid, he or she can reject all of those bids, and the seller retains the property.

Bait-and-Switch Confidence Games The **bait-and-switch confidence game** is a deliberately deceptive practice that entices buyers into a place of business when the seller actually has no intention of selling the item at the price stated in the advertisement. The practice has been outlawed by the Federal Trade Commission. In addition, many, and perhaps most, states have similar laws prohibiting bait-and-switch confidence games.

---

quick quiz 8-1

1. The person who freely makes an offer is called an offeree.	true | false
2. An offer is valid only if it has (a) serious intent, (b) clear and reasonably definite terms, and (c) communication to the offeree.	true | false
3. No valid offer will exist when terms are indefinite, inadequate, vague, or confusing.	true | false

---

8-2 Acceptance of an Offer

The second major element in a binding contract is acceptance of the offer. As previously stated, **acceptance** means that the offeree agrees to be bound by the terms set up by the offeror. Only the offeree, the one to whom the offer is made, has the right to accept the offer. If another party attempts to accept, that attempt would actually be a new and independent offer.

Unilateral contracts do not usually require oral or written communication of an acceptance. When the offeror makes a promise in a unilateral contract, the offeror expects an action, not another promise in return. Performance of the action requested within the time allowed by the offeror and with the offeror's knowledge creates the contract.

In bilateral contracts, unlike unilateral ones, the offeree must communicate acceptance to the offeror. Bilateral contracts consist of a promise by one party in return for a promise by the other. Until the offeree communicates a willingness to be bound by a promise, there is no valid acceptance.

Conditions of Performance
Some offers include conditions or terms that determine the rights and duties of the parties before performance, during performance, and following performance. These conditions may be classified as conditions precedent, conditions concurrent, or conditions subsequent. A **condition precedent** is a condition that requires the performance of certain acts or promises before the other party is obligated to pay money or provide any other agreed to consideration. In a *unilateral contract,* the performance of a condition precedent serves as the offeree's acceptance of the offer. In a *bilateral contract,* it is a promise that, if not performed, leads to either rescission or termination of the entire

THE OPENING CASE *Round 4*
Conditions Precedent, Loan Applications, and Good Faith

In the opening case, we learned that the Sharps had their house for sale and Andisman and Blakeley made an offer to purchase that house for $1.2 million. The offer was written and dated November 2. Blakely, who had promised to pay cash for this $1.2 million home, was not listed on the offer. Andisman's name was listed but she never signed it. A purchase agreement was then signed by the Sharps on November 7. Later, despite Blakely's promise to pay cash, an addendum was drawn up stating that agreement was contingent on Andisman getting a loan. This document was labeled Addendum A and later signed by Andisman. On November 22 Andisman's loan was preapproved, then returned unapproved, because the application was incomplete. The missing information was never supplied by Andisman. In June, a new addendum (Addendum C) removed the loan contingency, made Blakely party to the agreement, and changed the closing date to June 28. Both Andisman and Blakely signed Addendum C and faxed it to the Sharps. The new closing date came and went, with no action from the buyers.

Eventually, the sellers filed suit. The trial court found for the Sharps. Andisman and Blakeley argued on appeal that the trial court judge had erred in deciding the case for the Sharps because Addendum A set up a condition precedent that made the agreement dependent upon the approval of her loan application. Since the loan application had not been approved, the contract had never been finalized and, therefore, they cannot be held liable for breaching a contract that never existed. The court of appeals rejected this argument out of hand. The appellate court noted that Andisman had short-circuited the loan application herself by not supplying the extra material requested by the mortgage broker. Moreover, evidence demonstrated that Andisman never intended to obtain the loan. In fact, it appears that she did not even believe that she could obtain the loan, despite starting the application process. The appellate court concludes that Andisman cannot profit from her own refusal to meet the terms of the condition precedent. [See: *Sharp v. Andisman*, Nos. 24999, 25005 (2010-Ohio-4452).]

agreement. A common condition precedent is one that declares that the agreement will not be finalized and the contract will not exist until the buyer can obtain acceptable financing.

A condition that requires both parties to perform at the same time is a **condition concurrent**. A promise to deliver goods supported by the buyer's promise to pay on delivery is a very common condition concurrent. Real estate sales agreements, by custom, usually state that the owner–seller will deliver a good and complete deed to the real property on the buyer's presentation of either cash or a certified check for the amount of the purchase price. Failure of either to do as promised concurrently would be a breach of the express contract condition. A **condition subsequent** is one in which the parties agree that the contract will be terminated when a prescribed event occurs or does not occur. An agreement between a builder and a client stating that contract performance would terminate if required building permits were not obtained from the issuing public authority within 60 days after the contract is signed is a condition subsequent.

Communication of Acceptance

The communication of the acceptance of an offer may be either express or implied. In an express acceptance, the offeree chooses any method of acceptance, unless the offer states that the acceptance must be made in a particular manner. A stipulation such as "reply by fax" or "reply by e-mail" included in the offer must be carried out to achieve acceptance.

THE OPENING CASE *Round 5*
Faxing Does "In Fax" Work

In the opening case, we learned that the Sharps put their house up for sale and Andisman and Blakeley made an offer to purchase that house for $1.2 million. The offer was dated November 2. However, for personal reasons involving a pending divorce, Blakely, who had promised to pay cash for this $1.2 million home, was not listed on the offer as one of the buyers. Andisman's name was printed on the offer, but she never signed it. A purchase agreement was signed by the Sharps on November 7. Later, an addendum was drawn up stating that agreement was contingent on Andisman getting a loan. This document was labeled Addendum A and later signed by Andisman. In June, long after the closing date had passed, a new addendum was added to the agreement. This new addendum (designated Addendum C) removed the loan contingency, made Blakely party to the agreement, and changed the closing date to June 28. Both Andisman and Blakeley signed Addendum C and faxed it to the Sharps. The faxed document was accepted just as if it had been hand-delivered. Of all the things that went wrong in this case, and we have seen there were quite a few, the use of a fax machine to deliver Addendum C was not one of them. [See: *Sharp v. Andisman,* Nos. 24999, 25005 (2010-Ohio-4452).]

Face-to-Face and Telephone Communication No special problem as to the timing of acceptance usually arises if the parties are dealing face-to-face. The acceptance becomes complete and effective as soon as the offeror hears the words of acceptance spoken by the offeree. In a similar vein, if the parties are negotiating over the telephone, the acceptance becomes effective when the offeree speaks the words of acceptance into the telephone receiver (see Table 8-2). When the parties negotiate by mail, private courier, e-mail, or fax, problems may arise, and the law provides certain rules as to when acceptance occurs.

Table 8-2 Communication of Acceptance

Method Used	Legal Effect
Face-to-face communication	Acceptance is complete and effective when offeror hears the words of acceptance.
Telephone communication	Acceptance is complete and effective when offeror hears the words of acceptance.
Text messages	Acceptance is complete when text message is sent, if offeror has asked for a text response. If not, the acceptance is complete when sent, only if a text message is faster than the requested method.
Authorized means of communication	Acceptance is complete and effective when given by that same medium (e.g., mailed offer is accepted when acceptance is dropped in the mail).
Acceptance improperly dispatched	Acceptance is complete and effective when it actually reaches offeror.

Long-Distance Communication Under traditional common law principles, if a long-distance acceptance is made by an authorized method of communication, the acceptance is effective when it is sent. An authorized means of communication is one that has been endorsed by the offeror. The endorsement can be made either expressly or by implication. An acceptance is expressly endorsed by the offeror if he or she specifies the means of acceptance to be used by the offeror. Under traditional common law rules, an authorization of an acceptance is implied when the offeree accepts by the same means or by a means that is faster than that used to make the offer. Thus, an offer made through the mail is accepted when the acceptance is mailed or sent by a faster means such as a private courier (DHL, FedEx, or UPS), a fax, a phone call, an e-mail, or an in-person visit.

Text Messages Text-messages have become an integral, accepted method of communicating in many people's daily routine. It is quite common for people to "text" one another about informal, personal matters. However, texting business colleagues is another matter entirely. While text messages are efficient and fast, they are also, by nature and design, without detailed content. These shortcomings probably explain why texting is still not the usual way to communicate in the business world. Nevertheless, should an offeror ask for a text message acceptance, the offeree should not hesitate to respond as requested. An acceptance will be valid when sent if the offeree uses a technique requested or endorsed by the offeror. However, it is also good practice to follow up such an acceptance with something more detailed and more permanent, such as a confirmation letter.

The offer can dictate the form of acceptance required. If using an e-mail or text message to accept an offer, always follow up with a written and signed correspondence to create a permanent record.

The Uniform Commercial Code The Uniform Commercial Code asserts that a contract comes into existence if any reasonable means is used to communicate the acceptance. The UCC is quite explicit in noting that to establish a contract for the sale of goods, unless otherwise indicated by the offeror or by the circumstances, the offeree may accept the offer in any manner and by any medium that is reasonable. A contract for the sale of goods then comes into existence when the acceptance is sent, as long as the method used to send is reasonable. The actual text of this rule is found in UCC 2-206 (1) (a).

Unequivocal Acceptance

To be effective, an acceptance must be *unequivocal,* which means that the acceptance must not change any of the terms stated in the offer. Under common law, this requirement is known as the mirror image rule.

The Mirror Image Rule Under the mirror image rule, the terms as stated in the acceptance must exactly "mirror" the terms in the offer. If the acceptance changes or qualifies the terms in the offer, it is not an acceptance. A qualified acceptance is actually a counteroffer. A counteroffer is a response to an offer in which the terms of the original offer are changed. No agreement is reached unless the counteroffer is accepted by the original offeror.

Counteroffers under the UCC The UCC has changed the mirror image rule for sale-of-goods contracts. Under the UCC, as long as there is a definite expression of acceptance, a contract will come into existence, even if an acceptance has different or additional terms. If the parties are not both merchants, the different or additional terms are treated as proposals for additions to the contract. If both parties are merchants however, the

UCC 2-207 (see page 925)

different or additional terms become part of the contract unless (1) they make an important difference to the contract, (2) the offeror objects, or (3) the offer limits acceptance to its terms. This exception is discussed further in Chapter 13.

Implied Acceptance

Acceptance may result from the conduct of the offeree. Actions and gestures may indicate the offeree's willingness to enter into a binding agreement.

Unordered merchandise delivered by mail can be treated as a gift by the recipient. If a package is delivered by an agency other than the post office, the disposition of the merchandise is determined by state law.

Unordered Merchandise According to the Postal Reorganization Act, the recipient of unordered merchandise through the mail may treat such goods as a gift. The receiver has no obligation to pay for or return the goods or to communicate with the sender in any way. When unordered merchandise is delivered by agencies other than the post office, the common law rule is usually followed. Under the common law rule, the receiver is not obligated to contact the sender or to pay for the goods. There is, however, an implied obligation to retain the good and give them reasonable care over a reasonable period of time. After that time, the receiver may consider that the sender no longer claims the goods and may use or dispose of them as desired. Some states, however, have laws similar to the postal law that allows recipients of unordered goods to consider them as gifts no matter who delivers them.

Silence as Acceptance

As a general rule, in most situations, the offeror cannot bind the offeree just by declaring that the offeree's silence will signal an acceptance. However, should both parties agree that silence on the part of the offeree will be regarded as an acceptance, then the offeree's silence would operate as a valid acceptance.

A QUESTION OF ETHICS

Suppose, after conducting a survey that revealed most people did not know about their rights under the Postal Reorganization Act, a company began a mailing campaign that sent unordered merchandise to certain targeted groups. Would such a move be ethical? Explain.

Another exception to the general rule occurs when the offeree has allowed silence to act as an acceptance. The offeror cannot force the offeree into a contract by saying silence will mean acceptance. The offeree, however, can force the offeror into a contract if the offeror set up the silence condition.

EXAMPLE 8-1: Who Can Make Silence Acceptance?

Jason Riley wanted to sell his 1962 Volkswagen. He wrote a letter to Rita Tenpenny offering to sell the Volkswagen to Tenpenny for $25,000. Riley ended the letter by stating, "If I don't hear from you by December 3 of this year, I will take your silence to mean you accept my offer." Tenpenny received the letter and did not reply. Although Riley could not bind Tenpenny to this contract, Tenpenny could hold Riley to his offer because Riley set up the silence condition himself.

Rejection and Revocation

A **rejection** comes about when an offeree expresses or implies a refusal to accept an offer. Rejection terminates an offer and all negotiations associated with it. Further negotiations could commence with a new offer by either party or a renewal of the original offer by the offeror. Rejection is usually achieved when communicated by the offeree. A **revocation** is the calling back of the offer by the offeror. With the exception of an option contract and a firm offer, an offer may be revoked any time before it is accepted. The offeror has this right, despite what might appear to be a strong moral obligation to continue the offer. An offer may be revoked by the following methods and circumstances: communication, death or insanity of the offeror, automatic revocation, destruction of the subject matter, passage of time, and the subsequent illegality of the contract.

Option Contracts

An **option contract** is an agreement that binds an offeror to a promise to hold open an offer for a predetermined or a reasonable length of time. In return for this agreement, the offeror receives money or something else of value from the offeree. Parties to an option contract often agree that the consideration may be credited toward any indebtedness incurred by the offeree in the event that the offer is accepted. Should the offeree fail to take up the option, however, the offeror is under no legal obligation to return the consideration. An option contract removes the possibility of revocation through death or insanity of the offeror. The offeree who holds the option contract may demand acceptance by giving written notice of acceptance to the executor or administrator of the deceased offeror's estate or to the offeror's legally appointed guardian.

About the Law

Although the Ch'ing Dynasty, which ruled China from 1644 to 1911, codified the law of criminal offenses, it left civil law, for the most part, in the hands of the family and clan.

EXAMPLE 8-2: Who Controls an Option Agreement?

Takashi Osaka offered to sell Andras Galai a collection of rare Japanese prints for $755,000. Galai requested time to consider the offer, and Osaka agreed to hold the collection for Galai for one week in return for Galai's payment of $755. Osaka died several days later. When Galai tendered the $755,000, the executor refused to deliver the collection, claiming that death had revoked the offer. The court ruled otherwise, with judgment given to the offeree based on the option agreement between Galai and the deceased.

Firm Offers and Sale of Goods Contracts A special rule that involves the creation of a firm offer has been developed under the Uniform Commercial Code. A **firm offer** is created when a merchant agrees in writing to hold an offer open. Under this condition, no consideration is needed to hold the offer open. A firm offer may be made for a specified period of time. If no time limit is specified, then the offer may remain open for a reasonable amount of time. However, the upper limit for a firm offer is three months. Remember that a firm offer under the UCC involves only sale-of-goods contracts.

UCC 2-205 (see page 925)

Lease Options and Real Property A **lease option** is a contract that permits a party to lease real property while at the same time holding an option to purchase that property. Generally, to hold open the option to purchase the leased property, the person leasing the property will make an additional deposit beyond the amount that an ordinary renter would make, so that he or she retains the opportunity to purchase that property at a later time. Because a lease option involves two separate contracts, the lease contract and the option contract, it is often divided into two documents. The lease contract will detail the terms of the lease, whereas the option contract will outline the terms under which the renter can exercise the option to purchase the property.

8-3 Mutual Assent in Cyberspace

The legal system, as we have seen, operates as a complex adaptive system (CAS) that emerges from a network of interacting conditions that reinforce one another while, at the same time, adjusting to change from agents outside and inside the system. These systems, however, do not act independently of one another. Rather, they overlap, interact, and sometimes compete with one another. The technological CAS has interacted with the law to produce a new subset in the legal system called cyber-law or e-law. Cyber-law helps integrate the use of computers with the orthodox operation of the legal CAS. In many situations, the courts and the legislatures have *proactively integrated* the orthodox legal system with cyber-contracts, electronic contracts, or e-contracts, that is, contracts that are made with computers or that involve computer-related products. This active approach is seen in new developments in the Uniform Commercial Code and the Restatement of the Law of Contracts. This proactive process is also seen in several laws passed by Congress and others sponsored by National Conference of Commissioners on Uniform State Laws. The new rules are found in the federal Electronic Signatures in Global and National Commerce Act (E-Sign Act), the Uniform Electronic Transactions Act, and the Uniform Computer Information Transactions Act. At other times, however, the law has simply *passively reacted* to innovative cyber breakthroughs, such as those that involve social media and cloud storage techniques.

The E-Sign Act

The E-Sign Act was passed by Congress several years ago and represents an effort to make certain that commercial cyber-documents are given the same credence as their paper counterparts. Simply stated, the act provides that cyber-contracts that are entered into over the Internet or via e-mail will be valid, provided that the parties to the e-contract have agreed that electronic signatures will be used. As long as the cyber-contract can be duplicated and stored, it will have the same validity as a paper contract. The act expressly applies to Article 2 (Sale of Goods Contracts) and Article 2A (Leases) of the UCC.

The Uniform Electronic Transactions Act

The Uniform Electronic Transactions Act (UETA) was written by the NCCUSL to ensure that cyber-contracts are given the same legal effect as their paper equivalents. The act does not create any new rules applying to mutual assent, consideration, capacity, and legality but instead makes certain that the laws that govern these elements apply to cyber-contracts just as they apply to paper contracts. There are three basic elements under the UETA. First, the participants must concur on the use of an electronic medium to create their contractual relationship. This agreement is usually not a problem, because the parties to a cyber-contract are generally aware of the nature of their relationship when they sit down at a computer. Second, once the first requirement is met, the act says that the electronic record generated by the computerized transaction will have the same weight that a paper document would have in a traditional transaction. Third, once the first requirement is met, the act acknowledges that an cyber-signature is just as effective as a written signature on a paper document.

The Uniform Computer Information Transactions Act

The Uniform Computer Information Transactions Act (UCITA) arose when the Uniform Law Commission (ULC) and the ALI attempted to revise Article 2 (Sale of Goods Contracts) and Article 2A (Leases) of the UCC. Revising these articles to meet the demands of cyber-commerce and cyber-contractual relationships proved very difficult. In fact, the attempt was so difficult that the ALI dropped out of the process, leaving the ULC on its own. The ULC then elected to write an entirely new act that came to be known as UCITA. One of the problems encountered by the ULC in the writing of the new act was that many of the contracts that are entered into in cyberspace are more akin to licensing agreements than sale-of-goods contracts. The UCITA therefore covers such diverse areas as database contracts, software licensing agreements, customized software formulation, and the rights to multimedia commodities.

Many of the legal questions associated with Internet-made cyber-contracts are answered by the new act. For example, Section 102 of UCITA makes it clear that a license is to be considered "a contract that authorizes access to, or use, distribution, performance, modification, or reproduction of, information or information rights, but expressly limits the access or uses authorized or expressly grants fewer than all rights in the information, whether or not the transferee has title to a licensed copy." The UCITA has unified, streamlined, and refined the legal principles regarding such diverse areas as reverse engineering, consumer protection, shrink-wrap licenses, fair use, and consumer warranties. Despite all of this effort, the UCITA has been an extremely controversial act because many groups see it as increasing the rights and protections of software manufacturers rather than those of consumers.

Offer and Acceptance in Cyberspace

In addition to the terms included in most other offers, a cyber-offeror should insert the following terms in his or her offer: (1) payment criteria, (2) remedies that can be used by the offeree, (3) refund policies, (4) return procedures, (5) dispute settlement instructions, (6) the applicability of cyber-signatures, (7) liability disclaimers if needed, and (8) provisions relating to the offeree's manner of acceptance. In general, the offeree's acceptance in a cyber-contract is referred to as a "click-on acceptance" or a "click-on agreement." A click-on acceptance or a click-on agreement is one that is created by having a party click on a box on the computer screen that states he or she agrees to be bound by the terms of the contract. Otherwise, it is important to recall that, as explained previously, when the agreement deals with goods, the provisions of Article 2 of the UCC will apply.

Social Media, Offers, and Advertising

The proliferation of social media, including Facebook, Twitter, LinkedIn, websites, blogs, and so on, has led to interesting and unintended consequences in the world of cyber-contracts. Social media, when used properly and with appropriate caution, can be just as harmless as talking to someone at a ball game or after church. However, if handled improperly, the misuse of social media can inadvertently lead to unintended offers and perhaps, even worse, to accusations of fraud or misrepresentation. As a general rule, it is best to think of social media as a way of interacting with others unofficially. This is not to say that social media cannot be used as advertising, or as a way to make or accept an offer. On the contrary, it is good business to have a visible presence online. In the 21st century, shoppers and clients no longer run to the Yellow Pages or to the newspaper to search for professionals. Instead, they look to the Web. However, professionals who use the Web must do so in a carefully planned way.

Businesspeople, such as accountants, architects, financial advisors, and attorneys, who are regulated by professional organizations must be especially careful about their use of social media. Attorneys, for example, must pay special attention to what the Model Rules of Professional Conduct say about advertising and soliciting business and then apply those rules on an ad hoc basis to social media. For instance, under Rule 7.2 lawyers are permitted to advertise but under Rule 7.1 those advertisements must not be "false or misleading." Lawyers must, therefore, be especially careful not to cross these sometimes vague rules when constructing profiles on LinkedIn and Facebook, when blogging, when texting, and when using Twitter. Exaggerating or making unsubstantiated claims in an offhanded way on a Facebook page may come very close to crossing that invisible line between an informal and harmless chat and a false advertisement.

Professionals are not the only ones who need to be careful when using social media for business purposes. Commercial speech is constitutionally protected, but to earn that protection all commercial speech must be truthful. Blogs that guarantee the outcome of a case or that fabricate untrue stories about products and services have probably crossed the line. Creating a false identity when blogging or when offering testimonials, a practice known as **sock puppetry**, is also not a good idea. [See: Josh King, "Being Smart with Social Media: Ethics and Effectiveness when Engaging Online," Ohio State Bar Association 2014 Annual Convention (April 30 to May 2, 1014).]

Managing "The Cloud" When Making and Accepting Offers

Cloud storage (or cloud computing) is a cyber-technique that preserves electronic data without using local hard drives and flash drives. Instead the data is transferred to a data center that stores the data on a remote database. The data owner (or data depositor) can then access the data from anywhere by request through the Internet. Since the data is not kept on the data owner's hard drive, the owner is not tied to his or her own computer or storage device and thus gains a great deal of flexibility. Generally, the data center's storage capacity is also much greater than the storage ability of the data owner. Data centers also tend to keep current with the latest developments in Web applications. Moreover, the data is accessible no matter what electronic device (smartphones, tablets, laptops, and so on) the data owner might use. All of this sounds quite good, until we recall that often the information contained in an offer, such as the asking price, the details of the negotiation process, the price mentioned in counteroffer, the nature, timing, and technique of the acceptance must be kept secure and confidential.

Such might be true if the transaction involves a bidding contest for a construction contract or the auctioning of a unique item, such as a rare antiquity or an original work of art. This fact means that businesspeople using the cloud during the offer and acceptance steps in the creation of a contract should take the necessary steps to preserve the confidentiality of such data while it is kept within the cloud. Often data can be kept secure by using encryption measures, a list of sanctioned users, and a verification process. Data centers should also protect stored e-data with redundancy procedures that back up the data and thus protects it from theft, hacking, and a loss of electrical service. [See: Jonathan Strickland, "How Cloud Storage Works," *How Stuff Works* (2008), retrieved on January 11, 2013, from http:/computer.howstuffworks.com; Barron Henley, "Legal Technology Tips, Tricks, Gadgets, and Websites," Ohio State Bar Association 2013 Annual Convention (May 8-10, 2013).]

CLASSIC CASE From Invitation, to Offer, to Acceptance

The Great Minneapolis Surplus Store published the following advertisement in a Minneapolis newspaper:

> Saturday 9 A.M. Sharp 3 Brand New Fur Coats Worth to $100.00. First Come First Served $1 Each.

On April 13, the store published another advertisement in the same newspaper:

> Saturday 9 A.M. 2 Brand New Pastel Mink 3-Skin Scarfs
> Selling for $89.50
> Out they go Saturday. Each . . . $1.00
> 1 Black Lapin Stole Beautiful, worth $139.50 . . . $1.00
> First Come First Served

Following the clear instructions in the advertisement, Mr. Lefkowitz traveled to the Great Minneapolis Surplus Store and arrived early enough to be the first customer to enter the store at 9 A.M. He had his dollar in hand and was ready to purchase the black lapin stole. However, he was informed that the sale was designed only for the store's women customers. Lefkowitz protested, but was unable to get satisfaction from the store. Accordingly, he did what any red-blooded American would do—he filed a lawsuit. The store

argued, rather convincingly, that a newspaper advertisement like the one run by the store was not an offer but was, instead, only an invitation to make an offer. The advertisement was like the "For Sale" sign in front of a house or the price posted on a motor vehicle at a used car lot. In all such cases, the buyer is the offeror and the seller is the offeree. That permits the Great Minneapolis Surplus Store to refuse to honor the customer's offer—end of story. Lefkowitz disagreed. To prove his point he submitted the following argument. The advertisement in the newspaper is definite enough to pinpoint every element necessary in a contract. The advertisement identifies the subject matter (one black lapin stole), the price (one American dollar), the place of the sale (the department store), the day and time of the sale (Saturday morning at 9), and the buyer as the first person to show up at the store (first come, first served). That much detail turns the invitation into an offer that he, Leftkowitz, accepted. Therefore, the store could not at that point refuse to sell, at least not without some sort of legal consequences. The court agreed. [See: *Lefkowitz v. Great Minneapolis Surplus Store, Inc.,* 86 N.W.2d 689 (Minn. 1957).]

quick quiz 8-3

1. The Uniform Electronic Transactions Act (UETA) was passed by Congress as a federal law.   true | false

2. The Electronic Signatures in Global and National Commerce Act was written by the Uniform Law Commission.   true | false

3. The process of accepting an online offer is often referred to as a "click-on agreement."   true | false

8-4 The Destruction of Mutual Assent

As is true of most other parts of the legal system, contract law seeks to balance the rights and the duties of two or more parties. In contract law those two parties are the offeror and the offeree and the rights and the duties are assumed voluntarily. The balance emerges from a dialectic that pairs the offer with the acceptance and sets the stage for the development of a synthesis between the two. That synthesis is referred to as mutual assent. As the first element of a contract, mutual assent must stand on its own, without being propped up by artificial supports. Mutual assent, however, can be elusive. Unfortunately, some emergent agreements that appear to be correctly constructed at first glance are, in fact, substantively false, despite the pretty picture that they might create. Those forces that destroy assent come in five flavors: fraud, misrepresentation, mistake, duress, and undue influence.

Fraud and Misrepresentation

Both fraud and misrepresentation disrupt mutual assent. They do so by sabotaging the essential component of trust upon which all agreements, but especially contracts, are based. This is what makes both fraud and misrepresentation so insidious. They are based on deceitful practice that makes a mockery of the entire commercial process. Of the two, fraud is the more serious and the more despicable because it is deliberate. It is also the more difficult of the two to prove. This may be why many cases that should be litigated as fraud, end up in court as misrepresentation lawsuits.

Fraud To destroy mutual assent through a claim of **fraud**, the complaining or innocent party must prove the existence of five elements.

1.   The complaining party will have to prove that the other party made false representations about some **material fact** (i.e., an important fact, a fact of substance) involved in the contract. A material fact is one that is very crucial to the terms of the contract.

2.   The plaintiff must demonstrate convincingly that the other party made the representations knowing that they were false.

3.   The plaintiff must show that the false representations were made with the intent that they be relied upon by the innocent party.

4.   The complaining party must establish that there was a reasonable reliance on the false representations.

5.   The plaintiff must verify that he or she actually suffered some loss by relying on the false representations after entering the contract.

A case involving either active or passive fraud must be based on these five elements.

About the Law

While the common law courts of England were quite willing to acknowledge fraud in tort law, they were not as willing to see its application in contract law.

Types of Fraud There is more than one way to commit fraud. The law distinguishes between fraud in the inception and fraud in the inducement. **Fraud in the inception** occurs when one party tricks another party into a contract by lying to the innocent party about the actual nature of the contract. In effect, because of false representations made by one party, the innocent party believes that he or she is doing "A" when he or she is actually doing "B." For example, if an insurance agent were to tell an accident victim that the paper she was signing was a privacy waiver, when it was actually an agreement releasing the insurance company from all liability, it would be fraud in the inception. **Fraud in the inducement** occurs when one party tricks another into a contract by lying about the terms of the agreement to get the innocent party to enter the contract under false pretenses. In this case, because of the false representations made by one party, the innocent party believes that he or she is doing "A," but "A" turns out to be actually "A−" or "A+" or "a" rather than simply "A." If, for instance, a loan officer at a bank were to tell a borrower that the interest rate on the loan would be 8 percent when it was actually18 percent, that officer would have committed fraud in the inducement.

EXAMPLE 8-3: *Rhodes v. Hayden*

Gabriel Hayden owned a motorboat that was docked at the Butler Reservoir. Hayden, however, was about to move to the city and so was anxious to get rid of a boat for which he would have no use in the city. Kelly Rhodes, who was new in town, wanted to purchase a motorboat quickly so that she would have several weeks of summer weather left to enjoy the boat. Sensing that he could make a real killing on the deal, Hayden told Rhodes about the boat. Rhodes was impressed by Hayden's sales pitch, but she wanted to see the boat first and take it for a test run on the reservoir. Hayden agreed. Before Rhodes arrived the next day for the test run, Hayden patched up several obvious holes in the bottom of the boat with putty and poster board. Hayden knew the repairs would not make the boat seaworthy for longer than 15 minutes, but he figured that would be enough time to fool Rhodes into thinking that the boat was in good condition. Deceived by the apparently good condition of the boat, Rhodes purchased it. The next time she took it out on the reservoir, the boat quickly sank. Even though Hayden never actually told any verbal lies to Rhodes, he would still have committed fraud.

To be fraudulent, statements must involve facts. Opinions and sales puffery consist of the persuasive words and exaggerated claims made by salespeople to induce a customer to buy their product. As long as the comments are reserved to opinion and do not misstate facts, they cannot be considered fraud in a lawsuit, even if they turn out to be grossly wrong.

EXAMPLE 8-4: *Oldacker v. Kellog Formal Wear Shoppe*

Fran Holiday, a sales clerk representing the Kellog Formal Wear Shoppe, was trying to sell a tuxedo to Ken Oldacker. During the sales discussion, Holiday told Oldacker that the tux (1) came with two pairs of pants, (2) was made of 100 percent wool, (3) had a very rich texture, (4) looked very good on Oldacker, and (5) would make him look like James Bond. The first two statements are statements of material fact and could be the basis of a lawsuit for fraud if they are proven false. The others are either opinions expressed by the seller or the persuasive puffery that might induce Oldacker to buy the tux and therefore could not be used as the basis of a lawsuit for fraud.

Active and Passive Fraud As noted previously, active fraud occurs when one party actually makes a false statement intended to deceive the other party in a contract. In contrast, passive fraud, which is generally called concealment or nondisclosure, occurs when one party does not say something about certain facts that he or she is under an obligation to reveal. If this passive conduct is intended to deceive and does in fact deceive the other party, fraud results. In general, a party is not required to reveal every known fact related to the subject matter of a contract. Certain facts may be confidential and personal. However, if the problem or defect is hidden and the other party cannot reasonably be expected to discover the defect, provided the problem involves some material fact, the offeror may be obliged to reveal it. Some states have held that sellers are legally bound to reveal only problems so hidden that even an expert would not be able to uncover them. In these states, problems such as insect or rodent infestation would not be hidden problems because an expert could easily uncover them.

Fraud can occur in many ways. A consumer's best defense is to be knowledgeable, listen, and ask questions

A **fiduciary relationship** is a relationship based on trust. Such relationships exist, for example, between attorneys and clients, guardians and wards, trustees and beneficiaries, and boards of directors and corporations. If one party is in a fiduciary relationship with another party, then an obligation arises to reveal what otherwise might be withheld when the two parties enter an agreement.

A QUESTION OF ETHICS

Suppose that you are showing your car to Tim Jorgenson, a potential buyer. You know that if Jorgenson takes your car for a drive, he will notice that the front end rattles at speeds in excess of 35 miles per hour and that the brakes grind badly. Jorgenson, however, does not take the car on a test drive and therefore fails to detect any defects. Would you have an ethical duty to tell Jorgenson about the car's problems? Explain.

EXAMPLE 8-5: *San Rafael Motor Corporation v. Groza*

Otto Groza was vice president of business and finance for the San Rafael Motor Corporation when he learned that Toth Properties Ltd. wanted to buy 12,000 acres of land owned by San Rafael. Groza was the only one at San Rafael who knew that a new extension of the interstate was going to be located on the acreage owned by the company. Moreover, Groza knew that Toth wanted the land for an outlet mall and an adjoining hotel and was willing to pay $19,000 per acre. Groza made a deal with Toth agreeing to sell the land at that price. He then went to the CEO and the board of San Rafael and offered to buy the farmland without revealing anything about the Toth deal. As a result, he purchased the acreage for $1,000 per acre and made an $18,000 profit on each acre he resold to Toth. Groza will be liable to San Rafael because he concealed a material fact that he was obligated to reveal because of his fiduciary relationship with the company.

Misrepresentation A false statement made innocently with no intent to deceive is **misrepresentation**. Innocent misrepresentation makes an existing agreement voidable, and the complaining party may demand rescission. **Rescission** means that both parties are returned to their original positions, before they entered into the contract. Unlike cases based on fraud, which allow rescission and damages, cases based on innocent misrepresentation allow only rescission, not monetary damages (see Table 8-3). If a party to an agreement makes an innocent misrepresentation and then later discovers that it is false, that party must reveal the truth. If the party does not reveal the truth, the innocent misrepresentation becomes fraud.

Mistake, Duress, and Undue Influence

When there has been no real meeting of the minds because of a mistake, mutual assent was never achieved, and the agreement may be rescinded. As in misrepresentation, mistake permits rescission. Both duress and undue influence rob a person of the ability to make an independent, well-reasoned decision to enter a contractual relationship freely. Both of these conditions therefore strike at the heart of contract law.

Table 8-3 Agreements Made Defective by Falsehood

Falsehood	Definition	Remedy
Active fraud	Active fraud occurs when one party to a contract makes a false statement intended to deceive the other party and thus leads that party into a deceptively based agreement.	Damages and Rescission
Passive fraud	Passive fraud occurs when one party does not say something about certain facts that he or she is obligated to reveal. Obligations arise in situations involving hidden problems and fiduciary relationships.	Damages and Rescission
Misrepresentation	Misrepresentation occurs when a false statement is innocently made.	Rescission

The Nature of Mistake A mistake made by only one of the contracting parties is a unilateral mistake and does not offer sufficient grounds for rescission or renegotiation. When both parties are mistaken, it is a bilateral mistake. A bilateral mistake, which is also called a mutual mistake, may permit a rescission by either the offeror or the offeree. Mutual mistakes are of several kinds (see Table 8-4). Some are universally accepted as grounds for rescission. Others are not grounds for rescission. Still others can give rise to lawsuits, but not in all courts or in all states. When both parties are mistaken in the identification and description of subject matter, there is a real mutual mistake, and rescission will be granted.

Proof that the subject matter had been destroyed before the agreement was made gives grounds for rescission. Thus, if one party accepted an offer to purchase a boat that both parties mistakenly believed to be berthed at a specified marina, the agreement would be voidable if it were proved that moments before acceptance, the boat had been destroyed. Had the boat been destroyed after final acceptance, there would have been no mutual mistake, and an enforceable contract would have resulted. When two parties agree on the value of the subject matter and later find they were both mistaken, it is a mutual mistake of opinion, not of fact. Mutual mistakes of opinion are not grounds for rescinding a contract.

The Nature of Duress In general, duress may be viewed as an action by one party that forces another party to do what need not otherwise be done. Duress forces a person into a contract through the use of physical, emotional, or economic threats (see Table 8-5). In contrast, undue influence merely involves the use of excessive pressure.

Table 8-4 Agreements Made Defective by Mutual Mistake

Mistake	Legal Effect
Mistake as to description	Rescission will be granted.
Mistake as to existence	Proof that subject matter was destroyed *before* the agreement was made gives grounds for rescission.
Mistake as to value	Rescission will not be granted since value is a matter of opinion, not fact.

Table 8-5 Agreements Made Defective by Force or Pressure

Type of Force or Pressure	Explanation
Physical duress	Violence or threat of violence to person, family, household, or property.
Emotional duress	Acts or threats that create emotional distress in the one on whom they are inflicted.
Economic duress	Threats of a business nature that force another party without real consent to enter a commercial agreement.
Undue influence	Dominant party in a special relationship uses excessive pressure to convince the weaker party to enter a contract.

Moreover, undue influence requires the existence of a special relationship, generally of a confidential or fiduciary nature. **Physical duress** involves either violence or the threat of violence against an individual or against that person's family, household, or property. If only threats are used, they must be so intense and serious that a person of ordinary prudence would be forced into the contract without any real consent. Threats of physical duress are relatively rare today. Perhaps more common are threats that create emotional duress. **Emotional duress** arises from acts or threats that would create emotional distress in the one on whom they are inflicted. It is generally necessary that the action threatened be either illegal or illicit.

Economic duress, also known as **business compulsion,** consists of threats of a business nature that force another party without real consent to enter a commercial agreement. To establish economic duress, the complaining party must demonstrate the existence of three elements:

1. The plaintiff must prove that the other party wrongfully placed the plaintiff in a precarious economic situation.
2. The plaintiff must show that he or she had no alternative other than to submit to the contractual demands of the wrongful party.
3. The plaintiff must demonstrate that he or she acted reasonably in entering the contract.

If the plaintiff can prove the existence of these three elements, the court will rule the contract voidable on grounds of economic duress.

EXAMPLE 8-6: *National Air Races Inc. v. Macon City Airport*

The owners and operators of National Air Races negotiated a seven-year lease with the City of Macon for use of the Macon City Airport. Each summer, during the Fourth of July weekend celebration, the National Air Races were held at the Macon City Airport. One week before the first race of the fourth year under the contract, Macon city officials informed the owners and operators of the National Air Races that they would no longer be able to use the Macon City Airport for the Fourth of July races unless they paid a substantial rent increase. The owners and operators of the Air Races, who had already sold at least 5,000 tickets per race, accepted entry fees from 95 pilots, and had contracts with 20 concessionaires, could not find any other suitable airport within 120 miles of Macon. As a result, they agreed to the terms. Later, the owners of the Air Races sued Macon to have the rent increase rescinded. The court ruled that the rent increase was voidable due to economic duress.

The Nature of Undue Influence The problem of **undue influence** occurs when the dominant party in a special relationship uses excessive pressure to convince the weaker party to enter a contract that greatly benefits the dominant party. A plaintiff who wants to demonstrate that he or she was enticed into a contract by undue influence must prove the existence of two elements.

1.   The plaintiff must show that a special relationship existed between the parties. A special relationship can generally be characterized as one that is fiduciary in nature or one that involves domination. Examples of fiduciary relationships include the relationships of parent to child, guardian to ward, attorney to client, physician to patient, pastor to parishioner, and so forth. Relationships that involve dominance frequently occur when the stronger of the two parties is acting as a caretaker of the weaker party.

2.   Second, the plaintiff must show that the other party used excessive pressure to take advantage of him or her to enter a contract that greatly benefits the party applying the pressure.

In most cases involving undue influence, one party in the special relationship has enough strength and leadership to dominate the other party, who is obviously weaker and dependent.

Did You Know?

It is possible for a party to ratify a contract made under duress if, after the duress has ended, the party makes a new promise to abide by the terms of the original agreement. In such a situation, the party ratifying the contract need not supply any new consideration.

quick quiz 8-4

1. Misrepresentation is a false statement made with no intent to deceive.	true	false
2. Mutual mistake is grounds for rescinding a contract.	true	false
3. Economic duress is also known as business compulsion.	true	false

Summary

8.1 If certain requirements are met, the court will conclude that the parties intended to make and accept an offer. Mutual assent is created when an offer is made by one party and accepted by the other party. An offer is valid if it is made with serious intent, displays clear and definite terms, and is communicated to the offeree.

8.2 The second major part of mutual assent is the acceptance of the offer. Communication of the acceptance may be either express or implied. Under the mirror image rule, an acceptance must not change any of the terms of the offer. The UCC has altered the mirror image rule. At any time prior to acceptance, the offeror can withdraw the offer. Still, some types of offers cannot be revoked by the offeror. These involve option contracts, firm offers, and lease option contracts.

8.3 The principal rules concerning the interpretation of the enforcement of cyber-contracts are found in the E-Sign Act, the Uniform Electronic Transactions Act (UETA), and the Uniform Computer Information Transactions Act (UCITA).

8.4 Fraud involves deliberate deception about some material fact that leads a party into an agreement that is damaging to that party. Misrepresentation is a false statement innocently made with no intent to deceive. A mutual mistake may allow for rescission by either party. Duress and undue influence rob a person of the ability to make an independent, well-reasoned decision to enter freely into a contract.

Key Terms

Questions for Review and Discussion

1. What is mutual assent?
2. What are the elements of an offer?
3. What is the UCC's concept of an offer?
4. How does an acceptance come about?
5. What is the mirror image rule?
6. What is revocation?
7. What statutes affect mutual assent in cyberspace?
8. What are the elements of fraud and misrepresention?
9. What are the effects of mistake on mutual assent?
10. What are duress and undue influence?

Cases for Analysis

1. The Lindbergh-Sikorsky Aircraft Corporation e-mailed an offer to Kenneth Hiebel, the owner of the Triple R-Bar Ranch in Idaho. The e-mail stated, "Please consider this our offer to purchase 20,000 acres of your 61,200-acre ranch land near Harrington, Idaho. Our offering price is between $60,000 and $65,000 per acre. Please respond soon." Look at the requirements of an offer and determine whether the e-mail quoted above constitutes a valid offer. Explain.

2. Patrick Barnes and George Layton were employed by the Sailors' Maritime Service. When they expressed dissatisfaction with their jobs, their employer offered them a new contract whereby they would receive a 10 percent bonus on company profits if they remained with the firm. Several times they discussed the terms of the new agreement with an official of Sailors' Maritime. Eventually, they decided that the offer was a good one, and they continued on the job as usual. Sailors'

Maritime later refused to pay the 10 percent bonus, claiming that its offer had never been accepted. Is Sailors' Maritime refusal to pay legally correct? Or, to pinpoint the issue more directly, was the offer accepted by Barnes and Layton? Explain. Now suppose that Sailors' Maritime had said to Barnes and Layton, "We will consider your written acceptance of this new proposal as binding us to the payment of the 10 percent bonus." Would these additional facts change your initial evaluation of this case? Why or why not?

3. Sarah Jameson read an advertisement in *The Independent* inviting her to become a member of the New Era DVD Club. Jameson chose several DVDs that were listed in the advertisement. She paid only $1 for those DVDs and became a member of the DVD club. In doing so, she also agreed to purchase four more DVDs in a year's time. Under terms clearly specified in the advertisement, Jameson knew she would receive a brochure 12 times a year listing selections. The brochure would also identify the main selections, which would be sent to her automatically unless she sent a reply form to stop the shipment. In effect, New Era has made Jameson's silence acceptance. Is this a legally effective tactic? Explain.

4. Anthony Sanderson was browsing on eBay when he located what was labeled as a 1932 edition of *Brave New World* by Aldous Huxley, produced by Chatto and Windus, the London publisher that had printed the first edition of that landmark novel. The book was advertised as coming along with a companion book by Julian Huxley, entitled *If I Were Dictator,* published in 1934 by the London-based Methuen. The seller was Juliette Straus, who set the minimum bid for the two volumes at GBP 8,700. Sanderson, who quickly bid on the two books, eventually won the auction with a successful bid of GBP 9,800. Later, after receiving the two books, Sanderson discovered that the copy of *If I Were Dictator* was actually a 1948 reprint of the original work. Is this a case of fraud or misrepresentation? Explain.

5. An advertisement appeared in the *Chicago Sun-Times* for the sale of a Volvo station wagon at Lee Calan Imports, Inc., for $1,095. The advertisement had been misprinted by the *Sun-Times*. The actual price of the automobile was $1,795. O'Keefe showed up at Lee Calan and said he would buy the Volvo for $1,095. Lee Calan refused to sell the car for $1,095. O'Keefe sued, claiming that the advertisement was an offer that he accepted, creating a binding agreement. Was O'Keefe correct? Explain. [See: *O'Keefe v. Lee Calan Imports,* 262 N.E.2d 758 (IL).]

6. Morrison wanted to sell a certain parcel of land to Thoelke. He decided to make an offer by sending Thoelke a letter. When Thoelke received the letter, he decided to accept. He wrote a letter to Morrison saying that he would buy the land at the price quoted in the letter. Thoelke then mailed the letter. Before he received the letter from Thoelke, Morrison changed his mind and withdrew the offer to Thoelke. When Thoelke found out Morrison would not sell the land to him, he sued. Was Thoelke's letter a valid acceptance, binding Morrison to the sale? Explain. [See: *Morrison v. Thoelke,* 155 So.2d 889 (FL).]

7. Wholesale Coal Company ordered 25 carloads of coal from Guyan Coal and Coke Company. Guyan could not come up with 25 carloads. However, it did have seven carloads available. Before shipping the coal, Guyan wrote back to Wholesale stating, "You can be sure that if it is possible to ship the entire twenty-five carloads, we will do so. But under the circumstances, this is the best we can promise you." When Guyan heard nothing from Wholesale, it shipped the seven carloads. When Wholesale did not pay for the seven carloads, Guyan brought suit to compel payment. Wholesale countersued, claiming Guyan had not yet delivered the remaining 18 carloads. Was Wholesale correct? Explain. [See: *Guyan Coal and Coke Company v. Wholesale Coal Company,* 201 N.W. 194 (MI).]

8. Boskett offered to sell a 1916 dime to Beachcomber Coins, Inc. Beachcomber examined the coin carefully and agreed to pay Boskett $500 for it. Later, Beachcomber asked a representative from the American Numismatic Society to examine the coin. The coin turned out to be counterfeit. No evidence existed to indicate fraud on Boskett's part. Beachcomber sued Boskett for rescission and a return of the $500. Beachcomber claimed this bilateral mistake of fact created grounds for a rescission. Was Beachcomber correct? Explain. [See: *Beachcomber Coins, Inc. v. Boskett,* 400 A.2d 78 (NJ).]

9. Prisoners rioted at the Iowa State Penitentiary and held prison staff members as hostages. The warden agreed in writing that no reprisals would be levied against the rioting inmates. In exchange, the

prisoners released the hostages. After the hostages were released, several of the prisoners were punished for the riot. One prisoner, Wagner, was placed in solitary confinement for 30 days. He also received 180 days of administrative segregation and the loss of 1,283 days of good time earned. On what legal grounds could the warden refuse to keep his promise to the inmates? Explain. [See: *Wagner v. State,* 364 N.W.2d 246 (IA).]

10. Loral Corporation had a contract with the U.S. government to manufacture radar sets. Loral subcontracted with Austin Instrument for the production of precision parts to be used in the radar sets. In the middle of production, Austin told Loral that it would deliver no more parts unless Loral agreed to pay Austin a good deal more than originally agreed upon. Loral could not obtain the same parts in time from any other company. As a result, Loral agreed to the price increase. After delivering the radar sets, Loral sued Austin and asked the court to rescind the price increase. Did the court grant Loral's request? Explain. [See: *Austin Instrument, Inc. v. Loral Corporation,* 272 N.E.2d 533 (NY).]

quick quiz Answers

8-1	8-2	8-3	8-4
1. F	1. T	1. F	1. T
2. T	2. T	2. F	2. T
3. T	3. T	3. T	3. T

THE OPENING CASE *Round 1*
The Ultimate Dispute: When Attorneys on the Same Side Do Battle

By now we have come to expect attorneys to disagree with one another. That is, after all, their job—to act as advocates for their clients. However, what happens when attorneys who are in the same firm and on the same side disagree? Who advocates for the advocates? In the case of *Lightbody v. Rust,* two attorneys in the same firm found themselves in the same courtroom on opposite sides of the aisle. Rust was a partner in the firm of Woodley, Krost & Rust. The partners hired Lightbody to do much of the heavy lifting for the firm. Lightbody, who had no written agreement with the partnership, worked for one-half of the billings that each of his clients paid to the firm. So, the amount of his take-home pay was basically unknown from paycheck to paycheck. The risk to Lightbody was increased by the fact that, if the client did not pay, Lightbody was not paid. One of Rust's clients ("the inventor") was in the middle of a nasty patent battle with Harris Company over an alleged infringement of one of the inventor's patents. The inventor was in a financially vulnerable position, and so, because he could not pay cash, set up a contingency fee arrangement under which Rust would not get paid unless the inventor's case was successful. The contingency fee would amount to 40 percent of the proceeds from the inventor's inventions. Rust decided that he needed assistance, and Lightbody agreed to

help. However, since the inventor was paying based on a contingency fee arrangement, there would be no billable hours. The solution was to pay Lightbody on a contingency arrangement under which he would receive half of whatever Rust received as his contingency fee. So, again the exact amount of Lightfoot's take-home pay was in dispute because it would be based on 20 percent of the proceeds from the inventor's inventions. Once again the agreement was not placed in writing. As things moved along, Lightbody ended up doing most of the work on the case. The inventor's lawsuit was settled out of court for a total of $225,000, plus the rights to 18 patents, from which the contingency fee would be paid. Lightbody received one check for $28,000 and a second check for $217,000. So far so good. However, when Lightbody received the second check, Rust said that it would be his last payment on the inventor's account. Lightbody said something like, "No it's not. The proceeds are still coming in from the inventor and I am due my percentage." Despite this protest, he cashed the second check. On the other hand, for the next 12 months, Lightbody continued to demand his portion of the contingency fee from the inventor's proceeds. For his part, Rust continued to refuse to pay Lightbody, while at the same time collecting his own portion of the proceeds, which, at last count, amounted to more than $1 million.

After leaving the firm, Lightbody sued. Who wouldn't? [See: *Lightbody v. Rust,* 2003-Ohio-3937, No. 80927.]

Opening Case Questions

1. What is consideration? Explain.

2. Is there any bargained-for exchange in the deals between Lightbody and Rust? Why or why not? Explain.

3. How is it possible to set consideration if the final amount of payment is not known? Explain.

4. What is accord and satisfaction? Explain.

5. What are the elements of accord and satisfaction?

 Learning Objectives

1. Define the term *consideration.*
2. Identify the different types of detriment.
3. Explain the characteristics necessary for valid consideration.
4. Define the term *unconscionable.*
5. Explain whether a promise not to sue can be consideration.
6. Explain whether a charitable pledge can be consideration.
7. Define accord and satisfaction.
8. Identify those enforceable contracts that lack consideration.
9. Explain *promissory estoppel.*
10. Describe the issues involved in cyber-payments.

9-1 Requirements of Consideration

In Chapter 8, we explored the nature of mutual assent, the first of the four elements of a contract. The second element is the mutual promise to exchange benefits and sacrifices among the parties. This exchange of things of value is called **consideration**. If an agreement has no consideration, it is not a binding contract. For example, a promise to give someone a ride to the campus in the morning is not a contract. Instead, it is simply a social arrangement because the rider has given nothing in exchange for the ride. In contrast, if the rider decides to take the bus, call a cab, or rent a vehicle to get to campus then a contract will exist. This is because, in the second case, the rider will have to transfer consideration in the form of a fare or a rental price in exchange for the ride to class.

The Nature of Consideration

Consideration consists of a mutual exchange of gains and losses between contracting parties. In the exchange, a gain by the offeree is at the same time a loss to the offeror. Likewise, the gain bargained for by the offeror will result in a loss or sacrifice by the offeree. The legal term used to designate the gain that each party experiences is that party's legal benefit. Similarly, the legal term used to describe the sacrifice that each party must experience is that party's **legal detriment**. A legal detriment can be any of the following: (1) doing something (or promising to do something) that one has a legal right not to do; (2) giving up something (or promising to give up something) that one has a legal right to

THE OPENING CASE *Round 2*
The Ultimate Dispute: Doing Something for Nothing

In the opening case, we learned that Rust was a partner in the firm of Woodley, Krost, & Rust. The partners hired Lightbody to take on yeoman's duties for the firm. Lightbody worked for one-half of the billings that each of his clients paid to the firm. This contract was never put in writing, but it seemed not to matter, because Lightbody was paid accordingly in an honorable manner. Still, the amount of his take-home pay was a mystery from paycheck to paycheck. Moreover, the risk to Lightbody was increased by the fact that, if the client did not pay, Lightbody was not paid. One of Rust's clients ("the inventor") was caught up in a very serious patent lawsuit with the firm of Harris Company. The suit focused on an alleged infringement of the inventor's patents. The inventor was fiscally strapped at that time, and so, in lieu of cash, Rust established a contingency fee arrangement, under which Rust would not get paid unless the inventor's case was successful. The contingency fee would amount to 40 percent of the proceeds from the inventor's inventions. Rust decided that he needed help unraveling the details of the inventor's case and so he enlisted Lightbody. Lightbody agreed to assist. However, since the inventor was paying based on a contingency fee arrangement, there would be no billable hours. The solution was to pay Lightbody on a secondary contingency arrangement under which he would receive half of whatever Rust received as his contingency fee. In this case the consideration that flows from Lightbody to the firm is taking on the extra duties in the inventor's case without receiving his usual pay of half his billable hours. As noted above, consideration can be doing something (or promising to do something) that one has a legal right not to do. That is exactly what happened in this case. Lightbody had the legal right to refrain from taking on the extra duties under an arrangement that was not part of his original contract with the firm. [See: *Lightbody v. Rust,* 2003-Ohio-3937, No. 80927.]

keep; and (3) refraining from doing something (or promising not to do something) that one has a legal right to do. This last type of detriment is known as **forbearance**.

Suppose Kurt promises his trainer that he will give up sugar for a year in exchange for a year of free training sessions. It is likely that Kurt improved his health by giving up sugar; however, the fact that Kurt gained a medical benefit does not eliminate his sacrifice. This "non-act" by itself is consideration. Kurt has suffered what the courts call a legal detriment, so giving up sugar has legal value, and the contract is valid.

The Characteristics of Consideration

Consideration has three characteristics: (1) The agreement must involve a bargained-for exchange; (2) the contract must involve adequate consideration; and (3) the benefits and detriments promised must themselves be legal.

Bargained-for Exchange   The law will not enforce an agreement that has not been bargained for. An agreement involves a **bargained-for exchange** when (1) a promise is made in exchange for another promise, (2) a promise is made in exchange for an act, or (3) a promise is made for forbearance of an act. The concept of bargaining means that each party will be hurt in some way if the other party fails to keep a promise. Conversely, each party gains something when the promises are kept and the exchange is made.

Adequacy of Consideration   The fact that a contract has legal value is not the same as saying that it has adequate consideration. However, there are no specific requirements, other than being legal, regarding what one party may promise the other party in return for a pledge to deliver goods and services. The promise itself is adequate consideration when it represents something of value. Thus, the promise to assist another to repair an

THE OPENING CASE *Round 3*
The Ultimate Dispute: Doing Nothing for Something

In the opening case, it was revealed that Rust was a partner in the firm of Woodley, Krost, & Rust. The partners hired Lightbody to work for the firm. For his part, Lightbody received half of the billable hours from each of his clients. This agreement remained oral for the rest of Lightbody's time with the firm. One of Rust's clients ("the inventor") was caught up in a very serious patent lawsuit with the firm of Harris Company. Rust established a contingency fee arrangement with the inventor, under which Rust would not get paid unless the inventor's case was successful. The contingency fee would amount to 40 percent of the proceeds from the inventor's inventions. Rust needed assistance with the case, and Lightbody agreed to help. Under a second contingency agreement, Lightbody would receive half of whatever Rust received as his contingency fee. As the case developed, Lightbody did most of the work in the suit. The inventor's case was settled out of court for $225,000 and control over 18 patents, which would pay the contingency fee. Lightbody received one check for $28,000 and a second check for $217,000. So far so good. However, when Lightbody received the second check, Rust said that it would be his last payment on the inventor's account. Lightbody said something like, "No it's not. The proceeds are still coming in

from the inventor and I am due my percentage." Eventually, after leaving the firm, Lightbody went to court with his claim. The judge in the case could have noted that consideration requires that both parties suffer a detriment and reap a benefit, and that Lightbody had suffered no additional detriment because all he was doing was his regular job, nothing more. This was never really an issue, however, because, when Lightbody agreed to alter his method of payment, he did something that he did not have to do. He had, therefore, suffered a detriment sufficient to provide consideration. He was putting his payment at risk, since it was based on a contingency fee and an unknown amount of return on the patents, which could have yielded zero. But what about Rust? Certainly he suffered a detriment in parting with half of his own fee, at least for the time that he actually paid Lightbody. However, what benefit did he receive in the contract? Can the court place a value on Lightbody's alteration in his agreement? Yes, whatever Lightbody did, Rust did not have to do, thus freeing Rust to attend to other clients. The fact that no one knew the exact monetary value of the work is of no concern to the court. And that, as they say in the law, was that. [See: *Lightbody v. Rust,* 2003-Ohio-3937, No. 80927.]

automobile would be something of value promised. The value placed on goods and services need not be street or market value. It is important only that the parties freely agreed on the value and the price. In general, the courts do not look into the adequacy of consideration; that is, they do not look to see whether the value of the consideration was fair to both parties. Ever since industrial capitalism became the primary economic system in the West, the courts no longer looked to see if the things exchanged in a contract are of equal value. Such a move would violate the profit-making principle of capitalism. Therefore, the courts let people make their own agreements, placing their own values on the goods or services exchanged. The court then enforces those agreements.

The price and value of the goods exchanged need not be equal as long as the agreement is voluntary.

There are, however, exceptions to this general rule. In one exception, the courts give a party relief when the consideration is so outrageous that it shocks the conscience of the court. A court may refuse to enforce a contract or any clause of a contract if it considers the contract or clause **unconscionable**, that is, the consideration is so ridiculously inadequate that it shocks the court's conscience. This designation usually happens when there is a great inequality in bargaining power between the two parties. In very specific matters, usually related to taxes, some states have adopted statutes dealing with adequacy. In general though, courts remain reluctant to disturb the promises made by parties to an enforceable contract.

CLASSIC CASE Healthy, Wealthy, and Wise?

Literature instructors are fond of saying that a poem, a play, a novel, or a short story is considered good, sometimes even great, if it has stood the "test of time." The same is true of many legal cases. Such is the situation with the long-standing case of *Hamer v. Sidway,* a lawsuit that most law students and paralegals encounter (or should encounter) at some time in their academic careers. *Hamer and Sidway* begins at a golden wedding anniversary celebration. At the party, Uncle William promised his nephew and namesake, William, the Younger, that if he, the nephew, would give up a long list of vices that included smoking and swearing, until his 21st birthday, he, the uncle, would pay his nephew, William, $5,000. The challenge was made in front of a room full of family members and close friends, and William, the Younger, agreed to the arrangement. Following this and in compliance with the agreement, William embarked on an extensive period of abstinence that lasted several years. Soon after his 21st birthday, William wrote to his uncle telling him of his accomplishments and asking for the $5,000 due to him under the contract. Uncle William wrote a lengthy letter back in which he praised his nephew for his perseverance. He also promised to pay the money that was due. Unfortunately, Uncle William passed away before sending the money to his nephew. Undeterred, the nephew petitioned the executor of Uncle William's estate for payment. The executor refused to pay and William brought this lawsuit. William argued that he had performed as promised and was, therefore, entitled to the money. The executor recognized that William had, indeed, refrained from smoking and swearing, but argued that, in contract law, both sides must suffer a detriment for consideration to be valid and for a contract to exist. In this case, the executor said, young William had not suffered a detriment. In fact, the opposite was true. He was much healthier than he would have been, absent the promise, and he had, therefore, benefited greatly from giving up his bad habits for such an extended period of time. In the absence of consideration, no contract ever existed and, as a result, the estate did not owe young William a single cent. The court disagreed with this analysis. The court noted that, when William gave up something that he had a legal right to do, he had suffered a detriment sufficient to provide the consideration needed to make the agreement into a *bona fide* contract. To prove its point the court referred to a standard treatise on contract law and noted that, consideration "means not so much that one party is profiting as that the other abandons some legal right in the present, or limits his legal freedom of action in the future, as an inducement for the promise of the first." End of story—period. [See: *Hamer v. Sidway,* 124 N.Y. 538, 27 N.E. 256 (Court of Appeals of New York).]

Legality of Consideration Consideration requires that the benefits and sacrifices promised between the parties be legal. Absence of legality renders the consideration invalid. Thus, a party cannot agree to do something that he or she does not have the legal right to do. Similarly, a party cannot promise not to do something that he or she has no legal right to do. Also, a party cannot make valid consideration out of a promise to stop doing something that was illegal to do in the first place.

quick quiz 9-1

1. The fact that each party has received a benefit and suffered a detriment means that the consideration has legal value.   true | false

2. The legal term used to designate the gain that each party experiences is the party's legal benefit.   true | false

3. Consideration does not require that the benefits and sacrifices promised between the parties be legal.   true | false

9-2 Types of Consideration

Generally, consideration takes the form of money, property, or services. In certain special kinds of agreements and promises, however, the benefits and sacrifices are in some manner unique and not immediately obvious to the casual observer. Significant among these agreements are promises not to sue and charitable pledges.

Money as Consideration

Money is so closely connected with global commerce that we forget that it was not always part of the marketplace. The shift from a barter to a cash economy occurred when transporting goods to the market became difficult and hazardous. By the ninth century, the use of cash as a medium of exchange had become prevalent in medieval Europe. This shift to a cash economy was also accelerated by the need for credit. Because goods are perishable and the quality of goods can vary from transaction to transaction, contracts that required future payments were more attractive to merchants when coins rather than goods were involved. Thus, agreements based on credit backed up by coins had become commonplace throughout Europe by the 11th century, as had the practice of lending coins in exchange for interest. By the 13th century, the use of mortgage agreements based on transferring the right to receive all of the cash income from a tract of land had become routine. Today, we are once again in an era of change as we move from a cash/credit economy to one based almost totally on electronic transfers. Nevertheless, when electronic transfers are involved, people still tend to think in terms of cash, even those who have not actually handled coins or currency for some time. For this reason, it is best to always remember that hidden at the foundation of all contracts is the idea of cash equivalency. [See: Rodney Stark, *The Victory of Reason: How Christianity Led to Freedom, Capitalism, and Western Success* (New York: Random House, 2005), pp. 60–61.]

Property and Services as Consideration

Before money in the form of cash was accepted as a medium of exchange, consideration consisted of property and services. Sometimes, even today during recessionary or inflationary cycles, parties find it more beneficial to enter into barter agreements than to base their promises on cash payments. The courts have held that barter agreements contain valid consideration. For example, the exchange of services in return for the use of another's car or a promise to paint a house in exchange for accounting services represent benefits and sacrifices that constitute valid consideration to support a legally binding contract.

Promises Not to Sue

A promise not to sue, when there is the right, or at least the apparent right, to sue, is enforceable when it is supported by consideration. Promising not to sue is a forbearance. A promise not to sue in exchange for an amount of money is a customary way to settle or prevent a pending lawsuit. Settlements of this type often are preferred to expensive and time-consuming litigation. Such settlements are also better than submitting a claim to alternate dispute resolution procedures, such as arbitration or mediation.

> **Did You Know?**
>
> Common law judges would rarely entertain arguments regarding the adequacy of consideration, even in unconscionable situations. One exception involved the promise to repay immediately a greater sum of money than that originally transferred. This is what happened in the case of *Schnell v. Nell,* an 1861 case, in which a man promised to pay $600 in return for the loan of one penny.

EXAMPLE 9-1: Releases and Promises Not to Sue

Danny Hollinger was injured when a delivery van ran a red light and collided with his vehicle. Hollinger discussed his legal rights with an attorney, who suggested that he might receive compensation from the delivery company if he brought suit against the driver and the company. When faced with the suit, the delivery company's insurance company elected to offer Hollinger $250,000 if he would agree not to bring suit against the company. Hollinger agreed to these terms and signed a release in exchange for the money. The "thing of value" that Hollinger transferred to the insurance company was his right to bring a lawsuit. A court would uphold this agreement on the basis of the promise between the parties.

Acceptance of an agreement not to sue, supported by consideration, terminates one's right to continue any lawsuit, presently or in the future, on grounds described in the agreement. A promise not to sue is commonly called a **release**. Agreements of this kind are usually negotiated and agreed upon before a suit is even filed; however, occasionally they are negotiated between attorneys after a lawsuit has been filed and sometimes even after a trial has begun. In such an event, the settlement is arranged in cooperation with the court and presiding judge. Interestingly enough, some states will uphold a promise not to sue exchanged for consideration, even if circumstances later indicate that the party granting the release did not have the right to sue in the first place, as long as at the time of the agreement, the exchange was made in good faith and fraud was not involved.

Charitable Pledges

Under traditional rules, charitable pledges are not enforceable as contractual obligations because they are not supported by consideration. The dependence of charitable institutions and nonprofit organizations on the solicitation of contributions has encouraged the courts to enforce charitable pledges as though they were contractual obligations. Basically, there are three ways that the courts can seek to uphold charitable pledges. The first way involves actual consideration, which occurs when charitable contributions are made on the condition that the promisor be remembered for the gift by having his or her name inscribed in some way on a memorial associated with the project. Some courts see this promise to install a memorial to the pledgor as consideration.

A more contemporary approach is to use either promissory estoppel or public policy to support the claim. Promissory estoppel involves the detrimental reliance on a promise made by another party. If in reliance on a pledge or a series of pledges, a charity goes forward with a project, such as building an addition to the church hall or adding a wing to the synagogue, the courts will see the commencement of the project as evidence that the charity relied on the promises and will stop the promisors from denying the effects of the promise. At times pledges are used for the general operation and maintenance of a charitable or nonprofit organization rather than for a specific project.

When there is no promise to carry out a specific project, the courts have held that each pledge made is supported by the pledges of all others who have made similar pledges. This concept of consideration is used in support of all promises of money for undefined causes. The ultimate argument in this situation is that it would violate public policy to allow one pledgor to get away with denying his or her pledge when the other promisors relied on one another in making their individual pledges.

Courts today enforce charitable pledges by applying promissory estoppel and public policy.

9-3 Problems with Consideration

Problems sometimes arise when the consideration involved in a contract is money and the parties disagree as to the amount of money that the debtor owes the creditor. The resolution of such problems depends on whether the transaction involves a genuine dispute as to the amount owed. One way such disputes can be settled is by an agreement known as accord and satisfaction. Additional problems arise when an agreement lacks consideration.

Accord and Satisfaction

A **disputed amount** is one on which the parties never reached mutual agreement. It may be difficult at first to see how the amount due under a contract can end up as the focal point of a dispute, until we recall that the law permits a certain degree of incompleteness in the final terms of an agreement, provided there is a way to settle on the eventual amount owed. For instance, when a contractor is hired to do work on a home or an accountant is retained to figure out a client's taxes, the final amount owed is rarely laid out in absolute terms. Instead, the custom is to settle on an amount per hour, estimate the number of hours that will be spent on the job, and then settle on the final amount once the job is finished.

If a creditor accepts as full payment an amount that is less than the amount due, the dispute has been settled by an **accord and satisfaction**. An accord and satisfaction is a new agreement resulting from a bona fide dispute between the parties as to the terms of their original agreement. The mutual agreement to the new terms is the **accord**; performance of the accord is the **satisfaction**—thus, accord and satisfaction. For accord and satisfaction to operate properly, certain elements are necessary. First, there must be a genuine dispute as to the amount due under the original agreement. Second, one of the parties, usually the one who owes the money, will suggest a way to settle the dispute, usually by tendering a lesser amount. Third, there must be acceptance of the lesser amount generally demonstrated by cashing a check for that lesser amount or some other act that signals acceptance.

In the classic accord and satisfaction scenario, the debtor tenders a check to the creditor. The check is marked "Payment in full for the amount owed on . . ." or words to that effect. At that point the ball is in the creditor's court, as it were. If the creditor cashes or otherwise negotiates the check, the debt has been satisfied. If the creditor does not cash the check, the debtor still owes the original amount. Great importance is placed on the written notation on the check. Generally an oral statement that goes something like "Here is your check. That is it. I am not paying any more" is insufficient, especially if the creditor replies, "Oh, yes you are! This is not enough!" Even without the return comment by the creditor, however, the oral statement by the debtor is generally not enough, and the creditor can negotiate the check and still come back for the rest of the debt.

THE OPENING CASE *Round 4*
Accord, Maybe. But Satisfaction? Not a Chance.

In the opening case we learned that Lightbody, who had no written agreement with the firm of Woodley, Krost & Rust, worked for one-half of the billings that each of his clients paid to the firm. Rust, one of the firm's partners, frequently handed work over to Lightbody. In this case, one of Rust's clients ("the inventor") was involved in a patent lawsuit with Harris Company over an alleged patent infringement problem. The inventor set up a contingency fee arrangement, under which Rust would get paid 40 percent of the proceeds from the inventor's inventions. Rust needed help with the case, and Lightbody agreed to lend a hand. However, since the inventor had a contingency fee arrangement, no billable hours would be counted. To deal with this issue Lightbody would also be paid on a contingency arrangement. Accordingly, Lightbody would receive half of whatever Rust received as his contingency fee. So, the exact amount of Lightfoot's take-home pay was in dispute because it would be based on 20 percent of the proceeds from the inventor's inventions. Once again the agreement was not placed in writing. The lawsuit was settled out of court for a total of $225,000 plus the rights to 18 patents, from which the contingency fee would be paid. Lightbody received one check for $28,000 and a second check for $217,000. When Lightbody received the second check, Rust said that it would be his last payment on the inventor's account. Lightbody said something like, "No it's not. The proceeds are still coming in from the inventor and I am due my percentage." Despite this protest, he cashed the second check. For the next 12 months, Lightbody demanded his portion of the fee from the inventor's proceeds. Rust continued to refuse to pay Lightbody, while collecting his own portion of the proceeds, which amounted to more than $1 million. After leaving the firm, Lightbody sued. Rust argued that the debt had been discharged under accord and satisfaction when he had tendered the second check for $217,000 and Lightbody had cashed that check. Lightbody argued that the check contained no written clause that would render it as full payment. Rust countered that he clearly told Lightbody orally that the check was full payment. Lightbody testified that he had told Rust repeatedly both before and after cashing the check that he was not about to accept that $217,000 as full payment. The lack of a written notation of "full payment" on the check and Lightbody's oral refusal to accept that check as the full amount were enough to convince the judge that accord and satisfaction did not apply here. The appellate court agreed. [See: *Lightbody v. Rust,* 2003-Ohio-3937, No. 80927.]

Enforceable Agreements

As a general rule, an agreement without consideration will not be an enforceable contract because consideration is so important as the binding element within a contractual relationship. Nevertheless, some states eliminate the requirement of consideration in specific types of agreements. Unfortunately, as is frequently the case in such matters, there is no uniformity among jurisdictions as to the types of agreements subject to such laws. Still, some typical agreements falling into this category include promises under seal, promises after discharge in bankruptcy, debts barred by the statute of limitations, promises enforced by promissory estoppel, and options governed by the UCC (see Table 9-1).

Promises under Seal
A **seal** is a mark or an impression placed on a written contract indicating that the instrument was executed and accepted in a formal manner. Today a seal is usually indicated by the addition of the word *seal* or the letters "L.S." (*locus sigilli*, meaning "place of the seal") following a party's signature. Years ago, contracts under seal required no consideration. Some states still honor a promise under seal, but most have abolished this concept especially in relation to sale of goods contracts. In fact, the UCC has

UCC 2-205 (see page 925)

Table 9-1 Agreements without Consideration

Agreement	Legal Status
Promises under seal	Enforceable in some states for contracts not involving goods; unenforceable under the UCC for contracts involving goods
Promises after discharge in bankruptcy	Enforceable in most states
Promise to pay debts barred by statute of limitations	Enforceable
Promises enforced by promissory estoppel	Enforceable only if offeror knew that offeree would rely on the promise and offeree places himself or herself in a different and difficult position as a result of that promise
Option	Enforceable under the UCC if made by a merchant, in writing, stating the time period over which the offer will remain open
Illusory promises	Unenforceable
Promise of a gift	Unenforceable
Past considerations	Unenforceable
Preexisting duties	Unenforceable as a consideration in a new contract

eliminated the use of the seal in all sale-of-goods contracts; however, a few states still require the use of the seal in real property and certain other types of transactions. Because there is no uniformity in this regard, it is advisable to research and consult the specific requirements in your jurisdiction.

Promises after Discharge in Bankruptcy

Persons discharged from indebtedness through bankruptcy may reaffirm their obligations, prompted perhaps by moral compulsion. In the past, reaffirmation has been the subject of abuse by creditors who used pressure against those whose debts have been excused. In response, Congress passed a bankruptcy reform act that makes it more difficult for creditors to extract such promises. The bankruptcy court must now hold a hearing when a reaffirmation is intended, informing the debtor that reaffirmation is optional, not required, and of the legal consequences of reactivating a debt. It is also up to the court to approve such reaffirmations. State laws, in most cases, provide that no new consideration need be provided in support of reaffirmation. Most states require that a reaffirmation be supported by contractual intent. Some states require the new promise to be in writing; however, when there is no such provision, an oral promise or reaffirmation is usually sufficient.

Debts Barred by Statutes of Limitations

State laws known as **statutes of limitations** limit the time within which a party is allowed to bring suit. The time allowed for the collection of a debt varies from state to state, usually from three to 10 years. Some states allow more time for collection when the document of indebtedness is under seal, as in the case of a promissory note containing the seal of the maker. Debtors may revive and reaffirm debts barred by the statutes of limitations without the necessity of new consideration. Affirmation will result from the part payment of the debt. When a debt is revived, the creditor again is permitted the full term, provided by the statute of limitations, to make collection. Some states require a written reaffirmation when a debt made unenforceable by the statute of limitations is reactivated. Consequently, it would be best to check the rule in your jurisdiction.

Promises Enforced by Promissory Estoppel   The doctrine of estoppel denies rights to complaining parties that are shown to be the cause of their own injury. Promissory estoppel is a legal doctrine that restricts a party from denying that a promise was made under certain conditions, even though consideration has not been exchanged to bind an agreement. To be effective, promissory estoppel requires that the party making the promise know, or be presumed to know, that the other party might otherwise make a definite and decided change of position in contemplation of those promises. In reaching this doctrine, courts have accepted the principles of justice and fairness in protecting the party receiving the promise from otherwise unrecoverable losses.

EXAMPLE 9-2: Raymond and Remington and Promissory Estoppel

Rachel Raymond was arrested for a crime she did not commit. Rick Remington, her supervisor at Anwar Enterprises, told her that he had to suspend her. However, he also told her that if she were later found not guilty and released, she would have her old job back with the same seniority and pay grade that she had when she left. Two months later, the charges were dropped when another person confessed to the crime, and Raymond tried to get her job back. Remington refused to let her return to work. It took Remington six months to secure suitable employment. In a suit brought by Raymond against Anwar to recover the pay she lost during those four months, the court ruled in her favor. Remington and Anwar were stopped from denying the promise they'd made to Raymond despite the absence of consideration from her because she had relied on that promise and had not looked for other work while suspended.

Option   An option is the giving of consideration to support an offeror's promise to hold open an offer for a stated or a reasonable length of time. The UCC has made an exception to the rule requiring consideration when the offer is made by a merchant. In such cases, an offer in writing by a merchant, stating the time period during which the offer will remain open, is enforceable without consideration. The offer, which is called a firm offer or an irrevocable offer, must be signed by the offeror, and the time allowed for acceptance may not exceed three months. When the time allowed is more than three months, firm offers by merchants must be supported by consideration to be enforceable.

Unenforceable Agreements

The promises just described are exceptions to the general rule that consideration must support a valid contract. The exceptions are allowed by state statute or because the courts, in the interest of fairness or justice, find it inappropriate to require consideration. There are certain promises, however, that the courts will not enforce because they lack even the rudimentary qualities of valid consideration. Included in this category are promises based on preexisting duties, promises based on past consideration, illusory promises, and promises of future gifts and legacies.

Preexisting Duties   A promise to do something that one is already obligated to do by law or by some other promise or agreement cannot be made consideration in a new contract. Such obligations are called **preexisting duties**. The same rule of consideration applies to police officers, firefighters, and other public servants and officials who may pledge what appears to be some special service in exchange for a monetary reward, when all they have actually promised is to execute the duties they are already obligated to perform. Suppose, for instance, that the local fire chief, in exchange for a monetary reward, promises an apartment owner that he or she will provide protection should a fire start in the owner's building. Neither the fire chief nor the apartment owner could enforce such an agreement in court. The promise is based on the chief's empty guarantee to do what is already his or her job.

Past Consideration A promise to give another something of value in return for goods or services rendered and delivered in the past, without expectation or reward, is **past consideration**. Only when goods or services are provided as the result of bargained-for present or future promises is an agreement enforceable.

EXAMPLE 9-3: Past Consideration Is No Consideration

Gale Hansen wanted to have her hair dyed before her college graduation party but could not afford to pay the $120 fee that was expected by the local hairdresser. Without any mention of payment, her friend Marianne Everett helped Hansen dye her hair. After seeing what a good job Everett did on her hair, Hansen told Everett that she'd give her $35 for helping. Hansen's promise to Everett is not enforceable because Everett has already completed the work. Her consideration is therefore in the past.

Illusory Promises An **illusory promise** is one that seems genuine but that on close examination actually fails to obligate the promissor to do anything. A party who makes an illusory promise is the only one with any right to determine whether the other party will benefit in any way. Illusory promises fail to provide the mutuality of promises required in establishing consideration.

EXAMPLE 9-4: As Many Illusory Promises as You Might Desire

Pemberton Grocery agreed to buy such fruits and vegetables as it "might desire" for one summer season from Enchanted Farms, Inc. In return for this promise, Enchanted negotiated terms whereby it would give Pemberton a special schedule of discounts for the fruits and vegetables. The promise to buy as much as it "might desire" had actually obligated Pemberton to do nothing. Its promise was illusory because Pemberton might desire absolutely no fruits and vegetables and still keep its promise. The benefits that Pemberton were to derive from the schedule of discounts were not supported by a real or enforceable promise on Pemberton's part. A suit brought by either party to enforce this agreement would fail for want of consideration.

Future Gifts and Legacies The promise of a gift to be given at some future time or in a will is not enforceable if no consideration is given for the promise. Included here are promises to provide gratuitous services or to lend one's property without expectation of any benefits in return.

quick quiz 9-3

1. If a creditor accepts as full payment an amount that is less than   true | false
   the amount due, the dispute has been settled by promissory
   estoppel.

2. An option is the giving of consideration to support an offeror's   true | false
   promise to hold an offer open for a stated length of time.

3. Although illusory promises provide the mutuality of promises   true | false
   required in establishing consideration, the courts will not enforce
   them due to the doctrine of unconscionability.

9-4 Cyber-Payment Tactics and Concerns

Cyber-buying and cyber-selling has become second nature to most American consumers. Part of this process involves setting prices that are attractive to the buyer and profitable for the seller. Since the price involved in a contract is a major part of the consideration equation, and since the online marketplace has affected the pricing process, it is appropriate that we pause at this point to consider the legal ramifications of this new approach to the making of a contract. We will examine two aspects of the online pricing process (1) cyber-price and competition and (2) cyber-payments. As these ideas develop, we will also cover several pieces of cyber-legislation.

Cyber-Price and Competition

Businesses that buy products, supplies, and services from one another have always held an advantage over the average consumer. In the commercial network of market competition, businesses could frequently negotiate with one another over the value of the consideration involved in their contracts. The same was not true of consumers who were generally paralyzed by the price set by the other party. Oddly, this was true whether the offeror was the buyer or the seller. Certainly, there have always been consumers who would comparison shop as they sought the best prices available to them. Most consumers, however, were not that ambitious. The Internet has helped improve the pricing process. Consumers can now use the Internet to seek out competitive prices, thus improving their ability to set the consideration at a level with which they are comfortable.

Cyber-Price Shopping Consumers have a wide variety of ways to comparison shop when it comes to establishing consideration in online contracts. Some online cyber-consumers now make regular use of electronic agents, referred to as a *bot* (*robot, shopping bot, cyber-bot or e-bot*) to comb the vast reaches of cyberspace to find the lowest price available on an item or a service. Cyber-consumers must be aware of the legal ramifications of this process. Two model acts that cover this process are the Uniform Computer Information Transactions Act (UCITA) and the Uniform Electronic Transactions Act (UETA).

Cyber-Shopping Costs Cyber-shopping is not without its drawbacks. One such drawback involves the danger of hidden costs. One hidden cost is the Internet access fee. Most of the time, however, Internet users can track the number of minutes, or more often the number of megabytes, that they have utilized under the contract so that they can pace their time on the net, and either cut back or renegotiate a new contract with their Internet service provider (ISP). Another "hidden" cost comes in the form of shipping and handling fees. Most sellers provide shipping and handling data at the outset or at least as the contract is finalized so that the consumer enters the contract knowing the full value of the consideration paid for the goods purchased on line. Some shippers, however, will overestimate the shipping costs just to make certain that they are not caught paying more for shipping than they are prepared to spend. Buyers should be aware of this unavoidable and often untraceable hidden cost, and be ready to absorb the extra cost if they really want the merchandise.

Cyber-Shopping and the Law
Cyber-shopping is not without its legal entanglements and its illegal practices. Cyber-buyers and cyber-sellers must both be attuned to the difficulties lying in wait when they enter the online cyber-commerce arena. Some traditional and reccuring illegal practices, such as discriminatory price-setting and credit card fraud, are still prevalent in cyberspace. Others, such as the bait-and-switch schemes that we discussed in the previous chapter, are almost impossible to detect online until the damage is done. While both buyers and sellers can be targeted, it is the sellers who are especially vulnerable to credit card fraud and identity fraud. This is because it is much easier for buyers to use stolen credit cards and identity information online. To protect consumers, Congress passed the Identity Theft and Assumption Deterrence Act (ITADA). Later, ITADA was amended by the Identity Theft Penalty Enhancement Act (ITPEA), which outlaws the unauthorized transfer, possession, or use of a means of identifying another person to violate federal law. The amendment adds a new crime, called *aggravated identity theft,* to the original statute.

Cyber-Payments and Cyber-Contracts

Shopping online has many advantages that make it one of the fastest-growing market places on record. Most people shop online because it is quick and efficient. In addition, as noted above, shopping online also permits consumers to compare prices and to settle on the amount of consideration that they can afford. Additionally, some products that are not available in stores, are accessible online. Hard-to-get products available online include out-of-print books, antiques, vintage clothing, rare works of art, hi-fi speaker systems, Polaroid cameras, obsolete auto parts, black-and-white TVs, rotary-dial phones, turntables and vinyl records, outdated appliances, old license plates, carbon paper, old-fashioned audio tapes, vacuum tubes, pulp magazines, out-of date VHS and Beta cassettes, Golden and Silver Age comics, and other vintage products. Despite these advantages, online shopping still has many difficulties, not the least of which is selecting a payment method.

Cyber-Payment Options
Online consumers can choose from several payment methods. One of the most popular methods is by credit card or debit card. It would be very rare today for an online seller to refuse to accept credit or debit card payments. Most online sellers will accept the major credit cards such as Visa, MasterCard, Discover, and so on. Many online cyber-sellers also are moving toward the use of direct online payment systems such as PayPal. This type of system protects both the buyer and the seller. The system is so effective that at some time in the future this may be the only way permissible to buy and sell in cyberspace. This may become the most acceptable process because most of the time when people buy and sell in cyberspace they are dealing with strangers. The issue is especially acute in the cyber-auction industry, involving firms such as eBay. The online payment process eliminates (well, almost nearly eliminates) the identity verification problem.

This is important because one of the biggest concerns about online shopping is security. Once a buyer and a seller have agreed on consideration, they both want to make certain that the contract is fulfilled as promised.

Cyber-Payment Security Update
Consumers who shop online must provide the seller with a means of payment. As we have seen, the most popular method of making payment online is through the use of credit and debit cards. Unfortunately, the ease and efficiency of using such cards is frequently offset by the security concerns associated with their use. Oddly, the United States is not as up-to-date as the European Union in providing data and privacy protection to its consumers. The **EU Data Protection Directive** along with the **EU E-Privacy Directive** guarantee the rights of European citizens while, at the same time, ensuring the smooth exchange of data among those nation-states that honor the privacy and data protection standards themselves. U.S. corporations that are involved with EU corporations must demonstrate that, despite the lack of legislation in the United States, the companies themselves will promise to honor the same degree of protection to data and to privacy as guaranteed by the EU.

These guarantees have been labeled the **Safe Harbor Principles**. They are enforced by the U.S. Department of Commerce. Ironically, this means that U.S. consumers who deal with European companies or with U.S. companies that follow the EU standards will have more security protection than those who deal with purely U.S. companies. Ironically, the safe harbor dispensation is at risk of being destabilized by blowback from the discovery of the U.S. PRISM program, a project run by the National Security Agency that permitted the governments of the United States and the United Kingdom to run an extensive Internet communication collection process that compromised Google and other Internet corporations. In the wake of the PRISM revelation, the European Union has threatened to make it even more difficult for non-European companies to qualify for safe harbor exemptions.

These changes will make it more burdensome for American companies to demonstrate to the EU's satisfaction that they honor the same degree of protection to data and to privacy as guaranteed by the EU. The EU has also threatened to impose more substantial fines on American companies that violate EU privacy standards. Moreover, the EU is also preparing to raise the bar on data protection by providing a strict model for non-European companies to emulate, making it more difficult for American companies to comply with those global standards, thus fortifying the position of European companies that do comply. The EU may also establish an exclusive European cloud to make European data more secure and less accessible by American companies (although, realistically, this will not stop American intelligence gathering). [See: "Charlemagne: Reaching for the Clouds: Europe Wants Tougher Data-Privacy Rules to Deter American Snooping," *The Economist*, July 20, 2014, p. 49.]

quick quiz 9-4

1. The Internet has helped to improve the transparency of the pricing process.	true	false
2. Bait and switch are almost impossible to detect online until the damage is done.	true	false
3. The European Union has provided greater protection for cyber-shoppers than the United States.	true	false

Summary

9.1 The fifth element necessary to any valid contract is consideration. Consideration is the mutual exchange or promise to exchange benefits and sacrifices between contracting parties. Consideration has three requirements: (1) promises made during bargaining depend on the consideration to be received, (2) the consideration must involve something of value, and (3) the benefits and detriments promised must be legal.

9.2 Generally, consideration takes the form of money, property, or services. There are certain special kinds of agreements and promises to which the benefits and sacrifices are unique. Among these are promises not to sue and charitable pledges.

9.3 Problems sometimes arise when the consideration involved in a contract is money and the parties do not agree on the amount of money owed. If there is a genuine dispute, a creditor can accept an amount as full payment even though it is less than the amount claimed. Once the creditor has accepted the lesser amount, the dispute is settled by an act of accord and satisfaction. If the dispute is not genuine, accord and satisfaction do not apply. As a general rule, contracts are not enforceable

without consideration; however, some states eliminate the need for consideration in some agreements. These agreements include promises bearing a seal, promises after discharge in bankruptcy, debts barred by the statute of limitations, promises enforced by promissory estoppel, and options governed by the UCC. Other agreements that seem to involve consideration but that the courts will not enforce involve preexisting duties, past consideration, illusory promises, and gifts.

9.4 The measurement of consideration has become an issue when consumers buy and sell online. Consumers can comparison shop online using shopping search engines, patronizing user-friendly industries, and shopping with companies that provide price comparisons on their websites. Cyber-shopping hidden costs include Internet access fees and shipping and handling costs. Some illegal practices involved in online shopping include discriminatory price-setting, credit card fraud, and bait-and-switch schemes. Online consumers can choose from several payment methods including credit cards, debit cards, smart cards, and alternative cyber-payment systems such as PayPal. Privacy protection and security, however, are limited.

Key Terms

accord, 225
accord and satisfaction, 225
bargained-for exchange, 220
consideration, 219
disputed amount, 225
estoppel, 228
EU Data Protection Directive, 232
EU E-Privacy Directive, 232

firm offer, 228
forbearance, 220
illusory promise, 229
irrevocable offer, 228
legal detriment, 219
locus sigilli, 226
option, 228
past consideration, 229

preexisting duties, 229
promissory estoppel, 228
release, 224
Safe Harbor Principles, 232
satisfaction, 225
seal, 226
statutes of limitations, 227
unconscionable, 221

Questions for Review and Discussion

1. What is consideration?
2. What are the different types of detriment?
3. What characteristics are necessary for consideration to be valid?
4. What is meant by the term *unconscionable*?
5. Can a promise not to sue be consideration?
6. How can a charitable pledge be consideration?

7. What is the procedure that a debtor and creditor may use to settle a claim by means of accord and satisfaction?
8. What agreements may be enforceable by a court of law even though they lack consideration?
9. What is the doctrine of promissory estoppel?
10. What issues are involved in the cyber-payment process?

Cases for Analysis

1. Twenty-two congressional representatives proposed a bill that would permit corporate shareholders to review the consideration packages that had been granted to key corporate executives of public corporations. The bill, which was named the Shareholder Vote on Executive Compensation Act, would empower the shareholders of public corporations to evaluate and vote on the appropriateness of the compensation packages that had been granted to the corporation's top five officers. The vote, however, would not obligate the corporation to change the compensation package if the shareholders disapproved of its terms. Would such a bill, if enacted into law, conflict with established contract law principles that permit parties to negotiate their own level of consideration? Explain. [See: Donna Block, "Proposal Seeks Shareholder OK on Executive Pay," *The National Law Journal,* March 12, 2007, p. 9.]

2. Consideration can serve as a strong motivator. At least this is what a newly founded shareholder forum believes. The forum was formed to monitor the salaries of top corporate executives, especially CEOs, by matching those salaries with the executive's incentive package, which includes the corporation's latest list of objectives and the number or the percentage of those objectives that the executive must meet to receive incentive pay. The goal of incentive pay is to motivate top executives to do more than sit in the CEO's office from 9:00 to 5:00 each day. Is incentive pay a violation of the principle that says that preexisting duties cannot be used as consideration in a new contract? Explain. [See: Gretchen Morgenson, "Hear Ye, Hear Ye: Coralling Executive Pay," *The New York Times,* June 17, 2007, sec 3, pp. 1 and 8.]

3. General Motors decided to move a car producing operation to Arlington, Texas, from a plant located in Ypsilanti, Michigan. As a result, the township of Ypsilanti brought a lawsuit to stop General Motors from making the move. Ypsilanti argued that GM had promised to keep the plant in Ypsilanti in exchange for certain tax privileges. The township argued further that it had relied on those promises when it granted that tax abatement to the corporation. Therefore, GM should be forced to keep its promise to maintain the Ypsilanti plant. Should the court stop this move based on the doctrine of promissory estoppel? Explain. [See: *Charter Township of Ypsilanti v. General Motors,* 508 N.W.2d 556 (Michigan Court of Appeals).]

4. Aviation Electronics entered a contract with Sky Train Institute of Montana in which Aviation agreed to supply the institute with 17,000 component parts for the development of the institute's remote control bomber. The bomber had to be operational by December 3; otherwise, the institute would lose a research grant from the Department of Defense. After delivering 5,000 parts, Aviation told Sky Train that it wanted an additional $4 million beyond the original price agreed upon to deliver the remaining parts. Sky Train attempted to obtain the parts from other firms, none of which could fill the order in the time limit required by the DOD contract specifications. To make the deadline stipulated in the government contract, Sky Train reluctantly agreed to the new price demanded by Aviation. What "thing of value," if any, has Aviation transferred to the institute that it did not already owe the institute under the original contract? Explain.

5. Savaretti offered to pay his niece, Wilma, $2,000 if she would agree to give up eating meat and pastries and drinking caffeinated beverages for six months. Wilma agreed and gave up these activities for six months. At the end of those six months, Savaretti refused to give Wilma the $2,000, arguing that because giving up caffeine, meat, and pastries was beneficial to her health, she suffered no detriment and was owed nothing. Wilma took Savaretti to small claims court and demanded payment of the $2,000. She argued that because

she had the legal right to consume the caffeine, meat, and pastries, she suffered a legal detriment and was entitled to her money. How should the referee rule in this case? Explain.

6. Daniel Davidson told Velma Evans that he would hire her to work on an architectural job. He gave her a date to show up for work and told her to leave her present job. Relying on Davidson's statements, Evans left her job. Davidson never let Evans begin work, and as a result, she was out of work for six months. Evans sued Davidson for the wages she lost during those six months. Davidson argued that because they'd never decided on the final terms of employment, no contract ever existed between the two of them. Evans argued that the principle of promissory estoppel should apply here. Is Evans correct? Explain.

7. The Mighty Fine Food Emporium agreed to buy such fruits and vegetables as it "might desire" for one summer season from Kennelsworth Farms and Vineyards. In return for this promise, Kennelsworth negotiated terms whereby it would give Mighty Fine a special schedule of discounts for the fruits and vegetables. Did the promise to buy as much as it "might desire" obligate Kennelsworth in any way? Are the benefits that Kennelsworth was to derive from the schedule of discounts supported by an enforceable promise on Kennelsworth's part? Would a suit brought by either party to enforce this agreement succeed? Explain each answer.

8. Graham O'Hanlon, without any mention of payment, helped his friend, Patricia Tippon, move from Westerville to Pepper Pike. The entire move took 48 hours to complete. At the end of the day, after she was in her new house, Tippon told O'Hanlon that she'd give him $200 for helping her move. Is Tippon's promise to O'Hanlon enforceable? Why or why not?

9. Vanoni Biological Supplies, Inc., contracted with the Hayden Institute to supply the Institute with 24,000 biological specimens for a series of experiments that the institute has agreed to perform for the Maritime University of Columbia. The institute must have the specimens by September 9 to meet the university's schedule. After delivering 12,000 of the specimens, Vanoni told the institute that it wanted an additional $1,600 to deliver the remaining 12,000 specimens. Can Vanoni make the delivery of the remaining 12,000 specimens consideration in a new agreement with the institute? Explain.

10. Seier agreed to pay $10,000 to Peek in exchange for all the stock in a corporation. The agreement was placed in writing. Nevertheless, when the time came for payment, Seier refused to live up to his end of the deal. His argument was that the stock was not worth the $10,000 that he had agreed to pay for it. Did the court listen to Seier's argument and attempt to determine the value of the consideration? Explain. [See: *Seier v. Peek,* 456 So.2d 1079 (AL).]

quick quiz Answers

9-1	9-2	9-3	9-4
1. F	1. F	1. F	1. T
2. T	2. F	2. T	2. T
3. T	3. F	3. F	3. T

THE OPENING CASE *Round 1*
Geographical Limits at Work: How Much Territory Is Too Much Territory?

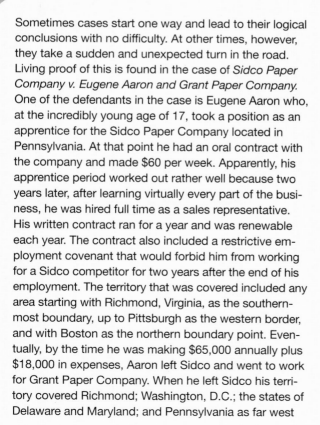

Sometimes cases start one way and lead to their logical conclusions with no difficulty. At other times, however, they take a sudden and unexpected turn in the road. Living proof of this is found in the case of *Sidco Paper Company v. Eugene Aaron and Grant Paper Company.* One of the defendants in the case is Eugene Aaron who, at the incredibly young age of 17, took a position as an apprentice for the Sidco Paper Company located in Pennsylvania. At that point he had an oral contract with the company and made $60 per week. Apparently, his apprentice period worked out rather well because two years later, after learning virtually every part of the business, he was hired full time as a sales representative. His written contract ran for a year and was renewable each year. The contract also included a restrictive employment covenant that would forbid him from working for a Sidco competitor for two years after the end of his employment. The territory that was covered included any area starting with Richmond, Virginia, as the southernmost boundary, up to Pittsburgh as the western border, and with Boston as the northern boundary point. Eventually, by the time he was making $65,000 annually plus $18,000 in expenses, Aaron left Sidco and went to work for Grant Paper Company. When he left Sidco his territory covered Richmond; Washington, D.C.; the states of Delaware and Maryland; and Pennsylvania as far west

as Chambersburg. Sidco filed a lawsuit asking for a preliminary injunction that would prevent Aaron from competing with Sidco in the protected territory. Aaron argued that the territory covered was much too vast and that it was drawn in a way that was not reasonably necessary to protect Sidco because Aaron was, after all, just one lone salesman. The law in this case is pretty straightforward. It says that restrictive employment covenants must be reasonably necessary to protect the former employer and must be limited in the type of work they prohibit, the length of time involved in the prohibition, and the geographical area covered by the prohibition. The case here does not involve type of work or duration of the covenant. The focus is on geography and whether the prohibition was a reasonable way to protect Sidco from this lone salesman. At first blush, the territory seems quite huge, covering as it does, much of Pennsylvania, Maryland, and Virginia, as well as Washington, D.C. However, the record also shows that Aaron was free to solicit business in New York, New Jersey, Delaware, Massachusetts, Philadelphia, four additional counties in Pennsylvania, and the rest of the country. Moreover, as far as reasonableness is concerned in the protected territory, Sidco's business dropped from $490,000 to $90,000 in the protected area in the year after Aaron left the firm. The trial court granted the preliminary injunction and so the question is what will the appellate court do now? [See: *Sidco Paper Company v. Aaron,* 465 Pa. 586, 315 A. 2d 250 (1976).]

Opening Case Questions

1. What is the age of majority in most states? Explain.

2. Can a 17-year-old make a valid, enforceable employment contract? Why or why not? Explain.

3. Why did the employer in this case wait for two years to give the employee a full-time contract? Explain.

4. What are the requirements of a reasonable restrictive employment agreement? Explain.

5. Are those limitations imposed by the employer reasonable in this case? Explain.

LO Learning Objectives

1. Identify the age of minority and the age of majority.
2. Explain the legal status of a contract made by a minor.
3. Differentiate between ratification and disaffirmance.
4. Identify the effects of mental impairment on a contract.
5. Discuss the contractual capacity of a drugged or intoxicated person.
6. Explain the legality of agreements to commit torts and crimes.
7. Identify those agreements made illegal under statutory law.
8. Enumerate those agreements contrary to public policy.
9. Explain what happens under the doctrine of *in pari delicto*.
10. Explain the effects of illegality.

10-1 The Final Elements

The final two elements of a contract are capacity and legality. A contract can have a valid offer, an effective acceptance, mutual assent, valid consideration, and still be void if it involves doing something illegal. An **illegal agreement** is one that violates criminal law or tort law, a statute, and/or public policy as established by the court. In general, the law will aid neither party involved in an illegal agreement. **Capacity** is the legal ability to enter a valid contract. Generally, a person has the ability to enter a contract if he or she possesses free will, displays a certain degree of self-knowledge and is informed about the nature, purpose, and effect of the agreement. The chapter here is designed to first explore the various factors that affect capacity and then look at what makes a contract illegal and what happens as a result of that illegality.

Minors are able to rescind most contracts; however, adults that contract with minors generally cannot.

The Nature of Capacity and Minority

Capacity is considered a **rebuttable presumption**. This means that, under the law, the parties to a contract are permitted to presume that each of them has the capacity to enter a contract. The term *rebuttable* means that presumption is not absolute. Rather, it can be challenged. Generally, in the case of capacity, the presumption is

challenged by the party claiming incapacity. In other words, that party is saying something like, "I know you presumed that I had capacity to enter the contract when we negotiated this agreement and thank you for that, but, guess what, I did not have capacity and I would, therefore, like to exit the agreement." So for example, under the current state of the law, for instance, when a minor enters a contract with an adult, and the minor seeks to void the contract, he or she is challenging the presumption of capacity.

The law allows minors the privilege to **disaffirm** (negate) a contract to protect them from unscrupulous adults (or unscrupulous minors for that matter) who might take advantage of the young people who might not fully comprehend the responsibilities that they are assuming. When a minor indicates by a statement or act an intent not to live up to a contract, that minor is entitled to a return of everything given to the other party. This right exists even when the property transferred to the minor under the contract has been damaged or destroyed. A few states will deduct something from the amount due back to the minor if the goods are damaged. Most states, however, deduct nothing.

In a sense then, minors actually have extra-capacity, that is, they have the capacity to enter a contract and the capacity to exit the contract by challenging that rebuttable presumption. This is unlike someone who uses mental impairment as the grounds for disaffirming a contract. The person using mental impairment is arguing that the mental impairment took away his or her capacity to enter a contract at the time of the agreement. In contrast, the minor is using a *legal fiction* that says minors lack capacity. Another way of saying this is to note that the person with a mental impairment really did not know the nature and the purpose and the effect of the agreement and, therefore, must not be held liable. The minor may or may not have real incapacity, that is, the actual real-life inability to understand the nature, purpose, and effect of the agreement, or the minor may have legal incapacity, which is a legal fiction that says we will lump all minors together and say that they do not have capacity until they cross a magical line called the age of majority.

About the Law

A rebuttable-presumption is also known as a "disputable presumption."

Definition of Minority

Under common law, **minority** was a term that described persons who had not yet reached the age of 21 years. Upon reaching that age, a person was said to have reached **majority**. Ratification and adoption of the 26th Amendment to the U.S. Constitution in 1971 lowered the voting age in federal elections from 21 to 18 years. To avoid the confusion that would result from having two voting ages, the states started to enact new laws that enabled 18-year-olds to vote in state and local elections. Then most states began to lower the age of majority to 18 years (note: Alabama and Nebraska use 19 and Mississippi and Puerto Rico use 21, but check the current law wherever you might live to make certain). Some states also tie the age of majority to high school graduation. As of the most recent check, these include Arkansas, Nevada, Ohio, Tennessee, Utah, and Wisconsin. Other age requirements differ from state to state in relation to matters such as the legal ability to purchase alcoholic beverages, enter a marriage, buy tobacco products, purchase firearms, and operate motor vehicles. Recently, for instance, in response to outside influences from a variety of social organizations and governmental institutions, many states have raised the legal age for purchasing and consuming alcohol to 21 years. Also, young men must register for selective service at 18 years of age.

U.S. Const.
Amendment 26
(see page 917).

Emancipation and Abandonment

In some jurisdictions, minors who become **emancipated**, that is, no longer under the control of their parents, are responsible for their contracts. This responsibility means that they cannot void a contract, despite their apparent minority. Emancipated minors include those who are married, those in the armed forces, and those who leave home and, in the process, give up all right to parental support. In certain states, minors are even allowed to ask the court for a legally sanctioned emancipation. In all these cases, emancipated minors are said to have

abandoned the usual protective shield given them. Although minors in these categories are no longer protected from liability on their contracts, merchants are still reluctant to deal with them on a credit basis, fearing that they may still attempt to disaffirm, or repudiate, their contracted debts. Again, for practical, not legal, reasons, merchants often require that minors get the signature of a responsible adult who will agree to guarantee payment of money owed.

Moreover, the hesitancy felt by some merchants in relation to emancipated minors is justified because a few states still hold to the opposite rule, that is, that emancipated minors do not give up the legal advantages associated with minority simply because they leave home or become married. To support this position, the courts in these jurisdictions note that the rule that allows minors to rescind contracts is based on the idea that minors are less experienced and less knowledgeable than adults about the consequences of their actions. It is therefore difficult to see why getting married or leaving home somehow bestows more common sense on a minor who does so. In fact, one court remarked that getting married and leaving home may actually indicate that a minor has less good sense than another minor who does neither. Because this rule differs from state to state, it would be a good idea to check the rule of law in your jurisdiction.

THE OPENING CASE *Round 2*
Capacity or Employment at Will? Which Dominates?

In the opening case we learned that Eugene Aaron, one of the defendants in the case of *Sidco Paper Company v. Eugene Aaron and Grant Paper Company,* at the age of 17, took a position as an apprentice for the Sidco Paper Company located in Pennsylvania. At that point he had nothing more than an oral contract with the company and he made $60 per week. However, Aaron's apprentice period must have worked quite well because after two years, he was given a full-time position as a sales representative. This time Sidco gave him written contract. The contract was only for a single year but it could be renewed annually. The written contract also included an interesting term that permitted each party to terminate the agreement provided that they gave 60 days' advanced notice. On the other hand, the contract also included a restrictive employment agreement that would be activated once Aaron's employment was terminated. The covenant would forbid Aaron from working for a Sidco competitor for two years after the end of his employment. The territory that was covered included any area starting with Richmond, Virginia, as the southern-most boundary, up to Pittsburgh as the western border, and with Boston as the northern boundary point. When Aaron was first hired as an apprentice at 17 he was still a minor. That meant that he could void any contact at any time with

no penalty. Another way to say this is that a contract made by a minor is voidable by the minor. The law allows minors to disaffirm contracts to protect them from unscrupulous adults who might take advantage of young people who might not fully comprehend the responsibilities that they are assuming. This explains why Sidco hired Aaron using only an oral agreement during his apprenticeship. Since he could leave at any time, there was no need for a written agreement. However, ironically, the written agreement that Sidco made with Aaron after he reached his majority is also one that he could disaffirm because, from all available evidence, it was an at-will agreement. Employment at will means that an employment contract can be terminated by either party at any time for any reason or for no reason, with or without notice. This also means that the notice provision in the contract was also unnecessary and unenforceable. After all, Sidco could not make Aaron work for the company if he did not want to. That would be involuntary servitude, something we outlawed in the United States some time ago. Of course, if Aaron's employment were not at-will, there might be some monetary penalty for violating the notice provision, but that would be the extent of the negative consequences for Aaron had that occurred. [See: *Sidco Paper Company v. Aaron,* 465 Pa. 586, 315 A. 2d 250 (1976).]

Misrepresentation of Age Minors sometimes lie about their age when making a contract. Despite this misrepresentation of age, most states will allow the minor to disaffirm or get out of the contract. Some jurisdictions, however, do not permit the minor to get away with the lie. Some states require the minor to place the adult party to the contract in the same situation that he or she was in before the contract. Others allow the adult to use tort law, rather than contract law, to sue the minor for fraud. Some states have also enacted statutes that allow recovery against a minor who is engaged in business and who misrepresents his or her age in a commercial contract. A number of states, for example, have statutes that deny disaffirmance if the minor has signed a written statement falsely asserting adult status. Without such a statute, the minor would be allowed to get out of the primary contract despite her or his signature on that primary contract or the contract asserting adult status.

Contractual Capacity of Minors

Executory contracts, those that have not been fully performed by both parties, may be repudiated by a minor at any time. A promise to deliver goods or render services at some future time need not be carried out by the minor who decides not to do so. This privilege is not available to an adult who contracts with a minor. If goods delivered to a repudiating minor are still in the minor's possession, it is the minor's duty to return them to the other party.

Did You Know?

Despite being designated as "necessaries," such things are not always needed to preserve or protect life. In fact, in one case the court held that funeral expenses were necessaries.

Contracts for Necessaries Goods and services that are essential to a minor's health and welfare are called **necessaries**. Thus, necessaries can include clothing, food, shelter, medical and dental services, tools and equipment needed for the minor to carry out his or her business, and even, in some cases, educational expenses. If a minor makes a contract for necessaries, he or she will be liable for the fair value of those necessaries. Despite the general tenor of this principle, if the necessaries have already been provided to the minor by parents or others, the rule does not apply. In addition, not everything that a party claims as a necessary will actually be a necessary. To determine whether goods and services qualify as genuine necessaries, the court will inquire into the minor's family status, financial strength, and social standing or station in life. Necessaries, then, are not the same to all persons.

Technically, a minor's contract covering necessaries is not enforceable against the minor in the truest sense of the term. Instead, the minor is required to pay the fair value of the necessaries that have been provided by the adult. The fair value is determined by the court. This approach to the law is an extension of the concept of quasi-contract. Remember that when applying the concept of quasi-contract, the court will require the parties to act as if there were a contract, even though a true contract does not exist. The point of requiring the minor to pay the fair value of the item is to play it straight with adults who carry the risk of dealing with minors in relation to necessaries. Allowing the minor to get away with completely rescinding such contracts would amount to unfair enrichment of the minor. The concept of quasi-contract is aimed at preventing this type of unjust enrichment.

Many people, including minors and the adults who deal with them, overlook an interesting corollary related to the concept of necessaries. This corollary is the standard that states that the rules related to necessaries apply only to executed contracts. An executed contract is one whose terms have been completely and satisfactorily carried out by both parties. In contrast, an executory contract is one that has not yet been fully performed by the parties. Wholly executory contracts calling for a future delivery or rendering of services may be repudiated by the minor.

Technically, parents are liable for a contract executed by a minor, even a contract for necessaries, *only* when they cosign the agreements. When a parent, or anyone else for that matter, cosigns for a loan or for a contract involving installment payments, the cosigner becomes a guarantor. A guarantor promises to pay the other party's debts if that party does not settle those debts personally. This promise is known as a guaranty of payment. In contrast, if parents do not cosign a contract, they are *not liable* for that contract, even though the contract was made by their minor child. As might be expected, there is an exception to this general rule. If a parent has neglected or deserted the minor, the parent may be held liable to a third person for the fair value of the necessaries supplied by the third party to the minor.

Other Contracts not Voidable   By statute and court decision, certain other types of contracts have been excepted from the general rule that the contracts of minors are voidable at the minor's option. For public policy reasons, minors may not at their option disaffirm a valid marriage or repudiate an enlistment contract in the armed forces based on a claim of incapacity to contract. Neither may a minor repudiate a contract for goods and services required by law; for example, minors may not repudiate payments for inoculations and vaccinations required for attendance at a university or college or required in securing a visa for travel in certain foreign lands. They may also be prevented from terminating contracts with banks and other financial institutions for educational loans. Some states bar minors from repudiating agency contracts and insurance contracts. Others prevent them from voiding contracts for psychological care, pregnancy care, the transfer of stocks and bonds, and contracts involving child support. These exceptions are state-by-state issues, so it is wise to check your own state statutes to determine which of these contracts are not voidable by minors in your jurisdiction.

Shield or Sword Doctrine   If tempted to see the rescission rights of minors as unfair, we must keep in mind the original intent of the court in granting this power. As noted previously, the right to rescind contracts was given to minors as a protective device or "shield" against those unscrupulous adults who might try to take unfair advantage of the immaturity and inexperience of minors. This type of situation is precisely what the law envisioned when it granted minors the "shield" that allows them to rescind contracts.

The problem with this protective device is that it can be exploited by minors who use it to rescind legitimate contracts. In effect, an unprincipled minor can take this safeguard, which is meant as a protective shield, and transform it into a sword that violates the rights of the other party. Fortunately, the courts are not oblivious to this type of abuse. Because the doctrine was never meant to allow minors to take advantage of innocent people, the courts have no difficulty denying rescission rights to minors when they use it as a weapon against another contracting party.

About the Law

Under the Napoleonic Code, people under 30 years of age could not marry without their father's permission. In addition, a father could have his child incarcerated for as long as six months on his word alone.

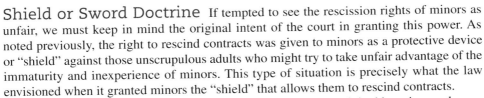

EXAMPLE 10-1: The Shield and Sword Doctrine

Amber Sampson, who was 16 years of age, purchased a round-trip ticket on New England Airlines for a trip from Portland, Maine, to San Diego, California, for spring break. When spring break was over, Sampson returned to Portland and, on arrival, demanded the return of all the money that she had paid for the round-trip ticket. Her demands were based on her rescission rights as a minor. Clearly, Sampson was using her right to rescind to take advantage of New England Airlines. She was not using her rights as a minor as a protective shield, as the law intended. It is doubtful that Sampson will be permitted to recover money for her ticket.

Voidable Contracts and Innocent Third Parties   Another curb on a minor's right to rescind contracts appears in the provisions of the UCC. These provisions protect the rights of an innocent third party who purchases goods from an individual who originally purchased those same goods from a minor. Although individuals who buy goods from minors have voidable ownership rights, under the UCC, those same individuals can transfer valid ownership rights to an innocent third-party purchaser of those goods. Thus, rescission by a minor will not require the innocent purchaser to return the goods.

EXAMPLE 10-2: Protecting the Innocent

David Wittmer, age 17 years, sold his laptop to Lustbader Electronics, LLC. Lustbader refurbished the ancient laptop and then sold it to Alex Myers, an innocent third-party buyer. Before Wittmer became an adult, he decided to get back his laptop from Myers by disaffirming his contract with Lustbader. Wittmer is out of luck here. He will not be able to recover the laptop by disaffirming his contract with Lustbader. Myers is an innocent third party and is thus protected by the UCC.

The UCC rule refers to the sale of personal property. In cases in which a minor has sold real estate to one who subsequently sells it to an innocent third party, the minor, on reaching adulthood, may disaffirm the sale and recover the real property.

Ratification and Disaffirmance People may ratify their contracts made during minority only after reaching their majority or within a reasonable time thereafter. **Ratification** or **affirmance** is the willingness to abide by contractual obligations. It may be implied by using the item purchased, making an installment payment, paying off the balance of money owed on a previously voidable contract, continuing to accept goods and services being provided under a contract, or just doing nothing about the contract after reaching majority. Affirmation may also result from the person's oral or written declaration to abide by the contract. These acts, as well as others, ratify an existing agreement and elevate it to the status of one that is enforceable against an adult.

THE OPENING CASE *Round 3*
Minority, Majority, and the Transformative Effect of Doing Nothing

In the opening case we learned that Eugene Aaron, at the age of 17, took a position as an apprentice for the Sidco Paper Company. The hiring process involved an oral contract with the company and he made no more than made $60 per week. Aaron's apprentice period worked quite well because after two years, he was given a full-time position as a sales representative. This time Sidco gave him a written contract that was for a single year, but that could be renewed annually. When Aaron was first hired as an apprentice at 17 he was still a minor. That meant that he could void any contact at any time with no penalty. Another way to say this is that the contract was made by a minor (Aaron) and was, therefore, voidable by the minor (Aaron). The law allows minors to disaffirm contracts to protect them from unscrupulous adults who might take advantage of young people who might not fully comprehend the responsibilities that they are assuming. This may be why Sidco hired Aaron using only an oral agreement during his apprenticeship. Since he could leave at any time, there was no need for a written agreement. Then again, the oral agreement made when Aaron was a minor might have changed into a valid, enforceable, adult-made contract. This transformation may have occurred because, after Aaron turned 18, he continued to work for Sidco, presumably under the same terms that they followed when the oral agreement was made when Aaron was 17. In this way, Aaron ratified that first contract. Ratification or affirmance is the willingness to abide by contractual obligations. In this case ratification was implied because Aaron did nothing differently after he turned 18. He continued to work for Sidco, signaling that the new "adult" Aaron passively consented to that original contract made by the now vanished "minor" Aaron. [See: *Sidco Paper Company v. Aaron,* 465 Pa. 586, 315 A. 2d 250 (1976).]

An individual may disaffirm an agreement made during minority before or within a reasonable time after reaching adulthood. The exact period of time will vary depending on the nature of the contract and on applicable state and local laws. Failure to disaffirm within a reasonable period of time would imply that the contract had been ratified. The method of disaffirmance is fundamentally the same as the method of ratification. Disaffirmance may be implied by the acts of the individual after achieving majority, such as by a failure to make an installment payment. Similarly, an oral or written declaration of disaffirmance would achieve the same end. In general, there are no particular protocols attached to the act of disaffirmance by a minor. However, it is generally a good idea to make the disaffirmance in writing so that there is a record of the transaction should questions arise later. This recommendation is especially true if the contract is disaffirmed after the minor has reached the age of majority.

---

quick quiz 10-1

1. Executory contracts, those which have not been fully performed by both parties, may be repudiated by a minor at any time.   true | false

2. Ratification is the willingness to abide by contractual obligations.   true | false

3. Necessaries are the same for all persons.   true | false

10-2 Other Capacity Problems

Persons deprived of the mental ability to comprehend contractual obligations have the right to disaffirm their contracts. Their rights are, in many respects, the same as the rights of minors. Agreements of mentally impaired persons are valid, voidable, or void, depending on the seriousness of their disability and whether they have been declared insane.

Persons Mentally Impaired

Under the orthodox rule of competency in contract law, a contract made by a person who is mentally infirm, has brain damage, is suffering from a physical illness such as Alzheimer's disease, or suffers from a psychological disorder may be voidable if the person's impairment is severe enough to rob that person of the ability to understand the nature, purpose, and effect of that contract. The question will be whether the mental problem existed at the time the contract was made and was so serious that the person did not understand the nature of the contract. If that is the case, the mentally impaired person may disaffirm any contract made under the influence of that mental impairment. The incompetent person must return all consideration received. This rule is true especially when the other party had no knowledge of the person's mental impairment. If, however, the other party knew about the person's mental impairment and took advantage of that knowledge, there is no requirement to return the other party to the identical place that he or she was in before the original agreement was established.

LO4

A second rule is also recognized by the Restatement of Contracts and by some states. That rule says that a person's contractual obligations may be voidable if that person suffers from a mental impairment that prevents him or her from acting in a reasonable manner. Under this version of the rule, a person may understand the nature of the contract but, because of his or her impairment, be unable to stop himself or herself from entering the contract. In such a situation, as long as the contract has yet to be executed or, if executed, can be shown to be very unjust, the impaired person may void the contract. If the contract is executed or fair, the impaired party may still void the contract but also must return the other party to the place he or she was in before the contract was entered. If returning the other party to his or her precontract condition cannot be done, the court will decide on a fair alternative.

A person declared to be insane by competent legal authority is denied the right to enter contracts. Such persons will be under the care of a guardian who acts on behalf of the impaired person, who has in effect become a ward of the court. Any contractual relationship with others results in nothing more than a void agreement. In most states, persons who knowingly take advantage of one declared insane are subject to criminal indictment and prosecution.

Persons Drugged or Intoxicated

A contract agreed to by someone under the influence of alcohol or drugs may be voidable. Incompetence related to either alcohol or drugs must be of such a degree that a contracting party would have lost the ability to comprehend or be aware of obligations being accepted under the contract. A person who enters into a contract while in this condition may either affirm or disaffirm the agreement later. Disaffirmance in such cases requires the return to the other party of all consideration that had been received. However, such a return may be refused when evidence indicates that the other party took advantage of the person's drunken or otherwise weakened condition.

EXAMPLE 10-3: Involuntary Intoxication Invalidates a Contract

Samuel K. Richardson III attended a reception at the Yakuza Gallery on Madison Avenue at 75th Street in Manhattan. Unknown to Richardson, the punch at the reception had been laced with alcohol. After drinking several glasses, Richardson became highly intoxicated. While intoxicated, he agreed to sell the original manuscript of the novel *The Bay Tree* to an antiquarian book dealer named Maynard Posner, who was also at the reception and who was quite sure that Richardson was "tipsy" at the time of the sale. When Richardson recovered, he sought to disaffirm the contract. Because his involuntary state of intoxication had robbed Richardson of his ability to comprehend the contract he was making with Posner, he would be allowed to get out of the agreement.

quick quiz 10-2

1. For a contract to be voidable by a person with a mental impairment, the mental problem must exist at the time the contract was made.   true | false

2. A person declared to be insane by competent legal authority cannot be denied the right to enter contracts.   true | false

3. A contract made by a person who is intoxicated is completely void.   true | false

10-3 Agreements to Engage in Unlawful Activity

The final element of a valid contract is legality. Ordinarily, the court will leave the parties to an illegal agreement where they placed themselves. If an illegal agreement is still executory, the court will not order it performed or award damages for breach of contract. If the illegal agreement has been executed, the court will not award damages or assist in having it annulled. The most obvious type of illegal contract is one in which parties agree to perform some sort of unlawful activity. This activity could be a crime or a tort, depending on the circumstances. However, when we use the term *unlawful activity* in this context, we are referring to activities that are clearly wrong in and of themselves. These unlawful activities include crimes and torts that most people would recognize as wrong, even if there were no statute, regulation, or court decision to tell them it was wrong.

Agreements to Commit Torts and Crimes

The law will not uphold any contract that obligates one of the parties to commit a tort. For example, a network television reporter who agrees to defame several politicians in return for a position as their opponent's press secretary would find no remedy in the law should her benefactor fail to follow through after the libelous story was printed. The agreement to commit a tort would be void in the eyes of the law. This approach only makes good sense. The law cannot lend its approval to a contract that breaks the law, no matter how complete it is in relation to the other three elements.

In like manner, the law cannot honor any agreement if the purpose of the agreement is to commit a crime. If, for example, a storekeeper would pay a known criminal to vandalize the shop of a competitor, that storekeeper would not be able to sue the criminal for breach of contract should the criminal take the money and run. As strange as it may seem, the nature of criminality is not always as clear as might be imagined. Because criminal law involves serious offenses that can result in the loss of a person's freedom or, more seriously, the loss of a person's life, all criminal statutes must be drawn as precisely and as clearly as possible. A statute that is obscure or outlines conduct that is ambiguous may be struck down by the court as void for vagueness. This ruling would mean that a contract that involves the conduct that is allegedly outlawed by a vague statute might not be void.

Agreements Illegal under Statutory Law

Most people of good faith would know, even in the absence of any statute, regulation, ordinance, rule, or court decision, that the behavior outlined in the previous examples would be wrong. It is difficult to imagine, for instance, that the shopkeeper would be surprised to discover that it is wrong to hire someone to destroy his competitor's property. Similarly, it is not easy to believe that the television reporter who agreed to lie in a television broadcast thought that her behavior was in any way admirable. In contrast, some activities that do not seem wrong on the surface may have been made wrong by specific statutory enactments. Therefore, the fact that some of these activities are illegal may catch us by surprise. For example, the shopkeeper knows vandalism is illegal but may be confused to learn that he cannot hold a garage sale without a license. Or the reporter who knows that libel is wrong may be amazed to learn that she cannot legally enforce the collection of her winnings from her Thursday night poker game (unless that game is run by a state sanctioned casino). For this reason, we will examine those activities that are wrong because a statute says they are wrong. These activities include usurious agreements, wagering agreements, unlicensed agreements, unconscionable agreements, and Sunday (Sabbath) agreements.

Usurious Agreements

The illegal practice of charging more than the amount of interest allowed by law is called **usury**. To protect borrowers from excessive interest charges, each state has passed laws that specify the rate of interest that may be charged in lending money. These interest rates vary from state to state. Agreements to charge more than is allowed by law are illegal. Special statutes, however, allow small loan companies, pawn shops, and other lending agencies that accept high-risk applicants for credit to charge a higher rate of interest.

Wagering Agreements

Any agreement or promise concerning a wager or some other form of gambling is invalid and may not be enforced. States make exceptions when bets are placed in accordance with laws that permit horse racing, state lotteries, church-related or charitable games of bingo, and gambling casinos regulated by state authority. However, even in states in which gambling is legal, borrowing money to gamble is frequently still illegal.

Unlicensed Agreements

Certain businesses and professions must be licensed before they are allowed to operate legally. One reason for requiring a license is to provide a source of revenue, part of which is used to supervise the business or profession being licensed. A city ordinance requiring all residents to obtain a license before holding a yard or garage sale would fall into this category. Another purpose that the government has in licensing individuals is to provide supervision and regulation of businesses and professions that might inflict harm on the public if they were allowed to operate without such controls. Physicians, nurses, dentists, attorneys, engineers, architects, public school teachers, and others in public service must be supervised for the protection of the public. The law distinguishes between licenses purely for revenue and licenses for protection of the public. If a license is required simply to raise revenue, the lack of a license will not necessarily make a contract void; if a licensing requirement is designed to protect the public, unlicensed persons will not be able to enforce their contracts.

Unconscionable Agreements

A court will not enforce a contract or any part of a contract that it regards as unconscionable. An agreement is considered unconscionable if its terms are so grossly unfair that they shock the court's conscience. When the court so desires, it will limit how the unconscionable clause in an agreement is carried out, provided it can do so without causing any unfair consequences.

Sunday Agreements

State statutes and local ordinances that regulate the making and performing of contracts on Sunday are called **blue laws** because one of the first laws banning Sunday or Sabbath contracts was written on blue paper. Today, the enforcement of restrictive blue laws varies in different geographical areas. Certain states have eliminated uniform statewide laws regulating Sunday activities but permit counties and incorporated cities, towns, and villages to adopt their own ordinances under a concept known as **local option**. Other states have rolled back these laws almost entirely, permitting most contracts while prohibiting or limiting only a few select Sunday contracts, such as those involving the sale of alcohol. Where laws do restrict Sunday business, two rules are usually observed. First, agreements made on Sunday or any other day requiring performance on Sunday may be ruled invalid. Exceptions to this rule are those agreements necessary to the health, welfare, and safety of the community and its residents. Second, agreements made on Sunday for work to be done or goods to be delivered on a business day are valid and enforceable. However, some states still require that there be an affirmation of such agreements on a day other than Sunday if such agreements are to be enforceable. The enforcement of blue laws varies widely from state to state, county to county, and village to village.

Agreements Contrary to Public Policy

The general legal principle of **public policy** says no one should be allowed to do anything that injures the public at large. Agreements most commonly invalidated as contrary to public policy are those to obstruct justice, interfere with public service, defraud creditors, escape liability, and restrain trade. Some of these agreements are prohibited by statute, such as those that suppress competition and those that interfere with public service. Consequently, they could have been listed and explained in the last section. Instead, these contracts are listed here with the other public policy–related contracts, because they share one thing in common, though such contracts are made between private individuals, they would hurt the entire social structure if the law enforced them in any way.

Agreements to Obstruct Justice Agreements to obstruct justice include agreements to protect someone from arrest, to suppress evidence, to encourage lawsuits, to give false testimony, and to bribe a juror. The category also includes a promise not to prosecute someone or not to serve as a witness in a trial. Any agreement promising to perform any of these activities would be void.

CLASSIC CASE Public Policy, Statutory Law, and Contract Validity

New England Surrogate Parenting Advisors (NESPA) is a nonprofit organization that seeks to match potential surrogate mothers with couples who are unable to have children of their own. In this case, a surrogate mother candidate and couple entered an agreement that stipulated that the father would pay for all pregnancy expenses plus a $10,000 fee to the mother for "conceiving, carrying, and giving birth to the child." The fee was to be transferred to the surrogate mother in installments based on a structured payment plan. The final $3,500 was to be paid to the surrogate mother when the child was born. All three parties to the agreement—the surrogate mother, the father, and the father's wife—underwent psychological screening by a psychologist. The psychologist reported that the surrogate mother was a stable, considerate, and knowledgeable woman who was aware of what she was doing and would be emotionally and psychologically capable of transferring custody to the child's biological father. For a while everything went according to the contract. The surrogate mother conceived a child by the father. The first two payments were sent and accepted by the mother. However, at the end of the sixth month, after receiving the third payment, the mother changed her mind, returned the third payment, and told the father's attorney that the contract was ended. That was the only money returned. She kept the first two payments and the expense money she had

received under the agreement. The father sued for custody, arguing that the surrogate mother had breached the contract. The judge agreed and transferred custody to the father based on the contract and because she believed such a move would ultimately be in the child's best interests. The surrogate mother appealed. The state supreme judicial court noted that, since the state had no statute covering this type of agreement, it would apply an adoption statute that was roughly analogous to the situation. Under that statute, a mother could not give up her child for adoption until four days after the child's birth. The statute also outlawed the payment of money to the mother for an adoption, although she could be paid pregnancy expenses. The state supreme court recognized that the legislature had a good reason for requiring a four-day waiting period before a mother could give up her child for adoption. The court took judicial notice of the fact that a mother comprehends the power of the connection between mother and child after the fourth day and is, therefore, in a better position to be fully aware what she is surrendering in an adoption. Using public policy, the court applied those same principles to the surrogate mother contract. In doing so, it concluded that, since the surrogate mother contract did not include a four-day waiting period, it was an illegal contract and was, therefore, void as a matter of law. [See: *R.R. v. M.H. and Another,* 426 N.E.2d 790 (Supreme Court of Massachusetts).]

Agreements Interfering with Public Service Agreements interfering with public service are illegal and void. Contracts in this group include agreements to bribe or interfere with public officials, to obtain political preference in appointments to office, to pay an officer for signing a pardon, or to illegally influence a legislature for personal gain.

A QUESTION OF ETHICS

In February 2011, the Egyptian people displayed their dissatisfaction with the government of Hosni Mubarak by demonstrating in Tahrir Square in Cairo and in the port city of Alexandria. The demonstrations led to Mubarak's abdication and to a military takeover of the government. The military leaders pledged to develop a new constitution and to turn the government over to civilian control as soon as possible. Nevertheless, despite the movement's victory over Mubarak and his government, many protestors continued to disrupt the peaceful transition to domestic peace. Chief among these demonstrators were members of the labor movement who had created a tightly knit network of agreements under which striking textile employees, airport workers, ambulance drivers, electrical engineers, and journalists continued to cause economic disruption. All of this continued to occur despite warnings by the military government that such actions should cease. Clearly the strikers believe that their cause is moral and their actions ethical despite their dubious legality. Under American law, agreements to strike illegally would violate public policy. Should the ethical motivation of the strikers trump the illegality of their actions? Defend your response using one of the ethical theories discussed in Chapter 1 of the text.

Agreements to Defraud Creditors An agreement that tends to remove or weaken the rights of creditors is referred to as an agreement to defraud creditors. Such agreements are void as contrary to public policy. Thus a debtor's agreement to sell and transfer personal and real property to a friend or relative for far less than actual value would be void if done for the purpose of hiding the debtor's assets from creditors with a legal claim to them.

Agreements to Escape Liability A basic policy of the law is that all parties should be liable for their own wrongdoing. Consequently, the law looks with disfavor on any agreement that allows a party to escape this responsibility. One device frequently used in the attempt to escape legal responsibility is the **exculpatory clause**. Such an agreement is usually found as a clause in a longer, more complex contract or on the back of tickets and parking stubs. The exculpatory clause will state that one of the parties, generally the one who wrote the contract, will not be liable for any economic loss of physical injury even if that party caused the loss or injury.

EXAMPLE 10-4: *Newsome v. Tibbs*

Pat Newsome, who worked for Van Sloane, Wentworth, and Michelson, was the chief architect on a project that involved building a new community center on the west side of Baltimore. Before the center could be built, a set of four high-rise apartment buildings, the Towers, had to come down. That job went to Tibbs TNT, LLC, an expert in razing ancient buildings. When Newsome arrived at the job, he was told by Elizabeth Tibbs, the owner of Tibbs TNT that he had to sign an additional contract with Tibbs. One of the clauses in the additional contract included an exculpatory clause that stated that Newsome would hold

Tibbs blameless should Newsome be injured during the tear down of the Towers. The actual implosion of the Towers went without incident; however, afterwards, Newsome was injured when the brakes on a Tibbs-owned truck failed and ran over Newsome. Newsome sued Tibbs. Tibbs pointed to the exculpatory clause and said she was not liable. The court disagreed, saying that the exculpatory clause could not protect Tibbs from liability for injuries that result from negligence on the part of Tibbs or her employees.

This exculpatory clause is an example of the type that the courts have found to be a violation of public policy. Such exculpatory clauses are not favored by the law because they permit behavior to fall below acceptable standards, which was what happened in the Newsome case. A clause simply disclaiming liability in general terms is often insufficient to release a party from his or her own negligence. Still, some courts will enforce exculpatory clauses if they do not offend public policy and there is no inequality of bargaining power between the parties. However, whenever an exculpatory provision is ambiguous, confusing, vague, incomplete, or can be interpreted in different ways, the court will construe the clause against the party it was designed to protect.

Sale of Business When a business is sold, it is common practice for the agreement to contain covenants that restrict the seller from entering the same type of business. Such restrictive covenants in a contract for the sale of a business will be upheld by the court if they are reasonable in time and geographical area. What is reasonable is determined by a careful examination of the business being sold. For example, an agreement by the seller of a barbershop not to open a similar shop in the same community for the next year would seem to be reasonable. In contrast, the opening of a different business, over a wider geographical area, or for a longer period of time might not be allowed by the court.

Restrictive Employment Covenants A restrictive employment covenant, or noncompete agreement as it is often called, limits a worker's employment options after leaving his or her present job. The idea is to protect the present employer from an employee who might take trade secrets, customer lists, or other confidential material to a competitor. In a typical restrictive employment covenant, an employee promises not to work for a competitor in the same field for a specified time period and within a specified geographical area after leaving the current job. Restrictive employment covenants must be reasonable in the type of work they prohibit, the length of time involved in the prohibition, and the geographical area covered by the prohibition.

Nondisclosure Agreements A nondisclosure agreement requires employees to promise that, should they leave their present place of employment, they will not reveal any confidential trade secrets that they might learn while on their current job. Because the limitation is placed on the use of confidential information rather than actual employment of the worker, such agreements do not deprive people of their employment and therefore do not constitute an extensive limit on competition. Although helpful, nondisclosure agreements are often not needed to protect trade secrets. The court will generally issue an injunction to prevent the revelation or the utilization of trade secrets if the employer can convince the court that (1) the information revealed by the former employee was actually a trade secret, (2) the secret information was crucial to the running of the employer's business, (3) the employer had the right to use the trade secret, and (4) the former employee came into possession of the trade secret while in a position of trust and confidence and in such a way that it would be unfair for the former employee to disclose that trade secret in a way that would hurt his or her former employer.

quick quiz 10-3

1. The illegal practice of charging more than the amount of interest allowed by law is called usury.   true | false

2. If a license is required simply to raise revenue, the lack of a license will make a contract void.   true | false

3. A restrictive employment covenant limits a worker's employment options after leaving his or her present job.   true | false

10-4 Consequences of Illegality

Illegality of contract, as in promises to commit criminal acts, not only serves to void existing agreements but may also lead to indictment and prosecution when sufficient evidence warrants such an action. Persons who agree to engage in criminal activity for a promised consideration are involved in what criminal law defines as a **conspiracy**. Agreements that do not violate criminal laws may still be invalid. Thus, many agreements considered contrary to public policy have been declared invalid as against the public good but not illegal in terms of criminal liability. Both types of agreements fail to have the characteristics that permit legal enforcement.

In Pari Delicto Contracts

When both parties to an illegal agreement are equally wrong in the knowledge of the operation and effect of their contract, they are said to be *in pari delicto* (in equal fault). In such cases, the court will give no aid to either party in an action against the other and will award no damages to either. When the parties are not *in pari delicto,* relief will often be allowed if sought by the more innocent of the two. Although this rule is not applicable when one may be less guilty of premeditation (plotting or planning an illegal act) and intent to achieve a gain through known illegal acts, it may be applied when one party is not aware that a law is being broken and there is no intent to do a wrong.

Partial Illegality in an Agreement

Sometimes an agreement will be partly legal and partly illegal. If the legal part of a contract can be removed from the illegal part, without changing the essential nature of the contract, then the agreement is said to be divisible. The court will enforce the legal part but not the illegal part. As long as the main purpose of the agreement can be reached without enforcing the illegal part, the courts are likely to uphold the agreement.

quick quiz 10-4

1. Persons who agree to commit criminal acts for a promised consideration are involved in a conspiracy.   true | false

2. When both parties to an illegal agreement are equally wrong in the knowledge of the operation and effect of their contract, they are said to be *in pari delicto.*   true | false

3. If the legal part of a contract can be removed from the illegal part, without changing the essential nature of the contract, the court will enforce both parts.   true | false

Summary

10.1 The third element essential to a legally effective contract is the legal ability to enter into a contractual relationship. This legal ability is known as capacity. Under the law, there is a rebuttable presumption that anyone entering a contract has the legal capacity to do so. Because the presumption is rebuttable, a party can attack it. Minors are allowed this privilege. Minority means that an individual has not yet attained the age of majority. An exception to the rule about minors and contracts involves necessaries. By statute and court decision, certain other types of contracts have been excepted from the general rule that the contracts of minors are voidable at the minor's option.

10.2 Contracts of persons who are mentally infirm or mentally ill, but not legally declared insane, may be valid or voidable, depending on the seriousness of the mental problem. Persons declared to be insane by competent legal authority are denied the right to enter into contracts, and contracts entered into may be declared void. Incompetence related to alcohol or drugs must be of such a degree that the contracting party has lost the ability to comprehend or be aware of the obligations being accepted under the contract.

10.3 An agreement might have offer, acceptance, mutual assent, competent parties, and consideration and still be invalid if the objective of the agreement is to do something that is illegal. These contracts include those to commit crimes, to commit torts, or to violate statutory law. Public policy is a general legal principle that says no one should be allowed to do anything that tends to hurt the public at large. Agreements found void for a violation of public policy include agreements to obstruct justice, agreements interfering with public service, agreements to defraud creditors, exculpatory agreements, and agreements in restraint of trade.

10.4 Contracts that involve illegal agreements are invalid. Moreover, promises to commit illegal acts may lead to indictment and prosecution. If an entire agreement is illegal, no binding contract results. If only part of an agreement is illegal, the court may rescind only those parts found to be illegal. When both parties are equally at fault in creating an illegal agreement, the court will award no damages to either. When the parties are not in equal fault, relief will often be granted if sought by the innocent party.

Key Terms

abandoned, 239
affirmance, 242
blue laws, 246
capacity, 237
conspiracy, 250
disaffirm, 238
emancipated, 238
exculpatory clause, 248

illegal agreement, 237
in pari delicto, 250
local option, 246
majority, 238
minority, 238
necessaries, 240
noncompete agreement, 249
nondisclosure agreement, 249

public policy, 247
ratification, 242
rebuttable presumption, 237
restrictive covenants, 249
restrictive employment covenant, 249
usury, 246

Questions for Review and Discussion

1. What is the age of minority and what is the age of majority?
2. What is the legal status of a contract made by a minor?
3. What is the difference between ratification and disaffirmance?

4. What are the effects of mental impairment on a contract?
5. What is the contractual capacity of a drugged or intoxicated person?
6. What is the legal status of an agreement to commit a tort or a crime?

7. What agreements are illegal under statutory law?

8. What agreements are contrary to public policy?

9. What happens under the doctrine of *in pari delicto?*

10. What are the effects of illegality?

Cases for Analysis

1. After she was married, Sherri Mitchell, a young woman of 17 years of age, was in an automobile accident in which she was hurt enough to require medical treatment. She was later approached by an insurance agent who offered her $2,500 as a settlement. All she had to do was sign a release that would absolve the insurance company of any complaint that she might have against it in regard to the accident. She agreed to accept the $2,500 and signed a release to that effect; however, she then changed her mind and decided to void the agreement. She argued that since she was 17 at the time she signed the release, she was a minor and could therefore void the contract. Is Mitchell correct? Explain. [See: *Mitchell v. State Farm Mutual Automobile Insurance Co.,* 963 S.W.2d (Ky. Ct. App.).]

2. Sperry Ford sold a car to Bowling when Bowling was only 16 years old. Once Bowling had paid the full purchase price in cash, Sperry turned over the car and the certificate of title. After driving the car for only a week, Bowling discovered that the main bearing was burned out. When Bowling found out that repair costs would almost equal the price he'd paid for the car, he left the car on Sperry's lot and asked for his money back. Sperry Ford refused to give Bowling his money. Was Sperry justified in this refusal? Explain. [See: *Bowling vs. Sperry,* 184 N.E.2d 901 (IN).]

3. Quality Motors, Inc., refused to sell a car to Hays because he was only 16 years old; however, Quality told Hays that they would sell the car to an adult and then show Hays how to transfer the title to his name. Hays agreed with the scheme and came back with a friend who was 23. Quality sold the car to Hays's friend. Quality then gave Hays the name of a notary public who would transfer the title to Hays. After the transfer was accomplished, Hays's father found out about the deal and tried to get Quality Motors to take the car back. Quality replied that the car had been sold to an adult, so Hays could not disaffirm the contract. Is Quality correct? Explain. [See: *Quality Motors v. Hays,* 225 S.W.2d 326 (AR).]

4. Lonchyna enlisted in the U.S. Air Force while he was still a minor. Three times he applied for and received educational delays that put off the beginning of his tour of duty. The last time, he claimed he could void the contract, because he'd entered into it when he was a minor. Was Lonchyna correct? Explain. [See: *Lonchyna v. Brown, Secretary of Defense,* 491 F. Supp. 1352 (N.D. IL).]

5. Darwin Kruse was a construction worker. He was injured while working for the Coos Head Timber Company. Subsequent to the accident, Kruse signed an agreement with his employer that granted Kruse compensation in exchange for his promise not to sue. Kruse is now trying to have the agreement voided. Evidence introduced proved that Kruse had an IQ of 83 and that he dropped out of school at age 18. When he dropped out of school, he was in the eighth grade but was doing less than sixth grade–level work. Will Kruse's "slowness" necessarily invalidate the contract? Explain. [See: *Kruse v. Coos Head Timber Co.,* 432 P.2d 1009 (OR).]

6. Clear Channel Broadcasting, Inc., required Diane Ignazio to sign a new contract that included an arbitration clause under which she agreed that all grievances that she might have with Clear Channel would be settled by arbitration. As part of the agreement, Ignazio gave up any right to bring a lawsuit against Clear Channel. When Ignazio was discharged, instead of moving to arbitration, she sued Clear Channel for discrimination and wrongful discharge. Clear Channel filed a motion to dismiss the case, arguing that Ignazio was bound by the arbitration agreement. Ignazio pointed to a clause in the agreement that rendered the entire agreement illegal. The clause allowed the arbitration award to be reviewed by a court based on the same broad standards used by an appeals court in reviewing a trial court's decision. This provision contradicts state law, which states that if an appeals court reviews an arbitration decision, it can only use a very limited approach to the appeal, including only such things as clerical error or misconduct. Clear Channel argued that even if the

clause was illegal, it could be severed from the agreement, and the rest of the agreement could be enforced. In fact, the contract even included a clause that stated that any clause found illegal ought to be removed from the contract, so that the rest of the contract could be upheld. The question before the court was whether the illegal clause could be removed from the agreement without changing the essential nature of the contract. Is it legally permissible to remove the illegal part of a contract so that the court can uphold the legal part? Should the court sever the illegal clause in this case? Explain. [See: *Ignazio v. Clear Channel*, 113 Ohio St.3d 276 (Ohio Supreme Court).]

7. Cyberian Enterprises and BrandAid Marketing Corporation entered a deal under which Cyberian was supposed to purchase $21 million in Brand-Aid's stock. Cyberian, however, did not have the funds available to make the actual purchase, a fact that was concealed by Cyberian representatives. When BrandAid discovered the lie, it filed a lawsuit against Cyberian for fraud, breach of contract, and breaking federal securities law. Cyberian brought a countersuit against BrandAid for fraud because BrandAid had apparently failed to tell Cyberian about its own financial difficulties. BrandAid's financial problems were on file with the Securities and Exchange Commission (SEC). When the case went to District Court, the judge dismissed the case because, citing the doctrine of *in pari delicto,* he stated that both parties were at equal fault in concealing their financial difficulties. The case then went to the Second Circuit Court of Appeals, which decided that the trial court had made a mistake in dismissing the case. Why did the appeals court overturn the decision of the trial court? Explain. [See: *BrandAid Marketing Corp. v. Biss*, 05-5243-cv (2d U.S. Cir. Ct. of App.). (See also Beth Bar, "Civil Practice: Finding of Equal Fault Is Overturned," *The National Law Journal,* September 11, 2006, p. 13.)]

8. Shannon Audley, a professional model, signed an agreement before starting work on a photo shoot at Bill Melton's studio. The agreement stated: "I, Shannon Audley, realize that working with wild and potentially dangerous animals (i.e., lion, white tiger, hawk) can create a hazardous situation resulting in loss of life or limb. I take all responsibility upon myself for any event as described above that may take place. I hold Bill Melton and T.I.G.E.R.S. or any of their agents free of any or all liability. I am signing this of my own free will." During the photo shoot, Audley was bitten on the head by the adult male lion with which she had been posing. Audley brought suit against Melton. Would the exculpatory clause be upheld by the courts? Explain. [See: *Audley v. Melton,* 640 A.2d 777 NH).]

9. Judy Myers and the Terminix International Company entered a contract in which Terminix agreed to inspect Myers's home and eliminate any termite problem found there. The service cost Myers an initial payment of $1,300 plus annual renewal fees of $85. Terminix failed to eradicate the termite infestation, causing more than $41,000 in damage to Myers's home. The contract contained a clause that required the parties to submit any disputes to arbitration under the American Arbitration Association (AAA). What the contract did not disclose was that Myers would be required to pay a filing fee to submit a claim to AAA. In this case, the filing fee amounted to $7,000. In a lawsuit filed for breach of contract, Myers asserted that the undisclosed filing fee requirement was unconscionable. Is Myers correct? Explain. [See: *Myers v. Terminix,* 697 N.E.2d 277 (OH).]

quick quiz Answers

10-1	10-2	10-3	10-4
1. T	1. T	1. T	1. T
2. T	2. F	2. F	2. T
3. F	3. F	3. T	3. F

Chapter 11

Written Contracts and Cyber-Commerce

THE OPENING CASE Round 1
"To Write or Not to Write"—For Attorneys that Is Never a Question

It helps to remember, as you read through the text, that what happens in these cases can happen to any one of us. Take, for example, the case of *Perez v. Schneider,* wherein all (well, most) problems could have been solved up front with one simple thing—a written agreement. The story begins when Josue Perez rented a building from Thomas Patrick without securing a written lease. Perez intended to open a bar and grill in the building and, to that end, made extensive revisions to accommodate that enterprise. For example, he installed sinks, refrigerators, freezers, coolers, furniture, and other related items. Perez also constructed a wooden bar and a back bar that would be used for storing the usual staples needed to properly operate a bar and grill. Moreover, he had an awning installed, as well as a fire-suppression system, a stainless-steel backsplash over the stove, and a ventilation hood. The bar and grill, named Josh's Place, opened and operated for 15 months before Perez also added a roof air conditioner for the bar. At one point he decided to eliminate the "grill" part of the "bar and grill" operation, and closed to make changes that included selling large portions of the restaurant and kitchen equipment. The items that he removed were to be sold on eBay, and Perez reported that he had sold some of the property and was finalizing several additional deals when

disaster struck. The disaster came when the owner of the building fell victim to a tax foreclosure sale. Patrick managed to short-circuit that action with a tax payment plan, but then fell behind on those payments and lost the building. The building was sold at sheriff's sale to Schneider. Schneider changed the locks on the building and claimed that the contents belonged to him. Perez yelled, "Foul!" and he asked, politely, that the bar, the back bar, the stove, the stove's equipment, the awning, the sinks, and the air-conditioning unit be returned to him immediately. Schneider, as expected, said, "No!" Moreover, he insisted that everything inside the building was his property. At that point, Perez should have produced a written lease to show Schneider that the trade fixtures still belonged to him. Of course, he could not do that because, well, he had no written lease. Perez was then forced to bring a lawsuit against Schneider to get his property back. The case went from the trial level to the appeals court. In a moment, the results of that appeal. [See: *Perez Bar & Grill v. Schneider,* 2012-Ohio-5820 (December 2012).]

Opening Case Questions

1. What law outlines those contracts that must be in writing to be enforceable? Explain.

2. What are those contracts that must be in writing to be enforceable? Explain.

3. Why should leases be placed in writing? Explain.

4. What are some special additional statutes that require a written version of a contract?

5. What are fixtures? What are trade fixtures?

 Learning Objectives

1. Identify the goals of the Statute of Frauds.
2. Identify those contracts that must be in writing.
3. List the information that must be in the writing.
4. Explain the Standard Construction Rule.
5. Discuss the Parol Evidence Rule.
6. Explain the exceptions to the Parol Evidence Rule.
7. Explain the Best Evidence Rule.
8. Discuss the Equal Dignities Rule.
9. Explain the problems associated with cyber-commerce.
10. Outline the latest cyber-commerce statutes.

11-1 The Statute of Frauds

Often when people hear the word *contract,* they immediately think of a piece of paper. Instead, they should think of an agreement, which may or may not be in writing. Many contracts do not have to be in writing to be enforceable. Most oral contracts are valid and upheld by the court. Although it may be desirable to put a contract in writing so that its terms are clear, only certain kinds of contracts are required to be in writing. This chapter discusses the **Statute of Frauds**, which is the law that requires certain contracts to be in writing to be enforceable.

Contracts that Must Be in Writing

According to the Statute of Frauds, applicable in most states, six types of contracts must be in writing to be enforceable:

1. Contracts that cannot be completed within one year.

2. Contracts transferring real property rights.

3. Contracts for the sale of goods of $500 or more.

4. Certain contracts entered into by executors and administrators.

5. Contracts by one party to pay a debt of another party.

6. Contracts in consideration of marriage.

The third contract on the list, contracts for the sale of goods of $500 or more, is actually included in the Uniform Commercial Code rather than the Statute of Frauds. This point is covered in depth in Chapter 13.

Contracts that Cannot Be Completed Within One Year If the terms of a contract make it impossible to complete the agreement within one year, the contract must be in writing.

Contracts Transferring Real Property Rights

Under the Statute of Frauds, conveyances of real property must be in writing to be enforceable. This provision covers the sale of land; however, it also covers trusts that are created by one party, the trustor, that permit a second party, the trustee, to possess and control the land for the advantage of a third party, the beneficiary. Whether the provision includes leases is problematic, because some jurisdictions permit short leases, generally those that last less than a year, to be oral. The parties to a lease are free to negotiate the time period for a lease, unless state law indicates otherwise. Most states, however, are relatively clear that leases that are designed to last longer than one year must be in writing to be enforceable. Written leases will also usually indicate what happens at the end of the time period covered in the lease. If the lease itself does not indicate what happens at the time that the lease expires, the state will generally lay down such a provision. Most states say that the lease transforms by law automatically to a month-to-month lease, although some states provide that the lease becomes valid for another year.

In addition to these provisions, the law often requires that other items be added to written leases. For example, most states require that a provision covering security deposits be added. State law also limits the amount that can be charged for security deposits. Most states limit this to one month's rent, but some can go as high as three months. States also require that security deposits be held in escrow and accrue interest that is then paid to

THE OPENING CASE *Round 2*

"To Write or Not to Write"—For Leases Check State Law and Check It Well

In the opening case, we learned the story behind *Perez v. Schneider* began when Josue Perez rented a building from Thomas Patrick without securing a written lease. Perez planned to open a bar and grill and modified the building to make it suitable for that purpose. The changes included adding sinks, refrigerators, freezers, coolers, furniture, a wooden bar, and a back bar for storing the usual staples needed to properly operate a successful bar and grill. He also had added an awning that prominently displayed the name of his new establishment. Inside, he added fire-suppression equipment, a stainless-steel backsplash for the stove, and a ventilation hood. The bar and grill, named Josh's Place, operated for 15 months. Perez then added a roof air conditioner for the bar. Later he decided to remove the restaurant portion of the bar. This meant closing the bar temporarily to make alterations. To that end, he removed and sold much of the unnecessary property on eBay. While Perez was occupied with this project, the building was sold at sheriff's sale to Schneider. One of the first things that Schneider did was change the locks on the building. Perez asked that his equipment, furniture, awning, stoves, coolers, sinks, refrigerators, and air-conditioning unit be returned to him. Schneider, however, refused to do so. At this point, we can see that Perez would have been much better off with a written lease in hand. Such a lease, if written properly, would have included a provision for the disposition of the fixtures. Fixtures are personal property items (goods, such as the appliances, awnings, air conditioners, sinks, and so on) that are later added to real property. Because such fixtures are usually attached in a way that makes them difficult to remove without damaging the real property, they normally stay with the property after a sale. An exception is made for trade fixtures. Trade fixtures are items of personal property that are needed for a business or profession. They remain with the seller of the property or, as in this case, with the tenant. Such a provision in a written lease would have covered the items Perez claimed were his. Unfortunately, the absence of a written lease made this situation much less clear. While it is true that a written lease might not have prevented the lawsuit, it might have created something more like an open and shut case than the one that Perez ended up facing here. [See: *Perez Bar & Grill v. Schneider,* 2012-Ohio-5820 (December 2012).]

the renters on the termination of the lease. These statutes also require that the landlord give tenants an itemization of the cost of all repairs that will be deducted from the security deposit when the lease ends. Most of these statutes also include provisions prohibiting discrimination based on race, color, creed, gender, national origin, parenthood, sexual orientation, family relationships, and even pet ownership. Another provision that should be included in any lease is the disposition of fixtures, including, especially, trade fixtures, when the lease terminates.

When a party owns land, he or she owns a bundle of rights that can be distributed among various other parties. Thus, it is possible, for example, for the owner of a parcel of land to divide the rights to that land among several different parties. One party might hold a lease to a house on the land allowing her to live there, a second could have an easement that permits him to cross the land, a third might own the right to mine the land, and so on. The Statute of Frauds requires a writing for each of these different transactions. The object of this requirement is to make certain that there is a way to follow the trail of each of these rights to determine who owns them, should a dispute arise concerning them.

An exception to the rule that contracts for the sale of land must be in writing is called **part performance** or **equitable estoppel**. The exception applies when a person relies on an owner's oral promise to sell real property and then makes improvements on the property or changes his or her position in an important way. The plaintiff in such a case must prove three elements to succeed in a lawsuit. First, the plaintiff must show that he or she made the improvement relying on the original promise and without suspecting that the other party intended to renege on the agreement. Second, the plaintiff must show that any other remedy, such as restitution for the amount spent, is not enough to satisfy his or her effort or outlay of funds. Third, the plaintiff must show that the part performance itself is evidence of the existence of the contract.

EXAMPLE 11-1: *Zuer v. Iafigliola*

Jake Iafigliola agreed in an oral contract to sell Dwight Zuer a run-down parcel of storefront property for $50,000. The storefront was located across the street from the site of a new Target that was about to be established in the neighborhood. Relying on Iafigliola's agreement, Zuer spent $20,000 improving the premises so that he could move his 24-7-365 fitness, wellness, and exercise business into the storefront. Iafigliola then backed out of the deal. Zuer sued, asking the court to order Iafigliola to go through with the contract. Iafigliola argued this was a real property contract and it had to be in writing to be enforceable. Zuer asked the court to apply the part performance doctrine. Zuer made the following case: First, he had made the improvements relying on the original promise. Second, he pointed out that any other remedy, such as restitution for the amount spent, would not be enough, because he clearly wanted the storefront in the lot across from the new Target. Third, Zuer argued that the fact that he spent $20,000 to improve the storefront could not be explained in any other way other than his reliance on the contract. The court agreed and allowed the lawsuit even without the writing.

The courts do not require a writing for a contract in which the owner of land agrees to improve the land for the use of another party who has already received a partial interest in the land. In such a situation, the courts believe that once the real interest in the land has been transferred, the contract to improve the land does not create a new interest. Instead, the new contract is solely a promise to provide labor and make changes in the land. It therefore falls outside the statute, and no writing is required.

EXAMPLE 11-2: *Dewey v. Collins*

Rene Collins owned a piece of land in rural Pennsylvania, just outside Streetsboro. Frederick Dewey received an easement across Collins's land. The easement, which was supposed to last for five years, was executed in a written document. After the first year, Dewey asked Collins to lay gravel on the small road that constituted the easement. Collins said that she would not lay the gravel herself but would permit Dewey to do so and reimburse him for the expense. Dewey laid the gravel and presented Collins with the bill. Collins refused to reimburse Dewey as agreed. Collins argued that because there was no writing, the contract, which involved land, was unenforceable. The referee disagreed, concluding that the agreement to lay gravel did not create a new interest. Instead, it simply involved a commitment to pay for improvements to land in which Dewey already owned an interest.

UCC 2-201 (see pages 924-925)

Contracts for the Sale of Goods of $500 or More Under the UCC, contracts for the sale of goods (movable items) for $500 or more must be in writing to be enforceable. However, there are four exceptions to this rule. Oral contracts for the sale of goods of $500 or more will be enforced in situations involving the following:

1. Oral contracts between merchants when a written confirmation has been received by one party and not objected to by the other party.
2. Specially manufactured goods that cannot be resold easily.
3. Admissions in court.
4. Executed agreements.

Certain Contracts Entered by Executors and Administrators

An **executor** is a person who is named in a will to oversee the distribution of the estate of a deceased according to the provisions outlined in the will. An **administrator** is a person named by the court to do the work of an executor if none is named in the will or if the executor cannot or will not perform those duties. As a general principle of law, neither an executor nor an administrator is personally liable for the debts of the decedent's estate. Executors and administrators must pay the debts of the estate, to be sure, but out of the assets of the estate, not out of their own pockets. Thus, any promise to pay the debts of the estate using the executor's or the administrator's own funds is unenforceable without a writing.

EXAMPLE 11-3: *Trautman v. Quinn*

Max Quinn was named the executor of his sister's estate. One of his sister's creditors, Nancy Trautman, demanded immediate payment of a debt of $6,600 owed by the deceased. To protect his sister's good name, Quinn promised Trautman that he would pay her the amount owed out of his own funds if the estate could not cover that amount. Trautman refused to agree unless Quinn placed the agreement in writing. Quinn agreed. After things calmed down, Trautman tried to collect the debt. Quinn refused to pay. Trautman was able to enforce the promise because she had written evidence of Quinn's agreement to pay the debt.

Contracts by One Party to Pay a Debt Incurred by Another Party A promise made by one party to pay another person's debts, if that person fails to pay the debt, falls within the statute and must be in writing to be enforceable. Several terms have been used to describe these types of transactions. They are alternately referred to as a guaranty of payment, a guaranty contract, or a collateral contract. The promisor is usually called a guarantor. Often in a commercial setting, the guarantor is referred to as a cosigner. The person to whom the promise is made is the obligee, and the person who owes the original debt is referred to as the obligor. It is crucial to distinguish between guaranty contracts and original contracts.

An exception to this rule is known as the primary objective test. Under the primary objective test (also referred to as the leading objective test and the main purpose test), if the promise to pay another party's debt is actually made to obtain a gain for the guarantor, there is no need for a writing to enforce the promise. Suppose, for instance, that Hans McKnight, the owner of Scottish Inn, depends on the Hometown Bakery for the inn's sub buns for its lunch trade. Suppose further that McKnight knows that the Hometown Bakery has had some financial trouble and may have to shut down its operations if it cannot pay Jakub's Supply for its regular flour shipment. If McKnight promises Jakub's that, if it continues to supply Hometown with flour, he will pay the bill, that promise falls under the primary objective test and need not be in writing to be enforceable.

Contracts in Consideration of Marriage Agreements made in consideration of marriage must be in writing to be enforceable. This part of the statute does not refer to the marriage contract itself or to engagement promises to marry, which are almost always oral. Rather, it refers to promises made by parties before marriage, in which they accept additional obligations not usually covered in the marriage vows. A prenuptial agreement (also referred to as a premarriage agreement and an antenuptial agreement) involves two people who are planning marriage and who agree to change the property rights they possess by law in a marriage. Such promises are enforceable only if they are in writing and agreed upon prior to the marriage. Many state legislatures, as well as the District of Columbia, have enacted the Uniform Premarital Ageement Act (UPAA). The UPAA supports the use of prenuptial agreements and provides for their enforcement.

Other Contracts Each state has enacted special statutes outlining other agreements that must be in writing. Other contracts that are usually required by special statutes to be in writing include the release of a party from debt (general release) and the resumption of obligations after bankruptcy. In addition, some states require real estate listing contracts and insurance binders to be in writing. Other contracts that require a writing under the UCC are contracts for the sale of securities (stocks and bonds) and agreements creating security interests.

The Contents of a Writing

The Statute of Frauds requires that the agreement be in writing—nothing more. The purpose of the writing is twofold. First, it proves that the parties entered an agreement. Second, it provides detailed information about the terms of that agreement. To accomplish these goals, the writing must be intelligible, but it need not follow any preset format. It can be found in letters, memos, documents, invoices, packing slips, and purchase orders that have been mailed, privately delivered, faxed, or sent electronically between the parties. It may be written on any surface suitable for the purpose of recording the intention of the parties, as long as all the required elements are present. A writing can even be placed in an e-mail, in a text message, or on a website, as long as it is possible to store and reproduce the electronic record of the agreement, and as long as the cyber-record includes an electronic signature as defined by the appropriate cyber-commerce statute.

Elements of a Writing

To be absolutely complete, a written agreement, or **memorandum**, as it is often called, should contain the following elements:

- Terms of the agreement.
- Identification of the subject matter.
- Statement of the consideration promised.
- Names and identities of the persons to be obligated.
- Signature of the party sought to be bound to the agreement.

quick quiz 11-1

1. A contract is said to be outside the statute if it must be in writing to show that the two objectives of the Statute of Frauds have been met.	true | false
2. An administrator is a person who is named in a will to oversee the distribution of the estate of a deceased person according to the provisions outlined in the will.	true | false
3. Agreements made in consideration of marriage must be in writing to be enforceable.	true | false

11-2 Legal Rules for Written Contracts

The legal system has developed certain basic criteria that make the construction and interpretation of written contracts as flawless as possible. These criteria act very much the way basic axioms or rules work in mathematics. Therefore, we could characterize these rules as unquestioned assumptions about the text of a writing that must be followed when an attorney, a magistrate, or a judge interprets a writing that claims to contain the terms of a contract. These four rules are (1) the standard construction rule, (2) the parol evidence rule, (3) the best evidence rule, and (4) the equal dignities rule. The first two rules cover the interpretation of contracts, whereas the latter two govern their enforcement.

The Standard Construction Rule

Appropriately, the first of the interpretation rules is the most critical and the most fundamental of the four. The **standard construction rule** guides the entire interpretation process by directing the interpreter of a contract to determine the principal objective of the parties in the making of the contract. The *principal objective* is the primary or main goal that the parties hoped to accomplish by entering the agreement in the first place. Once this principal objective is stated, everything else must be interpreted to promote that principal objective. In line with this rule, the law also says that common words used in the contract are given their expected, everyday definition, and technical terms or professional slang will be given their technical or professional definitions. The standard construction rule also says that any standard operating procedures that are used in the parties' professions or trades should be followed whenever there is any doubt about what procedure should be used in the contract.

Because the standard construction rule is the most fundamental guideline involved in the interpretation of written contracts, it also guides the interpreter on matters of ambiguity and misinterpretation. The rule says that whenever an ambiguous term, clause, or line is found in a prewritten or preprinted contract, that ambiguity is interpreted against the party who wrote the contract. This approach should encourage those people who draft contracts to do so in clear and unambiguous terms, because if they draft a clause that is ambiguous, it will be interpreted against them. Thus, there is no profit in making things difficult to understand in any written contract.

The Parol Evidence Rule

Under the **parol evidence rule**, evidence of oral statements made before signing a written agreement is usually not admissible in court to change or contradict the terms of a written agreement. Following oral discussion and negotiation, parties may reduce their agreements to some written form. When this is done, only the terms, conditions, and promises included in the writing will be allowed as evidence in court. This provision is enforced because the court presumes that the parties will have put everything they agreed to in the writing.

EXAMPLE 11-4: *Twaine v. Krell, Inc.*

Emily Twaine purchased a $745 tablet from Krell, Inc. Before all of the documents of sale were signed, the salesperson promised that she would get round-the-clock tech support from Krell technicians whenever she had a problem with her tablet or any of the software associated with the tablet. Krell subsequently refused to take care of any problems that Twaine had with the tablet. The court ruled that the salesperson's oral warranty statements were not admissible in court because they were not contained with the other conditions in the written sales agreement.

Exceptions to the Parol Evidence Rule The parol evidence rule will not apply when unfair and unjust decisions might result from its application. In cases in which a written agreement is incomplete, oral evidence may be used to supply the missing terms. Similarly, when a written contract is obscure or indistinct in certain of its terms, oral evidence may be used to clarify those terms. Also, if a written agreement contains a typographical or clerical error of some sort, the court will allow oral evidence as to the true intent of the parties.

EXAMPLE 11-5: *Bulwark v. Greene*

Edgar Bulwark was hired as an independent contractor to produce a series of magazine and journal articles that would appear under the name of a famous, and very busy, newspaper columnist named Arnold Greene. The written agreement had an error that indicated that Bulwark would receive $500 per article. The actual amount of consideration was supposed to be $5,000. The court would likely allow oral evidence to correct this obvious error.

In general, the courts allow a party to a written agreement to introduce oral testimony to show that the contract is void or voidable due to a lack of mutual assent or contractual capacity. The courts are willing to allow such testimony because it does not affect the terms of the agreement. Rather, it seeks to discredit the entire transaction. Thus, it is permissible to introduce oral evidence as to fraud, duress, misrepresentation, mistake, and undue influence. Similarly, it is appropriate to offer oral testimony as to a party's minority or mental incompetence.

EXAMPLE 11-6: *Staniland v. Morris*

James Staniland contracted with Richard Morris to purchase an original painting by Henrietta Stein, an artist who was part of the Dadaist movement in Paris during the 1920s. After signing the written contract, Staniland had the painting placed in the lobby of his business office. After one week, a customer spotted the painting and told Staniland that it was a forgery and that he had been defrauded by Morris. When Staniland took the witness stand during the trial, he was permitted to introduce evidence of the oral statements made by Morris that led him to the fraudulent conclusion that the painting was a genuine work by Stein. The court allowed the testimony because it did not affect the terms of the agreement. Rather, it sought to discredit the entire transaction.

If a written agreement depends on some event before it becomes enforceable, oral evidence may be offered regarding that condition precedent. A **condition precedent** is an act or promise that must take place or be fulfilled before the other party is obligated to perform his or her part of the agreement. The courts allow this type of oral evidence because, like the oral evidence involving assent and capacity, it does not have an impact on the terms of the agreement, but it does affect the enforceability of the entire contract.

EXAMPLE 11-7: *Lauretig v. Pierce*

Asa Pierce agreed to lease Jay Lauretig's warehouse. The terms of the lease were laid out in a lengthy, detailed written agreement. However, as a condition precedent, a credit history and background check by Lauretig on Pierce would have to come back flawless; otherwise, the deal would be canceled. When the Search and Discover Detective Agency reported that Pierce had both a bad credit rating and two criminal convictions on drug charges, Lauretig refused to go through with the contract. At court, the judge permitted oral testimony about the credit check and the criminal background search because they were precedent conditions that had to be met before the contract went into effect.

Oral evidence may be used to prove that the parties orally agreed to rescind or modify the terms of a written contract after entering into it. Subsequent negotiations to change or rescind the agreement are permitted, and evidence to that effect does not undermine the spirit of the parol evidence rule. However, if the change in the contract involves an agreement that would have to be in writing under the Statute of Frauds, then a writing would be required. Similarly, if the original written contract requires later modifications to be in writing, then that written requirement will rule.

EXAMPLE 11-8: *George Laurie Construction v. Popson*

George Laurie Construction entered into a contract with Terry and Sherrie Popson, the terms of which indicated that Laurie Construction was to place aluminum siding, downspouts, and gutters on the Popson vacation house on Kelley's Island. The agreement was written out in a long, preprinted contract with blanks for the pertinent individual information. All of the appropriate blanks were filled in, the contract was signed by all the parties, and the job began on schedule. Once Laurie was on the job for three days, Sherrie Popson decided that she wanted a window placed on the house. She discussed the cost of the additional work with George Laurie, who agreed to make the change indicated. The additional terms were not put in writing. After the job was completed, the Popsons paid the original amount but did not pay the added cost of the new window. The small claims court allowed testimony as to the terms involving the window because those terms represented negotiations subsequent to the original agreement to change the original terms.

As a final exception to the parol evidence rule, the UCC allows oral testimony about how the parties have done business together over a long time period. The UCC makes allowance for this type of testimony because, from a practical point of view, parties often get so used to dealing with each other in a particular way that they neglect to include certain terms in their written agreements. Similarly, some practices are so universal in a particular trade, business, or industry that the parties feel no need to include such universal practices in their written contracts. Accordingly, the UCC allows oral testimony to supplement a written agreement as to these practices.

UCC 1-205, 2-202, 2-208 (see pages 922 and 925)

EXAMPLE 11-9: *Commonwealth Chemical Company v. St. Clair Printing, Inc.*

St. Clair Printing, Inc., and the Commonwealth Chemical Company have been doing business for 20 years. St. Clair prints all labels, business cards, letterheads, invoices, and purchase orders for Commonwealth. During their long time working together, St. Clair has always delivered orders to Commonwealth. When a new foreman took over the bindery and delivery operation for St. Clair, he decided that there would be no deliveries to any customers outside a five-mile radius of the print shop. As a result, Commonwealth did not receive an important order of labels and lost several big orders. When Commonwealth sued St. Clair for breach of contract, St. Clair pointed out that there was nothing mentioned in the written contract about delivery responsibilities falling to St. Clair. However, because of their 20-year history of consistently dealing with each other, the court allowed oral testimony about past practices to supplement the written contract.

The Best Evidence Rule

Under the **best evidence rule**, the courts generally accept into evidence only the original of a writing, not a copy. Under this rule, a written instrument is regarded as the primary or best possible evidence. Thus, the best evidence rule concurs with and supports the parol evidence rule.

The Equal Dignities Rule

The **equal dignities rule**, which is followed in some states, provides that when a party appoints an agent to negotiate an agreement that must be in writing, the appointment of the agent must also be in writing. In contrast, the appointment of an agent to negotiate an agreement that the law does not require to be in writing may be accomplished through an oral agreement.

11-3 Formalities of Construction

Certain formalities are usually followed in the formation of anything other than the simplest kinds of written agreements. Although the Statute of Frauds may necessitate nothing more than the briefest written disclosure of promises, conditions, and terms, plus the signature(s) of the obligated party or parties, usually contracts in general commercial and consumer use are carefully written, researched for legal compliance, and signed. Furthermore, leases and contracts for the sale of real property may have additional requirements of content and formality that extend beyond these demands.

Signature Requirements

Written agreements should be, but need not be, signed by both parties. If signed by only one party, any obligation in the agreement would be limited to that party alone. Parties should use their usual signatures, that is, the signatures used in other matters in the regular course of business. However, any mark that the signer intends to be a signature will be the legal signature of that person. Although it is unusual, a party may adopt any name desired in creating a contractual obligation, as long as the party intends to be bound by that signature.

Facsimile Signatures With the increased use of facsimile (fax) machines, methods have been adopted to bypass the best evidence rule by giving authentication to signatures sent by way of facsimile machines. A facsimile signature will be acceptable on a contract if the contract states that facsimile signatures are valid. More commonly, however, people fax copies of signed documents to other parties, and follow it up by sending the original signed documents by overnight mail or express delivery. Some states have enacted statutes allowing certain facsimile signatures.

EXAMPLE 11-10: Massachusetts General Laws Chapter 92

Massachusetts has enacted the following statute relative to residence insurance agents: "A facsimile of a signature of any such resident agent imprinted on any property or casualty insurance policy issued by mail, computer modem or facsimile machine, so-called, shall have the same validity as a written signature." (Mass. Gen. Laws Chapter 92, s. 43.)

In addition, some states have adopted the **Uniform Facsimile Signatures of Public Officials Act.** This law allows the use of facsimile signatures of public officials when certain requirements are followed.

signature: *Daniel Colletti*

WITNESS: I hereby attest that Daniel Colletti was physically
           unable to sign his name and that his name was signed
           by me in his presence and at his request.

Jonas Abraham

Figure 11-1 The signature for an incapacitated person bears a witness's name.

In cases in which a party cannot sign the written agreement due to illness, physical disability, or some other physical reason, another person may sign for that person. The signature should be followed by a statement indicating that the contracting party was physically unable to sign the document and that a signature was placed on the document by another person in the contracting party's presence and at the request of the contracting party. The person who has signed for the contracting party then signs the document (see Figure 11-1). Persons who lack the ability to read or write are often obliged to sign contracts. In such situations, the law accepts the person's mark, usually an X, properly witnessed, as a valid signature (see Figure 11-2).

Witnesses and Acknowledgments

Witnesses are required in the signing of a will and sometimes a deed, but in most other documents, their signatures are at the option of the contracting parties. To ensure that no misunderstanding will arise as to the acceptance and signing of a written agreement, the use of witnesses is advised. Certain official documents, such as a certificate of title to a motor vehicle and a deed to real property, require the owner's signature and an

Her

Samantha X *Cunningham*

Mark

WITNESS: I hereby attest that Samantha Cunningham made her
           mark as her signature and that, at her request, I
           added her name to her mark.

Lindsay Quartermain

Figure 11-2 The signature (*X*) of a person who does not know how to write has been witnessed.

acknowledgment by a notary public that the signature was the person's free act and deed. The notary witnesses the signing of the document and then acknowledges this act by signing the document and adding the official seal to it. A notary is not authorized to read the document being signed and may be prevented from doing so.

Special Conditions and Circumstances

Recently several states have begun to revise the basic requirements for some written contracts involving real property. The two revisions involve (1) contracts for the sale or lease of residential real estate; and (2) real property construction projects, especially involving private homes.

Contracts for the Sale or Lease of Residential Real Estate The first type of contract that has been revised and updated by state law is a contract for the sale or lease of residential real estate. The difficulties inherent in these contracts involve their overall unpredictability. State law can outline most of the details that must be included within these agreements. However, some details depend upon local customs and traditions that are acknowledged by municipal, county, or regional real estate boards but which are foreign to brokers and attorneys who operate in other parts of the state. For example, Dayton, Ohio, was victimized by a massive flood in 1913 that led to the creation of the Miami Conservancy District, which is designed to maintain an extensive flood control system to prevent a similar disaster from happening in the future. More than a century after that flood, the conservancy district is still maintained by a yearly tax assessment on all property in the district. This tax assessment must be figured into all real property contracts in the Dayton area, something that is not involved in real property contracts in other parts of the state. Still, despite such regional differences there are some elements that must be in all real property contracts. State statutes that deal with such agreements will list the following items that must be in all real property transfer contracts.

1. A full description of the property that is the subject of the contract.
2. The price of the real property that is the subject of the contract.
3. The date of closing on the contract. Generally, there is a grace period added to this part of the agreement. The grace period can run up to 45 days.
4. An identification of the parties to the contract.
5. Any financing contingencies built into the agreement. Typically, this involves a condition precedent that the contract will not exist until the buyer has a financing plan in place.
6. An attorney approval clause that states that each party's attorney will have the power to make suggestions about any part of the contract that he or she feels might be detrimental to his or her client(s).
7. A detailed explanation of all tax assessments involved.
8. A list and description of all fixtures that stay with the property and those fixtures that can be removed. The list should also designate which fixtures are trade fixtures that can, therefore, be removed.
9. The timing of inspections. Generally, there is a statutory limit placed on this time period, something like, within 14 days of signing, or the like.
10. The home maintenance agreement. Normally, the seller warrants that a third party will fix any problems that occur within the first year of the sale.
11. A clause covering deed transfer and title insurance.
12. A clause that explains who is liable for destruction or damage to property after the inspections have occurred.

13. A statement of the earnest money put down by the buyer.

14. Any miscellaneous provisions that might be peculiar to this contract (such as a delayed possession process complete with a date of occupancy).

15. Dated and signed by all of the parties to the agreement.

The final requirement demands that all real property contracts must be written in plain English, with signed and dated duplicate originals retained by all parties. Generally, the law also requires that all alterations to the terms of the original written contract be in writing, initialed, and dated by all parties. [See: William Fergus, Deborah McDonald, and James Zitesman, "Contract and Closing Issues Relating to Residential Real Estate Transactions," Ohio State Bar Association Convention (April 30–May 2, 2014).]

Real Property Construction Projects

Anyone who has built a private residence or has been involved in a residential renovation project knows that such

THE OPENING CASE *Round 3*
"To Write or Not to Write"—Fixing the Identity of Fixtures

In the opening case, we learned that Josue Perez rented a building from Thomas Patrick without securing a written lease. Perez made comprehensive changes to the building to accommodate his plan for a bar and grill. The alterations included attaching sinks, refrigerators, freezers, coolers, furniture, and other items to the building. A wooden bar and a back bar for storing bar supplies were also added. In addition, Perez installed fire-suppression equipment, a stainless-steel backsplash for the stove, and a ventilation hood. Next, Perez added a roof air conditioner for the bar. Josh's Place opened and operated successfully for 15 months. Later, Perez decided to get out of the "grill" part of the "bar and grill" business. Accordingly, he closed the restaurant and began to sell the restaurant property online. When Patrick lost the building, it was sold at sheriff's sale to Schneider, who changed the locks and argued that everything in the building belonged to him. Perez asked that his equipment, furniture, awning, stoves, coolers, sinks, refrigerators, and air-conditioning unit be returned. Schneider refused, claiming, with some conviction, to own everything inside the building. At this point we can see that many of Perez's problems were caused by the fact that he had no written lease. If Perez had followed the rules and insisted on a written lease, the troublesome fixtures would have been a focal point of that agreement. In fact, had Perez designated certain pieces of equipment as *trade fixtures,* he might have escaped the inconve-

nience of a court appearance altogether. As it was, he ended up in court. Much of what Perez would have designated as trade fixtures turned out to be just that, but not all. The trial court used a line of precedent that explained a step-by-step procedure for identifying trade fixtures. As a result, the following items were characterized as trade fixtures: the bar and the back bar, the ventilation hood (along with the fire-suppression system and the stainless-steel backsplash), the sinks, and the awning (which included the name "Josh's Place). The air-conditioning unit on the roof was designated by the trial court as a trade fixture, but according to the appellate court, this was an error by the lower court. The refrigerators, freezers, coolers, furniture, and other bar and grill type items were not mentioned by the court. It may, therefore, be assumed that the restaurant furniture, the coolers, and the refrigerators, were removable and, in fact, had already been removed from the building. The appellate court also observed that a written contract for sale had been drawn up between Perez and Patrick, but had failed due to a lack of financing on the part of Perez. The fixtures were not mentioned in that agreement either. Perez and Patrick had discussed these improvements in general, but never in relation to their nature as fixtures. Again, following the requirements of a written agreement would have helped Perez avoid these problems. [See: *Perez Bar & Grill v. Schneider,* 2012-Ohio-5820 (December 190, 2012).]

undertakings are fraught with peril. Delays and errors are often caused by misunderstand-ings, mistakes, negligence, clumsiness, and impracticality. Cost overruns, time delays, work stoppages, equipment failure, property damage, alterations in materials or construc-tion plans can take their toll, if the project is not handled properly. There is probably no way to eliminate such gaps and turnarounds whenever someone is involved in lengthy and complicated construction deals. However, some of the intensity surrounding such dis-putes, disagreements, and debates can be assuaged if certain terms are included in a writ-ten agreement. The trend today is for the state legislatures to develop legally binding terms that must be included in all construction contracts but especially those involving private homes. Often state statutes that deal with such agreements will list the following items that must be in all real property construction projects contracts, but especially those involving private homes.

1. The builder and/or the construction company's name, address, phone number, e-mail address, insurance, bonding information, and tax identification number.
2. The homeowner's name, address, phone number, and e-mail address.
3. The address of the location where the home is to be constructed or the renovation, addition (shed, pool, garage, patio, deck, porch, etc.), or repairs are to be made.
4. A description of the goods and the services that will be provided by the contractor.
5. The anticipated date of completion, including cleanup.
6. The penalty for not meeting the anticipated date of completion (with some leeway built in [e.g., within two days of the anticipated date of completion]) often expressed in terms of dollars-per-day after the anticipated date of completion.
7. The estimated total cost of the project including parts, labor, subcontractors' costs, and so on.
8. Any added costs for delivering materials, installing items such as fixtures, taking paid breaks, traveling time to and from the job, and so on.
9. The contractor's certificate of insurance.
10. Signatures and dates added by all of the parties to the agreement.
11. An excess provision clause that indicates that, if there are added costs that are unex-pected but necessary and the total of these added costs exceeds a set level (generally something like $5,000 in total) that such added costs must be approved in writing by the homeowner before materials are purchased or construction work involving the extra added costs begins.

As is true of the requirements for contracts for the sale or lease of residential property, the last requirement in home construction contracts is that all real property contracts be written in plain English, with signed and dated duplicate originals retained by all the parties. Gen-erally, the law also requires that all alterations to the terms of the original written contract be in writing, initialed, and dated by all parties. These home construction contract statutes also often stipulate what cannot be in a written contract. Specifically, such statutes may define what is meant by "workmanlike conduct" or construction performed in workman-like manner. For example, Section 47022.01(G) of the Ohio Revised Code states that workmanlike manner "means the home construction service supplier has engaged in con-struction that meets or exceeds the minimum quantifiable standards promulgated by the Ohio home builders association." Since this duty is encoded within the statutory law of the state, the written agreement between the contractor and the homeowner cannot contain a clause in which the homeowner gives up the protection provided by the statute. Home con-struction contract statutes will also outline other activities that contractors cannot do, such as starting construction without a written contract, failing to provide the homeowner with copies of the written contract, failing to provide the homeowner with written estimates of excess costs, and so on. Strict requirements like these for residential real estate contracts and for home construction contracts will not eliminate disagreements, disputes, and debates in these projects. Such problems are inherent within these transactions. Nevertheless, the need to provide detailed written agreements will lessen the probability that such disputes will end up in court. [See: Andrew Fredelake, J. Bradley Leach, and Jon C. Walden, "Construction Law and Public Contracting Update," Ohio State Bar Association Convention (April 30–May 2, 2014).]

CLASSIC CASE The Evolution of a Fixture in Contract Law

The evolution of real estate contracts is part of the ongoing story of the overall nature of the complex adaptive system (CAS) that is the law. Each state can tell its own story about its evolutionary journey through real estate law, and most of these journeys will somehow touch upon the evolution of the trade fixture doctrine. The court in *Perez v. Schneider* was kind enough to give us a compact and streamlined view of this history starting with the classic case of *Teaff v. Hewitt.* In that landmark case, the court first defined a fixture. "A fixture," the court writes, "is an article [that] was a chattel, but [that] by being physically annexed or affixed to the realty, became accessory to it and part and parcel of it." [See: *Teaff v. Hewitt,* 1 Ohio St. 511, 527 (1853).] The court then outlines the basic elements of a fixture. In 1853, the justices brought in the following three elements: (1) "[a]ctual annexation to the realty, or something appurtenant thereto;" (2) "[a]ppropriation to the use or purpose of that part of the realty with which it is connected;" and (3) "[t]he intention of the party making annexation, to make the article a permanent accession to the freehold. . . . " As straightforward and unbreakable as these elements may sound, they were not difficult to change, as the courts moved on. The first element to be revised was, appropriately enough, the first element of "attachment." As cases came and went over a century, the court decided ultimately in *Masheter v. Boehm,* 37 Ohio St. 2d 68, 73 (1974), that attachment was the least significant of the three elements. The court declared that slight attachment would not necessarily defeat the idea that the item was not a fixture and a significant degree of attachment would not make an item a fixture if the other elements held sway. [See: *Trumbull Sav. & Loan Co.,* 135 Ohio St. 48, 53 (1939).] Next the court moved to gently refine the second element, that is, what is the use of the item compared to the overall use of the building to which it has been attached. The court employed a somewhat convoluted explanation of this second element. However, ultimately, in the case of *Zangerle v. Republic Steel Corp.,* 144 Ohio St. 529, paragraph seven of the syllabus (1945), the principle came down to this: If an item is used for the specific purpose of the business in the building, it will likely (though not definitely, remember the test is three pronged) be a trade fixture. However, if the attachment can be used by whatever business enters the premises and takes up residence there, then we have a "non-trade fixture." This is what happened to the air conditioner added by Perez. An air-conditioning unit can be used by a bar or a barbershop. The court sees the second element as a deal breaker. In fact, in the *Perez* case, the court writes, "If an item fails to meet the second prong of the *Teaff* test because it is peculiar to the business being operated on the premises, it is likely to be deemed a trade fixture" (Paragraph 19). That does not mean, however, that the third element carries no weight. On the contrary, it can overturn even element number two, if it is strong enough because it concerns the intent of the person who placed the item on the property to begin with. Interestingly enough, the court noted that it is not the actual goal of the party that matters, but how that attachment looks to an outsider given all of the circumstances in the case. The courts have observed that as far as the third element is concerned: "[I]t is not necessarily the real intention of the owner of the chattel which governs. His apparent or legal intention to make it a fixture is sufficient" and that "ought to be apparent, from the situation and surroundings." [See: *Holland Furnace Co. v. Trumbull Sav. & Loan Co.,* 135 Ohio St. 48, 53–54 (1939), as quoted in *Perez v. Schneider.*]

11-4 Cyber-Commerce and the Law

Cyber-commerce (computer commerce, electronic commerce, or e-commerce) involves transacting business by computer. One of the most common cyber-commerce techniques involves buying and selling directly on the Internet by accessing a company's website. Some companies, such as Amazon.com, have made a name for themselves by perfecting this e-commerce technique. Other enterprises, such as eBay, have made a business of providing a marketplace for putting buyers and sellers together in an electronic auction setting. Others, such as Orbitz and Priceline.com, have found a niche in the marketplace by providing bargain prices for airlines and hotels. There are, of course, problems associated with buying and selling on the Internet, one of which involves the difficulty of verifying the identity of the party on the other side of an Internet connection. Another problem involves how to make up for the lack of paper documents in cyber-commerce. In both cases, the law has provided a solution. We will look at the problems associated with verification first.

Verification Problems

Verification problems can be solved in a number of ways. In fact, the parties can avoid the problem by adding a term that delays the creation of the contract until the identities of the parties can be verified by some means other than computers. Or a business might elect to use its website only as an advertisement site. These solutions are unsatisfactory to most businesspeople, however, because they eliminate the advantages of doing business on the Internet. Another technique is for the parties to an Internet transaction to customize the verification process for each contract individually. However, in the interests of efficiency and cost, it would be preferable to have a process that applies to all contracts. A possible solution to this problem is the use of digital signatures. As we shall see, the Uniform Electronics Transactions Act defines a *digital signature* as "an electronic sound, symbol, or process attached to or logically associated with a record and executed or adopted by a person with the intent to sign the record." A digital signature is also referred to as a **cyber-signature**, an *electronic signature,* and an *e-signature.* Those businesses and legal practitioners who promote the use of digital signatures hope that the courts and/or the legislatures will institute a principle that states the use of a digital signature creates a rebuttable presumption that the signature is authentic and that the terms of the transaction have not been altered in transmission.

Offer and Acceptance Online An electronic party should always ensure that a copy of the contract is available on a hyperlink that will display the actual language of the agreement. The following terms should

Online shopping is fast, easy, and convenient. Utilizing digital signatures is an effective method used by businesses to verify the legitimacy of the transaction.

appear in any online agreement package: (1) payment procedures; (2) a limitation on the remedies that can be used by the parties; (3) refund policies; (4) the return process; (5) dispute settlement, forum selection, and choice-of-law provisions; (6) the applicability of cyber-signatures; (7) liability disclaimers; and (8) provisions relating to the offeree's manner of acceptance. In general, the other party accepts by clicking on a box on the computer screen that states that the party agrees to be bound by the terms of the contract. Sometimes this process is referred to as a *click-on acceptance* or *click-on agreement*. In a sense then, the *click* amounts to the party's signature. It is also critical to remember that when a cyber-agreement deals with goods, the provisions of Article 2 of the Uniform Commercial Code apply.

Cyber Contract Clauses and Hyperlinks As we have seen in this chapter, the Statute of Frauds requires that certain types of contracts must be in writing and that certain terms must be included in the writing. For example, the Statute of Frauds demands that each written contract include: the terms of the agreement, the subject matter, the consideration to be paid, the names and identities of the people to be obligated, and the signature of the party sought to be bound. In addition, the law requires that written contracts contain no ambiguity, misrepresentation, or uncertainty and that if such ambiguity, misrepresentation, or uncertainty enters a written contract, it will be interpreted against the party who wrote the contract. All of this sounds good, and it works quite well when dealing with paper contracts. However, when contracts are entered online through a website such as Amazon, Barnes & Noble, Dell, Best Buy, and so on, these terms may not be as clear to the unpracticed eye as they are on paper. In fact, some terms are hidden within the ether on one of those blue hyperlinks. With virtually no assistance from the legislatures, the courts have held, rather consistently, that, terms that are hidden behind one of those blue hyperlinks or their equivalent are roughly analogous to the pages of a long and drawn-out multipage paper contract. As long as the customer is notified on the screen about the clauses hidden by the hyperlink, and as long as the information in the link itself is neither ambiguous nor false nor uncertain, then the fact that the customer does not take advantage of the "click-here" invitation is no different from the customer who is told to read the unambiguous language on a multipage contract and fails to do so.

Online Advertisement "Click" Fraud One problem that arises in this area is verifying the identity of the "clicker." When companies are actually creating contracts, they police the process of verification rather closely. However, the click-on process functions not only in online contracts but also for online advertisements. Companies that advertise on the Internet often make contracts with search engines like Bing, Google, Yahoo, or America Online. The terms of these contracts generally include a provision that states that the company that places the advertisement online will pay the search engine on the basis of the number of clicks detected on that advertisement. The clicks are supposed to be a foolproof way to gauge interest in the advertiser's service or product. However, policing the exact nature of each click has proven difficult. Thus, hundreds of thousands of phony clicks have occurred in advertisements, inflating the bills of the advertisers that pay per click. The problem arises because the search engines often farm out the actual posting of the ads to intermediary companies, called *domain parkers,* that get paid on the basis of the number of clicks on the ads for which they are responsible. The domain parkers then transfer the ads to subsidiary websites. Some of these websites display advertisements and nothing more. This scenario provides a fertile ground in which the phony click campaigns grow. Some owners of these subsidiary websites pay fraudulent clickers a small amount to click on the ads, thus driving up the cost for the advertisers and increasing the site owner's split of the proceeds. Some even use "clickbot" software, capable of mechanically clicking on certain advertisements at programmed intervals. All of the major search engines have found themselves in litigation because of this new *cyber-confidence game*. [See: Brian Grow and Ben Elgin, "Click Fraud: The Dark Side of Online Advertising," *BusinessWeek,* October 2, 2006, pp. 46–57.]

Cyber-Commerce Legislation

Cyber-commerce legislation has taken many forms over the past decade. However, the three most influential acts have been the E-Sign Act, the Uniform Electronic Transactions Act (UETA), and the Uniform Computer Information Transactions Act (UCITA). A fourth new law that deals with a slightly different but no less serious problem, that of credit cards and identity theft, is the Fair and Accurate Credit Transactions Act (FACT).

The E-Sign Act The E-Sign Act is a federal act designed to deal with problems associated with cyber-commerce, especially those related to the recognition of electronic contracts and electronic signatures. Basically the act states that if the parties to a contract have voluntarily agreed to transact business electronically, the cyber-contract that results will be just as legally acceptable as a paper contract. The act also notes that the parties must be able to store and reproduce the cyber-record of the contract; otherwise, the cyber-record will not be legally sufficient under the act. The final word here is that under the provisions of the E-Sign Act, cyber-contracts and cyber-signatures are just as legitimate as their ink counterparts. A few documents are not covered by this statute, including court records, eviction notices, health insurance cancellations, wills, foreclosure notices, prenuptial contracts, and divorce papers. However, sale and lease of goods contracts as covered by the Uniform Commercial Code are included in the E-Sign Act.

The Uniform Electronic Transactions Act (UETA) The Uniform Electronic Transactions Act establishes the same type of legal parity between electronic records and paper records as does the E-Sign Act. It does not establish any new guidelines governing contracts just because they are entered electronically. The approach therefore is not to establish the differences between electronic contracts and paper agreements but instead to focus on the similarities. As a result, once the parties to a contract have voluntarily agreed to enter a transaction using an electronic medium, the agreement that results in electronic form, including the cyber-signatures, will be just as valid as a paper agreement. The UETA applies only to transactions that involve some sort of commercial, business, or governmental matter. The law also states that if an act, such as the Statute of Frauds, requires a writing and a signature, then a cyber-record and a cyber-signature will fulfill that requirement. Also, under provisions of the E-Sign Act, the UETA will trump the E-Sign Act provided that the state that has adopted the UETA has not altered its content. Most states, 48 at last count, have adopted the UETA. However, some states have altered provisions in the act and so it is best to check the version that has been enacted by your state. This is also why it would be smart to check the forum selection clause in any cyber-contract that you are about to enter. [See: The E-Sign Act, 15 USC Section 7002 9 (2) (A) (I).]

The Uniform Computer Information Transactions Act (UCITA)

The Uniform Computer Information Transactions Act (UCITA) focuses on contracts that involve the sale or lease of computer software, computer databases, interactive products, multimedia products, and any other type of computer information. The UCITA is in line with the basic provisions of the E-Sign Act and the UETA, in that it also declares that any transaction entered into using an electronic medium is just as valid as a paper agreement. Not all states have adopted the UCITA, so it is important to check on the applicability of the statute in your jurisdiction.

The Fair and Accurate Credit Transactions Act (FACT Act) The Fair and Accurate Credit Transactions Act (FACT Act) is Congress's antidote to one manifestation of the identity theft epidemic. The new law, which is actually an amendment to the Fair Credit Reporting Act (FCRA), is designed to cut down on identity theft related to the use of credit cards. The act prohibits merchants from using credit card receipts that show anything other than the last five credit card numbers. Receipts also cannot display credit card expiration dates. In effect, because the act outlaws such numerical displays, identity thieves will no longer be able to assume the identity of a consumer by obtaining a copy of a credit card receipt and using the credit card number and expiration date on the receipt to "verify their identity" over the phone or online.

quick quiz 11-4

1. The E-Sign Act is a model act designed to deal with problems associated with cyber-commerce.   true | false

2. The Uniform Electronic Transactions Act was passed by Congress to deal with the legality of electronic transactions.   true | false

3. The UCITA is not in line with any of the provisions of the E-Sign Act or the UETA.   true | false

Summary

11.1 The Statutes of Frauds outlines six types of contracts that must be in writing to be enforceable. These include contracts that cannot be completed within one year; contracts transferring real property rights; contracts for the sale of goods of $500 or more; certain contracts entered by executors and administrators; contracts by one party to pay a debt incurred by another party; and contracts in consideration of marriage.

11.2 The legal system has developed certain basic criteria that make the construction and interpretation of written contracts consistent. These four criteria are (1) the standard construction rule, (2) the parol evidence rule, (3) the best evidence rule, and (4) the equal dignities rule.

11.3 Certain formalities are followed in the formation of contracts. Written agreements need not be signed by both parties. However, any agreement signed by only one party would obligate only that party. Facsimile signatures are allowed on a contract if the contract states

that such signatures are valid. Some states have statutes allowing facsimile signatures. Persons who are illiterate usually sign written contracts with an X. Several states have begun to revise the basic requirements for the written expression of (a) contracts for the sale or lease of residential real estate; and (b) real property construction projects, especially involving private homes.

11.4 There are problems associated with buying and selling on the Internet. One of these problems involves the difficulty of verifying the identity of the person on the other side of an Internet connection. Another involves the question of how to deal with the fact that electronic transactions do not produce paper documents. In both cases, the law has provided some solutions to these difficulties. Three laws that address these problems include the E-Sign Act, the Uniform Electronic Transactions Act (UETA), and the Uniform Computer Information Transactions Act (UCITA). A fourth act that deals with the problem of identity theft is the Fair and Accurate Credit Transactions Act (FACT).

Key Terms

acknowledgment, 266
administrator, 258
antenuptial agreement, 259
best evidence rule, 263
collateral contract, 259

condition precedent, 262
cosigner, 259
cyber-signature, 270
equal dignities rule, 263
equitable estoppel, 257

executor, 258
guarantor, 259
guaranty contract, 259
guaranty of payment, 259
leading objective test, 259

Questions for Review and Discussion

1. What are the goals of the Statute of Frauds?
2. What contracts must be in writing under the Statute of Frauds?
3. What information must be in a writing under the Statute of Frauds?
4. What is the standard construction rule?
5. What is the parol evidence rule?
6. What are the exceptions to the parol evidence rule?
7. What is the best evidence rule?
8. What is the equal dignities rule?
9. What are the problems associated with cyber-commerce?
10. What are the latest cyber-commerce statutes?

Cases for Analysis

1. Several identity theft victims filed a series of class action lawsuits against firms that had not made the changes required by the Fair and Accurate Credit Transactions Act (FACT) by the statutory deadline. One of the issues before the court was whether the victims had to demonstrate that the offending company deliberately refused to comply or did so with reckless disregard for the new requirements. Which standard would be the appropriate one in this situation? Explain. [See: Amanda Bronstad, "Suits Multiply over Credit Card Exposure: Cash Registers Displaying Too Many Digits Spark Dozens of Class Actions," *The National Law Journal,* February 19, 2007, p. 4.]

2. Frank Strachan entered a contract with Wright Weber Construction for the building of an addition to his new home in Lakeside. The construction firm was to begin building the addition on April 2. Wright Weber agreed that the addition might be finished by March 1 of the following year, but also stipulated that May 1 of the following year was a more reasonable estimate. The details of the agreement were never reduced to writing. When Wright Weber ran into labor problems in August, it had to put the construction of the addition on hold. One month later, unable to resolve the labor dispute, Wright Weber shut the company down and abandoned the Strachan work site. As a result, Strachan had to negotiate a new contract with a new construction firm. The new contract cost $12,900 more than it would have had Weber completed the job as promised. In addition, because the Lakeside house could not be used during construction, Strachan incurred storage costs for his furniture because he had to move out of the home he was living in to accommodate the new owners. He also had to live in a hotel for four months while the Lakeside addition was completed. Strachan sued Wright Weber. Wright Weber moved for a dismissal because the contract was not in writing. Strachan argued that the contract could have been completed within one year and was therefore outside of the statute. How will the court decide the case? Explain your response.

3. Meng, a vice president at Boston University, resigned his position to protest what he regarded as the unethical and unprofessional behavior of the university's president, John Silber, in terminating a recently renewed contract with Linkage Corporation. Silber orally promised Meng, as a severance package when he resigned, 14 months of salary and benefits and free tuition for two of his children if either should attend the university. Was the oral promise enforceable? Explain. [See: *Meng v. Trustees of Boston University,* 96-9776 Appeals Court (MA).]

4. As part of an employment agreement, Bazzy orally promised to give Hall an option to buy 1,000 shares of company stock at $20 per share. Hall brought suit against the company when it refused to sell the stock to him. What legal argument may Bazzy's company use to refuse to sell the stock to Hall as agreed? [See: *Hall v.*

Horizon House Microwave, Inc., 506 N.E.2d 178 (MA).]

5. Anna Wilson was assistant manager of a Montgomery Ward store. When Montgomery Ward announced that it would be closing the store, the manager quit, leaving Wilson in charge. A district manager orally promised Wilson that if she stayed on and assisted in the closing of the store, she would receive a sum of money calculated according to a certain formula. Wilson stayed on and managed the closing of the store (which took two months) in addition to her regular duties. Montgomery Ward refused to pay her the money, claiming that the oral promise was unenforceable. Was the store correct? Why or why not? [See: *Wilson v. Montgomery Ward,* 610 F. Supp. 1035 (DC IN).]

6. Curtis Hendrix orally agreed to compensate Beverly Spertell for services rendered in connection with their living together out of wedlock. Later, when suit was brought to collect the money, Hendrix argued that the oral contract was unenforceable under the Statute of Frauds. Do you agree with Hendrix? Explain. [See: *Spertell v. Hendrix,* 461 N.Y.S.2d 823 (NY).]

7. Walt Nicklesworth entered a lease agreement with Marblehead Properties, under which Nicklesworth used the property located at 5293 Lake Shore Boulevard as a used bookstore. The terms of the lease included a right of first refusal, such that Nicklesworth could purchase the property if Marblehead ever decided to sell. Two years into the five-year lease, Marblehead sold the property to Daniel O'Donnell. Nicklesworth brought suit for breach of contract. At trial, no one could produce a written copy of the lease for the judge. The judge decided to dismiss the case. What justification did the judge use to dismiss the case? Explain.

8. Butler leased a certain piece of property from Wheeler with an option to purchase it at a later date. The agreement was handwritten and consisted of two separate documents, each listing part of the transaction. Butler later attempted to purchase the property but Wheeler refused to sell, claiming that the agreement was unenforceable because it was contained in two documents. Was Wheeler correct? Explain. [See: *Butler v. Lovoll,* 620 P.2d 1251 (NV).]

9. Ray's Motor Sales sold a mobile home to Hathaway. Before the written contract was signed, the salesperson told Hathaway that Ray's would take care of any problems that Hathaway might have with the mobile home. This promise was not included in the written document. When Hathaway had problems with the mobile home, he asked Ray's to take care of them. Ray's refused to be of any assistance. Could Hathaway enforce Ray's promise? Explain. [See: *Hathaway v. Ray's Motor Sales,* 247 A.2d 512 (VT).]

10. In 1919, Pasha Patel owned several acres of land in the Upper Peninsula of Michigan. Half a pond was located on Patel's land. The other half of the pond was located on land owned by Brooke Brookhaven. For a small consideration, Patel transferred the right to cut ice on her side of the pond each winter to Fred Xavier. The contract was oral and supposed to last for the next five winters. Each day from early October to late March, Xavier would cut the ice and remove it. He would carefully carve the ice into large cubes that fit perfectly into the ice boxes located in the rental cabins dotting the Upper Peninsula. (This was 1919, remember.) He then sold the ice to the cabin renters. One summer Brookhaven drained her part of the pond. In October, this action meant that ice was sparse, and what was available was sunk into the mud at the bottom of the lake and thus unusable for carving and sale. Xavier brought suit against Brookhaven, arguing that her action in draining the lake made his interest in the property worthless. The court asked for a copy of the written contract transferring the right to cut the ice to Xavier. When Xavier could not produce one, the judge dismissed the case. What will be the result of the case at this point? Explain.

quick quiz Answers

11-1	11-2	11-3	11-4
1. F	1. F	1. F	1. F
2. F	2. T	2. F	2. F
3. T	3. F	3. F	3. F

Chapter 12

Third Parties, Discharge, and Remedies

THE OPENING CASE Round 1
"Knock, Knock." "Who's There?" "Federal Home Loan Mortgage . . . Who?"

Most lawsuits represent the last stage in a complicated series of negotiations that begin when the two parties disagree. Sometimes, however, the other party just materializes out of nowhere. This is exactly what happened in the case of *Fed. Home Loan Mtge. Corp. (FHLMC) v. Schwartzwald.* The problems began when Duane and Julie Schwartzwald negotiated a mortgage agreement with Legacy Mortgage in the amount of $251,250 to help them purchase a home in Xenia, Ohio. As is often the case in these matters, the Schwartzwalds executed a promissory note and gave a security interest in the home to Legacy. Legacy quickly assigned the mortgage to Wells Fargo and, as part of that second deal, endorsed the promissory note, making it payable to Wells Fargo. Two years passed without incident during which the Schwartzwalds faithfully made their mortgage payments on a regular basis to Wells Fargo. Then Duane lost his job, which forced the family to move out of state. They maintained mortgage payments on the Xenia home for four months but then defaulted on the loan in January. A few months later, the Schwartzwalds negotiated a deal with Wells Fargo

under which the bank arranged to list the property for a short sale. In April the Schwartzwalds completed a sales agreement under which the house would be sold for $259,900. The closing date was scheduled for June. Everything seemed to be proceeding smoothly when the Schwartzwalds suddenly learned in April that a foreclosure action had been started by the Federal Home Loan Mortgage Corporation (FHLMC), a new player that had suddenly beamed down from . . . well . . . from out of nowhere, or so it seemed. As it turned out, along with the other papers filed with the court, the FHLMC had also appended a copy of the mortgage, which verified that the lender was Legacy, and that the borrowers were the Schwartzwalds. However, FHLMC did not attach a copy of the promissory note, which was reported as being "unavailable." (Julie had contacted Wells Fargo about all of this but was told it was just "standard procedure.") In April, FHLMC delivered to the court a copy of the Schwartzwalds' note with Legacy Mortgage that included a blank endorsement by Wells Fargo, placed above the endorsement by Legacy Mortgage, payable to Wells Fargo. The note itself, however, was not assigned to FHLMC until May, and the assignment itself was not filed in the court until June. All this time, Wells Fargo acted like the sale was going to go through, but the bank delayed so long that the buyers finally gave up. The Schwartzwalds asked that the action be dismissed because, when FHLMC filed the lawsuit in April, FHLMC had no standing to sue. The trial court and the appeals court ruled for FHLMC, but the case went to the State Supreme Court. How do you suppose the high court ruled on this issue? [See: *Fed. Home Loan Mtge. Corp. v. Schwartzwald,* 134 Ohio St.3d 13, 2012-Ohio-5017.]

Opening Case Questions

1. What is an assignment and how does it differ from a delegation? Explain.

2. What parties are involved in an assignment? Explain.

3. What party has the duty to notify the obligor of the assignment? Explain.

4. When does an assignment become effective? Explain.

5. What restrictions, if any, are imposed by law upon assignments? Explain.

 Learning Objectives

1. Explain the legal rights given to all beneficiaries.
2. Identify the legal rights given to incidental beneficiaries.
3. Explain the assignment of rights and the delegation of duties.
4. Explain the nature of a novation.
5. Relate what constitutes satisfactory performance of a contract.
6. Outline the difference between complete and substantial performance.
7. List the ways that a contract can be discharged by nonperformance.
8. Clarify the concept of anticipatory repudiation.
9. Enumerate the types of damages available in the event of a breach of contract.
10. Contrast specific performance with injunctive relief.

12-1 Contracts and Third Parties

A third party is a person who may in some way be affected by a contract but who is not one of the contracting parties. A third party, also known as an outside party, is at times given benefits from a contract made between two or more other parties. A third party receiving benefits from a contract made by others is known as a third party beneficiary or sometimes simply as a beneficiary to the contract. Although not obligated by the agreement made between those in privity, third parties may have the legal right to enforce the benefits given them by such agreements.

Intended Beneficiaries

A beneficiary in whose favor a contract is made is an intended beneficiary. With exceptions in some states, an intended beneficiary can enforce the contract made by those in privity of contract. Those who are most frequently recognized to be intended beneficiaries and have the right to demand and enforce the benefits promised are creditor beneficiaries, donee beneficiaries, and insurance beneficiaries.

Creditor Beneficiaries A creditor beneficiary is an outside third party to whom one or both contracting parties owe a continuing debt of obligation arising from a contract. Frequently, the obligation results from the failure of the contracting party or parties to pay for goods delivered or services rendered by the third party at some time in the past.

Donee Beneficiaries A third party who provides no consideration for the benefits received and who owes the contracting parties no legal duty is known as a donee beneficiary. However, the contracting parties owe the donee beneficiary the act promised; if it is not forthcoming, the donee beneficiary may bring suit. The consideration that supports this type of agreement is the consideration exchanged by the parties in privity of contract.

Insurance Beneficiaries An individual named as the beneficiary of an insurance policy is usually considered a donee beneficiary. The beneficiary does not have to furnish the insured with consideration to enforce payment of the policy. In some cases, an insurance beneficiary may also be a creditor beneficiary. This situation occurs in consumer or mortgage loans when the creditor requires the debtor to furnish a life-term insurance policy naming the creditor as the beneficiary. The policy will pay the debt if the debtor dies before the loan has been repaid.

Incidental Beneficiaries

An incidental beneficiary is an outside party for whose benefit a contract was not made but who would substantially benefit if the agreement were performed according to its terms and conditions. An incidental beneficiary, in contrast to an intended beneficiary, has no legal grounds for enforcing the contract made by those in privity of contract.

EXAMPLE 12-1: *Faber v. The Brotherhood of Aerospace Workers*

Mark Faber owned a hotel and restaurant in downtown Indianapolis. The Brotherhood of Aerospace Workers (BAW) had a contract with the city for the use of the municipal auditorium for the union's annual convention. One week before the convention, the union announced that it was canceling the meeting. The move was a clear violation of BAW's contract with the city. Faber brought suit against the BAW for damages due to lost business caused by the breach. The court dismissed the case on a motion for summary judgment. The court ruled that Faber was an incidental beneficiary and therefore had no grounds on which to bring the suit against the union.

---

quick quiz 12-1

1. A third party who provides no consideration and owes no legal duty to the contracting parties is a donee beneficiary.   true | false

2. A creditor beneficiary is an outside third party to whom one or both contracting parties owe a continuing debt of obligation arising from the contract.   true | false

3. Incidental and intended beneficiaries have the same rights.   true | false

12-2 The Law of Assignment

When people enter contracts, they receive certain rights and incur particular duties. It is completely accepted today that, with some exceptions noted subsequently and unless the contract itself provides otherwise, these rights and duties can be transferred to others. An **assignment** is a transfer of a contract right, and a **delegation** is a transfer of a contract duty.

Assignment and Delegation

In general, rights are *assigned,* and duties are *delegated.* In most cases, both are governed by the same rules. If A is owed money by B, A may assign to C the right to collect the money. However, if A has agreed to pay B to harvest 200 acres of wheat for a price, B may delegate the duty of harvesting to C. Restrictions against the delegation of duties are presented later in this chapter. Three parties are associated with any assignment. Two of the parties are the ones who entered the original agreement. The party who assigns rights or delegates duties is the **assignor**. The outside third party to whom the assignment is made is the **assignee**. The remaining party to the original agreement is the **obligor**. Consideration is not required in the assignment of a contract. When there is no supporting consideration, however, the assignor may repudiate the assignment at any time before its execution. In addition, when no consideration is given for an assignment, creditors of the assignor may have the assignment rescinded on the grounds that it is a fraudulent conveyance. A **fraudulent conveyance** is a transfer of property with the intent to defraud creditors. If a fraudulent conveyance occurs, the assignor's creditors could have the assignment rescinded.

THE OPENING CASE *Round 2*
Two Assignments Are Better Than One . . . Perhaps

In the opening case, we learned the story behind the case of *Fed. Home Loan Mtge. Corp. (FHLMC) v. Schwartzwald* began when Duane and Julie Schwartzwald negotiated a mortgage agreement with Legacy Mortgage in the amount of $251,250 to help them purchase a home. What followed was a series of assignments that greatly affected the outcome of the case for the Schwartzwalds. According to customary procedures, the Schwartzwalds executed a promissory note and gave a security interest in the home to Legacy. This is standard operating procedure in the industry. The next step was the *first assignment*. This step was also standard operating procedure, and the Schwartzwalds probably knew that this assignment was going to happen up front. The actual assignment occurred when Legacy assigned the mortgage to Wells Fargo and, as part of that second deal, endorsed the promissory note, making it payable to Wells Fargo. Two years passed without incident during which the Schwartzwalds made their mortgage payments on a regular basis to Wells Fargo. When Duane lost his job, however, and the family moved out of state, things got rough. The Schwartzwalds made mortgage payments on the house until January when they found that they could not continue. However, they negotiated a deal with Wells Fargo under which the bank arranged to list the property for a short sale. In April the Schwartzwalds completed a sales agreement under which the house would be sold for $259,900. The closing date was scheduled for June. Everything seemed to be proceeding smoothly when the Schwartzwalds learned in April that a foreclosure action had been started by the Federal Home Loan Mortgage Corporation (FHLMC). Unknown to the Schwartzwalds, Wells Fargo had negotiated a *second assignment* of the mortgage to FHLMC. Figure 12-1 gives a visual representation of the relationships that developed during this assignment process. [See: *Fed. Home Loan Mtge. Corp. v. Schwartzwald,* 134 Ohio St.3d 13, 2012-Ohio-5017.]

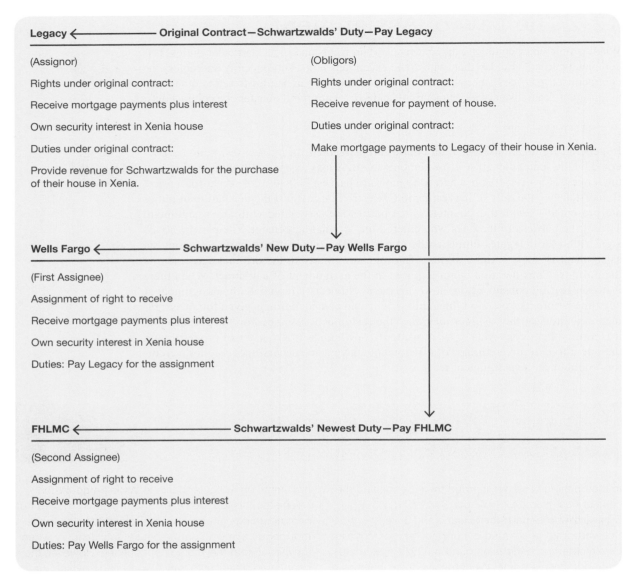

Legacy ←——————— Original Contract—Schwartzwalds' Duty—Pay Legacy

(Assignor)   (Obligors)

Rights under original contract: Rights under original contract:

Receive mortgage payments plus interest   Receive revenue for payment of house.

Own security interest in Xenia house   Duties under original contract:

Duties under original contract: Make mortgage payments to Legacy of their house in Xenia.

Provide revenue for Schwartzwalds for the purchase
of their house in Xenia.

Wells Fargo ←——————— Schwartzwalds' New Duty—Pay Wells Fargo

(First Assignee)

Assignment of right to receive

Receive mortgage payments plus interest

Own security interest in Xenia house

Duties: Pay Legacy for the assignment

FHLMC ←——————— Schwartzwalds' Newest Duty—Pay FHLMC

(Second Assignee)

Assignment of right to receive

Receive mortgage payments plus interest

Own security interest in Xenia house

Duties: Pay Wells Fargo for the assignment

Figure 12-1 The Legacy–Schwartzwald–Wells Fargo–FHLMC Assignment Maze

Assignment Methods

To be valid, an assignment must follow certain accepted procedures designed to protect all of the parties. Form of assignment, notice of assignment, and the rights of parties in successive or subsequent assignments must conform to practices established by case law and state statutes. Assignment may be accomplished through written, oral, or implied agreements between the assignor and the assignee. Parties to an assignment must observe the requirement provided by the equal dignities rule discussed in Chapter 11. Under that rule, the law requires that if the agreement by the original parties must be in writing, the assignment also must be in writing.

An assignment is valid at the time it is made. As a measure of protection against subsequent assignments, the assignee should give notice of the assignment to the obligor. Although this obligation falls to the assignee, either party may give notice. Once notice is received, the obligor should deal with the assignee. If notice is not given, it would be normal practice for the obligor to render performance to the original contracting party, the assignor. If due notice has been given and the obligor makes payment to the assignor, the obligor is not excused from making payment to the assignee.

Should the assignor make a subsequent assignment of the same right, the courts must decide which of the two assignees has a superior right and claim against the obligor. A majority of the states hold that the first assignee has a superior right, even if a later assignee was the first to give notice of the assignment to the obligor. A minority of courts hold that whichever assignee was first to give notice of assignment has a superior right and claim to any assigned benefits.

quick quiz 12-2

1. A delegation is the transfer of a contractual right.   true | false

2. The equal dignities axiom has no application in the law of   true | false
   assignment.

3. It is the responsibility of the assignor to give notice of the   true | false
   assignment to the obligor.

12-3 Assignment Rights, Duties, and Restrictions

Rights can be assigned, and duties can be delegated. Although this rule seems simple enough, disagreements still arise regarding both assignment and delegation. What is generally in dispute is whether a particular right or duty can be transferred and, if so, what legal effects arise from that transfer.

Rights and Duties of the Assignee

The rights and duties of the assignee are the same as those previously held by the assignor under the original contract. It is fair to say that the assignee "steps into the shoes" of the assignor. Claims the assignor may have had against the obligor now belong to the assignee. Also, defenses the obligor may have had against the assignor's claims may now be used against the assignee.

The assignee's duty in an assignment is to give notice of the assignment to the obligor. The obligor is allowed a reasonable time to seek assurance that an assignment has been truly made. Making the assignment in writing reduces the possibility of fraudulent representation as an assignee.

About the Law

An assignment, rather than a negotiation, occurs when a check is transferred to a third party without a required endorsement.

EXAMPLE 12-2: The Quitter–Stalker Assignment, Part I

Quitter appeared at the payroll department of the Meadville Delivery Company and told the paymaster that one of Meadville's drivers, Stalker, had made an assignment of part of his paycheck to her. Under terms of the assignment, Quitter was to receive $150 of the money that Meadville owed Stalker. Meadville, the obligor, would not have to pay Quitter the $150 until the paymaster had a reasonable amount of time to verify the assignment.

THE OPENING CASE *Round 3*
Ignorance Is Not Bliss: At Least Not When Assignments Are Involved

In the opening case, we learned Duane and Julie Schwartzwald negotiated a mortgage agreement with Legacy Mortgage in the amount of $251,250 so that they could buy a house in Xenia. The Schwartzwalds executed a promissory note and gave a security interest in the home to Legacy. Next, Legacy assigned the mortgage to Wells Fargo and endorsed the promissory note, making it payable to Wells Fargo. After Duane lost his job and the family moved out of state, the Schwartzwalds continued to make mortgage payments until January. They negotiated a deal with Wells Fargo under which the bank arranged to list the property for a short sale, and in April the Schwartzwalds completed a sales agreement under which the house would be sold for $259,900. The closing date was scheduled for June. Then suddenly in April, the Schwartzwalds learned that a foreclosure action had been started by the Federal Home Loan Mortgage Corporation (FHLMC). Unknown to the Schwartzwalds, Wells Fargo had negotiated a second assignment of the mortgage to FHLMC. However, the assignment seemed not to be complete when the foreclosure case was filed because, along with the other papers filed with the court, the FHLMC had appended a copy of the mortgage, which verified that the lender was Legacy and that the borrowers were the Schwartzwald, *but* failed to attach a copy of the promissory note, which it reported as being "unavailable." This is when one of the most troublesome parts

of the story begins. Julie had contacted Wells Fargo about all of this but was told it was just "standard procedure." She was also told by Wells Fargo "not to worry" because the short sale would take care of things. The Schwartzwalds relied on these representations from Wells Fargo and did not file an answer to the foreclosure filing, leaving them vulnerable to a default judgment in Common Pleas Court. In the meantime, Wells Fargo continued to work with FHLMC while also acting like the sale was going to go through. Moreover, Wells Fargo delayed so long that the buyers gave up. Now it is true that the assignor does not have the duty to inform the obligor of the assignment. However, Wells Fargo's actions here are suspect at best. There is, after all, a difference between failing to give notice and actively misleading an obligor by telling them that a foreclosure action is "standard procedure" and that they "should not worry." Moreover, continuing to work on a sale that they knew would not go through, also seems to cross some sort of invisible, but no less, real ethical line. The duty to notify the Schwartzwalds (the obligors) fell on the shoulders of FHLMC (the assignee) which seems to have ignored that duty, until the foreclosure notice, which would hardly constitute a valid notice in any body's book. [See: *Fed. Home Loan Mtge. Corp. v. Schwartzwald,* 134 Ohio St.3d 13, 2012-Ohio-5017.]

Liabilities and Warranties of the Assignor

The assignor is obligated to any express and implied warranties that serve to protect either the assignee or the obligor. A **warranty** is a promise, statement, or other representation that a thing has certain qualities.

Warranties to the Assignee
The assignor is bound by an implied warranty that the obligor will respect the assignment and make the performance, as required by the original agreement between the assignor and the obligor.

EXAMPLE 12-3: The Quitter–Stalker Assignment, Part II

Suppose, in the Quitter–Stalker assignment, that the Meadville Trucking Company had been either unwilling or unable to pay Quitter the $150. Stalker would be bound by an implied warranty to Quitter that the $150 would be paid. If the assignment were a gift to Quitter, there would be no enforceable warranty in the absence of consideration between the assignor and the assignee.

Warranties to the Obligor   If the assignor delegates to an assignee duties owed the obligor, there is an implied warranty that the duties delegated will be carried out in a complete and satisfactory manner.

Restrictions on Assignments

Although most contracts may be assigned, those for personal and professional services may not. The right of assignment may also be restricted by agreement of the original parties to the contract and, in certain cases, by law.

Restrictions on Personal and Professional Service Contracts   A
party may not delegate duties that are of a personal or professional nature. *Personal,* in this context, means "other than routine." Musicians or artists, for example, could not delegate their services to someone else. They are chosen for their ability or artistic talent. Professional services are those rendered by physicians, lawyers, certified public accountants, ministers, and others. People in these occupations are selected because of their special abilities, and their services could not be delegated to someone else. In contrast, routine services may usually be delegated. These are services performed by electricians, mechanics, woodworkers, plumbers, waitstaff, bankers, publishers, and others whose skills and abilities are judged according to the usual customs and standards of the marketplace.

Restrictions Imposed by Original Contract   Parties to a
contract may include a condition that will not allow its assignment. Some courts have held that a restriction against the assignment of a debt owed by the obligor robs the assignor of a property right guaranteed by law and would be contrary to public policy. Other courts have permitted this restrictive condition.

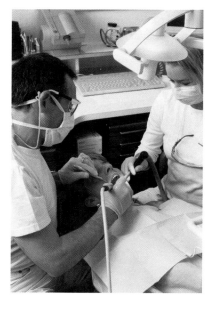

Professionals, like dentists, are chosen based on their particular skills and abilities and may not delegate their professional duties to another.

Restrictions Imposed by Law   Assignments, in special situa-
tions, may be restricted by law or declared void because they are contrary to public policy. Thus, members of the armed services may not assign any part of their pay except to a spouse or family member. Police officers, persons elected or appointed to public office, and others are likewise restricted from making assignment of their pay or of duties that they have been especially chosen to perform. Also, some states demand that, if an assignee wants to bring a lawsuit based on an assignment, as in a foreclosure action, that assignee must have already received the assignment. This is because, until the assignment has occurred, that party (assignee #2 as it were) has no personal stake in the lawsuit. Nor can the party transform itself retroactively into a party with standing after the action has begun. If the lawsuit is brought before the assignment is completed, the case will be dismissed because the

THE OPENING CASE *Round 4*
Standing Around in Court Is Not the Same as Having "Standing to Sue"

In the opening case, we learned Duane and Julie Schwartzwald negotiated a mortgage agreement with Legacy Mortgage in the amount of $251,250 so that they could buy a home in Xenia. The Schwartzwalds executed a promissory note and gave a security interest in the home to Legacy. Next, Legacy assigned the mortgage to Wells Fargo and endorsed the promissory note, making it payable to Wells Fargo. Duane lost his job and the family moved out of state, but the Schwartzwalds continued to make mortgage payments until January. They negotiated a deal with Wells Fargo under which the bank arranged to list the property for a short sale, and in April the Schwartzwalds completed a sales agreement under which the house would be sold for $259,900. The closing date was scheduled for June. Then suddenly in April, the Schwartzwalds learned that a foreclosure action had been started by the Federal Home Loan Mortgage Corporation (FHLMC). Unknown to the Schwartzwalds, Wells Fargo had negotiated a second assignment of the mortgage to FHLMC. However, the assignment seemed not to be complete when the foreclosure case was filed because, along with the other papers filed with the court, the FHLMC had appended a copy of the mortgage, which verified that the lender was Legacy and that the borrowers were the Schwartzwalds, but failed to attach a copy of the promissory note, which was reported as being "unavailable." Julie contacted Wells Fargo about all of this but was told it was just "standard procedure." In April, FHLMC delivered to the court a copy of the Schwartzwalds' note with Legacy Mortgage that included a blank endorsement by Wells Fargo, placed above the endorsement by Legacy Mortgage, payable to Wells Fargo. The note itself, however, was not assigned to FHLMC until May and the assignment itself was not filed in the court until June. The Schwartzwalds asked that the action be dismissed because, when FHLMC filed the lawsuit in April, it had no standing to sue. The trial court and the appeals court ruled for FHLMC, but the case went to the State Supreme Court. The high court saw things differently. Standing to sue, the court noted, requires that the party that brings the lawsuit have some real interest in the subject matter of that lawsuit. In other words, as the court put it, that party must have "a personal stake in the outcome of the controversy." Moreover, if that party does *not* have standing (a personal interest in the outcome of the controversy) when the action starts, that party cannot then provide a personal interest afterward. This is what FHLMC tried to do here, and the high court did not let FHLMC get away with it. Of course, that does not mean that any of the issues have been decided. It just means that FHLMC has to start the process from the beginning all over again. [See: *Fed. Home Loan Mtge. Corp. v. Schwartzwald,* 134 Ohio St.3d 13, 2012-Ohio-5017.]

party bringing lawsuit has no injury to vindicate. Once the action has been dismissed, it can be brought again, as long as the statute of limitations has not run out, the action was dismissed without prejudice, and the party obtains standing to sue. This situation must be distinguished from an action initiated by a legal representative, such as a guardian, an executor, an administrator, a trustee, and so on, brought on behalf of the real-party-in-interest. The *Schwartzwald* case illustrates the first situation, that is, a lack of standing to sue, rather than a case brought by an agent on behalf of a real-party-in-interest.

Novation and Assignment

Sometimes a party to a contract will assign all rights and delegate all duties to a third party (the assignee). Once this happens, the assignee will work directly with the obligor, performing the duties and receiving the benefits. Nevertheless, the assignor will remain in privity of contract with the obligor and be liable to the obligor if the assignee does not perform or performs improperly.

> ## EXAMPLE 12-4: *Superfine Market v. Allgood Canning Company*
>
> Allgood Canning Company entered into a contract to sell 1,000 cases of baked beans to Superfine Market for a specific price. Shortly thereafter, Allgood delegated its duty to ship the beans and assigned its rights to receive the money to Fastway Canning Company. The beans Fastway shipped were bad. If Superfine were to bring suit for damages, it would have to be brought against Allgood, because that was the company with which it had contracted. There was no privity between Superfine and Fastway.

In contrast, if all three parties agree, the assignor can be released from liability at the time of the assignment, and privity of contract can exist between the assignee and the obligor. Such an arrangement is called a **novation**, which is a substitution, by mutual agreement, of a new party for one of the original parties to a contract. If, in Example 12-4, Superfine and Fastway had agreed to release Allgood from responsibility under the original contract, a novation would have occurred. Privity of contract then would have been between Superfine and Fastway. Superfine's only recourse upon receiving the bad beans would have been to bring suit against Fastway because, by mutual consent, Allgood had been discharged.

quick quiz 12-3

1. The phrase "assignment of a contract" means the same thing as the phrase "assignment of rights." true | false

2. Personal and professional duties are just as transferable as all other duties. true | false

3. Novations have been outlawed under the Restatement of Contracts. true | false

12-4 Discharge by Performance

Most contracts are discharged by **performance**, which means that the parties do what they agreed to do under the terms of the contract. When performance occurs, the obligations of the parties end. Sometimes, however, the parties do not perform in a timely or satisfactory manner. At other times, they perform partially but not completely. At still other times, they do not perform at all.

Time for Performance

When the time for performance is not stated in the contract, the contract must be performed within a reasonable time. A **reasonable time** is the time that may fairly, properly, and conveniently be required to do the task that is to be done, considering attending circumstances. Whether a task is performed within a reasonable time is a question of fact to be decided by the jury in a jury trial or the judge in a nonjury trial.

EXAMPLE 12-5: *Rostow Aviation, Ltd. v. Futuregraphics, Inc.*

Rostow Aviation, Ltd., entered a contract with Futuregraphics, Inc., for the design and implementation of a new website for Rostow. The website was supposed to be up and operational within 60 days of the making of the contract. Futuregraphics was one week late in the completion of the site. Rostow attempted to rescind the agreement, claiming that time was of special importance. The court ruled that it had not been clearly established that time was essential for the completion of the website. Because time was not essential to the satisfactory performance of the agreement, Rostow was held to the contract.

A QUESTION OF ETHICS

The court held Rostow to the contract in Example 12-5 even though Futuregraphics was one week late in fulfilling its part of the agreement. Because time really was not essential to the agreement, and because Rostow presumably knew that, was it ethical for Rostow to raise the issue of Futuregraphics' lateness in the first place? If time had been important to the completion of the website, did Rostow have a responsibility to raise the issue of time before the contract was finalized? If Futuregraphics knew it was running behind schedule, did it have a duty to notify Rostow and offer some sort of compensation for the breach? Explain your answers.

When the time for performance is stated in the contract but there is nothing to indicate that time is of particular importance, the court will usually allow additional time to perform. When the time for performance is stated in the contract and there is something special about the contract that indicates time is essential, the time for performance will be strictly enforced.

EXAMPLE 12-6: *Carter City School System v. Spectrum Images, Inc.*

Spectrum Images, Inc., entered a contract with the entire Carter City school system for the design, production, and distribution of the yearbooks for each of the system's three high schools. A very strict schedule was developed for each high school yearbook staff, specifying when the manuscript, art, and photos had to be e-mailed to Spectrum; when the material had to be formatted and returned as pdf page proof files to the high schools; and when the pdf page proof files had to be read, corrected, and e-mailed to Spectrum. The yearbooks were to be delivered to each high school 90 days after Spectrum had received all pdf page proof files so that they would be ready for distribution on the graduation day for each of the high schools. In such a situation, it is clear that time is an important factor in this agreement. Unfortunately, the students at two of the three schools did not return the proofs on time, and the yearbooks were late. This missed deadline caused an extra expense for the city school system, which had to send the yearbooks to students by FedEx because they were no longer on campus to pick up their books personally. When Carter City sued Spectrum, the court ruled that because the students knew that time was of the essence and had not made the scheduled deadline, the city could not complain when Spectrum failed to meet the delivery date.

Similarly, when the phrase "time is of the essence" is included among the terms of a written contract, the time period will be enforced. The phrase makes it clear that the time element is of the utmost importance to the parties. Some contracts use a "best efforts" clause to avoid committing parties to a date but instead committing them to do their best to perform by a certain date.

Satisfactory, Complete, and Substantial Performance

Satisfactory performance exists when either personal taste or objective standards have determined that the contracting parties have performed their contractual duties according to the agreement. Satisfactory performance is either an express or implied condition of every contract. Sales agreements for consumer goods often note this condition by including the words: "money back if not entirely satisfied." In other contracts, satisfaction may be carefully defined according to the expectations of the parties. When there is no express agreement, the law implies that work will be done in a skillful manner and the materials or goods will be free of defects. Ordinarily, the parties may be discharged from a contract only if there has been satisfactory performance. Sometimes, one person will agree to do something to another person's satisfaction. Services rendered in a beauty salon or barbershop, photographs taken at a studio, and portraits painted by an artist fall within this classification. Regardless of the skill and application of the person doing the work, dissatisfied customers may, on the basis of their personal judgment and satisfaction, refuse to make payment.

Complete performance occurs when all the parties fully accomplish every term, condition, and promise to which they agreed. **Substantial performance** occurs when a party, in good faith, executes all promised terms and conditions with the exception of minor details that do not affect the real intent of their agreement. Complete performance terminates an agreement, freeing the parties of any further obligation. Ordinarily, substantial performance also serves to discharge the agreement but with one difference: A party who correctly complains that the other party's performance has been substantial but not complete has the right to demand reimbursement from the offending party to correct those details that were not performed.

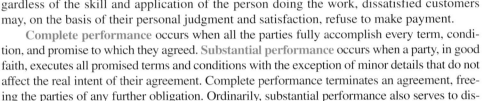

EXAMPLE 12-7: *South Central State College v. McLaughlin Construction, Inc.*

McLaughlin Construction, Inc., was the primary contractor for the construction of a new engineering center for South Central State College. The construction of the center was supposed to be completed within one year, and the doors were to open in time for the fall term. The building was completed by fall, but the architect for McLaughlin had committed an error. Apparently he had failed to take into consideration the stress that would be placed on the floor-to-ceiling windows in the building's lobby. As a result, several of those floor-to-ceiling windows developed cracks. An inspection by the state engineers demonstrated that the cracks posed no danger to anyone in or near the building. Nevertheless, the cracked windows were quite unsightly, and they leaked heavily when it rained, flooding the lobby. Consequently, the college demanded that the construction company make repairs at its own expense. The company refused, and the college threatened to rescind the entire contract. Instead, cooler heads prevailed, and the college hired another construction firm to make adjustments to the stress so that the floor-to-ceiling windows would be the showpieces they were supposed to be. When the college asked for and was refused reimbursement for the additional expense, it sued McLaughlin. The court held that there had been substantial performance of the original contract. However, because the cracked windows were caused by an error on the part of the McLaughlin architect, the court awarded reimbursement costs to the college.

Conditions and Tender of Performance

Some contracts have conditions or terms that determine the rights and duties of the parties prior to performance, during performance, and following performance. These conditions may be classified as conditions precedent, conditions concurrent, or conditions subsequent. Also, in most situations it is necessary for a nonbreaching party to continue to offer to perform as promised. This is referred to as a tender of performance. It is discussed below at length.

Conditions of Performance   A **condition precedent** is a condition that requires the performance of certain acts or promises before the other party is obligated to pay money or provide any other agreed to consideration. In a *unilateral contract,* the performance of a condition precedent serves as the offeree's acceptance of the offer. In a *bilateral contract,* it is a promise that if not performed leads to either rescission or termination of the entire agreement.

EXAMPLE 12-8: The Pressler Case

Pressler, a third-year law student, signed an agreement to accept a position with a law firm. The members of the firm agreed to hire Pressler on the condition that she receive her law degree and pass the bar examination in their state. Earning the law degree and passing the bar examination are conditions precedent to the performance of the obligation of the law firm in giving Pressler the position.

A condition that requires both parties to perform at the same time is a **condition concurrent**. A promise to deliver goods supported by the buyer's promise to pay on delivery is a very common condition concurrent. Real estate sales agreements, by custom, usually state that the owner–seller will deliver a good and complete deed to the real property on the buyer's presentation of either cash or a certified check for the amount of the purchase price. Failure of either to do as promised concurrently would be a breach of the express contract condition. A **condition subsequent** is one in which the parties agree that the contract will be terminated when a prescribed event occurs or does not occur. An agreement between a builder and a client stating that contract performance would terminate if a required building permit were not obtained from the issuing public authority within 60 days after the contract is signed is a condition subsequent. Some warranties included in contracts also illustrate these conditions.

EXAMPLE 12-9: *Graham v. Metcalf*

Luben Metcalf agreed to remodel Trisha Graham's back porch for $15,000. Both parties signed a written agreement. One clause in the agreement stated that Metcalf guaranteed the improvements would be free of defects for 12 months after the work was completed. Graham agreed to pay for the improvements upon completion. Metcalf's guarantee constituted a condition subsequent, that is, a condition that applies after both parties have performed their primary obligations under the contract. When, after only one month, the porch roof leaked, Graham demanded that Metcalf return and fix the problem. Metcalf repeatedly refused to do anything about the leaky roof. Graham was forced to hire another contractor to correct Metcalf's errors. Graham then successfully sued Metcalf and recovered the cost of the repairs.

Tender of Performance In contract law, **tender of performance** means to offer to do what one has agreed to do under the terms of the contract. If someone has agreed to sell a parcel of land for $40,000, for example, tender of performance would be offering to give a signed deed to the buyer at the agreed time. Similarly, **tender of payment** would be presenting the $40,000 to the seller at the agreed time. It is important to make tender even if one knows that the other party is not going to perform the contract. This provision is necessary in some states to test the other party's willingness and ability to perform. If neither party has made tender, the court would hold that a breach of contract has not been established. Thus, neither party would be in a position to bring suit against the other. People who must perform acts (e.g., selling goods, performing services) are excused from performing if they make proper tender and it is rejected. However, people who must pay money are not excused from paying if their tender of payment is rejected. They are merely excused from paying further interest.

---

quick quiz 12-4

1.	Very few contracts are discharged by performance.	true | false
2.	A condition precedent is a condition that requires the performance of certain actions before the other party to the contract is obligated.	true | false
3.	Tender of performance means to offer to do what one has agreed to do under the terms of the contract.	true | false

---

12-5 Discharge by Nonperformance

Nonperformance may be defined as failing to fulfill or accomplish a promise, contract, or obligation according to its terms. Sometimes the failure to perform makes a party vulnerable to legal action. However, not every instance of nonperformance results in a legal action. Sometimes, nonperformance results from mutual agreement between the parties. At other times, nonperformance is excused because of conditions that make performance impossible or by operation of law. Nevertheless, under certain circumstances, nonperformance will result in a breach of contract. Discharge by nonperformance often comes about in the following ways:

- Discharge by agreement.
- Discharge by impossibility and by operation of law.
- Discharge by breach of contract.

Discharge by Agreement

Parties to a contract may stipulate the time and conditions for termination and discharge as part of their agreement. They also may subsequently agree not to do what they had originally promised. The latter is the case when there is a mutual rescission of the contract, a waiver of performance by one or more of the parties, a novation, or an accord and satisfaction to liquidate an outstanding debt or obligation.

Termination by Terms of the Contract During contract negotiations, parties may agree to certain terms that provide for automatic termination of the contract. For example, a professional athlete may contract with management that the agreement will be terminated if for any reason the player becomes either physically or mentally incapable of rendering full performance.

Mutual Rescission Contracting parties may, either before or after performance commences, rescind their contract as a result of further negotiation and by their mutual assent. **Mutual rescission**, in the majority of cases, requires both parties to return to the other any consideration already received or pay for any services or materials already rendered.

Termination by Waiver When a party with the right to complain of the other party's unsatisfactory performance or nonperformance fails to complain, **termination by waiver** occurs. It is a voluntary relinquishing (waiver) of one's rights to demand performance. A waiver differs from a discharge by mutual rescission in that a waiver entails no obligation by the parties to return any consideration that may have been exchanged up to the moment of rescission. Discharge by waiver, when made, is complete in itself.

Novation By novation, the parties to a contract mutually agree to replace one of the parties with a new party. The former, original party is released from liability under the contract. Novation is discussed in detail earlier in the chapter.

Accord and Satisfaction An accord and satisfaction is a new agreement resulting from a bona fide dispute between the parties as to the terms of their original agreement. The mutual agreement to the new terms is the accord; performance of the accord is the satisfaction—thus, accord and satisfaction. The accord, though agreed to, is not a binding agreement until the satisfaction has been made. The original agreement therefore is not discharged until the performance or satisfaction has been provided as promised.

General Release A **general release** is a document expressing the intent of a creditor to release a debtor from obligations on an existing and valid debt. A general release terminates a debt and excuses the debtor of any future payment, without the usual requirement that consideration be given in return.

Discharge by Impossibility and by Law

Occasionally, it becomes impossible to perform a contract. For example, when the subject matter of a contract, without the knowledge of the parties, had been destroyed before the contract was entered into, the contract would be discharged. Sometimes a contract that is legal when it is originally entered into by the parties becomes illegal before it is performed. This leads to a discharge by operation of law.

Types and Conditions of Impossibility Conditions that arise subsequent to the making of a contract may either void the agreement or make it voidable by one of the parties. Discharge through impossibility of performance may, in some situations, be allowed only if the specific and anticipated impossibility has been made a condition to the agreement. When the exact subject matter of an executory contract has been selected by the parties and later is destroyed, the performance obligation is discharged. In contrast, when the contract is not specific in the description or the location of the subject matter, a promisor is not discharged if the subject matter intended for delivery is destroyed. In this case, the promisor is obligated to locate and deliver subject matter of the same kind and quantity that could be secured elsewhere. Any financial losses due to the misfortune must be borne by the promisor.

When the performance of a contract requires actions declared illegal because of existing common law, statute, or public policy, the contract is void from its inception. When the performance of a contract is made illegal through the passing of laws subsequent to the formation of the contract, the contract is likewise declared void, and the parties are discharged. The death, insanity, or disability of a party obligated to perform an act that requires a special talent or skill terminates and discharges an agreement, including promises to perform by musicians, artists, writers, skilled craftspeople, and certain professionals. When promised services are to be performed for the personal benefit of a promisee, the death of the promisee will also terminate the agreement. When the contract relates to services that may be performed by others and do not demand the personal services of the contracting party, performance is not excused through death, insanity, or disability. The guardian of the party involved or the estate of the deceased may be held liable for performance.

Frustration-of-Purpose Doctrine The *frustration-of-purpose doctrine* releases a party from a contractual obligation when performing the obligations would be thoroughly impractical and senseless. The doctrine is applied only in those cases in which a party recognizes and understands possible risks and accepts them in contemplation of performance.

EXAMPLE 12-10: *Stewart v. Gaverick*

George Gaverick rented a 50th-floor apartment from Thomas Stewart for the night of December 31. The apartment had a balcony overlooking Times Square in midtown Manhattan. The rental period was for only 24 hours, and the landlord knew that the purpose of the contract was to allow Gaverick an unrestricted view of Times Square for the city's New Year's Eve celebration. Unfortunately, a terrorist alert canceled the entire Times Square celebration that year. Stewart still demanded payment from Gaverick and brought a suit in small claims court to recover the amount due. The referee refused to force Gaverick to pay for the apartment. The referee concluded that, because the apartment was of no use to Gaverick, the purpose of the agreement was frustrated and Gaverick would not have to pay the rent.

Commercial Impracticability Although not identical to the frustration-of-purpose doctrine, a related concept is known as *commercial impracticability*. Under this doctrine, the courts may excuse the nonperformance of one party to a contract because an unforeseen and very severe hardship has arisen that would place an enormous hardship on that party. Commercial impracticability is not the same as impossibility, because the party still can perform the contract. It is just that the performance itself would cause a great deal of adversity. Also with commercial impracticability, the purpose of the contract is not undermined by the unforeseen event, so the frustration-of-purpose doctrine does not apply. Nevertheless, under this relatively modern doctrine, some parties may escape performance if the unforeseen event was truly unforeseen and not in any way the fault of the party seeking an escape from performance.

Operation of Law

The performance of a promised act may be discharged by operation of law. Some law that causes the parties to be discharged from their obligations, such as bankruptcy or the statute of limitations, comes into play in this case. Through the provisions of the Bankruptcy Reform Act, a discharge in bankruptcy from a court will be allowed as a defense against the collection of most, but not all, debts of the bankrupt. Therefore, most contractual obligations to pay money come to an end when a party files for bankruptcy. State statutes providing time limits within which suits may be brought are known as statutes of limitations. Each state sets its own time limits. In general, actions for collection of open accounts (charge accounts) must be brought within 3 to 5 years, written agreements within 10 years, and judgments from 10 to 20 years. Those states requiring a seal on certain contracts have still other limitations and requirements that are much broader than those applied to simple contracts. The time limit for bringing suit for breach of a sales contract is four years under the Uniform Commercial Code. The statute of limitations does not technically void the debt, but it gives the debtor a defense against any demand for collection.

Discharge by Breach of Contract

When there is a breach of contract, the injured party has the right to remedy in court. There are several ways in which a breach may occur.

Deliberate Breach of Contract   A breach of contract results when one of the parties fails to do what was agreed to under the terms of the contract. When time is of the essence, there is a breach if performance is not completed within the time limits agreed to by the parties. A breach also results if the performance has been negligent or unskillful. The services rendered must adhere to the standards of skill, as determined by the custom of the marketplace. Wrongful performance or nonperformance discharges the other party from further obligation and permits that party to bring suit to rescind the contract or recover money to compensate it for any loss sustained. Such compensation is known as *damages.*

Repudiation and Anticipatory Breach   An **anticipatory breach** occurs when a party to a contract either expresses or clearly implies an intention not to perform the contract, even before being required to act. The repudiation must indicate a deliberate refusal to perform according to the terms of the contract. Breaches of this kind are also called *constructive breaches.* The injured party may either commence suit at the time of the anticipatory breach or await the date agreed to for performance, thus giving the breaching party time to reconsider and begin performance. To succeed in a case based on anticipatory repudiation, the injured party must demonstrate that he or she was ready, willing, and able to comply with the contract but could not do so because of the other party's material breach. Anticipatory breach cannot be used if the only action repudiated was the promise to pay money to another party.

Abandonment of Contractual Obligations   Stopping performance once it has begun is called **abandonment of contractual obligations.** Leaving or deserting a party's obligations discharges the other party from any promises made and permits a suit for damages. A temporary, or short-lived, interruption of performance is not deemed abandonment. To constitute abandonment, the promisor must have inexcusably interrupted performance with the obvious intention of not returning to complete the obligations promised.

---

quick quiz 12-5

1. A general release is a document expressing the intent of a creditor to release a debtor from the obligations of an existing and valid debt.	true | false
2. With commercial impracticability, the purpose of a contract is undermined by an unforeseen event.	true | false
3. Stopping a performance once it has begun is called abandonment of contractual obligations.	true | false

---

12-6 Damages and Equitable Remedies

A breach of contract releases the injured party from any obligations under the contract and gives that party the right to ask a court of law for a remedy. The usual remedy for breach of contract is the payment of damages in the form of money. At times, however, the payment of monetary damages is not enough to satisfy the injured party. In such situations, the injured party will ask the court for rescission, specific performance, or an injunction.

Damages in Contract Law

Damages describe money awarded to parties who have been victimized or suffered injury to their legal rights by others. Damages are of different kinds, and the nature of a claim usually determines what type of damages will apply. In some states, by statute or judicial rule, juries are charged with two decisions: They must decide which party is to be given favorable judgment and determine how much is to be awarded in damages. Appeals to a higher court are allowed when the amount of damages awarded appears to be unreasonably low or excessively high.

Actual or Compensatory Damages Actual damages are the sum of money equal to the real financial loss suffered by the injured party. Because they are intended to compensate the injured party, actual damages are also called compensatory damages. Thus, damages awarded for nondelivery of promised goods or services would be an amount equal to the difference between the price stated in the contract and what the promisee would have to pay elsewhere. Should the same goods or services be conveniently available elsewhere at the same or at a lower price, no actual loss could be claimed.

Incidental and Consequential Damages Incidental damages and consequential damages are awarded for losses indirectly but closely attributable to a breach. Incidental damages cover any expenses paid out by the innocent party to prevent further loss. Consequential damages result indirectly from the breach because of special circumstances that exist with a particular contract. To recover consequential damages, the injured party must show that such losses were foreseeable when the contract was made.

Punitive or Exemplary Damages

Damages in excess of actual losses suffered by the plaintiff awarded as a measure of punishment for the defendant's wrongful acts are punitive damages, also called *exemplary damages*. They are a court-ordered punishment rather than compensation for a known loss. Punitive damages are awarded when a defendant is responsible for abusive and dishonest practices in consumer transactions that are unconscionable and contrary to the public good. Often such abusive and dishonest practices are associated with certain business-related torts, including fraudulent misrepresentation, disparagement, the violation of an implied covenant of fairness and honesty, and intentional interference with an existing contract.

Fraudulent Misrepresentation As noted previously, fraud, or fraudulent misrepresentation, occurs when one party makes false statements or commits some sort of false action that causes another party to rely on those falsehoods then experience an injury or loss as a result. Because fraud is a deliberate attempt to subvert proper business relationships, the court views it as especially reprehensible, and those that commit fraud will find themselves paying not only compensatory damages, if applicable, but also punitive damages. The idea of punitive damages is to punish the defrauding party to such an extent that he or she will be dissuaded from any future fraudulent conduct. Punitive damages are also supposed to serve as a deterrent so that other people do not even think about committing fraud. For this reason, punitive damages are also called *exemplary damages*. Exemplary damages are used as an example for other "would-be con artists" who ought to know better than to subvert the law through fraud.

Nominal Damages Token damages awarded to parties who have experienced an injury to their legal rights but no actual loss are nominal damages. Common law usually awarded six cents to the successful plaintiff when no actual losses were shown. In today's practice, the award is usually one dollar.

Present and Future Damages Damages may be awarded for present injuries and for others that might reasonably be anticipated in the future. Thus, a party charged with fraud in the sale of a building infested with termites may be held liable for all damages

CLASSIC CASE The Punishment Must Fit the Conduct

When one party breaks the terms of a contract, and the other party sues, the court will do its best to place the parties in as good a position as they would have been in had the contract been performed as promised. In this way contract law differs from other areas of the law, such as criminal law, which generally seeks to punish the wrongdoer and deter the criminal conduct in the future. Contract law also differs from tort law, which is designed to compensate the victim, punish the wrongdoer, and deter tortious behavior in the future. One reason for this policy is that people voluntarily assume responsibilities when they make a contract and those responsibilities affect only the parties and not the general public, as is the case with criminal law and, at times, tort law. All of this is fine as far as it goes, but what happens when the breaching party has deliberately undermined the basic intent of contract law by committing fraud not just in the contract at issue, but as a pattern of conduct, perhaps even an official policy, affecting hundreds and thousands of other contracts? This is precisely what happened in *State Farm Mutual v. Campbell.* In that case, the Campbells had been involved in an automobile accident and were being sued. Their insurer, State Farm, refused to settle out of court, despite the desires of the Campbells and the advice of State Farm's own investigators. The original accident case went to trial, and the Campbells lost. When State Farm refused to pay the full amount of the award, the

Campbells sued the insurer for bad faith, fraud, and intentional infliction of emotional distress. The Campbells offered evidence that the refusal to settle was not just fraudulent in relation to their contract, but was also part of a larger pattern of conduct planned and executed by State Farm over a 20-year period against hundreds of policyholders. The conduct involved a national campaign referred to as the Performance, Planning, and Review (PP&R) Policy. Once the jury heard evidence about the systematic execution of the PP&R Policy, they awarded the Campbells $145 million in punitive damages. The judge then reduced the punitive damages to $25 million. On appeal the Campbells stressed the fraudulent nature of the PP&R Policy, and State Farm argued that its conduct in relation to the other contracts should not be used to punish the company for its conduct in relation to the contract that it had with the Campbells. The Supreme Court of Utah agreed with the Campbells and reinstated the $145 million in punitive damages. The case made its way to the U.S. Supreme Court, which struck down that portion of the punitive damages that involved conduct unrelated to the Campbells' claim. The Court concluded that awarding punitive damage for conduct unrelated to the claim before the court in the present case violated the basic principles of due process. [See: *State Farm Mutual Automobile Ins. Co. v. Campbell,* 538 U.S. 408 (United States Supreme Court).]

revealed at the time of the suit and for damages that would reasonably be forthcoming as a result of the undisclosed and concealed infestation of the property.

Liquidated Damages
Parties may stipulate (agree) as a condition of their contract to the amount of damages that might be assessed if there is a breach. Damages agreed to in the initial contract are called liquidated damages. Liquidated damages must be realistic and in proportion to the losses that might be reasonably anticipated should there be a breach. When liquidated damages are found to be excessive or unreasonable, a court will disregard them and leave the matter of setting damages to the discretion of a jury.

Damages under *Quantum Meruit*
The doctrine of *quantum meruit* (i.e., as much as one had earned) is important in assessing damages in cases founded on contracts implied in law, or quasi-contracts. Thus, when there has been no express or implied mutual agreement, a court will at times impose an obligation against a party who has been unjustly rewarded at the innocent expense of another. Damages awarded are in an amount considered reasonable in return for the benefits the one party derived through the quasi-contract relationship.

Speculative Damages   Courts do not allow speculative damages. These damages are computed on losses that have not actually been suffered and that cannot be proved; they are damages based entirely on an expectation of losses that might be suffered from a breach. They differ from future damages in that speculative damages are not founded on fact but only on hope or expectation. Their basis is nothing more than a calculated guess as to the gains a party might have received had there not been a breach.

Mitigation of Damages   The injured party has an obligation to do what is reasonably possible to mitigate the damages, that is, to keep damages to a minimum. A party who has been wronged by another's breach must exercise reasonable precautions to prevent the damages from becoming unfairly and unreasonably burdensome to the other party.

Equitable Remedies

When money in the form of damages is not enough to provide a fair and just award to the injured party, the court may grant an equitable remedy. Rather than simply order the breaching party to pay damages, a court issuing an equitable remedy compels the breaching party to perform an act or refrain from performing an act. The two most common equitable remedies are specific performance and injunctive relief.

Specific Performance   A decree of specific performance is a court order calling for the breaching party to do what he or she promised to do under the original contract. The courts order specific performance only when the subject matter of a contract is unique or rare. The classic example of unique subject matter calling for specific performance is a contract for the sale and transfer of title to land, because each piece of land is unique. However, unique or rare subject matter could also include such items as antique, family heirlooms, original works of art, and special animals, such as a particular race horse. Obviously, an award of monetary damages would not provide the injured party satisfaction in any of these situations. Contracts for personal services are rarely enforced through specific performance. Demanding that an unwilling party perform promised personal services would be contrary to Amendment 13 of the U.S. Constitution, which prohibits human servitude. A remedy in cases of this kind, however, may be found through injunctive relief.

Injunctive Relief   An injunction is an order issued by a court directing that a party do or refrain from doing something. An injunction may be either temporary or permanent. A temporary injunction is issued as a means of delaying further activity in any contested matter until the court determines whether a permanent injunction should be entered or the injunction should be removed entirely. One who disobeys an injunction does so under threat of penalty of contempt of court.

quick quiz 12-6

1. Actual damages are also called compensatory damages.	true │ false
2. Punitive damages cover any expenses paid out by the innocent party to prevent further loss.	true │ false
3. The courts order specific performance only when the subject matter of a contract is unique or rare.	true │ false

Summary

12.1 Third parties are at times given benefits through a contract made between two other parties. Some contracts are made specifically to benefit a third party. Such a third party is known as a third party beneficiary. Three types of intended beneficiaries include creditor beneficiaries, donee beneficiaries, and insurance beneficiaries. Some third parties benefit from a contract even though the contract was not made for their benefit. These parties are known as incidental beneficiaries.

12.2 The transfer of contract rights to a third party outside of the original agreement is an assignment. In general, rights are assigned, and duties are delegated. However, the rules apply to both transfers in the same way. The party who assigns rights or delegates duties is the assignor. The outside third party to whom the assignment is made is the assignee. The remaining party to the original agreement is the obligor. The assignee must give notice of assignment to the obligor.

12.3 The rights and duties of the assignee are the same as those held by the assignor under the original agreement. Contracts for personal or professional services cannot be assigned. Assignments also can be limited by agreement. A novation occurs when two contracting parties agree to replace one of the parties with a new party.

12.4 Most contracts are discharged by performance, which means that the parties do what they agreed to do.

Unless the parties agree otherwise, satisfactory performance will be determined by objective standards. Substantial performance will discharge the agreement with the right to reimbursement for correcting details that were not completed. Conditions may determine the rights and duties of the parties prior to performance, during performance, and following performance. If neither party makes tender, a breach of contract is not established.

12.5 Nonperformance can discharge contractual obligations. Not every instance of nonperformance results in a breach of contract. Parties can agree to discharge a contractual obligation by terms in the contract, mutual rescission, waiver, novation, accord and satisfaction, or general release. Contractual obligations can also be discharged when it becomes impossible to perform a contract or under the frustration-of-purpose doctrine. These obligations can also be discharged by operation of law under principles of bankruptcy and the statute of limitations.

12.6 An injured party is released from any obligations under the contract following the other party's breach. In addition, the injured party has the right to ask a court of law for a remedy. The usual remedy is the payment of damages in the form of money. When the payment of monetary damages is not enough, the injured party will ask the court for rescission, specific performance, or an injunction.

Key Terms

abandonment of contractual obligations, 292
actual damages, 293
anticipatory breach, 292
assignee, 279
assignment, 279
assignor, 279
beneficiary, 277
commercial impracticability, 291
compensatory damages, 293
complete performance, 287
condition concurrent, 288
condition precedent, 288

condition subsequent, 288
consequential damages, 293
creditor beneficiary, 278
delegation, 279
donee beneficiary, 278
fraud (or fraudulent misrepresentation), 293
fraudulent conveyance, 279
frustration-of-purpose doctrine, 291
general release, 290
incidental beneficiary, 278
incidental damages, 293
injunction, 295

intended beneficiary, 277
liquidated damages, 294
mutual rescission, 290
nominal damages, 293
novation, 285
obligor, 279
outside party, 277
performance, 285
punitive damages, 293
reasonable time, 285
satisfactory performance, 287
specific performance, 295
speculative damages, 295

Questions for Review and Discussion

1. What are the legal rights given to all beneficiaries?
2. What are the legal rights given to incidental beneficiaries?
3. What is involved in an assignment of rights and a delegation of duties?
4. What is a novation?
5. What constitutes the satisfactory performance of a contract?
6. What is the difference between complete and substantial performance?
7. How can a contract be discharged by nonperformance?
8. What is anticipatory repudiation?
9. What types of damages are available in the event of a breach of contract?
10. What is the difference between specific performance and injunctive relief?

Cases for Analysis

1. Lee Wesley agreed to lay cement on the driveway leading up to Walter Lerro's house for $24,000. Plans and specifications were provided by Lerro. Wesley delegated the duties involved in laying the asphalt to Hanover Construction, Inc., another contractor. Hanover then assigned the right to collect the $24,000 from Lerro to Olsen Construction Supplies, Ltd. Lerro, who did not like the way his job and his money were being bounced all over the tri-county area, refused to pay Olsen. Lerro then called Wesley and ordered him to tear out the driveway because he was insulted by the fact that Wesley thought so little of his job that he had assigned it to Hanover. Identify each of the parties in this case as assignor, assignee, or obligor. Was Lerro within his rights when he refused to pay Olsen and when he ordered Wesley to remove the driveway? Explain.

2. Under a divorce decree, Blackston was ordered to pay $600 a month in child support to his former wife. The decree provided that the payments were to be paid to the clerk of the court's office. The clerk of the court assigned the right to receive the payments to the Department of Human Resources. Who was obligated to notify Blackston of the assignment? [See: *Blackston v. State Ex Rel. Blackston,* 585 So.2d 58 (AL).]

3. Gary Jones retained the law firm of Irace and Lowry after being injured in a motorcycle accident. Later, Jones required surgery after dislocating his shoulder in an unrelated incident. Having no money to pay the surgeon, Jones signed a letter requesting that the money from the accident settlement be assigned to Dr. Herzog for treatment of a shoulder injury that occurred at a different time. The law firm was notified of the assignment. When the settlement was received by the law firm, Jones instructed the firm to pay the money to him rather than to the surgeon. It did, and the surgeon was never paid. Could Dr. Herzog recover the money owed him from the law firm? Why or why not? [See: *Herzog v. Irace,* 594 A.2d 1106 (ME).]

4. Copeland contracted with McDonald's Systems, Inc., for a franchise. Copeland was granted the fast-food outlet franchise for Omaha. McDonald's also gave Copeland first refusal rights for any plans to open other franchise outlets in Omaha. Copeland exercised the right several times, opening several additional outlets. He then sold the franchise to Schupack and assigned to Schupack the right to open new McDonald's outlets in Omaha. When Schupack tried to exercise the first refusal right, McDonald's objected, claiming its relationship with Copeland developed through a special confidence in Copeland's ability to manage and promote its new franchise outlets. Was McDonald's correct? Explain. [See: *Schupack v. McDonald's Systems, Inc.,* 264 N.W.2d 827 (NE).]

5. Timbercrest built a house for the Murphys. After occupying the house for a while, the Murphys complained of several problems. Timbercrest fixed the problems, and the Murphys had no further

complaints. The Litwins bought the house from the Murphys three years later. When the house was sold, neither the Litwins nor the Murphys were aware of any problems. After living in the house for two years, the Litwins became aware of several problems. The Litwins then contacted the Murphys and had the Murphys assign them their rights under the original construction agreement with Timbercrest. The Litwins then sued Timbercrest, claiming Timbercrest had breached its contract with the Murphys by not providing them with a house free of defects. Were the Litwins correct? [See: *Litwins v. Timbercrest Estates, Inc.,* 347 N.E.2d 378 (IL).]

6. Nolan wrote the song "Tumbling Tumbleweeds" and, in an agreement with Sam Fox Publishing Company, transferred all rights to the song to the company. In return, Nolan was to receive royalties according to terms laid out in the agreement. Sam Fox later assigned all rights and interests in "Tumbling Tumbleweeds" to Williamson Music, Inc. Was it necessary for Sam Fox to obtain Nolan's consent before making the assignment to Williamson? Explain. [See: *Nolan v. Williamson Music, Inc.,* 300 F. Supp. 1311 (S.D. NY).]

7. When Kent contracted to have his new house constructed, he specifically noted that the plumbing must be made by Reading manufacturers. After the house had been completed, Kent did an inspection tour during which he discovered that, though much of the plumbing had come from Reading, some parts did not. After making his discovery, Kent demanded that the non-Reading plumbing fixtures be replaced with the supplies he had specified in the contract. In addition, Kent refused to pay the contractor until the proper plumbing supplies were added to the house. The contractor brought suit against Kent, arguing that though there were minor deviations from certain specified parts of the contract concerning the plumbing fixtures, he had nevertheless substantially performed his end of the deal. Kent stuck to his strict construction of the contract and labeled the contractor's performance unsatisfactory. He thus claimed to be released from the agreement unless the contractor lived up to every term in the original agreement. Who should prevail in this case? Explain. [See: *Jacob and Young v. Kent,* 129 N.E. 889.]

8. Sai Grafio agreed to paint Gerald Weaver and Katherine Brewer's house for $5,650. Weaver and Brewer paid for the paint job in installments but stopped payment on the final $1,845 check, claiming that Grafio had breached the contract by doing a poor job. The lower court judge found that the only defect in the paint job was a footprint left on the roof that would cost $50 to repair. How much money, if any, and under what legal theory, did the court allow Grafio to recover for the paint job? [See: *Weaver v. Grafio,* 595 A.2d 983 (DC).]

9. Arthur Murray, Inc., and Parker entered a series of contracts under which Arthur Murray agreed to teach Parker how to dance. Under the terms of each agreement, refunds were impossible, and the lessons could not be canceled. After the contracts were entered, Parker suffered a permanent disability that made it physically impossible for him to dance. When Arthur Murray refused to refund any part of Parker's money, he sued to rescind the contracts on grounds of impossibility. Arthur Murray claimed that the non-refund clause must be upheld by the court. Was Arthur Murray correct? Explain. [See: *Parker v. Arthur Murray, Inc.,* 295 N.E.2d 487 (IL).]

10. Bob Pagan Ford, Inc., hired Smith to work as a car salesperson in Galveston County. As part of his contract, Smith agreed not to work as an auto salesperson in Galveston County for three years after leaving his employment with Bob Pagan Ford. Smith worked for Bob Pagan for only a few months. He then left and took a sales job with another dealership in Galveston County. Was injunctive relief an appropriate remedy in this case? Explain. [See: *Bob Pagan Ford, Inc., v. Smith,* 638 S.W.2d 176 (TX).]

quick quiz Answers

12-1	12-2	12-3	12-4	12-5	12-6
1. T	1. F	1. F	1. F	1. T	1. T
2. T	2. F	2. F	2. T	2. F	2. F
3. F	3. F	3. F	3. T	3. T	3. T

Part 2 Case Study

Sylvia Burwell, Secretary of Health and Human Services, et al. v. Hobby Lobby Stores, Inc., et al. (AKA *The Hobby Lobby Case*)
United States Supreme Court
Nos. 13-354 and 13-356 (June 30, 2014)
573 U.S. _____ (2014)

Summary

This case, which is usually referred to as *The Hobby Lobby Case,* began before any of the corporations involved had any knowledge that a lawsuit was in their future. The events that precipitated the lawsuit began when Congress passed the Patient Protection and Affordable Care Act (ACA) in 2012. The goal of the act was to make certain that all (well, at least most) Americans had health care insurance. The mechanism by which this was to be accomplished was a mandate that all employers who had more than 50 workers employed on a full-time basis would have to provide "a group health plan or group health insurance coverage" that would give those employees "minimum essential coverage." [26 USC Section 5000 A (f) (2); Sections 4980 H (a) and (c) (2).] To enforce the law, Congress attached stiff penalties, in the form of heavy fines, for employers who failed to obey the law. (In the case of Hobby Lobby, for example, those fines would have been more than $1.3 million daily for a total of $475 million annually.) Part of this health care package required that the insurance plan provide "preventative care and screenings" for women that would be free from "any cost sharing requirements." [42 USC Section 300gg-13(a) (4).] The statute did not identify the kind of prevention; rather, it empowered the Department of Health and Human Services (HHS) acting through the Health Resources and Services Administration (HRSA), one of the department's subdivisions, to make that determination. The HRSA took immediate steps to fulfill that assignment by calling on the Institute of Medicine. The institute endorsed the idea that employers should be compelled to provide coverage for all contraceptive procedures approved by the Food and Drug Administration. Four of these methods are designed to stop the development of an already fertilized egg. These four methods are at the heart of this case.

The HHS also issued regulations that would exempt specific not-for-profit religious institutions from participating in the coverage of these contraceptive devices. Any nonprofit religious organization that had genuine religious convictions against such methods could notify their insurer of their objection, and the insurer would then eliminate that part of the plan from the institution's coverage and cover the cost with no cost sharing penalty for the employee. Other plans that did not cover contraceptive methods were grandfathered into the new act with no penalty. This provision allowed that coverage to continue without complying with the act's contraceptive provisions. Also, based on the fundamental requirements of the ACA, employers with less than 50 workers were also exempt. Those original provisions would not compel them to participate in the offering of such contraceptive methods to their employees.

These rules and the exemptions did not anticipate religious objections from certain closely held profit-making companies that are owned and operated by a few individuals who have strong, authentic religious objections to the use of the contraceptive methods in question here. Three corporations in particular fell into this category, and each one felt so strongly about the issue that they brought suit against the secretary of the Department of Health and Human Services. These three companies are Conestoga Wood Specialties, owned and operated by Norman and Elizabeth Hahn and their three sons, who belong to the Mennonite Church; Hobby Lobby, a national chain of arts and craft stores owned and operated by David and Barbara Green and their three children, all of whom are devoted Christians; and Mardel, a chain of Christian bookstores owned and operated by one of the Greens' sons. In each of these lawsuits the plaintiffs issued very clear and obviously sincere position statements defending their religious objection to being compelled to join in the coverage of what they considered a morally bankrupt practice. The lawsuit was brought under the authority of the Religious Freedom Restoration Act (RFRA) and the Free Exercise Clause of the Constitution.

The RFRA states that the government cannot "substantially burden a person's exercise of religion even if the burden results from a rule of general applicability" except when the government "demonstrates that the application of the burden to the person (1) is in furtherance of a compelling governmental interest; and (2) is the least restrictive means of furthering that compelling governmental interest." [42 USC Sections 2000bb-1(a)(b).] The threshold issue before the Court is whether the three corporate plaintiffs qualify as "legal persons" under the RFRA. The Court begins by noting that the goal of the RFRA is to make certain that a wide berth is given to individuals in the exercise of their religious beliefs. As the name of the act implies, congressional intent was to rebuild a layer of defense for religion that had been eroded over the years by the decisions of the judicial branch. In restoring the balance in favor of religious freedom rather than governmental power, Congress was, in essence, redirecting the courts to rebuild that lost defensive layer. Accordingly, that protection must be broadened, not narrowed. While it is true that the legal fiction of a corporation does create an entity that is separate from the founders, the purpose of that protective layer is not to protect the fiction in and of itself. Rather, that protection was built to defend real flesh and blood people. When the law defines the rights and duties of a corporation, it is actually defining the rights and duties of the people behind those corporations. They are the ones who must carry out corporate duties and who benefit from corporate rights. Thus, when the corporation is given property rights, those property rights really belong to the people. This is especially true when the right in question is a religious right. Thus, the Court in this case states with some conviction that the term *person* in the statute is not meant to protect corporate "persons" because the real protection flows to the people behind that corporate veil.

Having disposed of the "person" argument the Court moves on to the second argument made by the defense and supported by several lower court judges as well as by the principal dissent. That argument states that Hobby Lobby, Conestoga, and Mardel do not deserve the protection afforded by the RFRA because their principal objective is to earn a profit, not to promote religious values. The Court finds this argument weak at best. The Court acknowledges that it is conceivable that a law can be enacted by the government that makes the practice of a particular religion more expensive and thus more difficult. To demonstrate this point the Court refers to the case of *Braunfield v. Brown*, 366 U.S. 599 (1961), in which the Supreme Court acknowledged that forcing Jewish shop owners to remain closed on Sunday in addition to being closed on Saturday, which was required by their faith, might place an unfair burden on their constitutional right to the free exercise of their religion, even though the direct consequence of the prohibition was a loss of profits. Although the business owners lost the case, the right of profit making businesses to bring free exercise cases was affirmed by the Court. The Court also notes that the several lower courts have erroneously held that the Free Exercise Clause and the RFRA do not protect profit-making businesses because their only purpose is to earn a profit not to promote religious values. The Court points out that this is patently false in the modern view of corporate law, which has held repeatedly that corporations have civic and public duties beyond making a profit for their shareholders. Moreover, the plaintiffs in this case have repeatedly demonstrated that their corporations do have religious goals.

In a lengthy footnote, the court also makes a point that is directly related to our study of contract law. The Court notes that the dissent argues that the historical development of business in the common law does not support the notion that "lay corporations" (as opposed to ecclesiastical corporations) can have any religious function. This, as we saw in our lengthy examination of the historical development of the law merchant and its merger with common law, is simply not true. In fact, no matter which version of history we accept, the Church was closely allied with the development of the capitalist business system. Max Weber, for example, in *The Protestant Ethic: The Spirit of Capitalism,* defends the proposition that European capitalism began with the Protestant Reformation in the 16th century. Protestantism, primarily in the form of Puritanism, Separatism, and Calvinism, promoted the idea that the accumulation of wealth was a fairly good sign that the merchant who so prospered was among the elect, and, therefore, bound for heaven. In a similar vein, Rodney Stark in his book, *The Victory of Reason: How Christianity Led to Freedom, Capitalism, and Western*

Science, argues, rather convincingly, that one of the driving forces behind the growth of capitalism was the Roman Catholic Church. The medieval Church had the ability to redirect capitalism as it did because, as a system, the Roman Catholic Church had a strong central controlling agent and a concentration, rather than a dispersal, of power among various actors.

Thus, the Church helped provide a rational and moral foundation for the principles and procedures that guided the activities of merchants in their communities, their courts, and in the making of their contracts. The Church, which is directed by a central powerful leader, refused to condemn commercial activity. Instead, the Church monitored how those activities were carried out. In short, the Church encouraged this new class of sellers to establish guilds that followed the law of the Church, a legal tradition that is generally referred to as canon law. The Church also insisted that these emerging businessmen never engage in deceit or dishonesty and always follow a good faith approach to contract development. As long as they followed these basic precepts, the Church reassured the members of the new and expanding class of professional sellers that there was nothing inherently wrong with making a profit in their chosen profession. Finally, Berman in his study of the growth of the law merchant, *Law and Revolution: The Formation of the Western Legal Tradition,* states that, from the very beginning, merchants were involved in the courts that heard and settled contract disputes and commercial differences. Involvement meant that, as a system, the law merchant, like the Roman Catholic Church, had a strong central controlling agent and a concentration, rather than a dispersal, of power. This allowed the law merchant to direct, at least to a certain degree, the other characteristics of neutrality, universality, mutuality, integration, and evolution, all of which have an ethical basis. (Reproduced below is that portion of the Court's opinion that corresponds to this analysis. Footnote numerals are included but the citations themselves and explanatory notes are omitted.)

The Court's Opinion

Delivered by Justice Alito

At issue in these cases are HHS regulations promulgated under the Patient Protection and Affordable Care Act of 2010 (ACA), 124 Stat. 119. ACA generally requires employers with 50 or more full-time employees to offer "a group health plan or group health insurance coverage" that provides "minimum essential coverage." 26 U.S.C. §5000A (f)(2); §§4980H(a), (c)(2). Any covered employer that does not provide such coverage must pay a substantial price. Specifically, if a covered employer provides group health insurance but its plan fails to comply with ACA's group-health-plan requirements, the employer may be required to pay $100 per day for each affected "individual." §§4980D (a)–(b). And if the employer decides to stop providing health insurance altogether and at least one full-time employee enrolls in a health plan and qualifies for a subsidy on one of the government-run ACA exchanges, the employer must pay $2,000 per year for each of its full-time employees. §§4980H (a), (c) (1).

Unless an exception applies, ACA requires an employer's group health plan or group-health-insurance coverage to furnish "preventive care and screenings" for women without "any cost sharing requirements." 42 U.S.C. §300gg–13(a) (4). Congress itself, however, did not specify what types of preventive care must be covered. Instead, Congress authorized the Health Resources and Services Administration (HRSA), a component of HHS, to make that important and sensitive decision. *Ibid.* The HRSA in turn consulted the Institute of Medicine, a nonprofit group of volunteer advisers, in determining which preventive services to require. See 77 Fed. Reg. 8725–8726 (2012).

In August 2011, based on the Institute's recommendations, the HRSA promulgated the Women's Preventive Services Guidelines. *See id.,* at 8725–8726, and n. 1; online at http://hrsa.gov/womensguidelines (all Internet materials as visited June 26, 2014, and available in Clerk of Court's case file). The Guidelines provide that nonexempt employers are generally required to provide "coverage, without cost sharing" for "[a]ll Food and Drug Administration [(FDA)] approved contraceptive methods, sterilization procedures, and patient education and counseling." 77 Fed. Reg. 8725 (internal quotation marks omitted). Although many of the required, FDA-approved methods of contraception work by preventing the fertilization of an egg, four of those methods (those specifically at issue in these cases) may have the effect of preventing an already fertilized egg from developing any further by inhibiting its attachment to the uterus. Brief for HHS 9 Cite as: 573 U.S. ____ (2014) in No. 13–354, pp. 9–10, n. 4;[6] FDA, Birth Control: Medicines to Help You.[7]

HHS also authorized the HRSA to establish exemptions from the contraceptive mandate for "religious employers." 45 CFR §147.131(a). That category encompasses "churches, their integrated auxiliaries, and conventions or associations of churches," as well as "the exclusively religious activities of any religious order." See *ibid* (citing 26 U.S.C. §§6033(a) (3)(A)(i), (iii)). In its Guidelines, HRSA exempted these organizations from the requirement to cover contraceptive services. See http://hrsa.gov/womensguidelines.

In addition, HHS has effectively exempted certain religious nonprofit organizations, described under HHS regulations as "eligible organizations," from the contraceptive mandate. See 45 CFR §147.131(b); 78 Fed. Reg.39874 (2013). An "eligible organization" means a nonprofit organization that "holds itself out as a religious organization" and "opposes providing coverage for some or all of any contraceptive services required to be covered . . . on account of religious objections." 45 CFR §147.131(b). To qualify for this accommodation, an employer must certify that it is such an organization. §147.131(b)(4). When a group-health-insurance issuer receives notice that one of its clients has invoked this provision, the issuer must then exclude contraceptive coverage from the employer's plan and provide separate payments for contraceptive services for plan participants without imposing any cost-sharing requirements on the eligible organization, its insurance plan, or its employee beneficiaries. §147.131(c).[8] Although this procedure requires the issuer to bear the cost of these services, HHS has determined that this obligation will not impose any net expense on issuers because its cost will be less than or equal to the cost savings resulting from the services. 78 Fed. Reg. 39877.[9]

In addition to these exemptions for religious organizations, ACA exempts a great many employers from most of its coverage requirements. Employers providing "grandfathered health plans"—those that existed prior to March 23, 2010, and that have not made specified changes after that date—need not comply with many of the Act's requirements, including the contraceptive mandate. 42 U.S.C. §§18011(a), (e). And employers with fewer than 50 employees are not required to provide health insurance at all. 26 U.S.C. §4980H(c)(2).

All told, the contraceptive mandate "presently does not apply to tens of millions of people." 723 F. 3d 1114, 1143 (CA10 2013). This is attributable, in large part, to grandfathered health plans: Over one-third of the 149 million nonelderly people in America with employer-sponsored health plans were enrolled in grandfathered plans in 2013. Brief for HHS in No. 13–354, at 53; Kaiser Family Foundation & Health Research & Educational Trust, Employer Health Benefits, 2013 Annual Survey 43, 221.[10] The count for employees working for firms that do not have to provide insurance at all because they employ fewer than 50 employees is 34 million workers. See The Whitehouse, Health Reform for Small Businesses: The Affordable Care Act Increases Choice and Saving Money for Small Businesses 1.[11]

II A

Norman and Elizabeth Hahn and their three sons are devout members of the Mennonite Church, a Christian denomination. The Mennonite Church opposes abortion and believes that "[t]he fetus in its earliest stages . . . shares humanity with those who conceived it."[12]

Fifty years ago, Norman Hahn started a wood-working business in his garage, and since then, this company, Conestoga Wood Specialties, has grown and now has 950 employees. Conestoga is organized under Pennsylvania law as a for-profit corporation. The Hahns exercise sole ownership of the closely held business; they control its board of directors and hold all of its voting shares. One of the Hahn sons serves as the president and CEO.

The Hahns believe that they are required to run their business "in accordance with their religious beliefs and moral principles." 917 F. Supp. 2d 394, 402 (ED Pa. 2013). To that end, the company's mission, as they see it, is to "operate in a professional environment founded upon the highest ethical, moral, and Christian principles." *Ibid.* (internal quotation marks omitted). The company's "Vision and Values Statements" affirms that Conestoga endeavors to "ensur[e] a reasonable profit in [a] manner that reflects [the Hahns'] Christian heritage." App. in No. 13–356, p. 94 (complaint).

As explained in Conestoga's board-adopted "Statement on the Sanctity of Human Life," the Hahns believe that "human life begins at conception." 724 F. 3d 377, 382, and n. 5 (CA3 2013) (internal quotation marks omitted). It is therefore "against [their] moral conviction to be involved in the termination of human life" after conception, which they believe is a "sin against God to which they are held accountable." *Ibid.* (internal quotation marks omitted). The Hahns have accordingly excluded from the group health-insurance plan they offer to their employees certain contraceptive methods that they consider to be abortifacients. *Id.,* at 382.

The Hahns and Conestoga sued HHS and other federal officials and agencies under RFRA and the Free Exercise Clause of the First Amendment, seeking to enjoin application of ACA's contraceptive mandate insofar as it requires them to provide health-insurance coverage for four FDA approved contraceptives that may operate after the fertilization of an egg.[13] These include two forms of emergency contraception commonly called "morning after" pills and two types of intrauterine devices.[14]

In opposing the requirement to provide coverage for the contraceptives to which they object, the Hahns argued that "it is immoral and sinful for [them] to intentionally participate in, pay for, facilitate, or otherwise support these drugs." *Ibid.* The District Court denied a preliminary injunction, see 917 F. Supp. 2d, at 419, and the Third Circuit affirmed in a divided opinion, holding that "for profit, secular corporations cannot engage in religious exercise" within the meaning of RFRA or the First Amendment. 724 F. 3d, at 381. The Third Circuit also rejected the claims brought by the Hahns themselves because it concluded that the HHS "[m]andate does not impose any requirements on the Hahns" in their personal capacity. *Id.*, at 389.

B.

David and Barbara Green and their three children are Christians who own and operate two family businesses. Forty-five years ago, David Green started an arts and crafts store that has grown into a nationwide chain called Hobby Lobby. There are now 500 Hobby Lobby stores, and the company has more than 13,000 employees. 723 F. 3d, at 1122. Hobby Lobby is organized as a for-profit corporation under Oklahoma law.

One of David's sons started an affiliated business, Mardel, which operates 35 Christian bookstores and employs close to 400 people. *Ibid.* Mardel is also organized as a for-profit corporation under Oklahoma law.

Though these two businesses have expanded over the years, they remain closely held, and David, Barbara, and their children retain exclusive control of both companies. *Ibid.* David serves as the CEO of Hobby Lobby, and his three children serve as the president, vice president, and vice CEO. See Brief for Respondents in No. 13–354, p. 8.[15]

Hobby Lobby's statement of purpose commits the Greens to "[h]onoring the Lord in all [they] do by operating the company in a manner consistent with Biblical principles." App. in No. 13–354, pp. 134–135 (complaint). Each family member has signed a pledge to run the businesses in accordance with the family's religious beliefs and to use the family assets to support Christian ministries. 723 F. 3d, at 1122. In accordance with those commitments, Hobby Lobby and Mardel stores close on Sundays, even though the Greens calculate that they lose millions in sales annually by doing so. *Id.*, at 1122; App. in No. 13– 354, at 136–137. The businesses refuse to engage in profitable transactions that facilitate or promote alcohol use; they contribute profits to Christian missionaries and ministries; and they buy hundreds of full-page newspaper ads inviting people to "know Jesus as Lord and Savior." *Ibid.* (internal quotation marks omitted).

Like the Hahns, the Greens believe that life begins at conception and that it would violate their religion to facilitate access to contraceptive drugs or devices that operate after that point. 723 F. 3d, at 1122. They specifically object to the same four contraceptive methods as the Hahns and, like the Hahns, they have no objection to the other 16 FDA-approved methods of birth control. *Id.*, at 1125. Although their group-health-insurance plan predates the enactment of ACA, it is not a grandfathered plan because Hobby Lobby elected not to retain grandfathered status before the contraceptive mandate was proposed. *Id.*, at 1124.

The Greens, Hobby Lobby, and Mardel sued HHS and other federal agencies and officials to challenge the contraceptive mandate under RFRA and the Free Exercise Clause.[16] The District Court denied a preliminary injunction, see 870 F. Supp. 2d 1278 (WD Okla. 2012), and the plaintiffs appealed, moving for initial en banc consideration. The Tenth Circuit granted that motion and reversed in a divided opinion. Contrary to the conclusion of the Third Circuit, the Tenth Circuit held that the Greens' two for-profit businesses are "persons" within the meaning of RFRA and therefore may bring suit under that law.

The court then held that the corporations had established a likelihood of success on their RFRA claim. 723 F. 3d, at 1140–1147. The court concluded that the contraceptive mandate substantially burdened the exercise of religion by requiring the companies to choose between "compromis[ing] their religious beliefs" and paying a heavy fee—either "close to $475 million more in taxes every year" if they simply refused to provide coverage for the contraceptives at issue, or "roughly $26 million" annually if they "drop [ped] health-insurance benefits for all employees." *Id.*, at 1141.

The court next held that HHS had failed to demonstrate a compelling interest in enforcing the mandate against the Greens' businesses and, in the alternative, that HHS had failed to prove that enforcement of the mandate was the "least restrictive means" of furthering the Government's asserted interests. *Id.*, at 1143–1144 (emphasis deleted; internal quotation marks omitted). After concluding that the companies had "demonstrated irreparable harm," the court reversed and remanded for the District Court to consider the remaining factors of the preliminary injunction test. *Id.*, at 1147.[17]

We granted certiorari. 571 U.S. ___ (2013).

III A

RFRA prohibits the "Government [from] substantially burden[ing] a *person's* exercise of religion even if the burden results from a rule of general applicability" unless the Government "demonstrates that application of the burden to *the person*—(1) is in furtherance of a compelling governmental interest; and (2) is the least restrictive means of furthering that compelling governmental interest." 42 U.S.C. §§2000bb–1(a), (b) (emphasis added). The first question that we must address is whether this provision applies to regulations that govern the activities of for-profit corporations like Hobby Lobby, Conestoga, and Mardel.

HHS contends that neither these companies nor their owners can even be heard under RFRA. According to HHS, the companies cannot sue because they seek to make a profit for their owners, and the owners cannot be heard because the regulations, at least as a formal matter, apply only to the companies and not to the owners as individuals. HHS's argument would have dramatic consequences.

Consider this Court's decision in *Braunfeld* v. *Brown*, 366 U.S. 599 (1961) (plurality opinion). In that case, five Orthodox Jewish merchants who ran small retail businesses in Philadelphia challenged a Pennsylvania Sunday closing law as a violation of the Free Exercise Clause. Because of their faith, these merchants closed their shops on Saturday, and they argued that requiring them to remain shut on Sunday threatened them with financial ruin. The Court entertained their claim (although it ruled against them on the merits), and if a similar claim were raised today under RFRA against a jurisdiction still subject to the Act (for example, the District of Columbia, see 42 U.S.C. §2000bb–2(2)), the merchants would be entitled to be heard. According to HHS, however, if these merchants chose to incorporate their businesses— without in any way changing the size or nature of their businesses—they would forfeit all RFRA (and free-exercise) rights. HHS would put these merchants to a difficult choice: either give up the right to seek judicial protection of their religious liberty or forgo the benefits, available to their competitors, of operating as corporations.

As we have seen, RFRA was designed to provide very broad protection for religious liberty. By enacting RFRA, Congress went far beyond what this Court has held is constitutionally required.[18] Is there any reason to think that the Congress that enacted such sweeping protection put small-business owners to the choice that HHS suggests? An examination of RFRA's text, to which we turn in the next part of this opinion, reveals that Congress did no such thing.

As we will show, Congress provided protection for people like the Hahns and Greens by employing a familiar legal fiction: It included corporations within RFRA's definition of "persons." But it is important to keep in mind that the purpose of this fiction is to provide protection for human beings. A corporation is simply a form of organization used by human beings to achieve desired ends. An established body of law specifies the rights and obligations of the *people* (including shareholders, officers, and employees) who are associated with a corporation in one way or another. When rights, whether constitutional or statutory, are extended to corporations, the purpose is to protect the rights of these people. For example, extending Fourth Amendment protection to corporations protects the privacy interests of employees and others associated with the company. Protecting corporations from government seizure of their property without just compensation protects all those who have a stake in the corporations' financial well-being. And protecting the free-exercise

rights of corporations like Hobby Lobby, Conestoga, and Mardel protects the religious liberty of the humans who own and control those companies.

In holding that Conestoga, as a "secular, for-profit corporation," lacks RFRA protection, the Third Circuit wrote as follows:

> "General business corporations do not, *separate and apart from the actions or belief systems of their individual owners or employees,* exercise religion. They do not pray, worship, observe sacraments or take other religiously motivated actions separate and apart from the intention and direction of their individual actors." 724 F. 3d, at 385 (emphasis added).

All of this is true—but quite beside the point. Corporations, "separate and apart from" the human beings who own, run, and are employed by them, cannot do anything at all.

B 1

As we noted above, RFRA applies to "a person's" exercise of religion, 42 U.S.C. §§2000bb–1(a), (b), and RFRA itself does not define the term "person." We therefore look to the Dictionary Act, which we must consult "[i]n determining the meaning of any Act of Congress, unless the context indicates otherwise." 1 U.S.C. §1.

Under the Dictionary Act, "the wor[d] 'person' . . . include[s] corporations, companies, associations, firms, partnerships, societies, and joint stock companies, as well as individuals." *Ibid.*; see *FCC* v. *AT&T Inc.*, 562 U.S. ____, ____ (2011) (slip op., at 6) ("We have no doubt that 'person,' in a legal setting, often refers to artificial entities. The Dictionary Act makes that clear"). Thus, unless there is something about the RFRA context that "indicates otherwise," the Dictionary Act provides a quick, clear, and affirmative answer to the question whether the companies involved in these cases may be heard.

We see nothing in RFRA that suggests a congressional intent to depart from the Dictionary Act definition, and HHS makes little effort to argue otherwise. We have entertained RFRA and free-exercise claims brought by nonprofit corporations, see *Gonzales* v. *O Centro Spirit Beneficiate Union do Vegetal*, 546 U.S. 418 (2006) (RFRA); *Hosanna-Tabor Evangelical Lutheran Church and School* v. *EEOC*, 565 U.S. ____ (2012) (Free Exercise); *Church of the Lucama Babel Aye, Inc.* v. *Hialeah*, 508 U.S. 520 (1993) (Free Exercise), and HHS concedes that a nonprofit corporation can be a "person" within the meaning of RFRA. See Brief for HHS in No. 13–354, at 17; 20 Reply Brief in No. 13–354, at 7–8.[19]

This concession effectively dispatches any argument that the term "person" as used in RFRA does not reach the closely held corporations involved in these cases. No known understanding of the term "person" includes some but not all corporations. The term "person" sometimes encompasses artificial persons (as the Dictionary Act instructs), and it sometimes is limited to natural persons. But no conceivable definition of the term includes natural persons and nonprofit corporations, but not for-profit corporations.[20] Cf. *Clark* v. *Martinez*, 543 U.S. 371, 378 (2005) ("To give th[e] same words a different meaning for each category would be to invent a statute rather than interpret one").

2

The principal argument advanced by HHS and the principal dissent regarding RFRA protection for Hobby Lobby, Conestoga, and Mardel focuses not on the statutory term "person," but on the phrase "exercise of religion." According to HHS and the dissent, these corporations are not protected by RFRA because they cannot exercise religion. Neither HHS nor the dissent, however, provides any persuasive explanation for this conclusion.

Is it because of the corporate form? The corporate form alone cannot provide the explanation because, as we have pointed out, HHS concedes that nonprofit corporations can be protected by RFRA. The dissent suggests that nonprofit corporations are special because furthering their religious "autonomy . . . often furthers individual religious freedom as well." *Post*, at 15 (quoting *Corporation of Presiding Bishop of Church of Jesus Christ of Latter-day Saints* v. *Amos*, 483 U.S. 327, 342 (1987) (Brennan, J., concurring in judgment)). But this principle applies equally to for-profit corporations: Furthering their relegious freedom also "furthers individual religious freedom." In these cases, for example, allowing Hobby Lobby, Conestoga, and Mardel to assert RFRA claims protects the religious liberty of the Greens and the Hahns.[21]

If the corporate form is not enough, what about the profit-making objective? In *Braunfeld,* 366 U.S. 599, we entertained the free-exercise claims of individuals who were attempting to make a profit as retail merchants, and the Court never even hinted that this objective precluded their claims. As the Court explained in a later case, the "exercise of religion" involves "not only belief and profession but the performance of (or abstention from) physical acts" that are "engaged in for religious reasons." *Smith*, 494 U.S., at 877. Business practices that are compelled or limited by the tenets of a religious doctrine fall comfortably within that definition. Thus, a law that "operates so as to make the practice of . . . religious beliefs more expensive" in the context of business activities imposes a burden on the exercise of religion. *Braunfeld,* supra, at 605; see *United States* v. *Lee,* 455 U.S. 252, 257 (1982) (recognizing that "compulsory participation in the social security system interferes with [Amish employers'] free exercise rights").

If, as *Braunfeld* recognized, a sole proprietorship that seeks to make a profit may assert a free-exercise claim,[22] why can't Hobby Lobby, Conestoga, and Mardel do the same?

Some lower court judges have suggested that RFRA does not protect for-profit corporations because the purpose of such corporations is simply to make money.[23] This argument flies in the face of modern corporate law. "Each American jurisdiction today either expressly or by implication authorizes corporations to be formed under its general corporation act for any *lawful purpose* or business." 1 J. Cox & T. Hazen, Treatise of the Law of Corporations §4:1, p. 224 (3d ed. 2010) (emphasis added); see 1A W. Fletcher, Cyclopedia of the Law of Corporations §102 (rev. ed. 2010). While it is certainly true that a central objective of for-profit corporations is to make money, modern corporate law does not require for-profit corporations to pursue profit at the expense of everything else, and many do not do so. For-profit corporations, with ownership approval, support a wide variety of charitable causes, and it is not at all uncommon for such corporations to further humanitarian and other altruistic objectives. Many examples come readily to mind. So long as its owners agree, a for-profit corporation may take costly pollution-control and energy conservation measures that go beyond what the law requires. A for-profit corporation that operates facilities in other countries may exceed the requirements of local law regarding working conditions and benefits. If for-profit corporations may pursue such worthy objectives, there is no apparent reason why they may not further religious objectives as well.

HHS would draw a sharp line between nonprofit corporations (which, HHS concedes, are protected by RFRA) and for-profit corporations (which HHS would leave unprotected), but the actual picture is less clear-cut. Not all corporations that decline to organize as nonprofits do so in order to maximize profit. For example, organizations with religious and charitable aims might organize as for-profit corporations because of the potential advantages of that corporate form, such as the freedom to participate in lobbying for legislation or campaigning for political candidates who promote their religious or charitable goals.[24] In fact, recognizing the inherent compatibility between establishing a for-profit corporation and pursuing nonprofit goals, States have increasingly adopted laws formally recognizing hybrid corporate forms. Over half of the States, for instance, now recognize the "benefit corporation," a dual-purpose entity that seeks to achieve both a benefit for the public and a profit for its owners.[25]

In any event, the objectives that may properly be pursued by the companies in these cases are governed by the laws of the States in which they were incorporated—Pennsylvania and Oklahoma—and the laws of those States permit for-profit corporations to pursue "any lawful purpose" or "act," including the pursuit of profit in conformity with the owners' religious principles. 15 Pa. Cons. Stat. §1301 (2001) ("Corporations may be incorporated under this subpart for any lawful purpose or purposes"); Okla. Stat., Tit. 18, §§1002, 1005 (West 2012) ("[E]very corporation, whether profit or not for profit" may "be incorporated or organized . . . to conduct or promote any lawful business or purposes"); see also §1006(A)(3); Brief for State of Oklahoma as *Amicus Curiae* in No. 13–354.

ALITO, J., delivered the opinion of the Court, in which ROBERTS, C. J., and SCALIA, KENNEDY, and THOMAS, JJ., joined. KENNEDY, J., filed a concurring opinion. GINSBURG, J., filed a dissenting opinion, in which SOTOMAYOR, J., joined and in which BREYER and KAGAN, JJ., joined as to all but Part III-C-1. BREYER and KAGAN, JJ., filed a dissenting opinion.

Questions for Analysis

1. It should be clear that, contrary to the opinion offered by one of the dissents, that the Church played an enormous role in the development of contract law especially as it related to the growth of the law merchant. How does this realization support the majority opinion in relation to the purpose of a corporation and the relationship of that purpose to the RFRA? Explain.

2. In Chapter 7, "The Essentials of Contract Law," the feature *A Question of Ethics* asks the following question: "Should the Church, or perhaps religion in general, be given a stronger voice in the political and economic arena, to help redirect and perhaps even equalize the distribution of wealth?" After reading this case, how would you answer this question? Does this answer differ from the answer you offered when you first read Chapter 7? Why or why not?

3. The history of the law merchant offered by Harold J. Berman that we looked at briefly in Chapter 7 suggests that the law merchant always involved the merchants in the law-making process. In fact, the courts established by the guilds were run by elected guild members. It is likely that these guild leaders would have understood that the law can often make merchants choose between making a profit and following their religious beliefs. Given that knowledge, speculate on just how these guild members might have decided *The Hobby Lobby Case.*

4. Also in Chapter 7, we learned that one of the essential differences between contract law and the other areas of the law is that the duties assumed by the parties to a contract are voluntary. Use that knowledge to develop an argument that supports the dissenting justices in *The Hobby Lobby Case.* Explain.

5. Max Weber, in *The Protestant Ethic: The Spirit of Capitalism,* defends the proposition that European capitalism began with the Protestant Reformation in the 16th century. In a similar vein, Rodney Stark in his book, *The Victory of Reason: How Christianity Led to Freedom, Capitalism, and Western Science,* argues that one of the driving forces behind the growth of capitalism was the Roman Catholic Church. Which view is closer to your own view on the topic? Explain.

6. In Chapter 8, "Offer, Acceptance, and Mutual Assent," we learned that sometimes the law *acts proactively* and sometimes the law simply *passively reacts.* This knowledge helped explain why the law has acted (or reacted) as it has in the area of cyber-law. Does *The Hobby Lobby Case* reflect *proactive integration* or *passive reaction*? Explain.

7. In Chapter 10, "Capacity and Legality: The Final Elements," we learned that the most obvious type of illegal contract is one that is designed to obligate someone to commit a crime or a tort. Should there also be a prohibition against contracts that are designed to obligate the parties to do something unethical? Explain.

8. If corporations are legal persons, as Justice Alito suggests in the majority opinion, can they enter contracts that are binding on their shareholders, board members, and officers? Explain.

9. If corporations are legal persons, as Justice Alito suggests in the majority opinion, and if, in fact, they enter contracts that are binding on their shareholders, board members, and officers, what type of signature could they provide on any of those contracts that have to be in writing and signed by the party sought to be bound? Explain.

10. A complex adaptive system (CAS) is a network of interacting conditions that reinforce one another, while at the same time adjusting to change from agents outside and inside the system. In what ways does Justice Alito's opinion in this case reinforce the idea that the law works like a complex adaptive system? Explain.

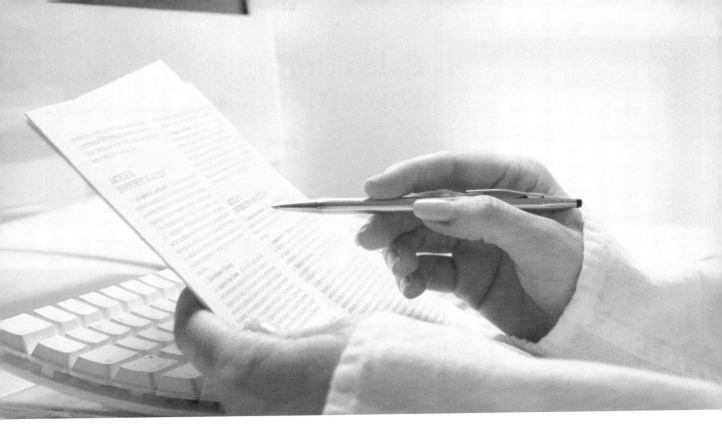

Part Three

Sales and Consumer Protection

Chapter 13

Sales Contracts: Formation, Title, and Risk of Loss

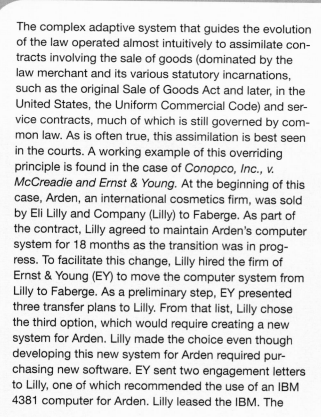

THE OPENING CASE Round 1
The Legal CAS in Action: Sales (the Law Merchant) or Services (Common Law)

The complex adaptive system that guides the evolution of the law operated almost intuitively to assimilate contracts involving the sale of goods (dominated by the law merchant and its various statutory incarnations, such as the original Sale of Goods Act and later, in the United States, the Uniform Commercial Code) and service contracts, much of which is still governed by common law. As is often true, this assimilation is best seen in the courts. A working example of this overriding principle is found in the case of *Conopco, Inc., v. McCreadie and Ernst & Young.* At the beginning of this case, Arden, an international cosmetics firm, was sold by Eli Lilly and Company (Lilly) to Faberge. As part of the contract, Lilly agreed to maintain Arden's computer system for 18 months as the transition was in progress. To facilitate this change, Lilly hired the firm of Ernst & Young (EY) to move the computer system from Lilly to Faberge. As a preliminary step, EY presented three transfer plans to Lilly. From that list, Lilly chose the third option, which would require creating a new system for Arden. Lilly made the choice even though developing this new system for Arden required purchasing new software. EY sent two engagement letters to Lilly, one of which recommended the use of an IBM 4381 computer for Arden. Lilly leased the IBM. The

second letter outlined nine sub-projects that EY would carry out to successfully move Arden onto the new system. In fact, as the project developed, EY went above and beyond these nine projects, but no one documented that extra work. Meanwhile, back at the ranch, Faberge sold Arden to Conopco (a subsidiary of Unilever), which then inherited (or was assigned) the EY contract. Ultimately, Conopco discovered a computer system that was (1) too slow, (2) unable to batch process at night, and (3) unable to run certain financial control and planning programs. Conopco sued EY arguing that (1) the work performed by EY was so poorly done that it amounted to malpractice, (2) EY was guilty of violating certain contract provisions (in other words it was liable for breach of contract), and (3) EY violated the implied warranty of fitness for use under the Uniform Commercial Code. EY filed a summary judgment motion to dismiss the case. The court dismissed the malpractice claim but allowed the breach of contract case to go to trial. That left the warranty claim. The first step in unraveling that claim was to determine whether the original contract was a sale-of-goods contract and, thus, subject to UCC principles or a service contract governed by common law. This issue was complicated; the court was not dealing with a simplified, one-dimensional contract but with something referred to as a mixed, blended, or hybrid contract. Such contracts are part sale-of-goods and part service. To unravel this identity crisis, the court must determine the goal of the original contract by examining certain factors. Read on to see what those factors turn out to be. [See: *Conopco, Inc., v. McCreadie and Ernst & Young,* 826 F. Supp. 855 U.S. District Court, New Jersey, 1993.]

Opening Case Questions

1. Is the agreement between Ernst & Young and Eli Lilly a sale-of-goods contract or a service contract? Explain.

2. What law will govern the details of the contract, if it is a sale-of-goods contract? Explain.

3. What law will govern the details of the contract if it is a service contract? Explain.

4. What difference does it make whether it is a service contract or a sale-of-goods contract? Explain.

5. In what way might following the dictates of the Statute of Frauds have solved all of these problems? Explain.

Learning Objectives

1. Define the term *goods* and explain the nature of a sale.
2. Explain how Article 2 of the UCC applies to contractual relationships.
3. Explain the UCC rules that relate to written contracts.
4. Explain the two laws related to cyber-sales contracts.
5. Contrast an auction with reserve with an auction without reserve.
6. Explain title, void title, and voidable title.
7. Determine when title of goods passes from seller to buyer.
8. Decide when the buyer or seller must bear the risk of loss.
9. Compare a sale on approval with a sale or return.
10. Define an insurable interest.

13-1 The Sale and Lease of Goods

Previously we discussed the general principles of contract law as they relate to common law principles regardless of what is being purchased or sold. Now we shift our focus to contracts that involve the sale or the lease of goods. Recall that goods are movable, tangible pieces of property such as vehicles, clothing, and electronic devices. As we saw in Chapter 7, much of the law regarding the sale of goods evolved from the law merchant on the European continent. With the Roman Catholic Church supplying political and social support, with canon law providing a moral framework, and with practicality guiding their activities over a 300-year period, the merchants developed a body of active law that was characterized by neutrality, universality, mutuality, involvement, integration, and evolution. The law of sales has gone through many changes over the years. However, throughout all these changes, even those that have integrated advanced cyber-technology into the sales contract, the people responsible for the Uniform Commercial Code (UCC) have attempted to preserve those six basic principles. The UCC, which has been adopted either

UCC 2-105(1) (see pages 923–924)

in whole or in part by every state in the United States, will, therefore, be the focal point of our study of sales law.

Sales of Goods

UCC 2-105(2) (see page 924)

UCC 2-106(2) (see page 924)

Some medieval version of a 21st century Madison Avenue advertising executive knew exactly what he was doing when he branded the subject matter of every sales contracts as "goods." It would hardly have attracted sales to call them "bads" or to settle on some other mundane label. Nevertheless, as we all know by the time we are old enough to read a Christmas catalogue, **goods** are things (other than money, stocks, and bonds) that are tangible, movable, and valuable (to someone). They include crops, timber, and minerals if they are to be sold separately from the real property. Office furniture, mobile homes, milk, wedding pictures, electricity, vehicles, computers, waste paper, kerosene, books, clothing, jewelry, horses, toys, candy, tablets, and baseball caps are all considered goods. Goods that are not yet in existence or under the control of people are called **future goods**. They include fish in the sea, minerals in the ground, goods not yet manufactured, and commodities futures. Whenever anyone buys food in a supermarket, gasoline at a gas station, clothing at a shopping mall, a meal at a restaurant, or even a daily newspaper, a sale of goods occurs. In fact, several sales contracts usually occur for a particular item before the item reaches the consumer and sometimes even after it reaches the consumer.

EXAMPLE 13-1: Sales Contracts at Different Levels

The Steven Andrew Corporation manufactures lawn mowers. The company enters into sales contracts with its suppliers every time it purchases parts and materials to make the mowers. In addition, the company enters into sales contracts with wholesalers when it sells the mowers. Similarly, wholesalers enter into sales contracts when they sell the mowers to retailers. In the same manner, retailers enter into sales contracts when they sell the mowers to consumers. Going even further, consumers enter into sales contracts when they sell their second-hand lawn mowers to other consumers. All of these contracts are governed by the UCC.

A gift is not considered a sale because, though title passes, it is not given for a price. Similarly, a bailment (e.g., when an item is left at a store to be sold on consignment) does not meet the definition of a sale because title does not pass between the parties. Article 2 of the UCC applies whenever people buy or sell goods, whether in person, online, over the telephone, or in any other manner. This law applies to sales of goods between private parties and sales of goods by businesspeople or merchants. To determine whether the UCC applies, ask if the contract is a contract for the sale of goods. If the answer is yes, apply the law under the UCC. If the answer is no, apply the common law of contracts. (See Table 13-1.)

UCC Article 2 (see pages 923–944)

Leases of Goods

UCC 2A-101-532 (see pages 944–964)

The leasing of goods is governed by Article 2A of the Uniform Commercial Code. This article includes leasing of such things as automobiles, trucks, machinery, computers, furniture, electronic equipment, and all types of tools. Many of the rules that are found in the UCC relating to the sale of goods (discussed in the following chapters) also apply to the leasing of goods under Article 2A of the UCC.

Table 13-1 Different Laws Apply to Different Transactions

Transaction	Applicable Law
Contract for the sale of real estate	General contract law (sometimes referred to as common law) and real property law
Contract for employment	General contract law and employment law
Sale of goods between two private parties	UCC (Article 2)
Sale of goods by a merchant to a consumer	UCC (Article 2) and state consumer protection laws
Sale of goods between two merchants	UCC (Article 2)
Contract for a mixture of goods and services—consisting mostly of goods	UCC (Article 2)
Contract for a mixture of goods and services—consisting mostly of services	General contract law
Sale of goods over the Internet	UCC (Article 2)
Sale of goods at an auction	UCC (Article 2)
The leasing of goods	UCC (Article 2A)
International sales of goods	United Nations convention on Contracts for the International Sale of Goods (CISG)
Sale of stock on the stock market	UCC (Article 8)
The writing of a check, promissory note, or draft	UCC (Article 3)

Goods and Services

When a contract includes both goods and services, it is referred to as a **mixed, blended, or hybrid contract**. Such contracts have just enough of the characteristics of both types of contracts to prevent them from being pure sales or service contracts. It is important to identify whether the contract is for goods or services, because the law that is applied to the contract will differ depending on the nature of the contract. Sale-of-goods contracts are governed under the UCC while service contracts are governed by common law rules. Most contracts are clearly one or the other. However, when faced with a genuine hybrid contract, the court will still have to determine which side dominates. To choose the dominant side, the court employs one simple and straightforward rule: Determine the ultimate goal of the parties when the contract was first made. If they wanted a sales contract, they get a sales contract. If they wanted a service contract, that is what they get. Of course, the judge cannot simply ask the parties which contract they wanted, because the parties will always (well usually) give conflicting answers. Instead, the court will look at three lines of evidence: (1) the language used in the agreement and the situation in which the contract was made; (2) the way that compensation was to be handled in the contract; and (3) the relationship between the goods and the services provided under the contract. If the sale of goods is dominant, as when someone

THE OPENING CASE *Round 2*
The Legal CAS in Action: The Rules for Hybrid Contracts

In the opening case we learned that Faberge purchased Arden from Eli Lilly and that Lilly agreed to maintain Arden's computer system for 18 months as the transition moved forward. To facilitate the transfer, Lilly hired Ernst & Young (EY) to supervise the details of the project. EY presented three options to Lilly, and Lilly picked the third option, which would require creating a new system for Arden. Lilly made the choice even though developing this new system required purchasing new software. EY sent two engagement letters to Lilly, one of which recommended the use of an IBM 4381 computer for Arden, which Lilly promptly purchased. The second letter outlined nine sub-projects that EY would have to carry out to successfully move Arden onto the new system. As the project developed, EY did more than these nine projects. While this was going on, Faberge negotiated the sale of Arden to Conopco (a subsidiary of Unilever), which was then assigned the EY contract. Once things became operational, Conopco discovered the computer system (1) was not fast enough, (2) was incapable of properly operating the batch processing system at night, and (3) was ill-equipped to run certain financial control and planning programs. To recover some sort of compensation to make up for all of the trouble caused by these delays and setbacks, Conopco sued EY. The case was complicated because at the outset the court was unaware what law to apply to the contract. If the contract involved only the sale or lease of a computer, then it

would be clear that the UCC would apply. Similarly, if the contract were limited to the purchase of a software package, again, the UCC would apply. If no hardware or software had been purchased, then the agreement made by EY would be labeled a service contract. The EY contract fell into none of these neat categories. Instead, it was a hybrid contract. Such contracts are part sale-of-goods and part service contract. To unravel this identity crisis, the court must determine the goal of the original contract by examining: (1) the language used in the agreement and the situation in which the contract was made; (2) the way that compensation was handled under the contract; and (3) the relationship between the goods and the services that were provided under the contract. Ironically, Conopco's own complaint sabotaged its claim that the EY contract was a sale-of-goods contract. Conopco argued that EY was at fault here for inadequately documenting the migration process, failing to properly test the system, and ignoring the need for certain quality-control procedures. All of these complaints involve *services*. Also, a close look at the two engagement letters noted above and the extra work done by EY all point directly at a service agreement not a sale-of-goods contract. The court agreed and granted the summary judgment motion in relation to the UCC warranty claim filed by Conopco. [See: *Conopco, Inc. v. McCreadie and Ernst & Young,* 826 F. Supp. 855 U.S. District Court, New Jersey, 1993).]

purchases a furnace and has it installed, the law under the UCC applies. In contrast, if the performance of services is dominant, as when someone has a furnace repaired and a few new parts are installed, the common law of contracts applies instead.

quick quiz 13-1

1. A gift is considered a sale.   true | false

2. Money, stocks, and bonds are movable items that are   true | false
   not goods.

3. The dominant element of a contract determines whether it is   true | false
   a sales contract or a services contract.

13-2 Rules for Sales Contracts

The fundamental rules of contract law, discussed in Part 2, serve as a foundation for the principles found in the UCC, but the UCC is often more flexible. This flexibility is built into the UCC in order to accommodate the day-to-day reality of the world of sales. The daily operation of the commercial world requires a rapid response to the demands of customers and the needs of suppliers. Unlike real property contracts, which sometimes seem to be moving in slow motion, sales contracts for goods often occur at a moment's notice with little or no preparation. Unlike collective bargaining contracts that require that all the parties agree to each word in each clause of each part of the agreement, purchase orders and invoices often have different terms hidden in the fine print, terms that might contradict one another, but which really do not matter to the actual completion of the contract. Unlike employment contracts, which will not begin until the parties know exactly what is expected of them, a shipment of goods might have to get started before all of the details of a deal are finalized. As we shall see, the UCC handles these realities in an effective and responsible way. In a very real sense, it is the almost universal adherence to the UCC that makes our commercial world work as well as it does. Some of these special rules for sales contracts are covered below.

UCC 1-203 (see page 922)

UCC 1-205 (see page 922)

UCC 2-204(1)(2) (see page 925)

Good Faith, Course of Dealings, and Usage of Trade

Under the UCC, every contract or duty imposes an obligation of good faith. In other words, the parties to a sales contract must act and deal fairly with each other. When the parties have dealt with each other before, their prior dealings give special meaning to sales contracts. Similarly, **usage of trade**, that is, any method of dealing that is commonly used in the particular field, is given special meaning. Unless the parties express otherwise, a course of dealings or usage of trade may be used to supplement or qualify the terms of a sales contract.

UCC 2-206(1)(a) (see page 925)

UCC 2-206(1)(b) (see page 925)

UCC 2-106(2) (see page 924)

Formation of a Sales Contract

A contract may be made in any manner that shows that the parties reached an agreement. It may be oral (with some exceptions) or in writing, or it may be established by the conduct of the parties. An enforceable sales contract may come about even if the exact moment of its making cannot be determined and even though some terms are not completely agreed upon.

Contracts may be formed either orally or in writing; however, a writing may be required by the Statute of Frauds for the contract to be enforceable.

Offer and Acceptance
To establish a contract for the sale of goods, unless otherwise indicated by the offeror or the circumstances, the offeree may accept the offer in any manner and by any medium that is reasonable. A contract for the sale of goods comes into existence when the acceptance is sent, as long as the method used to send it is reasonable. Unless the buyer indicates otherwise, an order or other offer to buy goods for prompt shipment may be accepted by either a prompt shipment or a prompt promise to ship. Under this rule, the goods that are shipped may be either conforming or nonconforming goods. **Conforming goods** are those that are in accordance with the obligations under the contract. **Nonconforming goods** are those that are not the same as those called for under the contract or that are in some way defective.

CLASSIC CASE Offer and Acceptance under the UCC

The Uniform Commercial Code (UCC) governs contracts that are made for the sale or the lease of goods. Goods, as we have seen, are movable tangible objects such as vehicles, electronic devices, and clothing. Many of the rules in the UCC are straightforward, unambiguous expressions of legal principles that have been imbedded in the law for centuries. This simple fact made the classic case of *XCEL v. DeVault* relatively easy for the court to solve. The facts in the case play out like this. DeVault Industries manufactures custom-built shotguns. XCEL had perfected a wire-cutting process that was ideally suited for the trigger assemblies in the DeVault shotguns. After an initial trial run, during which XCEL successfully produced six trigger assemblies, DeVault sent a purchase order (No. 27) to XCEL for 20 additional units (although there was enough material to produce 60 units), at a total cost of $1,080. XCEL received and accepted purchase order No. 27. Within a few days, however, Mr. Cain, the president of XCEL, phoned Mr. DeVault, the president of DeVault, and told him that XCEL could not manufacture the parts at that price. DeVault remembers the phone call differently, arguing that the two men did not talk price but, instead, discussed the quantity of the order, which was set at 20. However, DeVault did admit that Cain said he needed to produce more than 20 units to cover the setup costs for that initial 20 units. DeVault told him

not to worry because they would later figure out what a fair price would be. XCEL did, in fact, manufacture the units and sent them to DeVault. Once DeVault received the units, the company sent a check to XCEL for $1,080. The check included a clear notation that read, "pymt in full PO#27 60 pcs@18.00 ea." Someone at XCEL cashed the check and deposited the proceeds in an XCEL bank account. Nevertheless, Cain continued to claim that DeVault had not paid the full amount owed under the contract. Later XCEL sent its own check for $1,080 back to DeVault. By this time it was too late. DeVault would no longer listen to Cain, and Cain refused to hear DeVault. That was when the lawsuit erupted. The court using the UCC had no problem determining that a contract existed under the terms of the purchase order. As noted above, unless the buyer indicates otherwise, an order or other *offer to buy goods* for *prompt shipment* may be accepted by either a prompt shipment or a prompt promise to ship. The court identified DeVault's purchase order as the *offer to buy goods* and the XCEL's *prompt shipment* of the trigger assemblies as the acceptance. Moreover, since there was no indication that the goods were nonconforming, there could be no successful challenge to the existence of the contract. [See: *XCEL Mold & Machine v. DeVault Indus.* 146 Ohio Misc. 2d 32, 2008-Ohio-269.]

Firm Offer

The UCC holds merchants to a higher standard than nonmerchants. A **merchant** is a person who deals in goods of the kind sold in the ordinary course of business or who otherwise claims to have knowledge or skills peculiar to those goods. Although most rules under the UCC apply to both merchants and nonmerchants alike, some rules apply only to merchants. One such rule involves a firm offer.

No consideration is necessary when a merchant promises in writing to hold an offer open for the sale or lease of goods. Known as a **firm offer**, the writing must be signed by the merchant, and the time period for holding the offer open may not exceed three months. This rule differs from the general rule of contract law, which requires consideration in an option contract.

UCC 2-104(1) (see page 923)

UCC 2-205 (see page 925)

UCC 2-305(1) (see page 927)

Open-Price Terms

Another change that the UCC has made is that a contract for the sale of goods may be established even though the price is not settled. Such **open-price terms** may occur when the parties intend to be bound by a contract but fail to mention the price or decide to set the price later. Under non-UCC law, no contract would come about because the terms are not definite. The UCC allows such a contract to come into existence. If the parties cannot agree on the price at the later date, the UCC requires that the price will be reasonable at the time the goods are delivered.

Output and Requirements Terms

Sometimes, a seller will agree to sell "all the goods we manufacture" or "all the crops we produce" to a particular buyer. This agreement is known as an **output contract**. At other times, a buyer will agree to buy "all the oil we need to heat our building" (or some similar requirement) from a particular seller. This agreement is called a **requirements contract**. Such contracts often were not allowed under common law because the quantity of the goods to be bought or sold was not definite. The UCC allows output and requirements contracts for the sale of goods, as long as the parties deal in good faith and according to *reasonable expectations*.

UCC 2-306 (see page 927)

EXAMPLE 13-2: Unreasonable Expectations

Spencer Oil Co. agreed to sell to Lopaz Manufacturing Co. all the heating oil Lopaz would need during the next year. Spencer knew that Lopaz used about 5,000 gallons of oil each year. During the summer, Lopaz enlarged its building to an extent that it would require 25,000 gallons of heating oil during the next year. Spencer would not be bound to supply that amount of oil to Lopaz because it was far beyond the amount it expected to supply.

Additional Terms in Acceptance

Under the general rules of contract law, an acceptance of an offer must be an absolute, unqualified, unconditional assent to the offer. If the acceptance differs in the slightest from the offer, it is considered a rejection. The UCC changes this rule somewhat. A contract for the sale of goods occurs even though the acceptance states terms that are additional to or different from those offered or agreed upon (unless acceptance is made conditional on assent to the additional terms). The additional terms are treated as proposals for additions to the contract if the parties are not both merchants. If both parties are merchants, the additional terms become part of the contract unless they materially alter it, the other party objects within a reasonable time, or the offer limits acceptance to its terms. This rule is intended to deal with two typical situations. The first is when an agreement has been reached either orally or by informal correspondence between the parties and is followed by one or both of the parties sending formal acknowledgments or memos that contain additional terms not discussed earlier. The second situation in which this rule applies is one in which a fax or letter intended to be the closing or confirmation of an agreement adds further minor suggestions or proposals, such as "ship by Thursday" or "rush."

UCC 2-207 (see page 925)

EXAMPLE 13-3: Additional Terms in Acceptance

Cobb and Sons, Inc., reached an oral agreement with Valley Theatres, Inc., for the sale of an air-conditioning system. Later, Cobb put the agreement in writing, signed it, and sent it to Valley for its signature. Valley signed the writing but added additional terms relative to the date of completion of the contract. Because both parties were merchants, the additional terms would become part of the contract unless Cobb objected to them within a reasonable time. Had one of them not been a merchant, the contract would have to come into existence without the additional terms, and the added terms would have been treated as proposals for additions to the contract.

EXAMPLE 13-4: Different Terms in Acceptance

Cal-Cut Pipe and Supply, Inc., offered in writing to sell used pipe to Southern Idaho Pipe and Steel Co., specifying a delivery date. Southern Idaho accepted by sending a check but changed the delivery date. Cal-Cut mailed a confirmation containing the original delivery date with the postscript, "We will work it out." The court held that there was a binding contract between them despite the conflicting delivery terms.

UCC 2-209(1) (see page 925)

UCC 2-209(2) (see page 926)

Modification Under the general rules of contract law, if the parties have already entered into a binding contract, a later agreement to change that contract needs consideration to be binding. The UCC has done away with this rule in contracts for the sale of goods. An agreement modifying a contract for the sale of goods needs no consideration to be binding. Any such modification may be oral unless the original agreement is in writing and provides that it may not be modified except by a signed writing. Any such clause in a form supplied by a merchant to a nonmerchant, however, must be separately signed (such as in the margin) by the nonmerchant to be effective.

---

quick quiz 13-2

1. Under the UCC, a contract comes into existence when the acceptance is sent if the method used is reasonable.   true | false

2. No consideration is necessary to establish a firm offer when a consumer promises in writing to hold an offer open for the sale or lease of goods.   true | false

3. Under the UCC, a contract for the sale of goods may be established even though the price is not settled.   true | false

---

13-3 The Form of a Sales Contract

UCC 2-201(1) (see page 924)

The Uniform Commercial Code also outlines the rules that must be followed in relation to written sales contracts. This is critical because many contracts in the commercial world are written. Today many sales contracts are also made online, which has required some fine-tuning of the law. As we shall see, however, there are not quite as many changes in the law as one might expect because of the cyber-revolution in sales. This is a testimony to the law of sales, which has adopted a set of rules so well adjusted to its subject matter that it can adapt to even the most radical upheavals in the economic world without missing a beat. Some of this flexibility is made possible by the members of the Uniform Law Commission (ULC) who have been willing to accommodate the needs of those involved with the new technology

The Written Sales Contract

LO3

The Statute of Frauds outlines those contracts that must be in writing to be enforceable and what the writing must contain to be complete. As long as the value of the goods involved in a sales contract does not exceed $500, the contract can be oral and still be enforceable. Once the price is $500 or more, however, the contract must be in writing to be enforceable. Also under the UCC, a lease of goods must be in writing if the total payments to be made under the lease are $1,000 or more.

UCC 2A-201(1) (see page 947)

UCC 2-201(2) (see page 947)

Exceptions to the General Rule There are four exceptions to the requirement that contracts for the sale of goods for $500 or more and the lease of goods for $1,000 or more must be in writing to be enforceable. These exceptions involve the following:

1. Oral contracts between merchants in which a confirmation has been received by one party and not objected to by the other party.

2. Specially manufactured goods.

3. Admissions in court.
4. Executed contracts.

Most of the rules that involve written contracts and the sale of goods are covered in the UCC, but some contracts involving either sale-of-goods contracts or some other type of contract fall outside the UCC. For example, contracts that cannot be completed within one year and agreements to pay the debt of another party might both involve sale-of-goods contracts. First, let's look at contracts in which one party agrees to pay another party's debt. Several terms have been used to describe these types of transactions. They are alternately referred to as a guaranty of payment, a guaranty contract, or a collateral contract. The promisor is usually called a guarantor. Often in a commercial setting, the guarantor is referred to as a cosigner. The person to whom the promise is made is the obligee, and the person who owes the original debt is referred to as the obligor. It is crucial to distinguish between guaranty contracts and original contracts. An exception to this rule is known as the primary objective test. Under the primary objective test (also referred to as the leading objective test and the main purpose test), if the promise to pay another party's debt is actually made to obtain a gain for the guarantor, there is no need for a writing to enforce the promise. The other type of contract that might involve a sale-of-goods contract in need of a writing is a contract that cannot be completed within one year. While most sale-of-goods contracts can be completed within one year, this is not always the case. In fact, this is an issue in the opening case.

THE OPENING CASE *Round 3*
The Legal CAS in Action: The Rules Involving Written Contracts

In the opening case, we learned that Faberge purchased Arden from Eli Lilly and that Lilly agreed to maintain Arden's computer system for 18 months as the transition moved forward. To facilitate the transfer, Lilly hired Ernst & Young (EY) to supervise the details of the project. While the computer system was being replaced under EY's direction, Faberge negotiated the sale of Arden to Conopco (a subsidiary of Unilever), which was then assigned the EY contract. Once things became operational, Conopco discovered the new computer system (1) was not fast enough, (2) was incapable of properly operating the batch processing system at night, and (3) was ill-equipped to run certain financial control and planning programs. To recover some sort of compensation to make up for all of the trouble caused by these delays and setbacks, Conopco sued EY. The case was complicated because at the outset the court was unaware what law to apply to the contract. However, this did not stop Conopco from making a claim under the Statute of Frauds. Conopco asked the court to declare the contract unenforceable because it was not in writing as required by the statute. Conopco argued that, under the Statute of

Frauds, all contracts that cannot be completed within one year must be in writing to be enforceable. Since this contract was supposed to take 18 months and it was not in writing, it was not enforceable. The court did not waste much time rejecting this claim. The court provided two reasons to explain why this claim was spurious at best. First, the court noted that the Statute of Frauds requires a writing for contracts that *cannot* be completed within one year, but does not require a writing for contracts that *can* be completed within one year, even if that completion date is unlikely. Possibility is what rules here, not certainty or even probability. Thus, if it is possible that a contract can be completed within one year, no matter how unlikely, the contract need not be written to be enforceable. Second, the court also noted that the cases that have interpreted the Statute of Frauds on this point have consistently held that the one-year rule does not govern a contract that has actually been completed within one year. Since EY not only completed the job, but was also paid for it, the one-year rule does not apply. [See: *Conopco, Inc., v. McCreadie and Ernst & Young,* 826 F. Supp. 855 U.S. District Court, New Jersey, 1993.]

Oral Contracts between Merchants

An exception to the general rule occurs when there is an oral agreement made between two merchants. If either merchant receives a written confirmation of the oral agreement from the other merchant within a reasonable time and does not object to it in writing within 10 days, the writing is sufficient under the UCC even though it has not been signed by the other party. It is important to understand that this exception applies only to merchants, not to ordinary consumers. The UCC defines a merchant as "a person who deals in goods of the kind" that are the subject matter of the contract at hand. It is also crucial to note that any objection to the original written confirmation must be in writing. If that is not the case then the court will honor the original written confirmation, no matter how loudly and how persuasively the other party objected to the agreement.

UCC 2-201(3) (see page 924)

Specially Manufactured Goods

Another exception occurs when goods are to be specially manufactured for the buyer and are not suitable for sale to others in the ordinary course of the seller's business. If the seller has made either a substantial beginning in manufacturing the goods or commitments to buy them, the oral agreement will be enforceable.

EXAMPLE 13-5: Specially Manufactured Goods

Lifetime Windows, Inc., entered into an oral agreement to manufacture 15 oversized windows for Harold Cohen for the price of $6,000. The windows were such an odd shape that no one else would have a need for them. When the windows were manufactured, Cohen refused to take them on the ground that the oral contract was unenforceable. The court held against Cohen, however, and enforced the oral agreement. The windows were specially manufactured and were not suitable for sale to others.

UCC 2-201(3)(b) (see page 925)

Admissions in Court

If the party against whom enforcement is sought admits in court that an oral contract for the sale of goods was made, the contract will be enforceable. The contract is not enforceable under this exception, however, beyond the quantity of goods admitted.

UCC 2-201(3)(c) (see page 925)

Executed Contracts

When the parties carry out their agreement in a satisfactory manner, the law will not render the transaction unenforceable for want of an agreement in writing. Executed contracts (those that have been carried out) need not be in writing; the writing requirements apply only to contracts that are executory, that is, not yet performed. This provision means that contracts for goods that have been received and accepted need not be in writing. If there has been a part payment or a part delivery, the court will enforce only that portion of the agreement that has been performed.

UCC 2-201(1) (see page 924)

Requirements of Writing

The writing that is required to satisfy the UCC must indicate that a contract for sale has been made between the parties and mention the quantity of goods being sold. It must also be signed by the party against whom enforcement is sought (the defendant). A writing is acceptable even though it omits or incorrectly states an agreed-upon term. However, a contract will not be enforceable beyond the quantity of goods shown in such writing. For that reason, it is necessary to put the quantity of goods to be bought and sold in the written agreement. Although a paper similar to the one shown in Figure 13-1 may be used, an informal note, memorandum, fax, or sales slip will satisfy the writing requirements.

CONTRACT FOR SALE OF GOODS

AGREEMENT made by and between Ozzie Caldwell (Seller) and Geordi Hasenzahl (Buyer).

It has been agreed between the two parties that:

1. Seller agrees to sell, and Buyer agrees to buy, the following described property: one regulation-size pool table now located at the residence of Ozzie Caldwell, RD #1, Box 118, Ashberry, Kentucky.

2. Buyer agrees to pay Seller the total price of $850.00;

   payable as follows:

   $600.00 deposit herewith

   $250.00 balance by cash or certified check at time of transfer

3. Seller warrants he has full legal title to said property, authority to sell said property, and that said property shall be sold free and clear of all claims by other parties.

4. Said property is sold in "as is" condition. SELLER HEREBY EXCLUDES THE WARRANTY OF MERCHANTABILITY AND FITNESS FOR A PARTICULAR PURPOSE.

5. Parties agree to transfer title on February 7, 20 - -, at RD #1, Box 118, Ashberry, Kentucky, the address of the Seller.

6. This agreement shall be binding on the parties, their successors, assigns, and personal representatives.

7. This writing is intended to represent the entire agreement between the parties.

Signed under seal this nineteenth day of January, 20 - -.

Geordi Hasenzahl
_____
Buyer

Ozzie Caldwell
_____
Seller

Figure 13-1   With four exceptions, contracts for the sale of goods of $500 or more must be in writing to be enforceable. A formal writing such as this is not necessary to satisfy the writing requirements of the UCC, however.

UCC 1-201(39) (see
page 921)

Signature Requirements Under the UCC, a signature includes any symbol made with the intent to authenticate a writing. Thus, in addition to a handwritten signature, the courts have held various kinds of marks, including an X and a typewritten name, qualify as a signature as long as they were written with the intent to be signatures.

Cyber-Sales Contracts

Statutes covering the problems associated with cyber-sales contracts have taken many forms over the past decade. One of the problems that required a solution was how to treat an online contract that required a written form. Two acts that have dealt with that problem are the E-Sign Act and the Uniform Electronic Transactions Act (UETA).

The E-Sign Act Congress passed the E-Sign Act to address some of the difficulties associated with cyber-commerce, especially those that involve the recognition of electronic contracts and electronic signatures. In short, the statute declares that, as long as the parties to a cyber-contract have freely decided to conduct business electronically, the cyber-contract that results will have the same legal effect as a paper contract. The statute makes it clear that the parties to the contract must have some way to store and duplicate a cyber-record of the contract; otherwise, the cyber-record will not be legally sufficient under the act. It is also important to understand that some critical documents are not covered by the act. These include court records, eviction notices, health insurance cancellations, foreclosure notices, prenuptial contracts, and divorce papers. On the other hand, UCC contracts for the sale and lease of goods are included in the E-Sign Act.

The Uniform Electronic Transactions Act (UETA) The Uniform Electronic Transactions Act (UETA), which was produced by the Uniform Law Commission, is very similar to the E-Sign Act. The UETA promises the same legal parity between electronic records and paper records that is guaranteed by the E-Sign Act. However, the UETA applies only to transactions that involve a business, governmental, or commercial situation. Still, the statute does ensure that, whenever a writing is required under the Statute of Frauds, any electronic signature that results from a cyber-transaction will fulfill that requirement. Under the UETA an electronic signature is defined as "an electronic sound, symbol, or process attached to or logically associated with a record and executed or adopted by a person with the intent to sign the record."

International Law

Interestingly, the trend in other countries is to eliminate the requirement that a sales contract be in writing. Great Britain, for example, after having such a requirement for 277 years, did away with it in 1954. International sales law also has no writing requirements for a sales contract; instead, a sales contract may be proved by any means.

CISG Articles 1 and 2
(page 985)

CISG Articles 4 and 5
(page 985)

International sales law, called the United Nations **Convention on Contracts for the International Sale of Goods (CISG)**, applies only to sales between businesses whose places of business are in different countries that have adopted the law. It does not apply to sales of goods that are bought for personal, family, or household purposes. Also, the international law does not apply to auction sales; sales of stock, securities, negotiable instruments, or money; sales of ships or aircraft; or sales of electricity. The United States adopted the international sales law in 1988, and by 2007, 70 countries had made it part of their law.

UCC 2-328(2) (see
page 931)

UCC 2-328(3) (see
page 932)

The CISG is similar in many ways to the UCC. It also contains some differences. The CISG governs only the formation of a sales contract and the rights and duties of the parties that arise from it. The CISG is not concerned with the validity of a contract regarding, for example, the sale of illegal drugs, which would be governed by other laws. In addition, the CISG does not apply to the liability of the seller for death or personal injury caused by the goods to any person. In such a case, people would have to look to other laws for a remedy.

Auction Sales and Cyber-Auction Fraud

In an auction sale, the auctioneer presents goods for sale and invites the audience to make offers, which are known as bids. This process is similar to an invitation to trade. Bidders in the crowd respond with their offers. The highest bid (offer) is accepted by the auctioneer, usually by the drop of the gavel, together with the auctioneer's calling out the word *sold.* If, while the gavel is falling, a higher bid comes from those in the crowd, the auctioneer has two options: declare the goods sold or reopen the bidding.

UCC 2-328(4) (see page 932)

An auction sale is "with reserve" unless the goods are expressly put up without reserve. In an **auction with reserve**, the auctioneer may withdraw the goods at any time before announcing completion of the sale if the highest bid is not high enough. In an **auction without reserve**, after the auctioneer calls for bids on an article or lot, that article or lot cannot be withdrawn unless no bid is made within a reasonable time. In either case, a bidder may retract a bid until the auctioneer's announcement of completion of the sale. A bidder's retraction does not revive any previous bid.

The practice of planting persons in the crowd for the purpose of raising bids by innocent purchasers is not allowed. Except in a forced sale, such as by a sheriff, if a seller (or the seller's agent) makes a bid at an auction without notifying other bidders, a buyer has two options. Under the UCC, a buyer may either avoid the sale or take the goods at the price of the last good faith bid prior to the completion of the sale. In a forced sale, as when a sheriff auctions property on foreclosure or to satisfy a lien creditor, the owner is allowed to bid on the property being sold.

Auctions are frequently used to dispose of unwanted property, satisfy judgments, and liquidate foreclosed property.

Auctions on the Internet provide the opportunity to buy and sell goods worldwide as well as locally. An Internet auction (AKA a cyber-auction and an e-auction) can be either person-to person or business-to-person. In person-to-person auctions, sellers offer items directly to consumers. The highest bidder must deal directly with the seller to arrange for payment and delivery. In contrast, operators of business-to-person auctions have control of the items being offered and take charge of payment and delivery of goods bought and sold.

Cyber-auction fraud is alarming. Sometimes sellers don't deliver the goods or deliver something less valuable than they advertised. At other times, sellers don't disclose everything about a product or fail to deliver it when they say they will. The Federal Trade Commission (FTC) provides helpful information about cyber-auctions in its free brochures and on its website.

Did You Know?

The federal government auctions cars, trucks, real estate, airplanes, boats, jewelry, office equipment, heavy equipment, and many other items. For information about government auctions, log onto the Internet and, using the search engine Excite, type in the words "government auction." You may find something you need at a bargain price.

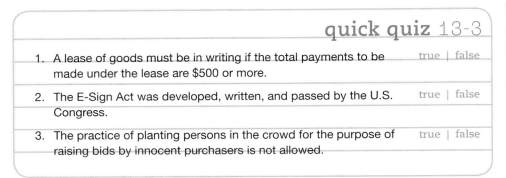

quick quiz 13-3

1. A lease of goods must be in writing if the total payments to be made under the lease are $500 or more.   true | false

2. The E-Sign Act was developed, written, and passed by the U.S. Congress.   true | false

3. The practice of planting persons in the crowd for the purpose of raising bids by innocent purchasers is not allowed.   true | false

13-4 Title, Passage of Title, and Risk of Loss

It is good for us to remember that the law of sales was born within the context of the law merchant and that the law merchant was closely associated with the development of capitalism. Moreover, it is also critical to recall that one of the driving forces behind the growth of capitalism was the Roman Catholic Church, which helped provide a rational and moral foundation for the principles and procedures that guided the activities of merchants in the making of their contracts. One of the things that the Church insisted upon was that merchants never engage in fraud and always follow a good faith approach to contract development. The problem of determining title to goods, especially determining just when title legitimately passes from one party to another, must be solved to ensure the basic fairness of the law of sales. After all, it is not only ownership that passes with title, but also the risk associated with that ownership. [See: Harold J. Berman, *Law and Revolution: The Formation of the Western Legal Tradition,* (Cambridge: Harvard University Press, 1983), pp. 336–341; and Rodney Stark, *The Victory of Reason: How Christianity Led to Freedom, Capitalism, and Western Science* (New York: Random House, 2005), p. xi. See also Henri Sée, *Modern Capitalism: Its Origin and Evolutions*, trans. Homer B. Vanderblue and Georges F. Doriot (New York: Adelphi Co. 1928), pp. 7–13.]

Valid Title, Void Title, and Voidable Title

Title, or **valid title**, is the right of ownership to goods. People who own goods have title to them. Sellers sometimes give a bill of sale to a buyer as evidence that the sale took place. A **bill of sale** is a written statement that provides evidence of the transfer of personal property from one person to another. It does not prove, however, that the seller had perfect title to the goods. The goods may have been stolen, obtained by fraud, purchased from a minor or an incompetent person, or entrusted with the seller by the true owner and sold by mistake. The question that arises in such cases is whether an innocent purchaser for value receives good title to the goods. The answer to this question depends on whether the seller's title to the goods was void or voidable and whether the goods had been entrusted to a merchant.

With the exception of voidable title, buyers of goods acquire whatever title their sellers had to the property. If a seller has **void title** (no title at all), a buyer of the goods obtains no title to them. The continued sale of the stolen property through several innocent buyers would not in any way defeat the real owner's right to the property. The rights of possession and title of successive buyers of stolen property can never be any better than the rights of the thief, who had no title. Of course, innocent purchasers may bring suit against the person from whom stolen goods were purchased for breach of warranty of title.

Anyone who obtains property as a result of another's fraud, misrepresentation, mutual mistake, undue influence, or duress holds only voidable title to the goods. **Voidable title** means title that may be voided if the injured party elects to do so. This kind of title is also received when goods are bought from a minor or a person who is mentally impaired. Some people refer to voidable title as title that is valid until voided. Anyone with voidable title to goods is able to transfer good title to others. According to the UCC, "A person with voidable title has power to transfer a good title to a good faith purchaser for value."

Entrusting Goods to a Merchant
People often entrust goods that belong to them to merchants. For example, they leave their watches with jewelers and their vehicles with the body shop to be repaired. When this occurs, if the merchant sells the goods in the ordinary course of business to a third party who has no knowledge of the real owner's

rights, the third party receives good title to them. The original owner who entrusted them to the merchant loses title to the goods altogether but may bring an action against the merchant for money damages caused by the loss. The reason for this rule of law is to give confidence to people who buy in the marketplace. People can be assured that they will receive good title to property (except stolen property) that they buy from a merchant who deals in goods of that kind in the ordinary course of business.

Passage of Title and Risk of Loss

It is not unusual for goods to be stolen, damaged, or destroyed while they are awaiting shipment, are being shipped, or are awaiting pickup after a sales contract has been entered. When something happens to the goods, it becomes necessary to determine who must suffer the loss: the seller or the buyer. The rules for determining the risk of loss are contained in the UCC. Except when goods are to be picked up by the buyer and in a few other cases, whoever has title to the goods bears the risk of loss. Goods must be identified in the contract before title can be transferred to the buyer. **Identified goods** are specific goods that have been selected as the subject matter of the contract. Once goods are identified, title passes to the buyer when the seller does whatever is required under the contract to deliver the goods. Contracts calling for the seller to deliver the goods are either *shipment contracts* or *destination contracts*.

Shipment Contracts

Shipment Contracts   A **shipment contract** is one in which the seller turns the goods over to a carrier for delivery to the buyer. The seller has no responsibility for seeing that the goods reach their destination. In a shipment contract, both title and risk of loss pass to the buyer when the goods are given to the carrier. Shipment contracts are often designated by the term *f.o.b. [the place of shipment]* (such as f.o.b. Chicago). The abbreviation **f.o.b.** means "free on board." When goods are sent **f.o.b. the place of shipment**, they will be delivered free to the place of shipment. The buyer must pay all shipping charges from there to the place of destination. The terms indicate that title to the goods and the risk of loss pass at the point of origin. Delivery to the carrier by the seller and acceptance by the carrier complete the transfer of both title and risk of loss. Thus, the buyer accepts full responsibility during the transit of the goods. (See Table 13-2.)

Destination Contracts

Destination Contracts   If the contract requires the seller to deliver goods to a destination, it is called a **destination contract**. Both title and risk of loss pass to the buyer when the seller tenders the goods at the place of destination. **Tender** means to offer to turn

Table 13-2	Abbreviations
Abbreviation	**Meaning**
f.o.b. New York	Free on board to New York (This would be a *shipment contract* if shipped from New York.)
f.o.b. Los Angeles	Free on board to Los Angeles (This would be a *destination contract* if shipped from New York.)
c.o.d.	Collect on delivery
c.i.f.	Cost of goods shipped, insurance, and freight
c.f.	Cost of goods shipped and freight
f.a.s.	Free alongside vessel or at a dock

CLASSIC CASE *(Revisited)*
Shipment and Destination Contracts

In the earlier Classic Case, we learned that DeVault, a shotgun manufacturer, sent a purchase order to XCEL for trigger-assembly units, at a total cost of $1,080. XCEL received and accepted purchase order No. 27. Within a few days, however, Mr. Cain, the president of XCEL, phoned Mr. DeVault, the president of DeVault, and told him that XCEL could not manufacture the parts at that price. DeVault told him not to worry because they would later figure out what a fair price would be. XCEL did, in fact, manufacture all 60 units and send them to DeVault. If the order had been a shipment contract, the seller, XCEL, would have turned the trigger-assembly units over to a carrier for delivery to DeVault. The seller, XCEL, would then have no responsibility for seeing that the trigger-assemblies reached DeVault. In a shipment contract, both title and risk of loss pass to the buyer when the goods are given to the carrier. In contrast, if the order had been a destination contract, then both title and risk of loss would have passed to the buyer, DeVault, when XCEL delivered the trigger-assemblies to DeVault's place of business, which was the final destination of the shipment.

the goods over to the buyer. Destination contracts are often designated by **f.o.b. the place of destination** (such as f.o.b. Tampa); goods shipped under such terms belong to the seller until they have been delivered to the destination shown on the contract. Similarly, the risk of loss remains with the seller until the goods are tendered at destination. Tender at destination requires that the goods arrive at the place named in the contract, the buyer is given notice of their arrival, and a reasonable time is allowed for the buyer to pick up the goods from the carrier.

When terms of shipment do not specify shipping point or destination, it is assumed to be a shipment contract. Adding the term **c.o.d.** (collect on delivery) instructs the carrier to retain possession until the carrier has collected the cost of the goods. The term **c.i.f.** (cost, insurance, and freight) instructs the carrier to collect all charges and fees in one lump sum. This sum includes the cost of goods shipped, insurance, and freight charges to the point of destination. The term **c.f.** means that insurance is not included in the sum. The term **f.a.s. vessel** (free alongside vessel) at a named port requires sellers to deliver the goods, at their own risk, alongside the vessel or at a dock designated by the buyer.

No Delivery Required When the contract calls for the buyer to pick up the goods, title passes to the buyer when the contract is made. Risk of loss, however, passes at different times depending on whether the seller is a merchant. If the seller is a merchant, the risk of loss passes when the buyer receives the goods. If the seller is not a merchant, the risk of loss passes to the buyer when the seller tenders the goods to the buyer (see Table 13-3).

Fungible Goods The UCC defines **fungible goods** as "goods of which any unit is, by nature or usage of trade, the equivalent of any like unit." Wheat, flour, sugar, and liquids of various kinds are examples of fungible goods. They have no important characteristics that identify them as coming from a particular supplier, and they are usually sold by weight or measure. Title to fungible goods may pass without the necessity of separating goods sold from the bulk. Under the UCC, "an undivided share of an identified bulk

Table 13-3 Passage of Title and Risk of Loss

Terms of Contract	Title Passes	Risk of Loss Passes
Shipment contract	When goods are delivered to carrier	When goods are delivered to carrier
Destination contract	When goods are tendered at destination	When goods are tendered at destination
No delivery required	When contract is made	*Merchant seller:* When buyer receives goods *Nonmerchant seller:* When seller tenders goods to buyer
Document of title	When document of title is given to buyer	When document of title is given to buyer
Agreement of the parties	At time and place agreed upon	At time and place agreed upon

of fungible goods is sufficiently identified to be sold although the quantity of the bulk is not determined."

EXAMPLE 13-6: Fungible Goods

Logan Trucking Co. owned a large fuel storage tank that was partially filled with diesel fuel. The exact quantity of fuel in the tank was not known. The company was going out of business. Interstate Trucking Co. contracted to buy half of the fuel in the tank, and Union Trucking Co. contracted to buy the other half. Both buyers agreed to send their own trucks to pick up the fuel. Title passed to the buyers when the contract was made even though the exact quantity of each sale was unknown and neither buyer had taken a share of the fuel from the entire lot.

Documents of Title Sometimes, when people buy goods, they receive a document of title to the goods rather than the goods themselves. They then give the document of title to the warehouse or carrier that is holding the goods and receive possession of them. A document of title is a paper giving the person who possesses it the right to receive the goods named in the document. Bills of lading and warehouse receipts are examples of documents of title. However, an automobile title certificate has not been given the legal status of a document of title, as the term is used in the UCC. When a document of title is used in a sales transaction, both title and risk of loss pass to the buyer when the document is delivered to the buyer.

Agreement of the Parties The parties may, if they wish, enter into an agreement setting forth the time that title and risk of loss pass from the seller to the buyer. With one exception, title and risk of loss will pass at the time and place agreed upon. If the agreement allows the seller to retain title after the goods are shipped, title will pass to the buyer at the time of shipment, regardless of the agreement, and the seller will have a security interest in the goods rather than title. A security interest gives the seller a right to have the property sold in the event that the buyer fails to pay money owed to the seller.

EXAMPLE 13-7: Security Interest

Raymond agreed to sell Glover her John Deere tractor for $12,000. The agreement called for Glover to pay $3,000 down and the balance in monthly installments for two years. Under the terms of the agreement, title to the tractor would not pass to Glover until the $12,000 was paid in full. Because Raymond delivered the tractor to Glover on the day that the agreement was signed, title passed to Glover at that time, regardless of the terms in the contract. The effect of those terms was to give Raymond a security interest in the tractor for the balance of the money owed to her.

Revesting of Title in Seller Buyers, after entering into sales contracts, sometimes refuse to accept the goods that are delivered or are otherwise made available to them. In all such cases, title to the goods returns to the seller. This reversion is true whether or not the buyer's rejection of the goods is justified. Similarly, title to goods returns to the seller when the buyer accepts the goods and then for a justifiable reason decides to revoke the acceptance. A justifiable reason for revoking an acceptance would be the discovery of a defect in the goods after having inspected them. When the seller sends goods to the buyer that do not meet the contract requirements and are therefore unacceptable, the risk of loss remains with the seller. For situations in which the buyer accepts the goods but later discovers some defect and rightfully revokes the acceptance, the passage of risk of loss depends on whether the buyer is insured. If the buyer has insurance, that insurance will cover the loss. If there is no insurance, the risk of loss remains with the seller from the beginning. When the buyer breaches the contract with regard to goods that have been identified to the contract, the seller may, to the extent of having no insurance coverage, treat the risk of loss as resting with the buyer.

International Sales The rules governing international sales are given in the United Nations Convention on Contracts for the International Sale of Goods (CISG). The international law does not address questions dealing with the passage of title because the laws of each country vary considerably. Instead, it leaves such questions to be decided by domestic law. This determination exists because third parties are usually involved in claiming title for themselves, and the laws of each country vary considerably. In contrast, the rules governing the passage of risk of loss are addressed in international law and are quite similar to those found in the UCC. The risk of loss passes to the buyer when the goods are handed over to the first carrier for transmission to the buyer unless the seller agrees to hand them over at a particular place. In that case, the risk of loss passes to the buyer at that time. Sometimes, goods are sold when they are in transit. When this kind of sale occurs (with some exceptions), the risk of loss passes to the buyer when the contract is made. In all other situations, the risk of loss, in general, passes when the buyer takes over the goods. The CISG has several exceptions in the contracts that it covers. It does not apply to goods bought for personal, household, or family use, or to contracts that mainly supply services. Nor does it cover the liability of the seller for death or injury caused by the goods sold.

quick quiz 13-4

1. *Void title* means title that may be voided if the injured party elects to do so.	true	false
2. *Voidable title* means no title at all.	true	false
3. Fungible goods must be separated from the bulk before title to them can pass to a buyer.	true	false

13-5 Sales, Returns, and Insurable Interest

Because of competition and a desire to give satisfaction, goods are sometimes sold with the understanding that they may be returned even though they conform to the contract. Determination of ownership and risk of loss while such goods are in the buyer's possession is sometimes necessary. Sales with the right of return are of two kinds: sale on approval and sale or return.

Sale on Approval

A sale that allows goods to be returned even though they conform to the contract is called a **sale on approval** when the goods are primarily for the buyer's use. When goods are sold on approval, they remain the property of the seller until the buyer's approval has been expressed. The approval may be indicated by the oral or written consent of the buyer or by the buyer's act of retaining the goods for more than a reasonable time. Using the goods in a reasonable and expected manner on a trial basis does not imply an acceptance. Grossly careless use and a failure to inform the seller of the buyer's intent to return, however, could constitute an acceptance. Goods held by the buyer on approval are not subject to the claims of the buyer's creditors until the buyer decides to accept them. In addition, the risk of loss remains with the seller until the buyer has accepted the goods.

Sale or Return

A sale that allows goods to be returned even though they conform to the contract is called a **sale or return** when the goods are delivered primarily for resale. When such a sale occurs, the buyer takes title to the goods with the right to revest (reinstate) title in the seller after a specified period or reasonable time. In such cases, the buyer must accept all of the obligations of ownership while retaining possession of the goods. Goods held on sale or return are subject to the claims of the buyer's creditors. While in the buyer's possession, the goods must be cared for and used in a reasonable manner, anticipating their possible return in the same condition as when received, after making allowance for ordinary wear and tear. Also, the goods must be returned at the buyer's risk and expense.

EXAMPLE 13-8: Consignment Contract

Butcher owned a gift shop in which she sold other people's goods on consignment. Hanson delivered a dozen handmade braided rugs to Butcher with the understanding that she would be paid for any that were sold. Any rugs that did not sell after three months would be returned to Hanson. This agreement was a sale or return because the rugs were delivered primarily for resale. Butcher would be required to pay Hanson for any rugs that were damaged, lost, or stolen while in Butcher's possession.

Insurable Interest

People must have an insurable interest in property to be able to place insurance on it. An **insurable interest** is the financial interest that an insured party has in the insured property. Buyers may place insurance on goods the moment a contract is made and the goods are identified to the contract. At this point, buyers receive an insurable interest in the goods they buy. They obtain an insurable interest even though they might later reject or return the goods to the seller. Notwithstanding the buyer's right to insure the goods, sellers retain an insurable interest in the goods as long as they have title to them.

EXAMPLE 13-9: Dual Insurable Interests

While shopping on vacation in an antique store in Connecticut, Maniff, who lived in Nevada, came upon a Native American totem pole she liked. She decided to buy the totem pole on the condition that the antique dealer would ship it f.o.b. Winnemucca, Nevada. The dealer agreed. Maniff received an insurable interest in the totem pole when it was identified to the contract. At the same time, the dealer retained an insurable interest in it until it was tendered at its destination in Winnemucca. Both Maniff and the antique dealer could insure the totem pole.

quick quiz 13-5

1. Goods that are sold on approval are subject to the claims of the buyer's creditors until the buyer decides to accept them.   true | false

2. Goods that are sold on approval remain the property of the seller until the buyer's approval has been expressed.   true | false

3. Goods that are sold on sale or return are not subject to the claims of the buyer's creditors.   true | false

Summary

13.1 The Uniform Commercial Code (UCC), which contains the law of sales, has been adopted, either in whole or in part, by every state in the United States. Article 2 of the UCC applies whenever people buy or sell goods. It applies to transactions between private parties as well as transactions by businesspeople or merchants. Article 2A applies to leases of goods.

13.2 The following rules that are different from general contract law apply to sales contracts:

- A sales contract may be made in any manner that shows that the parties reached an agreement.
- Unless otherwise specified, an offeree may accept an offer in any way that is reasonable, including a prompt shipment of the goods.
- A written promise by a merchant to hold an offer open needs no consideration to be binding.

- A sales contract may be made even though the price is not settled.
- Output and requirements contracts are allowed in sales contracts as long as the parties deal in good faith and according to reasonable expectations.
- A sales contract may result even when an offeree adds different or additional terms from those offered or agreed upon.
- No consideration is necessary to modify a contract for the sale of goods.

13.3 With four exceptions, a contract for the sale of goods for $500 or more and the lease of goods for $1,000 or more must be in writing. The exceptions are oral contracts between merchants in which a confirmation has been received by one party and not objected to by the other party, specially manufactured goods, admissions in court, and executed contracts. The United Nations

Convention on Contracts for the International Sale of Goods (CISG) applies to sales between U.S. businesses and foreign businesses.

In an auction sale, offers are made by the people in the audience. The acceptance takes place when the auctioneer bangs the gavel.

13.4 Title to goods can be either valid, void, or voidable. When a merchant sells goods without authority, the purchaser obtains good title. With few exceptions, such as when goods are to be picked up by the buyer, whoever has title to the goods bears the risk of loss. Once goods are identified, title passes to the buyer when the seller does whatever is required under the contract to deliver the goods. Title to fungible goods may pass without the need to separate goods sold from bulk. With a document of title, title and risk of loss pass to the buyer when the document is delivered. Title returns to the seller when the buyer refuses the goods. The risk of loss remains with the seller when the goods do not meet the requirements.

13.5 Goods sold on approval remain the property of the seller until the buyer approves. The seller retains the risk of loss. In a sale or return, the buyer takes title to the goods but is given the right to return the goods to the seller. The buyer must care for the goods in a reasonable manner and suffer the risk. Buyers have an insurable interest in goods the moment a contract is made and the goods are identified to the contract.

Key Terms

auction with reserve, 321

auction without reserve, 321

bill of sale, 322

blended contract, 311

c.f., 324

c.i.f., 324

c.o.d., 324

conforming goods, 313

Convention on Contracts for the International Sale of Goods (CISG), 320

destination contract, 323

document of title, 325

f.a.s. vessel, 324

firm offer, 314

f.o.b., 323

f.o.b. the place of destination, 324

f.o.b. the place of shipment, 323

fungible goods, 324

future goods, 310

goods, 310

hybrid contract, 311

identified goods, 323

insurable interest, 327

merchant, 314

mixed contract, 311

nonconforming goods, 313

open-price terms, 314

output contract, 315

requirements contract, 315

sale on approval, 327

sale or return, 327

shipment contract, 323

tender, 323

title, 322

usage of trade, 313

valid title, 322

void title, 322

voidable title, 322

Questions for Review and Discussion

1. What are goods and what is a sale?
2. When does Article 2 of the UCC apply to contractual relationship?
3. What are the UCC rules that relate to written contracts?
4. What are the two laws that relate to cyber-sales contracts and what do they accomplish?
5. What is the difference between an auction with reserve and an auction without reserve?
6. What are valid title, void title, and voidable title?
7. When does the title to goods pass from seller to buyer?
8. When must the buyer and when must the seller bear the risk of loss?
9. What is the difference between a sale on approval and a sale or return?
10. What is an insurable interest?

Cases for Analysis

1. Brenda Brandt had a medical device implanted as part of her treatment for a serious medical condition. A charge for the device was included in the hospital bill. Later, the device was recalled by its manufacturer as substandard. Brandt had suffered serious complications, and the device was removed. She brought suit against the hospital for, among other things, breach of warranty under the Uniform Commercial Code. Was the purchase of the medical device from the hospital covered under the Uniform Commercial Code? Explain. [See: *Brandt v. Boston Scientific Corporation,* Docket No. 93982, Illinois Supreme Court (IL).]

2. Alberto Parreira, a lobsterman, contracted in writing to sell Sam Adams 1,000 pounds of fresh lobsters at a particular price during the following season. A few months later, when lobsters became plentiful and the price went down, Adams tried to get out of the contract. He argued that the contract was not enforceable because the lobsters had not yet been caught when the contract was made. Do you agree with Adams? Why or why not?

3. Harnois entered into an oral contract with Neverson to lease a compact computer and a printer for three months for $600. In an attempt to rescind the contract, Harnois claimed that the contract was unenforceable because it was not in writing. Do you agree with Harnois? Why or why not?

4. Carolina Transformer Co., Inc., brought suit against Anderson for several thousand dollars owed it for the purchase of transformers. Anderson testified in court that he had orally negotiated the contract and reached a final agreement with Carolina for the purchase of the transformers. Anderson argued, however, that he was not responsible because under the UCC, a contract for the sale of goods of $500 or more is not enforceable unless it is in writing. Do you agree with Anderson? [See: *Carolina Transformer Co. v. Anderson,* 341 So.2d 1327 (MS).]

5. Representatives of a fish marketing association (AIFMA) and a fish company (NEFCO) met at Bristol Bay, Alaska, to negotiate a marketing agreement for the forthcoming fishing season. At this meeting, NEFCO's agent, Gage, signed an agreement that contained the price that was to be paid for the fish and other details about the transaction. It omitted the quantity of fish to be purchased. Later, when suit was brought on the agreement, NEFCO argued that it was unenforceable because the written agreement failed to mention the quantity. Do you agree with NEFCO? Explain. [See: *Alaska Indus Fish Mktg. Assoc. v. New England Fish Co.,* 548 P.2d 348 (WA).]

6. Wheel Sports Center entered into a sales contract agreeing to deliver a motorcycle to Ramos for the price of $893. Ramos paid the full price for the motorcycle and immediately had it insured and registered in his name. However, before it was delivered to Ramos, the motorcycle was stolen from Wheel Sports Center. Who must suffer the loss, Wheel Sports Center or Ramos? Why? [See: *Ramos v. Wheel Sports Center,* 409 N.Y.S.2d 505 (NY).]

7. Fanning, who was 17 years old, sold her bicycle to Gerard, an adult, for $75. The next day, Gerard advertised the bicycle for sale in the classified section of a local newspaper and sold it for $150. The person who bought the bicycle was unaware that it had belonged to Fanning. When Fanning discovered what Gerard had done, she attempted to get the bicycle back from the person who bought it, claiming that Gerard had voidable title to the bicycle. Does Fanning have the legal right to the return of the bicycle? Why or why not?

8. Harold Marcus entered into a contract with Corrigan's Yacht Yard & Marine Sales, Inc., to trade in his 34-foot Silverton power boat toward a later model Mainship boat. He delivered his Silverton boat to the yacht yard at the time of the contract in November. The new boat was not to be delivered until the following April. The yacht yard sold the Silverton boat to William Heiselman soon after receiving it. When the yacht yard was unable to deliver the Mainship boat to Marcus in April, Marcus took back his Silverton boat. Who had title to the boat, Marcus or Heiselman? Explain. [See: *Heiselman v. Marcus,* 488 N.Y.S.2d 571 (NY).]

9. Eberhard Manufacturing Company sold goods to Brown Industrial Sales Company without agreeing on who would bear the risk of loss. The contract contained no f.o.b. terms. Eberhard placed the goods on board a common carrier with instructions to deliver them to Brown. The goods were lost in transit. Who suffered the loss, Eberhard or Brown? Why? [See: *Eberhard Mfg. Co. v. Brown,* 232 N.W.2d 378 (MI).]

10. Henry Heide, Inc., received a warehouse receipt for 3,200 100-pound bags of sugar that it bought from Olavarria. The corporation withdrew 800 bags of the sugar from the warehouse (where thousands of pounds were stored), but when it returned for the balance, it discovered that the warehouse was padlocked and empty. Some 200,000 pounds of sugar had mysteriously disappeared from it. Henry Heide, Inc., carried insurance for such a loss, but its insurance company refused to pay, claiming that the corporation had no insurable interest in the sugar. Do you agree with the insurance company? Why or why not? [See: *Henry Heide, Inc., v. Atlantic Mut. Ins. Co.,* 363 N.Y.S.2d 515 (NY).]

quick quiz Answers

13-1	13-2	13-3	13-4	13-5
1. F	1. T	1. F	1. F	1. F
2. T	2. F	2. T	2. F	2. T
3. T	3. T	3. T	3. F	3. F

Chapter 14

Sales Contracts Rights, Duties, Breach, and Warranties

THE OPENING CASE Round 1
The Legal CAS in Action Once Again: When Is a Sale Really a Sale?

The complex adaptive system that directs the development of the law sometimes splits hairs in ways that are initially baffling, but that ultimately develop clarity of mission and purpose. Proof of this peculiar principle can be seen in the case of *Christine Seney v. Rent-A-Center, Inc.* The case began innocently enough when the Seneys rented a bed and mattress from their local Rent-A-Center (RC) outlet. The contract gave the Seneys possession of the bed for two weeks. At that time, they could rent the bed for an additional 120 days after which they would receive title to the bed. The contract also offered an opportunity to purchase the bed at any time before the 120-day period expired. Also included were several warranties established by RC—a promise to service the bed, to fix any problems with the bed, and to provide another bed if those repairs were ineffective. Other warranties that usually flow with a sale-of-goods contract were expressly retained by RC. The contract written by RC also stated that any dispute between the lessees and RC would be submitted to binding arbitration. The bed arrived as promised, was assembled by RC employees, and was set up in the bedroom of the Seneys' son. It did not take long, about seven days, before their son was diagnosed with bed-bug bites. The Seneys complained to RC, which sent a crew out to replace the mattress. That, however, did not

work because, apparently, the infestation had spread to the bed frame. RC employees removed the bed but in doing so made the situation worse by taking the unprotected, uncovered mattress and frame through several rooms in the house, resulting in a whole-house infestation. RC paid for a partial fumigation but drew the line at a plan to fumigate the entire residence. The Seneys filed a complaint in state court arguing that RC's actions breached RC's own warranties as well as provisions of the Magnusson-Moss Warranty Act (MMWA). The case was transferred to federal court, and RC asked the federal judge to force the Seneys into binding arbitration as per the contractual arrangement. The Seneys argued that the Federal Trade Commission had set up regulations under the MMWA that forbid binding arbitration until the parties have had an informal negotiation session, which in this case had not occurred. The lower court judge disagreed and ordered the arbitration to go forward. The Seneys, however, appealed. On appeal the Seneys argued that, while the FTC does allow binding arbitration, such binding arbitration cannot be initiated until after an informal negotiation session, which never took place. The appellate court agreed with the Seneys, which should have been good news. However, the court did not stop there. It also took judicial notice of a critical legal point that neither RC nor the Seneys seem to have noticed. That point involved the funda-mental question of whether the MMWA even applies to this situation. Or to put it more bluntly: When is a sale really a sale? Stay tuned for the answer to that question. [See: *Christine Seney v. Rent-A-Center, Inc.,* No. 13-1064 (December 11, 2013) (United States Court of Appeals for the Fourth Circuit).]

Opening Case Questions

1. Is the agreement between the Seneys and Rent-A-Center a sales contract or a lease agreement? Explain.

2. What rights and duties generally go along with the buyer in a sales contract? Explain.

3. What rights and duties generally go along with the seller in a sales contract? Explain.

4. What is the purpose of the Magnuson-Moss Warranty Act? Explain.

5. If the Seneys have no warranties in relation to the bed, other than the ones given to them by RC, who does own those original warranties? Explain.

LO   Learning Objectives

1. Describe what is meant by tender of performance.
2. Outline the rights and duties of sellers and buyers in a sales contract.
3. Explain the doctrine of anticipatory breach.
4. Discuss the seller's and the buyer's remedies in case of a breach.
5. Define the term *statute of limitations*.
6. Describe the three ways in which an express warranty may be created.
7. State the requirements of the Magnuson-Moss Warranty Act.
8. Differentiate among the implied warranties of fitness for a particular purpose, merchantability, and usage of trade.
9. Explain the meaning of a warranty of title.
10. Recognize the ways in which warranties may be excluded.

14-1 Rights and Duties of the Parties

The duties of the parties to a sales contract are simple and straightforward: The seller is obligated to turn the goods over to the buyer, and the buyer is obligated to accept and pay for the goods. In addition, all parties must act in good faith, which means that they must act honestly. The court need not enforce a contract or part of a contract that it finds to be unconscionable. An **unconscionable contract** is one that gives an unfair advantage to one of the parties. Unequal bargaining power, the absence of a meaningful choice by one party, and unreasonably one-sided terms, when put together, indicate unconscionability. When disputes arise between parties who have dealt together in the past, the court often looks to their past dealings to give meaning to the disputed transaction.

When interpreting the meaning of a contract, the court may also consider any usage of trade, that is, any particular methods of doing business that are commonly used in that field, and the way that the parties have dealt with one another in the past. Although terms that are expressly stated in a contract will usually control the contract's meaning, the parties' past dealings and usage of trade are often considered to supplement or qualify the express terms. Moreover, the UCC establishes a series of rights and duties that are key elements within all sales contracts. Most of these rights and duties are based on common

UCC 1-205 (see page 922)

sense and the practicality of the commercial world. Others have been uniquely created by the Uniform Law Commission (ULC) to ensure stability in the world of sales. These rights and duties include the tender of performance, the buyer's rights and duties upon delivery of improper goods, and the seller's right to cure improper tender.

Tender of Performance

When the seller offers to turn the goods over to the buyer and when the buyer offers to pay for them, **tender of performance** occurs. It is the offering by the parties to do what they have agreed to do under the terms of the contract. Tender is necessary to test the party's

THE OPENING CASE *Round 2*
The Legal CAS in Action Once Again: Usage of Trade and Unconscionability

In the opening case, we learned the Seneys rented a bed and mattress from their local Rent-A-Center (RC) outlet. Under the agreement, the Seneys had possession of the bed for two weeks. After two weeks, they could rent the bed for an additional 120 days, and then they would receive title to the bed. The contract included a chance to buy the bed before that 120-day period ended. The agreement also listed the following warranties promised by RC: a pledge to service the bed, to fix problems with the bed, and to provide another bed if those repairs were ineffective. All other warranties were expressly retained by RC. The contract written by RC also stated that any dispute between the lessees and RC would be submitted to binding arbitration. The bed arrived as promised, was assembled by RC employees, and was set up in the bedroom of the Seneys' son. When the Seneys discovered that bed was infested with bedbugs, they complained to RC, which sent a crew out to replace the mattress. That, however, did not solve the problem, and RC employees later removed the entire bed but in doing so the whole house became infested with bedbugs. RC paid for a partial fumigation but would not pay to fumigate the entire residence. The Seneys filed a complaint in state court arguing that RC's actions breached RC's warranties as well as provisions of the Magnusson-Moss Warranty Act (MMWA). The case was transferred to federal court, and RC asked the federal judge to force the Seneys into binding arbitration as per the contractual arrangement. The Seneys refused to engage in binding arbitration before going through an informal arbitration process.

The basic duties in the agreement had been met. The bed was delivered, and the Seneys made their payments. RC also lived up to its warranties by first seeking to fix the problem bed and then by removing the bed. However, once the trouble began, other problems emerged. Note that the writing of the contract was totally within the control of RC. Note also that the terms of the agreement seem to greatly favor RC. Is this a case of unconscionability? To determine this we must ask several questions. Was the agreement negotiated in a setting in which there was unequal bargaining power? Did the Seneys have no meaningful choice in the agreement? Were the terms unreasonably one-sided? In this case, the contract was written solely by RC, which appears to give RC most of the bargaining power. However, there was nothing in the arrangement or in the agreement that forced the Seneys to agree to those terms. The Seneys had one very meaningful choice to make, that was, to enter the agreement or to walk away. The fact that they chose to enter the agreement and the fact the initial term of contractual responsibility lasted only two weeks would seem to indicate that their free choice was intact. Indeed, the only clause that seems to be a problem is the one that compels binding arbitration. The fact that such a term is common usage in the trade and the fact that the Seneys could have objected before signing the agreement would seem to indicate that this agreement is not unconscionable. [See: *Christine Seney v. Rent-A-Center, Inc.,* No. 13-1064 (December 11, 2013) (United States Court of Appeals for the Fourth Circuit).]

ability and willingness to perform his or her part of the bargain. The seller must make tender of delivery, and the buyer must make tender of payment. If one party fails to make tender and the other breaches the contract, the one not making tender cannot bring suit. To be in a position to bring suit on a sales contract, the seller of goods must make **tender of delivery**, that is, offer to turn the goods over to the buyer. Failure to make this offer is an excuse for buyers not to perform their part of the bargain.

Making Proper Tender

To make proper tender, the seller must put and hold conforming goods at the buyer's disposition during a reasonable hour of the day. Sometimes goods are in the possession of a warehouse and are to be turned over to the buyer without being moved. When this situation occurs, tender requires that the seller either tender a document of title covering the goods or obtain an acknowledgment by the warehouse of the buyer's right to their possession. In a **shipment contract**, the seller must put the goods in the possession of a carrier and contract with that carrier for their transportation. Any necessary documents must be sent to the buyer, who must be promptly notified of the shipment.

UCC 2-507 (see page 935)

UCC 2-503(1)(b) (see page 933)

UCC 2-504 (see page 934)

UCC 2-503(4) (see page 934)

Tender of Payment by Buyer

Although the seller is obligated to deliver the goods to the buyer, this obligation stands on the condition that the buyer make tender of payment, unless otherwise agreed. **Tender of payment** means offering to turn the necessary money over to the seller. Such tender may be made by any means or in any manner that is commonly used in the ordinary course of business. The seller has the right to demand payment in legal tender but must give the buyer a reasonable time to obtain it. **Legal tender** is money that may be offered legally in satisfaction of a debt and that must be accepted by a creditor when offered. Payment by check is conditional under the UCC. If the check clears, the debt is discharged. If the check is dishonored, the debt is revived. When a contract requires payment before inspection, as when goods are shipped c.o.d., the buyer must pay for them first, even if they turn out to be defective when they are inspected. Of course, if the defect is obvious, the buyer would not have to accept or pay for the goods. Payment by the buyer before inspecting the goods does not constitute an acceptance of them. Upon discovering a defect and notifying the seller, the buyer may use any of the remedies that are mentioned later in the chapter against the seller for breach of contract.

UCC 2-511(1) (see page 935)

UCC 2-511(3) (see page 935)

UCC 2-512 (see page 935)

Buyer's Rights and Duties

Except when goods are shipped c.o.d. or when the contract provides for payment against a document of title, the buyer has the right to inspect the goods before accepting or paying for them. The inspection may take place after the goods arrive at their destination. Expenses of inspection must be borne by the buyer but may be recovered from the seller if the goods do not conform to the contract and are rejected by the buyer. Goods conform to a contract when they are in accordance with the obligations under the contract. When defective goods or goods not of the kind specified in the contract are delivered, the buyer may elect to reject them all, accept them all, or accept any commercial unit or units and reject the rest. A **commercial unit** is a single whole for the purpose of sale, the division of which impairs its character or value on the market. For example, a commercial unit may be a set of articles (e.g., suite of furniture, assortment of sizes), a quantity (e.g., bale, gross, carload), or a single article (e.g., a machine) treated in the marketplace as a single whole item.

UCC 2-513 (see page 936)

UCC 2-106(2) (see page 924)

Failure of the buyer to inspect goods upon delivery results in an acceptance of the goods, even if nonconforming.

UCC 2-601 (see page 936)

CISG Article 38 (see page 988)

UCC 2-602 (see page 936)

Rejection of Goods by the Buyer

A rejection occurs when a buyer refuses to accept delivery of goods tendered. A rejection must be done within a reasonable time after delivery or tender to the buyer. After a rejection, the buyer may not claim ownership of the goods. In addition, the buyer must notify the seller of the particular defect in the goods so as to give the seller an opportunity to correct the defect. If the goods are in the buyer's possession, the buyer must hold them with reasonable care long enough for the seller to remove them.

If the seller gives no instructions within a reasonable time after being notified of the rejection, the buyer may store the goods for the seller, reship them to the seller, or resell them for the seller. In all cases, the buyer is entitled to be reimbursed for expenses. A special duty comes into existence when a buyer who is a merchant rejects goods. Merchant buyers have a duty after the rejection of goods in their possession or control to follow any reasonable instructions received from the seller with respect to the goods. If there are no such instructions, they must make reasonable efforts to sell the goods for the seller if they are perishable or threaten to decline speedily in value. Merchants who sell rejected goods are entitled to be reimbursed either by the seller or from the proceeds of the sale for reasonable expenses of caring for and selling the goods. They are also entitled to such commission as is usual in the trade or, if none, a reasonable sum not exceeding 10 percent of the proceeds of the sale. A buyer who is not a merchant has no other obligation regarding goods that are rightfully rejected.

UCC 2-604 (see page 937)

Acceptance of Goods by the Buyer

UCC 2-603(1) (see page 936)

UCC 2-603(2) (see page 936)

UCC 2-606 (see page 937)

Once goods have been accepted, they cannot be rejected. Acceptance of goods takes place when the buyer, after a reasonable opportunity to inspect them, does any of the following:

- Signifies to the seller that the goods are conforming, that is, that they are in accordance with the obligations under the contract.
- Signifies to the seller a willingness to take them even though they are not conforming.
- Fails to reject them.
- Performs any act that is inconsistent with the seller's ownership.

When the buyer accepts goods and later discovers something wrong with them, the buyer must notify the seller within a reasonable time after the discovery. The failure to give proper notice will prevent the buyer from having recourse against the seller.

UCC 2-607(3) (see page 937)

Revocation of Acceptance

UCC 2-608 (see page 937)

If a buyer has accepted goods on the assumption that their nonconformity would be corrected by the seller and the seller does not do so, the buyer may revoke the acceptance. This revocation must be made within a reasonable time after the buyer discovers the nonconformity. A revocation of an acceptance is not effective until the buyer notifies the seller of it. Buyers who revoke an acceptance have the same rights and duties with regard to the goods involved as if they had rejected them.

Seller's Rights and Duties

UCC 2-508 (see page 935)

Sellers may sometimes **cure** an improper tender or delivery of goods; that is, they may correct the defect that caused the goods to be rejected by the buyer. When the time for performance has not yet expired, the seller has the right to cure the defect and make a proper tender within the contract time. If the time for performance has expired, the seller is allowed to have an additional amount of time to substitute a conforming tender if the seller has reasonable grounds to believe that the goods that were delivered were acceptable. In all cases, sellers have a duty to notify buyers that they are going to cure the improper tender or delivery.

EXAMPLE 14-1: Cure of Improper Tender

Caravan Motel ordered 10 dozen bath towels from samples shown by Fleming Towel Company's representative. The representative made a mistake in writing up the order. As a result, the towels that were delivered were inferior to those shown to Caravan at the time the order was given. Caravan rejected them. Because the Fleming Towel Company had reasonable grounds to believe that Caravan Motel would accept the towels that were delivered, it was allowed additional time to substitute correct towels for the ones that were delivered. When it learned of the rejection, Fleming Towel Company was required to notify the motel that it intended to cure the nonconforming delivery.

The seller does not have the right to cure improper tender when a buyer accepts nonconforming goods, even though the buyer may later sue the seller for breach of contract. The seller has this right only when the buyer either rejects the goods tendered or revokes an acceptance of the goods.

quick quiz 14-1

1. According to the law of sales contracts, all parties must act in good faith, which means they must act honestly.	true | false
2. Tender of performance is the offering by the parties to do what they have agreed to do under the terms of the contract.	true | false
3. Buyers have no right to inspect goods before paying for them when they are shipped c.o.d.	true | false

14-2 Breach of Contract

Breach of contract occurs when one of the parties fails to do what was agreed upon in the contract. When this happens, the other party to the contract has specific remedies available under the UCC. All parties must attempt to mitigate the damages, that is, to keep them as low as possible.

Anticipatory Breach

Sometimes, one of the parties will notify the other party before the time for performance that he or she is not going to conform. This notification is known as *anticipatory breach*. It is a breach committed before there is a present duty to perform the contract. Under older contractual law, the injured party in such a case had to wait until the actual time for performance before bringing suit or taking some other action. It was necessary to wait for the actual time for performance to know for sure that the other party was indeed not going to perform. Under the UCC, when either party repudiates the contract before the time for performance, the injured party may take action immediately if waiting would be unjust or cause a material inconvenience. Any of the remedies for breach of contract are available to the aggrieved party, in addition to the right to suspend his or her own performance.

UCC 2-610 (see page 938)

EXAMPLE 14-2: Anticipatory Breach

The Westwell Construction Company ordered 1,000 steel I-beams to be made to order from the Anaconda Steel Corporation for use in a building that Westwell was going to begin building in six months. Anaconda Steel agreed to deliver the I-beams on or before that date. Two months before the delivery date, Anaconda Steel notified Westwell that it would not be able to fill the order. Westwell could treat the contract as having been breached and use any of the buyer's remedies that are available to him under the UCC.

Seller's Remedies

When a buyer breaches a sales contract, the seller may select from a number of remedies. Table 14-1 lists six remedies that sellers may employ when the buyer breaches. These remedies include withholding the delivery of goods, stopping the delivery of the goods, reselling the goods, recovering damages, suing for the price of the goods, and simply canceling the contract. Of the six remedies, the last one, canceling the contract, is the simplest and the most pain-free solution. However, from a financial perspective, it is often the most damaging. On the other hand, the most difficult and time-consuming is initiating a lawsuit. However, if it is handled properly, a lawsuit can be the fairest and the most effective remedy available in the law today.

UCC 2-703(a) (see page 939)

Withhold or Stop the Delivery of Goods If the goods have not been delivered, the seller has a right to keep them upon learning of the buyer's breach. If, after shipping the goods, the seller discovers that the buyer is **insolvent** (unable to pay debts), the seller may have the delivery stopped. This right is known as **stoppage in transit** and is permitted after goods have been shipped but before they have reached their destination. The seller must give information to the **carrier** (the transportation company) to satisfy the latter that the buyer is insolvent. In addition, the seller must accept responsibility for any damage suffered by the carrier for not completing the shipment. If the insolvency information is incorrect, both the seller and the carrier could be sued for damages. The seller may also stop delivery of a carload, truckload, planeload, or larger shipments of express or freight when the buyer repudiates or fails to make a payment that is due before delivery or otherwise breaches the contract. If the seller has issued a document of title, the seller can stop delivery only by surrendering the document to the carrier. If the buyer has received the document, delivery of the goods cannot be stopped in transit.

UCC 2-705 (see page 940)

Table 14-1   Seller's Remedies When the Buyer Breaches

1. Withhold delivery of any goods not yet delivered.

2. If the buyer is insolvent, stop delivery of any goods that are still in the possession of a carrier.

3. Resell any goods that have been rightfully withheld, and then sue the buyer for the difference between the agreed price and the resale price.

4. If the goods cannot be resold, sue the buyer for the difference between the agreed price and the market price.

5. Sue the buyer for the price of any goods that were accepted by the buyer.

6. Cancel the contract.

Resell the Goods The seller may resell the goods or the undelivered balance of them. In the case of unfinished manufactured goods, a seller may either complete the manufacture and resell the finished goods or cease manufacture and resell the unfinished goods for scrap or salvage value. In such cases, the seller must use reasonable commercial judgment to avoid losses. After the sale, the injured party may sue the other for the difference between what the property brought on resale and the price the buyer had agreed to pay in the contract. Resale may be a public or private sale. If it is a private sale, the seller must give the buyer reasonable notice of its intention to resell the goods. If it is a public sale, it must be made at a place that is normally used for public sales, if such a place is available. In addition, if the goods are perishable or threaten to decline in value speedily, the seller must give the buyer reasonable notice of the time and place of resale. A purchaser who buys in good faith at a resale takes the goods free of any rights of the original buyer. Furthermore, the seller is not accountable to the buyer for any profit made on the resale. The seller who chooses to do so may buy the goods at resale.

UCC 2-706(1) (see page 940)

UCC 2-704(2) (see page 940)

UCC 2-706(4)(b) (see page 940)

UCC 2-706(4)(d) (see page 940)

Damages The seller may retain the merchandise and sue the buyer for either the difference between the contract price and the market price at the time the buyer breached the agreement or the profit (including overhead) that the seller would have made had the contract been performed. In either case, the seller is also entitled to *incidental damages*. These damages are reasonable expenses that indirectly result from the breach, such as expenses incurred in stopping delivery of goods, transporting goods, and caring for goods after the buyer's breach.

UCC 2-708 (see page 941)

UCC 2-710 (see page 941)

Sue for Price The seller may sue for the price of any goods that the buyer has accepted. Similarly, upon the buyer's breach, the seller may bring suit for the price of goods that cannot be resold at a reasonable price. In addition, the seller may sue the buyer for the price of any *lost* or damaged goods after the risk of their loss has passed to the buyer. In the commercial setting this remedy is sanctioned by the Uniform Commercial Code in UCC 2-709 (1) (a). The seller who sues the buyer for the price must hold for the buyer any goods that are under the seller's control. The goods may be sold, however, at any time resale is possible before the collection of a judgment in the case. The net proceeds of any resale must be credited to the buyer. Any goods that are not resold become the property of the buyer if the buyer pays for them as a result of a court judgment.

UCC 2-709 (see page 941)

Cancel the Contract The seller can cancel the contract. This cancellation occurs when the seller ends the contract because the other party breached. When cancellation takes place in this manner, the seller may use any of the remedies mentioned for breach of contract.

UCC 2-106 (see page 924)

Buyer's Remedies

When a seller breaches a sales contract, the buyer may select from a number of remedies. Table 14-2 lists six remedies that buyers may use whenever the seller breaches the sales contract. The first two remedies are relatively clear and straightforward. The buyer either tells the seller that the deal is off or demands a repayment of any money that has already been handed over to the seller as a down payment or some other type of monetary guarantee of performance. If the seller cooperates, there is no need to go any further. However, if the seller refuses to comply, the buyer has several additional options available. These include cover the sale, sue for breach, keep the goods and seek an adjustment, or, in some rare circumstances, sue for specific performance. Of these four remedies, the last one, suing for specific performance is the most difficult and the least applicable remedy because it can only be used when the subject matter of the sales contract is something unique, such

UCC 2-711 (see page 941)

UCC 2-712 (see page 942)

CLASSIC CASE The Case of the Disappearing Delivery or the Mystery of the Missing Merchandise

Any contract that involves clothing is covered by the Uniform Commercial Code (UCC). Keep in mind, as you read this case that the commissioners who wrote the UCC did their best to protect all the parties involved in a contract, even those who might not deserve that protection. In this case, the plaintiff is a Los Angeles clothing manufacturer, and the defendant is a retailer doing business in Westport, Connecticut, as a clothing store named The Rage. The manufacturer received an order from The Rage for a shipment of clothing that amounted to $2,216. The clothing was packaged carefully and then turned over to a reputable and dependable shipper, the Denver-Chicago Shipping Company (Denver). Denver gave a bill of lading to the manufacturer, and the manufacturer sent along four separate invoices to The Rage. The invoices stated explicitly that the shipment was "F.O.B. Los Angeles," that the shipper was Denver-Chicago, and that the buyer bore the risk of loss. Moreover, the bill of lading stated quite clearly that all shipping charges would be paid by The Rage. At some point between Los Angeles and Westport, exactly where is never made clear, Denver handed the shipment off to another trucking firm, the Old Colony Transportation Company of South Dartmouth, Massachusetts. When the Old Colony truck arrived at The Rage, the driver refused to deliver the goods inside the store, preferring to deliver them outside the premises. When the store manager refused to accept the eight cartons of clothing unless they ended up inside the store, the trucker drove off, still in possession of the shipment. The clothing was never seen again. The owner of The Rage sent an immediate letter of protest to the manufacturer, which filed a claim against Denver, which Denver refused to honor. Meanwhile, in Connecticut, the owner of The Rage continued to demand that the missing shipment be delivered inside the store. Whenever the manufacturer tried to contact the owner, he was unavailable. When the manufacturer finally sued, the owner of The Rage argued that he could not possibly be liable for goods he never received. Instead, he claimed that the manufacturer is responsible for the loss of the shipment because the manufacturer chose an unreliable shipper. In turn, the manufacturer argued that, since the risk of loss passed to the retailer when the shipment was delivered to the trucker, and since the retailer refused to accept a shipment that was quite literally on his doorstep, he must pay for the eight cartons of clothing whether he actually received them or not. The court agreed with the manufacturer. To prove its point, the court referred directly to UCC 2-709, which says quite clearly, "(1) When the buyer fails to pay the price as it becomes due, the seller may recover . . . the price (a) * * * of conforming goods lost or damaged within a commercially reasonable time after the risk of their loss has passed to the buyer." [See: *Ninth Street East, Ltd., v. Harrison,* 259 A.2d 772, 5 Conn.Cir.Ct. 597 (Connecticut Circuit Court, First Circuit).]

Table 14-2 Buyer's Remedies When the Seller Breaches

1. Cancel the contract.

2. Sue the seller for the return of any money that has been paid.

3. Cover the sale, that is, buy similar goods from someone else and sue the seller for the difference between the agreed price and the cost of the purchase.

4. Sue the seller for the difference between the agreed price and the market price at the time the buyer learned of the breach.

5. If nonconforming goods have been accepted, notify the seller that they do not conform to the contract. Then, if no adjustment is made, sue the seller either for breach of contract or for breach of warranty.

6. When goods are unique or rare, sue for specific performance.

as an original work of art, or when the subject is very rare, as with an antique, a family heirloom, or a vintage automobile. On the other hand, from a financial perspective, it is often a very rewarding process for buyers because, if they are successful, they receive exactly what they bargained for in the original contract.

Cover the Sale or Sue for Breach
The buyer may cover the sale, that is, buy similar goods from someone else. The buyer may then sue the seller for the difference between the agreed price and the cost of the purchase. Cover must be made without unreasonable delay. In the alternative, when a seller breaches a contract by not delivering the goods, the buyer may sue for damages if any were suffered. The measure of damages is the difference between the price that the parties agreed upon and the price of the same goods in the marketplace on the date the buyer learned of the breach. In addition, the buyer may sue for incidental and consequential damages. Damages for breach of contract may be liquidated, that is, agreed upon by the parties when they first enter into the contract. Liquidated damages will be allowed by the court if they are reasonable.

EXAMPLE 14-3: Cover of a Sales Contract
Flamme Bros. contracted to deliver a specific quantity of corn to Farmers' Union Co-op Co., a cooperative grain elevator. When Flamme Bros. failed to deliver the corn, Farmers' Union bought corn from its members over a two-week period. The court held that this purchase was cover of the contract without unreasonable delay. Farmers' Union recovered the difference between the agreed price of the corn from Flamme Bros. and the price it paid to the farmers for the corn it bought. In the alternative, Farmer's Union could have refrained from purchasing the grain from other suppliers and simply brought a lawsuit against Flamme Brothers for damages. The damages would be measured by the difference between the price that the parties agreed upon and the price of corn in the marketplace on the date Farmer's Union learned of the breach. In addition, Farmer's Union may sue for incidental and consequential damages.

Keep Goods and Seek Adjustment
When improper goods are delivered, the buyer may keep them and ask the seller for an adjustment. If no adjustment is made, the buyer may sue the seller for either breach of contract or breach of warranty, whichever applies. The amount of the suit would be the difference between the value of the goods contracted for and the value of the goods received. Warranties are discussed in later in this chapter.

EXAMPLE 14-4: Swimsuit Adjustment
The Jacobs Brothers Department chain of Omaha ordered 40 dozen swimsuits from Illumination Encore, Ltd., a clothing manufacturer in Fort Worth. The suits that were delivered were totally different from the samples shown by Illumination's sales rep. Because the Jacobs Brothers needed swimsuits for its spring trade show, Kenneth Jacobs, the CEO of the department chain, decided to keep them. If no adjustment is made by the manufacturer, Illumination Encore, Jacobs can sue the manufacturer for damages (including loss of profits) that were suffered because of the breach of the express warranty that the goods would be the same as the sample.

UCC 2-713 (see page 942)

UCC 2-715 (see page 942)

UCC 2-718(1) (see page 942)

UCC 2-714(2) (see page 942)

UCC 2-716(1) (see page 942)

Sue for Specific Performance   When the goods are unique or rare, the buyer may ask the court to order the seller to do what he or she agreed to do under the contract terms. This request is known as an action for specific performance of the contract. A decree of specific performance, if granted by the court, would require the seller to deliver to the buyer the goods described in the sales agreement. This type of action is permitted only when an award of money will not give the buyer sufficient relief. Contracts for *objets d'art,* rare gems, antiques, and goods described as one of a kind come within the scope of this type of action. Under the UCC, the decree of specific performance may include the payment of the price, damages, or other relief as the court may deem just. Buyers have a right of replevin for goods that have been identified to the contract if, after a reasonable effort, they are unable to buy the goods elsewhere. A **writ of replevin** is a court action that allows a person entitled to goods to recover them from someone who has them wrongfully.

The Commercial Docket

UCC 2-716(3) (see page 942)

UCC 2-725 (see page 944)

Commercial cases have become so numerous recently that a few states have taken the extraordinary step of establishing a separate court docket dedicated exclusively to commercial cases. Those commentators who support establishing a commercial docket argue that commercial lawsuits can be handled more effectively if they are assigned to judges who have been trained to manage such cases. For example, the State of Ohio recently inaugurated a commercial docket program. The **commercial docket** provides a legal forum that is limited to commercial lawsuits handled by judges and mediators who receive special education sessions devoted exclusively to commercial law. To implement the system, the chief justice of the Ohio Supreme Court chose five trial courts to lead the way by establishing a commercial docket within their jurisdictions. The chief justice then assigned several judges to handle every case that fit within the commercial docket in their court. The program limits the commercial docket to cases that involve disputes among two or more businesses, although the court also handles a long list of similar lawsuits, including such things as the formation or dissolution of a business, the rights and duties of business partners, and so on. Each commercial docket judge chooses a cadre of mediators, referred to in Ohio as **special masters,** who are trained to handle commercial lawsuits. The special masters are the first line of defense on the commercial docket. They handle cases and make rulings that are then passed on to the commercial docket judge for evaluation and approval. The judge can uphold, reject, reverse, or resubmit the case to the special master. [See: Ohio Rules of Superintendence for the Courts of Ohio, Rules 49-49.12.]

A QUESTION OF ETHICS

The Science Court v. The Commercial Docket

As noted earlier, a planned court system that is similar to the Ohio commercial docket is the proposed science court. The science court would act as a forum for cases involving scientific and technological disputes. Like commercial docket judges, the science court judges would be trained to deal exclusively with cases of a scientific and technological nature. The science court would focus on disputes involving genetic engineering; nuclear energy research; cyber-contract law; energy law; cloning; engineering, architectural, and technological projects; medical treatments; medical research; environmental law; birth control; health care wills; health care power of attorney disputes; abortion law disputes; intellectual property problems; surrogate parenting; and so on. The plan is to use specially trained judges with scientific and technological backgrounds who will be equipped to handle the complexities of today's science-related cases. The science court and the commercial docket look good on paper, but what would happen were the science court judges to face ethical issues? Would they be able to deal with such issues effectively? What would happen when the jurisdiction of the science court clashed with the jurisdiction of the commercial docket? How would such disputes be resolved?

ETHICAL QUESTIONS

1. What happens when a commercial contract involves an ethically questionable scientific issue, such as cloning or genetic engineering? Who should handle such a case? The science court judges or the commercial docket mediators? Or should there be a third court for purely ethical questions? Explain.

2. What would happen with a case involving a surrogate parenting contract? Is that a job for the science court or the commercial docket? Should an ethical philosopher or a theologian be involved in making such decisions? Explain.

3. Would commercial docket judges begin to lean toward the best interests of merchants rather than the consumer? Would such a course of action be ethical? Again, should an ethical philosopher or a theologian be involved in making such decisions? Explain.

4. Would science court judges begin to lean toward the best interests of scientists and engineers rather than the public? Would such a course of action be ethical? Should an ethical philosopher or a theologian be involved in making such decisions? Explain.

5. There is also the ethical question of equal protection of the law. Does the commercial docket violate equal protection by giving a special forum to businesspeople? Explain. Would the science court violate equal protection by giving special forum to scientists and engineers? Why or why not? Who gets the next special forum? Politicians? Educators? Lawyers? Civil servants? Police officers and firefighters?

Statute of Limitations

Nearly all lawsuits have a time limit within which a lawsuit must be brought. If the time limit is exceeded, the action is forever barred. In general, an action for breach of a sales contract must be brought within four years after the date of the breach. The parties may, if they wish provide for a shorter time period, not less than one year, in their sales agreement. They may not, however, agree to a period longer than four years.

LO5

CISG Article 49 (see page 990)

CISG Articles 61–64 (see page 991)

CISG Articles 74–77 (see page 993)

CISG Articles 79 (see page 993)

CISG Articles 81 (see page 993)

CISG Articles 85–88 (see page 994)

quick quiz 14-2

1. If the goods have not been delivered, the seller has a right to keep them upon learning of the buyer's breach.   true | false

2. The seller may sue the buyer for the price of any *lost* or damaged goods after the risk of their loss has passed to the buyer.   true | false

3. When the goods are unique or rare, the buyer may ask the court to order the seller to do what he or she agreed to do under the contract terms.   true | false

14-3 Warranty Protection

Until now in this chapter, we have focused on the actual sales agreement itself. We have looked at what constitutes performance, what constitutes nonperformance, and what happens when the seller does not deliver the goods, the buyer does not pay for the goods, or the trucking company loses the goods. Now we switch focus. Instead of looking at a contract that has not been performed, we will look at contracts that have been performed—sort of. Have you ever purchased an item that turned out to be damaged or broken when you opened the box? Have you ever paid for something that you wanted for a particular purpose, only to find that it would not do the job? Has a salesperson ever made a statement or a promise about a product that did not come true? Have you ever found an impurity or a foreign substance in food that you bought in a store or ate in a restaurant? The UCC gives you protection in all these situations under its law of warranties. A warranty is another name for a guarantee. Warranties come in all shapes and sizes. Still, in one way or another, all warranties fall into one of three categories: express warranties, implied warranties, and warranties of title.

Express Warranties

An **express warranty** is an oral or written statement, promise, or other representation about the quality of a product. Express warranties arise in three different ways: by a statement of fact or promise, by a description of the goods, or by a sample or model. In states that have adopted Article 2A of the UCC, express warranties arise when goods are leased in exactly the same way that they arise when goods are sold.

Statement of Fact or Promise Whenever a seller of goods makes a statement of fact to a buyer about the goods, that seller has created an express warranty. The seller's statement is treated legally as a guarantee that the goods will be as "they were stated to be." *This guarantee exists whether the seller is a merchant or not.* If the goods are not as they were stated to be, the seller has breached an express warranty. An express warranty also occurs when a seller makes a promise about the goods to a buyer. The promise must relate to the goods and be part of the transaction. Manufacturers often include express warranties with the products they sell. They are usually found inside the package containing the product and are sometimes referred to as *guarantees*. Formal words such as *warranty* or *guarantee* do not have to be used to create an express warranty. A seller may not intend to make a warranty, but if the language used by the seller is a statement of fact or a promise about the goods and is part of the transaction, an express warranty is created. Advertisements often contain statements and promises about goods that are express warranties.

Advertising Express Warranties The Federal Trade Commission has established specific rules for advertising express warranties on goods that are sold in interstate commerce:

- An advertisement stating that a product is warranted must tell you how to get a copy of the warranty before you buy the product.
- Advertisers who use expressions such as "Satisfaction Guaranteed," "Money-Back Guarantee," and "Free Trial Offer" must refund the full purchase price of their product at the purchaser's request. Any conditions, such as those limiting the return of the product, must be stated in the ad.
- Advertisers who warrant products for a lifetime must fully explain the terms of their promises, such as "Good for as long as you own the car."

Warranties are based on statements of fact. Therefore, the opinions of salespersons and their exaggerated and persuasive statements do not create express warranties. Courts have long indulged the temptation of salespersons to use sales puffery to extol their merchandise beyond the point of fact. Buyers must use common sense to recognize the difference between a salesperson's statements of fact from statements that are opinion or puffery. Such statements as "this is the best Hi Def screen on the market" or "this GPS system is a great buy" are examples of sales talk or puffery. They are not express warranties. Such statements as "this car has never been in an accident" or "this desk is made of mahogany' are factual statements that do create an express warranty.

Descriptions, Samples, and Models

Any description of the goods that is made part of the basis of the bargain creates an express warranty that the goods will be as described. It is a common practice of salespeople to show samples of their products to prospective buyers. When a sample or model becomes part of the basis of the bargain, an express warranty is created. The seller warrants that the goods that will be delivered are the same as the sample or model.

Magnuson-Moss Warranty Act

The federal Magnuson-Moss Warranty Act is designed to prevent deceptive warranty practices and provide consumers with more information about warranties that are made on products they buy. The act applies only when written warranties are made voluntarily for purchases of consumer products. These products are defined as tangible personal property normally used for personal, family, or household purposes. Because it is a federal law, the act affects only warranties on products that are sold in interstate commerce. Under the act, when a written warranty is given to a consumer on goods costing more than $10, the warranty must disclose whether it is a full or a limited warranty. When goods cost more than $15, the written warranty must be made available before the consumer decides to buy the product. The writing must express the terms and conditions of the warranty in simple and readily understood language.

A full warranty is one in which a defective product will be repaired without charge within a reasonable time after a complaint has been made about it. If it cannot be repaired within a reasonable time, the consumer may have either a replacement of the product or a refund of the purchase price. The consumer will not have to do anything unreasonable to get warranty service, such as ship a heavy product to the factory. A full warranty applies to anyone who owns the product during the warranty period, not only the original buyer. A full warranty must also state its duration, for example, a "full one-year warranty."

A limited warranty is any written warranty that does not meet all of the requirements for a full warranty. The consumer is not given the absolute, free-of-charge repair or replacement of a defective product, as in the full warranty. Something less than a complete remedy is given to the consumer. Examples of limited warranties are those that cover only parts, not labor; allow only pro rata (divided proportionately) refund or credit in the case of a defect rather than a full refund; require the buyer to return a heavy product to the store for service; or cover only the first purchaser.

Implied Warranties

Under the UCC, an implied warranty is a warranty that is imposed by law rather than by statements, descriptions, or samples given by the seller. It arises independently and outside the contract. The law annexes it, by implication, into the contract that the parties have made. Implied warranties are designed to promote high standards in business and to discourage harsh dealings. There are three types of implied warranties: the implied warranty of merchantability, the implied warranty of fitness for a particular purpose, and the implied warranty that is derived from a course of dealing or usage of trade.

THE OPENING CASE *Round 3*
The Legal CAS in Action Once Again: Sales and Leases and the WWMA

In the opening case, we learned *Christine Seney v. Rent-A-Center, Inc.,* started with the leasing of a bed at the local Rent-A-Center (RC) outlet. Under the lease agreement, the Seneys were given use of the bed for two weeks. After that, they could extend the lease for 120 days. When that time was up, they would have title to the bed. They also had an option to buy the bed at any time during that 120-day period. In addition, the agreement also listed the following warranties pledged by RC: a promise to service the bed; a promise to fix any and all problems with the bed; and a promise to provide another bed if those repairs were ineffective. RC retained all other warranties. The contract written by RC also stated that any dispute between the lessees and RC would be submitted to binding arbitration. Unfortunately, the bed was infested with bedbugs. RC sent a crew out to replace the mattress and, when that did not work, RC employees removed the bed. However, during the removal process the entire house was infested. RC paid for a partial fumigation but drew the line at a plan to fumigate the entire residence. The Seneys filed a complaint arguing that RC's actions breached RC's warranties as well as provisions of the Magnusson-Moss Warranty Act (MMWA). The case was transferred to federal court, and RC asked the federal judge to force the Seneys into binding arbitration as per the contractual arrangement. The Seneys argued that the FTC had set up regulations under the MMWA that forbid binding arbitration until the parties have had an informal negotiation session, which, in this case, had not occurred. The lower court judge disagreed and ordered the arbitration, but the appellate court agreed with the Seneys. This ruling should have been good news. However, the court did not stop there. The judge took judicial notice of a critical legal question that neither RC nor the Seneys had asked. Did the MMWA apply to this agreement in the first place? The court notes that the MMWA applies only to contracts involving a sale. The contract in this case was not a sale. It was a lease. While it is true, the judge said, that some courts have declared that certain lease agreements are covered by the MMWA, those lease agreements are not true lease agreements. They are, instead, the economic equivalent of a sale. To be the **economic equivalent** of a sale: (1) the lessee, in negotiating the lease, must agree to pay an amount up front that is equal to the amount that a buyer would pay plus interest, or (2) the lessee must agree to a payment schedule, while also taking possession of the item. Neither of these events took place in this case. The Seneys simply rented the bed for two weeks. That was it. RC actually retained title and, along with title, all the warranties that went along with it. Certainly the Seneys had the option to purchase the bed, but they never exercised that option (and why would they, the bed was infested with bedbugs). Since they never exercised the option, the lease is not a true sale and the MMWA does not apply. Consequently, the binding arbitration clause can be activated immediately. End of issue. [See: *Christine Seney v. Rent-A-Center, Inc.,* No. 13-1064 (December 11, 2013) (United States Court of Appeals for the Fourth Circuit).]

Merchantability One of the most beneficial warranties, from the point of view of a buyer, is the implied **warranty of merchantability**. This warranty provides that, unless excluded in one of the ways discussed, whenever a merchant sells goods, the merchant warrants that the goods are **merchantable**, that is, they are reasonably fit for the purpose for which they are sold. For example, merchantability means that a lawn mower will cut grass, a sailboat will not sink, an automatic dishwasher will wash dishes, and so on. This warranty is given when the seller is a **merchant** with respect to goods of that kind. It is given by manufacturers, wholesalers, and retailers whenever they sell goods to give assurance that products sold by them are fit for the purpose for which the goods are to be used. The warranty of merchantability is not given by someone who is not a merchant. To be merchantable, goods must at least pass without objection in the trade under the contract description; if fungible goods, be of fair average quality; be fit for the ordinary purposes for which such goods are used; be of the same kind, quality, and quantity; be adequately contained, packaged, and labeled as the agreement may require; and be in conformance with any promises or statements of fact made on the container or label. A claim for breach of warranty of merchantability can be made only when a defect exists at the time the goods are purchased.

EXAMPLE 14-5: No Defect at Time of Purchase

Haven Hills Farm purchased a truck tire from Sears, Roebuck. On a trip from Mississippi to Alabama, the tire blew out, causing the truck to turn on its side, destroying 11,862 dozen eggs. At the time of the blowout, the tire was-four-and-half months old and had been driven 30,000 miles. Haven Hills claimed that Sears was liable for breach of the implied warranty of merchantability. It argued that Sears sold the tire in a defective condition. In finding in favor of Sears, Roebuck, the court held that there was no evidence of a defect in the tire at the time it left the control of the manufacturer or seller.

Fitness for a Particular Purpose

Sometimes buyers will have the seller select goods for them rather than select them themselves. They rely on the seller's knowledge and experience to choose the product after telling the seller of the particular use they have for the goods. This arrangement creates an implied **warranty of fitness for a particular purpose**. When the buyer relies on the seller's skill and judgment to select the goods, the seller implicitly warrants that the goods will be fit for the purpose for which they are to be used.

Usage of Trade

Other implied warranties may arise from the ways in which the parties have dealt in the past or by usage of trade. For example, when a person sells a pedigreed dog, there is an implied warranty that the seller will provide pedigree papers to demonstrate the conformity of the animal to the contract. The reason this implied warranty arises is that providing such papers has become a well-established custom or practice of the trade.

Warranty of Title

Whenever goods are sold, either by a merchant or a private party, the seller warrants that the title being conveyed is good and that the transfer is rightful. This warranty is known as the **warranty of title**. It includes an implied promise that the goods will be delivered free of any liens (claims of others) about which the buyer has no knowledge. When anyone buys goods that turn out to be stolen, the rightful owner will be entitled to the return of those goods. The innocent purchaser may sue the seller for breach of warranty of title. When the buyer is aware that the person selling the goods does not personally claim title to them, the warranty of title is not made by the seller. Such is the case, for example, in sheriff's sales and sales by personal representatives of estates. To recover money damages for breach of warranty, buyers of defective goods must notify the seller of the defect within a reasonable time either after the discovery or after the defect should have been discovered. Failure to do so will prevent them from recovering damages for breach of warranty.

Warranty Exclusion

To exclude the implied warranty of merchantability in states that allow it, the word *merchantability* must be used in the disclaimer. If the exclusion is in writing, it must be in large, bold type so that it is conspicuous. To exclude the implied warranty of fitness for a particular purpose, the exclusion must be in writing and also be conspicuous. A common practice in the sale of used cars, lawn mowers, electrical appliances, and similar merchandise is for the seller to stipulate that the goods are being sold as is. The use of expressions such as *as is, with all faults,* and others is another way to exclude implied warranties. However, those words do not exclude express warranties or the warranty of title. Implied warranties may also be excluded under the UCC by having buyers examine the goods. When buyers have examined the goods, the sample, or the model as fully as they desire (or have refused to examine them when given the opportunity), there is no implied warranty as to defects that an examination would have revealed. Under the Magnuson–Moss Warranty Act, any clause purporting to exclude or limit consequential damages for breach of warranty must appear conspicuously on the face of the warranty. **Consequential damages** are losses that do not flow directly and immediately from an act but only from some of the consequences or results of the act.

EXAMPLE 14-6: Consequential Damages

Souci bought a freezer made by a reputable manufacturer. The freezer carried a full one-year warranty. The following sentence appeared in boldface type on the face of the warranty: "In no event shall this company be liable for consequential damages." Shortly after buying the freezer, Souci filled it with $1,500 worth of meat. Several days later, the freezer stopped working owing to a defect in its manufacture. Under the warranty, the company would have to repair or replace the freezer, but it would not be responsible for the loss of the meat. This loss would be considered consequential damage, which the company had effectively disclaimed.

Privity Not Required

Under earlier law, warranties extended only to the actual buyer of the product, that is, the one with whom the seller had dealt or was in privity of contract. People who were injured by defective products had no remedy against the seller for breach of warranty unless they themselves had purchased the goods. Thus, if children were injured by foreign objects in food that had been bought by their parents, the children could not recover for injuries because they had not purchased the goods. The UCC has abolished the requirement of privity. Instead, it provides three alternatives from which a state may choose. In all of the alternatives, warranties extend to people who would normally be expected to use the goods as well as to those who actually buy them.

Alternative A: A seller's warranty, whether express or implied, extends to any natural person who is in the family or household of his buyer or who is a guest in his home if it is reasonable to expect that such person may use, consume, or be affected by the goods and who is injured in person by breach of the warranty. A seller may not exclude or limit the operation of this section.

Alternative B: A seller's warranty, whether express or implied, extends to any natural person who may reasonably be expected to use, consume, or be affected by the goods and who is injured in person by breach of the warranty. A seller may not exclude or limit the operation of this section.

Alternative C: A seller's warranty, whether express or implied, extends to any person who may reasonably be expected to use, consume, or be affected by the goods and who is injured by breach of the warranty. A seller may not exclude or limit the operation of this section with respect to injury to the person of an individual to whom the warranty extends.

quick quiz 14-3

1. An express warranty is an oral or written statement, promise, or other representation about the quality of a product. true | false

2. An implied warranty is a warranty that is imposed by law rather than by statements, descriptions, or samples given by the seller. true | false

3. A warranty of title means that the seller warrants that the title for the goods being sold is good and that the transfer is rightful. true | false

Summary

14.1 Sellers and buyers must follow the terms of their contract and act in good faith. Tender of performance is necessary to test the other party's ability and willingness to perform. Tender of delivery requires the seller to make conforming goods available to the buyer at a reasonable hour of the day. Tender of payment may be made by any means that is commonly used in the ordinary course of business. Except when goods are shipped c.o.d. or when the contract provides for payment against a document of title, the buyer has the right to inspect goods before accepting or paying for them. When improper goods are delivered, the buyer may elect to reject all of them, accept all of them, or accept any commercial unit or units and reject the rest. Sellers may cure defects or nonconformities that caused the goods to be rejected by the buyer.

14.2 When a buyer breaches a sales contract, the seller may withhold delivery of any goods not yet delivered, stop goods that are in transit, resell the goods or the undelivered balance of them, retain the goods and bring suit for damages, bring suit for the price of any goods that the buyer has accepted, or cancel the contract. When a seller breaches a sales contract, the buyer may cancel the contract and recover any money paid out, buy similar goods from someone else and sue the seller for the difference in price, sue the seller for damages for nondelivery, keep the goods and deduct the cost of damages from any price still due, or sue for specific performance if the goods are rare or unique.

14.3 Express warranties arise by a statement of fact or promise, by a description of the goods, and by a sample or model. Other warranties may arise from the ways in which parties have dealt in the past. When goods are sold, either by a merchant or a private party, the seller warrants that the title is good and that there are no liens on the goods. Except when express warranties are made, sellers may exclude the warranties of merchantability and fitness for a particular purpose. Such an exclusion must be in writing and conspicuous. The words *as is* and *with all faults* serve to disclaim implied warranties but not the warranty of title. Warranties extend to people who would normally be expected to use the goods as well as to those who actually buy them.

Key Terms

carrier, 338

commercial docket, 342

commercial unit, 335

consequential damages, 348

consumer products, 345

cover, 341

cure, 336

economic equivalent, 346

express warranty, 344

full warranty, 345

good faith, 333

implied warranty, 345

insolvent, 338

legal tender, 335

limited warranty, 345

Questions for Review and Discussion

1. What is meant by tender of performance?
2. What are the rights and duties of sellers and buyers in a sales contract?
3. What is the doctrine of anticipatory breach?
4. What are the seller's and the buyer's remedies in case of a breach?
5. What is the statute of limitations?
6. In what three ways can an express warranty be created?
7. What are the requirements of the Magnuson–Moss Warranty Act?
8. What is the nature of each of the following warranties: merchantability, fitness for a particular purpose, and usage of trade?
9. What is meant by warranty of title?
10. How can warranties be excluded?

Cases for Analysis

1. Kathleen Liarkos purchased a used Jaguar XJS automobile from Pine Grove Auto Sales. After experiencing various mechanical problems, she discovered that the vehicle's odometer had been turned back. Liarkos notified the seller that she revoked her acceptance of the vehicle. When is this remedy available to a buyer? [See: *Liarkos v. Mello,* 639 N.E.2d 716 (MA).]

2. P&F Construction Corporation ordered 338 door units for an apartment condominium project from Friend Lumber Corporation. The doors were delivered to the job site three weeks after they were ordered. Each door unit came wrapped in clear plastic. Three and one-half months after receiving the door units, P&F Construction notified Friend Lumber that the doors were one-quarter inch off size. P&F refused to pay Friend Lumber the balance due. What rule of law may Friend Lumber use to recover the money owed? [See: *P&F Const. v. Friend Lumber Corp.,* 575 N.E.2d 61 (MA).]

3. William Young had cut evergreen boughs and sold them exclusively to Frank's Nursery & Crafts, Inc., for 10 years. Upon receiving a $238,000 order for 360 tons of boughs from Frank's, Young obtained cutting rights from many farmers, repaired his machinery, and made 75 new hand tiers to tie the evergreen bundles. Several months later,

Frank's reduced its order to less than $60,000 for about 70 tons of boughs. Young delivered the 70 tons of boughs and sued Frank's for breach of contract. How were Young's damages computed? [See: *Young v. Frank's Nursery & Crafts, Inc.,* 569 N.E.2d 1034 (OH).]

4. Herman Googe agreed to buy an automobile from Irene Schleimer. Later, Googe changed his mind and refused to buy the car. Schleimer, without making tender of delivery, brought suit against Googe for breach of contract. Did Schleimer recover damages? Explain. [See: *Schleimer v. Googe,* 377 N.Y.S.2d 591 (NY).]

5. Mr. and Mrs. Aldridge bought a motor home from Sportsman Travel Trailer Sales, located in Texas. Two years later, after traveling more than 14,000 miles on trips to Louisiana, Colorado, and California, they attempted to reject the motor home, claiming that it was defective. Could they return the vehicle and recover damages? Explain. [See: *Explorer Motor Home Corp. v. Aldridge,* 541 S.W.2d 851 (TX).]

6. DiCintio leased for a three-year period from Adzan Auto Sales a Jeep Grand Cherokee Laredo sport utility vehicle manufactured by DaimlerChrysler. Soon after accepting delivery, the automatic transmission failed to shift gears properly, and then the

vehicle started to pull to the left while being driven, after which it began to "idle rough" and stall while stopped at traffic lights. DiCintio took the vehicle to authorized dealers for repairs on six or seven occasions, but the defects persisted. When Adzan Auto Sales refused to terminate the lease or give him another car, DiContio brought suit against DaimlerChrysler for breach of the Magnuson-Moss Warranty Act. Does DiCintio have a cause of action under this law? Explain. [See: *Mark DiCintio v. DaimlerChrysler Corporation, et al,* 768 NE2d 1121 (NY).]

7. Lohr bought a mobile home from Larry's Homes. The home was damaged during delivery and never fully set up on Lohr's property. Larry's Homes attempted some repairs, but they were insufficient. An arbitrator found that the intended repairs would not have been enough even if they had been carried out. Lohr took the case to arbitration on the grounds of a breach of the warranty of merchantability under the UCC. Does the UCC apply to this case? Why or why not? [See: *Lohr v. Larry's Homes of Virginia.* Arbitrated by McCammon Group referred out of Cumberland County Circuit Court (VA).]

8. Caswell bought a gas grill to give to his friend, Kile, as a birthday present. The grill exploded the first time it was used due to a factory defect, and Kile was injured. The manufacturer of the grill argued that it was not responsible for Kile's injuries because Kile had not purchased the grill. There was no privity of contract between Kile and the manufacturer. How would you decide?

9. Shaffer ordered a glass of rosé wine at the Victoria Station Restaurant. As he took his first sip of wine, the glass broke in his hand, causing permanent injuries. Shaffer brought suit against the restaurant for breach of warranty of merchantability. The restaurant's position was that because it did not sell the wine glass to Shaffer (only its contents), it was not a merchant with respect to the glass and therefore made no warranty. Do you agree with the restaurant? Why or why not? [See: *Shaffer v. Victoria Station, Inc.,* 588 P.2d 233 (WA).]

10. McCoy bought an antique pistol from the Old Fort Trading Post for $1,000. Later, the gun was taken from McCoy by the police when they learned that it was stolen property. The police turned the gun over to the rightful owner. McCoy notified the Old Fort Trading Post of what had happened and asked for the return of his money, but the owner of the business refused to give him a refund. What remedy, if any, did McCoy have against the owner of the trading post? Explain. [See: *Trial v. McCoy,* 553 S.W.2d 199 (TX).]

quick quiz Answers

14-1	14-2	14-3
1. T	1. T	1. T
2. T	2. T	2. T
3. T	3. T	3. T

Chapter 15

Product Liability and Consumer Protection

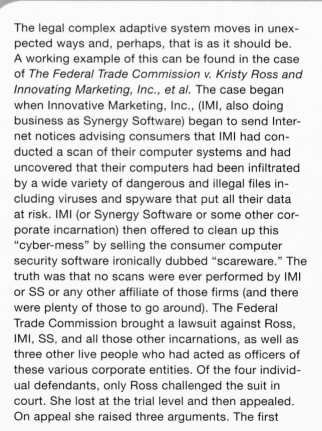

THE OPENING CASE *Round 1*
The Legal CAS as Social Engineer: Synergy Software's Sensational "Scareware" Scheme

The legal complex adaptive system moves in unexpected ways and, perhaps, that is as it should be. A working example of this can be found in the case of *The Federal Trade Commission v. Kristy Ross and Innovating Marketing, Inc., et al.* The case began when Innovative Marketing, Inc., (IMI, also doing business as Synergy Software) began to send Internet notices advising consumers that IMI had conducted a scan of their computer systems and had uncovered that their computers had been infiltrated by a wide variety of dangerous and illegal files including viruses and spyware that put all their data at risk. IMI (or Synergy Software or some other corporate incarnation) then offered to clean up this "cyber-mess" by selling the consumer computer security software ironically dubbed "scareware." The truth was that no scans were ever performed by IMI or SS or any other affiliate of those firms (and there were plenty of those to go around). The Federal Trade Commission brought a lawsuit against Ross, IMI, SS, and all those other incarnations, as well as three other live people who had acted as officers of these various corporate entities. Of the four individual defendants, only Ross challenged the suit in court. She lost at the trial level and then appealed. On appeal she raised three arguments. The first

challenged the FTC's authority and the third challenged the evidence. Neither of these is connected to our concerns in this chapter. In contrast, the second challenge is directly on point with determining responsibility for consumer fraud. In that challenge, Ross argued that she was not individually liable for IMI's deception because she lacked the authority to alter the practices complained of and that, in carrying out her duties, she was merely acting as an enthusiastic and skillful employee. Therefore, the standard that should be applied involves her authority to act. Backing up for a moment to the beginning, we find that Congress empowered the FTC to initiate a lawsuit against any individual (as well as corporations, partnerships, and so on) involved in the dissemination of false advertisements—period. Now the standard used to judge these individuals states that such officers, directors, managers, and so on will be held liable (1) if they deliberately directed or were empowered to direct the distribution of the deception *and* (2) they either knew about the deception or were "willfully blind" to it. (This is sometimes called building "plausible deniability.") Ross suggested a new standard, one that is used in securities fraud cases. That standard, she argued, reflects what actually happens in the real world of corporate activity. It takes into account the fact that officers sometimes see the big picture and enthusiastically move toward that picture, while being unaware of the day-to-day activities of their subordinates, who initiate these deceptive practices. Ross wanted to be held liable only if (1) she had the power to direct these deceptive campaigns *and* (2) had actual knowledge of their illegality. How will the court decide here? (Note: Compare the Ross standard to the standard suggested by the Supreme Court in *The Hobby Lobby Case* at the end of Part 2.) [See: *Federal Trade Commission v. Kristy Ross and Innovative Marketing, Inc., et al.,* No. 12-2340 United States Court of Appeals for the Fourth Circuit, February 25, 2014.]

Opening Case Questions

1. In what ways does the Federal Trade Commission protect consumers? Explain.

2. Should corporate officers be held liable for the deceptive practices of their subordinates? Explain.

3. What is meant by the term *willful blindness?* Explain.

4. Why would the new standard suggested by Ross weaken the power of the FTC? Or would it? Explain.

5. Why does the law have two standards for judging corporate wrongdoing, one for false advertising and one for securities fraud? Explain.

 Learning Objectives

1. Describe the link between social engineering and the law.
2. Explain the difference between public interest and public policy.
3. Explain the difference between negligence and strict liability.
4. State the purpose of the Consumer Product Safety Act.
5. Explain the enforcement of the Federal Trade Commission Act.
6. Develop a list of unfair or deceptive practices.
7. Identify several FTC rules designed to protect the consumer.
8. Identify the function of the Truth-in-Lending Act.
9. Explain the latest amendments to the Truth-in-Lending Act.
10. Explain the requirements of the Consumer Leasing Act.

15-1 Product Liability

One of the fastest growing areas of consumer law is known as **product liability**. Under product liability standards, a person harmed by a product's unsafe condition may recover damages from the manufacturer, the seller, or the supplier of the product. Product liability results from the court's willingness to react to social problems and, at times, use the law to engineer social results. Because of the court's flexibility in this regard, product liability suits can now be based on one of two legal theories, negligence or strict liability, both of which are tort actions.

Social Engineering and the Law

The German philosopher Max Weber saw the law as a combination of consensus and coercion. Consensus reveals the norms by which the people of a society live, while coercion clarifies the measures taken against those who violate the consensus. Some parts of the legal community, such as the legislature are designed to proactively shape social policy. Others, like the courts, passively deal with problems on a case-by-case basis. Still others, like the administrative agencies, operate as hybrids combining both consensus and coercion, by making regulations and then enforcing those regulations through administrative hearings or in the courts. Nevertheless, all three levels—active, passive, and hybrid—must understand consensus and must use coercion. To do this properly, the courts frequently call upon the doctrine of public policy, a concept based on the assumption that no one should be permitted to do anything that harms the public interest. [See: Gerald Turkel, *Law and Society: Critical Approaches* (Boston: Allyn and Bacon, 1996), pp. 8–9.]

Public Interest and Public Policy Public policy is not the same as public interest, although the two terms are very similar and at times are used interchangeably.

THE OPENING CASE *Round 2*
The CAS as Social Engineer: The Corporate
Veil–Protection or Deception?

Recall that in the opening case, the Federal Trade Commission brought a lawsuit against Ross, three additional officers, and a series of corporate entities. Ross challenged the suit in court, lost at the trial level, and filed an appeal. In her appellate brief she argued that she was not individually liable for the deceptive advertising campaign because she had no corporate authority to invade and change the deceptive practices and that, in exercising her official, corporate duties, she was simply acting as a passionate and practiced executive. Therefore, the standard that should be applied to her involved an examination of her authority to act. Recall that the standard that the FTC uses to judge officers, directors, and managers says that they will be held liable if (1) they deliberately directed or were empowered to direct the deception *and* (2) they either knew about that deception or were "willfully blind" to it. Ross suggested a new standard, one that is used in securities fraud cases. That standard, she argued, reflects what actually happens in the real world of corporate activity. It takes into account the fact that officers sometimes see the big picture and enthusiastically move toward that picture, while being unaware of the day-to-day activities of their subordinates, who initiate these deceptive practices. Ross wanted to be held liable only if she had the power to direct these deceptive campaigns *and* had actual knowledge of their illegality. Ross made a convincing argument, and yet the court denied her that protection. The question now on the table is whether the court was correct. This question is especially interesting, because the courts usually see the corporate veil as a way to protect officers. The courts have frequently ruled that the legal fiction of a corporation creates an entity that is separate from the founders. The

purpose of that corporate veil is not to protect the fiction of a corporate "person" but to protect the real *flesh and blood people* who own and operate it. In fact, in a recent decision known in the media as *The Hobby Lobby Case* (see the case study for Part 2), the Supreme Court said that, when the law defines the rights and duties of a corporation, it is actually defining the rights and duties of the people behind those corporations. They are the ones who must carry out corporate duties and who benefit from corporate rights. Thus, when the corporation is given property rights, those property rights really belong to the people. This is especially true when the right in question is a religious right. Thus, the court in *The Hobby Lobby Case* states, with some conviction, that the term *person* is not meant to protect corporate persons. Instead, the real protection flows to the people behind that corporate veil. Yet, in the Ross case, the court has no problem holding the executive in charge liable for the deception engineered by her subordinates (or so it seems). Is there an internal contradiction here, or is the legal CAS simply doing what it always does—adapting to a new set of circumstances that is unique and, therefore, worthy of a specialized exception? Which case is the exception—*Hobby Lobby* or *Ross*? Does the exception emerge in *Hobby Lobby* because religion is at issue or in *FTC v. Ross* because fraud is suspected? Is the ruling really fair to the defendant in the *FTC* case? [See: *Federal Trade Commission v. Kristy Ross and Innovative Marketing, Inc., et* No. 12-2340 United States Court of Appeals for the Fourth Circuit, February 25, 2014; *Sylvia Burwell, Secretary of Health and Human Services, et al. v. Hobby Lobby Stores, Inc., et al.* United States Supreme Court Nos. 13-354 and 13-356 (June 30, 2014) 573 U.S.—(2014).]

Public interest refers to the idea that certain activities affect the entire social structure and must, therefore, be regulated by the government. Public interest, then, is the equivalent of Weber's social consensus. It is in the best interests of society, for example, to have crime-free neighborhoods. **Public policy**, in contrast, seeks to implement behavior that promotes the public consensus and eliminates behavior that does not. Thus, any activity that somehow permits, encourages, or compels people to break the law and thus disrupt those crime-free neighborhoods would be against public policy and would, therefore, be outlawed. Public interest, then, is the ideal consensus, and public policy is the coercive social engineering strategy by which that consensus is implemented.

Social Engineering and Public Policy
Among the major actors in the field of social engineering and public policy are the administrative agencies. These agencies are created by the legislature and are empowered to create, enforce, and interpret regulations that carry the force of law. This legislative mandate makes these underrated and often berated agencies into hybrid operatives that use both proactive and reactive powers to engineer public policy. A case in point is the Federal Trade Commission, which shapes regulations on consumer issues and then judges whether those regulations have been followed. Often this means that the FTC will exercise a policy-making role that is just as influential as the courts and the legislature. In the opening case about *FTC v. Ross,* for instance, the FTC shaped the role of corporate officers and managers in relation to the corporate veil behind which they operate, in much the same way that the U.S. Supreme Court did in *The Hobby Lobby Case*. Nevertheless, the only case that received national attention was *The Hobby Lobby Case*. This is unfortunate because the vast majority of people do not appreciate the key role that these agencies pay in defining public interests and implementing public policy. The *FTC v. Ross* case demonstrates both functions rather well.

Public Policy and Product Liability
It is in the public interest to maintain a social structure that promotes health and safety and thus prevents illness and injury. To engineer this public interest goal, public policy promotes the making of safe products. To coerce this behavior, public policy demands that manufacturers, sellers, and distributors be held responsible for any injuries that result from their products. Therefore, public policy insists that manufacturers, sellers, and distributors compensate any innocent victim who is injured by an unsafe product, regardless of whether that victim purchased, used, or simply got in the way of that unsafe product. To meet the public interest goal of a safe society, the courts have produced two legal strategies, negligence and product liability. Nevertheless, of the two standards, strict liability is more effective in reaching that goal.

Negligence and Product Liability

One legal theory available to people who are injured by faulty products is negligence. Negligence results when an individual fails to exercise the degree of care that a reasonable person would have exercised under the same circumstances. To recover for negligence in a product liability case, the victim must prove (1) that the manufacturer or seller owed a duty to the victim; (2) that the manufacturer or the seller violated that duty by not following the appropriate standard of care; (3) that the victim suffered an injury because of that careless action; and (4) that the careless action was both the actual and the proximate cause of the victim's injury.

Strict Liability and Product Liability

The doctrine of **strict liability** holds manufacturers or suppliers liable for selling goods that are unsafe, without regard to fault or negligence. The principal consideration under the doctrine of strict liability is the safety of the product, not the conduct of the manufacturer or supplier of the goods. Under this rule, manufacturers have the duty to design reasonably safe

CLASSIC CASE Dangerous or Unsafe? One Is OK, the Other Is Not

Whether they admit to it or not, all legal professionals will, from time to time, use the law for social engineering purposes. One example of this social engineering function is found in the doctrine of product liability, and one clear example of product liability is seen in the automotive industry. *Huff v. White Motor Co.* started a trend toward a new standard of automotive product liability. Before this case, as strange as it may seem to us today, automotive manufacturers had successfully argued that "the intended purpose of an automobile does not include its participation in collisions." (Note: Exactly what this means is problematic, but let's just accept it as the standard offered by the car manufacturers and see where it leads us.) The pre-*Huff* rule stated that automobile makers had no responsibility to design and manufacture cars that would protect passengers and drivers from the effects of an accident. Since *Huff* started the ball rolling three decades ago, the courts and the legislatures have altered this standard and have declared that car manufacturers must now design vehicles that have a high level of "crashworthiness." Moreover, and perhaps more to the point, the crashworthiness standard is not based on warranties or negligence. Instead, the standard is based on strict liability. This means that the consumer in an automotive product liability lawsuit does not have to demonstrate that the manufacturer violated a warranty or behaved negligently. The simple fact that the automobile was unsafe beyond what would be expected by the ordinary consumer is enough to result in liability. Today the strict liability standard applies to all products not just vehicles. In addition, the standard extends beyond privity and can be used to hold both the manufacturer and the seller liable. Remember, though, that the law is a balancing act. The courts have also ruled, on the opposite end of the spectrum, that the manufacturers of dangerous products are permitted to promote the sale of their products even though they know that the products are dangerous (not unsafe, but dangerous; there is a difference). As long as the product itself is legal, the corporation can advertise and sell the product despite its dangerous nature. Thus, somewhere within the intangible dimension of legal niceties there exists an invisible, largely undetectable line between manufacturing products that are unsafe and selling products that are dangerous. Manufacturing "unsafe products" is wrong; selling "dangerous products" is not. As you read the rest of the chapter, see if you can detect just where that line might be drawn. [See: *Huff v. White Motor Co.,* 565 F.2d 104 (7th Cir. App. Ct 1977); David Lauter, "Automakers Face Strict Liability," *The National Law Journal,* December 21, 1981, p. 18; and Charles H. Moellenberg, Jr., and Leon F. DeJulius, Jr., "Remove the Tort Liability Muzzle," *The National Law Journal,* May 10, 2010, p. 34.]

products. They must also give proper instructions for the product's use and provide warnings of possible danger. People who are injured or suffer property damage from a defective product may recover from the manufacturer or seller only if they can prove all of the following:

1. The manufacturer or seller sold the product in a defective condition.
2. The manufacturer or seller was engaged in the business of selling the product.
3. The product was unsafe to an unreasonable degree to the user or the consumer.
4. The defective condition was the proximate cause of the injury or damage.
5. The defective condition existed at the time it left the hands of the manufacturer or seller.
6. The consumer sustained physical harm or property damage by use or consumption of the product.

The defective condition may arise through faulty product design, faulty manufacturing, inadequate warning of danger, or improper instructions for the product's use. The manufacturer's and seller's liability extends to all persons who may be injured by the product. Injured bystanders, guests, or others who have no relationship to the product, the seller, or the manufacturer may seek damages caused by defects in the offending product.

Duty to Warn Sometimes a duty is placed on manufacturers to warn consumers that harm may result from a product. Unavoidably dangerous products may require a warning to inform the consumer of possible harm. If the warning is adequate, consumers may be required to use the product at their own risk. A warning must specify the risk presented by the product and give a reason for the warning. When the danger that is presented by a product is obvious, however, no duty to warn exists because a warning will not reduce the likelihood of injury.

Punitive Damages In addition to recovering damages to compensate them for their losses, injured parties in strict liability cases sometimes recover punitive damages. These are monetary penalties imposed as a punishment for a wrongdoing.

A QUESTION OF ETHICS

Unsafe Products v. Dangerous Products

As we have seen many times throughout this text, the law is a balancing act. We have just examined how the courts have been willing (eager?) to use strict liability to hold manufacturers and distributors liable for injuries caused by unsafe products without any reference to negligence or warranties. Just how far will the courts go in this regard? What is the ultimate limit of strict liability as a coercive strategy of public policy? One answer to this question might be that there is no limit, that dangerous products, period, must be targeted by the law, at all cost no matter what. This is known as a *per se* rule. Literally translated from the Latin, *per se* means "in and of itself," and a rule that labels a product dangerous *per se* would assert that the product is dangerous in and of itself. In other words, such a product cannot be made "safe" because to make it "safe" would remove its basic function and render it useless. The prime target of the "dangerous *per se*" rule has been handguns. However, the rule could apply to any firearm or explosive device (read "bomb"). The argument goes something like this. Handguns, other firearms, and explosive devices are dangerous *per se* because their function is to kill. When a manufacturer designs, makes, and sells a handgun, any other firearm, or explosive device, that manufacturer knows that the product is designed to kill. Moreover, the only way to make a handgun safe is to render it unworkable, which makes it useless, and, therefore, is not an option. Moreover, there is no social benefit to the firearm or the explosive device that outweighs the potential harm that it can cause. Therefore, when a manufacturer places a firearm or explosive device in circulation, he or she is well aware of its potential (inevitable?) criminal use and, when such an event occurs, that manufacturer must be held strictly liable for the injuries and the harm that results—period. We will see the counterarguments to this position later in the text. For now, however, consider the "dangerous *per se*" rule and answer the following questions. [See: Donald E. Santarelli and Nicholas E. Calio, "Turning the Gun on Tort Law: Aiming at Courts to Take Products Liability to the Limit," *St. Mary's Law Journal* 14, no. 3 (1983), pp. 471–508.]

ETHICAL CONCERNS AND QUESTIONS

1. Is the function of a firearm or explosive device to kill? If you believe that the function is to kill, then what ethically justifiable reason is there for continuing to manufacture them? Explain.

2. If you believe that the function is *not* to kill, then what other ethical function does a firearm or explosive device possess? Explain.

3. Max Weber believes that the law can be used to coerce the members of a society into conforming to the general consensus. Will the "dangerous *per se*" rule eliminate killing and, thus, create crime-free neighborhoods? Explain.

4. The very first element of strict liability is that the plaintiff must prove that the manufacturer or seller sold the product in a defective condition. What is the defective condition of a firearm or explosive device that works exactly as it should? Explain.

5. What other products might be outlawed using the "dangerous *per se*" rule? Explain.

Aircraft Cases and Product Liability Despite the court's willingness to impose strict liability in product liability cases involving automobiles and despite the fact that the doctrine could easily be applied to other products, there has been a curious lack of activity in this area of the law. For example, there has been a reluctance on the part of both the courts and the legislature to apply strict liability, especially as it is expressed in the crashworthiness test, to aviation accident cases. Several reasons may explain the lack of movement in this area. One reason for this apparent inactivity is that aviation crashes are rare, at least when compared to automobile accidents. Another reason may be that most aviation cases are settled out of court before litigation even begins. However, probably the most significant reason is that aviation cases tend to be more complex and difficult than automobile cases. Typically, aviation cases will require a more in-depth understanding of and appreciation for the complexity of aircraft design and operation. It may be that product liability arguments in aviation cases will have to wait for the establishment of a science court, one version of which is discussed in two earlier A Question of Ethics features, one in Chapter 4 and the other in Chapter 14. [See: Scott G. Lindvall, "Aircraft Crashworthiness: Should the Courts Set Standards?" *William and Mary Law Review* 27, no. 2 (1986), pp. 371–408.]

The Consumer Product Safety Act

Product safety has not remained solely within the purview of the courts. Congress has also gotten into the act. In an attempt to protect consumers from dangerous products, Congress passed the Consumer Product Safety Act. The act established the Consumer Product Safety Commission (CPSC) to protect consumers from unreasonable risk or injury from hazardous products. The act covers products or component parts, American-made or imported, that are manufactured or distributed for sale to a consumer for personal use, consumption, or enjoyment. The commission can order the recall of products found to be inherently unsafe and dangerous. It has the authority to impose civil fines for violations of its standards and cease-and-desist orders. Private citizens, acting on their own behalf, may bring suit to establish or enforce a safety rule if the commission fails to act.

---

quick quiz 15-1

1. Public interest and public policy are the same thing. true | false

2. Negligence would usually be more effective as a legal theory in a product liability lawsuit than strict liability. true | false

3. In addition to recovering damages to compensate them for their losses, injured parties in strict liability cases sometimes recover punitive damages. true | false

---

15-2 Consumer Protection Laws

Consumer protection laws apply to transactions between business people and consumers. A **consumer** is someone who buys or leases real estate, goods, or services for personal, family, or household purposes. Thus, people who buy or rent things for personal use from a business are protected by consumer protection laws. However, if they buy the same things from another consumer or for business use, they are not, with some exceptions, protected by consumer protection law. State consumer protection offices provide information and help enforce state consumer protection laws. They sometimes assist consumers with individual problems. Consumer protection offices are located in state and county offices and, in some cities, the mayor's office.

Federal consumer protection law stems from the Federal Trade Commission Act (FTCA), which states that "unfair or deceptive acts or practices in . . . or affecting commerce are hereby declared unlawful." The act defines **commerce** as "commerce among the several states or with foreign nations or the District of Columbia." Thus, the act applies to businesses that sell real estate, goods, or services in interstate commerce or that somehow affect interstate commerce. **Interstate commerce** is business activity that touches more than one state. Purely local business activity, which has no out-of-state connections, called **intrastate commerce**, is not governed by the FTCA.

The Federal Trade Commission

The Federal Trade Commission Act transferred certain powers to the Federal Trade Commission, giving it the authority to oversee and eliminate deceptive and unfair practices in commerce. These powers include:

1. To conduct investigations into the practices of businesses.
2. To investigate possible antitrust violations.
3. To compel interstate businesses to file reports with the commission detailing their operations that fall within the FTC's jurisdiction.
4. To publish the results of the commission's investigation of interstate businesses.
5. To deal with disputes that emerge from the application of FTC regulations.
6. To deal with disputes that emerge from the application of federal antitrust law.
7. To make recommendations to Congress concerning new legislation.

In effect, the commission has become a coercive public policy instrument designed to promote the public interest. In doing so, the FTC must determine when a practice is unfair by balancing the harm that might affect consumers with the overall public good promoted by the activity under scrutiny.

If, after a thorough investigation, the FTC concludes that a violation of the law occurred, it may attempt to obtain voluntary compliance by entering into a consent order with the violating company. A **consent order** is an order under which the company agrees to stop the disputed practice without necessarily admitting that it violated the law. If an agreement cannot be reached, the FTC may issue a complaint. This action begins a formal hearing before an administrative law judge. If a violation of law is found, a cease-and-desist order or other appropriate relief may be issued. Consumers may bring individual or class-action lawsuits against businesses for violating FTC rules. A **class-action lawsuit** is one that is brought by one or more plaintiffs on behalf of a class of persons. Usually, a suit must be brought within one year after the violation. Alternate dispute resolutions are also available for resolving this type of problem.

Unfair or Deceptive Practices

The FTC Act prohibits unfair or deceptive practices. These practices include fraudulent misrepresentations, sending unordered merchandise, bait-and-switch schemes, and odometer tampering.

Fraudulent Misrepresentation
It is unfair or deceptive for a seller to make a fraudulent misrepresentation, that is, a statement that is designed to mislead the buyer. A misrepresentation usually occurs when the seller misstates facts important to the consumer. Making false statements about the construction, durability, reliability, safety, strength, condition, or life expectancy of a product is a deceptive practice. It is also deceptive to fail to disclose to a buyer any fact that would cause the buyer to walk away from the contract. You may see ads like the following in newspapers and magazines: "Would you like to earn hundreds of dollars a week at home in your leisure time? Many people are supplementing

their income in a very easy way. Let us tell you how. . . . " An offer like this may sound very attractive, particularly if you are unable to leave your home to work. Be cautious about work-at-home ads, especially ones that promise large profits in a short period of time. Although some work-at-home plans are legitimate, many are not. Home employment schemes are some of the oldest kinds of classified advertising fraud.

Unordered Merchandise   Except for free samples clearly and conspicuously marked as such and merchandise mailed by charitable organizations soliciting contributions, it is a violation of the postal law and the FTCA to send merchandise through the mail to people who did not order it. Similarly, it is illegal to send a bill for such unordered merchandise or to send dunning letters, that is, letters requesting payments. People who receive unordered merchandise through the mail may treat it as a gift. They may keep the merchandise or dispose of it in any manner they see fit without any obligation whatsoever to the sender. In addition, senders of unordered merchandise must attach a statement to the package informing recipients of their right to keep and use the goods.

THE OPENING CASE *Round 3*
The CAS as Social Engineer: Multiple Definitions for a Single Concept

In the opening case, we learned that the Federal Trade Commission brought a lawsuit against Ross, three additional officers, and a series of corporate entities. The case started when Innovative Marketing, Inc., (IMI, also doing business as Synergy Software) sent Internet notices that advised consumers that IMI had conducted a scan of their computer systems and had discovered that their computers had been infiltrated by a wide variety of dangerous and illegal files including viruses and spyware that put all their data at risk. IMI (or Synergy Software or some other corporate incarnation) then offered to clean up the "cyber-mess" by selling the consumer computer security software ironically dubbed "scareware." The truth was that no scans were ever performed by IMI or SS or any other affiliate of those firms. The Federal Trade Commission brought a lawsuit against Ross, IMI, SS, and all those other incarnations, as well as three other people who had acted as officers of these various corporate entities. The FTC defines fraud in the following way: "An act or practice is deceptive where: (1) A representation, omission, or practice misleads or is likely to mislead the consumer; (2) a consumer's interpretation of the representation, omission, or practice is considered reasonable under the circumstances; and (3) the misleading representation, omission, or practice is material." In the text we define fraud by noting, "It is unfair or deceptive for a seller to make a fraudulent misrepresentation, that is, a statement that is designed to mislead the buyer. A misrepresentation usually occurs when the seller misstates facts important to the consumer." In Chapter 8 we defined fraud in this way:

> To destroy mutual assent through a claim of fraud, the complaining or innocent party must prove the existence of five elements. 1. The complaining party will have to prove that the other party made a false representation about some material fact (i.e., an important fact, a fact of substance) involved in the contract. A material fact is one that is very crucial to the terms of the contract. 2. The plaintiff must demonstrate convincingly that the other party made the representation knowing that it was false. 3. The plaintiff must show that the false representations were made with the intent that they be relied upon by the innocent party. 4. The complaining party must establish that there was a reasonable reliance on the false representations. 5. The plaintiff must verify that he or she actually suffered some loss by relying on the false representation after entering the contract.

Why does the law provide three definitions for one concept (fraud)? Which definition of fraud applies in this case? Which definition is the correct definition? Which definition is the best definition? [See: *Federal Trade Commission v. Kristy Ross and Innovative Marketing, Inc., et al.* No. 12-2340 United States Court of Appeals for the Fourth Circuit, February 25, 2014.]

Bait-and-Switch Schemes

A bait-and-switch scheme is an alluring but insincere offer to sell a product or service that the advertiser does not really intend to sell. Its purpose is to switch customers from buying the advertised merchandise to buying something else, usually at a higher price or on a basis more advantageous to the advertiser. There is no question that the FTCA prohibits bait-and-switch schemes. The very nature of the strategy is to trick unwary consumers into purchasing something that they neither want nor need and that is more expensive than the original bait that snagged their interest and pulled them into the store. The statute states quite specifically that: "No advertisement containing an offer to sell a product shall be made when the offer is not a *bona fide* effort to sell the advertised product." Any of the following activities could indicate a bait-and-switch scheme:

- A refusal to show, demonstrate, or sell the product offered in accordance with the terms of the offer.
- A "put-down" of the product by the acts or words of the seller.
- Failing to have available at all outlets listed in the advertisement a sufficient quantity of the advertised product to meet reasonably anticipated demands.
- Refusing to take orders for the advertised product to be delivered within a reasonable period of time.
- Showing a product that is defective, unusable, or impractical for the purpose represented in the advertisement.

Odometer Tampering

The federal Odometer Law prohibits people from disconnecting, resetting, or altering the odometer of a motor vehicle in order to hide a vehicle's true mileage. Anyone who sells or gives away a car must provide the new owner with a written statement disclosing the odometer reading at the time of the transfer. If the seller believes that the mileage reading on the odometer is incorrect, the disclosure statement must indicate that the actual mileage is unknown. It is also a violation of the act to obtain a vehicle for resale without acquiring a finalized odometer statement from the seller. An odometer must be set at zero if it is repaired and cannot be adjusted to show the true mileage. In addition, the car owner must attach to the left doorframe a written notice showing the true mileage before the service, repair, or replacement and the date that the odometer was set at zero. It is illegal for anyone to alter or remove any such notice attached to the doorframe of a car.

Trade Regulation Rules

To correct wrongdoings in the marketplace, the FTC has also established trade regulation rules to govern the activities of interstate companies. These rules include the Used Car Rule, the Cooling-Off Rule, the negative option rule, the Mail and Telephone Order Rule, the telemarketing sales rule, and the rules connected with 900 numbers. Other rules are established by the antispam and the antislamming laws.

Used Car Rule

To remedy consumer complaints involving used car sales, the FTC established the Used Car Rule. This rule requires used car dealers to place a Buyer's Guide sticker in the window of each used car they offer for sale. The Buyer's Guide provides the following information:

- A statement that the car is sold *as is* if it is sold with no warranties. (Some states do not allow used cars to be sold "as is" by car dealers.)
- A statement that the car is sold with implied warranties only if that is the case.
- A statement telling whether the warranty is "full" or "limited" and citing the length of the warranty period if the car is sold with an express warranty. In addition, the guide must list the specific systems that are covered by the warranty and state the percentage of the repair costs that will be paid by the dealer.

- A statement that tells consumers not to rely on spoken promises.
- A suggestion that consumers ask whether they may have the vehicle inspected by their own mechanic either on or off the premises.
- A list of the 14 major systems of an automobile and some of the principal defects that may occur in these systems.
- Whenever the sale of a vehicle will be carried on in Spanish, a Spanish language version of the Buyer's Guide must be placed on the window before the vehicle is marketed.

A dealer is defined as anyone who sells more than five used cars in a 12-month period. The law covers the sale of automobiles, light-duty vans, and light-duty trucks. The Buyer's Guide sticker must be printed in black ink on a white sheet of paper that is at least $11 \times 7\frac{1}{4}$ inches in size. The guide becomes part of the sales contract and overrides any contrary provision that may be in the contract.

Cooling-Off Rule

The FTC has established the **Cooling-Off Rule** to give consumers an opportunity to change their minds after signing contracts with people who come to their houses. Under this rule, sales of consumer goods or services over $25 made away from the seller's regular place of business, such as at a customer's home, may be canceled within three business days after the sale occurs. This rule requires the seller to give the buyer two copies of a **cancellation form**, one of which the buyer may send to the seller any time before midnight of the third business day after the contract was signed. The law also applies to consumer product parties given in private homes and to sales made in rented hotel rooms or restaurants. There are, however, several exceptions to the rule. The rule does not apply to:

- Sales that are less than $25.
- Sales that involve items used for something other than personal, household, or family reasons.
- Sales that are entered completely by phone or by mail.
- Sales that begin at the seller's regular place of business and then are simply concluded at the buyer's home.
- Sales that are made under emergency conditions.
- Sales that are involved in the repair or maintenance of personal property.

In addition, the Cooling-Off Rule does not cover insurance, securities, real estate, or craft items sold at fairs, civic centers, schools, or shopping malls. Finally, the rule does not cover vehicle sales when the seller has set up a temporary location away from his or her permanent place of business. Under the laws of some states, such as New York, the three-day right to cancel does not begin until the seller gives the buyer a written notice of the right to cancel. Until such notice is given, the buyer may use any means to notify the seller of the cancellation of the contract.

Negative Option Rule

The negative option rule applies when a consumer subscribes to a magazine, or enters some other plan that sends products on a regular basis. Under such plans, the seller notifies the subscriber about the next selection before that selection is shipped. If the subscriber does nothing, the seller will ship the selection automatically. If the subscriber does not want the selection, he or she must tell the seller not to send the item before an agreed to deadline. The negative option rule does not outlaw such agreements but it does demand that sellers tell subscribers:

- The number of selections they must purchase, if any.
- The circumstances under which they can withdraw their membership.
- The notification process used to opt out of a selection.
- The timing for the return of the negative option cancellation forms.

- The circumstances under which subscribers qualify for credit in a return.
- The technique for determining postage and handling costs.
- The timing of each selection announcement.

The negative option rule does not apply to continuity plans. Under a **continuity plan**, the seller ships the goods to the subscriber on a regular basis without first sending an announcement of the upcoming delivery. While the negative option rule does not limit the use of such continuity plans, they are regulated by standard consumer protection rules. This means that the seller must notify the subscriber of all terms and conditions in a clear and unambiguous way.

The Mail and Telephone Order Rule

The FTC has established a rule to protect consumers who order goods by mail, telephone, Internet, or fax machine. Under the **Mail and Telephone Order Rule**, sellers must ship orders within the time promised in their advertisements. If no time period is promised, sellers must either ship the order within 30 days or send the consumer an option notice. The option notice informs consumers of any shipping delay and gives them a chance to cancel and receive a refund. Instructions on how to cancel orders must be included in the notice. In addition, the seller must provide a free means for consumers to reply.

Telemarketing Sales Rule

The FTC's Telemarketing Sales Rule is designed to protect consumers from abusive and unscrupulous telemarketers. The rule has established the *Do Not Call Registry* (see Figure 15-1) that makes it easier for consumers to reduce or eliminate unwanted sales calls. Under the Telemarketing Sales Rule:

- It is illegal for a telemarketer to call a consumer if the consumer has asked not to be called.
- Calling times are restricted to the hours between 8:00 A.M. and 9:00 P.M.
- Telemarketers must tell the consumer that it is a sales call, the name of the seller, and what they are selling before they make their pitch. If it is a prize promotion, they must tell the consumer that no purchase or payment is necessary to enter or win.
- It is illegal for telemarketers to misrepresent any information, including facts about their goods or services, earnings potential, profitability, the risk or liquidity of an investment, or the nature of a prize in a prize-promotion scheme.
- Before consumers pay, telemarketers must tell them the total cost of the products or services offered and any restrictions on getting or using them or that a sale is final or nonrefundable.

Consumers who have the slightest doubt about a telephone offer should ask for written information about the product, service, investment opportunity, or charity that is the subject of the call. They should resist high-pressure sales tactics and talk to a family member or friend before responding to the call. Consumers should never give out their bank account or credit card number to anyone who calls them. Similarly, they should never send money by courier, overnight delivery, or wire to anyone who insists on immediate payment.

900-Telephone Number Rules

Telemarketers sometimes use 900 telephone numbers as part of their strategy, because the consumer, rather than the seller, pays the phone charge. To combat the abusive use of 900 telephone numbers, the Federal Trade Commission has established a series of 900-Telephone Number Rules. These rules require telemarketers who use 900 numbers to warn callers of the cost of the calls and to give those callers a chance to hang up before being charged. Under the rules, customers are also permitted to ask telephone companies to block all 900-prefix number calls. In addition, the rules require telephone companies to send customers pay-per-call disclosure statements. The FTC also prohibits the use of any prefix other than 900 as a pay-per-call service. Moreover, the FTC will not permit

**NATIONAL
DO NOT CALL
REGISTRY**

Place your telephone number on the National Do Not Call Registry by calling toll-free 1-888-382-1222 (TTY: 1-866-290-4236) or going online to donotcall.gov. Registration is free.

Placing your telephone number on the Do Not Call Registry will stop all telemarketing calls except those from political organizations, charities, and people making surveys. You can expect fewer calls within three months of the date you sign up for the registry. Your number will stay in the registry for five years, until it is disconnected, or until you delete it from the registry. You may renew your registration after five years.

Telemarketers are required to search the registry every three months and avoid calling any phone numbers that are on the registry.

If you receive telemarketing calls after you have registered your telephone number and it has been in the registry for three months, you can file a complaint at donotcall.gov or by calling toll-free 1-888-382-1222 (TTY: 1-866-290-4236). You will need to provide the date of the call and the name or phone number of the company that called you. Telemarketers who disregard this law can be fined up to $11,000 for each call they make.

Figure 15-1 Once your number is registered, it will remain in the National Do Not Call Registry for five years.

telephone companies to disconnect phone service to customers who refuse to pay for 900-number calls. Finally, the FTC has established a series of rules for resolving billing disputes.

AntiSpam Law The **Can Spam Act** is an attempt by the federal government to reduce the use of unsolicited commercial e-mail, commonly known as **spam**, on the Internet. Under the law, unsolicited commercial e-mail messages must be truthful and cannot use misleading subject lines or incorrect return addresses. E-mail containing pornography must be specifically labeled in the subject line. In addition, spammers cannot harvest e-mail addresses from chat rooms and other sites without permission. The rule has also been amended to include messages that are intended for mobile phones, provided that a domain name is used as part of the Internet address. This ban does not include short phone-to-phone messages

AntiSlamming Law The illegal practice of changing a consumer's telephone service without permission is referred to as **slamming**. New consumer protection rules created by the Federal Communications Commission (FCC) provide a remedy for consumers who have been slammed. With these rules, the FCC has taken the profit out of slamming and protected consumers from illegal charges.

Cyber-law Developments and Updates

Cyber-commerce (computer commerce, electronic commerce, or e-commerce) involves transacting business by computer. One of the most common cyber-commerce techniques involves buying and selling directly on the Internet by accessing a company's website. One problem associated with buying and selling on the Internet involves the difficulty of verifying the identity of the party on the other side of an Internet connection. These problems have been exacerbated by the pervasive presence of handheld mobile computers such as smartphones and tablets. Two recent developments in this area involve the FTC's Children's Online Privacy Protection Rule and the Identity Theft and "Reclaim Your Name" Proposal.

Revised Children's Online Privacy Protection Rule The Children's Online Privacy Protection Rule (COPPR) has been part of the culture at the FTC since 1998 when the Children's Online Privacy Protection ACT (COPPA) was first made law. The rule mandates that website operators who have children (12 years old or younger) as their target market or who are aware that, as part of their website operation, children will provide them with personal data must inform parents and obtain consent before they are permitted to do anything with that data. The goal is to protect children and to keep the data collected from them confidential. As often happens, the rule has been updated, including a revision and an expansion of the rules for defining what is meant by personal data in relation to children. In an effort to keep pace with technology, personal data now includes information involving personal identifiers such as photos, videos, audio recordings, geolocation information, and cookies that track a child's online history. The FTC has also continued its safe harbor provisions that permit specific organizations to develop self-compliance programs. The FTC has also made available two documents designed to spread the word about the COPPA and its policies. The first document was written to help small businesses protect the privacy of the children that they deal with online. The second is designed to help parents keep up to date on COPPA protection methods for children operating online. [See: Jay Mayfield, "Revised Children's Online Privacy Protection Rule Goes Into Effect Today," Federal Trade Commission, July 1, 2013.]

Identity Theft and the "Reclaim Your Name" Program

In identity theft, a perpetrator uses an electronic system or technique to steal credit card information, PINs, financial data, access codes, passwords, or debit card information. The perpetrator then passes himself or herself off as the victim. Using this technique, the identity thief can clean out bank accounts, run up credit card debt, divert cash transfers, buy and sell stocks, enter electronic auction networks, approve or cancel shipments, make or revoke hotel and travel reservations, and disrupt the financial and the personal life of the victim. To combat identity theft the FTC is exploring the initiation of a new program titled, "Reclaim Your Name," which is designed to help consumers obtain the electronic ability to monitor the use of their own personal data. The goal of the program is to empower consumers with the ability to determine when and where to share information about their personal lives, finances, employment, buying habits, bank accounts, and so on. [See: Commissioner Julie Brill, "Keynote Address: Reclaim Your Name," 23rd Computers Freedom and Privacy Conference, Washington, D.C., June 26, 2013.]

State Consumer Law Developments and Updates

Most states have enacted statutes that supplement and enhance federal consumer protection laws. The Uniform Law Commission has helped in this regard by enacting a model law known as the Uniform Consumer Sales Practices Act (UCSPA), the purpose of which is to help states make adjustments to their own individual codes. State legislatures are free to adopt these statutes without change. Nevertheless, some states fashion their own statutes and others supplement the UCSPA with their own provisions that deal with some of the more troublesome aspects of consumer fraud in their own states.

Uniform Consumer Sales Practices Act

The Uniform Law Commission (ULC), which is also known as the National Conference of Commissioners of State Laws (NCCUSL), writes model laws that states are free to adopt. The ultimate goal is to develop a network of laws that are as similar as possible from state to state. As noted above, one such uniform law is the Uniform Consumer Sales Practices Act. The goal of this act is to streamline, refine, and update state statutes that regulate consumer sales contracts. The act is also designed to shield innocent buyers from unscrupulous sellers who engage in fraudulent practices. On the proactive side, the uniform law is also designed to foster the expansion of honest, impartial, and just sales techniques. Finally, the act is aimed at establishing a uniform set of laws that coordinate state laws with federal laws and state laws with one another. [See: Uniform Law Commission, Uniform Consumer Sales Practices Act, Legislative Fact Sheet and Final Act (2014).]

State Law Innovations States are free to add, reject, ignore, or modify the Uniform Consumer Sales Practices Act. Most modifications are made to address issues that are peculiar to individual states. Some states, for example, have crossed from civil to criminal law and have authorized the state attorney general to investigate consumer fraud that is criminal in nature. Sometimes these provisions permit the use of civil and administrative subpoenas in the investigative stage of any consumer fraud case. Some states have added their own cyber-law provisions that are aimed at investigating such things as telemarketing and telecommunications fraud. On the other side of the coin, some states have tried their best to balance the scales by providing some assistance to sellers, especially after a lawsuit has been initiated. One such measure might permit a seller who has been sued to offer a "cure" that will satisfy the consumer without having to go through a long and arduous legal battle. [See: Melissa Szozda, "ID Theft, Economic Crimes, and Case Updates," *Consumer Law,* Ohio State Bar Association (July 31, 2013); Helen M. MacMurray, "CSPA Right to Cure: Ohio's New Statutory Tool," *Consumer Law,* Ohio State Bar Association (July 31, 2013).]

State Lemon Laws State legislatures have also attempted to protect consumers from products that are so badly flawed that they are virtually worthless. State **lemon laws** will compensate buyers for losses that result from such defective products. Some states have statutes that force sellers to give the buyer his or her money back. Other states have lemon laws that compel the manufacturer to admit to the defect and provide the consumer with a substitute product or its equivalent. At the heart of any lemon law is the manufacturer's violation of warranty. Although when most people think of lemon laws they focus on automobiles, most lemon laws involve other products too, usually appliances, machinery, and other vehicles.

---

quick quiz 15-2

1. A consumer is someone who buys or leases real estate, goods, or services for personal, family, or household purposes.   true | false

2. The Federal Trade Commission Act transferred certain powers to the Federal Trade Commission, giving it the authority to oversee and eliminate deceptive and unfair practices in commerce.   true | false

3. To correct wrongdoings in the marketplace, the FTC has established trade regulation rules that must be followed by companies that transact business only in intrastate commerce.   true | false

---

15-3 Consumer Credit Laws

Most consumers today rely heavily on credit card transactions. For this reason, Congress has enacted several consumer credit protection laws.

Consumers need just as much protection (some experts would argue more protection) in their credit transactions as in their consumer product contracts. Most Americans use credit cards as a matter of course on a daily basis, almost without thinking about it. In addition, the average American makes an installment payment on a car loan (perhaps even two) every month, almost as if it were a civic duty, like paying taxes or voting. Due to this extensive use of credit, Congress has found it necessary to pass federal laws to protect the consumer.

The Federal Truth-in-Lending Act

Because lending institutions and businesses charge different rates of interest to consumers, it often pays to shop around before borrowing money or buying on credit. To help consumers know the truth about the cost of borrowing money, Congress passed the Truth-in-Lending Act. Under this act, lenders must disclose two important things to borrowers: the **finance charge** (the actual cost of the loan in dollars and cents) and the **annual percentage rate (APR)** (the true rate of interest of the loan). With this information, consumers can compare the cost of loans from different lenders before deciding from which to borrow. Surprisingly, the APR sometimes turns out to be greater than it would appear at first glance.

EXAMPLE 15-1: True Rate of Interest

Hana borrowed $100 for one year and agreed to pay a finance charge of $10. If she kept the $100 for the year and at the end of the year paid back the full amount, together with the $10 finance charge, the APR would be 10 percent. If, however, she paid the $110 in 12 monthly installments of $9.17 each, the APR would be 18 percent. The latter rate is higher because during the course of the year, she would have the use, on the average, of only about half of the $100.

Equal Credit Opportunity

The Equal Credit Opportunity Act was passed by Congress, as amendment to the Truth-in-Lending Act, to ensure that all consumers are given an equal chance to receive credit. The law makes it illegal for banks and businesses to discriminate against credit applicants because of their sex, race, marital status, national origin, religion, or age or because they get public assistance income. The law must be followed by anyone who regularly extends credit, including banks, credit unions, finance companies, credit card issuers, and retail stores. Some of the rights to consumers under the act are as follows:

1. People who apply for credit may not be asked to reveal their sex, race, national origin, or religion; whether they are divorced or widowed; their marital status, unless they are applying for a joint account or a secured loan; information about their spouse, except in community property states, unless the spouse is also applying for credit or will use the account; their plans for having or raising children; and whether they receive alimony, child support, or separate maintenance payments if they will not be relying on that income.

2. When deciding to extend credit, creditors must not consider the applicant's sex, marital status, race, national origin, or religion; consider the applicant's age, unless the applicant is a minor or is considered favorably for being over 62; refuse to consider public assistance income in the same manner as other income; and refuse to consider income from part-time employment, pensions, or retirement programs.

3. Applicants may apply for credit under the name given to them at birth, their married name, or a combination of both. They may receive credit without a cosigner if they meet the creditor's standards. In addition, applicants have a right to know within 30 days whether their application for credit has been accepted or rejected. If rejected, they have a right to know the reasons for the rejection within 60 days.

Unauthorized Use of Credit Cards

Sometimes credit cards are lost, stolen, or used by people who have no authority to use them. Under the Truth-in-Lending Act, credit cardholders are not responsible for any unauthorized charges made after the card issuer has been notified of the loss, theft, or possible unauthorized use of the card. Such notice may be given to the card issuer by telephone, letter, or any other means. Even then, credit cardholders are responsible only for the first $50 of any unauthorized charges. Debit cards do not have this built-in protection. The credit cardholder can avoid the $50 liability if the credit card issuer has not included on the card a method to identify the user of the card, such as a signature, a photograph, or other means of identification. Card issuers must notify cardholders in advance of the potential $50 liability. As an amendment to the Truth-in-Lending Act, Congress recently launched the Consumer Financial Protection Bureau, a new federal office that is deigned to act as a watchdog in the credit industry.

Fair Credit Reporting

The Fair Credit Reporting Act was passed by Congress to ensure that consumers are treated fairly by credit bureaus and consumer reporting agencies. A consumer has the right to know all information (other than medical information) that is in his or her files. A consumer also has the right to know, in most cases, the source of the information on file. In addition, a consumer has the right to be told the name of anyone who received a credit report in the past year (or two years if the credit report relates to a job application). If errors are found, credit bureaus must investigate and then correct or delete information that is inaccurate, incomplete, or obsolete. If the credit bureau retains information that the consumer believes to be incorrect, the consumer's version of the facts must be inserted in the file. Also, creditors are required to tell consumers the specific reasons for the denial of credit.

Billing, Collecting, and Leasing

Even with all of the consumer protection laws outlined above, there are still a variety of ways in which consumers can be victimized. The last of these areas include billing, collecting, and leasing. In billing, retail stores, credit card companies, and other businesses that extend credit sometimes make billing errors that threaten the reputation and the credit record of innocent consumers. To make it easier for billing errors to be corrected, Congress has passed the Fair Credit Billing Act (FCBA). Improper collection procedures can also hassle innocent consumers. Under the Fair Debt Collection Practices Act, specific rules must be followed by companies that are in the business of collecting debts for others. Finally, consumers who must rent or lease products sometimes find themselves victimized by unscrupulous leasing companies. The Consumer Leasing Act is a federal law requiring leasing companies to inform consumers of all of the terms of a lease of personal property.

The Fair Credit Billing Act
Under the Fair Credit Billing Act (FCBA), when consumers believe an error has been made in a bill, they must notify the creditor within 60 days after the bill was mailed. The notice must identify the consumer and give the account number, the suspected amount of error, and an explanation of why the consumer believes there is an error. The creditor must acknowledge the consumer's notice within 30 days. Then, within 90 days, the creditor must conduct an investigation and either correct the mistake or explain why the bill is believed to be correct. Another provision of the act gives consumers protection when they buy unsatisfactory goods or services with credit cards. If a consumer has a dispute with a credit card purchase, the consumer can disregard the bill for the disputed item and, instead, notify the credit card issuer of the error by telephone. The credit card issuer will put the disputed amount on hold and send the consumer a form to fill out explaining the dispute. The credit card issuer will attempt to resolve the dispute and inform the consumer of the results. Then, if the problem is not corrected and suit is brought by the credit card issuer, the consumer may use as a defense the fact that unsatisfactory goods or services were received. For this law to apply, the initial transaction must have taken place in the consumer's state or within 100 miles of the consumer's mailing address. Creditors may not give cardholders a poor credit rating for exercising their rights under this act.

Fair Debt Collection Practices

Under the Fair Debt Collection Practices Act, specific rules must be followed by companies that are in the business of collecting debts for others. Some of these rules are as follows:

1. When trying to locate someone, a debt collector may not communicate by postcard or tell others that the consumer owes money.

2. When the debt collector knows that the consumer is represented by an attorney, the debt collector may communicate only with the attorney.

3. A debt collector may not communicate with the consumer at any unusual or inconvenient time or place. Unless there are circumstances to the contrary, the convenient time for communicating with a consumer is between the hours of 8:00 A.M. and 9:00 P.M.

4. A debt collector may not communicate with the consumer at the consumer's place of employment if the debt collector knows that the employer prohibits such communication.

Under the Fair Debt Collection Practices Act, debt collectors must follow strict guidelines when contacting consumers.

5. A debt collector may not communicate, in connection with the collection of a debt, with any person other than the consumer, the consumer's attorney, the creditor's attorney, or a consumer reporting agency.

6. If a consumer notifies a debt collector in writing that the consumer refuses to pay the debt or wishes the debt collector to cease further communication, the debt collector must cease communication, except to notify the consumer of a specific action.

7. Debt collectors may not harass consumers or use abusive techniques to collect debts. The use or threatened use of violence or other criminal means to harm the person, property, or reputation of consumers is not allowed. In addition, debt collectors may not use obscene or profane language or publish a list of those who allegedly refuse to pay debts. It is also illegal for a debt collector to cause a telephone to ring or to engage in repeated telephone conversations with the intent to annoy the consumer.

Debt collectors who violate this law may be sued for actual damages, punitive damages, and attorneys' fees.

The Consumer Leasing Act

The Consumer Leasing Act is a federal law requiring leasing companies to inform consumers of all of the terms of a lease of personal property. Consumers can use the information to compare one lease with another or the cost of leasing with the cost of buying the same property. The law applies only to personal property leased by an individual for a period of more than four months for personal, family, or household use. It does not cover daily or weekly rentals, leases for apartments or houses, or leases to anyone for business purposes.

EXAMPLE 15-2: Businesses Not Protected

Guzman decided that her business could be managed much more efficiently if it had a computer. The cost of buying a computer, however, was more than Guzman could afford. She considered leasing one. The Consumer Leasing Act would not apply to Guzman's lease because the computer was for business rather than personal use. She would be able to make a better decision, however, if she asked the leasing company for the same information the company would be required to provide to a consumer.

The law requires that consumers be given a written statement informing them of the full cost of the lease, including the cost of any necessary licenses, taxes, or other fees. Consumers must be informed of any insurance requirements and penalties for late payment. They must also be told who is responsible for maintaining and servicing the property. In addition, they must be told whether they can buy the property and, if so, when and at what price. The law also places a limit on the amount of a **balloon payment** (a very large final payment) to no more than three times the average monthly payments. Advertisements of leases are also regulated by law. If an advertisement mentions the amount or number of payments, specifies a particular down payment, or states that no down payment is required; it must also disclose the total of regular payments, the consumer's responsibility at the end of the lease, and whether the consumer may purchase the property.

---

quick quiz 15-3

1. Under the terms of the Truth-in-Lending Act. Lenders need disclose only things to the finance charge to lenders. true | false

2. If a credit card or a debit card is lost, the cardholder is responsible only for the first $50 of any unauthorized charges. true | false

3. Debt collectors who violate the Fair Debt Collection Practices cannot be sued. true | false

---

Summary

15.1 Public interest refers to the idea that certain activities affect the entire social structure and must, therefore, be regulated by the government. Public policy, in contrast, seeks to implement behavior that promotes the public consensus and eliminates behavior that does not. Both concepts are inherent within the legal doctrines of product liability. Under the theory of product liability, a buyer or user of a product who is injured because of the product's unsafe or defective condition may recover damages from the manufacturer, the seller, or the supplier of the goods. Product liability suits can now be based on one of two legal theories, negligence or strict liability, both of which are tort actions. Public policy has not remained solely within the purview of the courts. Congress has also entered the product safety arena by establishing the Consumer Product Safety Commission (CPSC) to protect consumers from unreasonable risk or injury from hazardous products.

15.2 The Federal Trade Commission Act gave the Federal Trade Commission (FTC) the authority to oversee and eliminate deceptive and unfair practices in commerce. The FTC and the courts have determined that certain activities are unfair or deceptive. They include

fraudulent misrepresentations, sending unordered merchandise, bait-and-switch schemes, and odometer tampering. To correct wrongdoings in the marketplace, the FTC has also established trade regulation rules to govern the activities of interstate companies. These rules include the Used Car Rule, the Cooling-Off Rule, the negative option rule, the Mail and Telephone Order Rule, the telemarketing sales rule, and the rules connected with 900 numbers. Other rules are set up by the antispam law and the antislamming law.

15.3 Under the Truth-in-Lending Act, lenders must disclose the true nature of finance charges and the annual percentage rate. The Equal Credit Opportunity Act ensures that all consumers have an equal chance to receive credit. The Fair Credit Reporting Act guarantees fair treatment by credit bureaus and consumer reporting agencies. Under the Truth-in-Lending Act, credit card holders are not responsible for any unauthorized charges made after the card issuer has been notified of the loss, theft, or possible unauthorized use of the card. The Fair Credit Reporting Act promises that consumers will be treated fairly by credit bureaus and consumer reporting agencies. To make it easier to correct billing errors,

Congress has passed the Fair Credit Billing Act (FCBA). Under the Fair Debt Collection Practices Act, specific rules must be followed by companies that are in the business of collecting debts for others. The Consumer Leasing Act requires leasing companies to inform consumers of all of the terms of a lease of personal property.

Key Terms

Questions for Review and Discussion

1. What is the link between social engineering and the law?
2. What is the difference between the public interest and public policy?
3. What is the difference between negligence and strict liability?
4. What is the purpose of the Consumer Product Safety Act?
5. How is the Federal Trade Commission Act enforced?
6. What are some unfair or deceptive practices?
7. What are the FTC rules designed to protect the consumer?
8. What is the function of the Truth-in-Lending Act?
9. What are some of the latest amendments to the Truth-in-Lending Act?
10. What is required by the Consumer Leasing Act?

Cases for Analysis

1. Paul and Cynthia Vance invited Carl and Jeanne Leichtamer to go for a ride in the Vances' four-wheel-drive Jeep at an "off the road" recreation facility called the Hall of Fame Four-Wheel Club. The club had been organized by a Jeep dealer who showed films to club members of Jeeps traveling in hilly country. This activity was coupled with a national advertising program of American Motor Sales Corporation encouraging people to buy Jeeps that could drive up and down steep hills. As the Jeep went up a 33-degree sloped, double-terraced hill, it pitched over from front to back and landed upside-down. The Vances were killed, and the Leichtamers were severely injured. The Jeep was equipped with a factory-installed roll bar attached to the sheet metal that housed the rear wheels. When the vehicle landed upside down, the flat sheet metal gave way, causing the roll bar to move forward and downward 14 inches. The Leichtamers argued that the weakness of the sheet metal housing upon which the roll bar had been attached was the cause of their injuries. The manufacturer claimed that the roll bar was provided solely for side-roll protection, not pitch over, as occurred in this case. Did the Leichtamers recover against the manufacturer on a theory of strict liability? Why or why not? [See: *Leichtamer v. American Motors Corp.,* 424 N.E.2d 568 (OH).]

2. Michael P. Babine was injured when he was thrown from an "El Toro" mechanical bull that he rode at a nightclub. The club had placed mattresses around the bull to cushion the fall of riders, but the mattresses were not adequately pushed together. Babine was thrown off during his ride and hit his head on the floor where there was a gap between the mattresses. Before riding the bull, Babine had

signed a form releasing the nightclub from liability for injuries sustained from the activity. The mechanical bull had been manufactured for the purpose of being a training device for rodeo cowboys, and it was purchased second-hand by the nightclub. Babine sought to recover damages from the manufacturer under the theory of product liability. Did he succeed? Why or why not? [See: *Babine v. Gilley's Bronco Shop, Inc.,* 488 So.2d 176 (FL).]

3. Harriet Glantz lost her job. She was unable to find work for several months and fell behind in the payment of her debts. A debt collector telephoned her at 11:45 P.M., used profanity, and threatened to "take care of her" if she didn't pay the amount owed. Were Glantz's rights violated? Explain.

4. Ingram went to a used car lot in a large city and bought a used car. On his way home from the lot, the engine stopped running in the car he had just purchased. The used car lot refused to fix the car because the salesperson had written "as is" on the sales slip. Ingram had not been informed that the car was sold to him as is. Was a consumer protection law violated? Explain.

5. Prior to his marriage, Edward Garber had been in financial difficulty and had a poor credit rating. His wife, Natalie, applied for a credit card in her family name, fearing that she would be turned down if she used her married name of Garber. She was told that she must use her married name on a credit application. Could Natalie have used her family name when she applied for credit? Explain.

6. Horack bought a used Mustang from a used car lot. The odometer showed that the car had been driven only 30,000 miles. Later, while cleaning her car, Horack found a service receipt showing that the actual mileage on the car a year earlier was 45,000 miles. Was a law violated? Explain.

7. Carboni's MasterCard bill contained several charges that she had not made. Upon investigation, she discovered that her credit card was missing from her wallet. She immediately notified the bank

of the lost credit card. The unauthorized charges on the bill that she received amounted to $375. Did Carboni have to pay the full amount of the bill? Explain.

8. Delores Bierlein paid a $200 deposit toward the rental of the Silver Room at Alex's Continental Inn for her wedding reception. Later, Bierlein canceled the reception because her fiancé was transferred from Ohio to New York. The inn refused to refund Bierlein's deposit. The consumer protection law of that state requires suppliers to furnish receipts when they receive deposits. Bierlein was not given a receipt for her $200 deposit. When she sued for the return of the $200, the question arose as to whether this transaction fell within the consumer protection law. Do you think it does? Explain. [See: *Bierlein v. Alex's Continental Inn, Inc.,* 475 N.E.2d 1273 (OH).]

9. In response to a radio advertisement, Mr. and Mrs. Lancet telephoned Hollywood Decorators, Inc., and arranged for Mr. Wolff, a company representative, to visit their home. During Wolff's visit, the Lancets signed a contract for interior decoration and paid a $1,000 deposit. Two days later, the Lancets canceled the contract by telephone and asked for the return of their deposit. Twelve days after that, the Lancets' attorney wrote a letter to the company renewing the cancellation. Were they bound by the contract they signed? Why or why not? [See: *Hollywood Decorators, Inc., v. Lancet,* 461 N.Y.S.2d 955 (NY).]

10. After receiving an unsuccessful surgical procedure designed to facilitate weight loss, Gatten brought suit against the physician for violation of the state consumer protection law. That law read in part, "unfair methods of competition and deceptive practices in the conduct of any trade or commerce are unlawful." Gatten based her case on statements made to her about her course of treatment and the probable results of that treatment. Does the unsuccessful treatment by a physician fall within the consumer protection law? Explain. [See: *Gatten v. Merzi,* 579 A.2d 974 (PA).]

quick quiz Answers

15-1	15-2	15-3
1. F	1. T	1. F
2. F	2. T	2. F
3. T	3. F	3. F

Part 3 Case Study

Bill Parrot v. Daimler Chrysler Corporation
Arizona Supreme Court No. CV-05-0104-PR
Court of Appeals Division One No. 1 CA-CV 04-0121
Maricopa County Superior Court No. CV02-008392

Summary

The plaintiff in this case, Bill Parrot, leased a Jeep Eagle Cherokee, model year 2000, from a Chrysler dealer in Arizona named Pitre Chrysler. As is customary, the lease was then assigned to Chrysler Financial. The title to the car was retained by Pitre. The vehicle carried a standard limited warranty executed by Chrysler. From the outset, the vehicle performed poorly for Parrot. The vehicle was in the shop for repairs almost 20 times while in his possession. Some of these repairs were for minor flaws, such as a windshield leak, but others were for major items, including suspension and axle defects, brake problems, exhaust system defects, and alignment problems.

After repeated efforts to get satisfaction from Chrysler, Parrot gave up and brought a lawsuit against the manufacturer, claiming that Chrysler had violated its own written warranty multiple times. The suit was filed under provisions of the Magnuson-Moss Warranty Act (MMWA) and the Arizona Motor Vehicle Warranties Act (the lemon law). The defendant filed a summary judgment motion and the trial court granted that motion. The appellate court, however, reversed that ruling and the matter found its way into the Arizona Supreme Court.

The Arizona Supreme Court took the case to clarify certain discrepancies in the interpretation of the lemon law that had surfaced among the county courts and in the appellate divisions of the state. Specifically, the issue was whether the MMWA and the Arizona Lemon Law applied to lease agreements. In order to examine this problem, the court started at the beginning by defining the goal of the MMWA. The MMWA, the court noted, was created to deal with the avalanche of complaints from buyers about the fact that car companies and dealerships were ducking and weaving behind warranties and failing to follow the specific dictates of those warranties whenever those warranties would favor the consumer. The objective of the MMWA was (and still is, for that matter) to deal with this issue by outlawing deceptive warranties and fraudulent behavior and demanding that manufactures and dealers reveal the true "terms and conditions" of warranties in "simple and readily understood language."

To clarify such concepts, the MMWA defines certain terms including *consumer, consumer product, qualifying sale,* and *written warranty*. A consumer product is personal property, such as an appliance, a vehicle, a piece of furniture, and so on, that is used exclusively for personal, family, or household activities. 15 U.S.C. § 2301(1). *Consumer* is defined as (1) the actual buyer, (2) anyone to whom the product is transferred while the written warranty is in effect, or (3) any person entitled to enforce the written warranty. 15 U.S.C. § 2301(3). A qualifying sale is a situation in which a person buys a consumer product with no initial intent to resell that product. Finally, a written warranty is:

> (A) any written affirmation of fact or written promise made in connection with
> the sale of a consumer product by a supplier to a buyer which relates to the

nature of the material or workmanship and affirms or promises that such material or workmanship is defect free or will meet a specified level of performance over a specified period of time, or (B) any undertaking in writing in connection with the sale by a supplier of a consumer product to refund, repair, replace, or take other remedial action with respect to such product in the event that such product fails to meet the specifications set forth in the undertaking—

which written affirmation, promise, or undertaking becomes part of the basis of the bargain between a supplier and a buyer *for purposes other than resale of such product*. 15 USC Section 2301 (6) (emphasis added by the court).

Parrot claims to qualify as either (1) a person to whom the product is transferred while the written warranty is in effect, or (2) any person entitled to enforce the written warranty. 15 U.S.C. § 2301(3). A qualifying sale is a situation in which a person buys a consumer product with no initial intent to resell that product. In order to qualify as one of these two types of buyers, Parrot would have to be part of a deal in which there was no purpose of resale and within which there is a written warranty. Chrysler argues that Parrot is mistaken and the Supreme Court of Arizona seems to be willing to consider this argument. This is crucial because if, in fact, the transaction cannot be considered a qualifying sale, as defined by the act, then Parrot's case is not covered by the MMWA and that part of the suit must disappear.

That then becomes the key question in the case: Is the transaction between Parrot and Pitre a qualifying sale? The Arizona Supreme Court concludes that it is not a qualifying sale, which effectively short-circuits Parrot's entire MMWA case. The court's rationale is rather convoluted and indirect, but that is only because the bench feels compelled to examine the statutory definitions at length and in such a way to demonstrate that it is relying only on that language. However, at the heart of the matter is the question of whether this contract involves any intent to resell the jeep. The real focus then is actually a dual focus. The initial focus is aimed at (1) the Chrysler-Daimler contract and the second one is focused on (2) the Pitre-Parrot contract. Examining them in reverse order, the agreement between Pitre and Daimler is not a qualified sale because it lacks the central requirement of being a contract that involves no intent to resell. Whenever Pitre purchases a vehicle from Chrysler, it does so to make profit. Moreover, to make a profit the car must be resold. Since the contract is made with intent to resell, it is not a qualifying sale. This means, however, that the other contract,

the one that involves the lease to Parrot, also cannot be a qualifying sale, because the car will ultimately be returned to Pitre once the lease period is up and Pitre will resell the car for a profit. Pitre's intent to resell the car is made evident by the fact that Pitre retains the title to the Jeep, a title that was never transferred to Parrot and is needed for resale. Why does a dealership buy a car, then lease that same car while retaining the title? The answer to this is obvious. Ultimately, the dealership will resell the car. This transaction falls outside of the MMWA, and the case built on a violation of the MMWA must vanish.

Parrot fares no better under provisions of the Arizona Lemon Law, but for different reasons. The Arizona Supreme Court makes short order of this issue by examining the remedies offered under the Arizona law. The law offers two remedies. One is that the dealer will replace the "lemonized" vehicle for a properly running vehicle. This involves a change in ownership. The other remedy involves a refund of the money spent by the consumer on the "lemonized" vehicle in exchange for a return of the car. Both of these remedies require that the consumer have ownership of the car because both remedies require the transfer of the title. The dealer, however, has retained the title. Therefore, there is no remedy for the consumer and the statute is of no use to Parrot.

In both lines of reasoning here, the court rejects the idea that the deal is a *qualifying sale*. This decision contradicts the opening case in Chapter 14, *Christine Seney v. Rent-A-Center, Inc.* However, the contradiction comes not in the decision itself but in the way that the decision is made. In this case, *Bill Parrot v. Daimler Chrysler Corporation*, the decision is based on determining if any stage in the transaction entertained the possibility of resale. To determine this, the court focused on two things (1) which party held title and (2) the true intent of each contract. Since the title to the vehicle remained with the buyer in the first stage of the transaction, and since that party was a retailer, the true intent of the parties in the second stage would be to transfer the vehicle temporarily as part of a lease agreement with the understanding that the vehicle could be returned to the retailer for eventual resale. In the other case, *Christine Seney v. Rent-A-Center, Inc.*, the distinction turned on the fact that the lease could not be the economic equivalent of a sale. To be the economic equivalent of a sale: (1) the lessee, in negotiating the lease, must agree to pay an amount up front that is equal to the amount that a buyer would pay plus interest, or (2) the lessee must agree to a payment schedule, while also taking possession of the item. Now, ultimately, at some point in the future, these two tests may turn out to be the same test from two different perspectives. However, for now they appear to be two mutually exclusive and contradictory tests. This results, once again, because the law is a complex adaptive system that lacks a strong central controlling agent and in which power is dispersed among many interlocking and sometimes antagonistic agents. Thus, even when the court tries to unify the way the law is interpreted, it often falls short of the mark, as it does here. (Reproduced below is that portion of the court's opinion that reviews some of the counterarguments made to the court's MMWA decision and the rationale related to the court's analysis of the lemon law's the applicability to the case. Footnote numerals are included but the citations themselves and explanatory notes are omitted.).

The Court's Opinion

Delivered by Justice Michael D. Ryan

Parrot relies on several recent cases to support his claim that he is either a category two or three consumer. We do not find these cases persuasive. For example, in *Cohen v. AM General Corp.*, the court concluded that "the *purpose* of the transaction . . . was not for resale, but for the lease of the vehicle." 264 F. Supp. 2d 616, 619 (N.D. Ill. 2003). The court based its conclusion on the following factors: the leasing company would not have purchased the vehicle but for the fact that the car dealer had entered into a leasing agreement with the plaintiff; the leasing company did not "intend to add the vehicle to its inventory or advertise it for sale to other parties"; and it profited through the lease agreement. *Id.* In *Peterson v. Volkswagen of America, Inc.*, the court concluded that when a lessor purchased a vehicle for purposes of leasing the vehicle instead of reselling it, the lessee came within the purview of the Act as a category three consumer. 697 N.W.2d 61, 71-73, ¶¶ 33-37, 41-42 (Wis. 2005).

But here, Parrot conceded that Pitre, the dealer-lessor, had purchased the Jeep for resale. Thus, both *Cohen* and *Peterson,* in which the purpose of the purchase of the motor vehicle was found to be for leasing, are inapposite.

Parrot also relies heavily on opinions that have held that interpreting the Warranty Act as not applying to leases "is inconsistent with the purposes of the [Warranty] Act—to protect the ultimate user of the product." *Szubski v. Mercedes-Benz, U.S.A., L.L.C.*, 796 N.E.2d 81, 88, ¶ 28 (Ct. Com. Pl. Ohio 2003); *see also Cohen*, 264 F. Supp. 2d at 621 (holding that "[t]his reading . . . best serves Congress' goal of 'better protecting consumers'") (citation omitted); *Mesa v. BMW of N. Am., LLC*, 904 So. 2d 450, 458 (Fla. Dist. Ct. App. 2005) (same). Although this interpretation of the Act has a certain attraction, it does not comport with the plain language of the Act. As discussed above, a person must be a consumer as defined under the Warranty Act, which requires that there be a qualifying sale. *See* 15 U.S.C. § 2301(3), (6). In the absence of such a sale, Parrot simply does not qualify as a consumer under the Act.

Finally, a few courts, including our court of appeals, have concluded that if state law permits enforcement of a written warranty, then the Warranty Act governs that warranty even if the written warranty does not otherwise meet the requirements of the Warranty Act. *See, e.g., Voelker v. Porsche Cars N. Am., Inc.*, 353 F.3d 516, 525 (7th Cir. 2003); *Parrot*, 210 Ariz. at 148-49, ¶¶ 21-27, 108 P.3d at 927-28; *Mesa*, 904 So. 2d at 457; *Dekelaita v. Nissan Motor Corp.*, 799 N.E.2d 367, 372 (Ill. App. Ct. 2003).

We find the reasoning of these courts flawed in two respects. First, they rely upon an incorrect reading of 15 U.S.C. § 2301(6). Second, they rely upon the mistaken assumption that the use of the term "the warranty" in the second part of category three's definition of "consumer" means that the Warranty Act governs any warranty enforceable under state law.

For instance, in *Parrot,* the court mistakenly limited the qualifying phrase "which written affirmation, promise, or undertaking becomes part of the basis of the bargain between a supplier and a buyer for purposes other than resale of such product" to subsection (B) of 15 U.S.C. § 2301(6). *See* 210 Ariz. at 147, ¶ 15, 108 P.3d at 926.4 Instead, as set forth in paragraphs 13 and 14, above, the qualifying phrase applies to both subsection (A) and (B) of § 2301(6). *See also* 16 C.F.R. § 700.11(b) ("A written warranty must be 'part of the basis of the bargain.' This means that it must be conveyed at the time of sale of the consumer product . . . .").

This error led the court to conclude that, to be a category two consumer, one need only have a "written warranty . . . 'made in connection with the sale' of a consumer product by 'a supplier' to 'a buyer.'" *Parrot*, 210 Ariz. at 147, ¶ 15, 108 P.3d at 926 (citations omitted). Likewise, the court's conclusion that Parrot is a category three consumer rests in part on its mistaken reading of 15 U.S.C. § 2301(6). *See id.* at 148, ¶¶ 21-22, 108 P.3d at 927.

In *Dekelaita*, the court concluded that the lessee was a category three consumer because the lessee was entitled to enforce the warranty under state law. 799 N.E.2d at 372. This conclusion rested on the premise that "the third [category] does not exclusively require that the warranty meet the Act's definition if in fact it is enforceable under state law." *Id.* at 374.

But *Dekelaita* comes to this conclusion without any discussion of the statute or reference to "warranty" as

375

used in the definition of a category three consumer. *See id.* at 372. Instead, the court simply assumed that a category three consumer may obtain remedies under the Warranty Act if a warranty is enforceable under state law. *See id.* But this is an incorrect reading of the reference to warranty in the definition of a category three consumer. Under 15 U.S.C. § 2301(6), for the Act to apply, a purchase for purposes other than resale is required. *Dekelaita* simply does not address these requirements.

The court in *Dekelaita* nevertheless went on to conclude that a written warranty, as defined by the Warranty Act, existed in that case. *See id.* at 372-74. This conclusion, however, relies upon the same mistaken reading of 15 U.S.C. § 2301(6) as was made in *Parrot*. *See Dekelaita,* 799 N.E.2d at 370.

Because the court in *Dekelaita* relied on this misreading of 15 U.S.C. § 2301(6), it ignored the issue of whether the sale was for purposes other than resale and whether the written warranty was part of the basis of the bargain between the supplier and the buyer.5 *See* 799 N.E.2d at 372-74. *Dekelaita*'s holding that all that is necessary to be a category three consumer is to have some warranty that is enforceable under state law is based upon a mistaken premise.

In *Voelker*, the court depended upon the holding in *Dekelaita* to conclude that because the lessee could enforce the warranty under state law, the lessee was a category three consumer. 353 F.3d at 524 (citing *Dekelaita,* 799 N.E.2d at 372). Because we do not find *Dekelaita* persuasive precedent for this proposition, we decline to follow *Voelker*.

We therefore hold that because Pitre purchased the vehicle for purposes of resale, and there is no other qualifying sale on the record before us, Parrot does not qualify as a consumer under the Warranty Act. As a result, he cannot maintain an action against DaimlerChrysler under the Warranty Act.6

IV

The Warranty Act "apparently was not successful in resolving consumer problems with chronically defective automobiles." *Abrams*, 899 F.2d at 1317. As a result, a number of states enacted so-called lemon laws. *Id.*; *see also* Joan Vogel, *Squeezing Consumers: Lemon Laws, Consumer Warranties, and a Proposal for Reform*, 1985 Ariz. St. L.J. 589, 592 ("Due to the inadequacy of the UCC and the Magnuson-Moss Warranty Act, thirty seven states have now passed lemon laws to deal with automobile warranty disputes."). Arizona enacted its version of a lemon law in 1984. *See* 1984 Ariz. Sess. Laws, ch. 265, § 1 (codified as amended at A.R.S. §§ 44-1261 to -1265).

The Lemon Law definition of "consumer" parallels the definition in the Warranty Act:

> "Consumer" means the purchaser, other than for purposes of resale, of a motor vehicle, any person to whom the motor vehicle is transferred during the duration of an express warranty applicable to the motor vehicle or any other person entitled by the terms of the warranty to enforce the obligations of the warranty.

A.R.S. § 44-1261(A)(1). An important difference between the Lemon Law and the Warranty Act is that the Lemon Law does not define the term "warranty." Accordingly, the requirement that there be a sale for purposes other than resale does not apply to warranties under the Lemon Law. Thus, although Parrot would not qualify as a category one consumer under the Lemon Law because he did not purchase the Jeep, he may qualify as a category two or three consumer under A.R.S. § 44-1261(A) (1). However, we need not decide whether Parrot would qualify as a category two or three consumer because of the limited remedies afforded by the Lemon Law.

The Lemon Law's remedies for the failure of a manufacturer "or its authorized dealers" to correct or repair "any defect or condition which substantially impairs the use . . . of the motor vehicle," are replacing the vehicle "or accept[ing] return of the motor vehicle from the consumer and refund[ing] to the consumer the full purchase price, including all collateral charges, less a reasonable allowance for the consumer's use of the vehicle." A.R.S. § 44-1263(A).

Both remedies assume that the consumer has the right to transfer title to the vehicle back to the manufacturer. Only the owner of the vehicle or holder of title can transfer title. *See* A.R.S. § 28-2058 (2004). This record, however, establishes that Pitre is the owner and title holder; at oral argument Parrot conceded that he did not have title in the vehicle. A person who neither owns a vehicle nor has title to it cannot return the vehicle to the manufacturer, nor is he entitled to have the defective vehicle replaced by another. Therefore, under the Lemon Law, Parrot has no remedy.

Questions for Analysis

1. As we have seen several times, *stare decisis* is at the central core of the authority of the judicial branch. How does this case contradict that description of core authority? Explain.

2. What is the Magnuson-Moss Warranty Act? What precipitated its passage in Congress? What is its purpose? Explain.

3. What are state lemon laws? What precipitated their passage in the states? What is the purpose of a typical lemon law? Explain.

4. Define the following legal terms using the MMWA: consumer, consumer product, qualifying sale, and written warranty.

5. What test is used by the court in *Christine Seney v. Rent-A-Center, Inc.*, to determine if the transaction is actually a sale? Explain.

6. What test is used by the court in *Bill Parrot v. Daimler Chrysler Corporation* to determine if the transaction is actually a sale? Explain.

7. Which of these two tests seems best suited to carry out the will of Congress in relation to automobile leases? Explain.

8. What two remedies are offered in the Arizona lemon law to rehabilitate consumers who have been victimized by a "lemonized" vehicle? Explain.

9. In what way does the court use these remedies to reject the plaintiff's claim under the Arizona lemon law? Explain.

10. A complex adaptive system is a network of interacting conditions that reinforce one another, while at the same time adjusting to change from agents outside and inside the system. In what ways do the two cases, *Christine Seney v. Rent-A-Center, Inc.*, and *Bill Parrot v. Daimler Chrysler Corporation*, reinforce the idea that the law works like a complex adaptive system? Explain.

Part Four

Negotiable Instruments and Banking

The Nature of Negotiable Instruments

THE OPENING CASE *Round 1*
When Should Stop Payment Orders Themselves Be Stopped? Or Should They Ever Be Stopped?

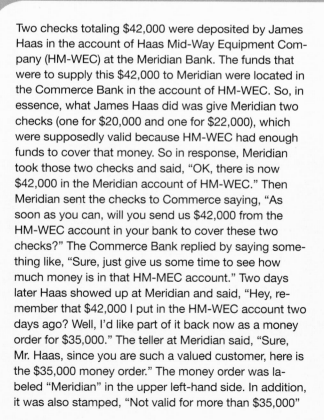

Two checks totaling $42,000 were deposited by James Haas in the account of Haas Mid-Way Equipment Company (HM-WEC) at the Meridian Bank. The funds that were to supply this $42,000 to Meridian were located in the Commerce Bank in the account of HM-WEC. So, in essence, what James Haas did was give Meridian two checks (one for $20,000 and one for $22,000), which were supposedly valid because HM-WEC had enough funds to cover that money. So in response, Meridian took those two checks and said, "OK, there is now $42,000 in the Meridian account of HM-WEC." Then Meridian sent the checks to Commerce saying, "As soon as you can, will you send us $42,000 from the HM-WEC account in your bank to cover these two checks?" The Commerce Bank replied by saying something like, "Sure, just give us some time to see how much money is in that HM-MEC account." Two days later Haas showed up at Meridian and said, "Hey, remember that $42,000 I put in the HM-WEC account two days ago? Well, I'd like part of it back now as a money order for $35,000." The teller at Meridian said, "Sure, Mr. Haas, since you are such a valued customer, here is the $35,000 money order." The money order was labeled "Meridian" in the upper left-hand side. In addition, it was also stamped, "Not valid for more than $35,000"

and made payable to James Haas. In the bottom right-hand corner, Haas signed the money order. He then took the money order to Trump Plaza and cashed it for "use" in the casino. (Note: It is not clear from the records what kind of day Haas had at the casino, but the progress of this case would seem to indicate that Haas either did poorly or did very well but took his winnings to neither Meridian nor Commerce.) In the meantime, Meridian received those two original checks back from Commerce with a friendly note saying something like, Sorry, Meridian, as much as we would like to honor these checks, we cannot send you any money from the HM-WEC account because, well, because the cupboard is bare. In fact, the account was closed some time ago." Meridian then turned around and took that $42,000 out of the HM-WEC account. Nevertheless, since Hass drew out $35,000 for that money order, the account was now overdrawn by $38,584. When Trump Plaza shows up with that $35,000 money order, Meridian returned it to Trump Plaza noting that the HM-WEC account at Meridian had insufficient funds to cover it. Trump Plaza then brought a lawsuit against Haas and Meridian for the missing money. Trump Plaza argues that (1) the casino is a "holder in due course" and, therefore, must be paid by Meridian; (2) the money order was already accepted by Meridian because its name is on it and it marked it "payment stopped," indicating Meridian recognized it as its own instrument; (3) if, in fact, the cupboard is bare, it is Meridian that should suffer the loss because it was negligent in figuring out that Hass had no money in the HM–WEC account; and (4) the court relied on a case that is inappropriate, inapplicable, or is so out of touch with reality, that it must be overturned. Meridian a summary judgment motion arguing that the suit should be dismissed because the money order is really the equivalent of a personal check and that it was not liable until it accepted it, and just because the bank's name was on the check and it wrote "payment stopped" does not mean that Meridian has accepted it. The trial court agreed and dismissed the action. Trump Plaza appealed. Will Trump Plaza succeed or "be fired"? (Get it?) [See: *Trump Plaza, v. Haas and Meridian Bank,* 692 A. 2d 86 (Superior Court of New Jersey, Appellate Division).] (Note: Please, do not take the dramatic license that we took in structuring the bank dialogue too literally.)

Opening Case Questions

1. What type of lawsuit did Trump bring against Haas and Meridian? Was this a tort case, a contract case, or something else? Explain.

2. Is the money order really the equivalent of a personal check or is it more like a certified check? Explain.

3. What constitutes acceptance in a case like this one? Explain.

4. What constitutes negligence in a case like this? Explain.

5. If the case against Meridian fails, what additional recourse might Trump have, if any? Explain.

(LO) Learning Objectives

1. State the purpose of a negotiable instrument.
2. Explain those negotiable instruments that contain a promise to pay money.
3. Explain those negotiable instruments that contain an order to pay money.
4. Differentiate among the different types of checks and money orders.
5. Identify the requirements of a negotiable instrument.
6. Explain an assignment and a negotiation of an instrument.
7. Name and describe four kinds of indorsements.
8. Identify the implied warranties related to indorsements.
9. Explain the contract that is made when people indorse negotiable instruments.
10. Describe the legal effect of a forged indorsement.

16-1 The Essentials of Negotiable Instruments

Throughout history, people have had a need to transact business without carrying around large sums of money. Moreover, people have also borrowed money from one another, necessitating an orderly system of procedures and laws to govern credit transactions. The law of negotiable instruments has developed to meet these needs. Checks, drafts, and notes are used conveniently and safely as a substitute for money and to obtain credit in today's society. With the rapid development of cyber-commerce and electronic banking, online payments are now being used as a substitute for checks and other paper transactions, as well as for actual check processing through the banking system. As a result, it is estimated that the number of checks written in the United States will decline greatly during the next decade. Still, even without paper checks, the principles underlying the process of transferring funds will remain the same. It is an effective process that has stood the test of time. Sometimes, however, it is beneficial to remember just how long this financial process has been part of our culture.

CLASSIC CASE The Birth of Banking and the Knights Templar

The financial world owes its very existence to the work of the medieval Knights Templar. Recent popular knowledge of the Knights Templar can be attributed to Dan Brown's novel *The Da Vinci Code* and Ron Howard's film of the same name. The legends attached to the Templars are many and varied. They are pictured as the discoverers of the Holy Grail, the defenders of the Priory of Scion, a branch of the Illuminati, the forerunners of the Freemasons, and the military arm of the Cathars. Most of these legends bear no resemblance to the truth, although they do make good stories. This is unfortunate because the mystique that has been built around the Templars interferes with an understanding of their true contribution to European history and that is in the development of the European banking system. The Templars probably began as an order of knights about 1118 or 1119. Some experts report that they were founded by Hugh de Payns (or Hugues de Payens) as an order of knights dedicated to protecting Christian pilgrims who needed armed guards to defend them as the traveled to and from the Holy Land during the Islamic occupation of that area in the Middle Ages. As their reputation grew, they attracted new members to their ranks, many of whom were wealthy men with extensive land holdings and rich treasuries. Often, when these men joined the Templars, they would transfer their property and money to the control of the knights. In this way, the wealth of the Templars grew to such an extent that, at their peak, they controlled thousands of estates across Europe. Some knights and noblemen who were supportive of the Templar mission also made annual donations to the order. Eventually, the Templars would also hold the

wealth of knights and other noblemen who would travel to the Holy Land and would not want to leave their valuables unattended while they were on their journeys. The Templars also established banks in their various monasteries throughout Europe and would store the riches in those banks in much the same way that safe deposit boxes do today. The Templars also devised a way by which a traveler could present a paper, called a note, to merchants and innkeepers at various points on their journey that would be redeemable for the amount of wealth that those documents represented on deposit at a Templar monastery bank. These documents are the forerunners of the modern negotiable instruments used today. Eventually, the wealth stored in the monastery banks also became the basis for a lending system that was used by several monarchs to finance their foreign wars. Some historians argue that it was this habit of lending money to the kings of Europe that led to the downfall of the Knights Templar at the hands of Philip the Fair of France in 1313. Philip had taken out extensive loans from the Templars to fight his wars with England and when he asked for another loan, despite having not paid back what he already owed, the Templars refused. Philip then trumped up charges against the Templars, allowing him to arrest, imprison, and execute them and then confiscate their great wealth. [See: Jefferson P. Webb, "The Knights Templar: Fathers of Modern Banking," *New Ulster Steel Fighting: Academy of European Martial Arts;* and Piers Paul Read, *The Templars: The Dramatic History of the Knights Templar, the Most Powerful Military Order of the Crusades* (New York: St. Martin's Griffin, 1999).]

Promise and Order Instruments

The law of negotiable instruments is found in Article 3 of the UCC. This article was originally drafted in 1952. Since that time, many new developments have occurred in the commercial field. To adapt to modern technology and contemporary practices, Article 3 of the UCC has been extensively revised over the last six decades. Today under the UCC, a **negotiable instrument** is a written document signed by the maker that contains an unconditional promise *or* order to pay a fixed amount of money on demand or at a definite time to the bearer or to order. There are two basic kinds of negotiable instruments: promise instruments (including notes and certificates of deposit) and order instruments (including drafts and checks).

UCC Revised (1990) 3-104(e)-(j) (see page 966)

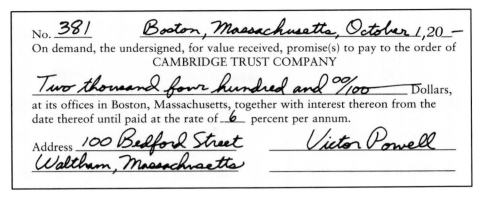

No. **381**   Boston, Massachusetts, October 1, 20 —

On demand, the undersigned, for value received, promise(s) to pay to the order of

CAMBRIDGE TRUST COMPANY

Two thousand four hundred and 00/100 ——————Dollars,

at its offices in Boston, Massachusetts, together with interest thereon from the
date thereof until paid at the rate of **6** percent per annum.

Address 100 Bedford Street   Victor Powell
Waltham, Massachusetts

Figure 16-1 A demand note is payable whenever the payee demands payment.

Promise Instruments: Notes

A **note** (often called a promissory note) is a written promise by one party, called the *maker,* to pay money to the order of another party, called the *payee.* People who loan money or extend credit use notes as evidence of debt. When two or more parties sign a note, they are called *comakers.* A **demand note,** as its name implies, is payable whenever the payee demands payment (Figure 16-1). A holder of a demand note may decide to collect the balance due at any time and for any reason. A time note, in contrast, is payable at some future time, on a date named in the instrument. Unless a note is payable in installments, the principal (face value) of the note plus interest must be paid on the date that it is due. In an **installment note,** the principal together with the interest on the unpaid balance is payable in a series of payments at specified times.

UCC Revised (1990)
3-104(e) (see page 966)

Promise Instruments: Certificates of Deposit

A **certificate of deposit (CD)** is an instrument containing an acknowledgment that a bank has received a sum of money and a promise by the bank to repay the sum of money. A CD is a note of the bank, and CDs are written for a specific time period, such as six months, one year, two years, or five years. Banks pay higher interest for longer-term CDs and more interest than regular savings accounts because the depositor cannot withdraw the money before the due date without penalty. Some banks allow a one time early withdrawal from a CD without penalty.

UCC Revised (1990)
3-108(a) (see page 967)

UCC Revised (1990)
3-104(j) (see page 966)

Order Instruments: Drafts

In contrast to notes, which are *promises* to pay money, drafts are *orders* to pay money. They are more complicated than notes because they involve three parties rather than two. The most common type of draft in use today is the check, but this was not always the case. For example, in Ernest Hemingway's *A Farewell to Arms,* a novel set in Italy during World War I, one of the characters, an American major, discusses with his friend Rinaldi the possibility of going to Milan:

LO3

UCC Revised (1990)
3-104(e) (see page 966)

> The tickets are very expensive. I will draw a sight draft on my grandfather, I said. A
> what? A sight draft. He has to pay or I go to jail. Mr. Cunningham at the bank does it. I
> live by sight drafts. Can a grandfather jail a patriotic grandson who is dying that Italy
> may live? Live the American Garibaldi, said Rinaldi. Viva the sight drafts, I said.

A **draft** (also called a **bill of exchange**) is an instrument in which one party writes an instrument ordering a second party to pay money to a third party. The one who draws the draft (that is, the one who orders money to be paid) is called the *drawer.* The one who is ordered to pay the money is called the *drawee.* The one who is to receive the money is known as the *payee.*

UCC Revised (1990)
3-409 (see page 977)

EXAMPLE 16-1: Sight Draft

In Hemingway's novel, the major would be the drawer of the draft, and his grandfather would be the drawee. The story does not name the payee of the draft, but it could be the railroad ticket office or a bank in Italy—whoever is to receive the money. If this situation involved a check, the person who signed the check would be the drawer, the bank would be the drawee, and the one to whom the check were written would be the payee.

About the Law

A **trade acceptance** is a draft used by a seller of goods to receive payment and extend credit. Drafts are often used in combination with bills of lading, which are receipts given by freight companies to people who ship goods. A seller will ship goods to a buyer and send a bill of lading, with a trade acceptance attached, to a

(continued)

A draft may be presented by the holder to the drawee for payment or for acceptance. When a draft is presented for payment, the drawee may decline to pay it unless it has been accepted. If the drawee refuses to pay an unaccepted draft, the draft is dishonored, and the drawee has no liability for refusing to pay it. In contrast, when a draft is presented for acceptance, the drawee is asked to become liable on the instrument. **Acceptance** is the drawee's signed agreement to pay the draft as presented. If the drawee refuses to accept the draft, it is dishonored, and again, the drawee has no liability.

Drawees are liable on drafts only when they accept them, that is, agree to become liable on them. To accept a draft, the drawee need only sign the draft across the face of the instrument. It is customary, however, when accepting a draft, for the drawee to write "accepted" across the face of the instrument, followed by the date and signature. An acceptance must be written on the draft itself; it may not be written on a separate piece of paper. By accepting a draft, the drawee agrees to pay the instrument at a later date when it became due.

Sight and Time Drafts A **sight draft** (Figure 16-2) is payable as soon as it is presented to the drawee for payment. A **time draft** (Figure 16-3) is not payable until the lapse of a particular time period stated on the draft. Drafts that are payable "30 days after sight" and "60 days after date" are examples of time drafts.

Domestic and International Bills of Exchange A **domestic bill of exchange** is a draft that is drawn and payable in the United States. A draft that is drawn in one country but payable in another is called an **international bill of exchange** or **foreign draft**.

Order Instruments: Checks

A **check** is a draft drawn on a bank and payable on demand. It is the most common form of a draft. It is drawn on a bank by a drawer who has an account with the bank and is made to the order of a specified person or business named

Figure 16-2 A sight draft is payable as soon as it is presented to the drawee for payment. How do you know that this draft has not been accepted by the drawee?

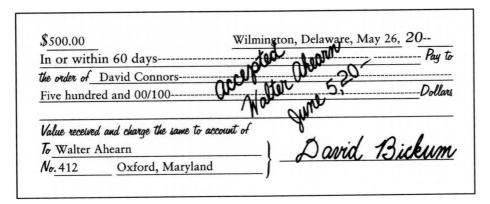

Figure 16-3 A time draft is not payable until the lapse of a particular time period stated on the draft. How do you know that this draft has been accepted by the drawee?

on the check or to the bearer. A check is a safe means of transferring money, and it serves as a receipt after it has been paid and canceled by the bank. In the check shown in Figure 16-4, Margaret Evans is the drawer; she has an account with the Western National Bank. Alicia Adams Fashions, Inc., is the payee. Western National Bank, on which the check is drawn, is the drawee. Ownership of a check may be transferred to another person by indorsement by the payee. In this manner, a check may circulate among several parties, taking the place of money. A bank must honor a check when it is properly drawn against a credit balance of the drawer. Failure to do so would make the bank liable to the drawer for resulting damages.

bank in the buyer's city. The trade acceptance orders the buyer to pay money to the seller or another party. The buyer must either pay the money or accept the draft to receive the bill of lading from the bank. The freight company will not release the goods to the buyer unless the buyer has possession of the bill of lading.

UCC Revised (1990) 3-104(f) (see page •••)

A QUESTION OF ETHICS

Along with their bill, credit card companies often include blank checks for customers to make payable to anyone they wish, thus increasing the amount owed the credit card issuer, usually at an exceptionally high rate of interest. The practice is legal; is it ethical?

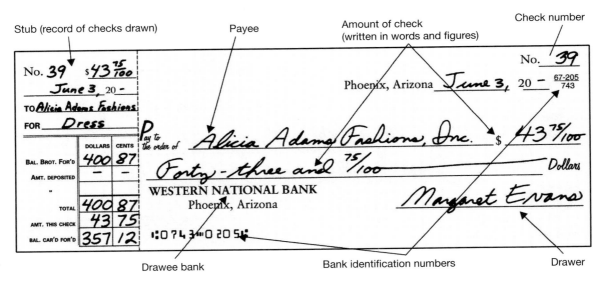

Figure 16-4 All elements of a sample check are identified.

UCC Revised (1990)
3-409(d) (see page 977)

Form for Checks Banks provide regular and special printed check forms. These check forms display a series of numbers printed in magnetic ink, which make it possible to process checks speedily and accurately by computer. The first set of figures is the bank's Federal Reserve number. This number is followed by the bank's own number. The second set of numbers is the depositor's account number. The use of printed forms is not required, however. Any writing, no matter how crude, may be used as a check if it is a draft drawn on a bank and payable on demand.

Certified Checks A **certified check** is a check that is guaranteed by the bank. At the request of either the depositor or the holder, the bank acknowledges and guarantees that sufficient funds will be withheld from the drawer's account to pay the amount stated on the check. A prudent person will request a certified check rather than accept a personal check when involved in a business transaction with a stranger. A certified check, under the UCC, is "a check accepted by the bank on which it is drawn." The UCC places no obligation on a bank to certify a check if it does not want to do so, and the refusal to certify is not a dishonor of the check. When a check is certified, the drawer is discharged regardless of when it was done or who obtained the acceptance. Figure 16-5 illustrates a certified check.

UCC Revised (1990)
3-414(c) (see page 978)

UCC Revised (1990)
3-104(g)(h) (see page 966)

Bank Drafts and Cashier's Checks A **bank draft**, sometimes called a **teller's check** or *treasurer's check,* is a check drawn by one bank on another bank in which it has funds on deposit in favor of a third person, the payee. Many banks deposit money in banks in other areas for the convenience of depositors who depend upon the transfer of funds when transacting business in distant places. When the buyer is unknown to the seller, such checks are more acceptable than personal checks. A **cashier's check** is a check drawn by a bank upon itself. The bank, in effect, lends its credit to the purchaser of the check. It is the equivalent of a promissory note of the bank. Courts have held that payment cannot be stopped on a cashier's check because the bank, by issuing it, accepts the check in advance. People who will not accept personal checks will often accept cashier's checks. Such a check may be made payable either to the depositor, who purchases it from the bank, or to the person who is to cash it. If the check is made payable to the depositor, it must be indorsed to the person to whom it is transferred.

Traveler's Checks A **traveler's check** is similar to a cashier's check, in that the issuing financial institution is both the drawer and the drawee. The purchaser signs the checks in the presence of the issuer when they are purchased. To cash a check, the purchaser writes the name of the payee in the space provided and countersigns it in the payee's presence. Only the purchaser can negotiate traveler's checks, and they are easily replaced by the issuing bank if they are stolen. Traveler's checks are issued in denominations of $10 and up, and the purchaser of the checks ordinarily pays a fixed fee to the issuer.

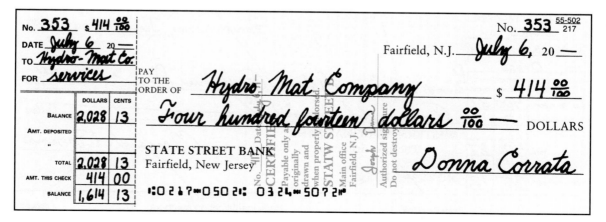

Figure 16-5 The State Street Bank became primarily liable when it certified this check.

Money Orders A **money order** is a type of draft that may be purchased from banks, post offices, telegraph companies, and express companies as a substitute for a check. Instead of being drawn on an individual's account as is a check, however, a money order is drawn on the funds of the organization that issues it. That organization promises payment from its own funds. Purchasers of money orders fill in their name and address and the name of the payee on the instrument. They are given a receipt along with the money order. If the money order is lost and the purchaser has the receipt, it will be replaced if it has not already been cashed. U.S. Postal Service money orders can be purchased for amounts up to $1,000. U.S. International Postal Service Money Orders are often used to send money to foreign countries. Telegraphic money orders may be used to send money quickly. Under the UCC, a *bank* money order is a check, even though it is described on its face as a money order, and payment can be stopped on it like an ordinary check.

Online banking and bill paying have replaced the need for paper transactions for many customers.

UCC Revised (1990) 3-104(i) (see page 966)

UCC Revised (1990) 3-104(f) (see page 966)

THE OPENING CASE *Round 3*
Money Orders Are Not What They Seem to Be

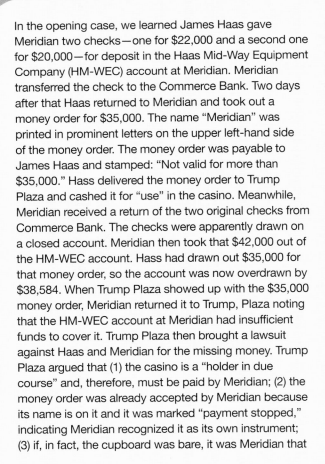

In the opening case, we learned James Haas gave Meridian two checks—one for $22,000 and a second one for $20,000—for deposit in the Haas Mid-Way Equipment Company (HM-WEC) account at Meridian. Meridian transferred the check to the Commerce Bank. Two days after that Haas returned to Meridian and took out a money order for $35,000. The name "Meridian" was printed in prominent letters on the upper left-hand side of the money order. The money order was payable to James Haas and stamped: "Not valid for more than $35,000." Hass delivered the money order to Trump Plaza and cashed it for "use" in the casino. Meanwhile, Meridian received a return of the two original checks from Commerce Bank. The checks were apparently drawn on a closed account. Meridian then took that $42,000 out of the HM-WEC account. Hass had drawn out $35,000 for that money order, so the account was now overdrawn by $38,584. When Trump Plaza showed up with the $35,000 money order, Meridian returned it to Trump, Plaza noting that the HM-WEC account at Meridian had insufficient funds to cover it. Trump Plaza then brought a lawsuit against Haas and Meridian for the missing money. Trump Plaza argued that (1) the casino is a "holder in due course" and, therefore, must be paid by Meridian; (2) the money order was already accepted by Meridian because its name is on it and it was marked "payment stopped," indicating Meridian recognized it as its own instrument; (3) if, in fact, the cupboard was bare, it was Meridian that

should suffer the loss because it was negligent in figuring out that Hass had no money in the HM-WEC account; and (4) the court relied on a case that was inappropriate, inapplicable, or so out of touch with reality it must be overturned. Meridian filed a summary judgment motion arguing that the suit should be dismissed because the money order is really the equivalent of a personal check and that it was not liable until it accepted it, and just because the bank's name was on the check or had written "payment stopped," did not mean that Meridian had accepted it. The trial court agreed and dismissed the action. Trump Plaza appealed. The court upheld the dismissal. In a lengthy opinion, the court disposed of each of Trump Plaza's arguments one by one: (1) the rights and protections of a holder in due course do not come into play unless and until the drawee bank accepts the instrument; (2) the fact that the check is imprinted with Meridian's name and has "payment stopped" written on it does not amount to an acceptance; (3) Trump Plaza has no negligence action against the bank because that cause of action is limited to the party who purchased the money order (Haas in this case). Finally, the appellate court seems to believe that Trump Plaza must have misread the case of *Newman v. First Nat'l State Bank of Toms River,* because in that case the court clearly said that a money order is the equivalent of a personal check. [See: *Trump Plaza v. Haas and Meridian Bank,* 692 A. 2d 86 (Superior Court of New Jersey, Appellate Division).]

Parties to Negotiable Instruments

UCC Revised (1990)
3-103 (see page 965)

UCC 1-201(5) (see page 919)

UCC Revised (1990)
3-109(a) (see page 967)

UCC 1-201(20) (see page 922)

UCC Revised (1990)
3-204 (see page 970)

The following are parties to negotiable instruments: maker or comaker; drawer; issuer; drawee; payee; bearer; holder; holder in due course; indorser; indorsee; and acceptor. One by one, step by step, this is what they look like. A **maker** is a person who signs a note, that is, a person who promises to pay. **Comakers** are two or more people who sign the same note promising to pay. A **drawer** is a person who signs a draft, that is, the one who orders payment. An **issuer** is either a maker or a drawer of an instrument. A **drawee** is a person ordered in a draft to make payment. A **payee** is a person to whom a note or draft is payable. A **bearer** is a person who is in possession of a negotiable instrument that is payable to the bearer or to cash. A person who is in possession of an instrument that has been indorsed in blank (by the payee's signature alone) is also a bearer.

A **holder** is a person who is in possession of a negotiable instrument that is issued or indorsed to that person's order or bearer. A **holder in due course** is a holder of a negotiable instrument who is treated as favored and given immunity from certain defenses. An **indorser** is a person who indorses a negotiable instrument, in most cases by signing one's name on the back of the paper. An **indorsee** is a person to whom a draft, note, or other negotiable instrument is transferred by indorsement. An **acceptor** is a drawee of a draft who has promised to honor the draft as presented by signing it on its face. (See Figure 16-6.)

Requirements of Negotiable Instruments

To be negotiable, instruments must: (1) be in writing; (2) be signed by the maker or drawer; (3) contain an unconditional promise or order to pay; (4) be made out for a fixed amount of money; (5) be payable on demand or at a definite time, and (6) except

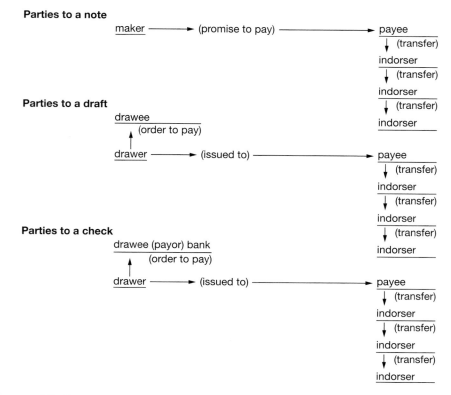

Figure 16-6 This diagram illustrates the relationship of the principal parties to negotiable instruments.

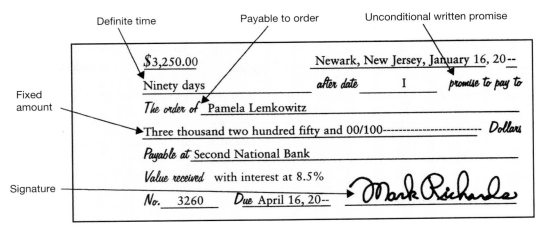

Definite time   Payable to order   Unconditional written promise

Fixed amount

Signature

$3,250.00   Newark, New Jersey, January 16, 20--

Ninety days _____ *after date*   I   *promise to pay to*

The order of Pamela Lemkowitz

Three thousand two hundred fifty and 00/100----------------------- *Dollars*

Payable at Second National Bank

Value received with interest at 8.5%   *Mark Richards*

No.   3260   *Due* April 16, 20--

Figure 16-7 The requirements of negotiability are indicated on this 90-day note.

for checks, be payable to order or to bearer. As will be discussed soon, instruments that do not meet all of these requirements can be transferred to others by assignment. They cannot, however, be transferred by negotiation. Let's look at these requirements one at a time.

Written Instrument
A negotiable instrument must be in writing (see Figure 16-7), which includes printing, word processing, pen or pencil writing, or any other tangible form of writing. Under the Uniform Electronic Transactions Act (UETA), an electronic record fulfills this requirement. Article 3 of the UCC has also been amended to permit electronic negotiable instruments. However, not all states have incorporated that amendment into their version of the statute and so it is best to check to see if your state has done so. Although it hardly seems worth mentioning, it is still a good idea to recognize that any negotiable instrument written in pencil is an invitation to alteration by forgery. If forgery should happen, the person who drew the instrument would be responsible for any loss caused by the negligent drawing of the instrument.

UCC Revised (1990) 3-104(a) (see page 966)

Signature of Maker or Drawer
To be negotiable, an instrument must be signed by the maker or drawer. Any writing, mark, or symbol is accepted as a signature as long as it is the writer's intent to be a signature. It may be handwritten, typewritten, printed, or produced by a machine. A signature may be made by an agent (one who represents and acts for another) or other representative. No particular form of appointment is necessary to establish such authority. Agents who sign their own names to an instrument are personally obligated if the instrument neither names the person represented nor shows that the agent signed in a representative capacity. The signature may appear in the body of the instrument as well as at the end.

UCC 1-201(46) (see page 921)

UCC Revised (1990) 3-401(a)(b) (see page 975)

UCC Revised (1990) 3-402 (see page 975)

UCC Revised (1990) 3-104(a) (see page 966)

Unconditional Promise or Order to Pay
To be negotiable, an instrument must contain no conditions that might in any way affect its payment. Statements requiring that certain things be done or that specific events take place prior to payment make the instrument a simple contract rather than negotiable paper. An instrument is conditional, and thus not negotiable, if it states that it is subject to any other agreement. The same is true if an instrument states that it is to be paid only out of a particular fund.

UCC Revised (1990) 3-106(b) (see page 966)

UCC Revised (1990) 3-104(a) (see page 966)

Did You Know?

In a step toward enforcing one currency for Europe, 11 members of the European Union introduced the euro in 1999. The euro replaced national currencies in 2002. The initial countries participating were Belgium, Germany, Spain, France, Ireland, Italy, Luxembourg, the Netherlands, Austria, Portugal, and Finland.

UCC 1-201(24) (see page 920)

UCC Revised (1990) 3-107 (see page 967)

UCC Revised (1990) 3-108(a) (see page 967)

UCC Revised (1990) 3-108(b) (see page 967)

This latter rule does not apply to instruments issued by government agencies. An instrument may state that it "arises out of" another agreement without being conditional. Similarly, a negotiable instrument may indicate a particular account that is to be charged. In addition to being unconditional, a negotiable instrument must contain a promise to pay (as in a note) or an order to pay (as in a draft). A writing that says "Due Karen Osgood $600" or "IOU $600" is not negotiable because it is neither a promise nor an order to pay.

Fixed Amount of Money A negotiable instrument must be payable in a fixed amount or sum certain of money. This stipulation means an amount of money that is clearly known. *Money* is defined as a medium of exchange adopted by a domestic or foreign government as part of its currency. Thus, a fixed amount of money need not be American dollars.

Payable on Demand or at a Definite Time Negotiable instruments must be made payable on demand or at a definite time. This requirement makes it possible to determine when the debtor or promisor can be compelled to pay. Without this information, the present value of an instrument cannot be determined.

Demand Paper An instrument is payable *on demand* when it so states or when it is payable "on sight" or "on presentation." The key characteristic of demand instruments is that the holder can require payment at any time by making the demand upon the person who is obligated to pay.

Definite-Time Paper Certainty as to the time of payment of an instrument is satisfied if it is payable on or before a stated date. Instruments payable at a fixed period after a stated date or at a fixed period after sight are also considered payable at a definite time. In each instance, a simple mathematical calculation makes the maturity date certain. The expressions "one year after date" and "30 days after sight" are definite as to time. An undated instrument payable 60 days after date is negotiable as a demand paper. A promise to pay only upon an act or event, the time of whose occurrence is uncertain, is not payable at a definite time. Thus, an instrument payable when a person marries, reaches a certain age, or graduates from college, or one payable within a specific period of time after a named person's death, is not negotiable.

Payable to Order or to Bearer Negotiable instruments, except for checks, must be payable to order or to bearer. The terms *to the order of* and *to bearer* are called words of negotiability. The most recent version of Article 3 of the UCC allows checks (but not other instruments) that are not payable to order or to bearer to be negotiable. Thus, a check, but no other instrument, payable "to Mary Harris" is negotiable in all states except those that have yet to adopt the revised Article 3.

Payable to Order An instrument is payable to order when it states that it is payable to the order of any person with reasonable certainty. The maker or drawer may state "Pay to the order of Mary Doe," "Pay to Mary Doe or order," or "Pay to Mary Doe or her assigns." An instrument may be payable to the order of the maker or drawer; the drawee; a payee who is not the maker, drawer, or drawee; two or more payees; an estate, trust, or fund; an office or officer by title; or a partnership or an unincorporated association.

Payable to Bearer An instrument is payable to bearer when it states that it is payable to bearer or the order of bearer, a specified person or bearer, cash or the order of cash, or any other indication that does not designate a specific payee. An instrument is payable to bearer when it does not state a payee. An instrument made payable to both, such as "Pay to the order of Anthony Andrews or bearer," is payable to order unless the word "bearer" is handwritten or word processed.

Dates and Controlling Words

The omission of the date does not affect the negotiability of an instrument. When the date is omitted, the date on which the instrument is received is considered to be the date of issue. An instrument may be predated or postdated without affecting its negotiability. Handwritten terms control word processed and printed terms, and word processed terms control printed terms. Words control figures, except when words are ambiguous (capable of being understood in more than one way). The numbering of, or the failure to number, an instrument does not affect its negotiability. The signature may appear in the body of the instrument as well as at the end.

---

quick quiz 16-1

1. Notes are promises to pay money and drafts are orders to pay money.   true | false

2. Checks are the least common form of a draft.   true | false

3. Under the Uniform Electronic Transactions Act (UETA) an electronic record fulfills the requirement that a negotiable instrument be in writing   true | false

---

16-2 Transferring Negotiable Instruments

When an instrument is first delivered by the maker or drawer for the purpose of giving rights to any person, it is said to be *issued*. When the person to whom it is issued delivers it to a third party, it is *transferred*. Instruments can be transferred by assignment or by negotiation. An **assignment** is the transfer of a contract right from one person to another. Negotiable instruments are assigned either when a person whose indorsement is required on an instrument transfers it without indorsing it or when it is transferred to another person and does not meet the requirements of negotiability. In all such transfers, the transferee has only the rights of an assignee and is subject to all defenses existing against the assignor. An assignment of negotiable instruments also occurs by operation of law when the holder of an instrument dies or becomes bankrupt. In such cases, title to the instrument vests in the personal representative of the estate or the trustee in bankruptcy.

A **negotiation** is the transfer of an instrument in such form that the transferee becomes a *holder* (a person in possession of an instrument issued or indorsed to that person, to that person's order, to bearer, or in blank). In contrast to an assignment, a negotiation gives greater rights to transferees. If an instrument is payable to order, such as "pay to the order of," it is known as **order paper**. To be negotiated, order paper must be indorsed by the payee and delivered to the party to whom it is transferred. If an instrument is payable to bearer or cash, it is called **bearer paper** and may be negotiated by delivery alone, without an indorsement. When order paper is indorsed with a blank indorsement, it is turned into bearer paper and may be further negotiated by delivery alone.

UCC Revised (1990)
3-104(c) (see page 966)

UCC Revised (1990)
3-109(b) (see page 967)

UCC Revised (1990)
3-109(a) (see page 967)

UCC Revised (1990)
3-113 (see page 968)

The payee is never guaranteed to receive payment on a check, so some small businesses choose not to accept personal checks.

The Concept of Negotiability

The concept of negotiability is one of the most important features of negotiable instruments. Largely because of this feature, negotiable instruments are highly trusted and used daily by millions of people. When an instrument is transferred by negotiation, the person receiving the instrument is provided with more protection than was available to the person from whom it was received. The person receiving the instrument is able, in many instances, to recover money on the instrument even when the person from whom the instrument was received could not have done so.

Instruments that do not meet all of the requirements of negotiability cannot be negotiated. However, they can be transferred by assignment, which is governed by the ordinary principles of contract law. People who receive instruments by assignment are not given the special protection provided those who receive instruments by negotiation, because they cannot be *holders in due course,* as explained in the next chapter.

Negotiation by Indorsement

An instrument is indorsed when the holder signs it, thereby indicating the intent to transfer ownership to another. Indorsements may be written in ink, typewritten, or stamped with a rubber stamp. They may be written or word processed on a separate paper (rider, or **allonge**), as long as the separate paper is so firmly affixed to the instrument that it becomes part of it. Although the UCC does not require indorsements to be on any particular side of the paper, for convenience, they are usually placed on the back of the instrument. Anyone who gives value for an instrument has the right to have the unqualified indorsement of the person who transferred it, unless it is payable to bearer.

Regulation CC, issued by the Federal Reserve Board under the Competitive Banking Act, has established standards for check indorsements (Figure 16-8). Under the regulation, the back of a check is divided into specific sections designed to protect the indorsement of the depositor bank (the bank of first deposit). The first one-and-a-half inches from the trailing edge of the check is reserved for the payee's indorsement. Negotiation is effective to transfer an instrument, even when it is transferred by a minor, a corporation exceeding its powers, or any other person without capacity; obtained by fraud, duress, or mistake of any kind; part of an illegal transaction; or made in breach of duty. Any such negotiations, however, may be rescinded except as against a holder in due course (defined and explained in the next chapter), who is given special protection. There are four commonly used types of indorsements: blank indorsements, special indorsements, restrictive indorsements, and qualified indorsements.

Blank Indorsements A **blank indorsement** consists of the signature alone written on the instrument. No particular indorsee (person to whom an instrument is indorsed) is named. When an instrument is indorsed in blank, it becomes payable to the bearer and may be transferred by delivery alone. If the instrument is lost or stolen and gets into the hands of another holder, the new holder can recover its face value by delivery alone. For this reason, a blank indorsement should be used only in limited situations, such as at a bank teller's window. A blank indorsement turns order paper into bearer paper and may be transferred by delivery alone. When an instrument is made payable to a person under a misspelled name or a name other than that person's own, the payee may indorse in the incorrect name, in the correct name, or in both. Signatures in both names may be required by a person paying or giving value for the instrument.

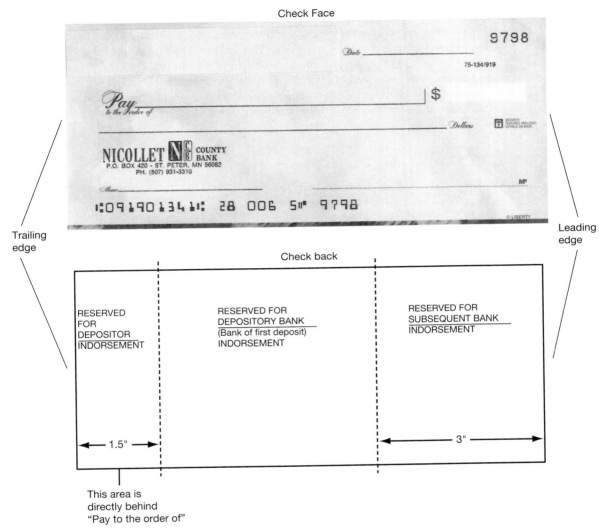

Figure 16-8 Regulation CC has issued check indorsement standards.

EXAMPLE 16-2: Blank Indorsement

Carol Barcley received her first paycheck from the restaurant where she worked as a part-time hostess. She took the check to the bank, where she indorsed it in blank at the teller's window. This was a proper time and place to use a blank indorsement because there was no likelihood that the check would get lost or stolen.

Special Indorsements A *special indorsement* (also called an *indorsement in full*) is made by writing the words *pay to the order of* or *pay to,* followed by the name of the person to whom it is to be transferred (the indorsee) and the signature of the indorser. When indorsed in this manner, the instrument remains an order instrument and must be indorsed by the indorsee before it can be negotiated further. The holder of an instrument may convert a blank indorsement into a special indorsement by writing the words *pay to the order of a person* or *pay to a person* above the indorser's signature.

EXAMPLE 16-3: Special Indorsement

Frank Cully withdrew $3,500 from his savings account to buy a car from Glendale Motors, Inc. When he made the withdrawal, Cully received a check from the bank payable to him for $3,500. He took the check to Glendale Motors, indorsed it with a special indorsement, and received title to the car. A special indorsement (indorsement in full) creates order paper, which requires the signature of the indorsee. Because the check could not be legally transferred or negotiated further until Glendale indorsed it, all parties were protected.

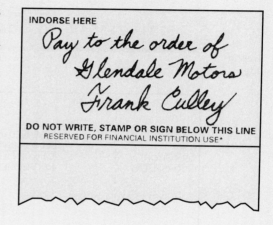

 Restrictive Indorsements A *restrictive indorsement* limits the rights of the indorsee in some manner to protect the rights of the indorser. Indorsements for deposit or collection are restrictive indorsements designed to get an instrument into the banking system for the purpose of deposit or collection. When a check is indorsed "for deposit only," as in Figure 16-9, the amount of the instrument is credited to the indorser's account before it is negotiated further. Retail stores often stamp each check "for deposit only" when it is received. This wording provides protection in the event the check is stolen. Checks mailed to the bank for deposit should always be indorsed in this way. An indorsement that purports to prohibit further transfer, such as "pay Olga Peterson only," may be further negotiated

Figure 16-9 A restrictive indorsement limits the subsequent use of the instrument.

after the directions in the indorsement are carried out. Thus, after Olga Peterson is paid, any holder of the instrument may continue to negotiate it. A restrictive indorsement does not prevent further transfer or negotiation of the instrument.

A **conditional indorsement**, a type of restrictive indorsement, purports to make the rights of the indorsee subject to the happening of a certain event or condition. A person paying the instrument or taking it for value, however, may disregard the condition.

EXAMPLE 16-4: Conditional Indorsement

Gallo wished to transfer a dividend check that he received to his grandson, James Ingram, as a birthday gift (see the indorsement in the illustration). Because Gallo did not want Ingram to cash the check before his 18th birthday, he issued a conditional indorsement. However, under the UCC, a bank or anyone else who gives Ingram money or value for the check will not be affected by the condition.

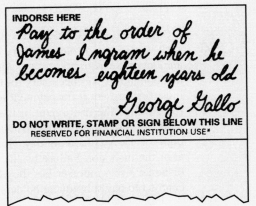

INDORSE HERE
Pay to the order of
James Ingram when he
becomes eighteen years old
George Gallo
DO NOT WRITE, STAMP OR SIGN BELOW THIS LINE
RESERVED FOR FINANCIAL INSTITUTION USE*

Qualified Indorsements A **qualified indorsement** is one in which words have been added to the signature that limit the liability of the indorser. By adding the words *without recourse* to the indorsement, the indorser is not liable in the event the instrument is dishonored, that is, not paid by the maker or drawer.

EXAMPLE 16-5: Qualified Indorsement

A $25,000 check was made payable to Attorney Samuel Brock in payment of a client's claim. Brock indorsed the check to the client, George Rose, "without recourse." By using this indorsement, Brock would not be responsible for payment if the check failed to clear, because a qualified indorsement limits the contractual liability of the indorser.

INDORSE HERE
Pay to the order
of George Rose without
recourse
Samuel Brock
DO NOT WRITE STAMP OR SIGN BELOW THIS LINE
RESERVED FOR FINANCIAL INSTITUTION USE*

Obligations of Indorsers

Indorsements have threefold significance. In addition to being necessary to negotiate order paper, they create obligations on the part of the indorser. These obligations come in the form of implied warranties and a contractual promise to pay subsequent holders of the instrument.

Warranties of Indorsers

An indorser who receives consideration for an instrument makes five warranties to subsequent transferees of the instrument. These five warranties are as follows. First, the indorser is entitled to enforce the instrument. This warranty gives assurances to subsequent holders that the person indorsing it did not steal it or come into possession of it in an unlawful manner. Second, the indorser warrants that all signatures are authentic and authorized. Third, the next warranty is that the instrument has not been altered. The indorser warrants that there has been no alteration or other irregularity. Fourth, the instrument is not subject to a defense of any party that can be asserted against the indorser. Fifth, the last warranty provides that the indorser has no knowledge of the bankruptcy of the maker, acceptor, or drawer.

Contract of Indorsers

Unless an indorsement states otherwise (e.g., by words such as *without recourse*), every indorser agrees to pay any subsequent holder the face amount of the instrument if it is **dishonored** (not paid by the maker or drawee). To enforce this obligation, it is necessary for the holder to do two things. The holder of an instrument must first present it for payment to the maker or drawee when it is due. If that person refuses to pay the instrument, it is said to be dishonored. The holder then must notify the indorser or indorsers of the dishonor. If the holder is a bank, notice must be given by midnight of the next banking day. Holders other than banks must give notice within 30 days after the dishonor. Failure by the holder to make presentment and give timely notice of dishonor to an indorser has the effect of discharging that indorser from liability on the contract to pay subsequent holders of the instrument.

Multiple Payees, Missing and Forged Indorsements

If an instrument is payable to either of two payees, as in "pay to the order of Eric Foss *or* Betty Foss," the indorsement of only one of the payees is necessary to negotiate it. However, if an instrument is payable to both of two payees, as in "pay to the order of Eric Foss *and* Betty Foss," the indorsement of both payees is necessary for a proper negotiation. A bank that has taken an instrument from a customer to send through the bank collection process may supply any indorsement of the customer that is necessary to title. This rule is designed to speed up bank collections by eliminating the necessity to return to a depositor any items that were not indorsed. Such an indorsement may not be supplied by a bank, however, if the instrument contains the words *payee's indorsement required*.

Unauthorized or Forged Indorsements

An unauthorized signature or indorsement is one made without actual, implied, or apparent authority. With three exceptions and unless ratified (approved afterward), an unauthorized or forged signature does not serve as the signature of the person whose name is signed. It has no effect. In addition, when an instrument is paid on a forged indorsement, the tort of conversion takes place. For example, when a bank pays proceeds to a forger and the payee's wishes are not carried out, the bank is held liable for converting the payee's funds. **Conversion** is the wrongful exercise of dominion and control over another's personal property.

Exceptions   There are three exceptions to the general rule that an unauthorized indorsement has no effect. The exceptions, shown in the following list, are designed primarily to promote negotiability of negotiable instruments.

1. ***Imposters***   An imposter is someone who impersonates another. When an instrument is issued to an imposter on the false belief that the imposter is the payee, the indorsement by any person in the name of the payee is treated as an effective indorsement. This rule places the loss, in such a case, on the one who is in the best position to prevent it—the maker or drawer of the instrument.

CLASSIC CASE Thrown by the Fictitious Payee Exception

Most of us are tempted from time to time to take the occasional shortcut or two to solve our problems. Fortunately, most of us also resist that temptation. Instead, we work for what we have; we pay our bills, and we wait patiently for our next paycheck. There are times, however, when the temptation is too great for some. An example involves Lorna Lewis, a supervisor in the credit department of Getty Petroleum. To appreciate what happened to Lewis we have to understand Getty's business. It worked something like this. Getty was in the business of distributing gasoline to its dealer-owned stations. The dealers accepted credit cards from motorists, who would pay at the pump or at the indoor cash register. The payments from the credit card companies would go directly to Getty, which would then generate checks that were made payable to the individual dealerships. The plan was foolproof—almost. There was one small glitch. The checks never went to the dealers. In a cleverly constructed accounting scheme, the checks were generated just to keep Getty's financial records straight. What actually happened was that Getty would void the checks and credit the accounts of the dealers against their future purchases. The plan might have worked well had it not been for Lewis. Lewis was charged with voiding the

checks. This gave her access to an enormous amount of money. At some point, Lewis decided to keep the checks and forge the indorsement of the payees. She then sent the checks to credit card companies to pay off her own credit card debt. The credit card companies forwarded the checks to Chemical Bank, which was where Getty kept its accounts. Eventually Lewis's game was discovered and Getty sued the credit card companies for the lost money. Getty argued that, whenever a credit card company pays money to a forger, that credit card company is liable for the lost money. Getty was correct too, well almost. Had it not been for a very important exception to the rule, the petroleum company might have actually won the case. The fictitious payee exception says that, when the maker or drawer of an instrument does not intend for the payee to have an interest in the instrument, any indorsement is effective. So, in this case, because the drawer (Getty) had no intent to transfer any interests to the payees (the service stations), anyone who signs those instruments (Lewis) has indorsed them properly and the loss falls on the shoulders of the drawer (Getty). [See: *Getty Petroleum Corp. v. American Express Travel Related Services, Co., Inc.* 683 N.E.2d 311 (New York Court of Appeals).]

2. ***Padded Payrolls*** When an agent or employee of the maker or drawer pads the payroll by supplying the employer with fictitious names, an indorsement by any person in the name of each fictitious payee is effective. This rule places the burden of preventing this type of fraud on the party who is in the best position to prevent it—either the drawer (if a draft) or the maker (if a note).

3. ***No Interest Intended; Fictitious Payee*** When the maker or drawer of an instrument intends the payee to have no interest in the instrument or the payee is a fictitious person, an indorsement by any person in the name of the payee is effective.

quick quiz 16-2

1. An instrument is indorsed when the holder signs it, thereby indicating the intent to transfer ownership to another.   true | false

2. Instruments that do not meet all of the requirements of negotiability cannot be negotiated nor transferred by assignment.   true | false

3. An unauthorized signature or indorsement is one made without actual, implied, or apparent authority.   true | false

Summary

16.1 The law of negotiable instruments is found in Article 3 of the UCC. Under the UCC, a negotiable instrument is a written document signed by the maker that contains an unconditional promise or order to pay a fixed amount of money on demand or at a definite time to the bearer or to order. There are two basic kinds of negotiable instruments: promise instruments (including notes and certificates of deposit) and order instruments (including drafts and checks). The following are parties to negotiable instruments: maker or comaker; drawer; issuer; drawee; payee; bearer; holder; holder in due course; indorser; indorsee; and acceptor. To be negotiable, instruments must: (1) be in writing; (2) be signed by the maker or drawer; (3) contain an unconditional promise or order to pay; (4) be made out for a fixed amount of money; (5) be payable on demand or at a definite time; and (6) except for checks, be payable to order or to bearer.

16.2 When an instrument is first delivered by the maker or drawer for the purpose of giving rights to any person, it is said to be *issued*. When the person to whom it is issued delivers it to a third party, it is *transferred*. Instruments can be transferred by assignment or by negotiation. An instrument is indorsed when the holder signs it, thereby indicating the intent to transfer ownership to another. Indorsements may be written in ink, typewritten, or stamped with a rubber stamp. There are four commonly used types of indorsements: blank indorsements, special indorsements, restrictive indorsements, and qualified indorsements. Indorsements have threefold significance. In addition to being necessary to negotiate order paper, they create obligations on the part of the indorser. These obligations come in the form of implied warranties and a contractual promise to pay subsequent holders of the instrument. An unauthorized signature or indorsement is one made without actual, implied, or apparent authority.

Key Terms

acceptance, 384
acceptor, 388
allonge, 392
assignment, 391
bank draft, 386
bearer, 388
bearer paper, 391
bill of exchange, 383
blank indorsement, 392
cashier's check, 386
certificate of deposit (CD), 383
certified check, 386
check, 384
comakers, 388
conditional indorsement, 395
conversion, 396

demand note, 383
dishonored, 396
domestic bill of exchange, 384
draft, 383
drawee, 388
drawer, 388
foreign draft, 384
holder, 388
holder in due course, 388
indorsee, 388
indorsement in full, 394
indorser, 388
installment note, 383
international bill of exchange, 384
issuer, 388
maker, 388

money order, 387
negotiable instrument, 382
negotiation, 391
note, 383
order paper, 391
payee, 388
qualified indorsement, 395
restrictive indorsement, 394
sight draft, 384
special indorsement, 394
teller's check, 386
time draft, 384
trade acceptance, 384
traveler's check, 386

Questions for Review and Discussion

1. What is the purpose of a negotiable instrument?
2. Which negotiable instruments contain a promise to pay money?
3. Which negotiable instruments contain an order to pay money?
4. What are the different types of checks and money orders?
5. What are the requirements of a negotiable instrument?
6. What is the difference between an assignment and a negotiation of an instrument?

7. What are the four kinds of indorsements?
8. What are the implied warranties that are related to indorsements?
9. What contract is made when people indorse negotiable instruments?
10. What is the legal effect of a forged indorsement?

Cases for Analysis

1. Gail Sak wanted to give her niece, Kim Ryan, a gift of money for her 21st birthday, which was two weeks away. Because she was leaving for a trip to Europe the next day, Sak gave Ryan a check dated that day reading, "Pay to the order of Kim Ryan when she reaches the age of twenty-one (signed) Gail Sak." Was the check negotiable? Why or why not?

2. In exchange for legal services rendered to her by the law firm of Westmoreland, Hall, and Bryan, Barbara Hall wrote the following letter: "I agree to pay to your firm as attorney's fees for representing me in obtaining property settlement agreement and tax advice, the sum of $2,760, payable at the rate of $230 per month for twelve (12) months beginning January 1, 1970. Very truly yours, Barbara Hall Hodge." Was the letter a negotiable instrument? Give the reason for your answer. [See: *Hall v. Westmoreland, Hall & Bryan,* 182 S.E.2d 539 (GA).]

3. Barton signed a promissory note promising to pay to the order of Scott Hudgens Realty & Mortgage, Inc., the sum of $3,000. The note stated, "This amount is due and payable upon evidence of an acceptable permanent loan . . . and upon acceptance of the loan commitment." Was the note negotiable? Why or why not? [See: *Barton v. Scott Hudgens Realty & Mortg.,* 222 S.E.2d 126 (GA).]

4. Melanie E. Regan wrote the following words on a sheet of notebook paper in her own handwriting: "Twenty years from date, I, Melanie E. Regan promise to pay to the order of Ryan M. Brown $10,000 without interest." She did not sign the paper at the end. Is the instrument negotiable? Why or why not?

5. David Shin, a silver collector, ran short of cash. He borrowed $1,500 from Vinnie Gaff, giving Gaff the following note: "Thirty days from date, I promise to pay to the order of Vinnie Gaff $1,500 worth of silver (signed) David Shin." Gaff indorsed the note and gave it to Kia Lai in exchange for services rendered by Lai. What legal term describes the transfer of the note from Gaff to Lai? Explain your answer.

6. Powell, intending to write a check to Thompson Electric, Inc., instead made it payable to the order of "Tompson Electric." Thompson Electric, Inc., indorsed the check with its name correctly spelled. Was the indorsement valid? Why or why not? [See: *State v. Powell,* 551 P.2d 902 (KS).]

7. Tufi forged the payee's name on the front of a U.S. Treasurer's check. When convicted of a forgery, he appealed, contending that a signature on the front of a check cannot be an indorsement. May an indorsement be written on the front of an instrument? Explain. [See: *United States v. Tufi,* 536 F.2d 855 (9th Cir.).]

8. Morse wrote a check for $2,500 payable to Reynolds for services rendered. Reynolds fraudulently raised the check to $5,500, indorsed it "without recourse," and deposited it in her bank account. Later, when the alteration was discovered, Reynolds argued that she was not responsible because her indorsement was qualified. Do you agree with Reynolds? Why or why not? [See: *Wolfram v. Halloway,* 361 N.E.2d 587 (IL).]

9. Sanders borrowed $5,000 from Waskow, giving Waskow a promissory note that read, "One year from date, I promise to pay to the order of James Waskow $5,000, without interest (signed) Mary Sanders." Six months later, Waskow died. The unindorsed note was in the possession of Waskow's landlord, who claimed that Waskow had given him the note in payment of back rent. Was the landlord a holder of the note? Why or why not? [See: *Smathers v. Smathers,* 239 S.E.2d 637 (NC).]

quick quiz Answers

16-1	16-2
1. T	1. T
2. F	2. F
3. T	3. T

Chapter 17

Holders in Due Course, Defenses, and Liabilities

THE OPENING CASE *Round 1*
Good Faith: Honesty in Fact or Reasonable Commercial Practices?

John Talcott, Jr., hired D. J. Rivera as an advisor to help him find investment opportunities. Talcott, who was 93 years old at the time, followed one of Rivera's suggestions and transferred $75,000 to Rivera to finance an investment opportunity. (The opportunity did not pan out as expected, but that is another story.) This story involves two additional checks that were made out by Talcott in support of this venture. These checks involve a third party named Salvatore Guarino who served as Rivera's assistant. In his role as Rivera's aide, Guarino opened an account with Any Kind Checks, Inc. (AKC). The account gave Guarino check cashing rights with AKC. To open the account, Guarino had to produce a driver's license, present a Social Security number, and fill out a card on which he identified himself as a "broker." Meanwhile, Rivera told Talcott that he could recoup some of Talcott's losses on that $75,000 if he could have an additional $10,000 in travel money so that his "associate" Guarino could take care of a few out-of-town details. Talcott sent a check for $10,000 via FedEx to Guarino. Next, Rivera called Talcott with Plan B, indicating that, after further consultation with "Mr." Guarino, he would need only $5,700 not $10,000. Accordingly, Talcott said that he would stop payment on check number one and make out check number two for $5,700. When Guarino received the first check (the $10,000 check) he immediately took it to AKC

along with his ID and the FedEx envelope. At AKC he worked with Nancy Michael who checked his card, which was on file at the office, and the FedEx envelope, and tried to call Talcott. She did not get Talcott on the phone but, based on the evidence on hand (the card and the envelope), she relied on her "experience" and cashed the check (minus AKC's 5 percent fee of $500). Five days later, Guarino returned to AKC with the check for $5,700. This time he talked to Joanne Kochakian. He presented to her a FedEx envelope and his other identification. She, however, had no authority to cash a check for that much. She called Michael. Michael told her to get Talcott on the phone. On the first try, she got no answer so Guarino said something like, "Let's try this number," and gave her a second number that was virtually identical to the first except that two numbers were reversed. (Stop and think for just a moment, and you'll get it.) This time she reached Talcott who OKd check number two. With Talcott's approval, the check was cashed. Two days later, Talcott heard from Rivera who told him that Guarino is a "thief." Talcott stops payment on check number two. It is easy to see that Rivera and Guarino scammed both Talcott and AKC. To get its money back, AKC sued Talcott and Guarino. To succeed in a case like this AKC must demonstrate that it is a holder in due course. To demonstrate that it is a holder in due course, AKC must prove that it took the instrument (1) for fair value, (2) in good faith, and (3) without notice that anything was wrong with it. Is AKC a holder in due course? Will the court decide differently between the $10,000 check and the $5,700 check? In a moment, the results of the court case will be made clear. [See: *Any Kinds Checks Cashed, Inc. v. Talcott, et al.* 830 So.2d 160 (2002).]

Opening Case Questions

1. Who is the drawer of the two checks? Explain.

2. What are the elements that make someone (or some entity) a holder in due course? Explain.

3. What constitutes "good faith" in a case like this one? Explain.

4. What party in this case has the burden of proof? Explain.

5. The court must review two checks in this case. Can the court decide differently in the case of each check? Explain.

 Learning Objectives

1. State the characteristics of being a holder in due course.
2. Describe the special protection given to a holder in due course.
3. Define holder.
4. Explain the protection given to a holder through a holder in due course.
5. Name six personal defenses.
6. Discuss the protection given to people who sign consumer credit contracts.
7. Name six real defenses and explain the significance of a real defense.
8. Explain primary liability.
9. Explain secondary liability.
10. Describe the conditions that must be met to hold a secondary party liable.

17-1 Holder in Due Course

A fundamental rule of contract law states that it is not legally possible for one party to transfer rights that are greater than they actually have themselves. A key exception to that rule is found in the law of negotiable instruments. One of the basic principles of the law of negotiable instruments says that a holder in due course of negotiable instruments can receive more rights than the party or parties who held the instrument before them. For this reason, negotiable instruments are used a lot and are passed openly from one party to another. Often the question of whether one of the parties in a lawsuit is a holder in due course will arise. Usually the party making this claim is the holder who is trying to elevate his or her status to that of a holder in due course (a title that even sounds more important than just a plain, run of the mill, "ordinary holder"). The UCC sets the standard for determining if an ordinary **holder** is really a holder in due course. In order to demonstrate that it is a **holder in due course**, the UCC says a party must demonstrate that it took the instrument (1) for fair value, (2) in good faith, and (3) without notice that anything is wrong with it. In general, in a case involving a holder in due course, one party (party A) is holding an instrument that says that party B should fork over the ready cash to cover the face value of that instrument. Party B then raises a defense and says, because of this defense, it does not have to pay party A. The burden switches to party A, which must now prove that it is a holder in due course.

UCC Revised (1990) 3-302(a)(2) (see page 971)

EXAMPLE 17-1: What It Takes to Be a Holder in Due Course

Mr. Harrison of Harrison Industries receives a check from Ms. Taft of Taft Consolidated for $50,897.77. He takes the check to Garfield National Bank to cash it. Garfield tries to contact Erie City Bank on which the check is drawn with no luck because of a computer problem. Later that "problem" turns out to have been an excuse from a not-so-industrious teller, who was outside on an extended "smoke break" when the request came across his desk. To its credit, the bank then tries to contact Ms. Taft, with no result. Because Mr. Harrison is such a good customer, Garfield still places the amount for the check in his account, which already contains $5,000. The next day, Mr. Harrison returns to Garfield National Bank and closes the account, taking out the full $55,897.77. That very afternoon, the Garfield National Bank discovers that the check has a stop payment order on it at Erie and Erie will not be sending the $50,897.77 to Garfield. After several attempts to recover the money peacefully from Harrison or Taft, Garfield National Bank sues Mr. Harrison and Ms. Taft for the $50,897.77 that it paid out beyond Mr. Harrison's original $5,000 despite the stop payment order. Ms. Taft demonstrates that she issued the stop payment order in a timely manner because Harrison had not performed the job that Mr. Harrison, as CEO of Harrison Industries, had promised. For Garfield to recover that $50,897.77 it will have to demonstrate that it is a holder in due course. In order to demonstrate that it is a holder in due course, the UCC says that Garfield must demonstrate that it took the instrument (1) for fair value, (2) in good faith, and (3) without notice that anything is wrong with it.

The Holder in Due Course Requirements

As we have seen frequently, the law operates as a complex adaptive system. Often this means that one agent within the system, a court or an agency, for example, will interact with the other agents to effect a change in the flow of information in that system, resulting in a new set of rules in that area of the law. Such was the case when the UCC was revised to take into account some of the changes in the way negotiable instruments were handled. One key target of the reform movement involved a revised explanation of the requirements needed to demonstrate the existence of holder in due course status. The requirements did not change. A holder still had to show that it took the instrument (1) for fair value, (2) in good faith, and (3) without notice that anything is wrong with it. However, measuring good faith became a bit more complicated and difficult than it had been in previous incarnations of the test.

The Value-Taking Requirement

The taking for value requirement differs little from the ordinary concept of consideration in general contract law. In essence, this means that the party who took the instrument and now holds it must have given something of value (or a promise of something of value) in exchange for that instrument. The UCC explains this requirement in simple and straightforward language in section UCC 3-303 when it says that a negotiable instrument is taken for value under the following circumstances:

1. A promise to perform has been fulfilled by the holder.
2. A security interest in or a lien on the instrument has been obtained by the holder.
3. A prior claim has been satisfied or been secured for the holder by taking the instrument.
4. A negotiable instrument is given by the holder in payment.
5. An irrevocable obligation is given by the holder in payment.

Recall that there are certain preordained situations in which consideration will never exist no matter whether the case involves negotiable instruments or regular garden-variety contracts. Gifts, for example, are not supported by consideration. That means if a party has received a negotiable instrument as a gift, that party has transferred nothing of value in exchange and, therefore, cannot be a holder in due course.

The Good Faith Requirement

The Good Faith Requirement   Good faith is the most fluid of the holder in due course requirements. The evolution of the requirement of good faith also exemplifies the evolutionary development of the law as a complex adaptive system. Like many of the concepts in modern contract law, the concept of good faith emerged from within the practices of the medieval principles of the law merchant. As noted in Chapter 7, four of the essential characteristics of the law merchant were (1) the involvement of the merchants in the operation of the law, the need for (2) neutral and (3) universal judgments, and support for the notion of (4) mutuality (AKA reciprocity). Nowhere in the law merchant are the elements more clearly seen than in the concept of good faith. This is, of course, quite understandable since the merchants themselves acted as judges and carried with them a consistent and straightforward understanding of the need for their fellow merchants to be fair and just to one another and to their suppliers and buyers. The concept of good faith carried within it an appreciation for neutrality, universality, and mutuality. Of course, an understanding of good faith did not guarantee that merchants acted with good faith. If that were the case, there would be no need of the courts. Nevertheless, understanding the concept meant that, ultimately, when merchants did not act in good faith they knew it. Ironically, it was that self-knowledge that made them effective judges in the mercantile court ("It takes a thief, to catch a thief"). [See: Harold J. Berman, *Law and Revolution: The Formation of the Western Legal Tradition* (Cambridge: Harvard University Press, 1983); and Roy Goode, "The Concept of 'Good Faith' in English Law," *Pace Law School Institute of International Commercial Law,* March 1992; updated, September 11, 2009.]

When the law merchant was merged with the common law and when parts of the common law were codified, one of the concepts that flowed along with it was the concept of good faith. The assimilation process, however, was not cut from whole cloth, and its evolution into the negotiable instrument law took some time. The concept of good faith has always involved two basic elements: (1) honesty in fact and (2) conforming to accepted commercial practices of fairness. These two sides of good faith, however, were not always used in tandem in all situations. Thus, when the Uniform Commercial Code was first codified, the two-prong test of honesty and commercial fairness was restricted to a few areas.

1. It was limited to agreements covered by Article 2 of the UCC.

2. It regulated the conduct of merchants, but no one else.

3. It involved only those situations in which the actual phrase *good faith* was mentioned in Article 2 of the UCC. [See: UCC Section 1-201 General Definitions-Official Comments.]

The first prong of the test, honesty, was always part of the holder in due course requirement. It represents probably what might be considered the lowest, or perhaps the simplest, type of good faith. In its barest form, the principle says that, on a purely subjective level, the party involved in the problematic transaction was trying to be honest, or intended to be honest, but out of habit, haste, or helplessness was, objectively (in reality), a liar, a cheat, or a thief. While this principle may appear to have emerged out of *Alice in Wonderland* ("sentence first … verdict afterward"), the idea of subjective honesty actually makes some sense when dealing with the banking system. One court explained it this way: "The check is the major method for transfer of funds in commercial practice. The maker, payee, and endorsers of a check naturally expect it will be rapidly negotiated and collected. The wheels of commerce would grind to a halt (if an objective standard were adopted)." [See: *Bowling Green Inc. v. State St. Bank & Trust,* 425 F.2d 81, 85 (1st Cir. 1970).]

This test, of course, was developed in the days before the computerized financial world had fully matured. Today, in the world of direct deposits, ATMs, debit cards, and so on, checks are no longer the "major method for the transfer of finds." Consequently, the standard was altered when the UCC was revised to include the second prong of the traditional test. Today, honesty in fact is not the only thing that is needed to create a holder in due course. Instead, a party claiming to be a holder in due course must also prove that it was acting in a way that demonstrates "conduct that meets reasonable commercial standards of fair dealing." This standard is also supported by a two-step test. Accordingly, to be operating in good faith from an objective perspective, a party who claims to be a holder in due course must act (1) according to the commercial standards of the industry, and (2) those commercial standards must themselves be reasonable. Moreover, any attempt to apply two requirements must be placed within the context of the individual transaction under scrutiny.

THE OPENING CASE *Round 2*
Good Faith: Honesty in Fact or Reasonable Commercial Practices?

In the Opening Case, we learned that Rivera convinced Talcott to place $75,000 in an investment opportunity that did not pan out. To help him recover from that original $75,000 loss, Rivera asked Talcott for an additional $10,000 for travel expenses. Talcott agreed and sent a check for $10,000 via FedEx to Guarino, Rivera's "assistant." A short time after that, Rivera told Talcott that Guarino would need only $5,700, not $10,000, for travel. In view of that, Talcott agreed to stop payment on check number one and made out a second check for $5,700. When Guarino received the first check (the $10,000 check) he took it to Any Kind Checks (AKC) where he had an account as a "broker." At AKC he worked with Nancy Michael who examined Guarino's file at the office and a FedEx envelope that he said had contained Talcott's check. Even though Michael could not reach Talcott on the phone, she cashed the check (minus AKC's 5 percent fee of $500). Five days later, Guarino returned to AKC with check number two for $5,700. This time he talked to Joanne Kochakian. He showed her a FedEx envelope and his other identification. She, however, had no authority to cash a check for that much so she called Michael. Michael told her to get Talcott on the phone. On the first try, Kochakian got no answer. However, when Guarino gave her a second number, she reached Talcott on the phone and he approved check number two. With Talcott's approval, the $5,700 check was cashed. Two days later, Rivera told Talcott that Guarino was a "thief." Talcott stopped payment on check number two. To get its money back, AKC sued Talcott and Guarino. To succeed in this lawsuit, AKC must prove that it is a holder in due course by showing that it took the instrument (1) for fair value,

(2) in good faith, and (3) without notice that anything is wrong with it. Under the former "honesty in fact" system, AKC would have succeeded in both instances, with both checks. In both cases, there was no doubt that Michael and Kochakian were acting honestly. Their actions were somewhat naïve, perhaps a bit careless, maybe even incompetent, but not dishonest. However, under the objective test, AKC will succeed with check number two (the $5,700 check) but fail with check number one (the $10,000 check). In the case of the second check, Kochakian called Talcott and received a verbal OK on that check and so, in relation to that check at least, AKC followed a reasonable commercial practice and was a holder in due course. In the case of check number one, however, AKC's actions did not pass the objective test. First, unlike Kochakian, Michael failed to get Talcott's permission on the first check. In fact, her only attempt to verify the validity of the check consisted of a single unsuccessful phone call. In addition, Michael should have been put on notice that the circumstances were suspicious because Guarino was a new customer and because the check was for an unusually high amount. (There also seems to have been some evidence that Guarino was in an unusual hurry to cash that check, which should have been another red flag.) Moreover, Michael should also have been put on notice by Guarino's claim to be a broker, since legitimate brokers rarely deal with fast-track check cashing outlets like AKC. As a result, the court had no difficulty concluding that AKC did not act in good faith in relation to the $10,000 check and, therefore, was not, in that case at least, a holder in due course. [See: *Any Kinds Checks Cashed, Inc. v. Talcott, et al.* 830 So.2d 160 (2002).]

The Without Notice of Defect Requirement

To be a holder in due course, a holder must not have notice of any claim or defense to an instrument or notice that an instrument is overdue or has been dishonored. A holder has notice of a claim or defense if the instrument bears visible evidence of forgery or alteration. The same is true if the instrument is so incomplete or irregular as to make its legal acceptance doubtful. Notice of a claim or defense is also considered given if the holder knows that the obligation of any party is voidable. A holder has notice that a demand instrument is overdue when more than a reasonable length of time has elapsed since it was issued. A check is overdue 90 days after its date. For other instruments, such as a note or draft, a reasonable time depends on the circumstances of each case. Knowledge of some facts does not in itself give the holder notice of a defense or claim. For example, the fact that an instrument is postdated or antedated

CLASSIC CASE "Pure Heart, Empty Head"—No More

The case at hand involves three life insurance checks that were delivered in Maine to Daniel, Joel, and Claire Guerrette, in the amount of $40,759.35 each. The checks were delivered to the Guerrette children by Steven Hall, an agent of the Sun Life Assurance Company of Canada, the insurance company that held the life insurance policy on Elden Guerrette, the father of the three adult children. The checks were drawn on Chase Manhattan Bank in Syracuse, New York. Instead of simply delivering the checks to the Guerrettes, Hall and his associate, Paul Richard, convinced the Guerrettes to endorse the checks over to them so that the money could be invested in an enterprise known as HER, Inc. Richard then took the three checks totaling $122,278.05 to the Maine Family Federal Credit Union (MFFCU). The MFFCU accepted the checks, deposited them in Richard's account, and then turned the cash over to him on the spot. Soon after this, the three Guerrettes decided that they had made a serious error in signing all that money over to Hall and Richard. Accordingly, they contacted Sun Life, which, in turn, contacted Chase, ordering the bank to stop payment on the checks, which it did. Ultimately Sun Life found itself out $42,366.56 that could not be recovered from Richard. MFFCU then filed a suit against Sun Life arguing that Sun Life was the drawer of the instruments and was, therefore, liable to the union for the outstanding amount. The case ultimately turned on the issue of whether MFFCU was a holder in due course. The court took this opportunity to explore the new good faith holder in due course requirement. The court openly admits that under the previous standard—the honesty in fact standard—MFFCU would be a holder in due course. This is because there was no question about the subjective honesty of the teller involved in handing the money over to Richard at the time that he took the checks into

the credit union. The court even uses a fairly colorful description noting that if it has used only the "pure heart, empty head" standard of the "honesty in fact" test, then MFFCU would clearly be a holder in due course. However, that is no longer the sole standard by which the good faith requirement is to be measured. The new standard quite clearly states that a party claiming to be a holder in due course must also prove that it was acting in a way that demonstrates "conduct that meets reasonable commercial standards of fair dealing." This standard is also supported by a two-step test. Accordingly, to be operating in good faith from an objective perspective, a party who claims to be a holder in due course must act (1) according to the commercial standards of the industry, and (2) those commercial standards must themselves be reasonable. Moreover, any attempt to apply the two requirements must be placed within the context of the individual transaction under scrutiny. In this case the court fixates on two commercial standards that the MFFCU did not follow properly. First, it was improper for the credit union to take a check of that amount (over $120,000) and to cash it without holding it for at least three days (although nine would have been more fitting). Moreover, the court also notes that, according to commercial practices in the banking industry, since the checks in question were all drawn on an out-of-state bank, the credit union should have been extra careful. As a result, the court decides that, in this case, because the credit union was dealing with several huge checks drawn on an out-of-state bank, it should have put a hold on the checks for at least three days. Moreover, had it done so, the stop payment order would have been activated and the entire problem short-circuited. [See: *Maine Family Federal Credit Union v. Sun Life Assurance Company of Canada* (Docket Number 98-324 (March 1999).]

does not prevent someone from being a holder in due course; neither does completing an incomplete instrument constitute having such notice, unless the holder has notice of any improper completion.

Holder through a Holder in Due Course

UCC Revised (1990) 3-304 (see page 972)

UCC Revised (1990) 3-203(b) (see page 969)

A holder who receives an instrument from a holder in due course acquires the rights of the holder in due course, even though he or she does not qualify as a holder in due course. This stipulation is called a **shelter provision**. It is designed to permit holders in due course to transfer all of the rights they have in the paper to others. The shelter does not apply to a holder who has committed fraud or an illegal act.

A QUESTION OF ETHICS

Michael Carrington, the CEO of the Ice-Fire Security Corporation, pushed his marketing division into developing a hard-hitting marketing campaign that included several new aggressive strategies. At one level the marketing executives launched a telemarketing promotion using a customer list that Ice-Fire had purchased from several publishers who kept track of buyers interested in the types of services and products provided by Ice-Fire. Whenever a potential customer responded favorably to the telemarketer's call, he or she was placed on the company's direct mail advertising list. The direct mail department then generated a series of mailings, each of which included a document that cleverly produced a sheet of paper about the size of a dollar bill that appeared to be a valid check but lacked one of the essential requirements of negotiability, such as the words, "Good only when applied to the purchase of . . ." Clearly then the entire direct mail campaign was designed to provoke the customer to open the mail, be duped by the imitation check, and make a purchase that ends up costing more than it appeared, because of the implied message induced by the fictitious check. Is this publishers' sale of the customer list ethical? Is Ice-Fire's purchase and use of the lists ethical? Is a campaign that targets susceptible customers ethical? Is the use of the simulated check ethical? Give reasons for each answer. Be consistent in your responses. If you have a difficult time being consistent, then your principle itself may be flawed. Try formulating a new guiding principle. If you're stumped on the nature of a guiding principle, look back to Chapter 1, "Ethics, Social Responsibility, and the Law." The information in that chapter should help you.

quick quiz 17-1

1. A holder is a person who is in possession of a negotiable instrument that is issued or indorsed to that person's order or to bearer.   true | false

2. Able bought a book from Baker and gave Baker a $25 check. Baker indorsed the check and gave it to Charlie in payment of a debt. Charlie was not a holder in due course of the check.   true | false

3. Charlie indorsed the check he received in Question 2 from Baker and gave it to David as a birthday gift. David had the rights of a holder in due course of the check.   true | false

17-2 Personal Defenses

The favorable treatment that holders in due course receive ensures that they take instruments free from all claims to them on the part of any person and free from all personal defenses of any party *with whom they have not dealt*. **Personal defenses** (also called **limited defenses**) are defenses that can be used against a holder but not a holder in due course of a negotiable instrument. (The terms *personal defense* and *limited defense* come from common law and are not used in the UCC.) The most common personal defenses are breach of contract, failure or lack of consideration, fraud in the inducement, lack of delivery, and payment (see Table 17-1).

UCC Revised (1990)
3-305(b) (see page 972)

Table 17-1 Most Common Personal Defenses	
Defense	**Description**
Breach of contract	One of the parties to a contract has failed to do what he or she has previously agreed to do.
Failure of consideration	One of the parties to a contract has failed to furnish the agreed consideration.
Lack of consideration	No consideration existed in the underlying contract for which the instrument was issued.
Fraud in the inducement	The drawer or maker of an instrument is persuaded to enter a negotiable instrument into a contract because of a misrepresentation of some fact regarding the item purchased.
Lack of delivery of a negotiable instrument	A payee forcibly, unlawfully, or conditionally takes an instrument from a maker or drawer. The maker or drawer did not intend to deliver the instrument.
Payment of a negotiable instrument	The drawer or maker of an instrument has paid the amount of the instrument.

Breach of Contract

Negotiable instruments are often issued in exchange for property, services, or some other obligation as part of an underlying contract. Sometimes, the party to whom the instrument was issued breaches the contract by failing to perform or by performing in an unsatisfactory manner. If suit is brought on the instrument by a holder against the maker or drawer, the latter may use breach of contract as a defense. Because breach of contract is a personal defense, however, it may not be used if the holder of the instrument is a holder in due course unless the parties dealt with each other.

Lack or Failure of Consideration

Lack of consideration is a defense that may be used by a maker or drawer of an instrument when no consideration existed in the underlying contract for which the instrument was issued. The ordinary rules of contract law are followed to determine the presence or absence of consideration in such a case.

EXAMPLE 17-2: Lack of Consideration

Lowell, without any mention of payment, helped his friend Ransom move from Cambridge to Gambier. At the end of the day, after he was in his new apartment, Ransom told Lowell that he'd give him some money for helping him move. The next day, Ransom gave Lowell a $200 check. Lowell cashed the check at a local market and promptly left town. Ransom then stopped payment on the check. Ransom's promise to pay Lowell was not enforceable because Lowell had completed the work when the promise was made—it was past consideration. The local market could recover the $200 from Ransom, however, because it was a holder in due course and was not subject to the personal defense of lack of consideration.

Failure of consideration is not the same as a lack of consideration, although many people confuse the two. **Failure of consideration** is a defense that the maker or drawer may use when the other party breaches the contract by not furnishing the agreed consideration. Both lack of consideration and failure of consideration are personal defenses. They may not be used against a holder in due course.

Fraud in the Inducement

There are two kinds of fraud: fraud in the inducement and fraud as to the essential nature of the transaction. The first is a personal defense; the second is a real defense, discussed later in the chapter. The five elements of fraud are explained in depth in the contract law unit. When someone is induced by a fraudulent statement to enter into a contract, that person may have the contract rescinded. However, he or she may not use that defense against a holder in due course. A holder in due course can cut through the defense of fraud in the inducement and collect from the person who was defrauded.

Lack of Delivery, Payment, and Consumer Protection

Every commercial instrument may be revoked by its maker or drawer until it has been delivered to the payee. *Delivery* is the voluntary transfer of possession of an instrument from one person to another. If the transfer of possession is not voluntary, the instrument has not been "issued." Thus, in the event a payee forcibly, unlawfully, or conditionally takes an instrument from a drawer, the drawer has the defense of lack of delivery. The payee therefore may be denied the right to collect on the instrument. If the payee negotiates the instrument to a holder in due course, however, this defense is removed.

EXAMPLE 17-3: Lack of Delivery

Morse wrote out a check payable to the order of Smith, intending to give it to Smith after Smith had completed a certain amount of work. Smith discovered the check on Morse's desk and took it without doing any work at all. Smith was not entitled to the check; however, if she negotiated the check to a bank, store, or private party for value, in good faith, and without notice (a holder in due course), Morse would have to honor the check even though Smith failed to do the required work.

Payment of an instrument by a maker or drawee usually ends the obligations of the parties. However, if a negotiable instrument is negotiated to a holder in due course after it has been paid, it will have to be paid again. This rule exists because payment is a personal defense, which cannot be used against a holder in due course. Because of this rule, anyone who pays a demand instrument should have it marked "paid" and take possession of it. This requirement is not as important with a time instrument, unless it is paid before its due date, because no one can be a holder in due course of a past due instrument.

The protection that is given to holders in due course was not always fair to consumers who bought on credit in the past.

EXAMPLE **17-4:** Former Law

In 1975, Ruby Merlin bought a car from a used car dealer. She paid a small amount down and signed a consumer sales contract agreeing to pay the balance in 24 monthly installments. The used car dealer negotiated the contract (which was actually a promissory note) to a finance company and received payment immediately. The next day, the car's transmission stopped working, and the dealer refused to fix it. Merlin would still have to pay the finance company the full amount due on the note because the finance company was a holder in due course and was not subject to personal defenses.

In 1976, the FTC adopted the holder in due course rule. Under this rule, holders of consumer credit contracts who are holders in due course are subject to all claims and defenses that the buyer could use against the seller, including personal defenses. Thus, if the situation described in Example 17-4 were to occur today, Merlin's defense that the car's transmission did not work could be used against the finance company, even though it was a holder in due course. When sellers of consumer products have arrangements with financial institutions to finance their customer's purchases, the financial institutions are subject to the customer's personal defenses. They lose their protection as holders in due course.

---

quick quiz 17-2

1. Personal defenses are defenses that can be used against a holder in due course but not a holder of a negotiable instrument.   true | false

2. The most common personal defenses are infancy and illegality.   true | false

3. If a negotiable instrument is negotiated to a holder in due course after it has been paid, it will have to be paid again.   true | false

---

17-3 Real Defenses

Some defenses can be used against everyone, including holders in due course. These defenses are known as real defenses or universal defenses. The terms *real* and *universal defense* come from the common law and are not used in the UCC. No one is required to pay an instrument when they have a real defense. Real defenses include infancy and mental incompetence, illegality and duress, fraud as to the essential nature of the transaction, bankruptcy, unauthorized signature, and alteration (see Table 17-2).

UCC Revised (1990) 3-305(a)(1) (see page 972)

Infancy and Mental Incompetence

A minor (person under the age of 18 years) or mental incompetent need not honor a negotiable instrument if it was given in payment for a contract that the minor or mental

Table 17-2 Most Common Real Defenses

Defense	Description
Infancy and mental incompetence	The maker or drawer of the instrument was a minor or mentally incompetent.
Illegality	The underlying contract for which the instrument was issued was illegal.
Duress	The instrument was drawn against the will of the maker or drawer because of threats of force or bodily harm.
Fraud as to the essential nature of the transaction	A false statement was made to the maker or drawer about the nature of the instrument being signed.
Bankruptcy	An order for relief was issued by the federal court that ended all the debtor's outstanding contractual obligations.
Unauthorized signature	Someone wrongfully signed another's name on an instrument without authority to do so.
Material alteration	The amount of the instrument or the payee's name was changed wrongfully after it was originally drawn by the maker or drawer.

incompetent may disaffirm on the grounds of minority or incompetency. This rule is true even if the instrument comes into the hands of a holder in due course. Similarly, persons who have been found insane by a court are not liable on a negotiable instrument, because their contracts are void.

Illegality and Duress

An instrument that is associated with duress or an illegal act, such as twisting one's arm or drug trafficking, would be void and uncollectible by anyone, even a holder in due course. This provision is true even if the holder in due course is unaware of the illegal acts or conditions.

EXAMPLE 17-5: Illegality—a Real Defense

The Condado Aruba Caribbean Hotel loaned Tickel, who resided in Colorado, $20,000. The money was loaned for the purpose of gambling at the hotel's casino in Aruba, Netherlands Antilles, where gambling is legal. Tickel wrote two checks to repay the debt, each of which was returned for insufficient funds. When suit was brought on the checks, the Colorado court held that gambling debts are unenforceable in that state even against a holder in due course. Tickel was not liable on the checks that he had written to the hotel.

Fraud as to the Essential Nature of the Transaction

Fraud as to the essential nature of the transaction is more serious than fraud in the inducement. When this type of fraud occurs, the defrauded party has no knowledge or opportunity to learn of the true character or terms of the matter. Because of its seriousness, it is a real defense and may be used against anyone, even a holder in due course.

EXAMPLE 17-6: Fraud as to the Essential Nature of the Transaction

Duffy, who was almost blind, was asked by Ingram to sign a receipt. Duffy signed the paper without having had it read to him. The paper was actually a note promising to pay Ingram $2,500. Duffy would not be required to pay the note, even to a holder in due course, because this kind of fraud is more critical than fraud in the inducement.

Bankruptcy

Bankruptcy may be used as a defense to all negotiable instruments, even those in the hands of a holder in due course. Holders of such instruments will receive treatment equal to that of other similar creditors when the debtor's assets are collected and divided according to the bankruptcy law.

Unauthorized Signatures

Whenever someone signs another's name on an instrument without authority, it is a forgery. Unless ratified, it does not operate as the signature of the person whose name is signed. Instead, it operates as the signature of the person who signed it, that is, of the wrongdoer.

UCC Revised (1990)
3-403(a) (see page 976)

EXAMPLE 17-7: Forgery—a Real Defense

With no authority to do so, Parks signed Brown's name on a note, promising to pay Rivera $3,000 in 90 days. The note was negotiated by Rivera to a holder in due course. Brown would not have to pay the money to the holder in due course because the unauthorized signature is a real defense. Parks had committed a crime. The holder in due course could recover from Rivera who, in turn, could recover from the wrongdoer, Parks.

Alteration

Sometimes negotiable instruments are altered after they leave the hands of the maker or drawer. Usually, the alteration involves changing the payee's name or increasing the amount of an instrument. The alteration of an instrument may be used as a real defense. Unless an instrument is written negligently so that it can be easily altered, makers and drawers are not required to pay altered amounts. They must pay only the amount for which the instrument was originally written.

Writing a check in pencil is legal, but not a good idea. It leaves the check vulnerable to alteration by a dishonest person.

EXAMPLE 17-8: Alteration—a Real Defense

Martinez wrote out a check in a proper manner for $315 and gave it to Video Sales in payment for a DVD player. Video Sales raised the check to read $815. Martinez's bank honored the altered check. Martinez could seek reimbursement from his bank for $500, the difference between the original and the altered amount.

UCC Revised (1990)
3-407 (see page 977)

UCC Revised (1990)
3-406 (see page 977)

Any person who negligently contributes to a material alteration of an instrument or an unauthorized signature may not exercise the defense of alteration or lack of authority against a holder in due course, a drawee, or other payor who pays the instrument in good faith. For example, using a pencil to write a check or not being careful to keep the figures compact and clear gives a dishonest holder an opportunity to alter the amount. The careless writer would be without defense.

quick quiz 17-3

1. No one with a real defense is required to pay an instrument.   true | false

2. Fraud in the inducement is more serious than fraud as to the   true | false
   essential nature of the transaction.

3. If a check is written with an erasable pen and later altered by a   true | false
   wrongdoer, the drawer of the check would not be responsible for
   any loss because alteration is a real defense.

UCC Revised (1990)
3-401 (see page 975)

UCC Revised (1990)
3-412, 3-413 (see
page 978)

17-4 Liability of the Parties

No person is liable on an instrument unless that person's signature or the signature of an authorized agent appears on the instrument. Parties to negotiable instruments have different liability depending on their function.

Makers, Acceptors, and Certain Drawers

The following are obligated to pay an instrument without reservations of any kind. They are said to be primarily liable: (1) the maker of a note; (2) the issuer of a cashier's check or other draft in which the drawer and the drawee are the same person; and (3) the acceptor of a draft.

Other Drawers and Indorsers

Other drawers and indorsers have limitations on their obligation to pay an instrument. They are said to be secondarily, or conditionally, liable. The drawer of a draft that has not been accepted is obligated to pay the draft to anyone who is entitled to enforce it; however, if a bank accepts a draft, the drawer is discharged. If a drawee other than a bank accepts a draft and it is later dishonored, the obligation of the drawer is the same as an indorser stated here.

UCC Revised (1990)
3-414, 3-415 (a)(c) (see
pages 978–979)

Indorsers are obligated to pay an instrument only when the following conditions are met: (1) The instrument must be properly presented to the drawee or party obliged to pay the instrument, and payment must be demanded; (2) the instrument must be dishonored, that is, payment refused; and (3) notice of the dishonor must be given to the secondary party within the time and in the manner prescribed by the UCC. If all three of these conditions are not met, drawers of drafts and indorsers are discharged from their obligations.

UCC Revised (1990) 3-501 (see page 981)

Presentment   Presentment means a demand made by a holder to pay or accept an instrument. Presentment may be made by any commercially reasonable means, including oral, written, or electronic communication. If requested by the person to whom presentment is made, the person making presentment must exhibit the instrument and provide identification.

UCC Revised (1990) 3-502 (see page 981)

Dishonor   *Dishonor* means to refuse to pay a negotiable instrument when it is due or to refuse to accept it when asked to do so. An instrument is dishonored when proper presentment is made and acceptance or payment is refused. Dishonor also occurs when

UCC Revised (1990) 3-503 and 3-504 (see page 982)

EXAMPLE 17-9: Dishonor

A note was presented to Baker for payment on the date specified. Baker refused to honor it, claiming the note was a forgery. The holder would have to proceed against the indorsers to obtain payment. The note was dishonored when Baker refused to pay it.

presentment is excused and the instrument is past due and unpaid. The presenting party has recourse against indorsers or other secondary parties after notice of dishonor has been given.

Notice of Dishonor   Obligations of indorsers and drawers of instruments may not be enforced unless they are given notice of the dishonor or notice is excused. Notice of dishonor may be given by any reasonable means, including oral, written, or electronic communication, and is sufficient if it reasonably identifies the instrument and indicates that the instrument has been dishonored or has not been paid or accepted. The return of an instrument given to a bank for collection is sufficient notice of dishonor.

Nonbank holders must give notice of the dishonor to the drawer and indorsers within 30 days following the day of dishonor. Banks taking instruments for collection must give notice before midnight of the banking day following the day the bank was notified of the dishonor. Delay in giving notice of dishonor is excused when the holder has acted carefully and the delay is due to circumstances beyond the holder's control. Presentment and notice of dishonor are also excused when the party waived either presentment or notice of dishonor.

About the Law

Formerly, it was necessary to send a protest to drawers and indorsers when a draft payable outside the United States was dishonored. A *protest* is a certificate of dishonor that states that a draft was presented for acceptance or payment and was dishonored, together with the reasons given for refusal to accept or pay, made under the hand and seal of a United States consul or notary public. Today, under the revised (1990) UCC, a protest is no longer required but may still be used.

quick quiz 17-4

1. Indorsers never have liability to pay.	true | false	
2. Presentment can be made by oral, written, or electronic communication.	true | false	
3. Notice of dishonor must be given by nonbank holders to indorsers within 30 days following the day of dishonor.	true | false	

Summary

17.1 A holder in due course is a holder who takes the instrument for value, in good faith, without notice that it is overdue or has been dishonored, and without notice of any defenses against it or claim to it. The concept of good faith involves two basic elements: (1) honesty in fact and (2) conforming to accepted commercial practices of fairness.

17.2 Personal defenses can be used against a holder but not a holder in due course. The most common personal defenses are breach of contract, lack or failure of consideration, fraud in the inducement, lack of delivery, and payment. Holders of consumer credit contracts who are holders in due course are subject to all claims and defenses that the buyer could use against the seller, including personal defenses.

17.3 Real defenses can be used against anyone, including a holder in due course. Real defenses are infancy and mental incompetence, illegality and duress, fraud as to the essential nature of the transaction, bankruptcy, unauthorized signature, and alteration.

17.4 Makers of notes and acceptors of drafts have an absolute liability to pay. Indorsers have a liability to pay only if an instrument is presented properly for payment, the instrument is dishonored, and proper notice of dishonor is given to the secondary party.

Key Terms

failure of consideration, 408

holder, 401

holder in due course, 401

holder in due course rule, 409

lack of consideration, 407

limited defenses, 407

personal defenses, 407

presentment, 413

real defenses, 409

shelter provision, 406

universal defenses, 409

Questions for Review and Discussion

1. What are the characteristics of being a holder in due course?
2. What special protection is given to a holder in due course?
3. What is a holder?
4. What protection is given to a holder through a holder in due course?
5. What are the six personal defenses?
6. What protection is given to people who sign consumer credit contracts?
7. What are the six real defenses and what is the significance of a real defense?
8. What is primary liability?
9. What is secondary liability?
10. What conditions must be met to hold a secondary party liable?

Cases for Analysis

1. Without authority to do so, Allen signed Baker's name on a note, promising to pay Cohen $5,000 in 30 days. The note was negotiated to Davidson who was a holder in due course. Will Davidson be successful in recovering the $5,000 from Baker in court? Why or why not?

2. Refrigerated Transport Co., Inc., employed a collection agency to collect some of its overdue accounts. The collection agency indorsed, without authority, checks made payable to Refrigerated Transport and deposited them in the agency's own checking account. Was the bank that accepted the checks for deposit a holder in due course? Why or why not? [See: *Nat'l Bank v. Refrigerated Transp.*, 248 S.E.2d 496 (GA).]

3. Andersen entered into a franchise agreement with Great Lake Nursery, under which Andersen was to grow and sell nursery stock and Christmas trees. Great Lake was to provide trees, chemicals, and other items. Andersen signed an installment note that read in part, "For value received, Robert Andersen promises to pay to Great Lake Nursery Corp. $6,412." Great Lake indorsed the note and transferred it to First Investment Company. Later, Andersen stopped making payments because Great Lake filed bankruptcy and failed to perform its part of the franchise

agreement. May Andersen use failure of consideration as a defense when sued by First Investment Company on the note? Why or why not? [See: *First Inv. Co. v. Andersen,* 621 P.2d 683 (UT).]

4. In exchange for an asphalt paving job, Paulick gave Bucci a note promising to pay to the order of Bucci $7,593 in six months with 10 percent per annum interest. Payment was not made on the due date, and Bucci brought suit. Paulick used failure of consideration as a defense, claiming that the paving job was improperly done. The court held that Bucci was a holder in due course because he had taken the instrument for value, in good faith, and without notice of any claims or defenses of Paulick's. Could Paulick use the defense of failure of consideration against Bucci? Why or why not? [See: *Bucci v. Paulick,* 149 A.2d 1255 (PA).]

5. Carolyn Brazil wrote a check to a contractor who agreed to make certain improvements on her home. She wrote the check in reliance on the contractor's false representation that the materials for the job had been purchased, when in fact, they had not. Brazil had the bank on which the check was drawn stop payment on it. Another bank, which cashed the check and became a holder in due course of the instrument, attempted to recover the amount of the check from Brazil. Could it do so? Explain. [See: *Citizens Nat'l Bank v. Brazil,* 233 S.E.2d 482 (GA).]

6. As part of the purchase price for a 9,040-acre ranch, Kirby gave Bergfield a $20,000 check drawn on the Bank of Bellevue. Bergfield had her banker telephone the Bank of Bellevue to inquire about Kirby's account balance to be sure that the check was good. It was learned that there was not enough money in Kirby's account to cover the check. Bergfield continued to hold the check and did not present it to the Bank of Bellevue for payment. Later, Bergfield argued that the telephone call to the bank was a presentment and demand for payment of the check. Do you agree? Why or why not? [See: *Kirby v. Bergfield,* 182 N.W.2d 205 (NE).]

7. Haik transferred his stock in Petrocomp, an oil exploration company, to Rowley in exchange for five $10,000 promissory notes. The notes were signed by Rowley and indorsed by Rowley's son, Stephen. Rowley failed to pay the notes when they became due. No presentment for payment was made by Haik on the due date, nor was a timely notice of dishonor given to Rowley's son, Stephen. Could Haik hold Stephen liable on the notes as an indorser? Explain. [See: *Haik v. Rowley,* 377 So.2d 391 (LA).]

8. David and Nettie Weiner signed seven promissory notes, totaling $89,000, in their capacity as president and secretary of NMD Realty Co. In addition, they indorsed each note on the reverse side with their individual signatures. Each note contained the following provision: "The Maker and indorser or indorsers each hereby waives presentment, demand, and notice of dishonor." The Weiners claimed that, because they are secondarily liable, the bank may not proceed against them individually until after presentment, notice of dishonor, and protest have occurred. Do you agree with the Weiners? Explain. [See: *Bank of Delaware v. NMD Realty Co.,* 325 A.2d 108 (DE).]

9. Rutherford purchased real property from Ethel Stokes for $35,000. He paid $5,000 down and signed a promissory note for the balance. The note was secured by a deed of trust (a type of security interest, discussed in detail in Chapter 31). When payments on the note were overdue, Stokes considered foreclosing on the property. Prior to doing so, however, she negotiated the note to Craig, who purchased it at a discount with notice that it was in default. Was Craig a holder in due course of the note? Why or why not? [See: *Matter of Marriage of Rutherford,* 573 S.W.2d 299 (TX).]

10. Bolton wrote a check for $20,000 to his daughter, Joyce, intending to make a gift. The check was drawn on the State Bank of Wapello and mailed to Joyce in Maryland, where she was living. Joyce received the check, indorsed it, and mailed it to her bank in Baltimore with instructions to use it to establish a certificate of deposit in joint tenancy with her father. Was Joyce a holder in due course of the check? Explain. [See: *Matter of Estate of Bolton,* 444 N.W.2d 482 (IA).]

quick quiz Answers

17-1	17-2	17-3	17-4
1. T	1. F	1. T	1. F
2. F	2. F	2. F	2. T
3. T	3. T	3. F	3. T

THE OPENING CASE *Round 1*
What Is a Bank? What Is a Forgery? When Is a
Depositor Liable?

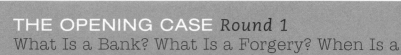

The case at bar began with the untimely passing of Arthur Woods. Woods had an annuity that was payable to Dorothy, his surviving wife. The annuity was controlled by MONY Legacy Life Insurance Company. Mrs. Woods directed her attorney, Cornelius Collins, to have MONY transfer the amount due on the annuity in a single payment. MONY followed these instructions and had the total amount of $24,900 deposited into a MONY checking account that was made out to Mrs. Woods. MONY then delivered the checkbook to Collins as per his instructions. Mrs. Woods was then sent a letter and a statement that informed her of this transaction including the transfer of the checkbook to Collins. About three weeks later, MONY also received a change of address request that asked that all future correspondence on Mrs. Woods's MONY account be sent to Collins. MONY agreed to do so and notified Mrs. Woods of the change. During the next four months, her signature was forged on six unauthorized checks that totaled $24,448.91, effectively draining most of the funds in the account. Five months' worth of statements were sent to Collins that showed the forged drafts. Mrs. Woods has stated that she did not even know about the MONY account until more than a year after it was opened in

her name. At that time she asked MONY for copies of the account and the allegedly forged checks. More than four months after receiving this information, she informed MONY that her signature had been forged. She then asked for her money back and MONY refused. Mrs. Woods, understandably upset by this strange turn of events, brought a lawsuit against MONY. Almost immediately, MONY filed a summary judgment motion to dismiss, which the trial court granted and which the court of appeals upheld. The case then went to the state supreme court. Ordinarily, under the UCC, a bank is liable whenever it takes money from a customer's account based on a forged check. However, under provisions in the UCC, the bank customer, Mrs. Woods in this case, also has a duty to examine any bank statements forwarded by the bank and a corresponding duty to report any irregularities (like, say, a forged signature or two) that she finds in that statement. If the customer does not perform these two duties within one year of receiving a statement from the bank, then the bank is under no legal duty to reimburse the customer for the loss. So far so good, for the bank, that is. However, Mrs. Woods raises two interesting points. First, she argues that MONY Legacy Life Insurance Company is not really a bank. It is, instead, an insurance company and, therefore, is not entitled to the protection provided by UCC Section 4-406. Second, even if MONY is a bank, Mrs. Woods did not receive any statements until one year after the original statements were sent to another party. Now, if we start the clock running at the moment she actually received the statements, she did, in fact, report the forgery within the statutory limit. So, is MONY a bank? Is delivery to Mrs. Woods's attorney, Collins, sufficient notification to her under the statute? Curious? Read on. [See: *Dorothy Woods v. MONY Legacy Life Insurance Company,* 84 N.Y.2d 280, 641 N.E.2d 1070, 617 N.Y.S. 2d 452 (New York).]

Opening Case Questions

1. What is a bank? Explain.

2. What evidence could be used to show that MONY qualifies as a bank? Explain.

3. Can a depositor designate another person to be the recipient of his or her bank statements? Explain.

4. When bank statements go to someone other than the depositor, when does the statutory time period begin to run? Explain.

5. How much time does a depositor have to report an alleged forgery? Explain.

LO Learning Objectives

1. Clarify the bank's duties in the bank–depositor relationship.
2. Clarify the depositor's duties in the bank–depositor relationship.
3. Explain a drawer's rights in relation to a stop-payment order.
4. Explain the extent of the insurance protection provided by the FDIC.
5. List the different terms used to describe banks during the bank collection process.
6. Outline a check's life cycle.
7. Describe the principal features of the Check 21 Act.
8. Describe the consumer protection features of the Check 21 Act.
9. Describe the process of an electronic fund transfer.
10. Discuss the protection given to consumers by the Electronic Fund Transfer Act.

18-1 The Bank–Depositor Relationship

We all believe that we know a bank when we see one. Banks are those respectable looking buildings, with drive-through windows and ATM machines outside, and huge, heavy-duty vault doors, inside. Right? Well, not always. The Uniform Commercial Code, requires us to stretch our imagination a bit and to expand our understanding of the nature of a bank. A **bank**, the UCC tells us is "any person engaged in the business of banking" (UCC section 1-201 [4]). Thus, if an institution collects money from its clients, provides those clients with checking accounts, issues checkbooks to those clients for use with those accounts, identifies their clients by signature cards that the clients have voluntarily completed, sends customers statements about those accounts, and pays out money from those accounts based on the orders contained within checks that are made out by and signed by those clients, then, by and large, that institution is a bank—period. This interpretation of the term *bank* is clearly in line with the objectives of the UCC, which, like almost any code, is to simplify, clarify, and modernize the law, in this case, "the law of commercial transactions" (UCC section 1-102 [2] [a]).

UCC 4-201*

UCC 4-212

The relationship between the drawee bank and its customer is that of both debtor and creditor and agent and principal. The relationship arises out of the express or implied contract that occurs when the customer opens a checking account with the bank. The bank becomes a debtor when money is deposited in the bank by the customer. At this time, the customer is

THE OPENING CASE *Round 2*
What Is a Bank?

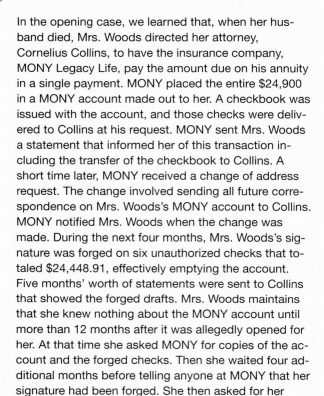

In the opening case, we learned that, when her husband died, Mrs. Woods directed her attorney, Cornelius Collins, to have the insurance company, MONY Legacy Life, pay the amount due on his annuity in a single payment. MONY placed the entire $24,900 in a MONY account made out to her. A checkbook was issued with the account, and those checks were delivered to Collins at his request. MONY sent Mrs. Woods a statement that informed her of this transaction including the transfer of the checkbook to Collins. A short time later, MONY received a change of address request. The change involved sending all future correspondence on Mrs. Woods's MONY account to Collins. MONY notified Mrs. Woods when the change was made. During the next four months, Mrs. Woods's signature was forged on six unauthorized checks that totaled $24,448.91, effectively emptying the account. Five months' worth of statements were sent to Collins that showed the forged drafts. Mrs. Woods maintains that she knew nothing about the MONY account until more than 12 months after it was allegedly opened for her. At that time she asked MONY for copies of the account and the forged checks. Then she waited four additional months before telling anyone at MONY that her signature had been forged. She then asked for her

money back and MONY refused. Mrs. Woods brought a lawsuit against MONY. In next to no time, MONY filed a summary judgment motion to dismiss, which the trial court granted and the court of appeals upheld. The case then went to the state supreme court. Ordinarily, under the UCC, a bank is liable whenever it takes money from a customer's account based on a forged check. However, banks are also provided some protection from this rule. Only truly authentic banks are entitled to this protection. Now we know (or should know) that the UCC defines a bank as "any person who engages in the business of banking" (UCC section 1-201 [4]). MONY, however, is a self-proclaimed insurance company. That does not sound like a bank. However, this seems not to matter to the highest state court in New York. The court says, "In basic respects, plaintiff's MONY account resembled an ordinary checking account. MONY, for example, provided and retained her signature card, issued a checkbook and sent its customer monthly statements." In this way, with these words, the court endorses the idea that the insurance company is a bank as defined by the UCC. [See: *Dorothy Woods v. MONY Legacy Life Insurance Company,* 84 N.Y.2d 280, 641 N.E.2d 1070, 617 N.Y.S.2d 452 (New York).]

---

owed money by the bank and is, therefore, a creditor. When an **overdraft** occurs, that is, when the bank pays out more than the customer has on deposit, the debtor–creditor role reverses, and the bank becomes the creditor. The bank acts as the customer's agent when it collects or attempts to collect checks or other negotiable instruments made payable to the customer. If the items are deposited in the customer's account, any settlement made by the bank with the customer is provisional. A provisional settlement may be revoked by the bank if an item that the bank is attempting to collect is dishonored. The bank may charge back the amount of any credit given for the item to its customer's account or obtain a refund from its customer.

The Bank's Duties

The bank owes a duty to its depositors to honor orders and to protect funds. However, these duties carry strict limitations.

UCC 4-401
UCC 4-402

Duty to Honor Orders   The drawee bank is under a duty to honor all checks drawn by its customers when there are sufficient funds on deposit in the customer's account. If there are insufficient funds on deposit, the bank may charge the customer's account even if it creates an overdraft. If a bank fails to honor a check because of a mistake on its part, the bank is liable to the customer for any actual damages the customer suffers. The drawee bank has no liability to the holder of the check, however, unless it is certified.

EXAMPLE 18-1: Bank's Liability Extends to Actual Damages Only

Rougier, who had $178 in her checking account, wrote a check for $78.42 and mailed it to the electric company in payment of a telephone bill. Due to a mistake on its part, Rougier's bank dishonored the check and returned it to the electric company marked "insufficient funds." As soon as the error was discovered, the electric company was notified, and the check was redeposited and honored by the bank. Because Rougier suffered no loss, the bank was not liable for dishonoring the check. Had Rougier's electricity been disconnected because of the dishonored check, the bank would have been liable to her for the cost of restoring service. The bank was not liable to the electric company.

A bank is under no obligation to a customer to pay a stale check unless it is certified. A **stale check** is a check that is presented for payment more than six months after its date. A bank, however, may honor a stale check without liability to its customer if it acts in good faith.   UCC 4-404

EXAMPLE 18-2: Bank Must Act in Good Faith

The Chemical Bank paid a check that had been written by New York Flameproofing Co. 10 years earlier on a check form no longer used by that company. The account on which the check was drawn had been closed for seven years, and the company's address written on the check had changed seven years earlier. In holding against the bank for paying the check, the court said that such payment was a reckless disregard of due care, so much as to constitute bad faith. The bank was liable for the amount paid.

The drawee bank is not liable to a holder of a check for dishonoring the instrument unless it is certified. The holder's recourse is against the drawer or indorsers on their secondary liability.

Death or Incompetence of Customer The drawee bank is not liable for the payment of a check before it has notice of the death or incompetence of the drawer. In any event, a bank may pay or certify checks for 10 days after the date of death of the drawer. This rule permits holders of checks that are drawn shortly before the drawer's death to cash them without the necessity of filing a claim with the court handling the deceased's estate.   UCC 4-405

Forged and Altered Checks A **forgery** is the fraudulent making or alteration of a writing. A forgery is committed when a person fraudulently writes or alters a check or other form of negotiable instrument to the injury of another. The commission of forgery is a crime, subject to a fine and imprisonment. The offering of a forged instrument to another person when the offeror knows it to be forged is also a crime, known as **uttering**. If a bank, in good faith, pays the altered amount of a check to a holder, it may deduct from the drawer's account only the amount of the check as it was originally written. The depositor is also protected against a signature being forged. When a checking account is opened, the depositor must fill out a signature card, which is permanently filed at the bank. Thereafter, the bank is held to know the depositor's signature. The bank is liable to the depositor if it pays any check on which the depositor's signature has been forged.

Despite this list of depositor rights, the banks are not without protection against forgery. For example, banks still control the contractual relationship that exists with their customers and can, thus, add a clause or two that protects them against certain types of forgery. For instance, a bank can add a clause to a contract stipulating that it will not be liable for forgeries that result from the customer's use of a facsimile or a nonmanual signature. So, if a customer uses a rubber stamp facsimile of his or her signature, as is a common practice among corporate

THE OPENING CASE *Round 3*
What Is a Forgery?

Mrs. Arthur Woods directed her attorney, Cornelius Collins, to have the annuity granted to her by her late husband paid to her in a lump sum by the insurance company, MONY Legacy Life. MONY had the total amount of $24,900 deposited into a MONY checking account made out to Mrs. Woods. MONY then delivered the checkbook to Collins. Mrs. Woods was notified about the transaction. A few weeks after this, MONY received a change of address request that asked the company to send all future correspondence on the account to Collins. MONY agreed and notified Mrs. Woods of the change. Over the next 16 weeks, Mrs. Woods's signature was forged on six unauthorized checks that totaled $24,448.91, effectively pulling the vast majority of the funds out of the account. Five months' worth of statements were sent to Collins that showed the forged drafts. Mrs. Woods, however, claims that she did not know about the MONY account until more than a year after it was opened. At that time she asked MONY for copies of the account and the allegedly forged checks. More than four months after receiving this information, she informed MONY that her signature had been forged. She then asked for her

money back and MONY declined to do so. Mrs. Woods brought a lawsuit against MONY. Almost immediately, MONY filed a summary judgment motion to dismiss, which the trial court granted and the court of appeals upheld. The case then went to the state supreme court. Recall that a forgery is the deceitful rendering or changing of a writing. A forgery is performed when a person falsely writes or modifies a check or other negotiable instrument, thus harming someone or some other entity. The act of forgery is criminal and can lead to imprisonment. The proper procedure for a bank to follow is to obtain a signature card from the customer when the account is opened. The card is then always on file at the bank. Thereafter, the bank is held to know the depositor's signature. Ordinarily, this means that, under the UCC, a bank is liable whenever it takes money from a customer's account based on a forged check. In fact, the UCC holds the bank liable for paying on a forged check based on strict liability. Yet, in this case, the court granted MONY's motion for summary judgment. Curious as to why? Read on. [See: *Dorothy Woods v. MONY Legacy Life Insurance Company,* b84 N.Y.2d 280, 641 N.E.2d 1070, 617 N.Y.S.2d 452 (New York).]

executives, and that stamp is used in a forgery scheme, the bank would not be liable. This is a contractual matter, however, making it something that the customer agrees to when he or she opens an account with that bank. If the customer is unhappy with that treatment, he or she is free to shop around for a bank that makes no such stipulation on their contracts.

On the other hand, banks sometimes put themselves at risk by permitting tellers to cash checks without verifying the depositor's signature. Many, perhaps most, banks actually have a formal policy in place that permits their tellers to cash checks under $2,500 without comparing the signature on the check with the signature on file. Most of the time this works. The checks are cashed, the funds are available, the signature is genuine, the transaction is completed and, most of all, the customer is pleased with bank's overall efficiency. When it does not work and a forged check slips through, the bank is responsible. In the long run, however, the amount of money saved by permitting the tellers to cash checks without verification far outweighs the amount of money lost on the occasional forgery.

Availability of Funds   In the past, banks were not uniform in the amount of time they required before they would make funds available to their depositors. Some banks held funds longer than others, and many banks did not disclose their holding policy to their customers.

To address the issue, Congress passed the Competitive Banking Act. Under the act, the Federal Reserve Board of Governors issued Regulation CC, which requires banks to make funds available to depositors according to a prescribed schedule (Table 18-1). With exceptions, funds from checks drawn on the U.S. Treasury or any state or local government and any bank draft, cashier's check, or postal money order must be made available on the next business day following the banking day of deposit; funds from checks drawn on banks

Table 18-1 Availability of Funds (Under $5,000) You Deposit in Your Bank	
Type of Check	**Funds Must Be Made Available for Withdrawal**
"On us" check [drawn on your bank]	1st business day* after the banking day[†] of deposit
Local check (except $100[‡]) [drawn on a bank in same check-processing region]	2nd business day* after the banking day[†] of deposit
Nonlocal (except $100[‡]) [drawn on a bank in a different check-processing region]	5th business day* after the banking day[†] of deposit
Electronic payment	1st business day* after the banking day[†] of deposit
Cashier's check	1st business day* after the banking day[†] of deposit
Certified check	1st business day* after the banking day[†] of deposit
Government check	1st business day* after the banking day[†] of deposit
U.S. Postal Service money order	1st business day* after the banking day[†] of deposit

*Monday through Friday except most federal holidays.

[†]Any business day (up to the bank's cut-off hour) when the bank is open for substantially all of its banking activities.

[‡]The first $100 (or the total amount of the deposit if less than $100) must be made available on the 1st business day after the banking day of deposit.

within the same Federal Reserve district must be made available within two business days following the banking day of deposit; and funds from checks drawn on banks outside the bank's Federal Reserve district must be made available within five business days following the banking day of deposit. A *business day* is defined under Regulation CC as Monday through Friday, except for most federal holidays. A *banking day* is any business day (up to the bank's cut-off hour) when the bank is open for substantially all of its banking activities.

EXAMPLE 18-3: Fund Availability

Edna Chase deposited a $500 local check that was payable to her in her bank at 3:00 P.M. on Monday. The bank's cut-off hour for the day's transactions was 2:00 P.M. Because the deposit was made after the bank's cut-off hour, it was considered received on Tuesday. The first $100 must be made available to Chase by Wednesday, and the remaining $400 must be made available by Thursday, the second business day after the banking day of deposit.

Exceptions are made for new accounts, deposits greater than $5,000, accounts that are repeatedly overdrawn, deposits of a suspicious nature, and emergency conditions. In addition, some state laws require even shorter time periods for banks to make funds available. Regulation CC also requires banks to disclose in advance their policy for making funds available to depositors. Such disclosures must be made when the account is initially opened and on conspicuously visible notices at teller stations in the bank.

Midnight Deadline Payor banks are required to either settle or return checks quickly. If they do not do so, they are responsible for paying them. If the payor bank is not the depositary bank, it must settle for an item by midnight of the banking day of receipt.

UCC 4-302

EXAMPLE 18-4: Bank's Midnight Deadline

LaPierre wrote a check to Kimberly Motors for $2,500 in payment for a secondhand car. The payor of the check (the bank on which it was drawn) was the National Bank & Trust Co. Kimberly Motors deposited the check into its account in the Southwest Mutual Bank (the depositary bank), which sent it on for collection. LaPierre's car broke down before she reached home that evening. She immediately stopped payment on the check. The National Bank & Trust Company must return the check to the Southwest Mutual Bank, with a notation that payment has been stopped, before midnight of the day that it received the check. If it keeps the check longer than that, it will be liable for payment.

UCC 4-104(h)

If the payor bank is also the depositary bank, it must either pay or return the check or send notice of its dishonor on or before its midnight deadline. In this case, the bank's **midnight deadline** is midnight of the next banking day following the banking day on which it receives the relevant item.

EXAMPLE 18-5: Longer Deadline for Depository Bank

If the National Bank & Trust Company in Example 18-4 had also been the depositary bank, it would have had an extra day to handle the check. The bank would have had until midnight of the next banking day to return the check to Kimberly Motors with the notation that payment had been stopped.

The Depositor's Duties

Depositors, in general, owe a duty to the banks in which they have checking accounts to have sufficient funds on deposit to cover checks that they write. They must also examine their bank statements and canceled checks promptly and with reasonable care and notify the bank quickly of any discrepancies.

Bad Checks Most states have statutes making it larceny or attempted larceny for a person to issue a check drawn on a bank in which the person has insufficient funds. Such statutes usually have the following provisions that must be observed in the prosecution of anyone issuing a *bad check,* sometimes called an *NSF check:* The payee has the obligation of informing the drawer of the nonpayment of the check, together with notice of the provisions of the bad-check law and of the party's legal rights and obligations. After receiving notice of nonpayment, or dishonor, the drawer is given a specified number of days, usually five or 10, in which to make the check good, without fear of prosecution. Failure to make full payment of the check within the number of days allowed by statute serves as presumption of guilt that the drawer issued the check with full knowledge of the facts and with intent to defraud.

Banks and their customers must both perform their responsibilities properly for the system to function effectively.

EXAMPLE 18-6: Bad Check Notice

State National Bank received Yoder's check for $120 due on an installment note it held. After it was deposited, the check was returned to State National with the notification "insufficient funds." The bank's collection department sent a certified letter to Yoder, which explained his responsibility under the bad-check statute. Failure on the part of Yoder to make the check good within the period of time indicated would result in a criminal complaint being lodged against Yoder through the office of the state's prosecuting attorney.

Bad-check statutes are effectively used as a means of collection. Most bad-check writers make an effort to make full payment of the check when advised that they are subject to prosecution. Many banks offer overdraft protection service to their depositors, which covers small overdrafts that are usually caused by the mistake of the drawer in balancing the checkbook. This service is important under the Check 21 Act, because checks may have a shorter float time than in the past. With this service, the bank honors small overdrafts and charges the depositor's account. This service saves the drawer the inconvenience and embarrassment of having a check returned to a holder marked "insufficient funds."

UCC 4-406

Duty to Examine Accounts The UCC imposes a duty on depositors to examine their bank statements and canceled checks promptly and with reasonable care when they are received from the bank. In the past, banks returned the canceled checks to their customers so that they could verify the authenticity of those checks and then balance their statements properly. Today, as we shall see shortly, as a standard operating procedure, banks send an electronic accounting to their customers. Banks will still send the paper checks to a customer if a customer demands that service; however, the bank will also charge the customer for that service. The electronic record that is sent to the customer will include the check number, the date the check was issued, and the amount charged to the customer's account. If, however, the customer pays bills online or has an automatic bill-paying plan in place, the bank statements will show the payees for each withdrawal.

Under common law, bank customers were responsible for examining bank statements to make certain that no forgeries passed through the bank undetected. The responsibility is based on the belief that the customer should know his or her signature better than anyone else, especially bank tellers who sometimes see dozens of signatures each day. This duty was codified when the UCC was finalized. The UCC provision reads in part, "Without regard to care or lack of care of either the customer or the bank, a customer who does not within one year after the statement or items are made available to the customer (subsection (a)) discover and report the customer's unauthorized signature on or any alteration on the item is precluded from asserting against the bank the unauthorized signature or alteration" (UCC 4-406[f]). The UCC also contains a provision that states, in the case of the same wrongdoer forging or altering more than one check, the bank must be notified of the wrongdoing within 30 days after the statement is made available to the depositor. One issue that sometimes emerges in a lawsuit involving forgery is the question of exactly when the statement has been "made available to the customer." This is a key issue because that one-year limit begins to run when the statement is "made available."

Antedated and Postdated Checks A check may be antedated or postdated. UCC 4-401(c)
It is antedated when it is written and dated on one day and delivered later. A check is postdated when the drawer delivers it before its stated date. However, a bank may charge a postdated check against a customer's account unless the customer has notified the bank of the postdated check within a reasonable time for the bank to act on it. Any such notice by a customer to a bank is effective for the same time periods allowed for stop-payment orders, discussed subsequently. If a check is undated, its date is the date that it was first given to someone.

Stop-Payment Rights

Drawers may order a bank to stop payment on any item payable on their account. The stop-payment order must be received in time and in such a manner as to afford the bank a reasonable opportunity to act on it. An oral order is binding upon the bank for 14 calendar days only, unless confirmed in writing within that period. A written order is binding for only six months, unless renewed in writing. The burden of establishing the fact and amount of loss resulting from the payment of an item contrary to a binding order to stop payment is on the customer.

UCC 4-403
UCC 4-403(3)

THE OPENING CASE *Round 4*
When Is a Depositor Liable?

Recall that the opening case began with the death of Arthur Woods, who left an annuity payable to his wife, Dorothy. Mrs. Woods directed her attorney, Cornelius Collins, to have the insurance company, MONY Legacy Life, pay the annuity in a single payment. MONY deposited $24,900 into a MONY checking account made out to Mrs. Woods. MONY delivered the checkbook to Collins according to his instructions. Mrs. Woods was sent a statement that informed her of this transaction. Shortly after, MONY also received a change of address request that asked that all future correspondence on Mrs. Woods's MONY account be sent to Collins. MONY agreed to do so and notified Mrs. Woods of the change. During the next four months, Mrs. Woods's signature was forged on six unauthorized checks that totaled $24,448.91, effectively draining most of the funds in the account. Five months' worth of statements were sent to Collins that showed the forged drafts. Mrs. Woods, however, has stated that she did not even know about the MONY account until more than a year after it was opened in her name. At that time she asked MONY for copies of the account and the allegedly forged checks. More than four months after receiving this information, she informed MONY that her signature had been forged. She then asked for her money back and MONY refused. Mrs. Woods brought a lawsuit against MONY. Almost immediately, MONY filed a summary judgment motion to dismiss, which the trial court granted and the court of appeals upheld. The

case then went to the state supreme court. Now as we have just seen, under the UCC, a bank is strictly liable whenever it takes money from a customer's account based on a forged check. However, under UCC section 4-406, the bank customer, Mrs. Woods in this case, also has a duty to examine any bank statements "sent or made available" by the bank and to report any irregularities found in that statement. Mrs. Woods makes a few creative arguments here. First she contends that, the checks that are handled by MONY are actually "payable through State Street Bank and it is State Street, not MONY that should be protected by UCC Section 4-406." The court disagrees noting that, "MONY, not State Street, opened Woods's account, retained the signature card, issued the checkbook, provided monthly statements and corresponded with the customer." Next Mrs. Woods argues that she did not receive her statements in a proper and timely fashion and so the time limit did not begin to run until she actually saw the statements. Therefore, she is well within the one-year limit. At this point the court looks at that "made available" language in the UCC and states, without hesitation, that, "the account statements were 'made available' to Woods, and the one-year period commenced, when Collins received the monthly statements." Sadly for Mrs. Woods, that ends the case. [See: *Dorothy Woods v. MONY Legacy Life Insurance Company,* b84 N.Y.2d 280, 641 N.E.2d 1070, 617 N.Y.S.2d 452 (New York).]

UCC 4-407

Bank's Right of Subrogation If a bank fails to stop payment on a check, it is responsible for any loss suffered by the drawer who ordered the payment stopped. The bank, however, may take the place of any holder, holder in due course, payee, or drawer who has rights against others on the underlying obligation. This right to be substituted for another is known as the bank's right of subrogation. It is designed to prevent loss to the bank and unjust enrichment to other parties.

Insured Accounts

The Federal Deposit Insurance Corporation (FDIC) insures deposits in banks as well as in savings and loan associations. The basic insurance coverage protects individual bank accounts for up to $250,000 and joint accounts for up to an additional $250,000. Revocable trust and payable-on-death bank accounts are protected for up to $250,000 for each beneficiary named in the account records. (See Table 18-2.)

CLASSIC CASE Distressed? Fear Not! At Times the Bank Must Face Reality

The case at hand involves a forgery that resulted in the plundering of an account owned by Abdul Matin and deposited at the Chase Manhattan Bank (Chase). When Matin returned to the United States after a long period overseas, he was surprised to learn that his account at Chase had been emptied. The culprit seems to have been an unknown person who managed to file a forged change of address card with Chase and to write multiple checks that resulted in the decimation of Matin's account. When Martin, understandably enough, asked for satisfaction from Chase he was, well, disappointed by the bank's refusal to do so. He then filed a lawsuit against the bank. Unperturbed, Chase filed one of those friendly neighborhood summary judgment motions arguing that the bank had "made available" statements to Matin who did not notify them of the forgery within the one-year statute of limitations established by UCC Section 4-406. Since Matin did not live up to his duty to report the forgery, the bank was off the hook. Unbelievably, the trial court granted Chase's motion. Stunned, Matin appealed. During that appeal, irritated and confused, and with a bit of frustration ringing in his voice, Matin could be expected to say something like (we are obviously paraphrasing here), "Now wait just a darn minute. Are you telling me that, you (the bank) made these statement available to me when you mailed them to another party?" The bank says, "Sure, how were we supposed to know it was forged?" At this point, the court of appeals steps into the argument and gently reminds the bank that, since it filed the summary judgment motion in the first place, it has the burden of demonstrating that there is no genuine issue as to any material fact. The court then says something like this to Chase, "Now, do you really think that you met that burden here, because, quite frankly, we don't." Chase, however, has another argument up its sleeve. Chase contends that it supplemented the protection given to the bank by the UCC by adding a clause to its account agreement that states that the customer, Matin in this case, must promptly and thoroughly examine any and all bank statements sent to him and to tell the bank about any and all irregularities, discrepancies, errors, and so on that are involved in those statements. Moreover, the duty emerges at the moment the statement is mailed to the customer. The court finds the argument weak at best and, thus, reverses the lower court's ruling on the summary judgment motion and sends the case back down for further deliberation. [See: *Matin v. Chase Manhattan Bank,* 10 A.S. 3d 447, 781 N.Y.S. 2d 158 (2004).]

Table 18-2 How a Husband, Wife, and One Child May Have Insured Accounts Totaling $2,500,000

Individual Accounts:

Husband	$ 250,000
Wife	$ 250,000
Child	$ 250,000

Joint Accounts:

Husband and Wife	$ 250,000
Husband and Child	$ 250,000
Wife and Child	$ 250,000

Revocable Trust Accounts:

Husband as Trustee for Wife	$ 250,000
Husband as Trustee for Child	$ 250,000
Wife as Trustee for Child	$ 250,000
Wife as Trustee for Husband	$ 250,000
	$2,500,000

18-2 Bank Deposits and Collections

The tremendous number of checks handled by banks and the countrywide nature of the bank collection process require uniformity in the law of bank collections. For this reason, Article 4 of the UCC* contains rules and regulations for handling bank deposits and collections.

Bank Descriptions

During the bank collection process, banks are described by different terms, depending on their particular function in a transaction. Sometimes a bank takes a check for deposit. At other times, it pays a check as a drawee. At still other times, it takes a check for collection only. The different terms that are used to describe banks and their meanings are as follows: A **depositary bank** is the first bank to which an item is transferred for collection, even if it is also the payor bank. The term **payor bank** describes a bank by which an item is payable as drawn or accepted. It includes a drawee bank. **Intermediary bank** defines any bank to which an item is transferred in the course of collection, except the depositary or payor bank. The **collecting bank** is any bank handling the item for collection, except the payor bank, and the **presenting bank** is any bank presenting an item, except a payor bank. **Remitting bank** describes any payor or intermediary bank remitting for an item.

UCC 4-105

A QUESTION OF ETHICS

Bethany Golemen was discharged from her job as an advertising executive at Farnsworth, Yardley, and Brook. Her credit cards were maxed out, her savings account depleted, and her rent was due. On the bright side, James Farnsworth, the senior partner in the advertising firm, had given Goleman a sizable severance check as she left the office on her last day. Goleman was feeling lucky until she tried to retrieve her car from the service station where Tommy Henderson had just finished fixing the brakes on her Saturn. When Goleman tried to pay by credit card her card was rejected. Henderson refused to allow her to take her car until she gave him some type of payment. To satisfy Henderson she wrote him a check for the new brakes, even though she knew that the account was empty. She fully intended to place the severance check into the account the next morning so that the check would not bounce. Unfortunately, when she arrived at her apartment, she found that the landlord had changed the locks because her rent was six months overdue. In order to get into her apartment, she signed the severance check over to the landlord. As a result she never deposited any money in her checking account and her check to Henderson bounced. Was it ethical for Goleman to write Henderson the check knowing there was no money in the account? Remember that, at the time she wrote the original check out to Henderson, she fully intended to place the severance check in the account the next day. From an ethical perspective, does her intent to deposit funds in her checking account tomorrow permit her to write the bad check today? Why or why not?

*To access the most recent version of the UCC and its Articles, please visit http://www.law.cornell.edu/ucc/ucc.table.html

A Check's Life Cycle

The life cycle of a check begins when the drawer writes a check and delivers it to the payee. The payee may take the check directly to the payor bank (the bank on which it was drawn) for payment. If that bank pays the check in cash, its payment is final, and the check is returned to the drawer with the next bank statement. However, it is more likely that the check will be deposited in the payee's own account in another bank. That bank, known as the depositary bank, acts as its customer's agent to collect the money from the payor bank. Any settlement given by the depositary bank in this case is **provisional** (not final). It may be revoked if the check is later dishonored. The check is sent (sometimes through an intermediary bank) to a collecting bank, which presents the check to the payor bank for payment. If it is honored by the payor bank, the amount will be deducted from the drawer's account, and a substitute check will be returned to the drawer with the next bank statement. If the check is dishonored for any reason, a substitute check will be returned to the payee via the same route that it was sent, and all credits given for the item will be revoked (see Figure 18-1).

UCC 4-213

UCC 4-201

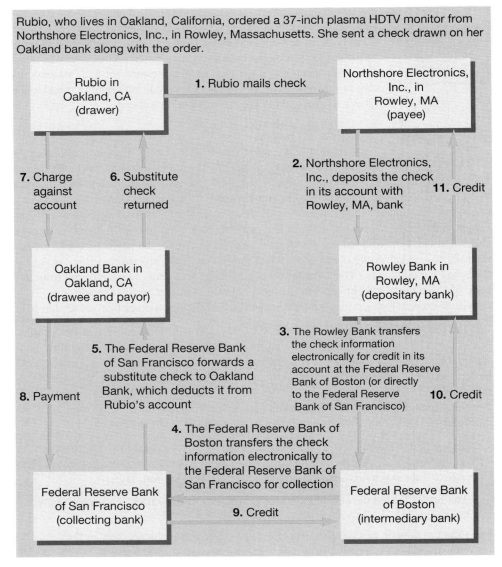

Figure 18-1
The life cycle of Rubio's check is traced through its collection and clearinghouse routes. Before the Check 21 Act became effective in October 2004, the check in this example would have had to be physically transported by plane or truck around its entire route.

18-3 Cyber-Banking

Like all of us, the world of banking has been forced to adapt to the global electronic revolution. The Internet has made the transfer of funds and the record keeping associated with

those funds easier, faster, and more efficient than ever before. The new system, however, is also filled with problems. In fact, the new electronic transfer process is more precarious than the traditional process. This is because the new system is subject to hacking, viruses, identity theft, and cyber-warfare. Consequently, as is true of all parts of the social system, the banking community has been forced to interface with several new statutes designed to monitor and influence its day-to-day operation. These statutes include but are not limited to the Check 21 Act and the Electronic Fund Transfer Act.

The Check 21 Act

Named for the 21st century, the **Check 21 Act** brings the check-clearing method into the modern age by the use of electronic check processing. Such processing could not be done prior to this 2004 law, because of the legal requirement that original checks be presented to the drawee bank for payment. Under this law, a new negotiable instrument called a substitute check is used. A **substitute check** (also called an *image replacement document,* or *IRD*) is a paper reproduction of both sides of an original check that can be processed just like the original check. Under the new law, banks are not required to use substitute checks, but when they do so for consideration, they make the following warranties: (1) The substitute check contains an accurate image of the front and back of the original check; (2) it is the legal equivalent of the original check; and (3) no drawer, drawee, indorser, or depositary bank will be asked to pay a check that already has paid.

Some banks prefer that customers use ATMs for their regular banking transactions, even featuring accounts that charge a fee for the use of live tellers.

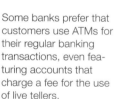

UCC 4-406 (a)(b)

Original Checks No Longer Returned As noted earlier in the chapter, many banks in the past automatically returned canceled checks with their monthly bank statements to their customers, even though the UCC does not require that original checks be returned unless a customer requests them. The Check 21 Act, which takes precedence over the UCC, changes this rule. Under the Check 21 Act, the customer has a right only to a paper substitute check that is a reproduction of the front and back of the original. Bank customers no longer have an absolute right to see their original canceled checks.

Consumer Protection To protect consumers from losses related to substitute checks, the Check 21 Act includes a consumer's right to claim an *expedited credit*. This right exists if the consumer asserts in good faith the following four facts:

- The bank charged the consumer's account for a substitute check that was given to the consumer.

- Either the check was not properly charged to the consumer's account, or the consumer has a warranty claim with respect to the substitute check.

- The consumer suffered a resulting loss.
- The production of the original check or a better copy of the original check is necessary to determine the validity of any claim.

If the consumer makes a claim within 45 days after receiving the bank statement or substitute check, the bank must investigate it and make any necessary recredit to the consumer's account. If the bank needs more than 10 days to investigate and resolve the complaint, it must recredit the consumer's account for an amount up to $2,500 while it completes its investigation. The bank must recredit any remaining balance greater than $2,500 no later than 45 days after the consumer submits the claim.

Electronic Fund Transfers

Electronic banking (also called an **electronic fund transfer** or **EFT**) uses computers and electronic technology as a substitute for checks and other banking methods. People can go to automatic teller machines (ATMs) 24 hours a day to make bank deposits and withdrawals. They can pay bills by phone, have deposits made directly to their bank accounts, and pay for retail purchases directly from their bank accounts. Some banks have arrangements for payment by **e-check** (sometimes called *electronic check conversion*), which is a system in which funds are electronically transferred from a customer's checking account, eliminating the need to process a paper check. Under one system, the customer writes out an ordinary check and gives it to a merchant when making a purchase. After obtaining the customer's written authorization, the merchant passes the check through an instrument that reads the information on the check and converts the payment from a paper check to an electronic funds transfer. The merchant then voids the check and returns it to the customer with a receipt. Payment by e-check is faster and less expensive, thus saving time and money for everyone involved.

ATM, Debit, and Combination Cards

An **ATM card** is used together with a personal identification number (PIN) to gain access to an automatic teller machine either on or off the bank premises. In contrast, a **debit card** (also called a *check card* or *cash card*) is used to subtract money electronically from a bank account to pay for goods or services. Debit cards are used at stores rather than at ATM machines and usually require the use of the customer's signature rather than a PIN. Many banks now use a combination ATM–debit card that performs both functions. There are two kinds of debit cards: online and offline. *Online* debit cards make an immediate transfer of money from the customer's bank account to the merchant's bank account. *Offline* debit cards record a debit against the customer's bank account, which is processed later. A debit card offers less protection than a credit card. Unlike a credit card, a debit card payment cannot be stopped if a purchase is defective or an order is not delivered. In addition, your liability for the unauthorized use of your ATM or debit card is limited to $50 only if you notify the issuer within two business days of the loss or theft of the card. Your liability increases to $500 if notice is delayed beyond that time, and it becomes unlimited when notice is not given within 60 days. The unauthorized use of an ATM card is a criminal offense punishable by fine and/or imprisonment.

EXAMPLE 18-7: Stolen ATM Card

A thief stole Hockmeyer's purse from a grocery store shopping cart. Three days later, Hockmeyer notified the bank that her ATM card was missing. By then, however, the thief had found the card along with Hockmeyer's secret identification number and withdrawn $800 from her account. Because the bank was notified within three days of the theft, Hockmeyer lost $500. Had she notified the bank within two business days of the theft, she would have lost only $50.

The Electronic Fund Transfer Act

UCC 4A-103-505

UCC 4A-104

UCC 4A-103

Regulation E, issued by the Federal Reserve Board under the Electronic Fund Transfer Act, establishes the basic rights, liabilities, and responsibilities of consumers who use electronic fund transfer services and financial institutions that offer these services. Transactions covered under the regulation include:

- Point-of-sale purchases.
- Automated teller machine transfers.
- Telephone-initiated transfers requiring an entry password (PIN).
- Transfers resulting from debit card transactions requiring an entry password (PIN).
- Internet banking.

Under the act, consumers are entitled to receive a written receipt whenever they use an ATM. In addition, the transaction must appear on the periodic statement sent to the consumer. The consumer has 60 days to notify the bank of any error on the periodic statement or terminal receipt. After being notified, the bank has 10 business days to investigate the error. If the bank needs more time, it may take up to 45 days to complete the investigation, but only if the money in dispute is returned to the consumer's account.

Because the Electronic Fund Transfer Act is a consumer protection law, it does not apply to transactions between banks and other businesses. A different law, Article 4A of the UCC, has been adopted by many states to govern EFTs made by banks and businesses. Under the UCC, a business that orders money to be sent electronically is called the *originator*. The business that is to receive the money is called the *beneficiary*. EFTs help businesses that deal with large sums of money make quick transfers to avoid a loss of interest.

EXAMPLE 18-8: Electronic Transfers by Banks

Data Control, Inc., sold a computer system to Western Sales, Inc., for $2 million. When the system was installed, Western Sales ordered its bank to pay $2 million to Data Control. Because both companies had accounts in the First National Bank, the bank simply debited Western Sales' account and credited Data Control's account for $2 million. Western Sales was the originator; Data Control was the beneficiary. If Data Control had used a different bank, the First National Bank would have ordered that bank, called the beneficiary's bank, to credit Data Control's account for $2 million.

Did You Know?

- A *credit* card is like a loan. You agree to pay the money back later at a high interest rate unless you pay the full amount when the bill arrives. A *debit* card, in contrast, means *(continued)*

The Global Financial Cyber-Crisis

The Internet provides us with an enormous amount of flexibility and efficiency in the transfer of funds and with the record keeping associated with those funds. However, as noted earlier, the system is also often at risk. Poorly written software, an incorrect file number, a solar storm, or inadequately maintained hardware can interrupt the operation of even the most secure system. Information technicians might enter an incorrect password, an inaccurate code, or the wrong PIN and the system might shut down or begin to act erratically. Most of these errors are handled easily enough. Other problems, those that are deliberate and knowingly target a computer system, are less easily solved.

Global Level Problems   For instance, a rival firm, an enemy nation, or a crime syndicate could send an e-mail with an attached PDF file that, when opened, will install a deadly virus into a corporate computer system. The software might command the system to shut down, delete data, or, perhaps worse, transfer control of the system to the hacker. What makes this type of attack so insidious is that no one knows about it until the damage is done. Thus, without so much as a digital alarm going off, a corporation might lose all of its data or a banking system might be wiped clean of all transactions. Constructing a plan for dealing with a deliberate computer attack is difficult at best. Nevertheless, steps must be taken to deal with such attacks. [See: "Briefing Cyber-war: War in the Fifth Domain," *The Economist,* July 3, 2010, p. 25.]

Global Cyber-Targets and Cyber-Tactics One step that has been suggested is to divide the data stream so that it travels along a variety of routes so that if one line is attacked the others can continue to transmit. This solution works most of the time. Unfortunately, there are bottlenecks along the global network at which the data streams intersect and fall under the control of a limited number of domain-name servers, making them tempting targets for cyber-criminals and cyber-terrorists. These main intersection points appear in the Middle East, in South East Asia, and along the Eastern seaboard of the United States, any one of which is an inviting target. [See: "Briefing Cyber-war: War in the Fifth Domain," p. 25.]

Cyber-Command (Cyber-com) The global response to such problems has been the establishment of a new cyber-command center. The task of the new command center is to protect the military's computer command system. The National Security Agency has been given control over this new center, which has been officially named Cyber-Command or Cyber-com. Cyber-com is designed to protect the American cyber-system from attack and to formulate plans to undermine the computer systems of enemy nations. Two of its goals might be to protect the "chokepoints" in the submerged fiber-optic system and to uncover effective ways to use the system in a way that benefits the American military [See: "Briefing Cyber-war: War in the Fifth Domain," p. 25.]

Domestic Cyber-Targets and Cyber-Tactics The tactics noted previously are needed to protect the global Internet, but they do not protect individuals except in an indirect way. This is crucial because cyber criminals also frequently target individuals. Such criminals can gain access to banks account, stock portfolios, and other financial records in order to drain funds from those accounts. Or they may steal an individual's identity in order to use that person's credit cards, debit cards, checking account, and other personal financial resources. Fortunately, the federal government has taken steps to protect your bank accounts and your identity from cyber criminal attacks. These steps include the establishment of the Internet Crime Complaint Center and the passage of legislation aimed at protecting Internet transactions.

Internet Crime Complaint Center (IC3) The federal government has set up the Internet Crime Complaint Center (IC3) which connects the National White Collar Crime Center (NW3C) with the Federal Bureau of Investigation (FBI). The IC3 handles complaints involving cybercrimes such as identity theft, cyber-extortion, and Internet fraud. Individuals and businesses can file complaints with the IC3 by accessing their website online. The IC3 also works closely with administrative agencies as well as with local, state, and federal law enforcement agencies. [See: *Internet Crime Complaint Center,* http://www.ic3.gov.]

Domestic Cyber-Legislation Congress has also passed legislation aimed at solving these problems. Two such acts are the Identity Theft and Assumption Deterrence Act (ITDA) and the National Stolen Property Act (NSPA). ITDA, which was amended by the Identity Theft Penalty Enhancement Act, outlaws the unauthorized transfer, possession,

"subtract"—when you use it, you subtract the money from your own bank account.

- If your *credit* card is lost or stolen, you can't lose more than $50. In contrast, if someone uses your *ATM* or *debit* card without permission, you can lose much more unless you notify your bank quickly.

- A *debit* card is often easier to obtain than a credit card and allows you to spend what is in your bank account.

- A *debit* card gives you less protection than a credit card when you purchase items that are defective or never delivered.

- Using a *debit* card instead of writing checks saves you from showing identification or giving out personal identification at the time of a transaction.

or use of a means of identifying another person to violate federal law. The amendment adds a new crime, called *aggravated identity theft,* to the original statute. The section on aggravated identity theft makes it clear that identity theft is much worse when it involves certain very serious felonies, including terrorism. Under the NSPA it is a federal crime to use interstate or foreign commerce to transport personal currency and securities that an individual is aware were stolen, were secured by fraud, or were taken by some other illegal method including an unauthorized electronic transfer.

---

quick quiz 18-3

1.	Consumers have 30 days to notify the bank of any error on the periodic statement received for the use of an ATM.	true | false
2.	A consumer's liability for the unauthorized use of an ATM card is limited to $500 if notice of the loss or theft of a card is given the issuer within two business days.	true | false
3.	The unauthorized use of an ATM card is a criminal offense punishable by a $500 fine and/or five years in prison.	true | false

---

Summary

18.1 The drawee bank must honor all checks (except stale checks) drawn by its customers when there are sufficient funds on deposit. Failure to do so makes the bank liable to the customer for any actual damages the customer suffers. The drawee bank has no liability to the holder of a check unless it is certified. Banks are responsible for paying altered or forged checks. Banks must make funds available to depositors according to a specific schedule. In addition, banks must pay or return checks on or before their midnight deadline. Depositors must examine their bank statements and canceled checks promptly. It is a crime to write a check with insufficient funds in the bank. Oral stop-payment orders are binding upon the bank for 14 days; written orders to stop payment are binding for six months.

18.2 During the bank collection process, banks are described by different terms, depending on their particular function in a transaction. Sometimes a bank takes a check for deposit. At other times, it pays a check as a drawee. At still other times, it takes a check for collection only. The different terms that are used to describe banks and their meanings are as follows: depositary bank, payor bank, intermediary bank, collecting bank, presenting bank, and remitting bank. The life cycle of a check begins when the drawer writes a check and delivers it to the payee. If a payee cashes a check at a payor (drawee) bank, the payment is final. If, instead, the payee deposits a check in his or her bank, which sends it to the payor bank for collection, any payment is provisional.

18.3 The Check 21 Act establishes substitute checks, which may be returned to bank customers in place of the canceled original check and thus make check clearing much quicker through the use of electronic processing. Consumers who use EFTs have 60 days to notify the bank of an error; thereafter, the bank must investigate. A consumer's liability for the unauthorized use of an ATM card is limited to $50 if notice of the loss or theft of a card is given the issuer within two business days. Article 4A of the UCC governs EFTs made by banks and businesses. The federal government has set up the Internet Crime Complaint Center, which handles complaints involving cybercrimes such as identity theft, cyber-extortion, and Internet fraud. Congress has also passed legislation aimed at solving these problems. Two such acts are the Identity Theft and Assumption Deterrence Act and the National Stolen Property Act.

Key Terms

ATM card, 429

bank, 417

Check 21 Act, 428

collecting bank, 426

debit card, 429

depositary bank, 426

e-check, 429

electronic fund transfers (EFTs), 429

forgery, 419

intermediary bank, 426

midnight deadline, 422

overdraft, 417

payor bank, 426

presenting bank, 426

provisional, 427

Regulation E, 430

remitting bank, 426

stale check, 419

subrogation, 424

substitute check, 428

uttering, 419

Questions for Review and Discussion

1. What are the bank's duties in the bank–depositor relationship?
2. What are the depositor's duties in the bank–depositor relationship?
3. What are a drawer's rights in relation to a stop-payment order?
4. What is the extent of the insurance protection provided by the FDIC?
5. What are the different terms used to describe banks during the bank collection process?
6. What are the steps in a check's life cycle?
7. What are the principal features of the Check 21 Act?
8. What consumer protection features are found in the Check 21 Act?
9. What happens during the process of an electronic funds transfer?
10. What protection is given to consumers by the Electronic Fund Transfer Act?

Cases for Analysis

1. Kelco bought a truck from Felton, paying for it with a cashier's check she had obtained from her bank. On her way home, the truck broke down. Kelco immediately telephoned her bank and told it to stop payment on the cashier's check. Later, Kelco discovered that her bank had not stopped payment on the cashier's check and instead had paid it. Did Kelco have a claim against the bank? Explain. [See: *Taboada v. Bank of Babylon,* 408 N.Y.S.2d 734 (NY).]

2. Granite Corp. sent a check to Overseas Equipment Co. When the check was reported lost, Granite wrote to its bank telling it to stop payment on the check. Granite then sent the money to Overseas Equipment Co. by wire. Thirteen months later, the check turned up, and Granite's bank paid it. Did the bank violate its duty to stop payment on the check? Explain. [See: *Granite Equip. Leasing Corp. v. Hempstead Bank,* 326 N.Y.S.2d 881 (NY).]

3. While in the hospital during his final illness, Norris wrote a check and gave it to his sister. She deposited it in her bank account. Norris died before the check cleared, and his bank refused to pay it. May a bank honor a check when it knows of the death of the drawer? Explain. [See: *In re Estate of Norris,* 532 P.2d 981 (CO).]

4. On June 18, Templeton deposited in his bank account a $5,000 check that was payable to his order. The check reached the drawee bank through normal banking channels on June 22. That bank had received a stop-payment order on the check on May 15 and, therefore, refused to honor it. It kept the check until June 28, when it returned it to Templeton with the notification that payment had been stopped. Did the drawee bank violate a duty it owed to Templeton? Explain. [See: *Templeton v. First Nat'l Bank,* 362 N.E.2d 33 (IL).]

5. In payment for services rendered, one of Stewart's clients gave him a check for $185.48 that had been drawn by the client's corporate employer and had been made payable to the order of the client. Although properly indorsed by the client, the

drawee bank flatly refused to cash the check for Stewart. The bank acknowledged that the check was good, that is, that there were sufficient funds in the account. Could Stewart sue the bank for refusing to honor the check? Why or why not? [See: *Stewart v. Citizens & Nat'l Bank,* 225 S.E.2d 761 (GA).]

6. Fitting wrote an $800 check on her account with Continental Bank. A bank employee had mistakenly placed a hold on the account, causing the bank to dishonor the check when it was presented for payment. Fitting was unable to prove that she suffered damages because of the dishonor. Could she recover damages from the bank? Explain. [See: *Continental Bank v. Fitting,* 559 P.2d 218 (AZ).]

7. Roberta Lunt deposited a $625 nonlocal check payable to her with a teller at her bank at 10:30 A.M. on Monday. The next day, Tuesday, she went to the bank to withdraw $300 and was told by the teller that she could have only $100 from the check she had deposited the day before. When must the funds be made available to Roberta? Explain why.

quick quiz Answers

18-1	18-2	18-3
1. F	1. T	1. F
2. T	2. T	2. F
3. T	3. T	3. F

Chino Commercial Bank v. Brian D. Peters
Court of Appeal, Fourth District, Division 2, California
No. E049170 (May 25, 2010)

Summary

The defendant in this case, Brian Peters, is the president of Faux Themes, Inc. (Faux). The corporation had a checking account with the Chino Commercial Bank. Peters and the treasurer of Faux, Marilyn Charlnoes, were authorized makers of the account and were, therefore, liable should there be any overdrafts (should any checks "bounce"). The account was a modest one, holding no more than $10,000 at any one time and usually only about $3,000 to $5,000 as a daily balance. In March 2009, Peters responded to an interesting e-mail that he received from a Malaysian citizen named Husaine Norman who needed someone in Canada or the United States to help him transfer large amounts of money. The e-mail indicated that Norman was a creditor for some people in both the United States and Canada who were reluctant to transfer the money that they owed him into any offshore accounts. Instead they insisted on using North American banks only. That was the point at which Peters could be of help (or so Norman claimed). All Peters had to do was allow him to use his bank account as a conduit. Norman's debtors would send him checks for the amounts that they owed Norman, and Peters would deposit them in his account and then wire that money to Asian accounts identified by Norman. In exchange for that minimal effort Peters would get a 12 percent fee. Since the amounts involved were quite high, his 12 percent would be very lucrative, just so long as things worked out as planned. Peters agreed to this arrangement.

When the first check arrived for $178,000, Peters (Charlnoes actually) deposited it as per Norman's original instructions. Nine days later, the bank confirmed that the check had cleared. On that same day, Peters sent $80,000 to a Hong Kong bank and received another check for $373,988, which was then deposited in the Faux account. Four days later another $71,000 went to Hong Kong. Three days later the bank notified Peters that the second check had cleared. Peters then sent another $317,000 to a Chinese bank, and six days later another check for $257,000 arrived for Peters. At this point things began to unravel. Chino notified Peters that the first check had been altered, changing the original payee to Faux. That meant those original checks had never been made to Faux but to someone else. As a result, all those deposits were dishonored. Now remember that a total of $458,782.60 went out of the Faux account, but since the checks from Norman's "debtors" were fake, none of that money had gone into the account and so the $458,782.60 that the bank wired to China was not Faux's but, well, the bank's, and now the bank wants all that money back. In effect, the $458,782.60 amounted to a spectacular overdraft and, as noted earlier, the bank wants its money. Well, it can't get it from Norman, who probably never existed in the first place, and so the bank turns to Peters, and Charlnoes, and Faux.

Peters admits to being scammed and, in fact, to his credit says he should have known better, but the money was so good that, well, he succumbed to the temptation of the "too good to be true" scheme handed to him by the fictitious Norman. Just to make certain that its hands are clean, the bank does a very close examination of the checks and finds that the alterations are so expertly done that they are virtually undetectable by using ordinary bank procedures common to the industry.

Satisfied that it was not to blame, Chino filed the present lawsuit against Peters, Charlnoes, and Faux. The case is based on breach of contract and fraud. As a remedy the bank wants to attach every bit of property belonging to Peters, Charlnoes, and Faux that it can get its hands on to make up for those monumental losses. Interestingly, the trial court's first inclination was to find the bank negligent and to let Peters, Charlnoes, and Faux off the hook. However, the burden does seem to rest with the defendants. Therefore, the trial court decides that the defendants must show that the bank was negligent. Accordingly, the court issues a right to attach order on the defendants' property.

Basically the issues in the case involve a close look at who was careful, who was careless, who acted reasonably, and who did not. Peters and Charlnoes, but especially Peters, admits to having been taken in by the promise of easy, quick money in amounts that were astronomically high. The bank, on the other hand, argues that it was as careful as it should have been, given the state of the checks and the clever forgery techniques used by the confidence men who engineered the con. In response, Peters argues that, no matter how careful the bank was, it was not careful enough because the con clearly went forward and the bank, therefore, failed in its responsibility. In short, Peters argues that the bank should have stopped him from wiring hundreds of thousands of dollars to some banks in China, when it was on notice that, historically, he and Faux carried a balance that rarely passed $5,000 at any given time. What we have here is a battle of responsibility. Who is more responsible for the alterations on the checks? The bank or Peters? The appellate court properly notes that the law by which this measurement is to be made is the UCC. The court also quite properly focuses on UCC Section 3-406 Negligence Contributing to Forged Signature or Alteration, which states:

(a) A person whose failure to exercise ordinary care substantially contributes to an alteration of an instrument or to the making of a forged signature on an instrument is precluded from asserting the alteration or the forgery against a person who, in good faith, pays the instrument or takes it for value or for collection.

(b) Under subsection (a), if the person asserting the preclusion fails to exercise ordinary care in paying or taking the instrument and that failure substantially contributes to loss, the loss is allocated between the person precluded and the person asserting the preclusion according to the extent to which the failure of each to exercise ordinary care contributed to the loss.

(c) Under subsection (a), the burden of proving failure to exercise ordinary care is on the person asserting the preclusion. Under subsection (b), the burden of proving failure to exercise ordinary care is on the person precluded.

In the present case, this comes down to the notion that any party that negligently contributes to any serious change in a negotiable instrument or whose conduct facilitates the paying or the taking of that altered instrument will have to be responsible for the consequences of that alteration. Let's look at how the appellate court dealt with this issue, and what it did with the trial court's position in support of the bank. (Reproduced below is a portion of the court's opinion. Footnote numerals are included but the citations themselves and explanatory notes are omitted.)

Procedural Background

The bank filed this action against defendants Faux, Peters, and Charlnoes, asserting causes of action for breach of contract and fraud. It then filed an application for a right to attach order, seeking to attach property of Peters and Charlnoes.

At the hearing on the application, the trial court noted that "[t]he recommendation from Research was to deny the [order] because of the allegations that Chino Commercial Bank was negligent." Nevertheless, it granted the right to attach order as to property of Peters (although it denied it as to property of Charlnoes).

The trial court essentially reasoned that Peters had the burden of proving that the bank had been negligent, particularly as he had been negligent himself. It was concerned that Peters, despite being culpably negligent, "then looks to the Bank and says, 'You should have prevented me from doing that.'"

It concluded that the bank had "met [its] burden to show that Mr. Peters was intricately involved in this." Peters, on the other hand, had not introduced sufficient evidence that the bank was negligent: "Unless I have some better evidence [than] you saying, 'Well, they're negligent, too' that doesn't prove anything."

The Trial Court Properly Found That the Bank Had Demonstrated the Probable Validity of Its Claim

To grant the right to attach order, the trial court had to find that the bank had established the "probable validity" of its claim. (Code Civ. Proc., § 484.090, subd. (a)(2).) "A claim has 'probable validity' where it is more likely than not that the plaintiff will obtain a judgment against the defendant on that claim." (Code Civ. Proc., § 481.190.)

Peters is essentially challenging the trial court's implied finding of probable validity. To the extent that this presents a question of fact, we apply the deferential substantial evidence standard of review. (*Crocker National Bank v. City and County of San Francisco* (1989) 49 Cal.3d 881, 888.) "If the trial court resolved disputed factual issues, the reviewing court should not substitute its judgment for the trial court's express or implied findings supported by substantial evidence. [Citations.]" (*People ex rel. Dept. of Corporations v. SpeeDee Oil Change Systems, Inc.* (1999) 20 Cal.4th 1135, 1143.) "'[W]e must consider the evidence in the light most favorable to the prevailing party, giving such party the benefit of every reasonable inference, and resolving all conflicts in support of the judgment. [Citation.]' [Citation.]" (*Gooch v. Hendrix* (1993) 5 Cal.4th 266, 279.) To the extent, however, that the trial court's finding presents a question of law, we review it independently. (*Crocker National Bank*, at p. 888.)

Surprisingly, Peters and, even more surprisingly, the bank both misidentify the applicable law. They cite and discuss *Pac. Coast Cheese, Inc. v. Sec.-First Nat. Bk.* (1955) 45 Cal.2d 75, *Basch v. Bank of America* (1943) 22 Cal.2d 316, and *Glassell Dev. Co. v. Citizens' Nat. Bk.* (1923) 191 Cal. 375 as if these were the leading authorities; the bank merely argues that they are distinguishable. These cases, however, have all been superseded by California's adoption of the Uniform Commercial Code, effective on January 1, 1965. (Stats.1963, ch. 819.)

The crucial provision here is California Uniform Commercial Code section 3406 (section 3406), which states:

> (a) A person whose failure to exercise ordinary care contributes to an alteration of an instrument or to the making of a forged signature on an instrument is precluded from asserting the alteration or the forgery against a person who, in good faith, pays the instrument or takes it for value or for collection.
>
> (b) Under subdivision (a), if the person asserting the preclusion fails to exercise ordinary care in paying or taking the instrument and that failure contributes to loss, the loss is allocated between the person precluded and the person asserting the preclusion according to the extent to which the failure of each to exercise ordinary care contributed to the loss.
>
> (c) Under subdivision (a), the burden of proving failure to exercise ordinary care is on the person asserting the preclusion. Under subdivision (b), the burden of proving failure to exercise ordinary care is on the person precluded.[1] (Reproduced below is that portion of the Court's opinion that corresponds to this analysis. Footnote numerals are included but the citations themselves and explanatory notes are omitted.)

It is undisputed that the bank is "a person who, in good faith, pa[id] the instrument or t[ook] it for value or for collection." "Good faith" simply means that the bank acted honestly and in accordance with "reasonable commercial standards of fair dealing." (Cal.U.Comm.Code, § 1201, subd. (b)(20).) Under an earlier version of the Uniform Commercial Code, which used a different definition of "good faith," negligence could be considered in determining good faith. (*Hollywood Nat. Bank v. International Business Machines Corp.* (1974) 38 Cal.App.3d 607, 613.) Under the current version, however, negligence does not defeat good faith. (2 White & Summers, Uniform Commercial Code (5th ed.2008) § 19-3(c), pp. 285–286.) Indeed, this follows from the structure of section 3406 itself; it contemplates that a person may have acted in good faith under subdivision (a), yet have failed to exercise ordinary care under subdivision (b).

Accordingly, if Peters's failure to exercise ordinary care contributed to the alteration of the instrument, he is at least partially precluded from asserting the alteration as a defense against the bank. The trial court found that Peters failed to exercise ordinary care. There is ample evidence to support this conclusion, and Peters does not challenge it; quite the contrary, he concedes that he "was, shall we say, less than smart in moving forward on the transaction."

Under section 3406, subdivision (b), however, if the bank failed to exercise ordinary care, and if that failure contributed to the loss, the loss must be allocated between the bank and Peters. Significantly, even if the bank was negligent, it is not wholly precluded from recovering against Peters. Its recovery is merely reduced, in accordance with principles of comparative negligence. (2 White & Summers, Uniform Commercial Code, supra, § 19-3(d), pp. 286–288.) Moreover, under section 3406, subdivision (c), it was Peters who had the burden of proving that the bank failed to exercise ordinary care. (See *Bank of Tex. v. VR Elec., Inc.* (Tex. Ct.App.2008) 276 S.W.3d 671, 680-681.)

The bank argues that the legal principles that would apply to a negligence action by a depositor against it are not controlling, because this is a contract action by it against a nondepositor. Section 3406, however, is not limited to negligence actions or to actions by a depositor. Everything we have said so far about the bank versus Peters applies equally to the bank versus Faux. Peters was Faux's agent; if Peters failed to exercise ordinary care, then so did Faux, and if not, not. Moreover, the bank could not contractually disclaim its duty of ordinary care. (Cal.U.Comm.Code, § 1302, subd. (b); see also Cal. U. Comm.Code, § 4103, subd. (a).) But if the bank is liable to Faux for its failure to exercise ordinary care, then there is, in effect, no overdraft in Faux's account and hence no overdraft for which Peters can be held contractually liable. Peters is, at most, a guarantor of Faux's liability.[2]

Peters argues that the trial court used the wrong burden of proof: It required him to prove the bank's negligence, when it should have required the bank to disprove its own negligence. As we have already discussed, however, under section 3406, subdivision (c), Peters did have the burden of proving the bank's negligence.

Alternatively, Peters also argues that there was evidence that the bank was, in fact, negligent. Basically, he claims it was negligent to allow Faux to make wire transfers to China totaling $468,000 when the balance in the account had historically been between $3,000 and $5,000.[3]

The California Uniform Commercial Code defines "'[o]rdinary care' in the case of a person engaged in business [as] observance of reasonable commercial standards, prevailing in the area in which the person is located, with respect to the business in which the person is engaged. In the case of a bank that takes an instrument for processing for collection, reasonable commercial standards do not require the bank to examine the instrument if the failure to examine does not violate the bank's prescribed procedures and the bank's procedures do not vary unreasonably from general banking usage not disapproved by this division or Division 4." (Cal.U .Comm.Code, § 3103, subd. (a)(7).)

There was absolutely no evidence that prevailing commercial standards required the bank to question the wire transfers. The bank even presented some evidence that it acted in accordance with prevailing commercial standards (although that evidence went largely to its acceptance of the checks for deposit, rather than to its making of the wire transfers). Even assuming the trial court could have concluded that the bank was negligent, in the absence of any evidence that the bank actually violated prevailing commercial standards, it was not required to do so.

We therefore conclude that Peters has not shown that the trial court erred by issuing the right to attach order.

Disposition

The order appealed from is affirmed. The bank is awarded costs on appeal against Peters. RICHLI, J We concur: HOLLENHORST, Acting P.J., and McKINSTER, J.

Questions for Analysis

1. As we have seen several times, *stare decisis* is at the central core of the authority of the judicial branch. Does this case support or contradict that description of core authority? Explain.

2. What is the Uniform Commercial Code? What goal does the Uniform Law Commission have in formulating the UCC? Explain.

3. What does UCC Section 3-406 say about altered checks and why is that section material to this case? Explain.

4. Define the following legal terms using the text: forgery, payee, overdraft, and negligence. How are these terms relevant in this case?

5. What test is used by the court in *Chino Commercial Bank v. Brian D. Peters* to determine responsibility? Explain.

6. How does the appellate court define the concept of "good faith" in *Chino Commercial Bank v. Brian D. Peters*? Explain.

7. How does the court's definition of "good faith" match up with the definition used in *Any Kinds Checks Cashed, Inc. v. Talcott?* (See Chapter 17.) Explain.

8. What remedy does Chino Commercial Bank seek in this case? Is that remedy a fair one considering its role in the con? Explain.

9. In what way does *Chino Commercial Bank v. Brian D. Peters* (the bank was exonerated) differ from the *Maine Family Federal Credit Union v. Sun Life Assurance Company of Canada* (the credit union may be liable)? Explain.

10. A complex adaptive system (CAS) is a network of interacting conditions that reinforce one another, while at the same time adjusting to change from agents outside and inside the system. In what ways do the two cases, *Chino Commercial Bank v. Brian D. Peters* and *Maine Family Federal Credit Union v. Sun Life Assurance Company of Canada,* reinforce the idea that the law works like a complex adaptive system? Explain.

Part Five

Insurance, Secured Transactions, and Bankruptcy

THE OPENING CASE *Round 1*
Liability Insurance: "Risks, and Umbrellas, and Dwellings, Oh My!"

Steve Granger, the plaintiff in the present case, along with a partner set up a trust to cover their resources, which involved, among other things, a piece of rental property in Akron, Ohio. Granger, his partner, and the trust took out a dwelling insurance policy on the rental property and Granger added an umbrella policy all his own. The policies were negotiated by the Church Agency and a broker named Mr. Coudriet, but the policies were actually held by Auto-Owners (Mutual) Insurance Company (AOMIC). Granger's problems started when he was approached by Valeria Kozera who asked about renting the Akron property. Kozera, the mother of a six-year-old, was turned away by Granger who, quite openly, told her that the property would not be leased to anyone with children. Kozera was insulted and personally humiliated by this treatment, and so she filed a report with the Fair Housing Contact Service (FHCS), which, after a thorough study of the incident, filed a federal lawsuit against Granger. The charges alleged that Granger had discriminated against Kozera in violation of federal and state law. More specifically the suit claimed that Granger's refusal to rent to Kozera was racially motivated and based on her family status. When AOMIC found out about the lawsuit, the company sent a letter to Granger indicating that the dwelling insurance policy on the Akron property did not

include claims of discrimination like the one filed by Kozera, and so it had no duty to defend Granger, his partner, or the trust. Accordingly, Granger and company settled with the FHCS and Kozera and handed over $32,500 as a settlement. Granger then turned around and sued AOMIC, Church, and Coudriet. As the case unfolded, it became clear that Granger's real claim was against AOMIC and the real grounds were based on the refusal of AOMIC to defend Granger, not based on the dwelling insurance policy, but on the umbrella policy. The trial court did not believe any of this and granted the insurance company's summary judgment motion. The appeals court, however, decided that the trial court had been just a bit too hasty and elected to hear the case, at least insofar as it addressed the discrimination claim under the umbrella policy that protected Granger. The appellate court began by examining the language used in the umbrella policy, specifically as that policy related to personal injury. Personal injury in the policy was defined in part as "mental anguish or mental injury," which Granger argued includes the humiliation that Kozera suffered when Granger refused to rent the Akron property to her because of her race and family status. AOMIC argued first, that "humiliation" did not rise to the level of either "mental anguish or mental injury," and so the company had no duty to defend Granger. Second, AOMIC claimed that, even if humiliation were within the parameters of mental anguish and mental injury, Granger's actions were not covered because Granger's statements were intentional and the policy did not cover intentional injuries. Now, remember this appeal was taken against the lower court's decision to grant a summary judgment motion and so if there were a genuine dispute as to any material fact, the order granting the motion should be reversed. The entire case boiled down to two simple questions. Is humiliation a personal injury? Is the intent to say "I do not rent to people with children" also the intent to humiliate? The answers to these questions are in the pages that follow. [See: *Granger, et al. v. Auto Owners, Insurance*

2013-Ohio-2792, Case. 26473, Court of Appeals, Ninth Judicial District (June 2013).]

Opening Case Questions

1. What is dwelling insurance? Explain.

2. What is an umbrella policy? Explain.

3. AOMIC wrote the policy. Now AOMIC is explaining what certain terms in the policy mean. Does this seem fair? Explain.

4. What is the difference between the duty to investigate and the duty to defend? Explain.

5. Did AOMIC fulfill either duty in this case? Explain.

Learning Objectives

1. Define and explain the purpose of insurance.
2. Identify the contractual elements of an insurance agreement.
3. Make clear the importance of insurable interest.
4. Differentiate among the different types of life insurance.
5. Explain how insurable interest differs with life insurance and property insurance.
6. Explain the coinsurance clause in most property insurance policies.
7. Describe coverage given by fire, marine, homeowner's, renter's, and flood insurance.
8. Differentiate among the principal kinds of automobile insurance.
9. Describe the benefits included in health insurance policies.
10. List the steps in applying for, obtaining, and maintaining an insurance policy.

19-1 Risk Assessment and Peril Management

The legal system is not a stand-alone network. Nor does it function in a void. The executive, legislative, judicial, and administrative agents often get overly connected with one another, while consistently acting at cross purposes. Yet, the emergent order within the network does exist. While this order is not always apparent on a daily basis, in the long run, the system does work, even when, logically, it should not. This paradox is especially true of the interface between insurance and the law. Strictly speaking, insurance is a business, not a branch of the law. Moreover, when insurance does interact with the law, at times it runs at counter purposes to the law. Insurance involves contracts made by agents to help people protect their lives, their health, their income, their savings, and their property against negligence, intentional torts, and criminal activity. Most insurance companies are large corporations, which themselves need protection. Some of the types of insurance available intersect with health law and property law. Others depend on an appreciation of and proper application of tort law and criminal law. Moreover, all insurance agreements are binding contracts, requiring the application of contract law. For all these reasons, and probably more, we cannot neatly package, divide, and classify insurance into well-ordered, unrelated topics. Keep this in mind and you will better understand some of the contradictory and overlapping topics that we are about to invade.

Risks and Perils: A Double-Sided Mirror

The problematic nature of insurance emerges because, at its core, it is built upon two conflicting sets of risks and perils. **Risks** are threats to those items (life, health, property, income, savings, investments, reputations, and so on) that a party wants to protect. **Perils** are the dangers that a party might pose to others and against which that party must shield itself. For example, from the risk side of the equation, when a party's life, health, property, income, savings, investments, and reputation are in danger, that party will purchase insurance to protect itself should the worst happen. So a party will purchase health insurance, home owner's insurance, automobile insurance, renter's insurance, and so on. Conversely, from the perils side of the issue, when a party's actions, business, and property endanger others, that party will buy insurance that will provide it with a legal defense team and with money to reimburse those it might injure. **Insurance**, then, is the transfer of the risk of economic loss, for a fee, from the insured to the insurer. Small contributions by a large number of people provide sufficient funds, with the help of properly managed investment opportunities, to protect the losses that are suffered by a few as they occur on an annual basis. The function of insurance then is to distribute each person's risk among all others who may not be imperiled that year or over many years. (See Table 19-1.)

The Insurance Contract: Parties, Elements, Interest

An insurance policy is actually a contract that follows the standard rules of regular contract law. This means that once you learn contract law, you already have a pretty good handle on the rules of making, writing, interpreting, enforcing, and terminating an insurance policy. That is the good news. The bad news is that you also have to learn a few things that

Table 19-1 Examples of Risk Management Strategies		
RISKS		**Strategies for Reducing Financial Impact**
Personal Event	**Financial Impact**	
Disability	• Loss of income • Increased expenses	• Savings and investments • Disability insurance
Death	• Loss of income	• Life insurance • Estate planning
Property loss	• Catastrophic storm damage to property • Repair or replacement • Cost of theft	• Property repair and upkeep • Auto insurance • Homeowner's insurance • Flood or earthquake insurance
Liability	• Claims and settlement costs • Lawsuits and legal expenses • Loss of personal assets and income	• Maintaining property • Homeowner's insurance • Auto insurance

Source: Gordon W. Brown, *Understanding Business and Personal Law,* 11e, p. 752. Copyright © 2006 Glencoe/McGraw-Hill. Reprinted with permission.

supplement contract law and are peculiar to insurance contracts (or policies, if you will). That includes the parties to a contract as well as the concept of insurable interests, and the duties of the insured and the insurer.

Insurance policies, like other contracts, require the four elements of a contract: mutual assent, capacity, consideration, and legality. The application filled in by an applicant is an offer to the insurer, who may then accept or reject the offer. When the insurer (the offeree) accepts the offer (the application) from the applicant (the offeror), mutual assent emerges between the parties. A party to a contract must also be capable of understanding the terms of the agreement. Consideration arises from the premiums paid by the insured and the promise of the insurer to pay money to the beneficiary if a certain event happens. Finally, the subject matter must not be tainted by illegality. For example, a fire insurance policy written on a building in which the owners permitted the illegal manufacture of fireworks would be void in the event of a fire.

THE OPENING CASE *Round 2*
The Language of the Insurance Contract

In the opening case, we learned that Steve Granger and his partner set up a trust to cover their holdings, which included rental property in Akron. Granger, his partner, and the trust took out a dwelling insurance policy on the rental property, and Granger added an umbrella policy all his own. The policy was held by Auto-Owners (Mutual) Insurance Company (AOMIC). Granger's problems started when he told Kozera, a potential renter, that he had no intention of renting the place in Akron to anyone with children. Kozera, the mother of a six-year-old, was insulted and humiliated by Granger's attitude and by his allegedly harsh, discriminatory words. Accordingly, she logged a complaint with the Fair Housing Contact Service (FHCS), which filed a federal lawsuit against Granger. The charges alleged that Granger's refusal to rent to Kozera was racially motivated and based on her family status. When AOMIC found out about the lawsuit, the company sent a letter to Granger indicating that the dwelling insurance policy on the Akron property did not include claims of discrimination like the one filed by Kozera, and so the company had no duty to defend Granger, his partner, or the trust. Backed into a corner, Granger settled and handed over $32,500 as compensation to Kozera. Granger then sued AOMIC. As the case unfolded, it became clear that Granger's claim against AOMIC was based on the company's refusal to defend Granger under the umbrella policy. The trial court granted the insurance company's summary judgment motion. The appeals court, however, elected to hear counterarguments, insofar as

they addressed the discrimination claim under the umbrella policy. The appellate court began by examining the language used in the umbrella policy, specifically as that language relates to the concept of personal injury. The appellate court noted at the outset that the goal of any court in the interpretation of language is to uncover the original intent of the parties. To do this the court had to focus on the plain and ordinary meaning of the words. Moreover, the court must also interpret any ambiguous terms strictly against the insurer (AOMIC) because the insurer is the party that actually wrote the agreement and, therefore, had the opportunity and the ability to make the terms as understandable (or as garbled) as it wanted. This rule of interpretation was very important in this case because AOMIC was trying to limit its responsibilities in relation to Granger. To get at the plain language of the policy, the court used *Black's Law Dictionary* and noted that emotional distress is defined as "[a] highly unpleasant mental reaction (such as anguish, grief, fright, *humiliation,* or fury) that results from another person's conduct[.]" After reading this definition, the appellate court decided that Kozera *could* have suffered emotional distress when Granger humiliated her. Since any emotional distress that results from humiliation is a personal injury covered under the policy, AOMIC should have defended Granger in the lawsuit. This round went to Granger. The score at this point was "Granger 1 – AOMIC 0." [See: *Granger, et al. v. Auto Owners, Insurance* 2013-Ohio-2792, Case. 26473, Court of Appeals, Ninth Judicial District (June 2013).]

In addition, the courts have ruled that, in the interpretation of contractual terms, the goal of the court must be to determine the original intent of the parties when they first sat down to enter the agreement. In order to accomplish this goal, the court will focus on the plain and ordinary meaning of the words in the agreement. Moreover, the court will also interpret any ambiguous terms strictly against the insurer because the insurer is the party that actually writes the agreement and, therefore, has the opportunity and the ability to make the terms as clear (or as obscure) as it wants. This technique is especially critical when the court interprets any clause that is designed to somehow limit or narrow the coverage that the insurer is granting to the insured.

The parties to an insurance contract are the insurer (sometimes called the *underwriter*), the insured, and the beneficiary. The **insurer** accepts the risk of loss in return for a **premium** (the consideration paid for a policy) and agrees to **indemnify**, or compensate, the insured against the loss specified in the contract. The **insured** is the party (or parties) protected by the insurance contract. The contract of insurance is called the **policy**. The period of time during which the insurer assumes the risk of loss is known as the life of the policy. A third party, to whom payment of compensation is sometimes provided by the contract, is called the **beneficiary**.

Insurable Interest and the Duties of the Parties

A person or business applying for insurance must have an insurable interest in the subject matter of the policy to be insured. An **insurable interest** is the financial interest that a policyholder has in the person or property that is insured. In the case of life insurance, all people have an insurable interest in their own lives as well as the lives of their spouses and dependents. Business partners have an insurable interest in each other because they could suffer a financial loss if a partner dies. A corporation can have a financial interest in its key employees for the same reason. In the case of property insurance, anyone who would suffer a financial loss from damage to property would have an insurable interest in that property. For life insurance, the insurable interest must exist at the time the insurance is purchased. In contrast, for property insurance, the insurable interest must exist at the time of loss.

As is true of all contracts, the parties to an insurance contract (policy) voluntarily adopt the duties that emerge from that agreement. At the same time, they receive certain benefits under the contract. The insured has an initial duty to inform the insured of everything the insurer asks so that the insurer can enter the policy agreement with full knowledge of the insured's situation. In the computer age, this means that some insurers may ask for full access to a client's computer records. This approach may seem intrusive and a bit extreme. However, the contractual relationship is voluntary and the insured can always seek out another insurer if the insured is uncomfortable with the arrangement. Once the contract has been entered, the insured has the duty to (1) pay the premiums on time and in the fashion prescribed by the insurer; (2) tell the insurance company about any claims in a timely and judicious manner; and (3) work together with the insurer when the time comes for an inquiry.

The insurer has a threefold duty. Once a claim has been placed on the table, the insurer has the **duty to investigate** the claim to determine all the facts and to decide in an appropriate manner if the client is entitled to payment. If the client is covered and the claim is authentic, then the insurer has the **duty to pay** the insured directly if the insured's property must be replaced or repaired or to pay any claim by a third party based on a liability clause. Finally, if the case is disputed by a third party, then the insurer has the **duty to defend** the client. Moreover, insurance companies have the right to step into the shoes of the party they compensate and sue any party the compensated party could have sued. This substitution of one person in place of another relative to a lawful claim is known as **subrogation**.

THE OPENING CASE *Round 3*
The Exclusion of the Duty to Defend?
Can You Really Do That?

In the opening case, we learned that Granger paid Kozera $32,500 as a result of a settlement agreement. Granger then sued AOMIC, Church, and Coudriet for not defending him. As the case unfolded, it became clear that Granger's real claim was against AOMIC and the real grounds were based on the *refusal of AOMIC to defend Granger,* under the umbrella policy. The trial court granted the insurance company's summary judgment motion, but the appellate court decided to hear Granger's counterargument, at least insofar as it addressed the discrimination claim under the umbrella policy. The appellate court began by examining the language used in the umbrella policy, specifically as that language related to the concept of personal injury. Personal injury in the policy was defined, in part, as "mental anguish or mental injury," which Granger argued includes the humiliation that Kozera suffered when he refused to rent the Akron property to her because of her race and family status. As noted in The Opening Case Round 2, the court, using the plain language of the contract (as well as *Black's Law Dictionary*), agreed that Kozera's claim of humiliation was a

personal injury under the policy. The court then turned to the exclusion clause. Remember that AOMIC argued, in the alternative, that, even if Kozera's humiliation was a personal injury, the insurance company still had no duty to defend Granger under the exclusion clause. The exclusion clause said that the insurance company would have no duty to defend the insured if the insured deliberately injured the victim. Turning to the facts in this case, if Granger did, in fact, intend to humiliate Kozera, then the insurance company no longer had the duty to defend him—end of story. Unfortunately for AOMIC, the court noted that the insurance company's argument on this issue was weak at best and the evidence was totally nonexistent. Therefore, the lower court's granting of the summary judgment motion was a mistake and the case must go trial. So, this round also went to Granger and the score at that point was "Granger 2 – AOMIC 0." However, two more issues are yet to be examined, so stay tuned for further developments. [See: *Granger, et al. v. Auto Owners, Insurance* 2013-Ohio-2792, Case. 26473, Court of Appeals, Ninth Judicial District (June 2013).]

quick quiz 19-1

1. The purpose of insurance is to spread losses among people who can most afford it.   true | false

2. An application filled in by an insurance applicant is a binding contract on the insurer.   true | false

3. Anyone can obtain insurance on another person or property, regardless of their relationship.   true | false

19-2 Types of Insurance

It is possible to obtain insurance against almost any risk if an individual or business is willing to pay the price. The premium charged will depend on the risk involved. Life insurance, property insurance, and health insurance are discussed here.

Life Insurance

Life insurance is an insurance contract that provides monetary compensation for losses suffered by another's death. Anyone has an insurable interest in the life of another if a financial loss will occur if the insured dies. For example, an insurable interest exists if the person who buys the insurance is dependent on the insured for education, support, business (partners), or debt collection. A life insurance policy will remain valid and enforceable even if the insurable interest terminates. It is necessary only that the insurable interest exists at the time the policy was issued.

Premiums for life insurance are based on several factors, including the age and health of the insured, the coverage, and the type of policy. It is less expensive to buy life insurance at a young age because the death rate for young people is very low, and their health is usually at its peak.

If an individual takes out insurance on him- or herself, it is not necessary for the beneficiary to have an insurable interest in the insured's life. However, if a person takes out life insurance on someone else, that person must have an insurable interest in the insured's life.

The principal types of life insurance are straight life, limited-payment life, term, and endowment insurance.

Straight Life Insurance
Straight life insurance, which is also known as **ordinary life insurance** or **whole life insurance**, requires the payment of premiums throughout the life of the insured and pays the beneficiary the face value of the policy upon the insured's death. The amount of the premium is determined by the age of the insured at the time of purchase and normally stays the same throughout the life of the policy. The younger the insured, the lower the premium, because the company expects to collect many years' worth of premiums.

Straight life insurance contains an investment feature known as the *cash surrender value*. The cash surrender value usually builds up slowly at first but in later years approaches the face amount of the policy. At some stated point (usually at the age of 95 or 100 years), it equals the face value of the policy. An insured can cancel a straight life policy at any time and receive its cash surrender value. Straight life insurance also contains a feature called a *loan value,* which is an amount of money that may be borrowed against the cash surrender value of the policy, usually at a relatively favorable rate of interest. During inflationary times, when bank interest rates are high, insurance policies are often excellent sources of loans at low interest rates.

EXAMPLE 19-1: Straight Life Insurance

At age 18 years, LaPlume purchased a straight life insurance policy with a face value of $20,000. The premiums were quite modest. At some later time, LaPlume could borrow on the policy or trade it in for its cash surrender value. Or, LaPlume could continue premium payments until death. If LaPlume died while a loan was outstanding, the insurance company would deduct the amount of the loan from the amount it paid to LaPlume's beneficiary.

A form of straight life insurance, called **universal life insurance**, allows the policy owner flexibility in choosing and changing terms of the policy. Within certain guidelines, the policy owner can modify the face value of the policy as well as the premiums in response to changing needs and circumstances in the policy owner's life. Under a typical universal life policy:

- Premiums may be increased or decreased within policy limits.
- The amount of insurance may be increased, subject to evidence of insurability, or decreased, subject to set minimums.

- The owner may borrow up to the maximum loan value at a prearranged interest rate. Policy loans reduce the cash surrender value and death benefit.

- Withdrawals may be made from the cash surrender value.

Limited-Payment Life Insurance
Limited-payment life insurance provides that the payment of premiums will stop after a stated length of time—usually 10, 20, or 30 years. The amount of the policy will be paid to the beneficiary upon the death of the insured, whether the death occurs during the payment period or after. Because of the limited number of payments made by the insured, the premiums are proportionately higher than those for straight life; however, the cash surrender value grows faster than that of straight life insurance.

Term Insurance
As the name suggests, **term insurance** is issued for a particular period, usually 10 or 20 years. The time period is known as the term. Term insurance is the least expensive kind of life insurance because term policies have no cash or loan value, as others do. Term insurance offers protection alone, in contrast to straight life, which combines protection with a savings plan. Term insurance can be renewable at the end of each period simply by paying the increased premium, without need for a new medical examination. *Convertible* term insurance policies can be converted to straight life policies without taking a new medical examination—allowing protection throughout the insured's lifetime. A modified form of term insurance is *decreasing term insurance*. The premium stays constant from year to year, but the amount of protection (death benefit) decreases over the years. This type of insurance is widely used to cover the outstanding balance of a home mortgage.

> **Did You Know?**
>
> Young families with large financial obligations are usually better off with term life insurance rather than whole life. The substantially lower premiums may enable them to purchase needed coverage to protect against loss of income at a time when they most need it.

Annuity
An **annuity** is guaranteed retirement income purchased by paying either a lump-sum premium or making periodic payments to an insurer. The insured may choose either (a) to receive an income for a certain fixed number of years, with a beneficiary receiving whatever is left of the annuity if the insured dies before the term expires, or (b) to receive payments as long as the insured lives and, upon death, relinquish whatever is left of the annuity, if anything.

Exemptions from Risk
Many life insurance policies contain clauses that exempt the insurance company from liability in certain situations. For example, policies often do not cover the insured when riding in an airplane, violating the law, or working in certain dangerous occupations.

Most policies provide that beneficiaries can recover for a death caused by suicide if the suicide occurs more than two years after the policy was taken out. They may not recover, however, when the policy contains a provision preventing such recovery or when the life insurance was purchased by someone planning suicide or who was insane. One example of a named beneficiary who could recover would be a creditor of the insured.

Life insurance policies usually include an exemption from liability in times of war. The exemption states that the insurer will not be liable on the policy if the insured is killed while a member of the armed forces, generally outside the continental United States, or by service-connected causes.

Optional Provisions
Life insurance policies have many optional provisions that may be purchased by the insured. Three popular options are double indemnity, waiver of premium, and guaranteed insurability.

For an additional premium, the insured may purchase a benefit known as **double indemnity**, or accidental death benefit. This option provides that if the insured dies from accidental causes, the insurer will pay double the amount of the policy to the beneficiary. Death must occur within 90 days of the accident for this benefit to apply.

The *waiver of premium* option excuses the insured from paying premiums if he or she becomes disabled. Some insurance policies automatically include the waiver in their provisions; others offer it as an extra-cost option.

A *guaranteed insurability* option allows the insured to pay an extra premium initially in exchange for a guaranteed option to buy more insurance at certain specified times later. The additional insurance can be purchased with no questions asked; thus, no new medical examination is required even if the insured develops a serious illness before exercising the option.

Property Insurance

Property insurance can be purchased to protect both real and personal property. To establish the existence of an insurable interest in property, the insured must demonstrate a monetary interest in the property. This monetary interest means that the insured will suffer a financial loss if the property is damaged or destroyed. Unlike life insurance, this insurable interest must exist when the loss occurs.

Property insurance can be made less expensive by the use of a **deductible**, which is an amount of any loss that is to be paid by the insured. It can be a specified dollar amount, a percentage of the claim amount, or a specified amount of time that must elapse before benefits are paid. The bigger the deductible, the lower is the premium charged for the same coverage.

Coinsurance Clauses   **Coinsurance** is an insurance policy provision under which the insurer and the insured share costs, after the deductible is met, according to a specific formula. Most property and inland marine policies have a coinsurance clause, which limits the insurance company's liability for a loss if the property is not insured for its full replacement value. For example, if a homeowner's insurance policy has an 80 percent coinsurance clause, the building must be insured for 80 percent of its replacement value to receive full reimbursement for a loss (see Figure 19-1).

Fire Insurance   A fire insurance policy is a contract in which the fire insurance company promises to pay the insured if some real or personal property is damaged or destroyed by fire. A fire insurance policy is effective on delivery to the insured, even before the premium is paid. Even an oral agreement will make fire insurance effective.

TYPICAL COINSURANCE CLAUSE

"The insurance company will pay that part of a loss that the insurance carried bears to 80 percent of the replacement cost of the building."

It would cost $100,000 to replace Felipe Garcia's house. If he insured it for $60,000, the insurance company would pay only three-fourths of any loss, computed as follows:

$$\frac{\text{Amount of insurance carried}}{\text{Percent of replacement cost}} \quad \frac{\$60,000}{80\% \text{ of }\$100,000} = \frac{\$60,000}{\$80,000} = \frac{3}{4}$$

A fire partially destroys the building, causing $40,000 worth of damage. Because of the co-insurance clause, Garcia would recover $30,000 (¾ of the loss) from the insurance company.

Figure 19-1   Here is a typical coinsurance clause found in an insurance policy. It limits the insurer's liability for a loss if the property is not insured for full, or at least 80 percent of, replacement value.

The insurer's liability under a fire policy usually covers losses other than those directly attributed to fire. Under most policies, claims may also be made for losses from water used to fight the fire; scorching; smoke damage to goods; deliberate destruction of property as a means of controlling a spreading fire; lightning, even if there is no resultant fire; riot or explosion, if a fire does result; and losses through theft or exposure of goods removed from a burning building.

Marine Insurance

Marine insurance is one of the oldest types of insurance coverage, dating back to Venetian traders who sailed the Mediterranean Sea. **Ocean marine insurance** covers ships at sea. **Inland marine insurance** covers goods that are moved by land carriers such as rail, truck, and airplane. Inland marine insurance also covers such items as jewelry, fine arts, musical instruments, and wedding presents. Customers' goods in the possession of bailees, such as fur-storage houses and dry cleaners, are also covered by inland marine insurance. A *floater policy* is one that insures property that cannot be covered by specific insurance because the property is constantly changing in either value or location. A personal property floater, for example, covers personal property in general, wherever it is located.

Homeowner's and Renter's Insurance

Many of the leading insurance companies offer a combination policy known as the **homeowner's policy**. This insurance gives protection for all types of losses and liabilities related to home ownership. Among the items covered are losses from fire, windstorms, burglary, vandalism, and injuries suffered by other persons while on the property. Losses from flooding generally are not covered under a homeowner's policy. **Renter's insurance** protects tenants against the loss of personal property, liability for a visitor's personal injury, and liability for negligent destruction of the rented premises.

Flood Insurance

Flooding can be caused by heavy rains, melting snow, inadequate drainage systems, failed protective devices such as levees and dams, and tropical storms and hurricanes. Nevertheless, most commercial, homeowner's, and renter's insurance policies do not cover flood damage. To obtain such coverage, special flood insurance must be obtained from an insurance agent.

Most flood insurance is backed by the National Flood Insurance Program (NFIP), established by Congress in response to the high cost of taxpayer-funded disaster relief for flood victims and the amount of damage caused by floods. Communities that agree to manage flood hazard areas by adopting minimum standards can participate in the NFIP. However, communities that do not participate in the program cannot receive flood insurance, federal grants and loans, federal disaster assistance, or federal mortgage insurance for the acquisition or construction of structures located in flood hazard areas of their community. Most lending institutions require borrowers to obtain flood insurance when they buy, build, or improve structures in Special Flood Hazard Areas (SFHAs). Lending institutions that are federally regulated or federally insured must determine if the structure is located in an SFHA and provide written notice requiring flood insurance.

Following Hurricane Katrina, which devastated the Gulf Coast in 2005, many insurance claims were delayed, and others were not paid on the grounds that damages were caused by water rather than by wind, though most homeowners had little or no flood insurance. Hundreds of lawsuits were brought by disgruntled homeowners against insurance companies, and some million-dollar jury verdicts against the companies were settled out of court. Some of the jury awards were for punitive damages because the companies failed to pay the claims quickly enough. A federal appeals court

Did You Know?

In the aftermath of Hurricane Katrina, insurers sharply boosted rates or even withdrew coverage in the most vulnerable coastal areas. In 2007, Allstate Floridian Insurance Co. notified more than 120,000 Florida residents that their home-owners' policies would not be renewed. But even in such areas, many people are seeing better rates and a wider choice of insurance carriers than in years past. One reason is that the insurance industry is enjoying *(continued)* an abundance of capital. No hurricanes struck the United States in 2006, so the nation's property-casualty industry posted a $31 billion net gain on underwriting—a sharp swing from the $6 billion net loss in 2005. Add investment income, and insurers had net income after taxes of nearly $64 billion, giving the industry its highest rate of return in 20 years. All that money expands the industry's underwriting wherewithal, driving down the price.

Source: Peter Coy and Adam Aston, "Hurricane Ahead, But Lower Insurance," *Business-Week,* May 14, 2007, pp. 68–69.

Without adequate insurance, most people would be unable to even approach status quo after suffering a catastrophic event.

found that many insurance policies covering property in New Orleans contained flood exclusions. The court said, "Regardless of what caused the failure of the flood-control structures that were put in place to prevent such catastrophe, their failure resulted in a widespread flood that damaged the plaintiffs' property. Their policies clearly excluded water damage caused by floods." One lower federal court case upheld the insurance company's view that homeowner policies cover damage from a hurricane's wind but not the rising water that ensues, including wind-driven surge. Several major insurers in Mississippi, which does not allow punitive damages in these cases, entered an agreement with the Mississippi attorney general to pay about $80 million to 639 policyholders whose claims were denied following Katrina. As part of the agreement, insurers were required to reopen and review claims filed by policyholders who live in that state.

Dwelling Insurance Most of the time, property insurance involves protecting property that the insured possesses and uses on a regular basis. However, some property, notably rental property, also demands protection, even though the owner may not set foot in the property for years. **Dwelling insurance** will provide this protection for the insured. A dwelling policy will protect the actual structure (a single family dwelling, an apartment building, and so on) from damage caused by fire, wind, snow, ice, lightning, and so on. However, it is also possible to add coverage for damage to the contents of the rental property. This coverage will be needed if the rental property is fully or partially furnished by the landlord or if the property contains appliances such as a range and refrigerator. Another clause can be added to a dwelling insurance policy to protect the landlord from lost rent. It is also possible, perhaps even advisable, for the insured to add liability coverage should a tenant or someone else, such as a postal worker, a contractor, or a visitor, be injured at the dwelling place. Liability insurance can also include coverage for medical payments.

THE OPENING CASE *Round 4*

Dwelling Insurance: "No Coverage Here, Friend. Move On!"

In the opening case, we learned that Granger and his partner set up a trust to cover their resources, which included a rental property in Akron, Ohio. Granger, his partner, and the trust took out a dwelling insurance policy on the rental property. The record does not tell much about that policy, except to describe what was not covered. Apparently, the policy did not cover such things as personal injuries that might result from emotional distress. The policy also did not provide a defense for

Granger when the FHCS and Kozera filed a discrimination lawsuit against him. Perhaps because he was an astute student of insurance, Granger had the foresight to buy an additional policy as protection. The umbrella policy did, in fact, provide a defense clause that should have protected him when he was sued. More on that umbrella policy is coming up soon. [See: *Granger, et al. v. Auto Owners, Insurance* 2013-Ohio-2792, Case. 26473, Court of Appeals, Ninth Judicial District (June 2013).]

Automobile Insurance

Automobile insurance provides for indemnity against losses resulting from fire, theft, or collision with another vehicle and damages arising out of injury by motor vehicles to the person or property of another. One thing to always remember about car insurance and about car accidents in general is that the law in relation to determining fault in such accidents differs a great deal from state to state. It is, therefore, always best to be very careful about choosing automobile insurance and in making certain that anyone involved in an accident contact an attorney in the state in which the accident occurs because it is the law of that state that generally applies to the accident. The following are the most common types of automobile insurance:

- Bodily injury liability insurance.
- Fault-based insurance.
- No-fault insurance.
- Add-on coverage.
- Threshold guidelines and choice-based jurisdictions.
- Uninsured-motorist insurance.
- Underinsured-motorist insurance.
- Medical payments insurance.
- Property damage liability insurance.
- Collision insurance.
- Comprehensive coverage.
- Substitute transportation insurance.
- Towing and labor insurance.

Bodily Injury Liability Insurance   The risk of bodily injury or death to pedestrians and the occupants of other cars arising from the negligent operation of the insured's motor vehicle is covered by **bodily injury liability insurance**. Under liability insurance, the insurer is liable for damages up to the limit of the insurance purchased. The insurance company must also provide attorneys for the insured's defense in any civil court action.

Fault-Based Insurance   Most states still base their car insurance and, therefore, the handling of car accident claims, on tort law. **Fault-based insurance** means that liability in an automobile accident will be measured by the degree of fault that can be assigned to each driver based on negligence principles. The level of fault that can be attributed to each party in the accident forms the basis for the insurance company's payment. In such a state, lawsuits may be necessary to determine damages based on pain and suffering, hospital expenses, lost wages, and so on.

No-Fault Insurance   Currently no-fault insurance is required, at least to some extent, in some states. **No-fault insurance** which is also called **personal injury protection (PIP)** places limitations on the insured's ability to sue other drivers but allows drivers to collect damages and medical expenses from their own insurance carriers, regardless of who is at fault in an accident. This coverage helps cut down on fraudulent and excessively high claims. It also eliminates costly litigation needed to determine the negligence or lack of negligence of people involved in automobile accidents. On the other hand, even in no-fault states, a victim must sue if he or she wants to be compensated for actual property damage to the automobile itself, or to the items in the car. Some states alter the no-fault formula by adding a new element called a **threshold**. When the damages go beyond this threshold, which is defined by a set dollar amount, by injury description, or by time, the victim can file a negligence based lawsuit. Threshold injuries based on description include very serious ailments such as a permanent disability. In contrast, time-based thresholds are ascertained by measuring the time that the victim is incapacitated. Moreover, some jurisdictions permit both descriptive and time-based thresholds.

Add-On Coverage

In some jurisdictions, add-on coverage is legally recognized. These jurisdictions currently include Arkansas, Delaware, Maryland, and the District of Columbia. Add-on coverage permits a driver to buy optional coverage such as personal injury insurance that would allow him or her to receive payment without bothering to determine fault. Add-on policies, however, would not prevent the insured from bringing a lawsuit for pain and suffering and other similar injuries. Generally, threshold provisions are included in these policies.

Threshold Guidelines and Choice-Based Jurisdictions

Some no-fault jurisdictions set threshold guidelines that must be met by everyone regardless of the nature of their insurance policy. Threshold guidelines determine when victims can bring a lawsuit for injuries that result from an auto accident. Several states apply a strict monetary threshold while some no-fault jurisdictions have descriptive thresholds. A few states permit drivers to choose between no-fault and tort-law based insurance.

Uninsured-Motorist Insurance

Essentially, uninsured-motorist insurance provides protection against the risk of being injured by an uninsured motorist. The coverage applies when the person who caused the accident was at fault and had no bodily injury liability insurance to cover the loss. It protects the insured, the insured's spouse, relatives in the same household, and any other person occupying an insured automobile. It also protects people who are injured by hit-and-run drivers. No coverage is provided to an automobile used without the permission of the insured or the insured's spouse. Uninsured motorist insurance provides no reimbursement for damages to the insured's property.

Underinsured-Motorist Insurance

Basically, underinsured-motorist insurance provides protection against the risk of being injured by an underinsured motorist. For an insured to collect this insurance, someone without enough bodily injury coverage must have caused the accident.

Medical Payments Insurance

In essence, medical payments insurance pays for medical (and sometimes funeral) expenses resulting from bodily injuries to anyone occupying the policyholder's car at the time of an accident. In some states, it pays for the medical bills of all family members who are struck by a car or who are riding in someone else's car when it is involved in an accident.

Property Damage Liability Insurance

In brief, property damage liability insurance provides protection when other people bring claims or lawsuits against the insured for damaging property such as a car, fence, or tree. The person bringing the claim or suit must prove that the driver of the motor vehicle was at fault.

Collision Insurance

Basically, collision insurance provides against any loss arising from damage to the insured's automobile caused by accidental collision with another object or with any part of the roadbed. Liability under collision insurance is limited to the insured's car.

Comprehensive Coverage

In short, comprehensive coverage provides protection against loss when the insured's car is damaged or destroyed by fire, lightning, flood, hail, windstorm, riot, vandalism, or theft. The insurance company's liability is limited to the actual cash value of the vehicle at the time of the loss.

Substitute Transportation Insurance   Essentially, substitute transportation insurance reimburses up to specified limits for car rental or transportation costs, including taxi, bus, and train fare, while the insured's car is undergoing covered repairs.

Towing and Labor Insurance   In essence, towing and labor insurance reimburses up to specified limits for towing and labor charges whenever the insured's car breaks down, whether or not an accident is involved.

Liability Insurance

As noted earlier in the chapter, perils are the dangers that a party might pose to others and against which that party must shield itself. When a party's actions, business, and property imperil others, that party should buy insurance that will provide it with a legal defense team and with the money to reimburse the victims, should the legal defense team fail to, well, to successfully defend that party. That type of coverage is generally referred to as liability insurance. Often liability insurance is attached to another larger, more comprehensive insurance contract. Thus, an automobile contract may include a liability clause to protect the driver from medical expenses that might occur as the result of an accident. Or, as noted earlier, a landlord should demand a liability clause in his or her dwelling insurance policies. Most of the time liability coverage focuses on negligence rather than intentional torts. However, businesses sometimes carry liability policies covering intentional torts. Thus, a tavern owner should demand liability protection from the consequences of an overenthusiastic bouncer. Similarly, a security company should insist on protection from invasion of privacy lawsuits, and a newspaper should have a liability clause protecting it against defamation suits. Professionals, such as lawyers, accountants, physicians, nurses, teachers, and so on, should carry liability contracts against lawsuits based on malpractice (professional negligence).

Health Insurance

With the increasingly high costs of prescriptions, other medical products, and services, affordable health insurance is a foremost need in today's society. Many people obtain health insurance through a group insurance plan from the company for which they work. Others have individual plans that they purchase directly from an insurer. Still others have government health insurance plans through government employment, Medicare, and Medicaid. Health insurance policies often include the following benefits:

- Physician care.
- Prescription drugs.
- Inpatient and outpatient hospital care.
- Surgery.
- Dental and vision care.
- Long-term care for the elderly.

Major medical coverage pays for expenses beyond those covered by a basic plan, including long-term hospitalization and catastrophic illness.

HMOs and PPOs   Health maintenance organizations (HMOs) contract with doctors and other health care professionals to provide health care services for their members. Members pay monthly premiums and must choose from a list of doctors provided by the HMO. HMOs encourage their members to have regular checkups, immunizations, and other forms of early treatment. In this way, it is hoped that people will be less likely to require more expensive kinds of treatment. Many different kinds of organizations sponsor HMOs, including doctors, community groups, insurance companies, labor unions, and corporations.

A preferred provider organization (PPO) is a group of health care providers, such as doctors or hospitals, that provide care for groups of employees at reduced rates. PPOs are usually sponsored as part of an employer's group health plan. Employees choose among the health care providers on the PPO list when they need treatment. Choosing a non-PPO provider reduces the benefits paid to the insured under the plan.

Medicare and Medicaid
Most people 65 years of age and older are eligible for Medicare, a federally funded health insurance program. Medicare Part A helps pay for inpatient hospital care. Medicare Part B pays for 80 percent of doctors' and other medical services. Many people buy their own medigap insurance to cover the 20 percent not covered by Medicare. Medicaid is a health care plan for low-income people. State governments administer Medicaid, which is funded by both state and federal funds.

Disability Insurance
Disability insurance pays benefits when a person cannot work because of a disability. Total, or long-term, disability pays if the insured cannot perform normal job duties for a year or longer; partial, or short-term, disability pays for shorter periods of time.

Long-Term Care Insurance
Long-term care insurance helps cover care received in adult day care, assisted-living facilities, and nursing homes. Benefits are usually payable when an insured is unable to perform certain daily living activities without assistance, such as eating, bathing, dressing, or using the bathroom.

Legal Protection
A variety of state and federal laws help make it easier for people with preexisting conditions to obtain and keep health insurance. A federal law known as HIPAA (Health Insurance Portability and Accountability Act) sets national standards for all health plans.

The Affordable Care Act
The Affordable Care Act (ACA), which became law in 2010, was designed to make sure that all Americans have health insurance. The goal is high-minded and optimistic, and it has had its problems. Still, as part of a complex adaptive system, it has become a workable part of the legal network and has been somewhat successful in reaching its goal.

The ACA has several features that make it a revolutionary element within the world of insurance and within the legal system. First, it has created a new document, called the Patient's Bill of Rights, which is designed to shield people from the errant practices of the health insurance trade. Another key feature related to the Patient's Bill of Right is the effort to provide as many cost-free preventative services as possible. The law also encourages the implementation of accountable care organizations that are designed to encourage health care professionals to cooperate with one another to help patients get the best care available. The ACA also authorized the development of the health insurance marketplace, a website that is designed to assist people in enrolling in a health insurance plan by helping them see differences and similarities among available health insurance plans. People with a household income between 100 percent and 400 percent of the national poverty level as calculated by the federal government can now take advantage of subsidies to purchase health insurance.

In 2013, the act introduced a pilot project labeled "bundling" under which health care providers will be paid per health care incident instead of by service rendered. The goal is to reduce costs by providing a flat rate per incident rather than an itemized step-by-step charge for each diagnostic test, each treatment, and each medication provided during that single incident. Also in 2013, the ACA instituted a funding program that will flow to state Medicaid plans to provide preventive care services. Starting in 2014, insurance providers are no longer permitted to discriminate based on preexisting conditions. Nor are they permitted to discriminate based on gender. Also in 2014, the law began to prohibit insurance companies from eliminating coverage for people who are enrolled in clinical trials for cancer treatments or treatments for other serious illnesses. In 2014, the law also provided a tax penalty for those without insurance. The maximum amount of the penalty tax is $95 for each adult not insured ($47.50 for each uninsured minor). However, the tax penalty gets worse after 2014, continuing to climb until it reaches a maximum in 2016. Federal tax forms were also revised in 2014 so that people now self-report a lack of insurance coverage. [See: "Key Features of the Affordable Care Act: Overview of the Health Care Law," U.S. Department of Health and Human Services, HHS.gov/HealthCare (August 31, 2014); Alexandra B. Jeanblanc, "The Affordable Care Act and You," Ohio State Bar Association 2014 Annual Convention, Columbus (April 30–May 2, 2014).]

Umbrella Insurance

Most insurance contracts have built-in ceilings to the coverage provided under the policy. Sometimes these restrictions will be expressed in terms of the risks that the insurer is willing to cover for the insured. More often, those limits will be expressed in a set limit on the funds that the insurance company is willing to pay out. An individual or a business can buy an **umbrella policy** that will grant coverage beyond the limits of the standard policy provided by the insurer in exchange for higher premium payments.

THE OPENING CASE *Round 5*
Umbrella Coverage for a Rainy Day?

In the opening case, we learned that the original policy taken out by Granger on the Akron rental property was for dwelling insurance only. The details of the coverage are never revealed in the case. However, if it is a standard dwelling contract, the insurance agreement likely protected the structure from damage caused by fire, wind, snow, ice, lightning, and so on. The contract could also have included coverage for damage to the contents of the rental property, for unpaid rent, and so on. We do know that the dwelling policy did not cover discrimination. We know this because AOMIC sent Granger a letter to that effect shortly after the FHCS suit was initiated. The letter, either by design or by accident, seems not to have mentioned the umbrella policy. Granger, however, did not forget that umbrella policy, and he raised that policy and its terms as he argued against the lower court's decision to grant the summary judgment motion. The appellate court closely examined this contract to determine whether (1) the humiliation claim was covered as a personal injury and (2) whether Granger's actions were intentional. The court examined the language of the contract and concluded (1) that humiliation could be a personal injury and (2) the issue of intent was still too unclear for a definitive court ruling. Therefore, the lower court's granting of the summary judgment motion was a mistake and the case would have to go trial. So, this round also went to Granger and the score at this point was "Granger 3—AOMIC 0." The moral of the story, at this point in the saga, seems to be that, sometimes, those umbrella policies are worth their weight in gold. [See: *Granger, et al. v. Auto Owners, Insurance* 2013-Ohio-2792, Case. 26473, Court of Appeals, Ninth Judicial District (June 2013).]

Umbrella policies rarely stand alone. Most insurance companies will not even think about issuing an umbrella except as a backup for existing insurance. Umbrella policies generally lie dormant until the standard policy runs out of coverage. Thus, to mix metaphors, umbrellas function as safety nets that are available only when all other coverage has vanished. An umbrella is generally an extravagant expense that does not pay out. However, when it does kick in, the coverage is well worth the expense as Granger learned in the opening case.

quick quiz 19-2

1. An insured can cancel a straight life policy at any time and receive its cash surrender value.	true | false
2. Term insurance is the most expensive kind of life insurance.	true | false
3. With property insurance, unlike life insurance, an insurable interest must exist when a loss occurs.	true | false

19-3 The Insurance Policy

In most states, the insurance policy (which is the insurance contract) comes in a standard form. These forms are carefully drafted by insurance commissioners with help from the states' legal advisors. In this way, the consumer-buyer is protected from deception or fraud. As an additional protection to consumers, some states now require that insurance contracts must be written in clear, understandable language and printed in a readable typeface. Insurance policies, nevertheless, are adhesion contracts; that is, contracts drawn by one party that must be accepted as is on a take-it-or-leave-it basis.

Application

The first step in obtaining an insurance policy is to fill in an application. The application is an offer made by the applicant to the insurance company. As with any offer, the offeree, in this case the insurance company, may accept or reject the offer.

Binders

The waiting period between the offer and the acceptance opens the insured to potential risk. To avoid this risk, the insured can arrange to have the insurer issue a binder. A binder, or binding slip, will provide temporary insurance coverage until the policy is formally accepted. The binder will include all of the usual terms that would be included in the actual policy to be issued.

Premiums

An insurance contract differs from many other contracts in that it requires the payment of premiums. The amount of the premium is determined by the nature and character of the risk and by how likely the risk is to occur. The premium increases as the chance of loss increases. Thus, a premium on a fireproof building in a city with a fire department will be much lower than the premium on a barn located where firefighting equipment is not available.

Lapse

When the insured stops paying premiums, an insurance contract is said to lapse. This feature may not mean, however, that the contract will terminate automatically on the date that the last premium is paid. It may also not lapse automatically if the insured makes a delayed payment. Although state laws differ, most states allow for a grace period in which the insured may make payments to keep life and health insurance policies in force. Beyond this period, however, the insurance contract will lapse, and the policy will terminate. Automobile and property insurance policies usually have no grace periods and will terminate when a premium is not paid when due.

quick quiz 19-3

1. An insurance binder provides permanent insurance coverage.   true | false

2. Insurance premiums increase as the chance of loss increases.   true | false

3. An insurance contract will terminate automatically if a premium   true | false
   payment is not paid on time.

19-4 Cancellation of Insurance by Insurer

Under certain conditions, the insurer is given a legal right to forfeit, or cancel, an insurance policy. Proof of a forfeiture permits cancellation either before a loss or at the time the claim is made on a policy. Among the grounds permitting forfeiture are a breach of warranty and a concealment or misrepresentation of a material fact by the insured (see Table 19-2). Neither the insured nor the insurer may deny statements or acts previously made or committed that might affect the validity of the policy.

Warranties

A *warranty* is an insured's promise to abide by restrictions, especially those written into a policy that are intended to be conditions precedent to the existence of coverage. By statute

Table 19-2 Cancellation of Insurance Policies

Grounds for Cancellation	Explanation
Warranty violation	Insured fails to abide by restrictions especially written into the policy
Concealment	Insured deliberately withholds fact of material importance to insurer's decision to issue a policy
Misrepresentation	Insured gives false answers to questions in the insurance application that materially affect the insurer's risk

in many states, an insurance company has the burden of proof in establishing that a warranty has been breached (broken) by the insured. If this breach is proved, the insurer may cancel the contract or refuse payment of loss to the insured or to a beneficiary.

EXAMPLE 19-2: Breach of Warranty

Nicole Duffy, a well-known NASCAR driver, applied for life insurance after being involved in several racing accidents. Community Life was aware of these accidents, and Duffy agreed not to race while the policy remained in force. Duffy was killed while racing in an important race. Community Life could rescind any obligation to pay Duffy's beneficiaries.

Concealment

Fraudulent concealment is any intentional withholding of a fact that would be of material importance to the insurer's decision to issue a policy. The applicant need only give answers to questions asked. However, the insured may not conceal facts that would be material in acceptance of a risk.

EXAMPLE 19-3: Concealment

VanDorn, an insurance agent for Canadian Life, inspected Kalintor's building before issuing a fire insurance policy. Kalintor did not show VanDorn the basement, which was filled with flammable chemicals. After the policy was issued, Kalintor's building burned to the ground. Canadian Life later learned of the secret lab and was permitted to cancel Kalintor's policy.

Misrepresentation

If an insured party gives false answers, or *misrepresentations,* to questions in an insurance application that materially affect the risk undertaken by the insurer, the contract is voidable by the insurer. A representation is material if the facts represented influence the insurer's decision to issue the policy or the rate of premium to charge.

EXAMPLE 19-4: Misrepresentation

The Clark family applied for fire insurance from the Alabama Farm Bureau Mutual Casualty Insurance Company. The Clarks answered no when asked whether they had ever been arrested. When their house was destroyed by fire and they attempted to collect under the policy, an investigation revealed that the Clarks had both been arrested on previous occasions. The court upheld the Farm Bureau's denial of benefits due to this deliberate material misrepresentation.

Although all jurisdictions agree on the effects of a deliberate deception, there is disagreement as to the effects of an innocent misrepresentation. A majority of the states hold that the intent of the insured is irrelevant. Even an innocent misrepresentation would make the policy voidable by the insurer. A minority of states would not allow the insurer to deny coverage to an insured whose misrepresentation was unintentional.

EXAMPLE 19-5: Innocent Misrepresentation

Folk took out an insurance policy with Countryside Casualty. When asked if he had any physical impairments, Folk, who suffered from epilepsy, said no. When Folk was killed in an automobile accident, his estate attempted to collect the insurance. Countryside, which had discovered Folk's epilepsy, refused to pay, claiming he had misrepresented his physical health. Evidence indicated that Folk genuinely did not consider his epilepsy, which was controlled by drugs, to be a physical impairment. In a majority of states, Folk's belief would make no difference. The policy would still be voidable by Countryside. In a minority of states, Folk's innocent misrepresentation would not allow Countryside to deny recovery under the policy.

Estoppel

An insurer may not deny acts, statements, or promises that are relevant and material to the validity of an insurance contract. This bar to denial is called an *estoppel*. When an insurer has given up the right to cancel a policy under certain circumstances by granting the insured a special dispensation, the insurer cannot deny that dispensation when the chance to cancel or deny liability arises.

EXAMPLE 19-6: Estopped from Denying Liability

Maxwell, an insurance agent for Fidelity, called on MacLaine, who wanted fire insurance to cover her new cabin. The cabin was heated by a woodburning stove that, according to Fidelity's specifications, was located too close to a wooden wall. Maxwell told MacLaine not to worry about those specifications. He then falsified the measurements on the application. Two weeks later, MacLaine's cabin burned to the ground. Due to Maxwell's behavior, Fidelity would be estopped from denying its liability to MacLaine under the policy.

When the insurance company gives up one of its rights to help the insured, the company has made a *waiver*. A waiver, which is actually a form of estoppel, can be implied from the conduct of the insurance company. For example, when an insurance company cashes the check of a lapsed policy, it has, in effect, given up or waived its right to cancel that policy. Once a right has been waived, the insurer may not later deny its waiver.

CLASSIC CASE Sometimes the Insurance Company Wins

The classic case at hand begins with a plane crash— well—sort of. The plane in question was owned by the plaintiff, Aviation Charters, Inc. At the time of the "crash" the plane had landed and was on the runway. Suddenly, the nose gear malfunctioned and the nose wheel of the plane collapsed, causing some $52,500 in damage to the plane. As a dutiful insured, Aviation Charters reported the incident to its insurance company, Avemco Insurance. The insurance company, following the duties of an insurer, investigated and discovered that the pilot of the plane (the plane that was already on the ground, mind you) did not meet the requirements spelled out in the policy. More specifically, the insurer looked at an exclusionary clause that said it would not be liable if the person piloting the craft at the time of the "crash" had less than 5,000 hours of flight time. Apparently to be "approved" under the policy, a pilot needed 5,000 hours of flight time (2,000 would not do, which was what this pilot had logged). The investigation demonstrated that no one was really very surprised by the collapsed gear because on this particular type of aircraft, the nose gear often collapsed, usually when the plane was in taxi mode. This meant that the pilot had nothing to do with the collapsed gear, the fallen nose, or the damage to the aircraft. He could have had 500,000 hours of flight time, and the nose gear would still have collapsed. Interestingly, the insurance company makes no effort to dispute this. However, it does file a summary judgment motion stating that the case must be dismissed.

The insurance company argues that it has no liability under the policy because the pilot was not "qualified." The lower court looked at the policy, interpreted the plain and ordinary language in the policy, and (probably with a resigned shrug) granted the motion for dismissal. Aviation Charters appealed. On appeal, the plaintiff, Aviation Charters, argued that the exclusionary clause is a technicality. The plaintiff points to the fact that the gear could have collapsed while no one was on the plane. Moreover, Aviation Charters also brings a number of cases to the court's attention, all of which demonstrate that the pilot qualification exclusion is a technicality that should not be honored by the court if there is clear evidence that there was no causal connection between the "unqualified" pilot and the "crash." The insurance company provides no evidence to dispute the fact that the pilot did not cause the "crash." Instead, it simply points to the language in the exclusion clause and states, in effect, "Sorry, but we win." The court of appeals looks at the language, looks at the facts, interprets the language using clear and simple definitions, and concludes that, well, the insurance company is correct. Going by the strict, easy to understand, and straightforward words in the clause, the fact that an unqualified pilot was in the left seat was the key to the case, and, as a result, the insurer did not have to pay that $52,500. [See: *Aviation Charters Inc. v. Avemco Insurance Company,* Superior Court of New Jersey, Appellate Division (December 21, 2000).]

A QUESTION OF ETHICS

The issues involved in the opening case at the start of this chapter present us with a perplexing ethical issue. Just in case you missed the irony of Granger's argument, let's review what happened. Remember that Granger's first policy with AOMIC was for dwelling insurance, nothing more. As a typical dwelling contract, the agreement probably covered damage to the building and the contents from fire, wind, snow, ice, lightning, and so on. The contract would also have included coverage for unpaid rent and the like. The dwelling policy, however, did not cover discrimination. Granger, however, took out a second policy to protect him from other risks. This was the umbrella policy that is the subject of the lawsuit. Now here is where things get interesting. Remember that the present case (*Granger, et al. v. Auto*

Owners, Insurance) is the second case in this scenario. The first case was the lawsuit that the FHCS and Kozera (the potential renter with the six-year-old child) brought against Granger. The second case does not give us a record of exactly what happened in that first lawsuit. However, it is likely that Granger argued that he did not discriminate against Kozera, but even if he did discriminate, the words that he spoke could not possibly have caused any type of personal injury to Kozera. In other words, Granger says something like, "I did not discriminate against Kozera and, even if I did (which I didn't) what I said did not hurt Kozera." Despite this, at some point in the process, Granger and his attorneys saw the writing on the wall and settled. Typically, a settlement, whatever else it says, will also indicate that the defendant is not admitting any fault despite his agreement to settle. So far so good. The next thing that Granger does is turn around and file a lawsuit against AOIMC. The lawsuit claims that AOMIC did not defend him as it should have. Then AOMIC says something like (this is a paraphrase), "Defend you for what?" To which Granger replies (paraphrasing), "For discriminating and for causing personal injury to Kozera." The insurance company says that its right to defend Granger only arises if he caused personal injury to Kozera, and humiliation does not constitute personal injury. To which Granger replies, "I'm covered by the umbrella policy if I cause personal injury to someone, and personal injury includes mental anguish and humiliation is mental anguish. Therefore, I caused Kozera mental anguish and you should have defended me for it." By now the irony should be clear. In the first case, Granger claims that he did not discriminate and did not injure Kozera. Why? That is simple—because he does not want to pay Kozera any money. In this case, *Granger, et al. v. Auto Owners, Insurance*, Granger says that he did discriminate and did, in fact, injure Kozera. Why? Why does he change his position in relation to his own behavior and his own culpability? That is also simple—because he wants to get the money that he paid to Kozera back from AOMIC. Is it ethical for Granger to reinterpret his own behavior out of hope for monetary gain? Also, and perhaps more importantly, how ethical is a judicial system that not only makes this sort of alternative arguing possible, but also awards it monetarily? Think about it. [See: *Granger, et al. v. Auto Owners, Insurance* 2013-Ohio-2792, Case. 26473, Court of Appeals, Ninth Judicial District (June 2013).]

quick quiz 19-4

1. An insurance company may refuse to pay for a loss if it can prove that the insured breached a warranty to abide by certain restrictions.   true | false

2. If an insured gives false answers to questions in an insurance application, the insurance company can do nothing about it unless it discovers the fraud before any loss.   true | false

3. An insurer may not deny acts, statements, or promises that are relevant and material to the validity of an insurance contract.   true | false

Summary

19.1 Insurance is a transfer of the risk of economic loss from the insured to the insurer. Insurance policies require the elements of a contract: offer, acceptance, mutual assent, capable parties, consideration, and legality. To be insured, one must have an insurable interest in the subject matter of the policy. The parties to an insurance contract include the insurer, the insured, and the beneficiary.

19.2 It is possible to obtain insurance for a variety of risks. Life insurance provides funds to a beneficiary on the death of the insured. A beneficiary must have an insurable interest when the policy is issued but need not have that interest when the insured dies. The principal types of life insurance are straight life, limited-payment life, term, and endowment insurance. Principal types of property insurance include fire, marine, homeowner's, flood, and automobile insurance. In the case of property insurance, the insured must have an insurable interest when the loss occurs. Health insurance helps pay for such things as physician care, prescription drugs, inpatient and outpatient hospital care, surgery, dental and vision care, and long-term care for the elderly.

19.3 The first step in obtaining an insurance policy is to fill in an application. A binder provides temporary insurance coverage between the time the application is made and the time the policy becomes effective. Premiums are the consideration or payment an insured gives the insurer for its acceptance of risk. A lapse occurs when the insured stops paying premiums.

19.4 Under certain conditions, the insurer is given a legal right to cancel an insurance policy. Grounds permitting cancellation include breach of warranty, concealment of material facts, and misrepresentation on an application. Under the estoppel rule, an insurer is not allowed to deny certain statements, activities, or waivers.

Key Terms

add-on coverage, 452

adhesion contracts, 456

annuity, 447

beneficiary, 444

binder, 456

bodily injury liability insurance, 451

coinsurance, 448

collision insurance, 452

comprehensive coverage, 452

deductible, 448

descriptive threshold, 452

double indemnity, 447

duty to defend, 444

duty to investigate, 444

duty to pay, 444

dwelling insurance, 450

fault-based insurance, 451

homeowner's policy, 449

indemnify, 444

inland marine insurance, 449

insurable interest, 444

insurance, 442

insured, 444

insurer, 444

liability insurance, 453

life insurance, 446

limited-payment life insurance, 447

Medicaid, 454

medical payments insurance, 452

Medicare, 454

monetary threshold, •••

no-fault insurance, 451

ocean marine insurance, 449

ordinary life insurance, 446

peril, 442

personal injury protection (PIP), 451

policy, 444

premium, 444

property damage liability insurance, 452

renter's insurance, 449

risk, 442

straight life insurance, 446

subrogation, 444

substitute transportation insurance, 453

term insurance, 447

threshold, 451

threshold guideline, 452

time-based threshold, 452

towing and labor insurance, 453

umbrella policy, 455

underinsured-motorist insurance, 452

uninsured-motorist insurance, 452

universal life insurance, 446

whole life insurance, 446

Questions for Review and Discussion

1. What is insurance and what purpose does it serve?
2. What are the contractual elements of an insurance agreement?
3. Why is insurable interest so important?

4. What are the differences among types of life insurance?
5. How does insurable interest differ with life insurance and property insurance?

6. What is a coinsurance clause?
7. What coverage is given by fire, marine, homeowner's, renter's, and flood insurance?
8. What differences exist among the principal kinds of automobile insurance?
9. What benefits are included in health insurance policies?
10. What are the steps in applying for, obtaining, and maintaining an insurance policy?

Cases for Analysis

1. Juan Ramos's wife, Maria, became concerned after a violent storm caused disastrous flooding in a community not far down the river from where their house was located. She felt comforted when her husband told her that they were fully protected against flooding by their homeowner's insurance policy. The following spring, a flood caused serious damage to their home, and Juan's insurance agent told him that his homeowner's policy did not cover flood damage. What recourse do the Ramoses have against the insurance company?

2. Al Zuni Trading, Inc., purchased a $1 million life insurance policy on the life of one of its officers, Thomas McKee. Three months later, McKee resigned from the company. Two years later, McKee died. Did Al Zuni Trading, Inc., have an insurable interest in the life of McKee, and thus, was it entitled to the million dollars? Explain. [See: *In re Al Zuni Trading, Inc.,* 947 F.2d 1403 (9th Cir.).]

3. U.S. Aviation Underwriters issued an aircraft insurance policy to Cash Air, Inc., covering its employees. The policy stated that to be covered under the policy, the aircraft must be "flown only by a pilot or pilots described on the Coverage Summary page." Each policy coverage page stated that a pilot not named in the policy must be one who holds "an AA commercial pilot certificate with AA multi-engine and instrument ratings who has flown a minimum of 2,500 hours as pilot in command, at least 1,000 hours of which shall have been in multi-engine aircraft and at least 25 hours of which shall have been in Piper PA 31-350 aircraft." Peter Covich, an employee of Cash Air, Inc., did not meet the pilot experience requirements when the Piper Seneca airplane he was piloting crashed, causing personal injuries and property damage. Must the insurance company pay for the loss? Explain. [See: *U.S. Aviation Underwriters v. Cash Air,* 568 N.E.2d 1150 (MA).]

4. Victory Container Corporation was owned by the three Radin brothers. Two of those brothers also owned the Warrensburg Paper and Board Corporation. Victory had no direct ownership of the Warrensburg plant, however. Nevertheless, Victory took out a fire insurance policy on the Warrensburg plant. When the Warrensburg property was damaged, Victory attempted to collect under the policy. Did Victory have an insurable interest in the Warrensburg property? Explain. [See: *Victory Container Corporation v. Calvert Fire Insurance Company,* 486 N.Y.S.2d 211 (NY).]

5. Avrit and Schuring entered an agreement to purchase a certain property. Each paid $1,000 as a down payment. They were later to pay an additional $25,000. The seller of the property was to maintain insurance until the deal was finalized. Avrit and Schuring also obtained an insurance policy on the property. Before the deal was finalized, fire damaged the property. Avrit and Schuring attempted to collect on their policy, but the insurance company claimed that Avrit and Schuring had no insurable interest at the time of the fire. Did Avrit and Schuring have an insurable interest between the time of the down payment and the time the deal was finalized? Explain. [See: *Avrit v. Forest Industries Insurance Exchange,* 696 P.2d 583 (OR).]

6. Martin Searle's life insurance policy contained a standard suicide clause. Under the clause, Allstate would not be liable to the beneficiary, Alice Searle, should Martin commit suicide within the first two years of the policy even if Martin were insane at the time of his death. Martin committed suicide 10 months after the policy went into effect. Allstate refused to pay Alice any benefits under the policy. Alice sued the company, claiming that her husband had been mentally deranged at the time of the suicide and did not realize the consequences of his action. Allstate argued that the sanity clause removed the issue of mental incapacity from the case. Who would prevail in a majority of states? Explain. [See: *Searle v. Allstate Life Insurance Company,* 212 Cal. Rptr. 466 (CA).]

7. Bayer took his car to Whitaker's auto repair shop for repairs. Whitaker took the car for a test drive, with Bayer seated in the passenger seat. During the test drive, a car operated by another person drove on the wrong side of the road and collided with Bayer's vehicle, injuring Bayer. Neither Bayer's vehicle nor the vehicle owned by the wrongdoer was insured. Whitaker carried insurance on his own vehicles, including uninsured-motorist insurance. Could Bayer recover from Whitaker's insurance company under the uninsured-motorist provision of the policy? Why or why not? [See: *Bayer v. Travelers Indemnity Co.*, 267 S.E.2d 91 (VA).]

8. Riggins contacted the Hartford Insurance Company and asked for an all-risk policy for his truck. An underwriter for Hartford agreed to the policy and issued a binder on March 28. On April 2, before the full policy had been executed, Riggins left on a trip, hauling liquor. Sometime during the trip, the liquor was stolen. Hartford refused to pay, arguing that the final policy that would have been issued would not have covered the hauling of liquor. Riggins argued that the all-risk binder was in effect at the time of the theft and that he was therefore covered, even though the final policy would not have covered him. Was Riggins correct? Explain. [See: *Hilt Truck Lanes, Inc., v. Riggins*, 756 F.2d 676 (8th Cir).]

9. When Sidney Henry applied for insurance with State Farm, he was asked whether he had ever had recurrent indigestion or a hernia. Henry answered no to each question. In fact, he had experienced recurring indigestion, and it had been diagnosed as either an ulcer or a hernia. The policy was issued. Eight months later, Henry died of cancer of the esophagus. When Eula Henry applied for benefits, State Farm denied her request. Eula argued that the misrepresentations were not material because her husband died from cancer, not the illnesses he was questioned about. Was Mrs. Henry correct? Explain. [See: *Henry v. State Farm*, 465 So.2d 276 (LA).]

10. On January 13, Lax made out a check to State Farm Insurance to pay for her automobile insurance, which had lapsed 62 days earlier. Unfortunately, she forgot to mail the check. On January 22, Lax was killed when trying to pass a truck. The check was found in the wreckage and taken to a State Farm agent who mailed it to the main office. The main office, with knowledge of the accident, cashed the check. The beneficiaries argued that State Farm's conduct in cashing the check with knowledge of the accident constituted a waiver of its right to cancel the policy due to her failure to pay by the due date. Were the beneficiaries correct? Explain. [See: *VanHulle v. State Farm*, 254 N.E.2d 457 (IL).]

quick quiz Answers

19-1	19-2	19-3	19-4
1. F	1. T	1. F	1. T
2. F	2. F	2. T	2. F
3. F	3. T	3. F	3. T

THE OPENING CASE *Round 1*
Who's on First? No . . . Who Filed first? That Is the Real Question

In any mortgage case there are at least two players, the sellers and the buyers. Sometimes (actually most of the time), a third party enters the fray—the mortgagor. In this case the sellers were Michael and Charles Hines (Hines and Hines); the buyers were Rhonda Gumm and Timothy McCord (Gumm and McCord), and the mortgagor was . . . no . . . the mortgagors were National City Bank and Hines and Hines. Gumm and McCord agreed to buy a house from Hines and Hines for $85,000 (sort of). However, what made the case interesting was the addendum in which Hines and Hines agreed to reduce the price to $73,000, by paying the buyers $12,000 and lending them $36,500. Do not gloss over this arrangement. Think about it for a moment. Hines and Hines, the sellers, lent Gumm and McCord the money to buy the house that Hines and Hines were trying to sell. In effect then, Hines and Hines became bankers for the buyers. The buyers (Gumm and McCord) also signed a note and mortgage for the $36,500 to be repaid over 30 years at 8 percent interest. The closing occurred June 6. During the closing, Gumm and McCord signed a promissory note in favor of National City Bank. The amount of the note was $68,000. They also executed a mortgage in the bank's favor for that amount. Deeds were signed and given to Gumm and McCord. On June 7, Gumm and

McCord executed a mortgage in favor of the seller to secure their promissory note for $36,500. Hines and Hines were not about to be caught watching the paint dry (especially paint on their own house), and so they recorded the mortgage on June 12. It was not until June 19 that the title company recorded both the deed and the mortgage on behalf of National City. About two years later, Gumm and McCord defaulted on the loan. National City foreclosed, and Hines and Hines jumped on board saying that their mortgage was recorded first and they were entitled to be paid first. Initially, the case went to a magistrate. The magistrate said that it was clear to him (and to the law, by the way) that the first mortgage filed is the mortgage that has a legal preference. Hines and Hines filed first and so they have preference The common pleas court, however, took issue with this conclusion, ruling that Gumm and McCord executed the promissory note and the mortgage with National City Bank first, and so the bank should be given preference. Hines and Hines appealed. The case went right to the court of appeals, which stated the problem very clearly. The issue is who holds the preference here? Who has first claim? Is it the party that executed first, or the party that filed first? Or is there some other formula that we are missing here? [See: *National City Bank v. Gumm, et al.*, 2004-Ohio-1263.]

Opening Case Questions

1. Who is the buyer in this case? Who is the seller? Explain.

2. Who or what is the mortgagor? Explain.

3. Who drew up the mortgage first? Explain.

4. What party filed the mortgage first? Explain.

5. Before reading ahead, make a guess. Who has preference here, National City or Hines and Hines? Explain.

 Learning Objectives

1. Differentiate between a secured and an unsecured loan.
2. Identify the types of mortgages that are available to borrowers.
3. Explain the legal effect of recording a mortgage.
4. Describe the rights and duties of the mortgagor and those of the mortgagee.
5. Differentiate between a financial recovery and a change in the initial conditions.
6. Identify short-term solutions to the 21st-century financial crisis.
7. Explain the long-term solutions to the 21st-century financial crisis.
8. Describe how a security interest is created for personal property.
9. Decide whether security interests are perfected.
10. Determine priorities when parties claim a security interest in the same property.

20-1 A Primer on Real Property Finance and Security

When encountering a subject like finance, mortgages, and security control, it is tempting to jump right into the crisis side of the issue, especially when that crisis has dominated the topic in the early 21st century. This temptation emerges from the dramatic nature of the subject, the seriousness of the issues at stake, and the apocalyptic aura that surrounds any crisis, but especially one that appears to have threatened the very social order upon which our culture is based. As always, however, the temptation must be resisted in favor of gathering basic ground rules, useful concepts, and helpful definitions. This observation is not made to downplay either the seriousness or complexity of the crisis. Rather, the idea is to emphasize that the complexity and seriousness of the crisis demands a measured and informed approach to unraveling its nature, causes, and consequences. As this study unfolds, we will learn that even the term *crisis* must be redefined and that the lessons of the recent past must not be ignored, especially as that past reveals what happens when super powers such as the United States and Russia, for example, ignore the telltale signs of that impending crisis. This chapter will explore introductory material to lay the groundwork, and then, so armed, enter the territory of the 21st-century financial crisis. After that we will see how personal property plays into the larger picture of American finance. Before diving off the deep end, however, let's look at some structural details that will help build a platform of financial concepts. These details include mortgage costs, types of mortgages, recording mortgages, and the rights and duties of the mortgagor and the mortgage.

Real Property as Security

Our economy is built upon credit, and credit is built upon trust. Trust is necessary to ensure that the money that the bank or the savings and loan company lends to the client will be

Did You Know?

The chances of a borrower defaulting on mortgage payments can increase dramatically with life-changing events. They jump:

- 54 percent if the borrower has an unexpected drop in income.

- 26 percent if the borrower gets divorced from his or her spouse.

- 6 percent for each additional household member after the first two.

repaid. Trust by itself, however, only goes so far. Bigger loans lead to a smaller level of trust, and, therefore, involve a higher need for some kind of security, or so the argument goes. Security is the assurance that a creditor will be paid back for any money loaned or for credit extended to a debtor. Debts are said to be secured when creditors know that somehow they will be able to recover their money. Lenders of money and people who extend credit often require a security device to protect their financial interests. A security device is a way for creditors to get their money back in case the borrower or debtor does not pay. A secured loan is one in which creditors have something of value, usually called collateral, from which they can be paid if the debtor does not pay. In general, if creditors are not paid the debt owed to them, they can legally gain possession of the collateral. The collateral is then sold, and the money is used to pay the debt. The right to use the collateral to recover a debt is called the creditor's security interest. If creditors lend money but do not require collateral, they have made an unsecured loan. An unsecured loan is one in which creditors have nothing of value that they can repossess and sell to recover the money owed to them by the debtor.

Both real property and personal property can be used to secure a debt. When real property is used as security for a loan, a device known as a mortgage is used to establish collateral for the loan. A mortgage is a transfer of an interest in property for the purpose of creating a security for a debt. The one who borrows the money (the mortgagor) conveys his or her interest in the property to the lender (the mortgagee) while at the same time retaining possession of the property. The borrower signs a promissory note as evidence of the loan in addition to a mortgage instrument. The mortgage creates a legal claim to the property. This legal claim, also called a lien, gives the lender the right to have the property sold if the debt is not paid. Once the land is sold and the debt is paid, the mortgagor's obligation to the mortgagee is over. However, if the sale of the property does not satisfy the whole debt, the mortgagor will still owe the balance.

THE OPENING CASE *Round 2*
Who's on Second? Mortgage Foreclosure, the Downside of the Mortgage Market

In the opening case, we learned that Michael and Charles Hines (Hines and Hines) sold a house to Rhonda Gumm and Timothy McCord (Gumm and McCord). The buyers were supported in their bid for the house by two mortgagees National City Bank and Hines and Hines. The double mortgages played out like this: Gumm and McCord agreed to buy the house from Hines and Hines for $85,000. In the addendum to the contract Hines and Hines agreed to reduce the price to $73,000, by paying the buyers $12,000 and lending them $36,500. In effect then, Hines and Hines became bankers for the buyers. Gumm and McCord also signed a note and mortgage for the $36,500 amortized over 30 years at 8 percent interest. The closing occurred June 6. During the closing Gumm and McCord also signed a promissory note in favor of National City Bank. The amount of that note was $68,000. They also executed a mortgage in the bank's favor for that amount. Deeds were signed and given to Gumm and McCord. On June 7, Gumm and McCord executed a mortgage in favor of the seller to secure their promissory note for $36,500. Hines and Hines recorded the mortgage on June 12. On June 19 the title company recorded both the deed and the mortgage for National City. About two years later, Gumm and McCord defaulted on the loan. National City foreclosed. Hines and Hines entered the case at this point claiming that their mortgage was recorded first and they were entitled to be paid first. The record in the case is unclear as to what happened after the court determined which mortgage superseded the other. However, once the dust clears and the house is sold, Gumm and McCord will be personally liable for any amount that exceeds the selling price of the house at auction. In fact, Gumm and McCord would be liable for that amount plus interest until the debt was fully paid. [See: *National City Bank v. Gumm, et al.*, 2004-Ohio-1263.]

Mortgage Costs

Many costs are associated with obtaining a mortgage. Initially, a potential borrower must pay a mortgage application fee, an appraisal fee, a credit report fee, and an inspection fee. Once the loan is approved, the borrower often pays an origination fee, which is a charge for issuing the loan. Sometimes, the borrower pays interest in a lump sum upfront, called points, to get a lower rate of interest. A point is a one-time charge equal to 1 percent of the principal amount borrowed. Thus, if three points are charged on an $80,000 mortgage, the borrower will be required to pay a one-time fee of 3 percent of $80,000, which amounts to $2,400. If all IRS requirements are met, points are tax deductible. Other items charged to the borrower include charges for document preparation, attorney's fees, title insurance, surveyor fees, termite inspections, mortgage insurance, and homeowner's insurance.

Types of Mortgages

There are many different types of real property mortgages (see Table 20-1). Some of the most common mortgages are conventional fixed rate, variable-rate, interest-only, graduated payment, balloon-payment, reverse, participation, construction, deeds of trust, subprime, junior, and home equity.

Conventional Fixed-Rate Mortgage   A **conventional fixed-rate mortgage** involves no government backing by either insurance or guarantee. The loan is made by private lenders, and the risks of loss are borne exclusively by them. Conventional mortgages have interest rates that stay the same during the life of the mortgage, regardless of fluctuations in the economy. Changes in recent years, however, have resulted in the creation of variations to the fixed-interest rate mortgage, including the variable rate mortgage.

Variable-Rate Mortgage   A **variable-** or **flexible-** or **adjustable-rate mortgage (ARM)** has a rate of interest that changes according to fluctuations in the index to which it is tied. The index rate may be the bank's prime rate or the Federal Reserve Board discount rate. As the index rate goes up and down, so does the rate of interest charged on the loan. This rate may be more or less than the index rate but always varies with it. The obvious advantage of the variable-rate mortgage is the drop in the amount of the mortgage payment when the rate drops. However, mortgage payments can also rise when the rate rises. In general, a change in payments, either up or down, does not occur without some advance warning. Also, variable-rate mortgages agreements must include a maximum rate that cannot be exceeded. In addition, the frequency of these changes in the rate is usually restricted by the terms of the mortgage agreement.

Interest-Only Mortgages   In some situations, a borrower might negotiate an **interest-only mortgage**. In such a situation, the borrower, who very often cannot afford a down payment on a house, will agree to pay only the interest on the loan for a set period of time, anywhere between one and three years or so, set by the agreement. The idea under this approach is to wait until the borrower's financial picture brightens, allowing him or her to make the higher payments that will eventually come due.

There are many different types of mortgages. Knowing which type fits your needs, both in the present and for the future, makes homeownership easier and more enjoyable.

Graduated-Payment Mortgage   A **graduated-payment mortgage** has a fixed interest rate during the life of the mortgage; however, the monthly payments made by the mortgagor increase over the term of the loan. In the first years of the mortgage, the

Table 20-1   Some Methods of Financing a House

Types of Mortgages	Description
Conventional Fixed-rate mortgage	Conventional fixed-rate mortgages have interest rates that are permanent, regardless of fluctuations in the economy.
Variable-rate mortgage	A variable- or flexible- or adjustable-rate mortgage has a rate of interest that changes according to fluctuations in the index to which it is tied.
Interest-only mortgage	With an interest-only mortgage, the borrower pays only the interest for a period of time, between one and three years or so, set by the agreement.
Graduated-payment mortgage	A graduated-payment mortgage has a fixed interest rate during the life of the mortgage; however, the monthly payments made by the mortgagor increase over the term of the loan.
Balloon-payment mortgage	A balloon-payment mortgage has comparatively low fixed payments during the life of the mortgage, followed by one large final (balloon) payment.
Reverse mortgage	A reverse mortgage is a loan that allows older homeowners to convert some of the equity in their home into cash while retaining ownership of their home.
Participation loans	In a participation loan, the borrower will transfer certain ownership (or equity) rights to the lender and in exchange, the borrower will negotiate lower interest rates or a lower down payment.
Construction loans	Construction loans authorize staggered payments at various stages of the process of building a home.
Deed of trust	Under a deed of trust, the mortgagor conveys his or her interest in the property to a trustee.
Subprime mortgages	Subprime loans are offered when a borrower does not qualify for one of the regular loans. To compensate, the lender demands that the borrower pay a much higher interest rate than more qualified lenders are required to pay.
Junior mortgages	A junior mortgage, also called a second (or subsequent) mortgage, is a mortgage subject to a prior mortgage.
Home equity loans	A home equity loan is either an outright loan or a line of credit made available to homeowners based on the value of the property over and above any existing mortgages. Home equity loans are often used to consolidate credit card balances or other debts that have higher interest rates.

payments are low. The payments gradually increase over time, usually reaching a plateau at which the payments remain fixed. This type of mortgage is advantageous for young people, whose income may be expected to increase as their mortgage payments increase.

Balloon-Payment Mortgage A **balloon-payment mortgage** has comparatively low fixed payments during the life of the mortgage, followed by one large final (balloon) payment. The mortgage has a fixed interest rate, but it is written for a short time period, such as five years. At the end of the time period, the mortgagor usually must find new financing, either with the same or with a different lender, at the current interest rate.

THE OPENING CASE *Round 3*
I Don't Know Is on Third! And the Type of Mortgage Here Is . . .

In the opening case, we learned Hines and Hines sold a house to Gumm and McCord. The buyers managed to negotiate twin deals with two potential mortgagees, National City Bank and Hines and Hines. The twin mortgage deal looked something like this: Gumm and McCord agreed to buy the house from Hines and Hines for $85,000. In the addendum to the contract, Hines and Hines agreed to reduce the price to $73,000, by paying the buyers $12,000 and lending them $36,500. In effect, Hines and Hines became bankers for the buyers. Gumm and McCord also signed a note and mortgage for the $36,500 repaid over 30 years at 8 percent interest. The record does not indicate what the terms were for the National City Bank part of the deal. However, there is no reason to believe from the content of the case that the loan between Hines and Hines, on one side, and Gumm and McCord, on the other, was anything other than a conventional fixed-rate mortgage. The fact that the buyers took out another mortgage with National City Bank would have had no effect on the terms of the Hines and Hines loan, unless it was specifically mentioned in the agreement. Still, the fact that there was a second mortgage floating out there does complicate things, especially since there is some discrepancy in relation to who filed first. More on that is about to be explored. [See: *National City Bank v. Gumm, et al.,* 2004-Ohio-1263.]

Reverse Mortgage A reverse mortgage is a type of loan that allows older home-owners to convert some of the equity in their home into cash while retaining ownership of their home. The loan is repaid when the property is sold, or on the occurrence of some other specified event.

Participation Loans A borrower who is shopping for a loan with terms that are more favorable than usual may request a participation loan. In such a loan, the borrower will transfer certain ownership (or equity) rights to the lender and in exchange, the borrower will negotiate lower interest rates or a lower down payment.

Construction Loans Sometimes a borrower wants to build a new home rather than to buy an existing one. In such a case, the borrower may wish to negotiate a construction loan that will authorize staggered payments at various stages of the building process. Thus, the loan will issue a payment at the time the borrower buys the land, when the foundation of the house is laid, when the framing is finished, when the exterior has been constructed, and when the entire house is completed. Construction loans come in a variety of flavors including both variable and fixed rate loans.

Deeds of Trust In some states, a deed of trust is used instead of a mortgage. In a conventional mortgage, the mortgagor conveys all or part of his or her interest in the property directly to the mortgagee. Under a deed of trust, the mortgagor conveys his or her interest in the property to a disinterested third party, known as a trustee. The mortgagor remains on the property, but the trustee holds certain rights to that property as security for the mortgagor's creditors. If the debtor defaults, the trustee can sell the property for the benefit of those creditors. The provisions of many deeds of trust allow the trustee to sell the property without going to court. For this reason, some legal authorities do not consider a deed of trust a true mortgage, because true mortgages require a foreclosure action for the sale of the property.

Subprime Mortgages When a borrower does not qualify for one of the regular mortgages just covered, he or she might ask for and receive a subprime loan. Generally, these borrowers have been disqualified from conventional loan because of a bad credit history or because of a low debt-to-income ratio. These loans generally have a much higher default rate than most of the conventional loans and are thus disfavored by lenders. This is true now more than ever before because of the recent mortgage crisis that has occurred during the last few years. To compensate for the risk involved in a subprime loan, the lender demands that the borrower pay a much higher interest rate than more qualified lenders are required to pay.

Junior Mortgages Sometimes an owner of real property may execute a junior mortgage on the property. A **junior mortgage**, also called a **second** (or subsequent) **mortgage**, is a mortgage subject to a prior mortgage. For example, if a homeowner wants to improve the mortgaged property and needs another loan to do so, he or she may use the property as security for another loan. If this transaction occurs, the mortgagor is said to have executed a second mortgage on the property. Some people have three or more mortgages on one parcel of property. If all the mortgages are recorded, the holders of second and subsequent mortgages may exercise their rights against the property only after prior mortgages have been paid off. Thus, if the first mortgagee causes the property to be sold and is paid off in full, the second and subsequent mortgages are paid out of the proceeds that remain. The first mortgagee acts as a trustee of the surplus funds for the benefit of the junior mortgagees.

Home Equity Loans A **home equity loan** is an example of a junior mortgage. It is either an outright loan or a line of credit made available to homeowners based on the value of the property over and above any existing mortgages. Such a loan takes advantage of the equity that has built up in a home over a period of time. Home equity loans are often used to consolidate credit card balances or other debts that have higher interest rates. Unlike interest paid on a credit card balance, interest paid on a home equity loan is tax deductible.

Recording the Mortgage

Like a deed, a mortgage must be in writing and delivered to the recorder's office in the county where the property is located. Recording a mortgage notifies any third party who may be interested in purchasing the property or in lending money to the owner that the mortgagee has an interest in the real property covered by the mortgage. If the mortgage is not recorded and a later mortgage is given on the same property, the new mortgage is superior to the first. The second mortgagee must not know about the first mortgage and must record the mortgage properly. A failure to record the first mortgage, however, would not remove the obligation of the mortgagor to the first mortgagee. The debt would simply be unsecured.

Rights and Duties of the Mortgagor

By law and by agreement, the mortgagor has certain rights and duties in conjunction with the mortgage. First, the mortgagor has the right to possess the property. Second, the mortgagor has the right to any income produced by the property. For instance, the mortgagor would be entitled to any rent proceeds gained from leasing all or part of the property. The mortgagor could, however, assign this right to the mortgagee, which is sometimes done as a condition of executing the original mortgage agreement. Third, the mortgagor has the right to use the property for a second or third mortgage. Fourth, the mortgagor has the **equity of redemption**, that is, the right to pay off the mortgage in full, including interest, and thus discharge the debt in total.

In addition to these rights, the mortgagor has certain duties. Chief among these duties is to make payments on time. Mortgagors must preserve and maintain the mortgaged property for the benefit of the mortgagee's interest and security. Similarly, the mortgagor is

THE OPENING CASE *Round 4*
Who's on First? It Looks Like Hines and Hines.

In the opening case, we learned about the case of *National City Bank v. Gumm.* Gumm and McCord agreed to buy a house from Hines and Hines for $85,000. Gumm and McCord negotiated an addendum to the contract under which Hines and Hines consented to lower the price to $73,000, by paying the buyers $12,000 and lending them $36,500. Essentially then, Hines and Hines turn into bankers for the buyers. Gumm and McCord signed a note and mortgage for the $36,500 amortized over 30 years at 8 percent interest. The closing occurred on June 6, during which Gumm and McCord signed a promissory note in favor of National City Bank. The amount of that note was $68,000. Gumm and McCord also set up a mortgage in the bank's favor for that amount. Deeds were signed and given to Gumm and McCord. On June 7, Gumm and McCord executed a mortgage in favor of the seller to secure their promissory note for $36,500. Hines and Hines recorded the mortgage on June 12. On June 19, the title company recorded both the deed and the mortgage for National City. About two years later, Gumm and McCord defaulted on the loan. National City foreclosed. Hines and Hines entered the case at this point claiming that their mortgage was recorded first and they were entitled to be paid first. Initially, the case went to a magistrate who ruled that the first mortgage filed is the mortgage that had a legal preference. Hines and Hines filed first and so they have preference. The common pleas court,

however, disagreed and held that Gumm and McCord executed the promissory note and the mortgage with National City Bank first, and so National City Bank should be given preference. Hines and Hines appealed. The case went right to the court of appeals, which stated that the issue is who holds the preference here? Who has first claim? Is it the party that executed first, or the party that filed first? The appeals court says that, while National City may have executed its mortgage first, the bank failed to record the mortgage even though it had ample time and every opportunity to do so. In fact, the record demonstrates that the bank waited seven days before bothering to make sure the mortgage was recorded. Since any recorded mortgage takes precedence, the bank's mortgage is subordinate to that of Hines and Hines. National City was not through arguing, however. The bank adds that it had no notice that there was going to be a second mortgage on the property. The appeals court finds this argument less than credible, since the addendum was clearly attached to the original paperwork. The bank could have added a clause to the original contract that would have subordinated the Hines and Hines mortgage to the bank's mortgage but it did not do so. Therefore, the court concludes that the magistrate was correct and that the mortgage that was recorded first, that is, the Hines and Hines mortgage, takes precedence—period. [See: *National City Bank v. Gumm, et al.,* 2004-Ohio-1263.]

often required to insure the property to the benefit of the mortgagee for the amount of the mortgaged debt. The mortgagor also must pay all taxes and assessments that may be levied against the property. Frequently, the mortgagor will ease the burden of these obligations by paying a percentage of the insurance premium and taxes each month along with the mortgage payment. The mortgagee holds the money in an escrow account. An escrow account is a special account into which money is deposited before the payment of the insurance or taxes is due. The money stays in the account until the time comes to pay the insurance or tax. The mortgagee then takes the money out of the account and makes the payments.

Rights and Duties of the Mortgagee

The mortgagee has the unrestricted right to sell, assign, or transfer the mortgage to a third party. Whatever rights the mortgagee had in the mortgage are then the rights of the assignee. The only way the mortgagor could stop the mortgagee from assigning the mortgage is to pay the mortgagee everything owed on the mortgage. Sometimes an assignment by the mortgagee to another mortgagee can cause unforeseen problems for the mortgagor.

Mortgagees have the right to receive each installment payment as it falls due. Frequently, mortgagees will include a term in the mortgage agreement allowing an **acceleration** of the debt if the mortgagor fails to meet an installment payment. This term means that a default on one installment payment will make the entire balance due immediately, giving the mortgagee the right to collect the full amount. In general, a clause allowing acceleration must be executed in good faith. In other words, before invoking the acceleration clause, the mortgagee must genuinely believe that the mortgagor will not be able to make good on the debt and that the mortgagee's security interest is therefore threatened. If the matter ends up in court, the mortgagor will have the burden of proving that the mortgagee did not act in good faith.

If the mortgagor has defaulted or has failed to perform some other agreement in the mortgage, the mortgagee has the right to apply to a court to have the property sold. This right is called **foreclosure**. It takes priority even when the mortgagor files for bankruptcy. Because, in a majority of jurisdictions, a mortgage is a lien on the land, a foreclosure is an equitable action. The mortgagor does not have a right to a jury trial in foreclosure action. A mortgage is foreclosed when the mortgagee proves the amount of the unpaid debt (including interest and other charges) and the property is sold by and under the direction of a court. The proceeds from the sale are then applied to the payment of the debt. Any money remaining after the claims of the mortgagee have been satisfied goes to the mortgagor or to the second and subsequent mortgagees. The mortgagee's financial interest in mortgaged property gives rise to certain constitutional rights. Under the 14th Amendment to the U.S. Constitution, mortgagees cannot lose their interest in property without due process of law.

U.S. Const. Amendment 14 (see page 914)

Purchase by Mortgage Takeover

Mortgages often contain a clause providing that if the property is sold, the mortgage becomes due and payable. If the mortgage does not contain such a clause, the property may be sold with the mortgage remaining on it. In such takeovers, the transfer of title to a new buyer is subject to the buyer's payment of the seller's mortgage at the existing rate of interest. In purchasing a property already mortgaged, the buyer will either **assume the mortgage** or take the property **subject to the mortgage**. When buyers decide to assume the mortgage, they agree to pay it. When they take the property subject to a mortgage, the seller agrees to continue paying the debt.

quick quiz 20-1

1. A security device is a way for creditors to get their money back in case the borrower or debtor does not pay.   true | false

2. A home equity loan is an example of a junior mortgage.   true | false

3. The mortgagor has the right to possess the mortgaged property and to any income produced by the property unless otherwise assigned.   true | false

20-2 The 21st-Century Financial Crisis

Before we look at the financial crisis of 2008, it might be a good idea to define the term *crisis*. In his book, *Time of Crisis*, Michel Serres, a French philosopher and writer, makes several interlocking observations about the nature of a crisis, any crisis, that are worth examining. After examining the history of the word, he concludes that any crisis (whether it involves medicine, law, politics, economics, and so on) implies that the system has reached a branch point (or flash point) of transition. In turn, the existence of a flash point within a system implies a shift in a new direction. Despite the vocabulary that we use rather habitually (and somewhat haphazardly), Serres argues, a crisis never has a real "recovery." According to Serres, the term **recovery** denotes a reversal to an earlier status. Such an about-face would actually threaten the security of the system in crisis, because it indicates that no progress had been made. A lack of progress ensures that the crisis will occur again. Thus, a system must not recover from a crisis; it must move away from the initial conditions that caused the crisis. Otherwise, the system remains volatile, a sure sign that "another" crisis will occur soon. This is true of the current 21st-century financial crisis just as it is true of any healthy complex adaptive system (CAS). Before delving into this crisis, Serres asserts, somewhat forcefully, that a proper study of the current financial crisis also requires an understanding of its deep roots. In fact, like the crisis of 1929, the crisis of 2008 is not simply a financial crisis. Rather, it is a global crisis that represents a series of tectonic shifts in agriculture, transportation, health, connections, and conflicts, demographics, all of which interact with one another to signal a multi-institutional crisis that goes, in the words of Serres, "far beyond the scope of normal history." [See: Michel Serres, *Times of Crisis: What the Financial Crisis Revealed and How to Reinvent our Lives and Future* (New York: Bloomsbury, 2014), pp. ix–xiii; 1–17.]

The Nature of the Crisis

From this observation, Serres makes an interesting leap—one worth contemplating as we attempt to deal with the crisis. Serres argues, rather convincingly, that these tectonic shifts are caused by human activity—nothing more. Agricultural production, for example, is now controlled by only 2 percent of the population, which has led to a shift in living space as people move from the country to the city. Advances in transportation (and communication, for that matter, which Serres chooses not to mention, perhaps because it is so obvious; perhaps because it is too complicated to explain in the short amount of space devoted to the issue) have created what amounts to a planetary city unprecedented in human history. Advances in health and medicine have lowered infant mortality and extended the average life span leading to a demographic leap in the size of our global population. [See: Serres, pp. 1–11.] Perhaps even more interesting, however, is Serres' observation that these tectonic shifts have given birth to a third player on the global scene, something that Serres refers to as the biogetic, a socioeconomic, cultural system created by humans, which has taken on a life of its own. Serres pictures this biogetic system as a third player in series of conflicts, each of which plays itself out with two sets of human players battling one another within that biogetic system. [See: Serres, pp. 25–44.]

Thus, in the current financial crisis, the politicians work to fix the system created by the economists, thus pitting the politicians and the economists against one another, both acting against the backdrop of the biogetic system. When politicians and lawyers pass a law (such as the Dodd–Frank Wall Street Reform and Consumer Protection Act), their opponents, the economists (and accountants, and bankers, and brokers, and CEOs, and investors and so on), react against that law. However, emerging from within this first level of interaction (people v. people; politicians v. economists) is a second, hidden level of interaction between the people and the system itself. The system, which has taken on its own separate existence, operates in a highly reflexive (even defensive) manner, leading to unpredictable, unintended consequences that we will be unable to evaluate fully until we develop a certain objective distance in time and space. It is for that reason that we discuss the recent measures taken to fix the crisis with a certain degree of cautious, but healthy skepticism.

The Economic-Political Dimension of the Crisis

It would be unfair and unwise to focus only on this picture of the crisis. For one thing the picture painted in *Times of Crisis* is based on philosophy and history rather than on economics and politics. When we shift to that base, the story of the crisis looks a bit more practical and, therefore, somewhat more manageable. This is the approach taken by Dmitry Orlov in his book, *Reinventing Collapse*. What Orlov suggests is that the economic crisis in the United States mirrors almost exactly the crisis that spelled the end of the Soviet Union. The Soviet Union collapsed, Orlov says, because five factors collided with one another at precisely the right place and time. These five factors are: (1) a rapid and unprecedented decline in the amount of energy resources (crude oil) available for production; (2) a rapid and uncontrolled widening of the international trade deficit caused by Russia's inability to produce food and goods; (3) an unrestrained level of spending on defense caused by the "star wars" initiative; (4) expanding foreign debt; and (5) a pervasive anxiety that anticipated impending disaster in the wake of the defeat in Afghanistan and the tragedy of Chernobyl. [See: Dmitry Orlov, *Reinventing Collapse: The Soviet Experience and American Prospects* (Gabriola Islands, BC, Canada: New Society Publishers, 2011), pp. 1–2.]

As a prelude to the financial crisis and as a foreshadowing of its ultimate economic collapse, Orlov declares that the United States spiraled through a series of similar events that will coincide to create the same type of disaster that the Soviet Union experienced. By 2005, the pattern of events looked like this: (1) crude oil fabrication was down in the United States; (2) the failure to keep abreast of technological advances threatened to intensify the inequity in foreign trade; (3) the American response to the "war on terror" caused a huge increase in military spending; (4) inflation had intensified the level of foreign debt; and (5) the setbacks in Iraq and the destruction caused by Hurricane Katrina sparked new waves of insecurity and angst at home. [See: Orlov, pp. 2–3.]

Each of these elements in and of itself did not create the type of crisis that emerged in 2008. However, when these events were stacked on top of one another and interlaced with other similar problems, they helped spark the type of situation that both Serres and Orlov warn about. As these elements combined, they eroded the confidence of the American people and led to reckless speculation in real property and foolish get-rich-quick schemes that typified the 21st-century financial crisis. People agreed to schemes that appeared to create wealth with little or no effort, that promised to make a lot of money rapidly with minimal risk, and that guaranteed a huge return on a small investment that did not have to be paid up front. Moreover, in each case the day of reckoning seemed so far removed as to be nonexistent. The problem was that the day of reckoning did arrive, and at that point scapegoats had to be found and quick-fix schemes established. People blamed Wall Street and Washington and focused on things like subprime mortgages and balloon payment schemes while ignoring the overarching big picture that set the stage for these abuses.

The Causes of the Crisis

As Nouriel Roubini and Stephen Mihm point out in their book *Crisis Economics,* "Subprime mortgages were but the most obvious sign of a deep and systemic rot. This fact underscores a cardinal principle of crisis economics: The biggest and the most destructive financial disasters are not produced by something so inconsequential as subprime mortgages or a few reckless risk takers. Nor are they merely produced by the euphoria of a speculative bubble. Rather, much as with earthquakes, the pressures build for many years, and when the shock finally comes, it can be staggering." [See: Nouriel Roubini and Stephen Mihm, Crisis Economics: A Crash Course in the Future of Finance (New York: Penguin, 2010), p. 62.] This diagnosis is not unlike those proposed by Serres and Orlov. The pressure in the financial sector had been building for years, even decades, caused by the laundry list of elements supplied by Orlov (energy shortfalls, trade imbalance, runaway military spending, climbing foreign debt, and so on) and by Serres (changes in agriculture, transportation, communication, and demographics) and leading to a mad scramble to get rich as quickly as possible in risk-free ways.

The pressure in the current crisis resulted from these big factors, but they led to a series of small mistakes that then combined, leading to the financial disturbance the impact of which is still felt today. The upcoming causes (revealed on the following pages) should be seen as secondary causes that spin off from the more fundamental causes outlined by Orlov, Serres, Roubini, and Mihm, in their respective studies. However, these smaller causes must be examined and then situated in their proper place in the overall financial puzzle. These factors include the creation and later mismanagement of Fannie Mae and Freddie Mac, the development of securitization (including both mortgage-backed securities and asset-backed securities), and the increased use of faulty loans (including subprime loans, liar loans, and NINJA loans).

Fannie Mae, Ginnie Mae, and Freddie Mac

The Federal National Mortgage Association (Fannie Mae) was chartered by the Reconstruction Finance Corporation during the Great Depression in 1938. Fannie Mae does not make mortgage loans. Rather, it purchases loans that were made based on strict guidelines set up by the Federal Housing Association (FHA) and the Veterans Administration (VA). Eventually Congress recognized a flaw in the Fannie Mae system caused by the fact that the agency had to borrow money to fund mortgages it purchased. That in and of itself was not the real problem, however. The real problem was that Congress had not properly anticipated the amount of debt that Fannie Mae would accumulate. To remedy this situation, Congress created another agency, the Government National Mortgage Association (Ginnie Mae), which then took over much of Fannie's debt, freeing Fannie to buy mortgages insured by the government. Around this same time Congress created the Federal Home Loan Mortgage Corporation (Freddie Mac), another government-sponsored enterprise (GSE) to help support the mortgage market. [See: Phil Angelides, et al., *The Financial Crisis Inquiry Report* (New York: Public Affairs, 2011), pp. 38–39; and Roubini and Mihm, pp. 61–63.].

Securitization and Mortgage Backed Securities

Slowly the government lifted some of the restrictions on Fannie and Freddie, first permitting them to buy loans that had not fallen within FHA or VA guidelines and then authorizing them to participate in securitization. The process of securitization works like this. [See: Angelides, et al., pp. 38–39 and 70–71; and Roubini and Mihm, pp. 62–65]. A bank or other lender lends money to a borrower who pays off the loan over time with interest. The lender makes money on the interest at a slow and steady rate over a period of years (decades actually when speaking of real property). Somewhere along the line some bright boy (or gal) decided that it would be better to bundle a bunch of these mortgages together and sell them as bonds (now called mortgage-backed securities) to big investors, like pension funds, which would then reap the benefit of the interest payments multiplied by the number of loans purchased in that bundle over a long period of time, while the lender received a big payment up front, allowing it to bundle more and more mortgages more and more rapidly. [See: Roubini and Mihm, p. 65]. As noted previously, Fannie, Ginnie, and Freddie were all authorized to purchase these mortgage backed securities.

Securitization and Asset-Backed Securities

Now three effects rolled off this set of circumstances. First, another bright gal (or boy) decided that, what worked for mortgages would work for car loans, furniture loans, boat loans, home improvement loans, student loans, construction loans, and so on. Thus, we witness the growing popularity of asset-backed securities. Second, the original lenders began to care less and less about whether the borrowers were financially qualified to pay back the loans because, well, the lenders were passing the risk on to those who purchased the securities. It was at this point that subprime loans, as well as other radical loan practices like the so-called liar loans and the NINJA ("no income, no job or assets") loans began to appear (see discussion that follows). Third, everybody got into the act, not only government-sponsored entities, like Fannie, Ginnie, and Freddie, but also commercial banks, investment banks, and dozens of private lending firms, such as Merit Financial, that appeared and vanished overnight. As a result the use of mortgage-and asset-backed securities grew by 230 percent between 2000 and 2006. This amounted to just about $2.7 trillion. [See: Charles Gasparino, *The Sellout* (New York: Harper, 2009), p. 158.] The final consequences were inevitable. The crash occurred when the high-risk borrowers could not make their payments. Land values collapsed and, in the wink of an eye, Roubini and Mihm's financial earthquake shook the very foundation of the economy.

Subprime Loans (Revisited) Before the collapse, the use of loans experienced a huge resurgence in the middle of the first decade of the 21st century. Some of this was due to technology that allowed loans to be processed faster and for approval to be based on a mathematical probability of repayment rather than the traditional criteria of credit, capacity, capital, and collateral. [See: Angelides, pp. 67–72.] However, some of it was also caused by a push toward deregulation. This encouraged the banks and other lenders to issue subprime loans as a way to bring new homeowners into the market while simultaneously helping the lenders build handsome portfolios. [See: Roubini and Mihm, pp. 73–76.]

Liar Loans and NINJA Loans (Also Revisited) An unintended consequence of this strategy was an increase in the number of liar loans and NINJA loans that appeared on the scene with increased regularity. **Liar loans** are those that deliberately misstate the qualifications of a borrower to push a loan through the approval process. A **NINJA loan** is one that has been negotiated by a borrower with "no income, no job, and no assets." Liar loans and NINJA loans actually come in many different shapes and sizes. They include both adjustable-rate and interest-only mortgages. The idea is to somehow make it easier for someone with little or no buying power to negotiate a mortgage. [See: Gasparino, p. 151; and Roubini and Mihm, pp. 65, 89]. Securitization made such loans possible and, in a strange retroactive way, encouraged many others to jump on the securitization bandwagon, thus accelerating the securitization process. Clearly this was a recipe for disaster although only a few people realized it at the time.

The Short-Term Solutions to the Crisis

The 21st-century financial crisis erupted when so many borrowers could not make mortgage payments that the mortgage securities market began to collapse. This collapse led to a rapid decline in the value of real property, which, like a line of dominoes (a snow ball rolling down a hill or a dam bursting, pick your metaphor), accelerated the breakdown. Those firms and individuals who had invested heavily in the mortgage-backed and asset-backed securities (and even those who had not invested all that heavily) began to experience unprecedented losses. The upcoming solutions (the short-term ones on the following pages) should be seen as quick-fix treatments that patched up the system without really targeting the underlying causes, at least as those causes are envisioned by Orlov, Serres, Rounini, and Mihm. These temporary measures include the takeover of Fannie and Freddie by the Federal Housing Finance Agency, the creation of HAMP and HARP, the establishment of the Troubled Asset Relief Program, and the passage of the Dodd–Frank Act. The first measure that we will look at is the takeover of Fannie and Freddie. This step was one of the most disheartening events that emerged from the crisis.

The Fannie and Freddie Takeover The risky mortgages purchased by Fannie and Freddie began to take their toll on the two GSEs. The purchasing power of the two GSEs had been exaggerated by the fact that their operation was supposedly supported by the U.S. Treasury. The apparently risk-free purchases that they made were focused on mortgaged-backed and asset-backed securities, both of which were much riskier than they had appeared. Then the bottom began to fall out from under them. The two GSEs were struck by enormous losses as the housing crisis hit and mortgages began to default. The fees that had been paid to Fannie and Freddie for backing these risky mortgages did not cover their losses. Nor could they cover those losses with insurance. Moreover, and perhaps more to the point here, their portfolios were filled to capacity with mortgages purchased by subprime borrowers, ARMs, and NINJAs, and everyone knew that as those mortgages failed, Fannie and Freddie's capital reserves would fall to zero. [See: Roubini and Mihm, p. 108; Angelides, pp. 309–23; and Gasparino, pp. 410–16.]

To prevent this disaster, and to restore confidence in the system, the government stepped in to save both institutions. The solution demanded radical steps, one of which was the formation of the **Federal Housing Finance Agency (FHFA)**. The FHFA was created in 2008 under the authority of the Housing and Economic Recovery Act of 2008. The new agency is the offspring of a merger between the Federal Housing Finance Board and the Office of Federal Housing Enterprise Oversight. In addition to its power to regulate the two wayward GSE's (Fannie and Freddie), the new group was also charged with reestablishing public faith in the mortgage market by restoring the stability, continuity, authority, and dependability of the entire lending system. The process of placing the popular and high-profile GSEs into what actually amounted to a conservatorship was deemed of critical importance to the survival of the economy. Two major programs that are operated under the auspice of the FHFA are the Home Affordable Refinance Program (HARP) and the Home Affordable Modification Program (HAMP). [See: "Who We Are and What We Do," Federal Housing Finance Agency (FHFA), http://www.fhfa.gov/.]

Home Affordable Modification Program

The **Home Affordable Modification Program (HAMP)** was established by the Department of the Treasury to support the efforts of homeowners who, though in default, wished to continue to make payments on their mortgages. The program provides help to the private banks and other lenders who own the mortgages and who must be convinced of the need and the value of restructuring the mortgages. Of course not every debtor will be qualified under the HAMP guidelines. In order to take advantage of HAMP, a debtor must owe no more than $729,750 on the mortgage; the property must be the debtor's primary residence; the mortgage must have been entered no later than January 1, 2009; and the debtor must also be at least 60 days behind on payments or close to losing the home. [See: "Who We Are and What We Do," Federal Housing Finance Agency (FHFA), http://www.fhfa.gov/.]

Home Affordable Refinance Program

The **Home Affordable Refinance Program (HARP)** is a sister program to HAMP that also operates under the authority of the Federal Housing Finance Agency. Unlike HAMP, however, HARP was designed for homeowners who are not in default on their mortgage payments but who have found themselves in the unfortunate position of owing more to the bank or mortgage company than the house is actually worth. HARP is open to homeowners whose loans are owned by Fannie or Freddie. The program permits qualified individuals to receive a break on out-of-pocket mortgage expenses by introducing a lower interest rate, reducing each monthly mortgage payment, obtaining a constant fixed-rate mortgage, or stockpiling equity at a more rapid rate. [See: "Who We Are and What We Do," Federal Housing Finance Agency (FHFA), http://www.fhfa.gov/.]

Recent Developments at the FHFA

Since their takeover by the FHFA in 2008, Fannie and Freddie, while still in conservatorship, have managed to carry the lion's share of financing of new mortgages. However, recently some key government officials, including the head of the FHFA, have determined that the time is ripe for a shift away from those rules that make financing more difficult. One step will be to reinforce the roles of

Fannie and Freddie, which, must be seen as the backbone of the lending market far into the future. This new policy is in contrast to the previous program that increased the cost of government financing through Fannie and Freddie in order to encourage borrowers to seek support in the private sector. This does not mean, however, that the government is abandoning confidence in the private sector. On the contrary, in addition to revitalizing Fannie and Freddie, new guidelines will be implemented to reassure private lenders that they need not be as strict in their mortgage application requirements as they have been thus far in the wake of the financial crisis of 2008. [See: Nick Timiraos and Deborah Solomon, "U.S. Backs Off Tight Mortgage Rules," *The Wall Street Journal,* May 14, 2014, pp. A1 and A2.]

Troubled Asset Relief Program (TARP)

Another government solution is the **Troubled Asset Relief Program**. This program was designed to allow the government to buy many of the so-called troubled assets that had resulted from the securitization epidemic. The program was funded at a level that topped $700 billion. Under provisions in EESA, the fund is managed by the secretary of the Treasury. The secretary has the duty to make certain that any institution that receives funds under this program agrees to permit the federal government to purchase non-voting stock in that institution. Not all of the assets, however, went to the purchase of these troubled assets, at least not directly. Instead, they went indirectly into the bailout of several large firms such as General Motors and Chrysler. Part of the funds also went to financial institutions such as AIG and Bank of America. Many people saw this as a move that bordered on a nationalization of these financial institutions. [See: Roubini and Mihm, pp. 168–69.]

Dodd–Frank Wall Street Reform and Consumer Protection Act

Undoubtedly the most sweeping reform bill enacted in this crisis is the **Dodd–Frank Wall Street Reform and Consumer Protection Act**. As might be expected, the Dodd–Frank Act is long, involved, and complicated. It consists of 16 separate titles, many of which are often referred to as separate acts. Thus, Title XIV of the Dodd–Frank Act is also called the Mortgage Reform and Anti-Predatory Lending Act. Title XIV is especially pertinent to our discussion of the 21st-century financial crisis because the new act is designed to prevent the problems noted earlier. Some of the new provisions include the following.

1. Lenders are now required to make a good faith attempt to insure that all borrowers have the financial ability to repay the loan taken out to finance the mortgage.

2. Lenders must also make a good faith attempt to determine whether the borrower can also pay all taxes, insurance, and all other assessments.

3. A good faith attempt must include an examination of specifically defined documents that provide concrete verifiable evidence of the borrower's income stream, credit history, debt-to-income situation, employment, and financial resources (not counting the equity in the real property involved in the current loan).

4. Lenders are required to use documentation supplied by the Internal Revenue Service (IRS) or some other comparable third party that is also regulated by the act.

5. Certain types of mortgage arrangements are either outlawed or limited by the act, including mortgages with balloon payments that more than double the previous payments.

The act also creates a category of mortgages called **qualified mortgages**, which have met the good faith requirements outlined in the act. Having a qualified mortgage bestows on the lender a safe harbor privilege that creates a presumption that the lender had ample evidence demonstrating that the borrower could satisfy the loan's repayment requirements. On the other hand, the act also outlaws certain types of lender-related compensation. Thus, mortgage originators cannot be compensated based on the loan's terms, except for terms related to the principal on the loan. Also, the mortgage originator cannot be paid an origination fee, with certain exceptions, unless that fee is paid by the borrower. [See: "Dodd–Frank Act Ushers in New Regulations for Mortgage Originators," *Day Pitney, LLP,* August 24, 2010, pp. 1–3; John ReVeal, "Mortgage Reforms Under the Dodd–Frank Act," *Bryan Cave LLP,* August 3, 2010, http://www.bankbryancave.com; "Summary of Mortgage Related Provisions of the Dodd–Frank Wall Street Reform and Consumer Protection Act," *Mortgage Bankers Association,* July 21, 2010, p. 1; and William Sweet, "Dodd–Frank Becomes Law," *The Harvard Law School Forum on Corporate Governance and Financial Regulation,* July 21, 2010, p. 2, http://blogs.law.harvard.edu.]

The Long-Term Solutions to the Crisis

The previous solutions (takeover of Fannie and Freddie by the Federal Housing Finance Agency, creation of HAMP and HARP, establishment of the Troubled Asset Relief Program, and passage of the Dodd–Frank Act) should be viewed as short-term therapy rather than a long-term cure for the problems that led to the 21st-century financial breakdown. These solutions may temporarily plug certain obvious leaks, but they cannot prevent the financial dam from bursting. To head off another collapse, the entire structure must be repaired from the ground up. The long-term solutions covered in this section address the underlying cracks in the foundation of the socioeconomic system that led, not just to this crisis, but to a series of overlapping disasters that have repeated themselves in a cyclical fashion over the past century.

A Philosophical Solution
A philosophical and somewhat optimistic long-term solution is offered by Serres in *Times of Crisis.* The most significant contribution that Serres makes to a long-term solution is his observation that, when a crisis occurs, there can be no true recovery if *recovery* is defined as a return to the set of original initial conditions. Such an approach is self-defeating, because those conditions triggered the problem. Instead of tinkering with a broken system, governmental and private authorities must alter or eliminate those initial conditions. The good news is that the initial conditions in this case were created, Serres tells us, by human activity in agriculture, transportation, health, demographics connections, and conflicts. [See: Serres, pp. 1–15.] The bad news is that the changes that have emerged from the development of these areas have generated a new relationship between the socioeconomic-biological-ecological system (Serres calls it Biogea and we have used the term the biogetic system) and the people who live and work within that system. [See: Serres, pp. 25–33.] Serres says we must re-immerse ourselves in the system in order to close the separation by abandoning the activities that created the initial separation. This is an interesting solution, but the law does not do well with such abstract programs. On the other hand, the notion that a new crisis will be prevented only by altering the initial conditions that led to the old crisis is a valuable observation that is related to the other two long-term solutions offered here. [See: Serres, pp. 48–72.]

An Economic-Political Solution
In *Reinventing Collapse,* Orlov also implies that a new crisis will occur unless the initial conditions that produced the current crisis are abolished. It is on this point that he and Serres agree. Where they differ is in the nature of the long-term changes. Orlov believes that economic collapse is inevitable. The initial conditions that gave birth to this crisis are grounded in a political and economic social system fed by five elements: (1) a decline in energy resources, (2) a serious trade deficit, (3) unrestrained defense spending, (4) expanding foreign debt, and (5) a pervasive psychosocial anxiety leading to erratic behavior. Once these elements are in place, collapse is inevitable. Consequently, we should be more concerned with what happens in the post-collapse era than during the collapse itself. Curiously, while the post-collapse era is to be avoided, the underlying principles of that era provide a template for long-term changes in the initial conditions. [See: Orlov, pp. 2–4.]

Those principles are best seen in a concrete example. Orlov suggests a new level of governmental regulation that, while severe, can actually do some practical good. For instance, in a post-collapse (or near-post collapse) world, energy resources in general and gasoline in particular will become so scarce that it will be rationed in a severely limited way. To address this problem, the government should prohibit the purchase of any new gas-powered vehicles—period. This prohibition would force industry to retool existing cars, making them more energy efficient. Banning new vehicles would also close all businesses related to the manufacture and sale of new vehicles, which itself results in a huge energy savings. It also leads to a drop in the use of vehicles by people; it encourages carpooling when possible and makes the development of alternative means of transportation necessary. People will ride bikes, take the bus, ride the train, develop solar-powered vehicles, fabricate steam-powered cars, and so on. [See: Orlov, pp. 132–33.]

Another measure that Orlov suggests is a post-collapse alteration in the very nature of the corporation, from one that is driven by the need for profit to one that is driven by the need to provide welfare and income for its employees. The corporation would then focus on becoming a self-perpetuating organization that does its own exploration for resources, its own manufacturing of a product, its own sales, and its own reapplication of the surplus into the development of a better corporation. Corporations become, in effect, self-perpetuating, self-sufficient communes in which people live, work, play, train, and so on, as a team. [See: Orlov, p. 129.] Both of these examples may seem highly implausible, perhaps even impossible. However, both examples focus on a solution that alters those dangerous initial conditions. Now, as we turn to Roubini and Mihm, we see how this principle can be used in the retooling of the current financial system to prevent a recurrence of an unending cycle of financial catastrophes.

A Quantifiable, Applied, Practical Solution

To summarize, the Serres principle promotes altering the initial conditions of the socioeconomic system to prevent a series of repeating financial disasters. Building on this, the Orlov principle promotes a radical rethinking of financial and corporate relationships to shake up those initial conditions. Roubini and Mihm apply these two principles, without naming them, to the work-a-day world of Washington and Wall Street and construct several proposals to make those radical adjustments a reality. In one proposal, they suggest that the government make it advantageous for our largest financial institutions to subdivide and reorganize themselves into smaller, independent units. The plan would make it illegal for large financial institutions to invest in any venture from which they cannot extricate themselves with the capital reserves that they have on hand. In essence, financial institutions would be legally compelled to maintain the ability to bail themselves out of financial danger. The need to maintain self-sustaining capital reserves discourages risk-intensive ventures and discourages unchecked institutional growth. Instead, the law would encourage financial institutions to downsize so they can properly control every investment they take on. In effect, the plan would eliminate the "too-big-to-fail" syndrome that has plagued the current financial system, thus attacking a key initial condition. No institution becomes too big to fail, because there is no value any longer in being quite that "big." [See: Roubini and Mihm, p. 226; Paul M. Barrett, "Prophet Making," *The New York Times Sunday Book Review*, June 27, 2010, p. BR13.]

In another proposal, Roubini and Mihm suggest a drastic reconfiguration of executive bonus packages. Oddly, they do not promote eliminating such bonuses. Such a move would be ill-advised. It is not "bonus as bonus" that is the problem. Rather, it is the bonus that is paid immediately with no concern for the long-term effects of the investment that earned that bonus. This technique encourages executives to support high-risk ventures that produce immediate dramatic results. Under the traditional bonus system, once an investment has produced a dramatically high return, the executive receives his or her bonus instantly. Should the investment later fail, the executive keeps that bonus. In contrast, Roubini and Mihm propose a bonus-escrow plan, referred to as the "bonus-malus" system, under which the bonus would be placed in an escrow account for several years to test the true value of the investment. The executive does not receive the bonus unless the investment demonstrates its staying power. If the investment loses money, then the bonus is reduced by an appropriate amount. Again, Roubini and Mihm have suggested a radical alteration of the initial conditions of the current system. Instead of encouraging risky "shoot-from-the-hip" investment opportunities, as the present system does, the new system encourages solid, long-term investment prospects that may even outlive the executive. [See: Roubini and Mihn, pp. 187–188; Barrett, p. BR13.]

These are only a few of the modifications that Roubini and Mihm have suggested to alter the initial conditions of the present financial situation. Others include changes in the method by which securities are approved, including a standardization of the process as well as heightened transparency that will allow investors greater access to investment ratings conducted by ratings agencies.

---

quick quiz 20-2

1. Subprime lending was the only cause of the 21st-century financial crisis.   true | false

2. To avoid a future crisis, the initial conditions of a financial system must be changed.   true | false

3. The federal government was forced to take over Fannie Mae but did not have to follow a similar strategy with Freddie Mac.   true | false

---

20-3 Personal Property as Security

Article 9 of the UCC* brings all personal property security devices, or security interests, together under one law. The property that is subject to the security interest is called collateral. A security interest is created by a written agreement, called a security agreement, which identifies the goods and is signed by the debtor. The lender or seller who holds the security interest is known as the secured party. A security interest is said to attach when the secured party has a legally enforceable right to take that property and sell it to satisfy the debt. It is said to be perfected when the secured party has done everything that the law requires to give the secured party greater rights to the goods than others have. The following definitions apply to secured transactions:

- Consumer goods are goods that are used or bought for use primarily for personal, family, or household purposes.

- Equipment is goods other than inventory, farm products, or consumer goods.

- Farm products are crops or livestock or supplies used or produced in farming operations.

- Inventory are goods other than farm products held for sale or lease or raw materials used or consumed in a business.

- Fixtures are goods that are so related to real estate that an interest arises in them under real estate law.

UCC 9-102(23)

UCC 9-102(33)

---

*To access the most recent version of the UCC and its Articles, please visit http://www.law.cornell.edu/ucc/ucc.table.html

UCC 9-102(34)

UCC 9-102(48)

UCC 9-102(41)

UCC 9-103

UCC 1-201(9)
(see page 919)

- **Purchase money security interest** is a security interest taken by a lender or a seller of an item to secure its price.
- **Buyer in the ordinary course of business** is a person who in good faith and without knowledge that the sale is in violation of ownership rights or security interest of a third party buys goods in ordinary course from a person in the business of selling goods of that kind, not including a pawnbroker.

Security Agreement

UCC 9-105(I)

A security agreement is an agreement that creates a security interest. It must be in writing, be signed by the debtor, and contain a description of the collateral that is used for security.

EXAMPLE 20-1: Security Agreement Must Describe Collateral

Moody Industries contracted to purchase certain robotics equipment from Universal. Moody's president signed a promissory note identifying Universal as a secured party. When Moody filed for bankruptcy, Universal claimed to have a security interest in the robotics equipment. Because the promissory note did not describe the collateral, Universal did not hold a valid security interest in the equipment.

If Universal had provided enough information about the collateral to allow the court to identify it without a detailed description, the result would have been different. Had Universal made reference to the equipment by including purchase order or invoice numbers, the court could have identified the equipment and would have upheld the validity of the security agreement.

Attachment of a Security Interest

To be effective, a security interest must be legally enforceable against the debtor. This enforceability is known as **attachment**. Attachment occurs when three conditions are met. First, the debtor has some ownership or possessive rights in the collateral. Second, the secured party (or creditor) transfers something of value, such as money, to the debtor. Third, the secured party takes possession of the collateral or signs a security agreement that describes the collateral.

UCC 9-203

EXAMPLE 20-2: Attachment of Security Interest

Conroy loaned Lightfoot $5,000 for six months at 8 percent interest. Lightfoot secured the debt by giving Conroy several uncut diamonds that Lightfoot owned. Conroy agreed to return the diamonds when Lightfoot paid the debt. The security interest was legally enforceable because all three conditions were met. First, Lightfoot had ownership rights in the diamonds. Second, Conroy gave Lightfoot something of value (the $5,000). Third, Conroy took possession of the diamonds. The security interest would also have attached if Lightfoot had kept the diamonds but signed a security agreement describing them.

Creditors may obtain security interests in property acquired by the debtor after the original agreement is entered. The creditor does so by placing a provision in the security agreement that the security interest of the creditor also applies to goods the debtor acquires at a later time. It is known as a **floating lien**. This lien is important to creditors who take security interests in goods, such as food items, that are sold and replaced within short periods of time. The lien is lost when the goods are sold but regained as soon as the debtor takes possession of the new property.

UCC 9-204

Perfection of a Security Interest

When a security interest attaches, it is effective only between debtor and creditor. Such creditors, however, want to make certain that no one else can claim that collateral before they do if the debtors fail to pay them back. To preserve the right to first claim on the collateral, creditors must perfect their interest. A security interest can be perfected in one of three ways: by filing a financing statement in the appropriate government office, by attachment alone, or by possession of the collateral.

Perfection by Filing
Security interests in most kinds of personal property are perfected by filing a financing statement in a public office. The office may be a central one (secretary of state's or secretary of the commonwealth's office) or a local one (county recorder or city clerk) where the debtor resides or has a place of business. The proper office for filing depends on the type of collateral and varies from state to state.

A financing statement must give the names of the debtor and the secured party. It must be signed by the debtor and give the address of a secured party from which information regarding the security interest may be obtained. It must also give a mailing address of the debtor and contain a statement indicating the types, or describing the items, of collateral. When the financing statement covers such things as fixtures, crops, timber, minerals, oil, and gas, the statement must also contain a description of the real estate concerned.

UCC 9-302

Perfection by Attachment Alone
A purchase money security interest in con*sumer goods* is perfected the moment it attaches, with the exception of motor vehicles and fixtures. Security interests on motor vehicles are perfected by making a note of the lien on the certificate of title issued by the state government. Security interests on fixtures are perfected by filing a financing statement with the registry of deeds where the land is located.

UCC 9-302(1)(d)
UCC 9-302(3)(b)

EXAMPLE 20-3: Perfection of Purchase Money Security Interest

Sabatini purchased a new 60″ Smart-4K Ultra HD TV for $1,999.99 from Steinbeck's TV Outlet. To pay for the TV, she borrowed money from the Atlantic Finance Company, which took a security interest in the TV by entering into a security agreement with Sabatini. Because this interest was a purchase money security interest and the TV set was a consumer good, the security interest would become perfected the moment it attached, that is, when Sabatini signed the agreement and received the TV set, and Steinbeck received payment from the finance company.

Perfection by Possession
A security interest may be perfected when the secured party (creditor) takes possession of the collateral. This possession is called a pledge. The borrower, or debtor, who gives up the property, is the pledgor. The secured party, or creditor, is the pledgee. A secured party who has possession of the collateral must take reasonable care of the property. The debtor must reimburse the secured party for any money spent to take care of the property.

UCC 9-313

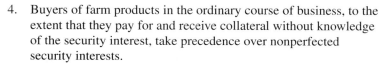

EXAMPLE 20-4: Pledge of Personal Property

After Sabatini paid off the debt to the Atlantic Finance Corporation, (See Example 20-3) she decided to buy a Kindle. This time, she borrowed the money from her cousin, Colter, who agreed to lend Sabatini the money only if he could have her Kindle as security until she repaid him. Colter's security interest in the Kindle became perfected when he took possession of it.

Priorities and Claims

UCC 9-312(3)

UCC 9-312(4)

UCC 9-307(1)

UCC 9-301(1)(c)

Sometimes, two or more parties claim a security interest in the same collateral. At other times, unsecured parties claim that they have better rights than secured parties. The UCC helps resolve these conflicts. The following are some of the provisions, stating who prevails over whom in particular situations:

1. A perfected purchase money security interest in inventory has priority over a conflicting security interest in the same inventory.

2. A purchase money security interest in collateral other than inventory has priority over a conflicting security interest in the same collateral if it is perfected when the debtor receives the collateral or within 10 days thereafter.

3. Buyers of goods in the ordinary course of business (except farm products) prevail over security interests in the seller's inventory.

4. Buyers of farm products in the ordinary course of business, to the extent that they pay for and receive collateral without knowledge of the security interest, take precedence over nonperfected security interests.

5. Buyers of consumer goods are not affected by perfected security interests of which they have no knowledge.

6. In all other cases, a perfected security interest prevails over an unperfected security interest.

7. Conflicting security interests rank according to priority in time of filing or perfection.

8. When two or more parties have unperfected security interests in the same collateral, the first to attach prevails over the other parties.

Collateral may be repossessed if the debtor defaults, but the repossession may not be conducted in a way that disturbs the peace.

UCC 9-307(2)

UCC 9-301

UCC 9-312(5)(a)

UCC 9-312(5)(b)

UCC 9-601

Default of the Debtor

If a debtor defaults by failing to make payments when due, the secured party may satisfy the debt by taking possession of the collateral. Because of the difficulties of doing this, the perfection of a security interest by possession, as in a pledge, is better than other types of perfection. Collateral may be repossessed without going through the court if it can be done without causing a disturbance; otherwise, the creditor must use legal processes.

After repossessing the goods, the secured party (the creditor) may sell them at a public auction or private sale. The terms of the sale must be reasonable, and the debtor must be given notice of the time and place of any public auction so that he or she may bid on them personally. If the goods are consumer goods and the debtor has paid 60 percent or more of the cash price of a purchase money security interest, the secured party cannot keep the goods. They must be sold.

quick quiz 20-3

1. A security interest is perfected when the secured party has a legally enforceable right to take that property and sell it to satisfy the debt. true | false

2. Security interests in most kinds of personal property are perfected by filing a financial statement in a public office. true | false

3. Buyers of goods in the ordinary course of business (except farm products) prevail over security interests in the seller's inventory. true | false

Summary

20.1 Individuals and institutions that lend money need some assurance that they will have their money returned to them. Security devices serve as this means of assurance.

20.2 A system must not recover from a crisis; it must move away from the initial conditions that caused the crisis in the first place. This is true of the current 21st-century financial crisis just as it is true of any healthy complex adaptive system (CAS). Like the crisis of 1929, the crisis of 2008 is a global crisis that must be fixed by reengineering the initial conditions that started the crisis. Some short-term solutions to the crisis include the takeover of Fannie and Freddie by the Federal Housing Finance Agency, creation of HAMP and HARP, establishment of the Troubled Asset Relief Program, and passage of the Dodd–Frank Act. Long-term solutions to the crisis must address the underlying cracks in the foundation of the socioeconomic system

that led not just to this crisis but to a series of overlapping disasters that have repeated themselves in a cyclical fashion over the past century.

20.3 When personal property is purchased on credit, the seller frequently retains a security interest in the property. Property that is subject to a security interest is called collateral. A security interest is created by a written agreement called a security agreement, which identifies the goods and is signed by the debtor. To be effective between debtor and creditor, a security interest must be made legally enforceable. This legality is known as attachment. To be effective against third parties who might also claim the secured property, the creditor must perfect the security interest. Perfection is accomplished by filing a financing statement, by attachment alone in certain cases, or by taking possession of the collateral.

Key Terms

acceleration, 474
adjustable-rate mortgage (ARM), 469
asset-backed security, 477
assume the mortgage, 474
attachment, 484
balloon-payment mortgage, 470
"bonus-malus", 483
buyer in the ordinary course of business, 484
collateral, 468
construction loan, 471
consumer goods, 483
conventional fixed-rate mortgage, 469
deed of trust, 471
Dodd–Frank Wall Street Reform and Consumer Protection Act, 480
equipment, 483
equity of redemption, 472
farm products, 483
Federal Housing Finance Agency (FHFA), 479
fixtures, 483
flexible-rate mortgage, 469
floating lien, 485
foreclosure, 474
government-sponsored enterprise (GSE), 477

Questions for Review and Discussion

1. What is the difference between a secured and an unsecured loan?
2. What types of mortgages are available to borrowers?
3. What is the legal effect of recording a mortgage?
4. What are the rights and duties of the mortgagor and those of the mortgagee?
5. What is the difference between a financial recovery and an alteration in the initial conditions of a system?
6. What short-term solutions to the 21st-century financial crisis have been implemented?
7. What long-term solutions to the 21st-century financial crisis have been proposed to alter the initial conditions of the economy?
8. How is a security interest is created for personal property?
9. When is a security interest perfected?
10. What priorities exist when parties claim a security interest in the same property?

Cases for Analysis

1. Sanchez bought a house for $100,000, paying $10,000 down and financing the balance through a local bank. As part of the closing costs, Sanchez was required to take out private mortgage insurance to protect the bank in case she defaulted on the mortgage. She had an excellent credit rating and always paid her mortgage payments when they were due. Two years after buying the property, she received an inheritance and used the money to pay an additional amount of $10,000 to the bank toward the principal of the loan. Hoping to cut down on her monthly payments, she asked the bank to cancel the mortgage insurance, but the bank refused. Does Sanchez have any rights in this situation? Explain.

2. Robert and Sherrell Bergeron gave a first mortgage on their property to First Colonial Bank and a second mortgage to Ford Motor Credit Company. When the Bergerons were unable to pay the mortgage, the bank foreclosed. The property was sold at a foreclosure sale for more money than the Bergerons owed the bank. The Bergerons claim that they are entitled to the surplus funds from the sale. Do you agree? Explain. [See: *First Colonial Bank for Savings v. Bergeron*, 646 N.E.2d 758 (MA).]

3. When the Prestons took out a variable mortgage with the First Bank of Marietta, their interest rate was 9 percent. The agreement allowed First Bank to raise or lower the interest rate at any time, provided

that the Prestons received 30 days' notice. When the bank raised the interest rate to 11 percent, the Prestons refused to pay, arguing that the agreement was unenforceable, because it set no limit on what interest rate they might be forced to pay. Were the Prestons correct? Explain. [See: *Preston v. First Bank of Marietta,* 473 N.E.2d 1210 (OH).]

4. The Woolseys ran a mink farm that was mortgaged to the State Bank of Lehi. The agreement included provisions that allowed acceleration and foreclosure if the Woolseys failed to pay their obligations under the contract. The Woolseys defaulted on several payments, and the bank foreclosed. The couple demanded a jury trial on the foreclosure action. They also argued that the bank had not acted in good faith in its acceleration and foreclosure. Were the Woolseys entitled to a jury trial? Explain. Who had the burden of proof in demonstrating the bank's good faith in accelerating payments and demanding foreclosure? [See: *State Bank of Lehi v. Woolsey,* 565 P.2d 413 (UT).]

5. Bloom executed a real estate mortgage in favor of Lakeshore Commercial Finance Corporation on September 16. On October 4, Bloom executed another mortgage on the same described real estate in favor of Northridge Bank. Northridge, without notice of the mortgage to Lakeshore, recorded its mortgage at 9:28 A.M. on October 25. On that same date, at 3:07 P.M., the prior mortgage executed in favor of Lakeshore was recorded. Bloom defaulted on the mortgages. The value of the real estate was insufficient to satisfy both mortgages fully. Which party had first rights to the property, Lakeshore or Northridge? Why? [See: *Northridge Bank v. Lakeshore Com. Fin. Corp.,* 365 N.E.2d 382 (IL).]

6. Cramer's mortgage contained a provision requiring her to pay monthly tax and insurance payments into an escrow account held by the bank in addition to principal and interest. Cramer paid the principal and interest regularly but refused to pay the tax and insurance escrow payments. The bank brought foreclosure proceedings. Did it have the right to foreclose on Cramer's mortgage? Explain. [See: *Cramer v. Metro. Sav. & Loan Ass'n,* 258 N.W.2d 20 (MI).]

7. Matthews Motors sold a Buick Riviera to Jenkins for $11,500. Matthews then borrowed money from Averysboro National Bank, using the Buick as collateral. When Matthews defaulted on the loan, the bank attempted to repossess the Buick from Jenkins. Jenkins refused to surrender the automobile, claiming that he and not Matthews owned it. The bank brought suit, asking the court to force Jenkins to turn over the Buick. Should the court grant the bank's request? Why or why not? [See: *Averysboro National Bank v. Jenkins,* 328 S.E.2d 399 (GA).]

8. Giant Wholesale agreed to supply Hendersonville Food Center with groceries if the owner, William Page, would guarantee all debts incurred by Hendersonville. Page agreed, and a security agreement was drawn up. The security agreement gave Giant a security interest in Hendersonville's groceries and equipment. Giant failed to file a financing statement properly. When Hendersonville ran into financial difficulty, Page turned over the checking account to Giant. When this maneuver did not work, Giant repossessed all of Hendersonville's inventory. Page later went bankrupt. Gray, the bankruptcy trustee, brought a suit against Giant, claiming that the inventory was part of Page's property and thus subject to the bankruptcy proceeding. Gray argued that because the financing statement had not been filed, Giant's security interest had not been perfected. Was Gray correct? Explain. [See: *Gray v. Giant Wholesale,* 758 F.2d 1000 (4th Cir.).]

9. U.S. Electronics, a Missouri corporation with a place of business in DeKalb County, Georgia, borrowed money from a Missouri bank. The corporation gave the bank a security interest in all of its machinery and equipment. The bank filed a financing statement in Fulton County rather than in DeKalb County, as required by law. U.S. Electronics defaulted on the loan and fell behind on its rent. The corporation's landlord obtained a judgment against it for past due rent, becoming a lien creditor. The landlord claimed priority over the bank for the proceeds of a sheriff's sale of the machinery and equipment, arguing that the bank's security interest was not perfected. Do you agree? Why or why not? [See: *United States v. Waterford No. 2 Office Center,* 271 S.E.2d 790 (GA).]

10. Lallana bought a car on credit from a dealer who assigned the contract and the security agreement to Bank of America. When Lallana failed to make several payments, the bank repossessed the car. The bank notified Lallana that if she did not redeem the car or reinstate the contract within

15 days, it would sell the car. The bank then sold the car at a public auction for $5,000 and sued Lallana for $11,249, the balance due on her loan. Kelley Blue Book's estimated retail value of the car at the time of the auction was $14,820. Did the bank give Lallana proper notice of the sale? Why or why not? [See: *Bank of America v. Lallana,* 960 P.2d 1133 (CA).]

quick quiz Answers

20-1	20-2	20-3
1. T	1. F	1. F
2. T	2. F	2. T
3. T	3. F	3. T

Chapter 21

Bankruptcy Law: In Theory, in History, and in Practice

THE OPENING CASE *Round 1*
Bankruptcy or Insolvency? Federal or State Control?
Traders or Traders Plus?

Once upon a time, in a kingdom far, far away, bankruptcy laws were not as clear cut, detailed, and accessible as they are today. In the past, 1902 to be exact, there was even some question, well many questions actually, about the advisability of having a federal bankruptcy law at all—period. The question of whether to establish a federal bankruptcy law was one of the issues in a case called *Hanover National Bank v. Max Moyses*. In this case, Moyses was the defendant debtor, and Hanover was the plaintiff creditor. The case was brought by Hanover in the federal court in New York in 1899 in an attempt to get satisfaction on a debt that Moyses owed the bank. Moyses, however, had been declared bankrupt in a federal court in Tennessee and had already discharged all of his debts, including the one owed to Hanover. The bank admitted that Moyses had been adjudicated bankrupt under the 1898 bankruptcy statute and that the law had been followed to the letter. So far so good, except for one minor point. Hanover argued that the bankruptcy act under which Moyses had been declared insolvent was unconstitutional. Hanover offered two reasons for the unconstitutionality of the federal bankruptcy law: (1) The law violated the Fifth Amendment prohibition against the taking of property

without due process, and (2) the law violated Article I, Section 8, Clause 4 of the U.S. Constitution. Let's look at each argument one at a time. Under the Fifth Amendment, the plaintiff claimed that the bankruptcy law was unconstitutional because, under its provisions, the process of distributing the debtor's property could be completed without notifying all those parties that had an interest in the property, Hanover being one such party. More specifically, Hanover claimed that the due process clause had been violated because: (a) the statute empowered the debtor to initiate the bankruptcy proceeding (AKA insolvency or voluntary bankruptcy) rather than the creditors, thus violating the creditors' due process rights; (b) the notice that was required under the act was so brief (10 days) that any distant creditors had no realistic chance of responding; and (c) if the creditor did manage to actually get to the bankruptcy court in a timely manner, the grounds for any objection were so limited that any retrieval of the property was almost nonexistent. As for Article I, Section 8, Clause 4, Hanover declared that the law was unconstitutional because (a) it failed to set up universal laws of bankruptcy for all states as required by the Constitution; (b) the act unconstitutionally delegated powers to the states that cannot be delegated to those states; and (c) the law unconstitutionally extended bankruptcy jurisdiction to individuals who were not traders as required by long-standing legal tradition in England and the United States. The case reached the U.S. Supreme Court, which agreed to hear the issues and to rule on those issues as soon as possible. Some of these questions were easy enough for the court to answer; others not so much. Working its way backward, the Court began with the question of the plaintiff's identity. Is Congress limited to passing bankruptcy legislation that protects traders alone? For the answer to this question, well, keep reading. [See: *Hanover National Bank of New York v. Max Moyses,* 186 U.S. 181, 22 S.Ct. 857, 45 L.Ed. 1113 (1902).]

Opening Case Questions

1. Who is the creditor in this case? Who is the debtor? Explain.

2. Was the lawsuit a state or federal case? Explain.

3. What two provisions of the constitution are under scrutiny here? Explain.

4. What court makes the final decision in issues of constitutionality? Explain.

5. Which issue does the court examine first? Why does it pick that particular issue? Explain.

 Learning Objectives

1. Summarize the history of bankruptcy law in the United States.
2. Discuss federal and state control of bankruptcy law.
3. State the criteria necessary to be eligible to file voluntarily for Chapter 7 bankruptcy.
4. Explain the "means test" that is required for filing Chapter 7 bankruptcy.
5. State the criteria necessary for creditors to force debtors into involuntary bankruptcy.
6. Distinguish between an *order for relief* and *automatic stay* in the bankruptcy process.
7. List the federal exemptions debtors can exclude from the bankruptcy process.
8. Recognize those debts that have priority payment status under the Bankruptcy Code.
9. Explain Chapter 11 bankruptcy, emphasizing the reorganization process.
10. Discuss the requirements for Chapters 12 and 13 bankruptcy.

21-1 The Checkered History of Bankruptcy in the United States

When the framers gathered in Philadelphia in 1787 to *revise* the Articles of Confederation they were troubled by the fragile and tentative nature of those articles and by the lack of power that had paralyzed the national government. Also on their minds was the recent rebellion led by Daniel Shays, Samuel Ely, and their fellow farmers in Massachusetts. The rebellion, which involved more than 2,000 angry farmers, may have been unsuccessful, but that did not diminish the impact that it had on the delegates, many of whom were nervous about a possible new revolution. [See: Walter A. MacDougal, *Freedom Just Around the Corner* (New York: Harper Collins, 2004), p. 295.] Fearing another rebellion, the framers did not want to make the same mistakes that had been made when the Articles of Confederation had been shaped. Consequently, the Framers did their best to provide a strong central government in the Constitution.

Reengineering the Constitution

As we saw in some detail in Chapter 2, the Framers of U.S. Constitution made a concerted effort to insulate the leadership of the new republic from the influence of the people. Several

U.S. Const., Article I, Sec. 8 (see page 910)

examples of this include: the Electoral College (Article II, Section 1); the election of senators (Article I, Section 3); the supremacy clause (Article VI); and the religion clauses of the First Amendment. The bankruptcy clause in Article I, Section 8, Clause 4, is also part of this effort. Curiously, the first version of the new Constitution made no reference to bankruptcy or insolvency laws. To remedy this oversight, a bankruptcy clause was prepared and submitted to the drafting committee. This initial draft of the clause declared that Congress would have the power "to establish uniform laws upon the subject of bankruptcies and respecting the damages arising on the protest of foreign bills of exchange." The clause was added to the Constitution after nine states had voted to approve it. The final version is found in Article I, Section, 8, Clause 4, which states that Congress has the power to, "establish . . . uniform laws on the subject of Bankruptcies throughout the United States." [See: Joseph Story, *Commentaries on the Constitution of the United States* (The Constitution Society) http://www.constitution.org/js/js_005htm.]

In his work *Commentaries on the Constitution,* Associate Justice Joseph Story of the Supreme Court wrote in 1833 that direct mention of bankruptcy in *The Federalist Papers* occurs only once. That passage states, "The power of establishing uniform laws of bankruptcy is so intimately connected with the regulation of commerce and will prevent so many frauds, where the parties or their property may lie, or be removed into different states, that the expediency of it seems not likely to be drawn into question." [See: Joseph Story, *Commentaries on the Constitution of the United States,* 4th ed., ed. Thomas Cooley (Boston: Little, Brown & Co., 1874), vol. 1.] Story also defends the addition of the bankruptcy clause. His defense is based on the idea that the bankruptcy process helps debtors to retain their ability to make a decent wage and thus to feed, clothe, and shelter their families. Story sees the bankruptcy process as a charitable system that helps the weak and powerless, and he seems convinced that the framers had this view also [See: Story, section 1100.]

Federal Control of Bankruptcy

Story then defends the use of a national law rather than a state statute to manage the distribution of a debtor's assets. First, he says that a uniform national law will foster consistency, uniformity, and justice in the distribution of a bankrupt's property. Second, he contends that a national law will avoid giving preference to one class of debtors' over another class. Third, Story argues that, as a matter of constitutional law, the states have no power to control the disposition of property that lies beyond their own borders and so, passing the responsibility of controlling bankruptcy on to them will create state statutes of limited jurisdiction. In contrast, the national government does have the power to cross state lines and create rules for the distribution of property that all states must observe. Fourth, similarly the states have no power to control the disposition of property beyond the borders of the United States, and so, once again, giving the states any authority over bankruptcy will result in statutes of dubious effectiveness. On the other hand, the national government does have that authority, under its ability to negotiate treaties, and so it makes sense to reserve that responsibility to Congress [See: Story, sections 1102–1104.]

All of this makes perfect sense, of course. However, what Story forgets (or conveniently ignores) is that the framers also added the bankruptcy provision as a protective measure that would ensure that the moneyed elite (the class to which the framers belonged) would have access to a legal process that would help them get their money back (or at least part of it) from delinquent debtors without having to take matters into their own hands. The motivation for exerting this control can be seen in Madison's *Federalist Papers,* especially Federalist No. 10. Madison does not write directly about bankruptcy in this essay, but he does defend republican government at the expense of democracy, using an argument based on economics, in general, and class distinctions in particular, both of which are related to bankruptcy legislation. His rhetoric, as always, sounds highly libertarian. He wants a republic because he fears that a direct democracy in a nation as large as the United States will empower the majority to control the minority. The words *majority* and *minority* are neutral enough to mislead us into thinking that Madison had noble motives (as Story implies) and that may be the case; however, we must also understand what he means by *minority* and *majority*. [See: Charles Beard, *An Economic Interpretation of the Constitution of the United States* (New York: Macmillan, 1913).]

By *minority* Madison meant the elite moneyed class (of which he and the other delegates were members) while by *majority* he meant the working class (the class involved in Shays' Rebellion). To see this more vividly, we need only turn to *The Federalist Papers* where Madison writes, "But the most common and durable source of factions has been the various and unequal distribution of property. Those who hold and those who are without property have ever formed distinct interests in society. *Those who are creditors, and those who are debtors.*" (emphasis added) [See: James Madison, *Federalist No. 10*, paragraph 6.] Moreover, we need not focus only on *The Federalist Papers*. The constitutional record itself can tell us something. In fact, in debate on June 26, 1787, Madison said that he feared a future in which "the property of the landed proprietors would be insecure" and that the government must be used "to support these invaluable interests, and to balance and check the other. They ought to be so constituted as to protect the minority of the opulent against the majority." [See: Robert Yates, "Notes of the Secret Debates of the Federal Convention of 1787, Taken by the Late Hon. Robert Yates, Chief Justice of the State of New York, and One of the Delegates from That State to the Said Convention," Yale Law Library, the Avalon Project, http://avalon.law.yale.edu/18th_century/yates.asp.]

The Growth of Federal Bankruptcy Law

As noted earlier, the bankruptcy clause is found in the U.S. Constitution in Article I, Section, 8, Clause 4, which states that Congress has the power to, "establish . . . uniform laws on the subject of Bankruptcies throughout the United States." In his commentaries, Justice Story reveals that the addition of this clause to the Constitution did not mean that everyone bowed to federal power. On the contrary, the issue of state-made bankruptcy laws continued to plague the legal system. Some experts in Story's era stated that the clause did, in fact, put the matter totally in the hands of the federal government. Others, however, argued that federal authority must be shared with the states. These experts claimed that, if the federal government had passed no bankruptcy laws, then the states were free to do so. Story, however, notes that any bankruptcy law passed by a state would apply only to contracts made between citizens of that state, made in that same state, after the law was passed. What happens to such laws after the federal government enacts a bankruptcy law remained uncertain. It was clear that should the federal government pass such a law, state power would be curtailed, but exactly how was not clear. As we shall see shortly the answer would not come until the 20th century. [Story, sections 1109-1110.]

Before answering that question, let's look at the checkered history of bankruptcy law at the federal level. The first federal bankruptcy law in the United States was enacted in 1800. Under that law, only creditors could begin a bankruptcy proceeding, and only merchants could qualify as debtors. That law lasted only three years before Congress repealed it. In 1840, debtor's prisons were abolished in the United States, and a year later, Congress passed a bankruptcy law that lasted only two years. Following the turmoil of the Civil War, Congress enacted a third bankruptcy law in 1867 that lasted 11 years. It wasn't until 1898 that permanent bankruptcy legislation came about in the United States with a law that gave businesses protection from creditors and lasted, with modifications during the Great Depression, for 80 years. The Bankruptcy Reform Act of 1978 again brought major changes, making it easier for businesses and individuals to obtain bankruptcy relief. It was in 1978 that Chapters 11 and 13 of the Bankruptcy Code (discussed later) were created, allowing businesses and individuals to reorganize and keep going. In addition, debtors were allowed to keep more of their assets, giving them a better chance to make a fresh start with their activities. The 1994 Bankruptcy Reform Act continued honing the law and created the National Bankruptcy Review Commission to study the subject and make recommendations. In 2005, following a period of easy credit with many people spending far above their means, Congress made it more difficult to declare bankruptcy by enacting far-reaching changes to the Bankruptcy Code. The current law is explained in this chapter.

State Control of Bankruptcy

By now it should be clear that the question of state control of bankruptcy in the absence of federal action was not an academic inquiry, but, instead, something of practical concern long into the 20th century. The courts were openly in favor of a universally applied bankruptcy statute that would unify the operation from state to state. However, being sympathetic to the concept of a universal federal bankruptcy law is not the same as mandating that Congress pass such an act, nor justification for declaring an inconsistent nonuniversal law as unconstitutional. Instead, the courts have held that, in the absence of any federal law covering bankruptcy, the states are free to enact their own bankruptcy laws. Moreover, since the time of *Hanover National City Bank v. Moyses,* the U.S. Supreme Court has also settled on several guidelines regarding this matter. First, the Court has ruled that once Congress passes a bankruptcy law, state laws are not declared null and void, but are, instead, subject to that federal law. Second, the states can plug their own provisions into state statutes that cover anything not covered by federal law, just so long as the state laws do not impair contracts (Article I, Section 10, Clause 1). Third, the states are without the power to create any bankruptcy law that impacts property outside their boundary lines or that diverges from federal bankruptcy laws. Fourth, state laws regarding exemptions may differ from state to state without violating the Constitution. Finally, service of process and personal notice are not needed in a federal bankruptcy proceeding, as long as proper notice is made according to the bankruptcy statute (which in this case involved notice by mail and by publication). [See: *Hanover National Bank of New York v. Max Moyses,* 186 U.S. 181, 22 S.Ct. 857, 45 L.Ed. 1113 (1902).]

quick quiz 21-1	
1. Congress passed one uniform bankruptcy statute in 1800 that has lasted until the present time.	true	false
2. The states have no power to pass any type of bankruptcy law at any time under any circumstances.	true	false
3. The bankruptcy clause in the U.S. Constitution seems to empower Congress to pass bankruptcy laws without actually requiring that Congress do so.	true	false

21-2 Liquidation—Chapter 7, Bankruptcy Code

Chapter 7 of the Bankruptcy Code, sometimes referred to as ordinary bankruptcy, provides a system in which debtors are forced to sell much of their property and use the cash to pay their creditors a portion of the amount owed each one. This process is also called liquidation. See Table 21-1 for a summary of different types of bankruptcy procedures.

Table 21-1 Types of Bankruptcy Procedures

Chapter	Who Can File?	When Used?	Special Features
Chapter 7: Ordinary Bankruptcy	Only those who (a) have income below the state's average family income for families of that size, (b) meet with an approved nonprofit credit counselor before filing, (c) provide a federal income tax return for the most recent tax year, and (d) take a course in financial management after filing.	Used when debtor wants to discharge most debts and begin with a clean slate	Debtor's property is liquidated; some property is exempt; some debts cannot be discharged
Chapter 11: Reorganization	Individuals, partnerships, and corporations can file; railroads can file; only commodity brokers and stockbrokers cannot; filing can be voluntary or involuntary.	Used when debtor, usually a business, wants to continue operating but needs to reorganize and liquidate debts	Debtor-in-possession feature; plan must be fair, equitable, and feasible; creditors can also file plans; confirmation needed
Chapter 12: Family Farmer or Fishing Business Debt Adjustment	Family farmer or fishing businesses that receive 50 percent of income from farming or fishing can file, including partnerships and corporations.	Used when debtor has a family farming or fishing business and needs a debt adjustment plan to keep running	Debtor-in-possession feature
Chapter 13: Individual Debt Adjustment	Individuals who meet with a credit counselor and have steady income only; no corporations or partnerships; no involuntary filings allowed.	Used when an individual debtor with a steady income voluntarily decides to adopt a debt adjustment plan	Only the debtor can file a plan; a few debts cannot be discharged; plan lasts three years (with two-year possible extension)

Commencing the Action

Under Chapter 7 bankruptcy, the debtor may be an individual, partnership, corporation, or other type of business. The process may be either voluntary or involuntary. With voluntary bankruptcy, the debtor files the bankruptcy petition. With involuntary bankruptcy, creditors file the papers to force the debtor into bankruptcy and pay them off.

Voluntary Proceedings Debtors sometimes realize that their financial position can never improve without some drastic action and decide to file a bankruptcy petition on their own. Under the most recent Bankruptcy Act, however, not everyone is allowed to file for Chapter 7 bankruptcy. To qualify, debtors must do all of the following:

- Satisfy the **means test**, discussed next.
- Meet with an approved nonprofit credit counselor before filing for bankruptcy.
- Provide a federal income tax return for the most recent tax year.
- Take a course in financial management after filing for bankruptcy.

The Means Test The means test consists of three steps, the passing of any one of which allows the debtor to file for Chapter 7 bankruptcy. The first step is to compare the debtor's average income during the previous six months with the median income for a family of that size in the debtor's state. If the debtor's income is less than the state's median

THE OPENING CASE *Round 2*
Traders or Traders Plus?

In the opening case, we learned that Moyses was the defendant debtor and Hanover was the plaintiff creditor in *Hanover National Bank v. Max Moyses*. Hanover brought the case in federal court in New York to get paid on a debt that Moyses owed the bank. Moyses, however, had been declared bankrupt in a federal court in Tennessee and had already discharged all of his debts, including the one owed to Hanover. The bank admitted that Moyses had been adjudicated bankrupt under the 1898 bankruptcy statute and that the law had been followed properly. In other words, the bank had no complaint about what had been done. Rather, at a more fundamental level, the bank argued that what had been done was illegal because the statute itself was unconstitutional. Hanover offered two reasons for the unconstitutionality of the federal bankruptcy law: The first argument is relevant to our present study. The bank claimed that the law violated the Fifth Amendment prohibition against the taking of property without due process. Under the bankruptcy law, as it existed at that time, the debtor was empowered to initiate his (or her) own bankruptcy case. The bank feared that allowing the debtor to decide who gets notified threatened the creditors' property rights. (Exactly why the bank had this misgiving is not clear from the record, but it probably had to do with a fear that the debtor might be selective in which creditors were notified.) Today, this would not

be an issue. However, in 1898 when this case was brought to court there was still some confusion about whether individuals could initiate their own bankruptcy process. The bank based its argument on an ancient English tradition that took for granted the notion that only traders, that is, businesspeople involved in buying and selling as a profession, could declare bankruptcy. As we can see here, Chapter 7 of the current bankruptcy statute allows (even at times encourages) individuals to file for bankruptcy when necessary. The ease by which such a provision could be added to the statute today, however, rests in part on the court's ruling in this case. The court decided that there is no need to limit bankruptcy laws to traders. In fact, such limits seem to be arbitrary and have more to do with the traditions of medieval England than with anything inherent within the process of bankruptcy in and of itself. Indeed, the court also takes judicial notice of the fact that there never really was any such restriction in the colonies, despite the model found in English law. The legislators in the colonies were not unaware of the English tradition and so it seems clear that they consciously decided that such a tradition would not be part of colonial law. The court sees no reason not to follow the colonial tradition and to reject the ancient English tradition (of traders only). [See: *Hanover National Bank of New York v. Max Moyses,* 186 U.S. 181, 22 S.Ct. 857, 45 L.Ed. 1113 (1902).]

income, the debtor is eligible to file for Chapter 7 bankruptcy. Every state's median income is provided by the U.S. Census Bureau and can be found at www.census.gov.

EXAMPLE 21-1: The Means Test—Step One

Raymond and Jessica Mattik lived with their two children in a house they owned in North Carolina. They were very much in debt. Not only were they behind in their payments for their late-model car and household furnishings, but they also owed the maximum amount on five credit cards. When the interest on their adjustable-rate mortgage increased dramatically, they considered filing for bankruptcy. Together, they earned $61,113 annually. They would be eligible to file for Chapter 7 bankruptcy because their income was less than $70,495—the median income for a family of four in North Carolina. Because they qualified under this first step, they are finished with the means test.

Suppose Raymond and Jessica, in Example 21-1, had income that exceeded their state's median income for a family of four. Then, they would have to go to step two of the means test, which is more complicated. Step two requires debtors to determine whether they have enough income to pay off some of their unsecured debts. This determination requires subtracting certain deductions, which vary according to where they live, and arriving at a figure called their **disposable income**. If their disposable income is less then $124.58 a month, they pass the means test and will be allowed to file for Chapter 7 bankruptcy. If it is more than $207.92 a month, however, they fail the means test and cannot file for Chapter 7. They may, however, be able to convert the case to Chapters 11, 12, or 13 of the Bankruptcy Code discussed subsequently.

EXAMPLE 21-2: The Means Test—Step Two

Robert and Carol Kling lived with their two children in Texas, where the median income for a family of four was $71,973. Because their combined income of $65,980 was greater than this median, they did not pass step one of the means test and had to go to step two. After deducting certain amounts prescribed for their geographical area, their disposable income was $277.43 a month—again, too high to pass the means test because it was over $207.92. They now must go to step three of the test.

The third step in the means test is taken only by debtors who do not qualify for Chapter 7 bankruptcy under the first two steps. Under this final step, a determination is made as to whether the debtor has the ability to pay unsecured debts over a five-year period. If a debtor's monthly disposable income is between $124.58 and $207.92 but not enough to pay more than 25 percent of outstanding unsecured debts over a five-year period, the debtor passes the means test and will be allowed to file for Chapter 7 bankruptcy. In contrast, if the disposable income is enough to pay those debts over five years, the debtor does not pass the means test and will be required to switch over to another bankruptcy chapter, such as Chapter 13, discussed later. [Note: These figures often change, so it is best to check the most up-to-date figures on the website of the federal courts (See: http://www.uscourts.gov/).]

To petition for bankruptcy, debtors file official forms with the nearest U.S. Bankruptcy Court. These courts are attached to district courts within the federal court structure (see Chapter 3). Official forms for filing bankruptcy can be obtained at legal stationery stores as well as www.uscourts.gov. The form asks debtors to name all of their creditors and indicate how much money they owe those creditors. The form also requires a listing of their property and a statement of income and expenses. Finally, the form asks debtors to list all of the property that they feel should be exempt from the sale when it comes time later in the bankruptcy proceeding to sell what they own.

Involuntary Proceedings Under Chapter 7 of the Bankruptcy Code, creditors may be able to force debtors, other than farmers, into involuntary bankruptcy if the debtor fails to pay bills generally as they become due. Creditors must prove that the outstanding debts are not subject to a bona fide dispute. Outstanding debt levels change every three years and so it is best to check the current amount of eligible debt on the federal court's website (See: http://www.uscourts.gov/).

Order for Relief

An **order for relief** is the court's command that the liquidation begin. In a voluntary filing, the bankruptcy petition itself becomes the order for relief and is effective the moment it is filed with the court. In an involuntary case, the court does not issue the order immediately because the debtor is allowed to contest the filing, after which a hearing is held to determine

THE OPENING CASE *Round 3*
Bankruptcy or Insolvency? Voluntary or Involuntary?

Let's return to the opening case to explore the historic controversy over the advisability of authorizing both voluntary and involuntary bankruptcy filings. The opening case was brought in federal court in 1899 in New York by Hanover National Bank to retrieve some money due under a debt that Moyses owed the bank. In Tennessee, however, Moyses had filed for bankruptcy voluntarily under the federal bankruptcy act that was on the books at the time. Moyses had followed every step in the process properly. The court had also followed every step properly. The result was a declaration of Moyses's bankruptcy and a distribution of his property. The bank was clearly disappointed with that distribution. The bank, however, could not complain about what Moyses had done or how the court ruled because everything had been done by the book. So, to get around this, the bank did the only thing that it could do. It attacked the statute itself, saying that it was unconstitutional. The argument was based on an idea that we would find somewhat bizarre today. The bank argued that the act violated due process because debtors were allowed to bring their own voluntary action for bankruptcy in federal court. According to the lawyers for the bank, this process amounted to an unconstitutional taking of their client's property under the Fifth Amendment. Exactly why the attorneys felt that voluntary bankruptcy threatened due process is unclear, except that they seemed to doubt the debtor's objectivity and to believe that the bank had the right to start (and presumably then control) the process from the outset. This right had evaporated with the bankruptcy statute. The court disagreed. In fact, the court says that there seems no practical or legal reason to make a distinction between voluntary and involuntary bankruptcy. The court does note that some cases in English law have made a distinction from time to time between insolvency and bankruptcy. Insolvency was an action initiated by an imprisoned debtor to discharge his debt, while bankruptcy was initiated by the creditors to obtain payment. The court saw such distinctions as buried in the traditions and history of England and found no need to make the distinction between insolvency (voluntary bankruptcy) and bankruptcy (involuntary bankruptcy) in American law. Thus, Congress may call the law whatever it wants and can allow either the debtor or the creditors to initiate the process, which is what happens today. [See: *Hanover National Bank of New York v. Max Moyses*, 186 U.S. 181, 22 S.Ct. 857, 45 L.Ed. 1113 (1902).]

whether an order for relief will be issued. When an order for relief is issued, a **case trustee** is named by the court. The trustee schedules a meeting of creditors, which the debtor is required to attend to answer questions about financial matters. Following the meeting, the trustee reports to the court as to whether the case should proceed.

The trustee is charged with the responsibility of liquidating the assets of the debtor for the benefit of all interested parties. Bank accounts, including debit cards, can no longer be used because they become the property of the bankruptcy trustee.

A QUESTION OF ETHICS

Carol and Michael Rothko created a limited liability company named Rosewood Acres, LLC, to buy, renovate, and flip homes in Sarasota, Florida. For the first four years of operation, the LLC made a neat little profit on each house flipped. At first the Rothkos had been cautious and had flipped one house at a time. When the market was at its peak, they purchased two homes to work on simultaneously. Then the market collapsed. Up until that time, contractors who worked for the Rothkos had been willing to let overdue payments slide because they knew that the Rothkos did a very good business and the contractors did not want to jinx a good thing. Similarly, the bankers who set up the mortgages in each case were willing to accept late payments because they also knew that the Rothkos had an excellent track record in the "flipping" business. However, when the market collapsed, the contractors found themselves losing jobs left and right and so they all pressed the Rothkos for more timely payments. The bank was also less forgiving about late payments. Eventually, the Rothkos found that they could not pay the contractors, the bank, or the utility companies. Nor could they pay property taxes on the three houses. Consequently, the Rothkos decided to file a voluntary petition for bankruptcy. The court appointed Arthur M. Dent as trustee to the debtor's bankruptcy estate. Dent decided to use his own real estate firm as a consultant to assist in the sale of the debtors' property. Consider each of the following ethical issues.

1.   First, was it ethical for the Rothkos to delay payments to the contractors?
2.   Second, was it ethical for the contractors to suddenly demand earlier payments just because the market had shifted?
3.   Third, was it ethical for the bank to demand on-time payments, after being so generous with the Rothkos?
4.   Fourth, was it ethical for the court to appoint a trustee to oversee the bankruptcy process of an LLC when the court knew that the trustee was a real estate agent?
5.   Finally, was it ethical for Dent to accept the position as trustee and to then use his own firm to assist in the sale of the debtors' property? Explain each point above using a consistent ethical standard.

Automatic Stay

When a voluntary or involuntary petition is filed, an **automatic stay** goes into effect. This stay is a self-operating postponement of collection proceedings against the debtor. Further efforts by creditors against the debtor to collect debts must stop immediately, except for debts caused by fraud, amounts owed for back taxes, family support, and student loans that do not impose a hardship on the debtor. Among other things, the stay prohibits creditors from beginning or continuing:

- Lawsuits to collect debts incurred before the filing of the petition.
- Attempts to enforce a judgment against the debtor.
- Foreclosure sales.
- Collection proceedings.
- Repossession activities.

As noted earlier, automatic stays apply to both voluntary and involuntary petitions. Creditors who knowingly ignore the stay can be held in contempt of court.

Federal Exemptions

As part of the fresh start approach under the Bankruptcy Code, debtors are permitted to exempt or exclude certain items of property from the bankruptcy process, which means that the property is kept by the debtor and cannot be sold to pay the debtor's outstanding bills. Exemptions can be doubled for married couples who file jointly.

Federal Homestead and Household Exemptions   The Bankruptcy Code allows debtors to keep a maximum amount set by law in equity in the debtor's place of residence and in property used as a burial ground. This allowance is known as the federal **homestead exemption**. Debtors can also keep a maximum amount set by law for any single item of furniture, household goods, clothes, appliances, books, crops, animals, or musical

THE OPENING CASE *Round 4*
Due Process and Proper Notice

Recall that in the opening case, Hanover National Bank argued that the bankruptcy act under which the defendant-debtor Moyses had been declared insolvent was unconstitutional. The bank argued that the 1898 bankruptcy statute violated the Fifth Amendment prohibition against the taking of property without due process because the type of notice given to creditors about the initiation of the bankruptcy proceeding was so brief (10 days) that any distant creditors had no realistic chance of responding. The court had little sympathy with the bank's complaint. In fact, the court seemed a bit irritated with Hanover. Accordingly, the court ran down several points. First, the debtor must file a petition for bankruptcy with the court and along with that petition include a list of his or her property, plus a list of creditors and amounts owed to those creditors along with addresses. Second, the petition also includes a statement that asserts that the debtor is willing to have his or her property confiscated to pay those debts (except what the law exempts). Third, the property then comes under the control of the court, which then distributes it to the creditors. At that point, the 10 days' notice goes out. Fourth, the notice is actually two notices, one by mail and the other by publication. Fifth, that notice is only the first step in a series of possible notices to creditors. Sixth, the court also noted that creditors get subsequent notices at every step in the administration and distribution of the property. Seventh, and finally, at that point the creditors get more time because the debt is not discharged for another month after the final distribution has been made, allowing more time for creditor input. The court was satisfied that this was enough time to account for due process. [See: *Hanover National Bank of New York v. Max Moyses,* 186 U.S. 181, 22 S.Ct. 857, 45 L.Ed. 1113 (1902).]

instruments. There is, however, a cap placed on these exemptions. Exemptions are also permitted for jewelry.

Necessities Congress allows debtors to maintain a minimum standard of living by exempting certain necessary items of property. For example, debtors are allowed to exclude a maximum of amount set by law in professional tools, instruments, and books. In addition, they can exempt a set maximum amount in a motor vehicle. Finally, medical supplies that have been prescribed for the health of the debtor can be excluded.

Benefits and Support Payments Again, to allow debtors to maintain a minimum standard of living, Congress allows the exclusion of certain benefits and support payments. For instance, alimony and child support payments can be excluded. Benefits received under Social Security or a disability program are also exempt. Profits that are due under profit-sharing, pension, and annuity plans may be excluded. Furthermore, debtors are allowed to protect payments due to them under certain court orders. For example, if someone owes a debtor damages resulting from a personal injury tort case, those damages are exempt up to a maximum amount set by law. Life insurance contracts carried for the benefit of a relative or approved beneficiary that have yet to mature are also protected. Finally, tax-deferred retirement funds are exempt under the bankruptcy act.

State Exemptions

The Bankruptcy Code allows states to use exemptions created by the state legislature rather than the federal exemptions. Often, the dollar amounts included in the state statutes will be a more accurate assessment of property values within each state, because the state legislators are more flexible in such matters than members of Congress, who must consider property values across the entire country. Every state has its own set of bankruptcy exemptions. States are permitted to give debtors a choice of using the state's exemptions or requiring debtors to take the state exemptions.

Trustee's Duties

After the order for relief is granted, a trustee will be appointed to take control of the debtor's property. One of the first things the trustee does is set aside, under the trustee's avoiding powers, certain sales and property transfers made by the debtor. The property is then returned to the estate of the debtor. Included in this "pull back" are any fraudulent transfers that the debtor might have made to temporarily hide property from creditors. If the debtor is a business, the bankruptcy court may authorize the trustee to operate the business for a limited period of time. In addition, the trustee sells the debtor's property to obtain cash. The trustee then distributes the cash among the creditors according to set priorities.

Property Distribution   The Bankruptcy Code provides a priority list that indicates which categories of debts are paid first (Table 21-2). Each category must be paid in full before moving on to the next category. As explained in Chapter 20, secured creditors have the right to take their collateral to satisfy the debt, and that collateral is not sold by the trustee. Although there are some narrow exceptions to this rule, most secured creditors are protected.

Table 21-2 Payment Priorities	
Debt	**Explanation**
Secured debts	Creditors with security interests take their collateral first.
Domestic obligations	Support obligations owed to a spouse or child.
Administrative expenses	Bankruptcy trustee and others involved in bankruptcy process are paid next.
Certain unsecured debts	All unsecured debts after an involuntary petition has been filed, but before order for relief has been granted, are paid next.
Wages	Employees are paid next; a maximum is set for each employee.
Benefit plans	Contributions owed on employee benefit plans are paid next; again, a maximum is set.
Deposits and advances	Deposits made for purchase or lease of property are paid next, as are advances made for personal, family, and household services.
Taxes	Certain taxes are paid next.
Death or injury claims	Some claims for death or injury caused by debtor.
Remaining unsecured creditors	All other unsecured creditors are paid from any balance remaining.
Debtor	If anything is left, it goes back to the debtor.

EXAMPLE 21-3: Secured Creditor Protected

Perez purchased a digital camera from Digicam Corp. Perez financed the deal by signing a security agreement with the company. Under the agreement, Digicam retained a security interest in the property, allowing it to repossess the camera if Perez defaulted on the loan. Digicam was a secured creditor. The digital camera was the collateral.

Exceptions to Discharge

Once the trustee has run through all the aforementioned creditors, the debtor's debts are said to be discharged, which means that the debts are wiped away, and the debtor is allowed to begin again. If the bankruptcy debtor does not have enough money to cover the debts, they are nevertheless considered discharged. However, there are some exceptions to this general rule. Some debts cannot be discharged. In other words, even though the debtor has gone through the entire bankruptcy proceeding, money may still be owed to certain creditors.

Debts Created by Misconduct Certain debts that have fallen into the debtor's lap because of misconduct cannot be charged in bankruptcy. For example, any debts that arose because of the debtor's fraudulent behavior cannot be discharged. Similarly, the debtor cannot escape legal liability for any debt that arose from willful and malicious misconduct. Finally, if the debtor knew about a debt that was not on the original list of debts, that unlisted debt cannot be discharged.

Debts Enforced by the Government Certain debts that the debtor owes the government remain on the books even after the bankruptcy proceeding has ended. These include certain back taxes, student loans that do not impose a hardship on the debtor, and many government fines and penalties. Similarly, several types of court-enforced debts cannot be discharged, including alimony and child support or any legal liability that resulted from a court-ordered judgment for driving while intoxicated. Finally, any debts that were not discharged under a previous bankruptcy cannot be discharged under the new bankruptcy proceeding.

Debts Created by Excessive Spending Congress also refuses to allow bankruptcy debtors to discharge any excessive expenditures that occur around the time of the bankruptcy filing. This measure prevents people from running up big bills unnecessarily because they think they will not have to pay the full amount due on these bills when their assets are finally distributed. Thus, debts for luxury items that exceed $650 in value cannot be discharged if those items were purchased within 90 days before the order for relief was granted. Likewise, the debtor cannot discharge any cash advances paid to a single creditor under an open-ended credit plan that total more than $925 if those advances were made within 70 days of the relief order.

EXAMPLE 21-4: Nondischargeable Debt

Caswell finally realized that his financial problems were out of control. Consequently, he decided to file for bankruptcy on the following Monday. That weekend, he charged $7,000 on his credit card on a weekend trip to Atlantic City before filing for bankruptcy on Monday. Caswell would not be allowed to discharge the $7,000 debt in bankruptcy.

Restoring Credit following Bankruptcy

A personal bankruptcy filing remains on a debtor's credit report for 10 years and has a detrimental effect on the ability to establish a line of credit. However, most debtors who file bankruptcy have already established a poor credit rating anyway, and filing bankruptcy gives them an opportunity to begin anew. A good number of their debts become discharged, which improves their debt-to-income ratio—a factor that potential creditors look at carefully. The more time that elapses after the bankruptcy filing, the easier it is to reestablish credit. Many people in this situation switch from credit cards to debit cards, which is like paying cash because instead of initiating a charge, debit cards withdraw money instantly from a bank account. Some banks offer *secured credit cards* in which customers deposit money in the bank to guarantee that their credit card charges will be paid. Until their credit is reestablished, their credit limit is the same as the amount of their bank deposit. Credit card issuers sometimes allow debtors to continue using their credit cards if they agree in writing, after the bankruptcy filing, to pay off the old debt. Often, this allowance also requires an agreement by the debtor to pay the credit card balance each month without carrying a balance. People who are able to make a down payment and have steady income may be eligible for a mortgage loan as soon as two years following a discharge in bankruptcy.

quick quiz 21-2

1. Congress no longer allows debtors to maintain a minimum standard of living by exempting certain necessary items of property.   true | false

2. Under Chapter 7 bankruptcy, debtors are forced to sell most of their property and use the cash to pay their creditors a portion of the amount owed each one.   true | false

3. The Bankruptcy Code allows states to use a list of exemptions created by the state legislature rather than the federal exemptions.   true | false

21-3 Reorganization—Chapter 11, Bankruptcy Code

LO9

Chapter 11 of the Bankruptcy Code provides a method for businesses to reorganize their financial affairs and still remain in business. If allowed to continue in operation, companies may be able to overcome their difficulties without having to sell most of their property. In a **reorganization**, a qualified debtor creates a plan that alters the repayment schedule. A Chapter 11 filing is available to sole proprietors, partnerships, and corporations and may be either voluntary or involuntary. Individuals who file must receive credit counseling from an approved credit counseling agency before doing so. Unlike Chapter 7, Chapter 11 also allows railroads to file. The only individuals specifically excluded from filing under Chapter 11 are commodity brokers and stockbrokers, who must use Chapter 7.

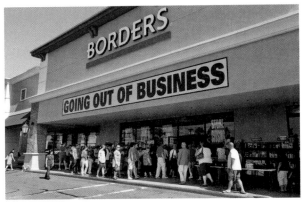

In February of 2011, Borders Group, Inc., announced that it was filing for Chapter 11 bankruptcy protection.

Special Features of Chapter 11

One of the most attractive features of Chapter 11 for business debtors is that the business continues to operate after the filing. A debtor is referred to as a **debtor in possession** under Chapter 11 because the debtor keeps possession and control of the assets, continues to run the firm, and performs most of the functions that a trustee performs in other types of bankruptcy. However, if the problems of the business have been caused by poor judgment, mismanagement, or dishonesty, a case trustee may have to step in to examine the debtor's financial position and provide the court, creditors, and tax authorities with financial information as necessary.

As with a Chapter 7 voluntary case, the bankruptcy petition itself becomes the order for relief. The moment it is filed, the debtor assumes the position of "debtor in possession." At the same time, an automatic stay goes into effect, stopping collection proceedings against the debtor. In an involuntary case, the order for relief comes later, because the debtor is allowed time to contest the filing.

THE OPENING CASE *Round 5*

Federal or State Control? Universal and Federal or Specific and Local?

Chapter 11 bankruptcy allows a business to reorganize its debts while continuing in operation. Often the business institutions that take advantage of this provision are large corporations that cross state lines. Such a provision would not be possible if individual states controlled the bankruptcy process. Still, it is neither advisable nor legally sound to take all such power away from the states. The case of *Hanover National Bank v. Moyses* gives us some insight into the value of permitting the states some ability to control bankruptcy procedures when necessary, just as long as the states stay within appropriate legal boundaries. To see this in more detail, let's return to the opening case one more time. The case was brought in federal court in New York in 1899 by Hanover National Bank to get back the money due to it on a debt that Moyses owed the bank. In Tennessee, however, Moyses had filed for bankruptcy voluntarily under the 1898 federal bankruptcy act. Moyses had followed every step in the process properly. The court had also followed every step correctly. The result was a declaration of Moyses's bankruptcy and a distribution of his property that did not please the bank. The bank, however, could not complain about what Moyses had done or how the court ruled because everything had been done by the book. So, to get around this, the bank did the only thing that it could do. It attacked the statute itself, saying that it was unconstitutional. The bank argued that the bankruptcy statute (a) failed to set up universal laws of bankruptcy for all states as required by the Constitution under Article I,

Section 8, Clause 4; and (b) unconstitutionally delegated powers to the states that cannot be delegated to those states. The court was sympathetic to the call for a universal bankruptcy statute passed by Congress to unify principles and procedures. However, that is quite different from saying that the Constitution mandates that Congress fashion such a law and that unless it does so, the statute that is in effect is unconstitutional. In fact the court indicates that, in the absence of any federal law covering bankruptcy, the states are free to enact their own bankruptcy laws. Moreover, since the time of *Hanover,* the U.S. Supreme Court has also settled on several guidelines regarding this matter. First, the Court has ruled that once Congress passes a bankruptcy law, state laws do not vanish into some legal purgatory. Instead, they remain subject to federal law. Second, the states can fill in gaps that are not covered by Congress in the federal law, provided that the state laws do not impair contracts (Article I, Section 10, Clause 1). Third, states cannot enact bankruptcy legislation that affects property outside their borders or that conflicts with federal bankruptcy laws. Fourth, state laws regarding exemptions may differ from state to state without violating the Constitution. Finally, service of process and personal notice are not needed in a federal bankruptcy proceeding, as long as proper notice is made according to the bankruptcy statute (which in this case involved notice by mail and by publication). [See: *Hanover National Bank of New York v. Max Moyses,* 186 U.S. 181, 22 S.Ct. 857, 45 L.Ed. 1113 (1902).]

The Reorganization Plan

When a Chapter 11 petition is filed, the debtor has 120 days, during which it has the exclusive right to file a reorganization plan. The 120-day period may be shortened or lengthened by the court. When the exclusive period ends, creditors (and the case trustee, if any) can file competing plans. The debtor also files a disclosure statement containing information about the debtor's assets, liabilities, and business affairs to allow creditors to make informed decisions about the reorganization plan. The disclosure statement must be approved by the court before there can be a vote by creditors on the reorganization plan.

Creditors' Committee A creditors' committee is appointed to investigate the operation of the business and assist the debtor in possession in developing and administering a reorganization plan. Membership on the committee normally consists of the creditors who hold the seven largest unsecured claims against the debtor.

Plan Qualifications The Bankruptcy Code requires fairness, equity, and feasibility in the creation of a reorganization plan. The plan will group claims against the debtor into the following classes:

- Secured creditors.
- Unsecured creditors entitled to priority (for such things as taxes and bankruptcy costs).
- General unsecured creditors.
- Equity security holders, such as shareholders and limited partners.

The law requires equal treatment for all creditors grouped in a class. In addition, the plan must be feasible; that is, there must be a good chance that the plan will actually work. The law does not require an absolute guarantee of success. A plan may be difficult to implement because of labor or supply problems and still be feasible within the meaning of the law.

A QUESTION OF ETHICS

The financial crisis that hit the United States and the international community in the early 21st century disrupted lives, ended careers, and depleted personal fortunes. It also led to a "bailout" mentality that insulated some financial institutions as untouchable while dooming others as expendable. This entire scene could have been avoided (not the crisis itself, but the bailouts) had the government "allowed" ordinary bankruptcy law to stay the course. This is the opinion offered by Michele Paige, a managing member of Paige-Capital Management, who in a *Barron's* article entitled, "A Most Useful Tool: Bankruptcy," argues quite convincingly that the American system of bankruptcy has served us well over the decades and should be allowed to do so again. This is a rather curious statement that deserves some clarification. Bankruptcy laws, Paige argues, are designed to encourage individuals to run businesses in an aggressive way that benefits not only the entrepreneur but also suppliers, customers, employees, and the community as a whole. Sometimes these businesses fail, it's true, but when they do, bankruptcy law gives them a second chance. This does mean that there are no victims—businesses that fall and never rise again. However, these failures testify to the effectiveness of a law that weeds out firms that probably should not have been formed in the first place. Paige contends that bankruptcy law, with a few minor tweaks, would work well in the current climate because the law would permit the owners of financial firms to operate the institution while the judicial system divides the losses among the firm's creditors. Should the court run into an institution so troubled that it cannot meet its obligations even using bankruptcy, then the government could step in as a last resort. Paige offers the savings and loan crisis in the 1990s as an example of how well bankruptcy can work when it is permitted to do so. The bankruptcy alternative is better than the current situation, which burdens a financial institution with one of two fates: federal control or benign neglect, leading inevitably to failure.

ETHICAL QUESTIONS

1. Do you agree or disagree with the premise that the purpose of bankruptcy law is to stimulate business? Is this an ethical purpose?

2. Should financial institutions be forced into bankruptcy by the government or is the current strategy (federal control or benign neglect) the ethically correct one to take?

3. What changes in the bankruptcy law would have to take place to implement the plan outlined earlier?

4. If you were a creditor of a financial institution which solution would you see as ethical? A bailout, failure, or bankruptcy?

5. If you were a shareholder of a financial institution which solution would you see as ethical?—a bailout, failure, or bankruptcy? Explain each point above using a consistent ethical standard.

See Michele Paige, "Other Voices—A Most Useful Tool: Bankruptcy," *Barron's*, May 3, 2010, p. 40.

Plan Approval If the plan has not changed the legal rights of the members of a class, then no approval is required from that class. However, impaired classes—those whose creditors receive less than full value of their claims—have the right to vote on the plan by ballot. More than one-half of the creditors who hold at least two-thirds of the amount of allowed claims in each class must accept the plan before it is approved. If there are impaired classes of claims, the plan must be approved by at least one impaired class. In addition, in the case of individual debtors, the plan cannot be confirmed over a creditor's objection without committing all of the debtor's disposable income over the next five years.

EXAMPLE 21-5: Plan Approval

The Miller Chemical Company filed for reorganization under Chapter 11 of the Bankruptcy Code. One class of creditors included unsecured creditors who were owed $2,000 or less. A second class included unsecured creditors who were owed more than $2,000. The plan called for a complete repayment of all Class 1 creditors, according to the terms of their original contracts. This provision made Class 1 an unimpaired class. The Class 2 creditors would have a choice: They could receive either a 60 percent repayment on the date of confirmation or 100 percent repayment extended over four years. The extended repayment plan called for a 30 percent repayment on the date of confirmation and seven 10 percent payments at six-month intervals. More than one-half of the Class 2 creditors would have to approve the plan. In contrast, the Class 1 creditors had no approval rights, because Class 1 was unimpaired.

Plan Confirmation The court will hold a hearing on the confirmation of the reorganization plan. A confirmation officially places a plan in operation. After confirmation, all property dealt with in the plan is free and clear of claims of creditors and equity security holders. The debtor is discharged from any debts that arose before the date of confirmation.

EXAMPLE 21-6: Citation Corp.'s Reorganization Plan

In 2007, Citation Corp. filed for Chapter 11 bankruptcy protection. In less than one month, the bankruptcy court confirmed the auto parts maker's reorganization plan. Under the plan, the company's lenders agreed to exchange $191 million in debt for a new $30 million loan and all of the company's stock. Claims by the company's unsecured creditors would be paid in full in the course of ongoing business, and stockholders were given warrants to buy new classes of stock.

quick quiz 21-3

1.	Chapter 11 of the Bankruptcy Code provides a method for businesses to reorganize their financial affairs and still remain in business.	true | false
2.	The automatic stay provision found in Chapter 7 of the Bankruptcy Code is not used in Chapter 11 proceedings.	true | false
3.	A trustee is appointed to run the firm when a business files a Chapter 11 bankruptcy petition.	true | false

21-4 Family Farmer or Fishing Business Debt Adjustment— Chapter 12, Bankruptcy Code

The Family Farmers and Family Fishermen Protection Act is designed to help farming and fishing proprietors, with regular income, create a plan for debt repayment that will allow them to keep their family businesses running. Thus, Chapter 12 is an alternative to the ordinary bankruptcy procedure provided for by Chapter 7. To be eligible, the operation must receive 50 percent of its total income from farming or fishing. Also, 50 percent of a farmer's debt must result from farm expenses, and 80 percent of a fishing business's debt must relate to either farming or fishing. Chapter 12 is voluntary—only the debtor may file a petition for this type of bankruptcy.

LO10

Chapter 12 has some important characteristics that allow individuals to file debt adjustment plans. First, Chapter 12 sets a $4,031,575 debt ceiling for farming and $1,868,200 for fishing. Second, in addition to individuals, Chapter 12 is open to partnerships and corporations as long as one-half of the outstanding stock or equity in the business is owned by one family or by one family and its relatives. Also, the family or the family and its relatives must conduct the farming or fishing undertaking.

The family farm gets preferential treatment in Chapter 12 bankruptcy filings.

Chapter 12 Procedures

Like a filing under Chapters 7 and 11, a filing under Chapter 12 creates an automatic stay of the collection of most debts. It is possible for creditors to ask the court to exempt them from the stay. However, a hearing on such a motion would have to be held, and the creditors would have to show why the court should grant exemptions.

As is the case in Chapter 7 and 11, the court will appoint a trustee to handle the farm's and fishing business's finances. The Chapter 12's trustee evaluates the case and serves as disbursing agent, collecting payments from the debtor and making disbursements to creditors.

The Chapter 12 Plan

Unlike the Chapter 11 debtor, who has a 120-day deadline to devise a reorganization plan, the Chapter 12 farming or fishing debtor is limited to 90 days. The clock starts running toward that 90-day deadline when the bankruptcy petition is filed. Debtors, however, can file for an extension.

Contents of the Plan
The Chapter 12 plan must include several provisions. First, the plan must provide for payment of fixed amounts to the trustee on a regular basis over a three-year period. The trustee then distributes the funds to the creditors according to the terms of the plan, which usually offers creditors less than the amount owed. Second, the plan must make certain that all priority claims, such as taxes and bankruptcy costs, are paid in full. Secured creditors must be paid at least the value of their collateral. Unsecured creditors must receive at least as much as they would if the debtor's nonexempt assets were liquidated under Chapter 7. The plan must not take longer than three years to complete, unless the time is extended by the court. The maximum extension is for two years.

Confirmation Hearing
After the plan's filing, the bankruptcy judge holds a confirmation hearing to decide whether the plan is feasible and follows the standards of the Bankruptcy Code. Creditors are notified and may appear to voice their approval or objections to the confirmation. If the judge confirms the plan, the trustee will begin disbursing funds according to the plan. If the judge does not confirm the plan, the debtor may file a modified plan, change to Chapter 7 bankruptcy, or allow the case to be dismissed and take some other course.

EXAMPLE 21-7: Court Approves Payment Plan

Bemis, who owned a dairy farm, filed for debt adjustment under Chapter 12. Bemis filed a payment plan with her bankruptcy petition. Under the plan, unsecured creditors owed more than $500 would receive 60 percent of the amount owed to them, payable monthly over a three-year period. Kimble Supply Co. objected to the plan, arguing that it would receive more if Bemis's assets were liquidated under Chapter 7 bankruptcy. Because Bemis was turning over 100 percent of her disposable income to the trustee for debt repayment, however, the court did not support Kimble's objection.

The debtor will receive a discharge after completing all payments agreed to and certifying that all domestic support obligations up to that time, if any, have been paid. The discharge releases the debtor from all debts listed in the plan.

21-5 Individual Debt Adjustment— Chapter 13, Bankruptcy Code

Sometimes debtors overextend their credit. They have regular income, but they cannot pay all their bills. If given time, they may eventually be able to pay at least part of the amount they owe to each creditor. Rather than selling the debtor's property, Chapter 13 of the Bankruptcy Code permits an individual debtor to put in place a repayment plan. Upon completion of payments under the plan, they receive a discharge from most remaining debt.

LO10

Only individual debtors, including sole proprietors and self-employed people, can take advantage of Chapter 13 provisions. Neither corporations nor partnerships can file.

To be eligible for Chapter 13, debtors must first meet with an approved nonprofit credit counselor. Their unsecured debts, such as credit cards and student loans, cannot exceed $383,175, and their secured loans, such as mortgages and car loans, cannot be more than $1,149,525 [Note: These amounts are adjusted for inflation periodically. Check the federal court's website for an update.]. Also, the debtor must have an already established steady income. Only voluntary filings are permitted under Chapter 13. The automatic stay provision clicks into place under Chapter 13 when the relief order is issued. A trustee oversees the Chapter 13 process. If Chapter 13 does not work out under certain circumstances, the individual may be allowed to convert to a Chapter 7 bankruptcy, which changes the repayment plan to a liquidation.

The Chapter 13 Plan

The debtor must file a repayment plan with the court, along with the Chapter 13 bankruptcy petition. Shortly thereafter, a trustee will be appointed and a meeting will be scheduled allowing the debtor to present the plan and be questioned by the trustee and creditors.

Excessive credit card debt is often a major contributory cause to consumer bankruptcy.

The plan must provide for payments of fixed amounts to the trustee on a regular biweekly or monthly basis. The trustee, in turn, distributes the money to creditors according to the terms of the plan. The payments must either satisfy all debts or consist of all the debtor's disposable income during the plan's period. The plan must make certain that priority debtors receive full payment.

Also, like Chapter 12, if the plan sets up groups of creditors, all group members must be treated equally. Finally, Chapter 13 debtors must abide by the rule requiring that the payment plan be completed within three to five years.

Plan Confirmation

Chapter 13 creditors have no prior input while the plan is being created. Secured creditors have approval powers, but unsecured creditors do not.

Unsecured creditors may of course object to the plan at the hearing. However, similar to Chapter 12, Chapter 13 will not allow the court to go along with an objection if the debtor plans to turn over 100 percent of all disposable income to the trustee for debt repayment.

Payments   The debtor must start payments within 30 days of submitting the plan to the court. If the court has yet to hold its hearing, the debtor pays the trustee. The trustee holds the money until the court upholds or rejects the plan.

Discharge   Once the amounts agreed to under the plan are paid, all remaining debts are discharged. The list of debts that cannot be discharged under Chapter 13 is much shorter than those included under Chapter 7. Only alimony, child support, retirement account payments, long-term debts covered in the plan, and some tax claims must be satisfied in full under Chapter 13. Every other debt may be discharged one way or another.

---

quick quiz 21-5

1. A trustee oversees the Chapter 13 process.   true | false

2. Sole proprietors can file for bankruptcy under Chapter 13 of the   true | false
   Bankruptcy Code, but corporations and partnerships cannot.

3. Under Chapter 13 of the Bankruptcy Code, secured creditors   true | false
   have approval powers of a repayment plan, but unsecured
   creditors do not.

Summary

21.1 The final version of the bankruptcy clause is found in the U.S. Constitution in Article I, Section 8, Clause 4, which states that Congress has the power to "establish . . . uniform laws on the subject of Bankruptcies throughout the United States." The clause empowers Congress to pass bankruptcy laws without actually requiring that Congress do so. The open-ended nature of the bankruptcy clause has led to periods in history during which no federal bankruptcy law was on the books. It wasn't until 1898 that permanent bankruptcy legislation came about in the United States, with a law that gave businesses protection from creditors and lasted, with modifications during the Great Depression, for 80 years. The Bankruptcy Reform Act of 1978 brought major changes, making it easier for businesses and individuals to obtain bankruptcy relief. In 1978, Chapters 11 and 13 of the Bankruptcy Code were created. The 1994 Bankruptcy Reform Act created the National Bankruptcy Review Commission. In 2005, following a period of easy credit with many people spending far above their means, Congress made it more difficult to declare bankruptcy by enacting far-reaching changes to the Bankruptcy Code.

21.2 Chapter 7 of the Bankruptcy Code covers ordinary bankruptcy, which is also called liquidation. To qualify, debtors must pass a means test, undergo counseling, provide a federal income tax return, and take a course in financial management. A case trustee sells the debtor's property and uses the cash to pay creditors a portion of the amount owed to each one. The process can be either voluntary or involuntary.

21.3 Reorganization under Chapter 11 of the Bankruptcy Code allows businesses to overcome financial difficulties without selling *all* their property. Instead, a reorganization plan is drawn up that changes the debtor's payment schedule. The new schedule allows the debtor to keep the business going while paying creditors.

21.4 Chapter 12 of the Bankruptcy Code applies to family farmer and fishing businesses in financial difficulty. Under Chapter 12, a family farmer or fishing business can maintain the activity while following a debt adjustment plan to satisfy creditors.

21.5 Chapter 13 of the Bankruptcy Code applies only to individual debtors with established steady incomes. Such debtors can prepare a debt-adjustment plan that will provide for repayment of outstanding debts.

Key Terms

automatic stay, 501

case trustee, 500

confirmation, 508

debtor in possession, 506

disposable income, 499

homestead exemption, 501

impaired classes, 508

liquidation, 496

means test, 497

order for relief, 499

reorganization, 505

Questions for Review and Discussion

1. What is the history of bankruptcy law in the United States?
2. What is the difference between federal and state authority to fashion bankruptcy law?
3. What criteria are necessary to be eligible to file voluntarily for Chapter 7 bankruptcy?
4. What is the "means test" that is required for filing Chapter 7 bankruptcy?
5. What criteria are necessary for creditors to force debtors into involuntary bankruptcy?
6. What is the difference between an *order for relief* and an *automatic stay*?
7. What are the federal exemptions debtors can exclude from the bankruptcy process?
8. Which debts have priority payment status under the Bankruptcy Code?
9. What is a Chapter 11 bankruptcy?
10. What are the requirements for Chapters 12 and 13 bankruptcy?

Cases for Analysis

1. Robert Marrama filed for Chapter 7 bankruptcy. In his petition, he did not disclose a vacation home that he had placed in trust. When Marrama discovered that the case trustee was going to take the vacation property as an estate asset, Marrama decided to convert his case to Chapter 13, which would allow him to keep the property and pay his debts over time. The bankruptcy court held that the failure to disclose the vacation home demonstrated bad faith by the debtor and refused to allow the conversion to Chapter 13. Do you agree with the bankruptcy court? Why or why not? [See: *Marrama v. Citizens Bank,* 05-996 U.S. Supreme Court.]

2. Soon after the birth of their second child, misfortune fell on the lives of Kurt and Leah Lyons. Kurt got laid off, the landlord raised their rent, they received notice that their car was about to be repossessed, and dunning letters arrived daily from credit card companies. Reluctantly, the couple filed for personal bankruptcy. Their disappointed parents told them that the bankruptcy would remain on their credit rating for the rest of their lives and that they would never again be able to establish a line

of credit or obtain a mortgage to buy a house. Were Kurt and Leah's parents correct? Explain.

3. Lisa and William Leeper filed a Chapter 13 bankruptcy petition. One of the unsecured debts they listed on their bankruptcy petition was an amount owed to the Pennsylvania Higher Education Assistance Authority to attend college under a guaranteed student loan program. Will the loan to attend college be discharged by the bankruptcy court? Explain. [See: *Leeper v. Pennsylvania Higher Education Assistance Agency,* 94-3372 & 94-3373, U.S. Court of Appeals (3rd Cir.).]

4. When a Florida court dismissed Nellie Cortez's voluntary bankruptcy petition, it ordered her not to file another petition "under any chapter of the Bankruptcy Code for a period of 12 months." Two months later, an involuntary bankruptcy petition was filed in California by Cortez's stepfather, Thomas Bronkovic. The California court dismissed that case, finding that Cortez had colluded with her stepfather and that the case was, in fact, her own "voluntary" petition rather than her stepfather's "involuntary" petition. While the California case was pending, the

FDIC brought suit against Cortez to enforce certain promissory notes. Did FDIC violate the automatic stay provision of the Bankruptcy Code? Why or why not? [See: *Federal Deposit Insurance Corporation v. Cortez*, 96-6047, U.S. Court of Appeals (2nd. Cir.).]

5. Dyana Landrin was convicted of grand larceny after she admitted she took nearly $19,000 from the Community Mutual Savings Bank while she was employed as a teller. The county court ordered her to pay restitution to the bank—that is, return the money. Before paying restitution, Landrin filed a petition for relief under Chapter 7 of the Bankruptcy Code. Is the money owed to the bank discharged by the bankruptcy petition? Explain. [See: *In re Landrin*, 93-B-20920 (Bankr. S.D. NY).]

6. Three creditors filed an involuntary bankruptcy petition against the Manchester Lakes Association, alleging that the association was not paying its bills when they came due. Manchester fought the petition, arguing that its general partner, Dominion Federal Savings and Loan, had enough money to pay these bills as they came due, even though it was not doing so. Should the court refuse to grant the order for relief if the debtor could prove it had the ability to pay its bills? Explain. [See: *In re Manchester Lakes Association*, 47 B.R. 798 (Bankr. E.D. VA).]

7. Finding itself in great financial difficulty, Fidelity Mortgage Investors filed a voluntary bankruptcy petition in a New York bankruptcy court. When the petition was filed, the automatic suspension went into effect. Ignoring the suspension, Camelia and Farnale, two of FMI's creditors, filed suit against FMI in a Mississippi federal court. As a result, FMI was forced to pay out enormous sums of money in its own defense on the Mississippi case. FMI then returned to the bankruptcy court in New York and asked that both Camelia and Farnale be held in contempt of court for ignoring the suspension. Should the New York bankruptcy court hold Camelia and Farnale in contempt? Explain. [See: *Fidelity Mortgage Investors v. Camelia Builders, Inc.*, 550 F.2d 47 (2nd Cir.).]

8. When the Rahls filed for bankruptcy, they attempted to exclude their entire silverware set from the bankruptcy sale by listing each piece at a value far under the $200 maximum allowed for each item of individual household goods at that time. Had they listed the silverware as one item, it would have been worth more than $6,000. Thus, the entire set would not have been exempt. By listing each piece of silverware separately, the total value did not exceed $4,000, and the entire set could be saved. Should the court force the Rahls to list the silverware set as one item, thus limiting the exemption to $200? Explain. [See: *In the Matter of Rahl*, 14 B.R. 153 (Bankr. E.D. WI).]

9. Dubuque stole more than $4,000 from his employer, U-Haul. He later pled guilty to "theft by unauthorized taking or transfer." The court sentenced him to pay back the stolen money. When Dubuque filed for bankruptcy, U-Haul claimed that this debt would qualify as an exception to discharge. Was U-Haul correct? Explain. [See: *In re Dubuque*, 46 B.R. 156 (NH).]

10. U.S. Truck Company, Inc., filed for a reorganization under Chapter 11 of the Bankruptcy Code. When the reorganization plan was presented for confirmation, one creditor objected to the plan. The creditor argued that the debtor was facing a possible strike and a new labor contract, both of which could place an additional strain on the debtor's finances. These potential labor problems, the creditor concluded, made the plan unfeasible. U.S. Truck admitted that the labor problems existed but noted that the company had recently rebounded from its financial problems to become very successful. Moreover, the labor union had just ratified two previous labor contracts by a 95 percent majority vote. U.S. Truck concluded that these factors made the plan workable, which was enough under the code, because the code did not require a guarantee of success. Was the conclusion correct? [See: *In the Matter of U.S. Truck Co., Inc.*, 47 B.R. 932 (Bankr. E.D. MI).]

quick quiz Answers

21-1	21-2	21-3	21-4	21-5
1. F	1. F	1. T	1. T	1. T
2. F	2. T	2. F	2. T	2. T
3. T	3. T	3. F	3. T	3. T

Part 5 Case Study

Superior Savings Association v. City of Cleveland

501 F. Supp. 1244 (U.S. District Court, Northern District of Ohio)

Summary

The Superior Savings Association, a reputable savings and loan institution with a long history of serving the Lithuanian community in Cleveland, owned a properly recorded first mortgage on a two-story brick building located at 6802 Superior Avenue in the city. The building was located just across the street from one of the branches of Superior Savings in the heart of the Lithuanian community, and one of the bank's officers passed the building every morning on his way to work. The building also held special significance in the neighborhood because it had once housed the main office of Cleveland's only Lithuanian newspaper and a neighborhood print shop owned and operated by a Lithuanian immigrant and his sons. You can, therefore, imagine the bank officer's surprise when he arrived at work one morning to find that the building had, to say it bluntly, vanished. As he gradually pieced together the story, the officer learned that the mortgagor, a fellow by the name of Hughes, had failed to keep the building in an appropriate state of repair, according to what was required by city ordinances. As a result, the city condemned the building. As a final warning, the city gave Hughes more than two months to make the needed repairs before the building would be demolished. When Hughes failed to comply, the building was torn down. At no time during the two-month grace period did anyone at Superior Savings receive any notice of the impending demolition of the building by the city. Superior Savings sued, arguing that the city had violated the association's constitutional rights by "taking away" its property without giving it proper notice. Attorneys for Superior Savings argued that the city, as an agent of the state, had deprived the banking institution of its constitutional rights under the due process clause of the 14th Amendment to the U.S. Constitution. In addition, the city had also violated its own ordinances, which also require that it give notice of the impending demolition to Superior Savings. Had the city followed its own procedures and complied with constitutional law, the bank would have been properly notified and could have taken steps to save what had become a local landmark in the Lithuanian neighborhood, despite its state of disrepair. At this point in the story, there is no way to undo the damage that has been done. The building was gone and there would be no bringing it back. Therefore, Superior Savings asked the court to grant the institution a monetary award that would provide it with money damages that would be equal to the amount that the mortgage was worth just before it was torn down and its value after being destroyed. The measurement of that value would, of course, take some fancy calculating, given the historical nature of the building, the cultural heritage of the neighborhood, and the memories that the print shop represented, but it would ultimately be worth it to Superior Savings. (Reproduced below is that portion of the Court's opinion that corresponds to this analysis. Footnote numerals are included but the citations themselves and explanatory notes are omitted.).

The Court's Opinion

Ben C. Green, Senior District Judge

Plaintiff is a savings and loan institution which holds a first mortgage on land located in the City of Cleveland, Ohio. Defendant is the City of Cleveland, which, plaintiff says, demolished a building on that land without notice to plaintiff. Plaintiff complains that the actions of the city deprived it of its property interest in the land without due process, and demands damages and attorney fees.

The city has not answered, but has filed a motion for summary judgment. That motion will be considered as a motion to dismiss for failure to state a claim upon which relief could be granted pursuant to Rule 12(b)(6), Federal Rules of Civil Procedure. Because the motion contains exhibits not part of the pleadings, the provisions of Civ.R. 56 regarding summary judgments will apply. Plaintiff has filed a brief opposing the city's motion, and has cross-moved for summary judgment.

This Court has jurisdiction to hear and decide this case pursuant to 42 U.S.C. § 1983, 28 U.S.C. § 1343.

The facts are not in dispute. In July 1977, plaintiff made a $12,000 loan to one George Hughes (who is not a party to this action), and secured the note resulting from the loan with a first mortgage on land and buildings located at 6802 Superior Avenue, Cleveland. Constructed on the land at the time was a two-story brick apartment building. The first mortgage was filed for record with the Cuyahoga County Recorder.

On October 19, 1979, the defendant, acting through its Department of Community Development, Division of Housing, inspected the subject premises and found 27 matters which were considered violations of the city's building and housing ordinances. A notice listing the violations was sent to Hughes, apparently by certified mail. The notice provided that, "This notice shall be complied with and all violations corrected by November 30, 1979." Typed in capital letters at the beginning of the itemization of the violations were the words: "THIS STRUCTURE SHALL BE DEMOLISHED AND ALL DEBRIS REMOVED FROM THE PREMISES OR THE VIOLATION SET OUT BELOW SHALL BE CORRECTED."

The notice also contains a reference that a copy thereof was to be sent to "Oper. Demo." Plaintiff did not receive a copy of the notice.

On December 14, 1979, the City's Division of Building inspected the structure, through Building Inspector John Capko and Registered Civil Engineer William L. Blankenburg. Photographs were taken at the time of the inspection and copies thereof were submitted as exhibits to the City's motion. Blankenburg's report, written that day and included as one of the exhibits, describes what is obvious from the photographs:

> The building was open, vacant, and partly vandalized. The building was only partly vandalized because the brick scavengers got there ahead of those looking for copper, and other metals. About 40 feet of brick bearing wall was removed for a height of two stories on the east side of the building. At the rear where the building juts out to the east, another 15 feet of a two-story brick bearing wall was removed from a north wall. Then at the rear, another 22 feet of a brick wall two stories high had been removed at the east wall. This last item (22 feet) was non-bearing as far as floor joists go, but it did carry parapet brick above the roof level. In every case where brick had been removed, the brick parapet was left in a dangerous condition. A heavy wind or a substantial snow load could bring down quite a bit of the building where floor or roof joists have no bearing wall to rest on.

Blankenburg concluded:

> In my opinion this building is beyond the point of economical repair. Furthermore, it is an attractive menace to the neighborhood children, and it should be torn down immediately.

In his affidavit, Inspector John Capko says that during his inspection he found a group of small children playing in and around the structure. In his handwritten report, made the day of the inspection, Capko writes:

> Comments: This structure should be razed forthwith . . . (I was informed that housing has this in demo. 12-79[)].

The city asserts in its brief that on "December 18, 19[79], the City's independent contractor . . . was authorized to demolish the subject property. . . ." The building was subsequently demolished.

From all of the above, the Court concludes that the building in question was in a manifestly deteriorated and dangerous condition from at least October 19, 1979, through the date of its demolition. The Court also concludes that the city seriously considered demolishing the building from that date onward. But at no time during that two and a half month period did the city notify the plaintiff of its intentions to raze the structure, even after the inspection of December 14 made apparent the course the city would take.

The Fourteenth Amendment to the United States Constitution reads, in pertinent part:

> "nor shall any State deprive any person of . . . property without due process of law . . ."

Under circumstances such as those presented here, communities have been held liable to landowners for destruction of buildings without either notice or opportunity for a hearing. *Miles v. District of Columbia,* 510 F.2d 188 (C.A.D.C., 1975). But the nature of the interests held by a mortgagor-landowner differs from those held by his mortgagee, and it has not been suggested that the interests of the mortgagor are subrogated to the mortgagee. Therefore, it will be necessary to examine the nature of the mortgagee's interests and determine to what extent constitutional protection should attach thereto.

In *Louisville Joint Stock Bank v. Radford,* 295 U.S. 555 at 594-95, 55 S.Ct. 854 at 865-866, 79 L.Ed. 1593 (1934), Justice Brandeis listed five property rights in a mortgage on real property which could not be taken from the mortgagee by Congress absent the due process required by the Fifth Amendment. Those attributes were set forth as follows:

> 1. The right to retain the lien until the indebtedness secured is paid; 2. The right to realize upon the security by a judicial public sale; 3. The right to determine when such sale shall be held, subject only to the discretion of the court; 4. The right to protect its interest in the property by bidding at such sale wherever held, and thus to assure having the mortgaged property devoted primarily to the satisfaction of the debt, either through receipt of the proceeds of a fair competitive sale or by taking the property itself; 5. The right to control meanwhile the property during the period of default, subject only to the discretion of the court, and to have the rents and profits collected by a receiver for the satisfaction of the debt.

In *W. B. Worthen Co. v. Kavanaugh,* 295 U.S. 56 at 59, 55 S.Ct. 555 at 556, 79 L.Ed. 1298 (1934), Justice Cardozo found unconstitutional a portion of a farmer's relief act, saying of Congress:

> With studied indifference to the interests of mortgagee or to his appropriate protection they have taken from the mortgage the quality of an acceptable investment for a rational investor.

And in *Wright v. Mountain Trust Bank,* 300 U.S. 440 at 457, 57 S. Ct. 556 at 559, 81 L. Ed. 736 (1937), the Court held that a federal statute violated the Fifth Amendment due process clause, since it effected a substantial impairment of the mortgagee's security. These concepts—that a mortgage confers upon the mortgagee certain specific rights of security for a debt as well as the right not to have the security impaired—remain valid today.

In *Board of Regents of State Colleges v. Roth,* 408 U.S. 564, 576-78, 92 S. Ct. 2701, 2708-2709, 33 L. Ed.2d 548 (1972), the Supreme Court held that:

> The Fourteenth Amendment's procedural protection of property is a safeguard of the security of interests that a person has already acquired in specific benefits. These interests—property interests—may take many forms.* * * * * * Property interests, of course, are not created by the Constitution. Rather, they are created and their dimensions are defined by existing rules or understandings that stem from an independent source such as state law—rules or understandings that secure certain benefits and that support claims of entitlement to those benefits.

In *Paul v. Davis,* 424 U.S. 693, 710-711, 96 S.Ct. 1155, 1164-1165, 47 L.Ed.2d 405 (1976), Justice Rehnquist further defined what interests may attain the status of "property" protected by the Fourteenth Amendment:

> It is apparent from our decisions that there exists a variety of interests which are difficult of definition but are nevertheless comprehended within the meaning of either "liberty" or "property" as meant in the Due Process Clause. These interests attain the Constitutional status by virtue of the fact that they have been initially recognized and protected by state law, and we have repeatedly ruled that procedural guarantees of the Fourteenth Amendment apply wherever the State seeks to remove or *significantly alter* that protected status. (emphasis added).

The law of Ohio recognizes and protects the status of mortgages, mortgagors, and mortgagees.[1] It is further recognized that an understanding, such as a contract, may create property protected by constitutional guarantees, provided that such understandings are mutually explicit, must be such that a person claiming the interest may invoke at a hearing, and must be defined with reference to state law. *Webster v. Redmond,* 599 F.2d 793 (C.A.7, 1979). A mortgage on real property such as the one in this case fits such criteria.

This Court thus concludes that the principles set forth in *Radford, Worthen,* and *Wright* have as much force today as when they were established. No state may deprive a mortgagee of the rights set forth in *Radford* without due process. A state may not, unless via due process, substantially impair the security of a mortgage by taking from it the quality of an acceptable investment for a rational investor.

Having determined that a mortgage contains property protectable by the Fourteenth Amendment, it now must be determined whether the demolition of a building located on land deprives a mortgagee of any of those interests.

It is now well established that the value of property and the rights protected by the Fourteenth Amendment arise not from the mere possession of the property but rather from its use. *Lake Country Estates v. Tahoe Regional Planning Agency,* 440 U.S. 391, 99 S.Ct. 1171, 59 L.Ed.2d rights in a mortgage arise not just from the lien in land, but also in the maintenance of the security which makes the mortgage an acceptable investment for the rational investor.

It seems also well established that state action which "frustrates distinct investment-backed expectations" of a property owner may form the basis for a finding of a "taking" barred by the Fifth Amendment. *Penn Central Transportation Corp. v. New York City,* 438 U.S. 104, 127, 98 S.Ct. 2646, 2660, 57 L.Ed.2d 631 (1978), citing *Pennsylvania Coal Co. v. Mahon,* 260 U.S. 393, 43 S.Ct. 158, 67 L.Ed. 322 (1922).

It is apparent from the language of the mortgage deed, a copy of which was made an exhibit by plaintiff, that plaintiff took pains to take as security for its loan not just the land at 6802 Superior Avenue, but any buildings on that land as well. Plaintiff had a distinct investment-backed expectation at the time the loan was made that the apartment building on the land would remain, so as to provide security for the debt and to provide a source of funds from which the loan could be repaid.

When the defendant city caused the destruction of the building, it irrevocably foreclosed the possibility that plaintiff's protected expectations arising from the building could be realized. The city therefore deprived plaintiff of some or all of its property interest in the mortgage.

Our inquiry does not end here, as not all deprivations of property interests by a state give rise to a finding of a constitutional violation. To give rise to such a finding, the deprivation must be the result of the denial of due process. It is the task now to assess the measure of protection due to plaintiff, and determine whether the city met its burden. *Board of Regents of State Colleges v. Roth,* 408 U.S. 564, 92 S.Ct. 2701, 33 L.Ed.2d 548 (1972); *Vruno v. Schwarzwalder,* 600 F.2d 124 (C.A.8, 1979); *Colm v. Vance,* 567 F.2d 1125 (C.A.D.C., 1977).

It has been held that when emergency conditions exist, a state may take action which deprives a person of a property interest without hearing or notice provided there is a special need for very prompt action. *Fuentes v. Shevin,* 407 U.S. 67, 92 S.Ct. 1983, 32 L.Ed.2d 556 (1972). It has also been held that when faced with conditions extremely dangerous to health and safety, a municipality may, pursuant to its police power, demolish a building summarily and without notice. *Miles v. District of Columbia,* 510 F.2d 188, 192 (C.A.D.C., 1975). But where a community allows an appreciable amount of time to elapse between an inspection and demolition, the actions of the city themselves demonstrate that the exigency does not exist. *Miles v. District of Columbia, supra; cf. Pioneer Savings and Loan Co. v. City of Cleveland,* 479 F.2d 595 (C.A.6, 1973). Under such circumstances—where the city has allowed several days to elapse between identification of the problem and its resolution by demolition—it cannot claim emergency as the reason for dispensing with notice and opportunity for a hearing.

It will not be necessary to determine here, however, whether the condition of the building at 6802 Superior Avenue justified demolition without notice as an exercise of the police power.

An administrative agency is bound to observe its own regulations, and denies due process if it does not. *Service v. Dulles,* 354 U.S. 363, 77 S.Ct. 1152, 1 L. Ed.2d 1403 (1957). "Statutory authority is as much a requirement for valid [administrative action] as is constitutional reasonableness." *Wilson v. Health and Hospital Corp. of Marion County,* 620 F.2d 1201, 1217 (C.A.7, 1980).

The city was required by its own ordinances to provide notice to plaintiff of its intent to demolish the building. Section 3103.08(f) of the codified ordinances of the city reads, in pertinent part:

> The Commissioner [of Building] shall . . . give written notice informing the owner or agent, *mortgagee of record,* and lien holders of record of the City's intention to demolish and remove the unsafe building or structure, at least 30 days prior to such intended action by the City. However, in cases of emergency as set forth in subsection (g) hereof, less than 30 days' notice may be given. (emphasis added).

The referenced subsection (g) authorizes the "prompt" demolition of buildings which in the opinion of the Building Commissioner present an "immediate" danger to the health and safety of others. Even though such prompt action is taken because of the emergent nature of the danger, *some* notice is required by the ordinance to be given to mortgagees of record.

When plaintiff filed the mortgage on 6804 Superior Avenue for record, it thereby gave notice to the City of

Cleveland and the whole world of its interest in the land and the buildings thereon. When the city failed to observe its own ordinances and did not give plaintiff notice of its intent to demolish the building, it denied plaintiff the due process of law. Since the denial of due process deprived plaintiff of a property interest protected by the Due Process Clause of the Fourteenth Amendment, the defendant city is liable to plaintiff for the damages caused.

In *Pioneer Savings and Loan Co. v. City of Cleveland,* 479 F.2d 595, 598 (C.A.6, 1975), a case involving circumstances similar to those here, the Sixth Circuit held:

> The City was guilty of violating the [plaintiff's] constitutional right to due process of law, under the Fourteenth Amendment, and is liable to [plaintiff] in the amount due and owing on its mortgage and note, including principal and accrued interest.

Three years later, however, the Supreme Court ruled, in *Carey v. Piphus,* 435 U.S. 247, 254-255, 98 S.Ct. 1042, 1047-1048, 55 L.Ed.2d 252 (1978):

> Rights, constitutional and otherwise, do not exist in a vacuum. Their purpose is to protect persons from injuries to particular interests, and their contours are shaped by the interests they protect. Our legal system's concept of damages reflects this view of legal rights. "The cardinal principle of damages in Anglo-American law is that of *compensation* for the injury caused to plaintiff by defendant's breach of duty." 2 F. Harper and F. James, Law of Torts, § 25.1, p. 1299 (1956) (emphasis in original).

It therefore appears that any award of damages in procedural due process cases must (1) be tailored to the interests protected by the right in question, and (2) be limited to the injury actually caused to those interests by the constitutionally tortious conduct. The damages formula set forth in *Pioneer Savings and Loan Co. v. City of Cleveland, supra,* does not reflect this standard for damages; rather it presumes that the loss to the mortgagee is the value of the mortgage. The *Pioneer Savings'* formula does not take into account any (1) loss in the security of the mortgage which may have taken place pursuant to the acts or omissions of the mortgagor-landowner or others, or (2) the residual value of the parcel (and the resulting value in the mortgage) after the demolition of the building and removal of debris.

It is axiomatic that the purpose of monetary damages is, to the extent that the payment of money can do it, to place the damaged party in the same position he would have been in had the wrongful act not occurred. *See* 22 Am.Jur.2d, *Damages,* § 12, n. 11, and cases cited therein. Where compensation and not punishment is the function, the law will not put him in a better position than he would be in had the wrong not been done. *See id.,* at § 13 and cases cited therein. "[T]he law . . . remains true to the principle that substantial damages should be awarded only to compensate actual injury. . ." *Carey v. Piphus, supra,* 435 U.S. at 266, 98 S.Ct. at 1054.

It thus appears to the court that the proper measure of damages in this case would be the difference in value of plaintiff's mortgage just prior to the demolition of the building and the value of that mortgage just after the structure was razed. The precise assessment of those damages is not possible on the present record. Further actions by the parties will be required to identify the standard by which that worth may be measured, and, through application of the standard through the fact-finding process, the measure of the loss.

An order will be entered granting partial summary judgment for plaintiff and against defendant on the issue of liability, reserving for later ruling the issues of the measure and amount of damages.

Questions for Analysis

1. How does the case of *Superior Savings Association v. City of Cleveland* support or contradict the core legal principle of *stare decisis*? Explain.

2. The judge in this case relies on the Supreme Court case *Louisville Joint Stock Bank v. Radford* to outline five property rights in a mortgage on real property that cannot be taken from a mortgagee by the government absent a following of the due process rights guaranteed by the Fifth Amendment. What are those five rights? Explain.

3. The judge also relies on *Paul v. Davis,* another Supreme Court case, this time to determine what property interests emerge from the 14th Amendment. What is that (are those) interest(s)? Explain.

4. As noted previously, the judge applies the 14th Amendment to this case to reach a conclusion. Why is it necessary to use the 14th Amendment when the Fifth Amendment already guarantees that private property will not be taken by the government for public use without due process? Explain.

5. In Chapter 2 of this book we learned that the framers added certain safeguards to the Constitution that were designed to insulate the leadership of the new republic from the influence of the people. Do the due process provisions in the Fifth and 14th Amendments support or discredit that supposition? Explain.

6. According to the judge in this case, in addition to the protections afforded by constitutional law, what other legal protections might exist for a mortgagee such as Superior Savings? Explain.

7. Would the outcome in this case have been any different had Superior Savings not properly recorded the mortgage on the property at 6802 Superior Avenue? Explain.

8. What was the net effect of recording the mortgage and how did that affect the outcome of this case? (Or did it?) Explain.

9. The judge believes that it is necessary to establish the existence of the plaintiff's (Superior Savings) rights before moving on with the case. Once that issue has been decided what is the next step that the court must take? Explain.

10. How can the injury that emerges from a violation of due process be measured in order to supply an appropriate monetary reward to the plaintiff in a case like this one? Explain.

Part Six

Agency and Employment

Chapter 22 Agency Law

THE OPENING CASE Round 1
Vicarious Liability, Negligent Hiring, Supervision, Retention, and the First Amendment

This case has two parts. The first part began when Liberatore, the defendant and a priest, was assigned as a diocesan vocations director. As part of the assignment, the defendant lived at a seminary and taught at a university. About 15 months after the defendant's assignment to the diocese, another priest at the seminary became concerned that the defendant might be involved in an improper sexual relationship with one of the seminarians, both of whom were supposed to be celibate. Although the seminarian was an adult, the defendant was in a position of authority in relationship to that seminarian, hence the concern. The priest informed the bishop of the diocese about his concerns. At the same time the priest also informed another bishop and three monsignors of his concerns. Several months later, another seminarian informed the rector of the seminary about an incident involving both the defendant and the first seminarian. The monsignor, in turn, reported the incident to the bishop. About the same time, the bishop was informed of another incident involving the defendant's improper sexual behavior. (The record is not clear which of these incidents occurred first, but they both took place in the spring of 1997. The bottom line is that the bishop was told about the defendant's "close relationships" with "several"

seminarians.) At that time, the bishop reassigned the defendant to one parish and shortly thereafter to another parish. where he became pastor. This reassignment began part two of the case. It was during this phase of the case that the bishop was informed in January of 2001 that the defendant appeared to be involved in a sexual relationship with a minor at the parish. In July of 2003, the diocese received a new bishop. Soon after his appointment, the new bishop heard rumors about the defendant's behavior. After learning that the defendant had been in a treatment facility the new bishop hired an investigator to get him the facts. By May of 2004, the defendant had been arrested and charged with sexual abuse. The defendant pleaded guilty. Shortly thereafter, the new bishop "dismissed the defendant from his clerical state." The case is disturbing because of the nature of the offenses and the identity of the defendant. What concerns us in this chapter especially is the question of the liability of the diocese under the doctrine of vicarious liability. We will explore the nature of agency, the nature of vicarious liability in tort law and criminal law, and the defenses associated with vicarious liability as they are related to this case and to similar cases. [See: *Doe v. Liberatore*, 478 F.Supp.2d 742 (2007).]

Opening Case Questions

1. What is agency? Explain.

2. What is vicarious liability? Explain.

3. What is negligent hiring? Explain.

4. What is negligent retention? Explain.

5. How might the First Amendment be involved in this case? Explain.

LO Learning Objectives

1. Describe the nature of the agency relationship.
2. Outline the doctrine of vicarious liability.
3. Distinguish among the different types of principals.
4. Distinguish among the different types of agents.
5. Distinguish among express, implied, and apparent authority.
6. Outline the duties of an agent to the principal.
7. Clarify the duties that a principal has in relation to an agent.
8. Name the ways that an agency relationship can be terminated.
9. Identify who is entitled to a notice that an agency has ended.
10. Explain electronic agency.

22-1 The Nature of Agency Law

In the essay "How Culture Changes," the anthropologist George Peter Murdock of Yale University explains, "It is a fundamental characteristic of culture that, despite its essentially conservative nature, it does change over time and from place to place." [See: George Peter Murdock. How Culture Changes. In *Man, Culture, and Society,* ed. H. L. Shapiro, 247–260. (New York: Oxford University Press, 1956), pp. 247–260.] The fact that the law is a part of this process of change has been a recurring theme throughout this book. The emergence of the law of agency within our culture is another example of this tendency toward change within the legal system. Many of the changes that we have seen throughout the book emerge because the law must adapt by striking a balance between or among competing interests.

Agency and Other Relationships

The emergence of the agency law demonstrates how the legal system works as it attempts to strike a balance between doing business on your own and having other people conduct certain aspects of your business for you. To create this balance, agency law has developed its own principles, rules, doctrines, and concepts, all of which emerged independently and belong only to agency. As a result, agency law is said to be *sui generis,* that is, a law unto itself.

Principal-Agent Relationship   **Agency** is a legal relationship in which one party, the **agent**, transacts business for and under the control of the second, the **principal**. The **third party** is that individual with whom the agent deals for the principal. The principal must indicate in some manner that the agent is to act for and under the control of the principal. (See Figure 22-1.) An agency relationship is always **consensual** because the agent must agree to act for the principal. The agency relationship is *fiduciary* because the agent and principal trust each other. All agency relationships are fiduciary relationships, although not all fiduciary relationships are agency relationships.

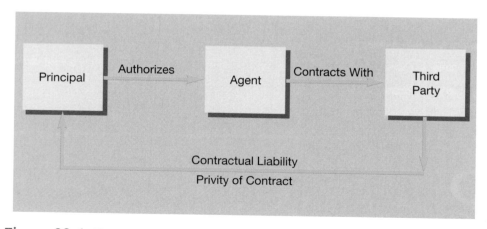

Figure 22-1 The agent has the authority to represent the principal in an agency relationship.

Employer–Employee Relationship The legal principles governing the relationship of principal and agent and of employer and employee are very similar. In fact, the two areas frequently intersect. Still, there are agency relationships that are not employment relationships so the two must *not* be thought of as equivalent. There are also employment relationships that are not agency relationships. The main distinction between the two relationships is that agent–employees have the authority to, and usually do, deal with third parties on behalf of the principal. Generally, we say that agent–employees conduct business for the principal, whereas non-agent–employees do not.

Master–Servant Relationship The terms *master* (employer) and *servant* (employee) continue to be used in some legal circumstances. A **master** is a person who has the right to control the activities of another person. The person whose activities are controlled is called the **servant**. A servant who has the right to conduct the business of the master is also an agent. In common usage, the terms *employer* and *employee* refer to the master–servant relationship. The terms *master* and *servant* are used instead of *employer* and *employee* in a legal setting when questions of tort liability arise.

Proprietor–Independent Contractor Relationship An **independent contractor** is a party who agrees to do a job and retains complete control over the methods employed to obtain final completion. The party for which an independent contractor works is often referred to as an employer or a **proprietor**. Independent contractors are not subject to the control of the proprietor. They maintain all required business licenses and permits and pay all job-related expenses; they are obligated only to get the job done. The proprietor has the right to specify the results of the job in question. Moreover, he or she has the right to inspect and approve, or disapprove, the results of the independent contractor's performance. Independent contractors are not employees; however, they may be agents. The distinction depends on whether the independent contractor deals with third parties for the proprietor.

Independent contractors are not employees of the homeowner.

The Question of Liability

The distinctions among these relationships frequently can be crucial in determining the nature and the extent of legal liability. It is important to note, however, that the names themselves are not controlling. Instead, it is the true nature of the relationship that is critical. Calling a servant an independent contractor does not transform the nature of the relationship if the master still controls the servant's conduct.

Contract Liability An agent is appointed by a principal to negotiate and enter into contracts on behalf of the principal. Therefore, the principal is bound to the terms of those contracts. Unless an employee is also an agent, he or she has no power to negotiate and enter contracts for the employer. Moreover, an independent contractor has no power to bind the proprietor to a contract, unless expressly authorized to do so.

Tort Liability The distinction between master–servant and proprietor–independent contractor relationships is especially critical in determining the nature and the extent of tort liability. This type of liability is called *vicarious liability*. Vicarious liability is based on the principle of *respondeat superior* (let the master, or the superior, respond). To apply the doctrine of *respondeat superior* in a tort case, two questions must be answered. First, is the alleged tortfeasor a servant? Second, was the servant's action within the scope of employment. (See Figure 22-2.)

Is the Alleged Tortfeasor a Servant? To establish the existence of the master–servant relationship, the court must decide whether the alleged tortfeasor (the hired person) is a servant or an independent contractor. The most widely accepted test for determining the existence of a master–servant relationship is the control test. The **control test** requires that we look at the degree of control, or right to control, that the hiring person exercises over the hired person. The more control, or right to control, that the hiring person has over the hired person, the more likely that the court will rule that a master–servant relationship exists. The question then is a simple one: Did the alleged master (employer) have control or the right to control the alleged servant (employee)?

When the degree of control is unclear or in dispute, the court has a series of factors that can be applied to bring the level of control into focus. These begin by reiterating the control test itself and then include the following additional factors:

1. Who decides the time period in which the job is performed?
2. Who owns the tools that are used on the job?
3. Who selects the overall length of the hired person's employment?
4. Who decides the method of compensating the hired person?
5. Who decides how the job is to be done?
6. What job skills are required to perform the tasks?
7. How much freedom does the hired person possess on the job?
8. Does the hired person operate a distinct business?

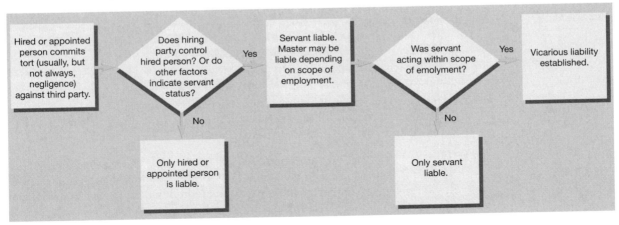

Figure 22-2 This chart shows the flow of master/servant tort liability under the *respondeat superior* doctrine.

THE OPENING CASE *Round 2*
Vicarious Liability? Control or the Lack Thereof?

When this case reached the court, the diocese did as expected, given the legal rules surrounding the doctrine of vicarious liability; it filed a summary judgment motion asking the court to dismiss the lawsuit. A summary judgment motion asks the court to dismiss a lawsuit because (a) there is no dispute as to any material fact, and (b) given this lack of dispute, when the law is applied to those undisputed facts, the moving party, in this case the diocese and certain named diocesan officials, will be entitled to a judgment in their favor. Therefore, there is no reason to proceed to trial, and the case should end now. Remember, the diocese itself did not commit the tort involving the sexual conduct. So, the fact that the tort involving the sexual conduct occurred is not at issue in relation to that conduct, at least as it applies to the question of vicarious liability. The issue in relation to the sexual conduct and vicarious liability is twofold: (1) Did the master–servant relationship exist; and (2) was the offense committed in pursuit of the servant's employment? (Note: The case does involve certain torts that are alleged to have been committed by the diocese, and others. For example, the plaintiff also argues that, once the diocese and certain named diocesan officials had actual knowledge of the defendant's behavior, they were negligent in their own capacity when they did not take

action to remove the threat to the plaintiff and, had they taken the action, the plaintiff would never have been injured. So far though, in our consideration of the case, the argument is focused only on whether the defendants were liable—vicariously. We will examine the torts allegedly committed directly by the diocese later in the chapter.) To determine vicarious liability, we first look at whether the diocese was the employer (master) and Liberatore its employee (servant). The strongest test for the existence of the master–servant relationship is the test of control. Simply stated the test asserts: Did the alleged employer have control or the right to control the alleged employee? In this case, the test can be stated in this way: Did the diocese and its attendant officials have control or the right to control the actions of the priest while he was on the job? The answer to this question is clearly, "yes." The diocese assigned Liberatore, first to the seminary, and later to two separate parishes. By the very nature of his position, Liberatore also took a vow of obedience to the church and its representatives. Given these facts alone, the existence of control and right to control are clear. The question of scope of employment is another situation, however. For the answer to that question, please keep reading. [See: *Doe v. Liberatore*, 478 F.Supp.2d 742 (2007).]

9. What was the understanding that existed between the parties?

10. What is the nature of the written agreement (if one exists)?

The first five questions are fairly straightforward. If the answer to a question is the hired person, then it is likely that he or she is an independent contractor (IC) at least for that question. The final five questions require a bit more analysis. For instance, in question six, the more skill involved on the job, the more likely the hired party is an IC. In question seven, the more freedom, the more likely the hired person is an IC. In question eight, a distinct business is indicative of an IC. Finally, the ninth and the tenth questions examine what transpired between the parties themselves. While the terms set up between the parties may provide evidence of an IC, those terms cannot alone prove the existence of an IC. Thus, the court will accept evidence about what the parties called themselves (IC or employee, for instance) but will not use it as final proof, absent some additional evidence.

Did the Servant Act within the Scope of Employment? If the court determines that a master–servant relationship exists, it will turn to the next question, that is, "Did the servant act within the scope of employment?" The scope of employment involves the range of activities for which the servant is engaged. For the doctrine of *respondeat superior* to apply, a tort must be committed while the worker was performing a task for which he or she was hired, or at least one that he or she was authorized to perform by his or her employer.

To determine whether a servant was operating within the scope of employment, the court will ask the following questions:

1. Was the action committed by the employee authorized by the employer?
2. Where did the action take place?
3. Were the employer's interests and goals promoted by the action?
4. Did the employer supply the instrumentality used in the action?
5. Was this action performed by other employees on a regular basis?
6. If the action involved force, was the use of force expected by the employee as part of the job?

The Intentional Tort Factor In some situations, the court may hold the master liable for the torts of the servant even when the tort is intentional. Most of the time, vicarious liability

---

THE OPENING CASE *Round 3*
Vicarious Liability? The Scope of Employment? The Intentional Tort Factor?

At the start of this action, the diocese filed a summary judgment motion asking the court to dismiss the lawsuit. Recall that a summary judgment motion asks the court to dismiss a lawsuit because (a) there is no dispute as to any material fact, and (b) given this lack of dispute, when the law is applied to those undisputed facts, the moving party, in this case the diocese and certain named diocesan officials, will be entitled to a judgment in their favor, and so the case should be thrown out of court. Also recall that the diocese did not commit the tort involving the sexual conduct. So, the fact that the tort occurred is not at issue, at least as it applies to the question of vicarious liability. The issue in relation to vicarious liability is twofold: (1) Did the master–servant relationship exist; and (2) was the offense committed in pursuit of the servant's employment? To determine vicarious liability, we first look at whether the diocese was the employer (master) and Liberatore its employee (servant). This was undisputed by the diocese and was not an issue for the court, and so we turn to the second part of the test. Was the offense committed in pursuit of the servant's employment? The court looks at the traditional test for determining scope of employment, saying that a servant's actions will be considered within the scope of employment if (a) the conduct at the focal point of the complaint involved actions that the servant was hired to carry out; (b) those actions were carried out where and when the work was supposed to take place; (c) those actions were carried out to further the goals of the employer, and (d) the conduct complained of involved

force, the force was expected by the employer as part of the job (as, for example, with a security guard or a bodyguard). The court, after looking in detail at these elements, concludes that the type of illegal sexual conduct involved in this case had absolutely nothing whatever to do with the job performed by a priest in pursuit of his duties in furtherance of the goals of the church. Moreover, as noted above, the doctrine of vicarious liability is not generally used to hold an employer liable for the intentional torts of the employee. The exception to that rule states that liability for intentional torts may be found if the employee commits a tort intending to further the master's business. Recall that the court has already concluded that the sexual conduct committed by the priest had absolutely nothing to do with the job performed by a priest in pursuit of his duties. In light of this conclusion, there is no possibility of finding the diocese liable for an intentional tort, using vicarious liability. As a result, in relation to the claims based on vicarious liability, the court concludes that the summary judgment motion must be granted, dismissing any claims based on that theory. The court writes, "No reasonable jury could find in favor of the Plaintiff on the vicarious liability claim. Therefore, the Court will grant summary judgment in favor of the diocese (the parish) and (the Bishop)." This decision, however, does not completely exonerate the defendants in relation to their own actions. For that decision, please continue reading. [See: *Doe v. Liberatore,* 478 F.Supp.2d 742 (2007).]

is applied to negligence cases, because workers are not usually hired to commit intentional torts. There are, of course, exceptions to this rule. If, for example, a servant commits a tort intending to further the master's business, as when a bouncer at a casino uses force to eject an unruly patron or when a security guard at a department store commits false imprisonment, while detaining a suspected shoplifter, the master may be liable. Moreover, if the master could reasonably foresee that the servant might commit the intentional tort, as might be the case with a bouncer in a casino or a security guard in a department store, the master may be liable for that tort.

Negligent Hiring, Supervision, and/or Retention In some situations, the court may also hold the master liable for the torts of the servant even when the tort is outside the scope of employment. For instance, in some jurisdictions, if an employer (master) is negligent in checking an employee's (servant's) qualifications and consequently hires

THE OPENING CASE *Round 4*
Negligent Hiring, Supervision, and/or Retention?

In the opening case, we learned the diocese filed a summary judgment motion asking the court to dismiss the lawsuit. The issue in relation to vicarious liability has already been decided in favor of the diocese and that claim has been dismissed. However, the plaintiff has also alleged that the diocese and certain named diocesan officials were liable directly for their own behavior, not because they were involved in any misconduct directly related to the acts of which Liberatore was accused, but because they had a responsibility to monitor his actions. To explain the standard by which the court must make this judgment, the court quotes an earlier case, that says, "A master has a duty to exercise reasonable care so to control his servant while acting outside the scope of his employment as to prevent him from intentionally harming others or from conducting himself as to create an unreasonable risk of bodily harm to them, if (a) the servant is upon the premises in possession of the master or upon which the servant is privileged to enter only as his servant, or is using a chattel of the master, and (b) the master knows or has reason to know that he has the ability to control his servant, and knows or should have known of the necessity and opportunity for exercising such control. R.A. ex rel. NA, 748 A.2d at 697 (citing Restatement (Second) of Torts section 317 (a), (b) (1965))." The same court adds in the same case that the master clearly possesses a responsibility "to exercise reasonable care in selecting, supervising, and

controlling employees." The court admitted openly that, when the diocese hired Liberatore it had no way of knowing of the problems that the former priest would present later in his career. So the court dismissed the part of the complaint that related to negligent hiring. However, concerning negligent supervision and negligent retention, the court was faced with a very different set of circumstances. This realization placed the court in a very delicate position. The court was quite clear that the actions that the priest committed with the adult seminarians involved consensual adult activities that would not, in any way, put the diocese on notice that Liberatore was a danger to the minor plaintiff. However, the diocese did have notice of the actions committed by Liberatore leading up to his relationships with the adult seminarians. These actions included expensive gift giving, overnight trips during which a room was shared, and sleeping together in the same room at the seminary. These actions became relevant when the diocese learned that the priest was engaged in similar conduct in relation to the minor plaintiff. It was at that point that the diocese may have known enough about Liberatore's conduct to take proper action. (Note: Again, the court did not find the diocesan defendants liable at this point. Rather, the court only decided not to grant the motion to dismiss on this count. In effect, the court is sending that issue to a jury.) [See: *Doe v. Liberatore,* 478 F.Supp.2d 742 (2007).]

someone who is incompetent, dangerous, or even aggressive, the employer may be held liable should an innocent third party be injured by the actions of the incompetent, dangerous, or aggressive employee. Should that happen, the court may hold the employer liable for the **negligent hiring** of the incompetent, dangerous, or aggressive employee. Similarly, an employer may be liable for the **negligent retention** of an incompetent, dangerous, or aggressive employee if, after hiring the employee, the employer learns that the employee is incompetent, dangerous, or aggressive and does not discharge that employee. Also, the employer may be liable if, during employee's time on the job, the employer fails to properly train, equip, and oversee the employee's activities and that lack of management injures an innocent person. This lack of proper management is referred to as **negligent supervision**. Some courts blend negligent retention and negligent supervision into a single tort, generally referring to it as negligent supervision. An employer may also be open to liability when the employer hires an independent contractor to perform a job that the law has not permitted the employer to delegate. This is referred to as a nondelegable duty. A **nondelegable duty** is one that the proprietor cannot delegate, or pass off, to another party. For example, an airline cannot delegate the responsibility it has for the safety of its passengers by hiring an independent contractor to do its maintenance work.

Fiduciary Duties   Some courts recognize that, when an employee breaches his or her fiduciary duty to a third party, the employer may also be liable for any injuries that result from that breach, if that employer had reason to believe that the employee might, in fact, breach that duty. In a breach of fiduciary duty lawsuit against an employer, the third party must present evidence showing that the fiduciary relationship (1) did exist; (2) was unequal in power, either (3) gave overwhelming control to the employee or (4) placed the third party in an especially vulnerable position (or both); and (5) actually injured the plaintiff. The courts generally reject such suits when the relationship is simply between a pastor and a parishioner. Instead, the relationship must have a more confidential and trusting dimension, as might exist between a counselor and a client. Moreover, the employer must have enough knowledge to reasonably believe that the third party is at risk. If all these elements fall into line, then a breach of fiduciary duty lawsuit may proceed against the employer. Such may have been the situation, in our opening case example of Doe v. Liberatore. In that situation, the court, or a jury, would have to decide whether (1) a fiduciary relationship existed between Doe and Liberatore; (2) that was unequal; (3) that gave Liberatore great influence over Doe; (4) that placed Doe in a very vulnerable position; and (5) that actually injured Doe. (Note: The court did not find the defendants liable at this point. Rather, the court only decided not to grant the motion to dismiss on this count. In effect, the court is sending that issue to a jury.) [See: *Doe v. Liberatore,* 478 F. Supp.2d 742 (2007).]

Criminal Liability   The principal or employer ordinarily is not liable for an agent's or employee's crimes, unless the principal or employer actually aids or participates in their commission. The commission of a crime usually requires a state of mind that is specified in the criminal statute. Thus, if the principal or employer had not authorized the crime, the courts would conclude that the requisite mental state has not been shown. A principal or employer will be held criminally liable for acts done by an agent or employee to further an illegal business. In addition, most states have enacted statutes that hold a principal or employer liable for certain crimes committed by their agents or employees, even though they acted disobediently. Examples of such statutes are those that penalize the sale of impure foods or alcoholic beverages.

THE OPENING CASE *Round 5*
Criminal Liability?

The opening case is grounded in tort law rather than criminal law. Recall that the doctrine of vicarious liability exonerated the diocese in tort law because the actions of Liberatore were clearly outside the scope of his employment. Even so, the diocese may still be held liable in tort law for its own negligent conduct for failing to properly supervise the defendant. Also remember that the defendant's actions in this case were both tortious and criminal. Moreover, under vicarious liability the employer can sometimes be held liable for criminal conduct. Here we know that the defendant pleaded guilty to the crime. So what about the diocese? Can diocesan officials be prosecuted for a crime indirectly under vicarious liability or directly for their own actions? As is often true in the law, the answer is "It depends." First, as noted previously under the guiding principles of vicarious liability, the principal or employer is ordinarily *not* liable for an employee's crimes, *unless* the employer actually aids or participates in their commission. The commission of a crime usually requires a state of mind that is specified in the criminal statute. Thus, if the employer did not authorize the crime, the requisite mental state does not exist. Since the diocesan officials did not authorize the defendant's actions, they would not be liable for the defendant's crimes under a theory of vicarious liability. However, sometimes employers can be held liable directly for their criminal failure to properly supervise their employees, especially when the employer has knowledge of the employee's criminal activity. However, that seems not to be the case here. It is true that certain diocesan officials had knowledge that suspicious actions were taking place (expensive gift giving, overnight stays, sharing hotel rooms, and so on), but the record does not indicate that they had any direct knowledge of actual sexual misconduct until after the defendant's arrest. This would not be enough information to rise to the level of actual knowledge of a criminal act. It may be enough evidence to proceed with a tort case based on negligent supervision and negligent retention, and it might be enough to hold the diocese liable for punitive damages, but it is not enough to impute criminal liability to the officials. While it is true that state law includes a statute prohibiting the corruption of a minor (18 Pa. Con. Stat. Section 6301) and a statute forbidding an individual to knowingly permit a minor to engage in any prohibited sexual conduct (18 Pa. Con Stat. Section 6312), both statutes require knowledge of the conduct in question, and no evidence is found in the record indicating that any diocesan official had actual knowledge. The court did examine the case in terms of criminal liability under federal law and concluded that no criminal liability existed. Here is the courts conclusion in that regard:

> While Plaintiffs evidence demonstrates that the Diocesan Defendants had reason to suspect that Liberatore was sexually abusing Plaintiff, there is nothing in the record demonstrating that the Diocesan Defendants consciously shared Liberatore's knowledge of the underlying substantive offenses, as well as the specific criminal intent to commit them. . . . Indeed, "[a] general suspicion that an unlawful act may occur" is not enough. . . . While it is possible to infer knowledge from a combination of suspicion and indifference to the truth, . . . there still remains no evidence even remotely suggesting that the Diocesan Defendants shared Liberatore's specific intent to commit the sexual offenses. While the Diocesan Defendants may have avoided learning of Liberatore's offenses, there is no evidence that the Diocesan Defendants desired that his crimes be accomplished. Also absent from the record is any evidence showing that the Diocesan Defendants actively participated in some manner to assist Liberatore in the commission of his offenses.

[See: *Doe v. Liberatore,* 478 F.Supp.2d 742 (2007).]

Independent Contractor Liability Recall that an independent contractor is someone who works for a proprietor but who maintains nearly total control over how the job is done. At the most, the proprietor can specify the outcome to be reached; the timing of that outcome; as well as the plans, materials, and colors to be used to reach that outcome. However, all other decisions are made by the contractor. Most of the time, any tort committed by an independent contractor is the responsibility of the independent contractor, not the proprietor. In fact, that is one of the advantages of hiring independent contractors rather than employees. However, this tactic does not always work. For instance, it is not legally possible for a proprietor to delegate certain duties. These duties, generally referred to as nondelegable duties, cannot be passed on to the contractor even if the contractor accepts those duties. For example, a common carrier, such as a ferry service, a bus company, or an airline, cannot delegate the responsibility it has for the safety of its passengers by hiring an independent contractor to do its maintenance work. Similarly, a hotel cannot delegate its responsibility to keep its guests secure in their rooms by hiring a private security firm. Also, proprietors can be held liable if they are not careful enough in hiring, training, supervising, and/or retaining an independent contractor. As noted above, like a negligent employer, a negligent proprietor can be held liable for the negligent hiring of the incompetent independent contractor. Similarly, a proprietor may be liable for the negligent supervision and the negligent retention of an incompetent independent contractor if, after hiring the independent contractor, the proprietor learns that the contractor is incompetent and does not dismiss the contractor.

Statutory Liability

One of the most heavily regulated segments of the social structure is employment. Both Congress and the state legislatures create agencies, commissions, and departments that make regulations governing workplace safety, wages and hours, unemployment compensation, workers' compensation, employment discrimination, health care, layoffs and plant closings, collective bargaining and labor unions, and so on. Such statutes include Title VII of the Civil Rights Act, the Age Discrimination in Employment Act, the Worker Adjustment and Retraining Notification Act, the Family and Medical Leave Act, ERISA, the Americans with Disabilities Act, the Internal Revenue Code, the Fair Labor Standards Act, and statutes related to workers' compensation, among others. Frequently, these statutes will be written so that they apply to employees and not to independent contractors. Or, as in the case of the Internal Revenue Code, the regulations will treat employees one way and independent contractors another. This has prompted employers to simply label workers as ICs to escape or minimize the effects of the law. Consequently, the courts have created a test, called the *economic reality test*, to uncover the true nature of the employment relationship.

The Economic Reality Test

The economic reality test is generally tailor made to reflect the goals of each statute and is, thus, a fairly flexible rule. Nevertheless, the rule is very similar to the control test used in *respondeat superior;* the economic reality test considers many of the same factors that are applied in the control test. These factors include determining the hired party's autonomy on the job, the length of time involved in the employment situation, and the level of skill needed to do the job. However, the economic reality test also adds some factors of its own. For example, in an attempt to determine the true nature of the financial arrangement between the parties, the economic reality test also asks about the hired party's investment in the employer's business and the degree to which the hired person's services were integrated into the employer's commercial activity.

Sovereign Immunity and the Federal Government

The doctrine of sovereign immunity prevents lawsuits against a government authority without the government's consent. The doctrine is no longer as important a defense for government torts as it once was. The Federal Tort Claims Act of 1946 limits the federal government's sovereign immunity. Whenever a federal employee harms a third party or private property while driving a motor vehicle in the course of employment, the federal government is liable. However, the 1946 law explicitly preserves governmental immunity for a vaguely defined category of "discretionary" actions by officials.

CLASSIC CASE The Free Exercise Clause of the First Amendment Does Not Shield All Behavior (or Does It?)

The defendants in this case include the pastor and the elders of a local community church. The plaintiff, is a past parishioner at the same church. When an individual joins the community church, he or she agrees to abide by the disciplinary rules and procedures of the church. The constitution of the church states that the members of the governing body of the church reserve the right to discipline any member who openly engages in a pattern of behavior that violates biblical principles and who remains "unrepentant" in regard to that behavior. Such discipline can ultimately include excommunication from the church. When such an event occurs, the removal of a member is announced to the congregation at a Sunday service "in a tenderhearted and discreet manner." The announcement is followed by prayer, presumably for that former member. Because she was having difficulties in her marriage, the plaintiff sought the pastor's advice. The pastor advised her in his capacity as a professional counselor. The counseling failed to help the plaintiff who separated from her husband and then decided to seek a divorce. When she told the pastor of her decision, she was told that she would have to give up her membership in the community church. The plaintiff says that she readily agreed to this ruling under the constitution and offered her resignation. Nevertheless, the pastor and the other elders wrote a letter that was sent to the congregation informing them of the plaintiff's situation. The letter included statements explaining that the plaintiff was leaving the congregation because she was divorcing her husband, despite the fact that she had no biblically sound reason for doing so, and, in addition, "she had engaged in a 'biblically inappropriate' relationship with another man." The letter also indicated that church members were to shun the plaintiff as a way to encourage repentance.

The plaintiff sued the pastor and the elders who had participated in the writing of the letter that was distributed to church members. The suit, which strictly speaking does not involve vicarious liability because the community church was unincorporated but can provide guidance on the limits of First Amendment protection, claimed that the pastor and the elders had committed the torts of intentional infliction of emotional distress, defamation, invasion of privacy, breach of fiduciary duty, and professional negligence. In response, the defendants filed motions to dismiss based on a lack of subject matter jurisdiction. In essence, by filing these motions, the defendants argued that the court had no power to hear the case, because the decisions made by the elders and the actions that came from those decisions were based on internal, church-related ecclesiastical decisions that were founded on a biblical interpretation made by the elders that the court, as an arm of the government, was not permitted to examine under the First and the Fourth Amendments of the Constitution. Any attempt to interfere would, therefore, violate the Free Exercise Clause. The court agreed with the defendants and dismissed the case. The plaintiff appealed. The appellate court concurred with the trial court on those claims that were related to the disciplinary letter. Those claims cannot be examined by the court because those matters and those decisions are all related to the church's constitution and its interpretation of biblical principles. Therefore, the trial court was correct in noting that it had no subject matter jurisdiction on which to base its authority.

However, the professional negligence claim against the pastor is another matter. When it comes to that claim, the court declares that the case has removed itself from any valid First Amendment claim. The conduct that the plaintiff complains of in relation to the counseling performed by the pastor is not related to the disciplinary letter but instead to his secular, professional treatment of the plaintiff, even though that counseling may have been indirectly related to the decision to write the letter. Quoting another case, the appeals court says, "The free exercise clause never has immunized clergy or churches from all causes of actions alleging tortious conduct," and it does not "necessarily bar all claims which may touch on religious conduct. *Tilton v. Marshall*, 925 S.W.2d 672, 677 (Tex.1996)." The court here concluded its consideration of this appeal by noting, "Having sustained (the plaintiff's) first issue, we reverse the trial court's dismissal for want of subject matter with respect only to the professional negligence claim against (the pastor) and remand that claim for trial on the merits. We affirm the trial court's dismissal in all other respects." [See: *Appellant, v. Appellee,* No. 2-02-260-CV (May 20, 2004).]

EXAMPLE 22-1: Above-Ground Radioactive Fallout

In 1982, a federal district court judge held that radioactive fallout from above-ground nuclear tests had caused at least nine people and perhaps dozens of others to die of cancer. The judge ruled that the federal government must pay damages under the Federal Tort Claims Act, explaining that while the high-level decision to conduct the tests had been discretionary, and thus was immune from liability, officials had conducted the tests in a negligent manner by failing to monitor radiation adequately or warn residents of neighboring areas in Nevada, southern Utah, and northern Arizona who lived downwind from the test site about radiation hazards and how to reduce them. A federal appeals court, however, held that all aspects of the testing program were conducted in accordance with discretionary decisions of the Atomic Energy Commission and were thus immune from liability. The U.S. Supreme Court in 1988 refused to hear an appeal from the appellate decision.

Sovereign Immunity, *Respondeat Superior*, and the States The formula for determining when a state government is liable for its own torts and for the torts of its employees, and when it retains its immunity, is often difficult to unravel. Generally, the starting point is to determine whether the state has a statute for preserving or eliminating sovereign immunity. If a statute exists that preserves immunity, the next step would be to determine whether the state has established any exceptions to the elimination of sovereign immunity. These exceptions would override sovereign immunity and permit a plaintiff to sue the state. For instance, even if immunity has been preserved in most cases, it might be forfeited if the action complained about involves a government employee's negligence while working for a state agency involved in the state's proprietary activities or its governmental functions. The final step would be to determine if any defenses are available to the state that would permit the state to escape liability, even though its sovereign immunity has been removed.

Charitable Immunity The doctrine of charitable immunity is designed to protect charitable institutions, including churches, from liability for lawsuits based on tort law. The **charitable immunity** principle, which finds its origin in English common law, is based on the belief that charities perform a useful purpose within the social network and should, therefore, not have their charitable funds diverted from charity work to tort law payments. The ultimate fear is that exposing charities to liability in tort law would impoverish many of those institutions, weaken others, and lead the rest to abandon their charitable work rather than end up on the wrong end of a lawsuit. Despite this rationale, the doctrine was eliminated in England but not before it was adopted and preserved by several jurisdictions in the United States. Since its inception in the United States in 1876, the doctrine has undergone a number of changes. Some jurisdictions, for instance, have transferred most issues surrounding the doctrine to the state legislature. Some states eliminated charitable immunity because of the widespread availability of insurance protection. In addition, many courts that kept the charitable immunity doctrine eliminated protection for charitable immunity for intentional torts. At last count, more than half of the states have eliminated charitable immunity completely. Other states, Massachusetts, for instance, have kept charitable immunity in the spirit, if not the letter, of the law, by limiting recovery in a tort law case against a charity to nominal amounts such as $20,000. Some jurisdictions have kept charitable immunity but have made an exception for the torts of negligent supervision, thus opening church officials to liability for those torts. However, this is not true in all jurisdictions. In fact, some jurisdictions still hold that, even in cases of negligent supervision, the protection of charitable funds as a social good outweighs the good that will come from denying clerical supervisors the protection of the charitable immunity doctrine. [See: Matthew Cobb, "A Strange Distinction: Charitable Immunity and Clergy Abuse in *Pincher v. Roman Catholic Bishop of Portland*," *Maine Law Review* 62, no. 2 (2010), pp. 703–16.]

A QUESTION OF ETHICS

Clergy Malpractice, the First Amendment, and Charitable Immunity

It may seem odd to focus on the First Amendment in a chapter devoted to agency law; however, as noted earlier, the intersection of agency and constitutional law is one of the unintended consequences of the attempt to prevent the involvement of religion in political affairs. The cases noted earlier (*Doe v. Liberatore* and *Penley v. Westbrook*) are only a small clue as to the extent of the problems associated with litigation that targets the work of the clergy. These complexities are highlighted in two law review articles— "Minimizing Liability for Church Related Counseling Services: Clergy Malpractice and First Amendment Religion Clauses," by Constance Frisby Fain, and "A Strange Distinction: Charitable Immunity and Clergy Abuse in *Pincher v. Roman Catholic Bishop of Portland*," by Matthew Cobb. The first article begins by defining clergy malpractice and by recounting a history of the First Amendment in relation to that tort. The elements of the tort of clergy malpractice are defined within the bounds of ordinary tort law, as a "breach of duty of professional care by the clergy person in providing pastoral counseling or other religious services, which is factually and legally the cause of the parishioner's or the claimant's injury." [See: Fain, pp. 230–231].

The article then examines several cases involving clergy malpractice, concluding that the case for the wholesale acceptance of the tort of clergy malpractice is problematic at best, especially when the counseling in question involves a religious interpretation of church doctrines, practices, beliefs, and so on. When this entanglement occurs, the court will be unable to establish a standard of care because such a standard would involve the court in the interpretation of those religious beliefs. However, when the counseling practices under fire step outside of those bounds, then the court can, on a secular basis, determine that standard of care. At that point, the clergy member is operating as a secular counselor and can be judged in the basis of professional counseling. This would seem to indicate that the tort of clergy malpractice does not exist. The article then examines the Establishment Clause and the Free Exercise Clause of the First Amendment. Under the Establishment Clause, if a tort claim cannot be settled without interpreting church doctrine, then excessive entanglement occurs and the case is at an end. On the other hand, if the tort claim against a clergy member does not involve the theology of the church, then the lawsuit may proceed. Similarly, under the Free Exercise Clause, a lawsuit will interfere with the free exercise of religion if the court interferes with (1) an individual's freedom to follow certain religious practices or (2) the church's power to guide its own in-house concerns. [See: Constance Frisby Fain, "Minimizing Liability for Church Related Counseling Services: Clergy Malpractice and First Amendment Religion Clauses," *Akron Law Review* 44, pp. 221–260. *Doe v. Liberatore*, 478 F.Supp.2d 742 (2007). In its discussion of fiduciary duties, the court does a good job explaining First Amendment issues related to clergy malpractice.]

The article concludes that, if a tort claim against a clergy member does not involve the theology of the church, then the lawsuit can proceed. [See: Fain, p. 251.] Does this mean that the tort of clergy malpractice does not exist? Probably. However, that does not eliminate the clergy member's or the church's liability, if the counseling "services" have crossed the line and become secular or, much worse, if the counseling becomes a tort in and of itself as when a "counseling" session turns into sexual harassment, sexual battery, or sexual abuse. In such a situation, the case no longer involves legitimate advice gone wrong but impermissible, tortious, and perhaps even criminal behavior. The interesting thing here is that, even in such a situation, the clergy member's supervisors may have a defense. That defense is charitable immunity. As noted in the second article, the doctrine of charitable immunity is designed to protect charitable institutions, including churches, from liability for lawsuits based on tort law under the notion that charities should not have their funds diverted from their charitable mission to pay the costs of a tort action. Although most states have eliminated the defense, it still exists in several states in one form or another. Thus, in relation to agency law, the defense might still work to protect clerical supervisors from liability. On the other hand, in most cases and in most states, including Maine which was the location of the case examined in this article, charitable immunity will not work as a defense for negligent supervision. [See: Matthew Cobb, "A Strange Distinction: Charitable Immunity and Clergy Abuse in *Pincher v. Roman Catholic Bishop of Portland*," *Maine Law Review* 62, no. 2 (2010), pp. 703–16.]

The following questions have not yet been answered. Before you consider each question, turn to Chapter 1 and review the various ethical theories noted there. Using one of those theories in a consistent way, answer the following questions on clerical malpractice, the First Amendment, charitable immunity, and the exceptions to charitable immunity. Is it ethical for clergy malpractice to be recognized as a viable tort in and of itself, despite the limits imposed by the religion clauses of the First Amendment? Is it ethical for clerical supervisors to be held liable in vicarious liability for the torts of their clergy members? Is there an ethical position that can be used to argue for the reinstatement of the defense of charitable immunity in the states to protect charitable funds from being used to pay damages in tort lawsuits? Is it ethical for the court to recognize an exception to the defense of charitable immunity when a clergy member's supervisor is being sued for negligent supervision?

quick quiz 22-1

1. An agency relationship is always consensual because the agent must agree to act for the principal.   true | false

2. All fiduciary relationships are agency relationships but not all agency relationships are fiduciary relationships.   true | false

3. Agency law is said to be *sui generis*, that is, a law unto itself.   true | false

22-2 Principles of Agency Law

LO3

LO4

Now that the different types of relationships involved in business have been discussed, the focus of the chapter can return to the principal–agent relationship. Several key guidelines help the courts distinguish among different types of principals and the different types of agents.

Types of Principals and Agents

There are three types of principals. A **disclosed principal** is one whose identity is known by third parties dealing with that principal's agent. When an agent does not reveal the existence of an agency relationship but appears to act on his or her own behalf rather than for another, an **undisclosed principal** exists. A **partially disclosed principal** exists when the agent, in dealing with third parties, reveals the existence of an agency relationship but does not identify the principal. Agents are generally classified according to the scope of their responsibility. A **general agent** is a person who is given broad authority to act on behalf of the principal in conducting the bulk of the principal's business activity on a daily basis.

A **special agent** is a person who is authorized to conduct only a particular transaction, conduct a series of related transactions, or perform only a specified act for the principal.

Examples are real estate brokers, lawyers, and accountants who are retained to do a specific job and whose authority is restricted to those acts necessary to accomplish it. A **factor**, or common merchant, is a special agent who is employed to sell merchandise consigned for that purpose. The factor has possession of the goods and sells them for and on behalf of a principal. A factor who guarantees the credit of a third party to a principal and guarantees the solvency of the purchaser and performance of the contract is known as a *del credere agent*. In the event of default, the *del credere* agent is liable to the principal.

EXAMPLE 22-2: The Antique Agent

Edna Freeman hired Leonard Tenpenny to act as her agent in the sale of several antiques. The contract of agency included a promise by Tenpenny that Freeman would not suffer any loss because of any sales on credit that Tenpenny made with third parties. Shortly after, Tenpenny sold a rare first edition of one of Louis Bromfield's novels, valued at $50,000, to Robert Fisher on credit. Fisher later declared bankruptcy. As a *del credere* agent, Tenpenny had guaranteed the credit of Fisher and is liable to Freeman for the value of the book.

Liability of Principals and Agents

The principal is liable for all contracts that a general or special agent may enter into with third parties, as long as the agent acts within the authority conferred by the principal. An undisclosed principal can be held liable for the acts of the agent once the identity of the principal is disclosed. Once the principal's identity is revealed, a third party may sue either the principal or the agent. Following this election, however, the third party cannot later decide to sue the other, unless the principal was undisclosed at the time the choice was made. When an agent is not known to be an agent and is acting as a principal, the agent can be held liable as a principal. When a person is known to be an agent, but it is not known for whom the agent acts, the third party can also hold the agent liable. In addition, when an agent exceeds the authority conferred by the principal, the agent can be made personally liable.

Scope of an Agent's Authority

Agents may perform only acts that have been authorized by the principal. Agents who exceed their delegated authority become personally liable. Unauthorized actions do not bind the principal unless those actions can be reasonably assumed by a third party to be within the scope of the agent's authority. Authority granted to an agent may be express, implied, or apparent.

Express, Implied, and Apparent Authority An agency is created by some action or conduct on the part of the principal. A would-be agent cannot by conduct alone or by any statement establish an agency relationship. It is therefore wise for a third party, when dealing with an agent, to determine the nature and extent of the agent's authority. An agency relationship is generally created by the following methods:

By appointment and implication.

By necessity and operation of law.

By estoppel and ratification.

The first way that a principal can create an agency relationship is by appointment. This occurs when the principal either orally or in writing creates the agency relationship. The agent's **express authority** is created at the same time that the principal appoints the agent and creates the agency relationship. This happens when the principal writes down (word processes, types out, e-mails, faxes, texts, and so on) the instructions or instructs the agent by saying the words of instruction aloud. In either case, the principal uses words to transfer authority to the agent. Sometimes referred to as *actual authority,* and sometimes even as *actual express authority,* express authority may also be indicated by conduct, as when a sales representative informs the principal of travel plans, and no objection to them is expressed.

Implied authority
The agent's authority to perform acts that are necessary or customary to carry out expressly authorized duties is referred to as implied authority and sometimes as *actual implied authority.* It stems from the reasonable effort of an agent to understand the meaning of the principal's words describing what the agent is to do. Implied authority can be described as *incidental authority* when the acts performed are reasonably necessary to carry out an express authority. For example, an agent might have incidental authority to contract for the repair of the principal's van that broke down while being used to deliver perishable products that the agent had express authority to sell and deliver. Implied authority may be described as *customary authority* when the agent acts in conformity with the general trade or professional practices of the business.

Apparent authority
When a principal, by words or actions, leads a third party to believe that a non-agent is an agent (or that a real agent has authority beyond that agent's actual authority), that principal has clothed that non-agent (or the over extended real agent) with apparent authority. Apparent authority is sometimes referred to as *agency by estoppel, apparent agency,* and *ostensible agency.* The principal may make known to the third party in a variety of ways that such authority exists. For instance, it may be generated by making a direct statement to the third party, permitting someone to have a meaningful business title, enabling someone to occupy a position of authority, or allowing someone to perform duties that give a third party reason to believe that the person has the authority to act for the principal. Sometimes apparent authority can even arise because the principal fails to act in some way. For example, apparent authority may be created if the principal terminates an agent's actual authority but fails to give proper notice of that termination to those who are entitled to receive such notice. Such apparent authority is sometimes referred to as lingering apparent authority. The party with whom the agent is dealing must reasonably believe that the agent has authority to so act, have had no notice of a lack of such authority, and act or rely on the agent's appearance of authority.

Agency by Ratification
Agents sometimes perform acts on behalf of the principal that exceed their authority. Also sometimes a person who has no authority to act as an agent does so without the principal's knowledge or permission. In such cases, the principal for whom the agent claimed to act may either ignore the transaction or affirm it by *ratification.* Ratification occurs when the principal approves the unauthorized act performed by an agent or by one who has no authority to act as an agent. Although an agent generally is personally liable to third parties for actions in excess of the agent's authority, this liability is not true when the third party knows that the agent has exceeded the proper level of authority. In addition to an intent to ratify, certain other conditions must be fulfilled for ratification to be valid. The principal must have the capacity to ratify and have knowledge of all the material facts. The act to be ratified must be legal and be done on behalf of the principal. Moreover, the ratification must apply to the entire act of the agent, and ratification must occur before the third party withdraws. The principal cannot accept the benefits of an unauthorized act and then refuse to accept the obligations that are part of it. The principal becomes bound as though the agent had authority to act.

Authority by Statute
In some cases, agency authority is bestowed upon employees by statutory law. Such authority carries with it the risk of liability for the illegal activities outlined by the statute. For example, the courts have held that some individual employees, such as corporate executives, who act as agents on behalf of the corporation, can be held personally liable for violations of the Fair Labor Standards Act. In contrast,

despite the fact that the word *agent* is included in the statutory definition of *employee* the courts have held that individual employees are not liable for violations of the Americans with Disabilities Act or for violations of Title VII of the Civil Rights Act.

Appointment of Subagents

Agents are appointed by principals because of their assumed fitness to perform some particular job. Because principals rely on the agent's personal skill and integrity, they do not ordinarily give agents the power to delegate someone else to do the job they have agreed to do. Should an agent delegate authority without authorization, the acts of the subagent do not impose any obligation or liability on the principal to third parties. In some instances, the agent is permitted to delegate authority, even if the agency agreement does not contain an express power of delegation. Such an intention may be implied from the nature of the employment or custom and usage. A real estate broker, for example, has the implied authority to delegate authority to salespersons. The nature of the business is such that it is presumed that the principal (seller) contemplates that the authority given to the agent (broker) would be exercised through the broker's agents (subagents).

Exceptions to the Delegation of Authority

The purpose of agency cannot be criminal or contrary to public policy. In addition, some acts must be performed in person, not delegated to an agent. Nondelegable acts include, but are not limited to, voting, serving on juries, testifying in court, making a will, and holding public office. However, forms required by law, such as tax returns and license applications, may be executed by an agent provided that the identity of the principal, as well as the identity and capacity of the agent, are clearly shown.

quick quiz 22-2

1. A disclosed principal is one whose identity is known by third parties dealing with that principal's agent.   true | false

2. A special agent is a person who is given broad authority to act on behalf of the principal in conducting the bulk of the principal's business activity on a daily basis.   true | false

3. A factor, or common merchant, is a special agent who is employed to sell merchandise consigned for that purpose.   true | false

22-3 Duties in Agency Law

The agency relationship between agent and principal establishes rights and obligations that may be expressed in the agreement or merely implied. An individual who acts as agent for another has a fiduciary relationship with the principal. This relationship implies the placement of trust and confidence in the agent that the agent will serve the principal's interests before all others. Thus, an agent may not enter any agency transaction in which the agent has a personal interest. An agent must also not take a position in conflict with the interest of the principal.

Agent's Obligations to a Principal

In compliance with the agency contract and the fiduciary relationship, various obligations are imposed on the agent. These obligations generally involve the following duties:

1.   To obey all instructions and be loyal to the principal.

2.   To exercise reasonable judgment, prudence, and skill and account for all property.

3.   To perform work personally and communicate fully with the principal.

Obedience and Loyalty

The agent, whether being paid or acting gratuitously, must obey all reasonable and legal instructions issued by the principal that relate to the agency agreement. In obeying the instructions of the principal, the agent is duty-bound to remain within the scope of authority (i.e., the range of acts authorized by the principal). For example, if the agent were to sell equipment to a third party in violation of the principal's instructions, the agent would be liable for any injury suffered by the principal. An agent may not engage in any activity that would result in a conflict of interest with the business of the principal. This duty of loyalty implies strict and continuing faithfulness to the principal's best interests at all times. Hence, the agent must resist any temptation to use acquired confidential information to advance the agent's own interest at the expense of the principal's.

Judgment, Prudence, Skill, and the Duty to Account

Agents imply that they possess the required knowledge, training, and skill to perform and carry out their agency obligations properly with reasonable care and diligence. Unless an agent claims to be an expert, the principal is entitled to expect that the agent has the degree of skill commonly displayed by others employed in similar work. An expert, such as a person in a profession requiring specific education and a special license, must use the expert judgment, prudence, and skill possessed by others who have been admitted to those professions. Whether an expert or not, the agent may be liable to the principal for losses resulting from personal neglect or incompetence.

The agent has a duty to keep a separate account of the principal's funds. Whatever money the agent receives during and as a result of the agency relationship is held in trust for the principal. An accounting must be given to the principal within a reasonable period of time after money or property is received or disbursed. Money collected by the agent must be held separate from funds belonging to the agent. If deposited in a bank, the money must be deposited in a separate account and so identified that a trust is apparent. Failure to keep such funds separate is known as *commingling,* and the agent may be held personally liable for any resulting losses.

Personal Service and Communication

The agency relationship is usually one involving an agreement for personal services. In the absence of the authority to do so, an agent may not delegate duties to others unless such duties are purely mechanical in nature and require no particular knowledge, training, skill, or responsibility. The agent is duty-bound to keep the principal fully informed of all facts that materially affect the subject matter of the agency because the law assumes that if an agent receives either notice or information, it was also communicated to the principal. Therefore, the rights and liabilities of the principal to any third party are the same as if the principal had personally received the notice or information that come to the agent's attention when acting within the agent's scope of authority.

EXAMPLE 22-3: A Commitment to Communicate

Marcy Magliozzi instructed Barbara Harrison to purchase a particular furnished house on Catawba Island for her. While examining the final contract, Harrison discovered that several thousand books that were in the house would not be considered as part of the "furnishings" that went along with the sale. Despite this exception, Harrison completed the purchase for Magliozzi. A little later, Magliozzi discovered that the books did not come with the "furnished" house. Magliozzi demanded that the contract be voided. Because in the course of carrying out her duties and before buying the house, Harrison learned that the books were not part of the deal, the law assumes that Magliozzi had the same information. She cannot use the loss of the books as the basis for voiding the contract.

Remedies Available to the Principal Remedies are always available when an agent fails to observe a duty owed to a principal. For instance, the principal may do one or more of the following:

1. Terminate the agent's contract of employment.
2. Withhold compensation otherwise due the agent.
3. Recover profit the agent made in violation of agency obligations.
4. Recover money or property gained or held by the agent to which the principal is entitled.
5. Restrain the agent from continuing to breach the agency obligations.
6. Recover damages from the agent for breach of the contract of employment or assessed against the principal for the agent's wrongdoing.
7. Rescind a contract entered into by the agent based on an improper relationship between the agent and the third party.

The Principal's Obligations to the Agent

The agreement between a principal and an agent creates the duties the principal owes to the agent. Even when the agency agreement is silent, there are implied obligations owed to the agent. Among the principal's actual and implied duties are the following obligations:

1. To compensate the agent.
2. To reimburse the agent.
3. To indemnify the agent.
4. To cooperate with the performance of the agent's duties.

Compensation The principal is under a duty to pay an agent an agreed amount or the fair value for work or services that the agent performs within the scope of authority or employment. In addition, the principal must make salary deductions and payments to the government as are required by law. All states have statutes that provide for the enforcement of the payment of wages and that place penalties on delinquent employers. The agent may not recover compensation for illegal services, even though they were rendered at the request of the principal. The agent may also forfeit rights to compensation when the agent breaches his or her duties to the principal. If an agency relationship does not result from a contract, it is a **gratuitous agency**, and the agent is a **gratuitous agent**.

Reimbursement The principal is obligated to reimburse the agent for any reasonable expenses incurred while working on the principal's behalf and within the scope of the agent's authority or employment. The agent cannot recover for expenses due to the agent's own negligence. Recovery is also barred when expenses incurred by an agent are unnecessary or unreasonable in the discharge of the agency.

Indemnification Agents are also entitled to **indemnification** (i.e., payment for loss or damage suffered) if they incur a loss or are damaged as a result of a request made by the principal. The obligation to pay for the agent's personal loss or damage, which may occur in the future or is already suffered, is avoidable if the loss or damage results from an action the agent knew to be illegal or from the agent's negligence. Public policy also requires employers to indemnify employees for personal injury sustained in the course of employment, except for self-inflicted injury or intoxication. State workers' compensation laws hold that the cost of paying for such injury should be a part of the operating expense of the business.

Cooperation with the Agent The principal, having granted the agent the duty to perform certain tasks, must not interfere with the performance of those tasks. Should the principal make the agent's job difficult or impossible, the principal has breached the duty of cooperation.

Remedies Available to the Agent The remedies of an agent against a principal are based on the principal's breach of express or implied contract obligations. Where appropriate, the agent has the option of exerting one or more of the agent's rights:

1. Leave the principal's employ.
2. Recover damages for the principal's breach of contract.
3. Recover the value of services rendered.
4. Obtain reimbursement for payments made for the principal.
5. Secure indemnity for personal liability sustained while performing an authorized act for the principal.

---

quick quiz 22-3

1. In obeying the instructions of the principal, the agent is duty-bound to remain within the scope of authority.	true | false
2. When the agency agreement is silent, there are no implied obligations owed to the agent.	true | false
3. If an agency relationship does not result from a contract, it is a gratuitous agency and the agent is a gratuitous agent.	true | false

---

22-4 A Final View of Agency Law

The agency agreement may be terminated by the acts of one or both parties to the agreement or by operation of the law. When the authority of the agent is terminated, the agent loses the right to act for the principal. The only exception to the rule that either the principal or the agent may terminate an agency relationship at any time arises in the situation of an agency coupled with an interest. The principal has the duty to inform certain third parties when an agency relationship is terminated.

Termination by the Acts of the Parties

Both principal and agent may terminate an agency relationship by their acts. Most agency relationships are terminated when the parties have satisfied their contractual obligations. The relationship also may be discharged by mutual consent, as well as when either the agent or the principal breaches the agency contract.

Fulfillment of Purpose or Mutual Agreement When the purpose for which the agency was created is achieved, the agency is terminated. If an agent is appointed for a specific period of time, the arrival of that time terminates the agency. In short, when the contract is performed, the agency is at an end. The parties to an agency relationship may terminate it at any time by agreement, even before the contract is fully performed. This is referred to as mutual agreement.

Revocation or Renunciation The principal or the agent usually has the power (if not necessarily the right) at any time to terminate the agency relationship. Acting with or without cause, the principal may terminate the agreement by simply recalling the agent's authority to act (i.e., **revocation**). Even though the principal's act of revocation may be a violation of contract, the agent's authority is terminated. Agents may terminate by simply giving notice to principals that they are quitting (i.e., **renunciation**). Unless the terms of the agency agreement permit termination "at will," agents and principals who end their relationship may be liable for damages resulting from the violation of the contractual promise. Nevertheless, one cannot be forced to work against one's will.

Termination by Operation of Law

The termination of the agency agreement by operation of the law results when significant events make the continuance of the agency impossible or impractical. Termination by operation of the law occurs in instances of death, insanity, bankruptcy, or impossibility of performance.

Death or Insanity
The death of the principal or agent ordinarily terminates the agency relationship automatically, even without notice. Hence, any agreement made between the agent and a third party is ineffective upon the death of the principal. Although the agent may be liable to third parties for breach of the implied warranty that the agent has authority to act, third parties cannot recover from the estate of the principal because the contract is not binding. The insanity of either the principal or the agent usually terminates the agent's authority. In some states, however, an agent has power to bind a principal who has become insane if the principal has not been legally declared insane and if the third party had no knowledge of the insanity. If the principal is only incapacitated briefly, the agent's authority may be suspended rather than terminated.

Durable Power of Attorney
Generally, an agency relationship is terminated upon the incapacity of the principal. However, the trend in many states has been to enact statutes that permit the creation of a durable power of attorney. Under such statutes, a person can appoint an agent by signing a written durable power of attorney. A **durable power of attorney** preserves the authority of an agent should the principal become incapacitated. In some cases, the durable power of attorney may even activate the agent's power once the principal is incapacitated. The durable power of attorney should contain the following words: "This power of attorney shall not be affected by subsequent disability or incapacity of the principal," or "This power of attorney shall become effective upon the disability or incapacity of the principal." The Uniform Law Commission also developed the **Uniform Durable Power of Attorney Act**. Many state legislatures are in the process of adopting either a complete or a modified version of this act and so it is best to check the most up-to-date version of the law in your state.

Bankruptcy
In the event of the bankruptcy of the principal, the agency is ended. All of the principal's ordinary contracts are canceled, and title to the principal's property passes to a trustee for the benefit of creditors. The bankruptcy of the agent sometimes terminates the agency for the same reasons, but the principal and the agent may continue the relationship if they choose. Usually, the bankruptcy of the agent does not prevent the agent from doing the job in the regular way, provided the agent is not using personal funds.

Impossibility of Performance
An agency relationship terminates when it is impossible for the agent to accomplish the purpose of the agency for any reason. Destruction of a house by fire ends the real estate broker's agency to sell the property. A broker authorized to sell a principal's boat loses that authority if the boat is destroyed in a storm. An agent's loss of a license required to conduct the principal's business ends the authority of the agent. A change in the law that causes authorized acts to be illegal terminates the agent's authority. The authority of the agent is also terminated by notice or knowledge of a change

in business conditions or values that substantially affects the agent's exercise of authority. For example, an agent hired to sell property at a specified price would have that authority terminated when the value of the property increases substantially because of zoning changes.

Agency Coupled with an Interest

The only exception to the rule that either the principal or the agent may terminate an agency relationship at any time arises in the situation of an agency coupled with an interest. An **agency coupled with an interest** is an agency agreement in which the agent is given an interest in the subject matter of the agency, in addition to compensation for services rendered to the principal. The concept protects the agent's interest in specific property belonging to the principal. The principal lacks power to revoke agencies of this kind without the consent of the agent.

EXAMPLE 22-4: An Agency Coupled with a Lot of Interest

James Heilman borrowed $9,000 from the National Security Specialty Bank of Louisville. He put up as security 200 shares of stock in the Actors' Theatre Group of Louisville. Heilman then authorized the bank to sell the shares to satisfy the loan obligation should he default on that loan. In the event that it becomes necessary to sell the stock, the bank serves as Heilman's agent. Heilman may not terminate the agency except by paying off the $9,000 loan (plus interest, as per his agreement with the National Security Specialty Bank).

Notice of Termination to Third Parties   The principal has the duty to notify third parties with whom the agent has done business when the agency relationship has been terminated by the act of the parties. The exception to this rule is when the agency is terminated by operation of the law. In such instances, the principal is not required to notify anyone, and no subsequent act by the agent will bind the principal. The type of notice required depends on how the former business relations were conducted. When the third party has given credit to the principal through the agent, the third party is entitled to actual notice of termination of authority, which may be done by regular mail or by telephone. The safest way, however, is by certified mail, because the post office provides a receipt of the notice. A notice in the classified advertisement section in a newspaper of general circulation is sufficient for third parties who have never given credit but who have had cash transactions with the agent or know that other persons have dealt with the principal through the agent. The failure to give third parties appropriate notice would make the principal liable on contracts made by a former agent with third parties.

Cyber-Agency Statutes

The Uniform Computer Information Transactions Act (UCITA) is valuable because it clearly establishes the nature of an electronic agent. According to UCITA, an *electronic agent* (also referred to as a *cyber-agent* or *e-agent*) can be characterized as a computer program that acts without human intervention to begin an activity, answer cyber-messages, deliver or accept *electronic mail,* or enter electronic contracts as a representative of an individual who does not intervene in the action taken by the electronic agent at the actual time of the electronic agent's activity. It is clear then that a *bot* (*robot, shopping bot, cyberbot,* or *e-bot*) that searches cyberspace for the lowest price in a contract, sifts through the Internet for the best accommodations, hunts cyberspace for the most economical plan, or spontaneously responds to a bidding process during an electronic auction is an electronic agent. The UCITA makes it clear that a principal, now termed an *electronic principal,* who places authority in the "hands" of an electronic agent will be liable for the electronic contracts entered by that electronic agent, even if the electronic principal remains ignorant of what the electronic agent has done because the electronic principal either ignores or forgets about the automated process.

Another model act, the Uniform Electronic Transactions Act (UETA), has legitimized the use of electronic agents by certifying that contracts made by electronic agents have the same binding effect as contracts created by human agents. The net effect of these provisions is to guarantee that a company that has used an electronic agent to receive and process an order sent by an electronic agent will not be able to deny the effectiveness of that electronic contract. The provisions also state that once an individual has received an e-mail, he or she is considered to have received notice of an e-contract, even if that person ignores or trashes the e-mail without opening or reading it. The UETA also says that e-agents must be programmed to give the other party a confirmation that the electronic contract has been entered. Otherwise, the e-contract is voidable by that party.

---

quick quiz 22-4

1. Most agency relationships are terminated when the parties have satisfied their contractual obligations.   true | false

2. The termination of the agency agreement can never happen solely by operation of law.   true | false

3. The principal has the duty to notify third parties with whom the agent has done business when the agency relationship has been terminated by the act of the parties.   true | false

---

Summary

22.1 Agency is the legal fiduciary relationship that exists when the principal authorizes the agent to represent the principal. The courts are often called upon to distinguish among relationships between principal and agent, employer and employee, master and servant, and proprietor and independent contractor. The terms *master* (employer) and *servant* (employee) are used when questions of tort liability arise. Even though all people are responsible for their own tortuous conduct, there are times when the law will hold not only the actual tortfeasor but also the person who engaged the tortfeasor liable for the tort. The name given to this type of liability is vicarious liability. Other liability questions include negligent hiring, negligent retention, negligent supervision, contract liability, criminal liability, statutory liability, sovereign immunity, clergy malpractice, and charitable immunity.

22.2 Any person legally capable of entering into a contract may be a principal. There are three kinds of principals—disclosed, undisclosed, or partially disclosed. Anyone may be appointed an agent. Agents are commonly classified as general agents, special agents, factor,

and *del credere* agents. A principal is liable on all contracts that a general or special agent enters into, as long as the agent acts with the authority of the principal. An agent's authority may arise expressly from the written or spoken words of the principal to the agent or implied from the agent's reasonable effort to understand the meaning of the principal's words describing what the agent is to do. Apparent authority results from actions by the principal that give a third party reason to believe that an agent has the authority to act for the principal. Ratification by the principal of an unauthorized act by another person does not create agency, but it has the effect of agency.

22.3 As a result of the fiduciary relationship, the agent owes the principal the duty of obedience to instructions; loyalty; reasonable judgment, prudence, and skill; accounting for agency money and property; personal performance of agency work; and communication of all facts that affect the subject matter of the agency. In addition to the duties that the principal owes to the agent under the agency agreement, there are certain implied obligations. These obligations include the duty to compensate the agent, reimburse the agent for authorized expenses incurred, indemnify the agent for losses caused by the agency relationship through no fault of the agent, and comply with the terms of the agency contract.

22.4 An agency agreement generally terminates when its purposes are accomplished. The agency may also terminate at any time by the principal's revocation of the agent's authority or by the agent's renunciation of the agency relationship. If either party dies, becomes insane, goes bankrupt, or ceases to be qualified to act, the agency relationship is terminated by operation of the law. The principal has the duty to notify third parties with whom the agent has done business when the agency relationship has been terminated by acts of the parties. Actual notice is required when the third party has given credit to the principal through the agent. A public notice in a newspaper of general circulation is sufficient for third parties who have never given credit but who have had cash transactions with the agent.

Key Terms

agency, 523

agency coupled with an interest, 543

agent, 523

apparent authority, 537

charitable immunity, 533

clergy malpractice, 534

consensual, 523

control test, 525

del credere agent, 536

disclosed principal, 535

durable power of attorney, 542

economic reality test, 531

express authority, 536

factor, 536

general agent, 535

gratuitous agency, 540

gratuitous agent, 540

implied authority, 537

indemnification, 540

independent contractor, 524

lingering apparent authority, 537

master, 524

negligent hiring, 529

negligent retention, 529

negligent supervision, 529

nondelegable duty, 529

partially disclosed principal, 535

principal, 523

proprietor, 524

ratification, 537

renunciation, 542

revocation, 542

scope of authority, 539

scope of employment, 526

servant, 524

sovereign immunity, 531

special agent, 536

sui generis, 523

third party, 523

undisclosed principal, 535

Uniform Durable Power of Attorney Act, 542

vicarious liability, 525

Questions for Review and Discussion

1. What is an agency relationship?
2. What is vicarious liability?
3. What are the different types of principals?
4. What are the different types of agents?
5. What is express authority? Implied authority? Apparent authority?
6. What are the duties of an agent to the principal?
7. What are the duties that a principal has in relation to an agent?
8. How can an agency relationship be terminated?
9. Who is entitled to a notice that an agency has ended?
10. What are the major electronic agency laws?

Cases for Analysis

1. During batting practice in the batting cages at Howland High School, while under the supervision of baseball coach Thomas Eschman, Jeffrey Elston was injured when a ball hit a protective screen, ricocheted, and struck him in the head. Elston was life-flighted to Cleveland by helicopter, where he was treated for head injuries at Rainbow Babies and Children's Hospital. Later Elston's parents brought suit against the high school. The school pointed to a state statute that granted state subdivisions, such as the school district, sovereign immunity. Elston's parents argued that the actions under scrutiny

involved a school-related activity located on government-owned property, which clearly made it one of the exceptions to the sovereign immunity rule. The school district defended itself by arguing that the coach's actions not only represented a legitimate exercise of his professional discretion but were also carried out in good faith and were free from wanton, reckless, or malicious conduct. Should the school district escape liability here? Explain. [See: *Elston v. Howland Local Schools,* 113 Ohio St.3d 314 (Ohio Supreme Court).]

2. A delivery truck driver who worked for the *Evening Star* in Washington, D.C., was on his route when he was commanded by a police officer to follow a traffic violator to apprehend him. The police officer then jumped onto the side of the truck and held on for the duration of the chase. During the high-speed pursuit, Balinovic was injured when the truck collided with his car. Balinovic wanted to sue both the driver and the *Evening Star* under the theory of vicarious liability. Would vicarious liability apply here? Was the driver a servant of the *Evening Star?* Was the driver operating within the scope of employment? Explain. [See: *Balinovic v. Evening Star Newspaper Co.,* 113 F.2d 505 (D.C. Cir.).]

3. Janet Young worked in an administrative capacity for the International Brotherhood of Locomotive Engineers. She was given a 10-year contract by John Sytsma, the president of the union. The president regularly engaged in hiring union employees without consulting with either the executive committee or the advisory board of the union. In addition, the president entered into other contracts on behalf of the union. Although these powers were not specified in the constitution, the union knew that he dealt with the hiring of employees and that he routinely entered nonemployment contracts on behalf of the union. Sometime after Sytsma was defeated in a reelection bid, Larry McFather, the new president, discharged Young. McFather argued that Sytsma did not have the capacity to enter a 10-year employment contract with Young because the authority to do so was not specified in the union's constitution. In addition, McFather pointed out that the contract had been entered during the union's convention, during which the power to govern the union falls to the delegates at the convention. In response, Young argued that the past practices of the union led her to the reasonable belief that the president had the power to grant her the employment contract. She also argued that even though the power to hire employees was not in the union constitution, the power to do so was implied by the powers of the president to preside over the union's administrative matters. Is Young correct on either of these points? Explain. [See: *Young v. International Brotherhood of Locomotive Engineers,* 683 N.E.2d 420 (OH).]

4. Mularchuk was employed as a part-time reserve police officer for the borough of Keansburg, New Jersey. He was never given any training, and he was not required to submit to any training with respect to the revolver he carried. A quarrel arose between McAndrew, who had car trouble, and a tow-truck driver whom McAndrew had called for assistance. Mularchuk proceeded to make arrests and, in the course of events, shot and seriously injured McAndrew. Was the borough of Keansburg liable to McAndrew under the doctrine of *respondeat superior?* Explain. [See: *McAndrew v. Mularchuk,* 162 A.2d 820 (NJ).]

5. Food Caterers, Inc., had a franchise agreement with Chicken Delight, Inc. Carfiro was employed by Food Caterers to deliver hot chicken bearing the trademark "Chicken Delight." While making a delivery, Carfiro was involved in an accident that killed McLaughlin. In a suit naming Chicken Delight, the franchiser, as defendant, the McLaughlin estate argued that Carfiro was an agent of Chicken Delight, because Carfiro was acting for the benefit of the company. There was no evidence, however, that Carfiro was hired, paid, instructed by, or even known by Chicken Delight. The decision was for whom, and why? [See: *Estate of McLaughlin v. Chicken Delight, Inc.,* 321 A.2d 456 (CT).]

6. While Elliot was an inmate at the state-run Chillicothe Correctional Institution, he was hit in the face by Turner, a corrections officer at the institution and therefore a state employee. Elliot brought a lawsuit against the state under the doctrine of *respondeat superior*. The state argued that because Turner had acted recklessly in striking Elliot, his actions were outside the scope of his employment. Therefore, the state concluded, the court should dismiss Elliot's claim against it. Were Turner's actions outside the scope of his employment as a prison guard? Explain. [See: *Elliot v. Ohio Department of Rehabilitation and Correction,* 637 N.E.2d 106 (OH).]

7. On April 11, Fred Chapman discharged Anna Savant, the manager of his store, the Super Electronic Supply Outlet. On April 12, Chapman called *The Barnard Crossings Chronicle* and had a notice

printed to the effect that Savant no longer worked for Super. On that same day, Savant ordered 12 electronic games, two computers, two laser printers, a fax machine, and a car stereo from the Global Electronic Components Corporation. As she had frequently done in the past while acting as manager for Super, she told George Pierce, the owner of Global, to send the bill to Super. Pierce did so. Savant then kept these items for herself. Pierce did not have actual notice of Savant's discharge until April 28, when he saw the notice as he was throwing out some old newspapers. Savant could not be located, so Pierce brought suit against Chapman and Super. Chapman argued that the newspaper notice was sufficient to warn Pierce not to deal with Savant. How would the court rule? Explain.

8. Stahl was having trouble with her Volkswagen. She brought it to the service station of LePage, where it was examined and the trouble was diagnosed. LePage informed Stahl that he would not be able to do the work, but that his employee Donley wanted to take the job on his own and could make use of the garage facilities for this purpose. A new engine was required, and Donley installed the wrong engine. The entire job had to be done over at a cost of hundreds of dollars. Stahl brought suit against LePage. She argued that she should be allowed to recover against LePage for the misdeed of Donley, because Donley had apparent authority to act as LePage's agent. LePage disputed this claim, arguing that the facts did not warrant a finding of agency under any theory. How did the court find in this dispute? Why? [See: *Stahl v. LePage*, 352 A.2d 682 (VT).]

9. Castle Fabrics, Inc., sold fabric to Fortune Manufacturers, Inc. A dispute arose as to the acceptability of the fabric received, and Fortune returned the fabric to Castle for full credit. Castle gave Fortune only partial credit and sued Fortune for recovery of its loss. In court, Fortune showed a credit memorandum from a Castle employee indicating that Fortune would be given full credit for the fabric. Although it was within the regular responsibility of the Castle employee to send the memorandum, on this occasion, management had specifically instructed the employee not to send one. Fortune argued that the employee was an agent of Castle and thus chargeable with any mistake the agent made. Castle claimed it was not chargeable with the action of its employee because the employee had disobeyed specific instructions not to send the memorandum. The judgment was for whom and why? [See: *Castle Fabrics, Inc., v. Fortune Furniture Mfrs. Inc.*, 459 F.Supp. 409 (N.D. MS).]

10. Lloyd, an attorney, was appointed guardian of Ernest Parker. Two years later, he was appointed guardian of Virginia Hockenberry. That same year, he agreed to represent David Isaac in the purchase of a plot of real estate from Debra Taylor. On several occasions, Lloyd deposited client settlement checks into his own account. The funds received were therefore commingled with the funds in his personal account. He later used these funds to pay for his student loans, his automobile loan, his insurance, his taxes, his outstanding credit card bills, and his barber. Identify the duties that Lloyd has violated in relation to his principals, Parker, Hockenberry, and Isaac. [See: *Office of Disciplinary Counsel v. Lloyd,* 643 N.E.2d 1086 (OH).]

11. Ross needed a grinding mill and consulted Clifton, who on occasion repaired such mills but did not sell them. Ross and Clifton together selected a mill from a catalog, which Clifton happened to have on hand, that they decided would meet Ross's purposes. Ross instructed Clifton to order the mill they had selected, and Clifton did so in his own name and with his own money. When the mill arrived, Ross refused to accept it, stating that it was too small and would not do the job he intended it to do. Clifton brought suit to recover the amount he had spent. The judgment was for whom and why? [See: *Clifton v. Ross,* 28 S.W. 1085 (AR).]

quick quiz Answers

22-1	22-2	22-3	22-4
1. T	1. T	1. T	1. T
2. F	2. F	2. F	2. F
3. T	3. T	3. T	3. T

Chapter 23 — Employment Law

THE OPENING CASE *Round 1*
Civil Rights? Public Policy? Retaliation? The First Amendment?

The First Amendment, civil rights legislation, and retaliation all play major roles in the case of Richard Ceballos and the Los Angeles County District Attorney's Office. When the case began, Ceballos was a 12-year veteran of the district attorney's office in LA. At the time of the lawsuit, he was a deputy district attorney for the City of Los Angeles. The problems for both Ceballos and Gil Garcetti, the district attorney, began when Ceballos became concerned about the efficacy of a search warrant that had been issued in a case on which he was working. Ceballos was alerted to the problem when a defense attorney filed a motion to suppress the warrant because it was allegedly founded on inaccurate information. Skeptical at first, Ceballos investigated the warrant on his own and, after talking to the deputy involved in obtaining the warrant, determined that the defense attorney was correct. Accordingly, Ceballos wrote a memo that recommended dismissing the case. The case and Ceballos's recommendation were discussed at a meeting, which became less than courteous. Notwithstanding Ceballos's warnings about the inaccuracies in the warrant, the case was not dismissed by the DA. In a

scene worthy of any number of *Law and Order* reruns, Ceballos testified for the defense about the problems with the warrant. Despite all this commotion about the warrant, the trial court refused to dismiss the case. The matter might have ended there had not Ceballos later been subjected to a number of apparently retaliatory moves by his supervisors. He was shipped to another court, refused a promotion, and denied access to murder cases (a requirement for promotions in the DA's office). At that point Ceballos filed a grievance, which was denied based on a finding that no one in the DA's office had really retaliated against him for the search warrant memo, the discussion in the meeting, or his testimony for the defense. At that point Ceballos filed a claim under Section 1983 of Title 42 of the United States Code (USC). The lawsuit went to the U.S. District Court, which dismissed the case, arguing that the First Amendment did not protect Ceballos in the writing of his memo because the memo was written as part of his duties as a public employee. The Ninth Circuit Court reversed the trial court after applying a free speech and public employee standard found in a U.S. Supreme Court ruling known as the Pickering Rule. The case went to the U.S. Supreme Court, which ruled that the Ceballos memo was not protected free speech because the First Amendment does not protect public employees when they make statements that are part of their employment duties. The case is troublesome in employment law for several reasons. First, how does Section 1863 of 42 USC fit into the flow of civil rights employment law? How does the Supreme Court's ruling impact public policy torts in employment law? What is retaliation in employment law? How does the case affect other public employees? [See: *Garcetti, et al. v. Ceballos,* 126 S. Ct. 1951 (U.S. Supreme Court).]

Opening Case Questions

1. What type of grievance was filed in this case? Explain.

2. What is the nature of retaliation in an employment case? Explain.

3. What type of civil rights action was filed in this case? Explain.

4. How was the First Amendment involved in this case? Explain.

5. What is the Pickering Rule? Explain.

 Learning Objectives

1. Explain the doctrine of employment at will.
2. Explain the contractual situations that fall outside employment at will.
3. Itemize the statutory situations that fall outside employment at will.
4. List the wrongful discharge exceptions to employment at will.
5. Explain the after-acquired evidence rule.
6. Explain the laws regulating employee working conditions.
7. Outline the laws providing worker benefits.
8. Explain the evolution of civil rights legislation.
9. Explain the protections provided by the Age Discrimination in Employment Act.
10. Explain the nature of and the need for a social media policy.

23-1 The Employment Relationship

An employment relationship may be formed in many ways. It may result from a simple oral agreement between two individuals, or it may be created by a detailed written contract that is finalized after complex negotiations between a union and a corporation. In the United States, the dominant legal doctrine governing most employment relationships is employment at will. Many states, however, have come to the conclusion that employment at will must be changed to ensure justice for employees. For this reason, the at-will doctrine has been modified by the addition of several wrongful discharge exceptions. Nevertheless, employment at will remains the dominant doctrine in the United States.

Employment at Will

As noted, most jurisdictions in the United States still follow the doctrine of employment at will, which says that an employer can dismiss an employee at any time for any reason. Under this doctrine, the employer does not even have to give a reason for the firing. The rationale for the employment-at-will doctrine is that both the employer and the employee must be free to terminate the employment relationship at any time. This principle allows both parties to end an unsatisfactory relationship or take advantage of new opportunities. Unfortunately, the principle can be abused by unscrupulous employers. Therefore, the law has created certain exceptions to the general rule. These exceptions fall into three categories:

contractual exceptions; statutory exceptions; and court-created wrongful discharge exceptions. Some of these exceptions modify parts of the at-will doctrine as it applies to an employee or a group of employees. Others actually eliminate an employee's at-will status.

Contractual Exceptions Individuals with unique abilities, special talents, or a highly specialized education often have the flexibility to negotiate their own **employment contracts**. Such individuals would not be affected by employment at will. Generally, such people are in demand and can thus be selective in the choice of employers. Professional athletes, established scientists, top business executives, famous entertainers, and well-known artists and writers belong in this category. In contrast to an individual employment contract, a collective bargaining agreement is negotiated by the employer and the labor union. A **collective bargaining agreement** is a contract that covers all issues related to employment. Such agreements, which are authorized under the National Labor Relations Act (NLRA), prevent the unfair discharge of employees. The employer needs some legitimate, employment-related reason, or just cause, for the release. In general, collective bargaining contracts also provide a grievance procedure. Under a **grievance procedure**, employees have the right to appeal any employer's decision that they think violates just cause. Often, economic conditions force layoffs or plant closings. When such events occur, some or all employees may lose their jobs. Still, most collective bargaining agreements provide a negotiated procedure by which such layoffs occur. In this way, employees are at least guaranteed that the layoffs will be handled in as fair a manner as possible.

Contractual Details For an employment contract to be valid and enforceable, it must contain some key details. These details add a level of certainty, honesty, and seriousness to the employment relationship that would not exist absent their presence in the agreement. The details include the following:

1. If appropriate, a provision that outlines the length of time that the employment relationship will last or a clear statement that, even given the establishment of a contract, the employment remains at will. This provision should also include an explanation of at-will employment and a list of the legal elements of employment at will.

2. A section that identifies the names of the parties to the contract and a clear identification of which party is the employer and which party the employee. Definitions of each (employer and employee) would also be appropriate.

3. A statement that demonstrates that the employer expects the employee to know and obey all rules, regulations, procedures, guidelines, and behavioral codes established by the employer.

4. For those employment arrangements that are not at will, the agreement should contain a specifically drawn list of all reasons for discipline, plus the nature and steps in any progressive disciplinary process, and for those employment arrangements that are not at will, an explicitly written list of all causes for discharge.

5. A clause that establishes the need for confidentiality during the entire employment period.

6. A section that explains the employee's access to and limitations in regard to all electronic systems including the employer's computer system, e-mail system, and so on. In addition, clauses must be included that stress the employer's ownership of those systems. The employer must also make certain that all employees understand that they have no expectation of privacy while working on those systems and that their work on those systems will be monitored and examined from time to time.

7. A statement that makes certain that the contract is assigned only to the employer's successors.

8. A provision specifying, in the event of a dispute, which jurisdiction will hear the case. This clause is usually called the choice-of-law provision.

9. A passage that indicates whether future disputes will be heard by an arbitrator, whether the arbitration will be binding, along with any and all additional details associated with a potential arbitration hearing.

10. An article that indicates the disposition of any and all tax issues associated with the employment agreement.

11. A section that covers the details of separation pay.

12. A segment that includes the details of compensation, including all stock option details, if applicable.

13. A policy outlining the procedure to be followed in any termination process, whether initiated by the employer or the employee, including the details of a termination interview, if applicable.

14. A statement explaining any change of control provisions.

15. A restrictive employment covenant (AKA noncompetition agreement) that includes protection for trade secrets and other confidential information, as well as provisions that include the type of work that is prohibited, the location, and the duration of the covenant.

16. A section that includes any indemnification provisions.

17. An article that permits the employee to take the agreement, examine it, and seek the advice of a lawyer about the details of the agreement before committing to the employment arrangement.

[See: Pamela S. Krivda, "Employment Contracts: Post Termination Issues," Ohio State Bar Association Convention, Columbus, Ohio (May 2, 2014).]

Statutory Exceptions The federal government has passed legislation that has altered the at-will doctrine in order to add a level of fairness to employment law that would not exist absent that legislation. In particular, the government has been interested in protecting employees from discrimination based on race, color, creed, national origin, and gender. Later, the legislature also developed statutory law to prevent discrimination based on age, disability, and service in the armed forces. Finally, Congress stepped in to protect workers from the hardship that results when a firm decides to close or move a business.

Civil Rights Laws The rule that says that an employer can discharge an employee at any time for any reason or for no reason is also limited by civil rights legislation, such as the Equal Pay Act and the various incarnations of the Civil Rights Act, as well as the Age Discrimination in Employment Act, the Uniformed Services Employment and Reemployment Rights Act, the Americans with Disabilities Act, and the Genetic Information Nondiscrimination Act. When most people consider the development of civil rights legislation, they usually think about the Civil Rights Act of 1964. This view ignores the importance of the 19th century civil rights acts that were passed by Congress in the wake of the Civil War and under the authority of the three Civil War amendments, the 13th, 14th, and 15th Amendments. These acts include especially (but are not limited to) the Civil Rights Acts of 1866 and 1871, which are now included in the United States Code in Title 42. While most of the "action" in civil rights litigation today is associated with

Employers with 100 or more full-time employees must provide a 60-day notice to the union, or if there is no union, to the individual employees, regarding any planned layoffs or closings.

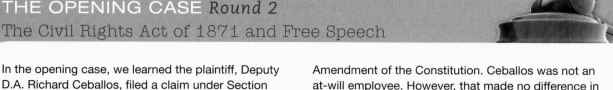

THE OPENING CASE *Round 2*
The Civil Rights Act of 1871 and Free Speech

In the opening case, we learned the plaintiff, Deputy D.A. Richard Ceballos, filed a claim under Section 1983 of Title 42 of the United States Code, which is the modern codification of the Civil Rights Act of 1871. The section declares that any person who is deprived of his or her constitutional rights by a person acting in an official government capacity will have grounds to bring a lawsuit against that government official. While Ceballos had not been discharged by the D.A. or his minions, they had made his job difficult, distasteful, and disagreeable because he had written a memo that showed the Sheriff's Department in a bad light. Ceballos argued that these actions, which had been carried out by individuals "acting in an official government capacity," violated his First Amendment Free Speech Rights as extended to the states by the 14th Amendment of the Constitution. Ceballos was not an at-will employee. However, that made no difference in this case. Even had he been an at-will employee, his employer, the State of California, could not dismiss him (or make his workplace experience miserable) in retaliation for the exercise of his First Amendment Rights. Well, at least, that was the position that Ceballos adopted in his lawsuit. As we saw in the abstract of The Opening Case at the beginning of this chapter, Ceballos failed in his lawsuit, thanks to the Supreme Court. Later we will examine the rationale used by the Court in reaching this surprising decision and the effects of that decision. For now, remember that, regardless of the outcome, Ceballos did have a valid cause of action under 42 USC Section 1983. [See: *Garcetti, et al. v. Ceballos,* 126 S. Ct. 1951 (U.S. Supreme Court).]

the 1964 act, some significant cases still emerge from time to time under these classic acts. Still, most of the focus today is on the 1964 act. As the modern prototype, the Civil Rights Act of 1964 provides a template that the other acts generally follow. The 1964 act acknowledges the existence of certain protected classes, including race, color, creed, gender, and national origin, and makes it illegal to use membership in one of those classes as a reason for employment-related decisions. Thus, it is not completely true to say that an employer can discharge an employee for "any reason or for no reason." Thanks to civil rights legislation, an employer *cannot* discharge an employee if the only reason for the discharge is membership in one or more of the protected classes. Civil rights legislation is covered at length later in this chapter.

Worker Adjustment and Retraining Notification Act Many employers who contemplate mass layoffs and/or plant closings must comply with the provisions of the Worker Adjustment and Retraining Notification Act (WARN). Under this federal statute, employers with more than 100 full-time employees must give written notice to a union official 60 days before any plant closing or mass layoff. If the employees are not represented by a union, the advance notice must go directly to all employees who will be affected by the layoff or closing. Written notice is not required if the layoff or closing is caused by a natural disaster, such as a flood or an earthquake. Notice is also not required if the closing is caused by an unpredictable business situation or if the notice might prevent the acquisition of business or capital that the employer is attempting to acquire.

Wrongful Discharge

Wrongful discharge, which is also referred to as *unjust dismissal* in some states, gives employees legal grounds for a lawsuit against employers who have dismissed them unfairly. The courts have used several theories to judge the injustice of a dismissal. These theories include promissory estoppel, fraud, implied contract, implied covenant, public policy tort, and the intentional inflection of emotional distress.

Promissory Estoppel

To make a case based on promissory estoppel, the employee must demonstrate that the employer or a representative of the employer, generally a supervisor or department head, promised the employee job security despite the apparent at-will nature of the employment relationship. In promissory estoppel cases, what matters is that someone in authority made a promise to the employee that the employee believed and relied on, to his or her detriment. Promissory estoppel thus involves four elements:

1. The employer makes a promise.
2. The employer can reasonably expect the employee to rely on the promise.
3. The employee really does rely on the promise and, as a consequence, does something or refrains from doing something.
4. The employee in turn is hurt by the action or inaction in reliance on the promise.

Under these circumstances, the employer cannot deny the promise made to the employee, and the doctrine of employment at will is unavailable as a defense.

EXAMPLE 23-1: The Power of Promissory Estoppel

Bennett worked for Jameson for three years without incident. Unfortunately, on the eve of the beginning of his fourth year, Bennett was arrested for a drug-related felony, allegedly committed during his free time. Sonja Gephardt, Bennett's supervisor, told him in front of several witnesses, "We have to lay you off now, but the company bosses have promised that you can have your job back at full seniority, once the case is over. They've also promised that you'll get back pay too." When Bennett was acquitted, he attempted to be reinstated as per Gephardt's promise but was told that he was no longer needed. When Bennett brought a wrongful discharge suit against Jameson, the company filed a summary judgment motion for dismissal noting that because Bennett was an at-will employee, the company could discharge him at any time for any reason or for no reason with or without notice. The court, however, refused to grant the summary judgment motion because the judge believed that Bennett had presented a *prima facie* case for promissory estoppel. This case was established because:

1. Gephardt, representing Jameson, had made a promise to Bennett that his job with full seniority and back pay would be waiting for him after the case was resolved.
2. Gephardt, and therefore Jameson, could have reasonably expected Bennett to rely on the promise.
3. Bennett really did rely on the promise and, as a consequence, did not look for employment elsewhere.
4. Bennett was hurt by not looking for another job because he lost money while he was unemployed and while he sought a new job.

Under the circumstances of this case, the company cannot deny the promise that its agent, Gephardt, made to the employee, Bennett, and the doctrine of employment at will will be unavailable to it.

Fraud-Related Employment Cases

Some states now permit an employee to bring a wrongful discharge based on fraud, a cause of action similar to promissory estoppel. A cause of action based on fraud generally applies only to false promises made by a prospective employer to a possible future employee who relies on those promises to his or her detriment. Often in such a situation, the employer induces a potential employee to take a job that the employer knows will last only a limited amount of time, without telling the employee about the short duration of that position. The employer thus exploits the employee for a limited period of time and then discharges the employee. Hiring an employee without informing him or her that the business is ending or that an office, store, or plant is about to close are circumstances that could provide the basis for employment-related lawsuits based on fraud.

Implied Contract The facts that support implied contract are similar to those that validate a promissory estoppel, so the two arguments often appear in the same case. However, there are major differences. Implied contract actually takes promissory estoppel several steps beyond a promise made by an employer and applies the principle to a general pattern of behavior by the employer that creates certain reasonable expectations on the part of the employees. Thus, **implied contract** involves an employment relationship that would have been at will had the employer or an agent of the employer not said, done, written, e-mailed, or printed something that created a workplace environment that implies the existence of a contract.

When examining a case to determine whether the employer has created an implied contract, the court can look at all of the facts involved in that employment arrangement. The court can consider, for example, spoken and written promises made by the employer, the nature of the employment relationship, the way the parties have dealt with each other in the past, the length of the employment relationship, the customary way the employer handles such situations, and the employer's policies and procedures. To determine the employer's policies and procedures, the court can examine various company documents, including the employee handbook; letters, memos, text messages, voice mail messages, and e-mails sent to the employee; the employee's evaluation record; and any spoken promises made in face-to-face situations between the employer and the employee. The creation of the implied contract exception gives employees a fighting chance to have their day in court, a chance that previously did not exist in pure employment-at-will jurisdictions.

EXAMPLE 23-2: A Prima Facie Case for Implied Contract

When Cynthia Montalbano went to work for Holmes Enterprises, she was required to read the entire employee handbook and sign an acknowledgment indicating that she had read and understood all of the terms in that manual. One of the procedures involved a progressive disciplinary process that promised, when employees were to be disciplined for any problem, they would first receive an oral warning, followed by a written warning. Only on the third offense would employees be penalized by a suspension, and only on a fourth offense would an employee be subject to a possible discharge order. The first time Montalbano was absent without permission, she was immediately discharged. When Montalbano filed a wrongful discharge suit against Holmes Enterprises, the company filed a summary judgment motion for dismissal, noting that because Montalbano was an at-will employee, the company could discharge her at any time for any reason or for no reason with or without notice. The court would not grant the summary judgment motion because the judge believed that Montalbano had presented a *prima facie* case for the creation of an implied contract, as established by Holmes clearly indicating that the handbook was to be considered a part of the employment relationship.

Many jurisdictions that have recognized the implied contract exception still allow employers to preserve an employment-at-will arrangement by using a disclaimer. In effect, a **disclaimer** says that, regardless of provisions or policies in the employee handbook and regardless of any oral promises to the contrary, an employment-at-will situation still exists between the employer and its employees. A legally effective disclaimer must include the following statements:

1. Neither the employee policy manual nor any other communication to employees is intended to create a contract between the business and its employees.

2. The employer reserves the right to dismiss an employee at any time with or without reason and with or without notice.

3. No one other than the president of the firm (or some other specified executive) can make any oral or written change in this disclaimer.

To be an effective attempt to preserve employment at will, a disclaimer also must be written in clear, unequivocal language. Moreover, it must be placed somewhere conspicuous, such as within the opening pages of the employee handbook or on a centrally located bulletin board. Finally, an effective disclaimer must be communicated to the employees or at least acknowledged by them in some way. Even then, a disclaimer might prove ineffective if the employer has made some sort of specific promise. For instance, if an employer adds a disclaimer to a handbook that also includes a very specific plan for progressive discipline, that employer might still be required to follow that disciplinary plan. Employers who fail to follow their own progressive disciplinary plan may find themselves in the midst of a wrongful discharge lawsuit, despite the disclaimer.

A QUESTION OF ETHICS

Beth Waid was to receive a 15 percent commission on all sales she made for her employer, the Jian Computer Corporation. Waid sold a $10,000,000 computer system to the Defense Department. To avoid paying $1,500,000 to Waid, Jian fired her, despite her record as a terrific salesperson. In an employment-at-will state that did not recognize the implied covenant exception, such a discharge would be legal. However, would such a termination be ethical? Explain.

Public Policy Tort In states that still adhere to the at-will doctrine, an employee who can prove that his or her discharge somehow violated public policy may recover damages in tort. Public policy is the broad legal principle that says that the courts will not allow anyone to do anything that injures the public at large. In many jurisdictions, if an employee is fired for refusing to violate the law, such a discharge would violate public policy. For example, if an employee refuses to dump toxic waste into a river and is then fired for insubordination, that employee would have public policy grounds for a wrongful discharge lawsuit.

Similarly, if the firing itself violates the law, public policy will provide a remedy for the employee. For instance, most jurisdictions have legislation that makes it illegal for an employer to terminate an employee for missing work in order to serve on a jury. Therefore, an employer who fires an employee for absenteeism, knowing that the absent employee is actually serving as a juror, would have violated public policy and could, therefore, be targeted in a wrongful discharge lawsuit.

To succeed in a wrongful discharge lawsuit grounded on the public policy tort exception to employment at will, the employee would have to prove clarity, jeopardy, causation, and the lack of an overriding business justification for the discharge.

1. Clarity requires the existence of a definite public policy, clearly created by the U.S. Constitution, the state constitution, a statute, an administrative regulation, a common law principle, or a general governmental policy.
2. Jeopardy requires that the public will be endangered if the court does not dissuade the type of firing involved in the case.
3. Causation requires that the discharge be induced by actions that are related to the stated public policy issue.
4. The lack of an overriding business justification means that the employer had no legitimate business reason for the discharge of the employee.

In a wrongful discharge lawsuit based on public policy, the judge is charged with determining whether the first two elements, clarity and jeopardy, exist. These two elements are considered questions of law. If the case is tried before a jury, the jurors, as the triers of fact, would determine the existence of causation and the absence of an overriding business justification. In the absence of a jury, the judge would make this determination.

THE OPENING CASE *Round 3*
Garcetti v. Ceballos and the Threat (Boost?) to Public Policy Tort Lawsuits

In his lawsuit, Deputy D.A. Ceballos argued that he had been unconstitutionally punished by his supervisors in the workplace because he had published an in-house memo (and filed an in-house employment-related grievance) that demonstrated that a deputy sheriff had obtained a search warrant in a criminal case based on an affidavit that contained allgedly inaccurate information. Ceballos filed a claim under Section 1983 of Title 42 of the United States Code. The case went to the U.S. Supreme Court, which ruled that the Ceballos memo was not protected free speech because the first amendment does not protect public employees *when they make statements that are part of their employment duties.* Now if we analyze this result in terms of public policy tort, we will see that the case may lead to some unintended consequences in wrongful termination lawsuits. Recall that in states that use at-will employment, an employee who can prove that his or her discharge somehow violated public policy may recover damages in tort. Public policy is the broad legal principle that says that the courts will not allow anyone to do anything that injures the public at large. Also recall that, to prove a public policy case, the employee must show: (1) that a definite public policy exists; (2) that the public will be endangered if the court does not dissuade the type of firing involved in the case; (3) that the discharge (or retaliation) was induced by actions that are related to public policy; and (4) that there is no justification for the firing (or retaliation). Now reconsider the facts in Ceballos. Deputy D.A. Ceballos is faced with knowledge that a search warrant may have been obtained by using inaccurate information.

Public policy would say that such search warrants should not be used by law enforcement officials. So Ceballos must do his best to stop the allegedly inaccurate search warrant from being used. Before this case, Ceballos (or any official in a similar position) would, following his duty as a public employee, write a memo and send it up the chain of command, confident that he is protected by the First Amendment. However, in the world after this case, Ceballos (or any official in a similar position) will probably reconsider his options. The Supreme Court has ruled that, as a public employee exercising his duties, Ceballos (or any official in a similar position) will not be protected by the First Amendment. Therefore, to protect himself (or herself), any public employee must adopt the persona of nonemployee before he (or she) speaks. So, instead of working in-house as a public employee where he (or she) has no protection, the public employee will be forced to work outside the office as a private citizen. To don this identity, he (or she) could send a letter to *The Los Angeles Times,* call a radio talk show, post an entry on a blog, send out a personal e-mail, and/or transmit a text with the details of the warrant. In this way, as a private citizen, the public employee is protected by the First Amendment and, if harassed or fired, he (or she) would have both a civil rights action under 42 USC 1983 and a public policy lawsuit in tort law. The Supreme Court probably did not intend to endorse this type of covert activity on the part of public employees. Nevertheless, it does seem to make good legal sense in the wake of *Garcetti, v. Ceballos.* [See: *Garcetti, et al. v. Ceballos,* 126 S. Ct. 1951 (U.S. Supreme Court).]

Implied Covenant The final wrongful discharge exception, **implied covenant**, holds that there is an implied promise in any employment relationship that the employer and the employee will be fair and honest with each other. Therefore, neither party will unfairly or dishonestly cheat the other out of anything due to the other party because of the employment relationship. The existence of an implied covenant has nothing to do with anything that the employer has said, written, or done. The implied covenant exists because the employment relationship exists. Several legal experts have argued convincingly that, once a jurisdiction embraces implied covenant, that jurisdiction is no longer an at-will jurisdiction. These experts contend that if a jurisdiction has said that a promise of fairness exists within any employment relationship, it becomes impossible to discharge an employee for "no reason" or "without notice." A discharge without cause or without notice would be inherently unfair and thus a clear violation of the ever-present, inescapable implied covenant.

Intentional Infliction of Emotional Distress Another tort claim that is being used more frequently in wrongful discharge lawsuits is the intentional infliction of emotional distress. An employee may attempt to recover damages for the intentional infliction of emotional distress if the conduct of the employer in the discharge of the employee caused serious mental and emotional suffering. To succeed in such a lawsuit, the plaintiff must prove that the employer's conduct was extreme, that the employer knew the conduct was extreme and would result in emotional distress, and that the conduct was the proximate cause of serious mental and emotional suffering.

After-Acquired Evidence Defense

A relatively new defense that employers have used successfully in wrongful discharge cases is called the *after-acquired evidence defense*. This defense is applied when an employer uncovers evidence, usually during the discovery process, that reveals that the employer could have legitimately discharged the employee, even if the employee's claims of wrongful discharge prove to be true. The defense is often raised as the grounds for the granting of a summary judgment.

EXAMPLE 23-3: An After-Acquired License Problem

Frank Handley was discharged from his position as a test pilot for Coastline Aviation, Inc., when he was absent from work on one occasion without notifying his superior. The company's employment manual, which had no disclaimer, indicated that an employee would receive three warnings, one spoken and two in writing, for unexcused absences before being suspended. Only after a fourth unexcused absence could an employee be discharged. Handley filed a wrongful discharge suit against Coastline based on a breach of the implied contract created by the promises in the employment manual. During the discovery process, attorneys for Coastline found out that Handley's pilot's license had been suspended several years before he was hired and that Handley had lied about his license on his job application. The court ruled that even though the lack of a license had not been the reason that he was discharged, under the circumstances, because he had falsified his application and was not qualified to fly an airplane, which is clearly the function of a test pilot, he would not be entitled to receive any damages.

The after-acquired evidence defense has also been used by defendants in discrimination lawsuits. Consequently, the Equal Employment Opportunity Commission has issued a special rule that is to be applied when such a defense is raised. This rule is discussed later in the chapter.

Retaliation and Constructive Discharge

So far we have discussed only wrongful discharge in cases that involve the actual separation of the employee from the employer's workplace. This is not the only kind of discharge, however. Sometimes employers will engage in conduct that adversely affects the employee's working conditions without actually terminating the employment relationship itself. This tactic is referred to as constructive discharge. For example, the employee may be relocated to less than desirable jobs at the workplace, be denied raises, be deprived of continuing educational opportunities, lose seniority, be stripped of promotions, lose vacation time, be reassigned to difficult and inconvenient hours, and so on. Thus, the employee continues to come to work and to draw a paycheck, but in conditions that slowly deteriorate, making the situation at work and on the job unbearably difficult for that employee. Often, as expected (even planned), the employee will "voluntarily" leave the job because the adverse conditions become intolerable. Nevertheless, there are states in which

THE OPENING CASE *Round 4*
Retaliation and Constructive Discharge

In the opening case, we learned that Deputy District Attorney Richard Ceballos became concerned about a warning from a defense attorney about an allegedly inaccurate search warrant in Los Angeles County, California. Ceballos investigated the warrant and decided that the defense attorney was correct. As a result, Ceballos wrote a memo that advised dismissing the case. During this time, Ceballos was accused of not doing his job properly. Even with Ceballos's warnings about the allegedly inaccurate warrant, the case went forward. Ceballos testified for the defense about the problems with the warrant. Despite his testimony, the judge did not dismiss the case. Things might have stopped there had not Ceballos been victimized by a pattern of retaliation. He was transferred, deprived of a promotion, and left with no access to murder cases (a requirement for promotions in the DA's office). At that point Ceballos filed an employment grievance, which was denied based on a finding that no one in the DA's office had really retaliated against him for the search warrant memo, the discussion in the meeting, or his testimony for the defense. At that point, even though Ceballos had not actually been fired, he was clearly the victim of a constructive discharge. Accordingly, Ceballos filed a claim under the Civil Rights Act of 1871. [See: *Garcetti, et al. v. Ceballos,* 126 S. Ct. 1951 (U.S. Supreme Court).]

constructive discharge, like constructive eviction, is actionable in court. Moreover, as explained later in this chapter, if the constructive discharge is conducted as **retaliation** for an employee's actions, the lawsuit may be found not only in tort law, as in public policy tort, but also in federal employment legislation, if the constructive discharge results from the filing of an employment-related claim involving federal employment legislation. Also, if the retaliation involves labor activities, recourse can be found in federal labor law (the Wagner Act, for instance), and in health and safety laws (OSHA for example), if the retaliation involves a complaint about health and safety issues.

quick quiz 23-1

1. Employment at will has virtually disappeared as a legal doctrine in most states thanks to the development of wrongful discharge.   true | false

2. Generally, collective bargaining agreements have eliminated grievance procedures as cumbersome and outdated because of the development of wrongful discharge.   true | false

3. Retaliation and constructive discharge are essentially the same cause of action or at least always occur in tandem with one another.   true | false

23-2 Laws Regulating Employment Conditions

Employment conditions can be divided into two distinct areas: the actual physical situation in which employees must work and the compensation received by employees. Moreover, there is a national employment verification system that affects all newly hired employees. The federal government regulates these working conditions to protect workers.

Health and Safety Laws

Various state and federal laws and administrative rules and regulations are designed to reduce preventable hazards to employees in the workplace and to provide for safe and helpful working conditions. On the state level, departments of labor and health may be charged with determining whether an employer is complying with state health and safety laws. On the federal level, the Occupational Safety and Health Act assures all workers in a business, in or affecting interstate commerce, a safe and healthful place of employment.

Occupational Safety and Health Administration

The Occupational Safety and Health Administration (OSHA), an agency responsible to the Department of Labor, establishes and enforces occupational health and safety standards with which employers must comply. To withstand a court challenge, however, it must be shown that the OSHA standards and regulations reasonably reduce the frequency or severity of employee injuries or illnesses. Employers are required to keep records of illnesses, injuries, and deaths suffered by employees and submit requested reports to the secretary of labor.

A team of OSHA inspectors enforces compliance with its many and varied health and safety regulations. Employees are permitted to request an inspection if they believe that a violation exists. The U.S. Supreme Court has ruled that an OSHA inspector must produce a search warrant if the employer refuses to admit an inspector to the job site voluntarily. When a violation of a standard is observed, the inspector issues a citation. A citation is a notice commanding the appearance of the employer in a proceeding. Employers may contest citations before the OSHA's Review Commission. If this effort fails, they may seek relief in the U.S. Court of Appeals.

Fair Labor Standards Act

The principal federal law affecting the wages and hours of employees is the Fair Labor Standards Act (FLSA), commonly referred to as the wage-hour law. Frequently amended, the act provides that workers in interstate commerce or in an industry producing goods for sale in interstate commerce must be paid no less than a specified minimum wage. Furthermore, it specifies that employees cannot work for more than 40 hours per week unless they are paid time and a half for overtime. The act prohibits the employment of children under the age of 14 years or the employment of "oppressive child labor" in any enterprise engaged in commerce or in the production of goods for commerce. Provisions of the FLSA have been duplicated by a number of states to regulate intrastate commerce and industries not covered by the federal law.

Wage and Hour Exceptions and Exemptions

The wage and hour provisions of the FLSA permit the employment of learners, apprentices, and messengers at less than the minimum wage. However, the employer must obtain express permission from the Wage and Hour Division of the Department of Labor and is subject to conditions set by it governing wages and hours. Full-time students are permitted to be employed under the same conditions in retail and service stores outside of school hours.

The wage and hour provisions of the FLSA, with certain exceptions, do not apply to people employed in an executive, administrative, or professional capacity. The exempt workers are generally identified as those who manage other employees. At least 50 percent of their primary duties must be in the performance of office or nonmanual work relating to the operations of the company or in the performance of work requiring scientific or specialized study. State, local, and federal employees; self-employed persons; and armed forces personnel are exempted from the wage and hour provisions. Also exempted are outside salespeople, employees of certain seasonal amusement or recreational businesses, and employees of small retail or service establishments.

Identity and Employment Eligibility

The federal Immigration Reform and Control Act of 1986 created a national employment verification system that placed responsibility for verification of the identity and employment of all employees on the employer. The act provided that alien workers hired on or before November 6, 1986, had until May 5, 1988, to seek temporary resident status. Those who do not have documentation of their right to work in this country are not entitled to help from the National Labor Relations Board (NLRB) in labor disputes.

Employers are required to request and examine documentation of identity and employment eligibility of all new hires and rehires, including U.S. citizens, permanent residents, and nonimmigrant visa holders. Job applicants must present original documentation. After the documents are reviewed by the employer, individuals who accept an offer of employment are required to complete and sign an employment eligibility verification form in the presence of a supervisor or a human resource officer.

quick quiz 23-2

1. The Occupational Safety and Health Act is a model law created by the American Law Institute.   true | false

2. The minimum wage is set by OSHA.   true | false

3. The Immigration Reform and Control Act of 1986 does not affect the job application process.   true | false

23-3 Worker Benefits

The law attempts to protect workers who have left a job because of retirement, injury, or disability. The law also assists workers who have been laid off or discharged. These objectives are accomplished through Social Security, unemployment insurance, and worker's compensation.

Social Security

Federal and state governments participate in programs designed to reduce the financial risk to workers caused by their unemployment, disability, hospitalization, retirement, or death. The primary federal law covering these risks is the Social Security Act of 1935. Under the Federal Insurance Contributions Act (FICA), both employers and employees are taxed equally to help pay for the worker's loss of income on retirement. The law provides that the employee's contribution is held back by the employer, who then provides a matching contribution. The amount that an employee is assessed is based on the employee's annual wage base. Each year the annual wage base is raised to accommodate changes that occur because of increases in the cost of living. The Social Security Administration will pay benefits to retired workers who are eligible under the plan. Each retired worker's benefit payments are set by law but are also raised automatically to match cost-of-living increases.

Unemployment Insurance

The unemployment insurance section of the Social Security Act provides for a joint federal and state system of unemployment insurance. Temporary financial assistance is available to individuals who are unemployed through no fault of their own and who have earned sufficient credits from prior employment. Under the Federal Unemployment Tax Act, each state operates its own unemployment insurance system, subject to conditions established by the federal government. In addition to meeting state requirements regarding length of time employed and amount of wages, former employees must be ready, willing, and able to take suitable full-time employment should it become available. Thus, claimants are ineligible to receive unemployment benefits when they refuse to work without good cause. Good cause for refusing to work must be real, not imaginary; substantial, not trivial; and reasonable, not whimsical. For example, a desire to avoid a small cut in pay does not constitute good cause to refuse an employer's offer of employment in a reasonably similar position.

An employee who quits a job without cause or is discharged for misconduct or theft generally does not qualify for unemployment benefits. Most states disqualify workers from receiving benefits if they are on strike because of a labor dispute. Domestic workers, agricultural workers, and state and local government employees are not governed by the federal–state program. Separate federal unemployment programs exist for railroad workers and federal civilian workers.

Unemployment benefits help those out of work; however, the recipient must be ready, willing, and able to work should suitable employment become available.

Workers' Compensation

Workers' compensation laws are in effect in all states. These statutes compensate covered workers or their dependents for injuries, disease, or death that occur on the job or as a result of it. One form provides a fund operated only by the state government. Employers pay into a state-controlled fund. When employees suffer injuries, they apply to the state to receive their benefits.

In another form of workers' compensation, companies are required to carry insurance for their workforce, but they have the option of contributing to the state fund or purchasing insurance from a private insurer. In the third form, all employers are required to purchase workers' compensation insurance from private insurers.

To recover for work-related injuries under workers' compensation, a worker must be injured on the job. A worker traveling to work, traveling home, or traveling to some other non-work-related destination cannot recover for injuries. This restriction is also true of lunches and breaks when a worker leaves the workplace. The result is different, however, when a worker leaves the work site on a *special mission* for the employer. Then the employee would be eligible to recover if he or she is injured, especially if the trip involved a business-related lunch that the employee was required to attend away from the job site.

If this worker is injured on the job, his state's workers' compensation insurance will pay benefits based on the severity and duration of the injury.

Pension Plan Regulation

The Employee Retirement Income Security Act (ERISA) provides necessary supervision over employee pension plans that are established by many employers. Under the act, employers must place their pension contributions on behalf of the employees into a pension trust, independent of the employer. Under the rules of vesting, workers are guaranteed the right to receive pension benefits, regardless of whether they are working under the plan at the time of retirement. The law requires all pension plans to have minimum vested benefits. All pension plans must provide vested benefits after a worker has been on the job for five years.

Family and Medical Leave Regulation

Under the provisions of the federal Family and Medical Leave Act (FMLA), employers who have 50 or more employees at the workplace (or within 75 miles of the workplace) must give those employees up to 12 weeks of leave time in a 12-month period for child, spousal, or parental care or for the employee's own serious medical condition if that condition necessitates either in-patient treatment or medical care on a continuing basis. The 12-month period can be calculated based on a calendar year or from the time the leave actually begins. The leave time may be unpaid, but it must not jeopardize the job of the employee. To qualify for the leave time guaranteed by the FMLA, the worker must have been employed by the firm for at least one year and worked for 1,250 hours over the 12-month period before the leave is requested. Employees can draw on the 12 weeks consecutively, at intervals, or as an adjusted work plan. For example, an employee might take a half-week of leave time now and another half-week later, or an employee might reduce his or her workweek from five to four days, or a worker might adjust his or her daily work schedule from eight to six hours, and so on.

Employer Responsibilities Both the employee and the employer have responsibilities under the FMLA. For instance, the employer must keep the employee's group health insurance in effect while the employee is on leave. Furthermore, when the employee returns to work, the employer must reinstate the employee to his or her former job or a job equal to the former job. In addition, the employer must make certain that, upon returning to work, the employee receives the same pay and the same benefits that he or she received before going on leave. Employers are also forbidden to dismiss an employee or discriminate against a worker who exercises his or her leave rights under the FMLA. Similarly, the employer cannot retaliate against a worker who protests the employer's attempt to bypass the rights granted to employees under this act. Employers are also responsible for informing employees, in writing, when leave time under the FMLA has been activated.

Employee Responsibilities The FMLA also imposes certain obligations on employees. For instance, employees are required by law to give notice of their intention to take an FMLA leave whenever they can foresee the need for the leave. This notice must be given to the employer at least 30 days before the employee intends to take the leave. If the need for a leave is unpredictable, the employee must give notice as soon as doing so is practical.

Enforcement of FMLA Rules Employees who believe that their employer has violated FMLA rules can file complaints with the Employment Standards Administration. Moreover, employees who believe that their rights have been violated may file a lawsuit against their employers. Finally, a state statute or a collective bargaining agreement that gives employees more comprehensive leave coverage would supersede FMLA.

Military Amendments to the FMLA Congress amended the FMLA in 2009 to accommodate military caregivers. Under these new provisions, an employer must give an employee up to 26 weeks of leave time in a 12-month period to care for a family member who has sustained a serious illness or injury that occurred because of military service. This new type of leave has been labeled **military caregiver leave**. In addition, employees are permitted to use as much as 20 weeks to take care of certain nonmedical emergencies during the time that a spouse, child, or parent is on active duty in the military. This is referred to as **qualifying exigency leave**.

quick quiz 23-3

1. Most states have eliminated workers' compensation laws because they are too expensive to maintain.   true | false

2. Under the Federal Unemployment Tax Act, all state unemployment compensation systems were dismantled.   true | false

3. The Family and Medical Leave Act provides for 12 weeks of paid leave for all employees in any 12-month period.   true | false

23-4 Equal Employment Opportunity

As noted earlier in the chapter, in recent years, the government has attempted to address the problem of discrimination in the workplace by fashioning statutes that promote equal employment opportunities. The most prominent of these statutes include Title VII of the Civil Rights Acts, the Equal Pay Act, the Age Discrimination in Employment Act, the Uniformed Services Employment and Reemployment Rights Act, the Americans with Disabilities Act, and the Genetic Information Nondiscrimination Act (GINA).

Civil Rights Legislation

Today we are so used to governmental efforts to promote equal employment opportunity that we forget that it was a long and hard struggle to reach the type of workplace equity that we enjoy today. The process began in the 19th century in the wake of the Civil War with the adoption of three major constitutional amendments. Amendment 13 abolished slavery; Amendment 14 guarantees due process and equal protection of the law; and Amendment 15 guarantees voting rights. Each of these amendments also ends with a key section that reads, "Congress shall have the power to enforce this article by appropriate legislation." Congress exercised that authority when it passed the initial civil rights legislation in the years following the war. The first such act was the Civil Rights Act of 1866, which officially bestowed citizenship on all people born in the United States and promised them equal citizenship rights. Because of the fear that the constitutionality of the act might still be challenged, given the imprecise nature of Amendment 13, Amendment 14 was enacted to solidify the principle of equal protection and due process. A new civil rights act, the Civil Rights Act of 1871, also known as the enforcement act, was enacted by Congress to make it clear that the states must also protect these rights. More specifically the act reads:

> Every person who, *under color of any statute, ordinance, regulation, custom, or usage, of any State or Territory or the District of Columbia,* subjects, or causes to be subjected, any citizen of the United States or other person within the jurisdiction thereof *to the deprivation of any rights, privileges, or immunities secured by the Constitution and laws*, shall be liable to the party injured in an action at law, suit in equity, or other proper proceeding for redress, except that in any action brought against a judicial officer for an act or omission taken in such officer's judicial capacity, injunctive relief shall not be granted unless a declaratory decree was violated or declaratory relief was unavailable. For the purposes of this section, any Act of Congress applicable exclusively to the District of Columbia shall be considered to be a statute of the District of Columbia. 42 United States Code, Section 1983. (Italics added)

While it took some time, it is now indisputable that all of the principles set forth in the Bill of Rights and all subsequent rights-oriented amendments must be protected by the states as well as by Congress. This is the act that Ceballos used to challenge the retaliatory action of his supervisors in his lawsuit against the District Attorney's Office in Los Angeles, California, outlined in the opening case.

The Equal Pay Act

The stage was set for the Civil Rights Act of 1964 by the Equal Pay Act of 1963. Under provisions of the federal Equal Pay Act, employers must pay women the same amount that they pay men for the same job. The underlying motto of those who support the Equal Pay Act is "equal pay for equal work." Such a rule is easy to follow when the work in question is exactly the same. Problems occur when the work done by the women in the workplace is comparable, but not identical, to the work done by the men. To deal with this issue, the courts have ruled that as long as the work in question requires the same level of effort, ability, and accountability and is rendered in a comparable work environment, it is considered substantially equal. Substantially equal work requires equal pay. Since 1979, the Equal Pay Act has been administered by the Equal Employment Opportunity Commission (EEOC).

THE OPENING CASE *Round 5*
The Civil Rights Act of 1871 (42 USC Section 1833)
and the First Amendment

In the opening case, we learned that Ceballos filed a claim under Section 1983 of Title 42 of the United States Code. Ceballos argued that he had been deprived of his constitutional right of free speech by being subjected to retaliatory moves for pointing out that some of his colleagues may have used inaccurate information to obtain a search warrant. The trial court believed that Ceballos had no case and dismissed the matter. The appeals court, however, believed that the state had, indeed, violated Ceballos's First Amendment rights and that he had the right to proceed to trial. The appellate court judges based their ruling on a standard that protects the free speech of public employees. The standard was created by the U.S. Supreme Court and is known as the Pickering Rule. The Pickering Rule is explained quite well by Justice Souter in his dissent in the Ceballos case. Souter writes:

> Where the employee speaks "as a citizen . . . upon matters of public concern," the First Amendment offers protection but only where the speech survives a screening test. *Pickering v. Board of Ed. of Township High School Dist.* 205, Will Cty., 391 U.S. 563, 568 (1968). That test, called, in legal shorthand, "Pickering balancing," requires a judge to "balance . . . the interests" of the employee *"in commenting upon matters of public concern* and *the interest of the State, as an employer, in promoting the efficiency of the public services it performs through its employees."* (Italics added)

The Supreme Court, in reaching its decision, in the Ceballos case, makes the following evaluation:

> The controlling factor in Ceballos' case is that his expressions were made *pursuant to his duties as a calendar deputy.* . . . That consideration—the fact that Ceballos spoke as a prosecutor fulfilling a responsibility to advise his supervisor about how best to proceed with a pending case—distinguishes Ceballos' case from those in which the First Amendment provides protection against discipline. We hold that when public employees *make statements pursuant to their official duties,* the employees are not speaking as citizens for First Amendment purposes, and the Constitution does not insulate their communications from employer discipline.

The Supreme Court has ruled that when public employees *"make statements pursuant to their official duties,"* they are not protected by the First Amendment. However, whenever public officials make statements *"pursuant to their official duties"* they are *"commenting upon matters of public concern."* It, therefore, appears that the Supreme Court has eliminated the first step of the Pickering balancing test and has overruled the Pickering case without expressly saying so. The best that can be said here is that the Court has left the matter in a state of confusion, at least for the present. [See: *Pickering v. Board of Ed. of Township High School Dist.* 205, Will Cty., 391 U.S. 563 (1968); *Garcetti, et al. v. Ceballos,* 126 S. Ct. 1951 (U.S. Supreme Court).]

Title VII of the Civil Rights Act of 1964   The Civil Rights Act of 1964 covers more than employment. It also outlaws discrimination in such things as housing, travel accommodations, and education. One of its primary features is the creation of the original five protected classes. Simply stated the act prohibits discrimination on the basis of race, color, creed, gender, and national origin. Employees who believe that they have been discriminated against can file complaints with the Equal Employment Opportunity Commission (EEOC). Moreover, some state governments have equal employment agencies that have been designated as deferral agencies under Title VII. In those states, all discrimination charges filed with the EEOC must be sent by the EEOC to the state equal employment agency. Even so, an employee who has filed such a claim can ask the EEOC, rather than the state agency, to conduct the inquiry. Discrimination claims must be registered with the EEOC no later than 180 days after the prohibited activity. In states with deferral agencies, that deadline is lengthened to 300 days. Discrimination can be committed in one of two ways: disparate treatment and disparate impact.

Disparate Treatment In cases of **disparate treatment**, the employer intentionally discriminates against an individual or a group belonging to one of the protected classes. For instance, a business that advertises for "salesmen" or "saleswomen" rather than "salespersons" would be practicing this type of discrimination. The act has had a profound effect on the language of the workplace. Words and phrases that reveal a certain bias (usually a gender bias) have largely disappeared from the language. We no longer see advertisements for "waiters," "stewardesses," "actresses," "salesmen," "busboys," or "girl Fridays." Instead, we read about "servers," "flight attendants," "actors," "salespersons," "bussers," and "administrative assistants." Nevertheless, a common misconception still exists that this type of brazen discrimination has been eliminated from the workplace. Such is not the case. Even in the present day, the United States Supreme Court is still reviewing cases that dealt with companies that continued to discriminate in direct and obvious ways.

EXAMPLE 23-4: The Johnson Battery Discrimination Case, Part I

Johnson Controls Inc., a battery manufacturer located in Wisconsin, had an employment policy that eliminated women younger than 70 years of age from performing certain jobs in the making of batteries unless they could produce proof that they were infertile. The company argued that it was just trying to protect its workers, because all the prohibited jobs involved prolonged exposure to lead. The U.S. Supreme Court disagreed and labeled the company's policy as a clear-cut example of sex discrimination.

Bona Fide Occupational Qualification Businesses have a defense against a charge of disparate treatment, called a *bona fide occupational qualification (BFOQ)*. The discrimination may be justified if the employer can prove that the job requirement is a BFOQ. Even so, a BFOQ defense can never be raised to justify racial discrimination. However, a BFOQ defense can work for some forms of sexual discrimination. For example, a requirement that all applicants for a job modeling women's bathing suits be female would be a BFOQ.

EXAMPLE 23-5: The Johnson Battery Discrimination Case, Part II

Could Johnson Controls Inc., in Example 23-4, argue that infertility in a woman is a valid BFOQ? The U.S. Supreme Court said no. A BFOQ must be related to the job performance. Both men and women can be competent battery makers, so excluding one sex or the other from that job cannot be justified.

Disparate Impact In contrast to disparate treatment, disparate impact is a more subtle form of discrimination. Discrimination through **disparate impact** or adverse impact occurs when an employer has a policy that on the surface seems neutral but that has an unequal and unfair impact on the members of one or more of the protected classes. For instance, an employer who requires all employees who work in the warehouse to be six feet tall and weigh at least 180 pounds may have discriminated against women under the doctrine of disparate impact. Although the criteria seem neutral on the surface, they would exclude women disproportionately and thus have an unfair impact on them.

Business Necessity Businesses have a defense against a charge of disparate impact known as **business necessity**. A qualification may be permitted despite its disparate impact on a

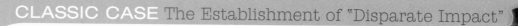

Every legal doctrine that is not specifically written into a statute must begin somewhere and that somewhere is, more often than not, the courts. Such was the case with creation of the doctrine of disparate impact. That doctrine—the one that says some employment policies may appear neutral on their face but still violate the law, because they have a disparate impact on a protected group—began in the following classic case. The facts are straightforward enough. A group of employees were upset about the promotion policies of their employer, Dan River Steam Station, a power-generating plant owned and operated by the Duke Power Company of Draper, North Carolina. The requirements for advancement included a high school education or successful completion of a standardized general education examination. The argument made by the petitioners was that neither of these requirements was actually related to doing an effective job at the plant; that both of the requirements had the adverse effect of eliminating black employees from hiring and promotions in a proportion that was at a substantially higher rate than white employees; and the positions that required the diploma or the test were filled only by white employees and had been dominated by white employees as part of a deliberate strategy to exclude blacks. The case went to the district court, which found that the company had indeed followed a deliberately discriminatory hiring and promotion process that was consciously designed to exclude blacks from the higher-paying positions. The plant had five departments: labor, coal handling, operations, maintenance, and the laboratory. Blacks worked exclusively in the labor department, which meant that all the high-paying jobs in the other departments were occupied by whites. Promotions in all departments were based on seniority alone. Starting in 1955 a high school diploma was needed for an initial assignment to any department

except labor. After the Civil Rights Act went onto effect in 1965, the company eliminated its deliberately discriminatory hiring policies. However, at that time, a high school diploma became a requirement for moving out of labor into any of the higher-paying departments. On July 2, 1965, the date that the Civil Rights Act went into effect, the company installed a new policy. The new policy required applicants to any department but the labor department to achieve a satisfactory score on two aptitude tests and to have a high school diploma. Later the requirement was modified somewhat to allow a transfer from the labor department or the coal department to a higher-paying department based on test scores alone. The district court ruled that the Civil Rights Act was not designed to pass judgment on past transgressions. The appeals court believed that the case should be decided based on the intent of the employer rather than on the actual results and, finding no intent to discriminate on the part of Duke, rejected the employees' charge of discrimination. At that point the case landed in the lap of the U.S. Supreme Court. The Supreme Court ruled that this apparently neutral policy established by the company violated the Civil Rights Act because it had a demonstrably disparate impact on blacks and was not really related to job performance. According to the Supreme Court: "What Congress has forbidden is giving these devices and mechanisms controlling force unless they are demonstrably a reasonable measure of job performance . . . Far from disparaging job qualifications as such, Congress has made such qualifications the controlling factor, so that race, religion, nationality, and sex become irrelevant. What Congress has commanded is that any tests used must measure the person for the job and not the person in the abstract." [See: *Griggs v. Duke Power Co.,* United States Supreme Court, 401 U.S. 424, 91 S.Ct . 849. 28 L.Ed . 158 (1971).]

protected class if the employer can show that the qualification is needed to perform the job. For example, a requirement that all job applicants have a law degree for a job as an attorney might have a disparate impact on one or more of the protected classes. However, because a law degree is needed for the job, it will be allowed. Naturally, the claimant has an opportunity to demonstrate that the challenged practice is not really needed to perform the job in question.

Workplace Harassment In recent years, the courts have witnessed an increase in the number of **workplace harassment** claims. The first type of harassment claims that appeared before the EEOC were sexual harassment claims. There is no question that sexual harassment is a type of sexual discrimination and that it is forbidden by the Civil Rights Act. However, exactly what constitutes sexual harassment is misunderstood by many people. Although most people recognize *quid pro quo* harassment, they do not realize that the creation of a *hostile work environment* also constitutes sexual harassment. **Quid pro quo sexual harassment** occurs when a supervisor makes unwelcome sexual advances toward a subordinate or suggests that the subordinate trade sexual favors for preferential treatment or to avoid the threat of an adverse employment decision such as a demotion, a pay cut, or termination. The Supreme Court has also made it clear that this type of discrimination can occur between individuals of the same gender.

A **hostile work environment** occurs when misconduct, such as sexually explicit comments, photographs, pictures, text messages, e-mails, Facebook postings, cartoons, jokes, posters, or gestures, pervade the workplace to the extent that conditions become distressing, offensive, or hostile. In recent years, the law has begun to recognize that a hostile work environment need not be limited to sexual situations. In fact, a hostile workplace can be created by misconduct that creates an environment that is so offensive that it interferes with the employee's work performance. This type of harassment can result from comments, jokes, cartoons, text messages, voice mails, e-mails, Facebook postings, and so on based upon insults, attacks, sarcasm, complaints, or inappropriate jokes because of another worker's religion, color, creed, gender or national origin. The law expressly forbids employers from retaliating against employees who file harassment complaints.

Affirmative Action The term **affirmative action** refers to a practice by which an employer actively pursues a policy that will reduce the effects of past discrimination in the workplace. The term *affirmative,* in this context, means to go forth actively, and the word *action* means a definitive plan. Affirmative action is neither mandated nor prohibited by the Civil Rights Act. Generally, affirmative action plans come from a court order but nothing prevents an employer from pursuing an affirmative action plan voluntarily. Some people are opposed to affirmative action because they see it as a form of reverse discrimination.

Reverse Discrimination Any practice that is designed to eliminate discrimination against the members of a protected class but that has the opposite effect on other members of that class or on the members of another protected class is called **reverse discrimination**. To prevent this, the Supreme Court ruled that affirmative action plans must promote a "compelling state interest" and must be finely drawn to minimize harm to those workers outside the plan. More specifically, to preserve an affirmative action plan, the government must show the plan is necessary to fight past discrimination, has a termination date, and is the only way to reverse the discriminatory practice.

Amendments to the Civil Rights Act
Congress has amended the Civil Rights Act many times since its original passage in 1964. One such amendment involving pregnancy occurred in 1978. Moreover, a major overhaul of the act took place in 1991. One goal of the 1991 amendments was to revitalize the doctrine of disparate impact. The second objective involves an expansion of the remedies available under civil rights legislation. The Equal Pay Act has also been amended recently.

The Pregnancy Discrimination Act This 1978 amendment to Title VII of the Civil Rights Act of 1964 makes it clear that employers cannot discriminate against women because of pregnancy or because they recently gave birth. Stated more positively, the act provides that pregnant women must be afforded the same treatment in all employment-related decisions, including health care, as any other employee.

Strengthening Disparate Impact The first goal of the1991amendments was to strengthen the doctrine of disparate impact that had been weakened by the U.S. Supreme Court. The amendments make it clear that in disparate impact cases, the employer has the burden of proving that a business necessity exists for the alleged discriminatory practice that forms the basis of the complaint. The law also makes it clear that the employer must prove that the hiring or promotion qualification is directly related to the specific job in question rather than to general business needs. The party who files a complaint in a disparate impact case may also be victorious if he or she can show that the same business goal can be reached by using a nondiscriminatory employment practice.

Compensatory and Punitive Damages A second objective was to expand the availability of compensatory and punitive damages. Prior to the passage of the new act, only victims of racial discrimination could collect compensatory and punitive damages. All other victims of discrimination were limited to collecting back pay only. Under the 1991 amendments, compensatory and punitive damages were made available to people who have been discriminated against because of their sex, religion, or national origin. Other remedies that are available under Title VII are back pay, reinstatement, and attorney fees.

Other Effects of the 1991 Amendments The 1991 amendments also added a few other critical provisions designed to reinstate the actual intent of Congress in creating the original statute in 1964. For instance, the new law mandates that American businesses must give U.S. citizens working abroad the same protection against discrimination that they give workers in the United States. In addition, the new act makes it clear that an employment practice is illegal even if only a portion of the practice is discriminatory.

Amendment to the Equal Pay Act The Equal Pay Act was designed to help women undo more than 45 years of continued paycheck discrimination. This discrimination had taken place, despite the passage of the Equal Pay Act in 1963. The amendments clarify that employers cannot discriminate against women in any gender-related capacity that might be related to education, training, or background. Moreover, the amendments also specify that the 180-day time limit for filing a claim with the EEOC begins to run every time the worker is paid. Thus, the paycheck is a continuing wrong that hurts the worker each time she receives it. Finally, the statute also adds compensatory and punitive damages to the remedies available in a gender-based wage discrimination case.

After-Acquired Evidence in Relation to Discrimination Cases The EEOC has adopted an approach for discrimination cases in which after-acquired evidence reveals that the employer had a legitimate reason for discharging the employee. The rule, which applies only to cases involving the EEOC, states that the commission will not require that the employer rehire the claimant, nor will the commission attempt to recover back pay or compensatory damages that arise after the time that the after-acquired evidence was obtained. However, to avoid squelching the effectiveness of the 1991 amendments, the EEOC will still seek punitive damages in such cases.

Age Discrimination in Employment Act

The Age Discrimination in Employment Act (ADEA) prohibits discrimination on the basis of age. ADEA covers employment agencies, employers of 20 or more employees, and labor unions of more than 25 members. This act protects any person aged 40 years or older from discrimination in hiring, firing, promotion, or other aspect of employment. Like the Civil Rights Act, the ADEA is administered by the EEOC. Age discrimination claims must be registered with the EEOC no later than 300 days after the prohibited activity. Naturally, if age is a true job qualification, the law does not apply. For instance, if the job involves the modeling of junior miss fashions, it would not be discrimination to hire someone of suitable age to model the clothes. The courts, however, will carefully scrutinize all such requirements and generally be able to detect those that are merely a pretense covering age discrimination.

Thomas Taggart, aged 58 years, lost his position when the subsidiary he worked for was disbanded by Time, Inc., the parent corporation. All of the employees who were laid off as a result of the closing were promised preferential treatment for other jobs at Time, Inc. Taggart applied for more than 30 of these positions. He was never rehired. Most of the time the reason given for his rejection was that he was overqualified. Taggart brought an age discrimination suit under the ADEA. Time, Inc., argued that Taggart was not rehired because of an overqualification barrier that had nothing to do with his age. The court disagreed. The court ruled that calling Taggart overqualified was just another way of saying he was too old.

In 1990, Congress amended the ADEA in response to a U.S. Supreme Court case that held that the original ADEA did not cover employee benefit plans. The amendment, which is called the Older Workers Benefit Protection Act (OWBPA), makes it clear that the ADEA forbids discrimination against older workers in the handling of their employee benefit and retirement plans. In addition, OWBPA gives older workers legal recourse if they are forced or tricked into giving up their rights under the ADEA. Usually this situation occurs when the employee is asked to sign a waiver. A waiver of rights is valid only if it is given freely and without force or coercion. The employer has the job of proving that the waiver is valid if it is introduced as evidence in court.

Uniformed Services Employment and Reemployment Rights Act

Under provisions of the Uniformed Services Employment and Reemployment Rights Act (USERA), an employee who has served in the armed forces and successfully completed his or her tour of duty is entitled, upon returning to work, to be reinstated in his or her previous position on the job. Unlike the Civil Rights Act, which is controlled by the EEOC, USERA is administered by the Veterans' Employment and Training Service (VETS). Also unlike the Civil Rights Act, under USERA, employees may file a complaint with VETS, or they can take the case directly to court. No statute of limitations is connected to USERA. However, employees are not permitted to hold back on the filing of a case for an unreasonable length of time. Employees who succeed in a case might receive damages, an injunction to prevent their termination, and sometimes, at the discretion of the judge, attorneys' fees.

Americans with Disabilities Act

The Americans with Disabilities Act (ADA) is designed to open the American workplace to this country's disabled citizens. The ADA is divided into several titles. Title I lays out the duties imposed on private-sector employers, whereas Title II covers public services and public transportation. The ADA is administered by the EEOC. The ADA carefully outlines what is considered a disability. It also explains who and what are covered by the act and what practices are specifically forbidden.

Disabilities The ADA defines disability as any physical or mental impairment that substantially limits one or more of the major life activities. This definition includes paralysis, blindness, deafness, cancer, mental retardation, learning disabilities, and AIDS, among others. Excluded from protection are people with kleptomania, pyromania, or gambling disorders. Nor does the act extend to people who use illegal drugs. The definition of disability also does not include homosexuality or bisexuality. However, because the act forbids discrimination against people who are associated with a particular disability, discrimination against homosexuals, on the basis of the claim that they are more likely to contract AIDS, would be forbidden.

Activities and Individuals Covered by ADA Discrimination is forbidden in the screening of applicants, initial hiring, and on-the-job treatment. This protection against discrimination also extends to apprenticeship programs, promotions, pay raises, and on-the-job-training opportunities. Individuals, including both employees and applicants for employment, cannot be segregated or classified because of a disability. The ADA also protects an individual from discrimination because that individual is associated with someone who has a disability. As is true of other situations, a state statute that gives individuals with disabilities more protection than the ADA would supersede the federal statute.

Forbidden Practices The ADA forbids discrimination on the basis of a disability if the disabled individual can do the essential functions of the job with "reasonable accommodations." Exactly what would qualify as a reasonable accommodation in a given set of circumstances is, at best, problematic. Nevertheless, the statute does give some guidance in determining the extent of a **reasonable accommodation**. An accommodation will be reasonable if it permits the disabled individual to accomplish the essential functions of the job without imposing an undue hardship on the employer. Factors used in determining whether a proposed accommodation will cause **undue hardship** include the type of accommodation needed, the expense involved in providing the accommodation, the financial ability of the company to provide the necessary accommodation, and the size and nature of the company involved. Because of the innovative nature of the law and the lack of precedent, the EEOC has decided to follow a case-by-case evaluation of all claims filed by disabled individuals against employers.

Genetic Information Nondiscrimination Act

Congress has become increasingly disturbed over the unauthorized use of generic information to invade the privacy of employees or to make employment decisions based on that information. To combat this threat, Congress passed the **Genetic Information Nondiscrimination Act (GINA)**. GINA was written to protect employees by making it unlawful for employers and health insurance companies to make decisions based on any genetic information that they have acquired due to any type of genetic testing. Under the statute, the purpose of the test is immaterial. GINA targets health insurance companies, forbidding them to use genetic information to make changes in premiums or in employee contributions. On the other hand, the new statute does permit medical professionals, such as physicians, nurses, therapists, technicians, and the like, to use genetic tests and to compile genetic information for health care reasons. In fact, the law even permits health insurance providers to establish payment schedules for their clients based on genetic information. Still, GINA demands that insurers use as little of the genetic information as possible to make such decisions. In contrast, employers are forbidden to use genetic information to make hiring, firing, promotion, vacation, continuing education, professional development, transfer, budgetary, work schedule, and salary decisions. The law also forbids unions, employment agencies, and joint labor–management committees from discriminating against individuals in any employment-related decisions related to genetic information. In fact, all employment-related decisions must be made free of any influence from the genetic information. Moreover, employers, unions, employment agencies, and joint labor–management committees cannot request, require, or purchase genetic information unless required by law, used to protect individuals from toxic substances, or as part of a forensic investigation for law enforcement purposes. [See: David J. Kovach, "GINA," Ohio State Bar Association: 2010 Annual Convention (May 5-7, 2010): 6.1-6.5. See also "The Genetic Information Nondiscrimination Act," *Department of Health and Human Services* (April 6, 2009), 1, retrieved on September 25, 2010, from http://www.genome.gov; and "H.R. 493: Genetic Information Nondiscrimination Act of 2008," *Congressional Research Service,* 1, retrieved on August 20, 2010, from http://www.gov.track.us/congress/bill.]

The Whistleblower Acts

A **whistleblower** can be defined as an individual who notifies official federal or state authorities about illegal activities that take place in business, government, and other similar settings. The fact that whistleblowers can often be subjected to retaliatory actions by employers, landlords, law enforcement officials, and other authority figures has prompted the passage of federal and state laws that protect individuals who have identified and reported cases of fraud, discrimination, cover-ups, and other similar illegal activities to the appropriate watchdog agencies. Many federal laws involving employment, including the Civil Rights Act of 1964, the Age Discrimination in Employment Act, the Employee Retirement Income Security Act (ERISA), the Family and Medical Leave Act, the Americans with Disabilities Act, the Equal Pay Act, the Wagner Act, the Fair Labor Standards Act, and the Occupational Safety and Health Act (OSHA), among others, contain whistleblower protection provisions. In addition, many states have enacted their own employment-related whistleblower protection acts.

Anti-Retaliation Safeguards

As noted earlier, one of the most troubling problems in employment is the danger of retaliation. Generally, employees face such retaliation after filing a complaint against an employer under the Civil Rights Act or in accordance with similar employment-related legislation. However, retaliation can also occur when employees cooperate with discrimination investigations or simply work against discrimination in the workplace. Title VII of the Civil Rights Act 1964 includes a protection against such employer retaliation. However, the EEOC has also ruled that anti-retaliation provisions can be invoked by individuals under the Americans with Disabilities Act and the Age Discrimination in Employment Act. Thus, the classes protected against retaliation include race, color, creed, national origin, gender, age, and disability. The act also protects people closely associated with people who file complaints as well as individuals who witness discrimination.

To demonstrate that retaliation has occurred, an individual must show: (1) that he or she is in a protected class; (2) that retaliation did take place; and (3) that the retaliation took place because of an action that is protected under the law. As noted earlier, the protected classes include race, color, creed, national origin, gender, age, and disability. Retaliation includes demotions, suspensions, adverse schedule changes, alterations in job descriptions, exclusion from job-related opportunities, such as continuing education, and so on. Finally, protected actions include filing discrimination claims, providing testimony and/or evidence in a discrimination case, helping in-house investigators in discrimination cases, making in-house grievances about discrimination, suggesting that official discrimination claims might be pursued with the EEOC or another official agency, and resisting employer suggestions to ignore other cases of discrimination in the workplace, among others.

quick quiz 23-4

1. The term *affirmative action* refers to a practice by which an employer actively pursues a policy that will reduce the effects of past discrimination in the workplace.   true | false

2. American businesses working in other countries need not give U.S. citizens the same protection against discrimination under the Civil Rights Act as those afforded workers in the United States itself.   true | false

3. The Uniformed Services Employment and Reemployment Rights Act (USERA) is administered by the EEOC.   true | false

23-5 Social Media Policies

There is no way to escape the social media craze that has swept through the business world in the 21st century. Employees and employers use computers as part of their jobs and they expect everyone else, customers and suppliers alike, to do the same. In fact, computers have become so commonplace in business that it is possible, perhaps even likely, that most business people no longer even notice then. Nevertheless, it is crucial to remember that computers are all around us, even in places and in devices that we do not usually think of as computers. Moreover, it is also important to recall that when people become too accustomed to technology they can become careless.

The Social Media Culture

Business people must remember that computers include not only mainframes, desktop PCs, tablet computers, and laptops, but also mobile phones, notebooks, personal digital assistants (PDAs), digital recorders, GPS units, smartphones, scanners, fax machines, and wireless reading devices (WRDs). It would also be helpful to remember that to the business person it is not just the devices that are important—it is the data itself. Keeping trade secrets and protecting a client's or an employee's privacy may also mean protecting data and, at times, metadata. Metadata is data about data and includes such things as archival metadata, administrative metadata, structural metadata, descriptive metadata, intellectual property rights, human resources metadata, planning metadata, management metadata, financial metadata, product metadata, architectural metadata, engineering metadata, research-related metadata, preservation metadata, and so on.

It is also crucial to see that employees have become so immersed in computers that they frequently act as if those computers have always been there and will always work flawlessly. They communicate with one another, customers, suppliers, wholesalers, and retailers online. They use conference calls and webinars on a daily basis. They make purchases, pay bills, and sell goods on line. They "talk" to one another on mobile phones, with text messages, by e-mail, and on Twitter. When they go home they jump on Facebook, YouTube, or LinkedIn. They make connections on dating websites; plan trips using Orbitz, Priceline, or Travelocity; purchase hard-to-get items on e-Bay or Craigslist; buy books from Amazon.com or Barnes and Noble online; they blog, read blogs, or tell others about their favorite blogs; and if that were not enough, they take college courses, attend webinars, take certification exams, and earn advanced degrees online.

The Nature of a Social Media Policy

In some ways this makes conducting business easier, more economical, and more efficient. However, the social media craze also causes problems, and a business person must be aware of the legal risks involved when employees use social media outlets and what to do about it when things go wrong. There is, therefore, no question that every business needs to write and enforce a social media policy. A social media policy (SMP) is a set of rules written by an employer telling employees what they can and cannot do when using electronic communication devices, formats, websites, and electronic messaging techniques, such as blogs, text messages, tweets, Skype transmissions, and e-mails. The only remaining questions are what are the risks involved in social media; what must be included in an SMP; what is the proper way to communicate an SMP to employees; and what is the most effective way to enforce an SMP?

The Hazards Involved in Social Media

As noted earlier, social media has a very important role in the business world. It can be used to communicate effectively, to contact customers and suppliers, to store data, to write proposals and reports, to conduct video conferences and webinars, to pay company bills online, to disseminate information, and so on. The purposes are limited only by the imagination of the business person at the keyboard. However, there are also risks involved. Social media can be used to disclose trade secrets, customer lists, or other company information that is best kept confidential. It can be used to harass fellow workers or customers or to defame them or perhaps to invade their privacy. There are also legal limits set down by the Federal Trade Commission that might be violated inadvertently by the improper use of social media. For these reasons, among others, it is best for every company to write, publish, distribute, and enforce a social media policy.

The Proper Way to Construct a Social Media Policy A social media policy must include certain features. First, the policy must be written in a language and a style that is precise, exact, plain, and explicit. There must be no room for misinterpretation, because if the court has to interpret an ambiguous clause, its decision will likely be against the party who wrote the policy to begin with. Second, the policy must be given to the employees with the understanding that they will read and comprehend the details of the policy. Moreover, as part of this disclosure process, employees must be told up front that the employer intends to monitor their e-mail accounts and all additional online work.

The Content of a Social Media Policy First, in order to play fair with employees, the employer must let the employees know what activities are forbidden. Forbidden activities would include: sending out trade secrets, customer lists, and other private business-related data; using sexual comments and discriminatory remarks about anyone, but especially other employees, supervisors, clients, and suppliers; making remarks that are libelous, invade privacy, create emotional distress, or constitute product or ownership disparagement; and distributing any communication about company products or services that is not accompanied by a clear statement distancing the company from the author. In addition, it would be helpful to also outline what activities are appropriate using social media in the workplace.

The Procedures Associated with a Social Media Policy Once the policy has been written and explained to the employees, each of them should be given two copies of the policy, one to sign and return for their personnel file and one to keep as a reminder of what is expected of them. The employer should reserve the right to make alterations in the policy as experience reveals situations and events that were not predicted by the original policy. It is also crucial for the employer to remember that, even after the policy is distributed and the employees have been warned, there are limits to what an employer can do about violations of the policy [See: Adrienne L. Rapp, "The Responsible Employer's Social Media Policy," *Labor and Employment Update,'* Ohio State Bar Association Annual Conference, (May 6, 2011).]

Bring Your Own Device Clauses Social media policies must also deal with the trend that some business have adopted permitting employees to use their personal smartphones, laptops, and tablets on the job. This trend was almost inevitable given the fact that most modern electronic devices are more portable, more user-friendly, and more compact than in the past (witness the recent development of wristwatches that operate as miniature mobile computers). In light of this trend, some (many?) employers are permitting, some even encouraging, their employees to bring their own devices to the workplace. These personally owned devices are then programmed by the firm's IT experts, who create secure work areas for e-mail, employee forms, and other work-related files. This approach to such devices works well because people are accustomed to using their own devices and so the learning curve for applying those devices to work-related situations is less time-consuming and, therefore, more efficient and economical than training employees to use new, unfamiliar devices. Still, some employers prefer to provide workers with company-owned devices that are programmed by the IT department to include separate areas for the employee's personal use. Whichever technique is adopted, the employer must make certain that the SMP makes it clear that these devices are subject to surveillance and that all work-related data on such devices is company-owned and must, therefore, remain confidential.

quick quiz 23-5

1. Metadata is data about data.   true | false

2. A social media policy must be given to the employees with the   true | false
   understanding that they will read and comprehend the details of
   the policy.

3. The employer should reserve the right to make alterations in the   true | false
   social media policy as experience reveals situations and events
   that were not predicted by the original policy.

Summary

23.1 The employment-at-will doctrine means that an employer can dismiss an employee at any time for any reason. Employees who belong to labor unions and individuals with the power to negotiate their own employment contracts would not be affected. Wrongful discharge gives employees legal grounds for a lawsuit against employers who have dismissed them unfairly. The courts have used several theories to judge the injustice of a dismissal. These include promissory estoppel, fraud, implied contract, implied covenant, public policy tort, and intentional inflection of emotional distress.

23.2 OSHA establishes and enforces occupational health and safety standards with which employers must comply. The principal federal law affecting the wages and hours of employees is the Fair Labor Standards Act. The act provides that workers in interstate commerce or in an industry that produces goods for sale in interstate commerce must be paid no less than a specified minimum wage. The federal Immigration Reform and Control Act of 1986 created a national employment verification system that placed responsibility on the employer for verifying the identity and employment of all employees.

23.3 Federal and state governments participate in programs designed to reduce the financial risk to workers by reason of their unemployment, disability, hospitalization, retirement, and death. The principal federal law covering these risks is the Social Security Act of 1935. Under the Federal Unemployment Tax Act, each state operates its own unemployment insurance system, subject to conditions established by the federal government. Workers' compensation laws are in effect in all states. These statutes compensate covered workers or their dependents for injuries, disease, or death that occurred on the job or as a result of it. ERISA provides needed supervision over employee pension plans established by many employers. Under provisions of the Family and Medical Leave Act (FMLA), employers who have 50 or more employees must give those employees up to 12 weeks of leave time for child, spousal, or parental care.

23.4 The Civil Rights Act of 1964 prohibits discrimination based on race, color, creed, gender, and national origin. Employees who believe they have been discriminated against can file a complaint with the EEOC. Discrimination can be committed in one of two ways: disparate treatment or disparate impact. Other steps toward equality in employment include the Age Discrimination in Employment Act, the Uniformed Services Employment and Reemployment Rights Act, and the Americans with Disabilities Act.

23.5 A social media policy must be written in a language and a style that is precise, exact, plain, and explicit. The policy must also be given to the employees with the understanding that they will read and comprehend the details of the policy. Moreover, employees must be told that the employer intends to monitor their e-mail accounts and their online work. The employer must also let the employees know what activities are forbidden. In addition, it would be helpful to outline what activities are acceptable when using social media in the workplace. Once the policy has been written and explained to the employees, they should be asked to sign a copy. The employer should reserve the right to make alterations in the policy. The employer needs to remember that even after the policy is distributed and the employees have been warned, there are limits to what an employer can do about violations of the policy.

Key Terms

affirmative action, 567

business necessity, 565

collective bargaining agreement, 550

constructive discharge, 557

disability, 569

disclaimer, 554

disparate impact, 565

disparate treatment, 565

employment at will, 549

employment contracts, 550

Genetic Information Nondiscrimination Act (GINA), 570

grievance procedure, 550

hostile work environment, 567

implied contract, 554

implied covenant, 556

metadata, 572

military caregiver leave, 562

qualifying exigency leave, 562

quid pro quo sexual harassment, 567

reasonable accommodation, 570

retaliation, 558

reverse discrimination, 567

social media policy (SMP), 572

undue hardship, 570

whistleblower, 571

workers' compensation, 561

workplace harassment, 566

wrongful discharge, 552

Questions for Review and Discussion

1. What is the doctrine of employment at will?
2. What contractual situations fall outside employment at will?
3. What statutory situations fall outside employment at will?
4. What are the wrongful discharge exceptions to employment at will?
5. What is the after-acquired evidence rule?
6. What laws regulate employee working conditions?
7. What laws provide worker benefits?
8. What are the key provisions of the Civil Rights Act?
9. What protections are provided by the Age Discrimination in Employment Act?
10. What is the nature of and the need for a social media policy?

Cases for Analysis

1. The Equal Employment Opportunity Commission (EEOC) recently has been hit with many newly filed cases that allege discrimination based on caregiver status. The cases involve, for example, a police officer who was not promoted because she had young children at home, a man who was fired for taking time off to care for his sick father, a class action case against an employer that discriminated against workers who had applied for FMLA leave, and a case filed by a man who took leave time to take care of his elderly parents. Caregiver discrimination, which is officially known as family responsibility discrimination, or FRD, has caused some experts to suggest that the EEOC should create guidelines that are specifically aimed at defining and outlining the elements of FRD. Others argue that there really is no such thing as FRD and that each case must be treated for what it really is, that is, gender discrimination, age discrimination, disabilities discrimination, family leave discrimination, or some other form of specifically delineated

discrimination. What existing statutes could be called upon to handle FRD cases, even if those cases must go by another, more traditional name? [See: Tresa Baldas, "EEOC Looks at Caregiver Bias: Suits Involving Family Care Rise," *The National Law Journal*, May 21, 2007, pp. 1 and 18.]

2. Eugene Meade was offered a job by Cedarapids, Inc. The job required moving to Eugene, Oregon, where Cedarapids, Inc., had a facility called the El-Jay Plant. To entice Meade to join the Cedarapids staff, management representatives told him that business was improving, that they believed in the potential of the El-Jay plant, that El-Jay sales were growing, that production at the plant was also increasing, and that there were plans to bring in even greater numbers of new employees. On the basis of these assurances, Meade left his job and moved to Oregon. He also signed an agreement that noted that he was an at-will employee who could be fired at any time. Meade later discovered that all of the statements about the financial health

of the El-Jay plant were false. Furthermore, Meade believed that the management had known all along that the statements were false. Meade learned that the El-Jay plant was actually caught in a downward economic spiral and was about to close. When Meade was discharged, he brought a lawsuit against Cedarapids, Inc., arguing that he had been defrauded into moving to Oregon. In response, the Cedarapids management team argued that they had no duty to disclose the plan to shut down the Oregon facility. The management team also pointed to the agreement that Meade had signed and concluded that, as an at-will employee, he could not complain about his firing. The trial court agreed and dismissed the case. Meade then filed an appeal. Is there enough evidence of fraud in this case to allow it to go to a jury? Explain. [See: *Meade v. Cedarapids, Inc.* Case No. 97-35836 (The United States Court of Appeals for the Ninth Circuit).]

3. Carla McFarland was an associate professor of English literature at Highland College. She was the only single person in her department. Consequently, she was frequently assigned classes late in the evening, on weekends, and during the summer semester. She was also called upon to pick up visiting professors and serve as their escort and guide during their stays at the college. She received extra duty as adviser to *The Highland Review,* the college's literary magazine. When McFarland complained about the unequal treatment, she was told that the married professors had family responsibilities that she did not have, which took up much of their time and prevented them from having the flexibility that she had. Thus, she would continue to carry the extra load. McFarland filed a complaint with the EEOC. Can discrimination based on an employee's status as a single person be considered unlawful under the Civil Rights Act? Explain. Is this a case of disparate impact or disparate treatment? Explain. [See: Robin Wilson, "Singular Mistreatment: Unmarried Professors Are Outsiders in the Ozzie and Harriet World of Academe," *The Chronicle of Higher Education,* April 23, 2004, pp. A10–A12.]

4. Henderson worked as a chemical engineer for the Wannisky Chemical Corporation. McGuire, Henderson's supervisor, ordered him to remove the labels from several hundred steel drums that had once contained a severely corrosive acid. McGuire told Henderson that they intended to reuse the drums to ship a new chemical fertilizer. Henderson refused to remove the labels because reusing the old drums would violate both state and federal laws. When McGuire told another employee to remove the labels and reuse the drums, Henderson reported the company's activities to the state and federal authorities. Henderson was fired for his refusal to follow orders and for notifying the authorities. In a lawsuit against Wannisky, which legal exception to the employment-at-will doctrine did Henderson use? Explain.

5. Bennerson was employed by the Checker Garage Service Corporation as an auto mechanic. His duties included both assisting mechanics in the garage and making road calls to service vehicles owned and operated by his employer. During his lunch hour, Bennerson used one of his employer's taxi cabs to drive to a restaurant. En route to the restaurant, he was seriously injured when the taxi struck a pole. Bennerson filed a claim before the workers' compensation board. His claim was granted. Checker Garage appealed, arguing among other things that the taxi that Bennerson drove did not "go out of control" but that Bennerson had lost control. Was Checker correct? Explain. [See: *Bennerson v. Checker Garage Service Corporation,* 388 N.Y.S.2d 374 (NY).]

6. Nancy Barillaro and Nancy Fotia were employed in the inspection and trimming departments of Elwood Knitting Mills for approximately 16 years. Barillaro was laid off in September and Fotia in November. Both were offered the option of returning to work in March of the following year as knitting machine operators, but at an 18 percent reduction in pay. Neither accepted the offer. They argued that the offered work would have involved a loss in seniority and a substantial reduction in pay. In addition, Fotia claimed that she was not familiar with the operation of the machine. Barillaro claimed that she was too short to operate the machine. The Pennsylvania Unemployment Compensation Board decided that neither claimant was eligible to receive benefits because they refused offers of suitable work without good cause. Was the board correct in its ruling? Explain. [See: *Barillaro v. Unemployment Compensation Bd. Of Review,* 387 A.2d 1324 (PA).]

7. The Wynn Oil Company, which conducted an enormous amount of business with Latin American companies, argued that being male was a bona fide occupational qualification (BFOQ) for the position of sales executive. Wynn contended that because of certain Latin American customs, the hiring of a female sales executive would have a serious detrimental effect on the company's business. The contention was challenged in federal court. Will

Wynn's argument succeed? Explain. [See: *Fernandez v. Wynn Oil Co.,* 653 F.2d 1273 (9th Cir.).]

8. The Spelling Entertainment Group hired actress Hunter Tylo to appear in the television show *Melrose Place.* Her role was to involve the seduction of another character's husband. When Tylo became pregnant, she dutifully reported her condition to Spelling. The entertainment company then discharged her, arguing that non-pregnancy was a bona fide occupational qualification (BFOQ) for the role designed for Tylo. Tylo challenged the contention that her condition disqualified her from performing her job. Can non-pregnancy be a BFOQ? Explain. [See: *Tylo v. Superior Court,* 55 Cal. App. 4th 1379 (CA).]

9. Rice, an African-American woman, was denied employment as a public health representative by the City of St. Louis for lack of a college degree. Failing to obtain relief after filing a complaint with the EEOC charging racial discrimination, she filed a lawsuit in the federal district court. Rice took the position that the degree requirement had a disparate impact on African-Americans and was invalid under the Civil Rights Act of 1964. She pointed out that blacks were only approximately 55 percent as likely as whites in the St. Louis area to have a college degree. Testimony showed that the satisfactory performance of public health representatives required the ability to communicate with others, frequently in emotional situations, and the ability to speak and write intelligibly. There was also a risk to the public health and safety in the employment of unqualified applicants. Did Rice prevail? Explain. [See: *Rice v. The City of St. Louis,* 607 F.2d 791 (8th Cir.).]

10. The Commonwealth of Virginia required all applicants for state troopers to be between 21 and 29 years of age, at least 5 feet, 9 inches tall, and at least 156 pounds. The height and weight requirements eliminated 98 percent of the female applicants. The basic employment requirements also made it mandatory that all applicants, including applicants for civilian dispatcher positions, complete and pass written mental ability tests. The tests for dispatcher positions were not valid predictors of job performance. The tests for the trooper positions also were shown not to be predictors of job performance. The United States brought suit, charging that Virginia engaged in a pattern and practice of discrimination against African-American applicants for the civilian positions and against both African-American and women candidates for the trooper positions. Did the United States prevail? Explain. [See: *United States v. Commonwealth of Virginia,* 620 F.2d 1018 (4th Cir.).]

11. Shirley Painter was the chief deputy clerk in the bookkeeping department of the Civil Division of the Municipal Court of the City of Cleveland. She decided to run for city council and asked for a leave of absence to pursue that goal. At first she was granted the leave. However, two months later, she was terminated. Painter brought a wrongful discharge lawsuit against Charles Graley, the assistant personnel director in the municipal court clerk's office. Painter asked to be reinstated. She also asked for back pay and punitive damages. Her wrongful discharge suit was based on a violation of public policy. She argued that she had appropriate grounds for the suit because her termination violated the state constitution. Graley argued that a plaintiff can bring a wrongful discharge lawsuit based on public policy only if a statute exists that prohibits the firing in question. Has Painter stated sufficient legal grounds for her wrongful discharge lawsuit? Explain. [See: *Painter v. Graley,* 639 N.E.2d 51 (OH).]

quick quiz Answers

23-1	23-2	23-3	23-4	23-5
1. F	1. F	1. F	1. T	1. T
2. F	2. F	2. F	2. F	2. T
3. F	3. F	3. F	3. F	3. T

Chapter 24   Labor Law

THE OPENING CASE *Round 1*
Northwestern (read "Employer" here) v. The College
Athletes Players Association (read "Union" here)

It was bound to happen one of these days, to one university or another, but it was Northwestern University (NU) that ultimately got the call—the call to enter uncharted territory. That call came when the College Athletes Players Association (CAPA) filed a petition with the National Labor Relations Board, asking the NLRB to permit the football players at NU to vote on whether to unionize. NU, of course, opposed the petition. The arguments put forth by the university can be summarized as follows: (1) The football players are not employees no matter how the term is defined but are, instead, students, as determined by an earlier case known as *Brown University,* 342 NLRB 483 (2004); (2) if the NLRB decides that the students are employees, they are, at best, temporary employees that have no right to unionize; and/or (3) even if the students are full-time employees, the potential bargaining unit, the CAPA, is not a "labor organization" under the Wagner Act and, therefore, has no standing to represent the players or to present the petition. The second and third arguments are easy enough to refute (and, in fact, were probably added as delaying tactics). Starting from the last and moving to the first argument, the university contended that CAPA is not a proper bargaining unit because it does not fit the definition found in the Wagner Act. The NLRB rejected the argument, saying that the CAPA clearly qualified as a union

because it "exists for the purpose . . . of dealing with employers on their (the employees) behalf regarding wages, hours of employment and other conditions of employment." As for the second argument, well, the NLRB easily ruled that the players are full-time employees, saying: (1) The players have a lengthy tenure at NU (four to five years); (2) they work more than 40 hours per week; (3) they work year round; and (4) they have a vested interest in their role as athletes (unlike others, such as student janitors, who focus on their studies and have no vested interest in their employment other than as a way to finance their student careers). The first argument is the real stumbling block. Are the players employees or are they students? This question was critical because the CAPA's entire case was based on the belief that the players were employees. If they were employees, then the rest of the arguments would easily fall into place. If they were not, the rest of the arguments fell apart. The problem was that the Wagner Act defines *employees* in a simple and, to be candid, a very unproductive way. The act says that the term *employees* includes "any employee." In order to unravel the true meaning of employee, the NLRB representative had to dive into case law and examine the common law definition of employee, a definition that was probably created by a medieval judge who did not even know what a football was, let alone a football player. How the NLRB answers this question is one of the key elements in this chapter. If you want to know, keep reading. [See: *Northwestern University, Employer v. College Athletes Players Association, Petitioner,* National Labor Relations Board, Region 13, Case Number, 13-RC-121359 (2014).]

Opening Case Questions

1. Who is the petitioner in this case? Explain.

2. What three issues are presented to the NLRB representative in this case? Explain.

3. Why are the second and third arguments characterized as delaying tactics? Explain.

4. How does the court rule on those two issues? Explain.

5. What is the remaining issue? How should the court rule on the remaining issue? Explain.

LO Learning Objectives

1. Relate the historical context in which unions developed.
2. Outline the congressional–judicial tug-of-war in union history.
3. Identify the major provision of the Norris–LaGuardia Act.
4. List the basic aims of labor unions.
5. Explain the nature of the 21st century crisis in labor law.
6. Indicate the primary tenets of the Wagner Act.
7. List the functions of the Taft–Hartley Act.
8. Explain the provisions of the Landrum–Griffin Act.
9. Describe the jurisdiction of the National Labor Relations Board.
10. Identify the possible results of a complaint filed with the NLRB.

24-1 Labor Law and the Economic Crisis

A labor union is an organization that acts on behalf of all employees in negotiations with the employer regarding the terms of their employment. It is a lawful assembly that is protected by the First Amendment to the U.S. Constitution and by federal and state statutes. Americans have always had a love–hate affair with unions. On the one hand, most Americans would like the marketplace to work without undue interference from the government. On the other hand, most Americans also acknowledge that businesses, when left unregulated, often take advantage of that freedom and exploit the labor market. This tension between a free market and a protective government is also seen in economics. The two dominant schools of economic thought in academia today are the Keynesians and the Austrians. At the risk of oversimplifying things (always a danger when speaking of economics) we can say that the Keynesians, named for their founder, the British economist John Maynard Keynes, push for governmental intervention into the economy in order to protect the workers, to control debt, to provide support for industry, and to control the money supply, while the Austrian school, notably Friedrich Hayek and Joseph Schumpeter, argue that government intervention does more harm than good because it permits weak financial firms to survive, thus postponing, but not eliminating, an economic crisis, a crisis that, as strange as it may seem, is necessary for the economy to correct itself.

Labor, unfortunately, falls in the middle of this mess and, at times, is sometimes supported and sometimes victimized by both sides. The Austrians would suspend or

John L. Lewis (left), founder of the Congress of Industrial Workers (CIO), and Samuel Gompers (right), founder of the American Federation of Labor (AFL), combined to form the AFL-CIO in 1955. Labor unions continue to shape the way companies operate.

eliminate labor unions and allow unprofitable companies to collapse to be replaced by profitable companies that rehire the unemployed workers of the collapsed firms, probably at better wages and in better workplace conditions than those that could be offered by collapsing firms. The Keynesians, in contrast, see unions as a necessary governmental control device, granting workers the power to determine their own wages and benefits, and thus permitting the government, in the form of the National Labor Relations Board, the courts, and Congress, to lawfully interfere in the operation of that business, thus preventing such economic implosions. This seesaw-like relationship is evident in the historical development of the union movement in the United States, and it provides a further example of the law as a balancing act. [See: Nouriel Roubini and Stephen Mihm, *Crisis Economics* (New York: Penguin Books, 2010), pp. 47–59.]

An Economic Tug-of-War

The history of union development in the United States provides us with a vivid example of the give and take between two economic theories: (1) the Keynesian strategy that approves of governmental control; and (2) the Austrian school that supports a laissez-faire approach to the economy. In this case, the legislature and the courts were at odds for a long period of time and played off one another in a complicated tug-of-war as they attempted to reestablish a balance within the law. Although this legal tug-of-war had no definitive beginning, for convenience, we can identify the passage of the Sherman Antitrust Act in 1890 as a logical starting point. This statute was designed to break up the great anticompetitive trusts of the 19th century. As such, the passage of the Sherman Antitrust Act was an Austrian-like tactic designed to encourage competition in the capitalist economy. Ironically, in fashioning the Sherman Act to promote Austrian-like competition, Congress used its power to interfere in the economic sector, a very Keynesian-like tactic. The courts responded by issuing injunctions that permitted the corporations to use the Sherman Act to break up unions, another Keynesian tactic that, strangely, promoted Austrian principles.

The Clayton Act of 1914 Congress reacted to this example of judicial activism by passing the Clayton Act in 1914, another Keynesian-like tactic that forced companies to cooperate with union organizers and thus helped keep people employed. One of the goals of the Clayton Act was to hamper the federal courts' ability to issue injunctions to stop union activities. This would force businesses to recognize the role of unions as a way for employees to protect their rights. The federal judicial system, however, again reflecting an Austrian-like desire to pull the government out of the economic sector, effectively destroyed the Clayton Act when the Supreme Court created two criteria that allowed the courts to issue injunctions freely to stop labor activities. The first test was *the objectives test*. Under this test, a court could issue an injunction if it determined that the goal of a strike was unlawful. Under the second test, *the means test,* the courts could stop a strike if it was conducted in an unlawful manner. The two tests were easily manipulated by big business and the courts cooperated by routinely issuing injunctions in ways that had not been foreseen nor intended by Congress. Once again a pro-Keynesian strategy (court-issued injunctions) had been used to reestablish an Austrian-like economy (a union-free, strike-free economic system).

A QUESTION OF ETHICS

Creative Destruction or Government Regulation: The Austrians v. The Keynesians

Recall that the leading schools in economic philosophy in intellectual circles in the modern age are the Keynesians and the Austrians. Predictably, the two schools agree on almost nothing, and so there is a clear dialectic split between the two groups, a split that inevitably affects labor, labor law, and the labor union concept. The two schools of thought do agree on one premise, however, and that is a belief that capitalism is unstable. Unfortunately, they disagree on what to do about that instability. The Keynesians advocate governmental involvement to protect the economy. The basic idea is that the best way to control an inherently unstable economy is to intervene in a rational way in order to reset the market's equilibrium. Conversely, the Austrians maintain that government intervention does more harm than good because it allows, even at times encourages, fragile businesses to continue, thus stalling, but not stopping, an economic collapse, a collapse that is needed for the economy to rebalance itself. To summarize, the Keynesians see instability as a harmful trend needing rational governmental correction, while the Austrians see it as the normal program of events that must remain unaffected by the government. Before you consider the following questions, turn back to Chapter 1 to review the various ethical theories noted there (market value ethics, social contract theory, utilitarianism, and rational ethics). Then, using one of those theories in a consistent way, answer the following questions on *creative destruction* and *government regulation* (or Austrianism v. Keynesianism). Is there a balancing principle hidden somewhere in this conflict or is the Keynesian-Austrian dialectic unresolvable? Which side (the Austrians or the Keynesians) seems to have the correct approach from an ethical perspective? Would you rather see the government step in or step out of the economy? [See: Nouriel Roubini and Stephen Mihm, *Crisis Economics* (New York: Penguin Books, 2010), pp. 47–59.]

The Norris–LaGuardia Act of 1932 Not to be outdone, Congress reacted to this subterfuge by passing another pro-Keynesian law, the Norris–LaGuardia Act, in 1932, the net effect of which was to prohibit the federal courts from issuing injunctions against union-organized strikes, thus forcing companies to do what Congress had wanted all along, to cooperate with union organizers and thus keep people working. The law also supported union activities by forbidding the courts from using injunctions to stop picketing or boycotts organized by unions, again forcing businesses to cooperate with union organizers.

The Goals of Labor Organizations

The Norris–LaGuardia Act was just one step down a long road of labor law development. Later labor laws both promoted the aims of labor unions while also preventing unions from becoming too powerful, thus perpetuating the Keynesian-Austrian balance (some might say tug-of-war). Many different types of unions have developed over the years since the advent of the Norris–LaGuardia Act. Whatever their form, however, labor unions have several objectives in common. These Keynesian-like goals include (1) creating a seniority system to protect workers' jobs from arbitrary layoffs and replacement with less demanding wage earners; (2) upgrading worker status through wage and fringe benefit increases; and (3) sponsoring laws that improve social, economic, and political conditions for worker.

The 21st Century Labor Crisis

Over the last few years, the battle over unions has started once again. Stymied by the recent economic meltdown caused by subprime loans, falling real estate prices, and uncontrolled debt, state governments have elected to use an odd hybrid of Keynesian-Austrian tactics on themselves. In a strangely schizophrenic pattern of activity, the state governments have decided that labor unions that represent state workers must be eliminated. In essence, the governors and the state legislatures of several midwestern states, notably Wisconsin, Ohio, and Michigan, created and passed legislation that was deliberately and unapologetically designed to eliminate the collective bargaining power of those unions that represent state workers (see Table 24-1). In theory, this plan would save the state governments a great deal of money, money that will not be paid in raises, health care benefits, and pension

Table 24-1 Provisions of Ohio's Antiunion Law (2011)

Provision	Explanation
Health Insurance	Employers cannot pay more than 80% into the cost of employee health insurance benefits.
Pension Plans	Stops public employers from paying employee contributions to state retirement systems.
Merit Pay	Mandates merit pay; takes step increases and all other automatic pay increases off the negotiating table.
Strikes and Mediation	Eliminates public employees' right to strike and to submit disputes to any agreed upon dispute resolution procedure.
Collective Bargaining I	Eliminates the collective bargaining rights of K-12 teachers in relation to class size, workload, and workforce size.
Collective Bargaining II	Eliminates collective bargaining completely for college and university faculty members.
Fiscal Emergencies	Municipalities, counties, school districts in fiscal emergency status can ignore past collective bargaining agreements. Also occurs if the state itself is in a fiscal emergency.

Sources: Nick Thomas, "Sub. S.B. 5 of the 129th G.A.," *Fiscal Note and Impact Statement: State and Local Fiscal Highlights, Ohio Legislative Service Commission* (February 2011); and Amanda Garrett, "Ohio's Senate Bill 5 Could End Collective Bargaining for Many Public College Professors," *Cleveland.com* (March 2011). See also Bill Analysis, Legislative Service Commission, Sub. S.B. 5, http://www/legislature.state.oh.us.)

contributions. Of course, this would also mean fewer dollars in the pockets of almost 360,000 workers in Ohio alone, which, of course, decreases the buying power of state citizens, citizens who will no longer be spending quite as much money in stores, restaurants, hotels, and shops in their home states. (Note: Ohio voters rejected the antiunion law by a 61-39 percent margin in November 2011.)

quick quiz 24-1

1. A labor union is an organization that acts on behalf of all employees in negotiations with the employer regarding the terms of their employment.   true | false

2. Labor union activity is not protected by the First Amendment.   true | false

3. The Norris–LaGuardia Act empowered the courts to issue injunctions to stop boycotts by workers.   true | false

24-2 Major Federal Labor Legislation

After the Norris–LaGuardia Act was passed by Congress in 1932, several tough labor laws were enacted. The three most important legislative enactments are the National Labor Relations Act of 1935 (generally referred to as the Wagner Act); the Labor-Management Relations Act of 1947 (popularly referred to as the Taft–Hartley Act); and the Labor

Table 24-2	Federal Laws Governing Labor-Management Relations	

Year	Law	Major Provisions
1914	Clayton Act	Exempted union activity from the antitrust laws
1926	Railway Labor Act	Provided for supervision of collective bargaining for railroads and airlines Established the National Mediation Board to conduct union elections and mediate employer-union disputes
1932	Norris–LaGuardia Act	Outlawed yellow-dog contracts Limited the power of federal courts to issue injunctions to halt labor disputes Guaranteed employees the right to organize into unions and to engage in collective bargaining
1935	Wagner Act	Created the National Labor Relations Board (NLRB) Authorized NLRB to conduct representative elections and to determine the bargaining unit Outlawed certain conduct by employers as unfair labor practices Authorized NLRB to hold hearings on unfair labor practice petitions
1947	Taft–Hartley Act	Outlawed certain practices by unions as unfair labor practices Allowed states to legislate right-to-work laws Provided an 80-day cooling-off period in strikes that endangered national health or safety Created a mediation and conciliation service to assist in the settlement of labor disputes
1959	Landrum–Griffin Act	Established a bill of rights for union members Required unions to adopt constitutions and bylaws Required unions to submit annual reports detailing assets, liabilities, payments, and loans Added further provisions to the list of unfair labor practices

Management Reporting and Disclosure Act of 1959 (often simply called the Landrum–Griffin Act). The first of these was designed to support labor's attempt to organize. The last two were designed to curb some unanticipated problems that accompanied the growth of unions in the United States. (See Table 24-2.)

The Wagner Act

The passage of the National Labor Relations Act in 1935 (commonly known as the Wagner Act) opened the door for the rapid growth of the union movement. It is probably the most significant U.S. labor relations statute in that it expressly sets forth the unfair labor practices prohibited for both employers and unions. The Wagner Act gives workers the right to organize by allowing them to form, join, or aid labor unions. It also establishes procedures for representative elections and collective bargaining. These basic rights are found in Title 29, Chapter 7, Subchapter II, Section 157, of the United States Code:

> Employees shall have the right to self-organization, to form, join, or assist labor organizations, to bargain collectively through representatives of their own choosing, and to engage in other concerted activities for the purpose of collective bargaining or other mutual aid or protection, and shall also have the right to refrain from any or all such activities except to the extent that such right may be affected by an agreement requiring membership in a labor organization as a condition of employment as authorized in section 158 (a) (3) of this title.

After a union has been chosen to represent the employees of a business, only that union can bargain with management. After the union has been set up at a business, individual workers cannot, on their own initiative, negotiate with management. The union has the exclusive right to bargain with the management of the business, even if the employees do not agree with how the union is handling a matter. The Wagner Act is also known for its creation of the National Labor Relations Board (NLRB), which hears and rules on charges that unfair labor practices have been committed by employers or by unions.

Employee and Labor Organization—Defined?

When first entering a subject as complex and multifaceted as labor law, and before describing the various provisions within that law, the legislature is usually very careful to define all relevant terms that will be used in that legislation. Sometimes such definitions take a great deal of space in the early sections of the law, and often people overlook these definitions. This is a mistake because the court will generally focus on such terms when litigation ensues. Unfortunately, sometimes the legislature is not much help. It may define a term in a simple and conservative way without providing much detail. In such cases, in trying to comprehend what the legislature means, the court will call on other sources such as the common law definition found in case law and those additional definitions that can be found in various restatements, legal treatises, law review articles, and so on. In the Wagner Act, for example, the legislature went to great lengths to define the term *labor organization* writing that a "'labor organization' means any organization of any kind, or any agency or employee representation committee or plan, in which employees participate and which exists for the purpose, in whole or in part, of dealing with employers concerning grievances, labor disputes, wages, rates of pay, hours of employment, or conditions of work." [See: 29 USC section 152 2(3).]

In contrast, when defining the term *employee,* the legislature was not quite as eloquent. The statutory definition of employee begins with a statement that says, quite simply, that an employee is "any employee." However, Congress then adds that the term *employee* shall:

> not be limited to the employees of a particular employer, unless this subchapter explicitly states otherwise, and shall include any individual whose work has ceased as a consequence of, or in connection with, any current labor dispute or because of any unfair labor practice, and who has not obtained any other regular and substantially equivalent employment, but shall not include any individual employed as an agricultural laborer, or in the domestic service of any family or person at his home, or any individual employed by his parent or spouse, or any individual having the status of an independent contractor, or any individual employed as a supervisor, or any individual employed by an employer subject to the Railway Labor Act [45 U.S.C. 151 et seq.], as amended from time to time, or by any other person who is not an employer as herein defined.

As can be seen here, most of the definition is devoted to covering what an employee is not. Consequently, whenever a court must define the term *employee,* that court must search through case law to find the common law definition as well as any other definitions that have been offered by various restatements, legal treatises, law review articles, and so on. In the case of the word *employee,* the courts have relied upon the common law definition as taken from the Restatement (Second) of Agency Section 2(2). That definition states, "An employee is a person who performs services for another under a contract of hire, subject to the others' control or right to control and in return for payment." [See: *Brown University,* 342 NLRB 483 49o, fn. 27 (2004) (citing *NLRB v. Town & Country Electric,* 516 U.S. at 94).]

Prohibited Activities: Unfair labor Practices

Various activities are prohibited by the Wagner Act as **unfair labor practices**, that is, improper employment practices by either an employer or the union. These activities include the following:

- Interference with employees' right to organize.
- Domination or interference with the formation or administration of any union.

THE OPENING CASE *Round 2*
Students or Employees? Academic Club or Labor Organization?

In the opening case, we learned that a local chapter of the College Athletes Players Association at Northwestern University filed a petition asking that a vote be permitted to see if the football players at NU would authorize the formation of a union. The university opposed the petition. The arguments put forth by NU were threefold: (1) The football players are not employees no matter how the term is defined but are, instead, students, as determined by an earlier case known as *Brown University,* 342 NLRB 483 (2004); (2) if the NLRB decides that the students are employees, they are, most certainly, temporary employees since they work for no more than four or five years, and are primarily students, who have no right to unionize; and/or (3) even if the students are full-time employees, the potential bargaining unit, the CAPA, is not a labor organization under the Wagner Act and, therefore, has no standing to represent the players or to present the petition. The first and the last arguments required that the NLRB representative at the hearing refer to the definition of *employee* (argument 1) and that of a *labor organization* (argument 3). The second argument depended on the first argument. To put it another way, if the NLRB ruled that the players are employees, moving one step further and ruling that they are full-time employees would be not be too hard. Now, returning to the question of whether the CAPA is a "labor organization," the NLRB decided that it is clearly a labor organization. In making its decision, the NLRB cited the statutory language of the Wagner Act, noting that the CAPA qualified as a union because it "exists for the purpose . . . of dealing with employers on their (the employees) behalf regarding wages, hours of employment and other conditions of employment." That leaves the question of whether the players are employees. Calling upon the common law definition found in case law and in the Restatement (Second) of Agency, the NLRB said, "An employee is a person who performs services

for another under a contract of hire, subject to the others' control or right to control and in return for payment." Looking at the evidence, the NLRB found that the coaching staff at NU uses a wide variety of techniques to control the activities of the players before, during, and after the season. Such areas of control include where they live, what vehicles they drive, whether they can leave the campus, whether they speak to the press, what they can place on the Internet, and so on. The players have a lengthy tenure at NU (four to five years) and work more than 50 to 60 hours per week before the season starts, 40 to 50 during the season, and 20 to 25 after the season. They can also receive as much as $250,000 in pay (although not as a salary, but in terms of overall financial perks) over a tenure of four to five years. This evidence was enough for the NLRB to declare that the players were employees. However, just to add icing to the cake, the NLRB also used the Brown University case as further authority. In that case, the NLRB ruled that graduate students are not employees and could not unionize. However, the NLRB makes several distinctions here, all of which underline the differences between graduate students and football players. They include that: (1) the players are not primarily students (the grad students are primarily students); (2) their athletic duties are not part of their curricular requirements for graduation (the grad students' duties are part of their core requirements for their degrees); (3) the academic faculty do not supervise the players (grad students are supervised by the faculty); and (4) the compensation received by the players is not like the financial aid received by the grad students. [See: *Northwestern University, Employer v. College Athletes Players Association, Petitioner,* National Labor Relations Board, Region 13, Case Number, 13-RC-121359 (2014); John Wolohan, "College Athletes Players Association v. Northwestern University," *Law In Sport,* April 25, 2014.]

- Discrimination to encourage or discourage union membership.
- Discharge for charges filed or testimony given.
- Refusal to bargain collectively.

Interference with Employees' Right to Organize An employer cannot interfere with employees when they are forming a union, selecting their representatives, voting, striking, picketing, or engaging in any other protected and legal acts. For example, an employer cannot threaten to fire or discipline a worker for union activity or reward workers who do not participate in union activities. Threats to eliminate certain benefits or privileges, to close the business, or to discharge workers for union activity also are prohibited.

EXAMPLE 24-1: Insubordination or Inconsistency: Which One Trumps the Other?

In his 10 years as a chef at the Imperial National Hotel in Houston, James Kirby might have been fired several times for violating work rules. He frequently refused to follow orders, disobeying direct instructions from his supervisor. When a union began organizing the kitchen service and housekeeping staff, Kirby strongly supported the effort. During the organizing campaign, Kirby apparently acted in an insubordinate manner and was discharged. At a subsequent NLRB hearing, his discharge was found to be tainted. On appeal, the court reasoned that, though Kirby was far from the valued and trusted employee the union claimed he was, the hotel had tolerated his insubordination for 10 years. The court held that Kirby's discharge was more the result of his union activities than his work performance and reinstated him with back pay.

Domination or Interference with the Formation or Administration of Any Union An employer cannot form a company-run union for its employees. The purpose of this prohibition is to bar company-run unions from bowing to the wishes of management. It is also an unfair practice to aid one union over another, place employer spies at union meetings, reward some union officials, or agree with a union that a closed shop will be maintained. A closed shop is a work site in which the employer, by agreement, hires only union members in good standing. It is usually lawful, however, to have a provision allowing a union shop in the employment contract. A union shop is a place of employment in which nonunion workers may be employed for a trial period of not more than 30 days, after which the nonunion workers must join the union or be discharged.

Discrimination to Encourage or Discourage Union Membership Intentional discrimination by the employer toward an employee to encourage or discourage union membership is an unfair labor practice. Such discrimination may involve assigning an employee to less desirable work or denying an employee the opportunity to participate in overtime work. Also viewed as discriminatory is constructive discharge, which occurs when an employee is demoted to a job with lesser pay or authority or poorer working conditions than a previously held job or when the employee is subjected to supervisory harassment. To avoid employee complaints of intentional discrimination, employers must rely on meaningful business reasons when bestowing or denying employment opportunities.

EXAMPLE 24-2: Constructive Discharge: Nothing Trivial About It

Teresa Remington was chosen by union members to serve as their representative in collective bargaining meetings with the Harrisburg Construction Company. After her selection, Remington was harassed by the general manager of her department for trivial matters pertaining to scheduled lunch breaks and the cleanliness of her locker in the break room. Remington has the right to file a complaint with the NLRB, charging constructive discharge due to her union activities.

Discharge for Charges Filed or Testimony Given It is unlawful for employers to discharge or otherwise discriminate against employees because they file charges or give testimony under the Wagner Act. The courts interpret discrimination under this provision to include discharge, layoff, failure to rehire or recall, and transfer of covered employees.

Refusal to Bargain Collectively An employer must negotiate with employee representatives over wages, hours, the effects of business changes on employees, grievance procedures, health benefits, seniority systems, dues check-offs, and vacations. Issues must be discussed willingly, free of delaying tactics, coercion, or harassment by both sides. The employer has no duty to agree to any union demands but must meet with employee representatives at reasonable times and places to bargain in good faith. Neither party can bargain about a closed shop contract, politics, religious issues, management functions, or foreign affairs. The NLRB has no jurisdiction over religious schools, both on labor relations grounds and by virtue of the religion clauses of the First Amendment of the U.S. Constitution. The U.S. Supreme Court has ruled that the requirements of collective bargaining would represent an encroachment upon the freedom of church authorities to shape and direct teaching in accordance with the requirements of their religion. Finally, the Wagner Act does not apply to most federal employees. Nor does it apply to state or local government employees. This is why it is possible for the state governments in Wisconsin, Ohio, and Michigan to attempt to alter the collective bargaining rights of firefighters, police officers, and teachers.

The Taft–Hartley Act

The Labor-Management Relations Act of 1947, popularly named the Taft–Hartley Act, established a means to protect employers in collective bargaining and labor organization matters. The act also prohibits union officials from using coercive or abusive tactics against its own members. A detailed list of unfair labor activities that unions, as well as employers, were forbidden to practice was added to those of the Wagner Act.

State Right-to-Work Laws State laws that prohibit labor–management agreements requiring union membership as a condition of getting or keeping a job are called right-to-work laws. These laws, in effect, outlaw both the closed shop and the union shop. Ordinarily, state labor laws have not applied to unions and businesses that are involved in interstate commerce and that are governed by federal labor laws. In fact, as noted earlier in the chapter, state labor laws generally focus only on those employees whose union activities are not regulated by federal labor law, such as state government workers. Nevertheless, the Taft–Hartley Act has created special rules with regard to state right-to-work laws. It provides that union shop contracts are legal only in states that do not forbid them. As a result, state right-to-work laws, where they exist, are applicable to most unions and businesses. All employees in the bargaining unit (i.e., a unit formed for the purpose of collective bargaining) are benefited by the collective bargaining agreement negotiated by the union, even if they have not paid union dues. However, nonunion employees lose all right to vote on union officers or collective bargaining agreements.

Limiting the Power of the NLRB Some members of Congress recently proposed limiting the power of the National Labor Relations Board to pressure an employer into keeping his or her business located in a particular state. Recall that some states have passed right-to-work laws that allow employees to opt out of union membership when a union is formed or presently operates in their workplace. This feature makes such states

attractive to businesses that would rather keep union membership in their business to a minimum. Some businesses have gone so far as to decide to move a plant or office from a non-right-to-work state into a state with a right-to-work law. In one case, the National Labor Relations Board issued an order that would have prevented a business from setting up a new facility in a right-to-work state. This order by the NLRB prompted some members of Congress to mount a campaign to amend the Wagner Act to limit the power of the board to frame such orders. Like the actions by the governors and the state legislatures in Wisconsin, Ohio, and Michigan, a proposal like this one in Congress further demonstrates the antiunion sentiment that has been growing within the government in the 21st century.

Free Speech Provision The Taft–Hartley Act includes a free speech provision that allows employers to comment freely on union organizing activities. The provision states that employers do not commit an unfair labor practice by speaking to employees about unions unless they threaten reprisal or promise some benefit to employees. For instance, an employer might properly inform its employees that they should not vote for a union, but a threat to fire anyone for favoring a union shop would be an unfair labor practice.

Employee Anti-Coercion Provision It is also an unfair labor practice for a labor union to try to coerce employees to join the union, block the employment of individuals who refuse to support a union, or encourage an employee to withdraw an unfair labor practice charge. A union can set rules for its internal operations and punish any member who refuses to follow them, but it cannot use force, violence, or intimidation against an employee. A union is also not permitted to discipline one of its members without good cause. The union has a duty to represent all of its members on an equal basis.

Secondary Boycott It is also prohibited for a union to engage in a **secondary boycott**. This action is a conspiracy in which a union places pressure on a neutral customer or supplier with whom the union has no dispute to cause the neutral entity to cease doing business with the employer with whom the union has a dispute. Under the Taft–Hartley Act provision, it is an unfair labor practice for a union (1) to strike against an employer because another employer uses nonunion employees, (2) to strike against a general contractor to force the contractor to stop dealing with a subcontractor, (3) to ask employees of another company not to load trucks carrying the products of a company the union is striking, or (4) to refuse to work on products made by nonunion employees.

EXAMPLE 24-3: Secondary Boycotts: Of Primary Concern

The Benning Oil Company sold fuel oil to the Monarchy Empire Hotel chain. The oil was shipped on tankers owned by the Metroliner Transport Corporation, whose employees were nonunion. The union representing Benning instructed its members to refuse to ship the fuel oil to the docks where the Metroliner tankers were docked to force Benning to stop using a nonunion shipper. This form of secondary boycott is an unfair labor practice because it involved an innocent employer in a union tactic intended to harm another employer.

National Emergency Strikes The Taft–Hartley Act gives the president of the United States special powers to deal with actual or threatened strikes that affect interstate

commerce or that endanger the nation's health and safety. On the basis of a board of inquiry's findings, the president can order the attorney general to petition a federal district
court to issue an injunction, stopping the strike for 60 days. The board of inquiry may then
require the union members to vote on the most recent offer within an additional 15-day
period and to send the results to the attorney general within five days after balloting.
When the injunction ends after this 80-day period, the employees may strike. However,
the president can then make legislative recommendations to Congress that would resolve
the dispute.

Other Prohibited Union Practices   Under other provisions of the Taft–Hartley
Act, unions cannot refuse to bargain collectively with an employer and must give notice to
the employer of an intention to strike prior to the termination date of a collective bargaining contract. It is also an unfair labor practice for a labor union to require an employer to
keep unneeded employees, pay employees for not working, or assign more employees to a
given job than are needed (i.e., **featherbedding**). Another provision of the law prohibits a
union from requiring employees who join a union to pay excessively high dues, fees, and
related expenses. To determine what is excessive, the courts consider the amounts other
unions charge and the employee's wages.

The Landrum–Griffin Act

The Labor Management Reporting and Disclosure Act of 1959, known as the Landrum–
Griffin Act, is a tough anticorruption law. It is designed to clean up the corruption and violence that had been uncovered in the internal affairs of unions. The law requires all unions
to adopt constitutions and bylaws and to register them with the secretary of labor. In addition, unions are required to submit annual reports detailing assets, liabilities, receipts,
sources, payments to union members exceeding $10,000, loans to union members and
businesses, and other monies paid out.

Bill of Rights Provision   An important part of the Landrum–Griffin Act is the
bill of rights provision for union members. This provision assures all union members of
the opportunity to participate in the internal affairs of their union. They are guaranteed
the right to vote in union elections, to speak at union meetings, and to receive union
financial reports.

Hot-Cargo Agreement   The Landrum–Griffin Act amended the Taft–Hartley Act,
making it an unlawful labor practice to become involved in a **hot-cargo contract**. In this
type of agreement, an employer voluntarily agrees with a union not to handle, use, or deal
in nonunion-produced goods of another employer.

quick quiz 24-2

1. The Wagner Act allowed unions to organize but did not identify any unfair labor practices.	true	false
2. Right-to-work laws were outlawed by the Landrum–Griffin Act.	true	false
3. The Taft–Hartley Act outlawed secondary boycotts.	true	false

24-3 The Collective Bargaining Process

The Taft–Hartley Act established a system for helping labor and management settle their disputes without causing a major disruption in the economy or endangering the public health and safety. Central to this collective bargaining process is the NLRB and the procedures it follows in settling labor–management disputes.

The National Labor Relations Board

The NLRB is a governmental commission that has the exclusive jurisdiction to enforce the Taft–Hartley Act and related laws. It has the power to act when cases are brought before it, but only in cases in which the employer's operation or the labor dispute affects commerce. Like most government regulatory agencies, the NLRB has investigative, regulatory, administrative, enforcement, and judgmental powers. It can make its own rules of procedure, conduct investigations into unfair labor practice charges, compel individuals to appear with papers relevant to the controversy, hold hearings, and issue orders. Appeals from the five-member board go first to the appropriate U.S. Court of Appeals and then to the U.S. Supreme Court.

Unfair Labor Practice Procedure

A person, union, or employer can file notice with the NLRB of an alleged unfair labor practice within six months after it occurs. It is important to remember that unfair labor practices include not only those practices that occur between management and the labor union but also those between a union and its own members. This point is a crucial part of the union representation process, because once a collective bargaining unit is formed, the employees have only one recourse when they have a grievance, and that is through the union. Consequently, the law imposes an affirmative duty on the unions to be fair in their representation of all members. This rule does not mean that the union cannot monitor its own internal affairs, nor does it mean that unions must represent those outside of the bargaining unit. However, once a worker becomes a member of a union, he or she has the right to expect fair and equal treatment, and the union has the duty to deliver such treatment or be liable for not doing so.

If the charge has merit, a complaint is issued to notify the offending party that a hearing is to be held concerning the charges. Efforts are made through arbitration to resolve the dispute before the hearing date. **Arbitration** involves the submission of the dispute to selected persons and the substitution of their decision for the judgment of the NLRB. If arbitration efforts fail, the hearing is held. In the event that the complaint is found to be valid, a cease-and-desist order may be issued, restoring the parties to the state that existed before the unfair practice began. For example, wrongfully discharged employees may be reinstated with or without back pay. Evidence at the hearing that does not support the complaint is dismissed. Either party to the hearing may subsequently appeal the NLRB action to the appropriate U.S. Court of Appeals and then to the Supreme Court.

Mediation The Taft–Hartley Act encourages labor and management to agree freely on the settlement of disputes. To further this effort to preserve labor peace and promote prompt settlements, Congress has formed the Federal Mediation and Conciliation Service. This body can act by itself or upon the request of either side to a labor dispute. Its mediation role is to offer nonbinding suggestions for settling the dispute, require the parties to negotiate, and force a vote by employees on an employer's offers.

Strikes, like the 2010 nurses' strike in Minnesota, can cause major inconvenience and hardship for the general public. Unions often count on public pressure to get favorable concessions from management.

CLASSIC CASE Social Media Policy as a Balancing Act: Employee Rights v. Company Protection

In the last chapter, we looked at what happens when an employer fails to implement a social media policy. Sometimes, however, the tables are turned and the mismanagement of an existing social media policy puts the employer on the spot. Such a situation occurred when an employee's use of Facebook violated her employer's social media policy. The question that emerged from the case focused on a section of the National Labor Relations Act (NLRA) that shields the speech of unionized employees who are engaged in "concerted activities for the purpose of . . . mutual aid and protection" [See: Title 29, Chapter 7, Subchapter II, Section 157 of the United States Code.] The exact meanings of the term "concerted activities" and the phrase "mutual aid and protection" were a bit uncertain until the case mentioned earlier brought Dawnmarie Sousa, an EMT employed by American Medical Response (AMR), to the National Labor Relations Board. Apparently, Sousa was fired for making disparaging remarks about her supervisor on Facebook. These remarks inspired several online responses from Sousa's co-workers. Evidently, Sousa had been the target of a customer complaint. Standard operating procedure at AMR required Sousa to write a response to that complaint. Sousa asked her supervisor to allow her to get help from a Teamsters' representative in writing her response. Simply stated, her supervisor said "no." At this point, or shortly thereafter, Sousa accessed Facebook and complained about her boss. At one point she wrote that she loved "how the company allows a 17 to become a supervisor." (It was later revealed that, at AMR, the number 17 refers to psychiatric patients.) When AMR learned about the Facebook discussion, Sousa was discharged because she had disobeyed an AMR rule that forbids workers from making unflattering remarks about AMR online. Sousa went to the National Labor Relations Board, and the agency filed a complaint on her behalf. The NLRB ruled against AMR, stating that Sousa's remarks were protected by the NLRA precisely because she had discussed working conditions with co-workers. According to the NLRB, this activity is protected by the NLRA as "concerted activities for the purpose of . . . mutual aid and protection." The NLRB also chastised AMR for developing a social media policy that was open ended and, as a result, violated NLRA rules. It was not just the employee's termination that bothered the NLRB; it was also the entire social media policy that AMR had created. The lesson to learn from this case is that a social media policy must be tailored very carefully as a balance between protecting the company and protecting free speech rights guaranteed to workers. [See: *In re American Medical Response of Connecticut,* as discussed in Steven Greenhouse, "Company Accused of Firing Over Facebook Posting," *The New York Times,* August 11, 2010; and Adrienne L. Rapp, "The Responsible Employer's Social Media Policy," *Labor and Employment Update,* Ohio State Bar Association Annual Conference (Columbus, Ohio, May 6, 2011).]

The Right to Strike in the Public Sector

In the public sector, when the general welfare, safety, health, and morals of the public are involved, the right to strike is restricted. Consequently, strikes by police, firefighters, refuse collectors, air traffic controllers, postal workers, and other public employees who perform vital services are generally illegal, unless specifically authorized by statute. The U.S. Code states that "an individual may not accept or hold a position in the government of the United States or the government of the District of Columbia if he participates in a strike or asserts the right to strike against the government." The U.S. Supreme Court has affirmed lower court rulings that there is no constitutional right to strike against the federal government. Thus, strikes by federal employees are substantially more than merely unfair labor practices; they are crimes.

A QUESTION OF ETHICS

Freedom of Speech for Public and Private Employees: An Unequal Standard

In the opening case in Chapter 23, Los Angeles County Deputy D.A. Richard Ceballos challenged a search warrant in a memo and during a meeting of law enforcement officers in the D.A.'s office. Subsequently, Ceballos was subjected to a number of retaliatory moves by his supervisors. After having a grievance rejected, Ceballos filed a claim under Section 1983 of Title 42 of the United States Code. In that case, Ceballos argued that he had been deprived of his constitutional right of free speech by being subjected to retaliatory moves for pointing out the conduct of some of his colleagues in obtaining a search warrant based on allegedly inaccurate information. Eventually, the U.S. Supreme Court ruled that when public employees *"make statements pursuant to their official duties,"* they are not protected by the First Amendment.

The problem is that, whenever public employees are on the job, they are generally *"commenting upon matters of public concern,"* and are, therefore, making statements *"pursuant to their official duties."* As a result, it appears that the Supreme Court has overruled the Pickering Rule and eliminated the right of public employees to speak freely on the job. The Ceballos case, then, amounts to an official gag order for public employees unless they are saying what their supervisors have told them to say. Now let's look at the recent public labor law crisis and combine what is happening there with the implications of the Ceballos case. Recall that the governors and the state legislatures of several Midwestern states, notably Wisconsin, Ohio, and Michigan, attempted (often unsuccessfully) to eliminate the collective bargaining power of public employee unions. Abolishing collective bargaining is not the same as placing a gag order on public employees, but such a move does eliminate the protection that unions give employees who want to speak out about conditions on the job.

Now, taking all this into consideration, contrast these events with those noted in *Sousa v. American Medical Response of Connecticut* and the Northwestern University case. In both these cases, the NLRB protected the free speech rights of private employees: The EMT was protected in the American Medical Response case and the football players were protected in the Northwestern University case. To summarize and simultaneously point out the contradictions among these cases, we can say the following: The private EMT has the right to text about her employer and the NU football players have the right to unionize, while the DA has no right to complain about allegedly inaccurate warrants, and police officers, firefighters, and teachers have no right to unionize in those states where the antiunion legislation is in effect. Is there an inherent unfairness within these governmental decisions? Before answering the next few questions, reconsider the different ethical theories mentioned in Chapter 1. Then, applying one, and only one, of those theories in a uniform way, respond to these questions.

1. What is the essential difference between a public worker and a private worker? Explain.
2. Should public workers have fewer rights than private sector workers? If so, why? If not, why not?
3. Does the profession of the public worker matter in determining the extent of protection for the worker's free speech rights? If so, what professionals deserve to have their freedom of speech protected and what professionals forfeit that First Amendment protection? Explain.
4. What trends in the sociopolitical economic sectors might account for this recent anti-public employee rights campaign? Explain.
5. If public workers have no right to free speech, but must remain within the "talking points" set up by their public employers, why are public officials (such as the secretary of State or the U.S. ambassador to the United Nations, for instance) subject to investigation when they simply repeat the "talking

points" given to them by that employer? Ceballos is punished for speaking his mind, while other public officials are penalized for not speaking their minds but, instead, saying whatever their superiors told them to say. How can these ethical inconsistencies be solved? Or can they be? Explain.

[See: *Pickering v. Board of Ed. of Township High School Dist.* 205, Will Cty., 391 U. S. 563 (1968); *Garcetti, et al. v. Ceballos*, 126 S. Ct. 1951 (U.S. Supreme Court; *In re American Medical Response of Connecticut,* as discussed in Steven Greenhouse, "Company Accused of Firing Over Facebook Posting," *The New York Times,* August 11, 2010; Adrienne L. Rapp, "The Responsible Employer's Social Media Policy," *Labor and Employment Update,* Ohio State Bar Association Annual Conference (Columbus, Ohio, May 6, 2011); *Northwestern University, Employer v. College Athletes Players Association, Petitioner*, National Labor Relations Board, Region 13, Case Number, 13-RC-121359 (2014).]

quick quiz 24-3

1. There is no appeal permitted after a decision has been rendered by the National Labor Relations Board. true | false

2. If a complaint is found valid under the NLRB procedures, a cease-and-desist order may be issued, restoring the parties to the state that existed before the unfair labor practice began. true | false

3. The United States Supreme Court has repeatedly affirmed that federal employees have a constitutionally protected right to strike. true | false

Summary

24.1 The first federal statute relating to labor was the Clayton Act, which attempted to prohibit federal courts from forbidding activities such as picketing and strikes. The Norris–LaGuardia Act specified acts, such as striking, picketing, and boycotting, that were not subject to federal injunctions.

24.2 The Wagner Act opened the door for the growth of labor unions. It set forth specific labor practices that were prohibited for employers and unions, established procedures for representative elections and collective bargaining, and created the NLRB. The Taft–Hartley Act outlaws specific conduct by unions as unfair labor practices and provides for an 80-day cooling off period in strikes that endanger national health or safety. The act also provides a mediation and conciliation service to assist in the settlement of labor disputes.

The Landrum–Griffin Act provides a bill of rights for union members, requires unions to report to the secretary of labor, and has added to the list of unfair labor practices.

24.3 The NLRB has exclusive jurisdiction to enforce labor–management relations laws with investigative, regulatory, administrative, enforcement, and judgment powers. Any person, union, or employer can file notice with the NLRB of an alleged unfair labor practice. If the complaint has merit, a hearing is held before the NLRB. If the complaint is found to be valid, an order may be issued restoring the parties to the state existing prior to the unfair practice. Appeals of NLRB actions can be taken to the appropriate U.S. Circuit Court of Appeals and then to the U.S. Supreme Court. The Federal Mediation and Conciliation Service was formed to encourage labor and management to agree freely on the settlement of their disputes. Its mediation role is to offer nonbinding suggestions for settling the dispute, require the parties to negotiate, and force a vote by employees on employers' offers. In the public sector, the right to strike is restricted. The U.S. Code states that "an individual may not accept or hold a position in the government of the United States or the government of the District of Columbia if he participates in a strike or asserts the right to strike against the government."

Key Terms

arbitration, 590

bargaining unit, 587

closed shop, 586

constructive discharge, 586

featherbedding, 589

hot-cargo contract, 589

labor union, 579

right-to-work laws, 587

secondary boycott, 588

unfair labor practices, 584

union shop, 586

Questions for Review and Discussion

1. What is the historical context in which unions developed?
2. What is the congressional–judicial tug-of-war in union history?
3. What are the major provisions of the Norris–LaGuardia Act?
4. What are the basic aims of labor unions?
5. What is the nature of the 21st century crisis in labor law?
6. What are the primary tenets of the Wagner Act?
7. What are the functions of the Taft–Hartley Act?
8. What are the provisions of the Landrum–Griffin Act?
9. What is the jurisdiction of the National Labor Relations Board?
10. What are the possible results of a complaint filed with the NLRB?

Cases for Analysis

1. Nine longshoremen, all of whom were members of Local 13 of the International Longshoremen's and Warehousemen's Union, found that they were having difficulty getting jobs. The problem seemed to be that Local 13 had refused to place them on a hiring list at the union's hiring hall. Because this list was the only way that union members could get jobs as longshoremen, the nine union members were in effect being boycotted by the union and, as a result, by all potential employers. When the out-of-work union members filed grievances with Local 13, they were effectively ignored. To challenge these actions (as well as others not covered here), the out-of-work longshoremen filed a complaint with the National Labor Relations Board (NLRB). The NLRB and the District Court dismissed the complaint, and the longshoremen appealed. The union argued that the question of whether to place certain members on the hiring list was a purely internal union affair that could not be challenged by the NLRB or the courts. The longshoreman contended that by refusing to place them on the list and ignoring their grievances, the union was being unfair to them. Should the appeals court overturn this ruling by the NLRB and the District Court? Explain. [See: *Richard Diaz, et al. v. International Longshoremen's and Warehousemen's Union, Local 13*, Case No. 04-56957 (U.S. Court of Appeals for the Ninth Circuit).]

2. The union representing employees of the Consolidated Manufacturing Company elected Franco and Allanson to act on their behalf at a collective bargaining session with management. At the session, Franco and Allanson demanded that the new collective bargaining agreement include terms that would require management to hire only union members in good standing. Management disagreed with this proposal. Instead, management offered a term in the agreement that would allow the company to hire nonunion workers for a trial period

lasting no more than 30 days. After the 30-day trial period, the nonunion worker would have to join a union. Which of these terms in the proposed collective bargaining agreement would be allowed under federal labor law? Explain. Management also proposed that the employee union be disbanded and replaced by a company-run union. Management argued that the new company-run union would not only be more efficient but also more economical than the current union. Would this proposal be allowed under federal labor law?

3. An employee was discharged for violating the company's no-solicitation rule in its factory and offices. The employee had persisted in soliciting union membership on company property during lunch periods. The company argued that its no-solicitation rule would have been enforced against not merely union solicitation but any solicitation. How would you decide? Why? [See: *Republic Aviation Corp. v. NLRB,* 324 U.S. 793 (U.S. Sup. Ct.).]

4. Having advised Exchange Parts Co. that it was conducting an organizational campaign, the union petitioned the NLRB for an election to determine whether it would be certified as the bargaining agent of the company's employees. During the organizational campaign, while the granted certification election was pending, the company announced five additional benefits for the employees, two of which were announced only a few days before the election. In the election, the employees voted against being represented by a union. The union then filed a complaint with the NLRB, charging the company with an unfair labor practice because it granted benefits while the campaign was taking place and the election was pending. The union argued that the company's actions interfered with the freedom of choice of the employees to determine whether they wished to be represented by the union. For whom would you decide? Why? [See: *NLRB v. Exchange Parts Co.,* 375 U.S. 405 (U.S. Sup. Ct.).]

5. Darlington Manufacturing Co. operated one textile mill that was controlled by Deering Milliken, which operated 27 other such mills. The union began an organizational campaign, which Darlington resisted. The employees filed charges of unfair labor practices with the NLRB. The board found in a subsequent hearing that the different mills controlled by Deering Milliken represented an integrated enterprise and that the closing of the

Darlington mill was due to the antiunion hostility of Deering Milliken. The NLRB ordered Deering Milliken to provide back pay to the workers until they obtained similar work. The court of appeals denied enforcement of the NLRB order, holding that an independent employer has an absolute right to close a business, regardless of notice. On review by the U.S. Supreme Court, how should the Court rule on the question of whether an employer has the absolute right to close part of a business, no matter what the reason? Why? [See: *Textile Worker's Union v. Darlington Mfg. Co.,* 380 U.S. 263 (U.S. Sup. Ct.).]

6. The NLRB conducted an election among employees of Savair Manufacturing Co. to determine whether the union would represent the employees. During the election, recognition slips were distributed. The employees were told by the union that if they signed the slips before the election, they would not have to pay an initiation fee if the union won. At least 35 employees signed the slips before the election, which the union won by a vote of 22 to 20. The company refused to bargain with the union, contending that the union, by offering possible benefits to employees for signing the recognition slips, was guilty of an unfair labor practice. Did the practice of the union prevent a fair and free choice of a bargaining representative? Why or why not? [See: *NLRB v. Savair Mfg. Co.,* 414 U.S. 270 (U.S. Sup. Ct.).]

7. The Department Store Employees Union was selected by the employees of the Emporium Capwell Company as their exclusive bargaining unit. Charges of discrimination in the workplace were levied against the company through the union. The union followed the grievance procedure, as established in the collective bargaining agreement. Some of the employees became dissatisfied with the union's handling of the case. Accordingly, they asked the union to begin to picket the company. Union officials advised these dissatisfied employees that according to the collective bargaining agreement, the union was bound to follow the established grievance procedure. The employees refused to cooperate with the grievance procedure and demanded that company management deal with them directly to establish an overall anti discrimination policy. Later the employees also picketed the store. Written notices were given to the picketing employees, telling them that they could be discharged if they repeated the conduct. The

employees ignored the notices and, after picketing on the following weekend, were discharged. The employees filed a complaint with the National Labor Relations Board, which found that it could not support the employees. The NLRB believed that such support would challenge the exclusive bargaining power of the union and thereby subvert the statutory intent of Congress. The appeals court hearing the case reversed the board's findings, stating its belief that discrimination cases had a special position and thus fell outside the guarantee to the union of exclusive bargaining power. The case was appealed to the United States Supreme Court. Should the Supreme Court uphold the union's exclusive right to engage in collective bargaining with the company? Explain. [See: *Emporium Capwell, Co. v. Western Addition Community Organization,* 420 U.S. 50. (U.S. Sup. Ct.).]

quick quiz Answers

24-1	24-2	24-3
1. T	1. F	1. F
2. F	2. F	2. T
3. F	3. T	3. F

Part 6 Case Study

Renken v. Gregory
No. 07-3126 U.S. Court of Appeals,
Seventh Circuit (2008)

"It would be so nice if something made sense for a change," Alice from *Alice in Wonderland* by Lewis Carroll

Summary

The case revolves around a dispute over the spending of grant money at the University of Wisconsin-Milwaukee's College of Engineering and Applied Sciences. The plaintiff, Dr. Kevin Renken, a tenured professor at the university, along with six other colleagues worked on a grant from the National Science Foundation. The grant would finance a project aimed at integrating laboratory sessions into those undergraduate science courses at the university that did not, up to that time, include practical applied lab experience. Renken led the project, acted as the primary investigator, and presented the proposal to the NSF. As is customary in such projects, the budget included compensation for undergraduates who would help in the project as well as a "buyout" clause for the instructors who would receive a smaller course load so that they could devote more time to the project's rigorous work schedule. The NSF approved the grant for a total of $66,499, as long as the university met a cost-sharing element amounting to $222,667.

Following this, Dean William Gregory sent a proposal to Renken explaining how the university's matching funds portion of the grant would be met. Renken signed that proposal indicating that he had agreed to those terms. Apparently, however, Renken had second thoughts (or first thoughts that he did not voice at the time of the signing). To remedy this error, Renken and another professor involved in the project sent a report to Gregory listing a set of grievances about how the project was being run. The list included: (1) a lack of lab space; (2) a protest about the way that some of the grant money would be spent on lab funds; (3) a delay in paying undergraduates; (4) several delays in sending out purchase orders vital to the project; (5) violations of NSF regulations as listed in Gregory's original letter; and (6) a failure to honor the teaching load reduction agreement. Renken then contacted the University Committee and initiated a complaint against Gregory, specifically complaining about the failure to pay the undergraduates their compensation and characterizing that failure as retaliation.

Gregory responded with a new proposal altering the lab space provisions, but changed nothing else. When Renken and his fellow professor would not sign the revised proposal, Gregory threatened to cancel the NSF grant. Renken did not sign and, instead, sent another complaint/request about the buyout provision. Gregory then notified Renken that the NSF money would be returned and the grant would be cancelled.

Not to be deterred, Renken filed a complaint with the University Board of Regents specifically focusing on the lab space problems, the course buyout issue, and the alleged violations of NSF regulations. Renken then sent another letter to the University Committee, which was now under new leadership, listing the same complaint about the failure to pay the undergraduates. Renken also added a report about a disturbing voice mail he had received, and about Gregory's continued effort to get

597

him to sign the proposal, a proposal that Renken maintained included provisions that violated NSF policy.

These events were followed by a compromise proposal submitted by a third party, the dean of the Graduate School. This compromise was rejected by Renken and his colleague. In reaction to Renken's rejection of the compromise, the university officially canceled the NSF grant and refunded the award to the government. Deciding that enough was enough, Renken initiated a civil rights lawsuit against Dean Gregory and others in positions of authority at the university, under 42 U.S.C. § 1983. The suit, which was filed in the Eastern District of Wisconsin, argued that Renken had been retaliated against for exercising his First Amendment rights. The retaliation consisted of a reduction in pay and the termination of the NSF grant. The university filed a summary judgment arguing that Renken was not entitled to the protection of the First Amendment because, in his role as a university professor, he had been speaking, not as a private citizen, but as a public employee as a part of his official duties. The district court granted the motion and dismissed the case, saying that Renken was not protected by the First Amendment when he spoke as a public employee about his official duties. Going even further, the court also found, in the alternative, that, even if Renken was speaking as a private citizen, he still had no First Amendment rights in this case because he was talking about a private, not a public, matter. The ruling by the District Court may be a bit confusing at this point, and so, it will be helpful to see what the Court of Appeals had to say about the case.

(Since the facts have been covered in this summary, only the Court's analysis is reproduced here. This analysis includes only sections II and III of the opinion. Some footnote numerals are included. Others, those located in the omitted material, are not included. In either case, the citations themselves and explanatory notes are omitted.)

The Court's Opinion

Manion, Circuit Judge

II

We review a district court's grant of a motion for summary judgment de novo. *Sigsworth v. City of Aurora,* 487 F.3d 506, 508 (7th Cir.2007). Summary judgment is appropriate if "the pleadings, depositions, answers to interrogatories, and admissions on file, together with the affidavits, if any, show that there is no genuine issue of material fact and that the moving party is entitled to a judgment as a matter of law." Fed.R.Civ.P. 56(c).

In order for a public employee to raise a successful First Amendment claim, he must have spoken in his capacity as a private citizen and not as an employee. "[W]hen public employees make statements pursuant to their official duties, the employees are not speaking as citizens for First Amendment purposes, and the Constitution does not insulate their communications from employer discipline." *Morales v. Jones,* 494 F.3d 590, 595 (7th Cir. 2007) (quoting *Garcetti v. Ceballos,* 547 U.S. 410, 126 S.Ct. 1951, 1960, 164 L.Ed.2d 689 (2006)). Determining what falls within the scope of an employee's duties is a practical exercise that focuses on "the duties an employee actually is expected to perform." Id. at 596 (quoting *Garcetti,* 126 S.Ct. at 1962). "Formal job descriptions often bear little resemblance to the duties an employee actually is expected to perform, and the listing of a given task in an employee's written job description is neither necessary nor sufficient to demonstrate that conducting the task is within the scope of the employee's professional duties for First Amendment purposes." *Garcetti,* 126 S.Ct. at 1962. Only if Renken was speaking as a citizen and not as an employee, will we "inquire into the content of the speech" to ascertain whether his speech touched on a matter of public concern to determine whether it is protected speech. *Spiegla v. Hull,* 481 F.3d 961, 965 (7th Cir.2007) (citations omitted).

Renken argues that the tasks that he conducted in relation to the grant were implemented at his discretion "while in the course of his job and not as a requirement of his job." As a professor, Renken was responsible for teaching, research, and service to the University. In fulfillment of his acknowledged teaching and service responsibilities, Renken acted as a PI, applying for the NSF grant. This grant aided in the fulfillment of his teaching responsibilities because, as Renken notes in his reply brief, the grant was an education grant for the benefit of students as "undergraduate education development." Moreover, because of his responsibilities as PI, Renken was entitled to a reduction in his teaching course load. In his capacity as PI, Renken administered the grant by filing a signed proposal, including a budget regarding the proposed grant and University funds involved in the project, seeking compensation for undergraduate participants, applying for course releases, and noting what appeared to be improprieties in the grant administration. Renken complained to several levels of University officials about the various difficulties he encountered in the course of administering the grant as a PI. Thereby, Renken called attention to fund misuse relating to a project that he was in charge of administering as a University faculty member. In so doing, Renken was speaking as a faculty employee, and not as a private citizen, because administering the grant as a PI fell within the teaching and service duties that he was employed to perform. See *Garcetti,* 126 S.Ct. at 1960; *Tamayo v. Blagojevich,* 526 F.3d 1074, 1092 (7th Cir.2008) (noting that an "official, in so informing the legislators [of irregularities], was discharging the responsibilities of her office, not appearing as 'Jane Q. Public.' Reporting alleged misconduct against an agency over which one has general supervisory responsibility is part of the duties of such an office."), *Spiegla,* 481 F.3d at 967.

We note, too, that whether Renken was explicitly required to apply for grants does not address whether his efforts related to the grant, including his complaints, were a means to fulfill his employment requirements, namely teaching and research. Moreover, Renken chose to exercise whatever discretion he had in this regard. See *Morales,* 494 F.3d at 598 n. 3 (7th Cir.2007). Contrary to Renken's urging, "focus[ing] on 'core' job functions is too narrow after *Garcetti,* which asked only whether an 'employee's expressions [were] made pursuant to official responsibilities.'" *Spiegla,* 481 F.3d at 966 (quoting *Garcetti,* 126 S.Ct. at 1961).

Along the same lines of his initial argument, Renken asserts that his speech was outside his employment because it was "[s]olely by the terms of the Grant, not his job, [that he] was required to complain if money was taken by the University." As we have noted above, the proper administration of an educational grant fell within the scope of Renken's teaching duties at the University, so much so that he would receive a reduction in his teaching load for serving as a PI for the project. Moreover, in his affidavit filed with the district court, Renken, himself acknowledged the import of the NSF grant to his job, stating, "My grants and the projects I develop from them must be documented and are a major factor considered in earning Full Professorship at [the University]."

Renken cites *Morales v. Jones,* 494 F.3d 590 (7th Cir.2007), in support of his contention that his speech was protected because his job duties did not extend to making formal complaints. In *Morales,* we held that the statements a police officer made to an assistant district attorney regarding the harboring of a fugitive by the chief of police was within the officer's employment, but the officer's statements on the same subject in the course of a civil lawsuit deposition were made as a private citizen. Specifically, we stated that "[b]eing deposed in a civil suit pursuant to a subpoena was unquestionably not one of Morales' job duties because it was not part of what he was employed to do." Id. at 598. Here, by Renken's own admission, his employment status as a full professor depended on the administration of grants, such as the NSF grant. It was in the course of that administration that Renken made his statements about funding improprieties within the confines of the University system and as the principal PI. Therefore, *Morales* does not support Renken's contention that his speech is protected. Because Renken's speech is not protected, his First Amendment claim fails.

III

Renken made his complaints regarding the University's use of NSF funds pursuant to his official duties as a University professor. Therefore, his speech was not protected by the First Amendment. The district court properly granted summary judgment in favor of the University, and we Affirm.

Questions for Analysis

1. How does the case of *Renken v. Gregory* support or contradict the core legal principle of *stare decisis*? Explain.

2. In what way is the case of *Renken v. Gregory* similar to and different from *Ceballos v. Garcetti* The Opening Case (in Chapter 23)? Explain.

3. What evidence does the court rely upon as it attempts to determine whether Renken, in his complaint about the university's handling of the NSF grant, was speaking as a faculty employee or as a private citizen? Explain.

4. What decision does the court arrive at as it considers that evidence? Explain. Is that decision in line with or does it contradict *Ceballos v. Garcetti*? Explain.

5. What is the essential difference between a public worker and a private worker? Should public workers have fewer rights than private-sector workers? If so, why? If not, why not?

6. Does the profession of college professor matter in determining the extent of protection for a public employee's free speech rights? If so, would the same consideration extend to high school teachers or to middle school teachers or to elementary school teachers? Explain.

7. Should members of the clergy be judged by a different standard when free speech under the First Amendment is at issue in a case? Explain.

8. What is academic freedom? What is academic freedom supposed to protect? Should the concept of academic freedom play a role in this case? Explain.

9. Could the plaintiff have filed a constructive discharge case based on retaliation in common law using the same arguments? Explain.

10. Look more closely at the decision of the District Court (not the Court of Appeals) in this case. The court ruled that the plaintiff is not protected by the First Amendment because he made his complaint in his role as a public employee and was, therefore, speaking about his official duties. However, in the alternative, the court says that, even if the plaintiff is a private citizen he is still not entitled to constitutional protection because his speech is about a private concern. Does this strike you as odd? It seems that the plaintiff is not protected as either a private citizen or a public employee because when he claims to be a public employee his complaints are about public matters but when he claims to be a private citizen, the same complaints change into a matter of private concern. Explain this apparent contradiction, using the case of *Ceballos v. Garcetti*, or, if it is easier, use *Alice in Wonderland* by Lewis Carroll. ("'When *I* use a word,' Humpty Dumpty said in rather a scornful tone, 'it means just what I choose it to mean—neither more nor less.'")

Note: The appellate court decided not to address this issue. However, the appellate court did mention the issue in its decision: "The district court granted the University's motion for summary judgment, concluding that Renken's complaints about the grant funding were made as part of his official duties, rather than as citizen, and therefore were not protected by the First Amendment. Alternatively, the district court concluded that if Renken spoke as a citizen and not as part of his official duties, his speech was still not protected because it related to a matter of private interest, namely Renken's teaching and research, and not a matter of public concern." "Curiouser and curiouser!"—Lewis Carroll (one more time) in *Alice in Wonderland.*

Part Seven

Business Organization and Regulation

Chapter 25 — The Business Entity: An Introduction

THE OPENING CASE *Round 1*
The Management of Managing Partners, the Liability Blues, and a Tale of Two Statutes

Some critics claim that the law has three speeds: slow, slower, and stopped. This is not always true; however, even if it were true, it would not necessarily be a bad thing. The legal process often moves slowly to give people time to adjust to changes made in the law. In fact, sometimes people also need a chance to say, "I think that I will sit this one out and not make the changes that you have suggested." A case in point is a lawsuit that featured a battle between PNC Bank and the partners of Washington Square Enterprises (WSE). Founded in 1978, WSE consisted of eight partners including Michael A. Farinacci, who acted as the firm's general manager. In his role as a managing partner, Farinacci was the central target of a lawsuit filed by PNC. (The other partners named in the suit were San Strano and Claire Gruttadauria. Strano, however, seems to have vanished and is not part of the judgment.) In the year 2000, WSE opened a line of credit with PNC for $35,000 to help in the operation of the partnership's shopping mall. For nine years, WSE drew upon the account in order to maintain and repair the mall. Then disaster struck; WSE plunged into insolvency and could not repay the $33,522.65 that it owed to PNC.

At that point, PNC elected to sue. As the suit progressed, it became clear that PNC had made a huge mistake by not adding the missing partners to the mix. When PNC tried to add those partners as defendants, the court refused to do so. Initially, PNC was confident that the failure to add the other partners would not be fatal to the outcome of the case, because, under the provisions of the Revised Uniform Partnership Act, partners are jointly and severally liable for both contract and tort debts. Farinacci disagreed and argued that the new law did not apply to WSE because the partnership had been formed in 1978 under the original Uniform Partnership Act (UPA) and that, as a result, UPA provisions, rather than those found in the RUPA, applied to WSE. In particular, section 1776.14 held that partners are jointly liable for the debts of the partnership that arise in contract law. Under that provision, PNC must be paid for the outstanding debt, but the court will order Farinacci and Gruttadauria to pay only their proportional share of the debt. This would amount to two-eighths of the debt or $4,190.33 each, which is considerably less than the full $33,522.65 that PNC wanted. To correct this judgment, PNC appealed. The

question presented to the appellate court was: Should the defendants be held jointly liable under the old law (UPA) or jointly and severally liable under the new law (RUPA)? To discover what happened on appeal, continue reading. [See: *PNC Bank v. Michael Farinacci,* Eighth Appellate District, County of Cuyahoga) Case Number 96134 (2011).]

Opening Case Questions

1. Why, after the state legislature has gone through all the trouble of passing a new law, would it permit a business entity to follow the old law? Explain.

2. What is the difference between joint liability and joint and several liability? Explain.

3. Why did the defendants want to be judged under the old law, the UPA, rather than the new law, the RUPA? Explain.

4. If the appellate court rules in favor of the defendants in relation to their payments, the bank will not have the full amount owed to it. What recourse would PNC have then, if any? Explain.

5. Why would the trial court judge refuse to add the remaining partners as defendants in this case? Explain.

LO Learning Objectives

1. List the most common forms of business associations.
2. Outline the advantages and disadvantages of a sole proprietorship.
3. Identify the two model acts that govern partnership law.
4. Describe the differences between the aggregate and the entity theories of partnership.
5. Explain the nature of a partnership agreement.
6. Explain when profit sharing does not create a partnership.
7. Explain what constitutes a person in partnership law.
8. Identify the different views of specific partnership property in partnership law.
9. Distinguish between dissociation and dissolution in partnership law.
10. Distinguish between a registered limited liability partnership and a limited partnership.

25-1 Sole Proprietorships and Other Business Entities

Multiple forms of doing business are available to people who are about to enter the economic arena. Here are some of the most common forms:

1. Sole proprietorships
2. General partnerships
3. Limited partnerships
4. Limited liability partnerships
5. Private corporations
6. Public (or state-owned) corporations
7. Quasi-public corporations
8. Limited liability corporations
9. Joint ventures
10. Franchises

This chapter will focus on sole proprietorships, general partnerships, limited partnerships, and limited liability partnerships as a way of initiating our exploration of business entities and the legal rules that apply to such entities. The next three chapters will focus on the nature, organization, operation, and regulation of the corporate entity. Before that, however, this chapter will examine a series of traditional and nontraditional business persons.

Formation of a Sole Proprietorship

The easiest business organization to form is a **sole proprietorship**. In most cases, businesspeople can initiate a sole proprietorship by simply opening their doors for business. Depending on the nature, location, and extent of the business, the sole proprietor may have to check zoning restrictions, licensing laws, and filing requirements. For example, some states require a formal filing if a sole proprietor chooses to use a fictitious name.

Advantages and Disadvantages of a Sole Proprietorship

Perhaps the greatest advantage to a sole proprietorship is that the owner has complete control over the business. Another major advantage is that the owner may keep all of the profits made by the sole proprietorship. A third advantage is that a sole proprietorship is relatively simple to begin and to end.

A major disadvantage to this type of business is that the owner of a sole proprietorship is subject to unlimited liability. For example, the sole proprietor is responsible for all of the debts incurred in running the business. This liability may even extend to the owner's personal assets. Another disadvantage is that the sole proprietorship's existence depends entirely upon the sole proprietor. Finally, owners of sole proprietorships often find it difficult to raise a lot of cash quickly for expansion purposes.

quick quiz 25-1

1. Businesspeople can form a sole proprietorship only by going through the attorney general's office in the state capital.	true | false	
2. The greatest advantage of a sole proprietorship is that the owner has complete control over the operation of the business.	true | false	
3. A major disadvantage of a sole proprietorship is unlimited liability.	true | false	

25-2 General Partnership Characteristics

Often a sole proprietor will decide to extend his or her business venture by joining with other people to create a partnership. The law of partnership has integrated principles associated with tort law, contract law, and agency law. However, because of its unique characteristics, it has also developed its own separate and distinct legal principles.

Revised Uniform Partnership Act

One of the most dependable sources of law affecting partnerships has been the Uniform Law Commission (ULC) which, when it was still known as the National Conference of Commissioners on Uniform State Laws, developed the **Uniform Partnership Act (UPA)** in 1914. The

UPA was so successful that it was put into practice by every state in the union but one. Only Louisiana, which is devoted to the Napoleonic Code, did not adopt the UPA. Nevertheless, the UPA has been the mainstay of partnership law, in relation to general partnerships, for more than 90 years. It does, however, have its limitations and shortcomings. For instance, the act never made it clear whether a partnership should be considered an entity with an existence separate from the partners or whether it was simply an aggregate of all of the partners. These problems motivated two agents within the complex adaptive legal system, the ULC and the American Bar Association (ABA), to collaborate to develop an updated set of rules for partnerships, named the **Revised Uniform Partnership Act (RUPA)**.

The ULC offers several reasons to support states' adoption of the RUPA. Chief among those reasons is that the new act solves several problems with the UPA, not the least of which is the old act's ambiguity about the status of a partnership as an entity or an aggregate. The new act also clarifies the nature of a partner's interest in partnership property, explains the duties partners have in relation to one another, and gives partners the power to pursue a remedy when those duties are violated. It grants partnerships continuity of life, a feature that is similar but not identical to the one enjoyed by corporations. Finally, the revised act solves one of the most troubling problems of the old partnership structure, that of joint and several liability. For these reasons, among others, the RUPA has been implemented in more than half the states. The RUPA will therefore be the basis of discussion for the remainder of this chapter.

Elements of a Partnership

The RUPA says that a **partnership** is "an association of two or more persons to carry on as co-owners a business for profit." The RUPA definition emphasizes the two most essential elements of a partnership. First, partnerships must involve at least two persons. As is often the case with legal terms, *person* can have multiple meanings. In this case, the term can refer to a flesh-and-blood individual, a corporation, other partnerships, joint ventures, trusts, estates, and other commercial or legal institutions. Second, a partnership must involve a sharing of profits. This last point is so crucial that the sharing of profits is considered *prima facie* evidence of the existence of a partnership. *Prima facie* evidence in this context means that the law presumes, in the absence of evidence to the contrary, that an individual receiving profits is a partner.

Entity and Aggregate Theories

Under the Uniform Partnership Act, there was room to dispute whether a partnership should be considered an aggregate or an entity. According to the **entity theory**, a partnership exists as an individual person with its own separate identity. This unique, individual entity is separate from the identities of the partners. In contrast, under the **aggregate theory**, the partnership is seen simply as an assembly or collection of the partners who do business together. The RUPA has settled this dispute. Under the RUPA, a partnership is considered an entity in most situations. Thus, a partnership is an entity in its ability to own title to property, to sue or be sued, and to have its own separate bank accounts in its own name. Under the RUPA, partnerships also have continuity of existence. **Continuity of existence** permits a partnership to continue to operate as an entity even after the individual partners are no longer associated with it. In addition, the partners are considered agents of the partnership. However, the RUPA still considers a partnership an aggregate in relation to liability. Thus, even under the RUPA, partners still have unlimited liability for the obligations of the partnership. It is, however, possible to avoid even this problem if the partners elect to form a registered limited liability partnership. The concept of registered limited liability partnerships is discussed subsequently in this chapter.

THE OPENING CASE *Round 2*
A Tale of Two Statutes

Recall that in the opening case, the general partnership of WSE opened a line of credit with PNC for $35,000. For almost a decade, the partnership used the account to maintain and repair its shopping mall. Then WSE became insolvent and could not repay the $33,522.65 that it owed to PNC. In order to recover the money it was owed, PNC sued WSE. Initially, PNC was confident it would prevail in the case because, under the provisions of the Revised Uniform Partnership Act, partners are jointly and severally liable for both contract and tort debts. Farinacci disagreed and argued that the new law did not apply to WSE because the partnership had been formed in 1978 under the original Uniform Partnership Act (UPA) and that, as a result, UPA provisions, rather than those found in the RUPA, applied to WSE. In particular, section 1776.14 held that partners are jointly liable for the debts of the partnership that arise in contract law. The trial court found that (1) since WSE was formed in 1978 (31 years before the new statute was enacted); (2) since there was no agreement among the partners to be held to the statute that went into effect in 2009; and (3) since the debt was incurred while the old statute was in effect (in 2000), the RUPA did not apply to it in this case. PNC

appealed the decision of the trial court to the court of appeals. The appellate court supported the trial court writing, "Washington Square was formed in 1978 with eight partners. There is no evidence that the partners agreed to be governed by the Ohio Uniform Partnership Act. PNC commenced this action in November 2009. Therefore, R.C. 1776.36 does not apply to Washington Square to extend the partners' liability. The law in effect at the time the obligation accrued governs the action. . . . Evidence in the record indicates that Washington Square defaulted on the line of credit in June 2002. Thus, the court properly applied R.C. 1775.14, which was in effect at the time of Washington Square's default. Under R.C. 1775.14, partners are jointly, not jointly and severally, liable for the ordinary debts of the partnership." The appellate court supported the trial court's order that compelled Farinacci and Gruttadauria to pay their proportional share of the debt. This would amount to two-eighths (or one-quarter) of the debt, or $4,190.33 each. So, while technically PNC won the case, the institution received considerably less than the full $33,522.65 that it wanted. [See: *PNC Bank v. Michael Farinacci*, Eighth Appellate District, County of Cuyahoga) Case Number 96134 (2011).]

Alternative Business Entities

As noted earlier, potential partners who are considering a business plan should think about forming a registered limited liability partnership rather than a general partnership. This simple statement, however, reveals only a very small part of the story. Starting a business, regardless of the final form of that business, is a risky endeavor. Accumulating the necessary start-up capital before opening the business and writing a comprehensive and complete operational agreement are only two of the many tasks facing new entrepreneurs. While risky, these projects are not hopeless. On the contrary, most problems can be anticipated and properly handled with well-directed, advanced research. The problems associated with the start of new business are not unlike the problems associated with establishing a stable national economy. In fact, the parallels are so close, it is worth spending a few moments considering them before moving forward.

National Economic Reform Movements
According to Adam Przeworski of the University of Chicago, the goal of any national economic reform movement (NERM) is to organize the national economy so that all available funds and properties are wisely utilized in order to develop a nation-state that is economically prosperous. Przeworski notes that any properly run NERM requires (1) the development of fresh marketplaces, (2) the

relaxation of prices, (3) the reduction of monopolies, and (4) the elimination of protection measures. Initiating such reforms, however, always results in unintended negative consequences (UNCs). Among these UNCs is a short-term decrease in the rate of spending that results from a transitory but seriously felt economic disruption within the nation-state, which leads to opposition from the people affected the most by the reforms. The pattern is inevitable. The relaxation of prices, for instance, leads to price increases, which leads to the decreased spending noted earlier. As competition rises, jobs are lost and people, again, spend less. The results may be so severe, Przeworski argues, that the entire reform movement may collapse under pressure for a return to the old days. However, a collapse is not inevitable as long as the managers of the NERM remember that the movement must be preceded by a fact-finding mission that uncovers the cost of the NERM, the political conditions under which the reform will be taken, and the effects of reform on the constituencies affected. [See: Adam Przeworski, *Democracy and the Market: Political and Economic Reforms in Western Europe and Latin America* (Cambridge, UK: Cambridge University Press, 1991).]

Unorthodox Business Entities
Like the goal of a NERM, the goal of any business plan is to organize a group of entrepreneurs and to use the capital (money and talent) provided by those entrepreneurs to fashion a product or service that is affordable and practical, the sale of which produces a profit. Like the development of a new state economy, the development of a new business requires (1) recognizing a target set of customers (fresh marketplaces), (2) developing a competitive cost structure (the relaxation of prices), and (3) outbidding of competitors (the reduction of monopolies), by selling the best product or set of services on the market. (Note: We removed the fourth factor here, the elimination of protective measures, because in the 21st century this job is reserved for the government.) Again, like the reform of a state economy, the initiation of a new business always results in unintended negative consequences. Among the possible UNCs facing a new business are a short-term decrease of capital available for discretionary spending, a loss of time available for other activities, a series of profitless days (weeks, months), extended loans, increased indebtedness, discouragement among the partners (investors, employees, and so on), and the temptation to dump the entire project as a mistake. The consequences may be so hard to bear that the entire entity may collapse under the overwhelming desire to escape. Once again, the end of the business can be avoided if the managers of the new business, like the managers of a NERM, remember that the establishment of the business must be preceded by a fact-finding mission that uncovers the cost of the business, the market conditions under which the business will operate, the effects of business on the partners, and the type of business entity that is best suited for the endeavor.

Additional Business Entities
So far we have discussed the parallels that run between creating a reformed national economy and developing a start-up plan for a new business. One of the major characteristics of any successful economic plan, whether that plan is to reform the economy or start a new business, is the ability to adapt. The development of national economic reform requires the capacity to adjust to the use of one of several orthodox business entities. Similarly, the development of a successful start-up plan requires the ability to adapt to the possibility of forming a nontraditional, or unorthodox, business entity. Before looking at the unorthodox business entities, let's review the more conventional entities. The orthodox (or traditional) business entities include the following:

1. **Sole proprietorship** is a business operation owned and operated by one person.

2. A **general partnership** is two or more persons operating a business entity as co-owners in order to make a profit.

3. A **limited partnership** is one or more general partners joined with one or more limited partners to operate a business entity for profit.

4. A **limited liability partnership** is a general partnership in all respects except one—liability.

5. A **private corporation** is an entity formed by private persons to carry out a task best undertaken by an organization that can raise large amounts of capital quickly and that can grant the protection of limited liability.

6. A **public (or state-owned) corporation** is an entity set up by the federal, state, or local governments for governmental purposes usually involving public health, safety, or welfare.

7. A **quasi-public corporation** is a privately organized entity that makes a profit but that provides a service on which the public depends.

8. A **limited liability corporation** is a cross between a partnership and a corporation, offering the protection of limited liability like a corporation and the tax benefits of a partnership.

9. A **joint venture** (or joint undertaking) involves a contractual arrangement by which individuals unite for a limited amount of time to create a new entity in which the founders share control, expenses, and profits.

10. A **franchise** is a business arrangement that permits an individual, a group of investors, or another entity to lease the right to use a parent entity's business operation, trademark, goods, services, and goodwill under a fee arrangement provided to the parent.

Some of the unorthodox (or the nontraditional) business entities, suggested by Adam Przeworski in *Democracy and the Market,* include the following:

1. A **failure-proof public corporation** is an entity operated by an autonomous board of directors, owned by the state, and protected from failure by the government.

2. A **public-private corporation** is an entity that is owned and operated by the state but that is not protected from failure by the government.

3. A **cross-owned corporation** is a business entity that is a public corporation owned and operated by another public corporation.

4. A **public bodies corporation** would not be a single corporation but would involve a project that would transform public corporations, making them into profit-making entities.

5. A **social corporation** is an entity run by a diverse board of directors with representatives from the employees, the state, and the general public.

6. A **cooperative corporation** is a business entity owned and operated by the employees or patrons of that corporation.

7. A **cooperative corporation with wage-earning employees** is a business owned and operated by the employees who hire nonowner employees to perform work beyond the expertise and/or availability of the owner-employees.

8. A **cooperative with nonemployee owners** is a business entity owned and operated by employees with some nonemployee shareholders.

One of the most interesting aspects of these business entities is that no one single entity can be labeled as the best or the worst. Often the success or the failure of a business entity depends not as much on the structure itself, as on the preliminary work done by those who plan the entity from the ground up. Again, this planning includes the ability of the members of the entity to adapt as the market, the competition, the availability of resources, and the law change. For the moment though, let's return to the formation of the more conventional general partnership.

25-3 Partnership Formation

The problem with a partnership is that it can emerge simply because of the way that two or more parties are doing business with one another. That is why it is essential that businesspeople be aware of their relationships with other businesspeople with whom they work on a daily basis (see Table 25-1). Certainly the best way to form a partnership is to enter a contractual relationship by drawing up a partnership agreement. Consequently, we will examine this approach first. However, we will also look at the circumstances that can automatically create a partnership as a matter of law.

Formation of a Partnership by Contract

One of the most common ways to form a partnership is by an express agreement between the parties. Although the agreement can be oral, it is generally best to put the terms in writing to prevent misunderstanding and disputes that might arise later in the life of the partnership. The written agreement that establishes a partnership is called a partnership agreement. The RUPA is quite specific about the nature of a partnership agreement. In fact, the RUPA defines a partnership contract as "the agreement, whether written, oral, or implied, among the partners concerning the partnership, including amendments to the partnership agreement." It is of course still possible for the partners to enter agreements subsequent to the creation of a partnership that would not be considered part of the partnership agreement. Thus, partners might enter a loan or a rental agreement that would be separate from the partnership agreement itself.

Both the RUPA and UPA are default statutes, which means that the partners are free to enter any type of agreement that they desire. However, if the partners neglect to include something in the agreement or are unsure of the interpretation of some point, the RUPA (or

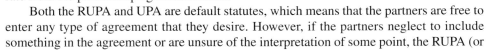

Form	Definition
Table 25-1 Partnership Formation	
Partnership by contract	Express agreement drawn up by partners
	Articles of partnership
Partnership by proof of existence	Individuals form partnership because of their method of doing business
	Sharing of profits is *prima facie* evidence

UPA in those states that still follow it) will "fill in the gaps." It is advisable for a partnership agreement to include the following provisions:

1. The name and duration of the partnership.
2. The names of the partners.
3. The amount of capital that each partner has contributed to the partnership.
4. The character and the extent of the business of the partnership.
5. The way that profits will be divided.
6. The way that any loss will be shared.
7. The duties of the partners.
8. Any limitations placed on the partners.
9. A section on salaries, if so desired.
10. An explanation of the dissolution process, if it is to be different from the process outlined in the RUPA.
11. A provision for determining the value of a partner's interest in the partnership.

It is also wise to recall that, though the RUPA does not require that a partnership agreement be in writing, the Statute of Frauds does dictate that certain types of contracts, such as those that will take longer than one year to complete, must be in writing. Thus, it is best to cross-reference with the Statute of Frauds just to make certain that none of those provisions apply.

Formation of a Partnership by Proof of Existence

The definition of a partnership offered by the RUPA establishes the parameters within which a partnership will be formed. The definition states that a business arrangement will be considered a partnership if it involves two or more persons, in association with one another, who are carrying on a business as co-owners for profit. Therefore, to show that a business is operating as a partnership by proof of existence, we must be able to point to three elements: (1) an association of two or more persons, (2) who are co-owners of (3) a business for profit.

An Association of Two or More Persons In the case of a partnership, a "person" can be a living flesh-and-blood individual, a corporation, another partnership, a joint venture, a trust, an estate, or some other commercial enterprise or legal institution. Any two of these persons working together would be sufficient to create an association.

Co-Ownership of the Business There are certain signs that indicate that the parties in a venture are co-owners. One such sign is the existence of management power. Of course, management power by itself is not enough. Employees who are not partners and even independent contractors who have control over certain projects conducted for the business may have management power without being co-owners. Still, the power to make management decisions is a persuasive piece of evidence that is helpful in establishing co-ownership. Co-ownership is also established by the sharing of profits among the partners. However, the RUPA also says that certain types of profit sharing, though real enough, will not rise to the level needed to create a partnership. These profit-sharing activities include the following:

1. The repayment of a debt.
2. Wages to an employee.
3. Payments to an independent contractor.

4. Rent payments to a landlord.

5. Annuity payments or health benefit payments to a beneficiary, representative, or designee of a retired or deceased partner.

6. Interest payments on a loan, even if the level of payments is tied to profit fluctuations.

7. Consideration for the sale of goodwill or for the sale of other property even if the payments are made in installments.

Although the sharing of profits is *prima facie* evidence of the existence of a partnership, parties can receive profits in any of the ways on this list without being saddled with the label of partner.

Carrying on a Business for Profit   Finally, it is not enough for two or more persons to simply be co-owners of property, even if the property does make a profit. The association must also have the goal of running the business together. It is, of course, essential that the business in question be run for a profit. This point means that the venture cannot involve an unincorporated nonprofit venture. It is also unlikely that a solitary profit-making business transaction by itself will be enough to establish a partnership.

---

quick quiz 25-3

1. A partnership can emerge simply because of the way two or more parties are doing business with one another.   true | false

2. A "person" can be a living flesh-and-blood individual, a corporation, another partnership, a joint venture, a trust, an estate, or some other commercial enterprise or legal institution.   true | false

3. The sharing of profits is *prima facie* evidence of the existence of a partnership.   true | false

---

25-4 Partnership Property Rights and Duties

Property is an extremely critical element in partnership law, because virtually every decision made by a partner deals with the disposition of partnership property. Decisions involving the use of partnership property, such as machinery, equipment, furniture, and vehicles; the purchase of raw materials; and the sale of finished products all involve the disposition of property. Even service-oriented partnerships such as shipping firms and restaurants involve the disposition of property in one way or another. Therefore, partnership duties and rights always involve partnership property. This point is also why it is critical to determine whether a given piece of property belongs to the partnership entity or to an individual partner as his or her personal property. At times it is relatively easy to distinguish between partnership property and property that belongs to individual partners. For instance, the capital contributions of all partners are considered the property of the partnership. **Capital contributions** are sums that are contributed by the partners as permanent investments and that the partners are entitled to have returned when the partnership is dissolved. In contrast, loans or later advances that partners make to the partnership and accumulated but undivided profits belong to the partners on an individual basis. Other forms of partnership property belong only to the partnership in its status as an entity.

Partnership Liability

Passage of the Revised Uniform Partnership Act has altered the type of liability that is levied against partners. **Joint liability** means that, when the partners are sued, liability will be spread among them equally. In contrast, **joint and several liability** means that the partners can be sued apart or together. Under the original Uniform Partnership Act, partners were jointly liable for contract obligations, but jointly and severally liable for any tort obligations. Under the Revised Uniform Partnership Act, liability was altered so that joint and several liability applies to suits in both contract and tort law. Basically this means that each

THE OPENING CASE *Round 3*

The Liability Blues

The opening case explained that WSE, a general partnership that owned and operated a shopping mall, opened a line of credit with the PNC Bank for $35,000. The funds were earmarked by the partnership to help in the operation and maintenance of the mall. For almost 10 years, the account was properly maintained. Then WSE ran into financial difficulties that made it impossible for the firm to repay the $33,522.65 that it owed to PNC. In order to recoup its losses, PNC brought a lawsuit against WSE. Rather than suing the partnership, PNC sued the individual partners directly. The bank also sued only three partners, Michael Farinacci, Sam, Strano, and Claire Gruttadauria, leaving the others untouched. As we shall see shortly, that was a serious error that would leave the management of the bank singing the liability blues. The first negative consequence of this decision was the disappearance of one of the defendants, leaving only Farinacci and Gruttadauria in the case. The second negative consequence was the refusal of the trial judge to add any of the other partners, beyond Farinacci and Gruttadauria, to the lawsuit. At first, the management of PNC was confident that the failure to add the other partners would not affect the outcome of the case because, under the provisions of the Revised Uniform Partnership Act, partners are jointly and severally liable for both contract and tort debts. The defendants, however, argued that the plaintiff had made a crucial mistake. This mistake was grounded in the failure to realize that, since the WSE had been formed in 1978, since the partners did not agree to be held to the new statute, and since the debt was incurred while the old statute was in effect, the RUPA did not apply in this case. Since the RUPA did not apply, the UPA had to be used to determine liability. The trial court, and later the appellate court, agreed

with the defendants. That was the third negative consequence. Under the new Revised Uniform Partnership Act, joint and several liability applies to suits in both contract and tort law. Under the original Uniform Partnership Act, the one that both courts said applied here, partners were jointly liable for contract obligations and jointly and severally liable for any tort obligations. Since this was a contract case, under the UPA, only joint liability would apply. This meant that, even though both courts decided that PNC could collect from both defendants, under the UPA, the bank could collect only each partner's proportionate share. Thus, under the UPA, the partners are jointly, not jointly and severally liable, for the debts of WSE. To emphasize this result, the trial court quoted the state supreme court in another case, wherein the court explained, "Joint liability apportions responsibility for a contractual debt equally, in the absence of a partnership agreement to the contrary, among the partners and thereby limits the creditor's execution on an individual partner's property to a *pro rata* share of the debt. Joint and several liability, on the other hand, allows for disproportionate satisfaction of the partnership obligation by rendering each general partner responsible for the entire amount of the partnership debt." [See: *Wayne Smith Constr. Co., Inc. v. Wolman, Duberstein & Thompson* (1992), 65 Ohio St.3d 383, 388.] The net result was that Farinacci and Gruttadauria had to pay only their proportional share of the debt. This amounted to two-eighths of the debt, or $4,190.33 each. So, while technically PNC won the case, the institution received considerably less than the full $33,522.65 that it wanted, leaving PNC management singing the liability blues. [See: *PNC Bank v. Michael Farinacci,* Eighth Appellate District, County of Cuyahoga) Case Number 96134 (2011).]

partner could find himself or herself sued separately and could be individually liable for the entire judgment, rather than simply a proportional amount. However, because the revised act emphasizes the entity nature of the partnership, the entity itself must satisfy any judgment, contract or tort, before an individual partner can be held personally responsible. These responsibilities can, however, be altered by the partners in the partnership agreement. Also remember that some states add provisions to the revised act to restrict the application of the new law so that it applies only to partnerships formed after the date of the law's enactment.

Partnership Property

The fact that the RUPA has established the existence of a partnership as an entity has alleviated some of the difficulties once associated with identifying partnership property. The RUPA states that partnership property is any and all property that has been obtained by the partnership itself. For instance, if the property was obtained in the partnership's name, it is partnership property. If the property was obtained by a partner in his or her role as a partner, it is partnership property. If the instrument of title for the property includes the name of the partnership, it is partnership property. Finally, if the instrument of transfer indicates that the property was obtained by a partner in his or her role as a partner or if the partnership is referred to in the instrument, the property belongs to the partnership.

When it is difficult to determine whether a piece of property belongs to the partnership or to a partner, the court may ask the following questions: Has the partnership included the property in its account books? Has the partnership expended its own funds to improve or repair the property? Has the partnership paid taxes on the property? Has the partnership paid other expenses, such as maintenance costs, for the property? The more of these questions that can be answered in the affirmative, the more likely it is that the property is partnership property.

Specific Partnership Property

The RUPA has made a significant change in the rule with regard to individual pieces of partnership property. Under the UPA, each partner had a property interest in all specific items of partnership property. Each partner was therefore a co-owner of that property. This form of ownership was known as tenancy in partnership. Under the UPA, a tenancy in partnership had the following characteristics:

1. A partner had an equal right with all other partners to possess and use specific partnership property for partnership purposes but not for that partner's personal use.

2. A partner's interest in partnership property could not be assigned (i.e., transferred by sale, mortgage, pledge, or otherwise) to a nonpartner, unless the other partners agreed to the transfer.

3. Partners' rights in partnership property were not subject to attachment (i.e., taking a person's property and bringing it into the custody of the law) for personal debts or claims against the partners themselves.

4. A deceased partner's interest in real property held by the partnership passed to the surviving partners.

5. Partners' rights in specific partnership property were not subject to any allowances or rights to widows, heirs, or next of kin.

Under the RUPA, all of this has changed. The RUPA states, "A partner is not co-owner of partnership property and has no interest in partnership property which can be transferred, either voluntarily or involuntarily." Of course, partners will still be able to use partnership property. However, their right to hold and use such property is limited to partnership purposes. This significant change in relation to partnership law actually brings partnership property rights in relation to individual pieces of partnership property in line with the way property rights operate for other business associations, such as corporations.

Interest in the Partnership

The RUPA establishes that a partner has an interest in the partnership as a firm. That right consists of two parts: (1) a transferable economic interest and (2) a nontransferable interest in management rights.

Transferable Economic Interest
The partner's economic interest is his or her share of the profits and losses and his or her share of the surplus. **Surplus** includes any funds that remain after the partnership has been dissolved and all other debts and prior obligations have been paid. Partners can voluntarily assign their economic interest to another party. The assignee in such an action, however, is not entitled to take part in the management of the partnership. The assignee also cannot gain access to the partnership books or the partnership financial records. Nor can an assignee demand to receive information concerning the transactions of the partnership.

Management of the Firm
Participation in management decision making is not limited to the partner's proportional share of the firm. Instead, all partners have equal rights in the management of the partnership business. The day-to-day decisions of the firm are decided by a majority vote of the partners. If a vote is split evenly, then the status quo remains. If such deadlocks persist, and the very operation of the business is threatened, it may be time to dissolve the partnership. Occasionally, a unanimous vote is required in a business decision. However, such decisions must involve actions that fall outside the regular, daily operation of the business. Decisions that involve amendments to the partnership agreement also require unanimous consent.

It is, of course, possible for a partner to reduce his or her part in management voluntarily by becoming a silent partner. A **silent partner** is one who does not participate in the day-to-day business of the firm. This role is in contrast to a **secret partner**, whose identity and existence are not known outside the firm but who nevertheless can participate in the management of the firm. Some partnerships create their own hierarchy of partners. Thus, a firm may be divided into *junior* and *senior partners* or into *managing* and *nonmanaging partners*.

Partnership Rights and Duties

We have already pinpointed most of the individual rights that partners possess by virtue of their participation in the partnership. These rights include: (1) the right to use partnership property, as long as the property is held and used for partnership purposes; (2) the right to receive the partner's share of the profits (and losses) and his or her share of the surplus; (3) the right to manage the regular day-to-day operation of the partnership business; (4) the right to approve of serious matters outside the ordinary course of business; and (5) the right to approve of amendments to the partnership agreement. In addition, partners have certain enforcement rights, should the need arise to implement the other rights.

Enforcement Rights
Under the UPA, a partner's enforcement rights are few. In fact, partners have only three enforcement rights: (1) the right to see the firm's financial records, (2) the right to compel an accounting, and (3) the right to compel a dissolution of the entire partnership. Under the RUPA, those enforcement rights are enhanced. The three rights previously noted are retained, but in addition, a partner can sue another partner directly or, under the entity theory, the partnership itself to enforce his or her partnership rights as expressed in the RUPA or granted by the partnership agreement. In such an action,

THE OPENING CASE *Round 4*
The Management of Managing Partners

Recall that in the opening case, the general partnership of Washington Square Enterprises (WSE) opened a line of credit with PNC for $35,000 to help in the operation of the partnership's shopping mall. The partnership of WSE consisted of eight general partners. However, only one of the general partners, Michael A. Farinacci, acted as the managing partner. Farinacci's status as managing partner is indicated by the fact that the partnership's business seems to have been conducted out of Farinacci's home. The firm received all of its correspondence at Farinacci's home address, and he was responsible for making all payments to PNC. Even so, the partnership was treated as a separate entity by Farinacci and the other partners. Still, in his role as a managing partner, Farinacci was the central target of the lawsuit filed by PNC. (The other partners named in the suit were San Strano and Claire Gruttadauria. Strano, however, seems to have vanished and was not part of the final judgment.) This left Farinacci, the managing general partner, and Gruttadauria, one of the non-managing general partners, as the only defendants in the lawsuit. Under the original Uniform Partnership Act, the one that both courts said applied here, all of the partners were jointly liable for the contract negotiated with PNC. This sounds like a fairly good deal for PNC. However, even though both courts decided that PNC could collect from all the partners, only Farinacci and Gruttadauria were named as defendants in this lawsuit. Consequently, under the UPA, the court ordered Farinacci and Gruttadauria to pay their proportional share of the debt. This amounted to two-eighths of the $33,522.65 owed to the bank, or $4,190.33 each. Significantly, Farinacci's role as a managing partner did not, in any way, alter (raise or lower) his proportionate share of the debt owed to the bank. The management role was one that he assumed voluntarily and, presumably, with the consent of the other partners. However, it had nothing to do with his status as a general partner. Nor did it affect the status or the indebtedness of the other partners. Nor did it add any more money to PNC's bank account. [See: *PNC Bank v. Michael Farinacci,* Eighth Appellate District, County of Cuyahoga) Case Number 96134 (2011).]

the partner can ask for damages or for an equitable remedy, such as an injunction or specific performance. Of course, the reverse is also true; that is, the partner can be sued by another partner or by the partnership itself.

Partnership Duties
The RUPA notes that partners have three critical duties: (1) loyalty, (2) obedience, and (3) due care. The first of these three, the duty of loyalty, is based on the fact that the partners are in a fiduciary relationship.

The Duty of Loyalty The duty of loyalty has become centrally important under the RUPA, unlike its position under the UPA, which devoted only a very small amount of space to the topic. According to the RUPA, the duty of loyalty includes the following items:

1. To account to the partnership for any property, profits, or benefit that comes from the partner's use of partnership property or from the winding up process after dissolution.

2. To refrain from dealing with people who may have an interest that is adverse to the best interests of the partnership.

3. To refrain from entering any competition with the partnership in the operation of partnership business.

A partner does, however, retain the right to look after himself or herself during the formation of the partnership, because the duty of loyalty does not arise until the partnership entity actually exists.

The Duty of Obedience Simply stated, the duty of obedience means that a partner must follow faithfully all the arrangements made in the partnership agreement. The partner must also honor all decisions made by the partnership, provided those decisions were made following proper protocols. If a partner disobeys the partnership agreement or disregards a decision lawfully made by the other partners, he or she will be liable for any loss that befalls the partnership as a result of that disobedience.

A QUESTION OF ETHICS

The End of Capitalism?

One of the premiere economists of the last century was a Harvard professor named Joseph Schumpeter, who wrote a treatise titled *Capitalism, Socialism, and Democracy* in which he foretold the ultimate end of the capitalist economic system. Oddly, Schumpeter was himself a confirmed capitalist, and a dedicated member of the Austrian school of economics, so when he predicted the end of the capitalist economy, it was without joy or pleasure. In fact, it was more of a warning than a prediction, offered with the hope that something could be done to divert the path away from destruction. Schumpeter's affection for capitalism is described in the following passage, penned by Allen M. Sievers in his study, *Revolution, Evolution, and the Economic Order:*

> The capitalist, for one thing, wishes to provide for his family, and indeed capitalism is really not individual-centered but family-centered. Further, the capitalist shares in lesser degree the romantic adventuresomeness which characterized feudal society, or there would be no risky innovation or entrepreneurial exploit. Capitalism also requires a kind of symbiosis with the aristocracy and other non-bourgeois elements to run the state, and this depends on a kind of loyalty by these classes to capitalism. The masses must also be awed by the glamor or prestige of capitalist success in order to submit to the discipline necessary for business production. The business classes themselves must have an *esprit de corps* and a devotion to their way of life, as well as a code of ethics if the contract and property system is to work. We might say in sum, that Schumpeter believed that capitalist civilization is based on a rationalism qualified just a bit by other human qualities.
>
> Allen M. Sievers, *Revolution, Evolution, and the Economic Order,* p. 41

We can distill from this quotation five essential qualities of the capitalist: (1) family-centeredness, (2) a willingness to take risks, (3) loyalty to the capitalist ideal, (4) awe at the success of capitalistic ventures, and (5) a code of ethics that permits the rules of contract and property law to work.

ETHICAL CONCERNS AND QUESTIONS

1. Which of the business organizations described in this chapter is best suited for realizing Sievers's capitalistic ideals? Explain. Which Business entity is the most and which the least ethical? Explain.

2. According to Sievers, capitalism requires an integration of the aristocratic and the working class elements of society. Is such an integration promoted or hampered by the partnership form of doing business? Explain. Is such an integration of the aristocratic and the working class elements of society ethical? Explain.

3. Do the alternate forms of partnership such as the limited partnership structure prove or disprove Sievers's theory? Explain.

4. Recall that Schumpeter, like F.A. Hayek, opposes governmental interference in the economy. Does this not mean that the sole proprietorship would be the perfect Schumpeter business? Why or why not?

5. Is the Austrian strategy of allowing economic collapse ethical? Explain.

The Duty of Due Care   Basically, the duty of due care means that partners must do their best in the business, based on their talents, education, and abilities. It does not mean that partners must be infallible. On the contrary, the standard recognizes that a partner may make mistakes and allows for those mistakes, provided the partner acted with an ordinary level of skill and competence and in the best interests of the partnership.

---

quick quiz 25-4

1. Under the RUPA, each partner has a property interest in all spe-   true | false
   cific items of partnership property.

2. The RUPA states that partnership property is any and all property   true | false
   that has been obtained by the partnership itself.

3. A partner's economic interest in the partnership is nontransferrable.   true | false

---

25-5 Dissociation and Dissolution

One of the objectives of the Uniform Law Commission and the American Bar Association in rewriting the UPA and developing the RUPA was to make certain that the new law coincided as much as possible with commercial realities. Under the UPA, whenever a partner ceased to be associated with the partnership, technically, that partnership went through the dissolution process. In present commercial realities, it no longer makes sense for partners to have to deal with the dissolution technicalities when the only thing that is really happening is the buyout of a partner who wants to leave the firm. Consequently, the RUPA now includes two methods by which a partner becomes dissociated with partnership: dissociation and dissolution.

Dissociation of a Partnership

Under the RUPA, a **dissociation** takes place whenever a partner is no longer associated with the running of the firm. It is always possible for partners to leave a partnership firm when they want. However, sometimes, a partner leaves the firm wrongfully when he or she does not have the legal right to do so. A partner's right to withdraw from a partnership may depend on whether the partnership is a term partnership or a partnership at will. A **term partnership** is one that has been set up to run for a certain set time period or to accomplish a task of some sort. A partner who leaves a term partnership before the term expires or before the task is accomplished has acted wrongfully. A **partnership at will** is one that any partner may leave without liability. The RUPA establishes the circumstances in which it is proper to leave a partnership. Some rules affect both types of partnerships; others apply only to partnerships at will. These include (1) a partner's death in either type of partnership; (2) a partner's leave-taking from a partnership at will; (3) a partner's leave-taking from either type of partnership under the rules set up by the partnership agreement; or (4) a partner's leave-taking from either type of partnership, if a court has decided that a partner cannot do what he or she is supposed to do under the partnership agreement.

Dissolution of a Partnership

The **dissolution** of a partnership occurs when a partner ceases to be associated with the partnership and the partnership ends. The dissolution of a partnership can occur in one of three ways: (1) by an action committed by the partners, (2) by operation of law, or (3) by the decree of a court of law.

This partnership is in the "winding up" stage and is selling its assets and inventory to satisfy creditors and hopefully distribute surplus to the former partners.

An Action by the Partners Whenever a partnership at will exists, that partnership can be dissolved whenever a partner notifies the other partners that he or she intends to leave the firm. Partnerships at will, however, are not dissolved when a partner dies or enters bankruptcy. Whenever a term partnership is involved, the RUPA says that there are several ways to dissolve the firm: (1) when the time limit has passed; (2) when the task of the partnership has been accomplished; (3) when there is express agreement among all partners to end the partnership; (4) when a partner dies; (5) when a partner becomes incapacitated; (6) when a partner goes bankrupt; and (7) when a partner produces a wrongful dissociation from the partnership and, within 90 days of that leave-taking, at least half the other partners agree to end the business.

By Operation of Law Dissolution becomes effective by operation of law if some event occurs that makes it illegal to continue the business of the firm. If, for instance, at some time in the distant future it became illegal to manufacture and sell tobacco products, a partnership formed to produce and market cigarettes would dissolve by operation of law.

By a Court Order When a partner has engaged in some sort of wrongdoing and, on those grounds, another partner petitions the court for a dissolution, the court may dissolve the partnership by court order. When a continuation of the business would be economically foolish, the court may dissolve the firm. Finally, when a partner does something that makes it impractical to continue the business with that partner, the court may order the dissolution of the business.

Winding Up the Partnership Business When a partnership terminates, there must be a winding up of the partnership affairs. This action includes the orderly sale of the partnership's assets, the payment of creditors, and the distribution, if any, of the remaining surplus to partners according to their profit-sharing rations.

quick quiz 25-5

1. The RUPA includes two methods by which a partner becomes dissociated with a partnership: dissociation and dissolution.   true | false

2. A partnership at will is one that any partner may leave without liability.   true | false

3. When partnership terminates, there must be a winding up of the partnership affairs.   true | false

25-6 Other Forms of Partnership Business

The changing needs of the modern marketplace and the development of new ideas in the law have combined to allow for a new form of partnership, the registered limited liability partnership. Those same forces have also cooperated to update one of the more traditional forms of the partnership business, the limited partnership.

Registered Limited Liability Partnerships

Statutory developments in several states have produced a new type of business organization known as the registered limited liability partnership (RLLP or LLP). A **registered limited liability partnership** is a general partnership in all respects except one—liability. In a traditional general partnership, the liability for the torts committed by a partner or an employee of the partnership is joint and several. This stance means that each partner is liable and may be sued in a separate action or in a joint action. A judgment may be levied against one or more partners. The release of one partner in one action does not necessarily release the others.

The statutes usually require that the registration statement be filed by all of the partners or at least by those partners holding a majority interest in the partnership. Limited liability partnerships must update their registration statement each year or risk the loss of registration. As far as the tax laws are concerned, LLPs are considered general partnerships. When an LLP has been created, partners can no longer be held jointly or severally liable for the torts, wrongful acts, negligence, or misconduct committed by another partner or by any representative of the partnership. Naturally, partners would still be liable for their own wrongful acts and for the wrongful acts committed by other partners or employees who are under the direct control of that partner. The Revised Uniform Partnership Act includes the provisions necessary for obtaining limited liability status. Thus, states that have adopted the RUPA in its entirety do not need to pass a separate statute to allow for the creation of an LLP.

Limited Partnerships

Limited partnerships are governed by the Revised Uniform Limited Partnership Act (RULPA). The revised act defines a **limited partnership** as "a partnership formed by two or more persons . . . having one or more general partners and one or more limited partners." **General partners** take an active part in the management of the firm and have unlimited liability for the firm's debts. **Limited partners** are nonparticipating investors. They contribute cash, property, or services to the partnership but do not take part in the management of the firm.

A limited partnership is advantageous for both the limited partner and the general partner. The general partner can accumulate additional capital without admitting another general partner who would be entitled to management rights. Thus, the general partner maintains control while strengthening the firm's treasury. The limited partner also benefits because a limited partnership means limited liability. **Limited liability** in turn means that the limited partner's nonpartnership property cannot be used to satisfy any debts owed by the partnership. Thus, limited partners receive a return on their investment while risking only that original investment.

Limited partnerships must follow strict filing requirements. Usually, a certificate of limited partnership must be filed with the secretary of state's office. The purpose of the certificate is to warn third parties of the limited liability of some partners. However, some state statutes indicate that neither the names of the limited partners nor the amounts of their capital contributions must be included in the certificate. This provision simplifies the formation of a limited partnership because it allows limited partners to remain anonymous.

Failure to file a certificate of limited partnership will deprive a limited partner of limited liability if third parties attempting to hold the limited partner liable did not know that they were dealing with a limited partnership. Moreover, if in the certificate of limited partnership, a limited partner is incorrectly identified as a general partner, he or she would not have limited partner status. To correct such an error, the limited partner would have to refile an amended certificate of limited partnership or leave the limited partnership altogether. Such drastic actions would be necessary unless the state statute under which the limited partnership was formed allows a limited partner who has been incorrectly named as a general partner to file with the appropriate state office a unilateral **disclaimer of general partner status**. Limited partners must also guard against becoming too involved in the

Did You Know?

Because the dissolution of a partnership occurs whenever a partner becomes disassociated with the carrying on of partnership business, the dissolution of every partnership is inevitable. Therefore, the dissolution of a partnership is not a question of "if" but of "when."

business. A limited partner who exercises too much control over partnership affairs may lose the protective mantle of limited liability. Recently, however, many state legislatures have greatly expanded the types of activities that a limited partner can perform without losing the shelter provided by limited partnership status.

quick quiz 25-6

1. A registered limited liability partnership is like a general partnership in all respects except liability. true | false

2. In most states, to become a registered limited liability partnership, the partners must file with the auditor's office in the county courthouse. true | false

3. Limited partnerships must have at least three limited partners and no general partners. true | false

Summary

25.1 The easiest business organization to form is a sole proprietorship. All that businesspeople have to do is open their doors for business, and a sole proprietorship is created. The greatest advantage to a sole proprietorship is that the owner has complete control over the business. The major disadvantage is that the sole proprietor is subject to unlimited liability.

25.2 The Revised Uniform Partnership Act states that a partnership is "an association of two or more persons to carry on as co-owners a business for profit." Under the RUPA, a partnership is considered an entity, or an individual unit that exists separate from the partners. A partnership is an entity in its ability to own title to property, sue or be sued, and have its own separate bank accounts in its own name. Under the RUPA, partnerships also have continuity of existence.

25.3 One of the most common ways to form a partnership is by an express agreement between the parties. It is generally best to put the terms in writing to prevent misunderstanding and disputes that might arise later in the life of the partnership. The written agreement that establishes a partnership is called a partnership agreement. To show that a business is operating as a partnership by proof of existence, three elements must exist: (1) an association of two or more persons (2) who are co-owners of (3) a business for profit.

25.4 Capital contributions are sums that are contributed by the partners as permanent investments and that the partners are entitled to have returned when the partnership is dissolved. Loans or later advances that partners make to the partnership and accumulated but undivided profits belong to the partners on an individual basis. Other forms of partnership property belong only to the partnership in its status as an entity. The RUPA states that "A partner is not co-owner of partnership property and has no interest in partnership property which can be transferred, either voluntarily or involuntarily." Partners can use a partnership only for partnership purposes. The RUPA establishes that a partner has an interest in the partnership as a firm. That interest consists of two parts: (1) a transferable economic interest and (2) a nontransferable interest in management rights.

25.5 Under the RUPA, a dissociation takes place whenever a partner is no longer associated with the running of the firm. Partners can leave a partnership firm whenever they want. A partner leaves a firm wrongfully if he or she does not have the legal right to do so. The dissolution of a partnership occurs when a partner ceases to be associated with the partnership and the partnership ends. The dissolution of a partnership can occur in one of three ways: (1) by an action committed by the partners, (2) by operation of law, or (3) by the decree of a court of law.

25.6 The changing needs of the modern marketplace and the development of new ideas in the law have combined to allow for a new form of partnership, the registered limited liability partnership. Those same forces have cooperated to update one of the more traditional forms of the partnership business, the limited partnership.

Key Terms

aggregate theory, 605
capital contribution, 611
continuity of existence, 605
cooperative corporation, 608
cooperative corporation with wage-earning employees, 608
cooperative with nonemployee owners, 608
cross-owned corporation, 608
disclaimer of general partner status, 619
dissociation, 617
dissolution, 617
entity theory, 605
failure proof corporation, 608

franchise, 608
general partner, 619
general partnership, 607
joint liability, 612
joint and several liability, 612
joint venture, 608
limited liability, 619
limited liability corporation, 608
limited liability partnership, 608
limited partner, 607
limited partnership, 607, 619
partnership, 605
partnership at will, 617
private corporation, 608
public corporation, 608

public bodies corporation, 608
public-private corporation, 608
quasi-public corporation, 608
registered limited liability partnership, 619
Revised Uniform Partnership Act (RUPA), 605
secret partner, 614
silent partner, 614
social corporation, 608
sole proprietorship, 604
surplus, 614
term partnership, 617
Uniform Partnership Act (UPA), 604

Questions for Review and Discussion

1. What are the most common forms of business associations?
2. What are the advantages and disadvantages of a sole proprietorship?
3. What are the two model acts that govern partnership law?
4. What are the differences between the aggregate and entity theories of partnership?
5. What is the nature of a partnership agreement?
6. When does profit sharing not create a partnership?
7. What constitutes a person in partnership law?
8. What are the different views of specific partnership property in partnership law?
9. What is the difference between dissociation and dissolution in partnership law?
10. What is the difference between a registered limited liability partnership and a limited partnership?

Cases for Analysis

1. Jennifer Yauger owned a loft in uptown Silverton. Robert Tomba and Gary Jorgen were partners in a mail-order business in Middletown called NASCAR Collectibles. To open an outlet in Silverton, Tomba and Jorgen leased the loft from Yauger. As part of the agreement, Yauger received $2,650 in rent each month. Later Tomba and Jorgen set up a website and began an online auction house for NASCAR collectibles, similar to eBay. They were successful beyond their highest expectations, making over $2 million in their first year of operation. When another online auction house offered Tomba and Jorgen $60 million for their site, they accepted the offer without hesitation. When Yauger heard about

the deal, she claimed that she was a partner and demanded a $20 million payment, a sum equal to a one-third share of the sale price. When the case went to court, Yauger pointed to her monthly payments and labeled those payments a share of the profits. She argued that this payment demonstrated that she was a partner, based on proof of existence. Should the court grant Yauger partner status and give her a share of the proceeds from the sale of the business? Explain.

2. Kerry Taylor owned a warehouse in the industrial flats of Parke Central City. Yale Roberts and William Hull were partners in a chain of restaurants called Pirate's Seafood Carousel. Roberts and Hull leased Taylor's warehouse for their restaurant. As part of the agreement, Taylor received $7,500 in rent each month. Taylor retained office space on the top floor of the warehouse. She also agreed to allow Roberts and Hull to remodel the rest of the warehouse to meet the needs of their new restaurant. Taylor occasionally offered advice about the remodeling of the warehouse. In addition, after the restaurant opened for business, Taylor frequently signed for shipments that Roberts and Hull had ordered for the restaurant. After five years in this location, and after selling their other restaurants, Roberts and Hull decided to dissolve their partnership. During the winding up process, they were surprised to learn that Taylor claimed that she should receive a share of the surplus cash after the dissolution of the partnership, because she claimed to be a partner in Pirate's Seafood Carousel. Is Taylor correct in her claim? Will Roberts and Hull have to pay her a share of their surplus cash? Explain.

3. When the father of Stephen and Chris Nuss died, the two boys, aged 15 and 12 years, began to work the family farm. While the boys were still under the age of majority, their mother, Lois, kept the books for the farm. As the boys grew older, they took more and more responsibility in running the farm. They also rented and worked additional acres of farmland. They financed these rental agreements on their own, but their mother cosigned for the arrangements. The boys also purchased additional farmland. Again, their mother helped in this purchase by cosigning. When Chris decided to leave farming, Stephen paid him $100,000, and in exchange, Chris signed over the deed to the newly purchased land. Lois was not involved in this transaction. Stephen's farming business grew. He eventually amassed more than 1,200 acres. He and his wife, Linda, kept their own financial records and maintained their own checking account for the running of the farm. Stephen's mother was not involved in any of this detail. However, Stephen continued to pay many of the expenses involved on the original farm, where his mother still maintained her residence. Stephen also paid the insurance, maintenance, and repair expenses on all buildings and equipment on the original farm. Because Stephen continued to farm this land, in addition to the land he had subsequently purchased, these payments were always characterized as rent. No other payments went to Stephen's mother. When Stephen died, Linda, his widow and executor, claimed that a partnership existed and that the farm equipment on the original acreage and original acreage itself belonged to that partnership. Lois argued that no partnership between Stephen and her existed. Is Linda or Lois correct? Did a partnership exist? Explain. [See: *In re Estate of Nuss,* 646 N.E.2d 504 (OH).]

4. McCoy and Gugelman borrowed money from State Security Bank for their partnership, Antiques, Etc. When McCoy and Gugelman failed to pay back the debt, the bank sued them as individuals. At trial, McCoy and Gugelman argued that their partnership, Antiques, Etc., was an entity, not an aggregate, of the partners. Therefore, they concluded, the bank would have to show that the partnership funds were insufficient to answer the judgment before it could proceed against them individually. Are they correct? Why or why not? [See: *Security State Bank v. McCoy,* 361 N.W.2d 514 (NE).]

5. Shane ran a liquid fertilizer business. As part of the operation of the business, Shane paid Svoboda a specified amount per acre to spread the fertilizer on his clients' crops. Svoboda's per acre payments remained steady, despite Shane's profits or losses. Frisch was injured while filling a tank truck that was supposed to haul the fertilizer to Svoboda's tractor. Frisch sued both Shane and Svoboda, claiming that Svoboda was sharing in Shane's profits and was therefore a partner. Was Frisch correct? Explain. [See: *Frisch v. Svobada,* 157 N.W.2d 774 (NE).]

6. Summers and Dooley formed a partnership for the purpose of operating a trash collection business.

The business was operated by the two men, and when either was unable to work, the nonworking partner provided a replacement at his own expense. Summers approached Dooley and requested that they hire a third worker. Dooley refused. Notwithstanding Dooley's refusal, Summers, on his own initiative, hired a worker. Summers paid the employee out of his own pocket. Dooley, upon discovery that a third person had been hired, objected. He stated that the additional labor was not necessary and refused to allow partnership funds to be used to pay the new employee. After paying out more than $11,000 in wages without any reimbursement from either partnership funds or his partner, Summers brought suit in the Idaho state courts. The trial court held that Summers was not entitled to reimbursement for the wages he had paid the employee. On appeal, did the Supreme Court of Idaho uphold the trial court's decision? Explain. [See: *Summers v. Dooley,* 481 P.2d 318 (ID).]

quick quiz Answers

25-1	25-2	25-3	25-4	25-5	25-6
1. F	1. F	1. T	1. F	1. T	1. T
2. T	2. F	2. T	2. T	2. T	2. F
3. T	3. T	3. T	3. F	3. T	3. F

Chapter 26 The Corporate Entity

THE OPENING CASE Round 1
Disregarding the Corporate Entity: Limited Liability and the Corporate Veil

This strange but weird case began when William Stewart, doing business as Stewart Coal Company entered a contract with R.A. Eberts, Inc., in which Stewart sold his coal mining operation to Eberts, Inc., for the tidy sum of $3,500,000. The agreement included these critical clauses: (1) Stewart would receive $475,000 up front; (2) Eberts, Inc., would owe Stewart Coal $1,588,195; (3) out of the $1,436,895 left over, Eberts, Inc., would make royalty payments of $1 for each ton of coal, but not less than $5,000 each month and (4) pay the total amount remaining by June 30, 2003. This all seemed to go pretty well until 2003 rolled around and Eberts, Inc., stopped royalty payments to Stewart and then missed the final payout due June 30, 2003. Accordingly, Stewart sued Eberts, Inc., for breach of contract. However, Stewart did not stop there. He later amended his complaint and sought to *pierce the corporate veil* of Eberts, Inc., in order to hold its officers, directors, and shareholders personally liable. After the discovery stage in the lawsuit, Stewart found out that the shareholders, officers, and directors of Eberts, Inc., had transferred all the company's assets and liabilities to Waterloo Coal Company. Waterloo and Eberts, Inc., shared the same officers, directors, and shareholders.

These same officers, directors, and shareholders later transferred all of the liabilities to a newly created LLC named Eberts, LLC. Eberts, Inc., was then liquidated. In fact, evidence indicates that the officers, directors, and shareholders of Eberts, Inc., simply closed one day and then reopened almost immediately as Eberts, LLC. The new LLC had two of the original owners of Eberts, Inc. (William Parks and T.L. Darlington) and two new owners (Scott Parks and Denton Bowman). The two new owners acquired Phil Bowman's interest. Bowman, a former owner of the dismantled Eberts, Inc., then left the firm. With all of this new information in mind, Stewart amended the complaint again, this time to hold the two additional companies, Waterloo and Eberts, LLC, liable and to also pierce the veil of these corporations in order to hold their officer, directors, and shareholders liable too. (Actually, in an LLC the owners and officers are referred to respectively as members and managers, but we will cover that later.) Undaunted, the defendants filed a summary judgment motion asking the court to dismiss the case because Stewart had not demonstrated that the veil-piercing doctrine could be applied in this case, specifically because Stewart had failed to demonstrate the first two elements of the veil-piercing test: (1) complete control of the alleged corporate entity, and (2) the use of that control by the real beneficiaries (here the officers, directors, and shareholders) to commit fraud against the plaintiff. The trial court agreed with the defendants, granted the summary judgment motion, and dismissed the case. Unsatisfied with being so curtly dismissed, Stewart appealed. On appeal, Stewart showed that Eberts, LLC, the new corporate person, had the same officers, directors, and shareholders as Eberts, Inc.; that both Eberts, Inc., and Eberts, LLC, had been badly undercapitalized to the point of insolvency; and that the other corporate person involved in this game, Waterloo, had been the recipient of all of the tangible assets of Eberts, Inc., while Eberts, LLC (the insolvent company), had received the intangible assets including the debt owed to Stewart, a debt that it clearly could not pay. How should the appeals court rule in this case? [See: *William Stewart d/b/a Stewart*

Coal Co. v. R. A. Eberts Company Inc., et al, Case Number 08CA10 (August 8, 2009).]

Opening Case Questions

1. Why was the plaintiff forced to amend his complaint twice in this case? Explain.

2. What is the difference between a corporation and an LLC? Explain.

3. Does an LLC possess the same corporate personhood status as that enjoyed by a corporation? Explain.

4. If the judge rules in favor of the defendants in relation to the money owed to the plaintiff, what recourse would the plaintiff have, if any? Explain.

5. What are the three elements needed to allow the court to pierce the corporate veil? Explain.

 Learning Objectives

1. Describe some strategies for avoiding a new 21st century economic crisis.
2. Explain what is meant by the term *corporation*.
3. List the four methods of protecting a corporation.
4. Describe the differences among a private, a public, and a quasi-public corporation.
5. Distinguish between a close and an S corporation.
6. List the typical elements within the articles of incorporation.
7. Distinguish between the articles of organization and the operating agreement of a limited liability company.
8. Distinguish between a *de jure* and a *de facto* corporation.
9. Identify the goal of piercing the corporate veil.
10. Distinguish between common and preferred stock.

26-1 The Economic Crisis and the Corporate Entity

In Chapter 20, we analyzed the nature of the 21st century economic crisis as it related to the financial issues of runaway mortgages and overextended lending practices, all of which led to the monetary disaster of 2008. While examining these issues, we called upon the wisdom of several modern thinkers, including Michel Serres in *Times of Crisis*, Dmitry Orlov in *Reinventing Collapse*, Nouriel Roubini and Stephen Mihm in *Crisis Economics*, and Paul M. Barrett in "Prophet-Making." To summarize their work (or our take on their work), in *Times of Crisis*, Serres argues, rather persuasively, that the only way to avert any future crisis is to avoid returning to the initial conditions that created that crisis. Serres also notes that the latest economic crisis has been caused by human tampering in agriculture, transportation (communication), health, demographics connections, and conflicts. This tampering, he argues, created a biogetic (his word) system that is unstable, leading to a series of unintended consequences.

Crisis Management and the Corporate Entity

In *Reinventing Collapse,* Orlov points out that, in the Soviet Union, several factors collided that led to that nation's economic crisis. Those factors include: (1) a decline in energy resources; (2) a serious trade deficit; (3) unrestrained defense spending; (4) expanding foreign debt; and (5) a pervasive psychosocial anxiety leading to erratic behavior. Without mentioning Serres but following a strategy that seems to heed his warnings, Orlov promotes two radical strategies designed to deal with some of the most serious results of that collision. These strategies include a governmental ban on the production of any new gas-powered vehicles and a radical alteration in the nature of the corporation, two measures that are original and thought-provoking but ultimately too idealistic and impractical for adoption in the real world of American capitalism. Again without referring directly to either Orlov or Serres, Roubini and Mihm appear to apply a set of integrated Serres-Orlov principles to the political and economic world of Washington and Wall Street in order to construct several proposals to make those radical adjustments a reality. In doing so, they propose two strategies, both of which focus on limiting corporate protection measures. To accomplish this objective, Roubini and Mihm suggest that Congress mandate the subdivision and reorganization of the nation's largest financial institutions into smaller, independent units. This plan would make it illegal for large financial institutions to invest in any venture from which they cannot extricate themselves with the capital reserves that they have on hand. In essence, financial institutions would be legally compelled to maintain the ability to bail themselves out of financial danger. Roubini and Mihm also propose a bonus-escrow plan, referred to as the "bonus-malus" system, under which the bonuses paid to top executives would be placed in escrow accounts for several years to test the true value of the programs and projects instituted by each executive. The executive does not receive the bonus unless the investment programs and projects demonstrate their staying power and profitability. If those investments lose money, then the bonus is reduced by an appropriate amount. [See: Dmitry Orlov, *Reinventing Collapse: The Soviet Experience and American Prospects* (Gabriola Islands, BC, Canada: New Society Publishers, 2011); Michel Serres, *Times of Crisis: What the Financial Crisis Revealed and How to Reinvent our Lives and Future* (New York: Bloomsbury, 2014); and Nouriel Roubini and Stephen Mihm, *Crisis Economics* (New York: Penguin, 2010).]

Capitalism and the Corporate Entity

Whether these strategies would actually be adopted by Congress is problematic. It is, after all, difficult to get politicians to do really risky things like break up corporations or freeze corporate payouts to executives (especially in election years). That is the bad news. The good news, however, is that corporate leadership does not have to wait for a congressional mandate to take the radical steps that might be needed to dodge the next financial crisis. This is because the corporation lies at the heart of the American economy and, as such, can orchestrate such changes on its own. To see why this is so, we need to examine the characteristics and the power of the corporation. A **corporation** (aka **corporate person** and **corporate entity**) is a legal entity created under the authority of a state or federal statute that gives certain individuals the capacity to operate an enterprise. As such, corporations are products of capitalism. Although capitalism originated in Europe, it flourished in the United States in the 19th century because the American economic system at that time provided the perfect engine for capitalistic progress. Much of this progress occurred because there was an enormous amount of land that needed to be developed in the United States and an influx of energetic immigrants who were willing to improve that land. Capitalism grew because those businesspeople who worked the land as farms, factories, railroads, and stores needed an efficient and rapid way to raise capital to finance land development projects. The corporate entity was the perfect means of raising capital quickly and using it effectively. The corporation of today, however, bears little resemblance to the corporate entity as it emerged in the 19th century. (Note: For detailed discussion if these radical differences, see Chapter 28.) Nevertheless, the corporate structure that exists today provides the needed power, protection, and protocols to deal with future economic problems and to profit from future economic opportunities.

Stabilizing Corporate Legal Principles

The capitalistic economic system has operated in a manner that has ensured that corporations are protected in a variety of ways. However, the basis of that protection lies within four fundamental legal principles that are designed to safeguard the corporate entity. These four principles are corporate limited liability, free transfer of ownership, central management, and the corporate person, itself.

LO3

Corporate Limited Liability
Today one of the most attractive features of the corporate way of doing business is its limited liability. **Limited liability** means that the corporate investors cannot be held personally liable for the debts of the corporation. Thus, the most that an investor can lose is the amount of money used to purchase his or her **shares** of the corporation. This liability is maintained indefinitely just so long as the corporation actually maintains its status as a self-governing, self-contained corporate person.

U.S. Const.
Amendment 14

THE OPENING CASE *Round 2*
Disregarding the Corporate Entity: Limited Liability?

Recall that in the opening case, the shareholders, officers, and directors of Eberts, Inc., transferred all the company's assets and liabilities to the Waterloo Coal Company. Recall also that Waterloo and Eberts, Inc., shared the same officers, directors, and shareholders. These same officers, directors, and shareholders later transferred all of Eberts' liabilities to a newly created LLC named Eberts, LLC. Eberts, Inc., was then liquidated. In fact, evidence indicates that the officers, directors, and shareholders of Eberts, Inc., simply closed Eberts, Inc., and then reopened almost immediately as Eberts, LLC. The new LLC had two of the original owners of Eberts, Inc. (William Parks and T.L. Darlington) and two new owners (Scott Parks and Denton Bowman). The two new owners acquired Phil Bowman's interest. Bowman, a former owner of the dismantled Eberts, Inc., then left the firm. It is important to understand that, as a newly existing corporation, Eberts, LLC, was a legally incorporated entity with its own separate identity and its own independent corporate status. It had its own articles of organization; its own operating agreement; its own owners (called

members); and its own officers (called managers). It looked, acted, and operated like a stand-alone corporate person. One of the advantages to the members and managers of Eberts, LLC, in the creation of the new company is that those members and managers would have *limited liability*. However, in order for the members and managers of Eberts, LLC, to take advantage of this arrangement, they would have to permit Eberts, LLC, to have a certain degree of independence so that, if they were ever asked to account for Eberts, LLC's actions, they could legitimately claim that, throughout all of the financial maneuvering that went on, the LLC remained an independent entity. That is what the court had to determine in this case—was Eberts, LLC, a separate corporate entity or simply a clone of Eberts, Inc., created to escape paying the money Eberts, Inc., owed to Stewart under a contract made for the sale of Stewart Coal Company, a contract that now seems to have gone sour. [See: *William Stewart d/b/a Stewart Coal Co. v. R. A. Eberts Company Inc., et al,* Case Number 08CA10 (August 8, 2009).]

CLASSIC CASE The *Hobby Lobby* Case: A New Spin on Corporate Personhood

The ink was hardly dry on the paper that printed the first copies of the Supreme Court's *Hobby Lobby* decision when it became clear that this case would become a classic. The case involves an insurance plan under the Affordable Care Act that would have provided "preventative care and screenings" for women employees free of "any cost sharing requirements." [42 USC Section 300gg-13(a) (4).] The statute empowered the Department of Health and Human Services (DHHS) to identify prevention techniques that would be covered under the act. To make that determination, the department enlisted the support of the Institute of Medicine, which declared that employers should provide coverage for all contraceptive procedures approved by the Food and Drug Administration. Four of these methods are designed to stop, potentially at least, the development of an already fertilized egg. These four methods violated the religious principles of the owners of Hobby Lobby, who believe that life begins at conception. Three corporations, including Hobby Lobby, brought lawsuits against the DHHS, arguing that they cannot be compelled by the government to participate in a practice that violates their religious beliefs. The lawsuit was brought under the authority of the Religious Freedom Restoration Act (RFRA) and the Free Exercise Clause of the U.S. Constitution.

Religious Freedom Restoration Act (RFRA)   The RFRA states that the government cannot "substantially burden a person's exercise of religion even if the burden results from a rule of general applicability" except when the government "demonstrates that the application of the burden to the person (1) is in furtherance of a compelling governmental interest; and (2) is the least restrictive means of furthering that compelling governmental interest." [42 USC Sections 2000bb-1(a) (b).] The first issue that the Court addresses in the opinion in *Hobby Lobby* is whether the three corporate plaintiffs qualify as "legal persons" *under this particular congressional statute.* The U.S. Supreme Court opens its opinion by making it absolutely clear that the purpose of the RFRA is to protect a person's right to exercise religious beliefs. The statute was named the Religious Freedom Restoration Act because Congress intended to reinstate a defense for religious expression that had been repeatedly weakened by the courts over the past several years (decades?). Clearly, then, the purpose of the mandate is to broaden religious protection guaranteed to all persons under the U.S. Constitution. The question then is whether a *profit-oriented* corporation qualifies as a "person" under the RFRA.

Corporate Personhood: The New Spin   In this case, the Supreme Court takes the first steps toward carrying

Free Transfer of Ownership   Corporate financing begins when the original investments are made to set up the corporation. Once the corporate person is operating, additional corporate financing may be obtained from earnings, loans, and the issuance of additional shares of stock. The issuing and selling of shares of stock to raise capital is known as *equity financing* and equity securities give their owners a legal interest in the assets, earnings, and control of the corporation. The part of a corporation's net profits or surplus set aside for the shareholders is known as dividends. The number of shares and classes of stock that a corporation is authorized to issue are established in its certificate of incorporation. A shareholder who purchases corporate stock invests money or property in the corporation and receives a stock certificate. A **stock certificate** is written evidence of ownership of a unit of interest in the corporation.

Central Management   Most state incorporation statutes provide that a corporation's business affairs are to be managed under the direction of a board of directors. The board of directors establishes broad policies, and the officers and other employees implement those policies. The shareholders are the owners of the corporation. How to keep the role of the board separate from that of executive management and that of shareholders is related to the challenge of how best to organize the board and select its members. The out the RFRA mandate and, in doing so, gives new life to the Free Exercise Clause of the First Amendment. However, the Court also puts a new spin on the concept of *corporate personhood.* The Court begins with the standard legal doctrine that establishes that a corporation exists as a person that is separate from its promoters, shareholders, employees, directors, and officers. So far so good. However, as its next step, the Court applies (invents?) a novel reinterpretation of the nature of corporate personhood. The Court says that, while the corporate identity is constructed to defend the corporation, it is also created to protect the flesh-and-blood people behind that corporation. Accordingly, when the law defines the rights and duties of a corporate person, it is actually defining the rights and duties of the people behind that corporation. These people are the ones who actually carry out corporate duties and who benefit from corporate rights. Thus, when the corporation is recognized as having rights, those rights really belong to the people behind the corporate veil. This is especially true when the "right" in question is a religious right. Thus, the Supreme Court concludes that the term *person* in the statute is meant to protect corporate "persons" *only because* the real protection flows to the people behind that corporate veil. It may be a bit hard to believe that someone on the Supreme Court actually said this, so let's take a brief look at exactly what Justice Alito states in his opinion. Alito writes:

> (I)t is important to keep in mind that the purpose of this fiction is to provide protection for human beings. A corporation is simply a form of organization used by human beings to achieve desired ends. An established body of law specifies the rights and obligations of the *people* (including shareholders, officers, and employees) who are associated with a corporation in one way or another. When rights, whether constitutional or statutory, are extended to corporations, the purpose is to protect the rights of these people. For example, extending Fourth Amendment protection to corporations protects the privacy interests of employees and others associated with the company. Protecting corporations from government seizure of their property without just compensation protects all those who have a stake in the corporations' financial well-being. And protecting the free-exercise rights of corporations like Hobby Lobby, Conestoga, and Mardel protects the religious liberty of the humans who own and control those companies.

This interpretation will undoubtedly spark controversy among corporate lawyers who are not used to such a revolutionary way of looking at the relationship between the corporate person and the people behind that person. In fact, this new way of looking at corporate identify may inspire a new wave of veil-piercing cases. [See: *Sylvia Burwell, Secretary of Health and Human Services, et al. v. Hobby Lobby Stores, Inc., et al.* United States Supreme Court, Nos. 13-354 and 13-356 (June 30, 2014) 573 U.S. — (2014).]

issues are even more complex today because a single individual often functions as a director, an officer, and a shareholder. Nevertheless, the three roles have distinct functions and should operate separately.

Corporate Personhood A corporation exists apart from its owners and is taxed directly on the income it earns. As a legal entity, a corporate person can own property and sue or be sued, just as an individual can. Moreover, the existence of a corporation is not affected by the death, incapacity, or bankruptcy of a manager or shareholder. A corporation is also considered an artificially created legal person under provisions of the U.S. Constitution. Within the context of the 14th Amendment, a corporate person—like a natural person—may not be deprived of life, liberty, or property without due process of law. Also, a corporation may not be denied equal protection of the laws within the jurisdiction of the state. A corporate person is considered a citizen of both the state in which it is incorporated and the state where it has its principal place of business. It can also be sued as a citizen of both these states. By virtue of the *due process clause* of the 14th Amendment, a state court may also exercise jurisdiction over a noncitizen corporate defendant, as long as that corporate person has had an appropriate contact with that state. Such contact can include owning property within the state, doing business in the state, or committing a tort within the state.

The Corporate Balancing Act

As we have seen at various intervals throughout the text, the law must balance several opposing factors: The letter of the law must be balanced with its spirit; the language of the law must be balanced with its interpretation; abstract legal principles must be balanced with the concrete application of those principles; and the intent of the law must be balanced with the results that emerge from the work of the lawmakers. In many ways, the corporate structure is a vivid manifestation of these balancing acts. Corporations are governed by their own bylaws, which must be balanced with federal statutes, state corporate law, and court decisions that govern the operation of those corporations. As a direct result of this, corporate officers will at times follow the letter of the law while skirting its spirit, as when they make corporate decisions that technically ought to go to the board of directors for a vote. Or they will at times interpret that language of the law to their own advantage as the big corporations did in the 19th century, when they used the Sherman Antitrust Law, specifically designed to end corporate monopolies, to break up union organizing activities and thus protect their corporate structure. None of this is to say that corporations or their officers are lawless or unethical. On the contrary, most of them are doing what they are supposed to do. They are protecting their own best interests and the best interests of their shareholders. Much of this is expressed in the balancing act among the legal watchdogs that make certain (or should make certain) that corporate officers, directors, and shareholders do not abuse the power and the privileges granted to them by the law and by the very nature of the capitalist economic system. This precarious balancing act is based upon the intervention of Congress at the federal level, the legislature at the state level, and the courts as they apply the common law.

A QUESTION OF ETHICS

The Spirit or the Letter of the Law?

As noted earlier, the law is frequently described as a balancing act. Perhaps one of the most-often-quoted segments of this concept of balancing is seen in the attempt to balance the *spirit* of the law with the *letter* of the law. It now appears, however, that this simple and, heretofore, rarely challenged concept has several new adversaries. Supreme Court Justice Antonin Scalia and his co-author Bryan A Garner, distinguished research professor of law at Southern Methodist University, have breathed new life into a form of legal interpretation referred to alternately as *textualism* and *originalism* that may demonstrate the naïveté of attempting to balance the spirit with the letter of the law.

THE TEXTUALIST APPROACH

In general, the idea behind textualism (also originalism) is for judges and attorneys to look at constitutions and statutes as literary works or as verbal icons that stand as separately created artifacts that must be judged, much like a poem or a short story, by its words and its word alone. The intent of textualism is to have legal interpreters bypass the generally biased and self-serving explanations found in legislative histories and committee reports and instead rely upon the meaning of the words that the legislators actually wrote and placed in the text of the constitution or the statute in question. Scalia and Garner explain the details of textualism in *Reading Law: The Interpretation of Legal Texts*. Much of the book is devoted to a detailed examination of 57 canons of interpretation and 13 false beliefs that they discredit. The very first attack on these false statements targets the idea that "the spirit of a statute should prevail over its letter." Scalia and Garner argue that the idea that the spirit of the law can somehow magically trump the letter of the law was probably born sometime in the Middle Ages when the chances of finding statutory law in England were unlikely at best. Moreover, they note that, since no one has ever identified any standards by which to deduce, measure, and apply this mysterious "spirit of the law," it was most likely used as a technique to grant judges the unrestricted ability to pay no attention to the language of the law. Scalia and Garner also point out that even those judicial and philosophical giants who are alleged to have supported the spirit over letter principle really did no such thing. The leading example of those distortions is Chief Justice John Marshall who is supposed to have depended on the spirit of the Constitution, when what he really said was that the spirit of the law should be respected just as much as the letter, and (here is the key) that the spirit itself was to be "collected chiefly from its letter." [See: Antonin Scalia and Bryan Garner, *Reading Law: The Interpretation of Legal Texts* (St. Paul, MN: West, 2012).]

THE PRAGMATIC APPROACH

On the other side of this issue are a number of legal experts, not the least of which is Richard Posner, chief justice of the U.S. Court of Appeals for the Seventh Circuit and the author of *Overcoming Law*. Posner's book predates Scalia and Garner's text by some 17 years. However, Posner devotes an entire chapter to textualism, largely fashioned as a critique of another champion of that theory, Robert Bork, the author of *The Tempting of America: The Political Seduction of the Law*. In *Overcoming Law*, Posner argues that textualism, whether supported by Bork or Scalia, is fine as far as it goes, but it cannot be considered as the only arrow in a judge's quiver. Textual criticism will help to get at the meaning of the words in the law; that much is true. However, to rely solely on this approach is to ignore the consequences of the law or of a singular and narrowly drawn interpretation of that law. Posner prefers, instead, a process that he labels *pragmatism*. In a nutshell, pragmatism involves an approach by judges that considers the consequences of a decision to be the single most important guideline in the development of that decision. In applying a pragmatic approach, the judge must attempt to get into the mind of the framer of that law and, in doing so, see how that framer would respond to the modern circumstances in which the judge finds himself or herself. The law, Posner believes, is not static nor should it be. Moreover, in making his or her determination, the judge must not focus alone on a single interpretation but must consider multiple interpretations in order to sort out the one that makes the most sense. This technique, Posner argues, is not "judicial lawlessness," but is, instead, an approach that looks both forward and backward and does so with a mind toward the consequences based on multiple forms of input. [See: Richard Posner, *Overcoming Law* (Cambridge, MA: Harvard University Press, 1995); Robert Bork, *The Tempting of America: The Political Seduction of the Law* (New York: Simon and Schuster, 1990).]

QUESTIONS YET UNANSWERED

The following questions have not yet been answered. Before you consider each question, turn to Chapter 1 to review the various ethical theories noted there (market value ethics, social contract theory, utilitarianism, and rational ethics). Then using one of those theories in a consistent way, answer the following questions. Is it ethical for *textualist* judges to ignore certain categories of legal research, such as legislative histories and committee reports, in their attempt to unravel the true meaning of a statute? Is it ethical for pragmatic judges to consider legislative histories and committee reports when evidence and experience have demonstrated that such reports and histories tend to be biased and prejudiced toward the position of the individual writer? Scalia and Garner argue that the spirit of the law is an invalid measuring stick because legal scholars have yet to detect any standards by which to deduce, measure, and apply this enigmatic "spirit of the law." Is this a valid argument? Why or why not? Assist Scalia and Garner by developing a standard or two that might help them identify those intangible "spiritual" standards. Posner argues that judges should always look at the possible consequences that may result from a statute once that statute goes into effect. At one level this sounds like a common-sense approach, but at another, more fundamental level, it looks like a recipe for disaster. A judge must troll through mountains of material when trying to interpret the Constitution, a statute, or a regulation. Moreover, looking backward is hard enough, but looking forward to consequences can sometimes amount to an exercise in judicial fortune-telling. That is why these results are often called "unintended consequences." Advise Posner by demonstrating the folly of trying to predict the future.

Federal Congressional Action: Congress and the Dodd-Frank Act The federal government's power to regulate business emerged directly (and quite quickly for that matter) out of the commerce clause of the U.S. Constitution. The commerce clause is found in Article I, Section 8, Clause 3. The wording of the clause is a study in simplicity. The clause reads, "Congress shall have Power To . . . regulate Commerce with foreign Nations and among the several states." One of the first commentators to recognize the full import of these words was Supreme Court Justice William Johnson who, in his concurring opinion in *Gibbons v. Ogden* 22 U.S. 1 (1824), wrote, "The power of a sovereign state over commerce therefore amounts to nothing more than a power to limit and restrain . . . that . . . power must be exclusive; it can reside but in one potentate, and hence the grant of this power carries with it the whole subject, leaving nothing for the State to act upon." Despite the fact that Johnson denies that he is a textualist, his study of the commerce clause in *Gibbons v. Ogden* is, nevertheless, a model of textual analysis. The words are plain and Johnson passes that plain meaning along to us.

Following Johnson's lead, the Supreme Court quickly recognized the federal government's power to regulate business. The power to regulate is so broad today that the federal government can regulate any business activity that affects interstate commerce, even if that activity takes place solely within the borders of a single state. Just about the only thing that the U.S. Supreme Court has not yet allowed the government to do is to force citizens, or anyone else for that matter, to participate in an activity whether they want to or not. In contrast, the states do sometimes order their citizens to engage in some forms of commerce, as when they require automobile owners to buy insurance. Such legislation, however, is permitted under the state's police power. On the other hand, even that power is limited. The state can require insurance but only if a citizen actually wants to own a car. It is unlikely that a state can order a person to engage in a business activity merely because that person exists.

In Chapter 20 we learned that, in response to the 21st century financial crisis, Congress passed several pieces of legislation, including the **Dodd-Frank Wall Street Reform and Consumer Protection Act**, aimed at fixing current economic problems and preventing such events from happening again. The problems that we discussed in Chapter 20 were related to mortgages. The mortgage industry, however, was only part of the problem. Another industry involved in the crisis was the securities industry. For that reason, Congress also included provisions in the Dodd-Frank Act to deal with the shortcomings and the errors of the securities industry, which stands at the heart of corporate ownership. As might be expected, the Dodd-Frank Act is long, involved, and complicated. It is, in fact, divided into 16 titles, many of which are named as individual acts. Two titles that affect the Securities Exchange Commission are Title VII, the Wall Street Transparency and Accountability Act, and Title IX, the Investor Protection and Securities Reform Act of 2010.

State Legislative Action: The Model Business Corporation Act

The states have the power to regulate business under their inherent police power, a power that the federal government does not have. As noted earlier, a corporation is a legal entity created under the authority of a state or federal statute that gives certain individuals the capacity to operate an enterprise. The statutory template that most states follow in developing their corporate law statutes is the Model Business Corporation Act, often referred to as the Model Corporation Act and sometimes simply as the MBCA. The MBCA is a relatively young statute and is therefore not quite as settled as older, more traditional statutes, such as the Uniform Commercial Code and the original Uniform Partnership Act. In addition, the model act has been revised since its inception, making some of its provisions even more recent and therefore less fully developed than similar provisions in other comparable statutes.

Judicial Action: State Common Law Decisions
Also, many states have a long history of common law decisions in relation to corporate law, some of which must be

preempted when a state legislature adopts the MBCA. Even in the face of explicit instances of preemption, however, some state courts have been reluctant to surrender long-term common law principles and sometimes have found creative ways to interpret the MBCA within the context of that state's long-standing legal tradition. Therefore, the study of corporate law must always be tempered by a look at the state law of the jurisdiction in which a dispute is located. The process of doing business as a self-governing business association, that is, as a corporate person, is called **associative corporativism**, or simply **corporativism**. In the 19th century, each corporation was individually created by a unique legislative enactment. Each corporation had its own charter that outlined the powers and abilities of that corporation. (Note: For a more detailed analysis of the nature and the limits of the state's power to regulate commerce, see Chapter 28.)

---

quick quiz 26-1

1. A corporation is a legal entity created by either a state or federal statute authorizing individuals to operate an enterprise.   true | false

2. A corporation may not be deprived of life, liberty, or property without due process of law.   true | false

3. Limited liability means that the corporate investors rather than the corporation will be held liable for corporate debts.   true | false

---

26-2 Types of Corporate Entities

The previous chapter focused on sole proprietorships, general partnerships, limited partnerships, and limited liability partnerships as a way of initiating our exploration of business persons and the legal rules that apply to such persons. This chapter focuses on the nature, the formation, the identity, and the financing of the corporate entity. Before that, however, we will review the various types of traditional corporate entities . These types include:

1. Private corporations
2. Public (or state-owned) corporations
3. Quasi-public corporations
4. Domestic corporations
5. Foreign corporations
6. Alien corporations
7. Close corporations
8. S Chapter corporations
9. Limited liability corporations
10. Joint ventures
11. Franchises

Private, Public, and Quasi-Public Corporate Persons

A **private corporation** is a corporation formed by private persons to accomplish a task best undertaken by an entity that can raise large amounts of capital quickly or that can grant the protection of limited liability. Private corporations can be organized for a profit-making business purpose or for a nonprofit charitable, educational, or scientific purpose. If the

Google, Inc., headquartered in Menlo Park, California, maintains 17 corporate offices in the United States and 38 corporate offices in 23 countries throughout Asia, Europe, and North and South America.

corporation is organized for profit-making purposes, those profits may be distributed to the shareholders in the form of dividends. **Dividends** are the net profits, or surplus, set aside for the shareholders. **Shareholders** (or stockholders, as they are also known) are those individuals who own units of interest (shares of stock) in a corporation. Large private corporations generally sell their stock to the public at large and are, therefore, often referred to as public corporations. When the owners of a private corporation decide to sell stock to the public at large, financial experts report that the corporation is about to "go public." This designation can be confusing because the term **public corporation** is more properly used to describe a corporation created by the federal, state, or local government for governmental purposes. When used in the latter sense, the term includes incorporated cities, sanitation districts, school districts, transit districts, and so on. Corporations that are privately organized for profit but also provide a service on which the public depends are generally referred to as **quasi-public corporations**. In most instances, they are public utilities, which provide the public with such essentials as water, gas, and electricity. (Note: Unless specified otherwise, the discussion in this chapter and those that follow will focus on private corporations.)

Domestic, Foreign, and Alien Corporate Persons

A corporation is a **domestic corporation** in the state that grants its charter. It is a **foreign corporation** in all other states. The right to do business in other states (subject to reasonable regulation) is granted by the commerce clause of the U.S. Constitution. To qualify to do business in another state, a foreign corporation must obtain a certificate of authority by providing information similar to the information provided by a domestic corporation applying for a charter. A **certificate of authority** is a document that grants a foreign corporation permission to do business in another state. A registered office and agent must be maintained within the state upon which service of process (notice of a lawsuit) may be made on behalf of the corporation. An **alien corporation** is one that, though incorporated in a nation-state other than the United States, is, nevertheless, doing business in the United States.

Close and S Corporations

A business corporation may be designated as a **close corporation** when the outstanding shares of stock and managerial control are closely held by fewer than 50 shareholders (often members of the same family) or by one person. State business corporation statutes generally accommodate closely held corporations by allowing them to have a few directors or a sole director and president, with no voting shares in the hands of the public. The Subchapter S Revision Act of 1982 gives small, closely held business corporations the option of obtaining special tax advantages by becoming an S corporation. An **S corporation** is a corporation in which shareholders have agreed to have the profits (or losses) of the corporation taxed directly to them rather than to the corporation. In this way, they avoid double taxation. There are, however, several restrictions on S corporations. These restrictions include limits on the number and types of owners that can be involved in such an entity. Consequently, many individuals now look to limited liability companies to escape double taxation.

Limited Liability Companies, Joint Ventures, and Franchises

The **limited liability company (LLC)** is best thought of as a cross between a partnership and a corporation. Like a corporation, the LLC offers the protection of limited liability to its owners. However, unlike a corporation, the LLC's tax liability flows through the LLC and to the owners. In this way, an LLC, like a partnership and an S corporation, escapes the double taxation penalty that falls on corporate entities. In addition, LLCs are statutory, which means that they may come into existence only if the owners follow the precise steps laid out in the state code by the state legislature. The owners of an LLC are called **members**. The people who run the LLC are called **managers**. Later in this chapter, we discuss the formation details of an LLC. Chapter 27 also includes a discussion of the duties and responsibilities of the members and the managers of an LLC. A **joint venture** (or **joint undertaking**) involves a contractual arrangement by which individuals unite for a limited time to create a new entity in which the founders share control, expenses, and profits. A **franchise** is a business arrangement that permits an individual, a group of investors, or another entity to lease the right to use a parent entity's business operation, trademark, goods, services, and goodwill under a fee arrangement provided to the parent.

quick quiz 26-2

1.	A private corporation is one that is formed under the authority of a state statute to perform a governmental function.	true | false
2.	A certificate of authority is issued only to S corporations that have passed the test of associative liability.	true | false
3.	Limited liability companies have been outlawed in most states because they limit the tax revenue that is due to the government.	true | false

26-3 Formation of the Corporate Entity

A corporation may be incorporated in any state that has a general incorporation statute. Keep in mind that corporations are also subject to court decisions and the state constitution. Federal agencies such as the Securities and Exchange Commission (SEC) also regulate corporate activity. A proper understanding of effective corporate formation necessitates an examination of promoters, the articles of incorporation, the corporate name, the approval of the articles, and commencement of business. Figure 26-1 illustrates the steps of the incorporation process.

Promoters

The people who want to begin a new corporation or incorporate an existing business are called **promoters**. These people do the actual day-to-day work involved in the incorporation process. **Incorporators** are the people who actually sign the articles of incorporation and submit them to the appropriate state officials. The promoters may also be the incorporators, who later become shareholders and directors of the corporation. Promoters occupy a fiduciary relationship with the nonexistent corporation and its future shareholders. Therefore, the promoter must act in the best interests of the new corporation and its shareholders. The promoter must be honest and loyal and fully reveal all information about any contracts made for the corporation.

Preformation Contracts   Often, promoters will enter contracts for the unborn corporation. For example, it may be necessary to lease office and warehouse space, purchase equipment, and hire employees as preliminary steps in preparing the way for the new corporation. A corporation is not bound by any of the promoter's contracts unless it adopts

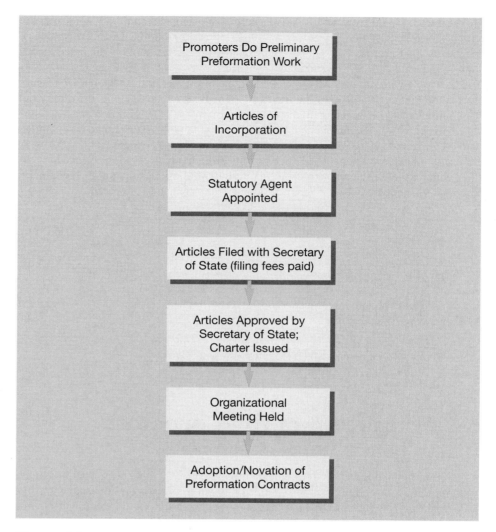

Figure 26-1 This chart shows the steps in the incorporation process.

those contracts. Adoption occurs expressly if the directors pass a resolution agreeing to be bound by a contract. Adoption can also occur implicitly if the corporation accepts the benefits of a contract or makes any payments called for by the agreement.

Novation Even after adoption of the contracts, promoters are still potentially liable under the preincorporation contracts. One way for promoters to escape potential liability is to have the corporation and the third party agree to release them. The agreement releasing a promoter is known as a **novation**. The promoter may also include an automatic release clause in all contracts negotiated for the unborn corporation. However, the release clause must do more than simply include the corporation as a party to the contract. It must also specifically release the promoters from liability.

Articles of Incorporation

The **articles of incorporation** are the written applications to the state for permission to incorporate. This written application is prepared by the corporation's incorporators. The articles, together with the state incorporation statute, represent the legal boundaries within which a corporation must conduct its business. Some state incorporation statutes are very strict, requiring detailed information in the articles of incorporation. Typically this information includes the following:

- The corporation's name.
- The duration of the corporation.
- The purpose(s) of the corporation.
- The number and classes of shares.
- The shareholders' rights in relation to shares, classes of shares, and special shares.
- The shareholders' right to buy new shares.
- The addresses of its original registered (statutory) office and its original registered (statutory) agent.
- The number of directors plus the names and addresses of the initial directors.
- Each incorporator's name and address.

The newer version of the MBCA has simplified this list somewhat, requiring only the name of the corporation, the number of shares originally authorized, the address of the original registered (statutory) office, the address of the original registered agent, and the incorporators' names and addresses.

The Corporate Name

One of the first steps in forming a corporation is to choose a corporate name. Usually, the words or an abbreviation of the words *corporation, company,* or *incorporated* must appear somewhere in the corporate name. Also, the corporation cannot choose a name that some other corporation already uses or a name that would confuse the new corporation with one already in existence. Even in situations in which a specific state statute does not prohibit the use of similar names, the courts will prevent such duplication if confusion or unfair competition results. Often the secretary of state's office can tell promoters whether a name has been taken. It is also possible to reserve a name. Usually, there is a small fee for this service. Promoters also must make certain that they check the availability of a corporate name in not only the state of incorporation but also any state within which they plan to have the corporation do business.

Approval of Articles

After the articles of incorporation are submitted to the state, the appropriate state officer, often the secretary of state, will examine them to make certain that they meet all legal requirements. The secretary of state will also make certain that all filing fees have been paid and that a registered or statutory office and a registered or statutory agent have been appointed. The registered or **statutory agent** is an individual who is designated to receive service of process when a lawsuit is filed against the corporation. Once satisfied that all legal formalities have been met, the secretary of state will issue the corporation's charter, or certificate of incorporation. The charter, or **certificate of incorporation**, is the corporation's official authorization to do business in the state. After the charter is issued, the corporation becomes a fully and legally incorporated entity. The work of the promoters and incorporators ends, unless they become directors or officers of the corporation.

Did You Know?

A quick reference to corporate law is a book titled *Corporations: Laws of the United States,* published by Nova Publishing.

Commencement of the Business

Most state statutes provide that the first order of business upon incorporation is holding an organizational meeting. Some states require that the meeting be run by the initial directors designated in the articles. In contrast, those states that do not require naming the directors in the articles allow the organizational meeting to be run by the incorporators. Neverthe-less, the first order of business at an incorporator-run meeting is to elect the directors. In addition to the appointment of the first directors, the adoption of bylaws, or regulations, also occurs at the organizational meeting. **Bylaws** or **regulations** are the rules that guide the corporation's day-to-day internal affairs. Bylaw provisions usually stipulate the time and place of shareholders' and directors' meetings, quorum requirements, qualifications and duties of directors and officers, and procedures for filling board vacancies.

Formation of a Limited Liability Company

Similar to a corporation, a limited liability company requires only one person to incorpo-rate. However, the term *person* is liberally defined to include not only people but also cor-porations and other legal entities, such as partnerships, limited partnerships, trusts, estates, and so on. The term can even include another LLC. Because not all states recognize the tax advantage usually granted to limited liability companies, it is wise for persons contemplat-ing the formation of an LLC to check the legal status of such entities in all of the states in which they intend to do business.

The Articles of Organization
The **articles of organization** are the written ap-plication to the state for permission to form a limited liability company. These articles must include the name of the LLC, the duration of the LLC, and the address where the LLC's operating agreement and bylaws are to be kept. If neither the articles nor the operating agreement, as discussed later, include a duration statement, then some state statutes set an automatic duration period, generally of 30 years. In contrast, in the absence of a duration statement, other state statutes set an unlimited duration. The name of the LLC must include "Limited Liability Company" or those words abbreviated, or be followed by "Limited" or the abbreviation "Ltd." In addition, the name of the LLC must not be the same as the name of another LLC or corporation.

However, a problem may arise when a general partnership is transformed into an LLC. An existing general partnership may discover that it has been using a name that is reserved for a corporation or for an already existing LLC. This transformation will require changing the name of the existing partnership before it becomes an LLC. Such a change can be both-ersome and complicated, not to mention expensive. The only other alternatives in such a situation would be to acquire authorization to use the common name or to abandon the ef-fort to form an LLC. In addition, a statutory agent for the service of process must be named at the time that the articles are filed in the office of the secretary of state. Finally, proper filing fees must also be paid. Such fees are generally not exorbitant.

The Operating Agreement
It is also beneficial for the members of an LLC to draw up an **operating agreement**. Such an agreement, though not required by law in all states, is still very helpful in establishing the bylaws of the LLC, which outline the struc-ture and operation of an LLC. Typically the articles of organization include formation provisions, operating provisions, the nature of the business to be conducted by the LLC, distribution of profits and losses, the powers of the managers, voting rights of the mem-bers, admission and withdrawal procedures, provisions regarding the transfer of a mem-ber's interest in the LLC, and provisions involving the termination of the LLC, among others. Provisions not covered by the operating agreement are determined by the statute authorizing the creation of LLCs in that state.

Oral Modifications of the Operating Agreement
Some state LLC statutes specify that operating agreements can be spoken. Under such a provision, cer-tain procedures may inadvertently be added to the operating relationship between the

members simply because of a conversation among those members. For this reason, operating agreements should be written even if state law does not require a writing. Moreover, it is wise to add a provision to the written operating agreement that asserts there can be no spoken modifications to the agreement. Fortunately, even those statutes that allow spoken. additions to the operating agreement specify that certain things, such as an agreement to make a capital contribution to the LLC, must be in writing to be binding on the members.

Taxation of an LLC Under Internal Revenue Service (IRS) regulations, the status of a business under state law is not the determining factor in establishing whether a firm, such as an LLC, should be taxed as a partnership or a corporation. Rather, the tax status of such an entity depends on an election made by the owners of that entity. Under the regulations, an entity with two or more members can elect to be treated for tax purposes as an association or as a partnership. An entity owned by one person can elect either association status or a status that will, in effect, hold that the owner and the entity are identical. Election as an association in either situation means that the entity will be taxed as a corporation. The other choice will avoid the corporate tax status.

---

quick quiz 26-3

1. An agreement that releases a promoter is called a novation.   true | false

2. Bylaws are the rules that guide the corporation's day-to-day internal affairs.   true | false

3. Operating agreements for LLCs are required in all states.   true | false

---

26-4 Corporate Identity

Corporations have a life of their own; or at least they are supposed to have such a life. That life begins when they are incorporated by their owners and continues through the choosing of a name, the appointment of an agent for service of process, the election of directors, the hiring or the appointment of managers, the selling of shares, and the paying of dividends. As we have seen, corporations have constitutional rights, citizenship (sometimes even dual citizenship), and limited liability. They are entities that can own property, buy and sell that property, sue and be sued. All of this is true, of course, provided that they are legally formed and are permitted by their owners to develop their own corporate identities. A legally formed corporation is referred to as a *de jure* corporation. A *de jure* corporation is one that has been formed properly by incorporators who followed all of the steps outlined by the state incorporation statute. Most corporations are *de jure* corporations. There are times, however, when the incorporation process is flawed or when the corporation loses its corporate standing. In those cases, the corporation may or may not be a *de facto* corporation, that is, one that exists in fact, but not in law. As strange as it may seem, there are even times when a group of people never intends to incorporate but acts like a corporation to such an extent that they create a **corporation by estoppel**. Finally, there are situations when a corporation is created legally but is held back by its owners and prevented from becoming an independent entity. In that case, if the subsidiary commits a wrongful act the victim may want to pierce the corporate veil of the subsidiary to reach the parent.

De Jure and De Facto Corporation

A corporation whose existence is the result of the incorporators having fully or substantially complied with the relevant corporation statutes is a *de jure* corporation. Its status as a corporation cannot be challenged by private citizens or the state. Sometimes an error is made in the incorporation process. When this occurs, the corporation does not exist legally. Nevertheless, as long as the following conditions have been met, a *de facto* corporation (a corporation in fact) will exist:

1. A valid state incorporation statute must be in effect.
2. The parties must have made a *bona fide* (good faith) attempt to follow the statute's requirements for incorporation.
3. The business must have acted as if it were a corporation.

Usually, if only some minor requirement has been left unsatisfied, the court will hold that there has been a good faith attempt to incorporate. Only the state can directly challenge the existence of a *de facto* corporation. Thus, a *de facto* corporation has the same rights, privileges, and duties as a *de jure* corporation as far as anyone other than the state is concerned. The doctrine of *de facto* corporation is in a state of flux at the present time. The doctrine is itself a common law principle and, as such, can be altered by the courts and by statutory law. Moreover, it seems that the Model Business Corporation Act eliminates the doctrine altogether. Nevertheless, some states have either altered that proposition or ignored it. A state could, for example, add a section to its own version of the MBCA, which states that a corporation that forfeits its corporate status, and then recovers it, will be treated as a corporation retroactively to the day that it lost its corporate status. In effect, what this statute does is to validate the use of the *de facto* doctrine when the secretary of state retroactively reactivates a corporation's corporate status. This application is not exactly the reestablishment of the *de facto* doctrine, but it is a reasonable facsimile. Other states have found other ways around the MBCA by reinstituting a frequently ignored doctrine called corporation by *estoppel*. Given the uncertainty surrounding this issue, however, it is best to check the most recent version of a state's corporate law statute should the question ever arise.

Corporation by Estoppel

In some states, if a group of people act as if they are a corporation when in fact and in law they are not, any parties who have accepted that counterfeit corporation's existence will not be allowed to deny that acceptance. Similarly, individuals who acted as if they were a corporation will not be able to deny that the corporation exists. This doctrine has been labeled corporation by estoppel. Corporation by estoppel does not create a real corporation. Instead, it is a legal fiction used by the courts on a case-by-case basis to prevent injustice. Generally, but not always, it is applied in contract cases rather than in tort cases. Some states may have also abolished corporation by estoppel, and so, as with *de facto* corporation, it is best to check the most recent version of a state's corporate law statute.

EXAMPLE 26-1: *Valley Victory Church v. Darvin Struck and Bonnie Struck*

The Valley Victory Church lost its *de jure* corporate standing when the attorney who was responsible for filing the church's yearly reports with the secretary of state's office left the state without filing that crucial report. When the report was not filed, the secretary of state revoked Valley Victory's corporate standing and sent a letter to that effect to the truant attorney. The attorney, of course, neither received the letter nor alerted church officials, who continued to act as if the church were a corporation. In the middle of a lawsuit involving the church, Darvin Struck, one of the parties to the suit, discovered this oversight. He argued that the church had no corporate existence at the time of his gift and so the property at the heart of the dispute was still his. Church officials made two counterarguments. First, they said that at the time of the gift, they had a good faith belief that the church was a corporation operating under the authority of a valid state incorporation statute. Therefore, under the doctrine of *de facto* corporation, they continued to operate as a corporation. Second, church officials argued that the Strucks had given the land to the congregation, not to the church. Although the court clearly wanted to accept the church's first argument, it reluctantly rejected that line of reasoning. The court, however, did decide that, under state statutory law, once the secretary of state had restored the church's corporate status, all previous corporate acts were ratified. That meant that the church's acceptance of the land was valid when it had occurred. The court also supported the church's second argument as far as it could, saying that under corporation by estoppel, the Strucks could not recognize the church as a corporation when they transferred the land and then change their minds when it suited them.

Piercing the Corporate Veil

Sometimes the courts will disregard corporate status to impose personal liability on those shareholders who have used the corporation to commit fraud or crimes or to harm the public. In such cases, the court will **pierce the corporate veil** and hold the wrongdoers (usually the controlling shareholders) personally liable for activities committed in the corporation's name. The corporate veil test has three incarnations: the alter ego test, the instrumentality test, and the three-step test for control, fraud, and injury.

The Alter Ego Test The shareholders of small close corporations are more likely to fall victim to piercing the corporate veil than are the shareholders of large corporations because the shareholders of a close corporation are often also the original incorporators, as well as the directors and officers of the corporation, and thus may neglect to follow the corporate formalities required by statute and may fail to keep corporate property and business separate from their personal property and business. Thus, the court will sometimes find that the corporation is nothing more than the **alter ego** (other self, you know, like Clark Kent is Superman's alter ego or Oliver Queen is the Arrow's alter ego) of the original incorporators. Veil piercing by the courts is less likely to occur with an LLC because corporate formalities are not required by law for LLCs as they are with a corporation. However, in many states, the shareholders of a small corporation can enter a close corporation agreement, which would allow them to escape the need to follow many corporate formalities.

The Instrumentality Test Large corporations can also fall victim to piercing the corporate veil if they set up subsidiaries, completely control those subsidiaries, and then commit fraud through those subsidiaries. In such cases, however, it is the parent corporation, rather than the individual shareholders, that the courts will hold liable. The test used to determine whether the corporate veil should be pierced to reach the parent corporation is called the **instrumentality test**. This test requires that the parent corporation so dominate the subsidiary that the subsidiary has become a "mere instrumentality of the parent." In this situation, the courts will allow the veil of the instrumentality to be pierced to reach the dominant corporation and to hold that corporation liable for any harm that has been committed through the instrumentality. The courts, however, do not engage in such veil piercing lightly. Still, while the courts respect the separate corporate identity of most subsidiaries, they cannot allow a subsidiary to be used by the parent so that the parent can escape liability, especially if the instrumentality was set up in the first place to commit fraud. When a corporation is set up as a mere instrumentality of a parent, it is sometimes referred to as a **dummy corporation** or a **corporate shell**.

The Three-Step Test

Regardless of the size or the configuration of a corporation, however, some courts have simplified matters by ignoring the distinction between large and small corporations and instead applying a three-step veil piercing test. This approach is common when the corporation has committed fraud in a fairly straightforward and obvious way. The stages in the **three-step test** for veil piercing are (1) complete control of the alleged corporate person by the owners (shareholders or members in an LLC); (2) the use of that control by the shareholders to commit fraud against the plaintiff; and (3) that fraud has caused the plaintiff to undergo some sort of injury or loss. Often *undercapitalization*

THE OPENING CASE *Round 3*
Disregarding the Corporate Entity: The Corporate Veil

Recall that the opening case began when William Stewart, d/b/a Stewart Coal Company, entered a contract with R.A. Eberts, Inc., in which Stewart sold his coal mining operation to Eberts, Inc., for $3,500,000. The terms of the agreement were fulfilled until 2003 when Eberts, Inc., stopped royalty payments to Stewart and failed to pay the final amount due under the contract. Stewart sued for breach of contract. Stewart later amended his complaint and sought to *pierce the corporate veil* of Eberts, Inc., to hold its officers, directors, and shareholders personally liable. During discovery Stewart found out that the shareholders, officers, and directors of Eberts, Inc., had transferred all the company's assets and liabilities to Waterloo Coal Company (Waterloo). He also found out that Waterloo and Eberts, Inc., shared the same officers, directors, and shareholders. These same officers, directors, and shareholders later transferred all of Eberts' liabilities to a newly created LLC named Eberts, LLC. Eberts, Inc., was then liquidated. Taking all this new information into account, Stewart amended his complaint in order to hold the two additional companies, Waterloo and Eberts, LLC, liable and to pierce the veil of those corporations in order to hold their officers, directors, and shareholders liable. The defendants filed a summary judgment motion to dismiss the lawsuit, arguing that Stewart had failed to demonstrate that the three steps in the veil-piercing test applied to the facts in this case. Those three steps are (1) complete control of the alleged corporate person by the owners; (2) the use of that control by the owners to commit fraud against the plaintiff; and (3) that the

fraud caused the plaintiff to undergo some sort of injury or loss. The trial court granted the summary judgment motion and dismissed the case. Stewart appealed. On appeal, Stewart contended that he should be permitted to argue his case in front of a jury. Specifically, to fulfill the first step in the test, Stewart showed that Eberts, LLC, the new corporate person, had virtually the same officers, directors, and shareholders as Eberts, Inc., and that both Eberts, Inc., and Eberts, LLC, had been managed to benefit those owners, to the detriment of the corporations themselves. Second, he argued that both corporations had been badly undercapitalized to the point of insolvency, and that the other corporation involved in this game, Waterloo, had been the recipient of all the tangible assets of Eberts, Inc., while Eberts, LLC (the insolvent company) had received only intangible assets, including the debt owed to Stewart, a debt that it clearly could not pay, thus defrauding the plaintiff. Third, as a result of these fraudulent activities, the LLC did not pay the money owned under the contract, thus leading to a substantial loss of revenue for the plaintiff. The appeals court had little problem determining that the trial court had made an error in its application of the law. Accordingly, the appellate court reversed the decision of the lower court, noting that the case had to go trial so that a jury could determine if the veil-piercing steps applied. (Note: The court would not indicate whether it felt that Stewart's claims had merit. What do you think?) [See: *William Stewart d/b/a Stewart Coal Co. v. R. A. Eberts Company Inc., et al,* Case Number 08CA10 (August 8, 2009).]

will be considered convincing evidence that the corporate owners intended to use the corporate façade to escape liability. However, by itself undercapitalization is not enough to pierce the corporate veil successfully. The court requires that the corporation's interests cannot be distinguished from those of the shareholders.

The Effects of the *Hobby Lobby* Case   In *William Stewart v. R. A. Eberts, Company, Inc.*, detailed in the opening case, the court was charged with determining whether to pierce the corporate veil of the company and to hold its owners liable for ignoring the terms of a contract that had been made several years earlier. It is important to note that the courts do not engage in veil piercing carelessly. Veil piercing is an extraordinary action because it requires the court to disregard the essential nature of the corporate person and to hold the owners and/or the officers and directors responsible for a level of legal liability they believed had been transferred to the corporate person. Consequently, veil piercing is, or at least should be, difficult. The *Hobby Lobby* case, which we reviewed previously as the one of the newest and most significant classic cases in recent memory, seems to have changed all of this. In *Hobby Lobby*, the Supreme Court treats corporate personhood as a suggestion or an option, rather than a mandate. In the *Hobby Lobby* case itself, the Court's decision to disregard the corporate person helped the owners of Hobby Lobby because their religious rights were vindicated. However, when we transform this case into a straight veil-piercing case, the legal result is the same, but the help to the owners has vanished. Once a judge rules that the law that defines the rights and duties of a corporation *also* defines the rights and duties of the people behind that corporation, he or she has placed the owners on the same level as the corporation. The whole point of corporate personhood is to separate the owners from the corporate person so that the owners can have the protection of the corporate veil and the corporation can have a life of its own (a life that includes its own "personal" rights). Now that the corporate person and the owners are to be equated, veil piercing becomes quite easy, in fact, unnecessary, because the veil has vanished and those behind the veil are revealed as the true corporate persons (entities?).

---

quick quiz 26-4

1. The doctrine of the *de facto* corporation requires that there be a *bona fide* attempt to incorporate under an existing incorporation statute and an exercise of corporate power.	true	false
2. Corporation by estoppel does not create a real corporation.	true	false
3. The three techniques used by the courts to determine whether the corporate veil should be pierced include the alter ego test, the instrumentality test, and the three-step test of control, fraud, and injury.	true	false

---

26-5 Financing the Corporate Entity

Corporate financing begins when the original investments are made to set up the corporation. Once the corporation is operating, additional corporate financing may be obtained from earnings, loans, and the issuance of additional shares of stock. The issuing and selling of shares of stock to raise capital is known as *equity financing,* and equity securities give their owners a legal interest in the assets, earnings, and control of the corporation. The part of a corporation's net profits or surplus set aside for the shareholders is known as dividends.

Classes of Corporate Stock

The number of shares and classes of stock that a corporation is authorized to issue are established in its certificate of incorporation. A shareholder who purchases corporate stock invests money or property in the corporation and receives a stock certificate. A **stock certificate** is written evidence of ownership of a unit of interest in the corporation.

Dividends

The most common type of dividend is the **cash dividend**, declared and paid out of current corporate earnings or accumulated surplus at regular intervals. A corporation's board of directors has the sole authority to determine the amount, time, place, and manner of dividend payment. Typically, the directors' declaration of a dividend sets a cutoff date—the date by which a shareholder must hold corporate stock of record to receive payment. In a few instances, a distribution of earnings is made in shares of capital stock, called a **stock dividend**.

Common Stock   The most usual type of corporate stock is **common stock**. Common stock carries with it all the risks of the business, inasmuch as it does not guarantee its holder the right to profits. The shareholder is usually entitled to one vote for each share of stock held. The holders of common stock are paid dividends when the corporation elects to make such a distribution. Holders of common stock risk whatever they invest.

Preferred Stock   Those classes of stock that have rights or preferences over other classes of stock are known as **preferred stock**. These preferences generally involve the payment of dividends and/or the distribution of assets on the dissolution of the corporation. Preferred stock may be either cumulative or noncumulative. Generally, dividends on cumulative preferred stock are paid every year. However, if the dividends are not paid in one year, they will be paid in later years if any dividends at all are paid by the corporation. Dividends on noncumulative preferred stock are also usually paid each year. However, with noncumulative preferred stock, dividends that are not paid in one year are lost forever.

Stock Valuation   **Par value** is the value placed on the shares of stock at incorporation. This value, which is the same for each share of stock of the same issue, is stated on the corporation's certificate of incorporation. In the case of par value shares, the amount of the capital stock or stated capital is the total par value of all the issued stock.

The practice of placing a par value on a share of stock has been criticized as misleading. Uninformed buyers often interpret par value printed on the face of the certificate as the actual market value of the shares. To correct this condition, all states have authorized the issuance of no par value stock. *No par value stock* is corporate stock issued without any stated price. In fact, par value stock has been eliminated under provisions found in the newest version of the MBCA.

---

quick quiz 26-5

1. Corporate financing cannot begin until six months after the certificate of incorporation has been issued.	true | false	
2. The most common type of dividend is the stock dividend.	true | false	
3. The practice of placing a par value on a share of stock has been approved of and is now mandated by the American Federated Banking Commission.	true | false	

Summary

26.1 The corporate entity lies at the heart of the American economy and, as such, can orchestrate change on its own. To see why this is so, we need to examine the characteristics and the power of the corporate entity. A corporation is a legal entity created under the authority of a state or federal statute that gives certain individuals the capacity to operate an enterprise. As such, corporations are products of capitalism. The capitalistic economic system has operated in a way that has ensured that corporations are protected in a variety of ways. However, the basis of that protection lies within four fundamental legal principles that are designed to protect the corporate structure. These four principles are corporate limited liability, free transfer of ownership, central management, and corporate personhood itself.

26.2 Corporations can be classified in many ways, including private, public, and quasi-public corporations; domestic and foreign corporations; and close and S corporations. The limited liability company offers the protection of limited liability but allows tax liability to flow through the LLC and to its owners.

26.3 A corporation can be incorporated in any state that has a general incorporation statute. The people who actually start the corporation are the promoters. Promoters are liable on preformation contracts until those contracts are adopted by the corporation. The articles of incorporation are drawn up by the corporation's incorporators. After reviewing the articles of incorporation, the secretary of state will issue a corporate charter, and the corporation becomes a legally incorporated entity. The members of a limited liability company must also follow precise formation procedures.

26.4 A *de jure* corporation is a legally formed corporation. Two doctrines, *de facto* corporation and corporation by estoppel, have been developed to deal with the problem of defective incorporation. A *de facto* corporation exists if there has been a good faith attempt to comply with an existing incorporation statute and an exercise of corporate power. The doctrine of corporation by estoppel prevents later denial of corporate existence by parties willing to deal with an entity as if it were a corporation. Under the doctrine of piercing the corporate veil, courts can refuse to recognize a legally formed corporation to prevent injustice and to impose liability on the wrongdoers.

26.5 Corporate financing begins when the incorporators give money to set up the business. Subsequent financing takes many forms. The issuing and selling of shares of stock to raise capital is called equity financing. The two most popular classes of stock are common stock and preferred stock. Stock can also be par value or no par value stock. Dividends can be issued as cash or as stock.

Key Terms

alien corporation, 634
alter ego, 641
articles of incorporation, 636
articles of organization, 638
associative corporativism, 633
bylaws, 638
cash dividend, 644
certificate of authority, 634
certificate of incorporation, 637
close corporation, 634
common stock, 644

corporate entity, 626
corporate person, 626
corporate shell, 642
corporation, 626
corporation by estoppel, 639
corporativism, 633
de facto corporation, 639
de jure corporation, 639
dividends, 634
Dodd Frank Wall Street Reform and Consumer Protection Act, 632

domestic corporation, 634
dummy corporation, 642
foreign corporation, 634
franchise, 635
incorporators, 635
instrumentality test, 641
joint undertaking, 635
joint venture, 635
limited liability, 627
limited liability company (LLC), 634

Questions for Review and Discussion

1. What are some of the strategies that may avoid a new 21st century economic crisis?
2. What is meant by the term *corporation*?
3. What are the constitutional rights of a corporation?
4. What are the differences among a private, a public, and a quasi-public corporation?
5. What is the difference between a close and an S corporation?
6. What are the typical elements within the articles of incorporation?
7. What is the difference between the articles of organization and the operating agreement of a limited liability company?
8. What is the difference between a *de jure* and a *de facto* corporation?
9. What is the objective of piercing the corporate veil?
10. What is the difference between common and preferred stock?

Cases for Analysis

1. Dr. Steven A. Pottschmidt was employed by Dr. Thomas J. Klosterman, who was doing business as a corporation named Thomas J. Klosterman, M.D., Inc. Once Pottschmidt's original employment agreement ended, he decided to bring a breach of contract suit against Klosterman alleging that he, Pottschmidt, had not been paid the amount that was actually owed him under the agreement. Within two months of the lawsuit, Klosterman created a new corporation, called Klosterman Family Practice, Inc. Klosterman Family Practice, however, did not employ anyone other than the staff of the first corporation, Thomas J. Klosterman, M.D., Inc. In addition, the second corporation had not moved from the original office, had not changed its phone number, had not purchased new equipment or new furniture, and had not taken on any new patients. For a while, the two corporations held separate accounts at one bank. Eventually, however, the first company's bank account was terminated, and income for bills sent out by the first company were placed in the account of the second company. Pottschmidt wants the court to permit him to pierce the corporate veil of both Thomas J. Klosterman, M.D., Inc., and Klosterman Family Practice, Inc., to hold Dr. Klosterman directly liable for the money owed to him. Is there enough evidence here to permit the veil piercing requested by the plaintiff? Explain. [See: *Pottschmidt v. Thomas J. Klosterman, M.D., Inc.*, 169 Ohio App.3d 824 (Court of Appeals of Ohio, Ninth District, Medina County).]

2. The Aerenthal Financial Loan Corporation lent $578,000 to Raymond Viviani and secured the loan with a mortgage on Viviani's ski lodge, which was located south of Burlington, Vermont. Vermont decided to build a new state highway along a route that cut right through Viviani's lodge. Viviani contested the state's decision and attempted to get the

highway rerouted. After several months of unsuccessful battles with the state, Viviani decided to settle for the offer from the government. The state then paid Viviani the market value for the property. Unfortunately, the state failed to notify Aerenthal Financial Loan Corporation about the transaction. When Aerenthal discovered that it had not been notified, it filed a formal protest with the state. The state sent its apologies but argued that Aerenthal had no right to be notified about what was essentially a contractual matter between Viviani and the government. Aerenthal disagreed, arguing that the government had violated its constitutional right not to be deprived of property without due process of law. The state responded by noting that under the state constitution, it had operated properly and Aerenthal was not entitled to due process. Who is correct here? Explain.

3. General Housing Assistance was incorporated as a nonprofit organization that provides low-cost housing for families who have been economically dislocated because of the downsizing of a company or the outsourcing of jobs. One year after the formation of General Housing Assistance, General Mutual Housing Assistance was incorporated in the same state. General Mutual Housing Assistance sold housing shares in condominiums to subscribers. General Mutual ran an aggressive, often obnoxious advertising campaign. After this campaign, General Housing found that people were confusing the two entities. The resulting mix-up damaged General Housing Assistance's image and threatened its charitable funding sources. Consequently, it filed suit to stop General Mutual from using the name because of the confusion between the two entities. Are the names similar enough to cause the court to order General Mutual to change its name? Explain.

4. Through Langham Engineering, Michael Langham marketed his invention, the cross-slope monitor (CSM), as an accessory to John Deere equipment. He had a plan to expand his business to include the CSM as an accessory to Caterpillar Tractor (CAT) equipment. To do this, Langham and Clark Balderson of Balderson, Inc., entered a preincorporation agreement (PIA), in which Langham agreed to contribute his technical abilities, and Balderson agreed to contribute his leadership capabilities to manufacture and market the CSM to CAT. No release clause was included in the PIA. The resulting corporation was named Illinois Controls, Inc. Balderson was designated the president and chairman of the board, and Langham was named vice president. Over the next two years, Balderson failed to train and motivate the sales staff about the proper techniques for selling the CSM to CAT dealers. Balderson also neglected to arrange demonstrations and consignment sales, failed to employ properly trained personnel, and disregarded the need to develop, print, and distribute installation manuals for the CSM. Finally, Balderson set up another corporation named the Dymax Corporation, which dealt with CAT's competitors, thereby undermining Illinois Control's relationship with CAT. As a result, Illinois Controls was forced to shut down operations. Langham sued Balderson personally for the losses that he incurred as a result of Balderson's failure to meet his obligations as outlined in the PIA. Balderson argued that the PIA was a promoter's contract and that the corporation had adopted it. Therefore, Illinois Controls should be held liable. Was Balderson correct? Explain. [See: *Illinois Controls, Inc., v. Langham,* 639 N.E.2d 771 (OH).]

5. Harry and Kay Robinson of New York purchased a new Audi automobile from World Wide Volkswagen (WWV) in New York. After having an accident in Oklahoma, they brought a product liability action against WWV. The case was brought to court in Oklahoma. The Robinsons claimed that the injuries they suffered were caused by the defective design and placement of their automobile's gas tank and fuel system. WWV, which was incorporated in New York and did business there, contended that the Robinsons could not sue WWV in Oklahoma because it was not a citizen of Oklahoma. WWV further contended that it performed no services, owned no property, and closed no sales in Oklahoma. It solicited no business in Oklahoma either through salespersons or through advertising. It also did not indirectly through others serve or seek to serve the Oklahoma market. Did the Oklahoma state court have jurisdiction over WWV? Explain. [See: *World Wide Volkswagen Corporation v. Woodson,* 100 S.Ct. 559 (U.S. Sup. Ct.).]

6. Spence was a promoter in the incorporation of a new business. The new corporation had not yet been formed when he bought Huffman's

employment agency to serve as the nucleus of that corporation. Eventually, the corporation was formed, but it never generated enough cash to pay Huffman for the employment agency. Huffman sued Spence, attempting to hold him personally liable for the amount due. Spence claimed that the corporation was liable and that his personal assets were not a proper target of the suit. Was Spence correct? Explain. [See: *Spence v. Huffman*, 486 P.2d 211 (AZ).]

7. MBI filed its original articles of incorporation under the name Montana Public Employees Benefit Services Co., Inc. After filing the articles, the corporation entered a contract with the Montana Department of Administration. Under the contract, the new corporation would have exclusive administrative control over Montana's public employee deferred-payment pension plan. The articles were not approved by the secretary of state, who requested a name change. After the corporation's name was changed to MBI, the charter was issued, and the corporation became a legal entity. The Montana Association of Underwriters, a private corporation that wanted a share in administering the state pension plan, challenged the validity of the contract, arguing that at the time the contract was signed, MBI did not legally exist. Was the Montana Association of Underwriters correct? Explain. [See: *Montana Association of Underwriters v. Department of Administration and MBI*, 563 P.2d 577 (MT).]

8. Lamas Company, Inc., was incorporated in Georgia. Baldwin negotiated with Lamas, sole owner of Lamas Company, Inc., to finish some electrical work on a construction site. When Baldwin was dissatisfied with the work, he decided to sue. Unfortunately, the statute of limitations ran out before he could sue Lamas Company, Inc., so he sued Lamas individually. Baldwin argued that he had dealt only with Lamas, that he did not know Lamas was an agent of the company, that Lamas did not tell him about the company, and that he understood the contract to be with Lamas individually. Lamas pointed out that Baldwin made out and sent checks directly to Lamas Company, Inc., and that Lamas Company, Inc., always appeared as the payee on those checks. Lamas claimed that this evidence alone would be enough to stop Baldwin from denying that he had dealt with Lamas Company, Inc. The trial court rendered

judgment against Lamas. On appeal, did the appellate court reverse? Explain. [See: *Lamas v. Baldwin*, 230 S.E.2d 13 (GA).]

9. Boafo was allegedly injured while giving birth at Parkway Regional Hospital. Boafo sued both Parkway Regional and Hospital Corporation of America (HCA), asking the court to pierce the corporate veil to reach HCA, which Boafo claimed was a parent company. Boafo showed that the two corporations shared the same offices, that they purchased hospital equipment together, that HCA owned 100 percent of Parkway stock, that major financing for Parkway was performed by HCA through a national accounting system, and that Parkway was insured by another wholly owned subsidiary of HCA. In answer, HCA emphasized that Parkway handled its own daily financing, that it was free to negotiate and enter its own contracts, that it had an adequate amount of money in its treasury, and that it was not formed to promote fraud, conceal crime, or evade legal liability. The trial court granted summary judgment, dismissing the claim against HCA. Did the appellate court uphold the trial court's ruling? Explain. [See: *Boafo v. Hospital Corporation of America*, 338 S.E.2d 477 (GA).]

10. The Northeastern Corporate Institute of Technology (NCIT), a profit-oriented corporation engaged in nuclear research projects, owned and operated an experimental station in a remote region of Alaska. The Alaskan Chemical Disposal Corporation, a subsidiary of NCIT, disposed of all chemical and nuclear waste products produced by NCIT's experimental station. On a routine disposal route, an Alaskan Chemical Disposal transport convoy collided with a North Coast moving van. The lead truck in the convoy spilled chemical waste into a lake owned by Kenneth Ridgeway. Ridgeway sued both NCIT and Alaskan Chemical Disposal. NCIT argued that the disposal of NCIT's chemical was the sole responsibility of Alaskan Chemical Disposal, which it characterized as an independent contractor. Ridgeway's attorney, however, had discovered that Alaskan Chemical Disposal had no business other than providing waste disposal services to NCIT. The attorney also discovered that Alaskan Chemical Disposal was listed as a division of NCIT, was financed by NCIT, and shared the same board of directors and officers as NCIT. Moreover, the

attorney found out that Alaskan Chemical Disposal was badly undercapitalized. In addition, all decisions in the running of Alaskan Chemical Disposal were made by NCIT. In light of all of this evidence, Ridgeway's attorney began to suspect that Alaskan Chemical Disposal might have been formed to allow NCIT to escape liability in just this type of situation. Will Ridgeway be allowed to maintain its suit against NCIT? Explain.

quick quiz Answers

26-1	26-2	26-3	26-4	26-5
1. T	1. F	1. T	1. T	1. F
2. T	2. F	2. T	2. T	2. F
3. F	3. F	3. F	3. T	3. F

Managing the Corporate Entity

THE OPENING CASE *Round 1*
Derivative Suits, the Demand Futility Doctrine, and the Business Judgment Rule

Generally, the courts are tasked with operating as the passive element within the legal system. This role is not a flaw, although at times it may seem to be. Rather, it is a necessary brake on the more energetic and often hasty actions of the legislative and executive branches. On the other hand, sometimes the courts preemptively create new doctrines that have a serious and long-lasting effect on the law. To see this aspect of the court's operation up close, let's look at the case of *Aronson v. Lewis*. The facts in the case involve a series of transactions between Meyers Parking Systems, Inc., and Leo Fink, one of its directors. Fink entered a five-year contract with Meyers, which was renewed automatically each year, and which permitted Fink to end the contract at will. The contract also included a provision allowing Fink to assume consulting duties at Meyers after the contract ended. After the contract terminated and Fink retired, he would be paid $150,000 for the first three years, $125,000 for the next three, and then $100,000 each year for life. Now the interesting thing about this arrangement, at least the one that concerned Lewis (the shareholder who filed the suit), was that Fink did not actually perform any duties for the money (at least according to Lewis). The plaintiff brought this suit arguing that the contract is "grossly excessive" because, allegedly, Fink did almost nothing for the money that he "earned" and that, because of his age, he might not be able to perform those duties if he were asked to actually do so. In addition, another agreement that Fink had with Prudential, a former owner of Meyers, would prevent Fink from devoting a full-time effort to his "duties" at Meyers. The bottom line of Lewis's case was that the payments to Fink represented a waste of corporate funds, for which the directors were personally liable. In response, the board argued that, in any derivative lawsuit, the plaintiff must exhaust internal remedies before running to the courts. Since the plaintiff did not consult the board about the issues involved in the lawsuit, the suit must be dismissed. Answering this allegation, the plaintiff argued that the board was completely controlled by Fink and, as a result, the directors do whatever Fink demands. The plaintiff argued further that, since it would be futile for him to ask the board for help, he can skip over that troublesome and difficult step, and bring the suit directly. As evidence for this claim, the plaintiff revealed that Fink had appointed every member of the board himself and that each board member was, therefore, indebted to Fink. Moreover, since all of the board members had been named as defendants in the lawsuit, they would not endorse the plaintiff's effort because, in effect, by supporting the case, they would be suing themselves. The court found the plaintiff's arguments interesting and, to make things just a bit clearer, labeled the idea as the doctrine of *demand futility*. Was the plaintiff correct? Was Fink an autocrat who exercised complete control over the board? If so, just how do we know that to be the case? If it were the case, which rule would the court use to judge the board of directors? The business judgment rule? Or the fairness rule? To uncover the *futility* of the *demand futility doctrine*, keep reading. [See: *Aronson v. Lewis*, 473 A.2d 805 (March 1, 1984).]

Opening Case Questions

1. Why was the plaintiff forced to bring the lawsuit himself, instead of giving it to the board of directors? Explain.

2. What is the *demand futility doctrine*? Explain.

3. Does the plaintiff in a corporate lawsuit always have to exhaust internal remedies before bringing a lawsuit against a corporate board? Explain.

4. What is the business judgment rule? Explain.

5. What is the fairness rule? Explain.

LO Learning Objectives

1. Explain the central dilemma of corporate governance.
2. Describe the functions of directors, officers, and shareholders.
3. List the five theories of corporate governance.
4. Describe cumulative voting and proxy solicitation.
5. Explain shareholder proposals.
6. Distinguish between voting trusts and pooling agreements.
7. Explain shareholder direct suits, shareholder derivative suits, and the demand futility doctrine.
8. Contrast the business judgment rule with the fairness rule.
9. List the rights that belong to shareholders.
10. Explain the management of a limited liability company.

27-1 Management of the Corporate Entity

Most state incorporation statutes provide that a corporation's business affairs are to be managed under the direction of a board of directors. The board of directors establishes broad policies, and the officers and other employees implement those policies. The shareholders are the owners of the corporation. How to keep the role of the board separate from that of executive management and that of shareholders is related to the challenge of how best to organize the board and select its members. The issues are even more complex today because a single individual often functions as a director, an officer, and a shareholder. Nevertheless, the three roles have distinct functions and should be examined separately.

Directors of the Corporation

The business affairs of a corporation are managed by a board of directors elected by the shareholders. The board's responsibility is to take whatever actions are appropriate, in keeping with the corporation's rules and regulations, to further the corporation's business.

Individual board members are supposed to use their own judgment in the corporate decision-making process.

Qualifications of Directors

State law and corporate rules set up the qualifications that a person must have to be a corporate director. Unless prohibited by the corporation's certificate of incorporation, membership on the board of directors can be extended to anyone, including aliens, minors, and nonshareholders. Often the certificate stipulates that at least one director must be a state resident and at least one must be a shareholder.

Time Commitment of Directors

Directors are elected at the annual meeting of the shareholders. Generally, directors hold office for one or two years. The number of directors on the board varies between 8 and 12. Usually, several directors are elected as a group to maintain continuity; this procedure permits one-third of the board to be elected annually. The basic time commitment for a director is approximately 30 days per year, but depending upon need, availability, and interest, it can be 40, 60, 80, or even more days. Naturally, directors can resign from the board. However, many states require written notice of the director's resignation to the corporation.

Meetings of Directors

The directors of most large corporations meet on a regular basis at a precise time and place of their choosing. The directors of many smaller corporations meet only when specific items are to be considered. Some states allow small corporations with fewer than 50 shareholders to eliminate the board of directors, as long as someone is assigned the duties that the board would have performed.

Directors are not entitled to be notified about regular board meetings unless notice is required by the corporation's bylaws. (The bylaws, or regulations of a corporation, determine how that corporation will operate.) However, directors must be notified of special meetings of the board. For example, a special meeting of the directors might be called to decide whether the corporation should institute a lawsuit. If any director is not notified of a special meeting, all actions taken at the meeting are void. A director may not specify another person to vote in her or his place. The quorum, or minimum number of directors necessary to conduct business, is usually one more than half of the total number of directors. Bylaws may require more than a quorum, perhaps 70 percent of the directors, to conduct certain types of business. This supermajority might be needed, for instance, to remove a director or sell a significant portion of the business. Generally though, the actions of a quorum constitute the official actions of the board.

EXAMPLE 27-1: Meeting the Quorum

The board of directors of Barber Enterprises, Inc., consisted of seven persons. At a properly called meeting, one of the directors presented a motion calling for a stock-option purchase plan for Barber's president, vice presidents, secretary, and treasurer. Five directors attended the meeting. This constituted a quorum. Three of the five voted for the plan. This vote would constitute an official act by the board.

Officers of the Corporation

Directors are not expected to spend all of their time and energy managing the corporation. They have the authority to appoint officers and agents to run the day-to-day affairs of the corporation. By statute, the usual officers are a president, several vice presidents, a secretary, and a treasurer. Other officers, such as a comptroller, cashier, and general counsel, are often provided. The bylaws of the corporation describe the duties of each officer. Officers have the authority of general agents for the operation of the normal business of the corporation. They in turn delegate duties to various department heads. Although the roles of directors and officers differ, they are frequently assumed by the same people. An individual may be both chief executive officer and chair of the board of the same corporation. Directors and officers can also be shareholders in the corporation.

Shareholders of the Corporation

The shareholders are the owners of the corporation. The more shares that a shareholder owns, the more voting power that shareholder has in the running of the corporation. Therefore, the most effective way for a shareholder to obtain corporate power is to purchase more stock. Unfortunately, purchasing additional stock is not always possible, either because the shareholder does not have the financial leverage needed to purchase enough shares to gain corporate control or because there are no shares available to purchase. Another way to gain operating power is to work with the shares that the shareholder already owns but increase voting power in other ways. Before looking at those voting techniques, it is important to remember that though many shareholders are individuals, others are institutions such as union pension funds that have invested large sums of money in corporate stock to gain a return for their retirees.

Stakeholders of the Corporation

Over the past few decades, corporate law has evolved significantly to now include the stakeholders of the corporation in the decision-making process. **Stakeholders** are those individuals and coalitions who, while officially outside of the corporate decision-making structure and outside the corporate ownership establishment, are dramatically affected by the results of corporate decision making. Included in this number are representatives from employees' unions; consumer protection organizations; suppliers; customers; clients; environmental protection groups; and the local, state, national, and international communities.

---

quick quiz 27-1

1. The business affairs of a corporation are managed by a board of directors elected by the shareholders.   true | false

2. Membership on a board of directors can never be extended to aliens, minors, or nonshareholders.   true | false

3. Directors have authority to appoint officers and agents to run the day-to-day affairs of the corporation.   true | false

---

27-2 Issues in Governing the Corporate Entity

Under the original concept of a corporation, the shareholders are the primary reason that a corporation exists. This image has evolved over the years, so that now shareholders often take a backseat to consumers, employees, environmentalists, politicians, social science engineers, and economists. For this reason, the corporate landscape has come to resemble a battlefield in recent years. There are those who believe that the battle is a good

Did You Know?

Although the shareholders of a corporation are the actual owners of the corporation, they are not agents of the corporation, as are the directors and officers, and therefore cannot commit the corporation to any contractual arrangements.

thing because it helps make corporations more responsible. Others, however, believe that the battle has weakened, and in some cases completely dismantled, corporate power.

The Corporate Balancing Act Revisited

A more productive way of looking at the issue might be to see, not a battlefield, but an extension of the corporate balancing act that we discussed in the previous chapter. We have noted repeatedly throughout the text that the law must balance several opposing factors. For instance, we have noted that the intent of the law must be balanced against the results that emerge from the work of lawmakers; the letter of the law must be balanced with its spirit (although there is some debate about the merits of the "spirit v. letter" approach); the language of the law must be balanced with its interpretation (there is also some quarrel about the wisdom of taking a "language v. interpretation" view of the law); abstract legal principles must be balanced with the concrete application of those principles; and so on. The issue of corporate leadership is just one more aspect of this legal balancing act. Thus, as we will see in this section, the needs of the shareholders must be balanced against the needs of the stakeholders, while the needs of the stakeholders must be balanced against the needs of the economic agenda of the state and the nation. Similarly, the expertise of the managers must be balanced against the profit motive of the shareholders, the regulatory agenda of the government, and the individual needs of the stakeholders. Each group has offered a different solution to the problem. Which group, if any, has correctly diagnosed the problem remains to be seen. For the present, we can examine five corporate control paradigms—governmental control, independent director control, managerial control, stakeholder control, and shareholder democratic control.

Theories of Corporate Governance

Legal scholars and business experts have put forth five theories regarding how corporations should be managed: governmental control, independent director control, managerial control, stakeholder control, and shareholder democratic control.

Governmental Control Support for the **governmental control** theory of corporate management is based on the belief that because corporate decision making influences more individuals and groups than just the shareholders and the managers, corporate decisions should be made by an impartial group of corporate outsiders. Usually, the corporate outsiders named are government officials. These specially educated government officials would make corporate decisions in an objective manner, based on the needs of the entire society and the economy as a whole. Opponents of this theory label such an approach socialistic and point to the relatively poor record of many socialist economies as evidence of the impracticality of this approach.

Of course, those who support governmental control do not always go so far as to demand that the government have a seat in every corporate boardroom in America. A less dramatic and perhaps more effective technique is to use governmental control indirectly through regulatory legislation. One particularly effective piece of congressional legislation in this regard is the **Sarbanes–Oxley (SarbOx) Act** of 2002. SarbOx was passed by Congress in the wake of a series of corporate scandals, some of which were caused by the failure of the board and the chief corporate officers to oversee activities properly within their corporations. Thus, Congress placed certain strict requirements on officers and directors and added severe penalties for the failure to meet those requirements. For example, under SarbOx, chief executive officers (CEOs), chief operating officers (COO's), and chief financial officers (CFOs) are required to present declarations that confirm the accuracy of their corporation's financial statements. They must indicate that the statements do not misrepresent the company's economic situation. The penalties for violating this particular provision include possible incarceration and monetary penalties that run into the millions.

Not everyone in the corporate community is happy about the passage of SarbOx or about the extra regulatory responsibilities that it places on corporate directors, officers, and auditors. Some financial experts, for instance, predict that the United States will soon experience a loss of foreign business because of the strict rules enforced under SarbOx. These pundits fear that some global alien corporations that have the chance to place their stock for sale on an American stock exchange will move instead to a foreign exchange in search of a more lenient approach to corporate governance. Although some evidence of this trend has been detected, other causes may explain why a foreign corporation might choose to list in London rather than New York. Some analysts argue that the epidemic of anti corporate lawsuits rather than regulatory legislation is what actually drives foreign firms away from the United States. Others suggest that the American insistence that all disputes be fashioned under American law, a trend known as **legal imperialism**, makes listing in the United States unpopular today. In contrast, some experts see no crisis at all, and still others suggest that the problem of attracting foreign firms to an American exchange is less troublesome than dealing with the type of widespread corruption that sparked the passage of SarbOx in the first place.

A QUESTION OF ETHICS

Legislating Morality: Rendering to Caesar the Things That Are Caesar's and . . .

The Sarbanes-Oxley Act (SarbOx) includes a long list of regulations that outlaw actions and procedures that most people would see as ethical problems rather than legal issues. For instance, SarbOx prevents individual loans from the corporation to board members or officers. It is difficult to see how anyone with a well-developed moral compass would even think about making or receiving such loans, let alone actually do it. Yet, here we have a federal statute that outlaws a clearly unethical practice. As if this were not surprising enough, Congress also felt the need to include a provision that expressly prohibits both altering evidence and revising, destroying, or suppressing any records needed in a government investigation of the corporation. Essentially, this is a statutory provision that tells corporate directors not to lie. It is sad to see that the Congress of the United States, of all bodies, must tell corporate managers that it is immoral to lie. Possibly even more disheartening is that the penalties for lying include incarceration. Perhaps most telling of all is that Congress believed it necessary to encourage corporate executives to develop ethical rules and regulations, as if corporate executives had never heard of the word *ethics* pre-SarbOx. Incredibly, Congress also found it necessary to remind executives that employees who provide information to federal authorities about any corporate violations are protected by the act. Finally, Congress did not trust corporate managers to follow the law on their own, and so SarbOx also set up the Public Company Accounting Oversight Board to regulate corporate auditing procedures.

QUESTIONS YET UNANSWERED

The following questions have yet to be addressed. Before you consider each question, turn to Chapter 1 to review the various ethical theories noted there (market value ethics, social contract theory, utilitarianism, and rational ethics). Then using one of those theories in a consistent way, answer the following questions.

1. In what way, if any, is SarbOx a reflection of general trends in this country concerning ethics and morality? Explain.
2. Should Congress also pass laws to regulate other institutions such as schools, churches, synagogues, and mosques, in the same way that SarbOx regulates corporations? Why or why not?

3. The text suggests that SarbOx is an example of government control over the corporate culture. In what way does SarbOx also promote independent director control and stakeholder control? Explain.

4. Is there any justifiable reason for congressional intervention into the world of ethics and morality, especially considering the Congress's poor track record in ethics? Explain.

5. In general, the trend demonstrated by SarbOx is called legislating morality. Is legislating morality ever an acceptable option? Before answering consider the rules that are promulgated by various religions. Is there a difference between Congress legislating morality and a religion teaching the Ten Commandments? Explain.

Independent Director Control A second theory of corporate control involves the establishment of independent directors. Those theorists who support the use of independent directors argue that the most effective way to ensure that corporate decisions are made in the best interests of those affected is to make certain that the decision makers themselves are not affected by those decisions. Some groups have already implemented requirements to ensure the addition of independent directors to the boards of many corporations. Independent directors are defined as directors who have no family members employed by the corporation, who are not themselves employed by the corporation, or, if they were at one time employed by the corporation, have not been on the staff for at least three years. There is, of course, an opt-out rule that permits some corporations to sidestep the independent directors' rule if they are a "controlled" company. A controlled company is one that has more than half its voting power concentrated in one individual or a small group of people who always vote together. The opt-out provision is designed to give parent companies that are already controlled by independent boards a technique for eliminating a duplication of the independence restriction in their subsidiaries.

Legislative Support for Independent Director Control Sometimes those people who support one method of corporate governance may inadvertently lend support for another form of government, often without being aware of the contradiction. Such is the case with congressional action in the passage of SarbOx. Although the main thrust of SarbOx is to facilitate governmental control of the corporate person, some provisions have given a boost to independent control. For example, SarbOx requires all U.S corporate persons that are publicly traded and all alien corporations included on an American stock exchange to set up an audit committee that consists of independent members. The audit committee has the duty to oversee the operation of each accounting firm that audits the company. The committee chooses the firm, sets the amount paid to the firm, and evaluates the work of the firm. Moreover, the independent auditing committee also has the job of establishing a process for handling grievances about accounting and auditing procedures. The committee is also empowered to hire outside attorneys and/or other counselors should that need arise. Also, the law does permit the entire board to serve as an audit committee, but only if the entire board consists of independent directors. [See: Margaret H. McFarland, Deputy Director, Securities Exchange Commission, 17 CFR Parts, 228, 229, 249, 274, Standards Relating to Listed Company Audit Committees, April 9, 2004.]

Managerial Control The third approach to corporate governance is managerial control. Those who favor managerial control point out that the officers and the directors of a corporation are in the best position for judging not only the needs of the corporation but also the needs of the community and the needs of society at large. Individuals who favor managerial control would insulate the managers from shareholders by limiting the shareholders' power to vote and making it difficult for shareholders to sue managers. Opponents of managerial control argue that corporate managers may tend to be self-interested and, as a result, make relatively shortsighted decisions.

Limitations on Managerial Control   The idea that management should have ultimate control over corporate decision making has been with us since the first corporations opened their doors. The argument that supports this notion states that management leaders are in the best position to make such decisions based on their education, experience, and place within the corporate culture. Yet, despite this, many people object to the power given to corporate management or at least to mega-giant corporations like Amazon and Wal-Mart. One such glaring example involves the power that has devolved to these giant corporate retailers over manufacturers. A shift in the power base began in 1975 when Congress passed the Consumer Goods Pricing Act of 1975 (CGPA). The critical feature of the CGPA, according to commentator Barry Lynn in the CNN story "Corporate Giants Have Too Much Power," was the ability passed on to retailers that allowed them to determine the amount charged for goods produced by manufacturers. This move, along with Reagan era policies based on "consumer welfare" in quotation marks. consumer welfare, led to a situation that empowers retail giants such as Walmart and Amazon to dictate prices at will. [See: Barry Lynn, "Corporate Giants Have Too Much Power," *CNN Opinions,* February 16, 2010, http://www.cnn.com/2010/OPINION/02/16/lynn.amazon.power/index.html.] Nevertheless, there are those who believe that the great power once wielded by corporations in general and by CEOs in particular has become a mere remnant of its former self. Much if this has to do with the fact that shareholder power has grown over the past decade or so, especially as that power is used by savvy investors that may hire expert firms to guide them through details of proxy battles. As noted earlier, the growing influence of independent board members has also played a role in this power shift. *The Economist* has reported in 2012, for example, that most corporate board members were no longer insiders but instead outsiders beyond the conventional influence of the CEO. [See: "The Shackled Boss: Corporate Bosses Are Much Less Powerful Than They Used to Be," *The Economist,* January 21, 2012, p. 76.]

Stakeholder Control   Stakeholder control is based on the idea that corporate decision making affects more individuals and groups than just the shareholders and the managers of the corporation. The people who have a stake in the corporate decision-making process, beyond shareholders, directors, and officers, argue that many corporate decisions, such as a decision to open or close a factory, affect the community through consumers, suppliers, employees, and community neighbors. Consequently, all of these stakeholders and more should be represented on the boards of directors of all major corporations. Individuals who support stakeholder control would like to see representatives from employees' unions; consumer protection organizations; suppliers; customers; clients; environmental protection groups; and local, state, national, and international communities.

Shareholder Democracy   Individuals who favor shareholder democracy, or corporate democracy as it is also known, believe that the shareholders have the right to run the corporation, because without their money, the corporation would not be able to survive. As the real owners of the corporation, the shareholders have a right to say how their money and their property should be used. Supporters of shareholder democracy would make management more responsive to shareholders by giving shareholders greater voting control and making it easier for them to take managers to court. Opponents of this theory point out that most shareholders are removed from the center of corporate activity and therefore cannot make the same type of informed decisions that the managers can make.

Today there is a delicate balance between the theories of managerial control and shareholder democracy. Therefore, this chapter will focus on the battle between these two positions as it examines the subject of corporate control. The two most significant areas of this conflict lie in shareholder voting control and shareholder lawsuits. Shareholders can influence corporate decision making through their voting powers and through their right to initiate a lawsuit against managers (see Table 27-1).

Shareholder Voting Control

Shareholders usually receive one vote per share of common stock held. Shareholders who are dissatisfied with management can attempt to buy more shares to increase their voting power. With this increased voting power, the dissatisfied or dissident shareholders can influence the election of the board of directors. However, shareholders are not always able to buy more shares of the corporation, either because they cannot afford them or because the other shareholders are not willing to sell. In such cases, shareholders can resort to one of the other voting methods available:

- Cumulative voting
- Proxy solicitation
- Shareholder proposals
- Voting trusts
- Pooling agreements
- Shareholder nominations
- Unanimous voting restrictions

Cumulative Voting Ordinarily, each share of common stock is worth one vote. Therefore, only a majority of shareholders can elect directors of the corporation. To give minority shareholders an opportunity to elect one or more directors, some states permit cumulative voting. This system allows shareholders to multiply the number of their voting shares by the number of directors to be elected. All these votes may be cast for one candidate or distributed among several candidates. This procedure allows minority shareholders an opportunity to be represented on the board of directors.

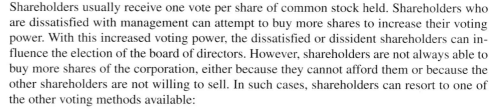

EXAMPLE 27-2: Cumulative vs. Straight Voting

Beth General, James Garrett, Ken Collins, and Heather Gilliam were presented to the shareholders as candidates for the board of directors of Shopton Enterprises, Inc. Three of the four were to be chosen. Because cumulative voting was authorized, the minority shareholders cast all their weighted votes for Gilliam, who had promised to represent the minority voice in corporate affairs. Had the minority voters been allowed only one vote for each share instead of three, they might have failed in their effort to elect a favored director.

Proxy Voting A proxy is the authority given to one shareholder to cast another shareholder's votes. Proxy solicitation is the process by which one shareholder asks another for his or her voting right. Proxy solicitation also refers to the actual document that is used to request the right to vote the other shareholders' votes. The minority shareholder's voting power increases as the number of proxies held rises. Because majority shareholders, including management, can also solicit proxies, a struggle between the two groups, known as a proxy contest, often results. Proxy contests involving large, publicly held corporations are closely regulated by the Securities and Exchange Commission (SEC). The primary federal law that controls the operation of a proxy contest is Section 14 (a) of the Securities Exchange Act of 1934. Section 14 (a) is designed to prevent fraud by requiring a complete revelation of certain facts by any individual or group that gets involved in the proxy solicitation process. Specifically, the law requires that anyone soliciting a proxy must disclose the identity of the solicitor, the reason behind the solicitation, and all other crucial facts that the shareholders will need to make an informed decision about the proxy. The document that communicates this information to the shareholders is called a **proxy statement**, which is delivered to the SEC and then sent to shareholders before the shareholders' annual meeting. Generally, the solicitation includes a card called a proxy card that can be returned to the solicitor. Rule 14 (a) of the Securities Exchange Act has recently become the focus of heated debate among shareholders and management alike. The dispute covers the question of what corporate management can and cannot exclude from proxy materials that are to be sent to shareholders.

The Securities and Exchange Commission recently enacted several new proxy solicitation rules that have answered a few of these questions. Specifically, the SEC now requires proxies to include additional information about manager-level compensation packages. This information includes (1) risk-related elements in corporate compensation packages; (2) equity awards added to corporate compensation packages; and (3) any conflicts of interest involved in the pay packages earned by compensation consultants. The first of these reflects the fact that corporate compensation packages sometimes involve risky investment opportunities that might have a long-term effect on the value of the shareholders' shares. Such risks must now be disclosed but only if the risks might have a "material adverse effect" on shareholders. The second disclosure reflects a change in the way that equity rewards are reported in proxy statements. Rather than the dollar figure called for under the old rules, the new rules require that the "fair value" of the award be reported. The final change requires the reporting of any money paid to consultants hired to evaluate nonexecutive-related salaries. The fear is that such consultants might be caught in a conflict of interest between the managers who pay their fees and the nonexecutives whose compensation packages are being evaluated. Not everyone believes that these changes will be helpful to shareholders. The fear is that the very nature of the new information (risk management, equity awards, and conflicts of interest) and the complex language needed to communicate the required facts might, at the very least, be useless to the shareholders and, at the worst, might confuse and mislead them, thus causing more harm than good. [See: Arden T. Phillips, "SEC Rules Bolster Compensation Disclosure," *The National Law Journal,* February 8, 2010, p. 7.]

Stockholders exercise their control through votes at annual meetings and through proxies.

Shareholder Proposals

Another way for shareholders to exercise their voting power to shape corporate decision making is the shareholder proposal. Because shareholder proposals are placed in the proxy materials that are sent from corporate management to shareholders, they are closely allied with the proxy solicitation process and also governed by the Securities Exchange Act of 1934. A shareholder proposal allows shareholders to influence corporate affairs because, under SEC guidelines, shareholders of large, publicly owned corporations can compel management to include their proposals in management's proxy solicitation prior to the next shareholder meeting. A **shareholder proposal** is a suggestion about a broad company policy or procedure that is submitted by a shareholder. The proposal cannot be about the ordinary business operation of the corporation. It must concern something that affects all shareholders. A proposal to hire or fire a particular employee would not qualify, whereas a proposal to amend the corporate charter would. The rules also prohibit proposals that concern only dividend payments.

To qualify as a valid shareholder proposal under SEC rules, the proposal must be no more than 500 words long and must be received by management at least 120 days before the date of the corporation's proxy statement released to shareholders in connection with last year's annual shareholder's meeting. In addition, the shareholder must have owned at least 1 percent or $2,000 in market value of the voting stock of the corporation for one year and may submit only one proposal at a time. Even then, managers can reject the proposal if they feel that it does not qualify as a valid shareholder proposal according to a lengthy list of disqualifying characteristics cataloged by the SEC. Included on this list are proposals that are personal grievances, those beyond the corporation's power, and proposals that relate to a corporate election. However, some of these limitations recently have been challenged in a series of lawsuits filed by high-powered corporate shareholders.

Shareholder proposals, sometimes referred to as **shareholder resolutions**, have traditionally been among the weakest of shareholder voting tactics. One reason is that for many years, such proposals were not taken seriously by the directors and officers of most corporations, a situation that was exacerbated by the fact that the courts did not appear to take them seriously either. Much of this attitude was caused by the open-ended nature of the rules which permitted the corporate directors to reject most proposals made by shareholders. Moreover, many of the proposals that did make it to the ballot were filed by people with a political agenda and demanded such things as a cessation of business dealings with South African companies, a boycott of Defense Department contracts, or a campaign to redistribute shareholder dividends among needy Third World nations.

The law of balancing forces has operated over the last few years to increase the power of shareholder proposals and decrease the ability of corporate managers to short-circuit such proposals. Part of this has emerged because the shareholder proposal itself has become less a soapbox for political dissidents and more a tool for large institutional shareholders, thus resetting a balance that had moved heavily toward politics. Institutional shareholders, such as the American Federation of State, County, and Municipal Employees or Boston Common Asset Management, have pressed claims against corporations asking not for political action but for a share in corporate governance. Typically, such proposals demand that the corporation make some sort of amendment in voting procedures, such as a change in the bylaws to require a majority rather than a plurality vote on directors, to allow shareholders to cast advisory votes on executive salaries, or to permit shareholders to vote on antitakeover tactics, such as the use of a white knight or a lockup agreement strategy (see Chapter 28). Corporate directors have become more amenable to such shareholder proposals in light of the SarbOx and the outside support that has been provided by newly formed expert support groups, such as the Institutional Shareholder Services and Global Advisors, Inc., to help shareholder activists.

Voting Trusts A **voting trust** is an agreement among shareholders to transfer their voting rights to a trustee. A **trustee** is a person who is entrusted with the management and control of another's property or the rights associated with that property. Sometimes, the trustee is one of the shareholders; at other times, the trustee is an outsider. The trustee votes those shares at the annual shareholders' meeting at the direction of the shareholders. Shareholders surrender only their voting rights. All other rights, including the right to receive profits, remain with them. Generally, once a voting trust has been created, it cannot be ended until the specified time period has run its course. However, state statutes usually place a maximum time limit on the duration of a voting trust. Most state time limits run from 10 to 21 years. Voting trusts must be in writing and must be filed with the corporation.

Pooling Agreements Sometimes, shareholders join in a temporary arrangement and agree to vote the same way on a particular issue. Such agreements are known as **pooling agreements**, shareholder agreements, or voting agreements. They differ from proxies and voting trusts because the shareholders retain control of their own votes. In this sense, pooling agreements are also the weakest voting arrangement because shareholders can change their votes at the last minute. If a member of a pooling agreement changes her or his vote, however, the other members may bring a lawsuit against the shareholder who broke the agreement. In general, pooling agreements are interpreted by the court under the principles of contract law.

Shareholder Nominations Another way to increase the voting power of shareholders is to augment their ability to elect a director or directors who will represent their point of view in crucial issues facing the company. Several ways to do this include enacting state statutes, altering SEC rules, or changing stock exchange regulations so that certain events will trigger the ability of shareholders to elect board members. One such triggering event might be coupled with a shareholder proposal to permit shareholders to nominate their own directors. The rules might permit this nomination process to go forward as long as 50 percent of the votes cast (not 50 percent of the available votes, but 50 percent of those votes actually used in an election) support such a proposal. Another triggering event might be the ability of the minority shareholders to reach a 35–50 percent (depending on how the rule is worded) margin of voters who block the election of a management-nominated board candidate. Should either of these events occur, the minority shareholders would be permitted to place their own director on the next ballot at the expense of the corporation.

Unanimous Voting Restrictions An additional approach to strengthening the power of the shareholders involves a change in the corporate bylaws that makes it more difficult for the board to approve crucial issues that affect the fate of the corporation. The new voting bylaws would require unanimous agreement among all directors when the issue before the board involves a critical matter such as a merger, the sale of corporate assets, or a large increase in the salary of a top officer. Under current bylaws, one director with one vote on a board of 12 persons is of little consequence. However,

Table 27-1 Shareholder Control	
Votes and Lawsuits	**Explanation**
Voting control:	
Cumulative voting	Each share of stock has as many votes as there are directors to be elected
Proxy voting	The right to vote another shareholder's stock
Voting trusts	An agreement among shareholders to transfer their voting rights to a trustee
Pooling agreements	Shareholders join in a temporary arrangement, agreeing to vote the same way on a particular issue
Shareholder proposals	A suggestion about a broad company policy or procedure submitted by a shareholder and included in management's proxy solicitation
Shareholder suits:	
Direct suit	A suit brought by shareholders who have been deprived of a right
Derivative suit	A suit brought by shareholders based on an injury to the corporation

under the revised regulations that require the unanimous approval of the board when major issues are decided, a single board member would have the power to block any material change contemplated by the rest of the board. The fact that a single director would have the power to stop major changes in corporate structure and policy might encourage minority shareholders to join forces in a campaign to elect their own director to the board.

Combinations Although each of these voting techniques has been discussed separately, in practice, they can be combined to increase shareholder voting power. For example, a group of minority shareholders could enter a pooling agreement in which they all agree to cast their cumulative votes for a single board candidate. It is even possible for one of the voting techniques to be used to institute another of those techniques.

Shareholder Lawsuits

The battle between management and dissident shareholders may also be waged on a front other than the annual shareholders' meeting. That front is the courtroom. Shareholders can sue management to compel a change in direction or to force management to overturn a decision. The two types of suits available to shareholders are direct suits and derivative suits.

Direct Suits A **direct suit** is brought by shareholders who have been deprived of a right that belongs to them as shareholders. These rights include the right to vote, the right to receive dividends, the right to transfer shares, the right to purchase newly issued stock, and the right to examine corporate books and records. If shareholders have been denied any of these rights, they can bring a direct suit to make up for any loss they have suffered.

Derivative Suits A **derivative suit** allows shareholders to sue corporate management on behalf of the corporation. Unlike a direct suit, a derivative suit is not based on a direct injury to a shareholder. Instead, the injury is to the corporation. The shareholders' right to sue is derived from the corporate injury. Shareholders who bring a successful derivative suit are entitled to recover attorney fees. To bring a derivative suit, shareholders must meet certain prerequisites. One prerequisite is the exhaustion of internal remedies. Before bringing suit, the shareholder must attempt to solve the problem by communicating with the board of directors and with other shareholders. In their original complaint commencing the derivative action, the shareholders must state the steps that they took to exhaust all internal remedies. If the shareholders have not exhausted internal remedies and still insist on bringing the lawsuit, the court will dismiss the case and deny any request from the shareholders for the payment of attorney fees. On the other hand, if the shareholders can show that, because of a director or officer's control of the board, any attempt to bring the matter to the board would have been futile, they may convince the court to waive the requirement to exhaust internal remedies. This rule is referred to as the **demand futility doctrine**. Some legal commentators refer to an officer who has total and unquestioned control of the board of directors as a corporate **monarch**. To bring a derivative suit, a shareholder must own stock at the time of the injury and at the time of the suit. This requirement is known as the **rule of contemporary ownership**. Frequently, state corporate laws also require derivative suit plaintiffs to pay a security deposit to cover the corporation's potential expenses in defending the derivative suits. All of these requirements make it difficult for a shareholder to bring a derivative lawsuit.

THE OPENING CASE *Round 2*
Derivative Suits and the Demand Futility Doctrine

In the opening case, we learned that *Aronson v. Lewis* concerned a series of arrangements between Meyers Parking Systems, Inc., and Leo Fink, one of its directors. For starters, Meyers granted Fink a contract that contained a condition that permitted Fink to become a consultant at Meyers after he retired. Additional stipulations within the agreement stated that Fink would be paid $150,000 for the first three years, $125,000 for the next three, and then $100,000 each year for life. Lewis, a shareholder, took offense at this arrangement, because, according to Lewis, Fink did not really perform any duties for the payments. Lewis was also upset because the board had ratified several interest-free loans to Fink. Altogether, the loans came to around $225,000. Lewis sued, asserting that the contract was "grossly excessive" and the "loans" were really just an extra added payment transferred to Fink. (Note: The defendant's attorney indicated later that these loans had been totally repaid.) The bottom line of Lewis's argument was that the payments to Fink represented a waste of corporate funds, for which the directors were personally liable. The board chose to challenge Lewis's right to bring the lawsuit. Specifically, they noted that, since this was a derivative lawsuit (true enough), Lewis had to exhaust internal remedies before bringing suit. This would have involved taking his complaints to the board. Lewis countered this challenge by arguing that Fink was a monarch, that is, a dictatorial officer who had complete control of the board. Therefore, the board did whatever Fink dictated. This rendered any demand on the board an exercise in futility. As evidence for this claim, the plaintiff revealed that Fink had appointed every member of the board and that each board member was, therefore, obligated to Fink. Furthermore, since all the board members had been designated as defendants in the suit, they would not approve Lewis's undertaking because, by assisting in the case, they would be suing themselves. The court christened Lewis's strategy the *doctrine of demand futility*. However, the court said that, to succeed under the futility demand doctrine, Lewis, or any similarly situated plaintiff, would have to present much more evidence than the court had before it at the present moment. First, the court noted that, the fact that an officer or director owns a lot of stock, when it is less than a majority of that stock, does not amount to complete control. Second, the court added, even majority ownership does not, by itself, amount to complete control, provided the directors exercise good judgment as they carry out their responsibilities. Third, the court noted the plaintiff had presented no evidence that the payments to Fink amounted to a waste of corporate assets. Fourth, the court declared that it is standard procedure for officers and directors to appoint new board members and that the performance of the board members is what matters, not their method of appointment. Finally, the court stated that the mere unsubstantiated claim that the directors would not sue themselves was by itself insufficient, but instead must be supported by evidence that the directors violated their corporate duties. [See: *Aronson v. Lewis*, 473 A.2d 805 (March 1, 1984).]

quick quiz 27-2

1. Under the original concept of the corporation, the shareholders are the primary reason that a corporation exists. true | false

2. Pooling agreements have been outlawed in all states. true | false

3. A controlled company is one that has more than half its voting power concentrated in one person or a small group of persons who always vote together. true | false

Table 27-2 Management Rule Situation Explanation

Business manager does *not* profit from decision.	**Business Judgment Rule** The decision stands if it is made (1) in good faith, (2) with due care (3) within the law, and (4) in the corporation's best interests.
Business manager profits from decision.	**Fairness Rule** The decision must be fair to the corporation decision because managers must remain loyal to the corporation.
Business manager exceeds authority.	**Actual Authority Rule** A manager may be held liable if he a corporate decision exceeds corporate authority and harms the corporation.

27-3 Governance Responsibilities

When a court hears a case challenging a manager's decision, that court will consider the following three rules in judging that conduct: the business judgment rule, the fairness rule, and the actual authority rule (see Table 27-2).

The Business Judgment Rule

Under the **business judgment rule**, the court will not interfere with most business decisions. The rule protects managers who act legally, with due care, and in good faith, as long as their decisions are in the best interests of the corporation. The rule results from the commonsense belief that based on their education, experience, and knowledge, managers are in the best position to run the corporation. In contrast, shareholders and judges are far removed from the day-to-day operations of the business and should not be allowed to second-guess most management decisions. Protecting directors and officers in this way encourages people to become corporate managers and reassures them that they will be protected when they make difficult business decisions. The business judgment rule emerges from the duty of due diligence that a manager owes to the corporation. The **duty of due diligence** consists of four parts. It says that, when acting on behalf of the corporation, a manager must act (1) legally, (2) in good faith, (3) using the same level of care that an ordinarily prudent individual would use in a comparable situation, and (4) in the reasonable belief that the best interests of the company are being met.

The Fairness Rule

The business judgment rule assumes that managers do not personally profit from business decisions. If managers do profit, then the decision is suspect because all managers owe a **duty of loyalty** to the corporation. To fulfill this duty, managers must place the corporation's interests above their own. When managers enter contracts with the corporation or when they are on the boards of two corporations that do business with each other, they are said to be self-dealing. Different standards are used to judge the conduct of **self-dealing managers**. For example, if a self-dealing manager seeks and obtains the approval of the board members who did not profit from the decision, or if that same manager seeks and obtains the approval of the shareholders who did not profit from the decision, then the

THE OPENING CASE *Round 3*
The Business Judgment Rule

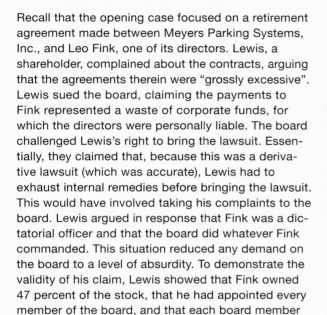

Recall that the opening case focused on a retirement agreement made between Meyers Parking Systems, Inc., and Leo Fink, one of its directors. Lewis, a shareholder, complained about the contracts, arguing that the agreements therein were "grossly excessive". Lewis sued the board, claiming the payments to Fink represented a waste of corporate funds, for which the directors were personally liable. The board challenged Lewis's right to bring the lawsuit. Essentially, they claimed that, because this was a derivative lawsuit (which was accurate), Lewis had to exhaust internal remedies before bringing the lawsuit. This would have involved taking his complaints to the board. Lewis argued in response that Fink was a dictatorial officer and that the board did whatever Fink commanded. This situation reduced any demand on the board to a level of absurdity. To demonstrate the validity of his claim, Lewis showed that Fink owned 47 percent of the stock, that he had appointed every member of the board, and that each board member

was, as a result, indebted to Fink. What's more, because the board members had been named as defendants in the case, they would not approve Lewis's undertaking because by supporting the case, they would have to sue themselves. The court dubbed Lewis's tactic the *doctrine of demand futility*. The court said that, to succeed under the futility demand doctrine, Lewis would have to present much more evidence than he had done thus far. First, the court noted that the fact that an officer or director owns a lot of stock, when it is less than a majority of that stock, does not amount to complete control. Second, the court noted that even majority ownership does not, by itself, amount to complete control. The court then called upon the business judgment rule, saying that, provided that the directors made their decisions in good faith and in the best interests of the corporation, the presumption of independence will stand. [See: *Aronson v. Lewis*, 473 A.2d 805 (March 1, 1984).]

manager's decision will be considered valid, despite the self-dealing. In the alternative, without board or shareholder approval, the manager's conduct will be judged by the fairness rule. The **fairness rule** requires managers to be fair to the corporation when they personally benefit from their business decisions. The fairness rule does not automatically declare managers disloyal if they profit from a corporate decision. Rather, it allows the court to examine the decision to determine its basic fairness to the corporation. How to measure fairness is, at best, problematic. At a minimum, it requires corporate managers to disclose all crucial information when they enter contracts with the corporation. Two rules that are offshoots of the fairness rule and the duty of loyalty are the insider trading rule and the corporate opportunity doctrine. Both rules give specific ways to measure a corporate manager's fairness in certain types of situations.

Insider Trading
Because of their role in corporate affairs, directors and officers often possess inside information. **Inside information** is material, nonpublic, factual data that can be used to buy or sell securities at a profit. Directors, officers, and other key individuals in a corporation, such as major shareholders who are not directors or officers, qualify as insiders. Insider trading may or may not be illegal. Corporate insiders who buy and sell stock in their own corporation are not trading illegally provided they report these transactions to the SEC. However, insiders who use material, nonpublic, factual data that they have in their possession by virtue of their corporate office to trade securities in violation of the fiduciary duties they owe to the corporation and its shareholders have engaged in illegal insider trading. Moreover, when a corporate insider "tips" an outsider about that

material, nonpublic, factual data, the "tipper" and the "tippee" who uses that data in a securities trade may both be liable for illegal insider trading. Moreover, a corporate outsider, such as a printer in a printing firm who, by virtue of his or her job, misappropriates such data and uses the data to make a securities trade is also engaged, at least potentially, in illegal insider trading. The SEC identifies the following classes of individuals who might be at risk of finding themselves on the wrong end of an insider trading case. Naturally, corporate directors, officers and employees can easily get themselves tangled in such cases if they use material, nonpublic, factual data in their trades. However, also at risk are family members, business colleagues, and friends, of such corporate insiders. Also in danger are employees who work for businesses, such as law firms, banks, brokerage houses, and printing companies, who have access to such material, nonpublic, factual data. Even government employees with ready access to such data are at risk. On the other hand, just being in these categories is not an offense. SEC Rule 10b-5-1 provides exceptions to insider trading liability when the tippees can show that, even though they had the material, nonpublic factual data, they did not use the information because the trade was already in the works before the information was obtained. [See: Electronic Code of Federal Regulations, Title 17, Chapter II, Part 240.10b-5-1 and 240.10b 5-2; see also US Securities and Exchange Commission, Investor Information: Fast Answers, January 15, 2013, http://www.sec.gov/answers/insider.htm.]

The Corporate Opportunity Doctrine As noted previously, along with the duty of due diligence and the duty of actual authority (see the next section), corporate managers also owe a duty of loyalty to the corporation. The duty of loyalty requires that corporate managers place the corporation's well-being ahead of their own interests. One offshoot of this duty is the idea of the corporate opportunity doctrine. The **corporate opportunity doctrine** states that corporate managers cannot take a corporate business opportunity for themselves if they know that the corporation would be interested in that opportunity as well. Before taking such an opportunity, a manager must first offer it to the corporation by informing other managers and shareholders. If the corporation rejects the opportunity, then the manager is free to take that opportunity.

The Actual Authority Rule

Corporate managers are also held to a third duty, that is, the duty to act within actual authority. The authority spoken of here includes those powers that have been granted to managers by virtue of their position within the corporation. The duties of the directors and officers of the corporation are outlined in the appropriate state statutes, in the articles of incorporation, in the regulations issued by government bodies such as the SEC, in relevant case law, and in the bylaws of the company. The **actual authority rule** states that a manager may be held liable if he or she exceeds his or her authority and the corporation is harmed as a result. Some states say that the managers will be liable for any violation of the limits of their authority on the basis of absolute or strict liability; some jurisdictions will consider the managers responsible only if the violation results in negligent or intentional conduct. This duty is also sometimes referred to as the **duty of obedience**. It is, of course, possible for a vote of the board or of the shareholders to approve a previously unauthorized act by a manager through the process of **ratification**.

Efforts to Limit Responsibility Corporate managers have come under scrutiny by regulators and the courts in recent years. As a result, many otherwise well-qualified individuals have avoided serving as corporate managers in general but, in particular, as corporate directors. To counteract this trend, some states have enacted legislation that is designed to help protect the good faith and due diligent activities of such managers. These legislative enactments take three forms: (1) voluntary protective measures, (2) automatic protective measures, and (3) protective measures that limit the amount of damages that can be recovered against directors. A voluntary protective measure is one that permits corporate shareholders to fashion their bylaws so as to limit or eliminate the liability of directors for decisions made while carrying out their duties. Such measures would allow recovery of damages only if the director deliberately broke the law, deliberately violated the duty of loyalty, deliberately violated the duty of good faith, or improperly benefited from the transaction in question. Automatic protective measures grant the same type of immunity by state law, regardless of the action or inaction of corporate shareholders. The final measure would allow lawsuits against managers even in the cases noted earlier but would place a cap on the amount of money damages that can be recovered against directors.

Efforts to Increase Responsibility

At the same time that state governments are attempting to ease the liability of directors, the federal government has enacted efforts to increase director responsibilities for catching and stopping the wrongdoing of others within the corporation. One such measure is SarbOx, which places an affirmative duty on the directors of publicly traded corporations to monitor whether their corporation is conforming to all legal requirements. A second measure involves the **United States Sentencing Commission**, which has issued a set of rules that control the discretion of the federal courts in issuing fines against corporations found guilty of criminal activities. Under the new rules, if the directors of a corporation did not do their best to discover and stop illegal activities, the court can place very severe penalties on the corporation, once it has been found guilty of those violations. The idea behind the new rules is to force directors to pay more attention to what is going on within their own companies, especially in relation to crime-stopping activities. The new rules have led some legal commentators to suggest a series of steps that corporate directors should take when faced with suspected wrongdoing within their company. Seven steps are recommended: (1) Once a legal violation has been uncovered (or even suspected), the activity must cease instantly; (2) any and all consequences that have flowed from the violation should be uncovered and stopped immediately; (3) any attempt to engage in a cover-up, and in fact any actions that can be remotely perceived as a cover-up, must be avoided religiously; (4) notification of the violation must be made to the proper authorities; (5) investigations must be made to uncover any similar or related activities that may be illegal; (6) the cause or causes of the legal violations must be determined; and (7) an action plan must be created and executed to punish the violators and to prevent any future violations.

---

quick quiz 27-3

1. The business judgment rule states that a manager's decision will stand as long as it was legal, was made with due care and in good faith, and was made in the best interests of the corporation.   true | false

2. The fairness rule states that a decision made by a manager will stand if it is fair to the corporation.   true | false

3. The business judgment rule is used by the courts when the manager is disinterested, that is, he or she does not personally gain from the decision.   true | false

27-4 Shareholder Rights

In addition to their voting rights and their right to sue, shareholders are entitled to examine certain corporate records, share in dividends, transfer shares of stock, and buy newly issued stock.

Right to Examine Corporate Records

A shareholder's right by statute to inspect the records of the corporation is usually limited to inspections for proper purposes at an appropriate time and place. Idle curiosity and an intent that unreasonably interferes with or embarrasses corporate management would prompt officers or directors to refuse shareholders' requests to examine corporate accounts, minutes, and records. When the purpose of inspection is proper, it may be enforced by a court order.

Right to Share in Dividends

Shareholders have the right to share in dividends after they have been declared by the board of directors. Once declared, a dividend becomes a debt of the corporation and enforceable by law, as is any other debt. However, shareholders cannot force the directors to declare a dividend unless the directors are not acting in good faith in refusing to do so. Courts are not inclined to order directors to meet and declare a dividend if the court must substitute its own business judgment for that of the directors.

Right to Transfer Shares of Stock

Shareholders have the right to sell or transfer their shares of stock. The person to whom stock shares are transferred has the right to have the stock transfer entered on the corporate books. The transferee becomes a **shareholder of record** and is entitled to vote, receive dividends, and enjoy all other shareholder privileges.

Preemptive Rights

Unless the right is denied or limited by the corporate charter or by state law, shareholders have the right to purchase a proportionate share of every new offering of stock by the corporation. This right is known as the shareholder's **preemptive right**. Preemptive rights are more prevalent in small, closely held corporations than in large, publicly owned corporations. This right prevents management from depriving shareholders of their proportionate control of a corporation simply by increasing the number of shares in the corporation.

---

quick quiz 27-4

1. Assuming a request by a shareholder to inspect the corporate books is a proper one, the courts will enforce that request.	true | false
2. Today the courts will readily substitute their own judgment and declare a dividend on corporate stock, even when the directors of the corporation have voted against such a move.	true | false
3. Preemptive rights are more common in large, publicly held corporations than in small, closely held corporations.	true | false

27-5 Governance of a Limited Liability Company

The members of a limited liability company can choose to manage the business themselves, or they can hire outside management. An LLC that is run by the members themselves is called a member-managed LLC, whereas one operated by outside managers is referred to as a manager-managed LLC.

LO10

Member-Managed LLCs

If the managers choose to run the LLC on their own, management rights are apportioned among the members, according to the capital contributions made by each member to the LLC. Like the partners in a general partnership, the members of the LLC act as agents of the LLC. Accordingly, whenever a member performs a function within his or her apparent authority, the LLC will be bound by that action. However, as is true of a partnership, some actions fall outside the member's apparent authority. These include but are not limited to disposing of the firm's goodwill and submitting a claim of the LLC to arbitration. Naturally, the operating agreement can alter any of these statutory provisions.

Manager-Managed LLCs

If the members hire outside managers, then the LLC is run like a corporation. In the absence of an operating agreement, a single manager operates much like the CEO of a corporation, while a group of managers acts as a board of directors. Nevertheless, regardless of the number of managers involved in an LLC, both the business judgment rule and the fairness rule apply to their decisions in the same way that those rules apply to the directors of a corporation.

Fiduciary Duties

Regardless of whether the members or the managers ultimately run the LLC, both groups have a fiduciary duty to the LLC and to its members. However, as noted in the previous chapter, it would be wise to outline the specific management duties in the written operating agreement.

Did You Know?

Limited liability companies became more popular in the United States in 1988 when a ruling by the Internal Revenue Service declared that they could be treated as partnerships for tax purposes.

---

quick quiz 27-5

1. The members of an LLC have no choice in the matter of who will manage their firm.   true | false

2. An operating agreement established by the LLC is not permitted to alter statutory provisions regarding governance in any way.   true | false

3. Regardless of whether the members or the managers ultimately run the LLC, fiduciary duties have been suspended by provisions outlined in the latest version of the Uniform Limited Liability Company Act.   true | false

Summary

27.1 The business affairs of a corporation are managed by a board of directors elected by the shareholders. The directors have the authority to appoint officers and agents to run the day-to-day affairs of the corporation.

27.2 Five theories have been put forth by legal scholars and business experts concerning how corporations should be managed. These theories are governmental control, independent director control, managerial control, stakeholder control, and shareholder democratic control. Shareholders can increase their voting power by purchasing additional stock. If they cannot purchase additional stock, they may use another device to increase their voting power, such as cumulative voting, proxies, voting trusts, pooling agreements, shareholder proposals, shareholder nominations, and unanimous voting restrictions. Shareholders can also sue the corporation. Direct suits are brought by shareholders to protect their own rights. Derivative suits are brought by shareholders when they feel that the corporation has been damaged by a management decision. Derivative suits are limited by certain rules including that shareholders must exhaust internal remedies before bringing such suits. However, the demand futility doctrine states that it is not necessary for a shareholder to exhaust internal remedies if that shareholder can demonstrate that because a manager controls the board such an approach would be futile.

27.3 Under the business judgment rule, the court will not interfere with most management decisions as long as those decisions are legal and are made with due care, in good faith, and in the best interests of the corporation. If the manager profits personally from a business decision, then the court will use the fairness rule to judge the manager's conduct.

27.4 Shareholder rights include the right to examine corporate records, the right to share dividends, the right to transfer shares of stock, and the right to buy newly issued stock.

27.5 The members of a limited liability company can choose to manage the business themselves or hire outside management. Regardless of whether the members or the managers ultimately run the LLC, both groups have a fiduciary duty to the LLC and to the members of the LLC. Nevertheless, it would be wise to outline specific management duties in the operating agreement.

Key Terms

actual authority rule, 667

audit committee, 656

business judgment rule, 664

controlled company, 656

corporate democracy, 657

corporate opportunity doctrine, 667

cumulative voting, 658

demand futility doctrine, 662

derivative suit, 662

direct suit, 662

duty of due diligence, 664

duty of loyalty, 664

duty of obedience, 667

fairness rule, 665

governmental control, 654

independent director, 656

inside information, 665

insider trading, 666

insider trading rule, 666

legal imperialism, 655

managerial control, 656

monarch, 662

opt-out rule, 656

pooling agreement, 661

preemptive right, 669

proxy, 658

proxy contest, 658

proxy solicitation, 658

proxy statement, 659

ratification, 667

rule of contemporary ownership, 662

Sarbanes–Oxley (SarbOx) Act, 654

self-dealing manager, 664

shareholder democracy, 667

shareholder of record, 669

shareholder proposal, 659

shareholder resolutions, 660

stakeholders, 653

trustee, 660

United States Sentencing Commission, 668

voting trust, 660

Questions for Review and Discussion

1. What is the central dilemma of corporate governance?
2. What are the functions of directors, officers, and shareholders?
3. What are the five theories of corporate governance?
4. What is the difference between cumulative voting and proxy solicitation?
5. What is a shareholder proposal?
6. What is the difference between a voting trust and a pooling agreement?
7. What is the difference between a shareholder direct suit and a shareholder derivative suit?
8. What is the difference between the business judgment rule and the fairness rule?
9. What are the rights that belong to shareholders?
10. How does the management of a limited liability company operate?

Cases for Analysis

1. United Missionary Baptist Church, a not-for-profit corporation, held an election for the new church pastor. Several members of the church were dissatisfied with the results of the election and with the procedures that were followed during the election. They claimed that the inclusion of absentee balloting violated the church's constitution. Without making any parliamentary moves to correct the alleged misapplication of the constitution, and despite the fact that they had used their own absentee ballots during the election, these unhappy members brought a derivative lawsuit, asking the court to compel the church to follow its own constitution. The suit was dismissed. However, the members who brought the lawsuit claimed that because the lawsuit was a derivative action, they were entitled to attorney's fees, just as the shareholders of a profit corporation were entitled to attorney's fees. The court agreed that the same rules that apply to profit corporations in derivative actions apply to derivative suits brought for nonprofit corporations. However, the court still refused to grant the request for attorney's fees. Why? [See: *Russell v. United Missionary Baptist Church*, 637 N.E.2d 82 (OH).]

2. The bylaws of Jameson Enterprises, Inc., required a 70 percent supermajority to establish a quorum sufficient to hold a meeting to remove a director from the board. The bylaws also designated a meeting with such a purpose as a special meeting. The board consisted of 10 directors. Six showed up at the meeting. Of the four who failed to attend, three were in Europe. The fourth, Weinberger, was not notified of the meeting because he was the one to be removed. The six directors attending the meeting first voted to change the bylaws to require only 60 percent of the directors to establish a quorum sufficient to hold a special meeting. The six directors then unanimously voted to remove Weinberger. When Weinberger found out about the meeting, he objected to the vote and claimed that the entire procedure was void. Was Weinberger correct? Explain.

3. Smith, a shareholder, filed suit against the board of directors of a corporation in which he had owned stock. Smith claimed that he and other shareholders had not received top dollar for their shares when their corporation had merged with another. Consequently, they sought either a reversal of the merger or payment from the directors to make up for their losses. The directors, Smith argued, had violated their duty of due care because they based their decision on a 20-minute speech by the CEO. Also, the directors had not even looked at the merger documents, let alone studied them. Furthermore, the directors had not sought any independent evaluation by outside experts. For their part, the directors argued that because their decision was made in good faith and was legal, they were protected by the business judgment rule. Were the directors correct? [See: *Smith v. Van-Gorkon*, 488 A.2d 858 (DE).]

4. Donald Lewis was a shareholder in S.L.&E., Inc., a corporation that owned land and a complex of buildings in Rochester, New York. The land and buildings were leased to LGT, a tire manufacturer. Lewis's brothers were shareholders and directors of both S.L.&E. and LGT. Lewis had no financial or managerial interest in LGT. S.L.&E. leased the land to LGT at a rate that Lewis considered

damaging to S.L.&E. He pointed out that S.L.&E. collected only $14,000 per year in rent from LGT while paying out $11,000 in taxes. This rate, he argued, meant that S.L.&E. could never be a profit-making corporation. Should the directors of LGT and S.L.&E. be judged by the business judgment rule or the fairness rule? Explain. [See: *Lewis v. S.L.&E., Inc.,* 629 F.2d 764 (2nd Cir.).]

5. Jackson set up a trust for his seven children. Most of the assets in the trust consisted of stock in the two newspapers owned and run by Jackson. Over the course of 18 years, Jackson transferred all but two shares of voting stock in the newspapers. The trustee was given full power to manage the assets in the fund and sell or otherwise dispose of the newspaper stock. State law places a strict 10-year limit on voting trusts. The plaintiffs claimed that the trust, which had lasted 18 years, was no longer valid, having passed the 10-year limit. The defendants claimed that the 10-year limit did not apply to this trust. Were the defendants correct? Explain. [See: *Jackson v. Jackson,* 402 A.2d 893 (CT).]

6. Klinicki and Lundgren incorporated to form an air taxi service known as Berlinair, Inc. Each of them owned one-third interest in the corporation. The final third was owned by Lelco, Inc., a company owned by Lundgren. In his capacity as president of Berlinair, Lundgren learned that the Berlinair Flug Ring (BFR), a business association of Berlin's travel agents, was looking for an air charter service. Lundgren incorporated a new corporate entity called Air Berlin Charter (ABC). ABC then negotiated an air charter contract with BFR. Klinicki brought suit, demanding that Lundgren reimburse Berlinair for any profits made by ABC on the BFR contract. Was this a direct or derivative suit? Explain. Should the business judgment rule or the fairness rule be used by the court to measure Lundgren's performance? Explain. Who should have won the suit? Defend your choice. [See: *Klinicki v. Lundgren,* 695 P.2d 906 (OR).]

7. Naquin, Dubois, and Hoffpauir incorporated to form Air Engineered Systems and Services, Inc. Dubois became president and Hoffpauir became secretary-treasurer. Naquin was employed by the company. Conflicts among the three caused a breakdown in the working relationship. Dubois and Hoffpauir offered Naquin $2,000 a month for 10 years for his share of the business if he would sign a noncompetition agreement. Naquin refused to sell until he could examine the corporate records. Dubois and Hoffpauir refused to allow Naquin to see the books until he signed the noncompetition agreement. Could Dubois and Hoffpauir attach such a condition to Naquin's request? Explain. [See: *Naquin v. Air Engineered Systems and Services, Inc.,* 463 So.2d 992 (LA).]

8. Snodgrass, a minority shareholder in the 21st Century Broadcasting Network, Inc., was dissatisfied with management's decision to cancel several long-running news shows and replace them with several sitcoms and talk shows. She was also disturbed that management had decided to discharge several editorial writers and newscasters, including one who had recently won a major award for investigative journalism. Finally, she believed that a change in policy that would phase out foreign broadcast efforts would eventually cost the company an enormous amount of money. Assuming that Snodgrass does not want to sue the corporation, what options does she have if she wants to increase her influence over the board of directors of 21st Century Broadcasting Network, Inc.? Explain.

9. Keith Harris, a shareholder of Fastway Airlines, Inc., discovered that Donald Fleure, chief executive officer of Fastway, had sold some of his own land to the corporation at what Harris believed to be excessive prices. Can Harris bring a direct or a derivative suit in this situation? Explain. Would the fairness rule or the business judgment rule be used to evaluate the activities of Fleure? Explain.

		quick quiz Answers		
27-1	**27-2**	**27-3**	**27-4**	**27-5**
1. T	1. T	1. T	1. T	1. F
2. F	2. F	2. T	2. F	2. F
3. T	3. T	3. T	3. F	3. F

Chapter 28

Government Regulation of the Corporate Entity

THE OPENING CASE *Round 1*
The Dodd–Frank Act (DFA), Whistleblowers, and Textualism

Three popular but conflicting theories of legal interpretation are textualism, purposivism, and pragmatism. *Textualism* requires judges to analyze legal documents as literary works, by focusing exclusively on each document's language. In contrast, *purposivism* insists that judges consider the legislative goals of a statute while *pragmatism* expects judges to focus on the consequences of a decision. Both pragmatism and purposivism seem to demand that judges investigate the circumstances behind the writing of the text. To see these techniques up close, let's look at the case of *Egan v. TradingScreen, Inc.* The case involved a series of transactions orchestrated by the CEO of two corporations, TradingScreen, Inc., (TSI) and TradingScreens Brokerage Services, LLC, (TSBS) in ways that allegedly violated both the Dodd–Frank Act (DFA) and the Securities Exchange Act (SEA). The plaintiff in the case was a former employee of TSI named Patrick Egan. Egan's starring role in the melodrama began when he discovered that the CEO of TSI and TSBS was diverting funds to another

company, a corporation named SpreadZero (Zero). So far so good, except that Zero was totally owned by the CEO and the amounts diverted to Zero topped hundreds of thousands of dollars. Egan believed these transfers represented an enormous risk to the financial health of TSI. Rather than running directly to the SEC, however, Egan reported his concerns to the president of TSI, who, in turn, reported the problem to the independent directors of TSI. The independent directors hired a firm named Latham and Watkins, LLP (LW), to examine the activities of the CEO. To accomplish this task, Egan was recruited to cooperate with the investigation. Subsequently, LW issued a report that clearly substantiated Egan's allegations. However, LW made no direct contact with the SEC about its conclusions. Instead, LW reported the results to the independent directors of TSI, who decided to move against the CEO on their own. Unfortunately, by the time the independent members of the board made their move, the CEO was in command of the board. With his newly found power, he blocked the attempt to force his resignation, fired the plaintiff, and cancelled the plaintiff's severance package. The plaintiff then sued the CEO, TSI, TSBS, and Zero under the whistleblower provisions of the Dodd–Frank Wall Street Reform and Consumer Protection Act (DFA). Specifically, he sued under an anti-retaliation section that creates a private cause of action against retaliatory firings. In analyzing the case, the court noted that the DFA will support any anti-retaliation case as long as the plaintiff can show that he was an authentic whistleblower. The DFA defines whistleblower in retaliation cases as one who "provides" or "acting jointly" with others provides "information relating to a violation of the securities law to the Commission." (That "Commission" is, of course, the SEC.) As the judge's opinion unfolds, he analyzes the DFA's language in order to determine whether the plaintiff qualified as a whistleblower. At one point, the judge considers looking at the legislative history behind the act in addition to examining the statutory language, but rejects the idea, because the record includes no relevant discussion of whether whistleblowers must talk directly to the SEC itself. Consequently, the judge, using a textual approach, focuses only on the words in the statute. In effect, the judge acts like a poetic critic, as he analyzes the words themselves to determine their meaning. The question that he is trying to answer is, given the statutory language (and only that language), does the plaintiff qualify as a "whistleblower" in a retaliation case like this one? [See: *Egan v. TradingScreen, Inc*. 10 Civ. 8202 (LBS), United States District Court for the Southern District of New York (2011).]

Opening Case Questions

1. What is the objective of the Dodd–Frank Act? Explain.

2. What is a whistleblower under terms of the Dodd–Frank Act? Explain.

3. What are textualism, purposivism, and pragmatism? Define each term.

4. In this case, did the judge use textualism, purposivism, or pragmatism? Explain.

5. Now, speculate on the judge's response. What do you think he will decide? Explain.

LO Learning Objectives

1. Describe the birth of the strong central government that evolved in American politics.
2. Describe the source of state power to regulate business.
3. Explain how the Securities and Exchange Commission prevents unfair practices.
4. Explain *per se* antitrust violations of antitrust law.
5. Explain the rule-of-reason standard in antitrust law.
6. Outline the general provisions of all post-Sherman antitrust laws.
7. Define the various techniques of corporate expansion.
8. Contrast the roles of the Securities and Exchange Commission with that of the Federal Trade Commission in corporate expansion.
9. Identify the two ways that a corporation may undergo dissolution.
10. Explain the circumstances under which a limited liability company may undergo dissolution.

28-1 The Constitution and the Corporate Entity

Federal power to control commerce is found in the commerce clause of the U.S. Constitution. The **commerce clause** is located in Article I, Section 8, Clause 3, of the Constitution. Clause 3 states, "Congress shall have the Power . . . to regulate Commerce with foreign nations, and among the several States." At first glance the clause appears to be an attempt by the Framers to limit the power of the central government and, conversely, to enhance the ability of the states to regulate their own internal economic activity. However, from the very beginning the courts identified the central national government as the favored source of commercial regulatory power in the United States.

The Federal Power to Control Commerce

The federal power to control commerce in the United States appeared so early in our history that it seems to have been woven into the very fabric of the Constitution. In the case of *Gibbons v. Ogden,* 22 U.S. 1 (1824), the first major commerce case to land in the Supreme Court, the Court declared that congressional power to regulate commerce included not only the authority to control navigation, but also the power to regulate activities that occurred within a single state. Nor was the decision a close one. Five of the seven justices joined in the majority opinion. Moreover, of the two remaining justices, one was not involved in the case at any level, and the other, William Johnson, sought to extend, not limit, congressional power over all commerce. Using textual criticism, Johnson states quite clearly that:

> [T]he plain and direct import of the words of the grant is consistent with this general understanding. The words of the Constitution are, "Congress shall have power to regulate commerce with foreign nations, and among the several States, and with the Indian tribes." It is not material, in my view of the subject, to inquire whether the article "a" or the should be prefixed to the word "power." Either or neither will produce the same result: if either, it is clear that the article "the" would be the proper one, since the next preceding grant of power is certainly exclusive, to-wit: "to borrow money on the credit of the United States."

While Johnson forswears the use of textualism, he nevertheless continues his argument by defining the word *power,* concluding that, "[t]he 'power to regulate commerce' here meant to be granted was that power to regulate commerce which previously existed in the States . . . The power of a sovereign state over commerce therefore amounts to nothing more than a power to limit and restrain . . . that . . . power must be exclusive; *it can reside but in one potentate,* and hence the grant of this power carries with it the whole subject, leaving nothing for the State to act upon." (Italics added.)

Over the next century or so, the Court generally avoided such explicit statements of full congressional power over commerce. However, in 1942 in the case of *Wickard v. Filburn,* the Court declared that the private use of wheat on a single family farm could be curtailed by the federal government. Still, the Court did manage to fashion a rationale to support this extension of power. The rationale focused on the real life problems of the American economy in the middle of the 20th century. The consumption of home-grown wheat seems to have been been the target of regulation because such consumption represented the most variable (and, therefore, the most volatile and, fortunately, most controllable) factor in the problem of the disappearing wheat crop in the U.S. at that time. In the majority opinion, the Court declared that the farmer's use of his own wheat on his own land to bake his own bread, nevertheless, affected interstate commerce. Taking all circumstances into account, the Court explained that, whenever any farmer uses his own wheat, he does not buy wheat in interstate commerce, thus weakening the entire interstate market. The justices emphasized that it was the cumulative effect of many such farmers that concerned them rather than the actions of a single farmer.

The Establishment of a Strong Central Government

The intent of the Framers to set up a strong federal government becomes clear when we place it within a proper historical context. We are generally accustomed to the childhood myth that the Framers were dedicated to individual freedom and personal liberty. As we saw in the early chapters of this book, however, the truth is almost entirely opposite to the myth. In Chapter 2, for example, we saw that James Madison, the undisputed father of the Constitution and one of the principal authors of the Bill of Rights, believed that the national government needed a free hand in determining most political questions and, therefore, could not risk contradiction from any factions, but especially factions within the states.

In addition, by 1787 on the eve of the Constitutional Convention, Madison was already campaigning for a strong central government. For example, in April of 1787 Madison wrote a lengthy analysis of the Articles of Confederation in a statement titled, "Vices of the Political System of the United States." In "Vices," Madison outlines 11 such "vices," including the fact that, under the Articles of Confederation, Congress had no power to create uniform laws to regulate commerce on a national basis. Madison continued his campaign by writing private letters to Thomas Jefferson, Edmund Randolph, and George Washington. In these letters, written during March and April of 1787, Madison announced his support for a unified system of federal laws to regulate trade, a federal veto by which Congress could void statutes passed by the state legislatures, and a strong central system under which the national government could force the states to do its bidding. [See: Richard K. Matthews, *If Men Were Angels: James Madison and the Heartless Empire of Reason* (Lawrence: University Press of Kansas, 1995), pp. 177–90.]

Nor was Madison alone in his convictions. Many of the delegates to the Constitutional Convention harbored similar concerns about the old system. For example, in his book, *An Economic Interpretation of the Constitution of the United States,* Charles Beard of Columbia University and Barnard College tells us that, in 1785, two years before the Constitutional Convention, several key entrepreneurs, including Thomas Fitzsimons and George Clymer, both of whom became delegates to the Constitutional Convention in Philadelphia, sent a lengthy statement to the Pennsylvania legislature in which they complained that, under the Articles of Confederation, Congress lacked "full and entire power over the commerce of the United States." In essence, they were supporting federalism, even if they did not yet use the word. Once this support for federalism is recognized as the pervading sentiment of the Framers, many of the puzzles within the Constitution, puzzles like the growth of congressional power in issues of commerce, corporate law, securities regulation, and antitrust law, for example, become quite clear. Separating myth from reality is important in the study of corporate law because, despite lip service to the opposite view, corporate law in this country is dominated (but not completely conquered) by the federal government. The states do retain some power, which is properly referred to as *residual power,* over commerce and corporate law. [See: Charles Beard, *An Economic Interpretation of the Constitution of the United States* (Mineola, NY: Dover Publications, 2004), pp. 40–41.]

Residual State Power over Commerce and Corporate Law

Despite the overwhelming power of the federal government in the regulation of corporate commercial activity, the states still retain some residual power in this arena. The power of the states to regulate commerce comes from a state's police power. **Police power** is the state's authority to restrict private rights to promote and maintain public health, safety, welfare, and morals. A state has police power simply by virtue of its existence as a legitimate governmental authority. The state government and the various subdivisions of the state government, from counties to cities to school boards to zoning districts, all play some role in the regulatory process. For example, the state grants incorporation status to corporate promoters and requires those promoters to appoint agents for the service of process. The state also collects incorporation fees, taxes corporate activities, regulates the assignment of corporate names, polices the actions of corporate managers, oversees corporate dissolutions, and creates new corporate entities, such as limited liability companies, franchises, and joint ventures. The states also police the assignment of permission for foreign and alien corporations to operate within the borders of the home state.

State Legislative Power: The Model Business Corporation Act

The states have the power to regulate business under their inherent police power, a power that, while less extensive than the constitutional power of the federal government does, nevertheless, have its place. As noted in Chapter 26, a corporation is a legal person created under the authority of a state or federal statute that gives certain individuals the capacity to operate an enterprise. Most states have contributed to a multi-state effort at establishing uniformity in corporate law by adopting the Model Business Corporation Act, often referred to as the Model Corporation Act and sometimes simply as the MBCA. The MBCA is a relatively young statute and is, therefore, not quite as settled as older, more traditional statutes, such as the Uniform Commercial Code and the original Uniform Partnership Act. In addition, the model act has been revised since its original inception, making some of its provisions even more recent and therefore less fully developed than similar provisions in other comparable statutes.

Judicial Power: Common Law Cases

Also, the common law tradition permeates the cases of many states in relation to the corporate person. While many of these cases are preempted when a state legislature adopts the MBCA, some state courts are understandably reluctant to surrender long-term common law principles and sometimes have found creative ways to interpret the MBCA within the context of that state's long-standing legal tradition. Therefore, the study of corporate law must always be tempered by a look at the state law of the jurisdiction in which a dispute is located. The process of doing business as a self-governing business association, that is, as a corporate person, is called associative corporativism, or simply corporativism.

Residual State Power

In the 19th century, each corporation was individually created by a unique legislative enactment. Moreover, the incorporation process did not follow the routine steps that are tracked today. On the contrary, each corporate entity had to be approved by the state legislature and that approval was sometimes at risk, as lengthy deliberations were conducted in the legislature to determine whether to accept this or reject that incorporation request. Each corporation had its own charter that outlined the powers and abilities of that corporation. Moreover, the officers and directors who managed the corporation could not step outside the carefully drawn bounds of that power and, if they did, the corporate charter could be revoked. Corporate managers who did exceed their authority were said to be operating *ultra vires*, that is, beyond their legal powers. Moreover, even if the corporation was never targeted for dissolution, the life of the corporation was limited to a set number of years as stated in the charter. [See: "Our Hidden History of Corporations in the United States," *Reclaim Democracy,* http://reclaimdemocracy. org/corporate-accountability-historycorporations-us/; Robert Charles Clark, "The Meaning of Corporate Personality," *Corporate Law* (Boston: Little, Brown, and Company, 1986), pp. 675–76.]

Corporate Law in Delaware

As corporate activity changed, state law changed along with it. However, the most revolutionary changes did not emerge until the waning years of the 19th century, specifically with the advent of Delaware's 1899 state corporate law statute. The Delaware statute was based on a corporate law statute in New Jersey. However, Delaware liberalized its law far beyond that of New Jersey's older law. For example, with the exception of banking, a Delaware corporation was permitted to conduct any legal business activity. Delaware incorporators were given the choice of setting a limited number of years for the existence of their corporation or accepting perpetual existence. A Delaware corporation was permitted to carry out business activities anywhere on the planet; to issue a variety of classes of stocks; to alter its charter; to unite with other corporations; to purchase other stock issued by other corporate entities; and to conduct director and shareholder meetings outside Delaware. In addition, the incorporation fee and corporate taxes were negligible, at least when compared to other states.

As a direct result of this relaxation in corporate law, out-of-state corporate promoters flocked to Delaware to incorporate. Today most states have recognized Delaware's advantage and refashioned their corporate laws to mimic the perks that were granted by Delaware to potential incorporators. Nevertheless, Delaware still holds the advantage. Even today the number of corporations that identify Delaware as their place of incorporation is astronomical. It is for that reason that most corporate case law that exists in the state courts today is found in Delaware. Moreover, more than anything else, Delaware corporate law focuses on the actions of the managers (officers and directors alike), and most of that activity involves the buying and selling of corporations. Also, the key focus of those decisions is on director responsibility and the primary vehicle for maintaining corporate objectivity is protecting the independent director corps. [See: Joel Seligman, "A Brief History of Delaware's General Corporation Law of 1899," *Delaware Journal of Corporate Law* 1, no. 2 (1976); and Steven Davidoff Solomon, "The Long Reach if Delaware's Corporate Influence," *The New York Times,* December 11, 2014, p. F2.]

---

quick quiz 28-1

1.	Federal power to control commerce is found in the commerce clause of the U.S. Constitution.	true | false
2.	In *Gibbons v. Ogden,* the Supreme Court declared that congressional power to regulate commerce included the authority to control navigation and the power to regulate activities that occurred within a single state.	true | false
3.	A state has police power only if that power is expressly granted to the state government in the state constitution.	true | false

28-2 Securities Regulation of the Corporate Person

Two pieces of federal legislation that affect business are the Securities Act of 1933 and the Securities Exchange Act of 1934 (see Table 28-1). The primary purpose of these acts is to protect business investors by making certain that they are informed about the securities they purchase. The independent regulatory agency that carries out this function is the Securities and Exchange Commission (SEC). The SEC regulates the issuance of securities by corporations and partnerships. A **security** has been defined as a monetary investment that expects a return solely because of another person's efforts. As the following example demonstrates, a security is a security even if it is called something else.

EXAMPLE 28-1: A Security by Any Other Name

Osgood Minerals, Inc., had to raise an enormous amount of capital quickly. One of the directors devised a scheme whereby Osgood would sell to investors parcels of land owned by the corporation and used for mining purposes. In return, the investors would be entitled to a return on their investment. The return would be calculated in relation to the amount of land owned by each investor. To avoid having to comply with SEC regulations, Osgood labeled each sale a land contract rather than a security. Because the sales were land contracts, Osgood argued, it did not have to follow SEC regulations. The SEC disagreed and brought suit to stop the sale of unregulated securities. The court held that because each investor's profits would be derived solely from the efforts of others, the investments were securities and therefore subject to SEC regulations.

Securities Act of 1933

The Securities Act of 1933 regulates the issuance of new securities by corporations and partnerships. Offers of securities by mail or through interstate or foreign commerce must be registered with the SEC. A registration statement and a prospectus must be filed with the SEC. A **registration statement** contains detailed information about the corporation, including data about its management, capitalization, and financial condition. A **prospectus** contains much of the same information but in a condensed and simplified form. The registration statement is designed for the experts at the SEC, whereas the prospectus is designed for potential investors.

Securities Exchange Act of 1934

The Securities Exchange Act of 1934, which actually established the SEC, deals with the subsequent trading in securities. It requires periodic reports of financial information

Table 28-1 Securities and Antitrust Regulations

Regulation	Explanation
Securities Regulation:	
Securities Act of 1933	Regulates the issuance of new securities
Securities Exchange Act of 1934	Established the Securities and Exchange Commission; act deals with subsequent trading in securities
Dodd–Frank Act Title VII	Title VII now requires that certain swaps be registered with the SEC and that they comply with certain principles enumerated in the act.
Dodd–Frank Act Title IX	Title IX creates the Office of Investor Advocate and authorizes the office to appoint an ombudsman; improves the regulation of credit rating institutions; alters the use of asset-backed securities; improves shareholder democracy; and enhances whistleblowing opportunities.
Antitrust Regulation:	
Sherman Antitrust Act	Prohibits contracts, combinations in restraint of trade; also prohibits monopolies, attempts to monopolize, and conspiracies to monopolize
Clayton Act	Prohibits specific practices such as tying agreements and interlocking directorates
Robinson–Patman Act	Deals with product pricing, advertising, and promotional allowances
Federal Trade Commission Act	Established the Federal Trade Commission

concerning registered securities, and it prohibits manipulative and deceptive actions in the sale and purchase of securities. The act prohibits insiders, including officers and directors, from realizing profit from any purchase and sale of securities within any period of less than six months. The courts have held that insiders are not permitted to trade on information until that information has been made available to the public.

According to Section 14 (a) of the 1934 act, shareholders, including majority shareholders, who solicit proxies (see Chapter 27) must also follow strict reporting requirements. The SEC requires a written proxy solicitation to include the identity of the individual or individuals seeking the proxy, any potential conflicts of interest, and specific information about any corporate changes to be voted on. When management solicits proxies, the solicitation must also include information about management salaries. The SEC regulations also state quite specifically that all material information must be stated in readable language and be displayed prominently, rather than buried in small type somewhere in the back of the document. The regulations also explicitly forbid false or misleading information.

The Securities and Exchange Commission (SEC) regulates the issuance of securities by corporations and partnerships and assures that the public is protected by enforcing mandatory reporting requirements and other 1933 and 1934 Act mandates.

Dodd–Frank Wall Street Reform and Consumer Protection Act

In Chapter 20 we learned that, in response to the 21st-century financial crisis, Congress passed several pieces of legislation, including the **Dodd–Frank Act**, aimed at fixing current economic problems and preventing such events from happening again in the future. The problems that we discussed in Chapter 20 were related to mortgages. The mortgage industry, however, was only part of the problem. Another industry involved in the crisis was the securities industry. For that reason, Congress also included provisions in the Dodd–Frank Act to deal with the shortcomings and the errors of the securities industry. As might be expected, the Dodd–Frank Act is long, involved, and complicated. It is divided into 16 different titles, many of which are named as individual acts. Two titles that affect the Securities Exchange Commission are Title VII, the Wall Street Transparency and Accountability Act, and Title IX, the Investor Protection and Securities Reform Act of 2010.

The Wall Street Transparency and Accountability Act The 21st-century financial crisis was caused in part by the reckless use of a financial instrument known as the derivative. A **derivative** (sometimes called a derivative contract and sometimes a derivative instrument) is a financial tool whose value emerges from a variable item, such as an interest rate, a stock index, or a commodity like fuel or crops. Derivatives can be used to manage risk as long as they are handled properly. In contrast, the misuse of derivatives can be disastrous, as was demonstrated during the 21st-century financial crisis. A **swap transaction** (or simply, a **swap**) is a derivative that is made in an over-the-counter market. The SEC has the power to regulate security-based swaps that are traded on the exchanges. According to the SEC, **security-based swaps** are "swaps based on (1) a single security, (2) a loan, (3) a narrow-based group or index of securities, or (4) events relating to a single issuer or issuers of securities in a narrow-based security index." The problem has been that, before Title VII of Dodd–Frank, the swap process was not well regulated. There was little or no transparency before, during, or after such transactions. Originally Dodd–Frank required that certain swap transactions comply with principles enumerated in the act. For example, the law required that banks place certain swaps into divisions that are not covered by federal

Financial institutions on Wall Street have come under increased regulation and scrutiny due to their reckless practices.

insurance programs and that are prevented from applying to the Federal Reserve Bank for loans in a crisis. The goal of these limitations was to insulate the taxpayers from being victimized by the type of governmental bailouts that occurred in 2008. The SEC and its sister regulating body, the Commodity Futures Trading Commission, have the power to make rules in consultation with one another on the swaps over which each agency has jurisdiction. [See: "SEC Proposes Rules for Securities-Based Swap Execution Facilities," *U.S. Securities and Exchange Commission* (February 2, 2011), http://www.sec.gov/news/press/2011/2011-35/htm; and Marl Jickling and Kathleen Ann Ruane, "The Dodd–Frank Wall Street Reform and Consumer Protection Act: Title VII Derivatives," *Congressional Research Service,* August 30, 2010, pp. i, 1–2; see also: Victoria McGrane, "A Primer on Derivatives Provision Banks Seek," *The Wall Street Journal,* December 11, 2014, p. A4.]

Changes in the Dodd–Frank Act

Some critics of the Dodd–Frank Act have long maintained that the swap limitation provisions discussed above actually threaten to cause more harm than good. These limitations, they argue, do not actually stop the swap process as intended. Instead, the provisions force those who configure swaps to utilize entities that are almost untouched by federal oversight provisions and, as a result, are not as well understood even by those who actually regulate them. Consequently, the provisions have merely shifted the risks to those investors who are involved in the swaps, rather than eliminating them. These same opponents also point to an increase in the cost of doing business that has resulted from implementing these provisions. Some experts also insist that these restrictions make it more difficult for American banks to compete with foreign banks that face no such limits. Those in favor of maintaining the swap limitation provisions argue that the goal is to prevent a repeat of the disastrous investments that led to the 2008 crisis and placed an undue burden on ordinary taxpayers, who bore the weight of the bailout provisions. Whatever the case, these changes were implemented as a rider to the 2015 spending bill passed by Congress in 2014. In effect, the rider to the spending bill repealed the Dodd–Frank provision requiring banks to place certain swaps in divisions that are not covered by federal insurance programs. [See: Victoria McGrane, "A Primer on Derivatives Provision Banks Seek," *The Wall Street Journal,* December 11, 2014, p. A4; and Victoria McGrane, "Swap Talk: Why Are People Fighting Over Dodd–Frank and Derivatives?" *The Wall Street Journal: Washington Wire,* December 10, 2014, http://blogs.wsj.com/washwire/2014/12/10/swap-talk-why-are-people-fighting-over-dodd-frank-and-derivatives/; see also "Dodd–Frank's 'Swaps Push-out Provision' Repealed in Omnibus Bill," *biz570.com: Northeast Pennsylvania Business Journal,* January 7, 2015, http://biz570.com/economy/dodd-frank-s-swaps-push-out-provision-repealed-in-omnibus-bill-1.1810394.]

Title IX Investor Protection and Securities Reform Act

The second area that Dodd–Frank now regulates more directly involves the day-to-day activities of corporations. Under Title IX, which is also known as the Investor Protection and Securities Reform Act, the rules governing the SEC have been revised so that the agency can better monitor the areas under its jurisdiction and provide more effective protection for investors. The act does several things: creates the Office of Investor Advocate and authorizes the office to appoint an ombudsman; improves the regulation of credit rating institutions; alters the use of asset-backed securities; improves shareholder democracy; and enhances whistleblowing opportunities.

The Office of Investor Advocate Subtitle A of Title IX of the Dodd–Frank Act creates a new agency, referred to as the **Office of Investor Advocate (OIA)**, the purpose of which is to help make the work of broker–dealers and investment advisors (IAs) more transparent.

The law also gives the SEC the power to make new regulations that will define the fiduciary relationship between IAs and broker–dealers, on the one hand, and their clients, on the other. Section A also empowers the OIA to appoint an ombudsman and reactivates the Investor Advisory Committee, which was originally authorized in 2009.

Regulation of Credit Rating Institutions   Subtitle C of Title IX authorizes the SEC to develop a new agency known as the **Office of Credit Ratings**, the purpose of which is to watch those organizations that issue credit ratings. These organizations, known in the industry as nationally recognized statistical rating organizations or NRSROs, are key elements in the financial structure of the U.S. economy because they open or close the door on the ability of investors and borrowers to enter the marketplace. Section C provides for better internal controls that will eliminate conflicts of interest and promote the reporting of irregularities, among other things.

Asset-Backed Securities   Subtitle D of Title IX of Dodd–Frank mandates more effective control over the issuance of asset-backed securities. Securitization became an issue during the 21st-century financial crisis because many institutions that issued asset-backed securities sold them almost immediately. This meant that they were unconcerned about the borrower's ability to pay back the loan. To minimize the risks associated with this practice, the new law requires institutions that engage in securitization to maintain an economic stake in the assets that they securitize. More specifically, the rules now state that institutions issuing asset-backed securities must keep a minimum of 5 percent of the credit risk, although there are exceptions to this rule built into the law.

Shareholder Democracy   One of the primary goals of Title IX of the Dodd–Frank Act is to enhance shareholder democracy. Recall that shareholder democracy demands that the shareholders of a corporation have more input into the decision-making process of the corporation, specifically as those decisions relate to the board of directors. To improve shareholder democracy, the following changes have been mandated by the act. The SEC is now required to make rules to ensure that shareholders have a continuing opportunity to review executive compensation. Moreover, the act specifically permits the shareholders to review and reject golden parachute contracts with executives. A **golden parachute** is a compensation package that protects executives who might lose their positions following a merger or consolidation, and so on. The SEC is also authorized to make new regulations that will empower shareholders to use management proxies to nominate board members in election contest. [See: David S. Huntington, "Summary of Dodd–Frank Financial Regulation Legislation," *The Harvard Law Forum on Corporate Governance and Financial Regulation* (July 7, 2010); and "Brief Summary of the Dodd–Frank Wall Street Reform and Consumer Protection Act," *U.S. Senate Committee on Banking, Housing, and Urban Affairs,* http://banking.senate.gov/public.]

Whistleblowing Enhancement   Perhaps the most controversial provision included in the new act is Subtitle B of Title IX, which permits the SEC to make regulations that will improve its enforcement powers by establishing rules to implement a "whistleblowing bounty" program analogous to the one that the IRS implemented in 2006. Whistleblowers, or SEC "bounty hunters," as they are sometimes called, must meet certain minimum requirements to qualify for their "bounty." For instance, it is necessary that the evidence provided by a bounty hunter concern a security law violation and include original information. (Apparently, *original* in this situation means that the SEC did not have the new evidence until the friendly neighborhood bounty hunter showed up.) Bounty hunting can be a very lucrative enterprise. Successful hunters can pull in somewhere between 10 and 30 percent of a sanction that is over $1 million. Because such well-paid rewards can be an irresistible temptation to some, cautionary steps must be taken to prevent would-be bounty hunters from reporting unsubstantiated accusations and then racing to the SEC for their "bounty" payments. Naturally, there is some disagreement about the best way to police the whistleblowing process. Some experts argue that whistleblowing bounty hunters should be required to exhaust internal remedies before going to the SEC. These experts contend that, since such reporting mechanisms are required, it makes sense to compel whistleblowers to go through those reporting systems first. On the other hand, those attorneys who have whistleblowing clients argue that such internal remedies are rarely, if ever, effective since the people who receive the complaints work for and report to the people accused in the complaint. This would be a little like requiring mugging victims to talk to a mugger's accomplice before going to the police, or so the argument goes. [See: David Ingram, "SEC Weighing How to Award Tipsters," *The National Law Journal,* May 16, 2011, pp. 1 and 4; *Egan v. TradingScreen, Inc.* 10 Civ. 8202 (LBS), United States District Court for the Southern District of New York (2011).]

THE OPENING CASE *Round 2*
The Dodd–Frank Act (DFA) and Whistleblowers

The opening case began when Patrick Egan (the plaintiff) discovered that the CEO of TSI and TSBS was sending assets that belonged to TSI to a corporation named SpreadZero (Zero), which was totally owned by that same CEO. Nor was this a minor transgression. The amounts diverted to Zero topped hundreds of thousands of dollars. Rather than reporting his suspicions to the SEC, Egan communicated his concerns to the president of TSI, who then informed the independent directors of TSI. The independent directors (IDs) then hired a firm named Latham and Watkins, LLP (LW), to examine the actions of the CEO. The facts indicate that Egan was involved in this investigative process. Shortly thereafter, LW issued a report that clearly substantiated Egan's allegations. Nonetheless, LW did not directly contact the SEC about its findings. Rather, LW reported the results to the IDs, who decided to take action against the CEO. Regrettably, by the time the IDs made their move, the CEO managed to block their attempt to force his resignation. He then fired the plaintiff and nullified his severance package. The plaintiff sued the CEO, TSI, TSBS, and Zero under the whistleblower provisions of the Dodd–Frank Wall Street Reform and Consumer Protection Act (DFA). More explicitly, he sued under an anti-retaliation section that creates a private cause of action against retaliatory firings. This would appear to be an open-

and-shut case. Egan blew the whistle on the CEO's antics; the CEO retaliated by firing him because of that report and then retaliated a second time by cancelling Egan's lucrative severance contract. Yet, the defendants still claimed that Egan was not a whistleblower. How could they make this argument? The answer lies in the statutory definition of *whistleblower.* Currently, the DFA defines a whistleblower as one who "provides" or "acting jointly" with others provides "information relating to a violation of the securities law to the Commission" (15 U.S. Code § 78u–6—Securities whistleblower incentives and protection). Egan, they argue, does not qualify as an official "whistleblower" under the act. It is true that Egan provided information to the investigative team. However, Egan did not hire the investigators or lead the investigation. Therefore, the defendants conclude that Egan did not act jointly with others in the investigation, and is, as a result, not a whistleblower. The court using a textual approach has no patience with this argument, concluding that such an interpretation would, "effectively rewrite the phrase 'acting jointly.'" Egan, the court concludes, is a whistleblower under that part of the law that "retaliates" against retaliation. [See: *Egan v. TradingScreen, Inc.* 10 Civ. 8202 (LBS), United States District Court for the Southern District of New York (2011).]

A QUESTION OF ETHICS

Whistleblowing from Another Angle

Despite (or perhaps because of) the defendants' unsuccessful attack against the plaintiff in The Opening Case at the beginning of this chapter, whistleblower vindication is still very much a part of the American legal system. A case in point is the multimillion-dollar whistleblower settlement in the lawsuits filed against the Bank of America, which ended up paying a $170 million penalty to four whistleblowers who filed suits against the bank for selling defective mortgage loans and for overvaluing mortgage properties, all of which contributed to the birth of the 21st-century financial crisis. The four record-breaking whistleblower rewards were part of a larger settlement package that was included within a variety of individual cases filed against Bank of America for financial wrongdoing. One of the lawsuits was filed by an ex-employee of a Bank of America affiliate, Land-Safe Appraisal Services, after his work time was reduced in reaction to his reservations about the possibility that borrowers and investors would be invited to purchase inflated properties. Another complaint was issued by an employee of Countrywide Financial Corp. (another company owned by the Bank of America) who reported that Fannie Mae and Freddie Mac were actually sold defective mortgages by the bank. A third allegation from another Countrywide Financial employee indicated that the Bank of America affiliate had routinely produced mortgage loans that were hugely under-valued. The program uncovered and reported by this third employee was nicknamed the Hustle because it systematically eliminated checkpoints and evaluation processes that slowed loan approv-als and rewarded brokers based on the number, rather than the quality, of the loans that they pushed through the system. The goal of the program, which was also christened the High Speed Swim Lane (HSSL) was not to produce solid mortgage loans but to increase Countrywide's bottom line. Fannie Mae and Freddie Mac then purchased the bad loans, which collapsed because the mortgagees de-faulted on their payments. Reports indicate that 57 percent of the Countrywide HSSL loans ended badly. Bank of America got into the act when it purchased a company it thought had the Midas touch, only to discover that Countrywide's success rate was a sham from day one. A fourth whistle-blower case features a New Jersey mortgage company named Mortgage Now, which complained that the Federal Housing Authority had received loans from Bank of America for which the values were badly distorted. All told, at the end of the day, Bank of America paid a $16.65 billion penalty, which included the whistleblower settlement of $1 billion, $170 million of which was parceled out to the whistleblowers themselves. [See: Christina Rexrode and Timothy Martin, "Whistleblowers Score Big," *The Wall Street Journal,* December 20-21, 2014, pp. B1–B2; and Kevin McCoy and Julie Schmit, "Jury: BofA Liable for Countrywide Mortgage Fraud," *USA Today*, October 23, 2013, http://www.usatoday.com/story/money/business/2013/10/23/bank-of-america-countrywide-mortgage-fraud/3172797/.]

QUESTIONS YET UNANSWERED

The following questions have not yet been answered. Before you consider each question, turn to Chapter 1 to review the various ethical theories noted there (market value ethics, social contract theory, utili-tarianism, and rational ethics). Then, using one of those theories in a consistent way, answer the following questions.

1. Is it ethical for the courts to award such enormous amounts of money in whistleblowing cases?
2. Do you believe that justice was done in the Bank of America case? Explain.
3. Would you change the decision in this case? Explain.
4. Is whistleblowing in general an ethical practice or does it encourage betrayal and entrapment? Explain.

28-3 Antitrust Regulation of the Corporate Person

Both the federal government and the states have antitrust laws to preserve the values of competition and to discourage monopolies. A **monopoly** is the exclusive control of a market by a business enterprise. At the federal level, the four principal antitrust statutes are the Sherman Antitrust Act, the Clayton Act, the Robinson–Patman Act, and the Federal Trade Commission Act.

Sherman Antitrust Act

The Sherman Antitrust Act (1890) prohibits contracts, combinations, and conspiracies in restraint of trade. It also prohibits monopolization, attempts to monopolize, and combinations or conspiracies to monopolize any part of interstate or foreign commerce. Violations of the Sherman Antitrust Act must involve at least two parties acting together. The courts use three standards to judge antitrust offenses: the *per se* violation standard, the rule-of-reason standard, and the quick-look standard. The three tests, however, sometimes represent moving targets that are easy to articulate but difficult to implement in a consistent and fair fashion.

The *Per Se* Standard Some restraint-of-trade practices are so serious that they are prohibited, whether or not they harm anyone. These practices are labeled *per se* **violations**, which means that the practice is so contrary to antitrust policy that harm is presumed and the practice is prohibited. For example, price fixing is inherently unreasonable and therefore considered a *per se* violation. An agreement between competitors to divide territories among themselves to minimize competition would also be unlawful, even if the agreement helps the parties compete against other parties outside the agreement. Similar unlawful activities include agreements among competitors to stop competing with one another in prices, customers, or products.

The Rule-of-Reason Standard If an alleged antitrust practice is not considered a *per se* violation, then the courts will judge the legality of that practice with the rule-of-reason approach. The **rule-of-reason standard** will stop certain practices only if they are an unreasonable restriction of competition. As a result, some practices that in fact limit competition may be legal. To determine if an anticompetitive practice is legal, the court considers such facts as the history of the restraint, the harm that results, the reason for the practice, and the purpose to be attained.

The Quick-Look Standard A third standard, the quick-look standard, has become a customary way for resolving those cases that fall into the slightly gray area

CLASSIC CASE Single Entity or Collection Point—
American Needle, Inc. v. The NFL

One of the primary money-making operations that the National Football League (NFL) has engaged in over the years has been the merchandising of goods, such as ball caps, jerseys, T-shirts, and so on, all of which bear the logo and/or colors of an NFL team. Throughout the 20th century, the NFL was satisfied to deal with a variety of vendors through a legal entity that it created known as National Football League Properties (NFLP). Then, in 2000, NFLP decided to award an exclusive contract to Reebok. One former NFL merchandiser, American Needle, was unhappy with the new arrangement. Consequently, American Needle brought a lawsuit against the NFL, arguing that the Reebok contract established a monopoly that was in violation of Section 1 of the Sherman Antitrust Law. Section 1 makes it illegal to enter a contract, combination, or conspiracy in order to restrain trade. Ordinarily under Section 1 the court would apply what is known as the rule-of-reason standard, which asks judges to balance the *pro*-competitive results of a challenged arrangement with the *anti*-competitive results. In this case, however, a different tactic was used. The Seventh Circuit Court of Appeals took a more fundamental approach and targeted the very ability of the NFL to enter a contract of any sort. The court ruled that the NFL was not a collection point around which a group of 32 teams joined forces but was, instead, a single entity. As a single entity, the NFL could not make any type of contract with itself, let alone a contract to restrain trade. This ruling means that Section 1 did not apply to the case and, as a result, the case was dismissed. The U.S. Supreme Court disagreed with the appellate court, however, and ruled that the NFL is not a single corporate person. The Court said that, although under corporate law, the NFL might be a single corporate person, under antitrust law, it is not. The NFL turns out to be, at least for purposes of antitrust law, a collection of 32 distinct constituent parts, referred to as teams and headquartered in different cities that make financial decisions on their own for their own purposes and benefit.

The case did not end here. Instead, it next went to the trial court where both sides filed motions for summary judgment. The plaintiff asked for summary judgment based on the idea that the case could be submitted to the court for a "quick look." Not to be outdone, the defendant also filed a summary judgment

motion arguing that American Needle had not built a sufficient case to demonstrate that the exclusive agreement with Reebok hurt competition. To bolster its claim, the NFL presented several pieces of evidence, including a claim that NFL apparel competes with apparel from other sports and from other activities outside of sports. America Needle presented counterevidence that indicated that the sale of NFL material tends to peak during the NFL season, indicating that the market for NFL products is a common market and, therefore, is a fitting object for the antitrust complaint. The court saw this as a reasonable argument and dismissed the defendant's summary judgment motion. However, the court also dismissed the plaintiff's summary judgment motion, noting the plaintiff's evidence was insufficient to allow a quick-look solution to decide that case. Moreover, the court dismissed all the defendant's other summary judgment motions as well, thus paving the way for a trial (or a settlement). Now, since the contract under consideration here does not appear to be a *per se* violation of the law, and since the quick-look standard cannot be applied, if the case reaches trial, the court will apply the rule-of-reason standard, which asks judges to balance the pro-competitive results of a challenged arrangement with the anti-competitive results. Take a moment to speculate on this. What might the pro-competitive results be from the single contract with Reebok? What might the anti-competitive results be? Now balance the two and predict how the court will rule. (Note: Of course, if you can find no appropriate balance here, you might just want to settle the case before going any further. After all, despite Jack McCoy's winning record on countless *Law and Order* reruns, sometimes surrendering is an option.) [See: *American Needle, Inc. v. New Orleans Saints, et al.,* No. 04-cv-7806, 2014 U.S. Dist. LEIXS 47527 (N.D. Ill. Apr. 4, 2014; *American Needle, Inc. v. National Football League,* 130 S.Ct. 2201 (2010). See also Gabriel Feldman, "The NFL Is Not a Single Entity," *The National Law Journal,* February 1, 2010, p. 35; and Michael P. Waxman, "*American Needle Inc. v. National Football League:* Surprise! The Supreme Court Upholds an Existing Antitrust Doctrine," *Marquette University Law School Faculty Blog,* October 29, 2010, http://law. marquette.edu.]

between *per se* violations and the rule-of-reason standard. Under the **quick-look standard**, a court will look at the evidence in an antitrust case and determine whether an objective observer with an elementary knowledge of the financial world would see that the arrangement under scrutiny could damage competition by hurting the consumer and impairing the marketplace itself. If the court decides that this is the case, then the defendant assumes the burden of demonstrating to the court or the jury that the harm is negligible, nonexistent, or permissible.

The Evolving Nature of the Triple Threat   The original *per se* and rule-of-reason standards have been part of antitrust law for decades, so the line of distinction between the two is usually very clear. However, sometimes, as the law evolves, that line of distinction becomes less and less distinct. A case in point involves the court's distinction between resale price maintenance (RPM) agreements and quasi-RPM arrangements. An **RPM agreement** occurs when a retailer and a manufacturer decide that the retailer will sell certain products at a price set by the manufacturer. These RPMs have been outlawed by the court as a *per se* violation of antitrust law. In contrast, a **quasi-RPM arrangement** occurs when a manufacturer lets retailers know the price that it expects to see on an item and then declines to sell that item to any retailer that does not list the item at that price. Such arrangements are legally permissible under antitrust law because the law cannot take away the rights of manufacturers to pick those sellers with which they want to deal. While the distinction between the two seems, at best, artificial and, at worst, nonexistent, it is the law. The differences have become somewhat clearer, however, with the advent of the "quick-look" standard, the third and the newest weapon in this triple-threat arsenal of antitrust law.

Post-Sherman Antitrust Legislation

Three principal antitrust statues made the Sherman Act more specific and, as a result, more effective. The Clayton Act of 1914, the Robinson–Patman Act of 1936, the Foreign Trade Antitrust Improvements Act, and the Federal Trade Commission Act of 1914 sought to prevent practices that reduced competition or favored the creation of monopolies.

Clayton Act   Congress passed the Clayton Act to police specific business practices that could be used to create a monopoly. One practice outlawed by the act is tying agreements. A **tying agreement** occurs when one party refuses to sell a product unless the buyer also purchases another product tied to the first product. The issue is the effect of the tie-in on the seller's competitors. Interlocking directorates are also outlawed by the Clayton Act. **Interlocking directorates** occur when individuals serve as directors of two corporations that are competitors. This provision is not entirely foolproof, however, because banks and common carriers are exempt. To fall under this part of the Clayton Act, at least one of the corporations must have an aggregate worth (capital, surplus, and individual profits) of more than $1 million.

Robinson–Patman Act   The Robinson–Patman Act deals with product pricing, advertising, and promotional allowances. It specifically prohibits a seller from charging different prices to different customers for the same product when such differences might injure competition. However, nothing in the law is intended to prevent price differences due to cost of manufacture, sale, delivery, or bulk purchases.

Federal Trade Commission Act   In addition to establishing the Federal Trade Commission (FTC), the Federal Trade Commission Act, as amended, declares that "unfair methods of competition, and unfair or deceptive practices in or affecting commerce are hereby declared unlawful." The act did not name specific unfair methods of competition.

Instead, it has allowed the courts and the FTC to determine those unfair practices. The Federal Trade Commission Act was amended by the Wheeler–Lea Act and amendments in 1938 and 1975. This legislation authorized the FTC to act against unfair or deceptive acts without first proving the existence of anticompetitive behavior. The FTC was also granted

A QUESTION OF ETHICS

Textualism and Pragmatism Revisited

As we've seen in this chapter and earlier in the text, three popular but conflicting theories of legal interpretation are textualism, purposivism, and pragmatism. Textualism requires judges to analyze legal documents as literary works, by focusing exclusively on each document's language. In contrast, purposivism insists that judges consider the legislative goals of a statute, while pragmatism expects judges to focus on the consequences of a decision. Both pragmatism and purposivism seem to demand that judges investigate the circumstances behind the writing of the text. One of the most baffling aspects of the ongoing debate involving these three techniques is that often, even when a judge would rather not identify his or her analytical technique as textualism, it is textualism toward which the judge inevitably gravitates. The explanation for this paradox probably may rest within the incontrovertible fact that legal analysis always involves a study of language. In simple, if somewhat facetious terms, until we all engage in non-local, quantum interconnected thought transfer at the subatomic level, we will have to work our way to an understanding of any written text through the use of language. For example, in his concurring opinion in *Gibbons v. Ogden,* William Johnson determined the extent of congressional power in business by dissecting the language of the commerce clause. By doing so he came unapologetically to the conclusion that congressional commercial power would always trump state power. What is most revealing about this analysis is that Williams specifically disavows the textual approach while at the same time using it quite thoroughly. Moreover, he does so because he is forced to admit that there are no outside sources that he can use beyond that actual words of the clause. Similarly, in *Egan v. TradingScreen, Inc.,* the judge uses a carefully orchestrated textual approach because there are no committee notes and no entries in the *Congressional Record* that will allow him to do otherwise.

QUESTIONS YET UNANSWERED

The following questions have not yet been answered. Before you consider each question, turn to Chapter 1 to review the various ethical theories noted there (market value ethics, social contract theory, utilitarianism, and rational ethics). Using one of those theories in a consistent way, answer the following questions.

1. Is it ethical for a pragmatic judge to abandon pragmatism and use instead a textual approach? Explain.

2. Answer the preceding question for purposivism.

3. One of the defenses given in support of textualism says that the consistent use of the textual approach by the courts will encourage legislators to write clear and unambiguous laws. Is this an ethical rationale in support of textualism? Explain.

4. Some people attack textualism because it narrows the interpretation strategies available to judges. Is this an ethical rationale in support of pragmatism? Explain.

5. Do you believe that Johnson has interpreted the language of the commerce clause correctly? Why or why not?

6. Do you believe that the *Egan* court interpreted the language of the whistleblower definition correctly? Why or why not?

the power to challenge false advertising of food, drugs, and cosmetics, regardless of the advertiser's knowledge of the advertisement's truth or falsity.

The Foreign Trade Antitrust Improvements Act (FTAIA)

Another antitrust measure passed by Congress is the Foreign Trade Antitrust Improvements Act (FTAIA). Unlike the other antitrust provisions supported by Congress, the FTAIA is designed to circumvent some of the restrictions placed on American companies by the Sherman Antitrust Act. The objective of the FTAIA is to permit American companies operating in foreign markets to have a fighting chance against foreign competitors that are not subject to the strict antimonopoly provisions of the act. Under terms of the bill, if an American company is operating totally in a foreign market, that company is not subject to American antitrust law.

In contrast, consumer advocates want to make it easier for plaintiffs to bring antitrust lawsuits against certain types of defendants, but especially against manufacturers. Plaintiffs frequently complain that retailers rarely bring antitrust claims against manufacturers, because retailers can avoid the effects of any antitrust scheme, such as a price-fixing conspiracy, by passing the increased cost of doing business on to the consumers. The consumers, who under current rules are frequently barred from bringing lawsuits against manufacturers, have no recourse other than to pay the higher prices. For this reason, consumer advocacy groups favor making it easier for plaintiffs to file class-action lawsuits against all manufacturing firms that violate antitrust law but especially against those large cartels that are the worst offenders. Finally, state and local regulators would also like to see changes in the law. These regulators favor changes that would transfer more antitrust enforcement authority from the federal government to the states.

---

quick quiz 28-3

1. Price fixing is an example of a rule-of-reason practice under the Sherman Antitrust Act.   true | false

2. *Per se* violations must involve actual harm to be actionable under the Sherman Antitrust Act.   true | false

3. The Robinson–Patman Act has been repealed by the United States Antitrust Modernization Committee.   true | false

---

28-4 Expanding the Corporate Person

No other area of corporate activity has been scrutinized by the government more closely in recent years than the area of corporate expansion (see Table 28-2). As noted previously, several governmental agencies may be involved in any given corporate expansion venture, including the Department of Justice and the Federal Communications Commission. However, the two agencies that have the primary responsibility for regulating this activity are the SEC and the FTC. The two commissions have different interests in the expansion process. The SEC is concerned with regulating the expansion tactics themselves, whereas the FTC is more concerned with the competitive effects of those expansion tactics.

Expansion Tactics and Securities Law

All corporations change in size. Some grow and expand, while others shrink until they dissolve or are absorbed by a larger, more successful enterprise. Like all other corporate activities, corporate expansions are looked at very closely by government. The primary

Table 28-2 Types of Corporate Expansion

Technique	Explanation	Regulation
Merger and Consolidation	In a merger, one company is absorbed by another; in a consolidation two companies join and a new company results	Most antifraud provisions of the SEC apply here
Asset acquisition	One corporation buys the property of another	SEC antifraud provisions apply if proxy solicitation or insider trading is involved
Stock acquisition	One corporation buys a majority of a target corporation's stock	Whenever a suitor makes an offer to acquire more than 5% of the target, the suitor must file with the SEC
Inversion	A U.S. corporation buys an alien corporation and then reincorporates in a foreign nation	New federal oversight rule in place

expansion techniques include mergers, consolidations, asset acquisitions, stock acquisitions, and inversions.

Merger and Consolidation

Traditionally, a **merger** involves two corporations, one of which is absorbed by the other. One of the two corporations continues to carry on business under its original name, and the other simply disappears into the first. In contrast, in a **consolidation**, both companies disappear, and a new company carries on the business under a new name. Today, most legal scholars do not make any distinction between merger and consolidation. In fact, many state incorporation statutes make no reference to consolidation, preferring the term *merger* instead. A merger requires advance approval from the boards and shareholders of both corporations. In general, a two-thirds majority vote of the shareholders will be required before a merger can be approved, though some states require a supermajority of four-fifths. Shareholders who dissent are entitled to be paid for their stock if they do not wish to be a part of the merger. Written notice of a dissent is required so that the cost of purchasing the dissenter's stock can be figured as a part of the expense involved in the merger.

Most antifraud provisions of the SEC apply to the merger process. Often the merger vote will be preceded by a proxy solicitation battle. All material facts about the merger must be included in the proxy solicitation. In addition, the solicitation must not contain any false or misleading information. Similarly, the SEC prohibits insiders who know of merger plans from taking advantage of that knowledge to profit personally before the knowledge is revealed to the public.

Some state statutes apply different rules to mergers that involve a limited liability company (LLC). Under some state statutes, a merger involving an LLC requires the unanimous approval of the members rather than the two-thirds majority required of corporations. However, as is true in other circumstances, the operating agreement of an LLC could cancel this unanimous vote requirement. If the operating agreement specifies that a merger vote may be approved by less than a unanimous vote, many states give those members who are opposed to the merger the right to withdraw from the LLC and receive the cash value of their investment. However, once again, the operating agreement can alter this statutory right.

Asset Acquisition

In an **asset acquisition**, one corporation purchases all the property of a second corporation. However, as in the case of mergers, SEC antifraud regulations can be applied to asset acquisitions if a proxy solicitation process is involved or if insider information is used to profit from the sale. Asset acquisition is easy and efficient, because the only formality required is approval by the directors and shareholders of the corporation that is selling its assets. A second advantage is that the buyer need not purchase all of the assets of the seller. The buyer may choose to purchase some assets while rejecting others.

Another advantage of asset acquisition is that, in general, no debts or other liabilities are transferred from seller to buyer. There are exceptions to this rule, however. In certain situations, the debts of the selling corporation will transfer to the buying corporation. For instance, if the buyer is simply a continuation of the selling corporation, the buyer will not escape the liabilities of the seller. Similarly, if the sale is structured fraudulently to escape the liabilities of the selling corporation, the debts will transfer to the buyer. It is also possible for the buyer to either expressly or implicitly assume the debts and liabilities of the seller. Finally, if, despite its label as an asset acquisition, the sale is actually a merger, the liabilities will transfer to the buyer.

Stock Acquisition

In a **stock acquisition**, the buyer purchases enough stock in a corporation to gain voting control of that corporation. Stock acquisitions come in many shapes and sizes (see Table 28-3). One type of stock acquisition is the **leveraged buyout (LBO)**. In a leveraged buyout, a controlling portion of the stock in a corporation is purchased by a group of shareholders, often several outsiders but sometimes a team of officers and directors of the company. The potential buyers can then collect the money needed to purchase the outstanding shares by enlisting the support of a bank. The bank will lend a good portion of the money to the buyers, taking an enormous payment to support that loan. If the amount produced by the bank proves inadequate, the buyers will seek the assistance of an investment firm. The investment firm produces the remainder of the needed money by issuing **junk bonds**, or bonds that are unstable but offer an elevated level of return to large, powerful investors. Because the stock purchase is made possible by these high-stakes loans, the buyout is referred to as "leveraged." The shareholders are motivated to sell because the buyout team offers them an inflated price for their shares. Sometimes after the buyers have purchased control of the corporation, they ensure their continued control by transforming the company into a private corporation. This action is referred to as "taking the company private."

A second form of stock acquisition is the tender offer. In a **tender offer**, the buyer or suitor, whether it is an individual, a consortium of like-minded individuals, or another corporation, makes a public offer to buy voting stock in a **target corporation**. A successful tender offer occurs once the buyer or buyers have purchased enough of the voting stock to satisfy the original goal, whatever that might have been. One advantage of the stock acquisition process is that it sidesteps the board of directors. The buyer deals directly with the

Table 28-3 Stock Acquisition Techniques

Technique	Explanation
Leveraged buyout	A controlling portion of stock purchased by shareholders; leveraged by loans and junk bonds.
Tender offer	Suitor makes a public offer to buy voting stock in a target corporation.
Takeover bid	Tender offer opposed by the management of the target corporation.
Corporate raid	Takeover bid opposed by management of target because corporate raider intends to dismantle target.

shareholders. Again, the shareholders are motivated to sell because the buyer has made an offer that is above the current market price of the stock.

Sometimes a tender offer is welcomed by the directors and the officers of the target because they see it as a way to strengthen the corporation and enhance their own positions within the company. At other times, however, the tender offer is seen as a corporate takeover bid by an unfriendly buyer. In a takeover bid, the unfriendly buyer, also known as an unfriendly suitor or a hostile bidder, intends to purchase enough stock to control the corporation. Often the goal of the hostile bidder is to change management and shake up the corporation after the takeover. If the suitor intends to dismantle the corporation totally or somehow integrate the target into an existing corporation to such an extent that the target ceases to exist, the suitor is referred to as a corporate raider and the tender offer a corporate raid. In both cases, hostile bidder and corporate raider, the target's management is expected to fight the takeover with every tactic available.

Inversions   An inversion typically occurs when an American corporation buys an alien corporation and then reincorporates in that alien's national base. However, it is also possible, and sometimes easier and less obvious, for an alien corporation to buy an American corporation under a deal that is engineered at the behest of, and largely for the benefit of, the American corporation. It seems not to matter whether the purchase involves an asset acquisition, a stock acquisition, or a combination of both. Whatever the actual process involved in the sale, inversions are generally constructed as a way for the U.S. corporations to sidestep certain tax laws that do not have the same impact on the aliens as they do on America corporations. For example, a newly inverted company (a corporate entity that has gone through the inversion process) may immediately take advantage of the hopscotch loan process, which permits a tax-free loan to flow from an established alien branch into the treasury of the new alien parent. Nothing is inherently illegal about the inversion strategy itself. There is, after all, no reason anyone, even an inverted company, must voluntarily pay a high tax bill if he or she (or it) can figure out a legal way to pay those same taxes at a lower rate.

However, the tactic does bother many critics who see it as an unfair loophole that some advantageously placed corporations can use, while most others cannot. It may be for that reason that the Treasury Department recently targeted inversions with a new set of tax-related rules. The new rules did not outlaw inversions as such, but they did declare that certain practices that roll off a completed inversion will no longer be tolerated. One targeted practice is the hopscotch rule noted earlier. These new rules may discourage future inversion schemes. On the other hand, the hopscotch loan is just one way for inverted companies to escape high tax rates. Thus, while future inversions may be curtailed, existing inverted companies are free to explore other loopholes in the tax laws. Moreover, since the new rules may discourage other corporate persons from using the inversion process, existing inverted companies may now have an unfair advantage over their competitors who have been discouraged from taking a similar path. [See: David Gelles, "A Brake on Reincorporating Abroad via Mergers," *The New York Times,* December 11, 2014, p. F14; and John S. Barry, "Corporate Inversions: An Introduction to the Issue and FAQ," *The Tax Foundation,* May 30, 2002, http://taxfoundation.org/article/corporate-inversions-introduction-issue-and-faq.]

Post-Offer Techniques   To avoid being taken over by a hostile bidder, the management of a corporation can institute both post-offer (see Table 28-4) and pre-offer tactics (see Table 28-5). Probably the least problematic post-offer technique is the public relations initiative. Such an initiative is aimed at convincing shareholders that it is in their best interests not to sell their shares to the hostile bidder. News releases, advertisements, press conferences, and even personal letters and e-mails would attempt to convince shareholders that present management should be retained. The difficulty with this approach is that many arguments pale to insignificance when placed alongside a bid that is above the current market price of the stock.

Sometimes the most effective way for a target to shake off a bidder's hostile suit is to offer the bidder greenmail. A corporation that activates the greenmail defense has offered to

Table 28-4 Post-Offer Antitakeover Tactics

Post-Offer Tactics	Explanations
Public relations campaign	Target corporation uses news releases, advertisements, and press conferences to convince shareholders to retain present management.
Greenmail	Target corporation offers to buy target's stock already owned by suitor.
White knight	Target corporation invites friendly suitor to outbid a hostile bidder.
Lockup agreement	Target corporation tags irreplaceable property for sale when hostile bidder succeeds in takeover.
Targeted shareholder agreement	Target corporation makes deal with suitor to protect management of target.

buy the portion of the target's stock that the bidder already owns. Naturally, such an approach will work only if the target's offer is significantly higher than the amount that the bidder paid for the stock in the first place. Such an approach is disfavored because it robs the shareholders of the opportunity to make a profit by selling their shares and may seriously devalue the target's remaining stock, thereby victimizing the shareholders a second time.

Another post-offer technique that can be used by the target company is the white knight gambit. To implement this tactic, the target invites another suitor to outbid the hostile bidder. The second suitor is known as a **friendly suitor** or a **white knight** because the invited suitor agrees that it will retain existing management. The white knight also frequently agrees not to disrupt the smooth running of the target by selling key assets, closing plants, or laying off employees. A takeover battle usually follows. The winner is generally the suitor that can offer the highest price for the target's outstanding stock.

A fourth post-offer technique is the **lockup agreement**. A lockup agreement might be used by target management if the target owns an irreplaceable piece of property, the sale of which would seriously devalue the overall worth of the target. Such property might include rich timberland or an extremely productive coal mine. Provided that the sale of that property does not deplete virtually all the assets of the target, management could enter a contract with a white knight, giving the knight an option to buy that valuable piece of property should the hostile bidder gain control of the target corporation. The idea is to discourage the hostile bidder from buying the now-devalued target.

A fifth post-offer technique is the **targeted shareholder agreement**. Strictly speaking, a targeted shareholder agreement is not an anti-acquisition tactic as much as it is an executive protection strategy. Under the provisions of a targeted shareholder agreement, the suitor negotiates a deal with certain targeted shareholders, generally the CEO, the CFO, the CTO, and other high-ranking officers. These agreements will provide the officers/shareholders with handsome employment-related deals that supplement the price that they will receive for the sale of their stock. Such deals might include a salary increase, a severance package, a non-compete agreement, and so on. The strategy behind negotiating a targeted shareholder agreement is not to stop the acquisition but to protect key employees who might be financially damaged or even discharged in the post-acquisition culture.

Targeted shareholder agreements were hampered in the late 1990s and early in the 21st century by two rules instituted by the SEC. These rules, known collectively as the **best-price rule**, prohibited suitors from offering different prices to different shareholders during a tender offer process. Unfortunately, the best-price rule was interpreted differently by different federal courts. Some courts, using what was called the **integral-part test**, decided that any type of price enhancement, including employment-related packages, would violate the best-price rule—period. The other rule, known as the **bright-line test**, was used by those courts that saw a violation of the best-price rule only during the actual tender offer. Thus, if an employment agreement was negotiated with a targeted shareholder before or after the actual tender offer, and the actual price that the suitor paid for the stock remained unaffected, then there was no violation of the best-price rule. The SEC eventually amended the rule to make it clear that targeted shareholder agreements that involved *only* employment-related agreements would not be subject to the best-price rule.

Pre-Offer Techniques

Sometimes post-offer techniques are instituted too late to prevent takeover. For this reason, many corporations plan ahead by instituting certain pre-offer measures even before any unfriendly suitors have appeared on the horizon (see Table 28-5). For example, a corporation could institute a supermajority provision into its bylaws that would require a 90 percent affirmative vote by all shareholders for the approval of any merger. Such a move would mean that any suitor would have to acquire 90 percent of the stock of the target to assure a takeover. A back up provision requiring a supermajority to change the supermajority bylaws would also be necessary to ensure that the suitor does not simply take 51 percent of the target and then use that majority control to eliminate the supermajority merger vote provision.

An additional pre-offer technique involves the corporation in a series of accelerated loans. Under the provisions of an accelerated loan program, all major loans taken out by the corporation are due in full immediately upon the takeover of the target by an unfriendly suitor. The plan is to place the suitor in a precarious financial position because, once the target has been acquired, the suitor would be forced to pay off a series of expensive loans, thus straining the treasury of the target. The accelerated loan gambit is often unsuccessful because the financial institutions that made the loans are often willing to renegotiate the terms of the accelerated loans with the target's new owner to avoid getting a poor return on their investments.

Another pre-offer technique is the poison pill tactic. Generally, a poison pill defense is established as a pre-offer strategy that remains dormant until the right set of circumstances activates its operation. The **poison pill** defense is triggered when a potential hostile bidder manages to purchase a specified percentage (perhaps 10 to 20 percent) of the firm. At that point, the price of the remaining shares drops dramatically for all other shareholders. The hostile bidder, however, is blocked from purchasing the bargain-basement shares. The goal of this plan is to encourage existing shareholders to buy additional shares at the reduced rate in order to water down the value of the stock, thus scaring off the potential buyer. This explanation says it poorly, however, because the poison pill process can be implemented in a variety of complex modes. There are those who oppose the technique because it damages competition among potential buyers. Oddly, this is the same argument that can be used against any of the post-offer or pre-offer techniques enumerated here, and so it is unclear exactly why this technique is so targeted for criticism. On the other hand, the complaint about the poison pill may lodge within the fact that the hostile bidder is frozen out of the chance to buy the bargain stock, thus placing him or her at an unfair advantage (although that is really the point, isn't it?). Moreover, some critics are uncomfortable with the fact that the strategy can be revoked by the directors whenever it suits their agenda (which is, after all, their prerogative as directors). [See: Robert Charles Clark, "Control Shifts and Insider Resistance: Tender Offers," *Corporate Law* (Boston: Little Brown, 1986), pp. 574–76; and "Shareholder Rights Plan," *Knowledge Encyclopedia*, http://www.referenceforbusiness.com/knowledge/Shareholder_rights_plan.html.]

Takeover Bids and the SEC

Takeover bids are scrutinized by the SEC. Under recent amendments to federal securities law, whenever a suitor makes an offer to acquire more than 5 percent of a target, that suitor must file a statement with the SEC. The statement must indicate (1) where the money for the takeover originates, (2) why the suitor is buying the

Table 28-5   Pre-Offer Antitakeover Tactics

Pre-Offer Tactic	Explanation
Supermajority provision— for takeover bids	Target corporation rewrites bylaws to require 90% vote to approve any takeover.
Supermajority provision— For amendments	Target corporation rewrites bylaws to require 90% vote to amend the bylaws.
Accelerated loans	Target corporation enters loan agreements that are due in full the when target is subject to a successful takeover.
Poison pill	Existing shareholders are empowered to buy additional shares of a potential target at bargain basement prices.

stock, and (3) how much of the target the suitor already owns. These procedures are designed to let shareholders know the identity and intention of a takeover bidder. Bidders who falsify any information on their statement may find their takeover bid stopped by a court order.

Expansion Tactics and Antitrust Law

As noted previously, antitrust law is designed to preserve competition and discourage monopolies. One way that companies can create monopolies is through a corporate expansion effort. Antitrust law does not focus on corporate expansion techniques. Instead, it looks at how an expansion attempt will affect competition in the marketplace (see Table 28-6). Section 7 of the Clayton Act forbids any corporate expansion if that expansion sets up a monopoly or otherwise hurts competition. The Clayton Act applies to horizontal, vertical, or conglomerate expansion attempts.

Expansion Attempts   Because **horizontal expansion** occurs between companies that are involved in the same business, such attempts often result in monopolies. Consequently, horizontal expansion schemes are scrutinized by the FTC and are more likely to be labeled illegal. A **vertical expansion** occurs between companies that were in a customer–supplier relationship. If a manufacturer of designer jeans were to buy a chain of department stores that carried its jeans, a vertical expansion would result. A **conglomerate expansion** joins two companies that were not in competition with each other, either because they dealt in different products or services or because they operated in different geographical areas.

Hart-Scott-Rodino Antitrust Act   Like the SEC, the FTC has a chance to step into expansion situations even before they become an established fact. This opportunity is provided by the Hart-Scott-Rodino Antitrust Act. Hart-Scott-Rodino is designed to police any expansion attempts that might harm competition in the marketplace. The act requires corporations that are setting up an expansion attempt to notify the FTC before the deal is completed. This advance notice allows the FTC to investigate the anticompetitive effects of the planned expansion. Should the FTC decide that the expansion will hurt competition, it can go to court and ask for an injunction to prevent the expansion.

The Tunney Antitrust Act   The federal government also regulates corporate expansion through the activities of the Antitrust Division of the Department of Justice (DOJ) and through the activities of specialized agencies, such as the Federal Communications Commission (FCC). The DOJ's Antitrust Division is charged with policing mergers that affect antitrust law to ensure that in carrying out a corporate combination, the participants

Table 28-6 Antitrust Law and Corporate Expansion

Technique	Explanation	Regulation
Horizontal expansion	Occurs between companies that are involved in the same business	Scrutinized by the FTC because of the likelihood of a monopoly
Vertical expansion	Occurs between companies that are in a customer–supplier relationship	Less likelihood of monopoly, therefore less FTC scrutiny
Conglomerate expansion	Occurs between two companies that are not in competition with each other	Least likelihood of monopoly, therefore least FTC scrutiny

have not violated those laws. The primary goal of the DOJ, however, is not to stop such mergers outright but instead to help the parties negotiate a merger that can be completed without violating the law. Such agreements are referred to as **consent decrees**. The Justice Department's antitrust consent decrees are, in turn, regulated by a federal statute known as the **Antitrust Procedures and Penalties Act** or simply as the **Tunney Act**.

The Tunney Act requires that the DOJ defend its support of a consent decree by sending the decree to the federal court along with a complaint and a **competitive impact statement (CIS)**. The CIS is a document that clarifies any potential antitrust problems inherent within the expansion and the solutions to those problems suggested by the decree. The law requires that 60 days before concluding the agreement, the DOJ publish the complaint, the decree, and the CIS in the *Federal Register*. Publishing the documents gives people a chance to have input into the nature, purpose, and effects of the agreement. The *Federal Register* will then print these statements and observations. A judge must also approve the decree. In doing so, the judge takes into account two elements: (1) the effect of the decree on competition and (2) the decree's effect on the community and on any parties who might be hurt separately. The Tunney Act was amended in 2004 to make it clear that the courts have the authority to challenge consent decrees negotiated by the Justice Department.

The corporate expansion process is sometimes regulated by specialty agencies that are charged with overseeing the socioeconomic activities of the corporations involved in the expansion process. Thus, for instance, the Federal Communications Commission would be responsible for reviewing merger plans proposed by corporations involved in the communications industry. Some agency officials take this responsibility very seriously and use their power to negotiate concessions within merger agreements that permit the agency to engage in an unofficial, but effective, brand of social engineering. The FCC is one such agency. In recent years, it has exercised its review power in merger cases to protect consumers, set prices, and return jobs to the United States. Agencies that use their regulatory powers to advance social agendas that are technically outside their legislative authority are referred to as **activist agencies**.

quick quiz 28-4

1.	Most antifraud provisions of the Securities and Exchange Commission apply to the merger process.	true | false
2.	Greenmail is the least effective anti-hostile takeover technique.	true | false
3.	The Hart-Scott-Rodino Act is designed to police any expansion attempts that might harm competition in the marketplace.	true | false

28-5 The Government and the End of the Corporate Person

Just as the government is involved in the birth and growth (expansion) of a corporation, it is also involved in its death, or dissolution. Whether a corporation ends involuntarily or voluntarily, the government is somehow involved.

Involuntary Dissolution

If a corporation has repeatedly conducted business in an unlawful manner, the secretary of state can ask the state attorney general to bring a *quo warranto* action against that corporation. Under a *quo warranto* proceeding, the state revokes the corporation's charter. Common examples of illegal actions forming the grounds for revocation include a failure to file annual reports, a failure to pay franchise taxes, or a failure to maintain a registered or statutory agent for service of process. Corporations formed fraudulently and those exceeding their authority may also be subject to a *quo warranto* proceeding.

Courts have the power to liquidate the assets of a corporation when an action is brought by a shareholder. Grounds for involuntary dissolution at the request of a shareholder include the following:

- Evidence of illegal, oppressive, or fraudulent acts.
- A misapplication or waste of corporate assets.
- A deadlock of directors that threatens irreparable harm.
- Evidence that a dissolution is necessary to protect the rights of the complaining shareholder.

Voluntary Dissolution

Because the government grants corporate charters and regulates corporate activity, it must be informed when a corporation voluntarily dissolves. A corporation can be dissolved voluntarily by the unanimous approval of the shareholders or by a positive vote of the directors with the approval of two-thirds of the shareholders. Once the decision to dissolve has been approved, a statement of intent must be filed with the state government. The corporation will then cease business and notify creditors (by certified mail) and the public (by publication). After all claims have been received, corporate assets will be used first to pay creditors, with the surplus going to shareholders. If the existing assets cannot meet all claims, a receiver may be called in to handle matters. A *receiver* is a person appointed by law to hold property subject to diverse claims. The receiver would divide assets fairly among creditors. Following the distribution of all assets, the corporation must prepare articles of dissolution and present them to the secretary of state.

---

quick quiz 28-5

1. If a corporation has repeatedly conducted business in an unlawful manner, the secretary of state can require the federal Justice Department to revoke its charter.   true | false

2. Courts no longer have any power to liquidate the assets of a corporation when an action is brought by a shareholder.   true | false

3. Corporations are no longer permitted to engage in voluntary dissolution.   true | false

28-6 Dissolution of a Limited Liability Company

Because limited liability companies are created by state statutory law, the dissolution of a LLC is also regulated by state statutory law. Most state LLC statutes outline the circumstances that will trigger the dissolution of an LLC.

Circumstances of Dissolution

The dissolution of an LLC can be initiated by the unanimous agreement of all of its members. Similarly, the dissolution can be triggered by the expulsion, bankruptcy, or withdrawal of a member. However, many state statutes now declare that in both member-managed and manager-managed LLCs, a member may not leave the LLC unless such a departure is authorized by the operating agreement. Naturally, the articles of organization or the operating agreement can also specify other events that would cause a dissolution. Some state statutes also assert that the death of a member does not trigger a dissolution. Instead, the death of a member is classified as a disassociation.

Effects of Dissolution

As is true with a partnership, a limited liability company does not stop business immediately upon the dissolution event. Dissolution must be distinguished from the winding up of the LLC, which effectively puts it out of business. Winding up involves completing all of the business of the LLC and selling its property to satisfy all of the debts of the firm. As is the case with the dissolution of a partnership, the dissolution of an LLC need not be followed by a winding up of the LLC. If all of the remaining members of the LLC want to continue the LLC, they may do so. It is also possible for the operating agreement to specify that the vote to continue need not be unanimous among the remaining members. The operating agreement should also indicate that the LLC will dissolve when the number of members within the LLC falls below the number required by state law.

---

quick quiz 28-6

1. The dissolution of an LLC is regulated by the federal government only.   true | false

2. Once an LLC has engaged in a dissolution procedure, the business does not stop immediately.   true | false

3. If all the remaining members of an LLC want to continue the LLC, they may do so.   true | false

---

Summary

28.1 The commerce clause is located in Article I, Section 8, Clause 3, of the Constitution. Clause 3 states that "Congress shall have the Power . . . to regulate Commerce with foreign nations, and among the several

States." At first glance the clause appears to be an attempt by the framers to limit the power of the central government and, conversely, to enhance the ability of the states to regulate their own internal economic activity.

However, from the very beginning the courts identified the central national government as the true source of commercial regulatory power in the United States.

28.2   The primary objective of the Securities Act of 1933 and the Securities Exchange Act of 1934 is to protect investors by informing them about the securities they purchase. The Securities and Exchange Commission carries out this objective.

28.3   To preserve the value of competition and to discourage monopolies, the government has enacted several antitrust statutes. The Sherman Antitrust Act prohibits contracts, combinations, and conspiracies in restraint of trade. The Clayton Act, the Robinson–Patman Act, the Foreign Trade Improvements Act, and the Federal Trade Commission Act make the Sherman Antitrust Act more specific and more effective.

28.4   Although both securities law and antitrust law pertain to monopolies, they have different areas of focus. Securities law is concerned with regulating corporate expansion techniques, including mergers, consolidations, asset acquisitions, and stock acquisition. Antitrust law is concerned with how corporate expansion affects competition in the marketplace. Antitrust law applies to horizontal, vertical, or conglomerate expansion attempts.

28.5   Corporations can dissolve involuntarily or voluntarily. A corporation that has repeatedly conducted business in an unlawful manner may be subject to involuntary dissolution by the state. A corporation can be voluntarily dissolved by unanimous approval of the shareholders or by a positive vote of the directors with the approval of two-thirds of the shareholders. The government is involved in both involuntary and voluntary dissolution.

28.6   Because limited liability companies are created by state statutory law, the dissolution of a limited liability company is also regulated by state statutory law. Most state LLC statutes outline the circumstances that will trigger the dissolution of an LLC.

Key Terms

activist agencies, 697

associative corporativism, 678

Antitrust Procedures and Penalties Act, 697

asset acquisition, 692

best-price rule, 694

bright-line test, 695

commerce clause, 675

competitive impact statement (CIS), 697

conglomerate expansion, 696

consent decree, 697

consolidation, 691

corporate raid, 693

corporate raider, 693

corporativism, 678

derivative, 681

Dodd–Frank Act, 691

friendly suitor, 694

golden parachute, 683

greenmail, 693

hopscotch loan, 693

horizontal expansion, 696

hostile bidder, 693

integral-part test, 695

interlocking directorates, 688

inversion, 693

inverted company, 693

junk bonds, 692

leveraged buyout (LBO), 692

lockup agreement, 694

merger, 691

monopoly, 686

Office of Credit Ratings, 683

Office of Investor Advocate, 682

per se violation, 686

police power, 677

poison pill, 695

prospectus, 680

quasi-RPM arrangement, 688

quick-look standard, 688

registration statement, 680

RPM agreement, 688

rule-of-reason standard, 686

security, 679

security-based swaps, 681

stock acquisition, 692

swap, 681

swap transaction, 681

takeover bid, 693

target corporation, 692

targeted shareholder agreement, 694

tender offer, 692

Tunney Act, 697

tying agreement, 688

ultra vires, 678

unfriendly buyer, 693

unfriendly suitor, 693

vertical expansion, 696

white knight, 694

Questions for Review and Discussion

1. How did the federal government's power to regulate business develop?
2. What is the source of state power to regulate business?
3. How does the Securities and Exchange Commission prevent unfair practices?
4. What is a *per se* antitrust violation of antitrust law?
5. What is the rule-of-reason standard in antitrust law?
6. What are the general provisions of the post-Sherman antitrust laws?
7. What are the various techniques of corporate expansion?
8. How do the interests of the Securities and Exchange Commission differ from those of the Federal Trade Commission in corporate expansion?
9. What are the two ways that a corporation may undergo dissolution?
10. Under what circumstances might a limited liability company undergo dissolution?

Cases for Analysis

1. The following lead paragraph was published in an article titled, "Why the *Times* Could Go Private," in the December 11, 2006 issue of *BusinessWeek:* "Even before restive shareholders began ramping up pressure on The New York Times Co. and insurance mogul Maurice R. 'Hank' Greenberg started buying shares, Chairman Arthur O. Sulzberger Jr. was thinking about taking the company private. In recent months, he has been quietly soliciting advice from trusted friend and financial adviser Steven Rattner, according to sources familiar with those discussions." Later, the article adds that "Rattner met with members of the Ochs-Sulzberger family, who control the voting shares of the parent company through a trust and hold 9 of the company's 13 director seats. He offered various strategic alternatives, say sources, including a leveraged buyout." What does the phrase "taking the company private" mean? What is a leveraged buyout? [See: Tom Lowry and Jon Fine, "Why the *Times* Could Go Private: An LBO Would Be a Long Shot, but Sulzberger and an Adviser Are Talking It Over," *BusinessWeek*, December 11, 2006, p. 40.]

2. The W.J. Howey Co. owned a large citrus grove in Florida. The citrus grove was serviced by Howey-in-the-Hills, Inc., a corporation owned and operated by the same people who ran the Howey Co. When the Howey Co. needed money, it sold tracts of land in the grove. Each buyer had to purchase both land from the Howey Co. and a service contract from Howey-in-the-Hills. The purchasers had no right to enter the land or to market the crop. All cultivating and marketing was done by the service company. Most of the buyers were from out of state. In return for their purchase, they received a share of the profits after the crops were harvested and sold. The SEC brought suit against both companies, arguing that the land and service contracts were actually securities that should have been registered with the commission. Was the SEC correct? Explain. [See: *Securities and Exchange Commission v. W.J. Howey Co.,* 66 S.Ct. 1100 (U.S. Sup. Ct.).]

3. Topco Associates, Inc., is a cooperative association of small and medium-sized regional supermarket chains. Each of its member chains operates independently. All members are required to operate under exclusive territorial licenses issued by Topco. These licenses provide that members will sell Topco-controlled brands only within the marketing territory given them. The government filed suit in federal district court. It argued that this scheme of dividing markets among competing chains violated the Sherman Antitrust Act because it prohibited competition in Topco-brand products among grocery chains engaged in retail operations. Topco defended by arguing that the association actually increased competition between the smaller and the larger chains. Was Topco correct? Defend your answer. [See: *United States v. Topco Associates, Inc.,* 92 S.Ct. 1126 (U.S. Sup. Ct.).]

4. Enstrom purchased an aircraft from the Interceptor Corporation. When the aircraft crashed due to a design defect, Enstrom sued Interceptor. However, when Enstrom found out that Interceptor's assets

had been purchased by the Interceptor Company (IC), it asked the court to join IC as a new defendant. IC argued that it was a different corporation involved in a different business. IC further argued that it had simply purchased the assets of Interceptor and was now involved in selling those assets, like the aircraft, to other buyers, like Enstrom. IC concluded that it was therefore not liable to Enstrom. Was IC correct? Why or why not? [See: *R.J. Enstrom Corporation v. Interceptor Corporation,* 555 F.2d 277 (10th Cir.).]

5. C.E. Stumpf & Sons, Inc., was formed to conduct a masonry and general contracting business. The corporation was owned in equal shares by Stumpf and his two sons, who had previously operated the same business as partners. Hostility between the two sons grew so extreme that one, Donald, ended contact with his family and was allowed no say in the operation of the business. After Donald's withdrawal from the business, he received no salary, dividends, or other revenue from the company. He brought suit seeking involuntary dissolution of the corporation. Should the court of appeals of California uphold the trial court's dissolution order? Why or why not? [See: *Stumpf v. C.E. Stumpf & Sons, Inc.,* 120 Cal. Rptr. 671 (CA).]

6. Image Technical Services, Inc. (ITS), an independent service organization (ISO), provides services for companies with copying machines made by the Eastman Kodak Co. In response to such competition, Kodak tied the sale of any of its parts to an agreement not to contract for services from any ISO. Under the terms of such an agreement, a customer who wished to buy Kodak parts had to agree not to purchase service from an ISO. ITS brought a lawsuit against Kodak under the Sherman Antitrust Act. In the suit, ITS alleged that such arrangements amounted to the type of tying agreement that was specifically outlawed by the Sherman Act. Kodak filed a motion for a summary judgment, arguing that the purchase of parts and the service of the machines with those parts did not represent the purchase of two separate products. Kodak concluded that it was therefore entitled to a judgment as a matter of law. Should the Court grant the summary judgment motion, or is there enough evidence of a tying agreement here to allow the matter to proceed to trial? Explain. [See: *Eastman Kodak Co. v. Image Technical Services, Inc., et al.,* 504 U.S. 451 (U.S. Sup. Ct.).]

quick quiz Answers

28-1	28-2	28-3	28-4	28-5	28-6
1. T	1. T	1. F	1. T	1. F	1. F
2. T	2. T	2. F	2. F	2. F	2. T
3. F	3. F	3. F	3. T	3. F	3. T

Part 7 Case Study

Gries Sports Enterprises, Inc. v. Cleveland Browns Football Co., Inc.
Supreme Court of Ohio 496 N.E.2d 959

Summary

Arthur Modell, president, CEO, and a director of the Cleveland Browns Football Co., Inc., owned 53 percent of that corporation. Other members of the board at that time included Pat Modell, Modell's wife; James Bailey, who was also chief counsel for and an employee of the Browns; James Berick, who was outside counsel representing the corporation and a Browns shareholder; Richard Cole; and Nate Wallack, who was also an employee of the Browns. The final member of the board of directors was Robert Gries, who owned 43 percent of the Browns and also owned Gries Sports Enterprises, Inc. (GSE). Modell also owned 80 percent of the Cleveland Stadium Corporation (CSC), which leased Cleveland Stadium from the city and then subleased the Stadium to the Browns and the Cleveland Indians. Other shareholders of CSC included Berick, Bailey, Cole, Wallack, Gries, and GSE. Modell was also president of CSC, and Bailey was both secretary and general counsel of that corporation.

CSC purchased 190 acres of land in Strongsville, Ohio, from Modell for $3,000,000 in cash and a promissory note for $1,000,000. Although Modell later canceled the $1,000,000 note, CSC still had debts exceeding $4,000,000. Modell decided that it would be expedient for the Browns to purchase CSC. Accordingly, he had CSC appraised by the brokerage and investment banking firm of McDonald and Company. Modell and Bailey, along with Michael Poplar, chief financial officer of CSC, determined that the Browns should pay $6,000,000 for the purchase of CSC. After this decision had been made, Modell, Bailey, Berick, and Poplar told Gries and Cole that CSC would be purchased by the Browns for $6,000,000. The purchase plan involved a payment of $120 per share of CSC to the minority shareholders, among whom were Berick, Bailey, Wallack, and Cole. Modell, the majority shareholder in CSC, was to receive a payment of $4,800,000 for his shares.

Subsequently, Gries did his own investigation into the value of CSC and concluded that Modell, Bailey, and Poplar had seriously overvalued the worth of that corporation. When the board met to consider the purchase, Modell made a presentation in support of the plan, and Gries explained his opposition. When the matter came to a vote, Bailey, Berick, Cole, and Wallack all voted for the plan. Neither Arthur nor Pat Modell participated in the vote, and Gries voted against the transaction. The following day, Gries filed a derivative lawsuit, the objective of which was to compel a reversal of the decision to purchase CSC. Gries stated that the transaction was unfair to the corporation, in that CSC was worth only $2,000,000 at the time that the Browns purchased it for $6,000,000. Gries argued that the fairness rule rather than the business judgment rule should be used to evaluate the directors' conduct because the directors who voted for the purchase were either "interested" directors due to their stock ownership or were dominated by Modell and had simply "rubber-stamped" his decision.

Moreover, Gries contended that the overvaluation of CSC was prompted by Modell's need to secure the money to pay off outstanding debts to several banks. Modell and the other directors argued that the decision to buy CSC should be evaluated by the business judgment rule. The trial court agreed with Gries, but the appeals court reversed that decision. The case then went to the Ohio Supreme Court.

The Court's Opinion

Justice Wise

The appellees-directors herein claim that they are protected by the presumption of good faith and fair dealing that arises from the business judgment and, therefore, they do not have the burden of proving that their decision to purchase CSC was intrinsically fair to the Browns' minority shareholders.

The issue before us, then, centers on the applicability of the business judgment rule. The business judgment rule is a principle of corporate governance that has been part of the common law for at least one hundred fifty years. It has traditionally operated as a shield to protect directors from liability for their decisions. If the directors are entitled to the protection of the rule, then the courts should not interfere with or second-guess their decisions. If the directors are not entitled to the protection of the rule then the courts scrutinize the decision as to its intrinsic fairness to the corporation and the corporation's minority shareholders. . . . A party challenging a board of directors' decision bears the burden of rebutting the presumption that the decision was a proper exercise of the business judgment of the board. . . .

In a stockholders' derivative action challenging the fairness of a transaction approved by a majority of directors of a corporation a director must be (1) disinterested, (2) independent, and (3) informed in order to claim benefit of the business judgment rule. If a director fails to pass muster as to any one of these three, he is not entitled to the business judgment presumption. This does not mean that the director's decision is necessarily wrong; it only removes the protection provided by the business judgment presumption. Once this presumption is removed, the court must then inquire into the fairness of the director's decision.

(A) [A] director is interested if (1) he appears on both sides of the transaction or (2) he has or expects to derive a personal financial benefit not equally received by the stockholders; (B) a director is independent if his decision is based on the corporate merits of the subject before the board rather than extraneous considerations or influences; a director is not independent when he is dominated by or beholden to another person through personal or other relationship; and (C) a director is informed if he makes a reasonable effort to become familiar with the relevant and reasonably available facts prior to making a business judgment.

Browns' directors Modell, Gries, Bailey, Berick, Cole, and Wallack, were all stockholders in CSC. Modell was the fifty-three percent majority stockholder in the Browns and the eighty percent majority stockholder in CSC (one hundred percent after March 2, 1982). [These facts convinced the court that the directors were interested in the challenged decision and were therefore not entitled to the protection of the business judgment rule. The court then went on to apply the fairness rule to the purchase of CSC by the Browns.]

(W)hen the transaction ". . . involves insiders dealing with their corporation the test of validity of the transaction is fairness. That our courts have frequently so held is without question . . . the substance of our decisions that 'when the persons, be they stockholders or directors, who control the making of a transaction and the fixing of its terms, are on both sides, then the presumption and deference to sound business judgment are no longer present.'"

In the instant case, no arms length negotiations as to price, terms, the elements to be included (or not to be included), or any other aspect of the proposed acquisition ever took place between the Browns and CSC. The $6,000,000 price was arrived at by Messrs. AMA (Modell), Bailey and Poplar . . . prior to any disclosure to plaintiffs of the possibility of such an acquisition, and never changed despite plaintiff's objections and despite the valuations furnished the defendants by plaintiffs. The manner in which the subject transaction was initiated, structured and disclosed to plaintiffs therefore did not satisfy the reasonable concept of fair dealing. . . .

The judgment of the court of appeals is reversed, and the judgment of the trial court is reinstated.

Judgment reversed.

Questions for Analysis

1. Which party had the burden of proof in this case?

2. According to the court's opinion, what factors should be taken into consideration in determining whether a director has an interest in a transaction that is challenged by a shareholder in a derivative lawsuit?

3. According to the court's opinion, when is a director independent, and under what circumstances does the director lose that independence?

4. What circumstances does the court say will make a director informed?

5. When the business judgment rule cannot be used, as occurred in this case, what standard is applied by the court to determine whether to reverse a challenged decision made by the directors?

6. Did the court consider the purchase of the Cleveland Stadium Corporation by the Cleveland Browns to be fair to the corporation and the minority shareholders in this case? Why or why not?

Part Eight
Property Law

Chapter 29

Personal Property and Bailments

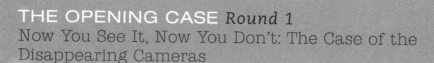

THE OPENING CASE Round 1
Now You See It, Now You Don't: The Case of the Disappearing Cameras

Here is a lesson for all college students: Keep track of your own stuff or . . . well read on. Richard Berglund was a full-time student at Roosevelt University where he was also an editor of the student newspaper and the paper's photographer. He was also paid by the university for his work on the paper. As editor and photographer he made frequent, one might say, habitual use of the campus newspaper offices, a practice that is common among student newspaper folks. In addition to the editorial offices, the newspaper's office suite included a darkroom and space to store cameras and other photography equipment. In addition to storing the university's camera equipment in the darkroom, Berglund also stored some of his own equipment there. When Berglund stored his cameras in the filing cabinet in the darkroom in the news offices he was doing exactly what most of his predecessors had done. The student activities coordinator at the university knew that Berglund was the newspaper's photographer, and she observed him at work multiple times. She also complimented him on the cameras that he used. However, Berglund did not go through proper channels, nor did he follow proper protocols to get permission to store his equipment in the newspaper offices. It also seems that the security guards at the university did not realize that Berglund's personal camera

equipment was stored in the offices. However, the university does employ a security staff that patrols the corridors of the building and that maintains a presence at the doors of the building. At the end of the day, all street doors to the building are locked and the overnight cleaning staff doubles as the security staff overnight. Regulations forbid the removal of any property from the building without written permission. Nevertheless, thefts did occur including a theft in the business manager's office just before Berglund's problems. Those problems began when Berglund left the newspaper office about 10:30 p.m. Friday, October 29. Berglund locked the office doors, but when he returned Monday morning (the Monday after Halloween by the way), he found the offices had been burglarized and his camera equipment was missing. Berglund brought a lawsuit to recover $1,789.15, the value of his camera equipment. The trial court found that a bailment existed between the school and Berglund, and that the university had been negligent in caring for that equipment, resulting in its loss. Accordingly, the court found for the plaintiff. The university appealed, arguing that the trial court had erred in its ruling. The university claimed that, since Berglund did not follow proper protocols, did not ask for permission, and did not inform university officials of the presence of the equipment in the office, no bailment had been created. The plaintiff argued that a constructive bailment had been created because of his discussions with the student activities coordinator and because past photographers had stored their equipment in exactly the same way, in exactly the same place. Will the appellate court uphold the trial court's ruling? [See: *Berglund v. Roosevelt University,* 310 NE 2d 773 Appellate Court of Illinois, First District, Third Division.]

Opening Case Questions

1. Who would be the bailor and who would be the bailee in this situation? Explain.

2. What elements are necessary to create a bailment? Explain.

3. Would this bailment (if one exists) be for the benefit of the bailor, for the benefit of the bailee, or for the mutual benefit of both parties? Explain.

4. What role does intent play in the creation of a bailment? Explain.

5. Would it make a difference if the court found that the student was also an employee of the university? Explain.

 Learning Objectives

1. Give examples of tangible and intangible personal property.
2. Describe the methods of owning property with others.
3. Differentiate among lost property, misplaced property, and abandoned property.
4. Identify the requirements of a completed gift.
5. Explain the law that applies to stolen property.
6. Determine when a bailment occurs.
7. Name and describe the principal types of bailments.
8. Discuss the burden of proof as it relates to bailments.
9. Make clear an innkeeper's duty to accept all guests.
10. Explain innkeepers' duties of care to their guests and their guests' property.

29-1 Personal Property

Broadly defined, **personal property** is everything that can be owned other than real estate. It is divided into two kinds, tangible and intangible. *Tangible* personal property is property that has substance and can be touched, such as a book, a pair of jeans, or a cell phone. Also called goods, or **chattels**, tangible personal property is movable and includes animals and crops. *Intangible* personal property, in contrast, is property that is not perceptible to the senses and cannot be touched. Accounts receivables and stock certificates are examples of intangible personal property. Another name for this type of property is **chose in action**, which means evidence of the right to property but not the property itself. In addition to the items mentioned, chose in action includes money due on a note or contract, damages due for breach of contract or tort, and rights under insurance policies.

Ownership of Personal Property

When personal property is owned solely by one person, it is said to be owned in **severalty**. When it is owned by more than one person, it is said to be held in **cotenancy**. The types of cotenancies discussed here are tenancy in common, joint tenancy, and community property. When two or more people own personal property as **tenants in common**, each cotenant's share of the property passes to his or her heirs upon death. In contrast, when two or more people own personal property as joint tenants (sometimes referred to as joint tenants with the right of survivorship), each cotenant's share of the property passes to the surviving joint tenants upon death. Nine states recognize community property, which is property (except a gift or inheritance) that is acquired by the personal efforts of either spouse during marriage and that, by law, belongs to both spouses equally. The states that recognize community property are: Arizona, California, Idaho, Louisiana, Nevada, New Mexico, Texas, Washington, and Wisconsin. Spouses can leave their half of the community property by will to whomever they choose. If they die without a will, their share passes to their surviving spouse.

Lost, Misplaced, and Abandoned Property

The finder of lost property has a legal responsibility, usually fixed by statute, to make an effort to learn the identity of the owner and return the property to that person. Advertising the property in a general circulation newspaper is usually evidence of the finder's honest effort to locate the owner, although today some sort of Internet posting might be even more effective. Statutes in many states provide that if the finder of lost property has made an effort to locate the owner and has not been successful within a period specified by law, the property belongs to the finder.

If lost property is found on the counter of a store, on a table in a restaurant or hotel, on a chair in a washroom, or in some similar public or semipublic place, it is considered not to be *lost* but to have been *misplaced*. It is reasonable to suppose that the owner will remember leaving it there and return for it. For this reason, the finder may not keep possession of the article but must leave it with the proprietor or manager to hold for the owner. If the property is found on the floor or in the corridor or any other place that would indicate it was not placed there intentionally, the finder may retain possession of the article while looking for the true owner. In this case, it is not likely that the owner would recall where it was lost.

EXAMPLE 29-1: Misplaced Property

While walking along a beach one morning, Carlow noticed a plastic bag near the edge of the water. She opened the bag and discovered that it contained a large sum of money. In the bag with the money was a bank deposit slip made out in the name of a nearby seafood restaurant. Carlow had a legal duty to return the money to the restaurant. Suppose the bank deposit slip had not been in the bag and Carlow was unsuccessful in an attempt to find the rightful owner. After making a sincere effort to locate the real owner, and after the period of time set by state statute, Carlow would become the owner of the money.

When property is found and turned over to officials of a state, without any claim registered by the finder, the property becomes the property of the state after a period of time set by statute. The same rule applies to bank deposits and other claims that have been abandoned by persons in whose names such claims were registered. In these latter instances, a period of up to 20 years may be required to establish the right of the state to take title. In some states, gift certificate money that is unclaimed after a certain number of years is supposed to be transferred to the state under the abandoned property law. When property reverts to the state, it is said to escheat. Some states have statutes that remove gift certificates from their abandoned property law, treating them in different ways.

Abandoned property is property that has been discarded by the owner without the intent to reclaim ownership of it. Courts require clear and convincing evidence of both the desertion of the property by the owner as well as the owner's intent not to return to it before determining that property was indeed abandoned. With some exceptions, anyone who finds abandoned property has the right to keep it and obtains good title to it, even against the original owner.

Old shipwrecks are often the subject of abandoned property cases. If an abandoned shipwreck is found outside the boundaries of a state, either the law of finds or the law of salvage applies under admiralty law. The *law of finds* gives ownership to the finder if all of the following apply: (a) the property is abandoned, (b) the finder intends to acquire the property, and (c) the finder has possession of the property. The *law of salvage* gives a **salvor** (one who salvages) the right to compensation for assisting a foundering vessel. **Salvage** is the reward given to persons who voluntarily assist a sinking ship or recover its cargo from peril or loss. In addition, the United Nations Convention on the Law of the Sea (UNCLOS) requires salvors to protect the historical character of shipwrecks. If an abandoned shipwreck is found in the submerged land of any state of the United States, the Abandoned Shipwreck Act of 1987 applies rather than the *law of finds* or the *law of salvage*. This act gives states the right of ownership to shipwrecks found beneath their waters.

EXAMPLE 29-2: Law of Finds

In 2004, the federal court awarded full ownership of a Civil War–era shipwreck to Odyssey Marine Exploration. The salvage company agreed to pay $1.6 million to an insurance company that had paid claims when the ship sank. The *SS Republic* was a side-wheel steamer that went down in 1865 while en route from New York to New Orleans after fighting a hurricane for two days. The salvage company discovered the shipwreck 1,700 feet below the surface of the Atlantic Ocean approximately 100 miles off the Georgia coast. Among other relics, the ship contained $400,000 (face value) of gold and silver coins, which may now be worth up to $180 million.

Gifts of Personal Property

People often make gifts of personal property. There are three requirements for a gift to be completed: the **donor** (the one giving the gift) must intend to make a gift, the gift must be delivered to the **donee** (the one receiving it), and the donee must accept the gift. Once all three requirements are met, the gift cannot be taken back by the donor. It is known as an absolute gift, or **gift** *inter vivos* (between the living). The gift of an engagement ring is a conditional gift, given in contemplation of marriage. Most courts hold that the donor of an engagement ring is entitled to its return if the engagement is broken by mutual agreement or by the donee. A few courts allow the return of the ring even when the donor breaks the engagement. These courts theorize that it is better to break the engagement without penalty than to have an unhappy marriage.

Uniform Transfers to Minors Act Problems can easily arise when gifts are given to minors. Sometimes, parents or guardians use such gifts for themselves rather than for the minor. At other times, donors make gifts to minors and then change their minds and take the gifts back. Gifts to minors are often used as tax shelters. Formerly, wealthy parents in high tax brackets often made gifts to their minor children as a way to shift unearned income to lower-bracket taxpayers. The IRS has changed this practice with the so-called kiddie tax. Unearned, income (dividends and interest) of a child under the age of 19 up to $2,000 is taxed at the child's income tax rate and, above that, at the parent's income tax rate. This rule also applies to college students under the age of 24 unless they provide over half of their own support from earned income (wages and salaries). (Note: The amount of unearned income that can be taxed at the child's income tax rate changes periodically so it is best to check the current dollar amount allowed under the law.)

The Uniform Transfer to Minors Act (UTMA), which has been adopted by most states, also prevents some of these problems. The act establishes a procedure for gifts to be made to minors. Under the procedure, minors are assured that gifts to them will either be used for their benefit or made available to them when they become adults. The income from gifts that are given to minors is taxable according to the kiddie tax rules mentioned previously. The UTMA allows money, securities, real property, and tangible and intangible personal property to be transferred to a custodian for the minor's benefit. The age of 21 rather than 18 years is used as the age when the custodianship terminates, because the IRS uses that age to terminate certain trusts.

Gift in Causa Mortis   A gift given during one's lifetime, in contemplation of death from a known cause, is a **gift** *in causa mortis*. A gift *in causa mortis* is conditional, and it is ineffective if the donor does not die as expected or if death is caused by circumstances other than those feared.

EXAMPLE 29-3: Void Gift *in Causa Mortis*

Rossano was seriously ill following an abdominal operation. Realizing that death might be near, Rossano signed over a savings account to Hall, giving Hall the savings book with necessary notations of assignment. Rossano did die three weeks later, not because of the surgery but because of a bacterial infection contracted in the hospital from contaminated surgical instruments. Rossano's executor may declare the gift *in causa mortis* void and demand the return of Rossano's savings for the benefit of the estate.

Anatomical Gifts   With so many medical advancements in recent years, there is an increased need in society for gifts of human bodies, tissues, and organs for medical education, research, and transplantation. The Uniform Anatomical Gift Act was revised in 2006 to help meet present-day needs.

Stolen Personal Property

Although a presumption of title to goods usually follows possession of them, it is possible for a person to have possession of goods without having title, just as it is possible for a person to have title without having possession. Thus, a thief acquires no title to goods that are stolen and therefore cannot convey a good title. The true owner never relinquished title to the goods, and even an innocent purchaser who acquired the goods in good faith and for value would be obliged to return the goods to the owner. Title to stolen goods never left the true owner, and possession can always be regained by that owner if the goods can be found, no matter in whose possession they may be at the time.

quick quiz 29-1

1. If lost property is found on a table in a restaurant, it is considered to be misplaced rather than lost.   true | false

2. Under the kiddie tax, a child's unearned income over $1,500 is taxable at the parent's income tax rate if the child has not reached age 14 years.   true | false

3. An innocent purchaser who buys stolen goods from a thief acquires good title to the stolen goods.   true | false

29-2 Bailments

Bailments happen all the time in everyday life. We just don't call them bailments. Ask your friend to watch your backpack in the cafeteria and you've created a bailment. Hand your keys to a valet at a parking garage and your car is in the hands of a bailee. Leave your computer at a nearby computer fix-it shop for repairs and, once again, you have set up a bailment. Most of the time this does not matter. However, when your backpack vanishes, or the valet bends a fender, or the repair shop gives you the wrong computer, then knowing about the elements, principles, and responsibilities attached to bailment comes in handy.

The Elements of a Bailment

A **bailment** is the transfer of possession and control of personal property (goods) to another with the intent that the same property will be returned later. Renting a vehicle, borrowing a friend's tablet, or leaving clothes at the cleaners are examples of bailment. The

THE OPENING CASE *Round 2*
One More Halloween Caper: The Case of the Missing Intent

Recall that in the opening case, Richard Berglund had assumed several roles during his tenure at Roosevelt University. He was a full-time student, an editor of the campus newspaper, a paid employee, and, most critical of all, the paper's photographer. In his role as a photographer, he had to have his cameras close by and ready to go. This explains his preference for keeping those cameras on hand in the newspaper office. Of course, he did not come up with that idea on his own. He kept his cameras in a certain drawer in a certain filing cabinet in the darkroom because most of his predecessors had done exactly the same thing. The newspaper office was housed in a building that had security, was locked to outsiders at night, and was policed by someone at all times, to the extent that no property could be removed without written permission. Nevertheless, somehow during Halloween weekend, Berglund's expensive personal camera equipment vanished. Since the cameras were stored on university property; since the cameras were in the darkroom because of his role as photographer, and since the student activities coordinator (SAC) (for all intents and purposes, his boss) knew that he owned and used his own private cameras, Berglund demanded reimbursement from the university. When that was not forthcoming, he brought this suit against the university, alleging that a bailment had been created and that the university had failed to protect his cameras as it was required to do as bailee. The trial court agreed with Berglund. If we look at the elements of a bailment, we might see why. The elements of

bailment include the intent to transfer and accept the property, thus creating the bailment; the actual delivery of the property to the bailee; and the bailee's acceptance of that property. Berglund certainly intended to transfer the property to the filing cabinet that was owned by the university; and he certainly delivered the cameras by placing them in the filing cabinet. Moreover, because the SAC had spoken to him about his cameras and because his predecessors had stored camera equipment in exactly the same place, the university's intent to act as a bailee can be inferred. As it turned out, the trial court agreed with Berglund that a bailment had been created. Yet something seems amiss. This is why the university appealed the case. What is missing is the university's true intent to accept and protect the cameras. Because Berglund did not follow protocol and did not ask permission to store the cameras in the office, neither the university nor any of its agents, including the security guards and the SAC, had any knowledge of the cameras and could, therefore, not intentionally accept the responsibilities of a bailee. As for Berglund's arguments about the SAC and the past practices of previous photographers, the appellate court decided that neither Berglund's conversations with the coordinator nor the past practices of other photographers could rise to the level of intent. For that reason, the appellate court reversed the decision of the trial court. The ruling was simple: No intent—no bailment. [See: *Berglund v. Roosevelt University*, 310 NE 2d 773 Appellate Court of Illinois, First District, Third Division.]

person who transfers the possession of the property to another is the **bailor**. The person to whom it is transferred is the **bailee**. The elements of bailment include the intent to transfer and accept the property, thus creating the bailment; the actual delivery of the property to the bailee; and the bailee's acceptance of that property. It is possible to create a bailment by expressly stated terms. A bailment can also be implied by circumstances. This is an **implied-in-fact bailment**, or an **implied-in-law** and/or a **constructive bailment**. To figure out whether a bailment actually exists, the facts and circumstances surrounding the transaction must be analyzed. The court will look at such issues as the intent on the part of both parties to be bound to the bailment, the benefits that accrue to each party, the nature of the property involved in the transaction, and who actually retains control. One additional element that is often unstated but is, nevertheless, essential to the creation of a bailment is knowledge. Both parties, but especially the bailee, who is, after all, accepting additional responsibilities, must know what is going on. Without knowledge, there can be no proper intent and no proper acceptance on the part of either party but especially on the part of the bailee. Thus, an individual cannot simply leave an item in your home without you knowing about it and then recover for damages for the loss of that hidden item. Nor can an individual take an item of property without the owner's knowledge and then charge the owner a handsome fee for protecting the item.

Principles of Bailment

In a bailment, neither the bailor nor the bailee intends any change in the title to the property involved in the bailment. The bailee has an obligation to return the same property to the bailor, or to someone the bailor designates, at a later time. A bailment does not occur when the person in possession of the property has no control over it. For example, it is not a bailment when someone parks a car in an unattended parking area. In contrast, courts have held it to be a bailment when someone parks a car in a garage or a parking lot that has an attendant present at all times to check cars going in and out. When an individual loans goods to another with the intention that the goods may be used and later replaced with an equal amount of different, but similar, goods, it is not a bailment. Instead, it is known as *mutuum*. For example, when you borrow a cup of flour from your neighbor, you will use the flour in a baking project of some sort. When you return the flour the next day, it is obviously not the same flour, but a substitute. You know this and so does your neighbor. The loan of the flour was a *mutuum* rather than a bailment because the parties did not expect that the identical particles of flour would be returned.

Bailments for Sole Benefit of Bailor

There are three principal types of bailments: bailments for the sole benefit of the bailor, bailments for the sole benefit of the bailee, and mutual-benefit bailments. In the first two types, called **gratuitous bailments**, property is transferred to another person without either party giving or asking for payment of any kind. Such bailments lack consideration; therefore, they may be rescinded at any time by either party. Parties to such agreements usually consider them only as favors. In reality, however, definite legal responsibilities are placed upon both the bailor and the bailee.

When possession of personal property is transferred to another for purposes that will benefit only the bailor, *bailments for the sole benefit of the bailor* result. In a bailment for the sole benefit of the bailor, the bailee owes a duty to use only *slight care*, because the bailee is receiving no benefit from the arrangement. The bailee is required only to refrain from **gross negligence**, or very great negligence—much more serious than ordinary negligence. In a bailment for the sole benefit of the bailor, the bailor has a duty to reimburse the bailee for any expenses the bailee might have in the care of the property.

However, the bailee has no implied right to use the bailor's property in a bailment for the sole benefit of the bailor. Use without permission is technically a tort of conversion on the part of the bailee; it would make the bailee liable for any damages that might result, even if the bailee had used great care and was not guilty of negligence. (Conversion is the civil wrong that arises when one unlawfully treats another's property as one's own.)

Bailments for Sole Benefit of Bailee

Transactions in which the possession of personal property is transferred for purposes that will benefit only the bailee are gratuitous *bailments for the sole benefit of the bailee*. In a bailment for the sole benefit of the bailee, the bailee is required to use *great care* because possession of the goods is solely for the bailee's benefit. The bailee is responsible for slight negligence, which is the failure to use that degree of care that persons of extraordinary prudence and foresight are accustomed to use. In this type of bailment, the bailee has the right to use the property for the purposes for which the bailment was created. Use for other purposes or over a longer period of time than provided for in the agreement will make the bailee responsible for any damages that may result to the property, regardless of the amount of care exercised.

Any *ordinary* and *expected expense* incurred in the use of another's property must be borne by the bailee. For example, if you borrow your friend's car, the use of gas and oil in the operation of the car would be ordinary and expected. You as the bailee would be expected to cover those expenses. However, repairs and adjustments not caused by ordinary use or damages not attributed to the bailee's negligence become the responsibility of the bailor. The bailee is not obligated to replace parts that break down because of the gradual use and depreciation of the other's property over an extended period. If a part of the car, let's say the serpentine belt, simply reaches the point of maximum wear and tears while you are using it, through no fault of your own, then you would not be responsible for the cost of repairing that belt, even if it snaps the next time your friend drives the car right after you've returned it.

When *unusual* and *unexpected* expenses result during a bailment that are not the result of any negligence on the part of the bailee, then the bailor will be responsible for any payments that might result. If, while you are using the car, the front tire has a blowout and it is evident that the tire was badly worn in many places due to your friend's long-term neglect, then you would not be responsible. Your friend would be responsible for any unusual and unexpected expenses that might result from this problem, including your friend's obligation to reimburse you should you pay to have the tire replaced. On the other hand, if while driving your friend's car you drive it for 70 miles without releasing the emergency brake, you will be liable for ruining the brake and will have to pay for having it replaced.

Mutual-Benefit Bailments

When personal property is transferred to a bailee with the intent that both parties will benefit, a *mutual-benefit bailment* results. Ordinary bailments involving business transactions are usually mutual-benefit bailments in which the businessperson is paid for his or her services. Renting an item such as a car or a moving van, leaving a car at a garage to be repaired or a suit to be cleaned at a cleaners, placing one's property in storage, and leaving a diamond ring at a pawn shop (a *pledge*) in exchange for a loan of money are examples of mutual-benefit bailments.

A consignment contract is a type of mutual-benefit bailment in which the consignor entrusts goods to the consignee for the purpose of selling them. If the goods are sold, the consignee, known as the *factor,* will forward the proceeds, minus a fee, to the consignor. If they are not sold, they will be returned. In a mutual-benefit bailment, the bailee owes a duty to use *reasonable care*. Reasonable care means the degree of care that a reasonably prudent person would use under the same circumstances and conditions. The bailee is responsible for ordinary negligence, which is the failure to use the care that a reasonable person would use under the same circumstances.

Many courts today apply the reasonable care standard to all types of bailments, including bailments for the sole benefit of the bailor and bailments for the sole benefit of the bailee. In a mutual-benefit bailment, the bailee must use the property only for the express purposes permitted by the bailor, as provided for in the contract of bailment. The rental of a car, tools, or formal wear, for example, implies the right of reasonable use. Failing to use the property as agreed makes the bailee responsible for any damages that might result, regardless of the degree of care exercised.

Burden of Proof

Sometimes items are damaged, lost, or stolen when they are in the possession of a bailee. In the past, the bailor had to prove that the bailee was negligent to recover against the bailee for damages. This proof was very difficult to obtain because the bailor was not in a

---

CLASSIC CASE   How Not to Meet the Burden of Proof: *American Ambassador Casualty Co. v. City of Chicago*

As any good citizen might do, Bruce Anderson took out an insurance policy on his automobile. The policy was taken out with American Ambassador Casualty Co. Anderson's policy insured his automobile against losses that might result if the vehicle were stolen. Moreover, the policy provided comprehensive coverage. As a result of a series of events not fully explained by the court in the case, somehow Anderson's car was impounded by officials operating under the authority of the City of Chicago. Apparently, the driver of the car had been arrested. The driver, however, was not Anderson. Therefore, Anderson was within his rights when he showed up at the impound lot and asked for his car. The city was either unwilling or unable to return Anderson's car. More than one month later Anderson was told by the police that his car had, well, vanished. Apparently, it had been stolen and, as far as the police were concerned, that was that. Anderson applied to his insurance company for compensation, and ultimately he received a check for $10,052. The insurance company then turned around, as was its right, and sued the city. The city asked the court to dismiss the action, arguing that no bailment existed and that it could, therefore, not be held liable. (Note: The city also argued that it was immune under the Tort Immunity Act, but that need not concern us here.) As we have seen and as the court explained in this case, a bailment is the transfer of possession and control of personal property (goods) to another with the intent *that the same property will be returned later* (italics added for ironic [satiric?] emphasis). The court also notes that

the elements of bailment include the intent to transfer and accept the property, thus creating the bailment; the actual delivery of the property to the bailee; and the bailee's acceptance of that property. Now it is interesting that the city did not contest the facts. Sure, the city said, we took the car and impounded it, and, yes, Anderson asked for it back, and, no, we did not return it. The only defense that the city offered was that the plaintiff was wrong in claiming that a bailment existed because none of its agents had agreed to the bailment, period. The case sounds eerily like *Berglund v. Roosevelt University* in the opening case. In both cases, we have defendants claiming that there was no agreement to create a bailment. However, there is a difference. In this case, the City of Chicago either misunderstands or just flat out twists the meaning of intent to meet its own agenda. In *Roosevelt,* neither the university nor its agents knew about the camera equipment until it came up missing. The university could not intend to keep something it did not know it had. Here city officials not only knew they had the car, but they also took the vehicle in the first place. Moreover, the city then kept the car, despite multiple requests for its return by the rightful owner, until the car just disappeared. The court sees this as the deciding factor in the case. The city implied its agreement to the bailment by taking and keeping the car. Those actions, therefore, created an implied bailment. Call it a constructive bailment, if you want; but it is a bailment, nonetheless. [See: *American Ambassador Casualty Co. v. City of Chicago*, 563 N.E.2d 882 (1990).]

position to know what caused the loss, because the bailee had possession of the property at the time. Most courts today shift the burden of proof in bailment cases to the one who is in the best position to know what happened—that is, to the bailee. Today, when items in the possession of a bailee are damaged, lost, or stolen, the burden is on the bailee to prove that it was not negligent.

Innkeepers, Carriers, Warehousers

Certain types of bailees, including innkeepers, common carriers, and warehousers, have extraordinary obligations in addition to the duties imposed on all bailees.

Innkeepers An **innkeeper** is the operator of a hotel, motel, or inn that holds itself out to the public as being ready to entertain travelers, strangers, and transient guests. A **transient** is a guest whose length of stay is variable. To assist travelers in obtaining accommodations, common law imposed the duty upon innkeepers to accept all people who requested a room if one was available. In addition, innkeepers were considered insurers of their guests' property. With some exceptions, these standards are still the law today. The Civil Rights Act of 1964 prohibits discrimination in the selection of guests for reasons of race, creed, color, gender, or ethnic background. People may be turned away when all rooms are occupied or reserved. In addition, innkeepers may refuse to accommodate people whose presence might endanger the health, welfare, or safety of other guests or the safety of the establishment itself.

Innkeeper's Duty of Care Innkeepers must use reasonable care in protecting their guests from harm. They are responsible for injuries to their guests caused by the inn's negligence or the negligence of employees. Innkeepers must respect their guests' rights to privacy. Guests are guaranteed exclusive and undisturbed privacy of rooms assigned by the hotel. Interruption of the guests' privacy through unpermitted entry by hotel employees or other guests creates a liability in tort for invasion of privacy.

Innkeepers' Eliminated Liability Innkeepers are not liable as insurers in four situations:

1. Losses caused by a guest's own negligence.
2. Losses to the guest's property due to acts of God or acts of the public enemy.
3. Losses of property due to accidental fire in which no negligence may be attributed to the hotelkeeper. This exception also includes fires caused by other guests staying at the hotel at the same time. Such persons, even though on other floors, are called fellow guests.
4. Losses arising out of characteristics of the property that cause its own deterioration.

Hotels hold great responsibility and must meet obligations when it comes to their guests and travelers.

Innkeeper's Lien and Credit Card Blocking Innkeepers have a lien on their guests' property. A lien is a claim that one has against the property of another. If a guest cannot pay the bill, the innkeeper is permitted to take possession of the guest's property as security for payment at some later date. Payment of the bill releases the property and terminates the right of lien. Credit card blocking is a common method used by hotels to secure payment for a room. Under this system, guests are asked for a credit card when they register. The hotel then contacts the card issuer electronically with the estimated cost of the bill. If the card issuer approves the transaction, the guest's available line of credit is reduced by the estimated amount. This procedure is known as a block (or authorization). The final

A QUESTION OF LAW AND ETHICS

Footsteps in the Night, Footprints in the Morning

The Mellings arrived at their hotel in Los Alamos to attend Mr. Melling's nephew's wedding. The couple checked into the inn and unpacked their luggage. After settling in, Mr. Melling decided to shower while his wife was out shopping. After taking a shower, he opened the bathroom door and discovered a couple bringing suitcases into his room. The desk clerk had assigned the room to another couple by mistake. Following the incident, Mr. Melling was embarrassed, humiliated, and angry with the inn's employees for making such a silly mistake, but there was nowhere else in town with vacancies and so the couple decided to stay. Meanwhile, while shopping, Mrs. Melling purchased a diamond ring, which she placed in the inn's safe deposit vault. Later, Mrs. Melling withdrew the ring from the vault to wear that evening at the rehearsal dinner. When she went to return the ring to the vault later that night, she was told by the desk clerk that the vault was closed until the next morning. Before retiring for the night, the Mellings locked their outside door but did not secure the chain latch. At about 5:30 a.m., they awoke to find a masked burglar in the room at the foot of their bed. The burglar escaped with Mrs. Melling's new diamond ring and Mr. Melling's wallet. After the police had been called and a report filed, the Mellings went to the wedding. Although they were advised to lock their room before going to the church, Mr. Melling was so upset with the inn staff that he just stormed off and drove away, leaving the room unlocked. While the couple was at the wedding and the reception, their luggage disappeared from their room. Later the couple brought suit against the Rosier Hospitality Corporation, which owned the hotel. Innkeepers have a greater duty of care toward their guests' property than is imposed in a usual mutual-benefit bailment. With exceptions (as described subsequently), innkeepers are held by law to be insurers of their guests' property. The insured property includes all personal property brought into the hotel for the convenience and purpose of the guests' stay. In the event of loss, the hotelkeeper may be held liable, regardless of the amount of care exercised in the protection of the guests' property.

A QUESTION OF LAW

Let's look again at the facts in this case and see the results of applying these principles to those facts. The inn will be held liable for the loss of the ring because it did not provide a place for its safekeeping, despite the fact that Mrs. Melling presented the ring to the staff and specifically asked for the protective measure that the staff should have been able to provide. On the other hand, the inn will not be held liable for the loss of the luggage because Mr. Melling had been specifically advised to lock the room and had failed to do so because of his inopportune temper tantrum. Moreover, in most states, innkeepers are further protected by laws limiting the amount of claim any guest may make for a single loss. The limit is usually $500 or less, depending on the state in which the hotel is located.

A QUESTION OF ETHICS

Let's look again at the facts in this case, only this time let's look at it from an ethical perspective. Before you consider each question, turn to Chapter 1 to review the various ethical theories noted there (market value ethics, social contract theory, utilitarianism, and rational ethics). Then using one of those theories in a consistent way, answer the following questions.

1. Is it ethical for an inn to set up an artificial time limit that will prevent some guests from getting the protection that they have come to expect while staying at hotels and motels? Explain.
2. Was it ethical for Mr. Melling to get angry with the hotel staff? Explain.
3. Was it ethical for Mr. Melling to storm off as he did leaving his room unlocked? Explain.
4. Was it ethical for the hotel staff to avoid checking Mr. Melling's room to see if it was locked? Explain.
5. Was it ethical for Mr. Melling to file this lawsuit given his own culpability in the situation (he did, after all, leave his own door unlocked)? Explain.

actual charge for the room will replace the block within a day or two after the guest checks out. If the guest pays the final charge with cash, check, or a different credit card, however, the block can remain on the original credit card for as long as 15 days.

Carriers The Transportation Security Administration (TSA) within the Department of Homeland Security protects the nation's transportation systems to ensure freedom of movement for people and commerce. Soon after the establishment of the TSA, Congress set up the Department of Homeland Security, which oversees the Coast Guard, Customs Service, Immigration and Naturalization Service, and TSA. Collectively, these organizations are responsible for protecting the nation's transportation system and supervising the entry of people and goods into the United States. **Carriers** are businesses that undertake to transport persons, goods, or both.

Common Carriers If a carrier holds itself out to the general public to provide transportation for compensation, it is called a **common carrier**. Like hotels, common carriers cannot turn away people who ask for their services, with exceptions for security reasons. Common carriers of goods are insurers of all goods accepted for shipment. They are liable as insurers regardless of whether they have been negligent. The Carmack Amendment to the Interstate Commerce Act states that a carrier is liable for damages to goods transported by it unless there is proof that the damage occurs because of one of the following exceptions:

- Acts of God (e.g., floods, tornadoes, cyclones, volcanoes, asteroid collisions, earthquakes).
- Acts of the public enemy (wartime enemies, terrorists, and the like).
- Acts of public authorities.
- Acts of the shipper.
- The inherent nature of the goods (e.g., perishable goods, evaporating and fermenting liquids, diseased animals).

EXAMPLE 29-4: Insurer of Goods

Whitehall Packing Co. engaged Amway Truck Lines to transport 40 barrels of fresh meat from its plant in Wisconsin to Howard Johnson's in New York. The federal government required plastic liners in the barrels, and Howard Johnson's would not allow dry ice in them. The refrigerator unit in Amway's truck operated properly. The truck experienced delays and took longer than its normal running time for the trip. When it arrived in New York, the meat in the barrels had a gassy odor and was not considered acceptable by the U.S. government inspector (no kidding!). An expert meat inspector testified that the barreled meat was smothered because of the use of the plastic liners and the absence of dry ice. Some hanging meat in the same truck was found to be in perfect condition. Although there was no evidence that Amway was negligent, the court held it responsible, saying that it was an insurer of the meat.

Antidiscrimination Provisions In addition to being insurers, common carriers of goods must accept *without discrimination* all goods offered to them for shipment. Under the Interstate Commerce Act, discrimination through either the selection of customers or the use of preferential rates is illegal. Exceptions to the rule against discrimination are as follows:

1. A common carrier is not required to accept goods of a type that it is not equipped to carry.
2. The carrier may refuse goods that are inherently dangerous and that would create hazard beyond the control of the carrier's usual safety facilities.
3. The common carrier may refuse goods that it does not represent itself as hauling.

4. The carrier may refuse goods that are improperly packed. Proper packaging is determined by the type of goods being shipped, the length of the haul, and the usual custom of the trade.

5. The carrier may refuse goods that are not delivered at the proper place and time.

Common carriers will not be excused from liability for losses due to strikes, mob violence, fire, and similar causes. Labor unions are required to give notice of impending strikes weeks in advance of the strike dates to allow carriers to reject shipments that might be damaged by delays caused by strikes. The carrier is required to ship goods by the proper route, protect them during shipment, and deliver them to the proper person. Carriers may limit the amount of their liability to the value stated on the bill of lading, which is the written contract between a common carrier and a shipper.

EXAMPLE 29-5: Failure to Read Contract

Bratton hired Allied Van Lines, Inc., to transport her household goods from Ohio to Florida. When the goods were picked up, Bratton signed a bill of lading that contained a provision limiting the carrier's liability to $1.25 per pound (which amounted to $4,500) or the actual value of the goods as written on the bill of lading. There was a place on the bill of lading for Bratton to fill in the actual value of the goods ($10,630). She failed to do so. The shipment was destroyed in transit. Bratton argued that because she did not read the document and was unaware of any provision affecting the carrier's liability, she was not bound by the words in the bill of lading. The court held that a bill of lading containing a limitation of the carrier's liability is binding, even though the shipper had not read it.

Carrier's Lien on Goods Shipped A common carrier has the right to the payment of fees agreed upon for the shipment of the goods and a lien on all goods shipped for the amount of the shipping charges due. Should the shipper or the party receiving the goods fail to pay the charges, the carrier has the right to sell the goods at public sale.

EXAMPLE 29-6: *Swift and Sure Shipping v. Harrison Printing*

The Harrison Printing Company ordered paper from the Metropolis Paper Company. The paper was shipped from Metropolis, Illinois, under terms that transferred title to the paper when delivered to the carrier, Swift and Sure Shipping. Harrison Printing refused to pay shipping costs when informed of the arrival of the shipment. Notice was finally given to both firms of the carrier's intention to sell the paper to recover shipping charges. At a public sale, the paper brought a high bid of $2,237. The carrier deducted shipping costs and turned over the balance to the Harrison Printing Company.

Common Carriers of Passengers A **passenger** is defined as a person who enters the premises of a carrier with the intention of buying a ticket for a trip. One continues to be a passenger as long as one continues the trip. This relationship is terminated after the person has reached the destination printed on the ticket and left the premises of the carrier. Prior to 9/11, common carriers had an obligation to accept all passengers who sought passage over their lines. This rule has changed. By order of the U.S. Congress, the Federal Aviation Administration (FAA) has established regulations that require the screening of passengers and property before they enter an aircraft to search for dangerous weapons, explosives, and other destructive substances. Passengers who do not consent to the screening must be refused transportation.

Functioning under the Department of Homeland Security, the TSA's mission is to prevent terrorist attacks and protect the U.S. transportation network. Its work encompasses all sectors of transportation, from container ships in harbors to trucks on highways to commuter trains in subways. The approach to security on aircraft includes thorough screening of baggage and passengers by highly trained screeners, fortified cockpit doors in all airliners, thousands of federal air marshals aboard a record number of flights, and armed federal flight deck officers. A list of items that cannot be taken on board an aircraft can be found on the Internet.

More Antidiscrimination Provisions Common carriers may not discriminate in the selection of passengers on the basis of race, color, national origin, religion, sex, or ancestry. **Racial profiling**, the act of targeting a person for criminal investigation primarily because of racial or ethnic characteristics, may not be a motivating factor in a carrier's decision to refuse transportation. However, carriers may refuse passengers (1) when all available space is occupied or reserved; (2) if they are disorderly, intoxicated, insane, or infected with a contagious disease; or (3) since 9/11, when the carrier decides a passenger "is or might be inimical to safety." Moreover, a passenger who has boarded a plane that has not taken off must leave the plane if told to do so by an authorized airline representative. This is because a carrier must exercise reasonable care in the protection of passengers. Injuries that are reasonably foreseeable or preventable and that result from the carrier's negligence give the passenger a right to sue for damages. However, if injuries are not reasonably foreseeable or preventable, the carrier is not responsible.

EXAMPLE 29-7: Carrier's Duty to Protect Passengers

Three men who were intoxicated boarded a commuter train around midnight. They were talking loudly and making a lot of noise. A conductor saw them and told them not to bother passengers. At the next stop, while the conductor let passengers on and off the train, the men went to another car. There, they assaulted, hit, and kicked a passenger. As soon as the conductor reboarded the train, he sought out the three men, discovered what they had done, and had them arrested. In a suit brought by the injured passenger against the carrier, the court held in favor of the carrier. The court said that the incident occurred so quickly and unexpectedly that the conductor, acting with the highest degree of care under the circumstances, could not have averted it.

Bumped Airline Passengers When an airline flight is overbooked, the airline must first find volunteers willing to give up their seats for ones on the next available flight. If there are not enough volunteers, other passengers may be denied a seat in accordance with the airline's priority rules. Airlines are required to establish and publish priority rules for determining which passengers holding confirmed reservation space will be denied boarding on an oversold flight.

Passengers who are denied boarding involuntarily, that is, bumped, may be entitled to compensation. If the airline can arrange alternate transportation that is scheduled to arrive at the passenger's destination within one hour of the original arrival time, there is no compensation. However, if the alternate flight gets to the destination between one and two hours late, the passenger is entitled to a cash payment. Passengers may refuse all compensation and bring private legal action. Federal regulations state: "The passenger may decline the payment and seek to recover damages in a court of law or in some other manner." The U.S. Supreme Court has confirmed that passengers who are bumped from a scheduled flight may sue the carrier for damages.

Passengers' Baggage Since 9/11, dangerous weapons, explosives, destructive items, and items that may be deemed to present a potential threat cannot be carried on board an aircraft.

Many items that cannot be hand-carried may, however, be carried in the luggage compartment of planes. The law has no requirement for returning banned items that are left at airport security checkpoints. In addition, those who attempt to bring banned items through airport checkpoints are subject to civil penalties and criminal penalties. Passengers must declare any hazardous materials that they are carrying. Violators of federal hazardous materials regulations may be subject to a civil and criminal penalties. In conjunction with the carrying of passengers, a carrier is obliged to accept a reasonable amount of baggage. Excess baggage may be shipped by a passenger or through payment of additional fees. Baggage limits vary with different airlines. Personal luggage carried aboard an airline and kept at one's seat does not generally fall within the baggage weight limits permitted each passenger. When a baggage car or baggage compartment is available for checking luggage, the carrier is considered an insurer of the luggage checked by the passengers and left in these places. Property kept by passengers at their seats or in overhead compartments places upon the carrier the obligation of exercising ordinary care for its safety. Federal rules place limits on the liability of airlines for lost luggage.

Warehousers

When goods are stored in a warehouse, the relationship of bailor and bailee is created between the owner of the goods and the warehouser. The UCC defines a warehouser as a person engaged in the business of storing goods for hire. A warehouse is a building or structure in which any goods, but particularly wares or merchandise, are stored. A *warehouse receipt* is a receipt issued by a person engaged in the business of storing goods for hire. Although both common carriers and warehousers are mutual-benefit bailees, they perform different functions. Common carriers are engaged in moving goods. Warehousers keep goods in storage. At times, however, one or the other will perform both functions.

Warehousers may be classified as public or private. A *public warehouser* is one that owns a warehouse in which any member of the public who is willing to pay the regular charge may store goods. Grain elevators in the Midwest, used to store farmers' grain, are sometimes established as public warehouses. A warehouser whose warehouse is not for general public use is a *private warehouser*. Most warehousers fall into this latter category. Sometimes, businesspeople will borrow money using goods that they have stored in a warehouse as security for the loan. The one who lends the money is given the warehouse receipt. If the debt is not paid, the holder of the receipt may obtain possession of the goods in storage. This practice is called *field warehousing*. A warehouser must use the amount of care that a reasonably careful person would use under similar circumstances. Failure to use such care is negligence and makes the warehouse liable for losses or damages to the goods.

EXAMPLE 29-8: Reasonable Care Required

Bekins Warehouse stored Keefe's household goods in its warehouse beneath some sprinkler system pipes. It did not inspect the area before placing the goods there. One of the pipes was unconnected, and water from the pipes leaked onto Keefe's goods, damaging them. Bekins's failure to inspect the area of storage was a negligent act that made Bekins responsible for the loss. The parties may limit the amount of liability of the warehouser by including terms to that effect in the storage agreement or warehouse receipt.

EXAMPLE 29-9: Contract Limitation

The warehouse receipt given by Bekins to Keefe in Example 29-8 limited Bekins's liability to 50 cents per pound per article. The limitation was enforceable even though it was not specifically called to Keefe's attention when the warehouse receipt was signed.

If goods are not removed from a warehouse at the end of a storage period, the warehouser may sell them. Before doing so, however, the warehouser must notify the owner that they are going to be sold and give that person the right to redeem them. If no time for storage is fixed in the agreement, the warehouser must give at least 30 days' notice to the owner before selling the goods. A warehouser has a lien on the goods that are in the warehouser's possession. A **warehouser's lien** is the right to retain possession of the goods until the satisfaction of the charges imposed on them. The lien is for the amount of money owed for storage charges, transportation charges, insurance, and expenses necessary for the preservation of the goods. The lien is a possessory one. It is lost when the warehouser voluntarily delivers the goods or unjustifiably refuses to deliver them. If the owner of the goods owes the warehouse money for the storage of other goods, the warehouser has a lien for the other debt only if it is so stated in the warehouse receipt.

If the person who stored the goods is a merchant in the course of business, the warehousers's lien may be enforced by a public or private sale at any time or place and on any terms that are commercially reasonable. Notice must be given to all persons known to claim an interest in the goods. The notice must include a statement of the amount due, the nature of the proposed sale, and the time and place of any public sale. If the person who stored the goods is not a merchant, more complicated rules must be followed to enforce the warehouser's lien. In addition to giving notice to all persons known to claim an interest in the goods, the nonmerchant must advertise the pending sale in a local newspaper. Notices and advertisements must contain specific information set forth in the UCC.

---

quick quiz 29-2

1. A bailment is the transfer of possession and control of personal property to another with the intent that the same property will be returned later. true | false

2. An innkeeper is the operator of a hotel, motel, or inn that holds itself out to the public as being ready to entertain travelers, strangers, and transient guests. true | false

3. If a carrier holds itself out to the general public to provide transportation for compensation, it is called a common carrier. true | false

---

Summary

29.1 Personal property is everything that can be owned except real estate. Anyone who finds lost property must make a reasonable effort to find the owner. Misplaced property must be turned over to the manager of the place where it is found. Abandoned property is property that has been intentionally discarded by the owner and may be kept by a finder. The Abandoned Shipwreck Act gives states the right to shipwrecks beneath their waters. For a gift to be completed, the donor must intend to make a gift, it must be delivered to the donee, and the donee must accept the gift. A thief acquires no title to goods that are stolen and therefore cannot convey a good title to others.

29.2 Bailment occurs whenever someone transfers possession and control of personal property to another with the intent that the same property will be returned later. The principal types of bailments are: bailments for the sole benefit of the bailor, bailments for the sole benefit of the bailee, and mutual-benefit bailments. Under modern law, bailees owe a duty to use reasonable care with the goods in their possession. When goods are lost or damaged while in the possession of a bailee, the burden is on the bailee to prove that no negligence was involved; if this proof cannot be made, the bailee will be held responsible for the loss. Innkeepers are required to accept all guests unless there are no vacancies. They must respect their guests' right of privacy. With some exceptions, innkeepers are insurers of their guests' property. The Transportation Security Administration (TSA), under the Department of Homeland Security, is responsible for protecting the United States' transportation system. Common carriers of goods are liable as insurers of the goods they ship regardless of whether they have been negligent. Public warehousers must accept goods for storage by any member of the public willing to pay for the service. Private warehouses are not for general public use.

Key Terms

abandoned property, 710
bailee, 714
bailment, 713
bailor, 714
carrier, 719
chattels, 709
chose in action, 709
common carrier, 719
community property, 710
consignee, 715
consignment contract, 715
consignor, 715
constructive bailment, 714
cotenancy, 709
donee, 711

donor, 711
escheat, 710
gift *in causa mortis,* 712
gift *inter vivos,* 711
gratuitous bailment, 714
gross negligence, 714
implied-in-fact bailment, 714
implied-in-law bailment, 714
innkeeper, 717
joint tenants, 710
joint tenants with the right of survivorship, 710
law of finds, 711
law of salvage, 711

mutuum, 714
ordinary negligence, 715
passenger, 720
personal property, 709
racial profiling, 721
salvage, 711
salvor, 711
severalty, 709
slight negligence, 715
tenants in common, 709
transient, 717
warehouse, 722
warehouser, 722
warehouser's lien, 723

Questions for Review and Discussion

1. What are some examples of tangible and intangible personal property?
2. What are the methods of owning property with others?
3. What are the differences among lost property, misplaced property, and abandoned property?
4. What are the requirements of a completed gift?
5. How does the law apply to stolen property?
6. When does a bailment occur?
7. What are the principal types of bailments?
8. What is the burden of proof as it relates to bailments?
9. What is an innkeeper's duty in relation to accepting guests?
10. What are innkeepers' duties of care to their guests and their guests' property?

Cases for Analysis

1. Susan Lacroix's Yerf-Dog go-kart was stolen from her driveway one evening when she went inside to have dinner. The thief placed an advertisement in the newspaper and sold it to Ronald Casey for half what it was worth. Later, Lacroix recognized the kart in Casey's yard and identified it as hers through its serial number. In a suit brought by Lacroix for the return of the go-kart, Casey argued that he now had title to the kart because he paid for it without knowledge that it had been stolen. Is Casey's argument sound? Explain.

2. David Bess rented three outdoor booth spaces at the Traders World flea market to display his inventory of Beanie Babies for sale. He stored his inventory in a locked trailer, which he left parked at the flea market overnight. When he returned the

next morning, he discovered that the padlock on his trailer had been changed. Upon forcing the trailer open, he found that his entire inventory of Beanie Babies, which he estimated had a value of $60,000 to $75,000, was missing. In a suit against Traders World, Bess argued that the transaction was a bailment. Do you agree with Bess? Why or why not? [See: *Bess v. Traders World, Inc.,* CA2001-06- 063 (OH).]

3. Schaeffer boarded a 30-passenger, single-aisle tur-boprop airplane carrying two pieces of baggage. When asked by a flight attendant to surrender one carry-on for proper storage, he refused and became verbally abusive. The captain of the plane decided not to depart with the disruptive passenger on board because he was concerned about the safety of the flight. When asked to leave the plane, Schaeffer refused, and the Port Authority police were called to remove him. Must a passenger who has boarded a plane that has not taken off leave the plane when told to do so by an authorized representative? Explain. [See: *Schaeffer v. Cavallero,* 54 F. Supp.2d 350 (S.D.N.Y.).]

4. Pollard found a valuable first edition that someone had dropped on the street. She took the book home, placing it with others in a collection of first editions. The owner's name could not be found in the lost book, and Pollard made no effort to locate the owner. Did she thus have title to the book? Explain. [See: *Doe v. Oceola,* 270 N.W.2d 254 (MI).]

5. Vincent Hartwell admired a valuable book collection on his uncle's bookshelf. To Hartwell's surprise, his uncle said that he planned to give the books to Hartwell as a gift and that he could have them at that moment. Hartwell replied that he was living in a dormitory and had no place to keep the collection. His uncle said, "Consider the books yours. I'll keep them here, and when you're ready for them, come and get them." Hartwell thanked his uncle and left for school. His uncle died a

week later. Hartwell's cousin, Kathleen Lane, inherited the uncle's entire estate. She claimed that the valuable book collection belonged to her. Who was the legal owner, Hartwell or Lane? Explain.

6. Torczyner, a diamond salesman, registered as a guest at the Hilton Hotel in Denver, Colorado. He placed his diamonds in the hotel safe when he did not need them for business purposes. On the last day of his visit, he removed the gems from the safe, left the hotel to make some business calls, and returned for the purpose of packing and checking out. Instead of placing the diamonds in the hotel safe, Torczyner carried them to his room. There, he was assaulted by two men who beat him and robbed him of the diamonds. Is the hotel responsible for the loss of the diamonds? Explain. [See: *Pacific Diamond Co. v. Superior Ct.,* 85 Cal. App. 3rd 871 (CA).]

7. In his will, Gavegnano left all his tangible personal property to his daughter, Caroline. At the time of his death, he owned 19 thoroughbred horses. In addition, a cashier's check made payable to him for $33,000 was found among his belongings. The lower court judge held that the horses and the check were tangible personal property and should be given to Caroline under the terms of the will. Caroline's brothers appealed the decision, claiming that neither the horses nor the check were tangible personal property. Were Caroline's brothers correct? Explain. [See: *Pagiarulo v. National Shawmut Bank,* 233 N.E.2d 213 (MA).]

8. Joe Scott left his automobile with Purser Truck Sales, Inc., to be repaired. Purser Truck Sales turned the automobile over to Lonz Radford to make the repairs. The car was demolished while in the possession of Radford. In a suit brought by Scott against Purser, the trial court held in favor of Purser, because Scott presented no evidence indicating that Purser was negligent. Was the trial court correct? Why or why not? [See: *Scott v. Purser Truck Sales, Inc.,* 402 S.E.2d 354 (GA).]

quick quiz Answers

29-1	29-2
1. T	1. T
2. T	2. T
3. F	3. T

Chapter 30

Real Property and Landlord and Tenant Law

THE OPENING CASE Round 1
If It's Not One Technicality, It's Another

This case begins with a contract between Wellington Resource Group (WRG) and Beck Energy Corporation (BEC). The agreement obligated WRG to find a well-financed buyer that would be able to purchase BEC's oil and gas interests on a tract of real property in the middle of Ohio. In exchange for finding a suitable buyer, BEC would pay WRG 5 percent of the final contract price. After a well-managed search, WRG found a firm named XTO Energy that had both the ready cash and the motivation to make the purchase. The final deal between XTO and BEC was for the tidy sum of $84,961,346. At a 5 percent commission, this meant that BEC owed WRG, $4,248,067.25. Unfortunately, when WRG asked for its payment, BEC refused to comply. BEC argues that WRG was in breach of the original agreement. WRG sued. That was when the fun began. Seemingly out of the blue, a new player appeared on the scene, Transact, a company from North Carolina that claimed its people, not WRG, actually found XTO. Transact claims to have a contract with WRG (and in some strange way with BEC), under which, Transact would be paid a 2 percent commission if it found a buyer for the BEC interests. Transact says that it provided the buyer, XTO, but has received nothing from WRG or BEC. Transact asks to be joined

to the lawsuit, an action that both WRG and BEC oppose. The court granted Transact's request to intervene and the case proceeded to the next stage. At that point, BEC filed a motion to dismiss that part of the case involving Transact. BEC did not dispute the facts. Yes, it admits that Transact may have found XTO and may have secured its involvement in the contract. However, even if all that is true, BEC says, Transact cannot recover one cent because the gas and oil lease that was negotiated is a real property contract and Transact is not a licensed real estate broker in the state of Ohio, which is a requirement to receive fees in such a deal. Since Transact does not have the necessary license, it cannot collect those fees and the case should be dismissed. (Note: BEC also argued that BEC and Transact did not enter a contract, despite Transact's claims to the contrary. The judge agreed that no contract existed and dismissed that part of the case. However, an equity claim of unjust enrichment kept the case alive.) BEC's claim may appear to be a mere technicality. After all, Transact seems to have secured the buyer for BEC, and so, it only seems fair that BEC would "share the wealth." However, there are some very good reasons for the state's licensing rule. Real estate negotiations are complicated, and detailed procedures that must be followed precisely to prevent errors in identifying real property boundaries, in securing inspections, in searching for deeds, in uncovering liens, in finding titles, and so on. That is why the state is so insistent that such contracts be negotiated by trained and experienced experts. The case, therefore, turns not on that technicality. Ironically, it turns on another technicality. Is the gas and oil contract negotiated here a real property contract or something else? If you want the truth here, keep reading. [See: *Wellington Resource Group, LLC. v. Beck Energy Corporation*, Case No. 2:12-CV-104 (United States District Court, Southern District of Ohio, Eastern Division (September 20, 2013).]

Opening Case Questions

1. How many contracts are actually involved in this case? Identify them all by naming the parties and discussing the subject matter.

2. Speculate on why XTO might want to purchase oil and gas rights in the middle of Ohio?

3. Why is it a good idea for real estate brokers to be licensed? Explain.

4. Speculate on whether the oil and gas contract is a real property contract. Explain.

5. If an oil and gas contract is not a real property contract, what kind of contract might it be? Explain.

 Learning Objectives

1. Explain what constitutes real property.
2. Differentiate between freehold and leasehold estates.
3. Describe the different types of co-ownership of real property.
4. Explain how oil and gas rights can be transferred.
5. Discuss the goal of the dormant minerals act.
6. Identify the methods of acquiring title to real property.
7. Explain eminent domain.
8. List the five elements necessary to create a landlord–tenant relationship.
9. Identify the essential requirements of a lease.
10. Make clear the duties of landlords and tenants.

30-1 The Rights Related to Real Property

Real property and real estate are not really the same thing, although they are often treated as if they were. When real estate agents, bankers, and attorneys use the term **real estate**, they are generally referring to the actual land itself as well as everything permanently attached to it. This would include buildings, fences, and trees on the surface; earth, rocks, and minerals under the surface; and the airspace above the surface. In contrast, the term **real property** refers to the ownership rights that go along with the real estate. The problem is that very few people know about this difference, and those who do know really do not care to make the distinction. For that reason, the two terms will be used alternately in the rest of the chapter, just as if they mean the same thing. The rights that are associated with real property generally include those rights related to trees and other vegetation, air rights, subterranean rights, water rights, and the rights associated with fixtures and easements

Trees and Vegetation

Trees, flowers, shrubs, vineyards, and field crops that grow each year without replanting (perennials) are considered real property. These plants have been planted and cultivated with the intention that they remain part of the real estate. Once planted and growing, such improvements to the land are called *fructus naturales* (fruit of nature). In contrast, crops or garden plantings that produce flowers, vegetables, or other harvest only for the year in which they are planted (annuals) are called *fructus industrials*. A tree belongs to the person on whose land the trunk is located. People who own adjoining land have the right to cut off trespassing tree branches in their airspace and trespassing roots at the boundary line of their property. Whenever property owners dig down at the very edge of their own property, however, they must provide support to their neighbor's land so that it does not cave in.

Air and Water Rights

In medieval England, landowners owned the airspace above their property to "as high as the heavens." This law changed with the increased use of the aircraft. Modern courts have held that landowners own the airspace above their land to as high as they can effectively possess or reasonably control. This height usually extends as high as the highest tree or structure on their property. It is a trespass for anyone to run wires through someone else's airspace or to use another's airspace in any way without permission. Electric and telephone companies must obtain easements for the right to run wires through the airspace of property owners.

Congress has enacted legislation that gives the public the right of freedom of transit through the navigable airspace of the United States. The **navigable airspace**, subject to FAA regulations, is the space above 1,000 feet over populated areas and above 500 feet over water and unpopulated areas. In airport cases involving planes landing and taking off, the courts try to strike a balance between the landowners' rights to the exclusive possession of their airspace, free from noise and exhaust fumes, and the public need for air travel.

Air rights are valuable and often sold to interested buyers, particularly in land-depleted metropolitan areas. For example, in New York City, developers bought air rights over the access to the George Washington Bridge and constructed multistory buildings. Two privately owned buildings have been constructed in the airspace over the Massachusetts Turnpike near Boston. Use of air rights becomes important when land is no longer available for new buildings. The private use of airspace also becomes a tax source for otherwise untaxable land owned by a city or state government.

People who own land along the bank of a river or stream are called **riparian owners**. They have certain rights and duties with respect to the water that flows over, under, and beside their land. Owners of land through which a stream flows own the soil beneath the water. If a nonnavigable stream is a boundary line between two parcels of land, the owner on each side owns to the center of the stream. If the stream is navigable, however, each owner owns only to the bank of the stream, and the bed is owned by the state. A navigable stream in some states is defined as one that ebbs and flows with the tide. In other states, it is defined as a stream that is capable of being navigated by commercial vessels. Although property owners may own the land under a stream, they do not own the water itself. Their right to the use of the water depends on the doctrine followed in their state.

Fixtures and Easements

Personal property attached to real property is known as a **fixture** and becomes part of the real property. Built-in stoves and dishwashers, kitchen cabinets, and ceiling light fixtures are examples of fixtures. If there is a question as to whether an item is a fixture, the courts ask the following questions: Has there been a temporary or permanent installation of the personal property? Can it be removed without damaging the real property? Has it been adapted to the intended use of the real property? Also, the court would ask what the intent of the party was at the time the personal property was attached to the real property. Trade fixtures are those items of personal property brought upon the premises by the tenant that are necessary to carry on the trade or business to which the premises will be devoted. Contrary to the general rule, trade fixtures remain the personal property of the tenant or occupier of the property and are removable at the expiration of the term of occupancy. Trade fixtures are not treated as part of the real property.

An easement (also called a right of way) is the right to use another's land for a particular purpose. Easements are used to give people the right to pass over another's land, to run wires through another's airspace, to drain water onto another's property, or to run pipes underneath someone else's ground. The one who enjoys the easement and to whom it attaches is called the dominant tenement. In contrast, the one on whom the easement is imposed is called the servient tenement.

EXAMPLE 30-1: Parties to an Easement

Hatfield owned a long, narrow strip of land that ran between a lake and a highway. She decided to sell the front half of the lot that bordered the highway to McCoy and keep the back half that bordered the lake for her own use. To give McCoy the ability to reach the lake, an easement was placed in the deed granting McCoy the right to "pass and repass" over Hatfield's property to reach the lake. In this easement, McCoy is the dominant tenement and Hatfield is the servient tenement. Also, to give Hatfield the ability to reach the highway, an easement was placed in the deed, reserving to Hatfield the right to "pass and repass" over McCoy's property to reach the highway. In this easement, Hatfield is the dominant tenement and McCoy is the servient tenement.

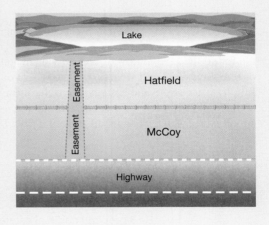

An easement may be created in three ways: by grant, by reservation, and by prescription. To create an easement by grant, the owner of the land signs a deed, giving the easement to the dominant tenement, and keeps the remainder of the land. To create an easement by reservation, the owner of the land grants to another person the entire parcel of land except for the easement that he or she keeps. An easement by prescription is an easement that is obtained by passing over another's property without permission, openly and continuously for a period of time set by state statute (20 years in many states). People claiming easements by prescription must show that they used (but did not possess) part of another's property openly, notoriously, and in a hostile manner for the prescribed period. This proof is similar to that used in adverse possession, discussed later in this chapter. A legal easement may exist even if it isn't written. For example, the law allows people access to their homes so, if the only access is by crossing through another land owner's property, the court may grant permission through an "easement by necessity." Once an easement is created, it runs with the land. This condition means that future owners will have the right to use the easement unless one of them gives it up by a deed or by not using it for a long period of time.

EXAMPLE 30-2: Easement Runs with Land

Jesse Horney conveyed the northern portion of his real estate to Wayne County Lumber Company by warranty deed in 1907. That deed included the following provision: "Said Jesse Horney hereby conveys to Wayne County Lumber Company the right of ingress and egress for teams and wagons in conducting their business through an open driveway along the South line to South Main Street." The property was conveyed to a different lumber company in 1930 and to a third lumber company in 1943. Later, in a dispute over the easement, the court held that the easement ran with the land and belonged to the third lumber company. In this case, Horney's property was the servient tenement. The lumber company's property was the dominant tenement.

A profit *à prendre* is a special type of easement with the added privilege of removing something of value from the servient property. For example, the right to enter another's property and remove sand, gravel, soil, or the like is called a profit *à prendre*. This right may be created by deed, will, or adverse use.

EXAMPLE 30-3: Profit *á Prendre*

The Bates Company and Sawyer executed an agreement that provided Bates could enter upon Sawyer's land and remove sand, gravel, and stone. Bates agreed to pay Sawyer a set rate per cubic yard or short ton for all the sand removed. The agreement stated, "Sawyer will not grant to anyone else the privilege of removing sand and stone from said parcel during the period hereof . . . but Sawyer reserves to herself, her successors and assigns, the right during said period . . . to go on and use said tract of land for any purpose they may desire, but without unreasonable interference with the rights of said Bates." The court held that Bates possessed a profit *á prendre* under the agreement.

quick quiz 30-1

1. Real property and real estate mean exactly the same thing.   true | false

2. In medieval England, landowners owned the airspace above   true | false
   their property to "as high as the heavens."

3. When personal property is attached to real property, it is known   true | false
   as a fixture and becomes part of the real property.

30-2 Estates in and Co-Ownership of Real Property

Most of the basic ownership rules regarding real property in the United States actually had their origin a millennium ago in England. After William the Conqueror won the English throne in the Battle of Hastings in 1066, he realized that he had an enormous amount of land to preserve and protect. Although he would have preferred to maintain and defend all the land on his own, he knew that he could not, and so he established a system by which he could retain the ownership of all the land in England while parceling out its maintenance and defense to the nobility. Those nobles who received large tracts of land from the king were said to hold estates, a term derived from the Latin word *status*. Although the rules that apply today emerged centuries ago on the other side of the Atlantic, they still affect us because of our English legal heritage. This heritage influences the rules that govern modern estates as well as those that relate to the co-ownership of land.

The Law of Estates

Most of the estates that were passed on to the nobility in medieval England could last infinitely because the nobles who held them were empowered to pass them on to their heirs. These estates were called **freehold estates**. Anyone with a freehold estate may transfer that interest to another by sale, gift, will, or by dying without a will. Freehold estates are either estates in fee simple or life estates.

Estates in Fee Simple
Anyone owning real property outright—that is, forever—is said to have an **estate in fee simple**. The estate descends, on the death of the owner, to the owner's heirs. The owner of an estate in fee simple has absolute ownership in the real estate, with the right to use or dispose of it as desired, so long as the use of it does not interfere with others' rights.

EXAMPLE 30-4: Fee Simple Estate

When the Landers bought the land on which to build their house, they received an estate in fee simple from the former owners. They thus received full rights to the property. They may sell it, give it away, or use it as they wish. The only restrictions are those contained in the deed or required of them by law.

Life Estates
A person who owns real property for life or for the life of another owns an interest in real property called a **life estate**. Such an estate may be created by deed, by will, or by law. When the terms of a deed or will state that the property is to pass at the end of a life estate to someone other than the grantor or the grantor's heirs, the future interest is a **remainder estate**.

EXAMPLE 30-5: Life Estate

Rosengard deeded her farm to Kinkaid for life. The deed stated that upon Kinkaid's death, the property was to pass to Honig in fee simple. Kinkaid owns a life estate in the farm. Honig owns a remainder estate until Kinkaid's death, then an estate in fee simple. The owner of a life estate may convey that interest to another. Thus, if Kinkaid conveys his interest to Jenkins, Jenkins will own a life estate for the duration of Kinkaid's life, after which the property will belong to Honig. When the terms of a deed or a will state that property is to return to the grantor or the grantor's heirs at the expiration of a life estate, the future interest is a **reversion estate**.

The Law of Co-Ownership

Often only one person owns a tract of real estate. This type of ownership is referred to as ownership in **severalty**. It is also very common, however, for two or more people to own the same tract of land. This type of ownership is referred to as **concurrent ownership**, although the more common term is **co-ownership**. Real property may be owned individually or by two or more persons known as **cotenants**. Cotenant relationships include: tenancy in common, joint tenancy, community property, and tenancy by the entirety.

Tenancy in Common When two or more persons own real property as **tenants in common**, each person owns an undivided share of the whole property. A cotenant's share of the property transfers to that cotenant's heirs upon his or her death rather than to the surviving cotenants. Each cotenant is entitled to possession of the entire premises. This rule is known as unity of possession. Tenants in common have the right to sell or deed away as a gift their share in the property without the permission of the other cotenants. When this action occurs, any new owner becomes a tenant in common with the remaining cotenants. One cotenant's interest is not necessarily the same as another cotenant's interest.

EXAMPLE 30-6: Tenants in Common

Ingalls and Carpenter owned a parcel of real property as tenants in common. When Ingalls died, his three children inherited his estate equally. The children became tenants in common (each owning a one-sixth interest) with Carpenter, who owned a one-half interest in the property.

Tenants in common may separate their interests in the property by petitioning the court for a partition of the property. If the court allows the petition, either it will divide the property into separate parcels so that each cotenant will own a particular part outright, or it will order the property sold and divide the proceeds of the sale among the cotenants. Creditors may reach the interest of a tenant in common by bringing a lawsuit against that particular cotenant and, if successful, having that cotenant's interest sold to pay the debt. By statute in most states, co-ownership of property by two or more persons is considered tenancy in common unless the relationship is expressly indicated as a joint tenancy or a tenancy by the entirety.

Joint Tenancy When two or more persons own real property as **joint tenants**, the estate created is a single estate with multiple ownership. Each tenant owns the entire estate, subject to the equal rights of the other joint tenants. Four unities must be present to create a joint tenancy: time, title, interest, and possession:

1. The unity of time means that all owners must take title at the same time.
2. The unity of title means that all owners must derive title from the same source.
3. The unity of interest means that all owners must have equal interests in the property.
4. The unity of possession means that all owners must have the equal right to possess the property.

Upon the death of one joint tenant, the entire ownership remains with the other joint tenants and does not pass to the heirs or devisees of the deceased cotenant. For this reason, joint tenants are often identified as joint tenants with the right of survivorship.

EXAMPLE 30-7: Joint Tenants

If Ingalls and Carpenter, in Example 30-6, had owned the parcel of real property as joint tenants instead of as tenants in common, Carpenter would have owned the entire property outright when Ingalls died. Ingalls's three children would not have been entitled to any interest in the real property whatsoever.

A joint tenant may deed away his or her interest to a new owner without permission of the other joint tenants. The new owner, in such a case, becomes a tenant in common with the remaining joint tenants. As in the case of a tenant in common, a joint tenant may petition the court for a partition of the estate, which would end the joint tenancy. Creditors may levy upon the interests of a joint tenant on execution and take over that particular joint tenant's interest as a tenant in common with the remaining joint tenants. To levy on execution means to collect a sum of money by putting into effect the judgment of a court.

Community Property Property (except a gift or inheritance) that is acquired by the personal efforts of either spouse during marriage is called community property. By law community property belongs to both spouses equally. The law originated in Spain, was embraced by Mexico, and is presently followed in Puerto Rico, in some Southern states, such as Texas and Louisiana, and in many Western states, such as California and Nevada. Although state laws differ, they all operate on the theory that both spouses contribute equally to the marriage—that all property acquired during the marriage is the result of the combined efforts of both of them. Although one spouse may earn all the money to acquire the property, all the property acquired is considered community property.

Tenancy by the Entirety A tenancy by the entirety may be held only by a husband and wife and is based upon the common law doctrine known as unity of person. Under this very old doctrine, a husband and wife were regarded, under the law, as one. In theory, each spouse owned the entire estate, and neither could destroy it by any separate act. The husband, however, had the entire control over the estate, including the exclusive right to possession and the right to all rents and profits. Many states have done away with the statute of tenancy by the entirety. Other states have enacted statutes giving equal rights to husbands and wives who own property as tenants by the entirety. Still other states require both spouses to consent to a valid mortgage on property owned as tenants by the entirety. See Table 30-1.

quick quiz 30-2

1. Most of the basic ownership rules regarding real property in the United States actually had their origin a millennium ago in France.   true | false

2. A person who owns real property for life or for the life of another owns an interest in real property called a life estate.   true | false

3. When two or more persons own real property as tenants in common, each person owns an undivided share of the whole property.   true | false

Table 30-1 Cotenant Relationships

	Tenants in Common	Joint Tenants	Tenants by Entirety	Community Property
1. Who can be cotenants	Any number of people	Any number of people	Only husband and wife	Only husband and wife
2. At death, deceased's share goes	To deceased's heirs*	To surviving cotenants	To surviving spouse	To deceased's heirs*
3. Title	Separate title for each cotenant	One title to the entire property	Husband has title (under the doctrine of unity)†	Title is in the community
4. Division of ownership interests	Cotenants can have equal or unequal interests	All interests must be equal	Interests equal; husband has the right to control and manage†	Both interests equal
5. Right to possession of entire premises	Equal with all cotenants	Equal with all cotenants	Husband only†	Equal with both spouses
6. Right to convey ownership interest	May convey to another without permission of cotenant	May convey to another but will end joint tenancy relationship	Husband may convey to anyone; wife's interest is protected†	May convey personal property without spouse's permission; must have written permission to convey real property
7. Right to partition the property	Yes	Yes	No	No
8. Owner's separate interest reachable by creditors	Yes	Yes	Husband's only†	No. Whole community only, depending on state law

*Either by will or the law of intestate succession if the deceased had no will.

† At common law. States have either abolished this type of tenancy or amended it to give equal rights to men and women.

30-3 Subterranean Rights: Oil and Gas Developments

Recently new technologies have enabled landowners (or, perhaps more correctly, land controllers) to access previously inaccessible reserve pockets of oil and gas (read "fracking" here). As is often the case, technology moves much faster than the law. Time and again technologists and investors move forward without noticing (or caring?) that certain legal difficulties have emerged. The law must, therefore, play a troublesome game of "catch-up." In this case, the very nature of the contractual relationship between landowners and gas and oil developers is unclear. Are these contracts simply leases or are they estates? Are there existing statutes such as the dormant minerals statute that impact these agreements? Solving these problems is critical because, as is often the case when technology moves forward, unintended and unforeseen consequences emerge. Someone must be responsible for dealing with such consequences. The recent rise in earthquake activity in the fracking areas of Oklahoma and Texas is one dramatic example of this problem. However, physical damage is not the only concern. Profit distribution, ownership rights, and contract duration are also of great interest to owners, leasees, and neighbors. For these reasons we must pause to look at this issue in some detail, even if the results uncover more questions than answers.

Subterranean Rights: The Basics

Unless excluded in the deed, the owner of land has exclusive title to material below the surface of the land. The right extends to the point determined to be the exact center of the earth. These **subterranean rights** are often sold to corporations exploring for coal, oil, or other mineral deposits. Taking out oil or minerals from below the surface would constitute trespass if such rights were not obtained from their owners. A landowner must not dig a cellar or other excavation so close to the boundary of a neighbor so as to cause the neighbor's land to cave in or the neighbor's building to be damaged. A person excavating who fails to properly shore up the adjoining land will, in all likelihood, be liable to the neighbor for damages. What happens when the damage that occurs impacts landowners, entrepreneurs, and renters who are on land not adjacent to the real property in question, but in distant areas that are affected by the search for oil and gas deposits? Or, to put it more bluntly, who pays for the earthquake damage in Fort Worth, when the oil and gas exploration takes place in Dallas County?

Oil and Gas Contracts: Lease, License, or Fee Simple?

Fracking (the more scientific term is hydrocarbon fracturing) is a technological practice that involves pumping highly pressurized, chemically treated water into rock formations that are located far under the surface of the earth in order to crack open fractures in the rock so that oil and gas deposits can be pulled to the surface where the gas or oil can be drawn from the water. The seismic activity, ground water depletion, air pollution, and noise pollution caused by fracking are troublesome enough to cause some states to build strict regulations around the operation itself. But not all questions associated with oil and gas leases involve fracking or some other new drilling technology. Sometimes the issue is whether a broker can obtain a fee or how an asset is affected in a bankruptcy situation. Nevertheless, one of the main problems that must be solved is the actual nature of the contract involved in transferring (or preserving) the subterranean rights of any sort, or to put it directly, is such a contract a real property lease, a license, or a fee of some sort? [See: Ryan Fisher, "Cleveland Law Firm Provides Expert Legal Help with Fracking Problems and Opportunities," *PR Newswire*, March 12, 2012, http://www. prnewswire.com/; "Hydraulic fracturing," *Wikipedia, the Free Encyclopedia*, January 11, 2015, http://en. wikipedia.org/wiki/Hydraulic_fracturing.]

Fee Simple Determinable

States differ on how they characterize a contract involving subterranean rights, especially as those rights relate to the extraction of gas, oil, and other minerals. Some states are quite unequivocal in declaring that a contract for oil and gas rights is neither a license nor a lease, but is instead, a fee simple determinable. As you will recall, anyone owning real property outright—that is, forever—is said to have an estate in fee simple. The estate descends, on the death of the owner, to the owner's heirs. The owner of an estate in fee simple has absolute ownership in the real estate, with the right to use or dispose of it as desired, so long as the use of it does not interfere with others' rights. Such rights can be altered by contract. In some states, for example, an oil and gas contract is considered a fee simple determinable. This is a fee simple that lasts as long as the ability to take the oil and gas from the earth continues. Once that ceases as an option, the fee simple reverts to the original owners. The original owners receive a royalty on the gas and oil produced by the drilling project. [See: Ryan Fisher, "Cleveland Law Firm Provides Expert Legal Help with Fracking Problems and Opportunities," PR Newswire, March 12, 2012, http://www. prnewswire.com/.]

Lease Agreements

In contrast, other states characterize oil and gas contracts as real property, lease agreements and others as a simple license. In a lease agreement, the lessees, those who purchase the right to enter the land from the lessors, those who owned the land outright, receive the ability to operate on the land as if it were their own, in exchange for an agreed to payment or a payment schedule. Thus, the lessees have the right to enter, leave, and move about the land as well as to construct the necessary drilling and extraction equipment, equipment such as derricks and pipelines, to perform their tasks. As the courts often say, in a lease agreement the lessees have been granted the ability to hold on to the land and to perform whatever tasks they reasonably need to perform in order to accomplish the objectives for which they wanted that land in the first place. Since the lease agreement is a real property contract, it must adhere to all of the legal requirements for such agreements, including the production of a written document, following all recording requirements, and so on. [See: Ryan Fisher, "Cleveland Law Firm Provides Expert Legal Help with Fracking Problems and Opportunities," PR Newswire, March 12, 2012, http://www. prnewswire.com/.]

A License to Search and Extract

In contrast, a license is a much more limited contract that bestows no property rights on the licensee. The only rights transferred are the right to enter the land, the right to search for the oil and gas, and the right to leave with a quantity of that oil and/or gas. No other property rights are transferred to the licensee. If we can use a simple analogy, the difference between a lease and a license is the difference between entering a tree farm to cut down a single evergreen to take home a Christmas tree (a license) and the right to plant, cultivate, nurture, and then cut down a tree (a lease). [See: Ryan Fisher, "Cleveland Law Firm Provides Expert Legal Help with Fracking Problems and Opportunities," PR Newswire, March 12, 2012, http://www. prnewswire.com/.]

A Lease that Establishes a Fee Simple Determinable

Some courts manage to mix and match a lease with a fee simple determinable. These courts would say that a lease agreement that empowers the lessees to hold on to the land and to perform whatever tasks they reasonably need to perform in order to accomplish the objectives for which they wanted that land actually creates a fee simple determinable. Ohio is one state that seems unable to make up its mind. The courts of Ohio, even the supreme court, seem

THE OPENING CASE *Round 2*
If It's Not One Technicality, It's Another

Recall in the opening case that WRG brought suit against BEC when BEC failed to pay WRG for obtaining XTO as a buyer for its oil and gas rights. Recall also that Transact, a company from North Carolina, asked to enter the lawsuit because its people, not WRG, had actually found XTO. The court granted Transact's request to intervene and the case proceeded to the next stage. At that point, BEC filed a motion to dismiss that part of the case involving Transact. BEC did not dispute the facts. Yes, it admits that Transact may have found XTO and may have secured its involvement in the contract. However, even if all that is true, BEC says, Transact cannot recover one cent because the gas and oil lease that was negotiated is a real property contract and Transact is not a licensed real estate broker in the state of Ohio, which is a requirement to receive fees in such a deal. Since Transact does not have the necessary license, it cannot collect those fees and the case should be dismissed. BEC's claim may appear to be a mere technicality. After all, Transact seems to have secured the buyer for BEC, and so, it only seems fair that BEC would pay Transact its fair share. However, there are some very good reasons for the state's licensing rule. Real estate negotiations are complicated and detailed procedures that must be followed precisely to prevent errors in identifying real property boundaries, in securing inspections, in searching for deeds, in uncovering liens, in finding titles, and so on. That is why the state is so insistent that such contracts be negotiated by trained and experienced experts. However, the case turns on another technicality. Is the gas and oil contract negotiated here a real property contract or something else? The question should have an easy answer and in many states it does. The State of Ohio, however, seems to have some difficulty in maintaining consistency in answering the question. But this time the court does not hesitate. An oil and gas contract like this one, it says, is not a real property contract. Therefore, a real estate broker's license is not needed. However, before you get too enthusiastic about this definitive and fearless answer by the court, look again. The case was brought in federal court and so what we have is a federal judge interpreting state law. Is that likely to stand? Your guess, quite frankly, is as good as anyone's. [See: *Wellington Resource Group, LLC. v. Beck Energy Corporation*, Case No. 2:12-CV-104 (United States District Court, Southern District of Ohio, Eastern Division (September 20, 2013).]

to hold at one time or another to all of these positions, not simultaneously, of course, but in waves of unpredictable and somewhat exasperating change. [See: Ilya Batikov, Kevin F. Eichner, Sheila Nolan Gartland, and Matthew W. Warnock, "Title Issues and Recent Cases Relating to Oil and Gas Developments in Ohio," Ohio State Bar Association Annual Conference, April 30 to May 2, 2014; [See: Ryan Fisher, "Cleveland Law Firm Provides Expert Legal Help with Fracking Problems and Opportunities," PR Newswire, March 12, 2012, http://www. prnewswire.com/.] Porter Wright, "What Is an Oil and Gas Lease? A Federal Court in Ohio Predicts Ohio Law," *Oil and Gas Law Report*, September 27, 2013, http://www.oil andgaslawreport.com/2013/09/27/; *Rayl v. E. Ohio Gas Co.*, 348 N.E.2d 385 (9th Dist.1973).]

Dormant Minerals Statutes

A **dormant minerals statute** is designed to permit the surface owner of a plot of land to recover mineral rights that have not been utilized by a purchaser of such rights for a long time, often a period of not less than 20 years. The use of such statutes has become more popular since landowners have become more aware of the lucrative contracts that can be negotiated for oil and gas rights as discussed earlier. Some dormant mineral rights statutes, those described as "use-it-or-lose-it" statutes, include provisions that assert that mineral rights revert to the original owner once the statutory time limit has passed and the mineral rights have not been exploited. The reversion in such statutes is inevitable, so the original owner need do nothing other than sit and wait for the clock to tick on. Other more strict statutes require a series of proactive stages on the part of the original owner to jump-start the statute's application to their land. These steps may include but are not limited to the following: the surface landowner must (1) serve notice by certified mail on the holders of the dormant mineral rights indicating the surface owner's intent to assert the rights available under the act or, if the holder cannot be found, publish notice of that intent, (2) check to see if the holder of the mineral rights has recorded any new agreements in the recorder's office that might affect the surface owner's intent to assert his or her rights, and (3) file a sworn statement of abandonment in the county recorder's office. Many older versions of dormant minerals statutes did not include oil and gas as minerals. This oversight has generally been remedied in most new statutes, which specifically include or exclude oil and gas deposits in their definitions of minerals. [See: Ilya Batikov, Kevin F. Eichner, Sheila Nolan Gartland, and Matthew W. Warnock, "Title Issues and Recent Cases Relating to Oil and Gas Developments in Ohio," Ohio State Bar Association Annual Conference, April 30 to May 2, 2014.]

quick quiz 30-3

1. A license is a limited contract that bestows no property rights on the licensee.	true	false
2. Lease agreements must adhere to all of the legal requirements for real property contracts.	true	false
3. A dormant minerals statute is designed to permit the surface owner of a plot of land to recover mineral rights that have not been used by a purchaser of such rights.	true	false

30-4 Acquiring Title to and Managing Real Property

Most of the time property owners, unless they are causing a nuisance of a danger to others, get to decide to use, manage, and transfer the title to their own property without undue interference from the government, except, of course, for the payment of taxes and fees. Sometimes, however, the government will decide how property will be used in certain parts of a city or town, and at other more extreme times, the government may actually confiscate property for the public good. Such governmental management is exercised through zoning ordinances and eminent domain.

Title to Real Property

Title to real property refers to the ownership of that property. Saying that someone has title to a piece of property is really just a quick way of saying that a person has the evidence needed to demonstrate that he or she is entitled to possess, use, and convey that property to another. Title to real property may be acquired by sale or gift, will or descent, or by neglect.

Title by Sale or Gift

Ownership and title to real property are most frequently transferred from one owner to another by sale or by gift. This action is done by transferring a written instrument called *a deed*. The person transferring title is the grantor. The person to whom the title is transferred is the grantee. A deed becomes effective when it is delivered to the grantee. A deed to real property may be bestowed as a gift from the owner or through a sale. In the case of a gift, consideration is not given by the grantee for the deed. There are four types of deeds:

1. General warranty deed.
2. Special warranty deed.
3. Bargain-and-sale deed.
4. Quitclaim deed.

A house deed is one example of a title to real property.

General Warranty Deed A general warranty deed, sometimes called a *full covenant and warranty deed,* contains express warranties under which the grantor guarantees the property to be free of encumbrances created by the grantor or by others who had title previously. It is the most desirable form of deed from the point of view of the grantee because it warrants (gives assurances) that title is good.

Special Warranty Deed A special warranty deed contains express warranties under which the grantor guarantees that no title defect arose during the time that the grantor owned the property, but not otherwise. No warranties are made as to defects that arose *before* the grantor owned the property.

EXAMPLE 30-8: Special Warranty Deed

Grant sold a vacant lot to Tuttle. The lot had been left to Grant through the will of a distant relative. Grant had never had the title searched, but she could guarantee Tuttle that no liens or claims against the property had been created since she inherited the property. Grant would be safe in granting title under a special warranty deed. The buyer would be protected only by making a title search that would disclose claims not covered by the seller's warranty.

Bargain-and-Sale Deed A bargain-and-sale deed is one that transfers title to property but contains no warranties. The form of the deed is the same as that of a warranty deed except that the warranties are omitted. Because a sale necessarily involves the idea of a valuable consideration, this type of deed is not valid without consideration. It could not be used to convey a gift of real property.

Quitclaim Deed A quitclaim deed (also called a *deed without covenants*) transfers to the buyer only the interest that the seller may have in a property. This type of deed merely releases a party's rights to the property. It contains no warranties. It is used when the seller gives up some right in the property, such as an easement or dower and courtesy, or to cure a defect in the chain of title.

Title by Will or Descent

When people die owning real property solely in their own name or with others as tenants in common, title passes to their heirs at the moment of death. If they die with a will, title passes to the people named in the will. If they die without a will, title passes to the heirs, as tenants in common, according to the laws of intestacy. A deed is not used when title passes to heirs in this manner. Instead, the records of the probate court establish title to the property. A deed may be used, however, by the personal representative of an estate to transfer title to real property to another. This transfer may be done in many states by authority granted in a will or by a license issued by the court.

Title by Adverse Possession Title to real property may be obtained by taking actual possession of the property openly, notoriously, exclusively, under a claim of right, and continuously for a period of time set by state statute. This method of obtaining title to real property is called adverse possession. To establish such ownership rights, claimants must prove the following:

- They have had continuous use of the property for 20 years (or a period set by state statute).
- This use has been without interruption by the owner.
- It was without the owner's permission.
- It was with the owner's knowledge.

Proof of these facts in court will give a person superior rights over the one in whose name a deed is recorded. A court of equity has the power to declare the one claiming under adverse possession to be the new owner.

EXAMPLE 30-9: Adverse Possession

Wilhelm and Kupersmith were next-door neighbors. Not realizing where the true property line was, Wilhelm built a garage and driveway two feet onto Kupersmith's land. He used the garage and driveway continuously, with Kupersmith's knowledge, for the next 22 years. The error was discovered when Kupersmith sold her property to a new owner, who had it surveyed. Wilhelm, through court action, was able to obtain title to the land on which the garage and driveway were located by adverse possession.

Governmental Management of Real Property

Thomas Jefferson once said that "the care of human life and happiness, and not their destruction, is the first and only legitimate object of good government." Ideally, the governmental management of real property should promote the "care of human life and happiness." Zoning laws, on the surface at least, have as their purpose the regulation, limitation, and planning of real property for the good of the entire society. Eminent domain goes a step further declaring that there are some instances in which the "care of human life and happiness" demands the confiscation of one person's property for the preservation and the promotion of the general good.

Zoning Laws Municipal zoning laws regulate the uses that may be made of properties within specified geographical areas or districts. Residential zoning prohibits properties from being used for commercial purposes within a given area. Multifamily zoning permits construction of apartment buildings. Limited-commercial zoning allows the construction of small stores but restricts the building of large shopping malls and commercial centers. Industrial zoning allows the building of factories, and agricultural zoning allows farming in a particular area. Zoning laws help keep property values from declining and protect against the undesirable use of neighboring property.

Newly passed zoning laws do not apply to existing uses of the land. Such uses are called **nonconforming uses** if they are not allowed under the new zoning law. They may continue in existence but may not be enlarged or changed in kind. By appeal to the local zoning board, variances may be given to individuals or businesses when justified and reasonable. A **variance** is an exemption or exception that permits a use that differs from those allowed under the existing ordinance. Variances are granted in special circumstances to protect property owners who might otherwise suffer a hardship if zoning laws were applied and enforced arbitrarily. Decisions of a local zoning commission may be appealed to county commissioners, a county court, or the highest court in the state.

Eminent Domain   All ownership of private property is subject to the government's superior rights if property is needed for a public purpose. **Eminent domain**, also called **condemnation**, is the right of federal, state, and local governments, or other public bodies, to take private lands, with compensation to their owners, for a public purpose. The right is

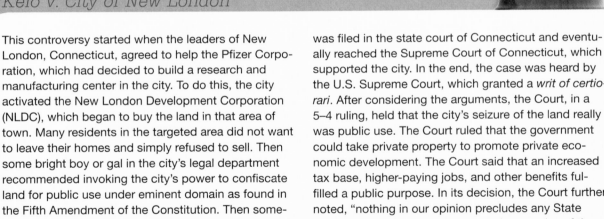

CLASSIC CASE Eminent Domain and All the King's Men: *Kelo v. City of New London*

This controversy started when the leaders of New London, Connecticut, agreed to help the Pfizer Corporation, which had decided to build a research and manufacturing center in the city. To do this, the city activated the New London Development Corporation (NLDC), which began to buy the land in that area of town. Many residents in the targeted area did not want to leave their homes and simply refused to sell. Then some bright boy or gal in the city's legal department recommended invoking the city's power to confiscate land for public use under eminent domain as found in the Fifth Amendment of the Constitution. Then somebody else in the city's legal department discovered that the power to exercise eminent domain in economic development situations was granted to the city by a Connecticut statute. A homeowner named Susette Kelo, along with several other owners, sued to end the unconstitutional seizure of their property. The homeowners argued that the taking of their land for private development purposes did not fall under the heading of "public use" as visualized by the Framers when they wrote the Fifth Amendment. The property owners also argued in the alternative that, even if the annexation of their property did qualify as public use, the city had to prove with "reasonable certainty" that the appropriation of their land really would result in the public benefits predicted by the development corporation. The suit

was filed in the state court of Connecticut and eventually reached the Supreme Court of Connecticut, which supported the city. In the end, the case was heard by the U.S. Supreme Court, which granted a *writ of certiorari*. After considering the arguments, the Court, in a 5–4 ruling, held that the city's seizure of the land really was public use. The Court ruled that the government could take private property to promote private economic development. The Court said that an increased tax base, higher-paying jobs, and other benefits fulfilled a public purpose. In its decision, the Court further noted, "nothing in our opinion precludes any State from placing further restrictions on its exercise of the takings power." Within two years after the unpopular decision in the *Kelo* case, more than 80 percent of U.S. states changed their laws on the subject, making it more difficult to take private property by eminent domain. Some states, including Florida, have taken a broad approach, such as forbidding the use of eminent domain for any kind of private development. Others, including Missouri, have made guarded changes, such as not allowing farmland to be classified as "blighted." In 2007, the New Jersey high court held that before invoking eminent domain, a municipality must prove a site is truly "blighted," not simply "not fully productive."[See: *Kelo v. City of New London,* 125 S. Ct . 2655 (U.S. Supreme Court).]

exercised for such purposes as new highway construction, public parks, and state hospitals, as well as to reinvigorate depressed areas.

Eminent domain is at times extended to public utilities when it can be shown that denial of a right of way for electric, telephone, gas, or other lines may interrupt construction of installations that provide needed services to an entire community. When private property is taken by eminent domain proceedings, the owner must be paid the fair value of what has been taken. The owner is not required to accept an amount offered by those assessing the value of the property. In fact, homeowners can also contest the government's decision to take their land, when they have reason to believe that the "taking' is not really for public purposes but is actual for private profit. This is precisely what happened in the classic *Kelo* case.

quick quiz 30-4

1. Title to real property may be acquired by sale or gift, will or ,descent, or by neglect.	true | false
2. Municipal zoning laws that regulate the uses that may be made of properties within specified geographical areas or districts have been declared unconstitutional.	true | false
3. Eminent domain is the right of federal, state, and local ,governments, or other public bodies, to take private lands, with compensation to their owners, for a public purpose.	true | false

30-5 The Landlord–Tenant Relationship

The landlord–tenant relationship is a contractual arrangement in which the owner of real property allows another to have temporary possession and control of the premises in exchange for consideration. The agreement that gives rise to the landlord–tenant relationship is called a lease. The property owner who gives the lease is the lessor or landlord, and the person to whom the lease is given is the lessee or tenant. Five elements are necessary for the creation of a landlord–tenant relationship:

1. Consent of the landlord to the occupancy by the tenant.
2. Transfer of possession and control of the property to the tenant in an inferior position (in subordination) to the rights of the landlord.
3. The right by the landlord to the return of the property, called the right of reversion.
4. The creation of an ownership interest in the tenant known as a leasehold estate.
5. Either an express or implied contract between the parties that satisfies all the essentials of a valid contract (mutual assent, capacity, consideration, legality).

Although rent is usually paid by the tenant to the landlord for the arrangement, it is not essential to the creation of the landlord–tenant relationship.

Leasing versus Other Relationships

Sometimes people confuse leasing with other relationships that are similar but convey different rights and, therefore, limit certain activities that would be permissible under a leasing arrangement. The two most common relationships that may be compared with the landlord–tenant relationship are licensing and lodging.

Leasing Compared with Licensing A lease differs from a license in that a lease gives an interest in real property and transfers possession, whereas a **license** gives no property right or ownership interest in the property but merely allows the licensee to do certain acts that would otherwise be a trespass.

EXAMPLE 30-10: License Rather than Lease

The city of Topeka was given a gift of 80 acres of land for use as a public park by the heirs of Guilford G. Gage. The deed signed by the heirs contained a condition that the property would revert to them if the property were ever deeded or leased to a third party. After the park was established, the city granted the exclusive right to McCall to construct and operate, for a period of five years, a miniature train on the premises. Under the agreement, McCall was subject in virtually all respects to the control of the city, and either party could terminate the arrangement by giving 30 days' notice. The heirs of Gage claimed that the transaction was a lease and that the property should be returned to them. In holding that McCall had a license rather than a lease, the court said that all McCall had was "the exclusive right to operate as the City may dictate."

Because a license confers a personal privilege to act and not a present possessory estate, it does not run with the land and is usually not transferable. It may be made orally or in writing and may be given without consideration. In addition, a license need not delineate the specific space to be occupied. In contrast, a lease gives the tenant exclusive possession of the premises as against all the world, including the owner. It describes the exact property leased and states the term of the tenancy and the rent to be paid. In addition, in some states, a lease must be in writing. Permission to sell Christmas trees at a gas station, to hold dance parties in a hall, and to place a sign on the outside of a building have all been held to be licenses rather than leases.

Leasing Compared with Lodging A **lodger** is one who has the use of property without actual or exclusive possession of it. A lodger is a type of licensee, with a mere right to use the property. The landlord retains control of the premises and is responsible for its care and upkeep. Unlike a tenant, a lodger has no right to bring suit for trespass or to eject an intruder from the premises. One who lives in a spare room of a house, for example, whose owner retains direct control and supervision of the entire house, is a lodger.

Types of Leasehold Interests

The interest conveyed by a lease is called a **leasehold estate** or a **tenancy**. There are four kinds of leasehold estates:

1. Tenancy at will.
2. Tenancy for years.
3. Periodic tenancy.
4. Tenancy at sufferance.

Tenancy at Will A **tenancy at will** is an ownership interest (estate) in real property for an indefinite period of time. No writing is required to create this tenancy, and it may be terminated at the will of either party by giving proper notice. The notice requirement to terminate a tenancy at will varies from state to state. It ranges from the time between rent periods to 30 days' written notice from the next day that rent is due. The rule generally followed in this country is that a tenancy at will comes to an end when the property is sold by the landlord to a third party. The notice required by state law must be given to the tenant in any event.

Tenancy for Years A tenancy for years is an ownership interest (estate) in real property for a definite or fixed period of time. It may be for one week, six months, one year, five years, 99 years, or any period of time, as long as it is definite. Such a tenancy automatically terminates on the expiration of the stated term. A tenancy for 100 years or more creates an estate in fee simple, transferring absolute ownership to the tenant. For this reason, leases are sometimes written for 99-year periods. In some states, a tenancy for years may be oral if the term is shorter than one year; otherwise, it must be in writing. Other states require all tenancies for years to be in writing. A tenant who remains in possession of the premises at the expiration of the term with permission of the landlord, but without a new lease, is a tenant at will in some states. In other states, such a tenant is known as a periodic tenant.

Periodic Tenancy A periodic tenancy, which is also known as a tenancy from year to year (or month to month or week to week), is a fixed-period tenancy that continues for successive periods until one of the parties terminates it by giving notice to the other party. Unless the landlord or tenant gives advance notice of an intention to terminate the lease, it will be automatically renewed at the end of each fixed period for the same term. Advance notice varies from state to state, but it generally is defined as a period of three months for periodic tenancies of one year or longer and "one period" for periodic terms of less than a year. The death of a tenant who holds a periodic tenancy does not terminate the tenancy. Rather, the interest of the tenant passes to the personal representative of the deceased's estate. A periodic tenancy may be created impliedly by a landlord accepting rent from a tenant for years whose lease has expired or who is wrongfully in possession. Some states treat the latter situation as a tenancy at will.

Tenancy at Sufferance A tenancy at sufferance arises when tenants wrongfully remain in possession of the premises after their tenancy has expired. It often comes about at the expiration of the term of a tenancy for years or when a tenancy at will has been properly terminated and the tenant remains in possession. Such a tenant is a wrongdoer, having no estate or other interest in the property. A tenant at sufferance is not entitled to notice to vacate and is liable to pay rent for the period of occupancy. A periodic tenancy or a tenancy at will may come about, however, instead of a tenancy at sufferance if a landlord accepts rent from a tenant whose tenancy has expired.

The Lease Agreement

The agreement between a lessor and a lessee, called a lease, creates the landlord–tenant relationship. It provides the tenant with exclusive possession and control of the real property of the landlord. Because the lease is a contract, the general rules of contract law apply to it. The essential requirements of a lease are: (1) a definite agreement as to the extent and bounds of the leased property, (2) a definite and agreed term, and (3) a definite and agreed price of rental and manner of payment (see Figure 30-1).

Rent Control Some large communities have passed rent control laws to keep rents within an affordable range. These laws limit what landlords can charge for rental property and often contain procedures that must be followed before tenants may be

LEASE

This lease made the 20th day of August, 2017, between ROBERT VICKERS, herein called Landlord, and ETHEL LOPAZ, herein called Tenant, witnesseth:

The Landlord leases to the Tenant the following described premises: Four rooms and a bath on the first floor of the premises located at 17 Rosebud Terrace, Ashmont, New Hampshire, for the term of one year commencing at noon on the first day of September 2017 and ending at noon on the 31st day of August, 2017.

The Tenant agrees to pay to the Landlord the sum of $6,000 for the said term, in eleven (11) monthly payments as follows: The first and last months' rent of $1,000, plus a security deposit of $500, payable on September 1, 2017, and $500 on the first day of each month thereafter.

The Landlord agrees that the Tenant on paying the said rent and performing the covenants herein contained shall peaceably and quietly have, hold, and enjoy the premises for said term.

The Tenant agrees that at the expiration of the time mentioned in this lease she will give peaceable possession of the said premises to the Landlord in as good a condition as they now are, the usual wear, unavoidable accidents, and loss by fire excepted, and will not make or suffer any waste thereof, nor assign this lease, nor sublet, nor permit any person to occupy the same, nor make or suffer to be made any alteration therein, without the consent of the Landlord in writing having first been obtained, and that the Landlord may enter to view and make improvements, and to show the premises to prospective tenants or purchasers.

The covenants herein shall extend to and be binding upon heirs, executors, and administrators of the parties to this lease.

IN WITNESS WHEREOF, the parties have hereunto set their hands and seals the day and year first above written.

Robert Vickers
Robert Vickers

Ethel Lopaz
Ethel Lopaz

Figure 30-1   This is an example of a lease.

evicted. In a number of areas, rent control laws have caused landlords to turn their apartments into condominiums, leading to shortages in rental apartments. Such laws differ from place to place. Some states, including Massachusetts, have done away with rent control laws.

Security Deposits In addition to the first month's rent, landlords often require either a security deposit or the last month's rent, or both, to be paid at the beginning of a tenancy. The deposit protects landlords against damages to their property as well as nonpayment of rent. Due to abuses of such deposits by landlords, state legislatures have passed laws regulating security deposits on residential property. Such laws spell out the rights of tenants and make it easier for tenants to prevail in court. Although these laws differ from state to state, most states limit security deposits to one, one and one-half, two, or two and one-half months' rent, and most states require that security deposits be placed in interest-bearing accounts. The interest is either paid to tenants on an annual basis or accrued in their favor. Security deposits may not be commingled with other money belonging to the landlord. Also, the landlord is given a specific period, usually 30 days after the lease ends, to account for the security deposit and return the balance due to a tenant. Many states have now "put teeth" into the law, providing for double or triple damages, court costs, and attorney's fees for tenants whose security deposits are wrongfully withheld.

EXAMPLE 30-11: Double Damages

Santos rented a $450-per-month apartment from Hollis for a term of two years. When Santos's tenancy ended, Hollis refused to return any of the $450 security deposit to Santos, claiming that the damages to the apartment fully offset the amount of the deposit. Santos hired a lawyer, who brought suit against Hollis. The landlord was able to demonstrate only $70 in damages to Santos's apartment. The court found that Hollis had wrongfully withheld $380 of Santos's security deposit. The court awarded Santos a judgment for double damages of $760 plus attorney's fees of $200. With court costs, the landlord was forced to pay over $1,000.

Option to Renew or to Purchase Many leases contain a provision allowing the lessee to have the option to renew the lease for one or more additional periods. An option to renew gives the lessee the right, at the end of the lease, to a new lease for an additional period. The new lease is on the same terms as the old one, with the possible exception of an increase in the rent. To exercise the option, the lessee must notify the lessor on or before the date set forth in the lease to do so. A lessee may, if the lease so provides, be given an option to purchase the property. This option is an agreement by the lessor to sell the property to the lessee for a stated price. To exercise the option, the lessee must notify the lessor, within the time period stated in the lease, of the decision to purchase the property.

EXAMPLE 30-12: Option to Purchase

Larson purchased a parcel of real property for $191,140 and leased it to the Panhandle Rehabilitation Center. The lease was for 10 years and contained an option to buy for $200,000. After leasing the premises for five years and spending $25,000 to improve it, Panhandle notified Larson of its intention to exercise its option. By this time, the property was worth $238,000. Larson refused to sell the property to Panhandle for $200,000. The court ordered her to do so.

Assignment and Subletting An assignment of a lease occurs when the interest in the leased premises is transferred by the lessee to another person for the balance of the term of the lease. The new party, called the *assignee*, steps into the shoes of the tenant, or assignor, and is liable for all of the original tenant's obligations and entitled to all the original tenant's rights under the lease. In contrast, it is called a sublease or underlease if the transfer is for a part of the term but not for the remainder of it. A lease may be assigned or sublet unless the lease states otherwise. Many leases are written so that they require landlord approval for an assignment or a sublease. However, in some states, the landlord cannot withhold such approval unreasonably. An assignment or sublease will be held valid if the landlord accepts rent over a period of time from either an assignee or a subtenant.

quick quiz 30-5

1. A license is just like a lease because it bestows upon the licensee the same type of property rights and ownership interests as those bestowed on a party with a lease. true | false

2. A tenancy at will is an ownership interest (estate) in real property for a definite period of time. true | false

3. An option to renew gives the lessee the right, at the end of the lease, to a new lease for an additional period. true | false

30-6 Duties of the Landlord and the Tenant

Like most of the legal relationships that we have examined in the book thus far, the landlord–tenant relationship is a balancing act that offsets the rights of one side against the duties of the other. In this case the rights are inherent within the very nature of the landlord–tenant relationship. The tenant is given the right to have temporary possession of the premises and the landlord has the right to receive consideration. The duties, in contrast, are not quite that clear.

Landlords must ensure that the property they rent out to tenants is habitable.

The Landlord's Duties

A good lease agreement will carefully spell out the respective rights and duties of the landlord and the tenant. However, state and local laws may restrict or expand upon what is set forth in the lease.

Duty to Refrain from Discrimination A landlord may not discriminate in selecting tenants on the grounds of race, creed, color, national origin, or gender. In most states, a landlord may restrict rentals to persons without children but may not restrict a married couple's freedom to bear children during the leasehold. It is permissible, however, for a landlord to set up a housing complex that is open only to people 62 years of age and older and not run counter to age discrimination prohibitions. Although not directly applicable to a lease agreement, the Americans with Disabilities Act does require that owners of public accommodations such as motels and hotels have handicapped accessibility.

Duty to Maintain the Premises When real property is rented for dwelling purposes, there is an implied warranty, called the **warranty of habitability**, that the premises are fit for human habitation. This provision

means that the landlord warrants there are no defects vital to the use of the premises for residential purposes. Examples of defects are unsafe electrical wiring, a malfunctioning heating or cooling system, broken windows, a leaking roof, and infestation of insects. Many municipalities have adopted ordinances to protect tenants from unsafe or unhealthy conditions created by a landlord's refusal to make necessary repairs. Building inspectors, health authorities, and other public officials are empowered to make inspections and demand improvements when they are contacted by dissatisfied tenants. In many cases, ordinances permit the tenant to cease payment of rent for the period during which the landlord fails to make the repairs or improvements needed. The majority of states hold that a landlord has a duty to clear common entryways of natural accumulations of snow and ice. Some states, nevertheless, still follow the older rule that the landlord owes no duty to tenants to clean common entryways of ice and snow unless there is an agreement on the part of the landlord to do so.

Duty to Deliver Peaceful Possession
The tenant is entitled to the exclusive peaceful possession and quiet enjoyment of the rental premises. **Quiet enjoyment** is the right of a tenant to the undisturbed possession of the property. The landlord may not interfere with the tenant's rights of possession as long as the tenant abides by the conditions of the lease and those imposed by law.

EXAMPLE 30-13: Breach of Quiet Enjoyment

Smith Grocery & Variety, Inc., leased one store in a two-store mall from Northern Terminals, Inc. The lease entitled Smith to the use of the parking areas (between 14 and 20 spaces) abutting the leased premises. Five months after Smith opened for business, Northern Terminals added an additional store to the mall without increasing the mall's parking facilities. Smith's business declined due to the severe parking shortage caused by the opening of a Triple-S Blue Stamp Redemption Center in the new addition. The court held that Northern Terminals, Inc., breached the covenant of quiet enjoyment. There was a substantial interference with the lessee's use of the premises, which was caused by the lessor's taking away of the parking spaces.

The right to exclusive possession by the tenant makes the landlord a trespasser should there be any unauthorized entry by the landlord into the rented premises.

EXAMPLE 30-14: Trespass

Benson & Childs rented a skylight suite for their architecture offices. The lease gave the owner permission to enter only when a request had been made or in the event of extreme emergency. The landlord entered the offices late one evening for what he termed was his regular safety and fire inspection. Benson & Childs may treat the landlord's trespass as a breach of their right to sole possession, giving them the right to terminate the lease and charge the landlord in either a civil or a criminal complaint.

A tenant who is wrongfully evicted is not required to return and may consider the lease as ended. An **eviction** is an act of the landlord that deprives the tenant of the enjoyment of the premises. It is called an **actual eviction** when the tenant is physically deprived of the leasehold. When the tenant is deprived of something of a substantial nature that was called for under the lease, it is termed a **constructive eviction**. The tenant is justified in abandoning the premises without paying rent when a wrongful eviction occurs. The tenant must mitigate (lessen) any damages, however, if possible.

EXAMPLE 30-15: Constructive Eviction

Sound City, U.S.A., was interested in renting space in a shopping center. An inspection of the premises disclosed portions of the ceiling tile missing or hanging loose, water marks on the ceiling, and bare fluorescent light fixtures. As a result, Sound City included in its one-year lease an addendum (addition), whereby the landlord agreed to repair and paint the ceiling tile, cover the lightbulb fixtures, panel the south wall, and erect a partition. Sound City moved into the shopping center, but after three months and many complaints, the repairs were never completed. It then moved out. The landlord brought suit for the remaining nine months' rent. The court held against the landlord, saying that there had been a constructive eviction. The physical appearance of the store was an important factor in the successful operation of Sound City's business. The failure to repair the premises properly in accordance with the lease rendered the premises unsuitable for the purpose for which they were rented.

The Tenant's Duties

The tenant has the duty to pay rent to the landlord. In addition, the landlord has the right to remove, through court procedures, a tenant for nonpayment of rent, disorderliness, or illegal or unpermitted use of the premises. A tenant has the duty to observe the valid restrictions contained in the lease. Leases may impose duties of all kinds as long as they are legal and do not deny a tenant's constitutional rights. Failure to abide by the restrictions agreed to at the time of the signing of the lease gives the landlord the right to seek the eviction of the tenant. Unless agreed otherwise, the tenant must turn over to the landlord all fixtures (except trade fixtures belonging to a business) that have been made a permanent part of the real property by the tenant during the leasehold. Tenants also have a duty to avoid damaging or destroying the property, that is, commit waste. **Waste** is defined as substantial damage to premises that significantly decreases the value of the property.

Tort Liability

When a person is injured on leased property, the one who is in control of the part of the premises where the injury occurs usually is responsible if the injury was caused by that person's negligence. The landlord, for example, is responsible for injury to others that may be caused by a defect in the common areas, such as hallways and stairways. Although landlords are not guarantors of the safety of persons in a building's common area, they are not free to ignore reasonably foreseeable risks of harm to tenants and others lawfully on the premises. Landlords must take reasonable steps to guard against foreseeable criminal acts of third parties.

Eviction Proceedings

States today do not allow landlords to use force to evict tenants. Instead, they must make use of statutory remedies that are available to them. Some states do, however, recognize the right of landlords to enter wrongfully held premises and take over possession if it can be done peacefully. **Ejectment** is the common law name given to the lawsuit brought by the landlord to have the tenant evicted from the premises. This older remedy is still available in many states; however, it is time consuming, expensive, and subject to long delays.

Unlawful detainer is a legal proceeding that provides landlords with a quick method of evicting a tenant. The proceeding is referred to by different names in different states, including the following: summary process, summary ejectment, forcible entry and detainer, and dispossessory warrant proceedings. The remedy provides landlords with a quick method of regaining possession of their property and protects tenants from being ousted by force and violence. Strict notice requirements must be followed by the landlord, after which both parties are given their day in court. If a forcible eviction becomes necessary, it is done by the sheriff under the supervision of the court.

quick quiz 30-6

1. A landlord may not discriminate in selecting tenants on the grounds of race, creed, color, national origin, or gender.   true | false

2. Tenants also have a duty to avoid damaging or destroying the property, that is, commit waste.   true | false

3. States today do not allow landlords to use force to evict tenants.   true | false

Summary

30.1 Real property is the ground and everything permanently attached to it. It includes the airspace above the surface to as high as the owner can use and the ground under the surface. Fixtures are personal property that are so permanently attached to real property that they become part of the real property. Easements give people the right to pass over another's land, to run wires through another's airspace, to drain water onto another's property, and to run pipes underneath another's ground. Easements run with the land.

30.2 An estate in fee simple is the greatest interest that one can have in real property. It descends to one's heirs upon death and can be disposed of in any manner during one's lifetime. In contrast, a life estate lasts only for someone's life. People may own real property individually or with others. When two or more people own real property as tenants in common, the interest of a deceased owner's share passes to the heirs upon death. In contrast, when two or more people own real property as joint tenants or tenants by the entirety, the interest of the deceased owner's share passes to any other cotenants upon death.

30.3 Subterranean rights are sold to corporations exploring for coal, oil, or other mineral deposits. States differ on how they characterize a contract involving subterranean rights especially as those rights relate to the extraction of gas, oil, and other minerals. Some states are quite unequivocal in declaring that a contact for oil and gas rights is neither a license nor a lease, but is instead a fee simple determinable. Other states characterize oil and gas contracts as real property, lease agreements, and others as a simple license. Some courts manage to mix and match a lease with a fee simple determinable. There are some states that seem unable to make up their minds. A dormant minerals statute is designed to permit the surface owner of a plot of land to recover mineral rights that have not been used by a purchaser of such rights for a long period as specified in the statute, often not less than 20 years.

30.4 A deed is used to transfer real property by sale or gift. The records of the probate court, instead of a deed, establish title to property when an owner dies. Title to real property may also be gained by adverse possession. Zoning laws regulate the uses that may be made of properties within specified geographical areas. Eminent domain is the right of federal, state, and local governments, or other public bodies, to take private lands for a public purpose. Owners must be paid the fair value of the property taken.

30.5 The landlord tenant relationship is a contractual arrangement whereby the owner of real property allows another to have temporary possession and control of the premises in exchange for consideration.

A lease is different from a license and from an agreement with a lodger. A tenancy at will is an ownership interest (estate) in real property for an indefinite period of time. A tenancy for years is an estate for a definite period of time, no matter how long or how short. A periodic tenancy is a tenancy that continues for successive periods until one of the parties terminates it by giving notice to the other party. A tenancy at sufferance arises when tenants wrongfully remain in possession of the premises after their tenancy has expired. A lease creates the landlord–tenant relationship. Because it is a contract, the general rules of contract law apply to it.

30.6 A landlord may not discriminate in selecting tenants on the grounds of race, creed, color, or gender. Landlords have the right to evict tenants for nonpayment of rent, disorderliness, and unpermitted use of the premises. Tenants must observe the valid restrictions in a lease and not commit waste. When someone is injured, the person in control of that part of the premises where the injury occurs is responsible if negligent. Peaceable entry, ejectment, and unlawful detainer are the principal methods available to landlords to regain possession of their premises.

Key Terms

actual eviction, 748

adverse possession, 740

bargain-and-sale deed, 739

community property, 733

concurrent ownership, 732

constructive eviction, 749

condemnation, 741

co-ownership, 732

cotenants, 732

dominant tenement, 729

dormant minerals statute, 737

easement, 729

easement by grant, 729

easement by prescription, 729

easement by reservation, 729

ejectment, 749

eminent domain, 741

estate in fee simple, 731

eviction, 748

fee simple determinable, 736

fracking, 735

freehold estates, 731

general warranty deed, 739

grantee, 739

grantor, 739

joint tenants, 732

landlord, 742

lease, 736

leasehold estate, 743

lessee, 736

lessor, 736

license, 736

life estate, 731

lodger, 743

navigable airspace, 728

nonconforming uses, 741

periodic tenancy, 744

quiet enjoyment, 748

quitclaim deed, 739

real estate, 727

real property, 727

remainder estate, 731

reversion estate, 731

right of way, 729

riparian owners, 728

servient tenement, 729

severalty, 732

special warranty deed, 739

sublease, 747

subterranean rights, 735

tenancy, 743

tenancy at sufferance, 744

tenancy by the entirety, 733

tenancy at will, 743

tenancy for years, 744

tenancy from year to year, 744

tenant, 742

tenants in common, 732

trade fixtures, 729

underlease, 746

unlawful detainer, 750

variance, 741

warranty of habitability, 747

waste, 749

zoning laws, 740

Questions for Review and Discussion

1. What constitutes real property?
2. What is the difference between freehold and leasehold estates?
3. What are the different types of co-ownership of real property?

4. What are the methods of transferring oil and gas rights?
5. What is the goal of the dormant minerals act?
6. What is eminent domain?
7. What are the methods of acquiring title to real property?
8. What are the five elements necessary to create a landlord–tenant relationship?
9. What are the essential requirements of a lease?
10. What are the duties of landlords and tenants?

Cases for Analysis

1. Aloi sold a section of her land to Bell, including in the deed an easement allowing Bell to cross Aloi's property to reach the newly acquired parcel. Three years later, Aloi sold his property to Cadd. Shortly thereafter, following an argument, Cadd put a chain across Bell's right of way, saying that he had not given permission for Bell to cross his land. How should the court rule on this case and why?

2. Alfonso DiFilippo and his brother, Pasquale, owned a parcel of real property as tenants in common. Pasquale died in 1961, leaving a life ,estate in the property to his widow, Annie, with the remainder estate when Annie dies to Alfonso. Annie died in 1985. Alfonso died in 1969, leaving his interest in the property to his wife, Maria. What interest did Maria own in the property when she died in 1981? [See: *DiFilippo v. DiFilippo*, 640 N.E.2d 1120 (MA).]

3. When its lease expired, Kingston Frameworks made plans to move to another building. Preparations were made to remove shelving, mat and glass cutters, display boards, benches, and other fixtures that had been built into the store when the lease first started. All the shelves and fixtures were specially designed for the picture-framing business. The landlord told the owners of Kingston Frameworks to stop removing the items from the property. Could they remove the shelves and other fixtures that were paid for and installed by them during their tenancy? Why or why not? [See: *George v. Town of Calais*, 373 A.2d 553 (VT).]

4. Smith and Dudley are next-door neighbors. The branches of a large maple tree on Smith's property hang over Dudley's driveway, dripping sap onto Dudley's car. Smith refuses to trim the branches overhanging Dudley's driveway, saying that she does not want to spoil the beauty of the tree. What are Dudley's legal rights in this situation?

5. Two years after Jean Russell was divorced from Billy Russell, Jean signed a quitclaim deed conveying her interest in their jointly owned real property to Billy. Later, she tried to have the deed set aside on the ground that Billy gave her no consideration. Was she successful? Why or why not? [See: *Russell v. Russell*, 361 So.2d 1053 (AL).]

6. Bech owned a building in which Cuevas resided as a tenant at will. Alleging that Cuevas had committed waste, Bech delivered a letter to Cuevas ordering her to vacate the premises in two days. The law of that state required 30-day notice to evict a tenant at will. Must Cuevas vacate the premises? Explain. [See: *Bech v. Cuevas*, 534 N.E.2d 1163 (MA).]

7. The following language was in a handwritten agreement signed by Harold and Saul and their respective wives: "Saul & Zelda get the option to rent the lower level of the Hope Chest store when their lease expires. If they do take it, they will pay the same rate of rent per square foot that Harold is paying for his store. Saul & Zelda will do all the fixing up at their expense. Entrance to upper level has to be maintained from Newbury Street—similar to how it is now. Saul and Zelda have to let Harold know six months ahead of time: (lease expires by May 31, 1987, so that Saul and Zelda have to let Harold know by Nov. 31, 1986). Saul and Zelda cannot use the name Simon or Simon's or anything with the Simon name as a name for their store. Too confusing." Does the language contain the essential elements of a lease? Explain. [See: *Simon v. Simon*, 625 N.E.2d 564 (MA).]

8. Goldstein rented an apartment from Dunbar as a tenant at will. She paid her rent on time and took good care of the premises; she was never disorderly. Dunbar decided to evict Goldstein and rent the apartment to a college friend who was moving to the area. He sent Goldstein a proper notice to quit. Goldstein claimed that she could not be asked to leave because she had done nothing wrong. Do you agree with Goldstein? Explain. [See: *Ralo, Inc., v. Jack Graham, Inc.*, 362 So.2d 310 (FL).]

9. Sarah H. Brown and Sandy F. Soverow agreed to rent separate apartments from Osborn, the owner of an apartment complex called Nob Hill Apartments, which was being constructed. Because their single apartments were not yet completed, Brown and Soverow agreed to rent one larger apartment in the complex and live in that until their separate apartments were finished. A fire occurred in the apartment shortly after Brown put some leftover liver and gizzards for her dogs on the electric stove and left the apartment. In the lawsuit that followed, the contention was made that Brown and Soverow were lodgers rather than tenants. Do you agree with the contention? Explain. [See: *Osborn v. Brown*, 361 So.2d 82 (AL).]

10. Alabama Outdoor Advertising Co., Inc., leased part of a lot from All State Linen Service Co. to erect a commercial advertising sign. The term of the lease was for "indefinite years, beginning 1st day of January, 1973, and ending year to year thereafter." When All State sold the lot, it was argued that Alabama's lease was a tenancy at will and therefore came to an end when the lot was sold. Do you agree with this argument? Why or why not? [See: *Industrial Mach., Inc., v. Creative Displays, Inc.*, 344 So.2d 743 (AL).]

quick quiz Answers

30-1	30-2	30-3	30-4	30-5	30-6
1. F	1. F	1. T	1. T	1. F	1. T
2. T	2. T	2. T	2. F	2. F	2. T
3. T	3. T	3. T	3. T	3. T	3. T

Chapter 31 — Wills, Trusts, and Advanced Directives

THE OPENING CASE *Round 1*

Windsor v. United States: A Landmark Case in ~~Domestic Relations~~ Law

More often than not, when the U.S. Supreme Court hears a case, that case involves some sort of abstract and academic issue, such as the establishment of a defendant's rights in court, the constitutionality of an anti-flag-burning statute, or the legality of American prisoner of war tribunals on foreign shores. Sometimes, however, even the Supreme Court must delve into matters that are generally seen as domestic, in-house, private matters, like, well, marriage. An example is the dispute in *Windsor v. United States*. This controversy started when an aging couple returned to their home in New York City after having been married in Ontario, Canada. Like Canada, the State of New York recognizes the legal validity of same sex marriages. That was not the trouble in this situation. The real trouble began when one of the two spouses, Thea Spyer, passed away and left her entire estate to the surviving spouse, Edith Windsor. In filing her federal income tax return, as required by law, Windsor characterized the inheritance as an exemption. Unfortunately, the Internal Revenue Service disallowed the exemption and demanded an estate tax payment of $363,053, arguing that Windsor was not really Spyer's spouse. The IRS based its claim on Section 3 of the federal Defense of Marriage Act (DOMA), which states that "In determining the meaning of any Act of Congress, or of any

ruling, regulation, or interpretation of the various administrative bureaus and agencies of the United States, the word 'marriage' means only a legal union between one man and one woman as husband and wife and the word 'spouse' refers only to a person of the opposite sex who is a husband or a wife." Since Windsor's Canadian marriage to Spyer was a union between two women, the IRS disallowed the exemption. Although this provision in DOMA does not stop a state (or, obviously, any foreign nation) from doing what it pleases in relation to the legality of same sex marriage, it does forbid any federal recognition of those marriages, which is what happened here. As a good citizen, Windsor dutifully paid the estate tax in full. However, she then filed a lawsuit against the United States, arguing Section 3 of DOMA is an unconstitutional deprivation of equal protection and due process under the Fifth Amendment of the Constitution, and asking for a return of that payment. It was at that point that the case became interesting (as if it were not interesting enough already). The Department of Justice informed Congress that it no longer felt comfortable defending the constitutionality of Section 3 and it would not do so in this case. Consequently, the Bipartisan Legal Advisory Group (BLAG) of the House of Representatives became involved in the case to defend DOMA. Ultimately, the Supreme Court ruled that Section 3 of DOMA is, indeed, an unconstitutional violation of equal protection and due process. The implications of this ruling were quite wide ranging at the time, and had a critically important impact on estate and trust planning. Read on to find out why and then read the Obergefell v. Hodges Case at the End of Part 8 to see how that case redirected most everything related to these issues. If that is not enough for you, read the dissents in Obergefell and see why the controversy continues. Read on to find out why. [See: *Windsor v. United States,* 570 U.S.___, 133 S.Ct. 2675, 186 L.Ed.2d 808 (2013).]

Opening Case Questions

1. Why did the Department of Justice refuse to participate in the case? Explain.

2. Why did the plaintiff decide to bring a lawsuit even after paying her estate tax? Explain.

3. All Supreme Court cases must involve an authentic controversy with parties that have a stake in the outcome. What legitimate stake in the outcome of this case can the Bipartisan Legal Advisory Group claim to have (if any)? Explain.

4. What areas of the law are affected by this ruling? Explain.

5. Read the Obergefell Case at the end of Part 8. How does the Obergefell Case impact the Windsor Case? (Or does it?) Explain.

 Learning Objectives

1. Give details about the sources of probate law and its relevance to business entities.
2. Identify the formal requirements for executing a will.
3. Determine whether a person who makes a will has the capacity to do so.
4. Explain how the Supreme Court's ruling involving DOMA affected the law.
5. List the different methods of revoking or changing a will.
6. Outline the three grounds for contesting a will.
7. Describe who will inherit the property of someone who dies without a will.
8. Understand the steps to be taken by an executor or administrator in settling an estate.
9. Discuss the types and purposes of advance directives.
10. Differentiate among the various types of trusts and determine when they might be used.

31-1 Sources and Relevance of Probate Law

The term **probate** refers to the process of handling the will and the estate of a deceased person. Each state has its own laws passed by its legislature, different from other states, governing the writing of wills and the settling of estates. For this reason, it is necessary to check one's own state law to ascertain the rules for writing a will and to determine how property passes when someone dies. In an attempt to standardize and modernize the different state laws on this subject, the Uniform Probate Code (UPC) has been set up by the Uniform Law Commission (ULC), formerly the National Conference of Commissioners on Uniform State Laws, however, the UPC does not enjoy the popularity and universal applicability of other model laws created by the ULC such as the Uniform Commercial Code and the Revised Uniform Partnership Act, and so not all states have made it part of their law. This reluctance to act may be due to the fact that each state jealously guards its own way of handling the distribution of the estates of its own citizens and is, thus, hesitant to pitch all of that in favor of a uniform standard, which may or may not reflect the traditions of that state. Moreover, unlike commercial law, which cannot operate without crossing state lines, issues in probate law can often be handled without leaving a jurisdiction and, thus, need not fit as neatly into the network of interstate legal matters.

Relevance of Probate to Business

Because probate matters deal with the handling of people's estates, and because all businesses are owned by people in one way or another, the subject of probate law is relevant to all forms of business entities. When sole proprietors die, for example, the assets of their businesses pass to their heirs according to their states' probate laws. When owners of a corporation—that is, stockholders—die, their solely owned shares of stock pass to their heirs in a similar fashion.

Probate Terminology

It is not uncommon for people to prepare for possible future misfortune by making advance arrangements while they are still mentally and physically able to do so. One such advanced arrangement is the making of a will. A **will**, also called a **last will and testament**, is a formal document that governs the transfer of property at death. A person who dies with a will is said to die **testate**. A person who dies without a will is said to die **intestate**. The giving away of one's property by will is known as testamentary disposition. A person who makes a will is called a **testator** if a man or a **testatrix** if a woman. (The masculine forms of terms like *testator* are used for purposes of discussion here. They refer to people of either sex.) Personal property that is left by will is called a **bequest** or legacy, except in states that have adopted the Uniform Probate Code.

Real property that is left by will is known as a **devise**. Those who receive property by will are referred to as beneficiaries. They are also known as **legatees** if they receive personal property and **devisees** if they receive real property under a will. In states that have adopted the Uniform Probate Code, the term *devise* refers to both real and personal property, and the term *devisee* refers to a person who receives a gift of either real or personal property. The term **heir** is a broader term referring to a person who inherits property either under a will or from a person dying without a will. A **durable power of attorney** is a document authorizing another person to act on one's behalf with words stating that it is to either survive one's incapacity or become effective when one becomes debilitated. This authorization is not the same as an ordinary *power of attorney*, which would have questionable effect upon one's incapacity.

quick quiz 31-1

1. The Uniform Probate Code (UPC) has been adopted by all 50 states and Puerto Rico.	true	false
2. A person who dies without a will is said to die testate.	true	false
3. A person who makes a will is called a *testator* if a woman or a *testatrix* if a man.	true	false

31-2 The Law of Wills

President John F. Kennedy once said, "Our problems are man-made; therefore, they can be solved by man. For in the final analysis, our most common link is that we all inhabit this small planet; we all breathe the same air; we all cherish our children's future, and we are all mortal." Kennedy was correct. As human beings we do cherish our children's future and we are all mortal. There is little we can do about the second proposition. However, the law of wills does give us some control over the first. As long as we are willing to follow the conditions set down by the law of wills, we should be able to transfer a good portion of our property to our spouse, to our children, and to others that we choose to remember.

Requirements for Executing a Will

The law governing the making and signing of wills is not uniform throughout the United States. Nevertheless, a will that is properly executed according to the laws of one state will be given full faith and credit in other states. The laws are highly technical and require strict adherence to detailed formalities. Many lawsuits have occurred over the years because people have attempted to make their own wills without consulting a lawyer. Often, in such cases, a technicality causes the will to be disallowed by the court, and the true wishes of the deceased are not carried out.

Soundness of Mind Any person who has reached the age of adulthood (18 years) and is of sound mind may make a will. The issue of soundness of mind is raised only when someone contests a will on that ground. In determining whether a testator was of sound mind when making a will, the court asks the following questions: When making the will, did the testator know, in a general way, the nature and extent of the property he or she owned? Did the testator know who would be the natural recipients of the estate? Was the testator free from delusions that might influence the disposition of the property? Did the testator know that he or she was making a will? If all of these questions are answered in the affirmative, the court will find that the testator was of sound mind when making a will.

EXAMPLE 31-1: Soundness of Mind

At the time of the execution of his will, Stein was suffering from loss of memory. His son observed his father's failing health and mental illness over a period of time. He once observed his father's failure to recognize his own wife. Stein's daughter once observed her father's failure to recognize her and another relative, both of whom he saw frequently. The court disallowed the will, saying, "The testator did not have mind and memory sound enough to know and understand the businesses upon which he was engaged at the time of execution."

Formal Requirements With the exception of a nuncupative will, discussed later, a will must be in writing, signed by the testator, and attested to in the testator's presence by the number of witnesses established by state law (see Figure 31-1). Each of the particular statutory requirements of the state where the will is made must be met for a will to be valid.

EXAMPLE 31-2: Improperly Signed and Witnessed

Dugan's will contained the following clause: "All United States Savings Bonds in safety deposit box #559 Farmers Bank 10th and Market Sts., Wilmington, Del., to be given to the people and places as marked." When Dugan died, a number of U.S. Savings Bonds were found in his safe-deposit box. There was also a handwritten list of the names of various individuals and organizations and, next to each name, serial numbers, dates, and face amounts corresponding to specific bonds. Further specific notations were written on small slips of paper and attached to each bond with a rubber band. The court held that there was no effective testamentary transfer of the bonds. Neither the list nor the envelopes nor the small slips of paper satisfied the statutory requirements for executing a will. They were not properly signed and witnessed. Dugan's wishes as stated in the will were never carried out.

LAST WILL AND TESTAMENT
OF
JUDITH M. DORE

I, JUDITH M. DORE, of Salem, County of Essex, Commonwealth of Massachusetts, make this my Last Will and Testament, hereby revoking all earlier wills and codicils.

ARTICLE I

I give, devise, and bequeath all my estate, real, personal, and mixed and wherever situated to my husband, PETER DORE, if he is living on the thirtieth day after my death.

ARTICLE II

If my husband, PETER DORE, is not living on the thirtieth day after my death, I give and devise all of my property of every kind and wherever located which I own at the time of my death or to which I am then in any way entitled in equal shares to my children, ALAINA DORE and DAVID DORE, but if either of them shall not be living, his or her share thereof shall pass to his or her issue then living by right of representation, and in default of such issue then his or her share shall pass to the survivor of them.

I, the undersigned testator, do hereby declare that I sign and execute this instrument as my last will, that I sign it willingly in the presence of each of said witnesses, and that I execute it as my free and voluntary act for the purposes herein expressed, this 15th day of January, 2015.

_____
Judith M. Dore

We, the undersigned witnesses, each do hereby declare in the presence of the aforesaid testator that the testator signed and executed this instrument as her will in the presence of each of us, that she signed it willingly, that each of us hereby signs this will as witness in the presence of the testator, and that to the best of our knowledge the testator is eighteen (18) years of age or over, of sound mind, and under no constraint or undue influence.

_____   _____
(Witness)   (address)

_____   _____
(Witness)   (address)

COMMONWEALTH OF MASSACHUSETTS
COUNTY OF ESSEX

On this 15th day of January, 2017, before me, the undersigned notary public, personally appeared JUDITH M. DORE, proved to me through satisfactory evidence of identification, which was a current Massachusetts driver's license, to be the person whose name is signed on this instrument, and acknowledged to me that she signed it voluntarily for its stated purpose.

_____
Charles E. Jones, Notary Public

Figure 31-1 These are sample portions of a formal will drafted according to Massachusetts law. The laws of each state are not the same on the subject of wills.

A will may be typewritten or handwritten, or it may consist of a filled-in form. It need not be under seal. The will offered for probate must be the original and not a copy. In a case in which a testator executed both an original and a carbon copy of a will and later canceled only the carbon, the court has held that it could be presumed that the testator also intended to cancel the original. Problems of this nature can be avoided by executing only an original will.

A will must be signed by the testator. The place of the signature on the will and the requirement as to who must be present at the signing vary from state to state. In some states, a will must be signed at the end of the instrument; in other states, the signature may be placed anywhere on the paper. Similarly, some states require a will to be signed in the presence of witnesses, whereas others allow a will to be signed privately if the testator acknowledges to the witnesses when they sign that it is his or her signature. Testators who are not able to write may make a mark, such as an X, attested to by the required number of witnesses. If the testator's condition makes movement impossible, as in paralysis, another person may sign for the testator. This signing must be done at the request of the testator, in the testator's presence, and in the presence of witnesses.

With the exception of some wills that are handwritten, wills must be witnessed by the number of witnesses prescribed by state law. Almost every state today requires that a will be witnessed by two witnesses. Witnesses must sign in the presence of the testator and, in some states, each other's presence. Because the witnesses may be called upon to attest to the genuineness of the testator's signature and soundness of mind, it is advisable that witnesses be younger than the testator. In some states, no age requirements are given for witnesses. Instead, minors may witness a will as long as they are of sufficient understanding and competent to testify in court as to the facts relating to the execution of the will. In other states, witnesses must have reached a certain age, such as 14, 16, or 18 years, to qualify as a witness. In many states, persons and their spouses who witness a will may not receive gifts under the will unless there are still other witnesses. The failure to observe this provision may result in their being disinherited. Some states protect beneficiaries who witness a will by allowing them to inherit up to the amount that they would have inherited had the deceased died without a will.

Need for Accuracy
Certain words often used in wills may have a legal interpretation that is different from their everyday meaning. Care must be taken to describe each bequest and devise in a manner that will satisfy the legal definition. For instance, a testator may use the word *heirs* when really meaning *children*. The differences in the meanings of the two words could result in much dispute and expensive litigation. It is also important to avoid ambiguous language.

Informal Wills
A *holographic will* is one that is not witnessed but is written entirely in the handwriting of the testator. About half the states in the United States treat holographic wills as valid. The other half do not recognize them because of the lack of witnesses.

EXAMPLE 31-3: Holographic Will

Sedmak resided in Pennsylvania. The following handwritten document was found among his papers when he died:

> My Brother Mil
> Please see that Zella Portenar receives $15,000 from my savings account it is in the Western Savings Bank.
> George A. Sedmak
> or Alexander Sedmak
> Oct 6, '02

The Pennsylvania court held the unwitnessed document to be a valid holographic will.

Oral wills made by persons in their last illness or by soldiers and sailors in actual combat are nuncupative wills. **Nuncupative wills** are valid only in some states and are restricted to the giving of personal property only. Testators must indicate their bequests and state that those hearing the statements are to be considered witnesses to the oral will.

Protection of Spouses and Children

Even though the law of wills differs from state to state, some provisions are consistent from jurisdiction to jurisdiction. Many of these identical provisions deal with the portion of an estate left to a spouse and that which is left to the children of the deceased. Most state laws contain a series of provisions that will protect the spouse. Similarly, most states have legal provisions that will protect the children. One major stipulation here is that children must have evidence that they were inadvertently left out of a parent's will. If they can do this, they are protected by state law in most jurisdictions.

Wills provide for the smooth transfer of property and assure the rights of the heirs and beneficiaries.

Protection of Spouses   As noted earlier, most state laws include various devices that are designed to protect all family members, but especially the spouse of the deceased. Some states provide for a **family allowance**, sometimes called a **widow's allowance**, which is an amount of money taken from the decedent's estate and given to the family to meet its immediate needs while the estate is being probated. The amount of the allowance is either a fixed, statutory amount or discretionary with the court and is not chargeable against other benefits given to the family members. Another family protection is the **homestead exemption**, which puts the family home beyond the reach of creditors up to a certain limit. Still another protective device provided by some states is known as **exempt property**, which is certain property of a decedent that passes to the surviving spouse or children and is beyond the reach of creditors. In some states, for example, $3,500 worth of personal property passes automatically to the surviving spouse or, if none, to surviving children equally. The rights of dower (for a widow) and curtesy (for a widower) are also available in some states, providing the surviving spouse with certain property rights in real property owned by the deceased spouse.

In addition to the rights mentioned, surviving spouses are assured a share of a deceased spouse's estate. A surviving spouse who does not like the provisions of a deceased spouse's will may choose to take a portion of the estate set by state statute rather than accept the amount provided in the will. In some states, this sum is referred to as a spouse's **forced share**. In other states, it is called a spouse's **elective share**. The amount the surviving spouse will receive varies from state to state. In some states, it is the amount the spouse would have received had the deceased spouse died without a will. In other states, the amount is computed by the use of a different formula.

Advantages and Disadvantages of the *Windsor* Ruling

As is often the case, when the Supreme Court rules in one area of the law other areas are affected. The *Windsor* case had a tremendous impact on financial planning. Some of these changes were improvements. For example, after *Windsor,* the surviving spouse of a same sex marriage could claim an inheritance as an exemption when paying federal taxes. This change represented progress. Another advantage was felt in health care.

THE OPENING CASE *Round 2*

Windsor v. United States: A Landmark Case in ~~Domestic Relations~~ Tax Law

Recall that in the opening case, Edith Windsor characterized the inheritance that she had received from her spouse, Thea Spyer, as an exemption. Not surprisingly, the Internal Revenue Service disallowed the exemption and demanded an estate tax payment of $363,053, arguing that Windsor was not really Spyer's spouse under the language found in Section 3 of the Defense of Marriage Act (DOMA). Section 3 of DOMA states, "In determining the meaning of any Act of Congress, or of any ruling, regulation, or interpretation of the various administrative bureaus and agencies of the United States, the word 'marriage' means only a legal union between one man and one woman as husband and wife and the word 'spouse' refers only to a person of the opposite sex who is a husband or a wife." Since Windsor's Canadian marriage to Spyer was a union between two women, the IRS disallowed the exemption. Windsor paid the estate tax, but then filed a lawsuit against the United States, arguing that Section 3 of DOMA is an unconstitutional deprivation of equal protection and due process under the Fifth Amendment of the Constitution, and asking for a return of that payment. Ultimately, the case arrived at the Supreme Court, which ruled that Section 3 of DOMA is, indeed, an unconstitutional violation of equal protection and due process. So far so good; however, when the Supreme Court ruled against the IRS in this case, it did more than simply return an estate tax payment to a single taxpayer. It also opened the way to altering, in a very fundamental way, the financial future of many same sex married couples. To grasp the significance of this ruling, it is first necessary to understand what the Court did *not* do. The Court did not, as many people

assume, uphold the legality of same sex marriage. Eventually, the Court would uphold the legality of same sex marriages, but that would not occur until the case of *Obergefell v. Hodges,* 576 U.S. ____ (2015) (see the Part 8 case study). In the *Windsor* case, the Court ruled that it is unconstitutional for the federal government to pass statutes that treat one class of citizens differently from another, by creating restrictions and limitations on that class in the face of a state law designed to protect that same class of citizens. The Court put it this way, "By seeking to injure the very class New York seeks to protect, DOMA violates basic due process and equal protection principles applicable to the Federal Government. The Constitution's guarantee of equality 'must at the very least mean that a bare congressional desire to harm a politically unpopular group cannot' justify disparate treatment of that group. *Department of Agriculture* v. *Moreno,* 413 U.S. 528–535." Perhaps without knowing it, but certainly without admitting it, the U.S. Supreme Court in *Windsor* initiated a wide range of legal consequences that would not be addressed until the *Obergefell v. Hodges* ruling in 2015. In particular, the case will have a considerable impact on estate planning. On the other hand, the Windsor case is still good law. While it is true that the Court in Windsor talks extensively about marriage and about the statutory effects on married couples, it also talks about protecting a "state-defined class" of people. Thus, it would be logical to use the Windsor rationale to protect other classes of people, such as veterans, seniors, priests, illegal immigrants, and so on. Think about it. [See: *Windsor v. United States*, 570 U.S.___, 133 S.Ct. 2675, 186 L.Ed.2d 808 (2013).]

Before *Windsor,* employer-provided health coverage for an employee's same sex spouse was taxable. Because of the Court's ruling in *Windsor,* that coverage was no longer taxable. However, as is often the case when a ruling comes down from the Supreme Court, some unanticipated drawbacks roll off that decision. For example, after *Windsor,* same sex married couples were no longer able to file income tax returns as single individuals. Whether the married couple files jointly or separately would depend upon a variety of tax consequences. In some cases, filing as a married couple will mean lower taxes, but in others it may result in a tax increase, regardless of whether the couple files jointly or separately. Predictably, the new difficulties discussed here merely scratch the surface.

Protection of Children

As mentioned earlier, children who can prove that they were mistakenly (rather than intentionally) left out of a parent's will are protected by the laws of most states. Forgotten children will receive the same share that they would have received had their parent died without a will. This situation does not mean that a parent may not disinherit a child. Parents are not obligated to leave children anything, but to avoid litigation, such an intention should be shown in the will. A testator who wishes to disinherit a child should name the child in the will and make the statement that the child was intentionally omitted. By doing so, the omitted child cannot claim to have been mistakenly omitted from the will. Adopted children, under modern laws, are given the same legal rights as natural children. They inherit from their adopting parents. In contrast, stepchildren, unless they have been adopted by a stepfather or stepmother, do not inherit from a stepparent. Children who have been taken into the family for one reason or another but never legally adopted have no right of inheritance.

The *Obergefell v. Hodges* Case

Windsor also had an impact on couples in those states that did not yet recognize same sex marriages as legally legitimate. What would happen to a same sex couple, legitimately married in a state that recognized same sex marriages, who moved to a state that did not? That question needed an answer because many people would find themselves in that predicament very soon. The Supreme Court answered that question and many related questions when, in the case of *Obergefell v. Hodges,* five justices ruled that any state action, legislative or constitutional, that limited the definition of marriage to opposite sex couples violated the due process and equal protection clauses of the 14th Amendment. *Obergefell v. Hodges* was actually a consolidation of four cases filed in Ohio, Michigan, Tennessee, and Kentucky. Each of these states officially defined marriage as the union of one man and one woman. The plaintiffs in these cases included 14 couples (and two individuals whose partners were deceased) who challenged the constitutionality of the laws defining marriage in those states. Their arguments were based on the Due Process and Equal Protection Clauses of the 14th Amendment to the Constitution, which have been interpreted by the Court over the last century and a half to require the states to guarantee the same rights upheld by the federal government in the Bill of Rights.

After recognizing the historical fact that the institution of marriage has changed over the centuries, the majority in *Obergefell* reviewed the evolution of our attitudes toward homosexuality, concluding that these attitudes have gradually relaxed to the extent that, in the early part of the 21st century many states began to legalize same sex marriage. Next the majority ran through a series of cases, each one ruling that under the Due Process Clause the fundamental right to be married cannot be procedurally dismantled or limited without some compelling state reason to do so, as in the case of minors. Despite (or perhaps because of) the fact that none of these cases redefine marriage or suppose that marriage means anything other than a lawful union between a man and a woman, the majority declares that "this analysis compels the conclusion same sex couples may exercise the right to marry."

The majority pulled the Equal Protection Clause into the argument by pointing to the "synergetic" relationship between the Equal Protection Clause and the Due Process Clause, concluding, "These considerations lead to the conclusion that the right to marry is a fundamental right inherent in the liberty of the person, and under the Due Process and Equal Protection Clauses of the Fourteenth Amendment, couples of the same sex may not be deprived of that right and that liberty." ***Obergefell, et al., v. Hodges, Director, Ohio Department of Health, et al.*** 576 U.S. ____ (2015).

Changes in Estate Planning

Spouses in a same sex marriage can now claim all of the protection methods available to traditional spouses in another area of the law, estate planning. This includes the family allowance, which, as noted earlier, is an amount of money taken from the decedent's estate and given to the family to meet its immediate needs while the estate is being probated. Also in estate planning, both the homestead exemption and the exempt property provision should be available to same sex married couples. It is important to note, until the *Obergefell* case, these protections were available only in states that had made same sex marriages legal. This changed with *Obergefell*. Now all states will be compelled to deal with these issues. In a wider sense though, the *Obergefell* ruling has simplified, perhaps even eliminated, many (most?) of these problem. Now any married couple, opposite sex or same sex, must be treated in the same way. No distinction can be made, based exclusively on the gender identities of the spouses. This rule is based on the Supreme Court's belief that "the right to personal choice regarding marriage is inherent in the concept of individual autonomy." This rationale seems eminently reasonable. However, some legal experts have suggested that the Court may have overlooked or ignored some of the consequences that emerge from this principle. If "the right to personal choice regarding marriage is inherent in the concept of individual autonomy," then the government should also honor an individual's personal choice to marry several people simultaneously, or to marry someone of a close genetic relationship, or someone who is under the age of consent, and so on. Of course, it is doubtful that the Court meant to go this far. However, because the decision in Obergefell is based on the "right to personal choice," these issues may face the Court in the future.

Revoking, Changing, and Contesting a Will

People often make promises that are later broken, forgotten, or ignored. Broken promises come with consequences, of course, many of them unpleasant. Nevertheless, when those consequences result in fines for overdue library books, late fees for tardy car payments, or low grades for forgotten homework, the pain is bearable. However, when the broken promises relate to a will, the consequences are far more hurtful and sometimes irreparable. This is why the law has a way for handling situations that involve revoking, changing, and contesting wayward wills.

Revoking a Will
With variations from state to state, a will may be revoked (canceled) in any of the following ways: (1) burning, tearing, canceling, or obliterating the will with the intent to revoke it; (2) executing a new will; and (3) in some states, the subsequent marriage of the testator. In most states, the divorce or annulment of a marriage revokes all gifts made under a will to the former spouse and revokes the appointment of the former spouse as executor of the will.

Changing a Will
Sometimes testators wish to make slight changes in a will. They may do so by executing a new will or executing a **codicil**, which is a formal document used to supplement or change an existing will. A codicil must be executed with the same formalities as a will. It must be signed by the testator and properly witnessed. In addition, it must refer to the existing will to which it applies.

EXAMPLE 31-4: Properly Executed Codicil

Rueda made a will giving her entire estate to her husband. Later, Rueda enjoyed unusual financial success and felt inclined to leave $100,000 toward a new church building under construction in her parish. Rueda's attorney prepared a codicil, which Rueda formally executed in the presence of two witnesses. The bequest to the church contained in the codicil became an integral part of the will itself.

A properly executed codicil has the effect of republishing a will. It is said that a codicil breathes new life into a will, which means that the codicil will reestablish a will that had been formerly revoked or improperly executed. If, for example, a will is witnessed by only one person in a state that requires two witnesses, the will is invalid. However, if a properly signed and witnessed codicil is added at a later date, the will becomes valid.

Contesting a Will Only persons who would inherit under an earlier will or under the law of intestacy (described later in this chapter) are allowed to contest a will. A will may be contested on any of three grounds: improper execution, unsound mind, and undue influence. *Improper execution* occurs when an individual has attempted to make a will but has not followed the formal requirements. Because laypeople are not usually aware of the formal requirements for executing a will, it can be risky for them to make their own. Another grounds to contest a will is to allege that the testator was of *unsound mind.* When such an allegation is made, the burden is on the person presenting the will to the court to prove that the testator was of sound mind. This proof may occur by testimony and affidavits of witnesses and by testimony of the deceased's physician. A will may also be attacked and held invalid if a probate court finds that the testator made the will under circumstances of *undue influence.* When persons come under the influence of another to the degree that they are unable to express their real intentions in a will, the will may be declared invalid. The court must distinguish between undue influence and the kindness, attention, advice, guidance, and friendliness shown toward the testator by the one named in the will.

EXAMPLE 31-5: Undue Influence

Smolak executed a will prepared by a lawyer whom he had selected and with whom he had conferred several times before the date on which the will was signed. His niece, Sandra, was the major beneficiary under that will. A week later, he executed another will under which his nephew Michael and Michael's brother were named principal beneficiaries. This will was executed at the same time that Smolak executed a deed conveying his farm to Michael and Michael's brother (which conveyance he later sought to rescind, claiming that it was procured by fraud). The second will was executed at the office of a lawyer employed by Michael. Michael had made arrangements for a conference between his lawyer and Smolak. Michael attended that conference and also attended the execution of the resulting will. Smolak never conferred privately with Michael's lawyer concerning the second will and therefore never had an opportunity to express his true intentions out of earshot of his nephew. The court held that the second will was procured through undue influence and was therefore void.

Dying without a Will

When people die without a will, they are said to have died **intestate**. The property of a person who dies intestate passes to others according to the various state laws of **intestate succession**. (See an example in Figure 31-2.) These state laws, which differ from state to state, contain the rules governing the allocation of intestate property. Personal property is treated differently from real property. *Personal property* is dispersed according to the law of the state where the deceased permanently resided (his or her domicile) at the time of death and passes to the personal representative to be distributed to the heirs. In contrast, *real property* passes according to the law where the property is located and passes directly to the heirs upon the death of the owner. The personal representative receives title to real property only when it must be sold to pay debts of the estate. The following steps are taken to ascertain who will inherit from someone who dies without a will:

- Determine the rights of the surviving spouse, if any.
- Determine the rights of the other heirs.

If the Deceased Is Survived by:	A Surviving Spouse (if any) Receives:	Any Remainder Is Distributed:
Issue (lineal descendants such as children, grandchildren, great-grandchildren)	One-half of the estate	Equally to the deceased's children. If any children are also deceased, their children divide their deceased parents' share equally.
No issue but by kindred (blood relatives)	$200,000 plus one-half of the remainder of the estate	Equally between the deceased's father and mother or to the survivor of them. *However, if both parents are deceased, then:* Equally among the deceased's brothers and sisters. If any brothers or sisters are also deceased, their children divide their deceased parents' share equally. *However, if there are no living brothers or sisters or nieces or nephews, then:* Equally among the deceased's *next of kin* (those who are most nearly related by blood, including aunts, uncles, and cousins).
No issue and no kindred	The entire estate *However, if there is no surviving spouse, issue, or kindred, then:* The entire estate *escheats* to (becomes the property of) the state.	

Figure 31-2 This is an example of the way intestate property is distributed under a typical state statute (Massachusetts).

Rights of the Surviving Spouse

Under a typical state statute, if a person dies intestate, the rights of the surviving spouse are as follows: If the deceased is survived by issue (children, grandchildren, great-grandchildren), the surviving spouse is entitled to one-half of the estate. If the deceased is survived by no issue but by blood relatives, the surviving spouse is entitled to $200,000 plus one-half of the remainder of the estate. If the deceased is survived by no issue and no blood relatives, the surviving spouse is entitled to the entire estate. Keep in mind that this particular formula will differ from state to state.

Rights of Other Heirs

Under the same typical state statute, if a person dies intestate, the property will pass, subject to the rights of the surviving spouse, as follows: If the deceased is survived by issue, the property passes in equal shares to the deceased's children, with the issue of any deceased child taking that child's share. If the deceased is survived by no issue, the property passes in equal shares to the deceased's father and mother or the survivor of them. If the deceased is survived by no issue and no father or mother, the property passes to the deceased's brothers and sisters, with the issue of any deceased brother or sister taking that brother's or sister's share. If the deceased is survived by no issue and no father, mother, brother, or sister, or issue of any deceased brother or sister, the property passes to the deceased's **next of kin** (those who are most nearly related by blood).

Simultaneous Death

When two people die in a common disaster so that it is impossible to determine who died first, the Uniform Simultaneous Death Act often comes into play. This law contains rules that are adhered to when the inheritance of property depends upon the time of death, and there is nothing to indicate that the parties died other than at the same time. The following rules are obeyed:

1.   The separately owned property of each person passes as if he or she had survived unless a will or trust provides otherwise. For example, if a husband and wife die together in a plane crash, the husband's individually owned property passes to his heirs as though his wife were not living at the time of his death. Similarly, the wife's individually owned property passes to her heirs as though her husband were not living at the time of her death.

2.   Property owned jointly by both of the deceased is distributed equally. In this example, half of the couple's jointly owned property passes to the husband's heirs; the other half passes to the wife's heirs.

3.   When the beneficiary of an insurance policy dies at the same time as the insured, the proceeds of the insurance policy are payable as if the insured had survived the beneficiary. Suppose, in the example, the wife was the beneficiary on the husband's life insurance policy. The wife would be regarded as deceased at the time of the husband's death. The proceeds of the policy would go to the husband's estate unless an alternate beneficiary is named in the policy.

EXAMPLE 31-6: Simultaneous Death Act Not Applicable

John F. Kennedy, Jr., and his wife, Carolyn Bessette Kennedy, were killed in 1999 when their plane crashed into the ocean off the coast of Martha's Vineyard. The Uniform Simultaneous Death Act did not apply because the gifts to the spouses in each will were prefaced by the phrase "if she (or he) is living on the thirtieth day after my death."

Settling an Estate

When people die owning assets, their estates must be **probated**, that is, settled under the supervision of the court. The court that supervises the procedure is called a probate court in some states and a surrogate court, or orphan's court, in others. The first step in probating an estate is to determine whether the deceased left a will. If a will exists, it usually names a personal representative called an **executor** (male) or **executrix** (female) who is the person named in the will to carry out its terms. If there is no will, or if the executor named in the will fails to perform, someone must petition the court to settle the estate. That person, if appointed, is called an **administrator** (male) or **administratrix** (female). In states that have adopted the Uniform Probate Code, executors and administrators are called **personal representatives**.

Before an executor or administrator is appointed, notice of the petition for appointment is published in a newspaper and sent to all heirs, legatees, and devisees. Anyone with grounds to object may do so. Witnesses are sometimes asked to testify or sign affidavits about their knowledge of the execution of the will. Testimony is not necessary when all heirs and next of kin assent to the allowance of the will and no one contests it.

To ensure faithful performance, the executor or administrator is required to post a bond. A **bond** is a promise by the executor or administrator (and the sureties, if any) to pay the amount of the bond to the probate court if the duties of the position are not faithfully performed. **Sureties** are persons or insurance companies that stand behind executors or administrators and become responsible for their wrongdoing. In some states, a bond is not required if the will indicates that the executor or administrator need not post bond. In other states, a bond is always necessary, but sureties are not required if the will so dictates.

When a satisfactory bond has been filed, the court issues a certificate of appointment, called letters testamentary, to an executor or letters of administration to an administrator. The executor or administrator, called a **fiduciary** (one in a position of trust), is then authorized to proceed. The fiduciary's job consists of gathering the assets, paying the debts and taxes, and distributing the remaining assets in accordance with the will or the law of intestate succession.

quick quiz 31-2

1. A will may be typewritten or handwritten, or it may consist of a filled-in form and, whatever the case, it must be under seal and notarized.	true	false
2. A will may be contested for only one reason: unsound mind.	true	false
3. When people die owning assets, their estates must be probated, that is, settled, under the supervision of the court.	true	false

31-3 Advanced Directives

It is not uncommon for people to prepare for possible future misfortune by making advance arrangements while they are still mentally and physically able to do so. A good time to do this is when a will is executed, because all the necessary documents can be prepared, signed, and witnessed simultaneously. Part of this procedure can involve advanced directives that include the making of a living will and the execution of a health care proxy.

Living Wills and Health Care Proxies

Advance directives are written statements in which people give instructions for their future medical care if they become unable to do so themselves. The most common type of advance directive is the **living will**, which is a written expression of a person's wishes to be allowed to die a natural death and not kept alive by heroic or artificial methods. Another vehicle that is used for this purpose is the **health care proxy**—a written statement authorizing an agent to make medical treatment decisions for another in the event of incapacity.

The Right to Die and the Supreme Court

In 1990, in *Cruzon v. Director, Missouri Department of Health,* the United States Supreme Court ruled that the right to die was guaranteed by the Due Process Clause of the Constitution. This was not the first time that the Supreme Court got into the business of mixing the law and science in relation to decisions regarding life and death.

The Government's Compelling Interest in Life Perhaps one of the most critical instances was the case of *Roe v. Wade,* in which the Supreme Court decided that the government does not have a compelling interest for interfering with a mother's own choices in relation to her pregnancy until the fetus becomes viable, that is, capable of living outside the mother's womb. At that point, the point of viability, the government has a compelling interest in preserving the life of the fetus that outweighs the mother's right to have an abortion. In 1972, the year of *Roe v. Wade,* the point of viability was after the pregnancy entered the third trimester. In a later case, the case of *Planned Parenthood v. Casey,* the Supreme Court eliminated the redline at the third trimester because medical advances allowed the fetus to become viable at an earlier time, one that could not now be drawn with any certainty. Indeed, because of scientific advances, the moment of viability had become a moving target.

Living Wills and the Right to Die

A curious disconnect exists among the use of a living will, the right to die, and the government's compelling interest in the preservation of life. On the one hand, the Supreme Court has said that the government has a compelling interest in preserving life and can, therefore, enact sanctions to stop the taking of a life by abortion while, on the other, it has said that the government has an interest in due process and cannot, therefore, enact sanctions that stop the taking of life by passive euthanasia. In short, the government cannot prevent passive euthanasia in accordance with a living will because it must protect due process, but it can prevent abortion because it has a compelling interest in preserving life. The next step in this controversy is represented by the classic case of *Gonzales, Attorney General v. Oregon.*

CLASSIC CASE Balancing the Right to Die with Federal Control: *Gonzales, Attorney General v. Oregon*

Sometimes the U.S. Supreme Court must dive into a controversy that has implications beyond the actual facts and issues in a particular case. In such situations, the Court may decide a case on what seems to be a narrow legal technicality but is actually a major policy shift that will shape the future of generations to come. A case in point is the dispute in *Gonzales, Attorney General v. Oregon.* This controversy started when the citizens of Oregon authorized the establishment of a radical new measure legalizing physician-assisted suicide. The unconventional measure, which had been dubbed the Oregon Death with Dignity Act (ODWDA), protected physicians from prosecution under criminal law and from litigation under civil law for prescribing drugs for terminally ill patients who wished to commit suicide. The problem arose because the drugs that would have been prescribed under the law were listed on the Controlled Substances Act (CSA) and are thus subject to federal scrutiny. The situation was, in fact, scrutinized by the U.S. Attorney General (AG), who issued an interpretive ruling that stated that any physician who prescribed such drugs under the authority of the act and with the intent to have those drugs used for suicide could lose his or her license to practice medicine. The AG reasoned that drugs controlled by the CSA were to be used only for legitimate medical purposes and, since suicide is not a legitimate medical purpose, a physician who prescribed controlled drugs for that purpose would be in violation of the act. Moreover, prescribing drugs for suicide was deemed by the AG to be "inconsistent with the public interest." A lawsuit was filed by several interested parties in the

Federal District Court in Oregon, which ruled in favor of the plaintiffs, and then enjoined the AG from enforcing his interpretation of the CSA. The appeals court agreed. The AG filed an appeal, which ended up in the U.S. Supreme Court. Sixteen years earlier, in a groundbreaking case known as *Cruzon v. Director, Missouri Department of Health* 110 S.Ct. 2841 (1990), the Supreme Court had ruled that the right to die was constitutionally preserved by the Due Process Clause. Consequently, the Court had little problem in this case telling the AG to, in effect, "mind his own business." The CSA is supposed to stop physicians from trafficking in illegal drugs. It is not supposed to give the federal government the power to police a state's authority to regulate the practice of medicine. Consequently, the AG clearly overstepped his authority when he tried to short-circuit the Oregon law. At least that is how the U.S. Supreme Court saw the case. Of course, in one sense the Court in *Gonzales, Attorney General v. Oregon* avoided the real issue, that is, the question of how to balance the right to die with the government's compelling interest in preserving life. Instead, ruling was actually based on two other issues: (1) the issue of the real purpose of the Controlled Substances Act (CSA), which is to prevent drug trafficking by physicians, and (2) the issue of the state's right to control the activities of the medical profession within its own borders. Therefore, the real problem, that is, the tug-of-war between the government's compelling interest in preserving life, and an individual's right to die as guaranteed by due process, has yet to be properly addressed. [See: *Gonzales, Attorney General v. Oregon,* 126 S.Ct. 904 (United States Supreme Court).]

A QUESTION OF ETHICS

The future that is outlined in the novel *Unisave* by Axel Madsen is dark, depressing, and discouraging. The novel is set in the 22nd century at a time when the planet's natural resources, its energy reserves, its agriculture, and its fresh water are depleted. The earth's population has surpassed the 24 billion mark. There is very little hope for the salvation of humanity. The planet has reached a tipping point. In a desperate attempt to stall the inevitable and perhaps reverse the slide toward disaster, the United Nations has come up with several plans. One of the chief plans is established under the authority of an all-powerful global agency known as Unisave. This agency has been granted the authority to enforce a population control program that will affect everyone. There are several aspects to this program. First, the agency is equipped with the power to set quotas to control the number of children permitted to each couple. That, however, is the least strict of the new controls implemented by Unisave. Second, the agency has developed a compulsory sterilization program for some people under some circumstances. Third, it has ordered the use of drugs to suppress the sex drive among young people. Fourth, it has instituted a global program of electronic surveillance to prevent the violation of its strict anti-sex laws. Finally, it has mandated a program of compulsory gericide, which involves the systematic killing of the elderly. Consider each of the following ethical and legal issues.

1. When the people of Oregon supported the so-called Death with Dignity Act, did they legalize *gericide* in Oregon? Explain.

2. Can the Supreme Court's "compelling interest" standard be used to argue that the United States *cannot* cooperate with Unisave? Explain.

3. Could that same standard be used to compel U.S. cooperation with Unisave? Explain.

4. Can the due process standard that upheld the right to die in *Cruzan v. Director, Missouri Department of Health* be used to argue that the United States must cooperate with the gericide program? Why or why not?

5. In what way can the ruling in *Gonzales, Attorney General v. Oregon* be used to support the implementation of a gericide program? Explain.

The Science Court Revisited In Chapter 4 on alternate dispute resolution, we discussed a proposal by the governor of Minnesota for the creation of a science court to resolve legal issues related to science, medicine, engineering, and technology. The science court would be made up of scientists, engineers, and other experts educated in the discipline and the industry involved in the dispute, thus allowing them to use their expertise in deciding the case. The science court would also permit the parties to avoid the long and involved process of litigation. Since living wills, the right to die, physician-assisted suicide, and gericide involve medical issues related to life and death, cases involving them would be perfect candidates for the future science court.

A QUESTION OF ETHICS

In *Dark Age Ahead,* Jane Jacobs argues that Western civilization in general and the United States in particular stand on the verge of cultural collapse. As the cause of this collapse, she focuses on the decline of five essential mainstays of society: the family and the community; colleges and universities; the productive use of science; the government and its taxing power; and the self-regulation of the learned professions. She ends her book with a final prognosis of our culture:

> Ironically, societies (including our own) that were great cultural winners in the past are in special peril of failing to adapt successfully in the face of new realities. This is because nothing

succeeds like success, and it follows that nothing hangs on past its prime like past success. Formerly vigorous cultures typically fall prey to arrogant self-deception for which the Greeks had a word, *hubris,* which we still use. Because a culture is all of a piece, tolerance of commercial false accounting for gaining profit has military equivalents in inflated reports or enemy casualties, along with wishful intelligence about disaffection in enemy ranks. The falsities merely feed hubris; the enemy is a "public" that knows quickly whether wartime false accounting and wishful intelligence are empty bragging. The Bay of Pigs fiasco in Cuba and false body counts in the Vietnam War demonstrated an American proclivity for deception. Worse, the incentives for deception—success at sycophancy and pursuit of specious careerism—imply civilian cultural expectations that are shameful whether or not they infect military capability. [See: Jane Jacobs, *Dark Age Ahead* (New York: Vintage Books, 2005), p. 175.]

Now consider each of the following ethical and legal issues.

1. When Attorney General Gonzales in the *Oregon* case argues that the government cannot be involved in supporting physicians who prescribe lethal drugs for terminally ill patients, is he "failing to successfully adapt in the face of new realities"? Explain.

2. When the Supreme Court supported the right to die in the *Cruzan* case was it exhibiting the type of self-deceptive hubris of which Jacobs writes in *Dark Age Ahead?* Why or why not?

3. Some people have argued that the Supreme Court justices used a "technicality" to avoid the real issue in Oregon and in doing so managed to support governmentally approved suicide without actually "sticking their necks out" in the *Gonzales* case. Is this action by the justices on the Supreme Court an example of the "American proclivity for self-deception"? Explain.

4. Are the rulings in *Roe v. Wade* and *Planned Parenthood v. Casey* two examples adapting successfully to changing circumstances or another case of self-deception? Explain.

5. Both *Roe v. Wade* and *Planned Parenthood v. Casey* use a standard for personhood based on science's ability to push viability closer and closer to conception. Is this faith in science an example of hubris? Explain.

quick quiz 31-3

1. Advance directives are oral statements in which people give instructions for their future medical care if they become unable to do so themselves.   true | false

2. A living will is a written expression of a person's wishes to be kept alive using heroic and artificial methods.   true | false

3. The U.S. Supreme Court has ruled that the right to die is guaranteed by the due process clause of the United States Constitution.   true | false

31-4 The Law of Trusts

A **trust** is a legal device by which property is held by one person (the **trustee**) for the benefit of another (the beneficiary). The person who sets up the trust is called the *settlor*. The property that is held in trust is the *corpus,* or *trust fund.*

When a trust is established, title is split between the trustee, who holds legal title, and the beneficiary, who holds equitable or beneficial title. This separation allows the trustee to manage the trust property for the benefit of the beneficiary. Trusts are established to save taxes, provide for the needs of young children, and prevent money from being squandered, among other reasons.

Property is often placed in trust so that it will be preserved for future generations. In such cases, only the income is given out during the life of the trust, with the principal held in relatively safe investments. The rule against perpetuities prevents trusts (except charitable trusts) from lasting indefinitely. This rule in many states requires trust property to become owned by the beneficiary outright not later than 21 years after the death of some person alive at the creation of the trust.

Types of Trusts

The two principal types of trusts are testamentary trusts and living trusts. A **testamentary trust** is a trust that is created by a will. It comes into existence only upon the death of the testator. The terms of the trust, together with the names of the trustee and beneficiaries, are set out in the body of the will itself.

EXAMPLE 31-7: Spendthrift Trust

Emile Hanson died, leaving four grown sons and daughters. His children had never demonstrated any real ambition and had depended heavily on their prospects of receiving large legacies from the estate. Hanson feared that his heirs would quickly spend their inheritances and have nothing to support themselves in the years ahead. He provided for this possibility in his will by placing all assets in trust. The assets would remain intact, safely invested, and a small income would be paid from the trust income to the children. Hanson's purpose was realized in that the estate would be preserved and the surviving children would not squander their inheritance.

In a trust, such as the one illustrated in Example 31-7, provision must be made for final distribution of the trust's assets when the purpose of the trust has been served. For example, Hanson could have the trust property go to a church, college, or some other worthy nonprofit organization on the death of the last surviving child. He also could have designated a grandchild or grandchildren as the ultimate beneficiaries.

A **living trust**, also called an *inter vivos* trust, comes into existence while the settlor is alive. It is established by either a conveyance in trust or a declaration of trust. In a **conveyance in trust**, the settlor conveys away the legal title to a trustee to hold for the benefit of either the settlor or another as a beneficiary. In a **declaration of trust**, the settlor holds the legal title to the property as trustee for the benefit of some other person (the beneficiary) to whom the settlor now conveys the equitable title. A living trust may be either irrevocable or revocable. If it is *irrevocable*, the settlor loses complete control over the trust and cannot change it. The advantage of an irrevocable trust is that the income from the trust is not taxable to the settlor, and estate and inheritance taxes are avoided. The disadvantage of such a trust is that it can never be rescinded. The settlor can never get back that which has been put in an irrevocable trust, regardless of the circumstances. A *revocable* living trust may be taken back or changed at any time during the settlor's lifetime. It has neither estate tax nor income tax advantages; however, it can serve the purpose of relieving the cares of management of money or property, as well as other purposes.

A spendthrift is one who spends money profusely and improvidently. A *spendthrift trust* is designed to provide a fund for the maintenance of a beneficiary and, at the same time, secure the fund against that person's improvidence or incapacity. In some states, all trusts are considered to be of this type. In others, a clause must be placed in the trust instrument to the effect that the beneficiary cannot assign either the income or the principal of the trust and neither the income nor the principal can be reached by the beneficiary's creditors. Spendthrift trusts are not permitted in some states.

A charitable, or public, trust is one established for charitable purposes, such as the advancement of education; relief to the aged, ill, or poor; or the promotion of religion. For the trust to be valid, the identity of the person to be benefited must be uncertain. The rule against perpetuities does not apply to a charitable trust.

A *sprinkling trust,* or *spray trust,* allows the trustee to decide how much will be given to each beneficiary rather than have the settlor make the decision. The advantage of this type is that the trustee can compare the tax brackets of the beneficiaries long after the settlor is dead and cause a smaller tax liability to occur by giving more money to those beneficiaries in the lowest tax brackets. It also has built-in spendthrift provisions. The chief objection to this type of trust is that it gives the trustee too much control.

Obligations of the Trustee

The trustee is obligated by law to use a high standard of care and prudence in the investment of funds held by the trust. If real property is held in trust, it is the trustee's obligation to supervise and care for the property. When economic and other reasons indicate the need to shift trust assets to safer areas of investment, it becomes the duty of the trustee to make such changes. If investments selected by the trustee fail, the trustee is held liable unless a court rules that the action was taken with prudence and caution.

The trustee relationship is one of great and continuing responsibility. Appointment as a trustee should not be accepted by those without the knowledge and background that would afford prudent and good management. Banks, trust companies, and other kinds of fiduciary corporations offer professional services in the administration of trusts. They provide professional investment services and generally give maximum security and benefit for the fees charged.

quick quiz 31-4

1. When a trust is established, title to the trust property is held completely by the trustee.   true | false

2. A *spendthrift* is one who is frugal and careful about spending money.   true | false

3. Trustees are obligated by law to use an average standard of care when investing funds for the trust.   true | false

Summary

31.1 Because each state's law is different on the subject of probate law, it is necessary to check one's own state law when dealing with probate matters. Furthermore, the subject of probate law is relevant to all forms of business entities.

31.2 The terms *will, last will and testament, testate, intestate, testator, testatrix, bequest, devise, legatees, devisees,* and *heir* are frequently used in the field of probate law. Any person who has reached adulthood and is of sound mind may make a will. Wills must be in writing, signed by the testator, and attested to in the testator's presence by two witnesses in most states. In some states, no formalities are necessary when a holographic will is made. Surviving spouses are given protection through such provisions as a family allowance, a homestead exemption, exempt property, and the rights of dower and curtesy. Spouses in states that recognize same sex marriages can now claim all of the protection methods available to traditional spouses regarding estate planning. Also, because of the Supreme Court's rulings in the *Windsor* and *Obergefell* cases, the surviving spouse of a same sex marriage can now claim an inheritance as an exemption when paying federal taxes. A will may be revoked by burning, tearing, canceling, or obliterating the will with the intent to revoke it; by executing a new will; and in some states, by the subsequent marriage of the testator. A will may be contested on the grounds of improper execution, unsound mind, and undue influence. When people die without a will, their property passes to others according to the law of intestate succession, which varies from state to state. Special rules apply when people die simultaneously. Separately owned property passes as if its owner had survived the other person. Property owned jointly by both decedents is distributed equally. Insurance proceeds are payable as if the insured survived the beneficiary when they both die at the same time. When people die owning assets, their estates must be probated. Heirs are notified, and an executor or administrator is appointed by the probate court.

31.3 Advance directives are written statements in which people give instructions for their future medical care if they become unable to direct their care themselves. The most common type of advance directive is the living will, which is a written expression of a person's wishes to be allowed to die a natural death and not kept alive by heroic or artificial methods. Another vehicle that is used for this purpose is the health care proxy—a written statement authorizing an agent to make medical treatment decisions for another in the event of incapacity.

31.4 Trusts are used, among other reasons, to save taxes, provide for the needs of young children, and prevent money from being squandered easily. They may be created to take effect while a person is alive or after a person dies. When a trust is established, title is split between the trustee, who holds legal title, and the beneficiary, who holds equitable or beneficial title. The trustee manages the trust fund for the beneficiary.

Key Terms

administrator, 766

administratrix, 766

advance directives, 767

bequest, 756

bond, 766

codicil, 763

conveyance in trust, 771

declaration of trust, 771

devise, 756

devisees, 756

durable power of attorney, 756

elective share, 760

executor, 766

executrix, 766

exempt property, 760

family allowance, 760

fiduciary, 767

forced share, 760

gericide, 769

health care proxy, 767

heir, 756

homestead exemption, 760

intestate, 756

intestate succession, 764

issue, 765

last will and testament, 756

legatees, 756

living trust, 771

living will, 767

next of kin, 765

Nuncupative wills, 760

personal representatives, 766

probate, 755

probated, 766

sureties, 766

testamentary trust, 771

testate, 756

testator, 756

testatrix, 756

trust, 770

trustee, 770

widow's allowance, 760

will, 756

Questions for Review and Discussion

1. What are the sources of probate law and why is it relevant to business entities?
2. What are the formal requirements for executing a will?
3. When does a person who makes a will have the capacity to do so?
4. How did the Supreme Court ruling involving the Defense of Marriage Act affect the law?
5. What are the different methods of revoking or changing a will?
6. What are the three grounds for contesting a will?
7. Who inherits the property of someone who dies without a will?
8. What are the steps to be taken by an executor or administrator in settling an estate?
9. What are the types and purposes of advance directives?
10. What are the various types of trusts and when might they be used?

Cases for Analysis

1. Miguel Ruiz, who had a wife and two small children, did not have a will. A friend told Miguel that he should have a will because if he died without one, everything he owned would go to the state. Was the friend correct? Explain.
2. Ling Lee, who had two children, made a will leaving $1 to her husband, Seung, and the balance in equal shares to her two children. When Ling died, her husband, Seung, claimed that he was legally entitled to more than $1. Do you agree with Seung? Explain.
3. D.W. Elmer, a hospital patient, was seriously ill and unable to write his name. He executed his will, however, by making a belabored X on the paper in the presence of witnesses. Can a signature on a will made by an X be valid? Explain. [See: *In re Estate of Elmer*, 210 N.W.2d 815 (ND).]
4. James and Wanda Barns, husband and wife, were killed in a head-on automobile collision. It was impossible to determine who died first, and neither one had a will. The couple owned the following items as joint tenants: the house in which they resided and its furnishings, a savings account, and a checking account. James owned a car and some Lucent stock separately in his name. Wanda owned a car and a certificate of deposit separately in her name. James was survived by two children of another marriage; Wanda was survived by one child of another marriage. Who will inherit their property?
5. Julia Dejmal executed her will while a patient in St. Joseph's Hospital. The will was witnessed by Lucille and Catherine Pechacek. Catherine was 19 years old and employed as an assistant X-ray technician at the hospital. The age of majority at the time in that state was 21. It was contended that the will was not valid because one of the witnesses to it was a minor. Do you agree with the contention? Why or why not? [See: *Matter of Estate of Dejmal*, 289 N.W.2d 813 (WI).]
6. Lazer, a wealthy 17-year-old, learned that he was suffering from AIDS. He wrote a will leaving everything he owned to a friend he had met in school. Two years later, when Lazer died, his parents claimed that the will was not valid. Do you agree with Lazer's parents? Explain.
7. Santiago, a widower, made a will leaving $1 to his son Carlos and the balance in equal shares to his other children, Benito and Angelita. The estate, after deducting debts, taxes, and expenses, amounted to $90,000. When Santiago died, Carlos claimed that he was legally entitled to $30,000 from his father's estate. Was Carlos correct? Why or why not?
8. Evidence was introduced in court to show that, at the time she executed her will, Blanch Robinson suffered from schizophrenia. She had delusions about having had a love affair with Nelson Eddy and was suspicious, mistrustful, and perhaps deluded about her friends and acquaintances. Dixon, who had been left out of the will, contended that Robinson lacked the mental capacity to make a will. Do you agree with Dixon? Explain. [See: *Dixon v. Fillmore Cemetery*, 608 S.W.2d 84 (MO).]
9. Walsh, as settlor, executed a declaration of trust, naming himself as trustee and giving himself the income from the trust during his lifetime. After his

death, the income was to be paid to his second wife for her life, and upon her death, to his two children, Edward and Margot. Upon their deaths, the income was to be paid to the children of Edward and Margot, after which it terminated. The trust expressly provided that the settlor had not made any provisions for his third child, Patricia, because "previous provisions had been made in her behalf." After executing the instrument, Walsh transferred to the trust the family residence, three farms, and a checking account. Patricia argued that the trust was testamentary and therefore invalid because it failed to comply with the statute of wills. Was this a testamentary or an *inter vivos* trust? Explain. [See: *First Nat'l Bank v. Hampson*, 410 N.E.2d 1109 (IL).]

10. Whitman Winsor's will read in part: "I give, devise, and bequeath all my property, real and personal, to my daughter Lucy T. Winsor. . . . I deem it only right and just that my said daughter Lucy T. Winsor shall have all my property . . . because she has lived with me and cared for me for many years, and it is my will that all shall be hers." Winsor had another daughter, Caroline, who was not provided for in the will. Is Caroline entitled to an intestate share of her father's estate? Why or why not? [See: *Hauptman v. Conant*, 400 N.E.2d 272 (MA).]

quick quiz Answers

31-1	31-2	31-3	31-4
1. F	1. F	1. F	1. F
2. F	2. F	2. F	2. F
3. F	3. T	3. T	3. F

Part 8 Case Study

Obergefell, et al., v. Hodges, Director, Ohio Department of Health, et al.

576 U.S. ____ (2015)

Summary

When the U.S. Supreme Court ruled that state statutes and constitutional provisions that limited marriage to opposite sex couples were an unconstitutional violation of the equal protection and due process clauses of the 14th Amendment to the Constitution, very few people were surprised. Most people, however, would be surprised if they actually read the majority opinion and discovered what the case was really all about from a legal, rather than a social and cultural, perspective. The case is, in reality, a triumph for the Madisonian belief in the need for a strong central government, which can, at will, veto state legislative and state constitutional enactments in order to control the debilitating effects of factionalism. Let's take a look at what the case was all about. Although the case will probably go down in the history books as *Obergefell v. Hodges* (576 U.S.____ [2015]), it was actually a consolidation of four cases filed in Ohio, Michigan, Tennessee, and Kentucky. Each of these states officially defined marriage as the union of one man and one woman. The plaintiffs in these cases included 14 couples (and two individuals whose partners were deceased) who challenged the constitutionality of the laws defining marriage in those states. Their arguments were based on the Due Process and Equal Protection Clauses of the 14th Amendment, which has been interpreted by the Court over the last 150 plus years to require the states to guarantee the same rights upheld by the federal government in the Bill of Rights.

Compared to some cases that we have examined in this text, the issues in this case are really quite simple. There are only two. (1) Does the 14th Amendment demand that state government license same sex marriage? (Michigan and Kentucky), and (2) Does the 14th Amendment demand that state governments uphold the legal validity of same sex marriages performed legally in other states? Justice Kennedy, who wrote the majority opinion in the case, begins his explanation by reviewing the history of marriage as a cultural and social institution. Kennedy then focuses on the facts in three of the cases before the Court. The facts differ in each, but the complaint is always the same: In refusing to recognize same sex marriage as a valid marriage, a state violates the basic rights of due process and equal protection of the law (pages 1–6 of the majority opinion). Remember what these two clauses mean. The Due Process Clause states that the government cannot deprive individuals of life, liberty, and property without following due process of the law. This does not mean that the government cannot deprive someone of life, liberty, or property, only that it cannot do it outside proper legal procedures. The Equal Protection Clause guarantees that the law shall protect everyone in the same way, barring some compelling state interest not to do so. These are not substantive rights, like the free exercise of religion or free speech. Rather they are procedural rights that promise that proper procedures will be used to protect substantive rights (freedom of religion, freedom of the press, and so on) in a fair and equitable way, barring a compelling reason (such as national security or crowd control) not to do so. (This distinction [procedural rights v. substantive rights] will become significant later.)

After recognizing the historical fact that the institution of marriage has changed over the centuries (although until 2000 never straying from its fundamental and universal definition as a union between a man and a woman), Kennedy reviews the historical evolution of our cultural, social, medical, and psychological attitudes toward homosexuality, concluding that these attitudes have gradually relaxed to the extent that, in the year 2003, the State of Massachusetts legalized same sex marriage. Shortly thereafter, in the case of the *United States v. Windsor,* the U.S. Supreme Court declared the federal Defense of Marriage Act unconstitutional to the degree that it discriminated against same sex marriage. Next Kennedy runs through a series of cases, each one ruling that, under the due process clause the fundamental right to be married cannot be procedurally dismantled or limited without some compelling state reason to do so, as in the case of minors (pages 6–11 of the majority opinion). Some of the cases that support Kennedy's position include *Loving* v. *Virginia*, 388 U.S. 1, 12 (1967), which ruled that there is no justifiable reason to outlaw interracial marriage; *Turner* v. *Safley*, 482 U.S. 78, 95 (1987), that concluded there is no justifiable reason to prevent a prison inmate from marrying; and *Zablocki* v. *Redhail*, 434 U.S. 374, 384 (1978), which ruled that there is no justifiable reason to stop a delinquent father (late on child support payments) from marrying (page 11 of the majority opinion). Despite (or perhaps because of) the fact that none of these cases redefine marriage or suppose that marriage means anything other than a lawful union between a man and a woman, Kennedy declares that "this analysis compels the conclusion same sex couples may exercise the right to marry" (page 12 of the majority opinion).

Next Kennedy structures a rationale that explains why this is so. He notes that he will present four principles that demonstrate that the fundamental right to marry is promised by the Constitution to same sex couples. The first premise is that the right to marry is "inherent in the concept of individual autonomy." The second principle states, "The right to marry is fundamental because it supports a two person union unlike any other in its importance to committed individuals." The third principle is based on the belief that marriage protects children and families and "the right of child bearing, procreation, and education." The final principle declares that marriage is important because it forms the glue that holds our society together (pages 12–19).

Kennedy then pulls the Equal Protection Clause into his argument by pointing to the "synergetic" relationship between the Equal Protection Clause and the Due Process Clause of the 14th Amendment, concluding, "These considerations lead to the conclusion that the right to marry is a fundamental right inherent in the liberty of the person, and under the Due Process and Equal Protection Clauses of the Fourteenth Amendment couples of the same sex may not be deprived of that right and that liberty. The Court now holds that same-sex couples may exercise the fundamental right to marry. No longer may this liberty be denied to them. *Baker* v. *Nelson* must be and now is overruled, and the State laws challenged by Petitioners in these cases are now held invalid to the extent they exclude same-sex couples from civil marriage on the same terms and conditions as opposite-sex couples" (pages 22–23).

Only then does Kennedy address the concerns of the appellate court, which focused on a belief that the process should wait for further debate and for legislative enactments as well as further litigation. Kennedy notes that those (see Roberts, Scalia, Thomas, and Alito) who argue for the legislative approach demanded by our democratic system ignore the fact that people who wish to exercise fundamental rights need not wait for the legislature to act, but can as a part of our republican form of government seek redress in the courts (which, by the way, is what happened here). Moreover, this principle is necessary as a way to protect the rights of a marginalized and victimized minority, which may not find support in the democratic principle of "majority rules" (pages 23–25).

The Court's Opinion

Justice Kennedy

. . . This analysis compels the conclusion that same-sex couples may exercise the right to marry. The four principles and traditions to be discussed demonstrate that the reasons marriage is fundamental under the Constitution apply with equal force to same-sex couples.

A **first premise** of the Court's relevant precedents is that the right to personal choice regarding marriage is inherent in the concept of individual autonomy. This abiding connection between marriage and liberty is why *Loving* invalidated interracial marriage bans under the Due Process Clause. See 388 U.S., at 12; see also *Zablocki, supra,* at 384 (observing *Loving* held "the right to marry is of fundamental importance for all individuals"). Like choices concerning contraception, family relationships, procreation, and childrearing, all of which are protected by the Constitution, decisions concerning marriage are among the most intimate that an individual can make. See *Lawrence, supra,* at 574. Indeed, the Court has noted it would respect to other matters of family life and not with respect to the decision to enter the relationship that is the foundation of the family in our society." *Zablocki, supra,* at 386.

. . . A **second principle** in this Court's jurisprudence is that the right to marry is fundamental because it supports a two-person union unlike any other in its importance to the committed individuals. This point was central to *Griswold* v. *Connecticut,* which held the Constitution protects the right of married couples to use contraception. 381 U.S., at 485. Suggesting that marriage is a right "older than the Bill of Rights," *Griswold* described marriage this way:

> "Marriage is a coming together for better or for worse, hopefully enduring, and intimate to the degree of being sacred. It is an association that promotes a way of life, not causes; a harmony in living, not political faiths; a bilateral loyalty, not commercial or social projects. Yet it is an association for as noble a purpose as any involved in our prior decisions." *Id.,* at 486.

And in *Turner,* the Court again acknowledged the intimate association protected by this right, holding prisoners could not be denied the right to marry because their committed relationships satisfied the basic reasons why marriage is a fundamental right. See 482 U.S., at 95–96. The right to marry thus dignifies couples who "wish to define themselves by their commitment to each other." *Windsor, supra,* at ___ (slip op., at 14). Marriage responds to the universal fear that a lonely person might call out only to find no one there. It offers the hope of companionship and understanding and assurance that while both still live there will be someone to care for the other.

. . . A **third basis** for protecting the right to marry is that it safeguards children and families and thus draws meaning from related rights of childrearing, procreation, and education. See *Pierce* v. *Society of Sisters,* 268 U.S. 510 (1925); *Meyer,* 262 U.S., at 399. The Court has recognized these connections by describing the varied rights as a unified whole: "[T]he right to 'marry, establish a home and bring up children' is a central part of the liberty protected by the Due Process Clause." *Zablocki,* 434 U.S., at 384 (quoting *Meyer, supra,* at 399). Under the laws of the several States, some of marriage's protections for children and families are material. But marriage also confers more profound benefits. By giving recognition and legal structure to their parents' relationship, marriage allows children "to understand the integrity

and closeness of their own family and its concord with other families in their community and in their daily lives." *Windsor, supra,* at ___ (slip op., at 23). Marriage also affords the permanency and stability important to children's best interests. See Brief for Scholars of the Constitutional Rights of Children as *Amici Curiae* 22–27.

As all parties agree, many same-sex couples provide loving and nurturing homes to their children, whether biological or adopted. And hundreds of thousands of children are presently being raised by such couples. See Brief for Gary J. Gates as *Amicus Curiae* 4. Most States have allowed gays and lesbians to adopt, either as individuals or as couples, and many adopted and foster children have same-sex parents, see *id.,* at 5. This provides powerful confirmation from the law itself that gays and lesbians can create loving, supportive families.

Excluding same-sex couples from marriage thus conflicts with a central premise of the right to marry. Without the recognition, stability, and predictability marriage offers, their children suffer the stigma of knowing their families are somehow lesser. They also suffer the significant material costs of being raised by unmarried parents, relegated through no fault of their own to a more difficult and uncertain family life. The marriage laws at issue here thus harm and humiliate the children of same-sex couples. See *Windsor, supra,* at ___ (slip op., at 23

. . . **Fourth and finally,** this Court's cases and the Nation's traditions make clear that marriage is a keystone of our social order. Alexis de Tocqueville recognized this truth on his travels through the United States almost two centuries ago:

> "There is certainly no country in the world where the tie of marriage is so much respected as in America . . . [W]hen the American retires from the turmoil of public life to the bosom of his family, he finds in it the image of order and of peace. . . . [H]e afterwards carries [that image] with him into public affairs." 1 Democracy in America 309 (H. Reeve transl., rev. ed. 1990).

In *Maynard* v. *Hill,* 125 U.S. 190, 211 (1888), the Court echoed de Tocqueville, explaining that marriage is "the foundation of the family and of society, without which there would be neither civilization nor progress." Marriage, the *Maynard* Court said, has long been "'a great public institution, giving character to our whole civil polity.'" *Id.,* at 213. This idea has been reiterated even as the institution has evolved in substantial ways over time, superseding rules related to parental consent, gender, and race once thought by many to be essential. See generally N. Cott, Public Vows. Marriage remains a building block of our national community.

For that reason, just as a couple vows to support each other, so does society pledge to support the couple, offering symbolic recognition and material benefits to protect and nourish the union. Indeed, while the States are in general free to vary the benefits they confer on all married basis for an expanding list of governmental rights, benefits, and responsibilities. These aspects of marital status include: taxation; inheritance and property rights; rules of intestate succession; spousal privilege in the law of evidence; hospital access; medical decision making authority; adoption rights; the rights and benefits of survivors; birth and death certificates; professional ethics rules; campaign finance restrictions; workers' compensation benefits; health insurance; and child custody, support, and visitation rules. See Brief for United States as *Amicus Curiae* 6–9; Brief for American Bar Association as *Amicus Curiae* 8–29. Valid marriage under state law is also a significant status for over a thousand provisions of federal law. See *Windsor,* 570 U.S., at ___ – ___ (slip op., at 15–16). The States have contributed to the fundamental character of the marriage right by placing that institution at the center of so many facets of the legal and social order.

There is no difference between same- and opposite-sex couples with respect to this principle. Yet by virtue of their exclusion from that institution, same-sex couples are denied the constellation of benefits that the States have linked to marriage. This harm results in more than just material burdens. Same-sex couples are consigned to an instability many opposite-sex couples would deem intolerable in their own lives. As the State itself makes marriage all the more precious by the significance it attaches to it, exclusion from that status has the effect of teaching that gays and lesbians are unequal in important respects. It demeans gays and lesbians for the State to lock them out of a central institution of the Nation's society. Same-sex couples, too, may aspire to the transcendent purposes of marriage and seek fulfillment in its highest meaning.

The limitation of marriage to opposite-sex couples may long have seemed natural and just, but its inconsistency with the central meaning of the fundamental right to marry is now manifest. With that knowledge must come the recognition that laws excluding same-sex couples from the marriage right impose stigma and injury of the kind prohibited by our basic charter.

Objecting that this does not reflect an appropriate framing of the issue, the respondents refer to *Washington* v. *Glucksberg,* 521 U.S. 702, 721 (1997), which called for a "'careful description'" of fundamental rights. They assert the petitioners do not seek to exercise the right to marry but rather a new and nonexistent "right to same-sex marriage." Brief for Respondent in No. 14–556, p. 8. *Glucksberg* did insist that liberty under the Due Process Clause must be defined in a most circumscribed manner, with central reference to specific historical practices. Yet while that approach may have been appropriate for the asserted right there involved (physician-assisted suicide), it is inconsistent with the approach this Court has used in discussing other fundamental rights, including marriage and intimacy. *Loving* did not ask about a "right to interracial marriage"; *Turner* did not ask about a "right of inmates to marry"; and *Zablocki* did not ask about a "right of fathers with unpaid child support duties to marry." Rather, each case inquired about the right to marry in its comprehensive sense, asking if there was a sufficient justification for excluding the relevant class from the right. See also *Glucksberg,* 521 U.S., at 752–773 (Souter, J., concurring in judgment); *id.,* at 789–792 (BREYER, J., concurring in judgments).

That principle applies here. If rights were defined by who exercised them in the past, then received practices could serve as their own continued justification and new groups could not invoke rights once denied. This Court has rejected that approach, both with respect to the right to marry and the rights of gays and lesbians. See *Loving* 388 U.S., at 12; *Lawrence,* 539 U.S., at 566–567.

The right to marry is fundamental as a matter of history and tradition, but rights come not from ancient sources alone. They rise, too, from a better informed understanding of how constitutional imperatives define a liberty that remains urgent in our own era. Many who deem same-sex marriage to be wrong reach that conclusion based on decent and honorable religious or philosophical premises, and neither they nor their beliefs are disparaged here. But when that sincere, personal opposition becomes enacted law and public policy, the necessary consequence is to put the imprimatur of the State itself on an exclusion that soon demeans or stigmatizes those whose own liberty is then denied. Under the Constitution, same-sex couples seek in marriage the same legal treatment as opposite-sex couples, and it would disparage their choices and diminish their personhood to deny them this right.

. . . There may be an initial inclination in these cases to proceed with caution—to await further legislation, litigation, and debate. The respondents warn there has been insufficient democratic discourse before deciding an issue as basic as the definition of marriage. In its ruling on the cases now before this Court, the majority opinion for the Court of Appeals made a cogent argument that it would be appropriate for the respondents' States to await further public discussion and political measures before licensing same-sex marriages. See *DeBoer,* 772 F. 3d, at 409.

Yet there has been far more deliberation than this argument acknowledges. There have been referenda, legislative debates, and grassroots campaigns, as well as countless studies, papers, books, and other popular and scholarly writings. There has been extensive litigation in state and federal courts. See Appendix A, *infra.* Judicial opinions addressing the issue have been informed by the contentions of parties and counsel, which, in turn, reflect the more general, societal discussion of same-sex marriage and its meaning that has occurred over the past decades. As more than 100 *amici* make clear in their filings, many of the central institutions in American life—state and local governments, the military, large and small businesses, labor unions, religious organizations, law enforcement, civic groups, professional organizations, and universities—have devoted substantial attention to the question. This has led to an enhanced understanding of the issue—an understanding reflected in the arguments now presented for resolution as a matter of constitutional law.

Of course, the Constitution contemplates that democracy is the appropriate process for change, so long as that process does not abridge fundamental rights. Last Term, a plurality of this Court reaffirmed the importance of the democratic principle in *Schuette* v. *BAMN,* 572 U.S. ___ (2014), noting the "right of citizens to debate so they can learn and decide and then, through the political process, act in concert to try to shape the course of their own times." *Id.,* at ___ – ___ (slip op., at 15–16). Indeed, it is most often through democracy that liberty is preserved and protected in our lives. But as *Schuette* also said, "The freedom secured by the Constitution consists, in one of its essential dimensions, of the right of the individual not to be injured by the unlawful exercise of governmental power." *Id.,* at ___ (slip op., at 15). Thus, when the rights of persons are violated, "the Constitution requires redress by the courts," notwithstanding the more general value of democratic decision making. *Id.,* at ___ (slip op., at 17). This holds true even when protecting individual rights affects issues of the utmost importance and sensitivity.

The dynamic of our constitutional system is that individuals need not await legislative action before asserting a fundamental right. The Nation's courts are open to injured individuals who come to them to vindicate their own direct, personal stake in our basic char-

ter. An individual can invoke a right to constitutional protection when he or she is harmed, even if the broader public disagrees and even if the legislature refuses to act. The idea of the Constitution "was to withdraw certain subjects from the vicissitudes of political controversy, to place them beyond the reach of majorities and officials and to establish them as legal principles to be applied by the courts." *West Virginia Bd. of Ed.* v. *Barnette,* 319 U.S. 624, 638 (1943). This is why "fundamental rights may not be submitted to a vote; they depend on the outcome of no elections." *Ibid.* (Bold face type added.)

Justice Roberts's Dissent

Robert begins his dissent with one generalized principle, that the United States Supreme Court is not a legislative body (although, it seems to think that it is). Roberts also wants to make sure that his position is clear. In no uncertain terms he says: "Understand well what this dissent is about: It is not about whether, in my judgment, the institution of marriage should be changed to include same-sex couples. It is instead about whether, in our democratic republic, that decision should rest with the people acting through their elected representatives, or with five lawyers who happen to hold commissions authorizing them to resolve legal disputes according to law. The Constitution leaves no doubt about the answer" (page 3 of the Roberts Dissent).

What becomes evident, as Roberts continues, is that his essential objection to the majority's opinion is that five justices have taken it upon themselves to sidestep any authentic attempt to interpret the Constitution and have, instead, imposed their individual beliefs on the state governments by eliminating a "universal definition of marriage" that "has existed for millennia across civilizations" (page 4). Roberts seems especially convinced that these five members of the court have acted as self-appointed social engineers who have substituted their own view of marriage for the judgment of the duly elected legislatures of the states involved in these lawsuits and have, in effect, marginalized the people who elected those legislators. He goes on to describe Justice Kennedy's opinion in the following way: "Stripped of its shiny rhetorical gloss, the majority's argument is that the Due Process Clause gives same-sex couples a fundamental right to marry because it will be good for them and for society" (page 10).

Moreover, Roberts notes that, while Kennedy chooses cases that interpret the right to marry in a fair and even-handed way, those cases do not stand for the proposition that anyone who wishes to marry has an automatic, unquestioned right to get married. What the Court actually does in all of those cases is demand that those states that want to limit the right to marry explain and defend those limits. However, most importantly of all, the cases cited by Kennedy assume that the fundamental and traditional definition of marriage stays unchanged (pages 15–16).

Justice Scalia's Dissent

Justice Scalia objects to the fact that the majority has conjured up "liberties" that are not included in the Constitution, or the Bill of Rights or any of the other Amendments. Incredibly, the majority makes this move while extoling the virtues of "liberty," oblivious to the fact that they are neither protecting liberty nor promoting rights, but are, instead, robbing the people of the power to govern themselves. In effect, the majority has told the People of the United States that their elected officials and their democratic processes do not matter (pages 1–2 of Scalia's Dissent). Scalia notes unapologetically and with great conviction that the Court, "ends this debate, in an opinion lacking even a thin veneer of law. Buried beneath the mummeries and straining-to-be-memorable passages of the opinion is a candid and startling assertion: No matter *what* it was the People ratified, the Fourteenth Amendment protects those rights that the Judiciary, in its 'reasoned judgment,' thinks the Fourteenth Amendment ought to protect" (page 4 of Scalia's Dissent). Scalia, as an avowed and dedicated textualist, recoils in horror as the majority concludes that they alone in the history of American jurisprudence have discovered a right that everyone else seems to have missed.

Justice Thomas's Dissent

It is Justice Thomas who is most concerned about the use of procedural rights to create substantive rights out of thin air in a way never envisioned by the Framers of the Constitution. Recall in the earlier summary of this case that the due process clause states that the government cannot deprive individuals of life, liberty, or property, without properly following due process. This does not mean that the government cannot deprive someone of life, liberty, or property only that it cannot do so outside proper legal procedures. Due process and equal protection are not substantive rights, like the free exercise of religion or freedom of speech. Rather they are procedural rights that promise that proper legal measures will be used to protect substantive rights in a fair and equitable way, barring a compelling reason not to do so. Justice Thomas notes that the truly insidious nature of this legal error is that it gives judges a green light to pull "rights" out of the Constitution at will based only

their personal opinion about what rights are guarded therein. Justice Thomas says it this way: "The majority's decision today will require States to issue marriage licenses to same-sex couples and to recognize same-sex marriages entered in other States largely based on a constitutional provision guaranteeing 'due process' before a person is deprived of his 'life, liberty, or property.' I have elsewhere explained the dangerous fiction of treating the Due Process Clause as a font of substantive rights. . . . It distorts the constitutional text, which guarantees only whatever 'process' is 'due' before a person is deprived of life, liberty, and property. . . . Worse, it invites judges to do exactly what the majority has done here—'roa[m] at large in the constitutional field' guided only by their personal views as to the 'fundamental rights' protected by that document" (page 2 of Thomas's Dissent).

Nor is Thomas dissuaded by the arguments put forth by the petitioners in the case, who contend that, when the voters place the time honored definition of marriage in a state constitution they have taken the issue outside the democratic system. Once the provision is in a state constitution it is out of bounds and off limits. Thomas argues, quite convincingly, that the alternative action contemplated by the petitioners does far more damage to the democratic process. Thomas, however, says it far more eloquently when he writes that, "the result petitioners seek is far less democratic. They ask nine judges on this Court to enshrine their definition of marriage in the Federal Constitution and thus put it beyond the reach of the normal democratic process for the entire Nation. That a 'bare majority' of this Court, *ante,* at 25, is able to grant this wish, wiping out with a stroke of the keyboard the results of the political process in over 30 States, based on a provision that guarantees only 'due process' is but further evidence of the danger of substantive due process" (page 3).

Justice Alito's Dissent

Alito, as a constitutional scholar, gets right to the point. He contends that the Court in the past (before this case) has held that the term *liberty* in the Due Process Clause protects rights that are "deeply rooted in this nation's history and traditions" (page 2 of Alito's Dissent). Having said this, he finds it difficult to understand how the right to engage in same sex marriage is a "deeply rooted right," especially since same sex marriage was not protected in any state prior to the year 2003 when Massachusetts passed the first law protecting that institution. Alito makes his point not to support or oppose same sex marriage but to demonstrate that the Constitution protects only "deeply rooted rights," not rights that are created by judicial belief alone (pages 2–3).

Questions for Analysis

1. How does the case of *Obergefell v. Hodges* support or contradict the core legal principle of *stare decisis*? Explain.

2. Throughout this textbook, but especially in Chapter 2, we examined the campaign waged by James Madison at the Constitutional Convention in Philadelphia and in the First Congress to create a strong central government under the banner of federalism (remember *The Federalist Papers*). In what way (or ways) does the *Obergefell v. Hodges* case verify the successful nature of Madison's campaign? Explain.

3. Madison wanted a federal veto added to the Constitution that would empower Congress to nullify any state legislative enactment that the federal government felt was unwise, dangerous, expensive, disruptive, or just plain inconvenient. Madison did not get his wish. Instead, he had to settle for the supremacy clause in Section VI of the Constitution. The supremacy clause was later interpreted by the Court to allow judges to invalidate statutes (executive actions, administrative regulations, and so on) that conflict with the Constitution or with federal laws made in line with the Constitution. In what way(s) has *Obergefell v. Hodges* demonstrated that the supremacy clause is even more powerful as a tool to abrogate state action than Madison's veto power would have been? Explain.

4. Justice Roberts's concern in his dissent about the decision in the case is that the five justices in the majority have acted as self-appointed social engineers who have substituted their own view of marriage for the judgment of the duly elected legislative representatives of the people in the states involved in these lawsuits. Although this may not have been the intent of the majority, Roberts is correct in pointing out that these justices have acted as social reconstructionists rather than as judges. Is it proper for judges, at whatever level, to act as social architects or should they stick to interpreting the law as it exists on the page? Explain.

5. Justice Scalia opposes the fact that members of the majority have stepped out of their traditional roles as judges and assumed the unconstitutional role of pseudo-legislators. This transgression is labelled poetically as "legislating from the bench." Legislating from the bench occurs when judges or, in this case, justices, stop interpreting the law and start creating it, which is the exclusive role of the legislature. The offense is compounded when a pseudo-legislative act sets aside a state statute or a state constitutional provision. Without using the phrase "legislating from the bench," Scalia, nevertheless, admonishes the five justices in the majority for overstepping their constitutional roles. Unfortunately, the fact that Scalia has chastised them will have little legal effect. The reality is that, in this case at least, the court has, in one fell swoop, struck down the legislative enactments and, in some cases, the constitutional provisions, of some 30 states. What proactive steps might be taken to prevent such "legislating from the bench" in the future? Should penalties be put in place for such misconduct? Should an extra-judicial reversal process be developed by Congress to nullify unauthorized legislative mandates issued from the bench? Explain.

6. Justice Scalia is also an unapologetic, premeditated textualist who believes that the true meaning of the law lies within the words of a statute or constitutional provision. Accordingly, he reprimands the majority for concluding that they alone in the history of American jurisprudence have discovered a right that everyone else seems to have missed. Scalia is correct in his observation that the word *marriage,* from a textualist perspective, has meant the same thing for the entire collective memory of the human race, at least up until the past few decades. Should an avowed textualist like Scalia take into consideration the evolving nature of cultural standards and the corresponding attitude changes that might alter the meaning of a text or should the text remain sacrosanct as written originally? Explain.

7. Justice Thomas is authentically disturbed by the confusion that exists between procedural and substantive rights. He correctly points out that neither the due process clause nor the equal protection clause creates a substantive right. Put simply, these two rights promise that the substantive rights—things like freedom of religion, freedom of the press, freedom of assembly, freedom of speech, and so on—cannot be disrupted without due process unless some compelling governmental reason (such as national security, for example) allows it. Is Thomas correct in his assessment? If he is correct, does it really matter? Isn't this just the same "end justifies the means" argument used for centuries by governmental officials to get their way? Explain.

8. Justice Alito begins his dissent by noting that the due process clause was designed to protect rights that are "deeply rooted in the nation's history and tradition." Rights that are "deeply rooted" in the nation's history would involve things like the rights listed in question 7— freedom of religion, freedom of the press, freedom of assembly, freedom of speech, and so on. Should the majority be congratulated for creating a new right or rebuked for violating tradition? Explain.

9. The case of *Obergefell v. Hodges* altered the definition of marriage on a national scale. This change clearly affects constitutional law and the law of domestic relations. Yet, as is true of many Supreme Court decisions, the consequences of *Obergefell v. Hodges* will be felt in many other areas of the law. What other parts of the legal landscape will feel the unintended consequences of the majority ruling? In what way does the case of *Obergefell v. Hodges* highlight the problem of unintended consequences? Explain.

10. A complex adaptive system (CAS) is a network of interacting conditions that reinforce one another, while at the same time adjusting to change from agents outside and inside the system. In what ways does Kennedy's majority opinion in this case reinforce the idea that the law works like a complex adaptive system? Explain.

Part Nine

The Legal Environment

Chapter 32　Professional Liability

THE OPENING CASE Round 1
Monday-Morning Quarterbacking: Actual Privity and Near-Privity

Liability is a tricky concept that must be handled with great precision by the courts. The legal doctrine itself always (well, "usually always," if there is such a thing) consists of two initial elements. (Note: Two additional elements are needed to establish liability—causation and injury—but these two elements will be discussed later.) For now the focus is on (1) the existence of a duty and (2) the fulfillment (or lack of fulfillment) of that duty. The two are not the same, but they are so closely related that it is often difficult to see the point at which one ends and the other begins. A working example is found in the case of *Delollis v. Friedberg*. The conflict in this case emerged from a pattern of fraudulent activities that made international headlines. The plaintiff, Empire State Carpenters Welfare, Annuity, and Pension Funds (of which Delollis was one of the trustees), invested heavily in a firm called Beacon Associates, LLC (BA), along with several additional incarnations of the same firm dubbed BA LLC I and BA LLC II. That was not the problem. The problem was that BA had invested Empire Funds' money in another firm named

Bernard L. Madoff Investment Securities LLC (BLM). The defendant in this case was the accounting firm of Friedberg, Smith & Co., P.C. (FSC), which served as the auditor for BA and issued annual auditing reports on BLM that stated BLM had "financial statements (that) fairly represented the financial position" of BA and of Empire Funds accounts with BLM. As every financial Monday-morning quarterback knows, this report was a bit less than accurate; BLM was virtually worthless and, as a result, Empire Funds suffered a staggering loss. Upset by this turn of events, Delollis and the other trustees brought this suit against FSC. The district court granted a motion to dismiss the claim against FSC. Empire Funds filed an appeal with the Second Circuit. The appellate court shaped the case around two basic questions: (1) Did FSC under the theory of near-privity, owe a duty of due care to Empire Funds, just as if it were in privity? and (2) Assuming that this duty does exist, did FSC meet the duty? As to the first question, it is interesting to note that no one, not even Empire Funds, claims that actual privity (read "real" privity here) exists. The absence of actual privity is not a barrier, however, when, under certain circumstances, a person (even a corporate person) acts "as if" privity does exist. This concept of privity comes in a variety of flavors, sometimes called quasi-privity or pseudo-privity. However, the most popular term is *near-privity*. In this case, "near-privity" may be established if FSC communicated directly with Empire Funds, knowing that Empire Funds would rely on its reports and would structure investment plans accordingly. If that is *not* the case, then the second question, the question of due care evaporates. Did FSC have to address that second critical question? Read on for the answer. [See: *Delollis v. Friedberg*, 12-1628-cv (Second Circuit 2015).]

Opening Case Questions

1. In what other area(s) of the law, outside of the law of accounting, are duty and breach of duty crucial? Explain.

2. What are the first two elements that must be established in order to determine liability in this case? Explain.

3. Why is it significant to determine whether the defendant communicated with the plaintiff? Explain.

4. Why is it important to prove whether the plaintiff relied on the communications received from the defendant? Explain.

5. What is actual privity? What is near-privity? Explain.

Learning Objectives

1. Distinguish between a certified public accountant and a public accountant.
2. Explain generally accepted accounting principles and generally accepted auditing standards.
3. Identify the types of auditing opinions that can be issued by auditors.
4. Distinguish between actual privity and near-privity in accounting.
5. Outline the registration requirements imposed on architects by the state.
6. Identify the duties that an architect owes to his or her clients.
7. Determine the duties that an attorney owes to his or her clients.
8. State the standard of care used to judge health care professionals.
9. Contrast the locality rule with the national standard.
10. Explain the limits of hospital liability for the torts of independent contractor.

32-1 The Liability of Accountants

As we've seen in the commercial world, the legal system and the economic culture interact with each other in such a way that they become, at times, one single system, the judicial–economic system. In the last chapter, we also examined how the judicial–economic system acts as another aspect of the balancing process within the law. Now we turn our attention to one of the key players in the judicial–economic system, the accountant.

The Regulation of Accounting and Auditing

Accountants, like all professionals, must meet certain basic standards that are defined by the nature of their profession. A **professional** is a person who can perform a highly specialized task because of his or her special abilities, education, experience, and knowledge. Often the term professional is reserved for those individuals who perform a service for the public good. An **accountant** is a professional who can plan, direct, and evaluate a client's financial affairs. Although many accountants are charged with keeping a client's financial records, their responsibilities often go far beyond such routine tasks. Moreover, the nature of accounting means that an accountant's activities may have an impact on investors who exist outside the accountant's inner circle of clients. For these reasons, among others, accountants are regulated by the government. The federal government's power to regulate business, in general, and accounting, in particular, emerges from the Commerce Clause of the Constitution. The regulation of accounting by the state is part of the state's police power. The state's police power permits the state to regulate various activities to promote the general health, safety, welfare, and morals of the people.

Accountant Registration

The regulation of accounting is part of the state's police power. There are many different types of accountants. Some accountants work only for one employer. British Petroleum, for example, employs hundreds of accountants to chart the financial fortunes of the corporation. Other accountants hire themselves out to work for a wide variety of different clients. Regardless of where they work, however, accountants generally belong to one of two categories: certified public accountants or public accountants.

Certified public accountants (CPAs) have met certain age, character, education, experience, and testing requirements. These requirements are generally established by the state. For example, the state government may require CPAs to be at least 18 years of age and of good moral character. The state may also require a bachelor's degree, two or more years of experience, and a passing score on a written examination that covers accounting, auditing, and other related subject areas. **Public accountants (PAs)** are accountants who work for a variety of clients but are not certified. Frequently, states will not allow individuals to call themselves public accountants unless they have met certain requirements that are not as strict as the requirements for CPAs. State registration requirements are designed to shield citizens against people who practice accounting without the education or experience necessary to do a competent job. The state cannot, however, prevent someone from practicing accounting as a profession. The state can only stop such individuals from calling themselves CPAs, PAs, or any other title that might mislead a client into thinking the nonregistered accountant is registered.

Accounting and Auditing

Accountants perform a number of functions for their clients. They may balance accounts, reconcile bank records with account books, handle the payroll, fill out income tax returns, and handle other tax matters. Another important job that falls to the accountant is the task of auditing.

Auditing   An **audit** is an examination of the financial records of an organization to determine whether those records are a fair representation of the actual financial health of the institution. To be effective, an audit is usually conducted by an outside, independent auditor. An **auditor** is an accountant who conducts an audit. The dilemma that auditors face is that they are responsible at two levels of accountability. Traditionally, auditors are hired by and work for the organization that is being audited. This is the first level of accountability. At the second level of accountability, auditors are responsible to the investors, lenders, shareholders, and others who rely on the financial statements made by those auditors. Ideally, auditors ought to be loyal to both groups of individuals. Realistically, auditors do not always overlook the fact that the organization is the one that hired them and that writes their paycheck. As a result, there is a tendency, probably unconscious in most cases, to help the organization rather than the outside investors.

Accounting Principles   An independent group known as the Financial Accounting Standards Board (FASB) has established generally accepted accounting principles (GAAP). The rules established by the FASB are followed by the American Institute of Certified Public Accountants (AICPA). The rules outline the procedures that accountants must use in accumulating financial data and preparing financial statements. In general, the procedures facilitate the preparation of reports that are useful, understandable, reliable, verifiable, and comparable.

Auditing Standards The Auditing Standards Board of the AICPA has set up generally accepted auditing standards (GAAS). These auditing standards measure the quality of the performance of auditing procedures. In short, the auditing standards explain how an auditor can determine whether proper accounting procedures have been used. Of the 10 auditing standards, three of them relate to the auditors, three relate to their work in the field, and four relate to the opinions that they issue.

Types of Opinion An auditor's opinions may be unqualified or qualified. When auditors conclude that the financial records of the company are an accurate reflection of the company's financial status, they will issue an unqualified opinion. When auditors issue a qualified opinion, they are saying that the books represent the company's financial health as of a given date. However, auditors may qualify the opinion in one of two ways. One type of qualified opinion is the "subject to" opinion. In this case, auditors state that the books represent the company's financial health subject to some uncertainty, such as a pending lawsuit, which may affect the company in the future. The second type of qualified opinion is an "except for" opinion. Such an opinion indicates that the financial statements are an accurate reflection of the company's financial health except for some minor deviation from GAAP, not serious enough to warrant an adverse opinion. Auditors may also issue adverse opinions and disclaimers. An adverse opinion is rendered when the deviations from GAAP are so serious that an unqualified opinion is impossible and a qualified opinion is not justified. An adverse opinion would be rendered in the following cases:

- The financial statements do not fairly present the financial health of the organization.
- Generally accepted accounting principles are consistently ignored.
- Financial information has not been adequately disclosed.
- There are major uncertainties that could have a serious impact on the organization, and the auditor disagrees with management's presentation of those uncertainties.

A disclaimer declares that the auditor has decided not to give any opinion on the company's financial records. This situation generally occurs because the auditor has not had enough time to examine the books properly or was denied access to crucial records. An auditor might also issue a disclaimer if the books indicate that the organization exercised no control over the accounting process.

Accountants have a fiduciary duty with their clients and must adhere to the AICPA Code of Professional Ethics as well as GAAP and GAAS standards for the profession.

Ethical Rules of Accountants The AICPA has also established a Code of Professional Ethics, which outlines rules that govern the ethical conduct of accountants. These rules are frequently used by the courts to determine whether an accountant has breached a duty to the client in nontechnical matters not covered by GAAP and GAAS. For example, the AICPA's code has established that accountants owe their clients a duty of confidentiality even after the relationship has terminated. In this regard, an accountant cannot reveal information about a client's business to anyone outside of

the accountant–client relationship unless authorized to do so by the client. Although this privilege does not extend to a court's request for information, it does cover most other situations. The ethical code also encompasses contingent fees, the independence of the auditor, promotional practices, operational practices, and quality reviews by peers.

The Sarbanes–Oxley Act

In response to some of the difficulties that can be traced to the dual identity that auditors must assume, Congress enacted the Sarbanes–Oxley Act. Although the Sarbanes–Oxley Act has many targets, one of the most crucial is to restore the confidence of the investment community. A key feature of the act is the creation of the Public Company Accounting Oversight Board (PCAOB). This new regulatory agency is charged with the task of making certain that correct, unbiased, and comprehensive data find their way to potential investors, so that they can make informed decisions about investment opportunities. To accomplish this task, Congress gave the board responsibility for the supervision of public accounting firms. With this power came the ability to set up practical instructions for auditing procedures and philosophical canons for the ethical values that such firms must follow. To give the new federal board proper authority, the act requires the registration of all public accounting firms that are involved in auditing publicly traded corporations. The board has the authority to inspect those companies and their procedures on a regularly established schedule. The board consists of five members, only two of whom are permitted to be certified public accountants. The hope is that this approach will keep the agency objective and unbiased as it evaluates both the accounting firms and the procedures by which they operate.

The Sarbanes–Oxley Act also enacted several additional features. For example, the act specifically prohibits conflicts of interest that might arise when former auditors are hired by a company, if that company is still being audited by the same firm that once employed the former auditor. The prohibition lasts for one year and covers only the uppermost management positions of the audited company. Sarbanes–Oxley also requires that corporate audit committees receive timely and comprehensive reports from the accounting firm that is auditing the company. Alternative approaches to the way that financial data is packaged must be included in these regular reporting sessions. Under the provisions of the act, Congress has probed the mergers that have occurred among various major accounting firms. The aim of such a probe would be to find out what led to the mergers, what fallout will result from the new configuration, and what ways exist to improve the competitive atmosphere in the accounting profession.

Conflicting Jurisdictional Problems

Although auditors and accountants are regulated by several different authorities, those authorities coexist peacefully as long as they agree with one another. Trouble results, however, when different agencies promote different agendas. This problem is further complicated whenever accountants interact with other professionals. Many of these professionals, notably attorneys, are also regulated by professional authorities, some of which promote duties that conflict with those of the accounting profession. Thus, for example, the FASB might require auditors to perform a task that calls for information that is in the hands of a client's attorney. The AICPA might support the auditor's need to obtain such information from the clients' attorneys, but the American Bar Association (ABA) might direct attorneys to withhold information from auditors to preserve attorney–client privilege or the work product privilege or both. At that point, no matter what happens, someone will violate his or her professional code and someone—the auditor, the attorney, or the client—will have to suffer the consequences.

EXAMPLE 32-1: The Hazards of Serving Too Many Masters

In the mid-1970s, in the midst of a growing litigation epidemic, the FASB released a decision that required auditors to make sure that they accrued certain losses to income while auditing any client's books, including losses that might result from possible lawsuits. To do this properly, the auditors had to get information from their clients' attorneys. To help auditors accomplish this task, the AICPA announced that auditors were now permitted to ask clients to obtain certain information from their attorneys. In reaction, the ABA declared that attorneys ought to be very careful about providing auditors with too much information, lest they violate the attorney–client or the work product privilege or both. The AICPA responded by assuring the ABA that their auditors would never go so far as to violate either the attorney–client or the work product privilege. Everything might have rested there, had the Public Company Accounting Oversight Board (PCAOB) of Sarbanes–Oxley not gotten into the act. The PCAOB muddied the waters considerably by warning auditors that they would be severely disciplined for not insisting that attorneys provide them with the necessary information, regardless of whatever arguments those attorneys might make. Does this conflict give the auditors a license to demand that attorneys violate the attorney–client privilege and the work product privilege? Certainly the ABA does not think so, but the PCAOB insists that it does. Whatever the ultimate outcome of this dispute might be, it serves to illustrate the problems that arise when too many governmental agencies regulate the same activity. [See: Peggy A. Heeg, "Auditors Are Increasingly at Odds with Attorneys," *The National Law Journal,* November 20, 2006, pp. S-1 and S-6–S-7.]

The Dodd–Frank Act

In Chapters 20 and 29 we learned that Congress attempted to deal with the 21st century financial crisis by passing the Dodd–Frank Act, the purpose of which is to rectify present economic problems and, thus, head off any future crisis. The problems that we discussed in Chapter 20 were related to mortgages. The problems that we looked at in Chapter 29 involved corporations. Mortgage lenders and corporate officers were not the only ones guilty of wrongdoing in the crisis. Accountants and auditors also had a hand in the mess. For that reason, Congress also included provisions in the Dodd–Frank Act for dealing with the problems peculiar to the accounting profession. As noted earlier in the book, the Dodd–Frank Act is a long, complex, and intricate statute covering over 2,000 pages. The provisions that we will concentrate on now are those that affect the potential liability of accountants.

Securities and Exchange Commission Jurisdiction
The Securities and Exchange Commission (SEC) has been charged with investigating the information that is given to investors. The goal of the study is to determine if such disclosures actually help investors. The ultimate goal of this program is to develop a new generation of literate investors who actually know what they are doing when they invest their money. (What a novel idea.) The SEC will report to Congress, specifically to the Senate Banking Committee and the House Financial Services Committee. As part of this investigation, the SEC will also look at the possibility of adding a private rights action section to the law, with an explanation of how such a proposal would affect institutional investors, among others.

Government Accountability Office/Public Company Accounting Oversight Board
The Government Accountability Office (GAO) has been charged with investigating how to regulate financial planners, especially those planners

who perform income tax planning services. Similarly, the Public Company Accounting Oversight Board (PCAOB) has been empowered to develop a plan to regulate and register auditors of nonpublic broker dealers. Accordingly, the PCAOB is also now considering the development of a fresh set of audit standards.

Duties Owed by the Accountant to the Client

The concept of duty in the law is slippery at best. Still, duty commonly emerges from within the context of rights. Some rights emerge simply because people exist within a sociocultural setting. The right to remain uninjured is one such right. The right to move about freely is another. However, not all rights arise automatically. Some duties emerge from within a voluntary relationship in which, at minimum, two parties expressly (or impliedly) agree to bind themselves to one another in order to receive mutual benefits. The agreement will always involve two complementary but essential elements, the right gained (which is generally the prime motivator for joining the game in the first place) and the newly acquired duty (the obligations adopted in exchange for the rights gained). The agreement involved in purchasing a vehicle, for instance, involves such elements. One party receives the right to possess and use the vehicle, yet simultaneously accepts the obligation to make regularly scheduled payments (the duty undertaken). Such arrangements exist at the heart of contract law. However, they also exist within corporate law, agency law, employment law, insurance law, and property law, among many others, including the law of accounting.

The problem here is that in many accounting arrangements, the levels of interaction among the parties are more complicated than in an ordinary straightforward contractual arrangement. Another difference is that within the law of accounting, multiple overlapping duties exist, all of which are interlaced and may emerge even when privity does not exist or when privity is so tenuous that it remains virtually unnoticed by most (perhaps even all) of the parties. Such entanglements rarely surface until something goes wrong, and then they emerge with a vengeance. These complex entanglements emerge when accountants seek to serve more than one master, something that is rarely advisable in the law (not to mention everyday life), but unfortunately inescapable in the accounting profession. A standard industry arrangement in accounting, an arrangement that we shall call a **type one arrangement**, exists between the accountant and a client and follows ordinary contract law principles. However, sometimes accountants must act in a dual capacity, as both accountants and as auditors. We will refer to such arrangements as **type two arrangements**. Since accountants must act in such dual positions, multiple connections emerge beyond the four walls of the original arrangement, thus complicating things. We will examine type one arrangements before advancing to the type two arrangement.

Type One Accounting Arrangements

In a standard type one accounting arrangement, the accountant enters an agreement with a client, sometimes to act as a financial manager, but more often as a tax preparer. If the accountant fails to fulfill the terms of the contract, then the client has a cause of action against the accountant. For this reason, it is very important that the terms of the contract include express duties that outline the task of the accountant and the time limits, if any, within which the tasks must be performed. Naturally, certain implied duties are included in any contract between an accountant and the client. These implied duties arise because the relationship exists. Thus, the accountant's agreement to work for the client implies an agreement to use the appropriate level of skill and due care that would be expected of any similarly situated accountant. An accountant might also be liable to clients under common law for negligence and fraud.

Negligence in Type One Arrangements The client has the right to expect the accountant to do a good job in whatever task has been assigned. From this right arises the accountant's duty of due care. The duty of due care means that the accountant must perform the job with the same skill and competence that a reasonable accounting professional would use in the same situation. Negligence, often called malpractice, occurs whenever an accountant fails to meet his or her duty of due care. Although the term *malpractice* is usually reserved for health care professionals and attorneys, it could also be applied to any form of professional negligence. How a reasonable accounting professional would handle a given situation, and thus avoid a charge of malpractice, would be determined by reference to GAAS or GAAP. Whenever accountants ignore the rules established by GAAS and GAAP, they do so at their own risk. It is fairly certain that ignoring or remaining ignorant of these principles and procedures is a one-way ticket to a malpractice suit, and there is little question that in such circumstances, the accountant would be found liable for negligence. Unfortunately, the opposite precept is not always true; that is, just because an accountant follows the GAAS or GAAP guidelines does not automatically lead to his or her vindication in a court of law. It is always possible that an accountant can follow the proper principles and procedures yet still make other errors that lead to liability. Thus, an accountant might follow GAAS, yet file a return after a required deadline, or the accountant might make a calculation error, or send the forms to the wrong agency, and so on.

THE OPENING CASE *Round 2*
Monday-Morning Quarterbacking: Type One or Type Two? Duty or No Duty?

Recall that in the opening case, the plaintiff, Empire State Carpenters Welfare, Annuity, and Pension Funds invested quite a bit of money in Beacon Associates, LLC (BA). Subsequently, BA invested Empire's money in a firm called Bernard L. Madoff Investment Securities LLC (BLM). As things turned out, this proved to be a mistake, and Empire lost a great deal of money. The case here, however, involves the auditing firm of Friedberg, Smith & Co., P.C. (FSC). FSC served as the auditor for BA, and as such issued annual auditing reports on BLM. These reports affirmed that BLM's "financial statements fairly represented the financial position" of BA and of Empire Funds accounts with BLM. As it turned out, BLM was virtually valueless. Consequently, as noted earlier, Empire Funds lost a large amount of money. Distressed by the enormity of the loss, the Empire trustees sued FSC. The district court granted a motion to dismiss the claim against FSC, and Empire Funds appealed. The Second Circuit Court of Appeals shaped the case around two questions, the first of which had to be

answered in the affirmative before the case could go forward: "Did FSC owe a duty of due care to Empire Funds?" We, however, should be able to see that an even more fundamental question sits at the base of the case and that question is: "What type of accounting arrangement exists between FSC and Empire?" Or perhaps, even more simply, "Is the arrangement between FSC and Empire a type one or a type two accounting arrangement?" If it is a type one arrangement, then duty flows automatically; however, if it is a type two arrangement, then the existence of duty is neither obvious nor direct. So which is it? Type one or type two? The answer should be obvious. Since the two firms, FSC and Empire had not entered a formal contract, we are dealing with a type two, rather than a type one arrangement. The question of duty was then still on the table. In a moment, the answer to that question will be revealed. To reach that answer, however, you must read on. [See: *Delollis v. Friedberg*, 12-1628-cv (Second Circuit 2015).]

Fraud Involving Type One Arrangements When an accountant enters a type one arrangement, he or she must perform all duties with the best interests of the client in mind. If an accountant *deliberately* misrepresents the client's financial condition or in some way *deliberately* falsifies a statement or an auditing report, that accountant will be liable to the client for fraud. Accountants may also be liable for fraud if they compile a financial report or conduct an audit recklessly. To make a proper case for fraud, it is not enough for the plaintiff to show that the accountant deliberately or recklessly attempted to falsify records and statements. In addition, the plaintiff must demonstrate that he or she actually relied on the false statements or reports. The extra effort is worth it, however, because if the plaintiff succeeds in proving that he or she was defrauded by the accountant, that plaintiff can ask for and will often be awarded punitive damages. Punitive damages, you will recall, are damages that exceed the actual financial harm to the plaintiff and are designed to punish the wayward defendant. The degree of difficulty involved in making such charges stick is directly related to whether the accountant has entered a type one or a type two arrangement.

Type Two Accounting Arrangements

As noted earlier, a type two accounting arrangement emerges when the accountant has a type one industry arrangement with one party that leads to a type two industry arrangement with at least one other party but also, frequently, with a variety of different parties. Under common law, an accountant can be held liable to some third parties who are damaged by a negligently prepared financial statement. Accountants are also liable to some third parties if they deliberately make fraudulent statements.

Negligence/Malpractice and Type Two Industry Arrangements The right to bring suit for a negligently prepared financial statement is not clear cut. In fact, the right varies from jurisdiction to jurisdiction, with some jurisdictions using more than one theory of recovery. The best that can be done is to present the various options on a track from the least to the most inclusive, or from the narrowest to the widest. The standards fall on the following spectrum: (1) actual privity (also called the Cardoza Standard); (2) near-privity (also referred to as the Actually Named Third-Party Standard); (3) near-privity plus (also dubbed the Specifically Foreseen Third-Party Standard); and (4) near-privity plus-2 (frequently named the Reasonably Foreseeable Third-Party Standard) and (5) the Platonic Stabilizing Standard (also called the Balancing Standard). (See Table 32-1.)

Actual Privity or the Cardoza Standard The Cardoza Standard of Actual Privity emerged from within the pages of a remarkable case decided in 1932 by Judge Benjamin Cardoza of New York. The Cardoza Standard is based on a strict interpretation of the nature of duty as it is relates to privity. As we have seen, privity is a relationship that emerges when two or more parties enter a contract. The parties to the contract are said to be *in privity* and it is the actual existence of that privity that creates the obligations that the parties owe to one another. Thus, under the Cardoza Standard, unless the parties have **actual privity**, that is, privity that results from a type one accounting contract, liability for negligence (aka malpractice) does not exist—period.

Near-Privity or the Actually Named Third-Party Standard If an accountant prepares a financial statement with the actual knowledge that the client is going to show the statement to a particular third party, then the accountant has entered a type two accounting arrangement. Since the accountant has actual knowledge of the existence and identity of

Table 32-1   Accountants' Liability to Third Parties under Common Law

Liability Theories and Explanations

Actual Privity (also the Cardoza Standard)	Privity is a relationship that emerges when two or more parties enter a contract. The parties to the contract are said to be *in privity,* and it is the actual existence of that privity that creates the obligations that the parties owe to one another. Thus, under the Cardoza Standard, unless the parties have actual privity, that is, privity that results from a type one accounting arrangement, liability does not exist.
Near-Privity (also the Actually Named Third-Party Standard)	To establish a condition of near-privity, the plaintiff must show that (a) the accountant knew that the reports would be shown to a third party, (b) the accountant knew the identity of the third party and that he or she would rely on the report, and (c) the accountant's conduct revealed that he or she had knowledge of the third party's reliance. The existence of near-privity means the plaintiff did, in fact and in law, owe a duty of due care toward the third party.
Near-Privity Plus (also the Specifically Foreseen Third-Party Standard)	Accountants can also be liable to the limited class of third parties that is specifically foreseen (not just actually known but specifically foreseen) when the financial statement is drawn up. Thus, an accountant who prepares a financial statement, knowing that the client intends to show it to some likely investors, would be liable to any investor in that same class of specifically foreseen third parties.
Near-Privity Plus-2 (also the Reasonably Foreseeable Third-Party Standard)	Some courts have become very broad in holding accountants liable to third parties. These jurisdictions have adopted a test that depends on whether the plaintiff in the case was *foreseeable* (not just foreseen but foreseeable) as a possible recipient of the accountant's report.
The Platonic Stabilizing Standard (also called the Balancing Standard)	Under the moderating influence of the Platonic Stabilizing Standard, the courts should consider the following elements to determine auditor–third party liability: (a) how extensive were the investments involved in the case; (b) how foreseeable was the injury that emerged from the conduct under scrutiny; (c) how certain is it that the auditor's behavior led to the injury: (d) how connected was the action of the auditor to the third party's financial injury; and (e) how high was the ethical responsibility of the auditor.

that third party, many courts will acknowledge that, even though a state of privity does not exist in this type two arrangement, the relationship between the accountant and the third party is one in which the parties acted as if privity existed, a condition referred to as one of near-privity. To establish a condition of near-privity, the plaintiff must show that (a) the accountant knew that the reports would be shown to a third party, (b) the accountant knew the identity of the third party and that he or she (or it?) would rely on the report, and (c) the accountant's conduct revealed that he or she had knowledge of the third party's reliance. The existence of near-privity means the plaintiff did, in fact and in law, owe a duty of due care toward the third party. The court can move to the second issue, and that is the question of whether the defendant acted in a dutiful manner toward the third party. Another way to put this is to ask, did the actions of the defendant conform to actions that are expected of a competent, law-abiding auditor in relation to the third party? Or, to phrase it a third way, did the activity complained of (or failure to perform that activity) by the plaintiff fall within the scope of the duty owed by the defendant to the plaintiff? If this question can be answered in the affirmative, then the defendant will be held liable for any actual financial

CLASSIC CASE Lack of Actual Privity: The Intolerable Indeterminacy of an Indeterminate Class

Fred Stern and Company applied to the Ultramares Loan Corporation for a credit advance in support of its import business. As was its custom, Ultramares asked Stern for a detailed financial statement that included an audited balance sheet. Stern agreed and supplied Ultramares with a report from its auditors, Touche, Niven, and Company. When Stern went to Touche, Niven, and Company, the import corporation did not reveal to the accounting firm that Ultramares would see the report. The only thing that the importers told the auditors was that the report would be shown to some possible creditors. Touche, Niven, and Company filed an audit report that stated Stern had a net worth of $1 million. Satisfied with the statement, Ultramares lent the money to Stern. The report turned out to be false. Fred Stern and Company was actually worth nothing at all, zero, zilch, zip, nada, nil, naught—nothing! The auditors had filed the erroneous report because Stern had shown them a record of a series of sales that had never taken place. The importer, of course, could not hope to pay Ultramares back for the money it had borrowed, so the loan company went after someone who actually had enough money to make up the loss, and that was the accounting firm of Touche, Niven, and Company. The firm argued that the report had been prepared for Stern, and because it had no

knowledge that Ultramares would see the report, it could not be liable for negligence to the loan company. Judge Cardoza ruled that the defendant accounting firm could be liable only if it were in a state of *actual privity* with the plaintiff. Such a state of actual privity would emerge only if a real contract existed between the plaintiff and the defendant. Since no such contract existed, liability for negligence could not emerge from the relationship. Ruling otherwise, Cardoza reasoned, would create an indeterminate class of persons, corporate and otherwise, to which the accounting firm might unexpectedly find itself liable, simply because its client decided to share the report with a group of outsiders. It was the *intolerable indeterminacy* of the class that bothered Cardoza who expressed his misgivings in the following way: "The remedy is narrower where the beneficiaries of the promise are indeterminate or general. Something more must then appear than an intention that the promise shall redound to the benefit of the public or to that of a class of indefinite extension. The promise must be such as to 'bespeak the assumption of a duty to make reparation directly to the individual members of the public if the benefit is lost' (*Moch Co. v. Rensselaer Water Co.*, 247 N. Y. 160, 164; American Law Institute, Restatement of the Law of Contracts, § 145)." [See: *Ultramares Corp. v. Touche,* 255 N.Y. 70, 174 N.E. 441 (1932).]

loss that occurred due to the defendant accountant's negligence (the causation and the harm spoken of earlier.) [See: *Delollis v. Friedberg,* 12-1628-cv (Second Circuit 2015); See also: *Credit Alliance Corp. v. Arthur Andersen & Co.,* Court of Appeals of New York, 65 N.Y.2d 536 (1985).]

The Near-Privity Plus or Specifically Foreseen Third-Party Standard Most states have extended this rule even further, holding that accountants are also liable to the limited class of third parties that is specifically foreseen (not just actually known but specifically foreseen) when the financial statement is drawn up. Thus, an accountant who prepares a financial statement, knowing that the client intends to show it to some likely investors, would *be liable* to any investor in that same class of specifically foreseen third parties. To recover from the accountant, the investors would have had to rely on the statements and suffer financial loss.

Near-Privity Plus-2 or the Reasonably Foreseeable Third-Party Standard Some courts have become very broad in holding accountants liable to third parties. These jurisdictions have adopted a test that depends on whether the plaintiff in the case was *foreseeable* (not just foreseen but foreseeable) as a possible recipient of the accountant's

THE OPENING CASE *Round 3*
Near-Privity and Actually Named Third Parties

Recall that in the opening case, Empire State Carpenters Welfare, Annuity, and Pension Funds, the plaintiff in the suit, invested in Beacon Associates, LLC (BA). Soon afterward, BA invested Empire's money in Bernard L. Madoff Investment Securities LLC (BLM). Unhappily, this move turned out to be a serious miscalculation. This lawsuit focuses not on BLM but on the auditors Friedberg, Smith & Co., P.C. (FSC). As BLM's auditor, FSC released yearly statements on BLM's financial health. These reports confirmed that BLM's "financial statements fairly represented the financial position" of BA and of Empire Funds accounts with BLM. As it happened, this description was incorrect, and BLM was effectively worthless. Unsettled by the scale of their loss, the trustees of Empire sued FSC. The trial court granted a motion to dismiss the claim against FSC, and Empire Funds appealed. The Second Circuit Court of Appeals focused on two questions, the first of which had to be answered in the affirmative before the case could go forward: "Did FSC owe a duty of due care to Empire Funds?" We, however, were able to see that an even more fundamental question sits at the base of the case and that question is: "What type of accounting arrangement exists between FSC and Empire?" Or perhaps even more simply, "Is the arrangement between FSC and Empire a type one or a type two accounting arrangement?" The question is easy enough to answer. Since the two firms, FSC and Empire, entered a type two, rather a type one arrangement, actual privity is nonexistent. In a court that follows the *Ultramares* case, the case would end at this point. In *Ultramares,* Cardoza ruled that the absence of actual privity would mean the auditor owes no duty to the third party. However, this court is just a bit more liberal and deals with the parties under a banner of near-privity. Near-privity can be established in a type two arrangement just so long as: (a) the accountant

knew that the reports would be shown to a third party, (b) the accountant knew the identity of the third party and that he or she (or it?) would rely on the report, and (c) the accountant's conduct revealed that he or she had knowledge of the third party's reliance. Such was the case here. The court put it this way: "We also agree that Empire has adequately pleaded near-privity between Empire and Friedberg (FSC) with regard to its Beacon investments. The proposed second-amended complaint alleges that Friedberg (FSC) addressed reports directly to Empire, that Friedberg (FSC) was aware that its reports would be used to make investments in Beacon, and that Empire would rely on its reports to do so . . . Cf. *Prudential Ins. Co. of Am. v. Dewey, Ballantine, Bushby, Palmer & Wood*, 80 N.Y.2d 377, 385 (1992)." Now that we know that near-privity exists (and with near-privity a duty of due care) we can ask if FSC violated its duty of due care to Empire. The court says, "No." This is because what Empire is asking is not that FSC perform an audit on BA because Empire knows that such an audit exists. Rather Empire is demanding that, in compiling its audit of BA, FSC also request additional information directly from BLM. This is outside the scope of its duties. The court says it this way: "Empire alleges that Friedberg was obliged to obtain additional information from BLMIS [sic] to verify the existence, accuracy, and value of Beacon's BLMIS investments. Friedberg's obligation, however, was to audit Beacon, not BLMIS [sic]. Empire fails to cite any provision of the Generally Accepted Auditing Standards (GAAS) or Generally Accepted Accounting Principles that would impose such a duty. While Empire is also careful not to allege that Friedberg had a duty to actually audit BLMIS [sic], this contention is at the foundation of its claims." [See: *Delollis v. Friedberg*, 12-1628-cv (Second Circuit 2015).]

report. For instance, if it is reasonable for the accountant to foresee that the financial statement would be shown to bankers, suppliers, and potential investors, then the accountant is liable to any of these reasonably foreseeable classes of individuals. This ruling would be true even if the class were not specifically mentioned when the accountant was hired by the client. This version is the widest of the three tests that the courts have adopted for determining the extent of an accountant's liability to third parties in negligence cases. Cardoza would be vindicated (unhappy but vindicated nevertheless) because what these courts have done is create a test that itself creates an indeterminate class of persons, corporate and otherwise, to which the accounting firm might unexpectedly find itself liable, simply because its client decided to share the report with a group of outsiders.

Platonic Stabilizing Standard   Some state courts have had a difficult time sticking to a single standard and, as a result, have a mixed bag of results with which to examine the auditor–third party liability issue. Perhaps the most effective way to deal with this dilemma is to use a Platonic Stabilizing Standard that balances the various liability standards and takes into account the individualized nature of each case. Like the ancient Greek philosopher Plato who saw the middle path of balance and moderation as the way to the good life, those judges who follow the balancing standard attempt to do likewise. Platonic-minded judges who mimic his path would say that the courts should take into consideration the following elements to determine third party liability: (a) how extensive were the investments involved in the case; (b) how foreseeable was the injury that emerged from the conduct under scrutiny; (c) how certain is it that the auditor's behavior led to the injury: (d) how connected was the action of the auditor to the third party's financial injury; and (e) how high was the ethical responsibility of the auditor. Two of the hopes implied by the stabilizing standard are that, by balancing the various factors, a fair and equitable result will emerge and such conduct will be deterred in the future.

Fraud   Because fraud involves a deliberate deception, the courts have no difficulty extending protection to a wide class of third parties. Thus, an accountant who prepares a fraudulent financial statement is liable to anyone who can be reasonably foreseen as relying on that statement.

An Accountant's Statutory Liability

Accountants may also be sued for violating statutory laws governing their activities. Such suits can arise under the Securities Act of 1933, the Securities Exchange Act of 1934, and various state laws.

Securities Act of 1933   Under the Securities Act of 1933, the first time a corporation issues stock for sale, it must file a registration statement (see Chapter 28). Such statements are prepared by accountants. The 1933 act allows purchasers who have lost money after buying corporate stock based on misleading or false registration statements to sue the accountants who prepared the statements. To succeed in such a lawsuit, the plaintiff must show that the registration statement included a false or misleading statement about a material matter and that he or she suffered a measurable financial setback as a result of relying on that statement. However, the accountant has a defense in such cases. Usually, if the accountant can show that he or she used due diligence in preparing the report, he or she will escape liability. Due diligence is generally demonstrated by reference to the proper application of GAAS and GAAP standards. However, the accountant will also have to show that he or she committed no additional negligent actions and made no other avoidable mistakes.

Securities Exchange Act of 1934   A second federal law, the Securities Exchange Act of 1934, also contains some provisions that affect accountants. These provisions are designed to prevent the fraudulent filing of various documents with the SEC and the fraudulent manipulation of the securities market. Both acts also contain provisions that impose criminal liability on accountants in some situations.

State Statutes   In addition to these federal statutes, most states have enacted similar statutes regulating the activities of accounts as they relate to the sale of stock. State statutes that regulate the sale of stock are frequently referred to as blue sky laws because they are set up to stop the sale of securities that are as empty as several feet of blue sky.

32-2 The Liability of Architects and Attorneys

In addition to accountants, two other frequently contracted business professionals are architects and attorneys. Both are regulated by the states, and both must follow certain clearly stated duties.

The Liability of Architects

An architect is a professional who plans the construction or alteration of a variety of structures, from small, single-family dwellings to enormous skyscrapers. Generally, architects do not actually construct the building. However, they may manage the construction according to their detailed plans.

State Regulation Under its police power, the state can regulate the conduct of architects. States often establish an agency that makes the rules that architects must follow to be officially recognized as professionals in their field of expertise. The state will usually establish age, character, education, experience, and testing requirements. Often a state will maintain a list of all architects officially registered as having met all of these legal requirements.

Duties of the Architect Like any other professional, an architect owes a duty to exercise due care and skill in carrying out professional duties. This standard of care requires the architect to use the same methods, techniques, and procedures that any architect of ordinary skill would use in a similar situation. The standard does not demand that the architect's design be perfect or that the execution of the design be faultless. Architects can make mistakes, as long as those mistakes do not result from a failure to use appropriate skill and good judgment according to accepted professional standards.

Contractual Liability Sometimes the final version of a building differs from the original plan at the time the contract was made. If the deviation is actually an error caused by the architect's failure to use due care and skill, the architect may have to reimburse the client for any extra money spent to correct the error. This requirement is known as the **cost of repair rule**. A different rule is followed if the design is so defective that the structure is unusable for its originally intended purpose. In such situations, the court may declare that the architect owes the client the difference between the market value of the building as it stands and the market value of the intended structure.

Tort Liability Unlike mistakes made by accountants, errors made by architects may injure people or damage property. If the architect has failed to exercise the appropriate standard of care and if, as a result, property is damaged or people are injured, the architect may have to compensate the victims. Note, however, that the architect's mistake must cause injury or damage.

EXAMPLE 32-2: The Ironic Puzzle of Causation

Architects Lefkowitz and Rudman were hired to plan the new convention center to be located in Las Vegas. Rudman failed to check the stress specs on a balcony on the second level of the convention center's main exhibition floor. Had he made the check, his inspection would have revealed that an error had been made that could cause the balcony to collapse under its own weight. The construction firm of McMahon-Fulton, Inc., ignored the Lefkowitz-Rudman specs and used their own plans. However, the McMahon-Fulton plan contained the same error that the architects' plan had contained. On the night that the convention center opened, the balcony suffered a partial collapse that injured several people. Because the contractor had ignored the Lefkowitz-Rudman plan, the architects were not held liable, despite their error.

The Liability of Attorneys

Next to the accountant, one of the most sought-after professionals by a businessperson is the attorney. An attorney is a professional because of expert knowledge, ability, and education in finding, understanding, interpreting, and applying the law. Attorneys advise their clients in a variety of different ways, all of which require good faith, loyalty, and the exercise of due care.

State Regulation of Attorneys Like accountants and architects, attorneys are regulated by the state's police power. Also like accountants and architects, attorneys are normally required to be of a certain age (usually 18) and of good moral character. They are required to possess a certain educational background and to pass a special examination, demonstrating minimum competency. Unlike architects and accountants, attorneys often do not have any experience requirements, because architects and accountants usually are required to have only a bachelor's degree, whereas attorneys obtain an advanced degree in law. This extra education often takes three to four years beyond the bachelor's degree. The experience requirement of architects and accountants frequently amounts to two years.

Ethical Rules of Attorneys The American Bar Association has established a set of ethical standards—the ABA Model Rules of Professional Conduct. These rules have been officially adopted and implemented in 49 states. Only California has rejected the new rules. California elected to create rules peculiar to their own jurisdictions. Professional Responsibility. The new Model Rules of Professional Conduct simplify the old rules by dividing professional responsibility into seven areas. These areas include the client–lawyer relationship, the lawyer's duty as a counselor, the lawyer's responsibilities as an advocate, the lawyer's obligations to third parties, the responsibilities of lawyers to one another in law firms and in partnerships, the lawyer's duty to perform public service, and the lawyer's responsibilities in relation to the legal profession.

Ethical Problems in Dodd–Frank One the most hotly debated provisions in the Dodd–Frank Act is Subtitle B of Title IX, which permits the SEC to develop regulations that will create a "whistleblowing bounty program" analogous to the one used by the IRS.

A QUESTION OF ETHICS

Indeterminacy from Another Angle

In his essay, "The Chaotic Indeterminacy of Tort Law: Between Formalism and Nihilism," Denis J. Brion, professor of law at Washington and Lee University School of Law, explains that two very distinct interpretations of the law have existed side by side for a number of years. He calls one of these two theories *formalism* and the other *nihilism*. Brion explains the two theories in the following way:

> In "Legal Formalism: On the Immanent Rationality of Law," Ernest Weinrib offers … the idea that the law can be accurately described in terms of … its "inner coherence." He argues that the law is altogether distinct from politics and that it can only be understood from within itself. The function of judges is to "make transactions and distributions" in the social world conform to the "latent unity" of the law. The function of legal scholars is to make explicit the internal coherence and intelligibility of the law. In *The Disorder of Law: A Critique of Legal Theory*, Charles Sampford sets out to criticize the various theories of law that seek to describe it as systematic. His principal thesis is that society itself is without system—his term is the "social melee"—and that the law, as an integral part of society, is correspondingly disordered—the "legal melee." He concludes that, because of this disorder, the impact of legal doctrine on social and individual practices is strongly attenuated.

A third alternative is offered by Lawrence Friedman in his treatise *Law in America*. The law, Friedman says, is not a separate autonomous system. Rather, the law "is, essentially, a product of society; and as society changes, so does its legal system. Feudal societies have feudal legal systems; socialist societies have socialist systems; tribal societies have tribal systems; capitalist societies have capitalist legal systems. How could it be otherwise?"

Of course, the German philosopher, Max Weber, would disagree with all three of these experts. Weber offers a fourth alternative in his essay, "Politics as a Vocation." in that essay, Weber argues that the type of legal system that a nation-state develops is based on the type of authority that shapes the government of that nation-state. Bureaucratic governments produce a rational system of hierarchical rules that are developed by a legislative process. The rules are written down and those rules bind everyone, even the leader. Patriarchal government are run by personal leaders who command authority by following traditional practices. There is no need to create new law because the law has existed from the very beginning of that socio-political system and must not be changed. In fact, changes in tradition may be grounds for revolution. Finally, governments led by charismatic leaders develop legal systems that emerge from the unique qualifications (and, mystical powers) of the leader and are developed on a case-by-case basis. So charismatic law is always changing.

QUESTIONS YET UNANSWERED

The following questions have not yet been answered. Before you consider each question, turn to Chapter 1 to review the various ethical theories noted there (market value ethics, social contract theory, utilitarianism, and rational ethics). Then in a consistent way, answer the following questions.

1. Of the four theorists, which one has the more ethical view of the legal system? Explain.

2. Which view supports the idea that the judicial–economic system is a balancing act that aims at creating a flexible and responsive system? Explain.

3. Which view is supported by the evidence in this chapter concerning the regulation of the legal profession? Explain.

4. Of the four theorists, which one reflects your own personal view? Explain.

5. Of the four views, which one best explains the need for laws such as Sarbanes–Oxley and Dodd–Frank? Explain.

Whistleblowers, or SEC "bounty hunters" as they are sometimes called, must qualify for their "bounty" by providing original evidence of a securities law violation. This is not always easy. Nevertheless, bounty hunters can be a very determined group because successful hunters can earn 10 to 30 percent of a penalty over $1 million. Unfortunately, for attorneys, there are ethical problems associated with bounty hunting. If an in-house counsel discovers evidence of an in-house securities violation, and if the SEC rules demand that bounty hunters circumvent internal remedies, then the attorney has an ethical choice to make. Does the attorney remain loyal to the client and not report the violation or does the attorney help the SEC and the public by reporting the violation according to "the new whistleblower rule system"? The answer should be obvious. Client loyalty always comes before any other loyalty. However, the whistleblowing system places an enormous temptation in the path of the unsuspecting attorney. It will be interesting to see how this all plays out in the future [See: David Ingram, "SEC Weighing How to Award Tipsters," *The National Law Journal,* (May 16, 2011), pp. 1 and 4.]

Negligence/Malpractice   An attorney has the duty to represent clients with good faith, loyalty, and due care. An attorney who does not fulfill these duties may be liable for malpractice. Usually, however, an attorney is not liable to a third party who is not a client.

Duties of the Attorney   When a client hires an attorney, the client has the right to expect the attorney to act in *good faith*, which means that the attorney's duty is to act in the best interests of the client. In the absence of such good faith conduct, the attorney may face a lawsuit brought by the client and disciplinary action brought by the state.

An attorney also has a duty of *loyalty* to protect the client and to make certain that the client receives advice and representation that is free of conflicting interests. Thus, an attorney cannot represent two clients on opposite sides of the same dispute, unless both sides have been completely informed of the dual representation and consent to it. Similarly, an attorney violates the duty of loyalty if he or she takes advantage of a client for personal profit. The duty of loyalty also gives rise to certain privileges that exist between clients and their attorneys. One of the most fundamental privileges is the attorney–client privilege. The attorney–client privilege guarantees that information that passes between clients and their attorneys will remain secret. The rationale that supports the attorney–client privilege is the belief that clients must feel free to tell their attorneys everything that is involved in a case so that the attorney can do his or her best as an advocate of that client. The privilege can be waived if a third party unrelated to the client is present during a discussion with the attorney, provided that third party is not a person involved in the case, such as another attorney in the firm, a paralegal, or a legal assistant.

Closely related to attorney–client privilege is the work product privilege. The work product privilege protects all notes, recordings, research documents, Q&As, voice mails, faxes, e-mails, computer records, memos, letters, flash drives, disks, DVDs, CDs, and so on that are prepared in anticipation of litigation. So, for instance, if an attorney interviews a client about the facts in a pending lawsuit and takes notes during that interview, those notes are protected by the work product privilege. Or if a client sends an e-mail to his or her attorney after an interview, saying something like, "Oh, by the way, when we talked yesterday, I forgot to tell you this or that about the lawsuit," that e-mail is also protected by the work product privilege. Like the attorney–client privilege, the work product privilege can be waived if the work product is revealed to a third party not related to the client or not involved in the preparation of the client's case. Moreover, the work product privilege is not an absolute privilege. This distinction means that the content of the work product may have to be disclosed if a party who needs the information wrapped up in that work product can convince a judge that he or she has a substantial need for that information and cannot obtain that information some other, more legitimate, less intrusive way.

Like all other professionals, an attorney owes a duty of *due care* to clients. This duty means that in giving legal advice, negotiating claims, litigating suits, making out wills, negotiating divorce settlements, and performing any number of other legal tasks, an attorney must exercise the same skill and care that would be expected of other attorneys in the same situation.

Steps in a Legal Malpractice Case

For a plaintiff to succeed in a malpractice case against an attorney, that plaintiff must demonstrate the existence of four specifically drawn elements. First, the plaintiff must show that the attorney owed a duty to that plaintiff. Generally, this proof is not a problem,

CLASSIC CASE Unconstitutional or Unethical: *State of Florida, et al. v. U.S. Department of Health and Human Services*

Almost immediately after the Patient Protection and Affordable Care Act became law, the attorney general of Florida, joined by AGs from 12 other states, filed a lawsuit asking the courts to declare the act unconstitutional. In essence, the AGs claimed that the law was an unconstitutional extension of federal power that violated the Commerce Clause, the 10th Amendment, and Article I, Sections 2 and 9 of the Constitution. Probably the most effective argument said that penalizing someone for inactivity (not having health insurance) could not be used to support a congressional invasion of the states. This might have been the end of it had it not been for the fact some experts began to suspect the AGs had no legal justification for bringing the lawsuit. Some experts even argued that the AGs should be made to pay for the cost of the lawsuit out of their own pockets and perhaps even be disbarred because they had violated Rule 11 of the Federal Rules of Civil Procedure. Rule 11 demands that an attorney certify that, in any lawsuit filed in federal court, the "claims, defenses, and other legal contentions are warranted by existing law." The claims brought in this case were not only unwarranted but also patently false, or so the argument goes. For one thing, the AGs had grossly misstated the law and had no evidence to support their factual contentions. The new law would not eliminate Medicare in noncomplying states, as the AGs contended; it would not require states to create an agency to help insurance consumers as the AGs said; and it would not impose a financial burden on the states, as the AGs argued, but would, instead, result in a huge savings for some states due to new federal money flowing into those states. Moreover, and perhaps more

to the point, the very filing of the lawsuit was an illegal exercise of state power since, as long ago as 1923, the Supreme Court ruled in *Massachusetts v. Mellon,* 262 U.S. 447, that the states have no standing to attack federal statutes on constitutional grounds. The consequences of this lawsuit went beyond the declaratory action requested by the AGs. It could have cost a fortune in taxpayers' money to argue the case; it could have delayed the law's implementation; and it could have eliminated many needed programs that would disappear along with any truly unconstitutional parts (if there really are any). On the other hand, despite these weighty and troubling accusations, it does appear that, under the new Model Rules of Professional Conduct, the AGs actually faced an authentic ethical dilemma in this case and others like it. The Ohio version of the model rules, for instance, demands that an attorney act as an advocate for his or her clients and, at the same time, "advance the administration of justice." When lawyers become the attorneys general of their states, their duty to their constituents comes first. They appear to owe a transcendent duty to the public in the home state and to the state itself. This direct and indisputable duty comes first. This may mean that the AGs must even challenge the authority of the federal government. After all, if they do not challenge the feds, who will? [See: *State of Florida, et al. v. U.S. Department of Health and Human Services,* 3:10-CV-91 RV/EMT; Timothy Stoltzfus Jost, "Sanction the 18 State AGs," *The National Law Journal,* April 12, 2010; "Preamble: A Lawyers Responsibilities," *Ohio Rules of Professional Conduct* (Columbus: Ohio Bar Liability Insurance Company, 2010), p. 1.]

because when the client consults the attorney, a contract is created by which the attorney assumes the duty to represent that client with the appropriate level of care. The question of duty can arise, however, when there is a factual discrepancy about whether the client actually hired the attorney to represent him or her. Thus, the duty clearly arises when the client comes to the attorney's office and asks the attorney to help him or her deal with a legal problem. In contrast, if a student were to ask a law professor a hypothetical question during a class discussion, then no duty has arisen because there is no client–attorney relationship created in such a situation.

Second, the attorney must have breached the duty that is owed to the client. The attorney's duty is measured by his or her compliance with a standard that holds that an attorney must represent a client in a way that demonstrates enthusiasm and dedication to the client's best interests. The attorney cannot, however, file claims or advance arguments that have no realistic chance of succeeding or that are not firmly grounded in acceptable legal principles. The attorney must act as a reasonable professional would in the same circumstances. This standard does not mean that attorneys are not permitted to make mistakes. On the contrary, mistakes are tolerated as an inevitable part of the legal profession, just as long as they do not result from carelessness, inattention, laziness, or ignorance. Third, the plaintiff must show that the attorney's questionable behavior caused the resulting harm to the plaintiff. Moreover, it is not enough that there is a factual connection between the behavior and the injury. There must also be a legal connection between the two. Such a legal connection requires foreseeability. Fourth, the plaintiff must show that he or she suffered actual harm as a result of the attorney's breach of duty.

Because attorneys are professionals and because the intricacies of the law are often mystifying to the layperson, the law requires that the elements of malpractice must be supported by expert testimony. Expert testimony can only be overlooked when the relationship between the injury suffered by the client and the behavior by the attorney is so obvious that the experience of the plaintiff is within the everyday experience of the jury. As we shall see, a very similar—in fact, an almost identical—standard is used to guide the question of whether expert testimony is needed in the case of malpractice claims that are filed against health care professionals.

Third-Party Liability
In contrast to accountants and architects, attorneys are rarely held liable to third parties because the attorney's responsibilities are tied closely to the interests of the client. On the other hand, this does not mean that an attorney can be disrespectful, cruel, or vindictive to a third party. In fact, in one instance, the Ohio version of the Model Rules of Professional Conduct state quite specifically that an attorney cannot, "embarrass, harass, delay, or burden a third person." The rules also stipulate that an attorney cannot with knowledge "make a false statement of material fact or law to a third person." [See: "Rule 4.1 Truthfulness in Statements to Others" and "Rule 4.4 Respect for Rights of Third Persons," *Ohio Rules of Professional Conduct* (Columbus: Ohio Bar Liability Insurance Company, 2010), pp. 133 and 139.]

Court-Driven Protection
As we've seen, attorneys who are negligent can be the target of a civil suit brought by a wronged client. There are other safeguards within the legal system, however, that are designed to make certain that attorneys do not file phony lawsuits, promote unwarranted legal arguments, conduct unnecessary investigations, file unjustifiable motions, or make allegations that lack evidentiary support. The Federal Rules of Civil Procedure, for example, specifically forbid such objectionable conduct and impose severe penalties should that rule be broken. Many states have similar civil rules that are designed to deter unprofessional conduct on the part of unscrupulous attorneys. Penalties can include a payment of money to the court or to the other party. These payments may even include attorneys' fees in appropriate cases.

Criminal Liability Attorneys are not immune to criminal liability, especially when they act in collusion with their clients. Fortunately, most of the time, attorneys know what is going on within the attorney–client relationship because they are responsible for most, if not all, of the legal decisions made in that relationship. Sometimes, however, an attorney, especially an in-house attorney, might not know everything about a transaction that he or she is handling for a client. An **in-house attorney** is one who is part of the officer corps of a business and, as an employee of that business, does what he or she is told to do by his or her supervisor. Therefore, the attorney might know very little about the details behind a particular deal. Thus, the attorney might draft a contract between a manufacturer and a retailer that appears legitimate but involves a series of unrecorded kickbacks about which the attorney knows nothing. Or an attorney might transcribe the details of a contract that involves a stock transaction based on insider trading without knowing anything about that insider's involvement in the deal. In the past, prosecuting attorneys were willing to give attorneys the benefit of the doubt. Today, however, such favoritism is fast becoming a thing of the past. In the current climate, prosecutors are less likely to be forgiving when an attorney should have known better about a suspicious contract or should have asked certain crucial questions that remained unspoken.

---

quick quiz 32-2

1. When an architect's plan is so defective that the structure he or she has designed is unusable, the courts will invoke the cost of repair rule.   true | false

2. For a plaintiff to fail in a malpractice case against an attorney, that attorney must disprove the existence of all four elements of malpractice.   true | false

3. Because attorneys are professionals and because the intricacies of the law are often mystifying to the layperson, the law requires that the elements of malpractice be supported by expert testimony.   true | false

---

32-3 The Liability of Health Care Providers

Health care providers are professionals who possess the specialized knowledge, abilities, education, and experience that make it possible for them to answer some aspect of a patient's health care needs. Some businesspeople must deal with health care providers on a daily basis. Such contact is routine for hospital administrators, risk-management experts, pharmaceutical salespeople, hospital accountants, insurance adjusters, and biomedical equipment salespeople. Even individuals who do not deal regularly with health care providers in the business world may one day have to deal with them as patients. Knowledge of the liability of such professionals may be helpful in these situations.

The Professional Status of Health Care Providers

It should be obvious that physicians are professionals, because they must possess the specialized knowledge, abilities, education, and experience needed to perform their jobs. Dentists, podiatrists, chiropractors, nurses, nurse practitioners, nurse technicians, radiologic technologists, respiratory therapists, and laboratory technicians are also considered health care professionals. All these professions are regulated by the state. In addition, most are regulated by independent professional organizations such as the American Society of Clinical Pathologists.

The Health Care Standard of Care

Unlike accountants, architects, and attorneys, health care professionals frequently must physically touch their patients. This physical touching can involve routine tests and examinations, as well as dangerous and painful procedures. To avoid liability for the intentional tort of battery, health care providers frequently must obtain the patient's written consent. In addition to intentional torts, health care providers might be vulnerable to charges of negligence if they do not follow the appropriate standard of care.

Consent Patients who undergo tests and treatment have the right to know about those procedures and the right to refuse to undergo them if they so desire. These rights impose a duty on the health care professional to seek the patient's consent. Consent takes two forms: general consent and informed consent. Upon entering a hospital, a patient automatically gives general consent for the routine tests and procedures that are needed for diagnosis and treatment. Although such consent is implied in the situation, many hospitals require patients to sign general consent forms (see Figure 32-1).

When a diagnostic test or a procedure will be dangerous or painful, the treating physician must obtain the patient's informed consent. For this type of consent, the physician

---

CONSENT UPON ADMISSION TO HOSPITAL

Patient _____ Date _____ a.m. _____ p.m. _____

(or _____ for _____)
knowing that I, or the patient (am) (is) suffering from an illness requiring hospital care do hereby voluntarily consent to such hospital care requiring an operation, diagnostic tests or therapeutic treatment by Dr. _____ , his/her assistant or his/her designee or as necessary according to his/her judgment.

I also recognize that during the course of my operation, tests, or therapy unforeseen conditions may necessitate additional or different procedures and I am aware that inasmuch as the practice of medicine and surgery is not an exact science, there have been no guarantees made to me as the result of treatments or examinations to be performed in this hospital.

I have read the above statements and I certify that I understand them.

_____   _____
Witness   Signature of Patient

Figure 32-1 Many hospitals today require patients to sign general consent forms like this one upon admission.

must tell the patient in advance about the procedure and the risks involved. Informed consent must be in writing on a form that is signed by the patient and witnessed by a third party. Generally, a written consent form is considered valid by the court and precludes any suit based on battery, unless the patient can prove a lack of understanding of the information on the form or a deliberate misrepresentation as to its content.

Negligence   For a patient to succeed in a negligence case against a health care professional, the patient must show that the four elements of negligence exist in the case. First, the patient must demonstrate that the health care provider owed a duty to that patient. Usually, the question of duty is not at issue in such cases. However, the question will arise whenever the relationship between the patient and the health care provider is not clear-cut or obvious. In such cases, the court may be asked to determine whether the health care provider owed a duty to the plaintiff.

Second, after establishing the existence of a duty between the health care provider and the patient, the plaintiff must show that the health care professional breached that duty. The health care professional's duty is measured by his or her compliance with a standard of care. The health care provider must act with the same level of skill, care, and knowledge that any reasonable health care provider would display in a similar situation. Determining how a reasonable health care provider would act in a given situation can be determined in several ways. One way is to refer to the hospital's policy and procedure manual. When professionals follow the standard policies and procedures as written in the manual, they are performing as any reasonable professional would, unless the procedure in the manual can be shown to be out of date, incompetently written, or incomplete in some way.

If a hospital's manual does not address a situation, if the manual is outdated, if the procedure is incompetently written, or if the steps in the procedure are incomplete, the court may judge the performance by going outside the hospital and looking at the manuals or procedures used at other hospitals. Many states today use a rule called the locality rule. The locality rule judges a health care provider's behavior on the basis of how other health care professionals in the same community would have acted in the same situation. Thus, rural physicians are compared to other rural physicians in the same rural community, city physicians with other city physicians in the same city, and so on. The rationale behind the locality doctrine is the commonsense notion that it is unfair to judge the professional conduct of a small-town general practitioner (GP) who is involved in a case involving a heart attack victim by comparing him or her to a big city cardiologist involved in a similar case. In such a comparison, the small-town GP will always be judged poorly, because he or she will have neither the educational opportunities nor the up-to-date facilities that are available to the big city cardiologist.

Despite the widespread use of the term *locality rule,* there is no single locality doctrine. Instead, there are variations on the same theme. The most rigorous version of the doctrine is the true locality rule. The true locality rule requires the court to look at the standard of care used in the exact locality of the physician. This standard makes it very difficult for the plaintiff, who must use an expert witness from the same area as the defendant. Such experts are rarely forthcoming because the fraternity of local physicians is generally a closed group. A second variation on the locality rule is the similar locality rule. This rule permits the court to judge the actions of a local physician against those of a physician in a community of comparable size and socioeconomic character. Thus, a physician in New York would be compared to one in Chicago or Los Angeles, a physician in Cleveland with one in Pittsburgh or Buffalo, and a physician in Green Bay, Wisconsin, with one in South Bend, Indiana, or Dayton, Ohio. This rule permits the plaintiff to find an expert in one of those analogous localities an easier task because there are fewer fraternal ties among that class of physicians.

The third version of the locality rule is the same state locality rule. This rule, perhaps the least logical of the four variations, ignores the socioeconomic character of the physician's home base and concentrates instead on the geographical limits of a state border. Thus, a plaintiff who finds him- or herself in a state that honors the same state locality rule can call an expert from any region in that state to testify as an expert witness. The final variation of the locality rule is known as the **similar practitioner rule**. This rule actually rests on a double standard that permits GPs to be judged by one criterion and specialists by another. Thus, GPs, who are apparently expected to stay close to home, are judged by other GPs in the same community, whereas specialists, who are expected to be more cosmopolitan and therefore more educated, more up-to-date, and more competent, are judged by a standard that can be applied anywhere in the country.

Those states that no longer use the locality rule have adopted another rule called the **national rule** or the **national standard**. These states have recognized that with the advent of continuing education requirements and the presence of mass communication, online continuing education programs, and the like, there is rarely any good reason for a health care professional to be unaware of the development of medical trends on a national, or, at times, even an international basis.

Causation in a Malpractice Suit A crucial element in any malpractice case is the issue of causation. In such a case, the plaintiff must prove not only that the defendant's conduct did not conform to acceptable medical practices but also that this failure to follow acceptable procedures was the cause of the plaintiff's injury. Much of the difficulty in supplying this proof arises because the fact finder in a malpractice case must attempt to understand medical evidence that is frequently beyond his or her experience.

Expert Testimony Because many of the tasks performed by the health care provider are highly specialized, determining how the professional should act often requires expert testimony. However, expert testimony is not required if the action under examination is within the common knowledge of all people.

EXAMPLE 32-3: Experts Need Not Apply

Nurse Noel Grady was called away from Kurt Yarborough's room by another nurse. Yarborough was sedated but restless. He was thrashing about and had attempted to leave the bed several times. Despite this state, Grady left him alone, failing to raise the siderails or restrain Yarborough in any way. While Grady was absent, Yarborough tried to get out of bed. He fell and broke his leg. At Grady's negligence trial, the judge ruled that no expert testimony was needed to measure Grady's standard of care. The judge felt that the issue of whether a sedated and restless patient should be left unsupervised and unrestrained was well within the common knowledge of the jurors.

Medical Records and the Patient's Rights

In recent years, concerns about privacy matters have come to the forefront of the law. In no area of the law is this truer than in health care law. Physicians once effectively guarded the secrecy of their files by arguing that patients were apt to misinterpret or misunderstand notations made in medical jargon or hospital shorthand. These arguments are no longer acceptable. To ensure the patient's right to see his or her records, Congress passed the **Health Insurance Portability and Accountability Act (HIPAA)**. Under HIPAA, Congress has guaranteed that patients have the right to see their medical records and parents have the right to see the medical records of their children. The act also gives both groups the right to obtain duplicates of the records. There are, of course, exceptions to this rule. For instance, records that result from psychotherapy sessions receive a higher level of protection under the act. Patients are permitted to see such records only if the patient has the physician's permission. Even with permission, the patient must look through the records along with the physician. These extra limitations are placed on psychotherapy records because they are seen as somewhat emotional and open to a wide variety of false impressions.

The Patient Protection and Affordable Care Act

Under provisions included in the federal Patient Protection and Affordable Care Act,

The Health Insurance Portability and Accountability Act (HIPAA) gives patients the right to review their medical records and the records of their children.

the Department of Health and Human Services has developed a set of new regulations on a trial basis to help support physicians, hospitals, clinics, and other health care establishments in the creation of a system of coordinated health care institutions for Medicare patients, known as accountable care organizations (ACOs). Under the new rules, an ACO can consist of a variety of formats including (1) ACO professionals, including physicians and hospitals in group practice arrangements; (2) networks of individual practices of ACO professionals; (3) partnerships or joint ventures between hospitals and ACO professionals; (4) hospitals employing ACO professionals; and (5) other Medicare providers and suppliers as determined by the secretary of health and human services.

The new regulations will measure the quality of an ACO under five criteria: (1) patient and caregiver experience, (2) care coordination, (3) patient safety, (4) preventative health, and (5) the handling of at-risk populations including the frail and elderly. The ACO program is administered by the Center for Medicare and Medicaid Services (CMMS). Under

CLASSIC CASE Unconstitutional or Unethical: *State of Florida, et al. v. U.S. Department of Health and Human Services—One More Time*

Let's look at the classic case of *State of Florida, et al. v. U.S. Department of Health and Human Services* one more time. Recall that a lawsuit was filed by the attorney general of Florida along with 12 additional state AGs, all of whom attacked the constitutionality of the Patient Protection and Affordable Care Act. When the case reached the district court, the judge decided that the act was indeed unconstitutional, at least in part. Unfortunately, the judge also ruled that the unconstitutional portions could not be separated

from the constitutional ones. Consequently, should one part of the act be lost, the entire act will be lost, including provisions like the one discussed earlier. What would then be the fate of an already established and operating accountable care organization? Explain your answer. [See: *State of Florida, et al. v. U.S. Department of Health and Human Services,* 3:10-CV-91 RV/EMT; and Timothy Stoltzfus Jost, "Sanction the 18 State AGs," *The National Law Journal,* April 12, 2010.]

the new rules, an ACO must have a board of governors with a wide-ranging membership including representatives of all the people affected by its operation. Specifically, the rules call for a membership that involves health care providers, suppliers, and Medicare beneficiaries. To be properly certified by the CMMS a new ACO must take responsibility for at least 5,000 beneficiaries for three years.

quick quiz 32-3

1. For a patient to succeed in a negligence case against a health care professional, the patient must show that the four elements of negligence exist in the case.   true | false

2. Today, most courts use a rule called the national rule or the national standard to make judgments in relation to the standard of care for health care providers in negligence cases.   true | false

3. To ensure the patient's right to see his or her records, the American Law Institute and the American Bar Association collaborated to create a model act called the Health Insurance Portability and Accountability Act (HIPAA).   true | false

32-4 Hospital Liability

Hospitals can be held liable for the negligence of a physician, even if that physician is not an employee of the hospital. Hospitals routinely grant physicians, who are not employed by the hospital, the privilege to treat their patients at that hospital. The granting of such **staff privileges** can be troublesome for the hospital if the staff physician becomes the defendant in a malpractice lawsuit, because the patient frequently sues not only the physician but also the hospital. Two legal theories that have been used successfully to add the hospital to the list of defendants in a malpractice lawsuit are ostensible authority and negligent credentialing.

Ostensible Authority and Hospital Liability

Ostensible authority, also known as agency by estoppel and apparent authority, has been successfully used by plaintiffs to hold the hospital, as well as the physician, liable for malpractice. **Ostensible authority** is created when a hospital presents itself to the public at large as a provider of health care services and in some way leads the patient to believe that a physician with staff privileges is an employee of the hospital. This authority can be shown if the hospital allows the physician to wear a hospital identification tag, use hospital equipment, dispense medication at the hospital, issue orders to hospital employees, and so on. Under such circumstances, the courts have been willing to hold that, because it is reasonable to believe that these representations would lead the patient to the conclusion that the physician is an employee of the hospital, the patient can add the hospital to the malpractice suit as a defendant.

Negligent Credentialing by Hospital Authorities

Negligent credentialing occurs if the hospital has retained a physician that the governing body of the hospital knew or should have known was incompetent. Another form of negligent credentialing occurs if a previously competent physician with staff privileges loses that competence and the hospital governing body knows or should have known about the changed circumstances but takes no remedial action. This form of negligent credentialing is sometimes referred to as **negligent retention**. In either situation, a patient injured by the malpractice of the incompetent physician can also hold the hospital liable.

Tort Reform and Litigation

In recent years, some states have attempted to lessen the burden placed on hospitals by ostensible authority and negligent credentialing. This movement has been motivated by the belief that such lawsuits frequently pull the hospital into a lawsuit unjustly. To alleviate this injustice, tort reform provisions often place the burden of proof on the plaintiff to prove both ostensible authority and negligent credentialing. For instance, in the area of ostensible authority, some states say that the plaintiff must prove that the hospital held itself out to the public at large as a provider of health care services and that the hospital gave no notice that nonemployee staff physicians, rather than hospital employees, would render services to the patient. Moreover, these statutes also allow the hospital to escape liability by posting notices that inform patients of the independent status of staff physicians. In states that have established such a statutory protection for hospitals, a patient can hold a hospital that posts such notices liable only if the hospital directed the negligent actions that injured the patient. In negligent credentialing, some states have created a rebuttable presumption that says a hospital is presumed to have properly credentialed staff physicians if the hospital is accredited by the Joint Commission of Accreditation of Health Care Organizations. If the hospital can show that it is accredited, the burden of proof shifts to the plaintiff to show that the hospital did not follow the credentialing procedures of the joint commission, that the hospital knew or should have known of the physician's incompetence and did nothing to limit the physician's privileges, or that the credentialing process did not apply to this hospital, this physician, or the type of case that formed the basis for the lawsuit.

quick quiz 32-4

1. A hospital can never be held liable for the torts of a physician unless that physician is an employee of that hospital.   true | false
2. Ostensible authority applies only to hospitals in large urban areas.   true | false
3. Negligent credentialing and negligent retention have been outlawed under the Restatement (Second) of Torts.   true | false

Summary

32.1 Accountants are business professionals who can plan, direct, and evaluate the complex financial affairs of their clients. The most common types of accountants are certified public accountants and public accountants. Accountants must follow generally accepted accounting principles. Auditors must follow generally accepted auditing standards. They must also follow the Code of Professional Ethics of the AICPA.

Accountants may be liable to both their clients and third parties. Making a determination of the extent of liability to third parties depends on understanding the nature of actual privity and near-privity.

32.2 Architects and attorneys are considered professionals and are regulated by the state. Architects may find themselves liable to clients and to third parties, whereas attorneys are generally responsible to their clients alone. Both architects and attorneys must exercise due care and skill in carrying out their professional duties.

32.3 The term *health care provider* includes physicians, dentists, chiropractors, podiatrists, nurses, nurse practitioners, nurse technicians, radiologic technologists, respiratory therapists, and laboratory technicians. Like other professionals, health care providers must act with the same skill, care, and level of knowledge that a reasonable health care professional would display in a similar situation.

32.4 Hospitals can be held liable for the negligence of a physician, even if that physician is not an employee of the hospital. The granting of staff privileges can be troublesome for the hospital if the staff physician becomes the defendant in a malpractice lawsuit, because the patient can sue both the physician and the hospital. Two legal theories that have been used successfully to add the hospital to the list of defendants in a malpractice lawsuit are ostensible authority and negligent credentialing.

Key Terms

accountant, 787

actual privity, 794

adverse opinion, 789

attorney–client privilege, 802

audit, 788

auditor, 788

certified public accountant (CPA), 788

Code of Professional Ethics, 789

cost of repair rule, 800

disclaimer, 789

general consent, 806

generally accepted accounting principles (GAAP), 788

generally accepted auditing standards (GAAS), 789

Health Insurance Portability and Accountability Act (HIPAA), 808

informed consent, 806

in-house attorney, 805

locality rule, 807

malpractice, 793

national rule, 808

national standard, 808

near-privity, 795

negligence, 793

negligent credentialing, 810

negligent retention, 811

ostensible authority, 810

professional, 787

public accountant (PA), 788

Public Company Accounting Oversight Board (PCAOB), 790

qualified opinion, 789

same state locality rule, 807

Sarbanes–Oxley Act, 790

similar locality rule, 807

similar practitioner rule, 808

staff privileges, 810

true locality rule, 807

type one arrangement, 792

type two arrangement, 792

unqualified opinion, 789

work product privilege, 802

Questions for Review and Discussion

1. What is the difference between a certified public accountant and a public accountant?
2. What is the difference between generally accepted accounting principles and generally accepted auditing standards?
3. What are the various types of auditing opinions that can be issued by auditors?
4. What is the difference between actual privity and near-privity?
5. What are the registration requirements imposed on architects?
6. What are the duties that an architect owes to his or her clients?
7. What are the duties that an attorney owes to his or her clients?
8. What is the standard of care used to judge health care professionals?
9. What is the difference between the locality rule and the national standard in determining a health care provider's liability?
10. What are the circumstances in which hospitals can be held liable for the torts of independent contractor physicians?

Cases for Analysis

1. While she was under investigation by a grand jury, Martha Stewart penned an e-mail that explained the circumstances that led to the ImClone scandal. Stewart then dispatched the e-mail to her attorney and sent a copy to her daughter, Alexis Stewart. The e-mail was inadvertently provided to the government, along with a number of other files that had been delivered in response to a subpoena. When the e-mail was identified, government attorneys went back to the court and asked the judge to decide whether they could use the e-mail as evidence. Stewart's attorneys argued that the e-mail was under the protection of the attorney–client privilege and the work product privilege. On the other side of that argument, it is clear that the intended recipient of the e-mail was Stewart's daughter, not her attorney. Should the judge uphold the protection granted by the attorney–client privilege and the work product privilege, or should she allow the government to use the e-mail, because Stewart sent it to a third party? Explain. [See: *United States v. Stewart,* 03 Cr. 717 (United States District Court Southern District of New York).]

2. The Consolidata Services Company (CDS) was established to provide small businesses with payroll services. All CDS clients were required to provide CDS with an advance deposit equal to the amount of one payroll. When CDS got into a cash flow problem, it tapped into some of this deposit money to cover its own debts. Eventually, the accounting firm of Alexander Grant, which had been hired by CDS to advise it on taxes and other financial matters, discovered that the deposit account was $150,000 short. CDS assured Grant that it was devising a plan to cover the missing $150,000. Accordingly, CDS asked Grant not to reveal the deficit. Nevertheless, Grant informed several of its own clients using the CDS payroll services and other nonclients of CDS's problem. Was Alexander Grant correct in revealing the information? What guidelines did the court use to answer this question? Explain. [See: *Wagenheim v. Alexander Grant and Co.,* 482 N.E.2d 955 (OH).]

3. Burke, an energy tycoon, hired the accounting firm of Arthur Young and Company to audit several of his operations. The SEC brought an action against Burke for fraud and for failure to meet certain SEC reporting requirements. The SEC also named Arthur Young as a defendant, claiming that the accounting firm should have discovered the fraud. Arthur Young argued that it had followed GAAS when it had audited Burke. The accounting firm concluded that this strict adherence to GAAS immunized it from liability under securities law. The SEC argued that Arthur Young should have done more to discover the fraud than what was required under GAAS. Was the SEC correct? Explain. [See: *Securities and Exchange Commission v. Arthur Young and Company,* 590 F.2d 785 (9th Cir.).]

4. Hutchins and O'Neil, as general partners in the Haddon View Investment Co., became limited partners in Car Wash Investments. The general partner in Car Wash was the Minit Man Development Company. Coopers and Lybrand accountants handled the accounting work for both Minit Man and Car Wash. They performed audits and prepared financial statements that allegedly revealed two healthy companies. Nevertheless, both Car Wash and Minit Man went out of business. As a result, Hutchins and O'Neil lost a total of $252,000. They sued Coopers and Lybrand, alleging malpractice, breach of contract, concealment, fraud, and deceit in the accountants' work for Car Wash and Minit Man. Coopers and Lybrand argued that Hutchins and O'Neil could not sue the firm because Car Wash and Minit Man were the clients, not Hutchins and O'Neil. Were the accountants correct? [See: *Haddon View Investment Co. v. Coopers and Lybrand,* 436 N.E.2d 212 (OH).]

5. Bainbridge hired the architectural firm of Seymour, Shaefer, and Lashutke to draw up plans for the alteration of Bainbridge's office building in Albuquerque, New Mexico. The plans called for the removal of the paneling in parts of the building and its replacement with Maxwell-Plus, a new, more durable material. Maxwell-Plus was specifically recommended by the architects as the best product on the market. From the beginning, the contractor had difficulty with the installation of Maxwell-Plus. In addition, two months after the work was completed, the new paneling began to deteriorate rapidly. Investigation indicated that Seymour, Shaefer, and Lashutke had failed to consider the dry, arid climate of Albuquerque, for which Maxwell-Plus was totally unsuitable.

Bainbridge had to have the paneling replaced at a cost of $122,532. Subsequently, he sued the architects. Seymour, Shaefer, and Lashutke argued that they were not liable to Bainbridge because the total value of the building had not been altered by their alleged error. Were the architects correct? Explain.

6. Malcolm was a physician who ran a small private practice in Harrison, Kansas. One evening, the Sandersons brought their young daughter in for treatment of what they thought was a minor throat infection. Dr. Malcolm treated her with a standard antibiotic and sent the child home. What neither Dr. Malcolm nor the Sandersons knew was that the child had contracted a rare and often fatal blood disease. The disease, Seballian Syndrome, could only be treated with a new antibiotic called Veritrium.

Had the Sanderson child been treated with Veritrium in a timely manner, her illness would have been short lived, and she would have suffered no permanent damage. As it was, the inaccurate diagnosis and the ill-advised treatment initiated by Dr. Malcolm actually made the child worse and almost caused her untimely death. Although the child eventually recovered, her hearing was permanently damaged. The Sandersons initiated a malpractice suit against Dr. Malcolm. The doctor argued that because of her location in the remote section of Kansas, she should not be expected to be as up to date on modern techniques as physicians who practice in large metropolitan areas. Furthermore, she argued that she could not have known about the new treatment and should therefore not be held liable. Is the physician correct? Explain.

quick quiz Answers

32-1	32-2	32-3	32-4
1. F	1. T	1. T	1. F
2. F	2. F	2. T	2. F
3. F	3. T	3. F	3. F

Chapter 33

Science, Technology, and Law in the 21st Century

THE OPENING CASE Round 1
The Ebola Case: When the Hospital Is Not Prepared and the Health Care Workers Suffer

Legal cases involving scientific issues are never easy, not for the parties, the lawyers, and certainly not for the judges. Such cases always involve complicated, highly specialized information that often requires expert witnesses to unravel and explain for just about everyone involved. An example is the first lawsuit filed in an American court involving the Ebola crisis. The lawsuit was filed by a nurse who contracted the Ebola virus while caring for a patient at Texas Health Presbyterian Hospital in Dallas. The suit was filed against both Texas Health Presbyterian and its corporate parent, Texas Health Resources. In the lawsuit, the plaintiff alleged that she was never properly trained for the task of dealing with such cases; that the hospital did not provide her with proper protective gear; that she was not trained in the gear that she was given, inadequate though it was; and that, after she contracted the

disease, she was treated in a way that violated her privacy. The hospital claimed that it did provide the nurse with an Ebola advisory from the Centers for Disease Control and Prevention in Atlanta, and that the hospital faithfully followed CDC and Texas state health care guidelines for handling such cases. Moreover, an official spokesperson also stated, allegations to the contrary notwithstanding, the hospital provided "full protective measures under the CDC protocols," although the same spokesperson also admitted that "there was an exposure somewhere, sometime." (Note: During the first days that the nursing staff, including the plaintiff, cared for the patient, the entire team wore inadequate gear that left skin exposed, and team members were not provided with full hazmat gear for several days. One is tempted to ask where those suits were before that time. It is also important to know that the nurse in this lawsuit was not the only nurse to contract Ebola while caring for the original patient.) The lawsuit also stated that the nursing staff was forced to create a makeshift waste disposal procedure on their own, and that the waste collected was not properly handled by the people at the hospital who were supposed to deal with it and so the nurses had to double as the janitorial clean-up staff during the crisis. The issues involved in a case like this focus on negligence to be sure (although fraud and invasion of privacy are also alleged). However, this type of situation elevates negligence to the level of professional malpractice, which means that experts must testify. The real question in such cases must focus on whether today's judges are qualified to make decisions in a case that involves detailed and complicated scientific and technological issues. The time may be upon us for the establishment of a special science court with scientifically trained and technologically savvy judges on the bench. [See: Richard Perez-Pena, "Nurse Who Contracted Ebola Sues Her Hospital Employer," *The New York Times,* March 3, 2015, p. A-18; Jennifer Emily, "Free of Ebola but Not

Fear: Nurse to File Lawsuit against Presby Parent, Worries about Continued Health Woes," *The Dallas Morning News,* February 28, 2015, http://res. dallasnews.com/interactives/nina-pham/.]

Opening Case Questions

1. Why are expert witnesses needed in a case like the lawsuit against Texas Health Presbyterian Hospital and Texas Health Resources? Explain.

2. What are the elements that the plaintiff must prove in any negligence case? Explain.

3. How does the jury unravel the technical aspects of such a case? Explain.

4. What type of scientific training is required for judges who handle scientific cases like this one? Explain.

5. What part of the U.S. Constitution authorizes Congress to create special courts and could that part of the Constitution authorize the creation of a science court? Explain.

LO Learning Objectives

1. Explain how the law permits the government to regulate science and technology.
2. Explain the purpose of the patent court pilot program.
3. Describe the function of the Office of Science and Technology Policy.
4. Outline the role of the National Science Foundation.
5. Define the function of the National Institutes of Health.
6. List Heilbroner's three challenges that face the modern world.
7. Identify the purpose of the Federal Energy Regulatory Commission.
8. Define the role of the Nuclear Regulatory Commission.
9. Describe the functions of the Clean Air Act and the Clean Water Act.
10. Explain how the law protects patents, trade secrets, and copyrights.

· 33-1 Governmental Authority Regulating Science and Technology

The law involves rules made by the government to promote order, stability, and justice. Science is an academic discipline that studies the natural universe with the goal of understanding the physical laws that guide the operation of the universe. Technology is the process of developing ways to enhance human control of those physical laws with the goal of extending human abilities. Science and technology, then, are involved in developing ways to create order and stability in the universe. For this reason, among others, science, technology, and the law often interact with one another. The point at which these three disciplines intersect can, for expediency, be referred to as jurriscience or, at times, as techno-jurriscience. Because the government produces and enforces the law, we must look to the sources of governmental power to determine just how much power the law has to control science and technology.

The powers to regulate, fund, and control science and technology in the United States are shared to a degree by the national government and the state governments and to a lesser extent by international convention. However, many of these functions are located in the federal government, and some of these powers and abilities reside exclusively within the federal government. For example, only the federal government is empowered to grant patents and copyrights. Some functions are shared by two levels of government, such as establishing departments, supporting education, and funding research programs. The national power emerges from the U.S. Constitution; the state power emerges from the states' residual police power. International power depends upon the type of international institution that is charged with oversight responsibilities. Depending upon which level a scientist has entered, he or she may find the road to governmental or international funding easy, difficult, or bureaucratically complex.

The Constitution and Science

It is often said that the Constitution revolves around two fundamental principles: (1) the separation of national powers among three distinct branches of government, and (2) a system of checks and balances to limit those powers. The principle of the separation of powers set up the three branches of the national government: the executive branch, the legislative branch, and the judicial branch. The principle of checks and balances allows each branch to share in the power of the other two branches. While all of this is true, we must also recall that the Constitution is filled with provisions designed to minimize the influence of political, social, economic, and religious factions on the national scene and to, thus, preserve the power of the central government. A faction is a special interest group that does its best to see that its point of view on certain issues is heard and acknowledged on Capitol Hill and in the White House. This concern over the influence of factions led the Framers (especially James Madison) to include several provisions in the Constitution to preserve and extend the power of the central government. In relation to science and technology, some of these enabling provisions are listed explicitly in Article I, such as the power "to promote the Progress of Science" by granting patents, while others have evolved over the past two centuries as the courts have interpreted the Commerce Clause, the Taxation Clause, the Supremacy Clause, the Necessary and Proper Clause, and the Treaty Clause.

The Legal Ecosystem as a Complex Adaptive System

Recall that a complex adaptive system (CAS) is a network of interacting conditions that reinforce one another, while at the same time adjusting to change from agents outside and inside the system. Any complex adaptive system includes a variety of agents with no central controlling agent, operating at multiple complex levels as it deals with and adapts to change by inferring the direction of future events. The purpose of a CAS is the survival and improvement of the system itself. As the law adapts to science and technology, it reinforces those practices that help the system adapt and survive, while downplaying or sidestepping those that do not. Here we see how five constitutional clauses have been interpreted to either support the expansion of federal power over techno-jurriscience or to reduce that expansion when necessary for the best interests of the entire system. In this complex adaptive tug-of-war, federal power over techno-jurriscience has been greatly expanded under the commerce, the taxation, and the supremacy clauses, and curbed somewhat under the necessary and proper clause and the treaty clause.

The Commerce Clause

By far the most powerful clause in Article I is the Commerce Clause (Article I, Section 8, Clause 3). The Commerce Clause has been used over the past two centuries to give Congress the power to create a national police force, the FBI; to prevent employment discrimination, the Civil Rights Act of 1964; and to regulate union activity, the Wagner Act. It has also been used to empower Congress to regulate science and technology. The actual text of the Commerce Clause is deceptively simple and innocuous. It says that Congress has the power "(T)o regulate Commerce with foreign Nations, and among the several States, and with the Indian Tribes." Early in the development of constitutional law, the courts created a very narrow interpretation of this clause, arguing that Congress could only regulate commercial dealings if they passed between two or more states.

This narrow interpretation, however, did not last long. The growth of the nation and the economic shift from an agrarian to a manufacturing economy demanded that the courts grant Congress more flexibility in handling economic issues. Part of this shift involved a distribution of land under the government's land-granting program. This program demanded that Congress have the power to enforce the allocation of this land. As a result, in a case known as *Gibbons v. Ogden,* the Supreme Court ruled that any commercial operation that touched on commerce among the states could be regulated by the federal government. The implications of this ruling were not immediately clear. However, eventually, lawmakers began to realize that any commercial activity affecting commerce, even an activity that took place totally within the borders of one state could be controlled by Congress. In the case of *Wickard v. Filburn,* the U.S. Supreme Court, acting as an important agent in the complex adaptive system of the law, expanded congressional power under the Commerce Clause to previously unimagined lengths. In that case the High Court ruled that a farmer's production of wheat for consumption on his own property in a single state had an impact on interstate commerce.

EXAMPLE 33-1: Strengthening the Commerce Clause

The federal power over science expanded in the case of *Gonzales v. Raich,* a case related to the federal government's science policy because it involved the regulation of marijuana use as a medical treatment. In *Raich,* the Supreme Court decided that Congress had the power to criminalize the sale and use of marijuana under the Controlled Substance Act, *even when the activity in question occurred completely within the borders of a single state.* The Court ruled, "One need not have a degree in economics to understand why a nationwide exemption for the vast quantity of marijuana (or other drugs) locally cultivated for personal use (which presumably would include use by friends, neighbors, and family members) may have a substantial impact on the interstate market for this extraordinarily popular substance. The congressional judgment that an exemption for such a significant segment of the total market would undermine the orderly enforcement of the entire regulatory scheme is entitled to a strong presumption of validity. Indeed, that judgment is not only rational, but 'visible to the naked eye,' *Lopez,* 514 U.S., at 563, under any common sense appraisal of the probable consequences of such an open-ended exemption." This case is also of critical importance because the majority opinion stresses that the Court's decisions in two high profile cases [United *States v. Lopez,* 514 U.S. 549 (1995) and *United States v. Morrison,* 529 U.S. 598 (2000)] have been repeatedly misinterpreted. In those cases, the Court struck down statutes authorized by Congress under the Commerce Clause. However, the majority expressly states that, it is a mistake to take either case for anything other than the Court's refusal to permit Congress to regulate activities under the authority of the Commerce Clause, when there is no commerce (the Court says "economic activity") involved in the prohibited conduct. [See: *Gonzales v. Raich,* 545 U.S. 1 (2005).]

Gonzales v. Raich underscored the almost unlimited authority of the federal government to control science policy at every level of the national system. However, the complex adaptive nature of the law meant that, at some other level within the legal CAS, the system would adapt to prevent an unhealthy concentration of power in the national government that could threaten the stability of the system itself. Such an adjustment occurred in a case in which the defense used an argument based on the Necessary and Proper Clause.

The Necessary and Proper Clause

The **Necessary and Proper Clause**, which is found in Article I, Section 8, Clause 18, of the U.S. Constitution, says that Congress has the power "(T)o make all Laws which shall be necessary and proper for carrying into Execution the foregoing Powers, and all other Powers vested by this Constitution in the Government of the United States, or any Department or Officer thereof." Generally, when Congress invokes the *Necessary and Proper Clause,* it specifically says so in the preamble to the legislative action. However, often when a case actually gets to court the interpretation of the Necessary and Proper Clause is tied to the court's need to pull several additional clauses into the rationale in order to arrive at a decision. Occasionally, for instance, the Necessary and Proper Clause is tied to the Commerce Clause as was the case in *People for the Ethical Treatment of Property Owners v. U.S. Fish and Wildlife Service,* No. 2:13-cv-00278-DB (D. Utah November 4, 2014). At the heart of this case is the federal government's attempt to control the treatment of the prairie dog population in the state of Utah (a case related to the federal government's science policy because it involves environmental regulation).

EXAMPLE 33-2: Challenging the Necessary and Proper Clause

In the 1970s, the Utah prairie dog was added to the endangered species list. Since that time a coalition consisting of government workers, property owners, and conservationists developed a suitable habitat for the prairie dog population. As a result of these efforts, the prairie dog population increased steadily over the next 40 years, resulting in the prairie dog's removal from that list. However, under provisions of the Federal Endangered Species Act, (ESA), as interpreted by by the U.S. Fish and Wildlife Service, among several additional defendants, the prairie dog was still entitled to certain protections that interfered with the plans of Utah property owners. Specifically, ESA Section 4(d) permits *only* a "regulated take of Utah prairie dogs," something the landowners wanted to avoid. The defense argued, in part, that the Necessary and Proper Clause empowered Congress to regulate the prairie dog population because managing the prairie dogs in Utah was part of a larger scheme by the federal government to protect those species in danger of being bought and sold into extinction. Therefore, since the wider plan was "necessary and proper," the subdivisions of that plan were too. The court, however, saw things differently. First, the court could see no market for prairie dogs so they could not be regulated directly. Second, the court could see no evidence that the loss of prairie dogs would affect those species, such as the bald eagle, that really were in danger of being bought and sold into extinction. Finally, the court could see no need for the government to merge the plan to regulate prairie dogs on non-federal land with other parts of its regulation scheme. Therefore, since the government's scheme was neither necessary nor proper to carry out its interstate objectives, it could not invoke the *Necessary and Proper Clause.* [See: *People for the Ethical Treatment of Property Owners v. U.S. Fish and Wildlife Service,* No. 2:13-cv-00278-DB (D. Utah November 4, 2014).]

This Utah prairie dog case, however, is not the end of the story because the complex adaptive nature of the law means that, at some other level within the legal CAS, the system will adapt to restore federal power over science. Such was the case in a lawsuit titled *State of Florida, et al. v. U.S. Department of Health and Human Services,* in which the Court was invited once again to deal with the general welfare clause.

The Taxation Clause The Taxation Clause is found in Article I, Section 8, Clause 1, of the Constitution. The clause declares, in part, that Congress is empowered to "lay and collect *taxes,* Duties, Imposts, and Excises, to pay the Debts and provide for the common defense and general welfare of the United States". Historically, the Taxation Clause was one of the first clauses used to justify the expansion of federal power over science and technology. Under that clause, Congress set up the Department of Agriculture in 1862 and, as part of the operation of that department, used federal money collected by taxes to hire scientists (botanists and chemists in particular) to work in that department. The power was challenged in the courts, and when the case known as *United States v. Butler* reached the Supreme Court, the court upheld (some experts say expanded) the taxing power of the court under the Taxation Clause despite the fact that it struck down the statute that was challenged in that case. Moreover, the taxing power of the federal government was strengthened once again in the case of *National Federation of Independent Business, et al., v. Sebelius,* 507 U.S._____, 132 S.Ct. 2566 (2012)

EXAMPLE 33-3: Preserving the Taxation Clause

The case of *National Federation of Independent Business, et al., v. Sebelius,* is related to the federal government's science policy because it involves the maintenance of the nation's health care system. In this case the plaintiffs challenged, as unconstitutional, that part of the Affordable Care Act that fined people who did not buy health insurance. The government defended that act, despite the fact that the law attempted to regulate non-action (not buying insurance). The government claimed that the act was valid under the Commerce Clause and the Necessary and Proper Clause. The Court refused to uphold the law under the Commerce Clause, arguing that the Framers did not give Congress the power to force people to engage in commercial activity. The Court also refused to sanction the act under the Necessary and Proper Clause. However, the Court did accept the government's third argument that the "fine" was not a penalty, but a tax. Accordingly, the Court ruled by a 5-4 margin that the "penalty" for not buying insurance, as required by the act, was not a penalty at all but was, instead, a tax issued under Article I, Section 8, Clause 1. Thus the act was a constitutional expression of the federal government's taxing power under the Taxation Clause. The Court's ruling was not surprising in this case because the Court has repeatedly strengthened the Taxation Clause of the Constitution in many cases throughout the years.

The Court has similarly strengthened the supremacy clause, which has empowered the federal government to, in effect, "veto" state law.

The Supremacy Clause The Supremacy Clause, which is found in Article VI, Clause 2, of the U.S. Constitution, says, "The Constitution, and the Laws of the United States, which shall be made in Pursuance thereof; and all Treaties made … shall be the supreme Law of the Land." Although it does not expressly say this, the Supremacy Clause has been interpreted to mean that the federal courts in general and the Supreme Court in particular have the legal authority to short-circuit state statutes, regulations, mandates, and executive orders that contradict the Constitution. The Supremacy Clause has also been interpreted to mean that federal law can preempt state law covering the same subject matter. State law can be preempted expressly if a preemption clause is added to a federal law or implicitly if the enforcement of the state statute makes the enforcement of the federal statute impossible. Otherwise, whenever a dispute over preemption arises the courts must determine if Congress intended to preempt. Such was the situation in the case of *Northern States Power Co. v. Minnesota* 447 F.2d 1143(1971), a case related to the federal government's science policy because it involves the building of a nuclear power plant.

EXAMPLE 33-4: Amplifying the Supremacy Clause

Northern States Power Company (NSPC), a Minnesota corporation, received permits from both the Atomic Energy Commission (AEC) and the Minnesota Pollution Control Agency to build a nuclear power plant in Minnesota. The Minnesota permit, however, required a more restrictive standard for waste disposal than the AEC's permit. In response. the power company sued the Minnesota agency, arguing that Minnesota had no authority to issue such a restrictive permit because, once Congress set up the AEC, it had preempted the state's authority to regulate the new facility. In response, Minnesota argued that the 10th Amendment to the Constitution gave it the right to stop pollution in its territory in order to protect the health of its people. None of this seemed to matter to the trial court, which ruled in favor of NSPC. Moreover, the appellate court upheld that decision, and the Supreme Court followed suit. [See: *Northern States Power Co. v. Minnesota* 447 F.2d 1143(1971); and Allen N. Elgart, "Constitutional Law—Federal Preemption of State Regulatory Authority," *Boston College Law Review* 13, no. 4 (1972), pp. 812–26.]

Despite this continued expansion of federal power, at times the legal CAS readjusts and, in a remarkable turnaround, ends up limiting itself. Such was the case when, under the authority of the treaty clause, the Senate short-circuited the administration's plan to endorse the Kyoto Protocol.

The Treaty Clause The Treaty Clause, which is found in Article II, Section 2, Clause 2, of the U.S. Constitution, says the president "shall have power to make Treaties with the Advice and Consent of the Senate." Generally, treaties have little to do with science, technology, and engineering. Instead, they are concerned with such things as fishing rights, trade agreements, boundary disputes, international law, disarmament, and mutual defense agreements. Occasionally, however, treaties deal with patent and copyright law, nuclear test ban agreements, genetic engineering agreements, and climate control. Although the president is not required to consult with the Senate before a treaty is negotiated or to have a senatorial representative on his or her diplomatic team, the president is required to obtain the Senate's approval before a treaty becomes the law of the land. Today, some of the most visible and controversial treaties that the president negotiates involve juriscientific matters, especially when such matters are related to climate change and environmental clean-up projects. Such has been the case with the Kyoto Protocol and its progeny.

EXAMPLE 33-5: Questioning the Treaty Clause

One of the most troublesome science-related laws to hit the newspapers in recent years was the Kyoto Protocol, a treaty negotiated by former President Bill Clinton and signed by him in November 1998. Among other things, the protocol called for the primary industrialized nations to reduce carbon dioxide emissions below levels recorded in 1990. Although the president had signed the protocol and repeatedly indicated his support for the measure, as a treaty, it had to be approved by the Senate. Unfortunately, the Senate was strongly opposed to the measure, indicating that it could not support any proposal that would not force developing nations to reduce pollution or that would damage the American economy. The bottom line was that, despite the support of the president of the United States, the Kyoto Protocol was dead in the water, so to speak, because, under Article II, Section 2, Clause 2, of the U.S. Constitution, the treaty needed Senate approval. The situation deteriorated even further after the election of George W. Bush, who, like Clinton, expressed support for pollution emission reduction but, unlike Clinton, would not underwrite such measures at the expense of the United States. President Obama also did not attempt to see the protocol ratified. The legal CAS had effectively readjusted itself once again. (See: Emily C. Barbour, "International Agreements on Climate Change: Selected Legal Questions," Congressional Research Service (2010) http://fpc.state.gov/documents/organization/142749.pdf.)

The Patent Court Pilot Program

So far we have examined just how complicated science-related cases can be when they touch even peripherally on constitutional provisions. We have not yet touched on laws related to the mechanism for funding science, except peripherally. Nor have we considered the question of residual state power in relation to scientific regulation, the complicated issues surrounding patent and copyright law, laws related to energy and the environment, nor issues related to international juriscience. These problems are made even more complicated when we consider the levels of the bureaucracy involved in science-related issues. These levels include the president, Congress, and a wide variety of administrative agencies. The courts are also involved in science and technology whenever a case includes a review of the right to die, a discussion of patient rights, an examination of patent law, an evaluation of genetic engineering laws, or an analysis of other cutting-edge technologies. Most of the time when such cases come before a judge at the trial level, the judge must unravel technical and scientific concepts for which he or she is neither educated nor experienced. This is a time-consuming and error-filled process. That is why some commentators have suggested the creation of a national science court.

Steps have been taken in that direction by the Federal Judicial Center. The center recently inaugurated a decade-long patent court pilot program aimed at improving the way that patent law cases are handled by the Federal Circuit. The pilot project will institute an education program for training judges in the intricacies of patent law that will help them develop a technique for effectively managing a patent law caseload. Under the guidelines set up for the program, 14 courts have been chosen to participate. Certain judges in each of these courts have been appointed to consider patent cases. Whenever a new patent case is added to the docket of a participating court, that new case is given to one of the judges in the district on an arbitrary basis. Those judges not in the patent law program can either keep the case or pass it along to the pool of patent law judges. The intent is that most of the cases will be passed on to these specially educated and scientifically trained judges. However, part of the program is also designed to determine the success rate, measured in terms of upheld and reversed cases, between trained and untrained judges. The program is being run under the auspices of the Judicial Conference Committee on Court Administration and Case Management. Status reports on the program will go to congress periodically. [See: Karen Redmond, "District Courts Selected for Patent Pilot Program," *The Third Branch News,* June 7, 2011; "The Patent Pilot Program Takes Off Around the Country," *Gibbons IP Law Alert,* October 20, 2011.]

A Federal Science Court

Should the patent court pilot program prove successful, it may lead to the development of a court that is fully dedicated to hearing all science- and technology-related cases from patent lawsuits to cases that involve regulation and funding. The federal science court would have exclusive jurisdiction over issues involving scientific, engineering, medical, and technological cases. All judges who sit on the national science court would be expected to have a scientific background or would be required to undergo special training sessions to get him or her up to speed on science and engineering matters. Each judge would be required to attend an internship program during which he or she would shadow a full-time science court judge to learn the ins and outs of all procedural and substantive issues peculiar to that court in regard to science and technology. The federal science court would deal with a wide variety of cases such as those involving nuclear power, cyber-terrorism, genetic engineering projects, medical malpractice suits, medical research issues, environmental protection law, intellectual property problems, and so on. As things develop, the court might even be subdivided into layers, each of which would be responsible for a different discipline. Thus, there might be a medical division, a scientific division, a technology division, and an engineering division.

THE OPENING CASE *Round 2*

The Ebola Case: Has the Time for the Science Court Finally Arrived?

Recall that in the opening case, a nurse who contracted Ebola sued her employer, Texas Health Presbyterian Hospital and its corporate parent, Texas Health Resources. In the lawsuit, the nurse alleged that she was never properly trained to deal with such cases; that the hospital did not provide her with proper protective gear; that the hospital did not train her properly in the gear that she was given, ineffective though it may have been; and that, after she contracted the disease, the hospital violated her privacy. In response, the hospital claimed that it did provide the nurse with the CDC's Ebola advisory and that the hospital faithfully followed CDC and state health care guidelines for handling such cases. Moreover, an official spokesperson also stated that the hospital had provided full protective measures under the CDC protocols, although the same spokesperson also admitted, "There was an exposure somewhere, sometime." Looking carefully at these issues we can see that they are filled with technical and scientific questions that must be answered before a decision can be reached. Recall that to succeed in any negligence case, a plaintiff must demonstrate the existence of four elements: (1) duty, (2) breach of duty by failing to meet the appropriate standard of care, (3) proximate cause, and (4) injury. The first and the fourth (duty and injury) are clear enough in this case. However, determining the appropriate standard of care will require expert knowledge about the exact nature of that level of care. Was the initial set of CDC protocols sufficient? If so, were those protocols followed? What constitutes following the protocols to begin with and were the protocols themselves sufficient? If they were sufficient, then why did the hospital not follow them? Was the hospital even capable of following the protocols? Perhaps the original patient should *not* have been taken to Texas Health Presbyterian Hospital. Maybe Johns Hopkins, the Mayo Clinic, the Cleveland Clinic, or the National Institutes of Health (NIH) in Maryland would have been more suitable. The nurse was, in fact, eventually transferred to the NIH, where she received a series of experimental drugs and plasma from Dr. Kent Brantly, an Ebola survivor. These are the types of questions that most judges are neither trained nor predisposed to deal with, and so, perhaps, it is time to set up that special science court to handle such complexities in a fair, effective, and efficient manner. [See: Richard Perez-Pena, "Nurse Who Contracted Ebola Sues Her Hospital Employer," *The New York Times,* March 3, 2015, p. A-18; Jennifer Emily, "Free of Ebola but Not Fear: Nurse to File Lawsuit against Presby Parent, Worries about Continued Health Woes," *The Dallas Morning News,* February 28, 2015, http://res.dallas-news.com/interactives/nina-pham/.]

Supporters and Detractors Commentators who support the national science court argue that the complex nature of today's scientific caseload is beyond the expertise of most judges who sit on the bench at the trial level. These experts argue that it would be more effective and economical to build an entirely new league of professional *science judges* to deal with these complexities. Those who oppose the national science court contend that the training sessions to bring judges up to speed would be cost-prohibitive. Moreover, the proposed subdivision of the court into subcourts handling different disciplines would create unnecessary and expensive duplication. As you read the following issues in relation to juriscience, see if you can decide whether the science court would be a help or a hindrance. [See: Barry Casper and Paul Wellstone, *Powerline: The First Battle of America's Energy War* (Amherst, MA: University of Massachusetts Press, 1981); and Barry Casper and Paul Wellstone, "Science Court on Trial in Minnesota," *Science in Context: Readings in the Sociology of Science,* ed. Barry Barnes and David Edge (Cambridge, MA: MIT Press, 1982).]

Residual State Regulatory Power

Notwithstanding the extensive control that the national government has over science, technology, and engineering, the states still maintain a certain level of residual power in this area. The capacity of the states to regulate science and technology emerges from the states' police power. **Police power** is the states' ability to uphold and sustain the public health, safety, welfare, and morals. Every state in the union possesses police power simply because it exists as the lawful governmental authority within its own territory. The state government along with its various departments and divisions from counties or parishes; to cities, towns, and villages; to zoning districts and school boards, all have some job to play in the regulatory process. The state creates colleges and universities with research programs; regulates hospitals and clinics; standardizes laboratories and testing facilities; designs science and engineering school curricula; runs state parks and conservation programs; controls state environmental, energy, and resource programs; and so on. The state also collects incorporation fees, taxes corporate activities, polices the actions of corporate managers, and creates new corporate entities, such as limited liability companies and joint ventures, all of which may have research and development departments.

Judicial Power and the Common Law

The tradition of common law fills the law books of many state court systems with cases related to science, technology, and engineering. While many of these cases are preempted when the federal courts overturn a case or when Congress passes a statute that preempts a state law, state courts are justifiably hesitant to relinquish long-standing common law values. Consequently, state courts frequently discover imaginative ways to interpret federal guidelines within the framework of that state's established legal institutions. Consequently, the study of juriscience must be moderated by the established principles of state law. As we have seen, that is what occurred in *People for the Ethical Treatment of Property Owners v. U.S. Fish and Wildlife Service*, No. 2:13-cv-00278-DB (D. Utah November 4, 2014); *Northern States Power Co. v. Minnesota*, 447 F.2d 1143(1971); *Gonzales v. Raich*, 545 U.S. 1 (2005); and *National Federation of Independent Business, et al., v. Sebelius*, 507 U.S._____, 132 S.Ct. 2566 (2012); all of which are covered earlier.

quick quiz 33-1

1. A faction is a special interest group that does its best to see that its point of view on certain issues is heard and acknowledged on Capitol Hill and in the White House. true | false

2. Congressional power to regulate science and technology is found only in the commerce clause. true | false

3. Police power is the state's ability to uphold and sustain the public health, safety, welfare, and morals. true | false

33-2 National Expenditures for Science and Technology

The federal government has been funding scientific and medical research for the past 150 years. That funding comes in many forms for a variety of purposes and with an enormously high price tag. Nevertheless, Congress and the president have agreed that the expenditure is necessary to provide for national security, to promote the health and welfare of American citizens, and to ensure the economic and social well-being of the nation. For this reason, the federal government has established a number of agencies and institutes that support, assess, coordinate, and fund scientific, medical, and technological research. The history of science funding at the national level reaches back to the 1800s and continues today at a very lucrative rate.

The History of Scientific Expenditures

Large expenditures for scientific research have a long history in the United States, extending back to the establishment of a group of land grant colleges launched in 1862 by Congress under the authority of the Morrill Act. The Morrill Act provided national monetary support for colleges and universities with the purpose of launching a set of partnerships among institutions of higher learning and the farming community. The textile industry also entered the race for progress by sending specialists into educational institutions with directions to help university researchers address issues related to technology and science in that business. Collaborations like this became so routine that they sparked the creation of huge scientific and technological educational institutions such as MIT. Paradoxically, the birth of big research universities also encouraged the establishment of research-based corporations like AT&T, Dow Chemical, Westinghouse, and GE [See: D. Dickson, "Universities and Industry: Knowledge as Commodity," *The New Politics of Science* (Chicago: University of Chicago Press, 1988), pp. 61–62.]

Another supply of funding emerged after the Second World War when Vannevar Bush, the director of the White House Office of Scientific Research and Development, delivered a report to the president titled *Science: The Endless Frontier,* but commonly referred to as *The Bush Report.* In *The Endless Frontier,* Bush pushed for the creation of a consolidated national research institution, the National Science Foundation (NSF). The purpose of the NSF would be to provide government dollars for technological and scientific research projects, many of which would be located in the nation's colleges and universities. [See: "Introduction and Overview," *Science for the 21st Century: The Bush Report Revisited,* Ed. C.E. Barfield (Washington: AEI, 1997), pp. 3–4; D.J. Kevles, "The Changed Partnership," *Wilson Quarterly* 19 (Summer 1995), p. 42; D.C. Mowery, "The Bush Report after Fifty Years—Blueprint or Relic," *Science for the 21st Century: The Bush Report Revisited,* Ed. C.E. Barfield (Washington: AEI, 1997), pp. 28–29.] Today the chief national scientific agencies for scientific, medical, and technological research are the Office of Science and Technology Policy, the National Science Foundation, and the National Institutes of Health.

Office of Science and Technology Policy

The Office of Science and Technology Policy originated in 1961 as the Office of Science and Technology under President John F. Kennedy. The primary purpose of the office under Kennedy was to keep the president apprised of developments in the space program. Eventually the purpose expanded to ensure that the president was informed about overall advances in technology and science as well as the impact that these developments might have on U.S. policy. In 1976 Congress expanded the scope and function of the office when it set up the Office of Science and Technology Policy under the National Science and Technology Policy Organization and Priorities Act. The goal of the new office is to advise the president on technological and scientific matters so that he can make informed decisions about federal programs that impact science and technology. The office is also responsible for managing science and technology policy, especially as that policy impacts the federal budget. In addition, the office integrates science policy at every level of governmental planning from the federal to the local level. This effort also includes coordinating governmental efforts with private industry to develop productive and efficient partnerships between the government and the private sector. Finally, its job is to assess the effectiveness of the overall federal science and technology program [See: "About OSTP," Office of Science and Technology Policy, The White House, http://www.whitehouse.gov/.]

Chief Technology Officer of the United States

In 2009, a new position was added to the office of the president known officially as the assistant to the president, associate director for the Office of Science and Technology Policy, but referred to generally as the chief technology officer (CTO) of the United States. The primary job of the CTO is to coordinate advances in technology and engineering as they relate to the practical jobs of improving the American economy, managing medical and health care costs, and preserving national security. The CTO works side by side with the United States chief information officer (CIO). The job of the CIO is to build an integrated technology policy designed to meet the needs of the national government. The position was created by Congress under the authority of the E-Government Act of 2002. All of these moves may seem new. However, even though none of these offices existed until recently, the president of the United States has had some sort of science and technology advisor on hand ever since Vannevar Bush worked for Franklin Delano Roosevelt and Harry S. Truman from 1939 to 1951. [See: "Chief Technology Officer," Office of Science and Technology Policy, The White House, http://www.whitehouse.gov/.]

National Institutes of Health

The National Institutes of Health (NIH) operate under the auspices of the Public Health Service of the Department of Health and Human Services. Their operational mission is to conduct research into all aspects of human life and health and to apply that understanding to cure illnesses, to alleviate disabilities, and to lengthen human life. The National Institutes also promote practical research that will reduce health care costs in order to improve the economic stability of the United States. The institutes also provide funding for research into the origin, prevention, and cure of diseases related to environmental problems. The institutes now invest over $21 billion each year in medical research. Eighty percent of that figure is awarded as grants to 350,000 recipients at over 3,000 universities, medical schools, and research organizations in the United States and around the globe. Ten percent of the original figure goes to funding the institutes' own operational laboratory in Bethesda, Maryland. The National Institutes of Health consists of 27 segments designated as institutes or as centers, each of which has an individualized research program. For example, the National Cancer Institute is charged with conducting cancer research. All but a few of these independent institutes receive their money directly from Congress. Nevertheless, the institutes handle their own administration. Funding decisions are delegated to institutes because such decisions are better handled by the experts who know how the money should be spent within their own areas of expertise. The system has the added benefit of preventing Congress from trying to use its influence to control the projects, the universities, and the individual scientists who receive the funding. The objective is to make sure the funds are spent where they should be spent. [See: "Mission," National Institutes of Health, United States Department of Health and Human Services, http://nih.gov.]

National Science Foundation

The National Science Foundation (NSF) is a federally funded agency that was created by Congress in 1950 to support scientific research, to stimulate the national economy, and to safeguard national security. The National Science Foundation has an annual budget that runs close to $7 billion. A substantial portion of that money is spent on scientific research

CLASSIC CASE Research: Driven by Science, Economics, Ethics, or Law?

The last-minute addition of an amendment to a congressional spending bill is usually seen, and rightly so, as an attempt to establish federal policy without seeming to do so. It is an effective but controversial strategy. However, generally, the controversy fades as public attention is drawn elsewhere. Such has not been the case with the Dickey-Wicker (DW) Amendment, which was added to the budget in 1998 and since then has been the subject of renewed attention again and again. The amendment forbids the National Institutes of Health (NIH) from funding "(1) the creation of a human embryo or embryos for research purposes; or (2) research in which a human embryo or embryos are destroyed, discarded, or knowingly subjected to risk of injury or death greater than that allowed for research on fetuses in utero under 45 C.F.R. 46.204(b) and [42 U.S.C. § 289g (b)]." *Id.* The NIH has interpreted that amendment to mean that any research that directly destroys a human embryo is forbidden but, and here is the rub, any research that uses cells that were already taken from an embryo through a process referred to as derivation, is permitted and, therefore, can be funded. The *Sherely v. Sebelius* lawsuit under consideration here was brought by two researchers who use adult stem cells in their projects rather than stem cells taken from embryos through derivation (or some other, similar technique). The plaintiffs claim that funding research that uses derivative cells violates the DW amendment's ban on the use of "embryos … destroyed, discarded, or knowingly subjected to risk of injury or death." The plaintiffs argue further that their research is in danger of being underfunded (or not funded at all) because NIH generally supports research using derivative cells rather than research that, in strict compliance with the law, uses nonderivative cells. The history of the case is long, involved, and somewhat convoluted but it

amounts to this. The trial court granted an injunction to the plaintiffs, which stopped the funding of projects using derivative cells. The defendants appealed the issuance of the injunction, and the appeals court agreed, overturning the injunction. This decision reopened the door to the use of derivative cells. The court's ruling turned on an interpretation of the language of the budget amendment. To interpret DW, the appeals court used a rule called the Chevron Doctrine. The Chevron Doctrine says that, when a congressional rule is truly ambiguous, a court must acquiesce to an agency's interpretation of that rule. If the ambiguity seems, let's say, "manufactured" by the agency to "get its way," the court will ignore the agency's self-serving interpretation and use a textualist approach to interpret the actual language of the congressional rule. The NIH's interpretation of DW said, in effect, that derivative cells do not qualify as having been "destroyed, discarded, or knowingly subjected to risk of injury or death" and, therefore, derivative cell research can be funded. The appellate court apparently saw some sort of ambiguity in DW and, following the Chevron Doctrine, acquiesced to the NIH interpretation. This decision lifted the trial court's injunction, which, to the plaintiffs' dismay, allowed derivative cell research to be funded once again. The questions on the table now are what, if anything, is ambiguous about the words "destroyed, discarded, or knowingly subjected to risk of injury or death" and should this case be passed onto the U.S. Supreme Court? What is your opinion and how did you formulate that opinion? [See: *Sherely v. Sebelius*, 1:09-cv-01575, U.S. District Court for the District of Columbia (2012). See also: *Sherely v. Sebelius*, No. 11-5241 (2012) Note: In the second appeal in the case, the Appellate Court did not revisit the issues discussed here. Therefore, this application of the Chevron Doctrine to the language of the amendment stands.]

in American colleges and universities. Grants from the National Science Foundation are available for practitioners in all fields of science, mathematics, and computer technology. The NSF, which is based in Arlington, Virginia, authorizes over 120,000 grants annually. These grants are approved by a merit-based assessment process. Most of these grants fund individuals or small teams of researchers. Some grants, however, are set aside for large institutions for the purchase of equipment, facilities, and hardware. Projects that are likely to be funded are those that are clearly on the cutting edge of scientific research and development. The goal of the NSF, however, is not only to support scientific research but also to enhance scientific education, while at the same time building a globally competent and internationally competitive scientific labor force. Over the past 30 years, NSF researchers have been awarded more than 180 Nobel Prizes. One of the most recent Nobel Prizes went to Richard Heck of the University of Delaware, Eiichi Negishi of Purdue University, and Skira Suzuki of Hokkaido University in Japan. They won the 2010 Nobel Prize for chemistry for developing an innovative technique for joining carbon atoms together to construct effective practical complex molecules. [See: "NSF at a Glance;" and "Nobel Prizes: The NSF Connection," National Science Foundation, http://nsf.gov.]

---

quick quiz 33-2

1. The federal government did not begin funding scientific and medical research until the 20th century.   true | false

2. The National Institutes of Health operates under the auspices of the Public Health Service of the Department of Health and Human Services.   true | false

3. The National Science Foundation (NSF) is a federally funded agency that was created to support scientific research and education, to stimulate the national economy, and to safeguard national security.   true | false

---

33-3 International Authority Regulating Juriscience

While we will discuss international law in detail in the next chapter, it will be helpful to look at it briefly before moving on. There are four types of international nongovernmental organizations (NGOs): (1) those that are completely dependent upon the nation-states that make up their membership; (2) those that are semiautonomous organizations; (3) those that are granted or earn entity status; and (4) those that are unaffiliated transnationals that act as rogues, outlaws, criminals, or terrorists.

International Nongovernmental Organizations

The NGOs that are completely dependent upon their member nations are aggregates or conglomerates of the membership. An organization such as the G-8, which is made up of the most powerful industrial nations of the world and has a floating leadership element that changes from year to year, is an excellent example. The second type is a semiautonomous organization that is initially made up of nation-states but which is actually more than the membership and is, therefore, capable of carrying out actions absent the consent of and sometimes in defiance of the members. Member nations might opt out of an action of which they disapprove, but the action might continue nevertheless. Member states might be able to stop some actions, depending on the structure of the organization. The United Nations is probably the best example of this type of semiautonomous international NGO.

    The third type is one that achieves or is initially granted entity status. NGOs with entity status act independently because they are not at the mercy of the member states. Some are formed by an independent membership, by corporations, or by other NGOs. The International Red Cross is a good example of an entity NGO. Some commentators say NGOs evolve; they may be originally formed as conglomerates but as they operate, they may change into semiautonomous organizations or even into entities. If in its early history the United States could have been conceived of as an NGO, then we can see how what was originally a loose confederation of independent states, under the Articles of Confederation, gradually evolved into a semiautonomous organization (before the Civil War the nation was referred to in the plural as in "the United States are . . .") and eventually became an entity (after the Civil War it becomes singular as in "the United States is . . ."). The European Union (EU) now appears to be going through a similar evolution. [See: Richard W. Mansbach and Kirsten L. Rafferty, *Introduction to Global Politics* (London: Routledge, 2008), pp. 403–04.]

Finally, some commentators would add a fourth category of NGO—the "transnats." *Transnats*, or transnational organizations, include terrorist groups, drug cartels, slave traders, and pirates. Transnats are unsanctioned bodies, such as al-Qaeda and ISIS, whose power comes from a willingness, some even say an eagerness, to break international law and who must, therefore, be taken into consideration when political leaders make strategic moves.

The United Nations

Despite the fact that the United Nations is a semiautonomous international NGO, it nevertheless wields a great deal of soft power on the international scene. *Soft power,* in contrast to *hard power,* which consists mostly of military force and economic influence, is waged at the emotional and psychological level. Soft power is used to persuade people, institutions, and nations that they have the same goals and objectives as the agency or person wielding the power. During the Vietnam era in the 1960s and '70s, soft power was described as the ability to earn the "hearts and minds" of the people. The United Nations has the ability to win the hearts and minds of many people in the international community. From an organizational perspective, the UN consists of three central governing agencies all located in New York City at its headquarters on the East River: the General Assembly, the Security Council, and the Secretariat.

The **General Assembly** consists of all UN member states. Each nation-state is empowered with a single vote on all matters presented to the assembly. The UN **Security Council** handles any crisis that threatens global peace. The Security Council is made up of 15 members. Five member states hold permanent seats: China, France, Russia, the United Kingdom, and the United States. The General Assembly elects the remaining 10 members for two-year terms. The **secretary general** is the chief administrator of the United Nations. He or she heads the **Secretariat**, which is the administrative bureaucracy of the UN. The secretary general also takes a leading role in promoting world peace. The Security Council recommends a candidate for the position of secretary general, but the General Assembly votes that person into office.

International Problems

The United Nations is a complicated and diverse organization. Many juriscientific issues related to international problems are handled by the Economic and Social Council (ECOSOC). This part of the UN is so big and so powerful that, after it takes its cut of the annual budget, only 30 percent is left to be divided among the remainder of the agencies. Another key agency is the UN Educational, Scientific, and Cultural Organization (UNESCO). UNESCO promotes integrated activities in science, education, and culture and is responsible for urging nations to preserve their cultural heritage. ECOSOC has an indirect nonreporting relationship with UNESCO and with the World Health Organization (WHO).

The WHO evolved out of a similar organization that was run under the auspices of the League of Nations, the precursor of the UN. WHO's job is to promote international health care and to help prevent the spread of illness and disease. It also supports programs in medical and health research in much the same way as the National Institutes of Health in the United States. The International Atomic Energy Commission (IAEC) is an independent agency that has oversight responsibilities in relation to nuclear energy programs, while the United Nations Environment Program, another independent agency, deals with pollution issues. The **World Intellectual Property Organization** is a specialized agency that has the job of shielding intellectual property from copyright infringement, patent violations, and IP theft. All these organization have parallels in the federal systems, and all deal with the juriscientific problems of the 21st century outlined subsequently.

UN Educational, Scientific, and Cultural Organization

UNESCO is a specialized agency of the United Nations run under the auspices of the ECOSOC. UNESCO is responsible for creating outreach efforts to develop educational, cultural, and scientific ties among the member nations of the UN. Initially, the objectives of UNESCO were seen as a function of the United Nations and were thus supported by the entire membership. Evidence of its key importance is the fact that the first head of UNESCO was the world-famous British author Julian Huxley. Unfortunately, because UNESCO's mission was to allocate funds to projects run by various member states, some of these states saw themselves being marginalized while others were being rewarded. This situation fostered jealousy and resentment. As a result, UNESCO became a highly politicized organization. Eventually it even went so far as to demand the redistribution of global resources from the developed to the underdeveloped world. In his book, *The Future of the United Nations,* Joshua Muravchik, resident scholar at the American Enterprise Institute, explains that UNESCO became more and more politicized when its leadership became tied to a bloc of underdeveloped nations within the UN.

UNESCO and The Group of 77   These underdeveloped nations referred to themselves as the Group of 77 (or just G-77). The G-77 appeared on the international stage after certain delegates attended a meeting sponsored by the United Nations Conference on Trade and Development (UNCTAD). At the time of that meeting, UNCTAD was under the leadership of the Argentine economist Raul Prebisch. Prebisch is best known as the father of dependency theory, an economic picture of the world that holds the developed world responsible for poverty in the underdeveloped world. Eventually, dependency theory became the official political position of the G-77, UNCTAD, and the United Nations. The result was a group of organizations that convinced the underdeveloped nations to adopt socialist economic structures. The G-77 also developed a manifesto called the New International Economic Order (NIEO), which was endorsed by UNESCO. [See: Linda Fasulo, *An Insider's Guide to the UN* (New Haven, CT: Yale University Press, 2004), p. 182; Robert Speaight, *Teilhard de Chardin: A Biography* (London: Collins, 1967), pp. 290–91; Joshua Muravchik, *The Future of the United Nations: Understanding the Past to Chart a Way Forward* (Washington, DC: The American Enterprise Institute Press, 2005), pp. 69–72.]

The World Health Organization and the Ebola Crisis

In 1948 the constitution of the World Health Organization (WHO) was ratified by the member nations of the United Nations. WHO's mission is to improve the health care available to all the people of the world, but especially to those most at risk because of poverty or special health-related threats. WHO's program is based on the following basic component parts: nutrition and food; sanitation and a healthy water supply; protection against contagious diseases; containment of local illnesses; effective handling of everyday injuries and familiar diseases; adequate supplies of critical pharmaceuticals; and family planning

A QUESTION OF ETHICS

Dependency Theory: A Blueprint for Injustice or a Blessing in Disguise?

The controversy surrounding UNESCO's politicization has caused an enormous amount of difficulty for the organization throughout the years. The commentators who say that UNESCO's bias in favor of the poorer nations is justified support UNESCO's critique of the developed world for exploiting the underdeveloped world, its support for dependency theory, and its adoption of the New International Economic Order (NIEO), including its demand that the rich nations compensate the poor nations. There is another side to the issue, however. The rich nations and the corporations that actually entered the underdeveloped world and drilled for oil, mined for diamonds, cut down timber, and dug for coal argue, rather convincingly, that it was their money, their equipment, and their employees that did the actual work. Their employees, with corporate money that came from investors, built roads, harbors, airports, power plants, sanitation systems, oil fields, refineries, communication systems, and so on. Moreover, the governments of the underdeveloped nations were all handsomely compensated for their fair share of the profits, or so the argument goes. Therefore, the government of each developing nation is at fault if that government failed to properly distribute a fair share of the profits to its citizens. Following this line of thought, the blessings brought by the corporations may have been disguised by the greed of the governments.

QUESTIONS YET UNANSWERED

The following questions have not yet been answered. Before you consider each question, turn to Chapter 1 to review the various ethical theories noted there (market value ethics, social contract theory, utilitarianism, and rational ethics). Then in a consistent way, answer the following questions.

1. Who is correct from an ethical perspective? Do the rich nations owe the underdeveloped nations because they, the rich, created the underdeveloped world's dependency on the developed world? Or does the fault lie in the hands of the governments of the underdeveloped world? Explain.

2. There is an interesting parallel situation in the operation of the National Institutes of Health and the National Science Foundation. In those institutions the complaint is that the best and the most lucrative grants go to researchers from the big, powerful, rich mega-universities, while the small schools and the unknown researchers are largely ignored. The other side of this argument states that the unknown researchers from the small schools actually self-select themselves out of the process, either by not applying or by giving up and withdrawing their applications before the final awards are made.

   Who is correct from an ethical perspective? Do the referees from the big schools owe the representatives from small schools special attention because they, the rich, created a peer-review merit-based process that favors the big schools and the big names? Or does the fault lie in the hands of the inexperienced researchers from the small schools who "get cold feet"? Explain.

efforts including especially the care of mothers and children. A good portion of the work done by the WHO is aimed at building up the medical and health care facilities and professionals in poor nations so that those nations can better handle the delivery of health care and medical services to the local people.

Education and Research Activities

Like the National Institutes of Health at the national level, the WHO supports health and medical research programs at the international level, all of which are aimed at promoting the basic component parts of medical and health care, that serve as its foundation. More specifically, the WHO has a special research program aimed at eradicating tropical diseases that it runs in cooperation with the UN Development Program (UNDP) and the World Bank. In addition, the WHO also works with the Food and Agriculture Organization of the UN, the World Bank, and the UNDP to fight a disease known as *onchocerciasis,* or river blindness, in West Africa. The WHO is also responsible for coordinating a global effort to control infection with human immunodeficiency virus (HIV) in an attempt to eradicate the acquired immune deficiency syndrome (AIDS). [See: *Basic Facts about the United Nations* (New York: The United Nations Department of Public Relations, 1992).]

Challenges and Achievements

Like UNESCO, the WHO has also had its fair share of controversy. In *The Future of the United Nations* (cited previously), Muravchik, reports a case involving allegations that the director of WHO in the 1990s had granted contracts to institutions that were tied directly to members of the WHO executive board. There were also allegations at the time that threats of economic sanctions were made against certain countries if the chief of the WHO, who had been charged with these irregularities, were not reelected. Muravchik also reports, however, that the WHO has had its share of successes and has accomplished a great deal in a variety of arenas. Specifically, he praises the WHO for dealing quickly with the severe acute respiratory syndrome (SARS) crisis in 2002–03 and thus preventing what could have been a devastating global epidemic. The WHO can also lay claim to playing a large role in the global elimination of both smallpox and polio.

The WHO and Ebola: International Health Regulations

Perhaps the most visible and active involvement of the WHO in international health care problems in recent years has concerned the Ebola epidemic. The Ebola virus was first identified in 1976 during two outbreaks, one near the Ebola River in the Congo and another in the Sudan. The epidemic surfaced in March 2014 when cases were reported in Guinea. The disease quickly spread to Sierra Leone, Liberia, Nigeria, Senegal, and Mali. Six months after the first outbreak was detected, the disease had reached such proportions that the director-general of WHO was compelled to label the situation an official public health emergency of international concern. Such a state of emergency is governed by protocols found in the International Health Regulations (IHR). All nations that are official members of the WHO are required to follow IHR protocols, which include reporting requirements, treatment procedures, and containment measures.

A public health emergency of international concern must be issued when an extraordinary public health event occurs: (1) that is determined to present a severe danger to the health of other nations because of the potential spread of the illness, and (2) that demands an effectively managed cooperative global effort to deal with the crisis. The problem with the rules and the protocols imposed by the IHR is that the WHO has no official enforcement mechanism. Thus, despite the details of the agreement, WHO depends upon peer pressure, the principle of reciprocity, international reputation, and good will to ensure compliance. [See: World Health Organization, "Frequently Asked Questions about the International Health Regulations (2005)," http://www.who.int/ihr/about/FAQ2009; WHO, "International Health Regulations (IHR)," http://www.who.int/topics/international health_regulations/en/; WHO, "Ebola Virus Disease," (Updated April 2015) http://www.who.int/mediacentre/factsheets/fs103/en/.]

The WHO and Ebola: Ethical Considerations

The global nature of the Ebola crisis raised a series of ethical concerns that officials at the World Health Organization were determined to manage quickly and effectively. For that reason, given the seriousness of the emergency, the World Health Organization convened a panel to consider the

THE OPENING CASE *Round 3*
The Ebola Case: Do Peer Pressure, Reciprocity, International Reputation, and Good Will Actually Work?

In the opening case we learned that a nurse who contracted Ebola sued her employer, Texas Health Presbyterian Hospital and its corporate parent, Texas Health Resources. Allegations made in the suit include arguments that the hospital health care staff was not suitably trained for the task of dealing with such cases; that the hospital failed to provide protective clothing; and that the hospital did not educate that staff appropriately in the protective clothing that was issued. As a defense, the hospital contended that it furnished the staff nurse with the CDC's Ebola advisory and that the hospital faithfully followed CDC and state health care guidelines for handling such cases. Now let's remember that the United States is a member state in the World Health Organization and is, therefore, obligated to follow International Health Regulations. The official *International Health Regulations: Guidance for national policy-makers and partners* published by the WHO lists the following "Key Obligations for States Parties":

1. Designate or establish a national IHR focal point.

2. Strengthen and maintain the capacity to detect, report, and respond rapidly to public health risks and public health emergencies of international concern.

3. Respond to requests for verification of information regarding potential public health emergencies of international concern.

4. Assess public health events by using the decision instrument and notify WHO, within 24 hours, of all events that may constitute a public health emergency of international concern.

5. Provide routine facilities, services, inspections, and control activities at international airports, ports, and ground crossings to prevent the international spread of disease.

6. Implement appropriate measures recommended by WHO.

7. Collaborate with other state parties and with WHO on IHR (2005) implementation. [See: *International Health Regulations: Guidance for national policy-makers and partners* (2008), pp. 10–11.]

Now consider the following: (1) Is the United States a state party to the International Health Regulations (extra research is required here)? (2) Has the United States established a national IHR focal point, and if so, what is it (extra research is required here)? (3) Based on your knowledge of the preceding case (and any additional research you might want to do on this issue), did the United States follow these obligations? (4) Is voluntary compliance on WHO regulations sufficient to convince nation-states to obey these regulations or should the WHO be given enforcement powers? [See: Richard Perez-Pena, "Nurse Who Contracted Ebola Sues Her Hospital Employer," *The New York Times,* March 3, 2015, p. A-18; Jennifer Emily, "Free of Ebola but Not Fear: Nurse to File Lawsuit against Presby Parent, Worries about Continued Health Woes," *The Dallas Morning News,* February 28, 2015, http://res.dallasnews.com/interactives/.]

ethical ramifications of using unregistered (read "experimental" here) treatments on the most severely affected patients. After due consideration, the panel approved the use of such experimental treatments. Nevertheless, the panel also recommended that such unregistered treatments be applied only under the following conditions: patients are to be informed about all aspects of the unregistered treatments used (including the fact that they are unregistered); patients are not to be treated until they give informed consent; patients are not to be coerced or unduly influenced into giving such consent; patients are to be promised confidentiality; patients are to be treated with dignity; and the community is to be informed about and involved in the program. The unregistered treatment programs are also to be conducted in a way that will allow for the collection and sharing of all data gathered as a result of the use of the unregistered treatments, even when that treatment occurs outside the actual clinical setting. [See: WHO, "Ethical Considerations for Use of Unregistered Interventions for Ebola Virus Disease (EVD): Summary of Panel Discussion," http://www.who.int/mediacentre/news/statements/2014/ebola-ethical-review-summary/en/.]

---

quick quiz 33-3

1. Five member states of the United Nations that hold permanent seats on the UN Security Council are: France, Russia, Japan, the United Kingdom, and the United States.   true | false

2. UNESCO is responsible for creating outreach efforts to develop educational, cultural, and scientific ties among the member nations of the UN.   true | false

3. After due consideration, a task force convened by the World Health Organization approved the use of unregistered experimental treatments on the most severely affected patients in the Ebola crisis.   true | false

---

33-4 Facing Global Challenges

The American bureaucratic system frequently appears complex and convoluted. The operation of the bureaucracy often seems erratic and directionless. The day-to-day activities appear to be designed to stall and block progress rather than to enhance it. The Federal Register, which produces a daily record of agency business, is so complex that it must include one section on rules and regulations, another on proposed rules, and one on notices of hearings, meetings, application deadlines, and administrative orders. There is also a section devoted to presidential orders and proclamations. The high level of activity within the bureaucracy could lead to the conclusion that the activity has become an end in itself, rather than the means to the end of running an efficient and effective government. While this evaluation may be discouraging, it may also be the price we pay for demanding a democratic government. Nevertheless, underneath, or perhaps above, all the activity is a series of challenges that funnel this activity in productive directions. All of the work done by the government, outside of the work needed to collect the money used to deal with the other problems themselves (think IRS here), relate in some way to four challenges: (1) the possibility of war, (2) the volatility of the marketplace, (3) the twin dangers of environmental deterioration and energy depletion, and (4) the demographic crisis. Dealing with all of these problems is part of the balancing act that is the law.

Heilbroner's Global Challenges

In 1974, the economist, author, and political scientist Robert Heilbroner wrote *An Inquiry into the Human Prospect*. In this pioneering book, Heilbroner argued that the planet Earth is faced with three challenges that must be met if humanity expects to continue into the 21st and the 22nd centuries. If these three problems are not handled, Heilbroner says with some degree of confidence, then humanity is doomed. The problems he focuses on are the possibility of war, especially nuclear war; the challenge of uncontrolled population growth (demographics), and the destruction of the environment. The list is slightly different from the one we compiled earlier. The one challenge he appears to miss is the challenge of a volatile economy. That challenge, however, is not actually missing from *An Inquiry into the Human Prospect*. In fact, the economy actually permeates the book because Heilbroner sees economic volatility as the challenge that underlies each of the other three and, ironically, is also the ultimate solution. In a sense, then, the economy is Heilbroner's mega-crisis [See: Robert Heilbroner, *An Inquiry Into the Human Prospect* (New York: Norton, 1991).] We have dealt with the legal handling of the economy since we began talking about contract law in Chapter 7. Moreover, and more to the point, we focused on much of it in Chapter 30 and 31 when we discussed the government's regulation of the economy especially as it relates to the stock market, the housing market, and corporate misconduct. In Chapter 34, we will deal at length with the challenge of war. It remains, then, for us to discuss the twin challenges of energy and the environment and the inescapable problem of overpopulation, both of which fall within the realm of juriscience.

Regulating Energy Problems

The Arab oil embargo of 1973 and the subsequent energy crisis focused national attention on the power industry. In answer to these concerns, Congress created the Department of Energy and the Federal Energy Regulatory Commission. National concerns with the problems of nuclear energy, especially after the disasters involving nuclear energy in Japan, have also recently focused attention on the Nuclear Regulatory Commission. The regulation of nuclear energy for peaceful uses on a global scale is charged to the United Nations International Atomic Energy Agency (IAEA).

The Federal Energy Regulation Commission   The Federal Energy Regulatory Commission (FERC) is responsible for regulating the transportation and the wholesale price of natural gas and electricity sold for use in interstate commerce. State utility commissioners regulate intrastate prices. Rates are calculated to allow companies a specific rate of return on investments (earnings divided by total assets), which they may not exceed. When utilities are confronted with increased costs due to higher fuel prices, they can apply to the commission for permission to pass these increased costs on to customers through fuel adjustment charges. The commission also licenses hydropower project proposals for the construction of interstate gas pipelines and liquefied natural gas terminals. In brief, a few of the additional duties of the FERC include regulating pipelines used in the interstate transport of oil; reviewing and approving interstate locations for natural gas lines; reviewing and approving the location of natural gas storage containers; reviewing applications for the placement of electricity transmission projects on a limited basis; licensing private and governmental (state and city) hydroelectric projects; producing mandatory standards for high-voltage interstate transmission systems; acting as a watchdog and overseeing accounting and financial reporting rules for companies regulated by the FERC; monitoring environmental risks in relation to hydroelectric and natural gas projects; and imposing civil penalties for violations of FERC regulations.

In 2005 Congress passed the Energy Policy Act which added a series of new tasks to the FRFC's already packed agenda. One of the top initiatives in the 2005 act involves the modernization of the nation's electric power grid. Specifically, the FERC is charged with the development of a smart grid that will make optimal use of state-of-the-art technology. The goal is to apply digital technology to the nation's power network to ensure a reliable, secure, and efficient electric grid. In addition, the FERC will ensure peak operation of the grid with protection from cyber-attacks of all kinds. Moreover, the FERC is charged with the task of implementing "smart technology in grid operations, including metering, communication, and distribution automation." Other new tasks involve removing unnecessary roadblocks that are currently preventing the implementation of the smart grid and developing standards for the interoperability of equipment connected to the grid, among many others. The FERC recently unveiled its new strategic plan outlining the outcomes that will be the focus of its program from now until the year 2018. Specifically, the commission has established three overall goals backed up by several objectives that explain the implementation of those goals. The goals include: (1) to ensure just and reasonable rates, terms, and conditions; (2) to promote a safe, reliable, secure, and efficient infrastructure; and (3) to support the commission's mission through organizational excellence. Each goal is further supported by (1) core functions that describe the actions and the tools needed to meet each goal, (2) a specific course of action detailing practical steps to deal with the challenges and opportunities that must be handled in carrying out each goal, and (3) strategic performance measures to rate the group's movement toward accomplishing each goal. [See: "Top Initiatives," "Smart Grid," and "Strategic Plan," Federal Energy Regulatory Commission http://ferc.gov. Federal Energy Regulatory Commission Strategic Plan (March 2014) FY 2014–2018.]

Nuclear Regulatory Commission Mandated by the Energy Reorganization Act, the Nuclear Regulatory Commission (NRC) is responsible for the licensing, construction, and operation of nuclear reactors. It is also responsible for regulating the possession, use, transportation, handling, and disposal of nuclear material. The NRC develops and implements rules and regulations governing licensed nuclear activities. Nuclear regulation actually began under the auspices of the Atomic Energy Commission, which was established by Congress under the Atomic Energy Act of 1946. The 1946 law was superseded by the Atomic Energy Act of 1954, which was designed to encourage the development of safe and reliable nuclear power plants. The AEC came under fire in the 1960s (What government agency didn't in the 1960s?) for developing lenient regulations regarding radiation protection, plant location, reactor safety, and protection of the environment. The AEC was eliminated in 1974 and replaced by a new agency, the current Nuclear Regulatory Commission under the authority of the Energy Reorganization Act of 1974. The NRC was charged with overseeing various aspects of the nuclear power industry, including especially radiation shielding and reactor safety. The Three Mile Island incident in Pennsylvania in1979 focused attention on the need for stricter regulations in relation to personnel training, energy planning, plant operation, plant operational records, and human involvement in plant operations, among several other things.

The NRC has evolved into an agency of rules and regulations for the security of nuclear materials to prevent the theft of that material, especially theft of that material by potential terrorists. The commission is also charged with developing and enforcing safety regulations in relation to radioactive waste materials. It also does its fair share of work in radiation medicine, developing standards and protecting patients from radiation overdoses. The NRC currently employs over 4,000 employees in Maryland and four regional offices in Georgia, Illinois, Pennsylvania, and Texas. NRC inspectors also visit nuclear power plant sites and various fuel facilities across the nation. It is important to note that the NRC does not regulate nuclear weapons, military reactors, or space vehicle reactors. It does not lobby Congress and it does not, contrary to popular opinion, operate its own reactors or its own power plants. It does, however, impose penalties for violations of its regulations. Penalties can be severe, up to $140,000 per day per violation. Licenses can also be revoked, changed, or suspended for especially egregious violations. It is even possible that a wrongdoer's violation is so severe that the violator's case is sent to the Justice Department for possible criminal proceeding. [See: "About NRC," United States Nuclear Regulatory Commission, http://www.nrc.gov.]

International Atomic Energy Agency On the international scene, the United Nations has an agency with oversight responsibility for matters dealing with nuclear power. The International Atomic Energy Agency (IAEA), which was created in 1957, is responsible for making certain that, on a global basis, nuclear energy is used only for peaceful purposes. Thus, under the statute creating the agency, there is an assumption that nuclear energy is both a useful and necessary source of energy production, especially for developing nations. Nevertheless, the IAEA also exhibits a healthy respect for the dangers associated with nuclear power. IAEA's program is based on four basic component parts:

setting up guidelines for the effective, economical, and environmentally safe production of nuclear energy; promoting the peaceful application of nuclear science technology; providing technical and engineering support on nuclear energy to member nations; and distributing scientific and technological knowledge about nuclear power. The agency must guard against the misplacement, loss, or theft of nuclear materials and equipment and make certain that such equipment and materials do not fall into the hands of those who would use them for military (or terrorist) operations. Much of this oversight is maintained by inspections, and by record-keeping procedures that can be verified by those inspectors. Such inspection and record-keeping strategies are involved in a variety of international agreements including: the Treaty for the Prohibition of Nuclear Weapons in Latin America and the Treaty on the Non-Proliferation of Nuclear Weapons, among others. [See: *Basic Facts about the United Nations* (New York: The United Nations Department of Public Relations, 1992).]

Unfortunately, in *The Future of the United Nations* (cited previously), Muravchik notes that such inspections and record-keeping processes are not foolproof. In fact, the IAEA inspection process has been less than 100 percent effective on a number of occasions, notably in the cases of Iraq, Iran, and North Korea. On a more positive note, other governments, in the peaceful pursuit of nuclear power, have come directly to the IAEA for equipment, for technical assistance, and for the education of its personnel. The IAEA is also responsible for setting up regulations that guide the requirements for radiation shielding and for the safe and efficient transport of nuclear materials. The agency also handles emergency operations in the case of a nuclear accident. The IAEA is also a clearinghouse of information, research, and data on all phases of nuclear energy. The clearinghouse, which is known officially as the International Nuclear Information System, is located in Vienna. The IAEA also runs the International Centre for Theoretical Physics in conjunction with UNESCO. [See: *Basic Facts about the United Nations* (New York: The United Nations Department of Public Relations, 1992).]

Regulating Environmental Problems

In his book, *An Inquiry into the Human Prospect,* Robert Heilbroner provides a succinct but poignant explanation for the nature of the environmental challenges that face the global community in the 21st century. Heilbroner writes: "Here we come to a crucial stage in our inquiry. For unlike the threats posed by population growth or war, there is an ultimate certitude about the problem of environmental deterioration that places it in a different category from the dangers we have previously examined. Nuclear attacks may be indefinitely avoided; population growth may be stabilized; but ultimately there is an absolute limit to the ability of the environment to support or tolerate the process of industrial activity, and there is a reason to believe that we are now moving to that limit very rapidly" (Heilbroner, 47). This is a scary thought. One that should give us pause. On the national level, the responsibility for the environment has been delegated to the Environmental Protection Agency. Important subsidiary legislation includes the Clean Air Act, the Clean Water Act, and the Oil Pollution Act. The regulation of the environment on a global scale is charged to the United Nations Environment Program (UNEP).

The Environmental Protection Agency
The Environmental Protection Agency (EPA) is an independent agency in the executive branch of the federal government. It was created to carry out the provisions of the National Environmental Policy Act and other major environmental laws and executive orders dealing with air, water, solid waste, toxic substance, and noise pollution. The purpose of the 1969 National Environmental Policy Act is to establish a national policy that will combat pollution and improve the environment. The legislation encourages efforts that prevent or eliminate damage to the environment and that stimulate the health and welfare of the public. The act requires a detailed statement of environmental consequences in every recommendation or proposal for legislation

and other major federal actions significantly affecting the quality of the human environment. These environmental impact statements describe in detail the expected adverse environmental consequences of a proposed action. The alternatives to the action are also described.

All major antipollution programs dealing with air, noise, solid wastes, toxic substances, and pesticides were placed under the administrative control of the Environmental Protection Agency in 1970. The EPA's primary responsibilities are to conduct research on all aspects of pollution, set and enforce pollution control standards, monitor programs to determine whether pollution abatement standards are being met, and administer grants to assist states in controlling pollution. The EPA has the power to enforce the standards and programs it initiates. It encourages voluntary compliance by industry and communities and supports state and local governments' efforts to conduct enforcement actions of their own. When such efforts fail, the EPA conducts enforcement proceedings. Moreover, state laws and local ordinances must be in line with federal regulatory policies and standards. The states and their subdivisions are not permitted to skirt federal law by creating statutes and ordinances that establish more lenient standards than those provided for in the federal statute. Congress can intentionally and expressly pass a statute or empower an agency to create regulations that are designed to preempt state law. On the other hand, it is permissible for states and their subdivisions to impose restrictions that are different from and perhaps stricter than those imposed by the federal government. Thus, it is legally permissible for a state to require special standards on resold vehicles or commercial vehicles, or to impose procedures enforcing federal standards.

The Clean Air Act In order to enforce the details of its overall environmental policy Congress has, over the years, passed subsidiary legislation regarding individual pollution problems. The three most visible acts are the Clean Air Act, the Clean Water Act, and the Oil Pollution Act. The Clean Air Act, for example, is designed to limit pollution from vehicles and from stationary sources such as factories and manufacturing centers. The act authorizes the EPA to initiate regulations to limit air pollution. Over the years, the government has added new standards that have gradually reduced the amount of pollution that can be released by vehicles. New emission control requirements were issued in 1990, regarding nitrogen oxide, hydrocarbon, and carbon monoxide. Additional emission control limits were introduced in 2009 ordering a reduction in pollution from a variety of vehicles including SUVs that must reach an 80 percent reduction level within 40 years. The penalties for violating the act are severe. Congress also added a unique feature to the Clean Air Act, which emphasizes the legislature's serious intent to see that the law is enforced. Under provisions in the act, private parties are empowered to sue violators. Private parties are also permitted to sue the act's administrator for not enforcing the act properly. There are limits to this right to bring a citizen's suit, however. The citizen bringing the suit must point to a definite violation by the perpetrator and must give advance notice to the administrator so that he or she has a chance to correct the problem before the lawsuit is initiated.

The Clean Water Act The Clean Water Act, which was passed by Congress in 1972 as an amendment to the Federal Water Pollution Control Act of 1948, sets requirements for limiting the pollution of the nation's water sources according to a schedule and based on the most effective technology currently available. The regulations set up a system for obtaining permits for the release of pollutants into the waterways. Permits are issued provided that the pollution emissions are within legal limits. Violations of the act are punished by fines up to $25,000 daily. Often the EPA must act against companies that pollute the environment, even if the pollution activity is unintentional. The courts have interpreted this broad prohibition to include even accidental pollution, because to hold otherwise would weaken the statute. The Clean Water Act also permits citizens suits against violators and against the administrator of the act for not properly carrying out his or her responsibilities under the act. The same definitive violation and notice provisions are applicable under this act as they are under the Clean Air Act. There is a difference between the two acts, however. Under the Clean Water Act, the party bringing the citizen's suit must be a person "having an interest which is or may be adversely affected" by the violation of the act. No such limit exists in the Clean Air Act.

The Oil Pollution Act The **Oil Pollution Act** was passed by Congress in 1990 in the wake of the 1989 Exxon Valdez Alaskan oil spill. The act is designed to encourage companies that ship, drill for, and store oil to develop and use the most up-to-date equipment and the most effective safety measures possible. Sometimes the act will require that specifically named technological and engineering steps be taken. For instance, the act mandates that, any oil tanker that wants to enter an American port must be equipped with double hulls to minimize any pollution damage should a spill occur. Under the act's provisions, any company responsible for a spill will be compelled to pay all expenses related to the clean up and will, in addition, be subject to a heavy fine. Depending on certain factors, such as the source of the spill, violators could end up paying up to $350 million.

United Nations Environment Program The United Nations Environment Program (UNEP) was created in 1972 as a consequence of work done at the United Nations Conference on the Human Environment in Stockholm that year. The UNEP, which has its central offices in Kenya, was the first UN institution located in a developing nation-state. The agency is responsible for stimulating global awareness of environmental issues and for coordinating international efforts to solve the tough problems associated with environmental deterioration. It organizes the efforts of several UN agencies as they interface with governments and private establishments, such as youth groups and women's organizations. UNEP's programs are based on 10 fundamental areas of concentration: (1) climate change; (2) the vanishing ozone layer; (3) atmospheric activity; (4) fresh water supplies; (5) desertification; (6) deforestation; (7) biological variety; (8) oceanic activity; (9) biotechnology and bioengineering; and (10) chemical safety and security. The UNEP works in a variety of ways to fulfill its environmental mission. A key activity is the Global Environmental Monitoring System (GEMS). This program controls an international system of monitoring centers run by over 30,000 scientists located in over 140 nation-states. The system monitors environmental activity in the oceans, in the atmosphere, in the climate, and in renewable resources. It also monitors pollution and pollution-related illnesses.

UNEP also monitors the work of INFOTERRA, a decentralized data clearing house that provides environmental information to institutions and individuals. Another source of environmental data monitored by UNEP is the Industry and Environment Office (IEO), which provides data to governments and industry. The IEO also promotes information and technology transfer between governments and industry dealing with environmental matters. The UNEP also develops action plans for dealing with problems in marine biology aimed at preserving marine resources. Such action plans have dealt with problems in the Mediterranean Sea, the Pacific Ocean, and the Black Sea. The UNEP also monitors a series of international agreements on the environment including the Vienna Convention and Montreal Protocol, the London Amendment to the Montreal Protocol, the Basel Convention on the Control of Transboundary Movements of Hazardous Wastes and their Disposal, and the Convention on International Trade in Endangered Species. [See: *Basic Facts about the United Nations* (New York: The United Nations Department of Public Relations 1992).]

United Nations Conference on Environment and Development
The UN has also taken steps to combine environmental and energy concerns together under the auspices of the United Nations Conference on Environment and Development (UNCED). UNCED, known more popularly as the Earth Summit program, is designed to integrate economic development and environmental protection into a single well-coordinated strategy

that will promote sustainable development in developing nations with the assistance and cooperation of the developed nations of the globe. The first UNCED Conference (Earth Summit I), which was held in Rio de Janeiro in 1992, resulted in an international agreement known as Agenda 21. The provisions of Agenda 21 established an in-depth set of tactics designed to activate sustainable development plans across the globe. Earth Summit I also resulted in the Rio Declaration, which defines a set of standards outlining the duties and the rights of nations in sustainable development. The summit also led to the creation of the Commission on Sustainable Development (CSD), which coordinates efforts to activate Agenda 21. The CSD also serves as a central clearing house for nations to report progress in the implementation of sustainable development plans.

A second international conference, known as the UN Framework Conference on Climate Change (UNFCCC), was held in Berlin in 1995. This conference involved 120 nations working to create a global strategy to stabilize growing levels of carbon dioxide and other greenhouse gases (GHGs) in the atmosphere. A plan was developed based on balancing (1) a timetable that will not endanger existing ecosystems; (2) a scientific strategy that will permit an adequate production of food; and (3) an economically feasible strategy that will support sustainable development. The plan, which was dubbed the Berlin Mandate, sets out a timetable for the reduction of carbon dioxide and other GHGs for various governments. The second Earth Summit held in 1997 revealed that very little progress had been made since the first conference. As a result Earth Summit II reconfirmed the goals, objectives, and plans of Agenda 21 and added a reconfirmation of the need to partner economic development with environmental protection. The new program, which was named Development Reconciling Environmental and Material Success (DREAMS), set a new set of priorities for the next five years.

A second meeting in 1997, under the auspices of UNFCCC, was held in Kyoto to discuss the lowering of greenhouse gas emissions during the first decades of the 21st century. Under terms of the agreement, known as the Kyoto Protocol, the primary industrial nations would be mandated to reduce carbon dioxide emissions below levels recorded in 1900. Unfortunately, the three major industrial nations on the planet, the United States, China, and India, refused to go along with the protocol. [See: *Basic Facts about the United Nations* (New York: The United Nations Department of Public Relations 1992); Derek Osborn and Tom Bigg, *Earth Summit II: Outcomes and Analysis* (London: Earthscan, 1998); and Christopher Flavin, "Facing Up to the Risks of Climate Change," in *State of the World 1996*, ed. Lester Brown (New York: Norton, 1996).]

The Copenhagen Accord   A new meeting under the auspices of the UN Framework Conference on Climate Change was held in Copenhagen in 2011. The meeting produced a new pact known as the Copenhagen Accord, which was negotiated by five nation-states, including the key nations that did not sign the Kyoto Protocol, the United States, China, and India. The accord actually operates outside the jurisdiction of the United Nations. In brief, the Copenhagen Accord includes a pledge made by the signatories to reduce greenhouse gases and to provide $30 billion annually to a fund designed to help developing nations balance sustainable development and environmental protection especially as it relates to GHGs. If things go according to plan, the Copenhagen Green Climate Fund will increase gradually, reaching $100 billion annually by the year 2020. There are, however, several weaknesses in the accord. First, the accord does not actually reduce any GHG emissions, at least before 2020. Second, the accord does absolutely nothing to reduce the Earth's future temperature problems. Third, from a legal perspective, the accord lacks "teeth." There is no way to enforce its provisions because it lies outside UN control. In this way, the Copenhagen Accord demonstrates the inherent drawbacks of semi autonomous organizations like the United Nations. Such international organizations are incapable of carrying out actions absent the consent of the members. In this case, the

United States, China, and India, all member states of the UN, decided, on their own authority, to ignore the Kyoto Protocol, to defy the other members of the UNFCCC, and to set up their own accord that they may or may not follow based on their own choice. [See: Lawrence Demase and Jennifer Smokelin, "After Copenhagen, It Is Clear There Will be Winners and Losers," *The National Law Journal,* February 2010, pp. 15 and 18.]

Regulating Population Growth

The third (our fourth) challenge that Heilbroner records in his book, *An Inquiry into the Human Prospect,* is the demographic challenge of runaway population growth. Heilbroner predicts that the population will pass its tipping point within a few generations. The tipping point will be reached when the planet can no longer support its people. What follows that tipping point is a downward slide characterized by famine, fresh water shortages, skyrocketing infant mortality rates, wars of redistribution, mega-city collapse, rolling blackouts, and a global economic depression. Heilbroner argues, rather convincingly, that this unchecked population explosion will continue unless two things happen: (1) those areas with the highest population growth rates impose strict birth control programs, and (2) strong "iron" governments rise to deal with the issues of birth control and social unrest.

Population Growth Figures

If we look at population growth figures, the United States, with a population of 322 million, a growth rate of 0.6 percent, and vast amounts of unsettled land, is not a threat. Neither is much of the developed world, including the EU, which has an even smaller growth rate of only 0.3 percent. In contrast, the least developed nations of the world have a population growth rate that reaches almost 2.32 percent. Moreover, if we put the growth rates together and project into the future, we can see that by the year 2048 the population will reach 9.0 billion. [See also: "U.S. and World Population Clock," U.S. Census Bureau (September 3, 2015) http://www.census.gov/popclock/; "Global Population Growth," U.S. Census Bureau, http://www.census.gov/population/international/files/wp02/wp-02003.pdf; "Population Change in U.S. and the World from 1950 to 2050," Pew Research Center: Global Attitudes and Trends (January 30 2014) http://www.pewglobal.org/2014/01/30/chapter-4-population-change-in-the-us-and-the-world-from-1950-to-2050/; The World Bank: Population Growth (Annual %) (2015); http://data.worldbank.org/indicator/SP.POP.GROW/countries/EU?display=graph.] The significance of these figures in relation to population growth rates is difficult to imagine. So, it might be helpful to make some reverse comparisons. If we look back to the 19th century, we would find that the Earth reached its first billion in the year 1825. By 1925, 100 years later, humans had managed to add a second billion. By 1976, the population doubled again, reaching 4 billion. [See: Paul Kennedy, *Preparing for the Twenty-First Century* (New York: Random House, 1993).]

Consequences of Uncontrolled Population Growth

What are the consequences of uncontrolled population growth? By the year 2050, predictions indicate a labor force of 3 billion. To employ the members of that labor pool, which is mostly in the developing world, would require the addition of 38 to 40 million jobs per year. [See: Paul Kennedy, *Preparing for the Twenty-First Century* (New York: Random House, 1993).] The result will be more workers than job openings. This leads to poverty in the mega-cities of the developing world. Poverty leads to disease as problems develop with sanitation and waste disposal. More out of work people means a higher crime rate, an increase in violence, and a threat of social disorder. For a while, science and technology may be able to feed and provide water for these people, but at some point the numbers will outstrip the scientific ability to provide sufficient food and water. Famine follows as well as wars of redistribution. The wars of redistribution are waged when a nation (or tribe or ethnic group or revolutionary movement or terrorist organization) looks across the border to another nation and, seeing the crops and the water that they need, simply moves in and takes what it can. Depending on who is doing what to whom, the struggle my even led to a nuclear confrontation, as might happen if the Arab states attack Israel again, Pakistan attacks India, or North Korea attacks South Korea.

The American Response

In light of all of this, we might believe that the United States would impose some legal incentives to participate in a birth control program that would, if nothing else, lead by example. Such a move, however, is not forthcoming. Return for a moment to Heilbroner's two solutions: (1) increased birth control and (2) the rise of iron governments to enforce both birth control and the civil peace. Neither of these is likely to emerge in the United States. First, the United States is not going to enforce birth control limitations on its citizens. The courts have a long and consistent tradition of avoiding any intrusion into the reproductive freedom of its citizens. The right to procreate without governmental interference was first recognized by the United States Supreme Court in the case of *Griswold v. Connecticut* when the justices ruled that the government could not prevent married couples from obtaining and using contraceptives. That right was extended to unmarried couples in the case of *Eisenstadt v. Baird*. In that case the Court wrote that "[i]f the right of privacy means anything it is the right of the individual married or single to be free from unwarranted governmental intrusion into matters so fundamentally affecting a person as the decision whether to bear or beget a child." The cap was put on the bottle, so to speak, when, in *Carey v. Population Services International*, the High Court ruled that selling and distributing contraceptives was protected by law. It is very important to note that the procreative freedom referred to by the High Court in all of these cases includes not only the right to avoid reproduction but also to have children without any interference by the government. Thus it is unlikely, first, that the United States will enforce birth control or, second, that it will evolve into one of Heilbroner's "iron" governments willing to violate those rights. [See: *Griswold v. Connecticut*, 381 U.S. 479, 85 S.Ct. 1678 (1965); *Eisenstadt v. Baird*, 405 U.S. 438 (1972); and *Carey v. Population Services International*, 431 U.S. 678 (1977).]

Nevertheless, there is always a difference between saying that the government *will not* do something and saying that it *cannot* do something. The flip side of the statement that the government *will not* interfere in procreative rights is that, given the right set of circumstances and the correct motivation, the government *can* interfere in procreative rights. Oddly enough that position was made clear in the case of *Roe v. Wade*. In that case the High Court supported laws that permit abortion as long as the abortion did not occur after the fetus becomes viable. In *Roe v. Wade* viability emerged in the third trimester, so laws that allowed abortion after that time were not permitted. According to *Planned Parenthood v. Casey*, viability comes earlier in a woman's pregnancy primarily because medical technology has pushed viability back further toward conception. Nevertheless, both cases say that the government can interfere in a woman's right to control her own body and both define that moment as the time at which the state has a compelling interest in the life of the child. In fact, *Planned Parenthood v. Casey* goes just a bit further noting that the state might even have an interest in the life of the fetus *before* viability and might even be able to pass legislature limiting the rights of the woman before viability, as long as those legal limits do not cause an undue burden on the woman. The important thing to note here is that the Supreme Court has said that the government *can* interfere in the child-bearing decision of a woman if it has a compelling interest to do so. Now, up until the present time, this has been assumed to mean that the government has a compelling interest to *stop* abortion. However, this same rationale could be made to enforce the idea that the government has a compelling interest in stopping runaway birth rates, that is, by forcing an abortion or birth control or perhaps even compulsory sterilization. If, for example, there is a national or a global crisis in relation to uncontrolled population growth, the government might find that it has a compelling interest in limiting population growth by any means available including coerced abortion, forced birth control, and so on. [See: *Planned Parenthood v. Casey,* 112 S.Ct. 2791 (1992).]

The International Response The international community seems more ready, willing, and able to deal with runaway population growth than the United States. In fact, the United Nations has been involved in such work since 1947 when the **Population Commission (PC)** was created under the auspices of the Economic and Social Council. The PC investigates demographic concerns and then consults with ECOSOC on a variety of population issues. These issues include compiling accurate demographic data; developing strategies to control population growth; and gauging the relationship between a growing population, on the one hand, and economic and social issues, on the other. The authority for the commission comes from the top down, flowing as it does through the Population Division of the Department of Economic and Social Development. Moreover, and perhaps more to the point, the PC is charged with helping to implement the UN World Population Plan of Action, which was developed in 1974 at the World Population Conference on Bucharest. The plan developed strategies based on the relationships between population growth and socio economic factors. The plan has been revised since that time and now publishes an extensive list of recommendations that suggest action in relation to population-related questions. To provide funding for population-related government projects, the United Nation's Population Fund (UNPF) was set up in 1966. The UNPF provides money for family planning projects and other work in population management. [See: *Basic Facts about the United Nations* (New York: The United Nations Department of Public Relations, 1992).]

---

quick quiz 33-4

1. The Federal Energy Regulatory Commission (FERC) is responsible for regulating the transportation and the wholesale price of natural gas alone.   true | false

2. The Nuclear Regulatory Commission owns and operates 104 civilian nuclear power plants and 63 military reactors.   true | false

3. The Clean Air Act is designed to limit pollution from vehicles but not from stationary sources such factories and manufacturing centers.   true | false

---

33-5 Protecting Intellectual Property

The authority of the government in the area of intellectual property has never been in doubt. However, as they say, "the devil is in the details." This is especially true of patents and copyrights because the very nature of an invention and a recorded work is originality. Originality means that every copyright and every patent application will present a new question for the patent office and, possibly, for the courts. For that reason alone the law of intellectual property is complicated and diverse. Nevertheless, the law of intellectual property plays an enormously important role in the development of scientific and technological advances that will help to combat Heilbroner's global challenges. In its most fundamental form, the entire idea behind the legal framework supporting intellectual property is that inventors, scientists, engineers, and writers must be encouraged to pursue their crafts so

CLASSIC CASE Act 1 JCVI and Patent Application US2007 0264688: "To Be or Not to Be . . . Alive"

Members of the J. Craig Venter Institute (JCVI) filed patent US 2007 0264688 with the U.S. Patent Office in an attempt to patent synthetic life. What JCVI had produced was a self-replicating bacterial cell completely under the control of a synthetic genome. The development of the synthetic self-replicating cell proved that such organisms can be planned by a computer, constructed chemically in a laboratory, and then placed in a bacterium from which the original DNA had been removed. The new cell then replicated itself 1 billion times. The process will make DNA synthesis more economical and more affordable, leading to possible breakthroughs in the development of new vaccines, innovative pharmaceuticals, clean water, new food products, innovative pollution filters, and possibly

even revolutionary new biofuel derivatives. This is not the first time that the legal system has faced this issue. In the case of *Diamond v. Chakrabarty*, the U.S. Supreme Court decided that it was possible to patent a life-form. Nevertheless, the issue of patenting a self-replicating completely synthetic life-form presents a new twist on that original theme. This is what intellectual property law is all about. [See: J. Craig Venter Institute, "First Self-Replicating Synthetic Bacterial Cell Constructed by J. Craig Venter Institute Researchers," May 20, 2010, http://www.jcvi.org; and Boonsi Dickinson, "Will Patents Give Craig Venter a Monopoly Over Synthetic Life?" *Smart Planet,* May 28, 2010, www.smartplanet.com; *Diamond v. Chakrabarty,* 447 U.S. 303, 100 S.Ct. 204 (1980).]

that the entire socioeconomic system can benefit from the advances that they produce. What the people at General Electric used to say about their own research and development applies equally well, perhaps even better, to the entire scientific community: "Progress is our most important product."

The Nature of Intellectual Property

Intellectual property involves an intangible ownership right in an invention, a process, a computer program, a chemical formula, an original recorded work such as a book or an article, and so on. The ownership rights bestowed on a person holding the property includes the right to give permission to use the property in exchange for some sort of consideration. This consideration is usually referred to as a **royalty**. The power of the government to grant the exclusive rights to intellectual property is expressly mentioned in Article I, Section 8, Clause 8 of the Constitution, where the framers gave Congress the authority to grant patents and copyrights. The clause reads that Congress has the power to "promote the Progress of Science and the useful Arts, by securing for limited Times to Authors and Inventors the exclusive Right to their respective Writings and Discoveries." The granting of patents and copyrights is one of the most direct and obvious entanglements of science and the law in juriscience.

Protecting Patents

A **patent** is a property right granted by the federal government to an inventor. A patent gives the inventor the exclusive right to make, use, and sell that invention for a period of 20 years (14 years if the patent covers a process). A patent is, in effect, a deal with the government. The inventor reveals the details of the invention in the patent application. In exchange, the inventor receives a guarantee from the government that it will protect the inventor's exclusive right to produce and profit from that invention for a specified period of time. As we shall see later, a trade secret is not revealed in any way in the open marketplace;

the holder of the trade secret receives no guaranteed protection from the government. A copyright differs from a patent in that a copyright protects only the expression of an idea, whereas a patent protects the idea itself.

The Patent Application Process Each patent application requires the creation of a unique technical document. The document is then filed with the Patent and Trademark Office. To qualify for a patent, an invention must meet three requirements. First, the invention must fall within the limits defined by the statute as "patentable subject matter." Second, the invention must consist of some nonobvious, new, and useful feature not known or understood before the invention of this particular device. Third, the patent application must be so specific that individuals who are educated and experienced in the field can create the device on their own.

Patentable Subject Matter The law states that for the subject of a patent application to be patentable, it must be a "process, machine, manufacturer or composition of matter." In contrast, such things as laws of nature, natural phenomena, and abstract ideas cannot be patented. Neither mathematical formulas nor mathematical algorithms are patentable because they are actually laws of nature. An algorithm is a series of steps that, if followed properly, will reach a desired goal. Because many computer software programs are based on mathematical algorithms, problems arose when inventors first attempted to patent computer software. In fact, when patent applications for computer software programs began to appear in the patent office in the 1970s, most software programs were eventually found to be unpatentable. However, during the 1980s and the 1990s, the trend reversed itself. Today, more than 80 percent of all patent claims involving computers have been upheld, including those involving software alone. However, the law in this area remains somewhat unclear. Fortunately, some general guidelines can be laid down. For example, if a software program is only one part of a larger, more conventional process, the courts will allow patent protection for the whole process.

EXAMPLE 33-6: Alison's Shatter-Proof Patent Problem

Alison Louise, the owner, operator, and CEO of Alison, Inc., "Home of the Best Shatter-Proof Glass Products in America," developed a new process for mass-producing shatterproof glass goods. The new process allowed Alison, Inc., to produce a better quality glass at about half the cost of its closest competitors. Part of Louise's success was due to the use of lasers in the process. However, the lasers had to be timed so precisely that each one was controlled by a computer, following the directions of a computer program. This portion of the process was only about one-fourth of the entire operation, the rest of which was relatively conventional. The patent examiner denied Louise's patent application because part of the process involved an unpatentable computer program. A federal court reversed the refusal because the process itself was new and could be patented. The use of the program was only one part of that process.

However, if the software stands alone, the question of whether the patent application will be granted is more difficult. The Court of Appeals for the Federal Circuit has addressed the issue in several cases and tends to affirm such patent applications. The appellate court generally upholds the patentability of software, even if it is based on a mathematical algorithm, because the software actually changes the operation of the computer. Thus, the software can be viewed as either a process or a change in the physical nature of the computer itself. To deal with the issue, the U.S. Patent and Trademark Office established a set of guidelines for computer-related inventions. The objective of the guidelines is to help eliminate ambiguity in the law regarding the patentability of software.

EXAMPLE 33-7: Cole's Infinity Bucks Tracker Tracks a Win

Cole Christopher, the owner-operator of Cole's Infinity Bucks, Inc., developed Cole's Infinity Bucks Tracker, a software program that allowed the user to overlay on a computer screen all available trajectories for any stocks that he or she wished to purchase or sell in the near future while simultaneously displaying all changes in the data related to each pictured stock. Such a program would be invaluable to investors as they planned investment strategies. The patent examiner refused to issue a patent, arguing that Christopher's program was simply the expression of a mathematical algorithm. The Board of Patent Appeals supported the examiner's position. The Court of Appeals for the Federal Circuit, however, reversed the decision and stated that in effect, Christopher's program transformed an ordinary, all-purpose computer into a specialized computer. Thus, the all-purpose computer had in effect become a new computer, capable of performing a new function by following the commands of the software program. Cole's Infinity Bucks Tracker can be viewed as either a process creating a change or an alteration in the physical nature of the computer itself.

Until recently a **business system** was also considered unpatentable because it was not a "process, machine, manufacturer, or composition of matter." However, in a recent court case, a computer system for analyzing information about a group of mutual funds was declared patentable by a federal court. This decision culminated in a slow erosion of the business systems category of unpatentable subjects. Even so, a computerized business system must still consist of some nonobvious, new, and useful feature not known or understood before the invention of this system. It must also be so specific that people who are educated and experienced in the field can re-create the system on their own.

Requirement 1: Usefulness The objective of patent law is to encourage inventiveness and promote progress for the benefit of all society. Thus, a device, to be patentable, must be useful, novel, and nonobvious. Many processes involving computer programs would pass the usefulness test. However, sometimes usefulness is not as clear as it seems on the surface. For an example, let's return for a moment to the requirement of "usefulness" and the classic case of the J. Craig Venter Institute and patent US 2007 0264688. Recall that the application filed with the patent office was an attempt to patent synthetic life. The development of the synthetic self-replicating cell proved that such organisms can be planned by a computer, constructed chemically in a laboratory, and then placed in a bacterium from which the original DNA had been removed. The new cell then replicated itself 1 billion times. All that is nice, but—so what? What can the synthetic life do that, well, "real" life cannot? The answer is that JCVI's new process will make DNA synthesis more economical and more affordable, leading to possible breakthroughs in the development of new vaccines, innovative pharmaceuticals, clean water, new food products, innovative pollution filters, and possibly even revolutionary new biofuel derivatives.

Requirement 2: Novelty Passing the usefulness test alone, however, is not enough to qualify for a patent. The new invention must also be novel and nonobvious. To pass the novelty test, the new device or process must be original. Copying someone else's innovation, even unintentionally, will disqualify an invention from patent eligibility.

Requirement 3: Nonobviousness

Passing both the usefulness and novelty tests is still not sufficient. To be patentable a new invention must also be nonobvious. To pass the nonobviousness test, the changes or improvements must not be apparent to a person of ordinary skill in the field. If the changes are evident, then a patent will not be issued. At least that is the way it used to be. Unfortunately, the patent review process became more difficult for patent holders recently when the U.S. Supreme Court revised the traditional test of nonobviousness. The traditional test, which was referred to as the **teaching, suggestion, or motivation test**, or the **TSM standard**, compelled those who challenged a patent to demonstrate that the so-called innovation would have been discernible to anyone exposed to the same *teaching* session, the same offhand *suggestion,* or perhaps even the same *motivation* that the inventor had experienced. In essence, the test rested on the belief that any small innovation based on prior art in the field would not be patentable but that other innovations, even small ones beyond prior art, would be (see Table 33-1). **Prior art** refers to all relevant technical knowledge about the field to which the invention belongs. The test was difficult, however, because it also required the challenger to produce some sort of firm evidence to support the TSM challenge. Generally, the only factual data that the court would accept as solid evidence was information that had been printed in a professional journal or data that rose to that same high level of credibility.

In creating a new, more lenient test, the Supreme Court stressed that previous courts had been too uncompromising in their use of TSM. Accordingly, the Court suggested that challengers ought to consider using other types of evidence to contest the validity of a patent claim. Such evidence might include economic conditions, the knowledge of other inventors in the same field, or progress in the relevant technology that might show that a person of ordinary skill could easily have developed the same innovation introduced in the challenged patent. If any of these features exist, the contested innovation would not be patentable. In addition, the Supreme Court reintroduced a variation on the TSM test called the obvious-to-try standard, a test that had been outlawed by previous precedent. Under the newly reinstated **obvious-to-try standard**, if the challenger can demonstrate that anyone of ordinary skill could see that it would have been obvious to try such an innovation, the innovation would be labeled as obvious, and the invention would not be patentable.

Table 33-1	Recent Developments in Patent Law
Standard	**Explanation**
Teaching, suggestion, motivation	An invention is obvious and not patentable if anyone exposed to the same teaching, suggestion, or motivation would have come up with the same invention.
Obvious-to-try standard	An invention is obvious and not patentable if the innovation was so obvious that anyone of ordinary skill could see that it was obvious to try that innovation.
Possible legislative changes	Some *possible* legislative changes slated for the future may be (1) increased ease in obtaining injunctions; (2) an 18-month publication rule; and (3) a change in the burden of proof

Nonobviousness and Cyber-Inventions

The new rulings make it more difficult for inventors to obtain patents and easier for challengers to demonstrate that an innovation is obvious and therefore not patentable. The decision to make the test of patentability harder will have a direct effect on computer-related cyber-inventions. Many innovations in computer technology that might have been patentable under the old rules will not be patentable under the new obviousness tests. For instance, under the old rules that dealt exclusively with TSM, a small innovation in the component parts of a laptop or a tablet might have been patentable if the new component was not made clear by teaching, suggestion, or motivation. Now, if the challenger can show that trends in engineering made the innovation a logical next step, or that it was obvious to try the change in the component parts of that tablet or laptop, the innovation, no matter how clever, will be unpatentable.

Specificity in the Application

Federal law states that a patent application must describe the nature of the invention in "full, clear, concise, and exact terms." In fact, the application must be so clear that any person educated and experienced in that field can re-create the invention without having to engage in an extensive trial-and-error period. This requirement causes some difficulty in computer software patent applications, because the surest way to guarantee that someone else will be able to re-create the invention is to provide the source code in the patent application. However, many inventors are

CLASSIC CASE Act 2 JCVI and Patent Application
US2007 026468: "To Be or Not to Be . . . Limited"

Members of the J. Craig Venter Institute were attempting to patent synthetic life after producing a self-replicating bacterial cell completely under the control of a synthetic genome. The development of the synthetic self-replicating cell proved that such organisms can be planned by a computer, constructed chemically in a laboratory, and then placed in a bacterium from which the original DNA had been removed. Not everyone was happy with this development, however. Some of JCVI's competitors accused the company of trying to corner the market with the patent application. The main objection to the JCVI patent application was that it was too broad. JCVI was not attempting to patent the synthetic self-replicating bacterium that the team actually created, but the process of planning, constructing, and creating any synthetic cell imaginable. Some legal experts argued that the problem may be that JCVI's patent application lacked appropriate specificity. These experts predicted that JCVI would get its patent, but not the way that it was originally written. Instead, JCVI would receive a patent for the process involving the bacterium used in the original process, or more likely, bacteria in general. JCVI would not earn a blank check to use the process on any cell imaginable. To deal with these issues, among many others associated with the development of synthetic life technologies, a presidential commission was formed in 2010 following JCVI's announcement. In the commission's report, *New Directions: The Ethics of Synthetic Biology and Emerging Technologies,* commission members acknowledged the problems associated with the overly broad nature of the JVCI patent application but proposed no recommendations of their own beyond offering a series of alternatives that might be used to address the concerns of all affected parties. [See: Presidential Commission for the Study of Bioethical Issues, *New Directions: The Ethics of Synthetic Biology and Emerging Technologies,* December 2010, pp. 119–21; J. Craig Venter Institute, "First Self-Replicating Synthetic Bacterial Cell Constructed by J. Craig Venter Institute Researchers," May 20, 2010, http://www.jcvi.org; and Boonsi Dickinson, "Will Patents Give Craig Venter a Monopoly Over Synthetic Life?" *Smart Planet,* May 28, 2010, http://www.smartplanet.com.]

A QUESTION OF ETHICS

The J. Craig Venter Institute classic case involved an application to patent synthetic life. JCVI had produced a self-replicating bacterial cell completely under the control of a synthetic genome. The development of the synthetic self-replicating cell proved that such organisms can be planned by a computer, constructed chemically in a laboratory and then placed in a bacterium from which the original DNA had been removed. This was not the first time that the legal system had faced this issue. In the case of *Diamond v. Chakrabarty,* the U.S. Supreme Court decided that it was possible to patent a life-form. As is often the case in sensitive issues like this, no one was happy with the Court's decision except, perhaps, the new patent holder. Some experts felt compelled to criticize the Court for stepping outside the bounds of its authority. Others accused the Court of a thoughtless ruling that would open the door to abusive use of biotechnology. However, one of the most interesting points was made when a commentator noted that it was strange that the Supreme Court was willing to grant a patent for a new life-form when, in the case of *Roe v. Wade,* the court had refused to define life.

A QUESTION YET UNANSWERED

The following question has not yet been answered. Before you consider the question, turn to Chapter 1 to review the various ethical theories noted there (market value ethics, social contract theory, utilitarianism, and rational ethics). Then answer the following question:

Is it ethical for the justices of the Supreme Court to avoid the definition of life when it comes to the rights of women and then turn around and permit a megacorporation, like General Electric, to reap potential profit from their decision? (The microbiologist who developed the DNA plasmid that was the subject of *Diamond v. Chakrabarty* was employed by General Electric.) Try to come up with a rationale for each side of the issue. [See: *Diamond v. Chakrabarty,* 447 U.S. 303, 100 S.Ct. 204 (1980); and *Roe v. Wade,* 410 U.S. 113, 93 S.Ct. 705 (1973).]

reluctant to include source code because such codes often contain trade secrets that they are unwilling to dump into the public domain. The usual compromise is to include in the patent application either a flowchart or some other visual diagram that reveals the details of the process.

The America Invents Act

Congress amended the patent law for the first time in over 60 years when, in 2011, it passed the America Invents Act (AIA). The new act is designed to do several things, not the least of which is to bring U.S. patent law in line with international patent law. The AIA does several important things in this regard. First, it has changed the basic principle of American patent law. The act adopts the "first-to-file" patent process, which replaces the "first-to-invent" process that had been the American standard for decades. Second, the new act has set up a series of innovative ways to dispute previous or pending patent claims.

The First-to-File Provision
As noted earlier, this is a key provision that will help bring U.S. patent law in line with international patent law. Some experts predict that this change will probably increase the practice of provisional filing. Provisional filing permits an inventor or company to "hold his or her place" in line as a first filer, without having to deal with some of the formalities involved in a full-fledged filing. The net effect will be that inventors and the companies that they represent will likely file more

patents earlier rather than later. The point of the early filing strategy will be to jump in line ahead of any other inventors who might be close to developing the same type of process or device that the first filer has developed, thus trumping the claims of all other inventors. The provision clearly gives the advantage to large corporate research and development departments. In contrast, those inventors who work in the family garage or in the basement of the family home and are more engrossed in the science and the technology than day-to-day business matters are likely to lose the race to the patent office. On the other hand, those inventors who are not certain about the profitability or perhaps even the marketability of their invention and, therefore, need more time to assess its cost-effectiveness can also "hold their place in line," by filing a provisional patent while they do the necessary research.

The New Dispute Resolution Process As indicated previously, the new law also sets up several new ways to call into question previous patent filings, including both those that have been completed and those that are still in the processing stage. There are several new ways to mount such challenges; however, the two most important are the (1) pre-issuance submission challenge and (2) the post-grant review process. The pre-submission disputes are permitted before the patent has been granted by the patent office. They can be submitted anonymously by third parties who seek to block the issuance of the patent. Naturally, proper documentation must be presented to demonstrate that the patent should not be granted. The new law also permits a post-grant review, which must be filed within nine months of the patent issuance. To be accepted for review the post-grant challenge must show either (a) the invention did not meet the requirements of patentability or (b) there are legal questions involved in the patent that will affect other patents and other patent applications that must be handled before proceeding further with the sale of distribution of the invention or process that is the subject of the challenged patent. [See: Ronald Abramson, et al., "First Major Revision in Nearly Six Decades Changes the Patent Landscape," *Hughes Hubbard and Reed, LLP,* (September 30, 2011), retrieved on October 11, 2011 from http://www.mondaq.com; and Chris Dixon, "Summary of New Patent Act," *Business Insider* (September 16, 2011), retrieved on October 11, 2011 from http://www.businessinsider.com.)

Protecting Trade Secrets

Sometimes an inventor or a discoverer refuses to apply for a patent. At first glance this may seem strange. After all, the patent protects the invention or the discovery so that no one else can use it except with the patent holder's permission, and then according to the owner's terms, which will generally include royalty payments of some sort. There are disadvantages to holding a patent, however. First, a patent expires at the end of a 20-year period, and for design patents, that period is only 14 years. At the end of that period the invention or the discovery is in the public domain and anyone can use and profit from it. Second, to be awarded a patent, the patent applicant must fill out the patent application with great specificity. This means that anyone can access the patent and see exactly what the inventor has developed. Certainly, most people will honor the patent. However, there are people who will try to copy the process or the invention and benefit from the patent owner's work without having to pay royalties. Finally, once the patent is a public record it is possible that someone who examines the patent might be clever enough to see the next leap in technology or science before the patent owner sees it. Thus, the work of the patent owner may inspire a competitor to take the next developmental leap before the original owner sees it, leaving the owner holding an outdated patent almost before it is approved by the patent office. For all of these reasons and probably more, many scientists and engineers who have invented or discovered something may try to keep that discovery or that invention as secret as possible. Juriscientific principles protect these efforts as long as the holder of the secret takes certain relatively easy but very important steps.

A Primer on Trade Secrets

A trade secret is a plan, process, device, procedure, formula, pattern, compilation, technique, program, design, method, or improvement used in a business and disclosed only to those employees who need to know it to do their jobs. The Uniform Trade Secrets Act sets up two conditions that must be met for a plan, process, program, and so on to gain trade secret status. First, the plan, process, or program must gain financial worth simply because it is a secret and cannot be applied by others who might use it to compete with the owner of the secret. Second, the alleged secret must be the subject of reasonable attempts to protect it from those who would use it in a way that would financially hurt the owner of the secret.

State Statutory Trade Secret Protection

Various states have enacted trade secret statutes designed to protect trade secrets within the state's borders. Many of these statutes are patterned after the Uniform Trade Secrets Act, written by the Uniform Law Commission (ULC). Typically, these statutes define a trade secret, describe transgressions of the act, and provide for both damages and injunctive relief when there has been a trade secret infringement. The statutes also generally include a statute of limitations, typically about four years, and indicate that continuing use of a trade secret is a single rather than a series of transgressions. Some state statutes also allow for attorney's fees.

The Economic Espionage Act

The federal government also entered the trade secrets' arena with the passage of the Economic Espionage Act in 1996. The act does not provide for any civil actions but instead outlines criminal sanctions for the theft of trade secrets and the use of fraud to obtain trade secrets. Persons convicted under the statute can face up to 10 years of imprisonment and fines that may reach as much as $500,000. The statute forbids the theft of trade secrets for distribution to a foreign government or an agent of a foreign government or for economic gain that does not benefit the actual owner of the trade secret.

Establishing Trade Secret Status

In the 21st century, many of the inventors, scientists, and engineers who apply for patents know that part of the patent application will include a step involving computers. For example the synthetic life process outlined in the JCVI case involves a computerized stage wherein the computer actually designs the synthetic genome before it is produced chemically and then placed in the bacterium. Scientists who are not overly concerned about the time limit placed on patents or with the specificity required in the patent application might file the patent application knowing full well that they have placed it at risk. Why do it then? The advantage to pursuing patent protection rather than trade secret protection is that the patent applicant can be almost certain that a patent can include a computer program. The same is not true of an engineer or a technician who wants to keep a computer program as a trade secret. The law at the moment is filled with ambiguities about the trade secret status of a computer program.

The right to characterize a computer program as a trade secret depends on the way the owners of the program treat it in relation to other people. In general, the easier it is for people to gain access to the program, the less likely it is that the program will be considered a secret should the matter be contested in court. Therefore, to protect trade secret status, the owners of a program must make certain that the program is treated as a secret from the very beginning. The goal is to grant access to the secret only to those people who need to know it to carry out their duties in the ordinary course of business. Steps that can be taken to increase the likelihood that a court will rule that a program is a trade secret include the following: (1) label the program as secret in all documents related to the program; (2) limit employee access to the program on a need-to-know basis; (3) maintain tight security in the business in general but especially in any area where the program is required to be out in the open for business purposes; (4) keep the program and all related material under lock and key when it is not in use; (5) require employees who work with the program to sign secrecy agreements; (6) require customers who purchase the use of the program to sign licensing agreements; and (7) be especially vigilant in limiting any access to the program by competitors.

Computer Programs Denied Trade Secret Status
Computer programs that have been transferred to software and then placed on the open market for wide distribution cannot claim trade secret status. Software that is widely distributed can be easily copied. Thus, it becomes difficult to demonstrate that the company has taken extensive measures to protect the information on the software. Moreover, because the purpose of placing the software on the open market is to sell it to as many people as possible, the seller must make the software readily available in bookstores and online. This availability on the open market defeats the whole trade secret concept.

Computer Programs Granted Trade Secret Status
Trade secret status is available to companies that distribute their software on a limited, highly selective basis. For example, a computer company that produces and sells a program used to control the distribution of drugs by pharmaceutical firms might be able to call that program a trade secret. Such a company would not actually sell the program to the pharmaceutical firm but would instead allow the firm to use the program through a licensing agreement. A licensing agreement occurs when the producer of a product, in this case a computer program, allows a purchaser to use the product only if the purchaser agrees to respect the producer's desire for secrecy. In this situation, to use the program, the pharmaceutical company would have to agree to respect the computer company's desire for secrecy. In this type of highly selective, strictly controlled transaction, trade secret status works.

Trademark Protection
Before moving on to copyright law, it would be a good idea to pause momentarily just to distinguish between trade secrets and trademarks. A trademark is a symbol, picture, image, name, device, color, or word that a business uses to distinguish itself from its competitors. Once a business has established that it owns a trademark, that business has the exclusive right to use that mark to identify its products and services, as well as the business itself. The law provides businesspeople with several ways to establish trademark ownership: common law, state law, and federal law. To claim that trademark ownership has been established by common law, the alleged owner must show that the trademark has been used with such intensity and for such a long time that the mark has come to be identified not only with the business's products but also with the business itself. Every state legislature has also passed state trademark laws to protect the use of trademarks in intrastate commerce. Despite the use of common law and state law to protect trademarks, most of the legal action in this area takes place at the federal level. The Trademark Protection Act, also known as the Lanham Act, was passed in 1946 to provide for the registration of trademarks with the federal government. The registration authority is the U.S. Patent and Trademark Office. Under the Lanham Act, once a trademark is properly registered with the office, it cannot be used by any other business. The act also protects trademark owners from businesses that use symbols, pictures, words, and so on that are so similar to the protected mark that consumers might be confused into thinking that the

secondary mark is actually the original mark, thus leading those consumers from the owner's product to those of the competitor.

Trademark Dilution   In 1995 Congress passed the Trademark Dilution Act to establish a standard for trademark infringement that would not involve direct and obvious consumer confusion. Unfortunately, the act has not always worked as well as it was supposed to, mainly because of the courts' often perplexing rules about how it ought to be interpreted. To remedy this situation, Congress amended the act in 2006. The new act, referred to as the Trademark Dilution Revision Act, established several new provisions. First, the new act allows trademark owners to obtain an injunction to stop the use of a trademark, simply by demonstrating that the effectiveness of the original mark would probably be diminished. Second, the act strengthens the eligibility of certain marks for protection, especially expressive trademarks such as Quick Lube, Fresh Way Cleaners, or Complete Comfort Heating. Third, the act provides a series of characteristics that the courts can apply to determine if the unauthorized use of a trademark really does obscure the effectiveness of the original mark.

Protecting Copyright

Copyright law is much more expansive than patent law because copyrights also protect the rights of nonscientific work. Therefore it encompasses an area of the law that goes beyond the bounds of normal juriscience. Nevertheless, there are two areas on which juriscience and copyright law intersect dramatically. The first is in the area of scientific writing. Perhaps more than any other academic discipline save perhaps law and literature, science communicates using the written word. Scientific ideas, claims, theories, antitheories, and arguments are all communicated by the written word. Scientific books, periodicals, articles, news releases, new stories, and conference poster presentations are the mainstay of the scientific community. Therefore, a clear connection exists between science and copyright law. The second, and perhaps more contemporary, way that science and copyright law intersect is in the world of computer advances. The law has had to play catch-up with scientific advances in computer technology. Scientists are responsible for these advances; they then communicate information about these advances using the advances themselves. The law must decide if the advances themselves and the way that those advances are communicated deserve copyright protection. A clear case exactly on point is the development and evolution of the computer program, something that scientists and information technologists took for granted but which the law struggled with for decades, literally.

A Primer on Copyright   A *copyright* is an intangible property right granted to authors of literary, artistic, and musical compositions. A copyright gives the owner the exclusive right to reproduce, publish, and sell his or her work in a fixed, tangible medium of expression. Most people are under the mistaken impression that obtaining a copyright is a long, involved, expensive bureaucratic nightmare. Nothing could be further from the truth. In fact, a copyright, unlike a patent, emerges once an idea is fixed in a set medium—period—that's it. No filing is necessary. In fact, according to the Berne Convention, an international agreement that the United States has approved, there is no longer any need to use the traditional copyright symbol or the word *copyright* on a copyrighted work. Still, it never hurts to place this notification on a work to short-circuit any attempts to "inadvertently" violate an owner's rights. The duration of a copyright is somewhat problematic, but in general, we can say that a copyright lasts for 70 years beyond the death of the owner. Business firms owning copyrights will hold on to the rights for 95 years from the time it is was first published or 120 years from the time it is first developed, whichever deadline is passed first.

Although it was not immediately obvious to lawmakers and judges 30 year ago, a computer program is a fixed medium of expression and is, therefore, subject to copyright protection. Today, the federal Copyright Act specifically lists the following as works that are subject to copyright protection: literary works, dramatic works, musical works, pantomimes, pictorial works, sculptures, graphic works, motion pictures, audiovisual works, sound recordings, architectural works, and choreographic works. Computer programs are also specifically covered by the Copyright Act of 1980, which includes computer programs in the category of "writings" or "literary" works to which exclusive rights can be granted.

The law allows some copying to be done without permission under the fair use doctrine. The doctrine provides that copyrighted material may be reproduced without permission if the use of the material is reasonable and not harmful to the rights of the copyright owner. Copying items for such purposes as criticism, comment, news reporting, teaching, scholarship, and research is permissible. The fair use doctrine was codified in Title 17 USC Section 107 of the United States Code, which tells us that four factors must be weighed when figuring out whether fair use is in effect: (1) the purpose and character of the use, including whether such use is of commercial nature or is for nonprofit educational purposes; (2) the nature of the copyrighted work; (3) the amount and substantiality of the portion used in relation to the copyrighted work as a whole; and (4) the effect of the use upon the potential market for, or value of, the copyrighted work.

Juriscience has finally responded to the unprecedented changes that have occurred in computer technology. To make up for lost time, many of the recent alterations in the law were specifically designed to keep abreast of the effects of electronic communication on copyright privileges. Despite this effort, the high-speed, global, interactive nature of the Internet has caused unforeseen problems in copyright law. For example, computer technology now makes it possible for a single copy of a computer program or an individual copy of a scientific paper to be made available to millions of computer users, simply by placing that single copy on a website that is accessible to other users. This advance in computer technology may have been predictable to cyberneticists, but it went virtually unnoticed for quite some time by jurists and legislators. Nevertheless, despite the unpredictability of the problem, juriscience has provided a few solutions.

The No Electronic Theft Act
One such solution came from Congress in the form of the No Electronic Theft Act (NET Act), a federal law that granted limited immunity to persons who duplicate copyrighted works on the Internet, as long as those users do not profit from the copying process. The statute does not simply grant immunity to infringers, however. Instead, it imposes criminal penalties for the violation of certain provisions. Specifically, it makes it illegal to create a duplication (including an electronic duplication) of a copyrighted work for commercial profit or private financial gain by copying or handing out one or more copies of one or more copyrighted productions within a single 180-day period.

The Digital Millennium Copyright Act
The Digital Millennium Copyright Act (DMCA) is designed to combat scientific and technological advances that permit users to override protection systems implanted on recorded materials to prevent that type of intellectual property theft. The law makes it illegal to use technological means to bypass, erase, or override programs specifically designed to prevent access to a copyrighted work. Another provision of the DMCA makes it illegal to use any means to circumvent a program intended to frustrate the copying of a copyrighted work.

The World Intellectual Property Organization
It would be unfair and incomplete to close any discussion of the Digital Millennium Copyright Act without mentioning its connection to the World Intellectual Property Organization (WIPO). WIPO is part of the United Nations and supported the development of two international treaties

specifically designed to deal with electronic copyright problems. Two separate but closely related treaties resulted from the efforts of the WIPO. The first treaty is known as the **World Intellectual Property Organization Copyright Treaty**. This treaty guarantees that copyright holders will be allowed to use the Internet to post their works with full copyright protection. The second WIPO treaty, the **World Intellectual Property Organization Phonograms Treaty**, gives copyright holders the right to copy, publish, and distribute their works in any way, including by making video copies, audio copies, and encrypted copies. The DMCA was written to implement the provisions of these treaties into law in the United States.

quick quiz 33-5

1. A patent gives the inventor the exclusive right to make, use, and sell that invention for a period of 20 years (14 years if the patent covers a process).	true	false
2. A trade secret is a plan, process, device, procedure, formula, pattern, compilation, technique, program, design, method, or improvement used in a business and disclosed only to those employees who need to know it to do their jobs.	true	false
3. A copyright is an intangible property right granted to authors of literary, artistic, and musical compositions.	true	false

33-6 Developing Global Solutions

The goal of this chapter has been to explore the relationship between science and the law and to look at how the law helps promote discoveries in science so that those discoveries can be directed toward social and economic improvements. A central function of the law is to contribute to the civic peace by securing order, stability, and justice. There can be no more serious threat to the global social system than the challenges that Heilbroner notes earlier. Some of these challenges can be met by promoting and awarding innovation and originality in science and technology by protecting intellectual property through patents, copyrights, and trade secrets. However, there is another way to help deal with these problems and that is to actively restructure the law to direct scientific and technological activities toward solving the problems.

Four Basic Requirements

In order to solve any problem, the first thing that the government must do is to identify the parameters of the problem. At the close of the 20th century, there was an enormous amount of work done by colleges and universities, governmental institutions, corporations, and private think tanks to identify the problems that will face humanity in the 21st century. One such study was conducted by the New York Academy of Sciences (NYAS). As a result, the NYAS published a report based on 20 case studies that examined the results of government-supported science and technology polices in the United States and around the globe. The studies examined a series of successful and "less-than-successful" projects in an attempt to identify those factors that made things work and those that made them fail. The results were compiled in "Lessons from Global Experiences in Policy for Science Based Development," by Susan U. Raymond, director of the policy programs at NYAS. In the article Raymond pinpoints six issues that became the focal point of these studies. There are, however, four main issues that we will examine here. They are (1) the necessity of focusing on long-range results; (2) the need to create partnerships among government, business, and the academic community; (3) the need to appreciate the key role played in these projects by human resources; and (4) the need to develop inventive ways to obtain capital investments in science and related projects. [See: Susan U. Raymond. "Lessons from Global Experiences in Policy for Science-Based Development," in *Science Based Economic Development: Case Studies Around the World* (New York: New York Academy of Sciences, 1996).]

Developing Long-Range Plans For decades American science and technology programs were based on the conclusions that were contained in a blue ribbon report compiled by a committee headed by Vannevar Bush, who served as the director of the White House Office of Scientific Research and Development under Presidents Franklin D. Roosevelt and Harry S. Truman. The report, which was cleverly dubbed *Science: The Endless Frontier,* emphasized the need for pure research, the kind conducted at colleges and universities and national think tanks. Pure research, or basic research as it is generally called, is aimed at understanding the laws of nature and the principles of the physical universe without any practical goals in mind. [See: Richard Nelson, "Why the Bush Report Has Hindered an Effective Civilian Technology Policy," in *Science for the 21st Century: The Bush Report Revisited* (Washington, DC: AEI, 1997).] The Bush report promoted pure research because the committee believed that it would contribute to American economic independence, promote technological developments, while preserving the cultural and artistic aspects of human life. [See: Claude E. Barfield, "Introduction and Overview," and David C. Mowery, "The Bush Report After 50 Years—Blueprint or Relic?" in *Science for the 21st Century: The Bush Report Revisited* (Washington, DC: AEI, 1997).]

The problem is that pure research is often underfunded because it is seen as impractical and unusable. As a result, for pure research to work it must be tied clearly to a set of long-range goals that show how such research can be applied in a practical real world setting. This is absolutely necessary in a capitalist democracy in which business people, politicians, consumers, and voters tend to look only as far as the next billing cycle or the next election. One way to do this is to create hybrid projects that include both short-term results and long-term goals. The immediate gains satisfy the politicians and the business people while the long-range goals serve to stimulate the researchers. Thus, the short-term gratification fuels support for the more long-range goals of the pure research program. Perhaps it will be of no surprise that this was the very technique used by the Benjamin Franklin Programs in Pennsylvania. Under the BF Programs, governmental long-term planning projects were designed to produce immediate results in entrepreneurship and education. The short-term accomplishments produced results that calmed critics and permitted the long-term goals to play themselves out successfully. [See: Walter H. Plosila and Susan U. Raymond, "Policies for Science Based Economic Development: The Experiences of Pennsylvania and Ohio," and Susan U. Raymond, "Lessons from Global Experiences in Policy for Science-Based Development," in *Science Based Economic Development: Case Studies Around the World* (New York: New York Academy of Sciences, 1996).]

Developing Partnerships The second requirement for a successful marriage between science and government is to develop partnerships among government, business, and the academic community. Such partnerships are valuable because they make use of the talents, abilities, and experience of researchers at various levels of the scientific community and in a wide variety of settings. This mixture promotes innovation, stimulates creativity, and ensures some level of success no matter what the task. Also a cross-fertilization of ideas takes place when scientists, engineers, and technicians are compelled to work together. Thus, the pure researchers in a university setting may see the practical applications of theories that they never considered before and the practical researchers in the corporations may learn about new theories that might guide them toward practical projects. Perhaps even more important is the fact that partnerships foster a sense of cooperation, camaraderie, and ownership that stimulates loyalty and motivates continued dedication to projects that, because of long-range planning, may take years to complete. [See: Walter H. Plosila and Susan U. Raymond, "Policies for Science Based Economic Development: The Experiences of Pennsylvania and Ohio," and Susan U. Raymond, "Lessons from Global Experiences in Policy for Science-Based Development," in *Science Based Economic Development: Case Studies Around the World* (New York: New York Academy of Sciences, 1996).] This is what happened in Ohio in the last decades of the 20th century when the state government established a program known as the Ohio Technology Transfer Organization (OTTO). Under the auspices of the OTTO program, the state established representatives at colleges and universities in nearly every major industrial and business center in the state. The job of these OTTO agents was to operate as a liaison between business and industry on the one hand, and the state's academic community on the other. When an OTTO agent uncovered a problem or a project at a business or a manufacturing firm that needed assistance, he or she would contact an expert in the academic community who would work with that business to solve the problem or to join the project team. As a result of this pairing process, all of the members of a project team felt a sense of buy-in in relation to the project and developed the sense of ownership that is so critical to success.

CLASSIC CASE Act 3 JCVI and Patent Application US2007 0264688: "To Be or Not to Be . . . a Not-for-Profit Institute"

Members of the J. Craig Venter Institute sought to patent a self-replicating bacterial cell under the control of a synthetic genome. The development of the synthetic self-replicating cell proved that such organisms can be planned by a computer, constructed chemically in a laboratory, and then placed in a bacterium from which the original DNA had been removed. The new cell then replicated itself 1 billion times. (Yes, that's billion with a "b.") The process makes DNA synthesis more economical and more affordable, leading to additional breakthroughs in the development of new vaccines, innovative pharmaceuticals, cleaner water, new food products, innovative pollution filters, and possibly even revolutionary new biofuel derivatives. The J. Craig Venter Institute is a privately funded organization, not a government institution. Plus, it's a *not-for-profit* institution. This was a very intelligent and informed way for Venter to finance the institute. Not-for-profit institutions, especially those organized as 501(c) (3) organizations, have a number of advantages. First, the surplus funds made by the institution are not distributed as dividends to shareholders or as a division of the profits to the partners. Instead, that money goes right back into the institution. Also, under federal law any 501 (c) (3) not-for-profit organization is eligible for certain tax exemptions under both federal and state tax law. Also, such institutions are eligible to receive donations that may double as tax breaks for contributors. All of these advantages would have provided Venter with a healthy source of capital for the business. All in all, the move to not-for-profit status under 501 (c) (3) was an extremely creative move on Venter's part, giving him a great source of revenue and giving us an excellent example of a creative way to develop capital resources. [See: J. Craig Venter Institute, "First Self-Replicating Synthetic Bacterial Cell Constructed by J. Craig Venter Institute Researchers," May 20, 2010, http://www.jcvi.org; and Boonsi Dickinson, "Will Patents Give Craig Venter a Monopoly Over Synthetic Life?" *Smart P Planet,* May 28, 2010, http://www.smartplanet.com.]

Developing Education and Human Resources If long-range plans and scientific partnerships are going to be effective, they must be run by people who are well educated, who work well together, and who have a sense of loyalty to the project and to the group. This is at least partly the government's job because, like it or not, the government is entangled within education. Education at the post-secondary level is entangled with the government that "pays the bills" at the state-run institutions and monitors the operation of the private schools, as well. Moreover, the boards of trustees at the private institutions must oversee the operation of their institutions to ensure that the curriculum includes a healthy dose of science and technology.

Nor is the government's involvement in education limited to the college and university level. Programs must be developed to promote science education as part of a continuing education program for graduate students and for adults on a non-degree-seeking path. All citizens, but especially those employed in research, development, and manufacturing, must be familiar with science, medicine, engineering, and technology, especially computer technology. The first goal of the government should be to help educators produce students who can think for themselves, who are articulate and well read, who are literate in science and technology, and who can cooperate as a member of a corporate or a scientific team. The second goal should be to keep those students in the state or at least within the United States. Homegrown scientists and researchers are always a country's best employees because they are motivated and inspired by a sense of loyalty and pride. [See: Susan U. Raymond, "Lessons from Global Experiences in Policy for Science-Based Development," in *Science Based Economic Development: Case Studies Around the World* (New York: New York Academy of Sciences, 1996).]

Developing Sources of Capital Perhaps the most important of the four requirements is that which encourages the development of creative capital sources. We have already noted how, in the United States, governmental institutions such as the National Science Foundation and the National Institutes of Health provide millions of dollars of support each year for cutting-edge scientific and medical research programs. The dollars spent by the NSF, for example, have resulted in thousands of successful projects, some of which have been recognized internationally for their accomplishments. Similar funding opportunities are available on a global level through institutions like the World Health Organization, which supports health and medical research programs at the international level, all of which are aimed at promoting advances in medical and health care. Similarly, part of UNESCO's mission is to allocate funds for educational, cultural, and scientific projects run by various member states. In the area of engineering and technology, the International Atomic Energy Agency provides funds to governments that come directly to the IAEA for equipment, for technical assistance, and for the education of its personnel in the peaceful pursuit of nuclear power. Capital sources are also available through creative arrangements with corporate sponsors. For example, in her article, "Lessons for Global Experience," Raymond cites an example of a funding program run by a consortium of Swiss entrepreneurs, who created a foundation named FUNDES, the purpose of which was to provide financial support to Latin American businesses involved in advanced research and development programs. Private foundations are also a source of funding for research and development projects. For example, in her article, Raymond also notes how Cambridge University created two foundations, the Cambridge Capital Development Fund and Cambridge Research and Innovation. The two foundations have received funds from Cambridge itself, from nine other institutions of higher education, the government, and several financial institutions. The two foundations disperse funds for projects run by the university and by local businesses. [See: Susan U. Raymond, "Lessons from Global Experiences in Policy for Science-Based Development," in *Science Based Economic Development: Case Studies Around the World* (New York: New York Academy of Sciences, 1996).]

UN Economic Security Council Proposed

While all of these projects are admirable and while many of them succeed, they all lack one thing. There is no centralized control point for the vast array of projects under way at any one time, at least not on the international scene. Some commentators insist that what is needed is a new way of integrating international efforts to pool global resources and to direct those resources toward solving Heilbroner's central modern challenges: environment, war, and unchecked population growth. A model of this type of organization exists if we combine the work of the Commission on Sustainable Development with the work done by the UN Security Council. The proposed institution that emerges from the marriage of these two institutions has been named the UN Economic Security Council. If we take a close look at how these two present-day institutions, the Commission on Sustainable Development (CSD) and the UN Security Council, work we will see how the proposed Economic Security Council might operate. First, recall how the CSD was created. The CSD was established after the first Earth Summit in 1992 in Brazil to administer Agenda 21, which established a set of tactics designed to activate sustainable development plans across the globe. The CSD also serves as a central clearinghouse for nations to report progress in the implementation of sustainable development plans. In this way the CSD just might be able to deal with Heilbroner's challenges were it not for two obvious drawbacks. First, the CSD deals only with the environment, while Heilbroner's challenges also deal with war, energy, and population. Second, the CSD lacks the power to enforce its recommendations under Agenda 21. In other words, the CSD has no "teeth". [See: Commission on Global Governance, *Our Global Neighborhood: The Report of the Commission on Global Governance* (Oxford: Oxford University Press, 1995).]

The second agency, the UN Security Council, provides a model for those missing teeth. The Security Council has the power to pass resolutions that have consequences for those who break those resolutions. Those consequence must be carried out by the military forces of member nations or by NATO, to be sure. However, the threat of those consequences is often enough to prevent a rogue or failed state from ignoring the decisions of the Security Council and its members. Some commentators have suggested that the UN Charter be amended to create a new Economic Security Council (ESC) that would utilize the best parts of the CSD and the Security Council to coordinate science and technology policy in order to solve the economic, environmental, and demographic problems of the globe. The ESC would first diagnose the condition of the world especially as it relates to the issues of environment, energy, and population. The council would then draw up some long-range plans that would involve specific projects for sustainable development, environmental cleanup, population control, and energy enrichment. Those plans would outline the roles that each member nation of the UN would play in the development plan, plus deadlines for those goals, plus funding resources, and, finally, consequences for noncompliance, consequences that would be carried out much like those carried out by the agents of the present Security Council.

Thus, the ESC would run much like the CSD in its planning and coordinating activities and much like the Security Council in its enforcement function, except that, instead of responding to short-range crises, as the Security Council does, the ESC would deal with long-range problems and long-range solutions. The ESC would be autonomous, much like the CSD and the Security Council. It would consist of the largest economic blocs on the planet. The blocs might be made up of a single nation such as China, India, or the United States, or by conglomerates such as the EU, or unified regions such as the Association of Southeast Asian Nations. The charter amendment creating the ESC would also include a provision to ensure that both developed and developing nations are represented proportionately based on a set formula agreed to by all member states. The ESC would not replace existing UN agencies, such as the ECOSOC. Rather, it would serve as a support mechanism that would make the projects and the plans of all agencies a reality. It might even take the UN from the level of a semi autonomous international NGO to a completely autonomous entity by giving it the teeth that it needs to be successful in its goals and objectives. [See:

CLASSIC CASE Act 4 JCVI and Patent Application US2007 026468: "To Be or Not to Be . . . the G-10's Action Plan"

The J. Craig Venter Institute had produced a self-replicating bacterial cell completely under the control of a synthetic genome. The development of the synthetic self-replicating cell proved that such organisms can be planned by a computer, constructed chemically in a laboratory, and then placed in a bacterium from which the original DNA had been removed. The new cell then replicated itself a billion times. The process will make DNA synthesis more economical and more affordable, leading to the development of new vaccines, innovative pharmaceuticals, clean water, new food products, innovative pollution filters, and possibly even revolutionary new biofuel derivatives. Now let's suppose that the United Nations Economic Security Council (ESC) had become a reality. Suppose further that the ESC has instituted an action plan that sets up a timetable for the reclamation of farmland, the recovery of clean drinking water, and the eradication of disease in a series of developing nations we will call the G-10 of the G-77. We know that the JCVI can probably use its patented process to create synthetic bacteria that can develop new vaccines and innovative pharmaceuticals to

cure disease. It might also be able to develop an organism to purify the water supply and perhaps to develop crops that can grow in and revitalize the depleted soil of the G-10. In other words, all of the problems targeted by the ESC in the G-10 might be solved by the JCVI's miracle synthetic life-forms. Should the ESC have the authority to force JCVI to hand over its work to activate the G-10 action plan? What if the ESC passed a resolution that it was ready to use military force to compel JCVI to cooperate? Does any of this seem fair to JCVI, which has put so much effort and funds into developing the synthetic life-forms? What should the United States do in such a situation? What should JCVI do? What recourse, if any, might JCVI have in the U.S. court system? The international court system? [See: J. Craig Venter Institute, "First Self-Replicating Synthetic Bacterial Cell Constructed by J. Craig Venter Institute Researchers," May 20, 2010, http://www.jcvi.org; and Boonsi Dickinson, "Will Patents Give Craig Venter a Monopoly Over Synthetic Life?" *Smart Planet*, May 28, 2010, http://www.smartplanet.com.]

Commission on Global Governance, *Our Global Neighborhood: The Report of the Commission on Global Governance* (Oxford: Oxford University Press, 1995).]

Positive Action Plans by the ESC

The JCVI Classic Case "Act 4" and the *Question of Ethics* exercise above paint a dark, dismal, and dangerous image of the proposed ESC. However, there is a positive side to the ESC proposal. An agency that is run by unbiased, well-trained, independent, and responsible individuals would be able to draw up tough but fair action plans that must be implemented to save the planet. The task would be difficult and thankless. However, at some time in the future (the very near future if we listen to Heilbroner) such drastic measures may be needed. Remember that it was Heilbroner who stated clearly and unapologetically that drastic measures by "iron" governments might be needed to save the planet. What if another great oil spill occurs under the watchful eye and the global jurisdiction of the ESC? Suppose further that the ESC has instituted an action plan that sets up a timetable for removing the oil spill and recovering clean drinking water. We know that the JCVI can probably use its patented process to create synthetic bacteria that can filter and eliminate the pollutants in the gulf and that can purify the water supply. To put it simply, all of the problems caused by the oil spill might be solved by the JCVI's genetically engineered synthetic life-forms. In this case, the ESC might pass a resolution compelling the responsible parties to cooperate with JCVI and to compensate the institute accordingly for the use of its patented process. Since the ESC has the necessary military might to enforce the order, it is likely that the project would be carried out in

A QUESTION OF ETHICS

One of the problems that the proposed UN Economic Security Council (ESC) would face early on is population growth. Remember that one reason for modeling the ESC after the Security Council is to provide teeth for the ESC's resolutions. Suppose that the ESC decided to enforce a vigorous program of population control and to use the power of the member nation's military forces to enforce its resolutions in this regard. This is what some critics of the ESC fear. They suspect that the inauguration of the ESC might usher in the same type of world that Axel Madsen imagined in his novel *Unisave*. The novel is set in the 22nd century at a time when the planet's natural resources, its energy reserves, its agriculture, and its fresh water are depleted. The Earth's population is more than 24 billion. The planet has reached a tipping point beyond which there seems to be nowhere to go. In a desperate attempt to reverse the slide toward disaster, the United Nations establishes an agency called Unisave. If we look at Unisave closely, we will see that it resembles a runaway ESC. First, Unisave has the authority to set quotas for family size. Second, Unisave has developed a compulsory sterilization program for some people under some circumstances. Third, it has ordered the use of drugs to suppress the sex drive among young people. Fourth, it has instituted a global program of electronic surveillance to prevent the violation of its strict anti-sex laws. Finally, Unisave has mandated a program of compulsory gericide, which involves the systematic killing of the elderly.

QUESTIONS YET UNANSWERED

The following questions have not yet been answered. Before you consider each question, turn to Chapter 1 to review the various ethical theories noted there (market value ethics, social contract theory, utilitarianism, and rational ethics). Then, in a consistent way, answer the following questions.

1. What must be done (if anything) to prevent the ESC from transforming itself into Unisave? Explain
2. Is there any way to effectively stop it? Explain
3. Is it better not to start in that direction in the first place? Explain
4. Is there a justification that would approve of, or perhaps even champion, the work of the ESC and that of Unisave? Explain

record time. The gulf would be cleaned up, JCVI would be justly compensated, and the environment would be safe again. The same technique could be used to compel a cleanup after a rogue military action such as those carried out by the terrorist groups like ISIS and al-Qaeda. Or such an action might be taken to force President Bashar al-Assad to rebuild the houses, schools, and hospitals that his military forces have destroyed in Syria. The point is that it is not the structure of the ESC that matters quite as much as the people who run it. It takes people with the proper motivation, the appropriate experience, the courage of their convictions, and just the right level of power to carry it off.

quick quiz 33-6

1. A central function of the law is to contribute to the civic peace by securing order, stability, and justice.	true	false
2. Scientific partnerships are valuable because they make use of the talents, abilities, and experience of researchers at various levels of the scientific community and in a wide variety of settings.	true	false
3. The UN Economic Security Council was established in 2010.	true	false

Summary

33.1 The point at which science, technology, and the law intersect can be referred to as juriscience. The power to regulate science and technology in the United States is shared by the national government and the state governments. The national power emerges from the U.S. Constitution. The five specific clauses that relate to the national power are the Commerce Clause, the Taxation Clause, the Supremacy Clause, the Necessary and Proper Clause, and the Treaty Clause. The Federal Judicial Center recently inaugurated a decade-long patent court pilot program aimed at improving the way that patent law cases are handled by the federal circuit. Another proposed solution that has been suggested for dealing with the problems related to the complicated nature of scientific cases is the establishment of a national science court. Once established, the federal science court would have exclusive jurisdiction over issues involving scientific, engineering, medical, and technological cases. On the state level, the capacity of the states to regulate science and technology emerges from the state's police power. Police power is the state's ability to uphold and sustain public health, safety, welfare, and morals. In the state courts, the tradition of common law fills many law books with cases related to science, technology, and engineering.

33.2 The federal government has been funding scientific and medical research for the past 150 years. That funding comes in many forms for a variety of purposes and with a high price tag. Nevertheless, Congress and the president have agreed that the expenditure is necessary to provide for national security, to promote the health and welfare of American citizens, and to ensure the economic and social well-being of the nation. The federal government has set up a number of agencies and institutes that support, assess, coordinate, and fund scientific, medical, and technological research. The chief national agencies for scientific, medical, and technological research are the Office of Science and Technology Policy, the National Science Foundation, and the National Institutes of Health.

33.3 There are four types of international nongovernmental organizations: (1) those that are completely dependent upon the nation-states that make up their membership; (2) those that are a semiautonomous organization; (3) those that are granted or earn entity status; and (4) those that are unaffiliated transnationals

that act as rogues or outlaws. International power depends upon the nature of the NGO itself. The primary international organizations under the umbrella of the UN are UNESCO and the World Health Organization. The United Nations consists of three major subdivisions, the General Assembly, the UN Security Council, and the Secretariat, which is the administrative bureaucracy of the UN. UNESCO is responsible for creating outreach efforts to develop educational, cultural, and scientific ties among the member nations of the UN. The World Health Organization's mission is to improve the health care available to all the people of the world, but especially to those most at risk because of poverty or special health-related threats.

33.4 All of the work done by the government relates in some way to four challenges: (1) the possibility of war, (2) the volatility of the marketplace, (3) the twin dangers of environmental deterioration and energy depletion, and (4) the demographic crisis. Dealing with all of these problems is part of the balancing act that is the law. The Federal Energy Regulatory Commission (FERC) is responsible for regulating the transportation and the wholesale price of natural gas and electricity sold for use in interstate commerce. State utility commissioners regulate intrastate prices. The Nuclear Regulatory Commission (NRC) is responsible for the licensing, construction, and operation of nuclear reactors. On the international scene, the International Atomic Energy Commission (IAEA) has oversight responsibility for matters dealing with nuclear power. On the national level, the responsibility for the environment has been delegated to the Environmental Protection Agency. Important subsidiary legislation includes the Clean Air Act, the Clean Water Act, and the Oil Pollution Act. The regulation of the environment on a global scale is charged to the United Nations Environment Program (UNEP).

33.5 Intellectual property involves an intangible ownership right in an invention, a process, a computer program, a chemical formula, an original recorded work such as a book or an article, and so on. A patent is a property right granted by the federal government to an inventor. A patent gives the inventor the exclusive right to make, use, and sell that invention for a period of 20 years (14 years if the patent covers a process). A trade secret is a plan, process, device, procedure, formula, pattern, compilation, technique, program, design, method, or improvement used in a business and disclosed only to those employees who need to know it to do their jobs. A copyright is an intangible property right granted to authors of literary, artistic, and musical compositions. A copyright gives the owner the exclusive right to reproduce, publish, and sell his or her work in a fixed, tangible medium of expression.

33.6 There are four factors to consider when attempting to solve the Heilbroner challenges. They are (1) the necessity of focusing on long range results; (2) the need to create partnerships among government, business, and the academic community; (3) the need to appreciate the key role played in these projects by human resources; and (4) the need to develop inventive ways to obtain capital investments in science and related projects. The primary job of the proposed UN Economic Security Council would be to assess the condition of the world economy especially as it relates to the issues of environment, energy, and population. The council would then draw up long-range plans that would involve specific projects for sustainable development, environmental cleanup, population control, and energy enrichment.

Key Terms

business system, 847

Clean Air Act, 839

Clean Water Act, 839

commerce clause, 819

compelling interest, 843

Copenhagen Accord, 841

copyright, 854

dependency theory, 831

Digital Millennium Copyright Act (DMCA), 855

Economic Espionage Act, 852

faction, 818

fair use doctrine, 855

General Assembly, 830

general welfare clause, 820

juriscience, 818

licensing agreement, 853

necessary and proper clause, 820

No Electronic Theft Act (NET Act), 855

obvious-to-try standard, 849

Oil Pollution Act, 840

patent, 845

police power, 825

Population Commission (PC), 844

prior art, 848

royalty, 845

Secretariat, 830

secretary general, 830

Security Council, 830

supremacy clause, 821

teaching, suggestions, or motivation test (TSM standard), 848

trade secret, 852

trademark, 853

transnats, 830

treaty clause, 822

Uniform Trade Secrets Act, 852

World Intellectual Property Organization (WIPO), 831, 855

World Intellectual Property Organization Copyright Treaty, 856

World Intellectual Property Organization Phonograms Treaty, 856

Questions for Review and Discussion

1. How does the law permit the government to regulate science and technology?
2. What is the purpose of the patent court pilot program?
3. What is the role of the National Science Foundation?
4. What is the function of the National Institutes of Health?
5. What does Heilbroner see as the three major challenges facing the modern world?
6. What is the purpose of the Federal Energy Regulatory Commission?
7. What is the role of the Nuclear Regulatory Commission?
8. What are the functions of the Clean Air Act and the Clean Water Act?
9. How does the law protect trademarks, trade secrets, and copyrights?
10. What are the four main issues that must be considered in developing a science policy?

Cases for Analysis

1. Earth Sciences, Inc., conducted gold-leaching operations in Colorado. The process involved spraying gold ore with a toxic substance. To prevent pollution, Earth Sciences had installed a reserve sump to catch any toxic runoff. An unexpected early thaw melted a snow bank, covering the ore heap. As a result, the reserve sump overflowed, dumping toxic waste into the Rito Seco Creek. The United States brought suit, alleging that Earth Sciences had violated pollution laws. Earth Sciences argued that it should not be held liable for an unintentional pollution accident. Was Earth Sciences correct? Explain. [See: *United States v. Earth Sciences, Inc.*, 559 F.2d 368 (10th Cir.).]

2. Gaskin, Ohio, is the home of Ransom College. Each August the population of the small village triples as the students return. When this happens, the traffic in the middle of town becomes congested and the exhaust from the cars chokes the entire downtown area. This year the Village Council of Gaskin passed an ordinance that required the installation of emission control devices in all vehicles as a new licensing requirement. A dozen students brought suit in the U.S. District Court in Columbus, asking the court to declare the new ordinance invalid and to prevent its enforcement. The students contended that the Clean Air Act, which did not make such demands, preempted the village ordinance. Under what circumstances will a federal law like the Clean Air Act preempt state and local law? Explain. Who will prevail in this case, the village or the students? Explain.

3. The Global Environment Resistance Movement (GERM) initiated a citizen's suit under the authority of the Clean Water Act asking the court to issue an order that would shut down a plant on the Kokosing River that was dumping waste into the navigable waterways of that river. The administrator responded that GERM had acted in haste and did not meet the statutory requirement of giving him 60 days' notice. GERM responded by noting that the notice requirement had been waived by the administrator when he announced in a press conference that he did not intend to shut down the Kokosing plant . . . ever! In its argument, GERM pointed to the Clean Air Act and used that as the template for its lawsuit. Do the Clean Air Act and the Clean Water Act have identical citizen suit provisions? If they are the same, why is this so? If they are different, what are the differences? Who should win this case, GERM or the administrator? Why?

4. Officials at Semco, Inc., believed that some of their most important computer files, which they characterized as trade secrets, had been appropriated by Terry Hildreth, a former vice president of Semco. Semco officials accused Hildreth of using these programs to run his new limited liability company, Hildreth Manufacturing, LLC. Semco engaged in a series of harassing tactics designed to stop Hildreth's use of the alleged trade secrets. To protect himself and his new firm, Hildreth brought a lawsuit asking for a declaratory judgment that no trade secrets had been taken, despite Semco's allegations to the contrary. Semco then brought a second lawsuit alleging, among other things, that trade secrets had indeed been misappropriated by Hildreth. After the suits were decided in favor of Hildreth, the results were appealed. During both suits, the following facts came to light: Material that described the manufacturing steps that Semco now claimed were trade secrets had been routinely made available to vendors. Semco also regularly provided information about its "secret" manufacturing processes to people outside the company. Semco did not require employees to file nondisclosure or secrecy agreements. Visitors were not screened, the building was locked only after regular business hours, and the plant was open for public tours. On the basis of these facts, how should the appeals court rule on the issue of trade secrets? Explain. [See: *Hildreth Mfg., LLC. v. Semco, Inc.*, 151 Ohio App. 3d 693.]

5. Parrish and Chlarson worked for J&K Computer Systems, Inc. Parrish was a computer programmer, and Chlarson was a trainee. In his capacity as programmer, Parrish wrote an accounts receivable program. Customers of J&K were granted licenses to use the program. A label on the program noted that it was J&K's property and that it could not be used without authorization under a licensing agreement. Parrish, Chlarson, and all other J&K employees were informed that the program was a secret. Nevertheless, Parrish copied it, left J&K's employ, and, along with Chlarson, opened a business similar to J&K. Parrish and Chlarson then

sold the copied program to various customers. When J&K sued, Parrish and Chlarson argued that the fact that J&K had revealed the program to customers meant it was no longer a trade secret. Were Parrish and Chlarson correct? Explain. [See: *J&K Computer Systems, Inc., v. Parrish,* 642 P.2d 732 (UT).]

6. Diehr and Latton applied for a patent to protect their development of a new process for molding raw, uncured synthetic rubber into cured products. Diehr and Latton argued that their unique contribution was to measure the temperature inside the mold and feed that temperature into a computer that was programmed to calculate the exact time needed for the curing process. The computer would then activate a mechanism to open the mold. The process, as conceived by Diehr and Latton, eliminated the guesswork usually associated with measuring the length of time for the mold to remain closed. The patent office denied the patent because it used a computer program in the process. The office said that the program was essentially a mathematical idea and was therefore unpatentable. Diehr and Latton argued that the mere fact that a computer program was used as part of a process did not mean that the whole process would be unpatentable. Were Diehr and Latton correct? Why or why not? [See: *Diamond v. Diehr,* 101 S.Ct. 1048 (U.S. Sup. Ct.).]

7. Hiroyuki Iwahashi, Yoshiki Nishioka, and Mitsuhiro Hakaridani applied for a patent for an autocorrelation unit for use in computers for pattern recognition, in this case to aid in voice recognition. To achieve this type of pattern recognition, computers must perform a lengthy multiplication cycle that requires intricate circuitry and a costly multiplier unit. The computer hardware involved in this process is also large and cumbersome. The purpose of the new invention is to streamline the multiplication cycle. The elimination of the multiplier and the intricate circuitry is made possible by an algorithm that allows the computer to obtain the needed result by detouring the time-consuming multiplication cycle and using instead the electronic equivalent of a multiplication table. The U.S. Patent and Trademark Office rejected the patent application, and the Board of Patent Appeals and Interferences upheld that decision. Both concluded that the alleged invention was nothing more than an algorithm and could not therefore be patented. The inventors appealed the decision,

arguing that the algorithm is simply part of the apparatus, which altered the operation of the computer and was therefore subject to patentability. Can a patent be rejected solely on the argument that the invention involves an algorithm? Explain. [See: *In re Iwahashi,* 888 F.2d 1370 (Fed. Cir.).]

8. Stern Electronics, Inc., entered a licensing agreement with Konami Industry Co., Ltd., granting Stern exclusive rights to market the video game Scramble in the United States. Omni Video Games, Inc., wrote a new program that duplicated the sights and sounds of Scramble. Stern sued Omni in federal court, asking for an injunction to prevent Omni from marketing its knockoff of Scramble. Omni argued that Stern could not get a copyright for the Scramble audiovisual display because every time a player plays the game, the display is different. The display is not fixed in a tangible medium, as required by law. Because Omni had written its own program, Stern could not stop it from marketing the duplicate Scramble games. Was Omni correct? Explain. [See: *Stern Electronics, Inc., v. Kaufman and Omni Video Games, Inc.,* 669 F.2d 852 (2nd Cir.).]

9. In *Kelo v. City of New London* the city fathers of New London agreed to help the Pfizer Corporation, which had decided to build a research and manufacturing center in the city. To do this, the city began to buy land in that area of town. Many residents in the targeted area refused to sell. The city invoked the government's power to confiscate land for public use under eminent domain. Kelo, along with several other owners, sued to end the unconstitutional seizure of their property. The homeowners argued that the taking of their land for private development purposes did not fall under the heading of "public use" as visualized by the founding fathers when they wrote the Fifth Amendment. The Court in a 5–4 ruling held that the city's seizure of the land really was public use. Now jump ahead in time and imagine that the ESC has been created under the UN. Could the ESC use this case as a precedent that would permit it to seize private land in the developed countries and then pass the rights and the possession of that land over to the underdeveloped countries? Explain your response. [See: *Kelo v. City of New London,* 125 S.Ct. 2655 (U.S. Supreme Court).]

10. The citizens of Oregon authorized the establishment of the Oregon Death with Dignity Act (ODWDA), which protected physicians from

prosecution under criminal law and from litigation under civil law for prescribing drugs for terminally ill patients who wished to commit suicide. The drugs would have to be prescribed under the Controlled Substances Act (CSA). The U.S. attorney general (AG) stated that any physician who prescribed such drugs with the intent to have those drugs used for suicide could lose his or her medical license. The attorney general argued that drugs controlled by the CSA could not be used for suicide because suicide is not a legitimate medical purpose. A lawsuit was filed by several interested parties in the federal district court in Oregon, which ruled in favor of the plaintiffs and which then enjoined the AG from enforcing his interpretation of the CSA. Could this case be used as precedent to promote or to fight government-enforced population control as imagined by Axel Madsen in *Unisave?* Explain. [See: *Gonzales, Attorney General v. Oregon,* 126 S.Ct. 904 (United States Supreme Court).]

quick quiz Answers

33-1	33-2	33-3	33-4	33-5	33-6
1. T	1. F	1. F	1. F	1. T	1. T
2. F	2. T	2. T	2. F	2. T	2. T
3. T	3. T	3. T	3. F	3. T	3. F

Chapter 34

International Law and the New World Order

THE OPENING CASE Round 1
China v. the United States: Friendly Rivalry or Global Judgment Day

Immediately after the fall of the Soviet Union in 1991, the United States, for the first time in its relatively short history, dominated the planet as the world's sole *superpower*. That role was comfortable until 1993 when American forces were ambushed in Somalia and 17 American servicemen were killed carrying out what had been characterized by the administration as a humanitarian mission. After this incident, the leadership of the United States seemed to freeze whenever foreign policy decisions had to be made, resulting in several subsequent missteps, not the least of which involved genocide in Rwanda. International mistakes continued to plague the United States for the next decades resulting in in two prolonged wars, a disintegrating Middle Eastern situation, the alienation of Israel, and unchecked aggression by a newly emboldened Russian Federation. However, at the present moment, the most significant threat to American dominance is the advance of China. Consider the following facts: (1) The United States depends upon China to purchase its Treasury bonds and to invest in American corporations by buying stock that allows these companies to continue to exist and to

place factories and retail outlets in China; (2) China owns about $1.2 trillion worth of U.S. treasury debt; (3) Chinese defense spending has risen precipitously over the last few years reaching, as high as 10 percent of its annual budget; (4) the Chinese have a standing army of more than 2.1 million active-duty personnel; and (5) between 1978 and 2005, 402 million Chinese people were lifted out of poverty by economic reforms. (Note: The entire population of the United States is about 322 million.) Some commentators believe that the unprecedented growth of China and its desire to control East Asia, the South China Sea, and the Western Pacific will lead to an inevitable conflict between the two nations. In fact, this inescapable clash has been foreseen by experts since Olaf Stapledon first predicted the encounter in his book *Last and the First Men* in 1931. Moreover, the certainty of such a collision looks more and more likely with every passing day. Still, such a battle may not be necessary. We just need to understand the flow of international events in order to head off the confrontation before it happens. Then again, can the future path of each of these two powerful nations and of the international community itself be predicted? In a peculiar way that is what international law is all about. [See: Noah Feldman, *Cool War: The Future of Global Competition* (New York: Random House, 2013); David C. Kang, *China Rising: Peace, Power, and Order in East Asia* (New York: Columbia University Press, 2007); Joyce P. Kaufman, *A Concise History of U.S. Foreign Policy* (New York: Rowman & Littlefield, 2006); Dan Smith, *The State of the World Atlas* (New York: Penguin, 2008); Olaf Stapledon, *Last and First Men* (New York: Dover, 1931).]

Opening Case Questions

1. What happened in Somalia and why is that significant to American foreign policy? Explain.

2. What happened in Rwanda and why is that significant to American foreign policy? Explain.

3. What facts support the idea that the United States and China are intertwined economically and militarily? Explain.

4. Why would China want to dominate East Asia, the South China Sea, and the Western Pacific (or would it)? Explain.

5. Are the United States and China headed to war? Explain.

Learning Objectives

1. Explain the process of predictive political history.
2. Identify and define the theories of international behavior.
3. Identify and define the various sets of global initial conditions.
4. Describe the mission of the International Criminal Court.
5. Identify the main goal of UNCITRAL.
6. State the differences between the UCC and the CISG.
7. Outline the structure of the World Trade Organization.
8. Relate the objectives of the Dispute Settlement Understanding.
9. Determine the major purpose of NAFTA.
10. Clarify the goals of the European Union.

34-1 The New World Order

The phrase *new world order* was used during the Paris peace talks in 1919 to describe the remaking of the world map following the Great War, and then again two decades later by H.G. Wells in a book that he published in 1939. George H.W. Bush used the term in the development of his defense planning document toward the close of the last century, and at the start of the 21st century, Daniel Drezner placed an original spin on the phrase when he penned an article for *Foreign Affairs* titled, "The New New World Order." The new world order, then, is a phrase frequently used to describe situations on the global stage that are unexpected, unusual, and unfamiliar. For that reason, among others, the phrase can be used to describe the situation in which we find ourselves today. The world order is a set of current initial conditions that describes how nation-states relate to one another on a global scale. The use of the word *new* to describe that world order reveals that these initial conditions have just emerged from a tectonic shift in international relations. Generally, because the conditions are so recent, no one is exactly certain what those conditions are and how they work. Thus, this changing environment must be unraveled if we are to understand the role of international law, if any, within that new environment. [See: Daniel Drezner, "The New New World Order," *Foreign Affairs*, March–April 2007; D.M. MacMillan, *Paris 1919: Six Months that Changed the World* (New York: Random House, 2001); and Zbigniew Brzezinski, *Second Chance: Three Presidents and the Crisis of American Superpower* (New York: Basic Books, 2007).]

Patterns within the New World Order

This description is not meant to imply that global conditions do not follow certain patterns, but in the new world order, those patterns have yet to be determined. These patterns are not rules exactly, but neither are they unpredictable chance events. Instead, they are indicators that are correct more often than not. The trick is to determine what the global initial conditions really are and what pattern those conditions can be expected to follow. What makes this trick so difficult is that the international players do not come into the game fresh; instead, they enter the new arena steeped in their own expectations of what the pattern should be. When the pattern shifts, sometimes the players do not, which causes diplomatic errors, international incidents, and global conflicts, some of which can be solved easily but many of which cannot. We are currently at the threshold of a changing global environment in which a volatile, unstable, yet predictable new world order is emerging.

Evidence of this emerging new world order can be seen (1) in the Arab Spring revolutions and their winter-like aftermath; (2) in the Russian invasion of Crimea and Ukraine and the threat that Russian troops still pose to Lithuania and Poland; (3) in the globalized entanglement of the United States and China as antagonistic trading partners; (4) in the rising economic dominance of Argentina, Brazil, and Chile in Latin America and the ensuing financial competition among them; and (5) in the disintegration of the Israeli-American partnership in the face of the growing power of a nuclear Iran. Our job during this chapter will be to determine the nature of this new world order.

It is not an easy task; not everyone agrees about what that order might be. Place 20 political commentators around a table and you'll get 25 versions of the new world order. Still, even within this confusing collection of political theories, common themes exist. Moreover, we suggest that there may be a hidden pattern within the disorder that can be used to give direction to our study. Accordingly, we will divide this section of the chapter into three parts: (1) the underlying technique for uncovering the new world order, something that we will refer to as predictive political history; (2) the theories of international behavior that tell us how nations act; and (3) the initial conditions (or new world orders, if you will) that offer to define the present alignment of states ranging from the most powerful nations (the United States, China, and Russia) to the most influential federation (the European Union) to failed states (Yemen, Libya, Somalia, and so on) to rogue states (North Korea and Iran) and including international nongovernmental organizations (the United Nations, the World Bank, the International Criminal Court, the Red Cross, NATO, and so on) and outlaw terror groups (such as al-Qaeda, ISIS, and Hezbollah, plus drug cartels, pirate bands, slave traders, and so on).

The Underlying Technique: Predictive Political History

Despite its name, predictive political history is not a technique for predicting the future. No such technique exists, except perhaps in the imagination of such notables as Auguste Comte, Pierre Laplace, G.W.F Hegel, and Isaac Asimov. Instead, predictive political history is a technique for determining how world leaders will probably act in a given world order when facing a crisis or mapping out a future global strategy. If a political scientist wants to apply predictive political history, he or she must first determine the present state of the global system (the international initial conditions or the new world order) and then match that system to the correct set of covering laws under an accurate theory of international behavior. Before exploring the implications of this proposition, it will be best to examine the operation of the theory.

As a process, predictive political history imitates science. A scientist might take the theory of gravity, for instance, and apply the covering laws of that theory to a set of initial conditions, including the positions of various celestial bodies, such as the Earth, the moon, the sun, the other planets, a cloud of interstellar dust, and so on, along with orbital paths, speeds, masses, directions, and so forth, of those bodies to predict when that invading interstellar dust cloud might pass between the Earth and the sun. Then, using the laws of physics, as applied to the composition of the cloud, its density, direction, speed, and so on, the scientists could predict the effects the cloud will have on the Earth as it blocks the light from the sun. (This scenario was imagined by the British astronomer Fred Hoyle in his book, The *Black Cloud* (New York: Signet Books, 1957). Similarly, a practitioner of predictive political theory can take a theory of human political behavior on the international level, the theory of *Realpolitik,* for instance, and apply the covering laws of that theory to a set of initial conditions (the new world order) on the international scene in order to predict the future of the global community or, more often, to diagnose the seriousness and the possible direction of an international crisis.

For example, how should the United States act when one nation invades another, as happened when Iraq invaded Kuwait and when Russia invaded Crimea? Should the United States intervene, back off, build a coalition, protest at the United Nations, use economic sanctions, and so on? The proper application of predictive political history will help the United States formulate an appropriate strategy. The theory of international behavior will predict how the leaders of the other nation will respond to an American move, and the set of global initial conditions will tell the Americans whether, from an American perspective, the invader and the target are friends, enemies, former allies, neutrals, and so on. So, if the set of global initial conditions identifies the aggressor as an ally and the relationship between the United States and the aggressor as one based on trade and economic dependence, then the United States will act differently than if the global initial conditions identify the aggressor as a failed state, an enemy nation, or a rogue state. The theory of international behavior will predict whether the leaders of the aggressor nation will act rationally in their nation's own best interests, by negotiating, for example, or by taking the case to the UN, or if they will seek alliances with other similarly situated rogue nations and escalate the aggression. Being able to visualize such future behavior, even in terms of probabilities, far outweighs simply "shooting in the dark" with no consistent strategy and just hoping for the best.

EXAMPLE 34-1: The Russian Invasion of Crimea

Early in 2014, Russia moved more than 2,000 military personnel into Ukraine's Crimean peninsula and took command of the two major airports there. Later, armed Russian troops occupied the Crimean Parliament. The Russians, of course, claim Crimea as their own, with some justification, since it is the home to almost 1.5 million Russians (about 60 percent of the population). The Russians also anchor their Black Sea naval fleet at a port in Crimea called Sevastopol. Yet, the current president of Ukraine called the placement of troops in Crimea an unlawful invasion, which it certainly seemed to be.

The theory of predictive political history should help us visualize what the Russians will probably do next and how the American president should probably react, if at all. To envision the next Russian move and to advise the American president how best to respond, we must first identify the theory of international behavior and the global set of initial conditions that we believe dominate the international community. For the sake of the example, we will use *Realpolitik* (rationalism) as our behavioral theory and the economic theory of Thomas Barnett as our set of initial conditions. Following the covering laws of *Realpolitik,* we can say that national leaders will generally act rationally with the best interests of their own nation in mind; and following Barnett's economic set of initial conditions, Russia and the United States, as members of the stable economic core, will both want to seek a rapid and definitive solution to the problem so as not to destabilize economic activity in the region.

Now taking these two elements, the rationality of *Realpolitik* and the economic ties of Barnett's set of initial conditions, we can conclude that the Russian invasion of Crimea is a rational move in economic terms on the part of Russia because it shields the Russian fleet at Sevastopol, which is used to protect Russian shipping in the Black Sea, and that Russian troops in Crimea can better defend a Russian natural gas pipeline that runs through Ukraine. What will the Russians do next? Well, from a rational perspective using *Realpolitik* covering laws and Barnett's set of economic initial conditions, we can predict that the Russians will stay in Crimea, that they may even set their sights on Ukraine, and perhaps on Lithuania and Poland. Why? Because when the Russian leaders apply *Realpolitik* and Barnett's economic initial conditions to the possible actions by the United States and the EU, they can predict that the EU will do nothing, because it is in the EU's best economic interests not to provoke Russia, which supplies the European nations with natural gas.

The Russians can also predict that the Americans will do nothing militarily because it is in their best interests to avoid military action anywhere in the world beyond the Middle East, because, economically, they cannot afford it. Also, from an economic perspective, the Americans do not want to destabilize their trading partners in the EU who need the natural gas supplied by Russia. In addition, the Russians know that, even if the EU and the United States do pressure them in some way, perhaps by economic sanctions, other consumer states need their natural gas and have the money (read China here) and are willing (read Turkey here) to pay a lot of money for it. To determine whether this scenario actually played itself out like this, and whether it was, in fact, the correct route to take, we must study the other theories of international behavior and the other sets of global initial conditions (AKA the other new world order options). However, for now you should have some idea of how this works.

The Theories of International Behavior

Having looked at the process of predictive political history and having studied an example of that process, it is time to step back and look at the four theories of international behavior, followed by an examination of the five sets of initial conditions. The four theories of international behavior are *Realpolitik;* idealism; neoconservativism; and neoliberalism. Each international behavioral theory can be summarized by reducing them to several covering laws. A **covering law** is a universal normative principle that follows a set pattern that can be used to understand natural processes or human behavior.

In physics, for example, a covering law, such as the law of action and reaction, identifies a physical pattern that can used to predict, in terms of probabilities, a future physical event. A series of interrelated covering laws will produce a theory, such as the theory of gravity. In predictive political history, a covering law identifies historical patterns that can be used to envision, in terms of probabilities, future international behavior. A series of interrelated covering laws will produce a theory of international behavior, such as *Realpolitik*. Some versions of these covering laws can be long and convoluted and so, in an effort to simplify each theory of international behavior, we will reduce them to four indispensable covering laws: (1) a characterization of the global scene, (2) a description of the chief actor on the global scene, (3) a claim as to how those chief actors make international decisions, and (4) a catalogue of special considerations that must be factored into any international study using the theory.

Realpolitik or **realism**, then, builds the four covering laws in this way: (1) characterization of the global scene: The international order can be described as a chaotic system (that is, a system that lacks a controlling agent) [see: Tim Dunne, Milja Kurki, and Steve Smith, *International Relations Theories: Discipline and Diversity* (Oxford: Oxford University Press, 2007), p. 73]; (2) chief actors: The chief actors on the global scene are nation-states, which have a high degree of autonomy that permits them to act independently; nonetheless, that authority is not shared uniformly among those nations, since some have more power and influence than others [see: Richard W. Mansbach and Kirsten L. Rafferty, *Introduction to Global Politics* (New York: Routledge, 2008), p. 20; and John J. Mearsheimer, *The Tragedy of Great Power Politics* (New York: Norton, 2014, pp. 17]; (3) decision making: National leaders customarily look for a rational (logical) way to sustain or widen their own power [see: Mearsheimer, *The Tragedy of Great Power Politics,* p. 17–18]; and (4) special considerations:

The power that leaders have is curbed by NGOs like the United Nations, the International Criminal Court, and so on; by international corporations; and by lower-level transnationals, such as terrorist groups, pirates, drug cartels, mercenaries, and so on.

Idealism or **liberal internationalism** constructs the four covering laws in the following way: (1) characterization: The global order is not fully chaotic but is instead controlled by the NGOs; (2) chief actors: Nation-states share power with the NGOs; (3) decision making: Nation-states and NGOs seek power and control but do so in the interests of international peace, by following international law and using military action only within international coalitions; and (4) special considerations: The final best state of affairs that all nation-states seek (or should seek) is the formation of a democratic or a republican world government.

Neoconservativism sets up the following covering laws: (1) characterization: The global landscape is chaotic; (2) chief actors: Nation-states are the chief actors and all foreign policy decisions must be made to echo the "deepest values of liberal democratic societies" [see: Francis Fukuyama, *America at the Crossroads: Democracy, Power, and the Neoconservative Legacy* (New Haven, CT: Yale University Press, 2006), p. 48]; (3) decision making: The United States must be involved in global affairs and, in doing so, must promote democratic principles; and (4) special considerations: Neoconservatives also voice a wariness for social reengineering missions, suspicion about the usefulness of NGOs, and a belief in the effectiveness of unilateral (as opposed to multinational) military crusades including especially pre-emptive and preventative strikes [see: Fukuyama, *America at the Crossroads*, p. 49].

Neoliberalism develops the four covering laws in this way: (1) characterization: The global community scene is largely chaotic; (2) chief actors: Nation-states and NGOs share the global power with international corporations; (3) decision making: International corporations cross frontiers and act to preserve their own existence, as do nation-states; however, internationals act reasonably as they work to generate higher profits; and (4) special considerations: Nation-states and international corporations act as collaborative partners and in doing so, follow the morality of profit.

When handling a crisis, the predictive political historian imitates the scientist by applying the best theory of international behavior to a set of global initial conditions that exemplify the present-day world order. In its most comprehensive version, the theory will include how a national leader will respond to and work within the initial conditions that describe the *global landscape*. The predictive history practitioner has several sets of initial conditions (new world orders) from which to choose. Still, to keep things as streamlined as possible, we will examine and explain four of these sets of initial conditions—economic, cultural, ideological, and hybrid. It is vital to determine how each set of conditions views the global order before considering international law. To study international law with no understanding of the environment in which it operates is like trying to teach the rules of baseball to someone who has never seen a baseball diamond. It can be done, but why try, especially if there is a real diamond on the next block.

The Global Initial Conditions

As noted previously, political scientists have offered four sets of initial conditions or new world orders for our consideration: the economic theory, the cultural theory, the ideological theory, and the hybrid theory. Each of these new world orders has several incarnations, each different from the others. Nevertheless, within each category, the variations share more characteristics than differences, so we will focus on those common denominators.

LO3

Economic Initial Conditions The economic new world order sees the international community as divided into two sectors: (1) those nations that are economically stable and secure and, thus, have healthy, functioning economies and (2) those nation-states that are economically dysfunctional. Thomas Barnett, senior strategic researcher at the Naval War College and author of *The Pentagon's New Map*, calls the functioning nations the Core" and the dysfunctional nations the Gap." Richard Haass of the Council on Foreign

Relations and author of *The Opportunity* refers to the economically secure nations as the "21st Century Concert." Haass does not directly name the economically unstable nations. However, given his overall theoretical bend, calling them the unintegrated nations would not be out of line. Traditionally, economically sound nations have been referred to as developed nations and economically fragile nations as developing nations. Developed nations include such nation-states as the United States, the countries in Western Europe, China, Russia, Japan, Australia, New Zealand, Canada, South Africa, Israel, India, and the ABC (Argentina, Brazil, Chile) countries of Latin America. The developing nations include nation-states in the Middle East, the Balkans, all of Africa except South Africa, South and Central America (except the ABCs), Indonesia, and Southeast Asia.

Both Barnett and Haass insist that Core nation-states must find ways to overcome or eliminate disconnectedness (Barnett's word) or to integrate (Haass's term) the Gap nations with the Core. Adopting this perspective dramatically alters the political map and, therefore, demands a change in tactics. Some nation-states, such as China and Russia, can no longer be seen by the United States as "the enemy" as they were during the Cold War. Instead, they are seen as allies within the Core, and as such, they share a common set of goals with all other Core nations. In contrast, the enemy is any individual, group, or set of circumstances that somehow separates a nation from the Core or prevents it from developing to the extent that it can become a self-sufficient member of the Core. Under this version of the new world order, international law has certain clear and decisive objectives, namely (1) to protect the Core nations from economic instability and political disruption; (2) to promote the integration of developing nations within the functioning Core; and (3) to fight the forces of disconnectedness that keep the Gap nations in poverty, whether those forces are terrorists in

THE OPENING CASE *Round 2*
Economic Initial Conditions—China v. the United States: Friendly Economic Allies

The opening case suggests that the biggest threat to American dominance of the globe is the advance of China. Consider the following statistics:

1. The United States depends upon China to purchase its treasury bonds and to invest in American corporations by buying stock that allows these companies to continue to exist and to place factories and retail outlets in China.

2. China owns about $1.2 trillion worth of U.S. treasury debt.

3. Chinese defense spending has risen precipitously over the last few years reaching, as high as 10 percent of its annual budget.

4. China fields a standing army of more than 2.1 million active-duty personnel.

5. Between 1978 and 2005, 402 million Chinese were lifted out of poverty by economic reforms.

Some experts preach that the upward curve of Chinese economic development and the Chinese goal to dominate East Asia, the South China Sea, and the Western Pacific will lead inevitably to a war between the China and the United States. If we take one of the theories of international behavior, *Realpolitik,* for example, and apply that theory to the economic set of initial conditions, we get the following results. Given that *Realpolitik* believes that national leaders will act rationally to protect their own power and the lives of their people, and given that both China and the United States are, using Barnett's terminology, Core nations, these two powerful nations are not enemies at all but economic allies that must cooperate to (1) protect the stability of the Core and (2) bring Gap nations into the Core in order to ensure global stability. [See: Noah Feldman, *Cool War: The Future of Global Competition* (New York: Random House, 2013); David C. Kang, *China Rising: Peace, Power, and Order in East Asia* (New York: Columbia University Press, 2007); and Dan Smith, *The State of the World Atlas* (New York: Penguin, 2008).]

al-Qaeda, warlords in Somalia, drug runners in Colombia, or rogue governments in Iran and North Korea. [See: T. Barnett, *The Pentagon's New Map: War and Peace in the Twenty-first Century* (New York: Berkley Books, 2004); and R.N. Haass, *The Opportunity: America's Moment to Alter History's Course* (New York: Public Affairs, 2005).]

Cultural Initial Conditions   The cultural new world order was developed by Samuel Huntington in his book, *The Clash of Civilization*. This view sees the globe as divided into eight distinct civilizations that are more or less autonomous and more or less incapable of successfully cooperating with more than one, or at the most two, other civilizations. A **civilization** is a group of people in a series of different nation-states that share common characteristics, including history, religion, tradition, beliefs, often language, and sometimes ancestry. Huntington identifies eight such civilizations: Western civilization (the United States, Canada, Western Europe, Israel, South Africa, Australia, and New Zealand); the Sinic civilization (China, North and South Korea, and most of Southeast Asia); the Orthodox civilization (Russia and other states in Eastern Europe); the Latin American civilization (South and Central America); the Islamic civilization (Middle Eastern nation-states, the nation-states of northern Africa, and Indonesia); the African civilization (the sub-Saharan regions of Africa); the Hindu civilization (India and Sri Lanka); and the Japanese civilization (Japan alone).

THE OPENING CASE *Round 3*
Cultural Initial Conditions—China v. the United States: Incompatible Civilizational Rivals

Recall that the conflict envisioned in the opening case involves a coming clash between the United States and China. Some commentators believe that the unprecedented growth of China and its desire to dominate, at minimum, East Asia, the South China Sea, and the Western Pacific will lead to an inevitable conflict between these two nations. To prevent this spiral into cultural war, Huntington suggests that those civilizations that can, should withdraw from the international community and, in a sort of self-imposed neo-isolationism, withdraw totally to within their civilizational community. In this case, the United States and China would belong to different civilizations. The United States would serve as the central controlling state of the Western civilization, while China would be the central controlling state of the Sinic civilization. Western civilization would also include Canada, Western Europe, Australia, New Zealand, South Africa, and Israel. China's civilization would include North and South Korea, and most of Southeast Asia, including the Philippines. The establishment of the new civilizational units would require a break in trade, manufacturing, investments, and banking ties with all other civilizations, but especially those whose customs and beliefs are as different as the Americans and the

Chinese. Can such disengagements actually be engineered? Huntington seems to think so. However, asking such a question is beside the point. Despite what we have just discussed here, we must realize that this take on Huntington actually misses the point. What Huntington really argues is not that the nation-states of the world should form such civilizations, but that such civilizations are already in place. The real problem is that we fail to recognize these cultural units and, as a result, we operate as if they do not exist. Moreover, Huntington adds, we do so at our own peril. When we fail to see that China exists in its own world, as do we, then we are doomed to repeat the errors of the past over and over again—errors caused, Huntington says, by operating as if no differences exist and by being surprised again and again when we find out that they do. [See: Noah Feldman, *Cool War: The Future of Global Competition* (New York: Random House, 2013); David C. Kang, *China Rising: Peace, Power, and Order in East Asia* (New York: Columbia University Press, 2007); S.P. Huntington, *The Clash of Civilizations and The Remaking of World Order* (New York: Simon & Schuster, 1996); Dan Smith, *The State of the World Atlas* (New York: Penguin, 2008); and Olaf Stapledon, *Last and First Men* (New York: Dover, 1931).]

Some of these civilizations contain powerful central states that serve as a sort of international "big brother" to the lesser states within a civilization. A civilization with a recognized central state is generally more stable, less warlike, and more economically prosperous than one without. The civilizations with central states include Western (the United States); Sinic (China); Hindu (India); Orthodox (Russia); and Japanese (Japan). Since most international conflicts occur between rather than within civilizations, each civilization is better off if it can limit its contact with other civilizations. To this end, Huntington has outlined a number of rules that each civilization should follow in dealing with all other civilizations. These rules include (1) the prime directive of the civilizational world order, that is, that each civilization should never interfere with the internal affairs of another civilization; (2) the rule of collective mediation, which calls for dialogue and negotiation among the central controlling states when possible whenever a dispute arises between civilizations; and (3) the commonalities rule, which encourages civilizations to emphasize those ideals that draw them together rather than those that drive them apart. Thus, it is healthier for Western civilization, for instance, to share its focus on self-determination, rather than to insist that all nations adopt Western-style democracy. Under this version of the new world order, international law has two goals: to promote civilizational autonomy and to protect civilizational rights. [See: S.P. Huntington, *The Clash of Civilizations and The Remaking of World Order* (New York: Simon & Schuster, 1996).]

Ideological Initial Conditions

The ideological new world order sees nation-states grouped based on politics. This view is promoted by Robert Kagan in his book, *The Return of History and the End of Dreams*. Kagan believes that the fall of the Soviet Union in 1991 led some political theorists to erroneously conclude that the ideological struggle among political systems had ended and that democracy had been victorious. These optimistic theorists announced the triumph of democracy and foresaw a cooperative world in which democratic nations worked together to promote freedom and free trade, the bedrocks of progress. They pointed to the transformation of the Soviet Union and the conversion of countries such as Poland, Lithuania, Latvia, and Estonia into democracies as evidence of this revolution. On the international scene, the United States, as the sole superpower, would keep the peace and would usher in a new age of goodwill and prosperity. These theorists, Kagan says, were wrong. The period of peace and prosperity in the 1990s was illusory at best. It represented a temporary respite in the eternal international struggle, a respite that would end as soon as the "losers" of the Cold War had a chance to pause, reassess their situation, regroup, and emerge as global powers once again.

This, Kagan argues, is precisely what happened when the Russian people, after their failed attempt at democracy, surrendered to the *de facto* dictatorship of a new Russian oligarchy and to the promise of a return to past days of imperial glory. The Russians, Kagan argues, believe that they were victimized by the United States and the European Union during the 1990s, and they are now determined to regain their place of power in the international community. Similarly, the Chinese, who also see themselves as victimized by the West (not without good reason), have decided to use their economic strength, their military power, and their political influence to rebuild alliances with the people of the Third World who need their help to resist the temptation of Western corporate domination. Both of these great powers, Russia and China, Kagan argues, have returned to a 19th century strategy of empire-building and both have the ideological structure to see those plans of empire succeed. Thus, Kagan envisions the globe divided into two political camps: (1) the democracies, led by the United States and the EU, and (2) the autocracies, led by Russia and China. In this international environment, the job of international law is to help build and protect a modern concert of democracies that would unite the democratic states into a treaty of mutual protection and act as a counterbalance to the new autocratic empires. [See: Robert Kagan, *The Return of History and the End of Dreams* (New York: Public Affairs, 2005).]

THE OPENING CASE *Round 4*
Ideological Initial Conditions—China v. the United States: Opposites or Capitalistic Democratic Twins?

The current relationship between China and the United States, as outlined in the opening case, indicates that Kagan may have misdiagnosed the global situation. Recall how much the United States relies on China economically to purchase its treasury bonds and to invest in American corporations by buying stock that allows these companies to continue to exist and to place factories and retail outlets in China. Note especially that this relationship between the United States and China is based on the economic strength of China. Some commentators who are opposed to Kagan's view might point to this situation as evidence that even China, which is still officially led by the Communist Party of China (CPC), may actually be a democratic capitalist state in disguise. It is true that, in the 1990s and the early years of the 21st century, China adapted well to capitalism, especially in the wake of the reacquisition of Hong Kong. However, despite its economic resurgence, China is still not truly a democratic state and, therefore, would never qualify for membership in Kagan's concert of democracies. Consider the following evidence. The Communist Party of China consists of some 75 million members. However, the government itself is run by a small group of people referred to as the Communist Party elites. The actual ruling members of the government come from the highest echelons of the elites, who number about 300 to 400. This figure rises from the core of elite members that number in the hundreds of thousands. However, even this figure seems small in a nation that has a population of 1.4 billion. The members of the elite (the "princelings" as they are called in China) inherit their positions from relatives who inherited their positions from other relatives or from sponsors. Young people with political ambition but no connections within the party are not likely to rise to power unless they can develop their own network of sponsors within the elite. It seems that more and more young outsiders are taking this route, thus expanding the number of newcomers outside the ranks of the princelings. These newcomers are part of what is referred to as the new meritocracy. This is a very good sign. However, even the meritocracy cannot be called democratic by even the most sympathetic Western observer. Still, this movement is encouraging. On the other hand, as Kagan has noted repeatedly, China still acts much like an autocratic state with territorial ambitions. China's belligerent attitude toward Taiwan and its insistence on establishing an Air Defense Identification Zone over the Senkaku Islands, despite the fact that the islands legally belong to Japan, makes China look very much like a 19th century empire. [See: Noah Feldman, *Cool War: The Future of Global Competition* (New York: Random House, 2013); Robert Kagan, *The Return of History and the End of Dreams* (New York: Public Affairs, 2005); Chelsea J. Carter and Kevin Wang, "U.S.: China Claim of Air Rights over Disputed Islands Creates Risk of Incident," CNN, November 24, 2013).]

Hybrid Initial Conditions
In *A Few Brass Tacks* and *A New Pattern for a Tired World,* the essayist Louis Bromfield develops a model for the new world order that anticipates a combined view of the work of Barnett, Haas, Huntington, and Kagan, and reflects the philosophical and ethical ideas of Max Weber, his contemporary. Taking a page from the ideology of *Realpolitik,* Bromfield declares unapologetically that American leaders have mismanaged their essential duties by concentrating on what Bromfield labels "world responsibility" rather than national responsibility. The United States intervenes in the affairs of other nations, intending to help but, instead, doing quite the opposite. Generally the target nation becomes dependent on American handouts, which damages the nation's independence and erodes its self-esteem. This means that the United States momentarily rescues failing nations by transferring billions of dollars into their treasuries, but never handles the real causes of the economic crisis itself. America's lack of skill in international affairs may be understandable given its youth and inexperience, but that does not excuse the repetition of the same mistakes over and over. Bromfield maintains that, to be genuinely responsible, American leaders must accept a long view of the future, one that determines what is best for the nation's citizens in

THE OPENING CASE *Round 5*

Hybrid Initial Conditions—China v. the United States: Coalition Leaders or Global Trade Rivals?

Louis Bromfield wrote his two major political narratives, *A Few Brass Tacks* and *A New Pattern for a Tired World,* in the years immediately following World War II, at a time when the United States was at the peak of its political, economic, and military power. As the only major nation untouched by the destruction of the war, the United States should have been able to manage the world's problems in a sensible, straightforward, and successful way. Unfortunately, as Bromfield has pointed out repeatedly, the United States did not live up to its potential. Instead of solving problems in Europe, Iran, Korea, Guatemala, and Viet Nam, the United States actually made things worse. Bromfield argues that America's failure to deal successfully with international problems is rooted in its inexperience and is manifested in its tendency to throw money at any problem in the hopes that money alone will make things better. As Bromfield writes in *A New Pattern*: "We pour billions of dollars into the nations of Europe, which has perhaps saved them from temporary bankruptcy, but has done nothing to solve the real and inevitable economic ills constituting the *real* causes of their decline." The United States, Bromfield says, is caught up in a repetition of past failures. As Bromfield notes: "The whole pattern of our interference and of our policies has included little but the old nineteenth-century political ideas which brought about two world

wars and are perhaps bringing about a third, which could easily mean the end of civilization or even of life upon this planet." Bromfield proposes that the United States abandon its Lone Ranger approach and, instead of trying to solve every nation's problems separately, lead a movement under which the major global powers, including the United States, Europe, Russia, China, Japan, and India, initiate economic coalitions with those nations closest to them, geographically and culturally. These economic zones would first trade among themselves until they were economically stable and would then explore relationships with other coalitions. How would this plan play out given the current relationship between the United States and China? Recall, again, that China and the United States are so intertwined economically that creating the type of economic zones that Bromfield suggests might not be possible unless the United States is prepared to renege on its trade, manufacturing, and investment contracts with China. Such a move in the present economic climate would lead to an international crisis at the Dispute Settlement Board (DSB) of the World Trade Organization or perhaps, even to a global, armed (nuclear?) conflict. (See Figure 34-1.) [See: Louis Bromfield, *A New Pattern for a Tired World* (New York: Harper, 1954).]

terms of what is best for the economic balance of the global community. Paradoxically, this means that the United States and other economically powerful nations must disengage from the global community and deal with the civic and economic well-being of their own people.

Bromfield proposes that the major global powers, including the United States, Europe, Russia, China, Japan, and India, establish regional economic zones among those nations closest to them. **Economic zones** are unified but isolated sectors of economic activity based on geographical areas designed to focus on the economic well-being of the nations in each zone. Bromfield's economic zones would conform to the following geographic arrangement: the Western Hemisphere: the United States, Canada, and Mexico (possibly also South America, led by Brazil): the European: essentially today's European Union; the East Asian: Russia, China and Japan (although at times Bromfield moves Russia into the European zone); and the South Central Asian: India, Pakistan (at times Bromfield adds "the rest of Asia" to this zone). Once

Figure 34-1 The China Economic Cycle.

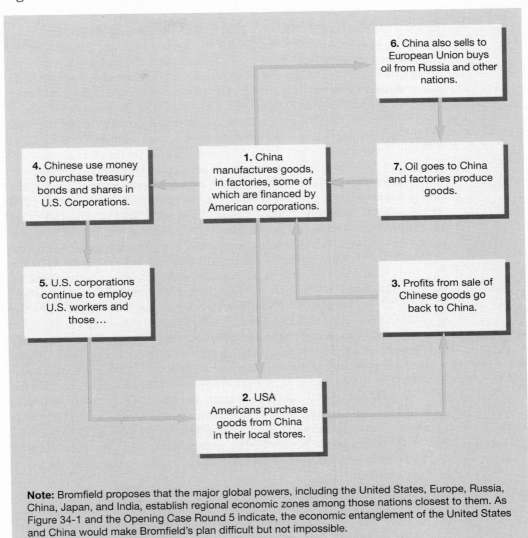

Note: Bromfield proposes that the major global powers, including the United States, Europe, Russia, China, Japan, and India, establish regional economic zones among those nations closest to them. As Figure 34-1 and the Opening Case Round 5 indicate, the economic entanglement of the United States and China would make Bromfield's plan difficult but not impossible.

these zones were economically and politically secure, the members of each zone would trade only with other nations within their respective zones. These exclusive trading arrangements would continue until the members of each zone developed economically secure relationships among themselves. The four major economic zones could then trade among themselves: the North American zone with the East Asian zone; the European zone with the South Central Asian zone, and so on. Eventually, each zone could enter open trade agreements with nations outside the four established zones, but only when those outside nations were ready to participate as economic equals. This strategy reflects an appropriate example of Weber's ethic of responsibility. The global giants will have demonstrated a responsible attitude toward their own people, and a mutually supportive relationship with the remainder of the globe. What's more, Bromfield foresees a future international community operating as a unified global economy. Although, he does not use the term *globalization* here, he certainly could have. [See: Louis

Bromfield, *A New Pattern for a Tired World* (New York: Harper, 1954); For an examination of the ethic of responsibility see also Max Weber, "Politics as a Vocation," in The Great Political Theories, Volume 2, Ed. Michael Curtis (New York: Harper, 2008), pp. 426–436.]

Variables, Uncertainty, and Unexpected Events

Predictive political history is not without its shortcomings and limitations. Chief among these is the realization that, unlike the laws of physics or those of chemistry, the covering laws of predictive political history are limited by the free will of the people who operate within that system. This limitation is referred to as the volition variable. The volition variable, which was identified, though not named as such, by Arthur Danto in his book, *Analytical Philosophy of History,* is an unstable element within the human decision-making process imposed by the fact that humans will use free will to inexplicably make arbitrary decisions that make the covering laws of predictive political history seem less than totally deterministic. On the other hand, if we do a careful study of the volition variable, we will see decision-making patterns that make even those apparently unpredictable moves predictable, at least in terms of probabilities. Still, Danto would say that to qualify as covering laws, the descriptions of such events must be stated using qualifiers such as "generally," "often," "usually," and so on. Such qualifiers allow for the fact that determinism is limited by free will and that the exercise of free can still be seen as determined by events. Thus, for example, a covering law in predictive political history can never state conclusively, "When nations feel threatened, they will strike preemptively." Instead, covering "laws" should be formulated as probabilities, such as, "(Generally) when nations feel (somewhat) threatened, they will (often) strike (more or less) preemptively. [See: Arthur Danto, *Analytical Philosophy of History* (New York: Rainbow-Bridge Book Company, 1965), pp. 183–187, 212–13.] For instance, during World War II, in June 1941, Joseph Stalin, in examining the political, military, geographical, and meteorological evidence, discounted speculation that the Germans would invade Russia. Stalin should have been correct. However, he failed to factor in the volition variable including evidence that Hitler tended to make unexpected and irrational decisions, as the German dictator did when he invaded Russia that year. On the other hand, Stalin had been warned that Hitler might make such an unexpected move, and Stalin, in exercising his own free will, chose to characterize those warnings as propaganda. [See: Richard Overy, *Atlas of 20th Century History* (New York: Harper Collins, 2004), pp. 74–75.]

Predictive political history might also be disrupted by the uncertainty principle. The uncertainty principle is an unstable element within the human decision-making process that emerges because the act of making a decision in a system often alters that system. This problem results because, whenever a decision maker is also a participant in a situation, the two roles (observer and actor) interfere with one another, producing unintended consequences. In his book, *The New Paradigm for Financial Markets,* the philosopher and financial analyst George Soros calls this tendency the reflexivity principle. The uncertainty (or reflexivity) principle is rarely a problem in science (unless we are dealing with quantum physics). Thus, when a scientist determines whether a passing celestial object will cross the orbit of the Earth and be suitable for telescopic observations, her decision has no effect on the orbit of that object, its speed, composition, mass, and so on. However, when a national leader must determine whether to launch a drone on a terrorist stronghold, he (or his advisors) must determine the payload, the trajectory, the timing, and so on. In such a situation, factors that appear to be objective are actually subjective because they require evaluation and judgment. Soros says that such factors do not qualify as knowledge because they are tainted by intentions and expectations. When decisions makers do not recognize this distinction, they see things as reliable facts that may actually be unreliable value judgments. This disconnect between what is true and what the decision maker believes is true means that the decision maker has changed the situation by adding his or her value judgments into the mix of fact and fiction. Such a mix can result in unintended consequences. [See: George Soros, *The New Paradigm for Financial Markets: The Credit Crisis of 2008 and What It Means* (New York: Public Affairs, 2008).]

Finally, predictive political history can also be disrupted by unexpected, uncontrollable chaotic events. In *Warrior Politics*, Robert Kaplan calls such occurrences sideswipes. **Chaotic events** consist of unpredictable and unexpected incidents, often with a natural origin, such as earthquakes, typhoons snowstorms, volcanic eruptions, plagues, and the like that come out of nowhere and have a debilitating effect on human decisions [See: Robert Kaplan, *Warrior Politics: Why Leadership Demands a Pagan Ethos* (New York: Random House, 2002).] Chaotic events, however, can also result from human activity, as with the advent of cloning, genetic engineering, fusion energy, drone warfare, computer viruses, and other scientific breakthroughs; unexpected political events such as the fall of the Soviet Union, the mortgage crisis of 2008, terror attacks such as 9/11, the London tube bombing, and the Spanish train attack; or unexpected and unpredicted cultural changes such as the drug crisis, immigration reform, campaign corruption, sex scandals, and governmental spying.

quick quiz 34-1

1. A world order is a set of initial conditions that describes how nation-states relate to one another on a global scale.   true | false

2. As a process, predictive political history imitates science.   true | false

3. The democracies have won the ideological battle and a cooperative world has emerged.   true | false

34-2 International Law and War

Karl von Clausewitz, a 19th century Prussian soldier and political scientist, is credited with one of the most often-quoted definitions of war. "War," Clausewitz claims, "is a continuation of politics by other means." In today's world of complex multinational corporations, delicate international relationships, and instantaneous Internet transactions, Clausewitz might have added that war is also the continuation of international business by other means. As we have seen recently, international business can be, affected profoundly by war, especially when it is an unpopular war that lacks international authorization and when it results in a protracted campaign of attrition that drags on for months with no clear goals and no end in sight. Such a situation can increase costs, cause shortages of raw materials, endanger shipping, and render the execution of a contract commercially impracticable, if not impossible to perform. This scenario may be true even if the parties to a war are not citizens of the nations that are at war. Some of these problems can be solved by the internal law of a particular nation-state.

EXAMPLE 34-2: The *S.S. Christos* and the Suez Crisis

The Transatlantic Financing Corporation operated the *S.S. Christos,* a cargo ship carrying wheat from Texas to Iran, for the United States government. While the *S.S. Christos* was en route to Iran, Israel invaded Egypt. Two days later, France and Great Britain invaded the Suez Canal Zone. The invasion and subsequent closing of the Suez Canal made it impossible for the *S.S. Christos* to use the canal. A 3,000-mile detour around the southern coast of Africa cost Transatlantic an unexpected $44,000 above the original estimated cost of $305,842.92. When the United States government refused to pay the additional amount, the company brought a lawsuit. Although the United States and Transatlantic were not directly involved in the Suez hostilities, their contract had been affected by the conflict. Nevertheless, the federal court did not allow Transatlantic to recover the additional payment from the government of the United States. The court's decision was based on a traditional rule of contract law in the United States. The court declared, "While it may be an overstatement to say that increased cost and difficulty of performance never constitute impracticability, to justify relief there must be more of a variation between the expected costs and the cost of performing by an available alternative than is present in this case."

The lesson to be learned from the case in Example 34-2 is a simple one: When entering a contract that relies on the international marketplace, it is wise for all parties to be aware of the international conditions in all areas of the globe that may affect the contract. This approach is crucial because courts in the United States will take into account the foreseeability of any international crisis, including not only war but also war-related events, such as blockades, quarantines, and border closings. If the court deems that the international crisis was foreseeable, the loss suffered by the parties affected by the crisis will not be offset by the court.

A QUESTION OF ETHICS

Delusional Fantasies and Foreseeable Wars

In her influential study of the Great War, the historian Barbara W. Tuchman writes in *The Guns of August* that in 1910 two very different, yet equally popular, views on the prospect of future wars existed within Europe. One of these views was represented by Norman Angell's book, *The Great Illusion*. Angell argued that war had become an untenable option because of the economic connections among the nations of the global community. Any war would have such devastating consequences that nations could no longer afford to engage in any sort of armed conflict. In support of this view, a key British military leader, Viscount Esher, contended that a combination of factors, including "commercial disaster, financial ruin, and individual suffering," made war in the 20th century "more difficult and improbable" than ever before in the history of civilization. A contradictory position was represented by a German general, Friedrich von Bernhardi, who, in a work titled *Germany and the Next War*, argued that war was inevitable. In fact, von Bernhardi argued, war was a consequence of "natural law." Von Bernhardi insisted that war was a "biological necessity" and actually the human expression of "the struggle for existence." Von Bernhardi wrote that, among nation-states, "there can be no standing still." He concluded that any country that fails to move up the evolutionary ladder of development faces inevitable destruction.

A QUESTION YET UNANSWERED

The following question has not yet been answered. Before you consider the question, turn to Chapter 1 to review the various ethical theories noted there (market value ethics, social contract theory, utilitarianism, and rational ethics). Then in a consistent way, answer the following question. Which view, the one promoted by Norman Angell and Viscount Esher or the one promoted by General von Bernhardi is morally correct? Explain. [See: Barbara Tuchman, "A Funeral," *The Guns of August* (New York: The MacMillan Company, 1962), pp. 10–11.]

The Just War Theory

One central question that cannot be answered solely by the law of a single nation-state is whether a war is just. Ethical and legal philosophers in the West have developed criteria for determining when a war can be considered legally and morally correct. This theory, termed the **just war theory**, has been invoked to defend and question the morality of many armed conflicts. In its traditional form, the theory focuses on two main areas. First, it establishes the criteria that would justify going to war. Second, it institutes criteria for the proper conduct of a war that is already in progress. A third modern feature of justifiability adds a set of criteria that establish the rules of conduct that must be followed after a war ends.

Criteria for Going to War

The just war theory endorses six criteria for deciding whether a war can be morally justified: (1) just cause, (2) right intention, (3) competent authority, (4) probability of success, (5) proportionality, and (6) last resort. The first criterion, **just cause**, says that to be morally permissible, a war must be waged for honorable motives. Included among these motives are self-defense and the defense of a fellow sovereign nation-state that has been targeted by an aggressor and is unable to, defend itself properly. The second criterion, **right intention**, declares that a war must be waged only if the combatant has the correct objective. The difference between the first and the second criteria is the difference between an objective justification for war and the subjective intent of the actual combatants. A war may have an objectively justifiable cause and yet be fought for the wrong reasons. This situation could happen, for instance, if one country goes to the defense of another country but then uses that defensive campaign as a pretext to destroy the government and subjugate the civilian population of the aggressor nation-state.

The third criterion, **competent authority**, states that war can be initiated only by legitimately recognized nation-states. This standard does not mean, however, as some people have suggested, that the United Nations must declare a war for that war to have been declared by competent authority. In fact, from a legal perspective, the UN cannot declare war at all. The UN Charter is founded on the belief that all member nations maintain their sovereign authority, including the authority to declare war. This criterion also means that it is not ethically permissible for individuals such as the late Osama bin Laden or a rogue terrorist group such as ISIS, to declare war on anyone, let alone the United States. War is a function of nation-states in their relationships with one another, not the purview of individuals, no matter how much outlaw groups like ISIS believe otherwise.

The fourth criterion, **probability of success**, declares that at the outset of a war, there must be a reasonable chance that the war will be successful; a suicidal war would fall outside this criterion. Fifth, **proportionality** holds that the good advanced by the war must exceed the negative consequences of entering the conflict. Thus, a war fought over an imaginary diplomatic insult must be considered unjust, because the objective of vindicating a spurious affront to national honor is not proportional to the death and destruction caused by war. Finally, the criterion of **last resort** means that a war can be fought only after all other means for the resolution of the dispute have been tried and failed. If both nations still have diplomatic options available for ending the crisis in a nonviolent way; if an international organization, such as the United Nations, is still willing to explore a negotiated settlement; or if time still exists to pursue a nonviolent solution, war cannot be waged as a solution to the conflict, and if one side insists on declaring war, that war will be an unjust conflict. However, the fact that all options have not been implemented is not decisive. What matters is that the nation-state that began the war gave authentic consideration to each available option, short of war.

Criteria for the Proper Conduct of War

It is not enough to advocate a set of ethical and legal criteria for entering war and then ignore the criteria for conducting the war or for conduct that must be followed after the end of a war. For this reason, many, modern, legal, and moral theorists suggest several additional criteria that should guide conduct during a war

CLASSIC CASE Act 1: The United States v. Bin Laden—Concerning the Just War Theory

Osama bin Laden and al-Qaeda were responsible for the 9/11 attacks on the World Trade Center in New York and the Pentagon in Washington that killed 2,996 people. Just short of a decade later, when U.S. military forces entered Pakistan for the express purpose of either capturing or killing Osama bin Laden, they were not concerned with legal niceties. They had a mission to accomplish and that was all that concerned them. Nevertheless, once the job was done, the legal questions emerged. In global operations such as the bin Laden mission, two legal spheres of influence must be addressed: the national and the international. In the international arena, there is the question of whether the uninvited use of American troops on foreign soil is legally permissible. One way to answer this question is to apply the principles of the just war theory. According to the theory, a military action is legally and morally correct, as long as it passes six tests: (1) just cause, (2) right intention, (3) competent authority, (4) probability of success, (5) proportionality, and (6) last resort. The bin Laden operation passes each of these tests. First, it was just in that it targeted the self-confessed, unrepentant mastermind of the 9/11 operation. Second, the action was fought with the right intention, bringing the man responsible for 9/11 to justice. Third, the operation was initiated by competent authority, in this case the authority of the president of the United States. Fourth, the operation had a great probability of success, given the experience, the training, and the planning used by the elite military team charged with mission. Fifth, the action was a limited operation with one primary objective in mind, the capture or elimination of bin Laden. Sixth, the action was a last resort, since all other efforts aimed at bringing bin Laden to justice had been for naught. [See: Dionne Searcey, "Killing Was Legal Under U.S. and International Law, Many Experts Say," *The Wall Street Journal,* May 6, 2011, p. A6; Jenna Greene, et al., "In Bin Laden Killing, Legal Clarity," *The National Law Journal,* May 9, 2011, pp. 1 and 4–5; Michael Byers, *War Law: Understanding International Law and Armed Conflict* (New York: Grove Press, 2005), p. 7.]

and behavior after a war. The first of the criteria for conducting a war requires that the warring factions use only those military means that are proportional to the ends that they wish to achieve. Thus, because it was possible for the international coalition to subdue and eject the invading Iraqi army from Kuwait in Gulf War I by using conventional weapons, the use of nuclear weapons would have been considered a disproportionate tactic. The second criterion states that the war must be fought with discrimination. This restriction means that only combatants should be targeted in the war and that civilians must be kept out of harm's way.

Criteria for Proper Postwar Conduct

Three just war principles have been established for gauging the morality of conduct following the cessation of hostilities. The first of these principles is the principle of repentance. The principle of repentance calls for a genuine expression of remorse by the combatants for the death and destruction caused by war. Conduct that expresses either joy or satisfaction at the death of enemy combatants, even combatants involved in a war of aggression, would violate this principle. The second criterion, the principle of honorable surrender, requires the victor in a war to accept the surrender of the enemy and treat the defeated combatants with dignity and respect. Refusing a genuine offer of surrender, violating that surrender after it has been implemented, or mistreating enemy combatants after surrender would all be violations of this principle. Actions that are motivated by revenge or retribution would also violate the principle of honorable surrender, as would conduct that injures or humiliates prisoners of war. Finally, the principle of restoration requires that the victor in a conflict act responsibly in rebuilding the defeated nation's physical environment, economy, and governmental structure.

Preemptive and Protective War

A nation-state starts a **preemptive war** to stop another nation-state's imminent attack on the first nation-state. A preemptive war is not the same as a preventative war, though the terms are often used as synonyms. A preemptive war is waged to stop an attack before it can begin. In contrast, a nation-state begins a **preventative war** to stop another nation-state from reaching a point that it would be capable of attacking the first nation. The doctrine adopted by the United States in 2002 was a doctrine of preemptive war, not one of preventative war. The concept of preemptive war goes back 500 years to Thomas More, who in his work *Utopia* noted that it would be wise to attack preemptively a force that was about to attack you. In the United States, two major military figures, General Leslie Groves, the head of The Manhattan Project, which developed the atomic bomb during World War II, and General Curtis LeMay, former commander of the Strategic Air Command (SAC), advocated preemptive war against the Soviet Union. In the 1950s, the Joint Chiefs of Staff commissioned a study that also recommended a preemptive strike against the Soviet Union. In all of these cases, cooler heads prevailed, and preemptive war was not at that time advocated as a strategic policy of the United States.

Times changed, however, when in 2002, preemptive war became an active, strategic policy of the United States and was the primary stated motivation for the invasion of Iraq in 2003. Although it is difficult to pinpoint the exact moment of this shift in policy, the move toward preemptive war as the national policy of the United States seems to have come about less than three months after September 11, 2001, when, in the aftermath of the attacks on the World Trade Center and the Pentagon, President George W. Bush asked then-Secretary of Defense Donald Rumsfeld about war plans for an attack against Iraq. Evidence indicates that President Bush had similar strategic planning discussions with Vice President Richard Cheney and National Security Advisor Condoleezza Rice. Nevertheless, the first conscious public declaration of this change in policy occurred in a presidential address to the graduating class of West Point on June 1, 2002.

Times changed again nine years later when, during the administration of President Barack Obama, the United States, in response to a series of human rights violations by the late Col. Muammar Gaddafi in Libya, launched a new type of war, a **protective war** aimed at providing aid and assistance to innocent civilians who are being victimized by the military of their own nation-state. Unlike preemptive war, which is designed as a tactic to shield one nation from the unwarranted and deadly attacks of another, a protective war is waged by a nation or a coalition of nations as an intervention in the internal affairs of a sovereign state to protect the civilians of that state from their own government. This is a crucial step away from the traditions inherent within the Treaty of Westphalia, which recognized the almost sacred right of a nation-state to do what it pleased within its own borders. Even the United Nations Charter, a document aimed at unifying the nation-states of the world in a global community, still holds sovereignty as one of its central premises. Consequently, while the theory is still in its formative stages, it might be a good idea to subject it to the tests of the just war theory as well as the test of international law and, in the case of the United States, to the test of domestic legality.

Protective War and the Just War Theory
The just war theory is designed to help individuals and governments make judgments about the justifiability of particular wars, rather than about the morality of war in general. Indeed, the very existence of a just war theory presumes that some wars are in fact justifiable and some are not. Therefore, it is difficult to characterize the morality of a war-making strategy, such as the strategy of protective war, without reference to the war's actual historical context. Nevertheless, all protective wars share certain characteristics that make it possible to judge such wars in theory. For example, all protective wars involve a situation in which the government of a

rogue or failed nation-state has somehow victimized its own people. This victimization might involve genocide, as in Rwanda; anarchy, as in Somalia; or, as in the cases of Libya and Syria, the use of the nation-state's military in an operation that targets its own people. Using this common context we can build a case in support of protective war using the just war theory. We will examine the criteria in reverse order: (1) last resort, (2) proportionality, (3) probability of success, (4) competent authority, (5) right intention, and (6) just cause.

First, the protector nations who initiate a protective war must demonstrate that the use of military force is a last resort. Basically, this would require the protector nations to use diplomatic channels and economic pressure to alter the behavior of the rogue nations before resorting to war. Second, a protective war should be, by definition, a war of proportional response. The object of such a war is to protect innocent civilians who have been victimized by their government. Thus, the war is not aimed at toppling the rogue government, gaining territory, aiding the rebels, or expanding the influence of the protector nations. Third, because protective wars are generally fought by coalitions with limited objectives, the probability of success is almost always ensured. Fourth, at least in the modern context, most protective wars will be channeled through the United Nations Security Council, which has a mechanism in place for dealing with such contingencies. Thus, there is little reason for a protective war to be launched outside competent authority. Fifth and sixth, as in the case of proportionality, the requirements of right intention and just cause are inherent within the reason for going to war in the first place. Protective wars, by definition "protect the innocent," a goal that involves both right intention and just cause. Thus, it is clear that a protective war like the one in Libya in 2011 or the one that could have been (or still could be) fought in Syria meet the criteria of a just war. However, this is only one-third of the battle. It is also necessary to examine the war from the perspective of international law and, in the case of the United States, from the perspective of domestic law.

Protective War and International Law   Immediately following the Second World War, the founders of the UN wrote a charter that provided for the possibility of future military action. The mechanism is found in Chapter VII of the United Nations Charter. Chapter VII places most of the decision-making process in the hands of the UN Security Council. Although the authority granted to the Security Council in Chapter VII falls short of permitting the UN to actually declare war on a sovereign state, it does outline a process that *approximates* that power. Chapter VII empowers the Security Council to first ascertain that a genuine danger exists that threatens the civil peace of a nation-state and then determine what actions must be initiated "to maintain or restore international peace and security" (UN Chapter VII). Before these actions can be taken, however, the charter stipulates that diplomatic and economic sanctions must be put into effect before resorting to military force. If such sanctions do not work, then member states may be authorized to carry out whatever military measures are deemed appropriate to restore order and stability within the nation-state and to the region affected by the actions of a rogue state, a failed state, or a self proclaimed empire.

In authorizing the protective war in Libya, the United Nations Security Council followed these steps religiously. First, the Security Council investigated the activities of the government in Libya and, following that investigation, issued UN Security Council Resolution 1970, which initiated economic and diplomatic sanctions against the Libyan government and referred the situation to the International Criminal Court. The next day the European Union officially approved the sanctions outlined in Resolution 1970. One day later the UN General Assembly, recognizing the human rights violations being carried out by the government of Libya, temporarily revoked Libyan membership in the Human Rights Council. Fifteen days after the initial resolution was passed and once it was clear that the diplomatic and economic sanctions had failed to deter Gaddafi and his governmental forces, the Security Council passed UN Resolution 1973. This new resolution authorized

NATO forces to take every means needed to protect civilians who had been endangered by the military onslaught carried out by Libyan governmental forces. The resolution included the establishment of a no-fly zone over Libya. Thus, it is quite clear that NATO's protective war in Libya is legal, based on international law. The final question remains. Is it legal under American domestic law? It is to that question that we now turn.

Protective War and U.S. Domestic Law

When dealing with questions concerning the legality of a war, the United States generally defers to the judgment of the United Nations. In fact, the United States has a fairly good (though certainly not a perfect) record of handling armed conflict through the UN Security Council. In 1950, for instance, after North Korea invaded South Korea, the United States and its allies went to the Security Council and sought a resolution to authorize military intervention against the North Koreans. Owing to the Soviet Union's decision to boycott the Security Council's vote on the issue, the United States succeeded in obtaining the required resolution. In October 1962 when President John F. Kennedy was contemplating a blockade against Cuba to stop the influx of offensive nuclear weapons being shipped there by the Soviets, the United States again went to the UN Security Council. Deference to the UN Security Council, however, is not identical to loyalty, obedience, or surrender, and so, at times, domestic law authorizes military action without forcing the president to go to the UN. Nevertheless, this does not mean that there is no oversight on the actions of the president in his role as commander-in-chief of the armed forces. In fact, Congress does play a role in this process—a big role.

The War Powers Resolution   In the 1970s after the problems associated with a president of the United States waging war without congressional approval, Congress enacted a law that would prevent a repeat of that type of activity. The **War Powers Resolution** of 1973 is designed to limit the power of the president as commander-in-chief of the armed forces to commit American troops to the field and to maintain those troops in the field contrary to congressional approval. The resolution also requires the president to communicate to Congress on a regular basis about the military action, once that action is approved by Congress. More specifically, the War Powers Resolution requires that the president inform Congress of his use of American troops within 48 hours of doing so. The notice must be in writing and must be delivered to the speaker of the House *and* the president pro tempore of the Senate. If Congress approves of the president's use of troops, he has 60 days to accomplish the mission. At that time, 60 days after the initial written notice was given to Congress, he must withdraw the troops within 30 days unless Congress authorizes a continuation of the action. All of this assumes, of course, that Congress can actually meet and has not somehow been compromised or eliminated by enemy action on American soil. In such a case, the president is authorized to continue whatever action is needed to protect the United States.

Authorization for the Use of Military Force of 2002   The **Authorization for the Use of Military Force** (AUMF) is an act passed in 2002 by Congress in the wake of the 9/11 attacks. The proper designation of the act is Public Law 107-40 [S.J. Res. 23]. Officially, it is a joint resolution passed by both the House and the Senate. The joint resolution begins by stating that the United States is justified in using self-defense to protect its citizens and territory. The resolution also recognizes that the 9/11 attacks were an instance of the "unusual and extraordinary threat to the national security and foreign policy of the United States" and that the president has the authority "under the Constitution to take action to deter and prevent acts of international terrorism against the United States." The resolution cites the War Powers Resolution [Section 8 (A) (1)] as the statutory authority upon which the new resolution is built. Like the action authorized by UN Article 51, the authorization act relies upon self-defense as justification for the use of force, so long as that military

CLASSIC CASE Act 2: The United States v. Bin Laden— Concerning the Authorization for the Use of Military Force

The U.S. military entered Pakistan to capture or kill Osama bin Laden. In Act 1, we asked and answered the question of whether the uninvited use of American troops on foreign soil was legally permissible. Applying the just war theory, we answered in the affirmative. Now, another unanswered question remains on the table: "Can the president of the United States use American forces *without* a congressional declaration of war in an operation aimed at capturing or assassinating a terrorist leader on foreign soil?" To answer this question in 2011 when the attack took place, we would have applied the basic principles of the original AUMF. As part of the original AUMF, Congress declared, "The president is authorized to use all necessary and appropriate force against those nations, organizations, or persons he determines planned, authorized, committed, or aided the terrorist attack that occurred on September 11, 2001, or harbored such organizations or persons, in order to prevent any future acts of

international terrorism against the United States by such nations, organizations, or persons." The resolution penned by Congress identifies Section 8 (A) (1) of the War Powers Resolution as the statutory foundation upon which the AUMF was established. Moreover, the AUMF also uses long-standing common law principles of self-defense as a valid justification for the application of military action in this case, provided the action taken is employed "to prevent any future acts of international terrorism" against the United States. So was the bin Laden operation legal under domestic statutory law? The answer is "yes"—at least under the AUMF of 2002. [See: Dionne Searcey, "Killing Was Legal Under U.S. and International Law, Many Experts Say," *The Wall Street Journal,* May 6, 2011, p. A6; Jenna Greene, et al., "In Bin Laden Killing, Legal Clarity," *The National Law Journal,* May 9, 2011, pp. 1 and 4–5; and Michael Byers, *War Law: Understanding International Law and Armed Conflict* (New York: Grove Press, 2005), p. 7.]

force is used "to prevent any future acts of international terrorism" against the United States. [See: Dionne Searcey, "Killing Was Legal Under U.S. and International Law, Many Experts Say," *The Wall Street Journal,* May 6, 2011, p. A6; Jenna Greene, et al., "In Bin Laden Killing, Legal Clarity," *The National Law Journal,* May 9, 2011, pp. 1 and 4–5; and Michael Byers, *War Law: Understanding International Law and Armed Conflict* (New York: Grove Press, 2005), p. 7.]

Authorization for the Use of Military Force of 2015 In 2015 after two extended military campaigns in Iraq and Afghanistan and in light of the new threat imposed by the Islamic State of Iraq and Syria (also known as ISIS and ISIL, and the Islamic State in Iraq and the Levant), the president presented a reengineered version of the AUMF Act of 2002 to Congress. The new plan, officially dubbed the Authorization for the Use of Military Force of 2015, was an attempt by the president to extend the military power of the commander-in-chief without appearing to do so. Under AUMF 2015, the president would be given the authority to use military action to oppose ISIS and any "associated persons and forces." In addition, the AUMF of 2015 would eliminate the existence of "enduring offensive ground combat operations," although it would still allow other types of smaller scale operations, such as those that the United States carried out in Libya. Moreover, as a safeguard, AUMF 2015 would also include a three-year expiration date for such campaigns. AUMF 2015 would officially terminate the 2002 authorization issued by Congress for the invasion of Iraq. Finally, the act would also expressly define **associated persons and forces** as "individuals and organizations fighting for, on behalf of, or alongside ISIL or any closely related successor entity in hostilities against the United States or its coalition partners." Despite vigorous on both sides if the political spectrum regarding the need for this resolution or one like it, as of

CLASSIC CASE Act 3: The United States v. Bin Laden—Concerning the Authorization for the Use of Military Force 2015 Style

The president in 2011 sent a group of Navy Seals into Pakistan to capture or assassinate Osama bin Laden, the man who had masterminded the 9/11 attacks and who had repeatedly promised to launch similar attacks against the United States in the future. In Acts 1 and 2 earlier, we asked and answered the question of whether the uninvited use of American troops on foreign soil was legally permissible under the just law theory and under the 2002 AUMF. In both cases the answer was "yes." One final question remains: "Would the president of the United States be permitted to use military forces, absent a congressional declaration of war, in a similar operation under AUMF 2015?" To answer this question, we must simply look at the wording of AUMF 2015. As noted earlier, AUMF 2015

recommends giving the president the power to use military action to oppose ISIS and "associated persons and forces." Taking even the most inflexible interpretation of the phrase "associated persons and forces," it is easy to see that bin Laden would fit in that category. Moreover, while AUMF 2015 would clearly abolish the use of "enduring offensive ground combat operations," it would still permit small-scale military campaigns, just like the one carried out in Pakistan against bin Laden. [See: 50 USC Sections 1541-48; Peter Baker, "News Analysis: A Dual View of War Power: Obama Is Proposing Limits and Leeway," *The New York Times,* February 12, 2015, pp. A-1, A-12; and "Presidential Power: A Law for War," *The Economist,* February 14, 2015, p. 28.]

this printing, Congress has yet to act on the AUMF of 2015. [See: 50 USC Sections 1541-48; Peter Baker, "News Analysis: A Dual View of War Power: Obama Is Proposing Limits and Leeway," *The New York Times,* February 12, 2015, pp. A1, A-12; and "Presidential Power: A Law for War," *The Economist,* February 14, 2015, p. 28. See also: Letter from the President—Authorization for the Use of United States Armed Forces in connection with the Islamic State of Iraq and the Levant, Office of the Press Secretary, The White House, February 11, 2015; See also: Lauren Leatherby, "Whatever Happened Tot The Debate Over Use Of Force Against ISIS?" NPR (June 17, 2015), http://www.npr.org/2015/06/17/415203016/whatever-happened-to-the-debate-over-use-of-force-against-isis.]

Substantive and Procedural Issues

Most of these just war requirements were established before the advent of contemporary warfare. In the modern age, the face of war has changed. Along with these changes have come alterations in the conduct of war, including ways of dealing with prisoners of war, occupation forces, and war crimes.

Substantive Legal Changes Following World War II, in 1949, a major effort involving most of the nations of the world and sponsored by the American Red Cross was held in Geneva, Switzerland, to address the issues of prisoners of war, occupation forces, and war crimes. Out of this series of international meetings came the Geneva Conventions. These conventions attempt to deal with many of the problems brought on by the nature of warfare in the modern era. For instance, the first, second, and third conventions are concerned with prisoners of war, and the fourth deals with occupation forces.

Procedural and Analytical Problems Substantive changes in the law of war and international relations, such as the Geneva Conventions, are frequently complicated by procedural and analytical questions. The mere fact that a convention has been written and adopted does not mean that it will be applied properly and consistently by the nations that signed the convention. Analytical questions nearly always plague any court faced with the application of an international agreement. To facilitate this analytical process, the U.S. courts have established some guidelines for interpreting international agreements such as the Geneva Conventions.

For instance, in determining the applicability of such international pacts, the courts will first look at the literal language of the agreement, especially any definitions contained within the agreement. Second, the court will examine any supporting documentation, such as the Red Cross Commentaries in the case of the Geneva Conventions, for assistance in interpreting the settlement. Third, U.S. courts will take a liberal view in the interpretation of such agreements. This guideline means that the court will broadly and openly interpret the convention to include as many cases and situations as are justly warranted.

quick quiz 34-2

1. One central question that cannot be answered solely by the law of a single nation-state is whether a war is just.   true | false

2. The just war theory was developed in the 21st century to deal with problems of modern warfare.   true | false

3. The Geneva Conventions attempt to establish rules involving, occupation forces and prisoners of war.   true | false

34-3 The United Nations and the Global Community

As World War II drew to a close, representatives of 50 nations met in San Francisco to work out the details of the formation of the United Nations. At that meeting, called the United Nations Conference on International Organization, the 50 nations adopted a charter that on June 26, 1945, established the United Nations. The stated purposes of the United Nations are to advance human rights, to end war, to enhance human achievement, to support peaceful international coalitions, and to promote truth, justice, and the rule of law. The promotion of international law has taken many forms within the structure of the United Nations, including the International Law Commission, International Court of Justice, the UN Commission on International Trade Law, and the UN Convention on Contracts for the International Sale of Goods. Although the International Criminal Court stands outside the official system of the UN, it nevertheless has an important role to play in the administration of global justice

The Structure of the United Nations

The United Nations is an enormous, complicated organization that consists of many agencies, organizations, courts, and commissions (see Table 34-1). The three major governing bodies are the Secretary General, the General Assembly, and the Security Council. The, **secretary general** is the chief administrator of the United Nations. He or she heads up the **Secretariat**, which is the administrative bureaucracy of the UN. The secretary general also takes a leading role in promoting world peace. The Security Council recommends a candidate for the position of secretary general, but the General Assembly votes that person into office. The **General Assembly** is made up of all the member nations of the UN. Each nation has one vote on resolutions and other matters presented to the assembly. The UN **Security Council** deals with crises that involve threats to international peace. The council consists of 15 members. Five of these members hold permanent seats: China, France, Russia, the United Kingdom, and the United States. The General Assembly elects the remaining 10 members for two-year terms.

The United Nations headquarters in New York City.

International Law and the United Nations

One of the strengths of the United Nations is that it is based on a platform that continues to respect the sovereignty of each member state. Without this express guarantee built into its founding principles, it is doubtful that the United Nations Charter would have been ratified, let alone developed into the symbol for international unity that it stands for today. As is often the case with such organizations, however, the UN's main strength is also its main weakness. The sovereign nature of each member state often means that the UN's power to enforce its decrees is a matter of voluntary acquiescence. Thus, the UN must make use of its soft power more than its hard power. The UN's soft power resides in its moral authority as a platform that speaks for all nations with equal objectivity. As we saw in Chapter 33, whether this unbiased attitude exists in reality is open to debate. Nevertheless, the ideal of objective representation stands as a central core belief of the UN, one that its various organizations cannot ignore, even when they want to. The legal organizations within the UN have a special duty to be as unbiased and impartial as possible. Those legal organizations include the International Law Commission, the International Court of Justice (known more popularly as the World Court), and the International Criminal Court.

The International Law Commission The authority to codify international law is the official mission of the International Law Commission. Because all UN member nations retain their sovereign identities, the codifications drawn up by the commission must be joined voluntarily by each nation-state. The commission meets every year at a time authorized by the General Assembly. A legal topic can make its way to the commission in one of two ways. Either the General Assembly submits a legal issue to the commission or the commission itself decides to pursue a legal problem. After the commission has examined a legal topic in depth, it may draw up a draft on that aspect of international law. That draft then goes to the General Assembly for further consideration. Once the General Assembly has accepted a draft, it is codified into a convention. That convention is then submitted to the member states for their adoption. Some of the conventions that have been suggested by the commission and adopted by the General Assembly include the Convention on the Law of Treaties and the Convention on Diplomatic Relations. The General Assembly elects each of the 34 members of the International Law Commission, who each remain on the commission for five years. [See: *Basic Facts about the United Nations* (New York: United Nations, 2003), pp. 269–70.]

The International Court of Justice One of the principal vehicles for the establishment of international law and justice is the **International Court of Justice (ICJ)**. Like many of the agencies of the UN, the ICJ, which is popularly referred to as the World

Table 34-1 The United Nations System

THE UNITED NATIONS SYSTEM

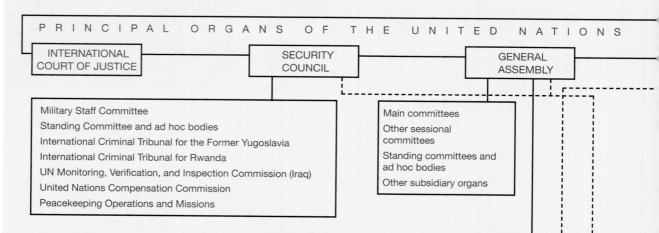

PRINCIPAL ORGANS OF THE UNITED NATIONS

| INTERNATIONAL COURT OF JUSTICE | SECURITY COUNCIL | GENERAL ASSEMBLY |

Military Staff Committee
Standing Committee and ad hoc bodies
International Criminal Tribunal for the Former Yugoslavia
International Criminal Tribunal for Rwanda
UN Monitoring, Verification, and Inspection Commission (Iraq)
United Nations Compensation Commission
Peacekeeping Operations and Missions

Main committees
Other sessional committees
Standing committees and ad hoc bodies
Other subsidiary organs

PROGRAMS AND FUNDS

UNCTAD
United Nations Conference on Trade and Development

ITC
International Trade Center
(UNCTAD, WTO)

UNDCP
United Nations Drug Control Program

UNEP
United Nations Environment Program

UNHSP
United Nations Human Settlements Program
(UN Habitat)

UNDP
United Nations Development Program

UNIFEM
United Nations Development Fund for Women

UNV
United Nations Volunteers

UNFPA
United Nations Population Fund

UNHCR
Office of the United Nations High Commissioner for Refugees

UNICEF
United Nations Children's Fund

WFP
World Food Program

UNRWA**
United Nations Relief and Works Agency for Palestine Refugees in the Near East

OTHER UN ENTITIES

OHCHR
Office of the United Nations High Commissioner for Human Rights

UNOPS
United Nations Office for Project Services

UNU
United Nations University

UNSSC
United Nations System Staff College

UNAIDS
Joint United Nations Program on HIV/AIDS

RESEARCH AND TRAINING INSTITUTIONS

INSTRAW
International Research and Training Institute for the Advancement of Women

UNICRI
United Nations Interregional Crime and Justice Research Institute

UNITAR
United Nations Institute for Training and Research

UNRISD
United Nations Research Institute for Social Development

UNIDIR†
United Nations Institute for Disarmament Research

*Autonomous organizations working with the United Nations and each other through the coordinating machinery of the Economic and Social Council.

†Report only to the General Assembly.

Source: Department of Public Information, *Basic Facts about the United Nations,* New York: 2003, p. 24.

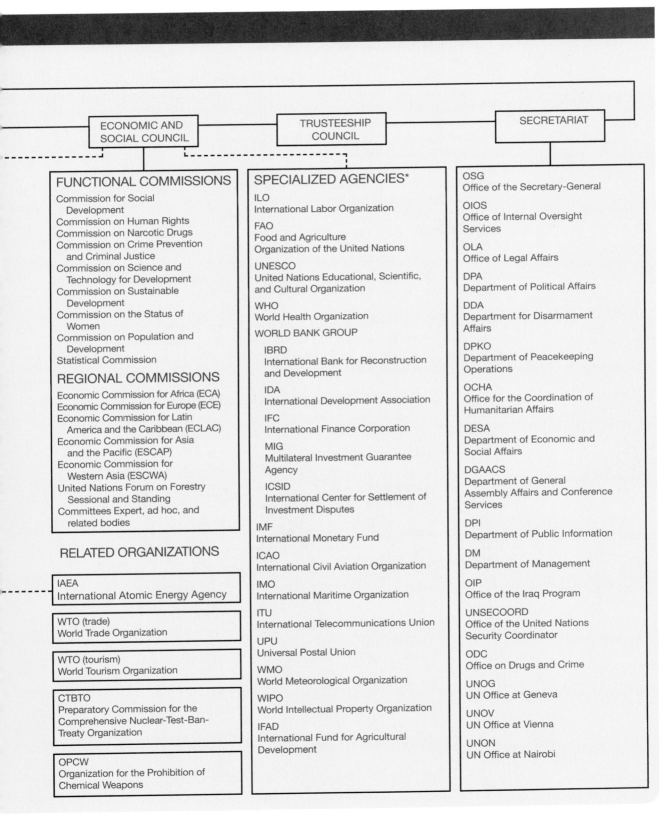

ECONOMIC AND SOCIAL COUNCIL

TRUSTEESHIP COUNCIL

SECRETARIAT

FUNCTIONAL COMMISSIONS

Commission for Social Development
Commission on Human Rights
Commission on Narcotic Drugs
Commission on Crime Prevention and Criminal Justice
Commission on Science and Technology for Development
Commission on Sustainable Development
Commission on the Status of Women
Commission on Population and Development
Statistical Commission

REGIONAL COMMISSIONS

Economic Commission for Africa (ECA)
Economic Commission for Europe (ECE)
Economic Commission for Latin America and the Caribbean (ECLAC)
Economic Commission for Asia and the Pacific (ESCAP)
Economic Commission for Western Asia (ESCWA)
United Nations Forum on Forestry Sessional and Standing Committees Expert, ad hoc, and related bodies

RELATED ORGANIZATIONS

IAEA
International Atomic Energy Agency

WTO (trade)
World Trade Organization

WTO (tourism)
World Tourism Organization

CTBTO
Preparatory Commission for the Comprehensive Nuclear-Test-Ban-Treaty Organization

OPCW
Organization for the Prohibition of Chemical Weapons

SPECIALIZED AGENCIES*

ILO
International Labor Organization

FAO
Food and Agriculture Organization of the United Nations

UNESCO
United Nations Educational, Scientific, and Cultural Organization

WHO
World Health Organization

WORLD BANK GROUP

IBRD
International Bank for Reconstruction and Development

IDA
International Development Association

IFC
International Finance Corporation

MIG
Multilateral Investment Guarantee Agency

ICSID
International Center for Settlement of Investment Disputes

IMF
International Monetary Fund

ICAO
International Civil Aviation Organization

IMO
International Maritime Organization

ITU
International Telecommunications Union

UPU
Universal Postal Union

WMO
World Meteorological Organization

WIPO
World Intellectual Property Organization

IFAD
International Fund for Agricultural Development

OSG
Office of the Secretary-General

OIOS
Office of Internal Oversight Services

OLA
Office of Legal Affairs

DPA
Department of Political Affairs

DDA
Department for Disarmament Affairs

DPKO
Department of Peacekeeping Operations

OCHA
Office for the Coordination of Humanitarian Affairs

DESA
Department of Economic and Social Affairs

DGAACS
Department of General Assembly Affairs and Conference Services

DPI
Department of Public Information

DM
Department of Management

OIP
Office of the Iraq Program

UNSECOORD
Office of the United Nations Security Coordinator

ODC
Office on Drugs and Crime

UNOG
UN Office at Geneva

UNOV
UN Office at Vienna

UNON
UN Office at Nairobi

Court, is not located in New York City (see Figure 34-2). Situated at The Hague in the Netherlands, the ICJ was established under provisions within the UN Charter. Key features of the court include its structure and its jurisdiction.

The Structure of the ICJ   The ICJ is made up of 15 judges. The Security Council and the General Assembly of the United Nations are jointly responsible for electing these judges, each of whom serves a nine-year term. All of the judges are also eligible for reelection. To ensure as much impartiality as possible, the UN Charter also specifies that no two judges can be citizens of the same country and that the judges may not have any additional employment while they sit on the court. Ideally, the judges are chosen because of their legal qualifications. Every attempt is also made to ensure that the judges exemplify the foremost legal institutions in the world. When a nation is involved in a case presented to the ICJ, that nation is permitted to appoint a single judge to the court on a temporary basis.

Standing within the ICJ   Only sovereign nations have legal standing to initiate a case before the ICJ. Included within this category are nations that are member states of the United Nations. Nations that are not member states, however, may also have cases heard before the court. Questions on the legal standing of nonmember states are left up to the determination of the General Assembly and the Security Council.

Subject Matter Jurisdiction in the ICJ   Subject matter jurisdiction in the ICJ is outlined within the UN Charter. This jurisdiction includes legal questions specifically referred to within the charter, as well as any legal question raised by a member nation before the court. Such legal questions may involve the interpretation of treaties and international conventions.

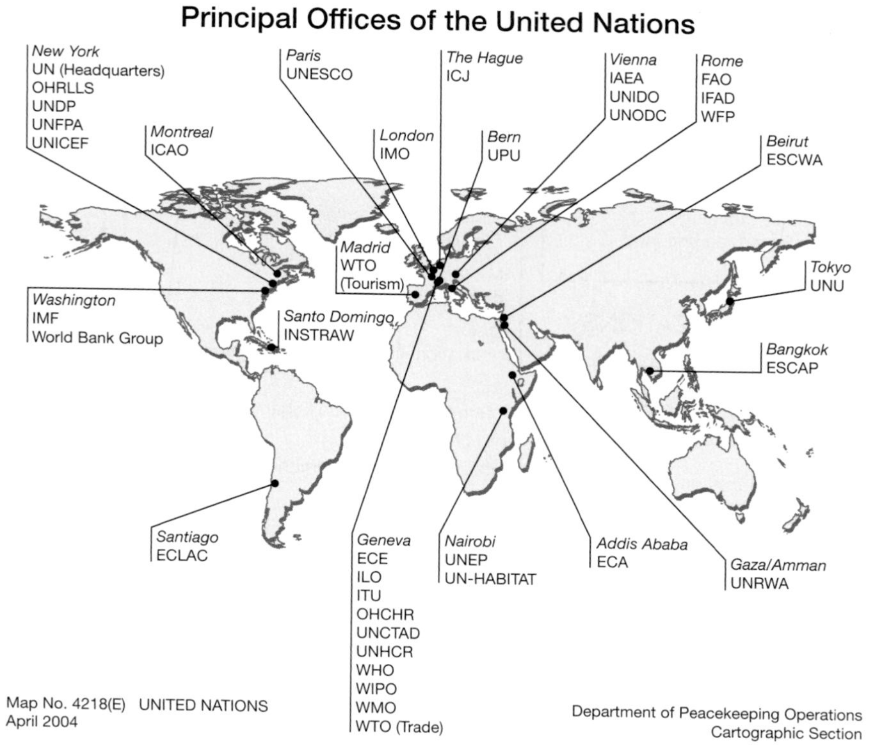

Principal Offices of the United Nations

New York
UN (Headquarters)
OHRLLS
UNDP
UNFPA
UNICEF

Montreal
ICAO

Paris
UNESCO

London
IMO

The Hague
ICJ

Bern
UPU

Vienna
IAEA
UNIDO
UNODC

Rome
FAO
IFAD
WFP

Beirut
ESCWA

Madrid
WTO
(Tourism)

Washington
IMF
World Bank Group

Santo Domingo
INSTRAW

Tokyo
UNU

Bangkok
ESCAP

Santiago
ECLAC

Geneva
ECE
ILO
ITU
OHCHR
UNCTAD
UNHCR
WHO
WIPO
WMO
WTO (Trade)

Nairobi
UNEP
UN-HABITAT

Addis Ababa
ECA

Gaza/Amman
UNRWA

Map No. 4218(E)   UNITED NATIONS
April 2004

Department of Peacekeeping Operations
Cartographic Section

Figure 34-2   The Principal Offices of the United Nations.
Source: Department of Public Information, *Basic Facts about the United Nations* (New York: United Nations, 2003), p. 24.

Unlike the courts in the federal system of the United States, which can render opinions only when faced with an actual case, the ICJ is permitted to issue advisory opinions when requested by nation-states, the General Assembly, the Security Council, or other authorized agencies within the structure of the United Nations. Those judges who disagree with the advisory opinion of the majority are empowered to issue dissenting opinions. In an advisory case, sometimes a dissenting opinion can be just as vital as the majority opinion, because the dissenter's rationale may be used in other venues.

EXAMPLE 34-3: Jurisdiction, Advisory Opinions, and the ICJ

One source of advisory opinions involves the question of how the corporate body of the United Nations relates to individual member nations. For instance, in 1949, the General Assembly solicited an advisory opinion from the ICJ concerning the assassination of a UN mediator. The mediator had been killed on a mission to Palestine. The issue before the court was whether the United Nations could hold a member state liable for any harm that befell an agent of the United Nations. The court found that the UN did indeed have that capacity.

The International Criminal Court To deal with crimes against humanity, an official **International Criminal Court (ICC)** was set up by the Rome Statute of the International Criminal Court in 1998. Unlike the ICJ, the ICC is not an official agency of the United Nations, though the UN was instrumental in its establishment. The objective of the new court, which actually began operation in 2002, is to preside over trials involving genocide, war crimes, and other human rights violations. The International Criminal Court itself and its prison are physically situated in The Hague, along with the International Court of Justice. Eighteen judges, no two of whom may be citizens of a single country, serve on the ICC for a term of nine years. The judges are elected by the states who are parties to the statute. The court also names one of the judges as president, as well as a registrar and an official prosecutor.

One of the key differences between the ICJ and the ICC is that the ICC has jurisdiction over individual defendants. On the other hand, the ICC does not have *original* jurisdiction over a defendant who has been charged with war crimes, genocide, or other offenses against humanity. Rather, the defendant's own government must prosecute the defendant before the ICC can claim original jurisdiction. Should the government fail to bring legal action against the defendant, the ICC can then step into the case. This feature has caused some concern among critics of the ICC, who argue that nation-states can protect their own citizens from prosecution in the ICC by prosecuting them in a home court that would intentionally acquit the defendant regardless of that defendant's real guilt or innocence. Supporters counter this concern by pointing out that the weight of world opinion will generally counteract this tendency of a nation-state to protect one of its own. Moreover, even though the ICC is not an official arm of the UN, the UN Security Council is empowered to intervene in a wrongful legal procedure perpetrated within or by the court. This safeguard should reassure a defendant's home nation that, once a defendant has been indicted, a strong case against that defendant has already been developed. One major drawback is that the court has very limited authority. Specifically, it can hear only cases that involve the citizens of those countries that ratified the original treaty that created the court. Several major countries, including the United States, have not ratified the treaty, which places their citizens outside the court's jurisdiction. [See: L. Fasulo, *An Insider's Guide to the UN* (New Haven, CT: Yale University Press, 2004), pp. 100–104; *Basic Facts about the United Nations* (New York: United Nations, 2003), p. 279.]

CLASSIC CASE Act 5: The United States v. Bin Laden— Concerning the International Criminal Court

The United States has repeatedly refused to ratify the Rome Statute of the International Criminal Court. Supporters of the international new world order might see this refusal as a puzzling development. After all, if the United States must act to defend itself and others in protective wars, it ought to benefit from any additional law enforcement support it can get. However, a closer look at this situation will reveal that this interpretation is not quite the case. If the United States must engage in protective wars from time to time and must, at other times, act as the *de facto* world government, the U.S. military must act as a *de facto* world police force. A police force, by its very nature, must enter dangerous, volatile, and potentially hazardous situations. Some of these police actions call for split-second decision making. Others may involve decisions that many people in the international community, especially those

who see the United States as the enemy, do not support and might even condemn. An example is when the United States sent military personnel into Pakistan with orders to capture or kill Osama bin Laden. Many individuals, groups, and nations opposed this action. However, this is often the case when the police, even the *de facto* global police, must perform unpopular actions. If the United States were a party to the Rome treaty, the Navy Seals who risked their lives to bring a sworn enemy of the United States to justice would be in danger of a politically motivated prosecution under the authority of the ICC. Since the United States must at times act as a global police force, then the members of its military, like the Navy Seals in the bin Laden operation, need the type of legal protection from political retribution that the ICC cannot now promise to deliver.

Economic Regulation and the United Nations

The United Nations does some of its best work in the area of economics and trade. It serves as a central clearing house for international treaties, trade proposals, conventions, and trade agreements, as well as for the development of the law as it relates to the making of international contracts. Some of the chief organizations and institutions of the UN that are involved in economics and trade include the UN Commission on International Trade, the UN Convention on Contracts for the International Sale of Goods, and the Commission on Science and Technology for Development.

The UN Commission on International Trade Law In 1996, the General Assembly of the United Nations authorized the creation of the **UN Commission on International Trade Law (UNCITRAL)**. The commission consists of 36 nations, chosen to represent the primary social, economic, legal, and geographical areas of the globe. The goal of the commission is to cultivate the organization and integration of international law in relation to international trade. To this end, it coordinates the activities of institutions involved in international trade, encourages continued commitment to current treaties and conventions, and constructs new agreements for the community of international trade.

The UN Convention on CISG One of these agreements is the **UN Convention on Contracts for the International Sale of Goods (CISG)**. This agreement became effective in 1988. It applies only to sales between businesses located in different countries. The agreement specifically excludes contracts involving goods purchased for use by individuals or families. The CISG affects the formation of an international trade contract, as well as the rights and duties that arise under such contracts. However, it deals neither with the, validity of such contracts nor with the liability of the seller for harm caused by the goods. Application of the CISG is limited to businesses that are located in countries that have ratified the agreement or those that create contracts that expressly stipulate that the CISG will apply to the agreement.

The CISG governs contracts for goods within the international community in much the same way that the Uniform Commercial Code (UCC) applies to sale-of-goods contracts within the United States. There are some significant differences, however. For example, the UCC applies to contracts between merchants and to those that involve nonmerchants. The CISG, in contrast, involves only contracts between merchants. The UCC also involves not only sale-of-goods contracts but also other commercial agreements, such as leases. The CISG, in contrast, applies only to sale-of-goods contracts. Also, the UCC has modified the traditional mirror image rule to overcome problems caused by the battle of the forms. The CISG still applies the mirror image rule to the acceptance of a contractual offer. Finally, the UCC has a provision that says that any contract for the sale of goods valued at over $500 must be in writing to be enforceable. The CISG has no such provision.

Additional UN Economic Agencies
The efforts extended by the United, Nations to monitor and regulate economic conditions in the global marketplace are evident in the existence of various organizations, each of which has its own mission in the financial structure of the worldwide economy. These agencies include global councils and conferences such as the Economic and Social Council (ECOSOC) and the UN Conference on Trade and Development (UNCTAD), as well as regional agencies such as the Economic Commission for Africa and the Economic Commission for Europe. Other agencies include the International Labor Organization; the World Health Organization; the United Nations Educational, Scientific, and Cultural Organization (UNESCO); the World Intellectual Property Organization (WIPO); and the Food and Agriculture Organization. Each organization makes assessments and enters judgments that influence how international business is conducted. One such organization that has special significance in this regard is the, Division for Science and Technology of UNCTAD.

The Commission on Science and Technology for Development
The **Commission on Science and Technology for Development** was created in 1992 as part of the Economic and Social Council (ECOSOC) of the United Nations. The job of the commission is (1) to act as a clearing house for issues concerning science and technology in relation to development, (2) to support progress in determining what must be done to advance science and technology policies in developing nations, and (3) to formulate recommendations and protocols for science and technology within the UN community. Many experts see this creation as a step in the right direction but urge an even more unified response in this regard. [See: Commission on Science and Technology for Development, UNCTAD, http://www.unctad.info/en/Science-and-Technology-for-Development—StDev/Science–Technology-on-the-UN-Agenda/CSTD/ (2009–2015).]

An Economic Security Council

The Commission on Global Governance, a 26-member international organization, has suggested streamlining the surveillance of international economic efforts under the auspices of an **Economic Security Council (ESC)**. The ESC would be a single, unified international agency under the management of the United Nations that would monitor the economic activities of the member nations of the UN. The ESC would evaluate the state of the international economy and implement long-term strategic planning to promote sustainable development across the planet. However, the ESC would not take the place of existing international agencies, such as the Economic and Social Council or the UN Conference on Trade and Development, but instead would coordinate their efforts in an efficient, effective, and economic manner.

quick quiz 34-3

1. The secretary general is the chief administrator of the United Nations.	true | false
2. When a nation is involved in a case presented to the ICJ, that nation must voluntarily eliminate any judge on the panel that is a citizen of that nation.	true | false
3. The UCC and the CISG are identical in every way.	true | false

34-4 International Law, Finance, and Trade

Not everyone who wants to enter a local business transaction has the ready cash to do so. This hurdle, however, does not necessarily prevent them from looking for ways to expand their, financial base. Therefore, by their very nature, business transactions often involve buying on credit, borrowing money, and investing in risky ventures designed to make a fast profit. The same thing can be said about international business transactions. To deal with issues of finance and trade on a worldwide scale, several international organizations and agreements have emerged that are designed to make global dealings work as smoothly as local ones.

The International Monetary Fund and the World Bank

Two organizations that emerged in the aftermath of the Great Depression and World War II were the International Monetary Fund and the World Bank. Both institutions came out of a series of meetings held in Bretton Woods, New Hampshire, in the final months of World War II. The **International Monetary Fund (IMF)** is designed to serve as a way for financially strapped nations to secure loans that will help them engage in programs of sustainable economic growth and development. The IMF has 188 members, each of which has pledged to act responsibly in the pursuit of economic and developmental goals.

The **World Bank** has a mission that is quite similar to the mission of the IMF. The difference is that the IMF is dedicated to helping all nations, developed, developing, and undeveloped, with fiscal problems, whereas the World Bank works exclusively with the poorest nations in the international community. Even this mission is split between the two arms of the World Bank. The International Bank for Reconstruction and Development (IBRD) handles more conventional loans based on normal market provisions, whereas the International Development Association (IDA) handles loans to the world's most economically challenged nations.

The World Trade Organization

After the end of World War II, the primary trading nations of the international community met to work out the details of a major trade agreement. The agreement, named the **General Agreement on Tariffs and Trade (GATT)**, had as part of its original plan the creation of an International Trade Organization (ITO). Although the ITO was never established, GATT continued to function, frequently holding international conferences on the formation and execution of international trade law. The eighth conference, which came to be known as the Uruguay Round Agreements, resulted in the creation of the **World Trade Organization (WTO)**.

The Structure of the World Trade Organization

The World Trade Organization was designed to serve as the corporate nucleus for the management of international trade relationships. As such, the WTO replaced GATT as the focus of world trade talks. However, all agreements, treaties, and trade obligations created under GATT have been included in the WTO and thus remain in force. The structure of the WTO involves three levels: the Ministerial Conference, the General Council, and the Secretariat. The power to make key determinations under the authority of multinational trade agreements falls to the Ministerial Conference, which meets every two years. The responsibilities of the Ministerial Conference pass to the General Council whenever the Ministerial Conference is not assembled. Finally, the Secretariat, which is headed by a director general, is responsible for the administration of the WTO.

The World Trade Organization is a constant target of controversy and its summits are frequently targeted by hostile and aggressive protesters.

The World Trade Organization Principles

The WTO has established certain overall principles that regulate how member nations must treat one another in the world of international trade. The first principle, the **national treatment principle**, states that WTO nations must apply the same standards to imports that they apply to domestic goods. The second principle, the **most-favored nation principle**, maintains that all member nations must apply the same privileges, advantages, and benefits to all other member nations in relation to similar imports. The third principle, the **tariff-based principle**, asserts that the only way that member nations can regulate the imports of other nations is through tariffs. This rule eliminates the use of more drastic techniques, such as boycotts, quotas, and quantitative limits.

The Dispute Settlement Board

The **Dispute Settlement Board (DSB)** of the WTO was established to provide a forum for settling trade disputes among member nations. The DSB follows a commonly adopted procedure known as the **Dispute Settlement Understanding (DSU)**. All member nations can be held accountable under DSU regulations. According to those regulations, only member nations have standing to initiate a case. The DSU implements a number of measures designed to improve the way that quarrels are handled. For instance, the DSU has set up a series of precise time limits for the stages in a trade conflict. The DSU ensures that a network of comprehensive guidelines is followed consistently in all such controversies. The DSU also allows effective retaliatory measures that can be implemented by one nation against another if the offending nation refuses to adhere to a decision rendered under the DSU.

Did You Know?

As of 2015, the World Trade Organization (WTO) had a membership that includes 161 nations. The United States joined on January 1, 1995.

EXAMPLE 34-4: The WTO, Germany, and the Korean Retaliation

Germany and Korea were involved in a dispute concerning trade in electronic appliances and, automobiles. Korea claimed that in violation of trade agreements, Germany imposed a tariff on certain electronic appliances manufactured in Korea and imported to Germany. Korea followed proper DSU procedures and received a ruling from a panel that was supported by an appellate board. The ruling indicated that Germany had indeed violated the agreement. The WTO could not directly sanction, Germany. Instead, it allowed Korea to impose an enormous tariff on luxury and sports model automobiles imported from Germany to Korea. This form of sanction is known as retaliation.

The North American Free Trade Agreement

The United States and many other similarly situated nations have entered comprehensive trade coalitions designed to open their borders to the free flow of international trade. The most famous of these comprehensive coalitions is the **North American Free Trade Agreement (NAFTA)**, a trading coalition that includes the United States, Canada, and Mexico. The goal of the coalition is to establish a trading market in North America, free from the burdens imposed by internal tariff barriers.

The European Union

One of the most significant events to affect international law and commerce lately has been the inauguration of the **European Union (EU)**. The creation of the European Union, the attempt to formulate a common European economic policy, and the introduction of a common currency for most of Europe may transform the EU into a major competitor with the power to challenge American business interests in the global marketplace. Moreover, because many businesses within the EU have embraced cyber-commerce, American firms may face unique challenges in that arena.

The Introduction of the Euro To adopt the **euro**, Europe's common currency, a country must first belong to the European Union. Membership in the EU alone, however, is not enough to allow a nation to adopt the euro. In addition, a nation must have a stable inflation rate, a history of interest rate convergence that falls within certain guidelines, and a pattern of fiscal responsibility. Of those nations that have qualified, 19 including Austria, Belgium, France, Germany, Ireland, Italy, Luxembourg, the Netherlands, and Spain, elected to join the effort. Several nations, including the United Kingdom, Denmark, and Sweden, opted out of the program. The use of the euro is designed to lower costs by eliminating the need to change currencies when firms in the member states deal with one another across national boundaries.

The euro became the common currency used by European Union member states in 2002, replacing many of the, individual currencies and providing consistency for the EU.

Electronic Commerce and the European Union The EU has been, active in the development of cyber-commerce directives in an attempt to head off proposed legislative initiatives in the individual member nations. Such individualized rules would complicate the rules of European cyber-commerce and defeat the purpose of a unified EU economic policy. One example of a unified directive is the Data Protection Directive. This directive assures all citizens of Europe that they will enjoy certain definitive privacy rights when they engage in cyber-commerce. Among the rights held by consumers in, Europe are the right to obtain any computer data stored about them, the right to adjust any incorrect data, the right to deny another party the use of computer data, and the right to a legal remedy for any unlawful activities in relation to computer data. Another EU directive that affects cyber-commerce is the Directive on the Protection of Consumers in Respect of Distance Contracts (ECD). This directive gives specifically enumerated privileges to consumers who deal with companies selling goods and services within the EU by electronic means. The ECD allows consumers to cancel any electronic commerce transaction without penalty within seven working days.

EXAMPLE 34-5: The Case of the Dissatisfied European Cyber-Consumer

Clay Joseph, a British citizen, was in the process of creating a new corporation that he hoped would revolutionize the comic book industry. To implement his business plan, he ordered a set of display cases from Volkmann Displays Unlimited, a German firm. On the same day, he also ordered a set of office furniture from IKEA in Sweden. When Joseph received the package from Volkmann, he discovered that the display cases could not hold the material that he wanted to store. One day later, the IKEA shipment arrived. Again he was dissatisfied, not because of any flaw in the furniture but because he had misjudged how the color of the chairs would fit into his office decor. As a European cyber-consumer, Clay Joseph's purchase of the books and the office furniture would be protected by the Directive on the Protection of Consumers in Respect of Distance Contracts (ECD), and he could rescind both deals within seven business days with no penalty whatsoever.

National and International Law Despite the importance of focusing on international law and the laws of other countries, businesses involved in international trade must always focus on the laws of their own nation. Sometimes national law will reach into the jurisdiction of a foreign country. Although such instances are rare, they may occur when one or more of the parties to a lawsuit are citizens of the country exercise jurisdiction and when the foreign activity somehow affects the welfare of that country.

Did You Know?

The official symbol for the euro looks like this: €. The symbol itself is usually printed in yellow with a blue background.

quick quiz 34-4

1. Two organizations that emerged in the aftermath of the Great Depression and World War II were the International Monetary Fund and the World Bank.   true | false

2. None of the agreements, treaties, or trade obligations created under GATT have been included in the WTO.   true | false

3. NAFTA is a trading coalition that includes the United States, the United Kingdom, and Greenland.   true | false

Summary

34.1 When a political scientist wants to use predictive political history to explain the past, to predict the future, or to handle an international crisis, he or she must first determine the present state of the global system (the international initial conditions or the new world order) and then match that system to the correct set of covering laws under an accurate theory of international behavior. The four theories of international behavior are *Realpolitik;* idealism; neoconservativism; and neoliberalism. Each international behavioral theory can be summarized by reducing it to several covering laws. A covering law is a rule of behavior that follows consistently predictable pattern such that it can be described as dictating normative decision-making processes. The four sets of initial conditions are (1) economic initial conditions, (2) cultural initial conditions, (3) ideological initial conditions, and (4) hybrid initial conditions.

34.2 War has many significant effects on the transaction of business in the international marketplace. One of the key questions concerning the nature of war as it relates to international business is whether the war is just. Ethical and legal philosophers in the West have developed criteria for determining when a war can be considered legally and morally correct. This theory is termed the just war theory.

34.3 The stated purposes of the United Nations are to advance human rights, to end war, to enhance human achievement, to support peaceful international coalitions, and to promote international fidelity to truth, justice, and the rule of law. The promotion of international law has taken many forms within the structure of the United, Nations, including the International Court of Justice, the UN Commission on International Trade Law, and the UN Convention on Contracts for the International Sale of Goods. The International Criminal Court also plays a key role in policing international justice.

34.4 To deal with issues of finance and trade on a worldwide scale, several international organizations and agreements have emerged that are designed to make global dealings work as smoothly as local ones. These include the International Monetary Fund, the World Bank, the World Trade Organization, the North American Free Trade Agreement, and the European Union.

Key Terms

associated persons and forces, 889

Authorization for the Use of Military Force, 887

chaotic events, 881

civilization, 874

Commission on Science and Technology for Development, 897

competent authority, 883

covering laws, 872

Dispute Settlement Board (DSB), 899

Dispute Settlement Understanding (DSU), 899

Economic Security Council (ESC), 897

economic zone, 880

euro, 900

European Union (EU), 900

General Agreement on Tariffs and Trade (GATT), 898

General Assembly, 881

Geneva Conventions, 889

idealism, 873

International Court of Justice (ICJ), 891

International Criminal Court (ICC), 895

international initial conditions, 870

International Monetary Fund (IMF), 898

just cause, 882

just war theory, 882

last resort, 883

liberal internationalism, 873

most-favored nation principle, 899

national treatment principle, 899

new world order, 870

neoconservativism, 873

neoliberalism, 873

North American Free Trade Agreement (NAFTA), 900

predictive political history, 870

preemptive war, 885

preventative war, 885

principle of honorable surrender, 885

principle of repentance, 884

principle of restoration, 885

probability of success, 883

proportionality, 883

protective war, 885

realism, 872

Realpolitik, 872

Questions for Review and Discussion

1. What is the process of predictive political history?
2. What are the theories of international behavior?
3. What are the various sets of global initial conditions?
4. What is the mission of International Criminal Court?
5. What is the main goal of UNCITRAL?
6. What are the differences between the UCC and the CISG?

7. What is the structure of the World Trade Organization?
8. What are the objectives of the Dispute Settlement Understanding?
9. What is the major purpose of NAFTA?
10. What is the European Union?

Cases for Analysis

1. After General Manuel Noriega had come under the authority of the United States forces following the invasion of Panama, his attorneys argued that he should be treated as a prisoner of war (POW) under the Geneva Conventions. The United States government agreed to treat Noriega as a POW but refused to give him official POW status. Noriega's attorneys argued that this treatment as a POW could be withdrawn by the government at any time. They asked the court to declare their client a POW under the Geneva Conventions. The government argued that the events in Panama were considered hostilities rather than a war. Consequently, the government pointed out, Noriega could not be a POW. Article II of Geneva Convention III states that "the present convention shall apply to all cases of declared war and of any other armed conflict which may arise between two or more of the High Contracting Parties, even if the state of war is not recognized by one of them." Moreover, the International Red Cross Commentary on Convention III says, "Any difference between two states leading to the intervention of the armed forces is an armed conflict within the meaning of Article II." Finally, Article IV of the convention defines POWs as "persons belonging to one of the following categories, who have fallen into the power of

the enemy: (1) members of the armed forces of a Party to the conflict. . . ." Taking all of this into account, as well as the United States courts' intent to construe the Geneva Conventions liberally, should the court declare Noriega a POW? Explain. [See: *United States of America v. Manuel Antonio Noriega,* 808 F. Supp. 791 (S.D. FL).]

2. American Rice, Inc., a U.S. corporation, sold its goods in Saudi Arabia under the trade name of ABU BINT, which means "of the girl." Another American corporation, the Arkansas Rice Growers Cooperative Association, marketed similar products in Saudi Arabia using the name BINT ALARAB, which in English means "Gulf Girl." American Rice sued Arkansas in federal district court under the Lanham Act, alleging an infringement by Arkansas of American Rice's exclusive trademark. None of the Arkansas rice products that American Rice complained of had entered any market within the United States. Arkansas argued that the federal district court had no extra-,territorial power to mediate this international trade dispute. Was Arkansas correct? Explain. [See: *American Rice, Inc., v. Arkansas Rice Growers Coop. Ass'n.,* 701 F.2d 414 (5th Cir.).]

3. Gulf Oil Corporation and Eastern Air Lines entered a contract under the terms of which Gulf Oil

was obligated to supply Eastern with jet fuel according to an established pricing system. In 1973, the Organization for Petroleum Exporting Countries (OPEC) established an oil embargo that precipitated the now-famous energy crisis of the 1970s. As a result of the oil embargo and the energy crisis, the price of crude oil skyrocketed. Gulf Oil asked Eastern to consent to a price increase over the price agreed to under the original contract. Eastern refused to comply with the increase. Gulf Oil then vowed to stop all jet fuel shipments to Eastern unless Eastern would reconsider its refusal to go along with the price increase. Eastern filed a lawsuit in federal district court alleging a breach of contract on Gulf Oil's part. Did the American court have jurisdiction over an exclusively American contract affected by an international incident, such as the 1973 oil embargo? Did the court agree that Gulf breached its contract with Eastern Airlines? Explain. [See: *Eastern Air Line, Inc., v. Gulf Oil Corporation,* 415 F. Supp. 429 (S.D. FL).]

4. Kenneth Armstrong, an American citizen, purchased the component parts of computers in Germany, Japan, and the United States. He took those parts to Bolivia, where he constructed the computers, stamped them with the name Starlight Computers, and sold them. Armstrong had a Bolivian registration that allowed him to use the trade name Starlight. Although none of the computers were imported into the United States by, Armstrong himself, many of the counterfeit computers eventually found their way into the U.S. marketplace. Starlight Computers, Inc., an American,

corporation, brought a lawsuit against Armstrong in United States District Court under the Lanham Act., Armstrong moved for a dismissal of the case, arguing that the American court did not have the, authority to enforce the Lanham Act against his, Bolivian, operation. Is Armstrong correct? Explain.

5. France and Japan are involved in a dispute regarding trade in aircraft parts. France claims that in, violation of certain trade agreements, Japan is, imposing a tariff on certain types of aircraft parts that are manufactured in France and imported to Japan. France follows proper DSU procedures and receives a ruling from a panel that is supported by an appellate board. The ruling indicates that Japan has indeed violated the agreement. France asks the WTO to apply punitive sanctions directly against Japan. Will France's request be granted? Explain.

6. Helga Godel, a German citizen, placed an order for certain software items from Pascal Enterprises, a French firm. On the same day, she ordered a, silverware set from Silverwings Ltd., an Austrian company. When Godel received the package from Pascal, she unwrapped the software and attempted to download the program into her computer. When she accessed the program, however, she found that though the program worked well, it was not what she had expected. Later that day, she received the silverware set. Again she was dissatisfied, this time with the quality of the product. As a European e-consumer, what rights does Godel have under the EU Directive on the Protection of Consumers in Respect of Distance Contracts? Explain.

quick quiz Answers

34-1	34-2	34-3	34-4
1. T	1. T	1. T	1. T
2. T	2. F	2. F	2. F
3. F	3. T	3. F	3. F

Part 9 Case Study

Legal Consequences of the Construction of a Wall in the Occupied Palestinian Territory (Request for Advisory Opinion)
The International Court of Justice
Order of 30 January 2004

Summary

The International Court of Justice is an agency of the United Nations, established under a statute within the UN Charter. Fifteen judges sit on the ICJ. The judges are elected by the Security Council and the General Assembly of the United Nations for nine years. The judges are also eligible for reelection. To ensure as much impartiality as possible, no nation-state can have more than a single judge on the court at the same time. The statute also says that judges must work exclusively for the court during their term on the bench. Ideally, the judges on the court are chosen because of their legal qualifications. Every attempt is also made to make certain that the judges exemplify the foremost legal institutions in the world.

The statute establishing the ICJ also includes provisions to ensure the impartiality of the judges. One such provision is Article 17, paragraph 2, which states, "No Member [of the ICJ] may participate in the decision of any case in which he has previously taken part as agent, counsel, or advocate for one of the parties, or as a member of a national or international court, or of a commission of enquiry, or in any other capacity."

The present case involves the question of whether one of the judges on the ICJ ought to be permitted to participate in the case or be disqualified under this provision because of his previous involvement in the issue before the court. The case was brought to the ICJ by the government of Israel in a letter addressed to the Court Registrar, dated December 31, 2003. In that letter, the government asserted:

> Resolution A/RES/ES-10/14 requesting the advisory opinion locates the request squarely in the context of the wider Arab-Israeli/Israeli-Palestinian dispute. The essentially contentious nature of the proceedings is also recognised by the Court's invitation to Palestine to participate in the case. It is inappropriate for a Member of the Court to participate in decisions in a case in which he has previously played an active, official and public role as an advocate for a cause that is in contention in this case. Israel will be writing to the President of the Court separately on this matter pursuant to Article 34 (2) of the Rules of Court.

Israel objected to the connection that Judge Nabil Elaraby of Egypt had to the case because of his involvement in a number of initiatives that touched on several sensitive issues involved in the dispute. Specifically, Israel pointed to the judge's contributions to the 10th Emergency Session of the General Assembly of the United Nations, his employment as a legal counselor to the Egyptian Ministry of Foreign Affairs, his work as a legal consultant to the Egyptian Delegates to the Middle East Peace Initiative at Camp David in 1978, and his connection to certain actions resulting from the 1979 Israeli–Egypt Peace Treaty, especially the development of independent West Bank and Gaza Strip territories. Finally, and perhaps most significantly, the government of Israel pointed to an interview printed in a newspaper in Egypt in which the judge discussed his personal political views in relation to the nation-state of Israel.

A majority of the judges on the ICJ saw no problem with Judge Elaraby's involvement in the activities to which Israel objected. Specifically, they saw no problem with his role as legal advisor for Egypt, because in that capacity, the judge had been speaking and acting as an agent of his government. In relation to the published interview, the majority pointed to the fact that Article 17, paragraph 2, detailed certain roles that a judge was prohibited from performing in a case that was before the court. Nothing on the list, the court concluded, mentioned giving interviews or publishing private political views. Therefore, the majority upheld the judge's participation in the case.

The sole dissenter was Judge Thomas Buergenthal of the United States. While Judge Buergenthal agreed with the court in relation to Judge Elaraby's official governmental roles, he disagreed about the private interview and objected to the court's strict and limited interpretation of Article 17, paragraph 2. This point is critical because, as noted previously, in an advisory case, a dissenting opinion can sometimes be just as vital as the majority opinion, because the dissenter's rationale may be used in other venues.

Dissenting Opinion of Judge Buergenthal

1. I have voted against the instant Order because I believe that the Court's decision is wrong as a matter of legal principle.

2. Israel challenges Judge Elaraby's participation in these proceedings on the ground that his previous professional involvement and personal statements on matters which go to the substance of the question before the Court in this advisory opinion request require that he not participate in these proceedings.

3. As far as Judge Elaraby's professional activities as diplomatic representative of his country and its legal adviser are concerned, the Court rejects Israel's objection by concluding that these activities, having been performed many years before the question of the construction of the wall now submitted to the Court first arose, do not fall within the activities contemplated by Article 17, paragraph 2, of the Statute to justify that he be precluded from participation in the case.

4. With regard to the newspaper interview that Judge Elaraby gave two months before his election to this Court at a time when he was no longer his country's diplomatic representative, the Court

finds no basis for precluding Judge Elaraby's, participation in these proceedings, because Judge Elaraby "expressed no opinion on the question put in the present case."

5. Israel seeks Judge Elaraby's disqualification on the ground, *inter alia,* that the views expressed by Judge Elaraby in the interview bear directly on issues that will have to be addressed in the advisory opinion request and that, given their nature, they create an appearance of bias incompatible with the fair administration of justice.

6. In principle, I share the Court's opinion that Judge Elaraby's prior activities, performed in the discharge of his diplomatic and governmental functions, do not fall within the scope of Article 17, paragraph 2, of the Statute of the Court so as to prevent his participation in these proceedings. . . .

7. I part company with the Court's conclusions, however, with regard to the interview Judge Elaraby gave in August of 2001, two months before his election to the Court, when he was no longer an official of his Government and hence spoke in his personal capacity. See *Al-Ahram Weekly Online,* 16–22 August 2001, issue No. 547. . . .

10. It is clear, of course, that the language of Article 17, paragraph 2, does not apply in so many words to the views Judge Elaraby expressed in the above, interview. That does not mean, however, that this provision sets out the exclusive basis for the disqualification of a judge of this Court. It refers to what would generally be considered to be the most egregious violations of judicial ethics were a judge falling into one of the categories therein enumerated to participate in a case. At the same time, Article 17, paragraph 2, reflects much broader conceptions of justice and fairness that must be observed by courts of law than this Court appears to acknowledge. Judicial ethics are not matters strictly of hard and fast rules—I doubt that they can ever be exhaustively defined—they are matters of perception and of sensibility to appearances that courts must continuously keep in mind to preserve their legitimacy.

11. A court of law must be free and, in my opinion, is required to consider whether one of its judges has expressed views or taken positions that create the impression that he will not be able to consider the issues raised in a case or advisory opinion in a fair and impartial manner, that is, that he may be deemed to have prejudged one or more of the, issues bearing on the subject-matter of the dispute before the court. That is what is meant by the

dictum that the fair and proper administration of justice requires that justice not only be done, but that it also be seen to be done. In my view, all courts of law must be guided by this principle, whether or not their statutes or other constitutive documents expressly require them to do so. That power and obligation is implicit in the very concept of a court of law charged with the fair and impartial administration of justice. To read them out of the reach of Article 17, paragraph 2, is neither legally justified nor is it wise judicial policy.

12. In paragraph 8 of this Order, the Court declares that, "whereas in the newspaper interview of August 2001, Judge Elaraby expressed no opinion on the question put in the present case; whereas consequently Judge Elaraby could not be regarded as having 'previously taken part' in the case in any capacity."

13. What we have here is the most formalistic and narrow construction of Article 17, paragraph 2, imaginable, and one that is unwarranted on the facts of this case. It is technically true, of course, that Judge Elaraby did not express an opinion on the specific question that has been submitted to the Court by the General Assembly of the United, Nations. But it is equally true that this cannot be examined by the Court without taking account of the context of the Israeli/Palestinian conflict and the arguments that will have to be advanced by the interested parties in examining the "Legal Consequences of the, Construction of a Wall in the Occupied Palestinian Territory." Many of these arguments will turn on the factual validity and credibility of assertions bearing directly on the specific question referred to the Court in this advisory opinion request. And when it comes to the validity and credibility of these arguments, what Judge Elaraby has to say in the part of the interview I quoted above creates an appearance of bias that in my opinion requires the Court to preclude Judge Elaraby's participations in the proceedings.

14. What I consider important in reaching the above conclusion is the appearance of bias. That, in my opinion, is what Article 17, paragraph 2, properly interpreted, is all about and what judicial ethics are all about. And that is why I dissent from this Order, even though I have no doubts whatsoever about the personal integrity of Judge Elaraby for whom I have the highest regard, not only as a, valued colleague but also a good friend.

(*Signed*) Thomas Buergenthal

Questions for Analysis

1. Why did Israel bring this case rather than a private party? Explain.

2. What is the central issue in this case?

3. What legal statutory provision provided grounds for the complaint lodged by Israel?

4. What was the decision of the majority? Explain.

5. On what point did the dissent contest the majority opinion? Explain.

Appendix A The Constitution of the United States

Preamble

We the People of the United States, in Order to form a more perfect Union, establish Justice, insure domestic Tranquility, provide for the common defence, promote the general Welfare, and secure the Blessings of Liberty to ourselves and our Posterity, do ordain and establish this Constitution for the United States of America.

Article I

Section 1. All legislative Powers herein granted shall be vested in a Congress of the United States, which shall consist of a Senate and House of Representatives.

Section 2. [1] The House of Representatives shall be composed of Members chosen every second Year by the People of the several States, and the Electors in each State shall have the Qualifications requisite for Electors of the most numerous Branch of the State Legislature.

[2] No Person shall be a Representative who shall not have attained to the Age of twenty-five Years, and been seven Years a Citizen of the United States, and who shall not, when elected, be an Inhabitant of that State in which he shall be chosen.

[3] Representatives and direct Taxes shall be apportioned among the several States which may be included within this Union, according to their respective Numbers, which shall be determined by adding to the whole Number of free Persons, including those bound to Service for a Term of Years, and excluding Indians not taxed, three fifths of all other Persons. The actual Enumeration shall be made within three Years after the first Meeting of the Congress of the United States, and within every subsequent Term of ten Years, in such Manner as they shall by Law direct. The Number of Representatives shall not exceed one for every thirty Thousand, but each State shall have at Least one Representative; and until such enumeration shall be made, the State of New Hampshire shall be entitled to chuse three, Massachusetts eight, Rhode Island and Providence Plantations one, Connecticut five, New York six, New Jersey four, Pennsylvania eight, Delaware one, Maryland six, Virginia ten, North Carolina five, South Carolina five, and Georgia three.

[4] When vacancies happen in the Representation from any State, the Executive Authority thereof shall issue Writs of Election to fill such Vacancies.

[5] The House of Representatives shall chuse their Speaker and other Officers; and shall have the sole Power of Impeachment.

Section 3. [1] The Senate of the United States shall be composed of two Senators from each State, chosen by the Legislature thereof, for six Years; and each Senator shall have one Vote.

[2] Immediately after they shall be assembled in Consequence of the first Election, they shall be divided as equally as may be into three Classes. The Seats of the Senators of the first Class shall be vacated at the Expiration of the Second Year, of the second Class at the Expiration of the fourth Year, and of the third Class at the Expiration of the sixth Year, so that one third may be chosen every second Year; and if Vacancies happen by Resignation, or otherwise, during the Recess of the Legislature of any State, the Executive thereof may make temporary Appointments until the next Meeting of the Legislature, which shall then fill such Vacancies.

[3] No Person shall be a Senator who shall not have attained to the Age of thirty Years, and been nine Years a Citizen of the United States, and who shall not, when elected, be an Inhabitant of that State for which he shall be chosen.

[4] The Vice President of the United States shall be President of the Senate, but shall have no Vote, unless they be equally divided.

[5] The Senate shall chuse their other Officers, and also a President pro tempore, in the Absence of the Vice President, or when he shall exercise the Office of President of the United States.

[6] The Senate shall have the sole Power to try all Impeachments. When sitting for that Purpose, they shall be on Oath or Affirmation. When the President of the United States is tried, the Chief Justice shall preside: And no Person shall be convicted without the Concurrence of two thirds of the Members present.

[7] Judgment in Cases of Impeachment shall not extend further than to removal from Office, and disqualification to hold and enjoy any Office of honor, Trust, or Profit under the United States: but the Party convicted shall nevertheless be liable and subject to Indictment, Trial, Judgment, and Punishment, according to Law.

Section 4. [1] The Times, Places and Manner of holding elections for Senators and Representatives, shall be prescribed in each State by the Legislature thereof; but the Congress may at any time by Law make or alter such Regulations, except as to the Places of chusing Senators.

[2] The Congress shall assemble at least once in every Year, and such Meeting shall be on the first Monday in December, unless they shall by Law appoint a different Day.

Section 5. [1] Each House shall be the Judge of the Elections, Returns, and Qualifications of its own Members, and a Majority of each shall constitute a Quorum to do Business; but a smaller Number may adjourn from day to day, and may be authorized to compel the Attendance of absent Members, in such Manner, and under such Penalties as each House may provide.

[2] Each House may determine the Rules of its Proceedings, punish its Members for disorderly Behavior, and, with the Concurrence of two thirds, expel a Member.

[3] Each House shall keep a Journal of its Proceedings, and from time to time publish the same, excepting such parts as may in their Judgment require Secrecy; and the Yeas and Nays of the Members of either House on any question shall, at the Desire of one fifth of those Present, be entered on the Journal.

[4] Neither House, during the Session of Congress, shall, without the Consent of the other, adjourn for more than three days, nor to any other Place than that in which the two Houses shall be sitting.

Section 6. [1] The Senators and Representatives shall receive a Compensation for their Services, to be ascertained by Law, and paid out of the Treasury of the United States. They shall in all Cases, except Treason, Felony and Breach of the Peace, be privileged from Arrest during their Attendance at the Session of their respective Houses, and in going to and returning from the same; and for any Speech of Debate in either House, they shall not be questioned in any other Place.

[2] No Senator or Representative shall, during the Time for which he was elected, be appointed to any civil Office under the Authority of the United States, which shall have been created, or the Emoluments whereof shall have been increased during such time; and no Person holding any Office under the United States, shall be a Member of either House during his Continuance in Office.

Section 7. [1] All Bills for raising Revenue shall originate in the House of Representatives; but the Senate may propose or concur with Amendments as on other Bills.

[2] Every Bill which shall have passed the House of Representatives and the Senate, shall, before it becomes a Law, be presented to the President of the United States; If he approve he shall sign it, but if not he shall return it, with his Objections to the House in which it shall have originated, who shall enter the Objections at large on their Journal, and proceed to reconsider it. If after such Reconsideration two thirds of that House shall agree to pass the Bill, it shall be sent together with the Objections, to the other House, by which it shall likewise be reconsidered, and if approved by two thirds of that House, it shall become a Law. But in all such Cases the Votes of both Houses shall be determined by yeas and Nays, and the Names of the Persons voting for and against the Bill shall be entered on the Journal of each House respectively. If any Bill shall not be returned by the President within ten Days (Sundays excepted) after it shall have been presented to him, the Same shall be a Law, in like Manner as if he had signed it, unless the Congress by their Adjournment prevent its Return in which Case it shall not be a Law.

[3] Every Order, Resolution, or Vote, to Which the Concurrence of the Senate and House of Representatives may be necessary (except on a question of Adjournment) shall be presented to the President of the United States; and before the Same shall take Effect, shall be approved by him, or being disapproved by him, shall be repassed by two thirds of the Senate and House of Representatives, accord-

ing to the Rules and Limitations prescribed in the Case of a Bill.

Section 8. [1] The Congress shall have Power To lay and collect Taxes, Duties, Imposts and Excises, to pay the Debts and provide for the common Defence and general Welfare of the United States; but all Duties, Imposts and Excises shall be uniform throughout the United States;

[2] To borrow money on the credit of the United States;

[3] To regulate Commerce with foreign Nations, and among the several States, and with the Indian Tribes;

[4] To establish an uniform Rule of Naturalization, and uniform laws on the subject of Bankruptcies throughout the United States;

[5] To coin Money, regulate the Value thereof, and of foreign Coin, and fix the Standard of Weights and Measures;

[6] To provide for the Punishment of counterfeiting the Securities and current Coin of the United States;

[7] To Establish Post Offices and Post Roads;

[8] To promote the Progress of Science and useful Arts, by securing for limited Times to Authors and Inventors the exclusive Right to their respective Writings and Discoveries;

[9] To constitute Tribunals inferior to the supreme Court;

[10] To define and punish Piracies and Felonies committed on the high Seas, and Offenses against the Law of Nations;

[11] To declare War, grant Letters of Marque and Reprisal, and make Rules concerning Captures on Land and Water;

[12] To raise and support Armies, but no Appropriation of Money to that Use shall be for a longer Term than two Years;

[13] To provide and maintain a Navy;

[14] To make Rules for the Government and Regulation of the land and naval Forces;

[15] To provide for calling forth the Militia to execute the Laws of the Union, suppress Insurrections and repel Invasions;

[16] To provide for organizing, arming, and disciplining, the Militia, and for governing such Part of them as may be employed in the Service of the United States, reserving to the States respectively, the Appointment of the Officers, and the Authority of training the Militia according to the discipline prescribed by Congress;

[17] To exercise exclusive Legislation in all Cases whatsoever, over such District (not exceeding ten Miles square) as may, by Cession of particular States, and the Acceptance of Congress, become the Seat of the Government of the United States, and to exercise like Authority over all Places purchased by the Consent of the Legislature of the State in which the Same shall be, for the Erection of Forts, Magazines, Arsenals, dock-Yards and other needful Buildings;—And

[18] To make all Laws which shall be necessary and proper for carrying into Execution the foregoing Powers, and all other Powers vested by this Constitution in the Government of the United States, or in any Department or Officer thereof.

Section 9. **[1]** The Migration or Importation of Such Persons as any of the States now existing shall think proper to admit, shall not be prohibited by the Congress prior to the Year one thousand eight hundred and eight, but a Tax or duty may be imposed on such Importation, not exceeding ten dollars for each Person.

[2] The privilege of the Writ of Habeas Corpus shall not be suspended, unless when in Cases of Rebellion or Invasion the public Safety may require it.

[3] No Bill of Attainder or ex post facto Law shall be passed.

[4] No Capitation, or other direct, Tax shall be laid, unless in Proportion to the Census or Enumeration herein before directed to be taken.

[5] No Tax or Duty shall be laid on Articles exported from any State.

[6] No Preference shall be given by any Regulation of Commerce or Revenue to the Ports of one State over those of another: nor shall Vessels bound to, or from, one State be obliged to enter, clear, or pay Duties in another.

[7] No money shall be drawn from the Treasury, but in Consequence of Appropriations made by Law; and a regular Statement and Account of the Receipts and Expenditures of all public Money shall be published from time to time.

[8] No Title of Nobility shall be granted by the United States: And no Person holding any Office of Profit or Trust under them, shall, without the Consent of the Congress, accept of any present, Emolument, Office, or Title, of any kind whatever, from any King, Prince, or foreign State.

Section 10. **[1]** No State shall enter into any Treaty, Alliance, or confederation; grant Letters of Marque and Reprisal; coin Money; emit Bills of Credit; make any Thing but gold and silver Coin a Tender in Payment of Debts; pass any Bill of Attainder, ex post facto Law, or Law impairing the Obligation of Contracts, or grant any Title of Nobility.

[2] No State shall, without the Consent of the Congress, lay any Imposts or Duties on Imports or Exports, except what may be absolutely necessary for executing its inspection Laws: and the net Produce of all Duties and Imposts, laid by any State on Imports or Exports, shall be for the Use of the Treasury of the United States; and all such Laws shall be subject to the Revision and Control of the Congress.

[3] No State shall, without the Consent of Congress, lay any Duty of Tonnage, keep Troops, or Ships of War in time of Peace, enter into any Agreement or Compact with another State, or with a foreign Power, or engage in War, unless actually invaded, or in such imminent Danger as will not admit of delay.

Article II

Section 1. **[1]** The executive Power shall be vested in a President of the United States of America. He shall hold his Office during the Term of four Years, and, together with the Vice President, chosen for the same Term, be elected, as follows:

[2] Each State shall appoint, in such Manner as the Legislature thereof may direct, a Number of Electors, equal to the whole Number of Senators and Representatives to which the State may be entitled in the Congress; but no Senator or Representative, or Person holding an Office of Trust or Profit under the United States, shall be appointed an Elector.

[3] The Electors shall meet in their respective States, and vote by Ballot for two Persons, of whom one at least shall not be an Inhabitant of the same State with themselves. And they shall make a List of all the Persons voted for, and of the Number of Votes for each; which List they shall sign and certify, and transmit sealed to the Seat of the Government of the United States, directed to the President of the Senate. The President of the Senate shall, in the Presence of the Senate and House of Representatives, open all the Certificates, and the Votes shall then be counted. The Person having the greatest Number of Votes shall be the President, if such Number be a Majority of the whole Number of Electors appointed; and if there be more than one who have such Majority, and have an equal Number of Votes, then the House of Representatives shall immediately chuse by Ballot one of them for President; and if no Person have a Majority, then from the five highest on the List the said House shall in like Manner chuse the President. But in chusing the President, the Votes shall be taken by States the Representation from each State having one Vote; A quorum for this Purpose shall consist of a Member or Members from two thirds of the States, and a Majority of all the States shall be necessary to a Choice. In every Case, after the Choice of the President, the Person having the greater Number of Votes of the Electors shall be the Vice President. But if there shall remain two or more who have equal Votes, the Senate shall chuse from them by Ballot the Vice President.

[4] The Congress may determine the Time of chusing the Electors, and the Day on which they shall give their Votes; which Day shall be the same throughout the United States.

[5] No person except a natural born Citizen, or a Citizen of the United States, at the time of the Adoption of this Constitution, shall be eligible to the Office of President; neither shall any Person be eligible to that Office who shall not have attained to the Age of thirty-five Years, and been fourteen Years a Resident within the United States.

[6] In case of the removal of the President from Office, or of his Death, Resignation or Inability to discharge the Powers and Duties of the said Office, the Same shall devolve on the Vice President, and the Congress may by Law provide for the Case of Removal, Death, Resignation or Inability, both of the President and Vice President, declaring what Officer shall then act as President, and such Officer shall act accordingly, until the Disability be removed, or a President shall be elected.

[7] The President shall, at stated Times, receive for his Services, a Compensation, which shall neither be increased nor diminished during the Period for which he shall have been elected, and he shall not receive within that Period any other Emolument from the United States, or any of them.

[8] Before he enter on the Execution of his Office, he shall take the following Oath or Affirmation: "I do solemnly swear (or affirm) that I will faithfully execute the Office of President of the United States, and will to the best of my Ability, preserve, protect, and defend the Constitution of the United States."

Section 2. **[1]** The President shall be Commander in Chief of the Army and Navy of the United States, and of the militia of the several States, when called into the actual Service of the United States; he may require the Opinion, in writing, of the principal Officer in each of the Executive Departments, upon any subject relating to the Duties of their respective Offices, and he shall have Power to grant Reprieves and Pardons for Offenses against the United States, except in Cases of Impeachment.

[2] He shall have Power, by and with the Advice and Consent of the Senate to make Treaties, provided two thirds of the Senators present concur; and he shall nominate, and by and with the Advice and Consent of the Senate, shall appoint Ambassadors, other public Ministers and Consuls, Judges of the supreme Court, and all other Officers of the United States, whose Appointments are not herein otherwise provided for, and which shall be established by Law; but the Congress may by Law vest the Appointment of such inferior Officers, as they think proper, in the President alone, in the Courts of Law, or in the Heads of Departments.

[3] The President shall have Power to fill up all Vacancies that may happen during the Recess of the Senate, by granting commissions which shall expire at the End of their next Session.

Section 3. He shall from time to time give to the Congress Information of the State of the Union, and recommend to their Consideration such Measures as he shall judge necessary and expedient; he may, on extraordinary Occasions, convene both Houses, or either of them, and in Case of Disagreement between them, with Respect to the Time of Adjournment, he may adjourn them to such Time as he shall think proper; he shall receive Ambassadors and other public Ministers; he shall take Care that the Laws be faithfully executed, and shall commission all the Officers of the United States.

Section 4. The President, Vice President and all civil Officers of the United States, shall be removed from Office on Impeachment for, and Conviction of, Treason, Bribery, or other high Crimes and Misdemeanors.

Article III

Section 1. The judicial Power of the United States, shall be vested in one supreme Court, and in such inferior Courts as the Congress may from time to time ordain and establish. The Judges, both of the supreme and inferior Courts, shall hold their Offices during good Behaviour, and shall, at stated Times, receive for their Services a Compensation, which shall not be diminished during their Continuance in Office.

Section 2. **[1]** The judicial Power shall extend to all Cases, in Law and Equity, arising under this Constitution, the Laws of the United States, and Treaties made, or which shall be made, under their Authority;—to all Cases affecting Ambassadors, other public Ministers and Consuls;—to all Cases of admiralty and maritime Jurisdiction;—to Controversies to which the United States shall be a Party;—between a State and Citizens of another State; between Citizens of different States;—between Citizens of the same State claiming Lands under the Grants of different States, and between a State, or the Citizens thereof, and foreign States, Citizens or Subjects.

[2] In all Cases affecting Ambassadors, other public Ministers and Consuls, and those in which a State shall be a Party, the supreme Court shall have original Jurisdiction, In all the other Cases before mentioned, the supreme Court shall have appellate Jurisdiction, both as to Law and Fact, with such Exceptions, and under such Regulations as the Congress shall make.

[3] The trial of all Crimes, except in Cases of Impeachment, shall be by Jury; and such Trial shall be held in the State where the said Crimes shall have been committed; but when not committed within any State, the Trial shall be at such Place or Places as the Congress may by Law have directed.

Section 3. **[1]** Treason against the United States, shall consist only in levying War against them, or, in adhering to their Enemies, giving them Aid and Comfort. No Person shall be convicted of Treason unless on the Testimony of two Witnesses to the same overt Act, or on Confession in open Court.

[2] The Congress shall have Power to declare the Punishment of Treason, but no Attainder of Treason shall work Corruption of Blood, or Forfeiture except during the Life of the Person attainted.

Article IV

Section 1. Full Faith and Credit shall be given in each State to the public Acts, Records, and judicial Proceedings of every other State. And the Congress may by general Laws prescribe the Manner in which such Acts, Records and Proceedings shall be proved, and the Effect thereof.

Section 2. **[1]** The Citizens of each State shall be entitled to all Privileges and Immunities of Citizens in the several States.

[2] A Person charged in any State with Treason, Felony, or other Crime, who shall flee from Justice, and be found in another State, shall on demand of the executive Authority of the State from which he fled, be delivered up, to be removed to the State having Jurisdiction of the Crime.

[3] No Person held to Service or Labour in one State, under the Laws thereof, escaping into another, shall, in Consequence of any Law or Regulation therein, be discharged from such Service or Labour, but shall be delivered up on Claim of the Party to whom such Service or Labour may be due.

Section 3. **[1]** New States may be admitted by the Congress into this Union; but no new State shall be formed or erected within the Jurisdiction of any other State; nor any State be formed by the Junction of two or more States, or Parts of States, without the Consent of the Legislatures of the States concerned as well as of the Congress.

[2] The Congress shall have Power to dispose of and make all needful Rules and Regulations respecting the Territory or other Property belonging to the United States; and nothing in this Constitution shall be so construed as to Prejudice any Claims of the United States, or of any particular State.

Section 4. The United States shall guarantee to every State in this Union a Republican Form of Government, and shall protect each of them against Invasion; and on Application of the Legislature, or of the Executive (when the Legislature cannot be convened) against domestic Violence.

Article V

The Congress, whenever two thirds of both Houses shall deem it necessary, shall propose Amendments to this Constitution, or, on the Application of the Legislatures of two thirds of the several States, shall call a Convention for proposing Amendments, which, in either case, shall be valid to all Intents and Purposes, as part of this Constitution, when ratified by the Legislatures of three fourths of the several States, or by Conventions in three fourths thereof, as the one or the other Mode of Ratification may be proposed by the Congress; Provided that no Amendment which may be made prior to the Year One thousand eight hundred and eight shall in any Manner affect the first and fourth Clauses in the Ninth Section of the first Article; and that no State, without its Consent, shall be deprived of its equal Suffrage in the Senate.

Articl e VI

[1] All Debts contracted and Engagements entered into, before the Adoption of this Constitution shall be as valid against the United States under this Constitution, as under the Confederation.

[2] This Constitution, and the Laws of the United States which shall be made in Pursuance thereof; and all Treaties made, or which shall be made, under the Authority of the United States, shall be the supreme Law of the Land; and the Judges in every State shall be bound thereby, any Thing in the Constitution or Laws of any State to the Contrary notwithstanding.

[3] The Senators and Representatives before mentioned, and the Members of the several State Legislatures, and all executive and judicial Officers, both of the United States

and of the several States, shall be bound by Oath or Affirmation, to support this Constitution; but no religious Test shall ever be required as a Qualification to any Office or public Trust under the United States.

Article VII

The Ratification of the Conventions of nine States shall be sufficient for the Establishment of this Constitution between the States so ratifying the Same.

Amendments

Articles in addition to, and in amendment of, the Constitution of the United States of America, proposed by Congress, and ratified by the Legislatures of the several States pursuant to the Fifth Article of the original Constitution.

Amendment 1 [1791]

Congress shall make no law respecting an establishment of religion, or prohibiting the free exercise thereof; or abridging the freedom of speech, or of the press; or the right of the people peaceably to assemble, and to petition the Government for a redress of grievances.

Amendment 2 [1791]

A well regulated Militia, being necessary to the security of a free State, the right of the people to keep and bear Arms, shall not be infringed.

Amendment 3 [1791]

No Soldier shall, in time of peace be quartered in any house, without the consent of the Owner, nor in time of war, but in a manner to be prescribed by law.

Amendment 4 [1791]

The right of the people to be secure in their persons, houses, papers, and effects, against unreasonable searches and seizures, shall not be violated, and no Warrants shall issue, but upon probable cause, supported by Oath or affirmation, and particularly describing the place to be searched, and the persons or things to be seized.

Amendment 5 [1791]

No person shall be held to answer for a capital, or other infamous crime, unless on a presentment or indictment of a Grand Jury, except in cases arising in the land or naval forces, or in the Militia, when in actual service in time of War or public danger; nor shall any person be subject for the same offence to be twice put in jeopardy of life or limb; nor shall be compelled in any criminal case to be a witness against himself, nor be deprived of life, liberty, or property, without due process of law; nor shall private property be taken for public use, without just compensation.

Amendment 6 [1791]

In all criminal prosecutions, the accused shall enjoy the right to a speedy and public trial, by an impartial jury of the State and district wherein the crime shall have been committed, which district shall have been previously ascertained by law, and to be informed of the nature and cause of the accusation; to be confronted with the witnesses against him; to have compulsory process for obtaining witnesses in his favor, and to have the Assistance of Counsel for his defence.

Amendment 7 [1791]

In Suits at common law, where the value in controversy shall exceed twenty dollars, the right of trial by jury shall be preserved, and no fact tried by jury, shall be otherwise re-examined in any Court of the United States, than according to the rules of common law.

Amendment 8 [1791]

Excessive bail shall not be required, nor excessive fines imposed, nor cruel and unusual punishments inflicted.

Amendment 9 [1791]

The enumeration in the Constitution, of certain rights, shall not be construed to deny or disparage others retained by the people.

Amendment 10 [1791]

The powers not delegated to the United States by the Constitution, nor prohibited by it to the States, are reserved to the States respectively, or to the people.

Amendment 11 [1798]

The Judicial power of the United States shall not be construed to extend to any suit in law or equity, commenced or prosecuted against one of the United States by Citizens of another State, or by Citizens or Subjects of any Foreign State.

Amendment 12 [1804]

The Electors shall meet in their respective states and vote by ballot for President and Vice President, one of whom, at least, shall not be an inhabitant of the same state with themselves; they shall name in their ballots the person voted for as President, and in distinct ballots the person voted for as Vice President, and they shall make distinct lists of all persons voted for as President, and of all persons voted for as Vice President, and of the number of votes for each, which lists they shall sign and certify, and transmit sealed to the seat of the government of the United States, directed to the President of the Senate;—The President of the Senate shall, in the presence of the Senate and House of Representatives, open all the certificates and the votes shall then be counted;—The person having the greatest number of votes for President, shall be the President, if such number be a majority of the whole number of Electors appointed; and if no person have such majority, then from the persons having the highest numbers not exceeding three on the list of those voted for as President, the House of Representatives shall choose immediately, by ballot, the President. But in choosing the President, the votes shall be taken by states, the representation from each state having one vote; a quorum for this purpose shall consist of a member or members from two thirds of the states, and a majority of all states shall be necessary to a choice. And if the House of Representatives shall not choose a President whenever the right of choice shall devolve upon them before the fourth day of March next following, then the Vice President shall act as President, as in the case of the death or other constitutional disability of the President.—The person having the greatest number of votes as Vice President, shall be the Vice President, if such number be a majority of the whole number of Electors appointed, and if no person have a majority, then from the two highest numbers on the list, the Senate shall choose the Vice President; a quorum for the purpose shall consist of two thirds of the whole number of Senators, and a majority of the whole number shall be necessary to a choice. But no person constitutionally ineligible to the office of President shall be eligible to that of Vice President of the United States.

Amendment 13 [1865]

Section 1. Neither slavery nor involuntary servitude, except as a punishment for crime whereof the party shall have been duly convicted, shall exist within the United States, or any place subject to their jurisdiction.

Section 2. Congress shall have power to enforce this article by appropriate legislation.

Amendment 14 [1868]

Section 1. All persons born or naturalized in the United States, and subject to the jurisdiction thereof, are citizens of the United States and of the State wherein they reside. No State shall make or enforce any law which shall abridge the privileges or immunities of citizens of the United States; nor shall any State deprive any person of life, liberty, or property, without due process of law; nor deny to any person within its jurisdiction the equal protection of the laws.

Section 2. Representatives shall be apportioned among the several States according to their respective numbers, counting the whole number of persons in each State, excluding Indians not taxed. But when the right to vote at any election for the choice of electors for President and Vice President of the United States, Representatives in Congress, the Executive and Judicial officers of a State, or the members of the Legislature thereof, is denied to any of the male inhabitants of such State, being twenty-one years of age, and citizens of the United States, or in any way abridged, except for participation in rebellion, or other crime, the basis of representation therein shall be reduced in the proportion which the number of such male citizens shall bear to the whole number of male citizens twenty-one years of age in such State.

Section 3. No person shall be a Senator or Representative in Congress, or elector of President and Vice President, or hold any office, civil or military, under the United States, or under any State, who having previously taken an oath, as a member of Congress, or as an officer of the United States, or as a member of any State legislature, or as an executive or judicial officer of any State, to support the Constitution of the United States, shall have engaged in insurrection or rebellion against the same, or given aid or comfort to the enemies thereof. But Congress may by a vote of two thirds of each House, remove such disability.

Section 4. The validity of the public debt of the United States, authorized by law, including debts incurred for payment of pensions and bounties for services in suppressing insurrection or rebellion, shall not be questioned. But neither the United States nor any State shall assume or pay any debt or obligation incurred in aid of insurrection or rebellion against the United States, or any claim for the loss or emancipation of any slave; but all such debts, obligations and claims shall be held illegal and void.

Section 5. The Congress shall have power to enforce, by appropriate legislation, the provisions of this article.

Amendment 15 [1870]

Section 1. The right of citizens of the United States to vote shall not be denied or abridged by the United States or by any State on account of race, color, or previous condition of servitude.

Section 2. The Congress shall have power to enforce this article by appropriate legislation.

Amendment 16 [1913]

The Congress shall have power to lay and collect taxes on incomes, from whatever source derived, without apportionment among the several States, and without regard to any census or enumeration.

Amendment 17 [1913]

[1] The Senate of the United States shall be composed of two Senators from each State, elected by the people thereof, for six years; and each Senator shall have one vote. The electors in each State shall have the qualifications requisite for electors of the most numerous branch of the State legislatures.

[2] When vacancies happen in the representation of any State in the Senate, the executive authority of such State shall issue writs of election to fill such vacancies: *Provided,* That the legislature of any State may empower the executive thereof to make temporary appointments until the people fill the vacancies by election as the legislature may direct.

[3] This amendment shall not be so construed as to affect the election or term of any Senator chosen before it becomes valid as part of the Constitution.

Amendment 18 [1919]

Section 1. After one year from the ratification of this article the manufacture, sale, or transportation of intoxicating liquors within, the importation thereof into, or the exportation thereof from the United States and all territory subject to the jurisdiction thereof for beverage purposes is hereby prohibited.

Section 2. The Congress and the several States shall have concurrent power to enforce this article by appropriate legislation.

Section 3. This article shall be inoperative unless it shall have been ratified as an amendment to the Constitution by the legislatures of the several States, as provided in the Constitution, within seven years from the date of the submission hereof to the States by the Congress.

Amendment 19 [1920]

[1] The right of citizens of the United States to vote shall not be denied or abridged by the United States or by any State on account of sex.

[2] Congress shall have power to enforce this article by appropriate legislation.

Amendment 20 [1933]

Section 1. The terms of the President and Vice President shall end at noon on the twentieth day of January, and the terms of Senators and Representatives at noon on the third day of January, of the years in which such terms would have ended if this article had not been ratified; and the terms of their successors shall then begin.

Section 2. The Congress shall assemble at least once in every year, and such meeting shall begin at noon on the third day of January, unless they shall by law appoint a different day.

Section 3. If, at the time fixed for the beginning of the term of the President, the President elect shall have died, the Vice President elect shall become President. If the President shall not have been chosen before the time fixed for the beginning of his term, or if the President elect shall have failed to qualify, then the Vice President elect shall act as President until a President shall have qualified; and the Congress may by law provide for the case wherein neither a President elect nor a Vice President elect shall have qualified, declaring who shall then act as President, or the manner in which one who is to act shall be selected, and such person shall act accordingly until a President or Vice President shall have qualified.

Section 4. The Congress may by law provide for the case of the death of any of the persons from whom the House of Representatives may choose a President whenever the right of choice shall have devolved upon them, and for the case of the death of any of the persons from whom the Senate may choose a Vice President whenever the right of choice shall have devolved upon them.

Section 5. Sections 1 and 2 shall take effect on the fifteenth day of October following the ratification of this article.

Section 6. This article shall be inoperative unless it shall have been ratified as an amendment to the Constitution by the legislatures of three fourths of the several States within seven years from the date of its submission.

Amendment 21 [1933]

Section 1. The eighteenth article of amendment to the Constitution of the United States is hereby repealed.

Section 2. The transportation or importation into any State, Territory, or possession of the United States for delivery or use therein of intoxicating liquors, in violation of the laws therefore, is hereby prohibited.

Section 3. This article shall be inoperative unless it shall have been ratified as an amendment to the Constitution by conventions in the several States, as provided in the Constitution, within seven years from the date of the submission hereof to the States by the Congress.

Amendment 22 [1951]

Section 1. No person shall be elected to the office of the President more than twice, and no person who has held the office of President, or acted as President, for more than two years of a term to which some other person was elected President shall be elected to the office of President more than once. But this Article shall not apply to any person holding the office of President when this Article was proposed by the Congress, and shall not prevent any person who may be holding the office of President, or acting as President, during the term within which this Article becomes operative from holding the office of President or acting as President during the remainder of such term.

Section 2. This article shall be inoperative unless it shall have been ratified as an amendment to the Constitution by the legislatures of three fourths of the several States within seven years from the date of its submission to the States by the Congress.

Amendment 23 [1961]

Section 1. The District constituting the seat of Government of the United States shall appoint in such manner as the Congress may direct:

A number of electors of President and Vice President equal to the whole number of Senators and Representatives in Congress to which the District would be entitled if it were a State, but in no event more than the least populous state;

they shall be in addition to those appointed by the states, but they shall be considered, for the purposes of the election of President and Vice President, to be electors appointed by a state; and they shall meet in the District and perform such duties as provided by the twelfth article of amendment.

Section 2. The Congress shall have power to enforce this article by appropriate legislation.

Amendment 24 [1964]

Section 1. The right of citizens of the United States to vote in any primary or other election for President or Vice President, for electors for President or Vice President, or for Senator or Representative in Congress, shall not be denied or abridged by the United States, or any State by reason of failure to pay any poll tax or other tax.

Section 2. The Congress shall have power to enforce this article by appropriate legislation.

Amendment 25 [1967]

Section 1. In case of the removal of the President from office or of his death or resignation, the Vice President shall become President.

Section 2. Whenever there is a vacancy in the office of the Vice President, the President shall nominate a Vice President who shall take office upon confirmation by a majority vote of both Houses of Congress.

Section 3. Whenever the President transmits to the President pro tempore of the Senate and the Speaker of the House of Representatives his written declaration that he is unable to discharge the powers and duties of his office, and until he transmits to them a written declaration to the contrary, such powers and duties shall be discharged by the Vice President as Acting President.

Section 4. Whenever the Vice President and a majority of either the principal officers of the executive departments or of such other body as Congress may by law provide, transmit to the President pro tempore of the Senate and the Speaker of the House of Representatives their written declaration that the President is unable to discharge the powers and duties of his office, the Vice President shall immediately assume the powers and duties of the office as Acting President.

Thereafter, when the President transmits to the President pro tempore of the Senate and the Speaker of the House of Representatives his written declaration that no inability exists, he shall resume the powers and duties of his office unless the Vice President and a majority of either the principal officers of the executive department or of such other body as Congress may by law provide, transmit within four days to the President pro tempore of the Senate and the Speaker of the House of Representatives their written declaration and the President is unable to discharge the powers and duties of his office. Thereupon Congress shall decide the issue, assembling within, forty-eight hours for that purpose if not in session. If the

Congress, within twenty-one days after receipt of the latter written declaration, or, if Congress is not in session, within twenty-one days after Congress is required to assemble, determines by two thirds vote of both Houses that the President is unable to discharge the powers and duties of his office, the Vice President shall continue to discharge the same as Acting President; otherwise, the President shall resume the powers and duties of his office.

Amendment 26 [1971]

Section 1. The right of citizens of the United States, who are eighteen years of age or older, to vote shall not be denied or abridged by the United States or by any State on account of age.

Section 2. The Congress shall have power to enforce this article by appropriate legislation.

Amendment 27 [1992]

No law varying the compensation for the services of Senators and Representatives shall take effect, until an election of Representatives shall have intervened.

Appendix B — Uniform Commercial Code (Articles 1, 2, 2a, and 3)*

Article 1: General Provisions

Part 1: Short Title, Construction, Application, and Subject Matter of the Act

§1-101. Short Title. This act shall be known and may be cited as Uniform Commercial Code.

§1-102. Purposes; Rules of Construction; Variation by Agreement.

(1) This Act shall be liberally construed and applied to promote its underlying purposes and policies.

(2) Underlying purposes and policies of this Act are

   (a) to simplify, clarify and modernize the law governing commercial transactions;

   (b) to permit the continued expansion of commercial practices through custom, usage and agreement of the parties;

   (c) to make uniform the law among the various jurisdictions.

(3) The effect of provisions of this Act may be varied by agreement, except as otherwise provided in this Act and except that the obligations of good faith, diligence, reasonableness and care prescribed by this Act may not be disclaimed by agreement but the parties may by agreement determine the standards by which the performance of such obligations is to be measured if such standards are not manifestly unreasonable.

(4) The presence in certain provisions of this Act of the words "unless otherwise agreed" or words of similar import does not imply that the effect of other provisions may not be varied by agreement under subsection (3).

(5) In this Act unless the context otherwise requires

   (a) words in the singular number include the plural, and in the plural include the singular;

   (b) words of the masculine gender include the feminine and the neuter, and when the sense so indicates words of the neuter gender may refer to any gender.

§1-103. Supplementary General Principles of Law Applicable. Unless displaced by the particular provisions of this Act, the principles of law and equity, including the law merchant and the law relative to capacity to contract, principal and agent, estoppel, fraud, misrepresentation, duress, coercion, mistake, bankruptcy or other validating or invalidating cause shall supplement its provisions.

§1-104. Construction against Implicity Repeal. This Act being a general act intended as a unified coverage of its subject matter, no part of it shall be deemed to be impliedly repealed by subsequent legislation if such construction can reasonably be avoided.

§1-105. Territorial Application of the Act; Parties' Power to Choose Applicable Law.

(1) Except as provided hereafter in this section, when a transaction bears a reasonable relation to this state and also to another state or nation the parties may agree that the law either of this state or of such other state or nation shall govern their rights and duties. Failing such agreement this Act applies to transactions bearing an appropriate relation to this state.

(2) Where one of the following provisions of this Act specifies the applicable law, that provision governs and a contrary agreement is effective only to the extent permitted by the law (including the conflict of laws rules) so specified:

Rights of creditors against sold goods. Section 2-402.

Applicability of the Article on Leases. Sections 2A-105 and 2A-106.

Applicability of the Article on Bank Deposits and Collections. Section 4-102.

Bulk transfers subject to the Article on Bulk Transfers. Section 6-102.

Applicability of the Article on Investment Securities. Section 8-106.

Perfection provisions of the Article on Secured Transactions. Section 9-103.

§1-106. Remedies to Be Liberally Administered.

(1) The remedies provided by this Act shall be liberally administered to the end that the aggrieved party may be put in as good a position as if the other party had fully performed but neither consequential or special nor penal damages may be had except as specifically provided in this Act or by other rule of law.

(2) Any right or obligation declared by this Act is enforceable by action unless the provision declaring it specifies a different and limited effect.

§1-107. Waiver or Renunciation of Claim or Right after Breach. Any claim or right arising out of an alleged breach can be discharged in whole or in part without consideration by a written waiver or renunciation signed and delivered by the aggrieved party.

§1-108. Severability. If any provision or clause of this Act or application thereof to any person or circumstances is held invalid, such invalidity shall not affect other provisions or applications of the Act which can be given effect without the invalid provision or application, and to this end the provisions of this Act are declared to be severable.

---

*To access the most recent version of the UCC and its Articles, please visit http://www.law.cornell.edu/ucc/ucc.table.html

§1-109. Section Captions. Section captions are parts of this Act.

Part 2: General Definitions and Principles of Interpretation

§1-201. General Definitions. Subject to additional definitions contained in the subsequent Articles of this Act which are applicable to specific Articles or Parts thereof, and unless the context otherwise requires, in this Act.

(1) "Action" in the sense of a judicial proceeding includes recoupment, counterclaim, set-off, suit in equity and any other proceedings in which rights are determined.

(2) "Aggrieved party" means a party entitled to resort to a remedy.

(3) "Agreement" means the bargain of the parties in fact as found in their language or by implication from other circumstances including course of dealing or usage of trade or course of performance as provided in this Act (Sections 1-205 and 2-208). Whether an agreement has legal consequences is determined by the provisions of this Act, if applicable; otherwise by the law of contracts (Section 1-103). (Compare "Contract".)

(4) "Bank" means any person engaged in the business of banking.

(5) "Bearer" means the person in possession of an instrument, document of title, or certificated security payable to bearer or indorsed in blank.

(6) "Bill of lading" means a document evidencing the receipt of goods for shipment issued by a person engaged in the business of transporting or forwarding goods, and includes an airbill. "Airbill" means a document serving for air transportation as a bill of lading does for marine or rail transportation, and includes an air consignment note or air waybill.

(7) "Branch" includes a separately incorporated foreign branch of a bank.

(8) "Burden of establishing" a fact means the burden of persuading the triers of fact that the existence of the fact is more probable than its non-existence.

(9) "Buyer in ordinary course of business" means a person who in good faith and without knowledge that the sale to him is in violation of the ownership rights or security interest of a third party in the goods buys in ordinary course from a person in the business of selling goods of that kind but does not include a pawnbroker. All persons who sell minerals or the like (including oil and gas) at wellhead or minehead shall be deemed to be persons in the business of selling goods of that kind. "Buying" may be for cash or by exchange of other property or on secured or unsecured credit and includes receiving goods or documents of title under a pre-existing contract for sale but does not include a transfer in bulk or as security for or in total or partial satisfaction of a money debt.

(10) "Conspicuous": A term or clause is conspicuous when it is so written that a reasonable person against whom it is to operate ought to have noticed it. A printed heading in capitals (as: NON-NEGOTIABLE BILL OF LADING) is conspicuous. Language in the body of a form is "conspicuous" if it is in larger or other contrasting type or color. But in a telegram any stated term is "conspicuous". Whether a term or clause is "conspicuous" or not is for decision by the court.

(11) "Contract" means the total legal obligation which results from the parties' agreement as affected by this Act and any other applicable rules of law. (Compare "Agreement".)

(12) "Creditor" includes a general creditor, a secured creditor, a lien creditor and any representative of creditors, including an assignee for the benefit of creditors, a trustee in bankruptcy, a receiver in equity and an executor or administrator of an insolvent debtor's or assignor's estate.

(13) "Defendant" includes a person in the position of defendant in a cross-action or counterclaim.

(14) "Delivery" with respect to instruments, documents of title, chattel paper or certificated securities means voluntary transfer of possession.

(15) "Document of title" includes bill of lading, dock warrant, dock receipt, warehouse receipt or order for the delivery of goods, and also any other document which in the regular course of business or financing is treated as adequately evidencing that the person in possession of it is entitled to receive, hold and dispose of the document and the goods it covers. To be a document of title a document must purport to be issued by or addressed to a bailee and purport to cover goods in the bailee's possession which are either identified or are fungible portions of an identified mass.

(16) "Fault" means wrongful act, omission or breach.

(17) "Fungible" with respect to goods or securities means goods or securities of which any unit is, by nature or usage of trade, the equivalent of any other like unit. Goods which are not fungible shall be deemed fungible for the purposes of this Act to the extent that under a particular agreement or document unlike units are treated as equivalents.

(18) "Genuine" means free of forgery or counterfeiting.

(19) "Good faith" means honesty in fact in the conduct or transaction concerned.

(20) "Holder" means a person who is in possession of a document of title or a certificated instrument or an investment security drawn, issued or indorsed to him or to his order or to bearer or in blank.

(21) To "honor" is to pay or to accept and pay, or where a credit so engages to purchase or discount a draft complying with the terms of the credit.

(22) "Insolvency proceedings" includes any assignment for the benefit of creditors or other proceedings intended to liquidate or rehabilitate the estate of the person involved.

(23) A person is "insolvent" who either has ceased to pay his debts in the ordinary course of business or cannot pay his debts as they become due or is insolvent within the meaning of the federal bankruptcy law.

(24) "Money" means a medium of exchange authorized or adopted by a domestic or foreign government as part of its currency.

(25) A person has "notice" of a fact when

    (a) he has actual knowledge of it; or

    (b) he has received a notice or notification of it; or

    (c) from all the facts and circumstances known to him at the time in question he has reason to know that it exists.

A person "knows" or has "knowledge" of a fact when he has actual knowledge of it. "Discover" or "learn" or a word or phrase of similar import refers to knowledge rather than to reason to know. The time and circumstances under which a notice or notification may cease to be effective are not determined by this Act.

(26) A person "notifies" or "gives" a notice or notification to another by taking such steps as may be reasonably required to inform the other in ordinary course whether or not such other actually comes to know of it. A person "receives" a notice or notification when

    (a) it comes to his attention; or

    (b) it is duly delivered at the place of business through which the contract was made or at any other place held out by him as the place for receipt of such communications.

(27) Notice, knowledge or a notice or notification received by an organization is effective for a particular transaction from the time when it is brought to the attention of the individual conducting that transaction, and in any event from the time when it would have been brought to his attention if the organization had exercised due diligence. An organization exercises due diligence if it maintains reasonable routines for communicating significant information to the person conducting the transaction and there is reasonable compliance with the routines. Due diligence does not require an individual acting for the organization to communicate information unless such communication is part of his regular duties or unless he has reason to know of the transaction and that the transaction would be materially affected by the information.

(28) "Organization" includes a corporation, government or governmental subdivision or agency, business trust, estate, trust, partnership or association, two or more persons having a joint or common interest or any other legal or commercial entity.

(29) "Party", as distinct from "third party", means a person who has engaged in a transaction or made an agreement within this Act.

(30) "Person" includes an individual or an organization (See Section 1-102).

(31) "Presumption" or "presumed" means that the trier of fact must find the existence of the fact presumed unless and until evidence is introduced which would support a finding of its non-existence.

(32) "Purchase" includes taking by sale, discount, negotiation, mortgage, pledge, lien, issue or re-issue, gift or any other voluntary transaction creating an interest in property.

(33) "Purchaser" means a person who takes by purchase.

(34) "Remedy" means any remedial right to which an aggrieved party is entitled with or without resort to a tribunal.

(35) "Representative" includes as agent, an officer of a corporation or association, and a trustee, executor or administrator of an estate, or any other person empowered to act for another.

(36) "Rights" includes remedies.

(37) "Security interest" means an interest in personal property or fixtures which secures payment or performance of an obligation. The retention or reservation of title by a seller of goods notwithstanding shipment or delivery to the buyer (Section 2-401) is limited in effect to a reservation of a "security interest". The term also includes any interest of a buyer of accounts or chattel paper which is subject to Article 9. The special property interest of a buyer of goods on identification of those goods to a contract for sale under Section 2-401 is not a "security interest", but a buyer may also acquire a "security interest" by complying with Article 9. Unless a consignment is intended as security, reservation of title thereunder is not a "security interest", but a consignment in any event is subject to the provisions on consignment sales (Section 2-326).

Whether a transaction creates a lease or security interest is determined by the facts of each case; however, a transaction creates a security interest if the consideration the lessee is to pay the lessor for the right to possession and use of the goods is an obligation for the term of the lease not subject to termination by the lessee, and

(a) the original term of the lease is equal to or greater than the remaining economic life of the goods,

(b) the lessee is bound to renew the lease for the remaining economic life of the goods or is bound to become the owner of the goods,

(c) the lessee has an option to renew the lease for the remaining economic life of the goods for no additional consideration or nominal additional consideration upon compliance with the lease agreement, or

(d) the lessee has an option to become the owner of the goods for no additional consideration or nominal additional consideration upon compliance with the lease agreement.

A transaction does not create a security interest merely because it provides that

(a) the present value of the consideration the lessee is obligated to pay the lessor for the right to possession and use of the goods is substantially equal to or is greater than the fair market value of the goods at the time the lease is entered into,

(b) the lessee assumes risk of loss of the goods, or agrees to pay taxes, insurance, filing, recording or registration fees, or service or maintenance costs with respect to the goods,

(c) the lessee has an option to renew the lease or to become the owner of the goods,

(d) the lessee has an option to renew the lease for a fixed rent that is equal to or greater than the reasonably predictable fair market rent for the use of the goods for the term of the renewal at the time the option is to be performed, or

(e) the lessee has an option to become the owner of the goods for a fixed price that is equal to or greater than the reasonably predictable fair market value of the goods at the time the option is to be performed.

For purposes of this subsection (37):

(x) Additional consideration is not nominal if (i) when the option to renew the lease is granted to the lessee the rent is stated to be the fair market rent for the use of the goods for the term of the renewal determined at the time the option is to be performed, or (ii) when the option to become the owner of the goods is granted to the lessee the price is stated to be the fair market value of the goods determined at the time the option is to be performed. Additional consideration is nominal if it is less than the lessee's reasonably predictable cost of performing under the lease agreement if the option is not exercised;

(y) "Reasonably predictable" and "remaining economic life of the goods" are to be determined with reference to the facts and circumstances at the time the transaction is entered into; and

(z) "Present value" means the amount as of a date certain of one or more sums payable in the future, discounted to the date certain. The discount is determined by the interest rate specified by the parties if the rate is not manifestly unreasonable at the time the transaction is entered into; otherwise, the discount is determined by a commercially reasonable rate that takes into account the facts and circumstances of each case at the time the transaction was entered into.

(38) "Send" in connection with any writing or notice means to deposit in the mail or deliver for transmission by any other usual means of communication with postage or cost of transmission provided for and properly addressed and in the case of an instrument to an address specified thereon or otherwise agreed, or if there be none to any address reasonable under the circumstances. The receipt of any writing or notice within the time at which it would have arrived if properly sent has the effect of a proper sending.

(39) "Signed" includes any symbol executed or adopted by a party with present intention to authenticate a writing.

(40) "Surety" includes guarantor.

(41) "Telegram" includes a message transmitted by radio, teletype, cable, any mechanical method of transmission or the like.

(42) "Term" means that portion of an agreement which relates to a particular matter.

(43) "Unauthorized" signature or indorsement means one made without actual, implied or apparent authority and includes a forgery.

(44) "Value". Except as otherwise provided with respect to negotiable instruments and bank collections (Sections 3-303, 4-208, and 4-209) a person gives "value" for rights if he acquires them

(a) in return for a binding commitment to extend credit or for the extension of immediately available credit whether or not drawn upon and whether or not a chargeback is provided for in the event of difficulties in collection; or

(b) as security for or in total or partial satisfaction of a pre-existing claim; or

(c) by accepting delivery pursuant to a pre-existing contract for purchase; or

(d) generally, in return for any consideration sufficient to support a simple contract.

(45) "Warehouse receipt" means a receipt issued by a person engaged in the business of storing goods for hire.

(46) "Written" or "writing" includes printing, typewriting or any other intentional reduction to tangible form. As amended 1962 and 1972.

§1-201. General Definitions *(1977 Amendments)*.

Subject to additional definitions contained in the subsequent Articles of this Act which are applicable to specific Articles or Parts thereof, and unless the context otherwise requires, in the Act:

* * *

1. (5) "Bearer" means the person in possession of an instrument, document of title or certificated security payable to bearer or indorsed in blank.

* * *

2. (14) "Delivery" with respect to instruments, documents of title chattel paper or certificated securities means voluntary transfer of possession.

* * *

3. (20) "Holder" means a person who is in possession of a document of title or an instrument or a certificated investment security drawn, issued or indorsed to him or his order or to bearer or in blank.

* * *

§1-202. Prima Facie Evidence by Third Party Documents.
A document in due form purporting to be a bill of lading, policy or certificate of insurance, official weigher's or inspector's certificate, consular invoice or any other document authorized or required by the contract to be issued by a third party shall be prima facie evidence of its own authenticity and genuineness and of the facts stated in the document by the third party.

§1-203. Obligation of Good Faith.
Every contract or duty within this Act imposes an obligation of good faith in its performance or enforcement.

§1-204. Time; Reasonable Time; "Seasonably".

(1) Whenever this Act requires any action to be taken within a reasonable time, any time which is not manifestly unreasonable may be fixed by agreement.

(2) What is a reasonable time for taking any action depends on the nature, purpose and circumstances of such action.

(3) An action is taken "seasonably" when it is taken at or within the time agreed or if no time is agreed at or within a reasonable time.

§1-205. Course of Dealing and Usage of Trade.

(1) A course of dealing is a sequence of previous conduct between the parties to a particular transaction which is fairly to be regarded as establishing a common basis of understanding for interpreting their expressions and other conduct.

(2) A usage of trade is any practice or method of dealing having such regularity of observance in a place, vocation or trade as to justify an expectation that it will be observed with respect to the transaction in question. The existence and scope of such a usage are to be proved as facts. If it is established that such a usage is embodied in a written trade code or similar writing the interpretation of the writing is for the court.

(3) A course of dealing between parties and any usage of trade in the vocation or trade in which they are engaged or of which they are or should be aware give particular meaning to and supplement or qualify terms of an agreement.

(4) The express terms of an agreement and an applicable course of dealing or usage of trade shall be construed wherever reasonable as consistent with each other; but when such construction is unreasonable express terms control both course of dealing and usage of trade and course of dealing controls usage of trade.

(5) An applicable usage of trade in the place where any part of performance is to occur shall be used in interpreting the agreement as to that part of the performance.

(6) Evidence of a relevant usage of trade offered by one party is not admissible unless and until he has given the other party such notice as the court finds sufficient to prevent unfair surprise to the latter.

§1-206. Statute of Frauds for Kinds of Personal Property Not Otherwise Covered.

(1) Except in the cases described in subsection (2) of this section a contract for the sale of personal property is not enforceable by way of action or defense beyond five thousand dollars in amount or value of remedy unless there is some writing which indicates that a contract for sale has been made between the parties at a defined or stated price, reasonably identifies the subject matter and is signed by the party against whom enforcement is sought or by his authorized agent.

(2) Subsection (1) of this section does not apply to contracts for the sale of goods (Section 2-201) nor of securities (Section 8-319) nor to security agreements (Section 9-203).

§1-207. Performance or Acceptance Under Reservation of Rights.
A party who with explicit reservation of rights performs or promises performance or assents to performance in a manner demanded or offered by the other party does not thereby prejudice the rights reserved. Such words as "without prejudice", "under protest" or the like are sufficient.

§1-208. Option to Accelerate at Will.
A term providing that one party or his successor in interest may accelerate payment or performance or require collateral or additional collateral "at will" or "when he deems himself insecure" or in words of similar import shall be construed to mean that he shall have power to do so only if he in good faith believes that the prospect of payment or performance is impaired. The burden of establishing lack of good faith is on the party against whom the power has been exercised.

§1-209. Subordinated Obligations.
An obligation may be issued as subordinated to payment of another obligation of the person obligated, or a creditor may subordinate his right to payment of an obligation by agreement with either the person obligated or another creditor of the person obligated. Such a subordination does not create a security interest as against either the common debtor or a subordinated creditor. This section shall be construed as declaring the law as it existed prior to the enactment of this section and not as modifying it. Added 1966.

Note: *This new section is proposed as an optional provision to make it clear that a subordination agreement does not create a security interest unless so intended.*

Article 2: Sales

Part 1: Short Title, General Construction, and Subject Matter

§2-101. Short Title. This Article shall be known and may be cited as Uniform Commercial Code—Sales.

§2-102. Scope; Certain Security and Other Transactions Excluded from This Article. Unless the context otherwise requires, this Article applies to transactions in goods; it does not apply to any transaction which although in the form of an unconditional contract to sell or present sale is intended to operate only as a security transaction nor does this Article impair or repeal any statute regulating sales to consumers, farmers or other specified classes of buyers.

§2-103. Definitions and Index of Definitions.

(1) In this Article unless the context otherwise requires

   (a) "Buyer" means a person who buys or contracts to buy goods.

   (b) [Reserved.]

   (c) "Receipt" of goods means taking physical possession of them.

   (d) "Seller" means a person who sells or contracts to sell goods.

(2) Other definitions applying to this Article or to specified Parts thereof, and the sections in which they appear are:

   "Acceptance". Section 2-606.

   "Banker's credit". Section 2-325.

   "Between merchants". Section 2-104.

   "Cancellation". Section 2-106(4).

   "Commercial unit". Section 2-105.

   "Confirmed credit". Section 2-325.

   "Conforming to contract". Section 2-106.

   "Contract for sale". Section 2-106.

   "Cover". Section 2-712.

   "Entrusting". Section 2-403.

   "Financing agency". Section 2-104.

   "Future goods". Section 2-105.

   "Goods". Section 2-105.

   "Identification". Section 2-501.

   "Installment contract". Section 2-612.

   "Letter of Credit". Section 2-325.

   "Lot". Section 2-105.

   "Merchant". Section 2-104.

   "Overseas". Section 2-323.

   "Person in position of seller". Section 2-707.

   "Present sale". Section 2-106.

   "Sale". Section 2-106.

   "Sale on approval". Section 2-326.

   "Sale or return". Section 2-326.

   "Termination". Section 2-106.

(3) "Control" as provided in Section 7-106 and the following definitions in other Articles apply to this Article:

   "Check". Section 3-104.

   "Consignee". Section 7-102.

   "Consignor". Section 7-102.

   "Consumer goods". Section 9-102

   "Dishonor". Section 3-502.

   "Draft". Section 3-104.

(4) In addition Article 1 contains general definitions and principles of construction and interpretation applicable throughout this Article.

§2-104. Definitions: "Merchant"; "Between Merchants"; "Financing Agency".

(1) "Merchant" means a person who deals in goods of the kind or otherwise by his occupation holds himself out as having knowledge or skill peculiar to the practices or goods involved in the transaction or to whom such knowledge or skill may be attributed by his employment of an agent or broker or other intermediary who by his occupation holds himself out as having such knowledge or skill.

(2) "Financing agency" means a bank, finance company or other person who in the ordinary course of business makes advances against goods or documents of title or who by arrangement with either the seller or the buyer intervenes in ordinary course to make or collect payment due or claimed under the contract for sale, as by purchasing or paying the seller's draft or making advances against it or by merely taking it for collection whether or not documents of title accompany or are associated with the draft. "Financing agency" includes also a bank or other person who similarly intervenes between persons who are in the position of seller and buyer in respect to the goods (Section 2–707).

(3) "Between merchants" means in any transaction with respect to which both parties are chargeable with the knowledge or skill of merchants.

§2-105. Definitions: Transferability; "Goods"; "Future" Goods; "Lot"; "Commercial Unit".

(1) "Goods" means all things (including specially manufactured goods) which are movable at the time of identification to the contract for sale other than the money in which the price is to be paid, investment securities (Article 8) and things in action. "Goods" also includes the unborn young of animals and

growing crops and other identified things attached to realty as described in the section on goods to be severed from realty (Section 2–107).

(2) Goods must be both existing and identified before any interest in them can pass. Goods which are not both existing and identified are "future" goods. A purported present sale of future goods or of any interest therein operates as a contract to sell.

(3) There may be a sale of a part interest in existing identified goods.

(4) An undivided share in an identified bulk of fungible goods is sufficiently identified to be sold although the quantity of the bulk is not determined. Any agreed proportion of such a bulk or any quantity thereof agreed upon by number, weight or other measure may to the extent of the seller's interest in the bulk be sold to the buyer who then becomes an owner in common.

(5) "Lot" means a parcel or a single article which is the subject matter of a separate sale or delivery, whether or not it is sufficient to perform the contract.

(6) "Commercial unit" means such a unit of goods as by commercial usage is a single whole for purposes of sale and division of which materially impairs its character or value on the market or in use. A commercial unit may be a single article (as a machine) or a set of articles (as a suite of furniture or an assortment of sizes) or a quantity (as a bale, gross, or carload) or any other unit treated in use or in the relevant market as a single whole.

§2-106. Definitions: "Contract"; "Agreement"; "Contract for Sale"; "Sale"; "Present Sale"; "Conforming" to Contract; "Termination"; "Cancellation".

(1) In this Article unless the context otherwise requires "contract" and "agreement" are limited to those relating to the present or future sale of goods. "Contract for sale" includes both a present sale of goods and a contract to sell goods at a future time. A "sale" consists in the passing of title from the seller to the buyer for a price (Section 2–401). A "present sale" means a sale which is accomplished by the making of the contract.

(2) Goods or conduct including any part of a performance are "conforming" or conform to the contract when they are in accordance with the obligations under the contract.

(3) "Termination" occurs when either party pursuant to a power created by agreement or law puts an end to the contract otherwise than for its breach. On "termination" all obligations which are still executory on both sides are discharged but any right based on prior breach or performance survives.

(4) "Cancellation" occurs when either party puts an end to the contract for breach by the other and its effect is the same as that of "termination" except that the

cancelling party also retains any remedy for breach of the whole contract or any unperformed balance.

§2-107. Goods to Be Severed from Realty: Recording.

(1) A contract for the sale of minerals or the like (including oil and gas) or a structure or its materials to be removed from realty is a contract for the sale of goods within this Article if they are to be severed by the seller but until severance a purported present sale thereof which is not effective as a transfer of an interest in land is effective only as a contract to sell.

(2) A contract for the sale apart from the land of growing crops or other things attached to realty and capable of severance without material harm thereto but not described in subsection (1) or of timber to be cut is a contract for the sale of goods within this Article whether the subject matter is to be severed by the buyer or by the seller even though it forms part of the realty at the time of contracting, and the parties can by identification effect a present sale before severance.

(3) The provisions of this section are subject to any third party rights provided by the law relating to realty records, and the contract for sale may be executed and recorded as a document transferring an interest in land and shall then constitute notice to third parties of the buyer's rights under the contract for sale.

Part 2: Form, Formation, and Readjustment of Contract

§2-201. Formal Requirements; Statute of Frauds.

(1) Except as otherwise provided in this section a contract for the sale of goods for the price of $500 or more is not enforceable by way of action or defense unless there is some writing sufficient to indicate that a contract for sale has been made between the parties and signed by the party against whom enforcement is sought or by his authorized agent or broker. A writing is not insufficient because it omits or incorrectly states a term agreed upon but the contract is not enforceable under this paragraph beyond the quantity of goods shown in such writing.

(2) Between merchants if within a reasonable time a writing in confirmation of the contract and sufficient against the sender is received and the party receiving it has reason to know its contents, it satisfies the requirements of subsection (1) against such party unless written notice of objection to its contents is given within 10 days after it is received.

(3) A contract which does not satisfy the requirements of subsection (1) but which is valid in other respects is enforceable

(a) if the goods are to be specially manufactured for the buyer and are not suitable for sale to others in the ordinary course of the seller's business and the seller, before notice of repudiation is received and under circumstances which reasonably indicate that the goods are for the buyer, has made either a substantial beginning of their manufacture or commitments for their procurement; or

(b) if the party against whom enforcement is sought admits in his pleading, testimony or otherwise in court that a contract for sale was made, but the contract is not enforceable under this provision beyond the quantity of goods admitted; or

(c) with respect to goods for which payment has been made and accepted or which have been received and accepted (Sec. 2–606).

§2-202. Final Written Expression: Parol or Extrinsic Evidence.
Terms with respect to which the confirmatory memoranda of the parties agree or which are otherwise set forth in a writing intended by the parties as a final expression of their agreement with respect to such terms as are included therein may not be contradicted by evidence of any prior agreement or of a contemporaneous oral agreement but may be explained or supplemented

(a) by course of performance, course of dealing, or usage of trade (Section 1-303); and

(b) by evidence of consistent additional terms unless the court finds the writing to have been intended also as a complete and exclusive statement of the terms of the agreement.

§2-203. Seals Inoperative.
The affixing of a seal to a writing evidencing a contract for sale or an offer to buy or sell goods does not constitute the writing a sealed instrument and the law with respect to sealed instruments does not apply to such a contract or offer.

§2-204. Formation in General.

(1) A contract for sale of goods may be made in any manner sufficient to show agreement, including conduct by both parties which recognizes the existence of such a contract.

(2) An agreement sufficient to constitute a contract for sale may be found even though the moment of its making is undetermined.

(3) Even though one or more terms are left open a contract for sale does not fail for indefiniteness if the parties have intended to make a contract and there is a reasonably certain basis for giving an appropriate remedy.

§2-205. Firm Offers.
An offer by a merchant to buy or sell goods in a signed writing which by its terms gives assurance that it will be held open is not revocable, for lack of consideration, during the time stated or if no time is stated for a reasonable time, but in no event may such period of irrevocability exceed three months; but any such term of assurance on a form supplied by the offeree must be separately signed by the offeror.

§2-206. Offer and Acceptance in Formation of Contract.

(1) Unless otherwise unambiguously indicated by the language or circumstances

(a) an offer to make a contract shall be construed as inviting acceptance in any manner and by any medium reasonable in the circumstances;

(b) an order or other offer to buy goods for prompt or current shipment shall be construed as inviting acceptance either by a prompt promise to ship or by the prompt or current shipment of conforming or non-conforming goods, but such a shipment of non-conforming goods does not constitute an acceptance if the seller seasonably notifies the buyer that the shipment is offered only as an accommodation to the buyer.

(2) Where the beginning of a requested performance is a reasonable mode of acceptance an offeror who is not notified of acceptance within a reasonable time may treat the offer as having lapsed before acceptance.

§2-207. Additional Terms in Acceptance or Confirmation.

(1) A definite and seasonable expression of acceptance or a written confirmation which is sent within a reasonable time operates as an acceptance even though it states terms additional to or different from those offered or agreed upon, unless acceptance is expressly made conditional on assent to the additional or different terms.

(2) The additional terms are to be construed as proposals for addition to the contract. Between merchants such terms become part of the contract unless:

(a) the offer expressly limits acceptance to the terms of the offer;

(b) they materially alter it; or

(c) notification of objection to them has already been given or is given within a reasonable time after notice of them is received.

(3) Conduct by both parties which recognizes the existence of a contract is sufficient to establish a contract for sale although the writings of the parties do not otherwise establish a contract. In such case the terms of the particular contract consist of those terms on which the writings of the parties agree, together with any supplementary terms incorporated under any other provisions of this Act.

§2-208. [Reserved.]

§2-209. Modification, Rescission, and Waiver.

(1) An agreement modifying a contract within this Article needs no consideration to be binding.

(2) A signed agreement which excludes modification or rescission except by a signed writing cannot be otherwise modified or rescinded, but except as between merchants such a requirement on a form supplied by the merchant must be separately signed by the other party.

(3) The requirements of the statute of frauds section of this Article (Section 2–201) must be satisfied if the contract as modified is within its provisions.

(4) Although an attempt at modification or rescission does not satisfy the requirements of subsection (2) or (3) it can operate as a waiver.

(5) A party who has made a waiver affecting an executory portion of the contract may retract the waiver by reasonable notification received by the other party that strict performance will be required of any term waived, unless the retraction would be unjust in view of a material change of position in reliance on the waiver.

§2-210. Delegation of Performance; Assignment of Rights.

(1) A party may perform his duty through a delegate unless otherwise agreed or unless the other party has a substantial interest in having his original promisor perform or control the acts required by the contract. No delegation of performance relieves the party delegating of any duty to perform or any liability for breach.

(2) Except as otherwise provided in Section 9-406, unless otherwise agreed all rights of either seller or buyer can be assigned except where the assignment would materially change the duty of the other party, or increase materially the burden or risk imposed on him by his contract, or impair materially his chance of obtaining return performance. A right to damages for breach of the whole contract or a right arising out of the assignor's due performance of his entire obligation can be assigned despite agreement otherwise.

(3) The creation, attachment, perfection, or enforcement of a security interest in the seller's interest under a contract is not a transfer that materially changes the duty of or increases materially the burden or risk imposed on the buyer or impairs materially the buyer's chance of obtaining return performance within the purview of subsection (2) unless, and then only to the extent that, enforcement actually results in a delegation of material performance of the seller. Even in that event, the creation, attachment, perfection, and enforcement of the security interest remain effective, but (i) the seller is liable to the buyer for damages caused by the delegation to the extent that the damages could not reasonably be prevented by the buyer, and (ii) a court having jurisdiction may grant other appropriate relief, including cancellation of the contract for sale or an injunction against enforcement of the security interest or consummation of the enforcement.

(4) Unless the circumstances indicate the contrary a prohibition of assignment of "the contract" is to be construed as barring only the delegation to the assignee of the assignor's performance.

(5) An assignment of "the contract" or of "all my rights under the contract" or an assignment in similar general terms is an assignment of rights and unless the language or the circumstances (as in an assignment for security) indicate the contrary, it is a delegation of performance of the duties of the assignor and its acceptance by the assignee constitutes a promise by him to perform those duties. This promise is enforceable by either the assignor or the other party to the original contract.

(6) The other party may treat any assignment which delegates performance as creating reasonable grounds for insecurity and may without prejudice to his rights against the assignor demand assurances from the assignee (Section 2–609).

Part 3: General Obligation and Construction of Contract

§2-301. General Obligations of Parties.
The obligation of the seller is to transfer and deliver and that of the buyer is to accept and pay in accordance with the contract.

§2-302. Unconscionable Contract or Clause.

(1) If the court as a matter of law finds the contract or any clause of the contract to have been unconscionable at the time it was made the court may refuse to enforce the contract, or it may enforce the remainder of the contract without the unconscionable clause, or it may so limit the application of any unconscionable clause as to avoid any unconscionable result.

(2) When it is claimed or appears to the court that the contract or any clause thereof may be unconscionable the parties shall be afforded a reasonable opportunity to present evidence as to its commercial setting, purpose and effect to aid the court in making the determination.

§2-303. Allocation or Division of Risks. Where this Article allocates a risk or a burden as between the parties "unless otherwise agreed", the agreement may not only shift the allocation but may also divide the risk or burden.

§2-304. Price Payable in Money, Goods, Realty, or Otherwise.

(1) The price can be made payable in money or otherwise. If it is payable in whole or in part in goods each party is a seller of the goods which he is to transfer.

(2) Even though all or part of the price is payable in an interest in realty the transfer of the goods and the

seller's obligations with reference to them are subject to this Article, but not the transfer of the interest in realty or the transferor's obligations in connection therewith.

§2-305. Open Price Term.

(1) The parties if they so intend can conclude a contract for sale even though the price is not settled. In such a case the price is a reasonable price at the time for delivery if
   (a) nothing is said as to price; or
   (b) the price is left to be agreed by the parties and they fail to agree; or
   (c) the price is to be fixed in terms of some agreed market or other standard as set or recorded by a third person or agency and it is not so set or recorded.

(2) A price to be fixed by the seller or by the buyer means a price for him to fix in good faith.

(3) When a price left to be fixed otherwise than by agreement of the parties fails to be fixed through fault of one party the other may at his option treat the contract as cancelled or himself fix a reasonable price.

(4) Where, however, the parties intend not to be bound unless the price be fixed or agreed and it is not fixed or agreed there is no contract. In such a case the buyer must return any goods already received or if unable so to do must pay their reasonable value at the time of delivery and the seller must return any portion of the price paid on account.

§2-306. Output, Requirements and, Exclusive Dealings.

(1) A term which measures the quantity by the output of the seller or the requirements of the buyer means such actual output or requirements as may occur in good faith, except that no quantity unreasonably disproportionate to any stated estimate or in the absence of a stated estimate to any normal or otherwise comparable prior output or requirements may be tendered or demanded.

(2) A lawful agreement by either the seller or the buyer for exclusive dealing in the kind of goods concerned imposes unless otherwise agreed an obligation by the seller to use best efforts to supply the goods and by the buyer to use best efforts to promote their sale.

§2-307. Delivery in Single Lot or Several Lots.

Unless otherwise agreed all goods called for by a contract for sale must be tendered in a single delivery and payment is due only on such tender but where the circumstances give either party the right to make or demand delivery in lots the price if it can be apportioned may be demanded for each lot.

§2-308. Absence of Specified Place for Delivery.

Unless otherwise agreed
(a) the place for delivery of goods is the seller's place of business or if he has none his residence; but
(b) in a contract for sale of identified goods which to the knowledge of the parties at the time of contracting are in some other place, that place is the place for their delivery; and
(c) documents of title may be delivered through customary banking channels.

§2-309. Absence of Specific Time Provisions; Notice of Termination.

(1) The time for shipment or delivery or any other action under a contract if not provided in this Article or agreed upon shall be a reasonable time.

(2) Where the contract provides for successive performances but is indefinite in duration it is valid for a reasonable time but unless otherwise agreed may be terminated at any time by either party.

(3) Termination of a contract by one party except on the happening of an agreed event requires that reasonable notification be received by the other party and an agreement dispensing with notification is invalid if its operation would be unconscionable.

§2-310. Open Time for Payment or Running of Credit; Authority to Ship under Reservation.

Unless otherwise agreed
(a) payment is due at the time and place at which the buyer is to receive the goods even though the place of shipment is the place of delivery; and
(b) if the seller is authorized to send the goods he may ship them under reservation, and may tender the documents of title, but the buyer may inspect the goods after their arrival before payment is due unless such inspection is inconsistent with the terms of the contract (Section 2-513); and
(c) if delivery is authorized and made by way of documents of title otherwise than by subsection (b) then payment is due regardless of where the goods are to be received (i) at the time and place at which the buyer is to receive delivery of the tangible documents or (ii) at the time the buyer is to receive delivery of the electronic documents and at the seller's place of business or if none, the seller's residence; and
(d) where the seller is required or authorized to ship the goods on credit the credit period runs from the time of shipment but post-dating the invoice or delaying its dispatch will correspondingly delay the starting of the credit period.

§2-311. Options and Cooperation Respecting Performance.

(1) An agreement for sale which is otherwise sufficiently definite (subsection (3) of Section 2–204) to be a contract is not made invalid by the fact that it leaves particulars of performance to be specified by one of the parties. Any such specification must be made in good faith and within limits set by commercial reasonableness.

(2) Unless otherwise agreed specifications relating to assortment of the goods are at the buyer's option and except as otherwise provided in subsections (1)(c) and (3) of Section 2–319 specifications or arrangements relating to shipment are at the seller's option.

(3) Where such specification would materially affect the other party's performance but is not seasonably made or where one party's cooperation is necessary to the agreed performance of the other but is not seasonably forthcoming, the other party in addition to all other remedies

    (a) is excused for any resulting delay in his own performance; and

    (b) may also either proceed to perform in any reasonable manner or after the time for a material part of his own performance treat the failure to specify or to cooperate as a breach by failure to deliver or accept the goods.

§2-312. Warranty of Title and against Infringement; Buyer's Obligation against Infringement.

(1) Subject to subsection (2) there is in a contract for sale a warranty by the seller that

    (a) the title conveyed shall be good, and its transfer rightful; and

    (b) the goods shall be delivered free from any security interest or other lien or encumbrance of which the buyer at the time of contracting has no knowledge.

(2) A warranty under subsection (1) will be excluded or modified only by specific language or by circumstances which give the buyer reason to know that the person selling does not claim title in himself or that he is purporting to sell only such right or title as he or a third person may have.

(3) Unless otherwise agreed a seller who is a merchant regularly dealing in goods of the kind warrants that the goods shall be delivered free of the rightful claim of any third person by way of infringement or the like but a buyer who furnishes specifications to the seller must hold the seller harmless against any such claim which arises out of compliance with the specifications.

§2-313. Express Warranties by Affirmation, Promise, Description, Sample.

(1) Express warranties by the seller are created as follows:

    (a) Any affirmation of fact or promise made by the seller to the buyer which relates to the goods and becomes part of the basis of the bargain creates an express warranty that the goods shall conform to the affirmation or promise.

    (b) Any description of the goods which is made part of the basis of the bargain creates an express warranty that the goods shall conform to the description.

    (c) Any sample or model which is made part of the basis of the bargain creates an express warranty that the whole of the goods shall conform to the sample or model.

(2) It is not necessary to the creation of an express warranty that the seller use formal words such as "warrant" or "guarantee" or that he have a specific intention to make a warranty, but an affirmation merely of the value of the goods or a statement purporting to be merely the seller's opinion or commendation of the goods does not create a warranty.

§2-314. Implied Warranty: Merchantability; Usage of Trade.

(1) Unless excluded or modified (Section 2–316), a warranty that the goods shall be merchantable is implied in a contract for their sale if the seller is a merchant with respect to goods of that kind. Under this section the serving for value of food or drink to be consumed either on the premises or elsewhere is a sale.

(2) Goods to be merchantable must be at least such as

    (a) pass without objection in the trade under the contract description; and

    (b) in the case of fungible goods, are of fair average quality within the description; and

    (c) are fit for the ordinary purposes for which such goods are used; and

    (d) run, within the variations permitted by the agreement, of even kind, quality and quantity within each unit and among all units involved; and

    (e) are adequately contained, packaged, and labeled as the agreement may require; and

    (f) conform to the promise or affirmations of fact made on the container or label if any.

(3) Unless excluded or modified (Section 2–316) other implied warranties may arise from course of dealing or usage of trade.

§2-315. Implied Warranty: Fitness for Particular Purpose.
Where the seller at the time of contracting has reason to know any particular purpose for which the goods are required and that the buyer is relying on the seller's skill or judgment to select or furnish suitable goods, there is unless excluded or modified under the next

section an implied warranty that the goods shall be fit for such purpose.

§2-316. Exclusion or Modification of Warranties.

(1) Words or conduct relevant to the creation of an express warranty and words or conduct tending to negate or limit warranty shall be construed wherever reasonable as consistent with each other; but subject to the provisions of this Article on parol or extrinsic evidence (Section 2–202) negation or limitation is inoperative to the extent that such construction is unreasonable.

(2) Subject to subsection (3), to exclude or modify the implied warranty of merchantability or any part of it the language must mention merchantability and in case of a writing must be conspicuous, and to exclude or modify any implied warranty of fitness the exclusion must be by a writing and conspicuous. Language to exclude all implied warranties of fitness is sufficient if it states, for example, that "There are no warranties which extend beyond the description on the face hereof."

(3) Notwithstanding subsection (2)

    (a) unless the circumstances indicate otherwise, all implied warranties are excluded by expressions like "as is", "with all faults" or other language which in common understanding calls the buyer's attention to the exclusion of warranties and makes plain that there is no implied warranty; and

    (b) when the buyer before entering into the contract has examined the goods or the sample or model as fully as he desired or has refused to examine the goods there is no implied warranty with regard to defects which an examination ought in the circumstances to have revealed to him; and

    (c) an implied warranty can also be excluded or modified by course of dealing or course of performance or usage of trade.

(4) Remedies for breach of warranty can be limited in accordance with the provisions of this Article on liquidation or limitation of damages and on contractual modification of remedy (Sections 2–718 and 2–719).

§2-317. Cumulation and Conflict of Warranties Express or Implied.
Warranties whether express or implied shall be construed as consistent with each other and as cumulative, but if such construction is unreasonable the intention of the parties shall determine which warranty is dominant. In ascertaining that intention the following rules apply:

(a) Exact or technical specifications displace an inconsistent sample or model or general language of description.

(b) A sample from an existing bulk displaces inconsistent general language of description.

(c) Express warranties displace inconsistent implied warranties other than an implied warranty of fitness for a particular purpose.

§2-318. Third Party Beneficiaries of Warranties Express or Implied.
Note: *If this Act is introduced in the Congress of the United States this section should be omitted. (States to select one alternative.)*

    Alternative A—A seller's warranty whether express or implied extends to any natural person who is in the family or household of his buyer or who is a guest in his home if it is reasonable to expect that such person may use, consume or be affected by the goods and who is injured in person by breach of the warranty. A seller may not exclude or limit the operation of this section.

    Alternative B—A seller's warranty whether express or implied extends to any natural person who may reasonably be expected to use, consume or be affected by the goods and who is injured in person by breach of the warranty. A seller may not exclude or limit the operation of this section.

    Alternative C—A seller's warranty whether express or implied extends to any person who may reasonably be expected to use, consume or be affected by the goods and who is injured by breach of the warranty. A seller may not exclude or limit the operation of this section with respect to injury to the person of an individual to whom the warranty extends.

§2-319. F.O.B. and F.A.S. Terms.

(1) Unless otherwise agreed the term F.O.B. (which means "free on board") at a named place, even though used only in connection with the stated price, is a delivery term under which

    (a) when the term is F.O.B. the place of shipment, the seller must at that place ship the goods in the manner provided in this Article (Section 2–504) and bear the expense and risk of putting them into the possession of the carrier; or

    (b) when the term is F.O.B. the place of destination, the seller must at his own expense and risk transport the goods to that place and there tender delivery of them in the manner provided in this Article (Section 2–503);

    (c) when under either (a) or (b) the term is also F.O.B. vessel, car or other vehicle, the seller must in addition at his own expense and risk load the goods on board. If the term is F.O.B. vessel the buyer must name the vessel and in an appropriate case the seller must comply with the provisions of this Article on the form of bill of lading (Section 2–323).

(2) Unless otherwise agreed the term F.A.S. vessel (which means "free alongside") at a named port, even though used only in connection with the stated price, is a delivery term under which the seller must

    (a) at his own expense and risk deliver the goods alongside the vessel in the manner usual in that port or on a dock designated and provided by the buyer; and

    (b) obtain and tender a receipt for the goods in exchange for which the carrier is under a duty to issue a bill of lading.

(3) Unless otherwise agreed in any case falling within subsection (1)(a) or (c) or subsection (2) the buyer must seasonably give any needed instructions for making delivery, including when the term is F.A.S. or F.O.B. the loading berth of the vessel and in an appropriate case its name and sailing date. The seller may treat the failure of needed instructions as a failure of cooperation under this Article (Section 2–311). He may also at his option move the goods in any reasonable manner preparatory to delivery or shipment.

(4) Under the term F.O.B. vessel or F.A.S. unless otherwise agreed the buyer must make payment against tender of the required documents and the seller may not tender nor the buyer demand delivery of the goods in substitution for the documents.

§2-320. C.I.F. and C. & F. Terms.

(1) The term C.I.F. means that the price includes in a lump sum the cost of the goods and the insurance and freight to the named destination. The term C. & F. or C.F. means that the price so includes cost and freight to the named destination.

(2) Unless otherwise agreed and even though used only in connection with the stated price and destination, the term C.I.F. destination or its equivalent requires the seller at his own expense and risk to

    (a) put the goods into the possession of a carrier at the port for shipment and obtain a negotiable bill or bills of lading covering the entire transportation to the named destination; and

    (b) load the goods and obtain a receipt from the carrier (which may be contained in the bill of lading) showing that the freight has been paid or provided for; and

    (c) obtain a policy or certificate of insurance, including any war risk insurance, of a kind and on terms then current at the port of shipment in the usual amount, in the currency of the contract, shown to cover the same goods covered by the bill of lading and providing for payment of loss to the order of the buyer or for the account of whom it may concern; but the seller may add to the price the amount of the premium for any such war risk insurance; and

    (d) prepare an invoice of the goods and procure any other documents required to effect shipment or to comply with the contract; and

    (e) forward and tender with commercial promptness all the documents in due form and with any indorsement necessary to perfect the buyer's rights.

(3) Unless otherwise agreed the term C. & F. or its equivalent has the same effect and imposes upon the seller the same obligations and risks as a C.I.F. term except the obligation as to insurance.

(4) Under the term C.I.F. or C. & F. unless otherwise agreed the buyer must make payment against tender of the required documents and the seller may not tender nor the buyer demand delivery of the goods in substitution for the documents.

§2-321. C.I.F. or C. & F.: "Net Landed Weights"; "Payment on Arrival"; Warranty of Condition on Arrival.
Under a contract containing a term C.I.F. or C. & F.

(1) Where the price is based on or is to be adjusted according to "net landed weights", "delivered weights", "out turn" quantity or quality or the like, unless otherwise agreed the seller must reasonably estimate the price. The payment due on tender of the documents called for by the contract is the amount so estimated, but after final adjustment of the price a settlement must be made with commercial promptness.

(2) An agreement described in subsection (1) or any warranty of quality or condition of the goods on arrival places upon the seller the risk of ordinary deterioration, shrinkage and the like in transportation but has no effect on the place or time of identification to the contract for sale or delivery or on the passing of the risk of loss.

(3) Unless otherwise agreed where the contract provides for payment on or after arrival of the goods the seller must before payment allow such preliminary inspection as is feasible; but if the goods are lost delivery of the documents and payment are due when the goods should have arrived.

§2-322. Delivery "Ex-Ship".

(1) Unless otherwise agreed a term for delivery of goods "ex-ship" (which means from the carrying vessel) or in equivalent language is not restricted to a particular ship and requires delivery from a ship which has reached a place at the named port of destination where goods of the kind are usually discharged.

(2) Under such a term unless otherwise agreed

    (a) the seller must discharge all liens arising out of the carriage and furnish the buyer with a direction which puts the carrier under a duty to deliver the goods; and

    (b) the risk of loss does not pass to the buyer until the goods leave the ship's tackle or are otherwise properly unloaded.

§2-323. Form of Bill of Lading Required in Overseas Shipment; "Overseas".

(1) Where the contract contemplates overseas shipment and contains a term C.I.F. or C. & F. or F.O.B. vessel, the seller unless otherwise agreed must obtain a negotiable bill of lading stating that the goods have been loaded in board or, in the case of a term C.I.F. or C. & F., received for shipment.

(2) Where in a case within subsection (1) a tangible bill of lading has been issued in a set of parts, unless otherwise agreed if the documents are not to be sent from abroad the buyer may demand tender of the full set; otherwise only one part of the bill of lading need be tendered. Even if the agreement expressly requires a full set

    (a) due tender of a single part is acceptable within the provisions of this Article on cure of improper delivery (subsection (1) of Section 2–508); and

    (b) even though the full set is demanded, if the documents are sent from abroad the person tendering an incomplete set may nevertheless require payment upon furnishing an indemnity which the buyer in good faith deems adequate.

(3) A shipment by water or by air or a contract contemplating such shipment is "overseas" insofar as by usage of trade or agreement it is subject to the commercial, financing or shipping practices characteristic of international deep water commerce.

§2-324. "No Arrival, No Sale" Term.
Under a term "no arrival, no sale" or terms of like meaning, unless otherwise agreed,

    (a) the seller must properly ship conforming goods and if they arrive by any means he must tender them on arrival but he assumes no obligation that the goods will arrive unless he has caused the non-arrival; and

    (b) where without fault of the seller the goods are in part lost or have so deteriorated as no longer to conform to the contract or arrive after the contract time, the buyer may proceed as if there had been casualty to identified goods (Section 2–613).

§2-325. "Letter of Credit" Term; "Confirmed Credit".

(1) Failure of the buyer seasonably to furnish an agreed letter of credit is a breach of the contract for sale.

(2) The delivery to seller of a proper letter of credit suspends the buyer's obligation to pay. If the letter of credit is dishonored, the seller may on seasonable notification to the buyer require payment directly from him.

(3) Unless otherwise agreed the term "letter of credit" or "banker's credit" in a contract for sale means an irrevocable credit issued by a financing agency of good

repute and, where the shipment is overseas, of good international repute. The term "confirmed credit" means that the credit must also carry the direct obligation of such an agency which does business in the seller's financial market.

§2-326. Sale on Approval and Sale or Return; Rights of Creditors.

(1) Unless otherwise agreed, if delivered goods may be returned by the buyer even though they conform to the contract, the transaction is

    (a) a "sale on approval" if the goods are delivered primarily for use, and

    (b) a "sale or return" if the goods are delivered primarily for resale.

(2) Goods held on approval are not subject to the claims of the buyer's creditors until acceptance; goods held on sale or return are subject to such claims while in the buyer's possession.

(3) Any "or return" term of a contract for sale is to be treated as a separate contract for sale within the statute of frauds section of this Article (Section 2–201) and as contradicting the sale aspect of the contract within the provisions of this Article on parol or extrinsic evidence (Section 2–202).

§2-327. Special Incidents of Sale on Approval and Sale or Return.

(1) Under a sale on approval unless otherwise agreed

    (a) although the goods are identified to the contract the risk of loss and the title do not pass to the buyer until acceptance; and

    (b) use of the goods consistent with the purpose of trial is not acceptance but failure seasonably to notify the seller of election to return the goods is acceptance, and if the goods conform to the contract acceptance of any part is acceptance of the whole; and

    (c) after due notification of election to return, the return is at the seller's risk and expense but a merchant buyer must follow any reasonable instructions.

(2) Under a sale or return unless otherwise agreed

    (a) the option to return extends to the whole or any commercial unit of the goods while in substantially their original condition, but must be exercised seasonably; and

    (b) the return is at the buyer's risk and expense.

§2-328. Sale by Auction.

(1) In a sale by auction if goods are put up in lots each lot is the subject of a separate sale.

(2) A sale by auction is complete when the auctioneer so announces by the fall of the hammer or in other customary manner. Where a bid is made while the hammer is falling in acceptance of a prior bid the

auctioneer may in his discretion reopen the bidding or declare the goods sold under the bid on which the hammer was falling.

(3) Such a sale is with reserve unless the goods are in explicit terms put up without reserve. In an auction with reserve the auctioneer may withdraw the goods at any time until he announces completion of the sale. In an auction without reserve, after the auctioneer calls for bids on an article or lot, that article or lot cannot be withdrawn unless no bid is made within a reasonable time. In either case a bidder may retract his bid until the auctioneer's announcement of completion of the sale, but a bidder's retraction does not revive any previous bid.

(4) If the auctioneer knowingly receives a bid on the seller's behalf or the seller makes or procures such a bid, and notice has not been given that liberty for such bidding is reserved, the buyer may at his option avoid the sale or take the goods at the price of the last good faith bid prior to the completion of the sale. This subsection shall not apply to any bid at a forced sale.

Part 4: Title, Creditors, and Good Faith Purchasers

§2-401. Passing of Title; Reservation for Security; Limited Application of This Section.
Each provision of this Article with regard to the rights, obligations and remedies of the seller, the buyer, purchasers or other third parties applies irrespective of title to the goods except where the provision refers to such title. Insofar as situations are not covered by the other provisions of this Article and matters concerning title become material the following rules apply:

(1) Title to goods cannot pass under a contract for sale prior to their identification to the contract (Section 2–501), and unless otherwise explicitly agreed the buyer acquires by their identification a special property as limited by this Act. Any retention or reservation by the seller of the title (property) in goods shipped or delivered to the buyer is limited in effect to a reservation of a security interest. Subject to these provisions and to the provisions of the Article on Secured Transactions (Article 9), title to goods passes from the seller to the buyer in any manner and on any conditions explicitly agreed on by the parties.

(2) Unless otherwise explicitly agreed title passes to the buyer at the time and place at which the seller completes his performance with reference to the physical delivery of the goods, despite any reservation of a security interest and even though a document of title is to be delivered at a different time or place; and in particular and despite any reservation of a security interest by the bill of lading

(a) if the contract requires or authorizes the seller to send the goods to the buyer but does not require him to deliver them at destination, title passes to the buyer at the time and place of shipment; but

(b) if the contract requires delivery at destination, title passes on tender there.

(3) Unless otherwise explicitly agreed where delivery is to be made without moving the goods,

(a) if the seller is to deliver a tangible document of title, title passes at the time when and the place where he delivers such documents and if the seller is to deliver an electronic document of title, title passes when the seller delivers the document; or

(b) if the goods are at the time of contracting already identified and no documents are to be delivered, title passes at the time and place of contracting.

(4) A rejection or other refusal by the buyer to receive or retain the goods, whether or not justified, or a justified revocation of acceptance revests title to the goods in the seller. Such revesting occurs by operation of law and is not a "sale".

§2-402. Rights of Seller's Creditors against Sold Goods.

(1) Except as provided in subsections (2) and (3), rights of unsecured creditors of the seller with respect to goods which have been identified to a contract for sale are subject to the buyer's rights to recover the goods under this Article (Sections 2–502 and 2–716).

(2) A creditor of the seller may treat a sale or an identification of goods to a contract for sale as void if as against him a retention of possession by the seller is fraudulent under any rule of law of the state where the goods are situated, except that retention of possession in good faith and current course of trade by a merchant-seller for a commercially reasonable time after a sale or identification is not fraudulent.

(3) Nothing in this Article shall be deemed to impair the rights of creditors of the seller

(a) under the provisions of the Article on Secured Transactions (Article 9); or

(b) where identification to the contract or delivery is made not in current course of trade but in satisfaction of or as security for a pre-existing claim for money, security or the like and is made under circumstances which under any rule of law of the state where the goods are situated would apart from this Article constitute the transaction a fraudulent transfer or voidable preference.

§2-403. Power to Transfer; Good Faith Purchase of Goods; "Entrusting".

(1) A purchaser of goods acquires all title which his transferor had or had power to transfer except that a purchaser of a limited interest acquires rights only to the extent of the interest purchased. A person with voidable title has power to transfer a good title to a good faith purchaser for value. When goods have been delivered under a transaction of purchase the purchaser has such power even though

   (a) the transferor was deceived as to the identity of the purchaser, or

   (b) the delivery was in exchange for a check which is later dishonored, or

   (c) it was agreed that the transaction was to be a "cash sale", or

   (d) the delivery was procured through fraud punishable as larcenous under the criminal law.

(2) Any entrusting of possession of goods to a merchant who deals in goods of that kind gives him power to transfer all rights of the entruster to a buyer in ordinary course of business.

(3) "Entrusting" includes any delivery and any acquiescence in retention of possession regardless of any condition expressed between the parties to the delivery or acquiescence and regardless of whether the procurement of the entrusting or the possessor's disposition of the goods have been such as to be larcenous under the criminal law.

[Legislative Note: If a state adopts the repealer of Article 6—Bulk Transfers (Alternative A), subsec. (4) should read as follows:]

(4) The rights of other purchasers of goods and of lien creditors are governed by the Articles on Secured Transactions (Article 9) and Documents of Title (Article 7).

[Legislative Note: If a state adopts Revised Article 6—Bulk Sales (Alternative B), subsec. (4) should read as follows:]

(4) The rights of other purchasers of goods and of lien creditors are governed by the Articles on Secured Transactions (Article 9), Bulk Sales (Article 6) and Documents of Title (Article 7).

For material relating to the changes made in text in 1988, see section 3 of Alternative A (Repealer of Article 6—Bulk Transfers) and Conforming Amendment to Section 2–403 following end of Alternative B (Revised Article 6—Bulk Sales).

Part 5: Performance

§2-501. Insurable Interest in Goods; Manner of Identification of Goods.

(1) The buyer obtains a special property and an insurable interest in goods by identification of existing goods as goods to which the contract refers even though the goods so identified are non-conforming and he has an option to return or reject them. Such identification can be made at any time and in any manner explicitly agreed to by the parties. In the absence of explicit agreement identification occurs

   (a) when the contract is made if it is for the sale of goods already existing and identified;

   (b) if the contract is for the sale of future goods other than those described in paragraph (c), when goods are shipped, marked or otherwise designated by the seller as goods to which the contract refers;

   (c) when the crops are planted or otherwise become growing crops or the young are conceived if the contract is for the sale of unborn young to be born within twelve months after contracting or for the sale of crops to be harvested within twelve months or the next normal harvest season after contracting whichever is longer.

(2) The seller retains an insurable interest in goods so long as title to or any security interest in the goods remains in him and where the identification is by the seller alone he may until default or insolvency or notification to the buyer that the identification is final substitute other goods for those identified.

(3) Nothing in this section impairs any insurable interest recognized under any other statute or rule of law.

§2-502. Buyer's Right to Goods on Seller's Repudiation, Failure to Deliver, or Insolvency.

(1) Subject to subsections (2) and (3) and even though the goods have not been shipped a buyer who has paid a part or all of the price of goods in which he has a special property under the provisions of the immediately preceding section may on making and keeping good a tender of any unpaid portion of their price recover them from the seller if:

   (a) in the case of goods bought for personal, family, or household purposes, the seller repudiates or fails to deliver as required by the contract; or

   (b) in all cases, the seller becomes insolvent within ten days after receipt of the first installment on their price.

(2) The buyer's right to recover the goods under subsection (1)(a) vests upon acquisition of a special property, even if the seller had not then repudiated or failed to deliver.

(3) If the identification creating his special property has been made by the buyer he acquires the right to recover the goods only if they conform to the contract for sale.

§2-503. Manner of Seller's Tender of Delivery.

(1) Tender of delivery requires that the seller put and hold conforming goods at the buyer's disposition and

give the buyer any notification reasonably necessary to enable him to take delivery. The manner, time and place for tender are determined by the agreement and this Article, and in particular

    (a) tender must be at a reasonable hour, and if it is of goods they must be kept available for the period reasonably necessary to enable the buyer to take possession; but

    (b) unless otherwise agreed the buyer must furnish facilities reasonably suited to the receipt of the goods.

(2) Where the case is within the next section respecting shipment tender requires that the seller comply with its provisions.

(3) Where the seller is required to deliver at a particular destination tender requires that he comply with subsection (1) and also in any appropriate case tender documents as described in subsections (4) and (5) of this section.

(4) Where goods are in the possession of a bailee and are to be delivered without being moved

    (a) tender requires that the seller either tender a negotiable document of title covering such goods or procure acknowledgment by the bailee of the buyer's right to possession of the goods; but

    (b) tender to the buyer of a non-negotiable document of title or of a record directing to the bailee to deliver is sufficient tender unless the buyer seasonably objects, and except as otherwise provided in Article 9 receipt by the bailee of notification of the buyer's rights fixes those rights as against the bailee and all third persons; but risk of loss of the goods and of any failure by the bailee to honor the non-negotiable document of title or to obey the direction remains on the seller until the buyer has had a reasonable time to present the document or direction, and a refusal by the bailee to honor the document or to obey the direction defeats the tender.

(5) Where the contract requires the seller to deliver documents

    (a) he must tender all such documents in correct form, except as provided in this Article with respect to bills of lading in a set (subsection (2) of Section 2–323); and

    (b) tender through customary banking channels is sufficient and dishonor of a draft accompanying or associated with the documents constitutes non-acceptance or rejection.

§2-504. Shipment by Seller.

Where the seller is required or authorized to send the goods to the buyer and the contract does not require him to deliver them at a particular destination, then unless otherwise agreed he must

    (a) put the goods in the possession of such a carrier and make such a contract for their transportation as may be reasonable having regard to the nature of the goods and other circumstances of the case; and

    (b) obtain and promptly deliver or tender in due form any document necessary to enable the buyer to obtain possession of the goods or otherwise required by the agreement or by usage of trade; and

    (c) promptly notify the buyer of the shipment.

Failure to notify the buyer under paragraph (c) or to make a proper contract under paragraph (a) is a ground for rejection only if material delay or loss ensues.

§2-505. Seller's Shipment Under Reservation.

(1) Where the seller has identified goods to the contract by or before shipment:

    (a) his procurement of a negotiable bill of lading to his own order or otherwise reserves in him a security interest in the goods. His procurement of the bill to the order of a financing agency or of the buyer indicates in addition only the seller's expectation of transferring that interest to the person named.

    (b) a non-negotiable bill of lading to himself or his nominee reserves possession of the goods as security but except in a case of conditional delivery (subsection (2) of Section 2–507) a non-negotiable bill of lading naming the buyer as consignee reserves no security interest even though the seller retains possession or control of the bill of lading.

(2) When shipment by the seller with reservation of a security interest is in violation of the contract for sale it constitutes an improper contract for transportation within the preceding section but impairs neither the rights given to the buyer by shipment and identification of the goods to the contract nor the seller's powers as a holder of a negotiable document of title.

§2-506. Rights of Financing Agency.

(1) A financing agency by paying or purchasing for value a draft which relates to a shipment of goods acquires to the extent of the payment or purchase and in addition to its own rights under the draft and any document of title securing it any rights of the shipper in the goods including the right to stop delivery and the shipper's right to have the draft honored by the buyer.

(2) The right to reimbursement of a financing agency which has in good faith honored or purchased the draft under commitment to or authority from the buyer is not impaired by subsequent discovery of defects with reference to any relevant document which was apparently regular.

§2-507. Effect of Seller's Tender; Delivery on Condition.

(1) Tender of delivery is a condition to the buyer's duty to accept the goods and, unless otherwise agreed, to his duty to pay for them. Tender entitles the seller to acceptance of the goods and to payment according to the contract.

(2) Where payment is due and demanded on the delivery to the buyer of goods or documents of title, his right as against the seller to retain or dispose of them is conditional upon his making the payment due.

§2-508. Cure by Seller of Improper Tender or Delivery; Replacement.

(1) Where any tender or delivery by the seller is rejected because non-conforming and the time for performance has not yet expired, the seller may seasonably notify the buyer of his intention to cure and may then within the contract time make a conforming delivery.

(2) Where the buyer rejects a non-conforming tender which the seller had reasonable grounds to believe would be acceptable with or without money allowance the seller may if he seasonably notifies the buyer have a further reasonable time to substitute a conforming tender.

§2-509. Risk of Loss in the Absence of Breach.

(1) Where the contract requires or authorizes the seller to ship the goods by carrier

    (a) if it does not require him to deliver them at a particular destination, the risk of loss passes to the buyer when the goods are duly delivered to the carrier even though the shipment is under reservation (Section 2–505); but

    (b) if it does require him to deliver them at a particular destination and the goods are there duly tendered while in the possession of the carrier, the risk of loss passes to the buyer when the goods are there duly so tendered as to enable the buyer to take delivery.

(2) Where the goods are held by a bailee to be delivered without being moved, the risk of loss passes to the buyer

    (a) on his receipt of possession or control of a negotiable document of title covering the goods; or

    (b) on acknowledgment by the bailee of the buyer's right to possession of the goods; or

    (c) after his receipt of possession or control of a non-negotiable document of title or other direction to deliver in a record, as provided in subsection (4)(b) of Section 2–503.

(3) In any case not within subsection (1) or (2), the risk of loss passes to the buyer on his receipt of the goods if the seller is a merchant; otherwise the risk passes to the buyer on tender of delivery.

(4) The provisions of this section are subject to contrary agreement of the parties and to the provisions of this Article on sale on approval (Sec,tion 2–327) and on effect of breach on risk of loss (Section 2–510).

§2-510. Effect of Breach on Risk of Loss.

(1) Where a tender or delivery of goods so fails to conform to the contract as to give a right of rejection the risk of their loss remains on the seller until cure or acceptance.

(2) Where the buyer rightfully revokes acceptance he may to the extent of any deficiency in his effective insurance coverage treat the risk of loss as having rested on the seller from the beginning.

(3) Where the buyer as to conforming goods already identified to the contract for sale repudiates or is otherwise in breach before risk of their loss has passed to him, the seller may to the extent of any deficiency in his effective insurance coverage treat the risk of loss as resting on the buyer for a commercially reasonable time.

§2-511. Tender of Payment by Buyer; Payment by Check.

(1) Unless otherwise agreed tender of payment is a condition to the seller's duty to tender and complete any delivery.

(2) Tender of payment is sufficient when made by any means or in any manner current in the ordinary course of business unless the seller demands payment in legal tender and gives any extension of time reasonably necessary to procure it.

(3) Subject to the provisions of this Act on the effect of an instrument on an obligation (Section 3–310), payment by check is conditional and is defeated as between the parties by dishonor of the check on due presentment.

§2-512. Payment by Buyer before Inspection.

(1) Where the contract requires payment before inspection non-conformity of the goods does not excuse the buyer from so making payment unless

    (a) the non-conformity appears without inspection; or

    (b) despite tender of the required documents the circumstances would justify injunction against honor under this Act (Section 5–109(b)).

(2) Payment pursuant to subsection (1) does not constitute an acceptance of goods or impair the buyer's right to inspect or any of his remedies.

§2-513. Buyer's Right to Inspection of Goods.

(1) Unless otherwise agreed and subject to subsection (3), where goods are tendered or delivered or identified to the contract for sale, the buyer has a right before payment or acceptance to inspect them at any reasonable place and time and in any reasonable manner. When the seller is required or authorized to send the goods to the buyer, the inspection may be after their arrival.

(2) Expenses of inspection must be borne by the buyer but may be recovered from the seller if the goods do not conform and are rejected.

(3) Unless otherwise agreed and subject to the provisions of this Article on C.I.F. contracts (subsection (3) of Section 2–321), the buyer is not entitled to inspect the goods before payment of the price when the contract provides

    (a) for delivery "C.O.D." or on other like terms; or

    (b) for payment against documents of title, except where such payment is due only after the goods are to become available for inspection.

(4) A place or method of inspection fixed by the parties is presumed to be exclusive but unless otherwise expressly agreed it does not postpone identification or shift the place for delivery or for passing the risk of loss. If compliance becomes impossible, inspection shall be as provided in this section unless the place or method fixed was clearly intended as an indispensable condition failure of which avoids the contract.

§2-514. When Documents Deliverable on Acceptance; When on Payment.
Unless otherwise agreed documents against which a draft is drawn are to be delivered to the drawee on acceptance of the draft if it is payable more than three days after presentment; otherwise, only on payment.

§2-515. Preserving Evidence of Goods in Dispute.
In furtherance of the adjustment of any claim or dispute

(a) either party on reasonable notification to the other and for the purpose of ascertaining the facts and preserving evidence has the right to inspect, test and sample the goods including such of them as may be in the possession or control of the other; and

(b) the parties may agree to a third party inspection or survey to determine the conformity or condition of the goods and may agree that the findings shall be binding upon them in any subsequent litigation or adjustment.

Part 6: Breach, Repudiation, and Excuse

§2-601. Buyer's Rights on Improper Delivery.
Subject to the provisions of this Article on breach in installment contracts (Section 2–612) and unless otherwise agreed under the sections on contractual limitations of remedy (Sections 2–718 and 2–719), if the goods or the tender of delivery fail in any respect to conform to the contract, the buyer may

(a) reject the whole; or

(b) accept the whole; or

(c) accept any commercial unit or units and reject the rest.

§2-602. Manner and Effect of Rightful Rejection.

(1) Rejection of goods must be within a reasonable time after their delivery or tender. It is ineffective unless the buyer seasonably notifies the seller.

(2) Subject to the provisions of the two following sections on rejected goods (Sections 2–603 and 2–604),

    (a) after rejection any exercise of ownership by the buyer with respect to any commercial unit is wrongful as against the seller; and

    (b) if the buyer has before rejection taken physical possession of goods in which he does not have a security interest under the provisions of this Article (subsection (3) of Section 2–711), he is under a duty after rejection to hold them with reasonable care at the seller's disposition for a time sufficient to permit the seller to remove them; but

    (c) the buyer has no further obligations with regard to goods rightfully rejected.

(3) The seller's rights with respect to goods wrongfully rejected are governed by the provisions of this Article on Seller's remedies in general (Section 2–703).

§2-603. Merchant Buyer's Duties as to Rightfully Rejected Goods.

(1) Subject to any security interest in the buyer (subsection (3) of Section 2–711), when the seller has no agent or place of business at the market of rejection a merchant buyer is under a duty after rejection of goods in his possession or control to follow any reasonable instructions received from the seller with respect to the goods and in the absence of such instructions to make reasonable efforts to sell them for the seller's account if they are perishable or threaten to decline in value speedily. Instructions are not reasonable if on demand indemnity for expenses is not forthcoming.

(2) When the buyer sells goods under subsection (1), he is entitled to reimbursement from the seller or out of the proceeds for reasonable expenses of caring for and selling them, and if the expenses include no selling commission then to such commission as is usual

in the trade or if there is none to a reasonable sum not exceeding ten per cent on the gross proceeds.

(3) In complying with this section the buyer is held only to good faith and good faith conduct hereunder is neither acceptance nor conversion nor the basis of an action for damages.

§2-604. Buyer's Options as to Salvage of Rightfully Rejected Goods.
Subject to the provisions of the immediately preceding section on perishables if the seller gives no instructions within a reasonable time after notification of rejection the buyer may store the rejected goods for the seller's account or reship them to him or resell them for the seller's account with reimbursement as provided in the preceding section. Such action is not acceptance or conversion.

§2-605. Waiver of Buyer's Objections by Failure to Particularize.

(1) The buyer's failure to state in connection with rejection a particular defect which is ascertainable by reasonable inspection precludes him from relying on the unstated defect to justify rejection or to establish breach

  (a) where the seller could have cured it if stated seasonably; or

  (b) between merchants when the seller has after rejection made a request in writing for a full and final written statement of all defects on which the buyer proposes to rely.

(2) Payment against documents made without reservation of rights precludes recovery of the payment for defects apparent in the documents.

§2-606. What Constitutes Acceptance of Goods.

(1) Acceptance of goods occurs when the buyer

  (a) after a reasonable opportunity to inspect the goods signifies to the seller that the goods are conforming or that he will take or retain them in spite of their non-conformity; or

  (b) fails to make an effective rejection (subsection (1) of Section 2–602), but such acceptance does not occur until the buyer has had a reasonable opportunity to inspect them; or

  (c) does any act inconsistent with the seller's ownership; but if such act is wrongful as against the seller it is an acceptance only if ratified by him.

(2) Acceptance of a part of any commercial unit is acceptance of that entire unit.

§2-607. Effect of Acceptance; Notice of Breach; Burden of Establishing Breach after Acceptance; Notice of Claim or Litigation to Person Answerable over.

(1) The buyer must pay at the contract rate for any goods accepted.

(2) Acceptance of goods by the buyer precludes rejection of the goods accepted and if made with knowledge of a non-conformity cannot be revoked because of it unless the acceptance was on the reasonable assumption that the non-conformity would be seasonably cured but acceptance does not of itself impair any other remedy provided by this Article for non-conformity.

(3) Where a tender has been accepted

  (a) the buyer must within a reasonable time after he discovers or should have discovered any breach notify the seller of breach or be barred from any remedy; and

  (b) if the claim is one for infringement or the like (subsection (3) of Section 2–312) and the buyer is sued as a result of such a breach he must so notify the seller within a reasonable time after he receives notice of the litigation or be barred from any remedy over for liability established by the litigation.

(4) The burden is on the buyer to establish any breach with respect to the goods accepted.

(5) Where the buyer is sued for breach of a warranty or other obligation for which his seller is answerable over

  (a) he may give his seller written notice of the litigation. If the notice states that the seller may come in and defend and that if the seller does not do so he will be bound in any action against him by his buyer by any determination of fact common to the two litigations, then unless the seller after seasonable receipt of the notice does come in and defend he is so bound.

  (b) if the claim is one for infringement or the like (subsection (3) of Section 2–312) the original seller may demand in writing that his buyer turn over to him control of the litigation including settlement or else be barred from any remedy over and if he also agrees to bear all expense and to satisfy any adverse judgment, then unless the buyer after seasonable receipt of the demand does turn over control the buyer is so barred.

(6) The provisions of subsections (3), (4) and (5) apply to any obligation of a buyer to hold the seller harmless against infringement or the like (subsection (3) of Section 2–312).

§2-608. Revocation of Acceptance in Whole or in Part.

(1) The buyer may revoke his acceptance of a lot or commercial unit whose non-conformity substantially impairs its value to him if he has accepted it

  (a) on the reasonable assumption that its non-conformity would be cured and it has not been seasonably cured; or

(b) without discovery of such non-conformity if his acceptance was reasonably induced either by the difficulty of discovery before acceptance or by the seller's assurances.

(2) Revocation of acceptance must occur within a reasonable time after the buyer discovers or should have discovered the ground for it and before any substantial change in condition of the goods which is not caused by their own defects. It is not effective until the buyer notifies the seller of it.

(3) A buyer who so revokes has the same rights and duties with regard to the goods involved as if he had rejected them.

§2-609. Right to Adequate Assurance of Performance.

(1) A contract for sale imposes an obligation on each party that the other's expectation of receiving due performance will not be impaired. When reasonable grounds for insecurity arise with respect to the performance of either party the other may in writing demand adequate assurance of due performance and until he receives such assurance may if commercially reasonable suspend any performance for which he has not already received the agreed return.

(2) Between merchants the reasonableness of grounds for insecurity and the adequacy of any assurance offered shall be determined according to commercial standards.

(3) Acceptance of any improper delivery or payment does not prejudice the aggrieved party's right to demand adequate assurance of future performance.

(4) After receipt of a justified demand failure to provide within a reasonable time not exceeding thirty days such assurance of due performance as is adequate under the circumstances of the particular case is a repudiation of the contract.

§2-610. Anticipatory Repudiation. When either party repudiates the contract with respect to a performance not yet due the loss of which will substantially impair the value of the contract to the other, the aggrieved party may

(a) for a commercially reasonable time await performance by the repudiating party; or

(b) resort to any remedy for breach (Section 2–703 or Section 2–711), even though he has notified the repudiating party that he would await the latter's performance and has urged retraction; and

(c) in either case suspend his own performance or proceed in accordance with the provisions of this Article on the seller's right to identify goods to the contract notwithstanding breach or to salvage unfinished goods (Section 2–704).

§2-611. Retraction of Anticipatory Repudiation.

(1) Until the repudiating party's next performance is due he can retract his repudiation unless the aggrieved party has since the repudiation cancelled or materially changed his position or otherwise indicated that he considers the repudiation final.

(2) Retraction may be by any method which clearly indicates to the aggrieved party that the repudiating party intends to perform, but must include any assurance justifiably demanded under the provisions of this Article (Section 2–609).

(3) Retraction reinstates the repudiating party's rights under the contract with due excuse and allowance to the aggrieved party for any delay occasioned by the repudiation.

§2-612. "Installment Contract"; Breach.

(1) An "installment contract" is one which requires or authorizes the delivery of goods in separate lots to be separately accepted, even though the contract contains a clause "each delivery is a separate contract" or its equivalent.

(2) The buyer may reject any installment which is non-conforming if the non-conformity substantially impairs the value of that installment and cannot be cured or if the non-conformity is a defect in the required documents; but if the non-conformity does not fall within subsection (3) and the seller gives adequate assurance of its cure the buyer must accept that installment.

(3) Whenever non-conformity or default with respect to one or more installments substantially impairs the value of the whole contract there is a breach of the whole. But the aggrieved party reinstates the contract if he accepts a non-conforming installment without seasonably notifying of cancellation or if he brings an action with respect only to past installments or demands performance as to future installments.

§2-613. Casualty to Identified Goods. Where the contract requires for its performance goods identified when the contract is made, and the goods suffer casualty without fault of either party before the risk of loss passes to the buyer, or in a proper case under a "no arrival, no sale" term (Section 2-324) then

(a) if the loss is total the contract is avoided; and

(b) if the loss is partial or the goods have so deteriorated as no longer to conform to the contract the buyer may nevertheless demand inspection and at his option either treat the contract as avoided or accept the goods with due allowance from the contract price for the deterioration or the deficiency in quantity but without further right against the seller.

§2-614. Substituted Performance.

(1) Where without fault of either party the agreed berthing, loading, or unloading facilities fail or an agreed type of carrier becomes unavailable or the agreed manner of delivery otherwise becomes commercially impracticable but a commercially reasonable substitute is available, such substitute performance must be tendered and accepted.

(2) If the agreed means or manner of payment fails because of domestic or foreign governmental regulation, the seller may withhold or stop delivery unless the buyer provides a means or manner of payment which is commercially a substantial equivalent. If delivery has already been taken, payment by the means or in the manner provided by the regulation discharges the buyer's obligation unless the regulation is discriminatory, oppressive or predatory.

§2-615. Excuse by Failure of Presupposed Conditions. Except so far as a seller may have assumed a greater obligation and subject to the preceding section on substituted performance:

(a) Delay in delivery or non-delivery in whole or in part by a seller who complies with paragraphs (b) and (c) is not a breach of his duty under a contract for sale if performance as agreed has been made impracticable by the occurrence of a contingency the non-occurrence of which was a basic assumption on which the contract was made or by compliance in good faith with any applicable foreign or domestic governmental regulation or order whether or not it later proves to be invalid.

(b) Where the causes mentioned in paragraph (a) affect only a part of the seller's capacity to perform, he must allocate production and deliveries among his customers but may at his option include regular customers not then under contract as well as his own requirements for further manufacture. He may so allocate in any manner which is fair and reasonable.

(c) The seller must notify the buyer seasonably that there will be delay or non-delivery and, when allocation is required under paragraph (b), of the estimated quota thus made available for the buyer.

§2-616. Procedure on Notice Claiming Excuse.

(1) Where the buyer receives notification of a material or indefinite delay or an allocation justified under the preceding section he may by written notification to the seller as to any delivery concerned, and where the prospective deficiency substantially impairs the value of the whole contract under the provisions of this Article relating to breach of installment contracts (Section 2–612), then also as to the whole,

(a) terminate and thereby discharge any unexecuted portion of the contract; or

(b) modify the contract by agreeing to take his available quota in substitution.

(2) If after receipt of such notification from the seller the buyer fails so to modify the contract within a reasonable time not exceeding thirty days the contract lapses with respect to any deliveries affected.

(3) The provisions of this section may not be negated by agreement except in so far as the seller has assumed a greater obligation under the preceding section.

Part 7: Remedies

§2-701. Remedies for Breach of Collateral Contracts Not Impaired. Remedies for breach of any obligation or promise collateral or ancillary to a contract for sale are not impaired by the provisions of this Article.

§2-702. Seller's Remedies on Discovery of Buyer's Insolvency.

(1) Where the seller discovers the buyer to be insolvent he may refuse delivery except for cash including payment for all goods theretofore delivered under the contract, and stop delivery under this Article (Section 2–705).

(2) Where the seller discovers that the buyer has received goods on credit while insolvent he may reclaim the goods upon demand made within ten days after the receipt, but if misrepresentation of solvency has been made to the particular seller in writing within three months before delivery the ten day limitation does not apply. Except as provided in this subsection the seller may not base a right to reclaim goods on the buyer's fraudulent or innocent misrepresentation of solvency or of intent to pay.

(3) The seller's right to reclaim under subsection (2) is subject to the rights of a buyer in ordinary course or other good faith purchaser under this Article (Section 2–403). Successful reclamation of goods excludes all other remedies with respect to them.

§2-703. Seller's Remedies in General. Where the buyer wrongfully rejects or revokes acceptance of goods or fails to make a payment due on or before delivery or repudiates with respect to a part or the whole, then with respect to any goods directly affected and, if the breach is of the whole contract (Section 2-612), then also with respect to the whole undelivered balance, the aggrieved seller may

(a) withhold delivery of such goods;

(b) stop delivery by any bailee as hereafter provided (Section 2–705);

(c) proceed under the next section respecting goods still unidentified to the contract;

(d) resell and recover damages as hereafter provided (Section 2–706);

(e) recover damages for non-acceptance (Section 2–708) or in a proper case the price (Section 2–709);

(f) cancel.

§2-704. Seller's Right to Identify Goods to the Contract Notwithstanding Breach or to Salvage Unfinished Goods.

(1) An aggrieved seller under the preceding section may

(a) identify to the contract conforming goods not already identified if at the time he learned of the breach they are in his possession or control;

(b) treat as the subject of resale goods which have demonstrably been intended for the particular contract even though those goods are unfinished.

(2) Where the goods are unfinished an aggrieved seller may in the exercise of reasonable commercial judgment for the purposes of avoiding loss and of effective realization either complete the manufacture and wholly identify the goods to the contract or cease manufacture and resell for scrap or salvage value or proceed in any other reasonable manner.

§2-705. Seller's Stoppage of Delivery in Transit or Otherwise.

(1) The seller may stop delivery of goods in the possession of a carrier or other bailee when he discovers the buyer to be insolvent (Section 2–702) and may stop delivery of carload, truckload, planeload or larger shipments of express or freight when the buyer repudiates or fails to make a payment due before delivery or if for any other reason the seller has a right to withhold or reclaim the goods.

(2) As against such buyer the seller may stop delivery until

(a) receipt of the goods by the buyer; or

(b) acknowledgment to the buyer by any bailee of the goods except a carrier that the bailee holds the goods for the buyer; or

(c) such acknowledgment to the buyer by a carrier by reshipment or as warehouseman; or

(d) negotiation to the buyer of any negotiable document of title covering the goods.

(3) (a) To stop delivery the seller must so notify as to enable the bailee by reasonable diligence to prevent delivery of the goods.

(b) After such notification the bailee must hold and deliver the goods according to the directions of the seller but the seller is liable to the bailee for any ensuing charges or damages.

(c) If a negotiable document of title has been issued for goods the bailee is not obliged to obey a notification to stop until surrender of possession or control of the document.

(d) A carrier who has issued a non-negotiable bill of lading is not obliged to obey a notification to stop received from a person other than the consignor.

§2-706. Seller's Resale Including Contract for Resale.

(1) Under the conditions stated in Section 2–703 on seller's remedies, the seller may resell the goods concerned or the undelivered balance thereof. Where the resale is made in good faith and in a commercially reasonable manner the seller may recover the difference between the resale price and the contract price together with any incidental damages allowed under the provisions of this Article (Section 2–710), but less expenses saved in consequence of the buyer's breach.

(2) Except as otherwise provided in subsection (3) or unless otherwise agreed resale may be at public or private sale including sale by way of one or more contracts to sell or of identification to an existing contract of the seller. Sale may be as a unit or in parcels and at any time and place and on any terms but every aspect of the sale including the method, manner, time, place and terms must be commercially reasonable. The resale must be reasonably identified as referring to the broken contract, but it is not necessary that the goods be in existence or that any or all of them have been identified to the contract before the breach.

(3) Where the resale is at private sale the seller must give the buyer reasonable notification of his intention to resell.

(4) Where the resale is at public sale

(a) only identified goods can be sold except where there is a recognized market for a public sale of futures in goods of the kind; and

(b) it must be made at a usual place or market for public sale if one is reasonably available and except in the case of goods which are perishable or threaten to decline in value speedily the seller must give the buyer reasonable notice of the time and place of the resale; and

(c) if the goods are not to be within the view of those attending the sale the notification of sale must state the place where the goods are located and provide for their reasonable inspection by prospective bidders; and

(d) the seller may buy.

(5) A purchaser who buys in good faith at a resale takes the goods free of any rights of the original buyer even though the seller fails to comply with one or more of the requirements of this section.

(6) The seller is not accountable to the buyer for any profit made on any resale. A person in the position of a seller (Section 2–707) or a buyer who has rightfully rejected or justifiably revoked acceptance must account for any excess over the amount of his security interest, as hereinafter defined (subsection (3) of Section 2–711).

§2-707. "Person in the Position of a Seller".

(1) A "person in the position of a seller" includes as against a principal an agent who has paid or become responsible for the price of goods on behalf of his principal or anyone who otherwise holds a security interest or other right in goods similar to that of a seller.

(2) A person in the position of a seller may as provided in this Article withhold or stop delivery (Section 2–705) and resell (Section 2–706) and recover incidental damages (Section 2–710).

§2-708. Seller's Damages for Non-acceptance or Repudiation.

(1) Subject to subsection (2) and to the provisions of this Article with respect to proof of market price (Section 2–723), the measure of damages for non-acceptance or repudiation by the buyer is the difference between the market price at the time and place for tender and the unpaid contract price together with any incidental damages provided in this Article (Section 2–710), but less expenses saved in consequence of the buyer's breach.

(2) If the measure of damages provided in subsection (1) is inadequate to put the seller in as good a position as performance would have done then the measure of damages is the profit (including reasonable overhead) which the seller would have made from full performance by the buyer, together with any incidental damages provided in this Article (Section 2–710), due allowance for costs reasonably, incurred and due credit for payments or proceeds of resale.

§2-709. Action for the Price.

(1) When the buyer fails to pay the price as it becomes due the seller may recover, together with any incidental damages under the next section, the price

   (a) of goods accepted or of conforming goods lost or damaged within a commercially reasonable time after risk of their loss has passed to the buyer; and

   (b) of goods identified to the contract if the seller is unable after reasonable effort to resell them at a reasonable price or the circumstances reasonably indicate that such effort will be unavailing.

(2) Where the seller sues for the price he must hold for the buyer any goods which have been identified to the contract and are still in his control except that if resale becomes possible he may resell them at any time prior to the collection of the judgment. The net proceeds of any such resale must be credited to the buyer and payment of the judgment entitles him to any goods not resold.

(3) After the buyer has wrongfully rejected or revoked acceptance of the goods or has failed to make a payment due or has repudiated (Section 2–610), a seller who is held not entitled to the price under this section shall nevertheless be awarded damages for non-acceptance under the preceding section.

§2-710. Seller's Incidental Damages.
Incidental damages to an aggrieved seller include any commercially reasonable charges, expenses or commissions incurred in stopping delivery, in the transportation, care and custody of goods after the buyer's breach, in connection with return or resale of the goods or otherwise resulting from the breach.

§2-711. Buyer's Remedies in General; Buyer's Security Interest in Rejected Goods.

(1) Where the seller fails to make delivery or repudiates or the buyer rightfully rejects or justifiably revokes acceptance then with respect to any goods involved, and with respect to the whole if the breach goes to the whole contract (Section 2–612), the buyer may cancel and whether or not he has done so may in addition to recovering so much of the price as has been paid

   (a) "cover" and have damages under the next section as to all the goods affected whether or not they have been identified to the contract; or

   (b) recover damages for non-delivery as provided in this Article (Section 2–713).

(2) Where the seller fails to deliver or repudiates the buyer may also

   (a) if the goods have been identified recover them as provided in this Article (Section 2–502); or

   (b) in a proper case obtain specific performance or replevy the goods as provided in this Article (Section 2–716).

(3) On rightful rejection or justifiable revocation of acceptance a buyer has a security interest in goods in his possession or control for any payments made on their price and any expenses reasonably incurred in their inspection, receipt, transportation, care and custody and may hold such goods and resell them in like manner as an aggrieved seller (Section 2–706).

§2-712. "Cover"; Buyer's Procurement of Substitute Goods.

(1) After a breach within the preceding section the buyer may "cover" by making in good faith and without unreasonable delay any reasonable purchase of or contract to purchase goods in substitution for those due from the seller.

(2) The buyer may recover from the seller as damages the difference between the cost of cover and the contract price together with any incidental or consequential damages as hereinafter defined (Section 2–715), but less expenses saved in consequence of the seller's breach.

(3) Failure of the buyer to effect cover within this section does not bar him from any other remedy.

§2-713. Buyer's Damages for Non-delivery or Repudiation.

(1) Subject to the provisions of this Article with respect to proof of market price (Section 2–723), the measure of damages for non-delivery or repudiation by the seller is the difference between the market price at the time when the buyer learned of the breach and the contract price together with any incidental and consequential damages provided in this Article (Section 2–715), but less expenses saved in consequence of the seller's breach.

(2) Market price is to be determined as of the place for tender or, in cases of rejection after arrival or revocation of acceptance, as of the place of arrival.

§2-714. Buyer's Damages for Breach in Regard to Accepted Goods.

(1) Where the buyer has accepted goods and given notification (subsection (3) of Section 2–607) he may recover as damages for any non-conformity of tender the loss resulting in the ordinary course of events from the seller's breach as determined in any manner which is reasonable.

(2) The measure of damages for breach of warranty is the difference at the time and place of acceptance between the value of the goods accepted and the value they would have had if they had been as warranted, unless special circumstances show proximate damages of a different amount.

(3) In a proper case any incidental and consequential damages under the next section may also be recovered.

§2-715. Buyer's Incidental and Consequential Damages.

(1) Incidental damages resulting from the seller's breach include expenses reasonably incurred in inspection, receipt, transportation and care and custody of goods rightfully rejected, any commercially reasonable charges, expenses or commissions in connection with effecting cover and any other reasonable expense incident to the delay or other breach.

(2) Consequential damages resulting from the seller's breach include

(a) any loss resulting from general or particular requirements and needs of which the seller at the time of contracting had reason to know and which could not reasonably be prevented by cover or otherwise; and

(b) injury to person or property proximately resulting from any breach of warranty.

§2-716. Buyer's Right to Specific Performance or Replevin.

(1) Specific performance may be decreed where the goods are unique or in other proper circumstances.

(2) The decree for specific performance may include such terms and conditions as to payment of the price, damages, or other relief as the court may deem just.

(3) The buyer has a right of replevin for goods identified to the contract if after reasonable effort he is unable to effect cover for such goods or the circumstances reasonably indicate that such effort will be unavailing or if the goods have been shipped under reservation and satisfaction of the security interest in them has been made or tendered. In the case of goods bought for personal, family, or household purposes, the buyer's right of replevin vests upon acquisition of a special property, even if the seller had not then repudiated or failed to deliver.

§2-717. Deduction of Damages from the Price.

The buyer on notifying the seller of his intention to do so may deduct all or any part of the damages resulting from any breach of the contract from any part of the price still due under the same contract.

§2-718. Liquidation or Limitation of Damages; Deposits.

(1) Damages for breach by either party may be liquidated in the agreement but only at an amount which is reasonable in the light of the anticipated or actual harm caused by the breach, the difficulties of proof of loss, and the inconvenience or nonfeasibility of otherwise obtaining an adequate remedy. A term fixing unreasonably large liquidated damages is void as a penalty.

(2) Where the seller justifiably withholds delivery of goods because of the buyer's breach, the buyer is entitled to restitution of any amount by which the sum of his payments exceeds

(a) the amount to which the seller is entitled by virtue of terms liquidating the seller's damages in accordance with subsection (1), or

(b) in the absence of such terms, twenty per cent of the value of the total performance for which the buyer is obligated under the contract or $500, whichever is smaller.

(3) The buyer's right to restitution under subsection (2) is subject to offset to the extent that the seller establishes

    (a) a right to recover damages under the provisions of this Article other than subsection (1), and

    (b) the amount or value of any benefits received by the buyer directly or indirectly by reason of the contract.

(4) Where a seller has received payment in goods their reasonable value or the proceeds of their resale shall be treated as payments for the purposes of subsection (2); but if the seller has notice of the buyer's breach before reselling goods received in part performance, his resale is subject to the conditions laid down in this Article on resale by an aggrieved seller (Section 2–706).

§2-719. Contractual Modification or Limitation of Remedy.

(1) Subject to the provisions of subsections (2) and (3) of this section and of the preceding section on liquidation and limitation of damages,

    (a) the agreement may provide for remedies in addition to or in substitution for those provided in this Article and may limit or alter the measure of damages recoverable under this Article, as by limiting the buyer's remedies to return of the goods and repayment of the price or to repair and replacement of non-conforming goods or parts; and

    (b) resort to a remedy as provided is optional unless the remedy is expressly agreed to be exclusive, in which case it is the sole remedy.

(2) Where circumstances cause an exclusive or limited remedy to fail of its essential purpose, remedy may be had as provided in this Act.

(3) Consequential damages may be limited or excluded unless the limitation or exclusion is unconscionable. Limitation of consequential damages for injury to the person in the case of consumer goods is prima facie unconscionable but limitation of damages where the loss is commercial is not.

§2-720. Effect of "Cancellation" or "Rescission" on Claims for Antecedent Breach.
Unless the contrary intention clearly appears, expressions of "cancellation" or "rescission" of the contract or the like shall not be construed as a renunciation or discharge of any claim in damages for an antecedent breach.

§2-721. Remedies for Fraud.
Remedies for material misrepresentation or fraud include all remedies available under this Article for non-fraudulent breach. Neither rescission or a claim for rescission of the contract for sale nor rejection or return of the goods shall bar or be deemed inconsistent with a claim for damages or other remedy.

§2-722. Who Can Sue Third Parties for Injury to Goods.
Where a third party so deals with goods which have been identified to a contract for sale as to cause actionable injury to a party to that contract

    (a) a right of action against the third party is in either party to the contract for sale who has title to or a security interest or a special property or an insurable interest in the goods; and if the goods have been destroyed or converted a right of action is also in the party who either bore the risk of loss under the contract for sale or has since the injury assumed that risk as against the other;

    (b) if at the time of the injury the party plaintiff did not bear the risk of loss as against the other party to the contract for sale and there is no arrangement between them for disposition of the recovery, his suit or settlement is, subject to his own interest, as a fiduciary for the other party to the contract;

    (c) either party may with the consent of the other sue for the benefit of whom it may concern.

§2-723. Proof of Market Price: Time and Place.

(1) If an action based on anticipatory repudiation comes to trial before the time for performance with respect to some or all of the goods, any damages based on market price (Section 2–708 or Section 2–713) shall be determined according to the price of such goods prevailing at the time when the aggrieved party learned of the repudiation.

(2) If evidence of a price prevailing at the times or places described in this Article is not readily available the price prevailing within any reasonable time before or after the time described or at any other place which in commercial judgment or under usage of trade would serve as a reasonable substitute for the one described may be used, making any proper allowance for the cost of transporting the goods to or from such other place.

(3) Evidence of a relevant price prevailing at a time or place other than the one described in this Article offered by one party is not admissible unless and until he has given the other party such notice as the court finds sufficient to prevent unfair surprise.

§2-724. Admissibility of Market Quotations.
Whenever the prevailing price or value of any goods regularly bought and sold in any established commodity market is in issue, reports in official publications or trade journals or in newspapers or periodicals of general circulation published as the reports of such market shall be admissible in evidence. The circumstances of the preparation

of such a report may be shown to affect its weight but not its admissibility.

§2-725. Statute of Limitations in Contracts for Sale.

(1) An action for breach of any contract for sale must be commenced within four years after the cause of action has accrued. By the original agreement the parties may reduce the period of limitation to not less than one year but may not extend it.

(2) A cause of action accrues when the breach occurs, regardless of the aggrieved party's lack of knowledge of the breach. A breach of warranty occurs when tender of delivery is made, except that where a warranty explicitly extends to future performance of the goods and discovery of the breach must await the time of such performance the cause of action accrues when the breach is or should have been discovered.

(3) Where an action commenced within the time limited by subsection (1) is so terminated as to leave available a remedy by another action for the same breach such other action may be commenced after the expiration of the time limited and within six months after the termination of the first action unless the termination resulted from voluntary discontinuance or from dismissal for failure or neglect to prosecute.

(4) This section does not alter the law on tolling of the statute of limitations nor does it apply to causes of action which have accrued before this Act becomes effective.

Part 1: General Provisions

§2A-101. Short Title. This Article shall be known and may be cited as the Uniform Commercial Code—Leases.

§2A-102. Scope. This Article applies to any transaction, regardless of form, that creates a lease.

§2A-103. Definitions and Index of Definitions.

(1) In this Article unless the context otherwise requires:

(a) "Buyer in ordinary course of business" means a person who in good faith and without knowledge that the sale to him [or her] is in violation of the ownership rights or security interest or leasehold interest of a third party in the goods buys in ordinary course from a person in the business of selling goods of that kind but does not include a pawnbroker. "Buying" may be for cash or by exchange of other property or on secured or unsecured credit and includes receiving goods or documents of title under a pre-existing contract for sale but does not include a transfer in bulk or as security for or in total or partial satisfaction of a money debt.

(b) "Cancellation" occurs when either party puts an end to the lease contract for default by the other party.

(c) "Commercial unit" means such a unit of goods as by commercial usage is a single whole for purposes of lease and division of which materially impairs its character or value on the market or in use. A commercial unit may be a single article, as a machine, or a set of articles, as a suite of furniture or a line of machinery, or a quantity, as a gross or carload, or any other unit treated in use or in the relevant market as a single whole.

(d) "Conforming" goods or performance under a lease contract means goods or performance that are in accordance with the obligations under the lease contract.

(e) "Consumer lease" means a lease that a lessor regularly engaged in the business of leasing or selling makes to a lessee who is an individual and who takes under the lease primarily for a personal, family, or household purpose [, if the total payments to be made under the lease contract, excluding payments for options to renew or buy, do not exceed $_____].

(f) "Fault" means wrongful act, omission, breach, or default.

(g) "Finance lease" means a lease with respect to which:

(i) the lessor does not select, manufacture, or supply the goods;

(ii) the lessor acquires the goods or the right to possession and use of the goods in connection with the lease; and

(iii) one of the following occurs:

(A) the lessee receives a copy of the contract by which the lessor acquired the goods or the right to possession and use of the goods before signing the lease contract;

(B) the lessee's approval of the contract by which the lessor acquired the goods or the right to possession and use of the goods is a condition to effectiveness of the lease contract;

(C) the lessee, before signing the lease contract, receives an accurate and complete statement designating the promises and warranties, and any disclaimers of warranties, limitations or modifications of remedies, or liquidated damages, including those of a third party, such as the manufacturer of the goods, provided to the lessor by the person supplying the goods in connection with or as part of the contract by which the lessor acquired the goods or the right to possession and use of the goods; or

   (D) if the lease is not a consumer lease, the lessor, before the lessee signs the lease contract, informs the lessee in writing (a) of the identity of the person supplying the goods to the lessor, unless the lessee has selected that person and directed the lessor to acquire the goods or the right to possession and use of the goods from that person, (b) that the lessee is entitled under this Article to the promises and warranties, including those of any third party, provided to the lessor by the person supplying the goods in connection with or as part of the contract by which the lessor acquired the goods or the right to possession and use of the goods, and (c) that the lessee may communicate with the person supplying the goods to the lessor and receive an accurate and complete statement of those promises and warranties, including any disclaimers and limitations of them or of remedies.

(h) "Goods" means all things that are movable at the time of identification to the lease contract, or are fixtures (Section 2A–309), but the term does not include money, documents, instruments, accounts, chattel paper, general intangibles, or minerals or the like, including oil and gas, before extraction. The term also includes the unborn young of animals.

(i) "Installment lease contract" means a lease contract that authorizes or requires the delivery of goods in separate lots to be separately accepted, even though the lease contract contains a clause "each delivery is a separate lease" or its equivalent.

(j) "Lease" means a transfer of the right to possession and use of goods for a term in return for consideration, but a sale, including a sale on approval or a sale or return, or retention or creation of a security interest is not a lease. Unless the context clearly indicates otherwise, the term includes a sublease.

(k) "Lease agreement" means the bargain, with respect to the lease, of the lessor and the lessee in fact as found in their language or by implication from other circumstances including course of dealing or usage of trade or course of performance as provided in this Article. Unless the context clearly indicates otherwise, the term includes a sublease agreement.

(l) "Lease contract" means the total legal obligation that results from the lease agreement as affected by this Article and any other applicable rules of law. Unless the context clearly indicates otherwise, the term includes a sublease contract.

(m) "Leasehold interest" means the interest of the lessor or the lessee under a lease contract.

(n) "Lessee" means a person who acquires the right to possession and use of goods under a lease. Unless the context clearly indicates otherwise, the term includes a sublessee.

(o) "Lessee in ordinary course of business" means a person who in good faith and without knowledge that the lease to him [or her] is in violation of the ownership rights or security interest or leasehold interest of a third party in the goods, leases in ordinary course from a person in the business of selling or leasing goods of that kind but does not include a pawnbroker. "Leasing" may be for cash or by exchange of other property or on secured or unsecured credit and includes receiving goods or documents of title under a pre-existing lease contract but does not include a transfer in bulk or as security for or in total or partial satisfaction of a money debt.

(p) "Lessor" means a person who transfers the right to possession and use of goods under a lease. Unless the context clearly indicates otherwise, the term includes a sublessor.

(q) "Lessor's residual interest" means the lessor's interest in the goods after expiration, termination, or cancellation of the lease contract.

(r) "Lien" means a charge against or interest in goods to secure payment of a debt or performance of an obligation, but the term does not include a security interest.

(s) "Lot" means a parcel or a single article that is the subject matter of a separate lease or delivery, whether or not it is sufficient to perform the lease contract.

(t) "Merchant lessee" means a lessee that is a merchant with respect to goods of the kind subject to the lease.

(u) "Present value" means the amount as of a date certain of one or more sums payable in the future, discounted to the date certain. The discount is determined by the interest rate specified by the parties if the rate was not manifestly unreasonable at the time the transaction was entered into; otherwise, the discount is determined by a commercially reasonable rate that takes into account the facts and circumstances of each case at the time the transaction was entered into.

(v) "Purchase" includes taking by sale, lease, mortgage, security interest, pledge, gift, or any other voluntary transaction creating an interest in goods.

(w) "Sublease" means a lease of goods the right to possession and use of which was acquired by the lessor as a lessee under an existing lease.

(x) "Supplier" means a person from whom a lessor buys or leases goods to be leased under a finance lease.

(y) "Supply contract" means a contract under which a lessor buys or leases goods to be leased.

(z) "Termination" occurs when either party pursuant to a power created by agreement or law puts an end to the lease contract otherwise than for default.

(2) Other definitions applying to this Article and the sections in which they appear are:

"Accessions". Section 2A–310(1).

"Construction mortgage". Section 2A–309(1)(d).

"Encumbrance". Section 2A–309(1)(e).

"Fixtures". Section 2A–309(1)(a).

"Fixture filing". Section 2A–309(1)(b).

"Purchase money lease". Section 2A–309(1)(c).

(3) The following definitions in other Articles apply to this Article:

"Account". Section 9–106.

"Between merchants". Section 2–104(3).

"Buyer". Section 2–103(1)(a).

"Chattel paper". Section 9–105(1)(b).

"Consumer goods". Section 9–109(1).

"Document". Section 9–105(1)(f).

"Entrusting". Section 2–403(3).

"General intangibles". Section 9–106.

"Good faith". Section 2–103(1)(b).

"Instrument". Section 9–105(1)(i).

"Merchant". Section 2–104(1).

"Mortgage". Section 9–105(1)(j).

"Pursuant to commitment". Section 9–105(1)(k).

"Receipt". Section 2–103(1)(c).

"Sale". Section 2–106(1).

"Sale on approval". Section 2–326.

"Sale or return". Section 2–326.

"Seller". Section 2–103(1)(d).

(4) In addition Article 1 contains general definitions and principles of construction and interpretation applicable throughout this Article.

§2A-104. Leases Subject to Other Law.

(1) A lease, although subject to this Article, is also subject to any applicable:

(a) certificate of title statute of this State: (list any certificate of title statutes covering automobiles,

trailers, mobile homes, boats, farm tractors, and the like);

(b) certificate of title statute of another jurisdiction (Section 2A–105); or

(c) consumer protection statute of this State, or final consumer protection decision of a court of this State existing on the effective date of this Article.

(2) In case of conflict between this Article, other than Sections 2A–105, 2A–304(3), and 2A–305(3), and a statute or decision referred to in subsection (1), the statute or decision controls.

(3) Failure to comply with an applicable law has only the effect specified therein.

§2A-105. Territorial Application of Article to Goods Covered by Certificate of Title.
Subject to the provisions of Sections 2A-304(3) and 2A-305(3), with respect to goods covered by a certificate of title issued under a statute of this State or of another jurisdiction, compliance and the effect of compliance or noncompliance with a certificate of title statute are governed by the law (including the conflict of laws rules) of the jurisdiction issuing the certificate until the earlier of (a) surrender of the certificate, or (b) four months after the goods are removed from that jurisdiction and thereafter until a new certificate of title is issued by another jurisdiction.

§2A-106. Limitation on Power of Parties to Consumer Lease to Choose Applicable Law and Judicial Forum.

(1) If the law chosen by the parties to a consumer lease is that of a jurisdiction other than a jurisdiction in which the lessee resides at the time the lease agreement becomes enforceable or within 30 days thereafter or in which the goods are to be used, the choice is not enforceable.

(2) If the judicial forum chosen by the parties to a consumer lease is a forum that would not otherwise have jurisdiction over the lessee, the choice is not enforceable.

§2A-107. Waiver or Renunciation of Claim or Right After Default.
Any claim or right arising out of an alleged default or breach of warranty may be discharged in whole or in part without consideration by a written waiver or renunciation signed and delivered by the aggrieved party.

§2A-108. Unconscionability.

(1) If the court as a matter of law finds a lease contract or any clause of a lease contract to have been unconscionable at the time it was made the court may refuse to enforce the lease contract, or it may enforce the remainder of the lease contract without the unconscionable clause, or it may so limit the

application of any unconscionable clause as to avoid any unconscionable result.

(2) With respect to a consumer lease, if the court as a matter of law finds that a lease contract or any clause of a lease contract has been induced by unconscionable conduct or that unconscionable conduct has occurred in the collection of a claim arising from a lease contract, the court may grant appropriate relief.

(3) Before making a finding of unconscionability under subsection (1) or (2), the court, on its own motion or that of a party, shall afford the parties a reasonable opportunity to present evidence as to the setting, purpose, and effect of the lease contract or clause thereof, or of the conduct.

(4) In an action in which the lessee claims unconscionability with respect to a consumer lease:

   (a) If the court finds unconscionability under subsection (1) or (2), the court shall award reasonable attorney's fees to the lessee.

   (b) If the court does not find unconscionability and the lessee claiming unconscionability has brought or maintained an action he [or she] knew to be groundless, the court shall award reasonable attorney's fees to the party against whom the claim is made.

   (c) In determining attorney's fees, the amount of the recovery on behalf of the claimant under subsections (1) and (2) is not controlling.

§2A-109. Option to Accelerate at Will.

(1) A term providing that one party or his [or her] successor in interest may accelerate payment or performance or require collateral or additional collateral "at will" or "when he [or she] deems himself [or herself] insecure" or in words of similar import must be construed to mean that he [or she] has power to do so only if he [or she] in good faith believes that the prospect of payment or performance is impaired.

(2) With respect to a consumer lease, the burden of establishing good faith under subsection (1) is on the party who exercised the power; otherwise the burden of establishing lack of good faith is on the party against whom the power has been exercised.

Part 2: Formation and Construction of Lease Contract

§2A-201. Statute of Frauds.

(1) A lease contract is not enforceable by way of action or defense unless:

   (a) the total payments to be made under the lease contract, excluding payments for options to renew or buy, are less than $1,000; or

   (b) there is a writing, signed by the party against whom enforcement is sought or by that party's authorized agent, sufficient to indicate that a lease contract has been made between the parties and to describe the goods leased and the lease term.

(2) Any description of leased goods or of the lease term is sufficient and satisfies subsection (1)(b), whether or not it is specific, if it reasonably identifies what is described.

(3) A writing is not insufficient because it omits or incorrectly states a term agreed upon, but the lease contract is not enforceable under subsection (1)(b) beyond the lease term and the quantity of goods shown in the writing.

(4) A lease contract that does not satisfy the requirements of subsection (1), but which is valid in other respects, is enforceable:

   (a) if the goods are to be specially manufactured or obtained for the lessee and are not suitable for lease or sale to others in the ordinary course of the lessor's business, and the lessor, before notice of repudiation is received and under circumstances that reasonably indicate that the goods are for the lessee, has made either a substantial beginning of their manufacture or commitments for their procurement;

   (b) if the party against whom enforcement is sought admits in that party's pleading, testimony or otherwise in court that a lease contract was made, but the lease contract is not enforceable under this provision beyond the quantity of goods admitted; or

   (c) with respect to goods that have been received and accepted by the lessee.

(5) The lease term under a lease contract referred to in subsection (4) is:

   (a) if there is a writing signed by the party against whom enforcement is sought or by that party's authorized agent specifying the lease term, the term so specified;

   (b) if the party against whom enforcement is sought admits in that party's pleading, testimony, or otherwise in court a lease term, the term so admitted; or

   (c) a reasonable lease term.

§2A-202. Final Written Expression: Parol or Extrinsic Evidence.
Terms with respect to which the confirmatory memoranda of the parties agree or which are otherwise set forth in a writing intended by the parties as a final expression of their agreement with respect to such terms as are included therein may not be contradicted by evidence of any prior agreement or of a contemporaneous oral agreement but may be explained or supplemented:

   (a) by course of dealing or usage of trade or by course of performance; and

(b) by evidence of consistent additional terms unless the court finds the writing to have been intended also as a complete and exclusive statement of the terms of the agreement.

§2A-203. Seals Inoperative.
The affixing of a seal to a writing evidencing a lease contract or an offer to enter into a lease contract does not render the writing a sealed instrument and the law with respect to sealed instruments does not apply to the lease contract or offer.

§2A-204. Formation in General.
(1) A lease contract may be made in any manner sufficient to show agreement, including conduct by both parties which recognizes the existence of a lease contract.

(2) An agreement sufficient to constitute a lease contract may be found although the moment of its making is undetermined.

(3) Although one or more terms are left open, a lease contract does not fail for indefiniteness if the parties have intended to make a lease contract and there is a reasonably certain basis for giving an appropriate remedy.

§2A-205. Firm Offers.
An offer by a merchant to lease goods to or from another person in a signed writing that by its terms gives assurance it will be held open is not revocable, for lack of consideration, during the time stated or, if no time is stated, for a reasonable time, but in no event may the period of irrevocability exceed 3 months. Any such term of assurance on a form supplied by the offeree must be separately signed by the offeror.

§2A-206. Offer and Acceptance in Formation of Lease Contract.
(1) Unless otherwise unambiguously indicated by the language or circumstances, an offer to make a lease contract must be construed as inviting acceptance in any manner and by any medium reasonable in the circumstances.

(2) If the beginning of a requested performance is a reasonable mode of acceptance, an offeror who is not notified of acceptance within a reasonable time may treat the offer as having lapsed before acceptance.

§2A-207. Course of Performance or Practical Construction.
(1) If a lease contract involves repeated occasions for performance by either party with knowledge of the nature of the performance and opportunity for objection to it by the other, any course of performance accepted or acquiesced in without objection is relevant to determine the meaning of the lease agreement.

(2) The express terms of a lease agreement and any course of performance, as well as any course of dealing and usage of trade, must be construed whenever reasonable as consistent with each other; but if that construction is unreasonable, express terms control course of performance, course of performance controls both course of dealing and usage of trade, and course of dealing controls usage of trade.

(3) Subject to the provisions of Section 2A–208 on modification and waiver, course of performance is relevant to show a waiver or modification of any term inconsistent with the course of performance.

§2A-208. Modification, Rescission, and Waiver.
(1) An agreement modifying a lease contract needs no consideration to be binding.

(2) A signed lease agreement that excludes modification or rescission except by a signed writing may not be otherwise modified or rescinded, but, except as between merchants, such a requirement on a form supplied by a merchant must be separately signed by the other party.

(3) Although an attempt at modification or rescission does not satisfy the requirements of subsection (2), it may operate as a waiver.

(4) A party who has made a waiver affecting an executory portion of a lease contract may retract the waiver by reasonable notification received by the other party that strict performance will be required of any term waived, unless the retraction would be unjust in view of a material change of position in reliance on the waiver.

§2A-209. Lessee under Finance Lease as Beneficiary of Supply Contract.
(1) The benefit of a supplier's promises to the lessor under the supply contract and of all warranties, whether express or implied, including those of any third party provided in connection with or as part of the supply contract, extends to the lessee to the extent of the lessee's leasehold interest under a finance lease related to the supply contract, but is subject to the terms of the warranty and of the supply contract and all defenses or claims arising therefrom.

(2) The extension of the benefit of a supplier's promises and of warranties to the lessee (Section 2A–209(1)) does not: (i) modify the rights and obligations of the parties to the supply contract, whether arising therefrom or otherwise, or (ii) impose any duty or liability under the supply contract on the lessee.

(3) Any modification or rescission of the supply contract by the supplier and the lessor is effective between the supplier and the lessee unless, before the modification or rescission, the supplier has received notice that the lessee has entered into a finance lease related to the supply contract. If the modification or rescission is effective between the supplier and the lessee,

the lessor is deemed to have assumed, in addition to the obligations of the lessor to the lessee under the lease contract, promises of the supplier to the lessor and warranties that were so modified or rescinded as they existed and were available to the lessee before modification or rescission.

(4) In addition to the extension of the benefit of the supplier's promises and of warranties to the lessee under subsection (1), the lessee retains all rights that the lessee may have against the supplier which arise from an agreement between the lessee and the supplier or under other law.

§2A-210. Express Warranties.

(1) Express warranties by the lessor are created as follows:

   (a) Any affirmation of fact or promise made by the lessor to the lessee which relates to the goods and becomes part of the basis of the bargain creates an express warranty that the goods will conform to the affirmation or promise.

   (b) Any description of the goods which is made part of the basis of the bargain creates an express warranty that the goods will conform to the description.

   (c) Any sample or model that is made part of the basis of the bargain creates an express warranty that the whole of the goods will conform to the sample or model.

(2) It is not necessary to the creation of an express warranty that the lessor use formal words, such as "warrant" or "guarantee," or that the lessor have a specific intention to make a warranty, but an affirmation merely of the value of the goods or a statement purporting to be merely the lessor's opinion or commendation of the goods does not create a warranty.

§2A-211. Warranties against Interference and against Infringement; Lessee's Obligation against Infringement.

(1) There is in a lease contract a warranty that for the lease term no person holds a claim to or interest in the goods that arose from an act or omission of the lessor, other than a claim by way of infringement or the like, which will interfere with the lessee's enjoyment of its leasehold interest.

(2) Except in a finance lease there is in a lease contract by a lessor who is a merchant regularly dealing in goods of the kind a warranty that the goods are delivered free of the rightful claim of any person by way of infringement or the like.

(3) A lessee who furnishes specifications to a lessor or a supplier shall hold the lessor and the supplier harmless against any claim by way of infringement or the like that arises out of compliance with the specifications.

§2A-212. Implied Warranty of Merchantability.

(1) Except in a finance lease, a warranty that the goods will be merchantable is implied in a lease contract if the lessor is a merchant with respect to goods of that kind.

(2) Goods to be merchantable must be at least such as

   (a) pass without objection in the trade under the description in the lease agreement;

   (b) in the case of fungible goods, are of fair average quality within the description;

   (c) are fit for the ordinary purposes for which goods of that type are used;

   (d) run, within the variation permitted by the lease agreement, of even kind, quality, and quantity within each unit and among all units involved;

   (e) are adequately contained, packaged, and labeled as the lease agreement may require; and

   (f) conform to any promises or affirmations of fact made on the container or label.

(3) Other implied warranties may arise from course of dealing or usage of trade.

§2A-213. Implied Warranty of Fitness for Particular Purpose.
Except in a finance lease, if the lessor at the time the lease contract is made has reason to know of any particular purpose for which the goods are required and that the lessee is relying on the lessor's skill or judgment to select or furnish suitable goods, there is in the lease contract an implied warranty that the goods will be fit for that purpose.

§2A-214. Exclusion or Modification of Warranties.

(1) Words or conduct relevant to the creation of an express warranty and words or conduct tending to negate or limit a warranty must be construed wherever reasonable as consistent with each other; but, subject to the provisions of Section 2A–202 on parol or extrinsic evidence, negation or limitation is inoperative to the extent that the construction is unreasonable.

(2) Subject to subsection (3), to exclude or modify the implied warranty of merchantability or any part of it the language must mention "merchantability", be by a writing, and be conspicuous. Subject to subsection (3), to exclude or modify any implied warranty of fitness the exclusion must be by a writing and be conspicuous. Language to exclude all implied warranties of fitness is sufficient if it is in writing, is conspicuous and states, for example, "There is no warranty that the goods will be fit for a particular purpose".

(3) Notwithstanding subsection (2), but subject to subsection (4),

   (a) unless the circumstances indicate otherwise, all implied warranties are excluded by expressions like "as is," or "with all faults," or by other language that in common understanding calls the lessee's attention to the exclusion of warranties and makes plain that there is no implied warranty, if in writing and conspicuous;

(b) if the lessee before entering into the lease contract has examined the goods or the sample or model as fully as desired or has refused to examine the goods, there is no implied warranty with regard to defects that an examination ought in the circumstances to have revealed; and

(c) an implied warranty may also be excluded or modified by course of dealing, course of performance, or usage of trade.

(4) To exclude or modify a warranty against interference or against infringement (Section 2A–211) or any part of it, the language must be specific, be by a writing, and be conspicuous, unless the circumstances, including course of performance, course of dealing, or usage of trade, give the lessee reason to know that the goods are being leased subject to a claim or interest of any person.

§2A-215. Cumulation and Conflict of Warranties Express or Implied.
Warranties, whether express or implied, must be construed as consistent with each other and as cumulative, but if that construction is unreasonable, the intention of the parties determines which warranty is dominant. In ascertaining that intention the following rules apply:

(a) Exact or technical specifications displace an inconsistent sample or model or general language of description.

(b) A sample from an existing bulk displaces inconsistent general language of description.

(c) Express warranties displace inconsistent implied warranties other than an implied warranty of fitness for a particular purpose.

§2A-216. Third-Party Beneficiaries of Express and Implied Warranties.

Alternative A—A warranty to or for the benefit of a lessee under this Article, whether express or implied, extends to any natural person who is in the family or household of the lessee or who is a guest in the lessee's home if it is reasonable to expect that such person may use, consume, or be affected by the goods and who is injured in person by breach of the warranty. This section does not displace principles of law and equity that extend a warranty to or for the benefit of a lessee to other persons. The operation of this section may not be excluded, modified, or limited, but an exclusion, modification, or limitation of the warranty, including any with respect to rights and remedies, effective against the lessee is also effective against any beneficiary designated under this section.

Alternative B—A warranty to or for the benefit of a lessee under this Article, whether express or implied, extends to any natural person who may reasonably be expected to use, consume, or be affected by the goods and who is injured in person by breach of the warranty. This section does not displace principles of law and equity that extend a warranty to or for the benefit of a lessee to other persons. The operation of this section may not be excluded, modified, or limited, but an exclusion, modification, or limitation of the warranty, including any with respect to rights and remedies, effective against the lessee is also effective against the beneficiary designated under this section.

Alternative C—A warranty to or for the benefit of a lessee under this Article, whether express or implied, extends to any person who may reasonably be expected to use, consume, or be affected by the goods and who is injured by breach of the warranty. The operation of this section may not be excluded, modified, or limited with respect to injury to the person of an individual to whom the warranty extends, but an exclusion, modification, or limitation of the warranty, including any with respect to rights and remedies, effective against the lessee is also effective against the beneficiary designated under this section.

§2A-217. Identification.
Identification of goods as goods to which a lease contract refers may be made at any time and in any manner explicitly agreed to by the parties. In the absence of explicit agreement, identification occurs:

(a) when the lease contract is made if the lease contract is for a lease of goods that are existing and identified;

(b) when the goods are shipped, marked, or otherwise designated by the lessor as goods to which the lease contract refers, if the lease contract is for a lease of goods that are not existing and identified; or

(c) when the young are conceived, if the lease contract is for a lease of unborn young of animals.

§2A-218. Insurance and Proceeds.

(1) A lessee obtains an insurable interest when existing goods are identified to the lease contract even though the goods identified are nonconforming and the lessee has an option to reject them.

(2) If a lessee has an insurable interest only by reason of the lessor's identification of the goods, the lessor, until default or insolvency or notification to the lessee that identification is final, may substitute other goods for those identified.

(3) Notwithstanding a lessee's insurable interest under subsections (1) and (2), the lessor retains an insurable interest until an option to buy has been exercised by the lessee and risk of loss has passed to the lessee.

(4) Nothing in this section impairs any insurable interest recognized under any other statute or rule of law.

(5) The parties by agreement may determine that one or more parties have an obligation to obtain and pay for insurance covering the goods and by agreement may determine the beneficiary of the proceeds of the insurance.

§2A-219. Risk of Loss.

(1) Except in the case of a finance lease, risk of loss is retained by the lessor and does not pass to the lessee. In the case of a finance lease, risk of loss passes to the lessee.

(2) Subject to the provisions of this Article on the effect of default on risk of loss (Section 2A–220), if risk of loss is to pass to the lessee and the time of passage is not stated, the following rules apply:

    (a) If the lease contract requires or authorizes the goods to be shipped by carrier

        (i) and it does not require delivery at a particular destination, the risk of loss passes to the lessee when the goods are duly delivered to the carrier; but

        (ii) if it does require delivery at a particular destination and the goods are there duly tendered while in the possession of the carrier, the risk of loss passes to the lessee when the goods are there duly so tendered as to enable the lessee to take delivery.

    (b) If the goods are held by a bailee to be delivered without being moved, the risk of loss passes to the lessee on acknowledgment by the bailee of the lessee's right to possession of the goods.

    (c) In any case not within subsection (a) or (b), the risk of loss passes to the lessee on the lessee's receipt of the goods if the lessor, or, in the case of a finance lease, the supplier, is a merchant; otherwise the risk passes to the lessee on tender of delivery.

§2A-220. Effect of Default on Risk of Loss.

(1) Where risk of loss is to pass to the lessee and the time of passage is not stated:

    (a) If a tender or delivery of goods so fails to conform to the lease contract as to give a right of rejection, the risk of their loss remains with the lessor, or, in the case of a finance lease, the supplier, until cure or acceptance.

    (b) If the lessee rightfully revokes acceptance, he [or she], to the extent of any deficiency in his [or her] effective insurance coverage, may treat the risk of loss as having remained with the lessor from the beginning.

(2) Whether or not risk of loss is to pass to the lessee, if the lessee as to conforming goods already identified to a lease contract repudiates or is otherwise in default under the lease contract, the lessor, or, in the case of a finance lease, the supplier, to the extent of any deficiency in his [or her] effective insurance coverage may treat the risk of loss as resting on the lessee for a commercially reasonable time.

§2A-221. Casualty to Identified Goods.
If a lease contract requires goods identified when the lease contract is made, and the goods suffer casualty without fault of the lessee, the lessor or the supplier before delivery, or the goods suffer casualty before risk of loss passes to the lessee pursuant to the lease agreement or Section 2A-219, then:

(a) if the loss is total, the lease contract is avoided; and

(b) if the loss is partial or the goods have so deteriorated as to no longer conform to the lease contract, the lessee may nevertheless demand inspection and at his [or her] option either treat the lease contract as avoided or, except in a finance lease that is not a consumer lease, accept the goods with due allowance from the rent payable for the balance of the lease term for the deterioration or the deficiency in quantity but without further right against the lessor.

Part 3: Effect of Lease Contract

§2A-301. Enforceability of Lease Contract.
Except as otherwise provided in this Article, a lease contract is effective and enforceable according to its terms between the parties, against purchasers of the goods and against creditors of the parties.

§2A-302. Title to and Possession of Goods.
Except as otherwise provided in this Article, each provision of this Article applies whether the lessor or a third party has title to the goods, and whether the lessor, the lessee, or a third party has possession of the goods, notwithstanding any statute or rule of law that possession or the absence of possession is fraudulent.

§2A-303. Alienability of Party's Interest Under Lease Contract or of Lessor's Residual Interest in Goods; Delegation of Performance; Transfer of Rights.

(1) As used in this section, "creation of a security interest" includes the sale of a lease contract that is subject to Article 9, Secured Transactions, by reason of Section 9–102(1)(b).

(2) Except as provided in subsections (3) and (4), a provision in a lease agreement which (i) prohibits the voluntary or involuntary transfer, including a transfer by sale, sublease, creation or enforcement of a security interest, or attachment, levy, or other judicial process, of an interest of a party under the lease

contract or of the lessor's residual interest in the goods, or (ii) makes such a transfer an event of default, gives rise to the rights and remedies provided in subsection (5), but a transfer that is prohibited or is an event of default under the lease agreement is otherwise effective.

(3) A provision in a lease agreement which (i) prohibits the creation or enforcement of a security interest in an interest of a party under the lease contract or in the lessor's residual interest in the goods, or (ii) makes such a transfer an event of default, is not enforceable unless, and then only to the extent that, there is an actual transfer by the lessee of the lessee's right of possession or use of the goods in violation of the provision or an actual delegation of a material performance of either party to the lease contract in violation of the provision. Neither the granting nor the enforcement of a security interest in (i) the lessor's interest under the lease contract or (ii) the lessor's residual interest in the goods is a transfer that materially impairs the prospect of obtaining return performance by, materially changes the duty of, or materially increases the burden or risk imposed on, the lessee within the purview of subsection (5) unless, and then only to the extent that, there is an actual delegation of a material performance of the lessor.

(4) A provision in a lease agreement which (i) prohibits a transfer of a right to damages for default with respect to the whole lease contract or of a right to payment arising out of the transferor's due performance of the transferor's entire obligation, or (ii) makes such a transfer an event of default, is not enforceable, and such a transfer is not a transfer that materially impairs the prospect of obtaining return performance by, materially changes the duty of, or materially increases the burden or risk imposed on, the other party to the lease contract within the purview of subsection (5).

(5) Subject to subsections (3) and (4):

    (a) if a transfer is made which is made an event of default under a lease agreement, the party to the lease contract not making the transfer, unless that party waives the default or otherwise agrees, has the rights and remedies described in Section 2A–501(2);

    (b) if paragraph (a) is not applicable and if a transfer is made that (i) is prohibited under a lease agreement or (ii) materially impairs the prospect of obtaining return performance by, materially changes the duty of, or materially increases the burden or risk imposed on, the other party to the lease contract, unless the party not making the transfer agrees at any time to the transfer in the lease contract or otherwise, then, except as limited by contract, (i) the transferor is liable to the party not making the transfer for damages caused by the transfer to the extent that the damages could not reasonably be prevented by the party not making the transfer and (ii) a court having jurisdiction may grant other appropriate relief, including cancellation of the lease contract or an injunction against the transfer.

(6) A transfer of "the lease" or of "all my rights under the lease", or a transfer in similar general terms, is a transfer of rights and, unless the language or the circumstances, as in a transfer for security, indicate the contrary, the transfer is a delegation of duties by the transferor to the transferee. Acceptance by the transferee constitutes a promise by the transferee to perform those duties. The promise is enforceable by either the transferor or the other party to the lease contract.

(7) Unless otherwise agreed by the lessor and the lessee, a delegation of performance does not relieve the transferor as against the other party of any duty to perform or of any liability for default.

(8) In a consumer lease, to prohibit the transfer of an interest of a party under the lease contract or to make a transfer an event of default, the language must be specific, by a writing, and conspicuous.

§2A-304. Subsequent Lease of Goods by Lessor.

(1) Subject to Section 2A–303, a subsequent lessee from a lessor of goods under an existing lease contract obtains, to the extent of the leasehold interest transferred, the leasehold interest in the goods that the lessor had or had power to transfer, and except as provided in subsection (2) and Section 2A–527(4), takes subject to the existing lease contract. A lessor with voidable title has power to transfer a good leasehold interest to a good faith subsequent lessee for value, but only to the extent set forth in the preceding sentence. If goods have been delivered under a transaction of purchase, the lessor has that power even though:

    (a) the lessor's transferor was deceived as to the identity of the lessor;

    (b) the delivery was in exchange for a check which is later dishonored;

    (c) it was agreed that the transaction was to be a "cash sale"; or

    (d) the delivery was procured through fraud punishable as larcenous under the criminal law.

(2) A subsequent lessee in the ordinary course of business from a lessor who is a merchant dealing in goods of that kind to whom the goods were entrusted by the existing lessee of that lessor before the interest of the subsequent lessee became enforceable against that lessor obtains, to the extent of the leasehold interest transferred, all of that lessor's and the existing

lessee's rights to the goods, and takes free of the existing lease contract.

(3) A subsequent lessee from the lessor of goods that are subject to an existing lease contract and are covered by a certificate of title issued under a statute of this State or of another jurisdiction takes no greater rights than those provided both by this section and by the certificate of title statute.

§2A-305. Sale or Sublease of Goods by Lessee.

(1) Subject to the provisions of Section 2A–303, a buyer or sublessee from the lessee of goods under an existing lease contract obtains, to the extent of the interest transferred, the leasehold interest in the goods that the lessee had or had power to transfer, and except as provided in subsection (2) and Section 2A–511(4), takes subject to the existing lease contract. A lessee with a voidable leasehold interest has power to transfer a good leasehold interest to a good faith buyer for value or a good faith sublessee for value, but only to the extent set forth in the preceding sentence. When goods have been delivered under a transaction of lease the lessee has that power even though:

    (a) the lessor was deceived as to the identity of the lessee;

    (b) the delivery was in exchange for a check which is later dishonored; or

    (c) the delivery was procured through fraud punishable as larcenous under the criminal law.

(2) A buyer in the ordinary course of business or a sublessee in the ordinary course of business from a lessee who is a merchant dealing in goods of that kind to whom the goods were entrusted by the lessor obtains, to the extent of the interest transferred, all of the lessor's and lessee's rights to the goods, and takes free of the existing lease contract.

(3) A buyer or sublessee from the lessee of goods that are subject to an existing lease contract and are covered by a certificate of title issued under a statute of this State or of another jurisdiction takes no greater rights than those provided both by this section and by the certificate of title statute.

§2A-306. Priority of Certain Liens Arising by Operation of Law.
If a person in the ordinary course of his [or her] business furnishes services or materials with respect to goods subject to a lease contract, a lien upon those goods in the possession of that person given by statute or rule of law for those materials or services takes priority over any interest of the lessor or lessee under the lease contract or this Article unless the lien is created by statute and the statute provides otherwise or unless the lien is created by rule of law and the rule of law provides otherwise.

§2A-307. Priority of Liens Arising by Attachment or Levy on, Security Interests in, and Other Claims to Goods.

(1) Except as otherwise provided in Section 2A–306, a creditor of a lessee takes subject to the lease contract.

(2) Except as otherwise provided in subsections (3) and (4) and in Sections 2A–306 and 2A–308, a creditor of a lessor takes subject to the lease contract unless:

    (a) the creditor holds a lien that attached to the goods before the lease contract became enforceable;

    (b) the creditor holds a security interest in the goods and the lessee did not give value and receive delivery of the goods without knowledge of the security interest; or

    (c) the creditor holds a security interest in the goods which was perfected (Section 9–303) before the lease contract became enforceable.

(3) A lessee in the ordinary course of business takes the leasehold interest free of a security interest in the goods created by the lessor even though the security interest is perfected (Section 9–303) and the lessee knows of its existence.

(4) A lessee other than a lessee in the ordinary course of business takes the leasehold interest free of a security interest to the extent that it secures future advances made after the secured party acquires knowledge of the lease or more than 45 days after the lease contract becomes enforceable, whichever first occurs, unless the future advances are made pursuant to a commitment entered into without knowledge of the lease and before the expiration of the 45-day period.

§2A-308. Special Rights of Creditors.

(1) A creditor of a lessor in possession of goods subject to a lease contract may treat the lease contract as void if as against the creditor retention of possession by the lessor is fraudulent under any statute or rule of law, but retention of possession in good faith and current course of trade by the lessor for a commercially reasonable time after the lease contract becomes enforceable is not fraudulent.

(2) Nothing in this Article impairs the rights of creditors of a lessor if the lease contract (a) becomes enforceable, not in current course of trade but in satisfaction of or as security for a pre-existing claim for money, security, or the like, and (b) is made under circumstances which under any statute or rule of law apart from this Article would constitute the transaction a fraudulent transfer or voidable preference.

(3) A creditor of a seller may treat a sale or an identification of goods to a contract for sale as void if as against the creditor retention of possession by the seller is fraudulent under any statute or rule of law, but retention of possession of the goods pursuant to a lease contract entered into by the seller as lessee and

the buyer as lessor in connection with the sale or identification of the goods is not fraudulent if the buyer bought for value and in good faith.

§2A-309. Lessor's and Lessee's Rights When Goods Become Fixtures.

(1) In this section:

   (a) goods are "fixtures" when they become so related to particular real estate that an interest in them arises under real estate law;

   (b) a "fixture filing" is the filing, in the office where a mortgage on the real estate would be filed or recorded, of a financing statement covering goods that are or are to become fixtures and conforming to the requirements of Section 9–402(5);

   (c) a lease is a "purchase money lease" unless the lessee has possession or use of the goods or the right to possession or use of the goods before the lease agreement is enforceable;

   (d) a mortgage is a "construction mortgage" to the extent it secures an obligation incurred for the construction of an improvement on land including the acquisition cost of the land, if the recorded writing so indicates; and

   (e) "encumbrance" includes real estate mortgages and other liens on real estate and all other rights in real estate that are not ownership interests.

(2) Under this Article a lease may be of goods that are fixtures or may continue in goods that become fixtures, but no lease exists under this Article of ordinary building materials incorporated into an improvement on land.

(3) This Article does not prevent creation of a lease of fixtures pursuant to real estate law.

(4) The perfected interest of a lessor of fixtures has priority over a conflicting interest of an encumbrancer or owner of the real estate if:

   (a) the lease is a purchase money lease, the conflicting interest of the encumbrancer or owner arises before the goods become fixtures, the interest of the lessor is perfected by a fixture filing before the goods become fixtures or within ten days thereafter, and the lessee has an interest of record in the real estate or is in possession of the real estate; or

   (b) the interest of the lessor is perfected by a fixture filing before the interest of the encumbrancer or owner is of record, the lessor's interest has priority over any conflicting interest of a predecessor in title of the encumbrancer or owner, and the lessee has an interest of record in the real estate or is in possession of the real estate.

(5) The interest of a lessor of fixtures, whether or not perfected, has priority over the conflicting interest of an encumbrancer or owner of the real estate if:

   (a) the fixtures are readily removable factory or office machines, readily removable equipment that is not primarily used or leased for use in the operation of the real estate, or readily removable replacements of domestic appliances that are goods subject to a consumer lease, and before the goods become fixtures the lease contract is enforceable; or

   (b) the conflicting interest is a lien on the real estate obtained by legal or equitable proceedings after the lease contract is enforceable; or

   (c) the encumbrancer or owner has consented in writing to the lease or has disclaimed an interest in the goods as fixtures; or

   (d) the lessee has a right to remove the goods as against the encumbrancer or owner. If the lessee's right to remove terminates, the priority of the interest of the lessor continues for a reasonable time.

(6) Notwithstanding subsection (4)(a) but otherwise subject to subsections (4) and (5), the interest of a lessor of fixtures, including the lessor's residual interest, is subordinate to the conflicting interest of an encumbrancer of the real estate under a construction mortgage recorded before the goods become fixtures if the goods become fixtures before the completion of the construction. To the extent given to refinance a construction mortgage, the conflicting interest of an encumbrancer of the real estate under a mortgage has this priority to the same extent as the encumbrancer of the real estate under the construction mortgage.

(7) In cases not within the preceding subsections, priority between the interest of a lessor of fixtures, including the lessor's residual interest, and the conflicting interest of an encumbrancer or owner of the real estate who is not the lessee is determined by the priority rules governing conflicting interests in real estate.

(8) If the interest of a lessor of fixtures, including the lessor's residual interest, has priority over all conflicting interests of all owners and encumbrancers of the real estate, the lessor or the lessee may (i) on default, expiration, termination, or cancellation of the lease agreement but subject to the agreement and this Article, or (ii) if necessary to enforce other rights and remedies of the lessor or lessee under this Article, remove the goods from the real estate, free and clear of all conflicting interests of all owners and encumbrancers of the real estate, but the lessor or lessee must reimburse any encumbrancer or owner of the real estate who is not the lessee and who has not otherwise agreed for the cost of repair of any physical injury, but not for any diminution in value of the real estate caused by the absence of the goods removed or by any necessity of replacing them. A person entitled to reimbursement may refuse permission to remove until the party seeking removal gives adequate security for the performance of this obligation.

(9) Even though the lease agreement does not create a security interest, the interest of a lessor of fixtures, including the lessor's residual interest, is perfected by filing a financing statement as a fixture filing for leased goods that are or are to become fixtures in accordance with the relevant provisions of the Article on Secured Transactions (Article 9).

§2A-310. Lessor's and Lessee's Rights When Goods Become Accessions.

(1) Goods are "accessions" when they are installed in or affixed to other goods.

(2) The interest of a lessor or a lessee under a lease contract entered into before the goods became accessions is superior to all interests in the whole except as stated in subsection (4).

(3) The interest of a lessor or a lessee under a lease contract entered into at the time or after the goods became accessions is superior to all subsequently acquired interests in the whole except as stated in subsection (4) but is subordinate to interests in the whole existing at the time the lease contract was made unless the holders of such interests in the whole have in writing consented to the lease or disclaimed an interest in the goods as part of the whole.

(4) The interest of a lessor or a lessee under a lease contract described in subsection (2) or (3) is subordinate to the interest of

   (a) a buyer in the ordinary course of business or a lessee in the ordinary course of business of any interest in the whole acquired after the goods became accessions; or

   (b) a creditor with a security interest in the whole perfected before the lease contract was made to the extent that the creditor makes subsequent advances without knowledge of the lease contract.

(5) When under subsections (2) or (3) and (4) a lessor or a lessee of accessions holds an interest that is superior to all interests in the whole, the lessor or the lessee may (a) on default, expiration, termination, or cancellation of the lease contract by the other party but subject to the provisions of the lease contract and this Article, or (b) if necessary to enforce his [or her] other rights and remedies under this Article, remove the goods from the whole, free and clear of all interests in the whole, but he [or she] must reimburse any holder of an interest in the whole who is not the lessee and who has not otherwise agreed for the cost of repair of any physical injury but not for any diminution in value of the whole caused by the absence of the goods removed or by any necessity for replacing them. A person entitled to reimbursement may refuse permission to remove until the party seeking removal gives adequate security for the performance of this obligation.

§2A-311. Priority Subject to Subordination.
Nothing in this Article prevents subordination by agreement by any person entitled to priority.

Part 4: Performance of Lease Contract: Repudiated, Substituted, and Excused

§2A-401. Insecurity: Adequate Assurance of Performance.

(1) A lease contract imposes an obligation on each party that the other's expectation of receiving due performance will not be impaired.

(2) If reasonable grounds for insecurity arise with respect to the performance of either party, the insecure party may demand in writing adequate assurance of due performance. Until the insecure party receives that assurance, if commercially reasonable the insecure party may suspend any performance for which he [or she] has not already received the agreed return.

(3) A repudiation of the lease contract occurs if assurance of due performance adequate under the circumstances of the particular case is not provided to the insecure party within a reasonable time, not to exceed 30 days after receipt of a demand by the other party.

(4) Between merchants, the reasonableness of grounds for insecurity and the adequacy of any assurance offered must be determined according to commercial standards.

(5) Acceptance of any nonconforming delivery or payment does not prejudice the aggrieved party's right to demand adequate assurance of future performance.

§2A-402. Anticipatory Repudiation.
If either party repudiates a lease contract with respect to a performance not yet due under the lease contract, the loss of which performance will substantially impair the value of the lease contract to the other, the aggrieved party may:

   (a) for a commercially reasonable time, await retraction of repudiation and performance by the repudiating party;

   (b) make demand pursuant to Section 2A–401 and await assurance of future performance adequate under the circumstances of the particular case; or

   (c) resort to any right or remedy upon default under the lease contract or this Article, even though the aggrieved party has notified the repudiating party that the aggrieved party would await the repudiating party's performance and assurance and has urged retraction. In addition, whether or not the aggrieved party is pursuing one of the foregoing remedies, the aggrieved party may suspend performance or, if the aggrieved party is the lessor, proceed in accordance with the provisions of this Article on the lessor's right to identify goods to the lease contract notwithstanding default or to salvage unfinished goods (Section 2A–524).

§2A-403. Retraction of Anticipatory Repudiation.

(1) Until the repudiating party's next performance is due, the repudiating party can retract the repudiation unless, since the repudiation, the aggrieved party has cancelled the lease contract or materially changed the aggrieved party's position or otherwise indicated that the aggrieved party considers the repudiation final.

(2) Retraction may be by any method that clearly indicates to the aggrieved party that the repudiating party intends to perform under the lease contract and includes any assurance demanded under Section 2A–401.

(3) Retraction reinstates a repudiating party's rights under a lease contract with due excuse and allowance to the aggrieved party for any delay occasioned by the repudiation.

§2A-404. Substituted Performance.

(1) If without fault of the lessee, the lessor and the supplier, the agreed berthing, loading, or unloading facilities fail or the agreed type of carrier becomes unavailable or the agreed manner of delivery otherwise becomes commercially impracticable, but a commercially reasonable substitute is available, the substitute performance must be tendered and accepted.

(2) If the agreed means or manner of payment fails because of domestic or foreign governmental regulation:

  (a) the lessor may withhold or stop delivery or cause the supplier to withhold or stop delivery unless the lessee provides a means or manner of payment that is commercially a substantial equivalent; and

  (b) if delivery has already been taken, payment by the means or in the manner provided by the regulation discharges the lessee's obligation unless the regulation is discriminatory, oppressive, or predatory.

§2A-405. Excused Performance. Subject to Section 2A-404 on substituted performance, the following rules apply:

(a) Delay in delivery or nondelivery in whole or in part by a lessor or a supplier who complies with paragraphs (b) and (c) is not a default under the lease contract if performance as agreed has been made impracticable by the occurrence of a contingency the nonoccurrence of which was a basic assumption on which the lease contract was made or by compliance in good faith with any applicable foreign or domestic governmental regulation or order, whether or not the regulation or order later proves to be invalid.

(b) If the causes mentioned in paragraph (a) affect only part of the lessor's or the supplier's capacity to perform, he [or she] shall allocate production and deliveries among his [or her] customers but at his [or her] option may include regular customers not then under contract for sale or lease as well as his [or her] own requirements for further manufacture. He [or she] may so allocate in any manner that is fair and reasonable.

(c) The lessor seasonably shall notify the lessee and in the case of a finance lease the supplier seasonably shall notify the lessor and the lessee, if known, that there will be delay or nondelivery and, if allocation is required under paragraph (b), of the estimated quota thus made available for the lessee.

§2A-406. Procedure on Excused Performance.

(1) If the lessee receives notification of a material or indefinite delay or an allocation justified under Section 2A–405, the lessee may by written notification to the lessor as to any goods involved, and with respect to all of the goods if under an installment lease contract the value of the whole lease contract is substantially impaired (Section 2A–510):

  (a) terminate the lease contract (Section 2A–505(2)); or

  (b) except in a finance lease that is not a consumer lease, modify the lease contract by accepting the available quota in substitution, with due allowance from the rent payable for the balance of the lease term for the deficiency but without further right against the lessor.

(2) If, after receipt of a notification from the lessor under Section 2A–405, the lessee fails so to modify the lease agreement within a reasonable time not exceeding 30 days, the lease contract lapses with respect to any deliveries affected.

§2A-407. Irrevocable Promises: Finance Leases.

(1) In the case of a finance lease that is not a consumer lease the lessee's promises under the lease contract become irrevocable and independent upon the lessee's acceptance of the goods.

(2) A promise that has become irrevocable and independent under subsection (1):

  (a) is effective and enforceable between the parties, and by or against third parties including assignees of the parties; and

  (b) is not subject to cancellation, termination, modification, repudiation, excuse, or substitution without the consent of the party to whom the promise runs.

(3) This section does not affect the validity under any other law of a covenant in any lease contract making the lessee's promises irrevocable and independent upon the lessee's acceptance of the goods.

Part 5: Default

A. In General

§2A-501. Default: Procedure.

(1) Whether the lessor or the lessee is in default under a lease contract is determined by the lease agreement and this Article.

(2) If the lessor or the lessee is in default under the lease contract, the party seeking enforcement has rights and remedies as provided in this Article and, except as limited by this Article, as provided in the lease agreement.

(3) If the lessor or the lessee is in default under the lease contract, the party seeking enforcement may reduce the party's claim to judgment, or otherwise enforce the lease contract by self-help or any available judicial procedure or nonjudicial procedure, including administrative proceeding, arbitration, or the like, in accordance with this Article.

(4) Except as otherwise provided in Section 1–106(1) or this Article or the lease agreement, the rights and remedies referred to in subsections (2) and (3) are cumulative.

(5) If the lease agreement covers both real property and goods, the party seeking enforcement may proceed under this Part as to the goods, or under other applicable law as to both the real property and the goods in accordance with that party's rights and remedies in respect of the real property, in which case this Part does not apply.

§2A-502. Notice after Default.
Except as otherwise provided in this Article or the lease agreement, the lessor or lessee in default under the lease contract is not entitled to notice of default or notice of enforcement from the other party to the lease agreement.

§2A-503. Modification or Impairment of Rights and Remedies.

(1) Except as otherwise provided in this Article, the lease agreement may include rights and remedies for default in addition to or in substitution for those provided in this Article and may limit or alter the measure of damages recoverable under this Article.

(2) Resort to a remedy provided under this Article or in the lease agreement is optional unless the remedy is expressly agreed to be exclusive. If circumstances cause an exclusive or limited remedy to fail of its essential purpose, or provision for an exclusive remedy is unconscionable, remedy may be had as provided in this Article.

(3) Consequential damages may be liquidated under Section 2A–504, or may otherwise be limited, altered, or excluded unless the limitation, alteration, or exclusion is unconscionable. Limitation, alteration, or exclusion of consequential damages for injury to the person in the case of consumer goods is prima facie unconscionable but limitation, alteration, or exclusion of damages where the loss is commercial is not prima facie unconscionable.

(4) Rights and remedies on default by the lessor or the lessee with respect to any obligation or promise collateral or ancillary to the lease contract are not impaired by this Article.

§2A-504. Liquidation of Damages.

(1) Damages payable by either party for default, or any other act or omission, including indemnity for loss or diminution of anticipated tax benefits or loss or damage to lessor's residual interest, may be liquidated in the lease agreement but only at an amount or by a formula that is reasonable in light of the then anticipated harm caused by the default or other act or omission.

(2) If the lease agreement provides for liquidation of damages, and such provision does not comply with subsection (1), or such provision is an exclusive or limited remedy that circumstances cause to fail of its essential purpose, remedy may be had as provided in this Article.

(3) If the lessor justifiably withholds or stops delivery of goods because of the lessee's default or insolvency (Section 2A–525 or 2A–526), the lessee is entitled to restitution of any amount by which the sum of his [or her] payments exceeds:

(a) the amount to which the lessor is entitled by virtue of terms liquidating the lessor's damages in accordance with subsection (1); or

(b) in the absence of those terms, 20 percent of the then present value of the total rent the lessee was obligated to pay for the balance of the lease term, or, in the case of a consumer lease, the lesser of such amount or $500.

(4) A lessee's right to restitution under subsection (3) is subject to offset to the extent the lessor establishes:

(a) a right to recover damages under the provisions of this Article other than subsection (1); and

(b) the amount or value of any benefits received by the lessee directly or indirectly by reason of the lease contract.

§2A-505. Cancellation and Termination and Effect of Cancellation, Termination, Rescission, or Fraud on Rights and Remedies.

(1) On cancellation of the lease contract, all obligations that are still executory on both sides are discharged, but any right based on prior default or performance

survives, and the cancelling party also retains any remedy for default of the whole lease contract or any unperformed balance.

(2) On termination of the lease contract, all obligations that are still executory on both sides are discharged but any right based on prior default or performance survives.

(3) Unless the contrary intention clearly appears, expressions of "cancellation," "rescission," or the like of the lease contract may not be construed as a renunciation or discharge of any claim in damages for an antecedent default.

(4) Rights and remedies for material misrepresentation or fraud include all rights and remedies available under this Article for default.

(5) Neither rescission nor a claim for rescission of the lease contract nor rejection or return of the goods may bar or be deemed inconsistent with a claim for damages or other right or remedy.

§2A-506. Statute of Limitations.

(1) An action for default under a lease contract, including breach of warranty or indemnity, must be commenced within 4 years after the cause of action accrued. By the original lease contract the parties may reduce the period of limitation to not less than one year.

(2) A cause of action for default accrues when the act or omission on which the default or breach of warranty is based is or should have been discovered by the aggrieved party, or when the default occurs, whichever is later. A cause of action for indemnity accrues when the act or omission on which the claim for indemnity is based is or should have been discovered by the indemnified party, whichever is later.

(3) If an action commenced within the time limited by subsection (1) is so terminated as to leave available a remedy by another action for the same default or breach of warranty or indemnity, the other action may be commenced after the expiration of the time limited and within 6 months after the termination of the first action unless the termination resulted from voluntary discontinuance or from dismissal for failure or neglect to prosecute.

(4) This section does not alter the law on tolling of the statute of limitations nor does it apply to causes of action that have accrued before this Article becomes effective.

§2A-507. Proof of Market Rent: Time and Place.

(1) Damages based on market rent (Section 2A–519 or 2A–528) are determined according to the rent for the use of the goods concerned for a lease term identical to the remaining lease term of the original lease agreement and prevailing at the times specified in Sections 2A–519 and 2A–528.

(2) If evidence of rent for the use of the goods concerned for a lease term identical to the remaining lease term of the original lease agreement and prevailing at the times or places described in this Article is not readily available, the rent prevailing within any reasonable time before or after the time described or at any other place or for a different lease term which in commercial judgment or under usage of trade would serve as a reasonable substitute for the one described may be used, making any proper allowance for the difference, including the cost of transporting the goods to or from the other place.

(3) Evidence of a relevant rent prevailing at a time or place or for a lease term other than the one described in this Article offered by one party is not admissible unless and until he [or she] has given the other party notice the court finds sufficient to prevent unfair surprise.

(4) If the prevailing rent or value of any goods regularly leased in any established market is in issue, reports in official publications or trade journals or in newspapers or periodicals of general circulation published as the reports of that market are admissible in evidence. The circumstances of the preparation of the report may be shown to affect its weight but not its admissibility.

B. Default by Lessor

§2A-508. Lessee's Remedies.

(1) If a lessor fails to deliver the goods in conformity to the lease contract (Section 2A–509) or repudiates the lease contract (Section 2A–402), or a lessee rightfully rejects the goods (Section 2A–509) or justifiably revokes acceptance of the goods (Section 2A–517), then with respect to any goods involved, and with respect to all of the goods if under an installment lease contract the value of the whole lease contract is substantially impaired (Section 2A–510), the lessor is in default under the lease contract and the lessee may:

(a) cancel the lease contract (Section 2A–505(1));

(b) recover so much of the rent and security as has been paid and is just under the circumstances;

(c) cover and recover damages as to all goods affected whether or not they have been identified to the lease contract (Sections 2A–518 and 2A–520), or recover damages for nondelivery (Sections 2A–519 and 2A–520);

(d) exercise any other rights or pursue any other remedies provided in the lease contract.

(2) If a lessor fails to deliver the goods in conformity to the lease contract or repudiates the lease contract, the lessee may also:

(a) if the goods have been identified, recover them (Section 2A–522); or

(b) in a proper case, obtain specific performance or replevy the goods (Section 2A–521).

(3) If a lessor is otherwise in default under a lease contract, the lessee may exercise the rights and pursue the remedies provided in the lease contract, which may include a right to cancel the lease, and in Section 2A–519(3).

(4) If a lessor has breached a warranty, whether express or implied, the lessee may recover damages (Section 2A–519(4)).

(5) On rightful rejection or justifiable revocation of acceptance, a lessee has a security interest in goods in the lessee's possession or control for any rent and security that has been paid and any expenses reasonably incurred in their inspection, receipt, transportation, and care and custody and may hold those goods and dispose of them in good faith and in a commercially reasonable manner, subject to Section 2A–527(5).

(6) Subject to the provisions of Section 2A–407, a lessee, on notifying the lessor of the lessee's intention to do so, may deduct all or any part of the damages resulting from any default under the lease contract from any part of the rent still due under the same lease contract.

§2A-509. Lessee's Rights on Improper Delivery; Rightful Rejection.

(1) Subject to the provisions of Section 2A–510 on default in installment lease contracts, if the goods or the tender or delivery fail in any respect to conform to the lease contract, the lessee may reject or accept the goods or accept any commercial unit or units and reject the rest of the goods.

(2) Rejection of goods is ineffective unless it is within a reasonable time after tender or delivery of the goods and the lessee seasonably notifies the lessor.

§2A-510. Installment Lease Contracts: Rejection and Default.

(1) Under an installment lease contract a lessee may reject any delivery that is nonconforming if the nonconformity substantially impairs the value of that delivery and cannot be cured or the nonconformity is a defect in the required documents; but if the nonconformity does not fall within subsection (2) and the lessor or the supplier gives adequate assurance of its cure, the lessee must accept that delivery.

(2) Whenever nonconformity or default with respect to one or more deliveries substantially impairs the value of the installment lease contract as a whole there is a default with respect to the whole. But, the aggrieved party reinstates the installment lease contract as a whole if the aggrieved party accepts a nonconforming delivery without seasonably notifying of cancellation or brings an action with respect only to past deliveries or demands performance as to future deliveries.

§2A-511. Merchant Lessee's Duties as to Rightfully Rejected Goods.

(1) Subject to any security interest of a lessee (Section 2A–508(5)), if a lessor or a supplier has no agent or place of business at the market of rejection, a merchant lessee, after rejection of goods in his [or her] possession or control, shall follow any reasonable instructions received from the lessor or the supplier with respect to the goods. In the absence of those instructions, a merchant lessee shall make reasonable efforts to sell, lease, or otherwise dispose of the goods for the lessor's account if they threaten to decline in value speedily. Instructions are not reasonable if on demand indemnity for expenses is not forthcoming.

(2) If a merchant lessee (subsection (1)) or any other lessee (Section 2A–512) disposes of goods, he [or she] is entitled to reimbursement either from the lessor or the supplier or out of the proceeds for reasonable expenses of caring for and disposing of the goods and, if the expenses include no disposition commission, to such commission as is usual in the trade, or if there is none, to a reasonable sum not exceeding 10 percent of the gross proceeds.

(3) In complying with this section or Section 2A–512, the lessee is held only to good faith. Good faith conduct hereunder is neither acceptance or conversion nor the basis of an action for damages.

(4) A purchaser who purchases in good faith from a lessee pursuant to this section or Section 2A–512 takes the goods free of any rights of the lessor and the supplier even though the lessee fails to comply with one or more of the requirements of this Article.

§2A-512. Lessee's Duties as to Rightfully Rejected Goods.

(1) Except as otherwise provided with respect to goods that threaten to decline in value speedily (Section 2A–511) and subject to any security interest of a lessee (Section 2A–508(5)):

(a) the lessee, after rejection of goods in the lessee's possession, shall hold them with reasonable care at the lessor's or the supplier's disposition for a reasonable time after the lessee's seasonable notification of rejection;

(b) if the lessor or the supplier gives no instructions within a reasonable time after notification of rejection, the lessee may store the rejected goods for the lessor's or the supplier's account or ship them to the lessor or the supplier or dispose of them for the lessor's or the supplier's account with reimbursement in the manner provided in Section 2A–511; but

(c) the lessee has no further obligations with regard to goods rightfully rejected.

(2) Action by the lessee pursuant to subsection (1) is not acceptance or conversion.

§2A-513. Cure by Lessor of Improper Tender or Delivery; Replacement.

(1) If any tender or delivery by the lessor or the supplier is rejected because nonconforming and the time for performance has not yet expired, the lessor or the supplier may seasonably notify the lessee of the lessor's or the supplier's intention to cure and may then make a conforming delivery within the time provided in the lease contract.

(2) If the lessee rejects a nonconforming tender that the lessor or the supplier had reasonable grounds to believe would be acceptable with or without money allowance, the lessor or the supplier may have a further reasonable time to substitute a conforming tender if he [or she] seasonably notifies the lessee.

§2A-514. Waiver of Lessee's Objections.

(1) In rejecting goods, a lessee's failure to state a particular defect that is ascertainable by reasonable inspection precludes the lessee from relying on the defect to justify rejection or to establish default:

 (a) if, stated seasonably, the lessor or the supplier could have cured it (Section 2A–513); or

 (b) between merchants if the lessor or the supplier after rejection has made a request in writing for a full and final written statement of all defects on which the lessee proposes to rely.

(2) A lessee's failure to reserve rights when paying rent or other consideration against documents precludes recovery of the payment for defects apparent on the face of the documents.

§2A-515. Acceptance of Goods.

(1) Acceptance of goods occurs after the lessee has had a reasonable opportunity to inspect the goods and

 (a) the lessee signifies or acts with respect to the goods in a manner that signifies to the lessor or the supplier that the goods are conforming or that the lessee will take or retain them in spite of their nonconformity; or

 (b) the lessee fails to make an effective rejection of the goods (Section 2A–509(2)).

(2) Acceptance of a part of any commercial unit is acceptance of that entire unit.

§2A-516. Effect of Acceptance of Goods; Notice of Default; Burden of Establishing Default after Acceptance; Notice of Claim or Litigation to Person Answerable Over.

(1) A lessee must pay rent for any goods accepted in accordance with the lease contract, with due allowance for goods rightfully rejected or not delivered.

(2) A lessee's acceptance of goods precludes rejection of the goods accepted. In the case of a finance lease, if made with knowledge of a nonconformity, acceptance cannot be revoked because of it. In any other case, if made with knowledge of a nonconformity, acceptance cannot be revoked because of it unless the acceptance was on the reasonable assumption that the nonconformity would be seasonably cured. Acceptance does not of itself impair any other remedy provided by this Article or the lease agreement for nonconformity.

(3) If a tender has been accepted:

 (a) within a reasonable time after the lessee discovers or should have discovered any default, the lessee shall notify the lessor and the supplier, if any, or be barred from any remedy against the party not notified;

 (b) except in the case of a consumer lease, within a reasonable time after the lessee receives notice of litigation for infringement or the like (Section 2A–211) the lessee shall notify the lessor or be barred from any remedy over for liability established by the litigation; and

 (c) the burden is on the lessee to establish any default.

(4) If a lessee is sued for breach of a warranty or other obligation for which a lessor or a supplier is answerable over the following apply:

 (a) The lessee may give the lessor or the supplier, or both, written notice of the litigation. If the notice states that the person notified may come in and defend and that if the person notified does not do so that person will be bound in any action against that person by the lessee by any determination of fact common to the two litigations, then unless the person notified after seasonable receipt of the notice does come in and defend that person is so bound.

 (b) The lessor or the supplier may demand in writing that the lessee turn over control of the litigation including settlement if the claim is one for infringement or the like (Section 2A–211) or else be barred from any remedy over. If the demand states that the lessor or the supplier agrees to bear all expense and to satisfy any adverse judgment, then unless the lessee after seasonable receipt of the demand does turn over control the lessee is so barred.

(5) Subsections (3) and (4) apply to any obligation of a lessee to hold the lessor or the supplier harmless against infringement or the like (Section 2A–211).

§2A-517. Revocation of Acceptance of Goods.

(1) A lessee may revoke acceptance of a lot or commercial unit whose nonconformity substantially impairs its value to the lessee if the lessee has accepted it:

(a) except in the case of a finance lease, on the reasonable assumption that its nonconformity would be cured and it has not been seasonably cured; or

(b) without discovery of the nonconformity if the lessee's acceptance was reasonably induced either by the lessor's assurances or, except in the case of a finance lease, by the difficulty of discovery before acceptance.

(2) Except in the case of a finance lease that is not a consumer lease, a lessee may revoke acceptance of a lot or commercial unit if the lessor defaults under the lease contract and the default substantially impairs the value of that lot or commercial unit to the lessee.

(3) If the lease agreement so provides, the lessee may revoke acceptance of a lot or commercial unit because of other defaults by the lessor.

(4) Revocation of acceptance must occur within a reasonable time after the lessee discovers or should have discovered the ground for it and before any substantial change in condition of the goods which is not caused by the nonconformity. Revocation is not effective until the lessee notifies the lessor.

(5) A lessee who so revokes has the same rights and duties with regard to the goods involved as if the lessee had rejected them.

§2A-518. Cover; Substitute Goods.

(1) After a default by a lessor under the lease contract of the type described in Section 2A–508(1), or, if agreed, after other default by the lessor, the lessee may cover by making any purchase or lease of or contract to purchase or lease goods in substitution for those due from the lessor.

(2) Except as otherwise provided with respect to damages liquidated in the lease agreement (Section 2A–504) or otherwise determined pursuant to agreement of the parties (Sections 1–102(3) and 2A–503), if a lessee's cover is by a lease agreement substantially similar to the original lease agreement and the new lease agreement is made in good faith and in a commercially reasonable manner, the lessee may recover from the lessor as damages (i) the present value, as of the date of the commencement of the term of the new lease agreement, of the rent under the new lease agreement applicable to that period of the new lease term which is comparable to the then remaining term of the original lease agreement minus the present value as of the same date of the total rent for the then remaining lease term of the original lease agreement, and (ii) any incidental or consequential damages, less expenses saved in consequence of the lessor's default.

(3) If a lessee's cover is by lease agreement that for any reason does not qualify for treatment under subsection (2), or is by purchase or otherwise, the lessee may recover from the lessor as if the lessee had elected not to cover and Section 2A–519 governs.

§2A-519. Lessee's Damages for Non-delivery, Repudiation, Default, and Breach of Warranty in Regard to Accepted Goods.

(1) Except as otherwise provided with respect to damages liquidated in the lease agreement (Section 2A–504) or otherwise determined pursuant to agreement of the parties (Sections 1–102(3) and 2A–503), if a lessee elects not to cover or a lessee elects to cover and the cover is by lease agreement that for any reason does not qualify for treatment under Section 2A–518(2), or is by purchase or otherwise, the measure of damages for non-delivery or repudiation by the lessor or for rejection or revocation of acceptance by the lessee is the present value, as of the date of the default, of the then market rent minus the present value as of the same date of the original rent, computed for the remaining lease term of the original lease agreement, together with incidental and consequential damages, less expenses saved in consequence of the lessor's default.

(2) Market rent is to be determined as of the place for tender or, in cases of rejection after arrival or revocation of acceptance, as of the place of arrival.

(3) Except as otherwise agreed, if the lessee has accepted goods and given notification (Section 2A–516(3)), the measure of damages for non-conforming tender or delivery or other default by a lessor is the loss resulting in the ordinary course of events from the lessor's default as determined in any manner that is reasonable together with incidental and consequential damages, less expenses saved in consequence of the lessor's default.

(4) Except as otherwise agreed, the measure of damages for breach of warranty is the present value at the time and place of acceptance of the difference between the value of the use of the goods accepted and the value if they had been as warranted for the lease term, unless special circumstances show proximate damages of a different amount, together with incidental and consequential damages, less expenses saved in consequence of the lessor's default or breach of warranty.

§2A-520. Lessee's Incidental and Consequential Damages.

(1) Incidental damages resulting from a lessor's default include expenses reasonably incurred in inspection, receipt, transportation, and care and custody of goods rightfully rejected or goods the acceptance of which is justifiably revoked, any commercially reasonable charges, expenses or commissions in connection with effecting cover, and any other reasonable expense incident to the default.

(2) Consequential damages resulting from a lessor's default include:

(a) any loss resulting from general or particular requirements and needs of which the lessor at the time of contracting had reason to know and which could not reasonably be prevented by cover or otherwise; and

(b) injury to person or property proximately resulting from any breach of warranty.

§2A-521. Lessee's Right to Specific Performance or Replevin.

(1) Specific performance may be decreed if the goods are unique or in other proper circumstances.

(2) A decree for specific performance may include any terms and conditions as to payment of the rent, damages, or other relief that the court deems just.

(3) A lessee has a right of replevin, detinue, sequestration, claim and delivery, or the like for goods identified to the lease contract if after reasonable effort the lessee is unable to effect cover for those goods or the circumstances reasonably indicate that the effort will be unavailing.

§2A-522. Lessee's Right to Goods on Lessor's Insolvency.

(1) Subject to subsection (2) and even though the goods have not been shipped, a lessee who has paid a part or all of the rent and security for goods identified to a lease contract (Section 2A–217) on making and keeping good a tender of any unpaid portion of the rent and security due under the lease contract may recover the goods identified from the lessor if the lessor becomes insolvent within 10 days after receipt of the first installment of rent and security.

(2) A lessee acquires the right to recover goods identified to a lease contract only if they conform to the lease contract.

C. Default by Lessee

§2A-523. Lessor's Remedies.

(1) If a lessee wrongfully rejects or revokes acceptance of goods or fails to make a payment when due or repudiates with respect to a part or the whole, then, with respect to any goods involved, and with respect to all of the goods if under an installment lease contract the value of the whole lease contract is substantially impaired (Section 2A–510), the lessee is in default under the lease contract and the lessor may:

(a) cancel the lease contract (Section 2A–505(1));

(b) proceed respecting goods not identified to the lease contract (Section 2A–524);

(c) withhold delivery of the goods and take possession of goods previously delivered (Section 2A–525);

(d) stop delivery of the goods by any bailee (Section 2A–526);

(e) dispose of the goods and recover damages (Section 2A–527), or retain the goods and recover

damages (Section 2A–528), or in a proper case recover rent (Section 2A–529);

(f) exercise any other rights or pursue any other remedies provided in the lease contract.

(2) If a lessor does not fully exercise a right or obtain a remedy to which the lessor is entitled under subsection (1), the lessor may recover the loss resulting in the ordinary course of events from the lessee's default as determined in any reasonable manner, together with incidental damages, less expenses saved in consequence of the lessee's default.

(3) If a lessee is otherwise in default under a lease contract, the lessor may exercise the rights and pursue the remedies provided in the lease contract, which may include a right to cancel the lease. In addition, unless otherwise provided in the lease contract:

(a) if the default substantially impairs the value of the lease contract to the lessor, the lessor may exercise the rights and pursue the remedies provided in subsections (1) or (2); or

(b) if the default does not substantially impair the value of the lease contract to the lessor, the lessor may recover as provided in subsection (2).

§2A-524. Lessor's Right to Identify Goods to Lease Contract.

(1) After default by the lessee under the lease contract of the type described in Section 2A–523(1) or 2A–523(3)(a) or, if agreed, after other default by the lessee, the lessor may:

(a) identify to the lease contract conforming goods not already identified if at the time the lessor learned of the default they were in the lessor's or the supplier's possession or control; and

(b) dispose of goods (Section 2A–527(1)) that demonstrably have been intended for the particular lease contract even though those goods are unfinished.

(2) If the goods are unfinished, in the exercise of reasonable commercial judgment for the purposes of avoiding loss and of effective realization, an aggrieved lessor or the supplier may either complete manufacture and wholly identify the goods to the lease contract or cease manufacture and lease, sell, or otherwise dispose of the goods for scrap or salvage value or proceed in any other reasonable manner.

§2A-525. Lessor's Right to Possession of Goods.

(1) If a lessor discovers the lessee to be insolvent, the lessor may refuse to deliver the goods.

(2) After a default by the lessee under the lease contract of the type described in Section 2A–523(1) or 2A–523(3)(a) or, if agreed, after other default by the lessee, the lessor has the right to take possession of the goods. If the lease contract so provides, the lessor

may require the lessee to assemble the goods and make them available to the lessor at a place to be designated by the lessor which is reasonably convenient to both parties. Without removal, the lessor may render unusable any goods employed in trade or business, and may dispose of goods on the lessee's premises (Section 2A–527).

(3) The lessor may proceed under subsection (2) without judicial process if it can be done without breach of the peace or the lessor may proceed by action.

§2A-526. Lessor's Stoppage of Delivery in Transit or Otherwise.

(1) A lessor may stop delivery of goods in the possession of a carrier or other bailee if the lessor discovers the lessee to be insolvent and may stop delivery of carload, truckload, planeload, or larger shipments of express or freight if the lessee repudiates or fails to make a payment due before delivery, whether for rent, security or otherwise under the lease contract, or for any other reason the lessor has a right to withhold or take possession of the goods.

(2) In pursuing its remedies under subsection (1), the lessor may stop delivery until

   (a) receipt of the goods by the lessee;

   (b) acknowledgment to the lessee by any bailee of the goods, except a carrier, that the bailee holds the goods for the lessee; or

   (c) such an acknowledgment to the lessee by a carrier via reshipment or as warehouseman.

(3) (a) To stop delivery, a lessor shall so notify as to enable the bailee by reasonable diligence to prevent delivery of the goods.

   (b) After notification, the bailee shall hold and deliver the goods according to the directions of the lessor, but the lessor is liable to the bailee for any ensuing charges or damages.

   (c) A carrier who has issued a nonnegotiable bill of lading is not obliged to obey a notification to stop received from a person other than the consignor.

§2A-527. Lessor's Rights to Dispose of Goods.

(1) After a default by a lessee under the lease contract of the type described in Section 2A–523(1) or 2A–523(3)(a) or after the lessor refuses to deliver or takes possession of goods (Section 2A–525 or 2A–526), or, if agreed, after other default by a lessee, the lessor may dispose of the goods concerned or the undelivered balance thereof by lease, sale, or otherwise.

(2) Except as otherwise provided with respect to damages liquidated in the lease agreement (Section 2A–504) or otherwise determined pursuant to agreement of the parties (Sections 1–102(3) and 2A–503), if the disposition is by lease agreement substantially similar to the original lease agreement and the new lease agreement is made in good faith and in a commercially reasonable manner, the lessor may recover from the lessee as damages (i) accrued and unpaid rent as of the date of the commencement of the term of the new lease agreement, (ii) the present value, as of the same date, of the total rent for the then remaining lease term of the original lease agreement minus the present value, as of the same date, of the rent under the new lease agreement applicable to that period of the new lease term which is comparable to the then remaining term of the original lease agreement, and (iii) any incidental damages allowed under Section 2A–530, less expenses saved in consequence of the lessee's default.

(3) If the lessor's disposition is by lease agreement that for any reason does not qualify for treatment under subsection (2), or is by sale or otherwise, the lessor may recover from the lessee as if the lessor had elected not to dispose of the goods and Section 2A–528 governs.

(4) A subsequent buyer or lessee who buys or leases from the lessor in good faith for value as a result of a disposition under this section takes the goods free of the original lease contract and any rights of the original lessee even though the lessor fails to comply with one or more of the requirements of this Article.

(5) The lessor is not accountable to the lessee for any profit made on any disposition. A lessee who has rightfully rejected or justifiably revoked acceptance shall account to the lessor for any excess over the amount of the lessee's security interest (Section 2A–508(5)).

§2A-528. Lessor's Damages for Non-acceptance, Failure to Pay, Repudiation, or Other Default.

(1) Except as otherwise provided with respect to damages liquidated in the lease agreement (Section 2A–504) or otherwise determined pursuant to agreement of the parties (Sections 1–102(3) and 2A–503), if a lessor elects to retain the goods or a lessor elects to dispose of the goods and the disposition is by lease agreement that for any reason does not qualify for treatment under Section 2A–527(2), or is by sale or otherwise, the lessor may recover from the lessee as damages for a default of the type described in Section 2A–523(1) or 2A–523(3)(a), or, if agreed, for other default of the lessee, (i) accrued and unpaid rent as of the date of default if the lessee has never taken possession of the goods, or, if the lessee has taken possession of the goods, as of the date the lessor repossesses the goods or an earlier date on which the lessee makes a tender of the goods to the lessor, (ii) the present value as of the date determined under clause (i) of the total rent for the then remaining lease

term of the original lease agreement minus the present value as of the same date of the market rent at the place where the goods are located computed for the same lease term, and (iii) any incidental damages allowed under Section 2A–530, less expenses saved in consequence of the lessee's default.

(2) If the measure of damages provided in subsection (1) is inadequate to put a lessor in as good a position as performance would have, the measure of damages is the present value of the profit, including reasonable overhead, the lessor would have made from full performance by the lessee, together with any incidental damages allowed under Section 2A–530, due allowance for costs reasonably incurred and due credit for payments or proceeds of disposition.

§2A-529. Lessor's Action for the Rent.

(1) After default by the lessee under the lease contract of the type described in Section 2A–523(1) or 2A–523(3)(a) or, if agreed, after other default by the lessee, if the lessor complies with subsection (2), the lessor may recover from the lessee as damages:

  (a) for goods accepted by the lessee and not repossessed by or tendered to the lessor, and for conforming goods lost or damaged within a commercially reasonable time after risk of loss passes to the lessee (Section 2A–219), (i) accrued and unpaid rent as of the date of entry of judgment in favor of the lessor, (ii) the present value as of the same date of the rent for the then remaining lease term of the lease agreement, and (iii) any incidental damages allowed under Section 2A–530, less expenses saved in consequence of the lessee's default; and

  (b) for goods identified to the lease contract if the lessor is unable after reasonable effort to dispose of them at a reasonable price or the circumstances reasonably indicate that effort will be unavailing, (i) accrued and unpaid rent as of the date of entry of judgment in favor of the lessor, (ii) the present value as of the same date of the rent for the then remaining lease term of the lease agreement, and (iii) any incidental damages allowed under Section 2A–530, less expenses saved in consequence of the lessee's default.

(2) Except as provided in subsection (3), the lessor shall hold for the lessee for the remaining lease term of the lease agreement any goods that have been identified to the lease contract and are in the lessor's control.

(3) The lessor may dispose of the goods at any time before collection of the judgment for damages obtained pursuant to subsection (1). If the disposition is before the end of the remaining lease term of the lease agreement, the lessor's recovery against the lessee for damages is governed by Section 2A–527 or Section 2A–528, and the lessor will cause an appropriate credit to be provided against a judgment for damages to the extent that the amount of the judgment exceeds the recovery available pursuant to Section 2A–527 or 2A–528.

(4) Payment of the judgment for damages obtained pursuant to subsection (1) entitles the lessee to the use and possession of the goods not then disposed of for the remaining lease term of and in accordance with the lease agreement.

(5) After default by the lessee under the lease contract of the type described in Section 2A–523(1) or Section 2A–523(3)(a) or, if agreed, after other default by the lessee, a lessor who is held not entitled to rent under this section must nevertheless be awarded damages for non-acceptance under Section 2A–527 or Section 2A–528.

§2A-530. Lessor's Incidental Damages.
Incidental damages to an aggrieved lessor include any commercially reasonable charges, expenses, or commissions incurred in stopping delivery, in the transportation, care and custody of goods after the lessee's default, in connection with return or disposition of the goods, or otherwise resulting from the default.

§2A-531. Standing to Sue Third Parties for Injury to Goods.

(1) If a third party so deals with goods that have been identified to a lease contract as to cause actionable injury to a party to the lease contract (a) the lessor has a right of action against the third party, and (b) the lessee also has a right of action against the third party if the lessee:

  (i) has a security interest in the goods;

  (ii) has an insurable interest in the goods; or

  (iii) bears the risk of loss under the lease contract or has since the injury assumed that risk as against the lessor and the goods have been converted or destroyed.

(2) If at the time of the injury the party plaintiff did not bear the risk of loss as against the other party to the lease contract and there is no arrangement between them for disposition of the recovery, his [or her] suit or settlement, subject to his [or her] own interest, is as a fiduciary for the other party to the lease contract.

(3) Either party with the consent of the other may sue for the benefit of whom it may concern.

§2A-532. Lessor's Rights to Residual Interest.
In addition to any other recovery permitted by this Article or other law, the lessor may recover from the lessee an amount that will fully compensate the lessor for any loss of or damage to the lessor's residual interest in the goods caused by the default of the lessee.

Article 3: Negotiable Instruments (Revised 1990)

Part 1: General Provisions and Definitions

§3-101. Short Title. This Article may be cited as Uniform Commercial Code—Negotiable Instruments.

§3-102. Subject Matter.

(a) This Article applies to negotiable instruments. It does not apply to money, to payment orders governed by Article 4A, or to securities governed by Article 8.

(b) If there is conflict between this Article and Article 4 or 9, Articles 4 and 9 govern.

(c) Regulations of the Board of Governors of the Federal Reserve System and operating circulars of the Federal Reserve Banks supersede any inconsistent provision of this Article to the extent of the inconsistency.

Note: The previous version of Article 3, Commercial Paper, is found in the Instructor's Resource Guide. You may wish to photocopy it for your students' use.

§3-103. Definitions.

(a) In this Article:

(1) "Acceptor" means a drawee who has accepted a draft.

(2) "Drawee" means a person ordered in a draft to make payment.

(3) "Drawer" means a person who signs or is identified in a draft as a person ordering payment.

(4) "Good faith" means honesty in fact and the observance of reasonable commercial standards of fair dealing.

(5) "Maker" means a person who signs or is identified in a note as a person undertaking to pay.

(6) "Order" means a written instruction to pay money signed by the person giving the instruction. The instruction may be addressed to any person, including the person giving the instruction, or to one or more persons jointly or in the alternative but not in succession. An authorization to pay is not an order unless the person authorized to pay is also instructed to pay.

(7) "Ordinary care" in the case of a person engaged in business means observance of reasonable commercial standards, prevailing in the area in which the person is located, with respect to the business in which the person is engaged. In the case of a bank that takes an instrument for processing for collection or payment by automated means, reasonable commercial standards do not require the bank to examine the instrument if the failure to examine does not violate the bank's prescribed procedures and the bank's procedures do not vary unreasonably from general banking usage not disapproved by this Article or Article 4.

(8) "Party" means a party to an instrument.

(9) "Promise" means a written undertaking to pay money signed by the person undertaking to pay. An acknowledgment of an obligation by the obligor is not a promise unless the obligor also undertakes to pay the obligation.

(10) "Prove" with respect to a fact means to meet the burden of establishing the fact (Section 1-201(8)).

(11) "Remitter" means a person who purchases an instrument from its issuer if the instrument is payable to an identified person other than the purchaser.

(b) Other definitions applying to this Article and the sections in which they appear are:

"Acceptance"	Section 3-409
"Accommodated party"	Section 3-419
"Accommodation party"	Section 3-419
"Alteration"	Section 3-407
"Anomalous indorsement"	Section 3-205
"Blank indorsement"	Section 3-205
"Cashier's check"	Section 3-104
"Certificate of deposit"	Section 3-104
"Certified check"	Section 3-409
"Check"	Section 3-104
"Consideration"	Section 3-303
"Draft"	Section 3-104
"Holder in due course"	Section 3-302
"Incomplete instrument"	Section 3-115
"Indorsement"	Section 3-204
"Indorser"	Section 3-204
"Instrument"	Section 3-104
"Issue"	Section 3-105
"Issuer"	Section 3-105
"Negotiable instrument"	Section 3-104
"Negotiation"	Section 3-201
"Note"	Section 3-104
"Payable at a definite time"	Section 3-108
"Payable on demand"	Section 3-108
"Payable to bearer"	Section 3-109
"Payable to order"	Section 3-109
"Payment"	Section 3-602
"Person entitled to enforce"	Section 3-301
"Presentment"	Section 3-501
"Reacquisition"	Section 3-207

"Special indorsement"	Section 3-205
"Teller's check"	Section 3-104
"Transfer of instrument"	Section 3-203
"Traveler's check"	Section 3-104
"Value"	Section 3-303

(c) The following definitions in other Articles apply to this Article:

"Bank"	Section 4-105
"Banking day"	Section 4-104
"Clearinghouse"	Section 4-104
"Collecting bank"	Section 4-105
"Depositary bank"	Section 4-105
"Documentary draft"	Section 4-104
"Intermediary bank"	Section 4-105
"Item"	Section 4-104
"Payor bank"	Section 4-105
"Suspends payments"	Section 4-104

(d) In addition, Article 1 contains general definitions and principles of construction and interpretation applicable throughout this Article.

§3-104. Negotiable Instrument.

(a) Except as provided in subsections (c) and (d), "negotiable instrument" means an unconditional promise or order to pay a fixed amount of money, with or without interest or other charges described in the promise or order, if it:

(1) is payable to bearer or to order at the time it is issued or first comes into possession of a holder;

(2) is payable on demand or at a definite time; and

(3) does not state any other undertaking or instruction by the person promising or ordering payment to do any act in addition to the payment of money, but the promise or order may contain (i) an undertaking or power to give, maintain, or protect collateral to secure payment, (ii) an authorization or power to the holder to confess judgment or realize on or dispose of collateral, or (iii) a waiver of the benefit of any law intended for the advantage or protection of an obligor.

(b) "Instrument" means a negotiable instrument.

(c) An order that meets all of the requirements of subsection (a), except paragraph (1), and otherwise falls within the definition of "check" in subsection (f) is a negotiable instrument and a check.

(d) A promise or order other than a check is not an instrument if, at the time it is issued or first comes into possession of a holder, it contains a conspicuous statement, however expressed, to the effect that the promise or order is not negotiable or is not an instrument governed by this Article.

(e) An instrument is a "note" if it is a promise and is a "draft" if it is an order. If an instrument falls within the definition of both "note" and "draft", a person entitled to enforce the instrument may treat it as either.

(f) "Check" means (i) a draft, other than a documentary draft, payable on demand and drawn on a bank or (ii) a cashier's check or teller's check. An instrument may be a check even though it is described on its face by another term, such as "money order".

(g) "Cashier's check" means a draft with respect to which the drawer and drawee are the same bank or branches of the same bank.

(h) "Teller's check" means a draft drawn by a bank (i) on another bank, or (ii) payable at or through a bank.

(i) "Traveler's check" means an instrument that (i) is payable on demand, (ii) is drawn on or payable at or through a bank, (iii) is designated by the term "traveler's check" or by a substantially similar term, and (iv) requires, as a condition to payment, a countersignature by a person whose specimen signature appears on the instrument.

(j) "Certificate of deposit" means an instrument containing an acknowledgment by a bank that a sum of money has been received by the bank and a promise by the bank to repay the sum of money. A certificate of deposit is a note of the bank.

§3-105. Issue of Instrument.

(a) "Issue" means the first delivery of an instrument by the maker or drawer, whether to a holder or nonholder, for the purpose of giving rights on the instrument to any person.

(b) An unissued instrument, or an unissued incomplete instrument that is completed, is binding on the maker or drawer, but nonissuance is a defense. An instrument that is conditionally issued or is issued for a special purpose is binding on the maker or drawer, but failure of the condition or special purpose to be fulfilled is a defense.

(c) "Issuer" applies to issued and unissued instruments and means a maker or drawer of an instrument.

§3-106. Unconditional Promise or Order.

(a) Except as provided in this section, for the purposes of Section 3-104(a), a promise or order is unconditional unless it states (i) an express condition to payment, (ii) that the promise or order is subject to or governed by another writing, or (iii) that rights or obligations with respect to the promise or order are stated in another writing. A reference to another writing does not of itself make the promise or order conditional.

(b) A promise or order is not made conditional (i) by a reference to another writing for a statement of rights with respect to collateral, prepayment, or acceleration, or (ii) because payment is limited to resort to a particular fund or source.

(c) If a promise or order requires, as a condition to payment, a countersignature by a person whose specimen signature appears on the promise or order, the condition does not make the promise or order conditional for the purposes of Section 3-104(a). If the person whose specimen signature appears on an instrument fails to countersign the instrument, the failure to countersign is a defense to the obligation of the issuer, but the failure does not prevent a transferee of the instrument from becoming a holder of the instrument.

(d) If a promise or order at the time it is issued or first comes into possession of a holder contains a statement, required by applicable statutory or administrative law, to the effect that the rights of a holder or transferee are subject to claims or defenses that the issuer could assert the original payee, the promise or order is not thereby made conditional for the purposes of Section 3-104(a); but if the promise or order is an instrument, there cannot be a holder in due course of the instrument.

§3-107. Instrument Payable in Foreign Money.
Unless the instrument otherwise provides, an instrument that states the amount payable in foreign money may be paid in the foreign money or in an equivalent amount in dollars calculated by using the current bank-offered spot rate at the place of payment for the purchase of dollars on the day on which the instrument is paid.

§3-108. Payable on Demand or at Definite Time.

(a) A promise or order is "payable on demand" if it (i) states that it is payable on demand or at sight, or otherwise indicates that it is payable at the will of the holder, or (ii) does not state any time of payment.

(b) A promise or order is "payable at a definite time" if it is payable on elapse of a definite period of time after sight or acceptance or at a fixed date or dates or at a time or times readily ascertainable at the time the promise or order is issued, subject to rights of (i) prepayment, (ii) acceleration, (iii) extension at the option of the holder, or (iv) extension to a further definite time at the option of the maker or acceptor or automatically upon or after a specified act or event.

(c) If an instrument, payable at a fixed date, is also payable upon demand made before the fixed date, the instrument is payable on demand until the fixed date and, if demand for payment is not made before that date, becomes payable at a definite time on the fixed date.

§3-109. Payable to Bearer or to Order.—

(a) A promise or order is payable to bearer if it:

(1) states that it is payable to bearer or to the order of bearer or otherwise indicates that the person in possession of the promise or order is entitled to payment;

(2) does not state a payee; or

(3) states that it is payable to or to the order of cash or otherwise indicates that it is not payable to an identified person.

(b) A promise or order that is not payable to bearer is payable to order if it is payable (i) to the order of an identified person or (ii) to an identified person or order. A promise or order that is payable to order is payable to the identified person.

(c) An instrument payable to bearer may become payable to an identified person if it is specially indorsed pursuant to Section 3-205(a). An instrument payable to an identified person may become payable to bearer if it is indorsed in blank pursuant to Section 3-205(b).

§3-110. Identification of Person to Whom Instrument is Payable.

(a) The person to whom an instrument is initially payable is determined by the intent of the person, whether or not authorized, signing as, or in the name or behalf of, the issuer of the instrument. The instrument is payable to the person intended by the signer even if that person is identified in the instrument by a name or other identification that is not that of the intended person. If more than one person signs in the name or behalf of the issuer of an instrument and all the signers do not intend the same person as payee, the instrument is payable to any person intended by one or more of the signers.

(b) If the signature of the issuer of an instrument is made by automated means, such as a check-writing machine, the payee of the instrument is determined by the intent of the person who supplied the name or identification of the payee, whether or not authorized to do so.

(c) A person to whom an instrument is payable may be identified in any way, including by name, identifying number, office, or account number. For the purpose of determining the holder of an instrument, the following rules apply:

(1) If an instrument is payable to an account and the account is identified only by number, the instrument is payable to the person to whom the account is payable. If an instrument is payable to an account identified by number and by the name of a person, the instrument is payable to the named person, whether or not that person is the owner of the account identified by number.

(2) If an instrument is payable to:

(i) a trust, an estate, or a person described as trustee or representative of a trust or estate, the instrument is payable to the trustee, the representative, or a successor of either, whether or not the beneficiary or estate is also named;

(ii) a person described as agent or similar representative of a named or identified person, the instrument is payable to the represented person, the representative, or a successor of the representative;

(iii) a fund or organization that is not a legal entity, the instrument is payable to a representative of the members of the fund or organization; or

(iv) an office or to a person described as holding an office, the instrument is payable to the named person, the incumbent of the office, or a successor to the incumbent.

(d) If an instrument is payable to two or more persons alternatively, it is payable to any of them and may be negotiated, discharged, or enforced by any or all of them in possession of the instrument. If an instrument is payable to two or more persons not alternatively, it is payable to all of them and may be negotiated, discharged, or enforced only by all of them. If an instrument payable to two or more persons is ambiguous as to whether it is payable to the persons alternatively, the instrument is payable to the persons alternatively.

§3-111. Place of Payment.
Except as otherwise provided for items in Article 4, an instrument is payable at the place of payment stated in the instrument. If no place of payment is stated, an instrument is payable at the address of the drawee or maker stated in the instrument. If no address is stated, the place of payment is the place of business of the drawee or maker. If a drawee or maker has more than one place of business, the place of payment is any place of business of the drawee or maker chosen by the person entitled to enforce the instrument. If the drawee or maker has no place of business, the place of payment is the residence of the drawee or maker.

§3-112. Interest.

(a) Unless otherwise provided in the instrument, (i) an instrument is not payable with interest, and (ii) interest on an interest-bearing instrument is payable from the date of the instrument.

(b) Interest may be stated in an instrument as a fixed or variable amount of money or it may be expressed as a fixed or variable rate or rates. The amount or rate of interest may be stated or described in the instrument in any manner and may require reference to information not contained in the instrument. If an instrument provides for interest, but the amount of interest payable cannot be ascertained from the description, interest is payable at the judgment rate in effect at the place of payment of the instrument and at the time interest first accrues.

§3-113. Date of Instrument.

(a) An instrument may be antedated or postdated. The date stated determines the time of payment if the instrument is payable at a fixed period after date. Except as provided in Section 4-401(c), an instrument payable on demand is not payable before the date of the instrument.

(b) If an instrument is undated, its date is the date of its issue or, in the case of an unissued instrument, the date it first comes into possession of a holder.

§3-114. Contradictory Terms of Instrument.
If an instrument contains contradictory terms, typewritten terms prevail over printed terms, handwritten terms prevail over both, and words prevail over numbers.

§3-115. Incomplete Instrument.

(a) "Incomplete instrument" means a signed writing, whether or not issued by the signer, the contents of which show at the time of signing that it is incomplete but that the signer intended it to be completed by the addition of words or numbers.

(b) Subject to subsection (c), if an incomplete instrument is an instrument under Section 3-104, it may be enforced according to its terms if it is not completed, or according to its terms as augmented by completion. If an incomplete instrument is not an instrument under Section 3-104, but, after completion, the requirements of Section 3-104 are met, the instrument may be enforced according to its terms as augmented by completion.

(c) If words or numbers are added to an incomplete instrument without authority of the signer, there is an alteration of the incomplete instrument under Section 3-407.

(d) The burden of establishing that words or numbers were added to an incomplete instrument without authority of the signer is on the person asserting the lack of authority.

§3-116. Joint and Several Liability; Contribution.

(a) Except as otherwise provided in the instrument, two or more persons who have the same liability on an instrument as makers, drawers, acceptors, indorsers who indorse as joint payees, or anomalous indorsers are jointly and severally liable in the capacity in which they sign.

(b) Except as provided in Section 3-419(e) or by agreement of the affected parties, a party having joint and several liability who pays the instrument is entitled to receive from any party having the same joint and several liability contribution in accordance with applicable law.

(c) Discharge of one party having joint and several liability by a person entitled to enforce the instrument does not affect the right under subsection (b) of a party having the same joint and several liability to receive contribution from the party discharged.

§3-117. Other Agreements Affecting Instrument. Subject to applicable law regarding exclusion of proof of contemporaneous or previous agreements, the obligation of a party to an instrument to pay the instrument may be modified, supplemented, or nullified by a separate agreement of the obligor and a person entitled to enforce the instrument, if the instrument is issued or the obligation is incurred in reliance on the agreement or as part of the same transaction giving rise to the agreement. To the extent an obligation is modified, supplemented, or nullified by an agreement under this section, the agreement is a defense to the obligation.

§3-118. Statute of Limitations.

(a) Except as provided in subsection (e), an action to enforce the obligation of a party to pay a note payable at a definite time must be commenced within six years after the due date or dates stated in the note or, if a due date is accelerated, within six years after the accelerated due date.

(b) Except as provided in subsection (d) or (e), if demand for payment is made to the maker of a note payable on demand, an action to enforce the obligation of a party to pay the note must be commenced within six years after the demand. If no demand for payment is made to the maker, an action to enforce the note is barred if neither principal nor interest on the note has been paid for a continuous period of 10 years.

(c) Except as provided in subsection (d), an action to enforce the obligation of a party to an unaccepted draft to pay the draft must be commenced within three years after dishonor of the draft or 10 years after the date of the draft, whichever period expires first.

(d) An action to enforce the obligation of the acceptor of a certified check or the issuer of a teller's check, cashier's check, or traveler's check must be commenced within three years after demand for payment is made to the acceptor or issuer, as the case may be.

(e) An action to enforce the obligation of a party to a certificate of deposit to pay the instrument must be commenced within six years after demand for payment is made to the maker, but if the instrument states a due date and the maker is not required to pay before that date, the six-year period begins when a demand for payment is in effect and the due date has passed.

(f) An action to enforce the obligation of a party to pay an accepted draft, other than a certified check, must be commenced (i) within six years after the due date or dates stated in the draft or acceptance if the obligation of the acceptor is payable at a definite time, or (ii) within six years after the date of the acceptance if the obligation of the acceptor is payable on demand.

(g) Unless governed by other law regarding claims for indemnity or contribution, an action (i) for conversion of an instrument, for money had and received, or like action based on conversion, (ii) for breach of warranty, or (iii) to enforce an obligation, duty, or right arising under this Article and not governed by this section must be commenced within three years after the [cause of action] accrues.

§3-119. Notice of Right to Defend Action. In an action for breach of an obligation for which a third person is answerable over pursuant to this Article or Article 4, the defendant may give the third person written notice of the litigation, and the person notified may then give similar notice to any other person who is answerable over. If the notice states (i) that the person notified may come in and defend and (ii) that failure to do so will bind the person notified in an action later brought by the person giving the notice as to any determination of fact common to the two litigations, the person notified is so bound unless after reasonable receipt of the notice the person notified does come in and defend.

Part 2: Negotiation, Transfer, and Indorsement

§3-201. Negotiation.

(a) "Negotiation" means a transfer of possession, whether voluntary or involuntary, of an instrument by a person other than the issuer to a person who thereby becomes its holder.

(b) Except for negotiation by a remitter, if an instrument is payable to an identified person, negotiation requires transfer of possession of the instrument and its indorsement by the holder. If an instrument is payable to bearer, it may be negotiated by transfer of possession alone.

§3-202. Negotiation Subject to Rescission.

(a) Negotiation is effective even if obtained (i) from an infant, a corporation exceeding its powers, or a person without capacity, (ii) by fraud, duress, or mistake, or (iii) in breach of duty or as part of an illegal transaction.

(b) To the extent permitted by other law, negotiation may be rescinded or may be subject to other remedies, but those remedies may not be asserted against a subsequent holder in due course or a person paying the instrument in good faith and without knowledge of facts that are a basis for rescission or other remedy.

§3-203. Transfer of Instrument; Rights Acquired by Transfer.—

(a) An instrument is transferred when it is delivered by a person other than its issuer for the purpose of giving to the person receiving delivery the right to enforce the instrument.

(b) Transfer of an instrument, whether or not the transfer is a negotiation, vests in the transferee any right of the transferor to enforce the instrument, including any right as a holder in due course, but the transferee cannot acquire rights of a holder in due course by a transfer, directly or indirectly, from a holder in due course if the transferee engaged in fraud or illegality affecting the instrument.

(c) Unless otherwise agreed, if an instrument is transferred for value and the transferee does not become a holder because of lack of indorsement by the transferor, the transferee has a specially enforceable right to the unqualified indorsement of the transferor, but negotiation of the instrument does not occur until the indorsement is made.

(d) If a transferor purports to transfer less than the entire instrument, negotiation of the instrument does not occur. The transferee obtains no rights under this Article, and has only the rights of a partial assignee.

§3-204. Indorsement.

(a) "Indorsement" means a signature, other than that of a signer as maker, drawer, or acceptor, that alone or accompanied by other words is made on an instrument for the purpose of (i) negotiating the instrument, (ii) restricting payment of the instrument, or (iii) incurring indorser's liability on the instrument, but regardless of the intent of the signer, a signature and its accompanying words is an indorsement unless the accompanying words, terms of the instrument, place of the signature, or other circumstances unambiguously indicate that the signature was made for a purpose other than indorsement. For the purpose of determining whether a signature is made on an instrument, a paper affixed to the instrument is a part of the instrument.

(b) "Indorser" means a person who makes an indorsement.

(c) For the purpose of determining whether the transferee of an instrument is a holder, an indorsement that transfers a security interest in the instrument is effective as an unqualified indorsement of the instrument.

(d) If an instrument is payable to a holder under a name that is not the name of the holder, indorsement may be made by the holder in the name stated in the instrument or in the holder's name or both, but signature in both names may be required by a person paying or taking the instrument for value or collection.

§3-205. Special Indorsement; Blank Indorsement; Anomalous Indorsement.

(a) If an indorsement is made by the holder of an instrument, whether payable to an identified person or payable to bearer, and the indorsement identifies a person to whom it makes the instrument payable, it is a "special indorsement". When specially indorsed, an instrument becomes payable to the identified person

and may be negotiated only by the indorsement of that person. The principles stated in Section 3-110 apply to special indorsements.

(b) If an indorsement is made by the holder of an instrument and it is not a special indorsement, it is a "blank indorsement". When indorsed in blank, an instrument becomes payable to bearer and may be negotiated by transfer of possession alone until specially indorsed.

(c) The holder may convert a blank indorsement that consists only of a signature into a special indorsement by writing, above the signature of the indorser, words identifying the person to whom the instrument is made payable.

(d) "Anomalous indorsement" means an indorsement made by a person who is not the holder of the instrument. An anomalous indorsement does not affect the manner in which the instrument may be negotiated.

§3-206. Restrictive Indorsement.

(a) An indorsement limiting payment to a particular person or otherwise prohibiting further transfer or negotiation of the instrument is not effective to prevent further transfer or negotiation of the instrument.

(b) An indorsement stating a condition to the right of the indorsee to receive payment does not affect the right of the indorsee to enforce the instrument. A person paying the instrument or taking it for value or collection may disregard the condition, and the rights and liabilities of that person are not affected by whether the condition has been fulfilled.

(c) If an instrument bears an indorsement (i) described in Section 4-201(b), or (ii) in blank or to a particular bank using the words "for deposit", "for collection", or other words indicating a purpose of having the instrument collected by a bank for the indorser or for a particular account, the following rules apply:

(1) A person, other than a bank, who purchases the instrument when so indorsed converts the instrument unless the amount paid for the instrument is received by the indorser or applied consistently with the indorsement.

(2) A depositary bank that purchases the instrument or takes it for collection when so indorsed converts the instrument unless the amount paid by the bank with respect to the instrument is received by the indorser or applied consistently with the indorsement.

(3) A payor bank that is also the depositary bank or that takes the instrument for immediate payment over the counter from a person other than a collecting bank converts the instrument unless the proceeds of the instrument are received by the indorser or applied consistently with the indorsement.

(4) Except as otherwise provided in paragraph (3), a payor bank or intermediary bank may disregard the indorsement and is not liable if the proceeds of the instrument are not received by the indorser or applied consistently with the indorsement.

(d) Except for an indorsement covered by subsection (c), if an instrument bears an indorsement using words to the effect that payment is to be made to the indorsee as agent, trustee, or other fiduciary for the benefit of the indorser or another person, the following rules apply:

(1) Unless there is notice of breach of fiduciary duty as provided in Section 3-307, a person who purchases the instrument from the indorsee or takes the instrument from the indorsee for collection or payment may pay the proceeds of payment or the value given for the instrument to the indorsee without regard to whether the indorsee violates a fiduciary duty to the indorser.

(2) A subsequent transferee of the instrument or person who pays the instrument is neither given notice nor otherwise affected by the restriction in the indorsement unless the transferee or payor knows that the fiduciary dealt with the instrument or its proceeds in breach of fiduciary duty.

(e) The presence on an instrument of an indorsement to which this section applies does not prevent a purchaser of the instrument from becoming a holder in due course of the instrument unless the purchaser is a converter under subsection (c) or has notice or knowledge of breach of fiduciary duty as stated in subsection (d).

(f) In an action to enforce the obligation of a party to pay the instrument, the obligor has a defense if payment would violate an indorsement to which this section applies and the payment is not permitted by this section.

§3-207. Reacquisition. Reacquisition of an instrument occurs if it is transferred to a former holder, by negotiation or otherwise. A former holder who reacquires the instrument may cancel indorsements made after the reacquirer first became a holder of the instrument. If the cancellation causes the instrument to be payable to the reacquirer or to bearer, the reacquirer may negotiate the instrument. An indorser whose indorsement is canceled is discharged, and the discharge is effective against any subsequent holder.

Part 3: Enforcement of Instruments

§3-301. Person Entitled to Enforce Instrument. "Person entitled to enforce" an instrument means (i) the holder of the instrument, (ii) a nonholder in possession of the instrument who has the rights of a holder, or (iii) a person not in possession of the instrument who is entitled to enforce the instrument pursuant to Section 3-309 or 3-418(d). A person may be a person entitled to enforce the instrument even though the person is not the owner of the instrument or is in wrongful possession of the instrument.

§3-302. Holder in Due Course.

(a) Subject to subsection (c) and Section 3106(d), "holder in due course" means the holder of an instrument if:

(1) the instrument when issued or negotiated to the holder does not bear such apparent evidence of forgery or alteration or is not otherwise so irregular or incomplete as to call into question its authenticity; and

(2) the holder took the instrument (i) for value, (ii) in good faith, (iii) without notice that the instrument is overdue or has been dishonored or that there is an uncured default with respect to payment of another instrument issued as part of the same series, (iv) without notice that the instrument contains an unauthorized signature or has been altered, (v) without notice of any claim to the instrument described in Section 3-306, and (vi) without notice that any party has a defense or claim in recoupment described in Section 3-305(a).

(b) Notice of discharge of a party, other than discharge in an insolvency proceeding, is not notice of a defense under subsection (a), but discharge is effective against a person who became a holder in due course with notice of the discharge. Public filing or recording of a document does not of itself constitute notice of a defense, claim in recoupment, or claim to the instrument.

(c) Except to the extent a transferor or predecessor in interest has rights as a holder in due course, a person does not acquire rights of a holder in due course of an instrument taken (i) by legal process or by purchase in an execution, bankruptcy, or creditor's sale or similar proceeding, (ii) by purchase as part of a bulk transaction not in ordinary course of business of the transferor, or (iii) as the successor in interest to an estate or other organization.

(d) If, under Section 3-303(a)(1), the promise of performance that is the consideration for an instrument has been partially performed, the holder may assert rights as a holder in due course of the instrument only to the fraction of the amount payable under the instrument equal to the value of the partial performance divided by the value of the promised performance.

(e) If (i) the person entitled to enforce an instrument has only a security interest in the instrument and (ii) the person obliged to pay the instrument has a defense, claim in recoupment, or claim to the instrument that may be asserted against the person who granted the security interest, the person entitled to enforce the instrument may assert rights as a holder in due course only to an amount payable under the instrument which, at the time of enforcement of the instrument, does not exceed the amount of the unpaid obligation secured.

(f) To be effective, notice must be received at a time and in a manner that gives a reasonable opportunity to act on it.

(g) This section is subject to any law limiting status as a holder in due course in particular classes of transactions.

§3-303. Value and Consideration.

(a) An instrument is issued or transferred for value if:

    (1) the instrument is issued or transferred for a promise of performance, to the extent the promise has been performed;

    (2) the transferee acquires a security interest or other lien in the instrument other than a lien obtained by judicial proceeding;

    (3) the instrument is issued or transferred as payment of, or as security for, an antecedent claim against any person, whether or not the claim is due;

    (4) the instrument is issued or transferred in exchange for a negotiable instrument; or

    (5) the instrument is issued or transferred in exchange for the incurring of an irrevocable obligation to a third party by the person taking the instrument.

(b) "Consideration" means any consideration sufficient to support a simple contract. The drawer or maker of an instrument has a defense if the instrument is issued without consideration. If an instrument is issued for a promise of performance, the issuer has a defense to the extent performance of the promise is due and the promise has not been performed. If an instrument is issued for value as stated in subsection (a), the instrument is also issued for consideration.

§3-304. Overdue Instrument.

(a) An instrument payable on demand becomes overdue at the earliest of the following times:

    (1) on the day after the day demand for payment is duly made;

    (2) if the instrument is a check, 90 days after its date; or

    (3) if the instrument is not a check, when the instrument has been outstanding for a period of time after its date which is unreasonably long under the circumstances of the particular case in light of the nature of the instrument and usage of the trade.

(b) With respect to an instrument payable at a definite time the following rules apply:

    (1) If the principal is payable in installments and a due date has not been accelerated, the instrument

becomes overdue upon default under the instrument for nonpayment of an installment, and the instrument remains overdue until the default is cured.

    (2) If the principal is not payable in installments and the due date has not been accelerated, the instrument becomes overdue on the day after the due date.

    (3) If a due date with respect to principal has been accelerated, the instrument becomes overdue on the day after the accelerated due date.

(c) Unless the due date of principal has been accelerated, an instrument does not become overdue if there is default in payment of interest but no default in payment of principal.

§3-305. Defenses and Claims in Recoupment.

(a) Except as stated in subsection (b), the right to enforce the obligation of a party to pay an instrument is subject to the following:

    (1) a defense of the obligor based on (i) infancy of the obligor to the extent it is a defense to a simple contract, (ii) duress, lack of legal capacity, or illegality of the transaction which, under other law, nullifies the obligation of the obligor, (iii) fraud that induced the obligor to sign the instrument with neither knowledge nor reasonable opportunity to learn of its character or its essential terms, or (iv) discharge of the obligor in insolvency proceedings;

    (2) defense of the obligor stated in another section of this Article or a defense of the obligor that would be available if the person entitled to enforce the instrument were enforcing a right to payment under a simple contract; and

    (3) a claim in recoupment of the obligor against the original payee of the instrument if the claim arose from the transaction that gave rise to the instrument; but the claim of the obligor may be asserted against a transferee of the instrument only to reduce the amount owing on the instrument at the time the action is brought.

(b) The right of a holder in due course to enforce the obligation of a party to pay the instrument is subject to defenses of the obligor stated in subsection (a)(1), but is not subject to defenses of the obligor stated in subsection (a)(2) or claims in recoupment stated in subsection (a)(3) against a person other than the holder.

(c) Except as stated in subsection (d), in an action to enforce the obligation of a party to pay the instrument, the obligor may not assert against the person entitled to enforce the instrument a defense, claim in recoupment, or claim to the instrument (Section 3-306) of another person, but the other person's claim to the instrument may be asserted by the obligor if the other person is joined in the action and personally asserts the claim against the person entitled to enforce the instrument. An obligor is not obliged to pay the instrument if the person seeking enforcement of the instrument does not have rights of a holder in due course and the obligor proves that the instrument is a lost or stolen instrument.

(d) In an action to enforce the obligation of an accommodation party to pay an instrument, the accommodation party may assert against the person entitled to enforce the instrument any defense or claim in recoupment under subsection (a) that the accommodated party could assert against the person entitled to enforce the instrument, except the defenses of discharge in insolvency proceedings, infancy, and lack of legal capacity.

§3-306. Claims to an Instrument.

A person taking an instrument, other than a person having rights of a holder in due course, is subject to a claim of a property or possessory right in the instrument or its proceeds, including a claim to rescind a negotiation and to recover the instrument or its proceeds. A person having rights of a holder in due course takes free of the claim to the instrument.

§3-307. Notice of Breach of Fiduciary Duty.

(a) In this section:

　(1) "Fiduciary" means an agent, trustee, partner, corporate officer or director, or other representative owing a fiduciary duty with respect to an instrument.

　(2) "Represented person" means the principal, beneficiary, partnership, corporation, or other person to whom the duty stated in paragraph (1) is owed.

(b) If (i) an instrument is taken from a fiduciary for payment or collection or for value, (ii) the taker has knowledge of the fiduciary status of the fiduciary, and (iii) the represented person makes a claim to the instrument or its proceeds on the basis that the transaction of the fiduciary is a breach of fiduciary duty, the following rules apply:

　(1) Notice of breach of fiduciary duty by the fiduciary is notice of the claim of the represented person.

　(2) In the case of an instrument payable to the represented person or the fiduciary as such, the taker has notice of the breach of fiduciary duty if the instrument is (i) taken in payment of or as security for a debt known by the taker to be the personal debt of the fiduciary, (ii) taken in a transaction known by the taker to be for the personal benefit of the fiduciary, or (iii) deposited to an account other than an account of the fiduciary, as such, or an account of the represented person.

　(3) If an instrument is issued by the represented person or the fiduciary as such, and made payable to the fiduciary personally, the taker does not have notice of the breach of fiduciary duty unless the taker knows of the breach of fiduciary duty.

　(4) If an instrument is issued by the represented person or the fiduciary as such, to the taker as payee, the taker has notice of the breach of fiduciary duty if the instrument is (i) taken in payment of or as security for a debt known by the taker to be the personal debt of the fiduciary, (ii) taken in a transaction known by the taker to be for the personal benefit of the fiduciary, or (iii) deposited to an account other than an account of the fiduciary, as such, or an account of the represented person.

§3-308. Proof of Signatures and Status as Holder in Due Course.

(a) In an action with respect to an instrument, the authenticity of, and authority to make, each signature on the instrument is admitted unless specifically denied in the pleadings. If the validity of a signature is denied in the pleadings, the burden of establishing validity is on the person claiming validity, but the signature is presumed to be authentic and authorized unless the action is to enforce the liability of the purported signer and the signer is dead or incompetent at the time of trial of the issue of validity of the signature. If an action to enforce the instrument is brought against a person as the undisclosed principal of a person who signed the instrument as a party to the instrument, the plaintiff has the burden of establishing that the defendant is liable on the instrument as a represented person under Section 3-402(a).

(b) If the validity of signatures is admitted or proved and there is compliance with subsection (a), a plaintiff producing the instrument is entitled to payment if the plaintiff proves entitlement to enforce the instrument under Section 3-301, unless the defendant proves a defense or claim in recoupment. If a defense or claim in recoupment is proved, the right to payment of the plaintiff is subject to the defense or claim, except to the extent the plaintiff proves that the plaintiff has rights of a holder in due course which are not subject to the defense or claim.

§3-309. Enforcement of Lost, Destroyed, or Stolen Instrument.

(a) A person not in possession of an instrument is entitled to enforce the instrument if (i) the person was in possession of the instrument and entitled to enforce it when loss of possession occurred, (ii) the loss of possession was not the result of a transfer by the person or a lawful seizure, and (iii) the person cannot reasonably obtain possession of the instrument because the instrument was destroyed, its whereabouts cannot be determined, or it is in the wrongful possession of an unknown person or a person that cannot be found or is not amenable to service of process.

(b) A person seeking enforcement of an instrument under subsection (a) must prove the terms of the instrument and the person's right to enforce the instrument. If that proof is made, Section 3-308 applies to the case as if the person seeking enforcement had produced the instrument. The court may not enter judgment in favor of the person seeking enforcement unless it finds that the person required to pay the instrument is adequately protected against loss that might occur by reason of a claim by another person to enforce the instrument. Adequate protection may be provided by any reasonable means.

§3-310. Effect of Instrument on Obligation for Which Taken.

(a) Unless otherwise agreed, if a certified check, cashier's check, or teller's check is taken for an obligation, the obligation is discharged to the same extent discharge would result if an amount of money equal to the amount of the instrument were taken in payment of the obligation. Discharge of the obligation does not affect any liability that the obligor may have as an indorser of the instrument.

(b) Unless otherwise agreed and except as provided in subsection (a), if a note or an uncertified check is taken for an obligation, the obligation is suspended to the same extent the obligation would be discharged if an amount of money equal to the amount of the instrument were taken, and the following rules apply:

(1) In the case of an uncertified check, suspension of the obligation continues until dishonor of the check or until it is paid or certified. Payment or certification of the check results in discharge of the obligation to the extent of the amount of the check.

(2) In the case of a note, suspension of the obligation continues until dishonor of the note or until it is paid. Payment of the note results in discharge of the obligation to the extent of the payment.

(3) Except as provided in paragraph (4), if the check or note is dishonored and the obligee of the obligation for which the instrument was taken is the person entitled to enforce the instrument, the obligee may enforce either the instrument or the obligation. In the case of an instrument of a third person which is negotiated to the obligee by the obligor, discharge of the obligor on the instrument also discharges the obligation.

(4) If the person entitled to enforce the instrument taken for an obligation is a person other than the obligee, the obligee may not enforce the obligation to the extent the obligation is suspended. If the obligee is the person entitled to enforce the

instrument but no longer has possession of it because it was lost, stolen, or destroyed, the obligation may not be enforced to the extent of the amount payable on the instrument, and to that extent the obligee's rights against the obligor are limited to enforcement of the instrument.

(c) If an instrument other than one described in subsection (a) or (b) is taken for an obligation, the effect is (i) that stated in subsection (a) if the instrument is one on which a bank is liable as maker or acceptor, or (ii) that stated in subsection (b) in any other case.

§3-311. Accord and Satisfaction by Use of Instrument.

(a) If a person against whom a claim is asserted proves that (i) that person in good faith tendered an instrument to the claimant as full satisfaction of the claim, (ii) the amount of the claim was unliquidated or subject to a bona fide dispute, and (iii) the claimant obtained payment of the instrument, the following subsections apply.

(b) Unless subsection (c) applies, the claim is discharged if the person against whom the claim is asserted proves that the instrument or an accompanying written communication contained a conspicuous statement to the effect that the instrument was tendered as full satisfaction of the claim.

(c) Subject to subsection (d), a claim is not discharged under subsection (b) if either of the following applies:

(1) The claimant, if an organization, proves that (i) within a reasonable time before the tender, the claimant sent a conspicuous statement to the person against whom the claim is asserted that communications concerning disputed debts, including an instrument tendered as full satisfaction of a debt, are to be sent to a designated person, office, or place, and (ii) the instrument or accompanying communication was not received by that designated person, office, or place.

(2) The claimant, whether or not an organization, proves that within 90 days after payment of the instrument, the claimant tendered repayment of the amount of the instrument to the person against whom the claim is asserted. This paragraph does not apply if the claimant is an organization that sent a statement complying with paragraph (1)(i).

(d) A claim is discharged if the person against whom the claim is asserted proves that within a reasonable time before collection of the instrument was initiated, the claimant, or an agent of the claimant having direct responsibility with respect to the disputed obligation, knew that the instrument was tendered in full satisfaction of the claim.

§3-312. Lost, Destroyed, or Stolen Cashier's Check, Teller's Check, or Certified Check.

(a) In this section:

   (1) "Check" means a cashier's check, teller's check, or certified check.

   (2) "Claimant" means a person who claims the right to receive the amount of a cashier's check, teller's check, or certified check that was lost, destroyed, or stolen.

   (3) "Declaration of loss" means a written statement, made under penalty of perjury, to the effect that (i) the declarer lost possession of a check, (ii) the declarer is the drawer or payee of the check, in the case of a certified check, or the remitter or payee of the check, in the case of a cashier's check or teller's check, (iii) the loss of possession was not the result of a transfer by the declarer or a lawful seizure, and (iv) the declarer cannot reasonably obtain possession of the check because the check was destroyed, its whereabouts cannot be determined, or it is in the wrongful possession of an unknown person or a person that cannot be found or is not amenable to service of process.

   (4) "Obligated bank" means the issuer of a cashier's check or teller's check or the acceptor of a certified check.

(b) A claimant may assert a claim to the amount of a check by a communication to the obligated bank describing the check with reasonable certainty and requesting payment of the amount of the check, if (i) the claimant is the drawer or payee of a certified check or the remitter or payee of a cashier's check or teller's check, (ii) the communication contains or is accompanied by a declaration of loss of the claimant with respect to the check, (iii) the communication is received at a time and in a manner affording the bank a reasonable time to act on it before the check is paid, and (iv) the claimant provides reasonable identification if requested by the obligated bank. Delivery of a declaration of loss is a warranty of the truth of the statements made in the declaration. If a claim is asserted in compliance with this subsection, the following rules apply:

   (1) The claim becomes enforceable at the later of (i) the time the claim is asserted, or (ii) the 90th day following the date of the check, in the case of a cashier's check or teller's check, or the 90th day following the date of the acceptance, in the case of a certified check.

   (2) Until the claim becomes enforceable, it has no legal effect and the obligated bank may pay the check or, in the case of a teller's check, may permit the drawee to pay the check. Payment to a person entitled to enforce the check discharges all liability of the obligated bank with respect to the check.

   (3) If the claim becomes enforceable before the check is presented for payment, the obligated bank is not obliged to pay the check.

   (4) When the claim becomes enforceable, the obligated bank becomes obliged to pay the amount of the check to the claimant if payment of the check has not been made to a person entitled to enforce the check. Subject to Section 4-302(a)(1), payment to the claimant discharges all liability of the obligated bank with respect to the check.

(c) If the obligated bank pays the amount of a check to a claimant under subsection (b)(4) and the check is presented for payment by a person having rights of a holder in due course, the claimant is obliged to (i) refund the payment to the obligated bank if the check is paid, or (ii) pay the amount of the check to the person having rights of a holder in due course if the check is dishonored.

(d) If a claimant has the right to assert a claim under subsection (b) and is also a person entitled to enforce a cashier's check, teller's check, or certified check which is lost, destroyed, or stolen, the claimant may assert rights with respect to the check either under this section or Section 3-309.

Part 4: Liability of Parties

§3-401. Signature.

(a) A person is not liable on an instrument unless (i) the person signed the instrument, or (ii) the person is represented by an agent or representative who signed the instrument and the signature is binding on the represented person under Section 3-402.

(b) A signature may be made (i) manually or by means of a device or machine, and (ii) by the use of any name, including a trade or assumed name, or by a word, mark, or symbol executed or adopted by a person with present intention to authenticate a writing.

§3-402. Signature by Representative.

(a) If a person acting, or purporting to act, as a representative signs an instrument by signing either the name of the represented person or the name of the signer, the represented person is bound by the signature to the same extent the represented person would be bound if the signature were on a simple contract. If the represented person is bound, the signature of the representative is the "authorized signature of the represented person" and the represented person is liable on the instrument, whether or not identified in the instrument.

(b) If a representative signs the name of the representative to an instrument and the signature is an authorized signature of the represented person, the following rules apply:

(1) If the form of the signature shows unambiguously that the signature is made on behalf of the represented person who is identified in the instrument, the representative is not liable on the instrument.

(2) Subject to subsection (c), if (i) the form of the signature does not show unambiguously that the signature is made in a representative capacity or (ii) the represented person is not identified in the instrument, the representative is liable on the instrument to a holder in due course that took the instrument, without notice that the representative was not intended to be liable on the instrument. With respect to any other person, the representative is liable on the instrument unless the representative proves that the original parties did not intend the representative to be liable on the instrument.

(c) If a representative signs the name of the representative as drawer of a check without indication of the representative status and the check is payable from an account of the represented person who is identified on the check, the signer is not liable on the check if the signature is an authorized signature of the represented person.

§3-403. Unauthorized Signature.

(a) Unless otherwise provided in this Article or Article 4, an unauthorized signature is ineffective except as the signature of the unauthorized signer in favor of a person who in good faith pays the instrument or takes it for value. An unauthorized signature may be ratified for all purposes of this Article.

(b) If the signature of more than one person is required to constitute the authorized signature of an organization, the signature of the organization is unauthorized if one of the required signatures is lacking.

(c) The civil or criminal liability of a person who makes an unauthorized signature is not affected by any provision of this Article which makes the unauthorized signature effective for the purposes of this Article.

§3-404. Impostors; Fictitious Payees.

(a) If an impostor, by use of the mails or otherwise, induces the issuer of an instrument to issue the instrument to the impostor, or to a person acting in concert with the impostor, by impersonating the payee of the instrument or a person authorized to act for the payee, an indorsement of the instrument by any person in the name of the payee is effective as the indorsement of the payee in favor of a person who, in good faith, pays the instrument or takes it for value or for collection.

(b) If (i) a person whose intent determines to whom an instrument is payable (Section 3-110(a) or (b)) does not intend the person identified as payee to have any interest in the instrument, or (ii) the person identified as payee of an instrument is a fictitious person, the following rules apply until the instrument is negotiated by special indorsement:

(1) Any person in possession of the instrument is its holder.

(2) An indorsement by any person in the name of the payee stated in the instrument is effective as the indorsement of the payee in favor of a person who, in good faith, pays the instrument or takes it for value or for collection.

(c) Under subsection (a) or (b), an indorsement is made in the name of a payee if (i) it is made in a name substantially similar to that of the payee or (ii) the instrument, whether or not indorsed, is deposited in a depositary bank to an account in a name substantially similar to that of the payee.

(d) With respect to an instrument to which subsection (a) or (b) applies, if a person paying the instrument or taking it for value or for collection fails to exercise ordinary care in paying or taking the instrument and that failure substantially contributes to loss resulting from payment of the instrument, the person bearing the loss may recover from the person failing to exercise ordinary care to the extent the failure to exercise ordinary care contributed to the loss.

§3-405. Employer's Responsibility for Fraudulent Indorsement by Employee.

(a) In this section

(1) "Employee" includes an independent contractor and employee of an independent contractor retained by the employer.

(2) "Fraudulent indorsement" means (i) in the case of an instrument payable to the employer, a forged indorsement purporting to be that of the employer, or (ii) in the case of an instrument with respect to which the employer is the issuer, a forged indorsement purporting to be that of the person identified as payee.

(3) "Responsibility" with respect to instruments means authority (i) to sign or indorse instruments on behalf of the employer, (ii) to process instruments received by the employer for bookkeeping purposes, for deposit to an account, or for other disposition, (iii) to prepare or process instruments for issue in the name of the employer, (iv) to supply information determining the names or addresses of payees of instruments to be issued in the name of the employer, (v) to control the disposition of instruments to be issued in the name of the employer, or (vi) to act otherwise with respect to instruments in a responsible capacity. "Responsibility" does not include authority that merely

allows an employee to have access to instruments or blank or incomplete instrument forms that are being stored or transported or are part of incoming or outgoing mail, or similar access.

(b) For the purpose of determining the rights and liabilities of a person who, in good faith, pays an instrument or takes it for value or for collection, if an employer entrusted an employee with responsibility with respect to the instrument and the employee or a person acting in concert with the employee makes a fraudulent indorsement of the instrument, the indorsement is effective as the indorsement of the person to whom the instrument is payable if it is made in the name of that person. If the person paying the instrument or taking it for value or for collection fails to exercise ordinary care in paying or taking the instrument and that failure substantially contributes to loss resulting from the fraud, the person bearing the loss may recover from the person failing to exercise ordinary care to the extent the failure to exercise ordinary care contributed to the loss.

(c) Under subsection (b), an indorsement is made in the name of the person to whom an instrument is payable if (i) it is made in a name substantially similar to the name of that person or (ii) the instrument, whether or not indorsed, is deposited in a depositary bank to an account in a name substantially similar to the name of that person.

§3-406. Negligence Contributing to Forged Signature or Alteration of Instrument.

(a) A person whose failure to exercise ordinary care substantially contributes to an alteration of an instrument or to the making of a forged signature on an instrument is precluded from asserting the alteration or the forgery against a person who, in good faith, pays the instrument or takes it for value or for collection.

(b) Under subsection (a), if the person asserting the preclusion fails to exercise ordinary care in paying or taking the instrument and that failure substantially contributes to loss, the loss is allocated between the person precluded and the person asserting the preclusion according to the extent to which the failure of each to exercise ordinary care contributed to the loss.

(c) Under subsection (a), the burden of proving failure to exercise ordinary care is on the person asserting the preclusion. Under subsection (b), the burden of proving failure to exercise ordinary care is on the person precluded.

§3-407. Alteration.

(a) "Alteration" means (i) an unauthorized change in an instrument that purports to modify in any respect the obligation of a party, or (ii) an unauthorized addition of words or numbers or other change to an incomplete instrument relating to the obligation of a party.

(b) Except as provided in subsection (c), an alteration fraudulently made discharges a party whose obligation is affected by the alteration unless that party assents or is precluded from asserting the alteration. No other alteration discharges a party, and the instrument may be enforced according to its original terms.

(c) A payor bank or drawee paying a fraudulently altered instrument or a person taking it for value, in good faith and without notice of the alteration, may enforce rights with respect to the instrument (i) according to its original terms, or (ii) in the case of an incomplete instrument altered by unauthorized completion, according to its terms as completed.

§3-408. Drawee Not Liable on Unaccepted Draft.
A check or other draft does not of itself operate as an assignment of funds in the hands of the drawee available for its payment, and the drawee is not liable on the instrument until the drawee accepts it.

§3-409. Acceptance of Draft; Certified Check.

(a) "Acceptance" means the drawee's signed agreement to pay a draft as presented. It must be written on the draft and may consist of the drawee's signature alone. Acceptance may be made at any time and becomes effective when notification pursuant to instructions is given or the accepted draft is delivered for the purpose of giving rights on the acceptance to any person.

(b) A draft may be accepted although it has not been signed by the drawer, is otherwise incomplete, is overdue, or has been dishonored.

(c) If a draft is payable at a fixed period after sight and the acceptor fails to date the acceptance, the holder may complete the acceptance by supplying a date in good faith.

(d) "Certified check" means a check accepted by the bank on which it is drawn. Acceptance may be made as stated in subsection (a) or by a writing on the check which indicates that the check is certified. The drawee of a check has no obligation to certify the check, and refusal to certify is not dishonor of the check.

§3-410. Acceptance Varying Draft.

(a) If the terms of a drawee's acceptance vary from the terms of the draft as presented, the holder may refuse the acceptance and treat the draft as dishonored. In that case, the drawee may cancel the acceptance.

(b) The terms of a draft are not varied by an acceptance to pay at a particular bank or place in the United States, unless the acceptance states that the draft is to be paid only at that bank or place.

(c) If the holder assents to an acceptance varying the terms of a draft, the obligation of each drawer and indorser that does not expressly assent to the acceptance is discharged.

§3-411. Refusal to Pay Cashier's Checks, Teller's Checks, and Certified Checks.

(a) In this section, "obligated bank" means the acceptor of a certified check or the issuer of a cashier's check or teller's check bought from the issuer.

(b) If the obligated bank wrongfully (i) refuses to pay a cashier's check or certified check, (ii) stops payment of a teller's check, or (iii) refuses to pay a dishonored teller's check, the person asserting the right to enforce the check is entitled to compensation for expenses and loss of interest resulting from the nonpayment and may recover consequential damages if the obligated bank refuses to pay after receiving notice of particular circumstances giving rise to the damages.

(c) Expenses or consequential damages under subsection (b) are not recoverable if the refusal of the obligated bank to pay occurs because (i) the bank suspends payments, (ii) the obligated bank asserts a claim or defense of the bank that it has reasonable grounds to believe is available against the person entitled to enforce the instrument, (iii) the obligated bank has a reasonable doubt whether the person demanding payment is the person entitled to enforce the instrument, or (iv) payment is prohibited by law.

§3-412. Obligation of Issuer of Note or Cashier's Check.

The issuer of a note or cashier's check or other draft drawn on the drawer is obliged to pay the instrument (i) according to its terms at the time it was issued or, if not issued, at the time it first came into possession of a holder, or (ii) if the issuer signed an incomplete instrument, according to its terms when completed, to the extent stated in Sections 3-115 and 3-407. The obligation is owed to a person entitled to enforce the instrument or to an indorser who paid the instrument under Section 3-415.

§3-413. Obligation of Acceptor.

(a) The acceptor of a draft is obliged to pay the draft (i) according to its terms at the time it was accepted, even though the acceptance states that the draft is payable "as originally drawn" or equivalent terms, (ii) if the acceptance varies the terms of the draft, according to the terms of the draft as varied, or (iii) if the acceptance is of a draft that is an incomplete instrument, according to its terms when completed, to the extent stated in Sections 3-115 and 3-407. The obligation is owed to a person entitled to enforce the draft or to the drawer or an indorser who paid the draft under Section 3-414 or 3-415.

(b) If the certification of a check or other acceptance of a draft states the amount certified or accepted, the obligation of the acceptor is that amount. If (i) the certification or acceptance does not state an amount, (ii) the amount of the instrument is subsequently raised, and (iii) the instrument is then negotiated to a holder in due course, the obligation of the acceptor is the amount of the instrument at the time it was taken by the holder in due course.

§3-414. Obligation of Drawer.

(a) This section does not apply to cashier's checks or other drafts drawn on the drawer.

(b) If an unaccepted draft is dishonored, the drawer is obliged to pay the draft (i) according to its terms at the time it was issued or, if not issued, at the time it first came into possession of a holder, or (ii) if the drawer signed an incomplete instrument, according to its terms when completed, to the extent stated in Sections 3-115 and 3-407. The obligation is owed to a person entitled to enforce the draft or to an indorser who paid the draft under Section 3-415.

(c) If a draft is accepted by a bank, the drawer is discharged, regardless of when or by whom acceptance was obtained.

(d) If a draft is accepted and the acceptor is not a bank, the obligation of the drawer to pay the draft if the draft is dishonored by the acceptor is the same as the obligation of an indorser under Section 3-415(a) and (c).

(e) If a draft states that it is drawn "without recourse" or otherwise disclaims liability of the drawer to pay the draft, the drawer is not liable under subsection (b) to pay the draft if the draft is not a check. A disclaimer of the liability stated in subsection (b) is not effective if the draft is a check.

(f) If (i) a check is not presented for payment or given to a depositary bank for collection within 30 days after its date, (ii) the drawee suspends payments after expiration of the 30-day period without paying the check, and (iii) because of the suspension of payments, the drawer is deprived of funds maintained with the drawee to cover payment of the check, the drawer to the extent deprived of funds may discharge its obligation to pay the check by assigning to the person entitled to enforce the check the rights of the drawer against the drawee with respect to the funds.

§3-415. Obligation of Indorser.

(a) Subject to subsections (b), (c), and (d) and to Section 3-419(d), if an instrument is dishonored, an indorser is obliged to pay the amount due on the instrument (i) according to the terms of the instrument at the time it was indorsed, or (ii) if the indorser indorsed an incomplete instrument, according to its terms when completed, to the extent stated in Sections 3-115 and 3-407. The obligation of the indorser is owed to a person entitled to enforce the instrument or to a subsequent indorser who paid the instrument under this section.

(b) If an indorsement states that it is made "without recourse" or otherwise disclaims liability of the indorser, the indorser is not liable under subsection (a) to pay the instrument.

(c) If notice of dishonor of an instrument is required by Section 3-503 and notice of dishonor complying with that section is not given to an indorser, the liability of the indorser under subsection (a) is discharged.

(d) If a draft is accepted by a bank after an indorsement is made, the liability of the indorser under subsection (a) is discharged.

(e) If an indorser of a check is liable under subsection (a) and the check is not presented for payment, or given to a depositary bank for collection, within 30 days after the day the indorsement was made, the liability of the indorser under subsection (a) is discharged.

§3-416. Transfer Warranties.

(a) A person who transfers an instrument for consideration warrants to the transferee and, if the transfer is by indorsement, to any subsequent transferee that:

(1) the warrantor is a person entitled to enforce the instrument;

(2) all signatures on the instrument are authentic and authorized;

(3) the instrument has not been altered;

(4) the instrument is not subject to a defense or claim in recoupment of any party which can be asserted against the warrantor; and

(5) the warrantor has no knowledge of any insolvency proceeding commenced with respect to the maker or acceptor or, in the case of an unaccepted draft, the drawer.

(b) A person to whom the warranties under subsection (a) are made and who took the instrument in good faith may recover from the warrantor as damages for breach of warranty an amount equal to the loss suffered as a result of the breach, but not more than the amount of the instrument plus expenses and loss of interest incurred as a result of the breach.

(c) The warranties stated in subsection (a) cannot be disclaimed with respect to checks. Unless notice of a claim for breach of warranty is given to the warrantor within 30 days after the claimant has reason to know of the breach and the identity of the warrantor, the liability of the warrantor under subsection (b) is discharged to the extent of any loss caused by the delay in giving notice of the claim.

(d) A [cause of action] for breach of warranty under this section accrues when the claimant has reason to know of the breach.

§3-417. Presentment Warranties.

(a) If an unaccepted draft is presented to the drawee for payment or acceptance and the drawee pays or accepts the draft, (i) the person obtaining payment or acceptance, at the time of presentment, and (ii) a previous transferor of the draft, at the time of transfer, warrant to the drawee making payment or accepting the draft in good faith that:

(1) the warrantor is, or was, at the time the warrantor transferred the draft, a person entitled to enforce the draft or authorized to obtain payment or acceptance of the draft on behalf of a person entitled to enforce the draft;

(2) the draft has not been altered; and

(3) the warrantor has no knowledge that the signature of the drawer of the draft is unauthorized.

(b) A drawee making payment may recover from any warrantor damages for breach of warranty equal to the amount paid by the drawee less the amount the drawee received or is entitled to receive from the drawer because of the payment. In addition, the drawee is entitled to compensation for expenses and loss of interest resulting from the breach. The right of the drawee to recover damages under this subsection is not affected by any failure of the drawee to exercise ordinary care in making payment. If the drawee accepts the draft, breach of warranty is a defense to the obligation of the acceptor. If the acceptor makes payment with respect to the draft, the acceptor is entitled to recover from any warrantor for breach of warranty the amounts stated in this subsection.

(c) If a drawee asserts a claim for breach of warranty under subsection (a) based on an unauthorized indorsement of the draft or an alteration of the draft, the warrantor may defend by proving that the indorsement is effective under Section 3-404 or 3-405 or the drawer is precluded under Section 3-406 or 4-406 from asserting against the drawee the unauthorized indorsement or alteration.

(d) If (i) a dishonored draft is presented for payment to the drawer or an indorser or (ii) any other instrument is presented for payment to a party obliged to pay the instrument, and (iii) payment is received, the following rules apply:

(1) The person obtaining payment and a prior transferor of the instrument warrant to the person making payment in good faith that the warrantor is, or was, at the time the warrantor transferred the instrument, a person entitled to enforce the instrument or authorized to obtain payment on behalf of a person entitled to enforce the instrument.

(2) The person making payment may recover from any warrantor for breach of warranty an amount equal to the amount paid plus expenses and loss of interest resulting from the breach.

(e) The warranties stated in subsections (a) and (d) cannot be disclaimed with respect to checks. Unless notice of a claim for breach of warranty is given to the warrantor within 30 days after the claimant has reason to know of the breach and the identity of the warrantor, the liability of the warrantor under subsection (b) or (d) is discharged to the extent of any loss caused by the delay in giving notice of the claim.

(f) A [cause of action] for breach of warranty under this section accrues when the claimant has reason to know of the breach.

§3-418. Payment or Acceptance by Mistake.

(a) Except as provided in subsection (c), if the drawee of a draft pays or accepts the draft and the drawee acted on the mistaken belief that (i) payment of the draft had not been stopped pursuant to Section 4-403 or (ii) the signature of the drawer of the draft was authorized, the drawee may recover the amount of the draft from the person to whom or for whose benefit payment was made or, in the case of acceptance, may revoke the acceptance. Rights of the drawee under this subsection are not affected by failure of the drawee to exercise ordinary care in paying or accepting the draft.

(b) Except as provided in subsection (c), if an instrument has been paid or accepted by mistake and the case is not covered by subsection (a), the person paying or accepting may, to the extent permitted by the law governing mistake and restitution, (i) recover the payment from the person to whom or for whose benefit payment was made or (ii) in the case of acceptance, may revoke the acceptance.

(c) The remedies provided by subsection (a) or (b) may not be asserted against a person who took the instrument in good faith and for value or who in good faith changed position in reliance on the payment or acceptance. This subsection does not limit remedies provided by Section 3-417 or 4-407.

(d) Notwithstanding Section 4-215, if an instrument is paid or accepted by mistake and the payor or acceptor recovers payment or revokes acceptance under subsection (a) or (b), the instrument is deemed not to have been paid or accepted and is treated as dishonored, and the person from whom payment is recovered has rights as a person entitled to enforce the dishonored instrument.

§3-419. Instruments Signed for Accommodation.

(a) If an instrument is issued for value given for the benefit of a party to the instrument ("accommodated party") and another party to the instrument ("An accommodation party") signs the instrument for the purpose of incurring liability on the instrument without being a direct beneficiary of the value given for the instrument, the instrument is signed by the accommodation party "for accommodation".

(b) An accommodation party may sign the instrument as maker, drawer, acceptor, or indorser and, subject to subsection (d), is obliged to pay the instrument in the capacity in which the accommodation party signs.

The obligation of an accommodation party may be enforced notwithstanding any statute of frauds and whether or not the accommodation party receives consideration for the accommodation.

(c) A person signing an instrument is presumed to be an accommodation party and there is notice that the instrument is signed for accommodation if the signature is an anomalous indorsement or is accompanied by words indicating that the signer is acting as surety or guarantor with respect to the obligation of another party to the instrument. Except as provided in Section 3-605, the obligation of an accommodation party to pay the instrument is not affected by the fact that the person enforcing the obligation had notice when the instrument was taken by that person that the accommodation party signed the instrument for accommodation.

(d) If the signature of a party to an instrument is accompanied by words indicating unambiguously that the party is guaranteeing collection rather than payment of the obligation of another party to the instrument, the signer is obliged to pay the amount due on the instrument to a person entitled to enforce the instrument only if (i) execution of judgment against the other party has been returned unsatisfied, (ii) the other party is insolvent or in an insolvency proceeding, (iii) the other party cannot be served with process, or (iv) it is otherwise apparent that payment cannot be obtained from the other party.

(e) An accommodation party who pays the instrument is entitled to reimbursement from the accommodated party and is entitled to enforce the instrument against the accommodated party. An accommodated party who pays the instrument has no right of recourse against, and is not entitled to contribution from, an accommodation party.

§3-420. Conversion of Instrument.

(a) The law applicable to conversion of personal property applies to instruments. An instrument is also converted if it is taken by transfer, other than a negotiation, from a person not entitled to enforce the instrument or a bank makes or obtains payment with respect to the instrument for a person not entitled to enforce the instrument or receive payment. An action for conversion of an instrument may not be brought by (i) the issuer or acceptor of the instrument or (ii) a payee or indorsee who did not receive delivery of the instrument either directly or through delivery to an agent or a co-payee.

(b) In an action under subsection (a), the measure of liability is presumed to be the amount payable on the instrument, but recovery may not exceed the amount of the plaintiff's interest in the instrument.

(c) A representative, other than a depositary bank, who has in good faith dealt with an instrument or its proceeds on behalf of one who was not the person entitled to enforce the instrument is not liable in conversion to that person beyond the amount of any proceeds that it has not paid out.

Part 5: Dishonor

§3-501. Presentment.

(a) "Presentment" means a demand made by or on behalf of a person entitled to enforce an instrument (i) to pay the instrument made to the drawee or a party obliged to pay the instrument or, in the case of a note or accepted draft payable at a bank, to the bank, or (ii) to accept a draft made to the drawee.

(b) The following rules are subject to Article 4, agreement of the parties, and clearing-house rules and the like:

(1) Presentment may be made at the place of payment of the instrument and must be made at the place of payment if the instrument is payable at a bank in the United States; may be made by any commercially reasonable means, including an oral, written, or electronic communication; is effective when the demand for payment or acceptance is received by the person to whom presentment is made; and is effective if made to any one of two or more makers, acceptors, drawees, or other payors.

(2) Upon demand of the person to whom presentment is made, the person making presentment must (i) exhibit the instrument, (ii) give reasonable identification and, if presentment is made on behalf of another person, reasonable evidence of authority to do so, and (iii) sign a receipt on the instrument for any payment made or surrender the instrument if full payment is made.

(3) Without dishonoring the instrument, the party to whom presentment is made may (i) return the instrument for lack of a necessary indorsement, or (ii) refuse payment or acceptance for failure of the presentment to comply with the terms of the instrument, an agreement of the parties, or other applicable law or rule.

(4) The party to whom presentment is made may treat presentment as occurring on the next business day after the day of presentment if the party to whom presentment is made has established a cut-off hour not earlier than 2 p.m for the receipt and processing of instruments presented for payment or acceptance and presentment is made after the cut-off hour.

§3-502. Dishonor.

(a) Dishonor of a note is governed by the following rules:

(1) If the note is payable on demand, the note is dishonored if presentment is duly made to the maker and the note is not paid on the day of presentment.

(2) If the note is not payable on demand and is payable at or through a bank or the terms of the note require presentment, the note is dishonored if presentment is duly made and the note is not paid on the day it becomes payable or the day of presentment, whichever is later.

(3) If the note is not payable on demand and paragraph (2) does not apply, the note is dishonored if it is not paid on the day it becomes payable.

(b) Dishonor of an unaccepted draft other than a documentary draft is governed by the following rules:

(1) If a check is duly presented for payment to the payor bank otherwise than for immediate payment over the counter, the check is dishonored if the payor bank makes timely return of the check or sends timely notice of dishonor or nonpayment under Section 4-301 or 4-302, or becomes accountable for the amount of the check under Section 4-302.

(2) If a draft is payable on demand and paragraph (1) does not apply, the draft is dishonored if presentment for payment is duly made to the drawee and the draft is not paid on the day of presentment.

(3) If a draft is payable on a date stated in the draft, the draft is dishonored if (i) presentment for payment is duly made to the drawee and payment is not made on the day the draft becomes payable or the day of presentment, whichever is later, or (ii) presentment for acceptance is duly made before the day the draft becomes payable and the draft is not accepted on the day of presentment.

(4) If a draft is payable on elapse of a period of time after sight or acceptance, the draft is dishonored if presentment for acceptance is duly made and the draft is not accepted on the day of presentment.

(c) Dishonor of an unaccepted documentary draft occurs according to the rules stated in subsection (b)(2), (3), and (4), except that payment or acceptance may be delayed without dishonor until no later than the close of the third business day of the drawee following the day on which payment or acceptance is required by those paragraphs.

(d) Dishonor of an accepted draft is governed by the following rules:

(1) If the draft is payable on demand, the draft is dishonored if presentment for payment is duly made to the acceptor and the draft is not paid on the day of presentment.

(2) If the draft is not payable on demand, the draft is dishonored if presentment for payment is duly made to the acceptor and payment is not made on the day it becomes payable or the day of presentment, whichever is later.

(e) In any case in which presentment is otherwise required for dishonor under this section and presentment is excused under Section 3-504, dishonor occurs without presentment if the instrument is not duly accepted or paid.

(f) If a draft is dishonored because timely acceptance of the draft was not made and the person entitled to demand acceptance consents to a late acceptance, from the time of acceptance the draft is treated as never having been dishonored.

§3-503. Notice of Dishonor.

(a) The obligation of an indorser stated in Section 3-415(a) and the obligation of a drawer stated in Section 3-414(d) may not be enforced unless (i) the indorser or drawer is given notice of dishonor of the instrument complying with this section or (ii) notice of dishonor is excused under Section 3-504(b).

(b) Notice of dishonor may be given by any person; may be given by any commercially reasonable means, including an oral, written, or electronic communication; and is sufficient if it reasonably identifies the instrument and indicates that the instrument has been dishonored or has not been paid or accepted. Return of an instrument given to a bank for collection is sufficient notice of dishonor.

(c) Subject to Section 3-504(c), with respect to an instrument taken for collection by a collecting bank, notice of dishonor must be given (i) by the bank before midnight of the next banking day following the banking day on which the bank receives notice of dishonor of the instrument, or (ii) by any other person within 30 days following the day on which the person receives notice of dishonor. With respect to any other instrument, notice of dishonor must be given within 30 days following the day on which dishonor occurs.

§3-504. Excused Presentment and Notice of Dishonor.

(a) Presentment for payment or acceptance of an instrument is excused if (i) the person entitled to present the instrument cannot with reasonable diligence make presentment, (ii) the maker or acceptor has repudiated an obligation to pay the instrument or is dead or in insolvency proceedings, (iii) by the terms of the instrument presentment is not necessary to enforce the obligation of indorsers or the drawer, (iv) the drawer or indorser whose obligation is being enforced has waived presentment or otherwise has no reason to expect or right to require that the instrument be paid or accepted, or (v) the drawer instructed the drawee not to pay or accept the draft or the drawee was not obligated to the drawer to pay the draft.

(b) Notice of dishonor is excused if (i) by the terms of the instrument notice of dishonor is not necessary to enforce the obligation of a party to pay the instrument, or (ii) the party whose obligation is being enforced waived notice of dishonor. A waiver of presentment is also a waiver of notice of dishonor.

(c) Delay in giving notice of dishonor is excused if the delay was caused by circumstances beyond the control of the person giving the notice and the person giving the notice exercised reasonable diligence after the cause of the delay ceased to operate.

§3-505. Evidence of Dishonor.

(a) The following are admissible as evidence and create a presumption of dishonor and of any notice of dishonor stated:

   (1) a document regular in form as provided in subsection (b) which purports to be a protest;

   (2) a purported stamp or writing of the drawee, payor bank, or presenting bank on or accompanying the instrument stating that acceptance or payment has been refused unless reasons for the refusal are stated and the reasons are not consistent with dishonor;

   (3) a book or record of the drawee, payor bank, or collecting bank, kept in the usual course of business which shows dishonor, even if there is no evidence of who made the entry.

(b) A protest is a certificate of dishonor made by a United States consul or vice consul, or a notary public or other person authorized to administer oaths by the law of the place where dishonor occurs. It may be made upon information satisfactory to that person. The protest must identify the instrument and certify either that presentment has been made or, if not made, the reason why it was not made, and that the instrument has been dishonored by nonacceptance or nonpayment. The protest may also certify that notice of dishonor has been given to some or all parties.

Part 6: Discharge and Payment

§3-601. Discharge and Effect of Discharge.

(a) The obligation of a party to pay the instrument is discharged as stated in this Article or by an act or agreement with the party which would discharge an obligation to pay money under a simple contract.

(b) Discharge of the obligation of a party is not effective against a person acquiring rights of a holder in due course of the instrument without notice of the discharge.

§3-602. Payment.

(a) Subject to subsection (b), an instrument is paid to the extent payment is made (i) by or on behalf of a party obliged to pay the instrument, and (ii) to a person entitled to enforce the instrument. To the extent of the payment, the obligation of the party obliged to pay the instrument is discharged even though payment is made with knowledge of a claim to the instrument under Section 3-306 by another person.

(b) The obligation of a party to pay the instrument is not discharged under subsection (a) if:

    (1) a claim to the instrument under Section 3-306 is enforceable against the party receiving payment and (i) payment is made with knowledge by the payor that payment is prohibited by injunction or similar process of a court of competent jurisdiction, or (ii) in the case of an instrument other than a cashier's check, teller's check, or certified check, the party making payment accepted, from the person having a claim to the instrument, indemnity against loss resulting from refusal to pay the person entitled to enforce the instrument; or

    (2) the person making payment knows that the instrument is a stolen instrument and pays a person it knows is in wrongful possession of the instrument.

§3-603. Tender of Payment.

(a) If tender of payment of an obligation to pay an instrument is made to a person entitled to enforce the instrument, the effect of tender is governed by principles of law applicable to tender of payment under a simple contract.

(b) If tender of payment of an obligation to pay an instrument is made to a person entitled to enforce the instrument and the tender is refused,. . . .

§3-604. Discharge by Cancellation or Renunciation.

(a) A person entitled to enforce an instrument, with or without consideration, may discharge the obligation of a party to pay the instrument (i) by an intentional voluntary act, such as surrender of the instrument to the party, destruction, mutilation, or cancellation of the instrument, cancellation or striking out of the party's signature, or the addition of words to the instrument indicating discharge, or (ii) by agreeing not to sue or otherwise renouncing rights against the party by a signed writing.

(b) Cancellation or striking out of an indorsement pursuant to subsection (a) does not affect the status and rights of a party derived from the indorsement.

§3-605. Discharge of Indorsers and Accommodation Parties.

(a) In this section, the term "indorser" includes a drawer having the obligation described in Section 3-414(d).

(b) Discharge, under Section 3-604, of the obligation of a party to pay an instrument does not discharge the obligation of an indorser or accommodation party having a right of recourse against the discharged party.

(c) If a person entitled to enforce an instrument agrees, with or without consideration, to an extension of the due date of the obligation of a party to pay the instrument, the extension discharges an indorser or accommodation party having a right of recourse against the party whose obligation is extended to the extent the indorser or accommodation party proves that the extension caused loss to the indorser or accommodation party with respect to the right of recourse.

(d) If a person entitled to enforce an instrument agrees, with or without consideration, to a material modification of the obligation of a party other than an extension of the due date, the modification discharges the obligation of an indorser or accommodation party having a right of recourse against the person whose obligation is modified to the extent the modification causes loss to the indorser or accommodation party with respect to the right of recourse. The loss suffered by the indorser or accommodation party as a result of the modification is equal to the amount of the right of recourse unless the person enforcing the instrument proves that no loss was caused by the modification or that the loss caused by the modification was an amount less than the amount of the right of recourse.

(e) If the obligation of a party to pay an instrument is secured by an interest in collateral and a person entitled to enforce the instrument impairs the value of the interest in collateral, the obligation of an indorser or accommodation party having a right of recourse against the obligor is discharged to the extent of the impairment. The value of an interest in collateral is impaired to the extent (i) the value of the interest is reduced to an amount less than the amount of the right of recourse of the party asserting discharge, or (ii) the reduction in value of the interest causes an increase in the amount by which the amount of the right of recourse exceeds the value of the interest. The burden of proving impairment is on the party asserting discharge.

(f) If the obligation of a party is secured by an interest in collateral not provided by an accommodation party and a person entitled to enforce the instrument impairs the value of the interest in collateral, the obligation of any party who is jointly and severally liable with respect to the secured obligation is discharged to the extent the impairment causes the party asserting discharge to pay more than that party would have been obliged to pay, taking into account rights of contribution, if impairment had not occurred. If the party asserting discharge is an accommodation party not entitled to discharge under subsection (e), the party is deemed to have a right to contribution based on joint and several liability rather than a right to reimbursement. The burden of proving impairment is on the party asserting discharge.

(g) Under subsection (e) or (f), impairing value of an interest in collateral includes (i) failure to obtain or maintain perfection or recordation of the interest in collateral, (ii) release of collateral without substitution of collateral of equal value, (iii) failure to perform a duty to preserve the value of collateral owed, under Article 9 or other law, to a debtor or surety or other person secondarily liable, or (iv) failure to comply with applicable law in disposing of collateral.

(h) An accommodation party is not discharged under subsection (c), (d), or (e) unless the person entitled to enforce the instrument knows of the accommodation or has notice under Section 3-419(c) that the instrument was signed for accommodation.

(i) A party is not discharged under this section if (i) the party asserting discharge consents to the event or conduct that is the basis of the discharge, or (ii) the instrument or a separate agreement of the party provides for waiver of discharge under this section either specifically or by general language indicating that parties waive defenses based on suretyship or impairment of collateral.

United Nations Convention on Contracts for the International Sale of Goods

THE STATES PARTIES TO THIS CONVENTION,
BEARING IN MIND the broad objectives in the resolutions adopted by the sixth special session of the General Assembly of the United Nations on the establishment of a New International Economic Order,
CONSIDERING that the development of international trade on the basis of equality and mutual benefit is an important element in promoting friendly relations among States,
BEING OF THE OPINION that the adoption of uniform rules which govern contracts for the international sale of goods and take into account the different social, economic and legal systems would contribute to the removal of legal barriers in international trade and promote the development of international trade,
HAVE AGREED as follows:

Part I Sphere of Application and General Provisions

Chapter I Sphere of Application

Article 1

(1) This Convention applies to contracts of sale of goods between parties whose places of business are in different States:
  (a) when the States are Contracting States; or
  (b) when the rules of private international law lead to the application of the law of a Contracting State. [Pursuant to the reservation permitted by Article 95, the United States has excluded applicability of the Convention under this subparagraph.]

(2) The fact that the parties have their places of business in different States is to be disregarded whenever this fact does not appear either from the contract or from any dealings between, or from information disclosed by, the parties at any time before or at the conclusion of the contract.

(3) Neither the nationality of the parties nor the civil or commercial character of the parties or of the contract is to be taken into consideration in determining the application of this Convention.

Article 2 This Convention does not apply to sales:

(a) of goods bought for personal, family or household use, unless the seller, at any time before or at the conclusion of the contract, neither knew nor ought to have known that the goods were bought for any such use;

(b) by auction;

(c) on execution or otherwise by authority of law;

(d) of stocks, shares, investment securities, negotiable instruments or money;

(e) of ships, vessels, hovercraft or aircraft;

(f) of electricity.

Article 3

(1) Contracts for the supply of goods to be manufactured or produced are to be considered sales unless the party who orders the goods undertakes to supply a substantial part of the materials necessary for such manufacture or production.

(2) This Convention does not apply to contracts in which the preponderant part of the obligations of the party who furnishes the goods consists in the supply of labour or other services.

Article 4 This Convention governs only the formation of the contract of sale and the rights and obligations of the seller and the buyer arising from such a contract. In particular, except as otherwise expressly provided in this Convention, it is not concerned with:

(a) the validity of the contract or of any of its provisions or of any usage;

(b) the effect which the contract may have on the property in the goods sold.

Article 5 This Convention does not apply to the liability of the seller for death or personal injury caused by the goods to any person.

Article 6 The parties may exclude the application of this Convention or, subject to Article 12, derogate from or vary the effect of any of its provisions.

Chapter II General Provisions

Article 7

(1) In the interpretation of this Convention, regard is to be had to its international character and to the need to promote uniformity in its application and the observance of good faith in international trade.

(2) Questions concerning matters governed by this Convention which are not expressly settled in it are to be settled in conformity with the general principles on which it is based or, in the absence of such principles, in conformity with the law applicable by virtue of the rules of private international law.

Article 8

(1) For the purposes of this Convention statements made by and other conduct of a party are to be interpreted according to his intent where the other party knew or could not have been unaware what that intent was.

(2) If the preceding paragraph is not applicable, statements made by and other conduct of a party are to be interpreted according to the understanding that a reasonable person of the same kind as the other party would have had in the same circumstances.

(3) In determining the intent of a party or the understanding a reasonable person would have had, due consideration is to be given to all relevant circumstances of the case including the negotiations, any practices which the parties have established between themselves, usages and any subsequent conduct of the parities.

Article 9

(1) The parties are bound by any usage to which they have agreed and by any practices which they have established between themselves.

(2) The parties are considered, unless otherwise agreed, to have impliedly made applicable to their contract or its formation a usage of which the parties know or ought to have known and which in international trade is widely known to, and regularly observed by, parties to contracts of the type involved in the particular trade concerned.

Article 10 For the purposes of this Convention:

(a) if a party has more than one place of business, the place of business is that which has the closest relationship to the contract and its performance, having regard to the circumstances known to or contemplated by the parties at any time before or at the conclusion of the contract;

(b) if a party does not have a place of business, reference is to be made to his habitual residence.

Article 11 A contract of sale need not be concluded in or evidenced by writing and is not subject to any other requirement as to form. It may be proved by any means, including witnesses.

Article 12 Any provision of Article 11, Article 29 or Part II of this Convention that allows a contract of sale or its modification or termination by agreement or any offer, acceptance or other indication of intention to be made in any form other than in writing does not apply where any party has his place of business in a Contracting State which has made a declaration under Article 96 of this Convention. The parties may not derogate from or vary the effect of this article.

Article 13 For the purposes of this Convention "writing" includes telegram and telex.

Part II Formation of the Contract

Article 14

(1) A proposal for concluding a contract addressed to one or more specific persons constitutes an offer if it is sufficiently definite and indicates the intention of the offeror to be bound in case of acceptance. A proposal is sufficiently definite if it indicates the goods and expressly or implicitly fixes or makes provision for determining the quantity and the price.

(2) A proposal other than one addressed to one or more specific persons is to be considered merely as an invitation to make offers, unless the contrary is clearly indicated by the person making the proposal.

Article 15

(1) An offer becomes effective when it reaches the offeree.

(2) An offer, even if it is irrevocable, may be withdrawn if the withdrawal reaches the offeree before or at the same time as the offer.

Article 16

(1) Until a contract is concluded an offer may be revoked if the revocation reaches the offeree before he has dispatched an acceptance.

(2) However, an offer cannot be revoked:

(a) if it indicates, whether by stating a fixed time for acceptance or otherwise, that it is irrevocable; or

(b) if it was reasonable for the offeree to rely on the offer as being irrevocable and the offeree has acted in reliance on the offer.

Article 17 An offer, even if it is irrevocable, is terminated when a rejection reaches the offeror.

Article 18

(1) A statement made by or other conduct of the offeree indicating assent to an offer is an acceptance. Silence or inactivity does not in itself amount to acceptance.

(2) An acceptance of an offer becomes effective at the moment the indication of assent reaches the offeror. An acceptance is not effective if the indication of assent does not reach the offeror within the time he has fixed or, if no time is fixed, within a reasonable time, due account being taken of the circumstances of the transaction, including the rapidity of the means of communication employed by the offeror. An oral offer must be accepted immediately unless the circumstances indicate otherwise.

(3) However, if, by virtue of the offer or as a result of practices which the parties have established between themselves or of usage, the offeree may indicate assent by performing an act, such as one relating to the dispatch of the goods or payment of the price, without notice to the offeror, the acceptance is effective at the moment the act is performed, provided that the act is performed within the period of time laid down in the preceding paragraph.

Article 19

(1) A reply to an offer which purports to be an acceptance but contains additions, limitations or other modifications is a rejection of the offer and constitutes a counter-offer.

(2) However, a reply to an offer which purports to be an acceptance but contains additional or different terms which do not materially alter the terms of the offer constitutes an acceptance, unless the offeror, without undue delay, objects orally to the discrepancy or dispatches a notice to that effect. If he does not so object, the terms of the contract are the terms of the offer with the modifications contained in the acceptance.

(3) Additional or different terms relating, among other things, to the price, payment, quality and quantity of the goods, place and time of delivery, extent of one party's liability to the other or the settlement of disputes are considered to alter the terms of the offer materially.

Article 20

(1) A period of time for acceptance fixed by the offeror in a telegram or a letter begins to run from the moment the telegram is handed in for dispatch or from the date shown on the letter or, if on such date is shown, from the date shown on the envelope. A period of time for acceptance fixed by the offeror by telephone, telex or other means of instantaneous communication, begins to run from the moment that the offer reaches the offeree.

(2) Official holidays or non-business days occurring during the period for acceptance are included in calculating the period. However, if a notice of acceptance cannot be delivered at the address of the offeror on the last day of the period because that day falls on an official holiday or a non-business day at the place of business of the offeror, the period is extended until the first business day which follows.

Artcle 21

(1) A late acceptance is nevertheless effective as an acceptance if without delay the offeror orally so informs the offeree or dispatches a notice to that effect.

(2) If a letter or other writing containing a late acceptance shows that it has been sent in such circumstances that if its transmission had been normal it would have reached the offeror in due time, the late acceptance is effective as an acceptance unless, without delay, the offeror orally informs the offeree that he considers his offer as having lapsed or dispatches a notice to that effect.

Article 22 An acceptance may be withdrawn if the withdrawal reaches the offeror before or at the same time as the acceptance would have become effective.

Article 23 A contract is concluded at the moment when an acceptance of an offer becomes effective in accordance with the provisions of this Convention.

Article 24 For the purposes of this Part of the Convention, an offer, declaration of acceptance or any other indication of intention "reaches" the addressee when it is made orally to him or delivered by any other means to him personally, to his place of business or mailing address or, if he does not have a place of business or mailing address, to his habitual residence.

Part III Sale of Goods

Chapter I General Provisions

Article 25 A breach of contract committed by one of the parties is fundamental if it results in such detriment to the other party as substantially to deprive him of what he is entitled to expect under the contract, unless the party in breach did not foresee and a reasonable person of the same kind in the same circumstances would not have foreseen such a result.

Article 26 A declaration of avoidance of the contract is effective only if made by notice to the other party.

Article 27 Unless otherwise expressly provided in this Part of the Convention, if any notice, request or other communication is given or made by a party in accordance with this Part and by means appropriate in the circumstances, a delay or error in the transmission of the communication or its failure to arrive does not deprive that party of the right to rely on the communication.

Article 28 If, in accordance with the provisions of this Convention, one party is entitled to require performance of any obligation by the other party, a court is not bound to enter a judgment for specific performance unless the court would do so under its own law in respect of similar contracts of sale not governed by this Convention.

Article 29

(1) A contact may be modified or terminated by the mere agreement of the parties.

(2) A contact in writing which contains a provision requiring any modification or termination by agreement to be in writing may not be otherwise modified or terminated by agreement. However, a party may be precluded by his conduct from asserting such a provision to the extent that the other party has relied on that conduct.

Chapter II Obligations of the Seller

Article 30 The seller must deliver the goods, hand over any documents relating to them and transfer the property in the goods, as required by the contract and this Convetion.

Section I. Delivery of the goods and handing over of documents

Article 31 If the seller is not bound to deliver the goods at any other particular place, his obligation to deliver consists:

(a) if the contract of sale involves carriage of the goods—in handing the goods over to the first carrier for transmission to the buyer;

(b) if, in cases not within the preceding subparagraph, the contract relates to specific goods, or unidentified goods to be drawn from a specific stock or to be manufactured or produced, and at the time of the conclusion of the contract the parties knew that the goods were at, or were to be manufactured or produced at, a particular place—in placing the goods at the buyer's disposal at the place;

(c) in other cases—in placing the goods at the buyer's disposal at the place where the seller had his place of business at the time of the conclusion of the contract.

Article 32

(1) If the seller, in accordance with the contract or this Convention, hands the goods over to a carrier and if the goods are not clearly identified to the contract by markings on the goods, by shipping documents or otherwise, the seller must give the buyer notice of the consignment specifying the goods.

(2) If the seller is bound to arrange for carriage of the goods, he must make such contracts as are necessary for carriage to the place fixed by means of transportation appropriate in the circumstances and according to the usual terms for such transportation.

(3) If the seller is not bound to effect insurance in respect of the carriage of the goods, he must, at the buyer's request, provide him with all available information necessary to enable him to effect such insurance.

Article 33 The seller must deliver the goods:

(a) if a date is fixed by or determinable from the contract, on that date;

(b) if a period of time is fixed by or determinable from the contract, at any time within that period unless circumstances indicate that the buyer is to choose a date; or

(c) in any other case, within a reasonable time after the conclusion of the contract.

Article 34 If the seller is bound to hand over documents relating to the goods, he must hand them over at the time and place and in the form required by the contract. If the seller has handed over documents before that time, he may, up to that time, cure any lack of conformity in the documents, if the exercise of this right does not cause the buyer unreasonable inconvenience or unreasonable expense. However, the buyer retains any right to claim damages as provided for in this Convention.

Section II. Conformity of the goods and third party claims

Article 35

(1) The seller must deliver goods which are of the quantity, quality and description required by the contract and which are contained or packaged in the manner required by the contract.

(2) Except where the parties have agreed otherwise, the goods do not conform with the contract unless they:
   (a) are fit for the purposes for which goods of the same description would ordinarily be used;
   (b) are fit for any particular purpose expressly or impliedly made known to the seller at the time of the conclusion of the contract, except where the circumstances show that the buyer did not rely, or that it was unreasonable for him to rely, on the seller's skill and judgment;
   (c) possess the qualities of goods which the seller has held out to the buyer as a sample or model;
   (d) are contained or packaged in the manner usual for such goods or, where there is no such manner, in a manner adequate to preserve and protect the goods.

(3) The seller is not liable under subparagraphs (a) to (d) of the preceding paragraph for any lack of conformity of the preceding paragraph for any lack of conformity of the goods if at the time of the conclusion of the contract the buyer knew or could not have been unaware of such lack of conformity.

Article 36

(1) The seller is liable in accordance with the contract and this Convention for any lack of conformity which exists at the time when the risk passes to the buyer, even though the lack of conformity becomes apparent only after that time.

(2) The seller is also liable for any lack of conformity which occurs after the time indicated in the preceding paragraph and which is due to a breach of any of his obligations, including a breach of any guarantee that for a period of time the goods will remain fit for their ordinary purpose or for some particular purpose or will retain specified qualities or characteristics.

Article 37 If the seller has delivered goods before the date for delivery, he may, up to that date, deliver any missing part or make up any deficiency in the quantity of the goods delivered, or deliver goods in replacement of any non-conforming goods delivered or remedy any lack of conformity in the goods delivered, provided that the exercise of this right does not cause the buyer unreasonable inconvenience or unreasonable expense. However, the buyer retains any right to claim damages as provided for in this Convention.

Article 38

(1) The buyer must examine the goods, or cause them to be examined, within as short a period as is practicable in the circumstances.

(2) If the contract involves carriage of the goods, examination may be deferred until after the goods have arrived at their destination.

(3) If the goods are redirected in transit or redispatched by the buyer without a reasonable opportunity for examination by him and at the time of the conclusion of the contract the seller knew or ought to have known of the possibility of such redirection or redispatch, examination may be deferred until after the goods have arrived at the new destination.

Article 39

(1) The buyer loses the right to rely on a lack of conformity of the goods if he does not give notice to the seller specifying the nature of the lack of conformity within a reasonable time after he has discovered it or ought to have discovered it.

(2) In any event, the buyer loses the right to rely on a lack of conformity of the goods if he does not give the seller notice thereof at the latest within a period of two years from the date on which the goods were actually handed over to the buyer, unless this time-limit is inconsistent with a contractual period of guarantee.

Article 40 The seller is not entitled to rely on the provisions of Articles 38 and 39 if the lack of conformity relates to facts of which he knew or could not have been unaware and which he did not disclose to the buyer.

Article 41 The seller must deliver goods which are free from any right or claim of a third party, unless the buyer agreed to take the goods subject to that right or claim. However, if such right or claim is based on industrial property or other intellectual property, the seller's obligation is governed by Article 42.

Article 42

(1) The seller must deliver goods which are free from any right or claim of a third party based on industrial property or other intellectual property, of which at the time of the conclusion of the contract the seller knew or could not have been unaware, provided that the right or claim is based on industrial property or other intellectual property:

   (a) under the law of the State where the goods will be resold or otherwise used, if it was contemplated by the parties at the time of the conclusion of the contract that the goods would be resold or otherwise used in that State; or

   (b) in any other case, under the law of the State where the buyer has his place of business.

(2) The obligation of the seller under the preceding paragraph does not extend to cases where:

   (a) at the time of the conclusion of the contract the buyer knew or could not have been unaware of the right or claim; or

   (b) the right or claim results from the seller's compliance with technical drawings, designs, formulae or other such specifications furnished by the buyer.

Article 43

(1) The buyer loses the right to rely on the provisions of Article 41 or Article 42 if he does not give notice to the seller specifying the nature of the right or claim of the third party within a reasonable time after he has become aware or ought to have become aware of the right or claim.

(2) The seller is not entitled to rely on the provisions of the preceding paragraph if he knew of the right or claim of the third party and the nature of it.

Article 44 Notwithstanding the provisions of paragraph (1) of Article 39 and paragraph (1) of Article 43, the buyer may reduce the price in accordance with Article 50 or claim damages, except for loss of profit, if he has a reasonable excuse for his failure to give the required notice.

Section III. Remedies for breach of contract by the seller

Article 45

(1) If the seller fails to perform any of his obligations under the contract or this Convention, the buyer may:

   (a) exercise the rights provided in Articles 46 to 52;

   (b) claim damages as provided in Articles 74 to 77.

(2) The buyer is not deprived of any right he may have to claim damages by exercising his right to other remedies.

(3) No period of grace may be granted to the seller by a court or arbitral tribunal when the buyer resorts to a remedy for breach of contract.

Article 46

(1) The buyer may require performance by the seller of his obligations unless the buyer has resorted to a remedy which is inconsistent with this requirement.

(2) If the goods do not conform with the contract, the buyer may require delivery of substitute goods only if the lack of conformity constitutes a fundamental breach of contract and a request for substitute goods is made either in conjunction with notice given under Article 39 or within a reasonable time thereafter.

(3) If the goods do not conform with the contract, the buyer may require the seller to remedy the lack of conformity by repair, unless this is unreasonable having regard to all the circumstances. A request for repair must be made either in conjunction with notice given under Article 39 or within a reasonable time thereafter.

Article 47

(1) The buyer may fix an additional period of time of reasonable length for performance by the seller of his obligations.

(2) Unless the buyer has received notice from the seller that he will not perform within the period so fixed, the buyer may not, during that period, resort to any remedy for breach of contract. However, the buyer is not deprived thereby of any right he may have to claim damages for delay in performance.

Article 48

(1) Subject to Article 49, the seller may, even after the date for delivery, remedy at his own expense any failure to perform his obligations, if he can do so without unreasonable delay and without causing the buyer unreasonable inconvenience or uncertainty of reimbursement by the seller of expenses advanced by the buyer. However, the buyer retains any right to claim damages as provided for in this Convention.

(2) If the seller requests the buyer to make known whether he will accept performance and the buyer does not comply with the request within a reasonable time, the seller may perform within the time indicated in his request. The buyer may not, during that period of time, resort to any remedy which is inconsistent with performance by the seller.

(3) A notice by the seller that he will perform within a specified period of time is assumed to include a request, under the preceding paragraph, that the buyer make known his decision.

(4) A request or notice by the seller under paragraph (2) or (3) of this article is not effective unless received by the buyer.

Article 49

(1) The buyer may declare the contract avoided:

(a) if the failure by the seller to perform any of his obligations under the contract or this Convention amounts to a fundamental breach of contract; or

(b) in case of non-delivery, if the seller does not deliver the goods within the additional period of time fixed by the buyer in accordance with paragraph (1) of Article 47 or declares that he will not deliver within the period so fixed.

(2) However, in cases where the seller has delivered the goods, the buyer loses the right to declare the contract avoided unless he does so:

(a) in respect of late delivery, within a resonable time after he has become aware that delivery has been made;

(b) in respect of any breach other than late delivery, within a reasonable time:

(i) after he knew or ought to have known of the breach;

(ii) after the expiration of any additional period of time fixed by the buyer in accordance with paragraph (1) of Article 47, or after the seller has declared that he will not perform his obligations within such an additional period; or

(iii) after the expiration of any additional period of time indicated by the seller in accordance with paragraph (2) of Article 48, or after the buyer has declared that he will not accept performance.

Article 50

If the goods do not conform with the contract and whether or not the price has already been paid, the buyer may reduce the price in the same proportion as the value that the goods actually delivered had at the time of the delivery bears to the value that conforming goods would have had at that time. However, if the seller remedies any failure to perform his obligations in accordance with Article 37 or Article 48 or if the buyer refuses to accept performance by the seller in accordance with those articles, the buyer may not reduce the price.

Article 51

(1) If the seller delivers only a part of the goods or if only a part of the goods delivered is in conformity with the contract, Articles 46 to 50 apply in respect of the part which is missing or which does not conform.

(2) The buyer may declare the contract avoided in its entirety only if the failure to make delivery completely or in conformity with the contract amounts to a fundamental breach of the contract.

Article 52

(1) If the seller delivers the goods before the date fixed, the buyer may take delivery or refuse to take delivery.

(2) If the seller delivers a quantity of goods greater than that provided for in the contract, the buyer may take delivery or refuse to take delivery of the excess quantity. If the buyer takes delivery of all or part of the excess quantity, he must pay for it at the contract rate.

Chapter III Obligations of the Buyer

Article 53 The buyer must pay the price for the goods and take delivery of them as required by the contract and this Convention.

Section I. Payment of the price

Article 54 The buyer's obligation to pay the price includes taking such steps and complying with such formalities as may be required under the contract or any laws and regulations to enable payment to be made.

Article 55 Where a contract has been validly concluded but does not expressly or implicitly fix or make provision for determining the price, the parties are considered, in the absence of any indication to the contrary, to have impliedly made reference to the price generally charged at the time of the conclusion of the contract for such goods sold under comparable circumstances in the trade concerned.

Article 56 If the price is fixed according to the weight of the goods, in case of doubt it is to be determined by the net weight.

Article 57

(1) If the buyer is not bound to pay the price at any other particular place, he must pay it to the seller:

    (a) at the seller's place of business; or

    (b) if the payment is to be made against the handing over of the goods or of documents, at the place where the handing over takes place.

(2) The seller must bear any increase in the expenses incidental to payment which is caused by a change in his place of business subsequent to the conclusion of the contract.

Article 58

(1) If the buyer is not bound to pay the price at any other specific time, he must pay it when the seller places either the goods or documents controlling their disposition at the buyer's disposal in accordance with the contract and this Convention. The seller may make such payment a condition for handling over the goods or documents.

(2) If the contract involves carriage of the goods, the seller may dispatch the goods on terms whereby the goods, or documents controlling their disposition, will not be handed over to the buyer except against payment of the price.

(3) The buyer is not bound to pay the price until he has had an opportunity to examine the goods, unless the procedures for delivery or payment agreed upon by the parties are inconsistent with his having such an opportunity.

Article 59 The buyer must pay the price on the date fixed by or determinable from the contract and this Convention without the need for any request or compliance with any formality on the part of the seller.

Section II. Taking delivery

Article 60 The buyer's obligation to take delivery consists:

    (a) in doing all the acts which could reasonably be expected of him in order to enable the seller to make delivery; and

    (b) in taking over the goods.

Section III. Remedies for breach of contract by the buyer

Article 61

(1) If the buyer fails to perform any of his obligations under the contract or this Convention, the seller may:

    (a) exercise the rights provided in Articles 62 to 65;

    (b) claim damages as provided in Articles 74 to 77.

(2) The seller is not deprived of any right he may have to claim damages by exercising his right to other remedies.

(3) No period of grace may be granted to the buyer by a court or arbitral tribunal when the seller resorts to a remedy for breach of contract.

Article 62 The seller may require the buyer to pay the price, take delivery or perform his other obligations, unless the seller has resorted to a remedy which is inconsistent with this requirement.

Article 63

(1) The seller may fix an additional period of time of reasonable length for performance by the buyer of his obligations.

(2) Unless the seller has received notice from the buyer that he will not perform within the period so fixed, the seller may not, during that period, resort to any remedy for breach of contract. However, the seller is not deprived thereby of any right he may have to claim damages for delay in performance.

Article 64

(1) The seller may declare the contract avoided:

    (a) if the failure by the buyer to perform any of his obligations under the contract or this Convention amounts to a fundamental breach of contract; or

    (b) if the buyer does not, within the additional period of time fixed by the seller in accordance with paragraph (1) of Article 63, perform his obligation to pay the price or take delivery of the goods, or if he declares that he will not do so within the period so fixed.

(2) However, in cases where the buyer has paid the price, the seller loses the right to declare the contract avoided unless he does so:

    (a) in respect of late performance by the buyer, before the seller has become aware that performance has been rendered; or

    (b) in respect of any breach other than late performance by the buyer, within a reasonable time:

        (i) after the seller knew or ought to have known of the breach; or

        (ii) after the expiration of any additional period of time fixed by the seller in accordance with paragraph (1) of Article 63, or after the buyer has declared that he will not perform his obligations within such an additional period.

Article 65

(1) If under the contract the buyer is to specify the form, measurement or other features of the goods and he fails to make such specification either on the date agreed upon or within a reasonable time after receipt of a request from the seller, the seller may, without

prejudice to any other rights he may have, make the specification himself in accordance with the requirements of the buyer that may be known to him.

(2) If the seller makes the specification himself, he must inform the buyer of the details thereof and must fix a reasonable time within which the buyer may make a different specification. If, after receipt of such a communication, the buyer fails to do so within the time so fixed, the specification made by the seller is binding.

Chapter IV Passing of Risk

Article 66 Loss of or damage to the goods after the risk has passed to the buyer does not discharge him from his obligation to pay the price, unless the loss or damage is due to an act or omission of the seller.

Article 67

(1) If the contract of sale involves carriage of the goods and the seller is not bound to hand them over at a particular place, the risk passes to the buyer when the goods are handed over to the first carrier for transmission to the buyer in accordance with the contract of sale. If the seller is bound to hand the goods over to a carrier at a particular place, the risk does not pass to the buyer until the goods are handed over to the carrier at that place. The fact that the seller is authorized to retain documents controlling the disposition of the goods does not affect the passage of the risk.

(2) Nevertheless, the risk does not pass to the buyer until the goods are clearly identified to the contract, whether by markings on the goods, by shipping documents, by notice given to the buyer or otherwise.

Article 68

The risk in respect of goods sold in transit passes to the buyer from the time of the conclusion of the contract. However, if the circumstances so indicate, the risk is assumed by the buyer from the time the goods were handed over to the carrier who issued the documents embodying the contract of carriage. Nevertheless, if at the time of the conclusion of the contract of sale the seller knew or ought to have known that the goods had been lost or damaged and did not disclose this to the buyer, the loss or damage is at the risk of the seller.

Article 69

(1) In cases not within Article 67 and 68, the risk passes to the buyer when he takes over the goods or, if he does not do so in due time, from the time when the goods are placed at his disposal and he commits a breach of contract by failing to take delivery.

(2) However, if the buyer is bound to take over the goods at a place other than a place of business of the seller, the risk passes when delivery is due and the buyer is aware of the fact that the goods are placed at his disposal at that place.

(3) If the contract relates to goods not then identified, the goods are considered not to be placed at the disposal of the buyer until they are clearly identified to the contract.

Article 70 If the seller has committed a fundamental breach of contract, Articles 67, 68 and 69 do not impair the remedies available to the buyer on account of the breach.

Chapter V Provisions Common to the Obligations of the Seller and of the Buyer

Section 1. Anticipatory breach and installment contracts

Article 71

(1) A party may suspend the performance of his obligations if, after the conclusion of the contract, it becomes apparent that the other party will not perform a substantial part of his obligations as a result of:

(a) a serious deficiency in his ability to perform or in his creditworthiness; or

(b) his conduct in preparing to perform or in performing the contract.

(2) If the seller has already dispatched the goods before the grounds described in the preceding paragraph become evident, he may prevent the handing over of the goods to the buyer even though the buyer holds a document which entitles him to obtain them. The present paragraph relates only to the rights in the goods as between the buyer and the seller.

(3) A party suspending performance, whether before or after dispatch of the goods, must immediately give notice of the suspension to the other party and must continue with performance if the other party provides adequate assurance of his performance.

Article 72

(1) If prior to the date for performance of the contract it is clear that one of the parties will commit a fundamental breach of contract, the other party may declare the contract avoided.

(2) If time allows, the party intending to declare the contract avoided must give reasonable notice to the other party in order to permit him to provide adequate assurance of his performance.

(3) The requirements of the preceding paragraph do not apply if the other party has declared that he will not perform his obligations.

Article 73

(1) In the case of a contract for delivery of goods by installments, if the failure of one party to perform any of his obligations in respect of any installment constitutes a fundamental breach of contract with respect to that installment, the other party may declare the contract avoided with respect to that installment.

(2) If one party's failure to perform any of his obligations in respect of any installment gives the other party good grounds to conclude that a fundamental breach of contract will occur with respect to future installments, he may declare the contract avoided for the future, provided that he does so within a reasonable time.

(3) A buyer who declares the contract avoided in respect of any delivery may, at the same time, declare it avoided in respect of deliveries already made or of future deliveries if, by reason of their interdependence, those deliveries could not be used for the purpose contemplated by the parties at the time of the conclusion of the contract.

Section II. Damages

Article 74 Damages for breach of contract by one party consist of a sum equal to the loss, including loss of profit, suffered by the other party as a consequence of the breach. Such damages may not exceed the loss which the party in breach foresaw or ought to have foreseen at the time of the conclusion of the contract, in the light of the facts and matters of which he then knew or ought to have known, as a possible consequence of the breach of contract.

Article 75 If the contract is avoided and if, in a reasonable manner and within a reasonable time after avoidance, the buyer has bought goods in replacement or the seller has resold the goods, the party claiming damages may recover the difference between the contract price and the price in the substitute transaction as well as any further damages recoverable under Article 74.

Article 76

(1) If the contract is avoided and there is a current price for the goods, the party claiming damages may, if he has not made a purchase or resale under Article 75, recover the difference between the price fixed by the contract and the current price at the time of avoidance as well as any further damages recoverable under Article 74. If, however, the party claiming damages has avoided the contract after taking over the goods, the current price at the time of such taking over shall be applied instead of the current price at the time of avoidance.

(2) For the purposes of the preceding paragraph, the current price is the price prevailing at the place where delivery of the goods should have been made or, if there is no current price at that place, the price at such other place as serves as a reasonable substitute, making due allowance for differences in the cost of transporting the goods.

Article 77 A party who relies on a breach of contract must take such measures as are reasonable in the circumstances to mitigate the loss, including loss of profit, resulting from the breach. If he fails to take such measures, the party in breach may claim a reduction in the damages in the amount by which the loss should have been mitigated.

Section III. Interest

Article 78 If a party fails to pay the price or any other sum that is in arrears, the other party is entitled to interest on it, without prejudice to any claim for damages recoverable under Article 74.

Section IV. Exemptions

Article 79

(1) A party is not liable for a failure to perform any of his obligations if he proves that the failure was due to an impediment beyond his control and that he could not reasonably be expected to have taken the impediment into account at the time of the conclusion of the contract or to have avoided or overcome it or its consequences.

(2) If the party's failure is due to the failure by a third person whom he has engaged to perform the whole or a part of the contract, that party is exempt from liability only if:
   (a) he is exempt under the preceding paragraph; and
   (b) the person whom he has so engaged would be so exempt if the provisions of that paragraph were applied to him.

(3) The exemption provided by this article has effect for the period during which the impediment exists.

(4) The party who fails to perform must give notice to the other party of the impediment and its effect on his ability to perform. If the notice is not received by the other party within a reasonable time after the party who fails to perform knew or ought to have known of the impediment, he is liable for damages resulting from such non-receipt.

(5) Nothing in this article prevents either party from exercising any right other than to claim damages under this Convention.

Article 80 A party may not rely on a failure of the other party to perform, to the extent that such failure was caused by the first party's act or omission.

Section V. Effects of avoidance

Article 81

(1) Avoidance of the contract releases both parties from their obligations under it, subject to any damages which may be due. Avoidance does not affect any provision of the contract for the settlement of disputes or any other provision of the contract governing the rights and obligations of the parties consequent upon the avoidance of the contract.

(2) A party who has performed the contract either wholly or in part may claim restitution from the

other party of whatever the first party has supplied or paid under the contract. If both parties are bound to make restitution, they must do so concurrently.

Article 82

(1) The buyer loses the right to declare the contract avoided or to require the seller to deliver substitute goods if it is impossible for him to make restitution of the goods substantially in the condition in which he received them.

(2) The preceding paragraph does not apply:

(a) if the impossibility of making restitution of the goods or of making restitution of the goods substantially in the condition in which the buyer received them is not due to his act or omission;

(b) if the goods or part of the goods have perished or deteriorated as a result of the examination provided for in Article 38; or

(c) if the goods or part of the goods have been sold in the normal course of business or have been consumed or transformed by the buyer in the course of normal use before he discovered or ought to have discovered the lack of conformity.

Article 83

A buyer who has lost the right to declare the contract avoided or to require the seller to deliver substitute goods in accordance with Article 82 retains all other remedies under the contract and this Convention.

Article 84

(1) If the seller is bound to refund the price, he must also pay interest on it, from the date on which the price was paid.

(2) The buyer must account to the seller for all benefits which he has derived from the goods or part of them:

(a) if he must make restitution of the goods or part of them; or

(b) if it is impossible for him to make restitution of all or part of the goods or to make restitution of all or part of the goods substantially in the condition in which he received them, but he has nevertheless declared the contract avoided or required the seller to deliver substitute goods.

Section VI. Preservation of the goods

Article 85

If the buyer is in delay in taking delivery of the goods or, where payment of the price and delivery of the goods are to be made concurrently, if he fails to pay the price, and the seller is either in possession of the goods or otherwise able to control their disposition, the seller must take such steps as are reasonable in the circumstances to preserve them. He is entitled to retain them until he has been reimbursed his reasonable expenses by the buyer.

Article 86

(1) If the buyer has received the goods and intends to exercise any right under the contract or this Convention to reject them, he must take such steps to preserve them as are reasonable in the circumstances. He is entitled to retain them until he has been reimbursed his reasonable expenses by the seller.

(2) If goods dispatched to the buyer have been placed at his disposal at their destination and he exercises the right to reject them, he must take possession of them on behalf of the seller, provided that this can be done without payment of the price and without unreasonable inconvenience or unreasonable expense. This provision does not apply if the seller or a person authorized to take charge of the goods on his behalf is present at the destination. If the buyer takes possession of the goods under this paragraph, his rights and obligations are governed by the preceding paragraph.

Article 87

A party who is bound to take steps to preserve the goods may deposit them in a warehouse of a third person at the expense of the other party provided that the expense incurred is not unreasonable.

Article 88

(1) A party who is bound to preserve the goods in accordance with Article 85 or 86 may sell them by any appropriate means if there has been an unreasonable delay by the other party in taking possession of the goods or in taking them back or in paying the price or the cost of preservation, provided that reasonable notice of the intention to sell has been given to the other party.

(2) If the goods are subject to rapid deterioration or their preservation would involve unreasonable expense, a party who is bound to preserve the goods in accordance with Article 85 or 86 must take reasonable measures to sell them. To the extent possible he must give notice to the other party of his intention to sell.

(3) A party selling the goods has the right to retain out of the proceeds of sale an amount equal to the reasonable expenses of preserving the goods and of selling them. He must account to the other party for the balance.

Part IV Final Provisions

Article 89

The Secretary-General of the United Nations is hereby designated as the depositary for this Convention.

Article 90

This Convention does not prevail over any international agreement which has already been or may be entered into and which contains provisions concerning the matters governed by this Convention, provided that the parties have their places of business in States parties to such agreement.

Article 91

(1) This Convention is open for signature at the concluding meeting of the United Nations Conference on Contracts for the International Sale of Goods and will remain open for signature by all States at the Headquarters of the United Nations, New York, until 30 September 1981.

(2) This Convention is subject to ratification, acceptance or approval by the signatory States.

(3) This Convention is open for accession by all States which are not signatory States as from the date it is open for signature.

(4) Instruments of ratification, acceptance, approval and accession are to be deposited with the Secretary-General of the United Nations.

Article 92

(1) A Contracting State may declare at the time of signature, ratification, acceptance, approval or accession that it will not be bound by Part II of this Convention or that it will not be bound by Part III of this Convention.

(2) A Contracting State which makes a declaration in accordance with the preceding paragraph in respect of Part II or Part III of this Convention is not to be considered a Contracting State within paragraph (1) of Article 1 of this Convention in respect of matters governed by the Part to which the declaration applies.

Article 93

(1) If a Contracting State has two or more territorial units in which, according to its constitution, different systems of law are applicable in relation to the matters dealt with in this Convention, it may, at the time of signature, ratification, acceptance, approval or accession, declare that this Convention is to extend to all its territorial units or only to one or more of them, and may amend its declaration by submitting another declaration at any time.

(2) These declarations are to be notified to the depositary and are to state expressly the territorial units to which the Convention extends.

(3) If, by virtue of a declaration under this article, this Convention extends to one or more but not all of the territorial units of a Contracting State, and if the place of business of a party is located in that State, this place of business, for the purposes of this Convention, is considered not to be in a Contracting State, unless it is in a territorial unit to which the Convention extends.

(4) If a Contracting State makes no declaration under paragraph (1) of this article, the Convention is to extend to all territorial units of that State.

Article 94

(1) Two or more Contracting States which have the same or closely related legal rules on matters governed by this Convention may at any time declare that the Convention is not to apply to contracts of sale or to their formation where the parties have their places of business in those States. Such declarations may be made jointly or by reciprocal unilateral declarations.

(2) A Contracting State which has the same or closely related legal rules on matters governed by this Convention as one or more non-Contracting States may at any time declare that the Convention is not to apply to contracts of sale or to their formation where the parties have their places of business in those States.

(3) If a State which is the object of a declaration under the preceding paragraph subsequently becomes a Contracting State, the declaration made will, as from the date on which the Convention enters into force in respect of the new Contracting State, have the effect of a declaration made under paragraph (1), provided that the new Contracting State joins in such declaration or makes a reciprocal unilateral declaration.

Article 95 Any State may declare at the time of the deposit of its instrument of ratification, acceptance, approval or accession that it will not be bound by subparagraph (1)(b) of Article 1 of this Convention. [The United States has made such reservation.]

Article 96 A Contracting State whose legislation requires contracts of sale to be concluded in or evidenced by writing may at any time make a declaration in accordance with Article 12 that any provision of Article 11, Article 29, or Part II of this Convention, that allows a contract of sale or its modification or termination by agreement or any offer, acceptance, or other indication of intention to be made in any form other than in writing, does not apply where any party has his place of business in that State.

Article 97

(1) Declarations made under this Convention at the time of signature are subject to confirmation upon ratification, acceptance or approval.

(2) Declarations and confirmations of declarations are to be in writing and be formally notified to the depositary.

(3) A declaration takes effect simultaneously with the entry into force of this Convention in respect of the State concerned. However, a declaration of which the depositary receives formal notification after such entry into force takes effect on the first day of the month following the expiration of six months after the date of its receipt by the depositary. Reciprocal unilateral declarations under Article 94 take effect on the first day of the month following the expiration of six months after the receipt of the latest declaration by the depositary.

(4) Any State which makes a declaration under this Convention may withdraw it at any time by a formal notification in writing addressed to the depositary. Such withdrawal is to take effect on the first day of the

month following the expiration of six months after the date of the receipt of the notification by the depositary.

(5) A withdrawal of a declaration made under Article 94 renders inoperative, as from the date on which the withdrawal takes effect, any reciprocal declaration made by another State under that article.

Article 98 No reservations are permitted except those expressly authorized in this Convention.

Article 99

(1) This Convention enters into force, subject to the provisions of paragraph (6) of this article, on the first day of the month following the expiration of twelve months after the date of deposit of the tenth instrument of ratification, acceptance, approval or accession, including an instrument which contains a declaration made under Article 92.

(2) When a State ratifies, accepts, approves or accedes to this Convention after the deposit of the tenth instrument of ratification, acceptance, approval or accession, this Convention, with the exception of the Part excluded, enters into force in respect of that State, subject to the provisions of paragraph (6) of this article, on the first day of the month following the expiration of twelve months after the date of the deposit of its instrument of ratification, acceptance, approval or accession.

(3) A State which ratifies, accepts, approves or accedes to this Convention and is a party to either or both the Convention relating to a Uniform Law on the Formation of Contracts for the International Sale of Goods done at The Hague on 1 July 1964 (1964 Hague Formation Convention) and the Convention relating to a Uniform Law on the International Sale of Goods done at The Hague on 1 July 1964 (1964 Hague Sales Convention) shall at the same time denounce, as the case may be, either or both the 1964 Hague Sales Convention and the 1964 Hague Formation Convention by notifying the Government of the Netherlands to that effect.

(4) A State party to the 1964 Hague Sales Convention which ratifies, accepts, approves or accedes to the present Convention and declares or has declared under Article 92 that it will not be bound by Part II of this Convention shall at the time of ratification, acceptance, approval or accession denounce the 1964 Hague Sales Convention by notifying the Government of the Netherlands to that effect.

(5) A State party to the 1964 Hague Formation Convention which ratifies, accepts, approves or accedes to the present Convention and declares or has declared under Article 92 that it will not be bound by Part III of this Convention shall at the time of ratification, acceptance, approval or accession denounce the 1964 Hague Formation Convention by notifying the Government of the Netherlands to that effect.

(6) For the purpose of this article, ratifications, acceptances, approvals and accessions in respect of this Convention by States parties to the 1964 Hague Formation Convention or to the 1964 Hague Sales Convention shall not be effective until such denunciations as may be required on the part of those States in respect of the latter two Conventions have themselves become effective. The depositary of this Convention shall consult with the Government of the Netherlands, as the depositary of the 1964 Conventions, so as to ensure necessary co-ordination in this respect.

Article 100

(1) This Convention applies to the formation of a contract only when the proposal for concluding the contract is made on or after the date when the Convention enters into force in respect of the Contracting States referred to in subparagraph (1)(a) or the Contracting States referred to in subparagraph (1)(b) of Article 1.

(2) This Convention applies only to contracts concluded on or after the date when the Convention enters into force in respect of the Contracting States referred to in subparagraph (1)(a) or the Contracting State referred to in subparagraph (1)(b) of Article 1.

Article 101

(1) A Contracting State may denounce this Convention, or Part II or Part III of the Convention, by a formal notification in writing addressed to the depositary.

(2) The denunciation takes effect on the first day of the month following the expiration of twelve months after the notification is received by the depositary. Where a longer period for the denunciation to take effect is specified in the notification, the denunciation takes effect upon the expiration of such longer period after the notification is received by the depositary.

DONE at Vienna, this day of eleventh day of April, one thousand nine hundred and eighty, in a single original, of which the Arabic, Chinese, English, French, Russian and Spanish texts are equally authentic.

IN WITNESS WHEREOF the undersigned plenipotentiaries, being duly authorized by their respective Governments, have signed this Convention.

A Bill Establishing a Provision for Teachers of the Christian Religion (The Tax Assessment Bill)

Submitted by Patrick Henry

Whereas the general diffusion of Christian knowledge hath a natural tendency to correct the morals of men, restrain their vices, and preserve the peace of society; which cannot be effected without a competent provision for learned teachers, who may be thereby enabled to devote their time and attention to the duty of instructing such citizens, as from their circumstances and want of education, cannot otherwise attain such knowledge; and it is judged that such provision may be made by the Legislature, without counteracting the liberal principle heretofore adopted and intended to be preserved by abolishing all distinctions of pre-eminence amongst the different societies or communities of Christians;

Be it therefore enacted by the General Assembly, that for the support of Christian teachers,—per centum on the amount, or—in the pound on the sum payable for tax on the property within this Commonwealth, is hereby assessed, and shall be paid by every person chargeable with the said tax at the time the same shall become due; and the Sheriffs of the several Counties shall have power to levy and collect the same in the same manner and under the like restrictions and limitations, as are or may be prescribed by the laws for raising the Revenues of this State.

And be it enacted, That for every sum so paid, the Sheriff or Collector shall give a receipt, expressing therein to what society of Christians the person from whom he may receive the same shall direct the money to be paid, keeping a distinct account thereof in his books. The Sheriff of every County, shall, on or before the __ day of __ in every year, return to the Court, upon oath, two alphabetical lists of the payments to him made, distinguishing in columns opposite to the names of the persons who shall have paid the same, the society to which the money so paid was by them appropriated; and one column for the names where no appropriation shall be made. One of which lists, after being recorded in a book to be kept for that purpose, shall be filed by the Clerk in his office; the other shall be the Sheriff be fixed up in the Court-house, there to remain for the inspection of all concerned.

And the Sheriff, after deducting five per centum for the collection, shall forthwith pay to such person or persons as shall be appointed to receive the same by the Vestry, Elders, or Directors, however, denominated of each such society, the sum so stated to be due to that society; or in default thereof, upon the motion of such person or persons to the next or any succeeding Court, execution shall be awarded for the same against the Sheriff and his security, his and their executors or administrators; provided that ten days previous notice be given of such motion. An upon every such execution, the Officer serving the same shall proceed to immediate sale of the estate taken, and shall not accept of security for payment at the end of three months, nor to have the goods forthcoming at the day of sale; for his better direction wherein, the Clerk shall endorse upon every such execution that no security of any kind shall be taken.

And be it further enacted, That the money to be raised by virtue of this Act, shall be by the Vestres, Elders, or Directors of each religious society, appropriated to a provision for a Minister or Teacher of the Gospel of their denomination, or the providing place of divine worship, and to none other use whatsoever; except in the denominations of Quakers and Menonists, who may receive what is collected from their members, and place it in their general fund, to be disposed of in a manner which they shall think best calculated to promote their particular mode of worship.

And be it enacted, That all sums which at the time of payment to the Sheriff or Collector may not be appropriated by the person paying the same, shall be accounted for with the Court in manner as by this Act is directed; and after deducting for his collection, the Sheriff shall pay the amount thereof (upon account certified by the Court to the Auditors of Public Accounts, and by them to the Treasurer) into the public Treasury, to be disposed of under the direction of the General Assembly, for the encouragement of seminaries of learning within the Counties whence such sums shall arise, and to no other use or purpose whatsoever.

Memorial and Remonstrance against Religious Assessments– Full Text

By James Madison

To the Honorable the General Assembly of the Commonwealth of Virginia A Memorial and Remonstrance

We the subscribers, citizens of the said Commonwealth, having taken into serious consideration, a Bill printed by order of the last Session of General Assembly, entitled "A

Bill establishing a provision for Teachers of the Christian Religion," and conceiving that the same if finally armed with the sanctions of a law, will be a dangerous abuse of power, are bound as faithful members of a free State to remonstrate against it, and to declare the reasons by which we are determined. We remonstrate against the said Bill,

(1) Because we hold it for a fundamental and undeniable truth, "that Religion or the duty which we owe to our Creator and the manner of discharging it, can be directed only by reason and conviction, not by force or violence." [Virginia Declaration of Rights, art. 16] The Religion then of every man must be left to the conviction and conscience of every man; and it is the right of every man to exercise it as these may dictate. This right is in its nature an unalienable right. It is unalienable, because the opinions of men, depending only on the evidence contemplated by their own minds cannot follow the dictates of other men: It is unalienable also, because what is here a right towards men, is a duty towards the Creator. It is the duty of every man to render to the Creator such homage and such only as he believes to be acceptable to him. This duty is precedent, both in order of time and in degree of obligation, to the claims of Civil Society. Before any man can be considered as a member of Civil Society, he must be considered as a subject of the Governour of the Universe: And if a member of Civil Society, who enters into any subordinate Association, must always do it with a reservation of his duty to the General Authority; much more must every man who becomes a member of any particular Civil Society, do it with a saving of his allegiance to the Universal Sovereign. We maintain therefore that in matters of Religion, no man's right is abridged by the institution of Civil Society and that Religion is wholly exempt from its cognizance. True it is, that no other rule exists, by which any question which may divide a Society, can be ultimately determined, but the will of the majority; but it is also true that the majority may trespass on the rights of the minority.

(2) Because if Religion be exempt from the authority of the Society at large, still less can it be subject to that of the Legislative Body. The latter are but the creatures and vicegerents of the former. Their jurisdiction is both derivative and limited: it is limited with regard to the co-ordinate departments, more necessarily is it limited with regard to the constituents. The preservation of a free Government requires not merely, that the metes and bounds which separate each department of power be invariably maintained; but more especially that neither of them be suffered to overleap the great Barrier which defends the rights of the people. The Rulers who are guilty of such an encroachment, exceed the commission from which they derive their authority, and are Tyrants.

The People who submit to it are governed by laws made neither by themselves nor by an authority derived from them, and are slaves.

(3) Because it is proper to take alarm at the first experiment on our liberties. We hold this prudent jealousy to be the first duty of Citizens, and one of the noblest characteristics of the late Revolution. The free men of America did not wait till usurped power had strengthened itself by exercise, and entangled the question in precedents. They saw all the consequences in the principle, and they avoided the consequences by denying the principle. We revere this lesson too much soon to forget it. Who does not see that the same authority which can establish Christianity, in exclusion of all other Religions, may establish with the same ease any particular sect of Christians, in exclusion of all other Sects? That the same authority which can force a citizen to contribute three pence only of his property for the support of any one establishment, may force him to conform to any other establishment in all cases whatsoever?

(4) Because the Bill violates that equality which ought to be the basis of every law, and which is more indispensable, in proportion as the validity or expediency of any law is more liable to be impeached. If "all men are by nature equally free and independent," [Virginia Declaration of Rights, art. 1] all men are to be considered as entering into Society on equal conditions; as relinquishing no more, and therefore retaining no less, one than another, of their natural rights. Above all are they to be considered as retaining an "*equal* title to the free exercise of Religion according to the dictates of Conscience." [Virginia Declaration of Rights, art. 16] Whilst we assert for ourselves a freedom to embrace, to profess and to observe the Religion which we believe to be of divine origin, we cannot deny an equal freedom to those whose minds have not yet yielded to the evidence which has convinced us. If this freedom be abused, it is an offence against God, not against man: To God, therefore, not to man, must an account of it be rendered. As the Bill violates equality by subjecting some to peculiar burdens, so it violates the same principle, by granting to others peculiar exemptions. Are the Quakers and Menonists the only sects who think a compulsive support of their Religions unnecessary and unwarrantable? Can their piety alone be entrusted with the care of public worship? Ought their Religions to be endowed above all others with extraordinary privileges by which proselytes may be enticed from all others? We think too favorably of the justice and good sense of these denominations to believe that they either covet pre-eminences over their fellow citizens or that they will be seduced by them from the common opposition to the measure.

(5) Because the Bill implies either that the Civil Magistrate is a competent Judge of Religious Truth; or that he may employ Religion as an engine of Civil policy. The first is an arrogant pretension falsified by the contradictory opinions of Rulers in all ages, and throughout the world: the second an unhallowed perversion of the means of salvation.

(6) Because the establishment proposed by the Bill is not requisite for the support of the Christian Religion. To say that it is, is a contradiction to the Christian Religion itself, for every page of it disavows a dependence on the powers of this world: it is a contradiction to fact; for it is known that this Religion both existed and flourished, not only without the support of human laws, but in spite of every opposition from them, and not only during the period of miraculous aid, but long after it had been left to its own evidence and the ordinary care of Providence. Nay, it is a contradiction in terms; for a Religion not invented by human policy, must have pre-existed and been supported, before it was established by human policy. It is moreover to weaken in those who profess this Religion a pious confidence in its innate excellence and the patronage of its Author; and to foster in those who still reject it, a suspicion that its friends are too conscious of its fallacies to trust it to its own merits.

(7) Because experience witnesseth that ecclesiastical establishments, instead of maintaining the purity and efficacy of Religion, have had a contrary operation. During almost fifteen centuries has the legal establishment of Christianity been on trial. What have been its fruits? More or less in all places, pride and indolence in the Clergy, ignorance and servility in the laity, in both, superstition, bigotry and persecution. Enquire of the Teachers of Christianity for the ages in which it appeared in its greatest lustre; those of every sect, point to the ages prior to its incorporation with Civil policy. Propose a restoration of this primitive State in which its Teachers depended on the voluntary rewards of their flocks, many of them predict its downfall. On which Side ought their testimony to have greatest weight, when for or when against their interest?

(8) Because the establishment in question is not necessary for the support of Civil Government. If it be urged as necessary for the support of Civil Government only as it is a means of supporting Religion, and it be not necessary for the latter purpose, it cannot be necessary for the former. If Religion be not within the cognizance of Civil Government how can its legal establishment be necessary to Civil Government? What influence in fact have ecclesiastical establishments had on Civil Society? In some instances they have been seen to erect a spiritual tyranny on the ruins of the Civil authority; in many instances they have been seen upholding the thrones of political tyranny: in no instance have they been seen the guardians of the liberties of the people. Rulers who wished to subvert the public liberty, may have found an established Clergy convenient auxiliaries. A just Government instituted to secure & perpetuate it needs them not. Such a Government will be best supported by protecting every Citizen in the enjoyment of his Religion with the same equal hand which protects his person and his property; by neither invading the equal rights of any Sect, nor suffering any Sect to invade those of another.

(9) Because the proposed establishment is a departure from that generous policy, which, offering an Asylum to the persecuted and oppressed of every Nation and Religion, promised a lustre to our country, and an accession to the number of its citizens. What a melancholy mark is the Bill of sudden degeneracy? Instead of holding forth an Asylum to the persecuted, it is itself a signal of persecution. It degrades from the equal rank of Citizens all those whose opinions in Religion do not bend to those of the Legislative authority. Distant as it may be in its present form from the Inquisition, it differs from it only in degree. The one is the first step, the other the last in the career of intolerance. The magnanimous sufferer under this cruel scourge in foreign Regions, must view the Bill as a Beacon on our Coast, warning him to seek some other haven, where liberty and philanthrophy in their due extent, may offer a more certain repose from his Troubles.

(10) Because it will have a like tendency to banish our Citizens. The allurements presented by other situations are every day thinning their number. To superadd a fresh motive to emigration by revoking the liberty which they now enjoy, would be the same species of folly which has dishonoured and depopulated flourishing kingdoms.

(11) Because it will destroy that moderation and harmony which the forbearance of our laws to intermeddle with Religion has produced among its several sects. Torrents of blood have been spilt in the old world, by vain attempts of the secular arm, to extinguish Religious discord, by proscribing all difference in Religious opinion. Time has at length revealed the true remedy. Every relaxation of narrow and rigorous policy, wherever it has been tried, has been found to assuage the disease. The American Theatre has exhibited proofs that equal and compleat liberty, if it does not wholly eradicate it, sufficiently destroys its malignant influence on the health and prosperity of the State. If with the salutary effects of this system under our own eyes, we begin to contract the bounds of Religious freedom, we know no name that will too severely

reproach our folly. At least let warning be taken at the first fruits of the threatened innovation. The very appearance of the Bill has transformed "that Christian forbearance, love and charity," [Virginia Declaration of Rights, art. 16] which of late mutually prevailed, into animosities and jealousies, which may not soon be appeased. What mischiefs may not be dreaded, should this enemy to the public quiet be armed with the force of a law?

(12) Because the policy of the Bill is adverse to the diffusion of the light of Christianity. The first wish of those who enjoy this precious gift ought to be that it may be imparted to the whole race of mankind. Compare the number of those who have as yet received it with the number still remaining under the dominion of false Religions; and how small is the former! Does the policy of the Bill tend to lessen the disproportion? No; it at once discourages those who are strangers to the light of revelation from coming into the Region of it; and countenances by example the nations who continue in darkness, in shutting out those who might convey it to them. Instead of Levelling as far as possible, every obstacle to the victorious progress of Truth, the Bill with an ignoble and unchristian timidity would circumscribe it with a wall of defence against the encroachments of error.

(13) Because attempts to enforce by legal sanctions, acts obnoxious to so great a proportion of Citizens, tend to enervate the laws in general, and to slacken the bands of Society. If it be difficult to execute any law which is not generally deemed necessary or salutary, what must be the case, where it is deemed invalid and dangerous? And what may be the effect of so striking an example of impotency in the Government, on its general authority?

(14) Because a measure of such singular magnitude and delicacy ought not to be imposed, without the clearest evidence that it is called for by a majority of citizens, and no satisfactory method is yet proposed by which the voice of the majority in this case may be determined, or its influence secured. "The people of the respective counties are indeed requested to signify their opinion respecting the adoption of the Bill to the next Session of Assembly." But the representation must be made equal, before the voice either of the Representatives or of the Counties will be that of the people. Our hope is that neither of the former will, after due consideration, espouse the dangerous principle of the Bill. Should the event disappoint us, it will still leave us in full confidence, that a fair appeal to the latter will reverse the sentence against our liberties.

(15) Because finally, "the equal right of every citizen to the free exercise of his Religion according to the dictates of conscience" is held by the same tenure with all our other rights. If we recur to its origin, it is equally the gift of nature; if we weigh its importance, it cannot be less dear to us; if we consult the "Declaration of those rights which pertain to the good people of Virginia, as the basis and foundation of Government," it is enumerated with equal solemnity, or rather studied emphasis. Either then, we must say, that the Will of the Legislature is the only measure of their authority; and that in the plenitude of this authority, they may sweep away all our fundamental rights; or, that they are bound to leave this particular right untouched and sacred: Either we must say, that they may controul the freedom of the press, may abolish the Trial by Jury, may swallow up the Executive and Judiciary Powers of the State; nay that they may despoil us of our very right of suffrage, and erect themselves into an independent and hereditary Assembly or, we must say, that they have no authority to enact into law the Bill under consideration. We the Subscribers say, that the General Assembly of this Commonwealth have no such authority: And that no effort may be omitted on our part against so dangerous an usurpation, we oppose to it, this remonstrance; earnestly praying, as we are in duty bound, that the Supreme Lawgiver of the Universe, by illuminating those to whom it is addressed, may on the one hand, turn their Councils from every act which would affront his holy prerogative, or violate the trust committed to them: and on the other, guide them into every measure which may be worthy of his blessing, may redound to their own praise, and may establish more firmly the liberties, the prosperity and the happiness of the Commonwealth.

Glossary

abandoned In contract law, the condition that exists when a minor has left home and given up all rights to parental support.

abandoned property Property that has been discarded by the owner without the intent to reclaim ownership of it. Courts require clear and convincing evidence of both the desertion by the owner and the owner's intent never to return.

abandonment of contractual obligations The situation that exists when a party to a contract stops performance once it has begun.

abuse of discretion The determination that the judge in the lower court has misused his or her authority.

abuse of process The use of a legal procedure for a purpose other than that for which it is legitimately intended.

acceleration A provision in a mortgage agreement that allows the mortgagee to demand the entire balance due when the mortgagor misses a single installment payment.

acceptance A promise or act on the part of an offeree indicating a willingness to be bound by the terms and conditions contained in an offer. Also, the acknowledgment of the drawee that binds the drawee to the terms of a draft.

acceptor A drawee of a draft who has promised to honor the draft as presented by signing it on its face.

accommodation party A person who signs an instrument in any capacity for the purpose of lending his or her name to another party to the instrument. That person then assumes the same liability as the marker.

accord The implied or expressed acceptance of less than what the creditor billed the debtor.

accord and satisfaction An agreement (accord) whereby a creditor accepts as full payment an amount that is less than the amount due.

accountant A professional who can plan, direct, and evaluate a client's financial affairs.

accounting A statement detailing the financial transactions of a business and the status of its assets.

acknowledgment The official recognition by a notary public that another's signature was made by that party's free will. The acknowledgment is accomplished when the notary has signed the document and added the official seal to it.

active data Data in a computer system that are actually being used at the present time.

active fraud A false statement made or an action actually taken by one party with the intent to deceive a second party and thus lead that second party into a deceptively based agreement.

activist agencies Agencies that use their regulatory powers to advance social agendas that are technically outside their legislative authority.

actual authority rule A rule that states a manager may be liable for exceeding his or her authority if the corporation is harmed as a result.

actual cause In tort law, the relationship between the unreasonable conduct and the injury to the innocent party, whether the injury was or was not foreseeable. Actual cause is also referred to as cause-in-fact.

actual damages A sum of money equal to the real financial loss suffered by an injured party. Also called *compensatory damages*.

actual eviction An eviction in which the tenant is physically deprived of the leasehold.

actual malice The legal test used by the courts to determine defamation against a public official or a public figure. The actual malice test requires the public official or public figure to prove not only that the statement was false, negative, and communicated to a third party, but also that it was made with the knowledge that it was false or with a reckless disregard for its truth or falsity.

actual malice test A defense against libel cases that states public officials must prove not only that the statement was false, negative, and communicated to a third party, but was also made with actual malice.

actual privity Privity between a client and an accountant that results from a type one accounting arrangements.

add-on coverage In insurance law, optional coverage, such as personal injury insurance, that allows a driver to receive payments without having to determine fault.

adhesion contract A contract drawn by one party that must be accepted on a take-it-or-leave-it basis.

adjustable rate mortgage (ARM) In property law, a variable or changing rate of interest in a mortgage agreement that fluctuates based on the index (the bank's prime rate or the Federal Reserve's discount rate, and so on) to which the mortgage is tied.

administrative law That body of law, including decrees and legal decisions, generated by administrative agencies.

administrator A person appointed by a court to by the court to manage the estate of a decedent.

administrator (male); administratrix (female) A person appointed by the court to do the work of an executor if none is named in a will or if the executor either refuses to perform or is incapable of performing the duties.

admiralty court In the historical development of the law merchant, a local court established by a coastal city, usually in Italy, to handle commercial disputes regarding goods carried as cargo by ships docked at the city's port.

ADR contract clause A clause that specifies that the parties to the agreement have promised to use an alternative dispute resolution technique when a disagreement arises rather than litigating the issue.

advance directives Written statement in which people gives instructions for their future medical care.

adversarial system The system on which the American legal process is built. An orderly and aggressive way to settle disputes in which attorneys for each side attempt to persuade a judge or jury of the veracity of his or her case.

adverse opinion An auditor's opinion that states that deviations from generally accepted accounting principles are so serious that an unqualified opinion is impossible and a qualified opinion is not justified.

adverse possession Title to real property obtained by taking actual possession of the property openly, notoriously, exclusively, under a claim of right, and continuously for a period of time set by state statute.

affirmance See *ratification*.

affirmative action A policy designed to reduce the effects of past discrimination.

affirmative defense A set of circumstances that indicates that a defendant should not be held liable, even if the plaintiff proves all of the facts in a complaint.

agency A legal agreement between two persons, whereby one is designated the agent of the other.

agency coupled with an interest An irrevocable agency agreement in which the agent is given an interest in the subject matter of the agency. Also called *irrevocable agency*.

agent A person authorized to act on behalf of another and subject to the other's control in dealing with third parties.

aggravated arson In criminal law, using fire or explosives to create a substantial risk of harm to an individual or an occupied structure, often also including the hiring of another person to carry out the offense.

aggravated burglary In criminal law, gaining unlawful entry to an occupied building by using a deadly weapon, inflicting actual harm, attempting to harm, or threatening to harm, with the intent to commit a crime.

aggravated murder In criminal law, killing someone with premeditation or with prior calculation and design, or while committing a serious felony such as rape, robbery, or kidnapping.

aggravated robbery In criminal law, attempting to commit or actually committing theft using a deadly weapon or a dangerous ordnance, or doing the same by inflicting harm on the victim.

aggregate theory A theory in partnership law that holds that a partnership is actually a conglomeration of the partners rather than a separate legal person with its own legal identity.

agreements in restraint of trade Agreements that remove competition, deny to the public the services it would otherwise have, or result in higher prices and hardship.

algorithm A series of mathematical steps that, if followed properly, will reach a desired goal.

alien corporation A corporation that though incorporated in a foreign country does business in the United States.

allonge A strip of paper attached to a negotiable instrument for the writing of indorsements.

alter ego In corporate law, a subsidiary corporation set up by a parent corporation to do the bidding of the original parent corporation.

alternative dispute resolution (ADR) A process that occurs whenever individuals attempt to resolve a disagreement by stepping outside the usual adversarial system and applying creative settlement techniques, many of which have fact finding and the discovery of truth as their goal.

alternative payment system A computer based payment system such as Pay-Pal that is not card dependent.

American Law Institute (ALI) test A test under which a criminal defendant will be judged not guilty by reason of insanity "as a result of mental disease or defect he lacks substantial capacity either to appreciate the criminality of his conduct or to conform his conduct to the requirements of the law."

annual percentage rate (APR) The true rate of interest on a loan.

annuity A guaranteed retirement income.

anomalous indorsement An indorsement made by an accommodation party.

answer A defendant's official response to a complaint.

antenuptial agreement In contract law, a written agreement between two people planning marriage, who agree in writing to change the property rights they possess by law.

anticipatory breach A breach that occurs when a party to a contract either expresses or clearly implies an intention not to perform the contract even before being required to act. Also called *constructive breach*.

Antitrust Procedures and Penalty Act In federal antitrust law, a federal statute that regulates the Department of Justice's antitrust consent decrees.

apparent authority An accountability doctrine whereby a principal, by virtue of words or actions, leads a third party to believe that an agent has authority but no such authority was intended. Also called *ostensible authority* and *agency by estoppel*.

appeal The referral of a case to a higher court for review.

appeal bond The payment of a set sum of money into a protected account to secure the payment of that money to the plaintiff should the defendant be defeated.

appellate jurisdiction The power of a court to review a case for errors.

arbitration The process by which an outside party settles a dispute between two other parties.

arbitrator The third party in the arbitration procedure whose job is to settle the dispute.

arraignment A formal court proceeding during which the defendant, after hearing the indictment or information read, pleads either guilty or not guilty.

arson The willful or malicious act of causing the burning of another's property.

Articles of Confederation The first constitution of the United States; replaced by the U.S. Constitution in 1787.

articles of incorporation A written application to a state for permission to incorporate.

articles of organization The written application to the state for permission to form a limited liability company.

articles of partnership A written agreement that establishes a partnership.

assault An attempt to commit a battery.

asset acquisition The purchase of all the property of a corporation by another corporation.

assign To transfer property by sale, mortgage, pledge, or otherwise.

asset-backed securities In property law, lending money by establishing a security interest in goods such as cars, furniture, boats, and so on.

assignee A person to whom an assignment is made.

assignment The transfer of a contract right from one person to another.

assignor A person who assigns rights or delegates duties under an assignment.

associated persons and forces According to AUMF-2015, "Individuals and organizations fighting for, on behalf of, or alongside ISIL or any closely-related successor entity in hostilities against the United States or its coalition partners."

associate corporatism The process of doing business as a self-governing association.

associative corporativism The process of doing business as a self-governing business association, that is, as a corporation. Also known as *corporativism*.

assume the mortgage An agreement whereby the buyer of real property already mortgaged agrees to pay the mortgage.

assumption of the risk A defense against negligence that states the victim voluntarily exposed him- or herself to a known risk.

ATM card A card used together with a personal identification number (PIN) to gain access to an automatic teller machine (ATM).

attachment The act of taking a person's property and bringing it into the custody of law.

attorney–client privilege The guarantee that information that passes between clients and attorneys remains secret.

auction A sale that is open to the public, during which potential buyers compete for the right to purchase certain items by placing higher and higher bids until the highest bid is reached and the auctioneer accepts on behalf of the seller

auction with reserve An auction at which the auctioneer has the right to withdraw goods and not sell them if acceptable bids are not made.

auction without reserve An auction at which the auctioneer cannot withdraw goods unless no bid is made within a reasonable time.

audit An examination of the financial records of an organization to determine whether those records are a fair representation of the actual financial health of the institution.

audit committee A corporate committee that consists of independent members who oversee the accounting firm that audits the corporation.

Auditing Standards Board A group of experts established by the American Institute of Certified Public Accountants (AICPA) to set up auditing standards.

auditor The accountant who examines the financial records of an organization to determine whether those records are a fair representation of the actual financial health of the institution.

authenticate (*a*) to sign; or (*b*) with the intent to sign a record, otherwise to execute or adopt an electronic symbol, sound, message, or process referring to, attached to, included in, or logically associated or linked with, that record.

Authorization for the Use of Military Force of 2015 (AUMF) An attempt by the President to extend the military power of the Commander-in-Chief.

automatic stay A self-operating postponement of collection proceedings against a debtor who has filed a petition for bankruptcy.

automatic suspension A court order that stops a debtor's creditors from making any further moves to collect the money that the debtor owes them.

backup data Data associated with a computer system that have been duplicated for safekeeping at another location.

bailee The person to whom personal property is transferred under a contract of bailment.

bailment The transfer of possession and control of personal property to another with the intent that the same property will be returned later.

bailment by necessity A bailment that arises when a customer must give up possession of property for the benefit of both parties; for example, when one purchases a suit or dress and is required to give up possession of one's own property while being fitted.

bailment for the sole benefit of the bailee A bailment in which the bailee receives all the benefits of the transaction.

bailment for the sole benefit of the bailor A bailment in which the bailor receives all the benefits of the transaction.

bailor The person who transfers personal property under a contract of bailment.

bait-and-switch confidence game An illegal promotional practice in which a seller attracts consumers by promoting a product (bait) that he or she does not intend to sell and then directs the consumers' attention to a higher-priced product (switch).

balloon payment A large final payment on a mortgage that has relatively low fixed payments during the life of the mortgage.

balloon-payment mortgage A mortgage that has relatively low fixed payments during the life of the mortgage followed by one large final (balloon) payment.

bank According to the Uniform Commercial Code a bank is "any person who engages in the business if banking." (UCC Section 1-201 (4)).

bank draft A check drawn by one bank on another bank in which it has funds on deposit in favor of a third person, the payee. Also called *teller's check.*

bankruptcy The legal process by which the assets of a debtor are sold to pay off creditors so that the debtor can make a fresh start financially.

bankruptcy trustee A person appointed by the court who is charged with the responsibility of liquidating the assets of the debtor for the benefit of all interested parties.

bargain-and-sale deed A deed that transfers title to real property but contains no warranties. This type of deed is not valid without consideration.

bargained-for exchange In reference to agreements, when a promise is made in exchange for another promise, in exchange for an act, or in exchange for a forbearance to act.

bargaining unit Employees joined together for the purpose of collective bargaining.

battered spouse syndrome A defense to criminal liability available to defendants if they can prove that they believed the only way to escape death or severe bodily injury was to use force against their tormentors.

battery The unlawful touching of another person.

bearer A person who is in possession of a negotiable instrument that is payable to the "bearer" or "cash" or that has been indorsed in blank.

bearer paper An instrument payable to bearer or cash that may be negotiated by delivery only.

beneficiary A third party receiving benefits from a contract made between two other parties. Also, the person named in an insurance policy to receive benefits paid by the insurer in event of a claim.

bequest Personal property left in a will. Also called *legacy*.

best evidence rule The legal rule that holds that the courts generally accept into evidence only the original of a writing, not a copy.

best-price rule Rules that prohibit suitors from offering different prices to different shareholders during a tender offer process.

bilateral contract A contract in which both parties make promises.

bilateral mistake In contract law, a mistake made by both parties to a contract. Bilateral mistake allows rescission by either party. Also called *mutual mistake*.

bill of exchange See *draft*.

bill of lading A document evidencing the receipt of goods for shipment and issued by a person engaged in the business of transporting or forwarding goods.

bill of sale A written statement evidencing the transfer of personal property from one person to another.

binder An oral or a written memorandum of an agreement for insurance intended to provide temporary insurance coverage until the policy is formally accepted.

binding precedent A previous case that a particular court must follow.

blank indorsement An indorsement made by a signature alone, with no particular indorsee, written on a negotiable instrument.

blended contract In contract law a binding agreement that has enough characteristic of a sales contract and a service contract to be considered a combination of both. See also mixed contract and hybrid contract.

blue laws State statutes and local ordinances that regulate the making and performing of contracts on Sunday.

bodily injury liability insurance A type of automobile insurance that covers the risk of bodily injury or death to pedestrians and to the occupants of other cars arising from the negligent operation of the insured's motor vehicle.

bond A certificate of indebtedness that obligates a government or corporation to pay the bondholder a fixed rate of interest on the principal at regular intervals and to pay the principal on a stated maturity date. Also, a promise by

the executor or administrator (and the sureties, if any) of a will to pay the amount of the bond to the probate court if the duties of the position are not faithfully performed.

bonus malum A plan under which an executive does not receive his/her bonus immediately but only when the investment he/she engineered proves to have appropriate profitability for the corporation.

bot A type of cyberagent that searches cyberspace for the lowest price in a contract, sifts through the net for the best accommodations, hunts cyberspace for the most economical plan, or spontaneously responds to a bidding process. Also known as *robot, shopping bot, cyberbot,* and *e-bot*.

boycott A concerted refusal to have dealings with someone to force the acceptance of certain conditions.

breach of contract The failure of one of the parties to a contract to do what was previously agreed upon.

breaking and entering In criminal law, using force, deceit, or cunning to trespass into an unoccupied building with the intent to commit a felony.

bribery The act of offering, giving, receiving, or soliciting something of value to influence official action or the discharge of a public duty.

bright-line test Test used by the courts that establishes violations of the best-price rule occur only during the actual tender offer.

bring your own device (BYOD) policy A procedure under which employees use their own electronic units at work on the job.

bulk transfer Any transfer of a major party of the materials, supplies, merchandise, or other inventory of an enterprise that is not in the ordinary course of the transferor's business.

burglary The break-in of a dwelling or building for the purpose of carrying out a felony.

business compulsion See *economic duress*.

business judgment rule The rule that a corporate manager's decisions will not be interfered with by a court as long as the decision was made with due care, is in good faith, is lawful, and is in the best interest of the corporation.

business system Until recently, business systems were considered unpatentable because they were not a "process, machine, or composition of matter." Recently, however, some computerized business systems have been patented if they consist of some nonobvious, new, and useful feature not known or understood before the invention of this system.

buyer in the ordinary course of business A person who in good faith and without knowledge that the sale is in violation of ownership rights or security interests of a third party buys goods in ordinary course from a person in the business of selling goods of that kind, not including a pawnbroker.

Buyer's Guide A window sticker that is required by the Federal Trade Commission Act to be placed in the window of each used car offered for sale by a used car dealer. The sticker discloses the warranties that are made with the sale of the car and other consumer protection information.

bylaws Rules that guide a corporation's day-to-day internal affairs. Also known as regulations.

c.f. Cost and freight. Terms instructing a carrier to collect the cost of goods shipped and freight charges.

c.i.f. Cost, insurance, and freight. Terms instructing a carrier to collect the cost of goods shipped, insurance, and freight charges.

c.o.d. Cash on delivery. Instructs a carrier to retain goods until he or she has collected the costs of the goods.

Can Spam Act A federal law designed to reduce the use of unsolicited e-mail, commonly known as spam, on the Internet.

cancellation form Under the Federal Trade Commission's Cooling-Off Rule, a document that can be filled out to terminate an order for consumer goods or services made at the buyer's home for consumer goods or services valued at $25 or more.

capacity In contract law, the legal ability to enter into a contractual relationship.

capital The money and property that a business needs to operate.

capital contribution The sum contributed by a business partner as a permanent investment in the business. It is then considered to be the property of the partnership.

carrier A business that undertakes to transport persons, goods, or both.

case in chief The collection of evidence that will prove a plaintiff's version of case to a jury.

case trustee A person appointed by a bankruptcy court to meet with creditors and report whether the case should proceed.

cash dividend Dividend paid to shareholders in the form of cash.

cashier's check A check drawn by a bank upon its own funds.

cause in fact In tort law, the relationship between the unreasonable conduct and the injury to the innocent party, whether the injury was or was not foreseeable. Cause in fact is also referred to as actual cause.

certificate of authority A document that grants a foreign corporation permission to do business within another state.

certificate of deposit (CD) An acknowledgment by a bank of the receipt of money and a promise to pay the money back on the due date, usually with interest.

certificate of incorporation A corporation's official authorization to do business in a state. Also called *charter* or *corporate charter*.

certification authority (CA) It is the job of the CA to provide businesses with digital signatures and to make certain that those signatures are kept current.

certified check A check that has been marked, or certified, by the bank on which it was drawn, guaranteeing payment to the holder.

certified public accountant (CPA) An accountant who has met certain age, character, education, experience, and testing requirements.

chaotic events Unpredictable and unexpected incidents, often with a natural origin, such as earthquakes, typhoons snowstorms, volcanic eruptions, plagues and the like that come out of nowhere and have a debilitating effect on human made decisions. (See also sideswipes)

charitable immunity A common law principle that grants immunity from tort law litigation to charities to protect the useful continuation of those services that such organizations make to society as a whole.

chattels Property that has substance and that can be touched.

check A draft drawn on a bank and payable on demand.

Check 21 Act A law that makes check clearing much quicker by the use of a *substitute check* in place of the original check for electronic check processing.

chemical abuse The use of drugs or alcohol to such an extent that a person's judgment is impaired or his or her physical body is harmed.

chemical dependency The state a person reaches when she or he can no longer function normally without regularly consuming drugs or alcohol.

chose in action Evidence of the right to property but not the property itself.

civil litigation The process of bringing a case to court to enforce a right.

civilization A group of people in a series of different nation-states that share common characteristics, including history, religion, tradition, beliefs, often language, and sometimes ancestry.

class action lawsuit A lawsuit that is brought by one or more plaintiffs on behalf of a class of persons.

Clean Air Act In environmental law, a federal statute designed to limit pollution from vehicles and from stationary sources such factories and manufacturing centers.

Clean Water Act In environmental law, a federal statute that sets requirements for limiting the pollution of the nation's water sources according to a schedule, based on the most effective technology currently available.

clearly erroneous standard The determination that the decision made in the lower court was undeniably wrong, given the facts and evidence in the case.

click-on acceptance A method of acceptance used in Internet contracts in which a party manifests acceptance by clicking on an icon on the computer screen that states that he or she agrees to the terms of the contract.

close corporation A corporation whose shares of stock and managerial control are closely held by fewer than 50 shareholders (often members of the same family) or by one person.

close-end credit Credit that is extended only for a specific amount of money, such as to buy a car or other expensive item.

closed shop A place of employment in which the employer, by agreement, hires only union members in good standing.

cloud storage A cyber-technique that preserves electronic data without using local hard drives or flash drives.

code A compilation of all the statutes of a particular state or of the federal government.

Code of Federal Regulations (CFR) Annual listing of finalized federal rules and regulations.

Code of Professional Ethics A set of rules established by the American Institute of Certified Public Accountants that outlines rules that govern the ethical conduct of accountants.

codicil A formal document used to supplement or change an existing will.

coinsurance An insurance policy provision under which the insurer and the insured share costs, after the deductible is met, according to a specific formula.

collateral The property that is subject to a security interest.

collateral contract In contract law, a contract by which one party agrees to pay the debt of another party if that party fails to meet that obligation.

collecting bank Any bank handling an item for collection except the payor bank.

collective bargaining A good faith meeting between representatives of employees and employers to discuss the terms and conditions of employment.

collective bargaining agreement A contract negotiated by an employer and a labor union that covers all issues related to employment.

collective science court A proposed judicial forum that would act as a legal clearing ground for disputes involving scientific and technological issues.

collision insurance A type of automobile insurance that protects the insured against any loss arising from damage to the insured's automobile caused by accidental collision with another object or with any part of the roadbed.

comaker A person obligated, along with at least one other person, as a payor on a promissory note.

commerce Trade among the several states or between any foreign country and any state or territory.

commerce clause The clause in the U.S. Constitution that gives the federal government the power to regulate business among the states.

commercial impracticability A doctrine under which the courts may excuse the performance of one party to a contract because an unforeseen and very severe hardship has arisen that would place an enormous amount of hardship on that party.

commercial unit A single whole for the purpose of sale, the division of which impairs its character or value on the market, such as a set of furniture.

commingled Mixed together, as in goods stored at a warehouse or funds in a bank account.

Commission on Science and Technology for Development A UN agency created in 1992 as part of the Economic and Social Council (ECOSOC) to act as a clearing house for issues concerning science and technology in relation to development; to support progress in determining what must be done to advance science and technology policies in developing nations, and to formulate recommendations and protocols for science and technology within the UN community.

common carrier A company that transports goods or persons for compensation and offers its facilities to the general public without discrimination. Compare *contract carrier.*

common law The body of recorded decisions that courts refer to and rely upon when making later legal decisions.

common stock The most usual type of corporate stock. It carries with it all the risks of the business and does not guarantee its holder the right to profits.

community property Property that is acquired by the personal effects of either spouse during marriage and which, by law, belongs to both spouses equally.

company-owned, personally enabled devices (COPE) policy A procedure under which employees use electronic units supplied and programmed by the employer.

comparative negligence A form of contributory negligence that requires the court to assign damages according to the degree of fault of each party.

compelling interest The inescapable, overriding interest that the government of a nation or state has in a particular issue, such as the state or the nation's interest in the lives of its own citizens, which the government cannot ignore, and which it must pursue and protect at the risk of losing its legitimacy as the proper governing body of that state or nation.

compensatory damages See *actual damages.*

competent authority The requirement that just war may be declared and run only by legitimately recognized nation-states.

competitive impact statement (CIS) In antitrust law, a decree that clarifies any potential antitrust problems inherent within a corporate expansion and the solutions to those problems.

complaint A legal document filed by a plaintiff to begin a lawsuit. The complaint sets forth the names of the parties, the facts in the case, the alleged legal violations by the defendant, and the relief sought by the plaintiff.

complete performance In contract law, the situation that exists when both parties to a contract have fully accomplished every term, condition, and promise to which they agreed.

comprehensive coverage A type of automobile insurance that provides protection against loss when the insured's car is damaged or destroyed by fire, lightning, flood, hail, windstorm, riot, vandalism, or theft.

computer firmware Computer software that is written to be used with only one type or brand of computer.

computer hardware The actual device known as a computer and its components, including the keyboard, screen, disk drive, and printer.

computer information Information in a form directly capable of being processed or used by, or obtained from or through, a computer.

computer package The combination of the computer hardware and the computer software when sold together.

computer program The instructions that tell the computer hardware what to do and when to do it.

computer software The card, tape, disk, or silicon chip that contains the computer program.

concealment In insurance, the intentional withholding of a fact that would be of material importance to the insurer's decision to issue a policy. In contract law, the intentional withholding of a material fact that the other party relies upon and which results in financial harm to the innocent party. See also *passive fraud.*

condemnation See *eminent domain.*

condition concurrent A condition in a contract that requires both parties to perform at the same time.

condition precedent In contract law, an act or promise that must take place or be fulfilled before the other party is obligated to perform his or her part of the agreement.

condition subsequent A condition in a contract in which the parties agree that the contract will be terminated depending on a prescribed event occurring or not occurring.

conditional indorsement An indorsement that makes the rights of the indorsee subject to the happening of a certain event or condition.

confidential relationship A relationship of trust and dependence between persons in a continued relationship, as between doctor and patient, between parent and child, or between a caretaker and a dependent person.

confirmation In bankruptcy law, the official approval of a reorganization plan.

conforming goods Goods that are in accordance with the obligations under the contract.

conglomerate expansion The joining of two companies that were not in competition with each other either because they dealt in different products or services or because they operated in different geographical areas.

consensual A freely given agreement to act.

consent decree Agreements created by the Department of Justice to help parties negotiate a legal merger.

consent order Under the Federal Trade Commission Act, an order under which a company agrees to stop a disputed practice without necessarily admitting that the practice violated the law.

consequential damages Losses that do not flow directly and immediately from an act but only from some of the consequences or results of the act.

consideration In contract law, the mutual promise to exchange benefits and detriments between parties.

consignee One to whom goods are entrusted under a *consignment contract* for the purpose of selling those goods.

consignment contract A type of mutual benefit bailment in which the *consignor* entrusts goods to the *consignee* for the purpose of selling them.

consignor One who entrusts goods under a *consignment contract* to a *consignee* for the purpose of selling them.

consolidation The joining of two corporations.

conspiracy The crime that occurs when people get together with others to talk about, plan, or agree to the commission of a crime.

constitution The basic law of a nation or state.

constitutional law That body of law that involves a constitution and its interpretation.

construction loan A loan for the building of a home that permits staggered payments that fall due at various stages in the building process.

constructive discharge Discriminatory action whereby an employee is demoted to a job with less pay, authority, or poorer working conditions than the job that person previously held or is subjected to supervisory harassment.

constructive eviction An eviction that occurs by the act of the landlord depriving the tenant of something of a substantial nature that was called for under the lease.

consumer Someone who buys or leases real estate, goods, or services for personal, family, or household purposes.

consumer goods Goods normally used for personal, family, or household purposes.

consumer products Tangible personal property normally used for personal, family, or household purposes.

continuity of existence A concept promoted by the Revised Uniform Partnership Act that permits a partnership to continue to operate as an entity even after individual partners are no longer associated with it.

continuity plan In sales law, an arrangement by which the seller of goods ships the goods to the subscriber on a regular basis without first sending an announcement of the upcoming delivery.

contract An agreement based on mutual promises between two or more competent parties to do or to refrain from doing some particular thing that is neither illegal nor impossible. The agreement results in an obligation or a duty that can be enforced in a court of law.

contract carrier A company that transports goods or persons for compensation only for those people with whom it desires to do business. Compare *common carrier.*

contract for sale Either a present sale of goods or a contract to sell goods at a future time.

contract of record A special type of formal contract usually confirmed by a court with an accompanying judgment issued in favor of one of the parties.

contributory copyright infringement A violation of copyright law in which one party provides a way for a second party to violate the copyright protection granted to the third party even though the first party never violates the copyright himself or herself.

contributory negligence A legal defense that involves the failure of an injured party to be careful enough to ensure personal safety.

control test In tort law and in agency law, the test within the doctrine of *respondeat superior* which asks that we determine the degree of control or right to control that the hiring person had over the hired person in order to determine liability.

controlled company A corporation that has more than half its voting power concentrated in one individual, or a small group of people, who always vote together.

Convention on Contracts for the International Sale of Goods (CISG) A United Nations treaty designed to govern commercial transactions between parties whose places of business are in different countries.

conventional mortgage A mortgage that involves no government backing by either insurance or guarantee.

conversion The wrongful exercise of dominion and control over another's personal property.

conveyance in trust A trust in which the settlor conveys away the legal title to a trustee to hold for the benefit of either the settlor or another as beneficiary.

Cooling-Off Rule A Federal Trade Commission rule under which sales of consumer goods or services over $25 made away from the seller's regular place of business may be canceled within three business days after the sale occurs.

cooperative corporation A business entity owned and operated by the employees of that corporation.

cooperative corporation with wage earning employees A business owned and operated by the employees who hire non-owner employees to perform work beyond the expertise and/or availability of the owner-employees.

cooperative with non-employee owners A business entity, owned and operated by employees with some non-employee shareholders.

Copenhagen Accord An agreement made under the auspices of the UN Framework Conference on Climate Change and entered by five nations, including China, the United States, and India, to reduce greenhouse gases and to provide $30 billion annually to help developing nations balance sustainable development with environmental protection.

copyright A right granted to an author, composer, photographer, or artist to exclusively publish and sell an artistic or literary work for the life of the author plus 70 years.

corporate democracy See *shareholder democracy.*

corporate entity A legal entity created under the authority of a state or federal statute that gives certain individuals the capacity to operate as an enterprise.

corporate opportunity doctrine A principle that states corporate managers cannot take a business opportunity for themselves if they know their corporation would be interested in that opportunity.

corporate person A legal entity created under the authority of a state or federal statute that gives certain individuals the capacity to operate as an enterprise.

corporate raid An unfriendly takeover, designed to dismantle the target corporation.

corporate raider An unfriendly suitor that intends to dismantle the target corporation after obtaining it.

corporate shell A subsidiary corporation set up as a mere instrumentality of a parent corporation.

corporation A legal entity (or a legal person) created by either a state or federal statute authorizing individuals to operate an enterprise.

corporation by estoppel The doctrine by which parties who have benefited by dealing with a business as though it were a corporation—though in law it is not—cannot deny its existence as a corporation. Similarly, individuals who have acted as if they were a corporation would not be able to deny that the corporation existed.

corporativism The process of doing business as a self-governing association.

cost–benefit thinking A system of thought that focuses on the consequences to one person or institution and then weighs the cost against the benefits of performing the action under scrutiny.

cost of repair rule The principle that states that an architect or contractor may have to reimburse a client for any extra money spent by the client to correct an error initially made by the architect or contractor.

cost-plus contract A contract in which the price is determined by the cost of labor and materials plus an agreed percentage markup.

cotenancy The quality or state of more than one owner of a single property.

cotenants Two or more persons who own real property together.

counteroffer A response to an offer in which the terms and conditions of the original offer are changed.

courts Judicial tribunals that meet in a regular place and apply the law in an attempt to settle disputes by weighing the arguments presented by advocates for each party.

cover Buying similar goods from someone else when a seller breaches a contract.

covering law A universal normative principle that follows a set pattern that can be used to understand and predict, in terms of probabilities, natural processes or human behavior.

creditor beneficiary A third party to whom one or both contracting parties owe a continuing debt of obligation arising from a contract.

crime An offense against the public at large punishable by the official governing body of a nation or state.

criminal simulation In criminal law, the altering or falsifying of art objects, antiques, photos, films, recordings, manuscripts, and/or antiquities with the intent to defraud.

cross-appeal An appeal filed by a party that has prevailed at trial.

cross-examination The questioning of witnesses by an opposing attorney.

cross-owned corporation A business entity that is public corporation owned and operated by another public corporation.

cumulative voting A system of voting for corporate directors that is designed to benefit minority shareholders by allowing shareholders to multiply their voting shares by the number of directors to be elected.

cure The correction of a defect in goods that caused the goods to be rejected by a buyer.

current market price contract An agreement in which the prices are determined with reference to the market price of the goods on a specified date.

curtesy Under common law, the right that a widower had, if children of the marriage were born alive, to a life estate in all real property owned by the wife during the marriage.

cyber-agent (a.k.a. electronic agent and e-agent) A computer program that acts without human intervention to begin an activity, to answer cybermessages, to deliver or accept cybermail, or to enter cybercontracts.

cyber-bulletin board An electronic message board.

cyber-commerce Involves transacting business by any one of several types of electronic communication, from debit card purchases to buying and selling goods on the Internet.

cyber-consumer Someone who buys something on the Internet.

cyber-contract A contract involving the sale or licensing of information in a digital format.

cybercrime Any criminal act that includes a computer.

cyber-defamation The communication of false and destructive information about an individual through the use of a computer or other electronic device.

cyber-discovery A search for evidence using a computer. Also called *cyberspace discovery*.

cyber-disparagement In tort law, disparagement committed using a computer system.

cyber-evidence Any and all types of computer-generated data.

cyber-germ warfare Using viruses to attack a computer system.

cyber-invasion of privacy The unwelcome intrusion into private matters initiated or maintained by a computer.

cyber-jurisdiction The authority of a court to hear a case based on Internet-related transactions.

cyber-pirate Someone who registers a trademark or trademarks as a domain name with little or no intention of actually using the domain name in the hope that the actual holders of the trademark will buy the domain name for enormous sums.

cyber-principal A principal who places authority in the hands of a cyberagent.

cyber-signature An electronic sound or process attached to or logically associated with a record and executed or adopted by a person with the intent to sign a record.

cyber-spoiler See *cyber-pirate*.

cyber-spoofing Falsely adopting the identity of another computer user or creating a false identity on a computer Web site to commit fraud.

cyber-spyware (a.k.a. cyber-snoopware) A program which, once it is installed in a computer, can keep a record of the keyboarding patterns established by the computer user.

cybers-stalking Targeting an individual for exploitation using that person's computer connections.

cyber-terrorism Using a computer to disrupt or destroy one of the critical elements of the nation's electronic infrastructure.

cybertort The invasion, distortion, theft, falsification, misuse, destruction, or financial exploitation of information stored in a computer.

cyber-trespass Gaining access to a computer with the intent to commit a crime.

cyber-vandalism Attacking a computer system so that a Web site is completely destroyed or paralyzed.

damage cap A limit on the amount of money that juries can award in certain types of tort law cases.

damages Money recovered by a party in a court action to compensate that party for injury or loss.

database The compilation of information in a form that can be understood and used by a computer.

de facto **corporation** A corporation defectively incorporated in good faith that exists in fact though not in law.

de jure **corporation** A corporation whose existence is the result of incorporators having fully or substantially complied with the relevant corporation statutes.

debit card A card used to electronically subtract money from a bank account to pay for goods or services.

debtor in possession A debtor who continues to operate his or her business after filing for bankruptcy.

declaration of trust A trust in which the settlor holds the legal title to the property as trustee for the benefit of some other person (the beneficiary) to whom the settlor now conveys the equitable title.

deductible An amount of any loss that is to be paid by the insured.

deed of trust A formal written instrument that transfers legal ownership of real property to a third party while the mortgagor remains on the property. The third party holds certain rights to that property as security for the mortgagor's creditors.

defamation The intentional tort that occurs when a false statement is communicated to others that harms a person's good name or reputation.

defective agreement An apparent contract in which mutual assent has been destroyed, thus rendering the alleged contract void.

defective condition A condition that makes a product unreasonably dangerous to the consumer, user, or property. See *product liability*.

defendant The person against whom a lawsuit is brought and from whom recovery is sought.

defense of others A defense to criminal liability to defendants if they can show they used force to rescue another person who was the victim of an apparent attack. The rescuer must have good reason to believe the victim was in danger of severe bodily injury or death.

del credere agent (del·KREH·de·reh) A factor who guarantees the credit of a third party to a principal and guarantees the solvency of the purchaser and the performance of the contract.

delegation The transfer of a contractual duty.

demand futility doctrine A corporate rule that says that a shareholder need not take a complaint to the board of directors before filing a derivative lawsuit if that board is controlled by the director that is the target of the suit.

demand note A promissory note that is payable whenever the payee demands payment.

demurrage charge A fee charged by a carrier for the storage of goods still remaining in its possession beyond the time allowed for unloading by the cosignee.

demurrer A motion for dismissal of a case on the grounds that a plaintiff has failed to state a claim for which relief can be granted.

dependency theory An economic picture of the world that holds the developed world responsible for the poverty and deprivation found in the developing world.

depositary bank The first bank to which an item is transferred for collection; the depositary bank may also be the payor bank.

deposition An oral question-and-answer session conducted under oath during which an attorney questions parties or witnesses from the opposition in a lawsuit.

dereliction of duty In criminal law, an activity that involves a law enforcement officer's failure to carry out his or her lawful duties.

derivative A financial tool the value of which emerges from a variable item, such as an interest rate, a stock index, or a commodity like fuel or crops. (See also derivative contract and derivative instrument.)

derivative contract A financial tool the value of which emerges from a variable item, such as an interest rate, a stock index, or a commodity like fuel or crops. (See also derivative and derivative instrument.)

derivative instrument A financial tool the value of which emerges from a variable item, such as an interest rate, a stock index, or a commodity like fuel or crops. (See also derivative contract and derivative.)

derivative suit A lawsuit brought by shareholders on behalf of the corporation.

descriptive theory A system of ethical thought that describes the values at work within a social system.

descriptive threshold In insurance law, a guideline that determines when a victim can bring a lawsuit for injuries that result from an auto accident.

destination contract A contract under which the seller is required to deliver goods to a place of destination. The title and risk of loss remain with the seller until the goods reach the place of destination.

devise Real property that is left in a will. In states that have adopted the Uniform Probate Code, the term refers to both real and personal property.

devisee One who receives the real property under a will. In states that have adopted the Uniform Probate Code, the term refers to a person who receives a gift of either real or personal property under a will.

devolution When courts redefine a right and transfer the power and the obligation to enforce that right from a higher legal authority to a lower one.

digital information contract A contract involving the sale or licensing of information in a digital format.

Digital Millennium Copyright Act (DMCA) A law that makes it illegal to use technological means to bypass or override programs designed to prevent access to a copyrighted work.

digital signature An encoded message that appears at the end of a contract created online.

direct examination The questioning of witnesses by the lawyer who has called them.

direct suit A suit brought by shareholders who have been deprived of a right that belongs to them as shareholders.

disability Any physical or mental impairment that substantially limits one or more of the major life activities.

disaffirm In contract law, to indicate by a statement or act an intent not to live up to the terms of the contract.

disclaimer In employment law, a statement that regardless of provisions or policies in an employment handbook and regardless of oral promises to the contrary, an employment-at-will situation still exists between an employer and its employees. In the accounting profession, a statement declaring that an auditor has decided not to give any opinion on a firm's financial records.

disclaimer of general partner status A document filed with the appropriate state office when a limited partner has been incorrectly named as a general partner.

disclosed principal The person known by a third party to be the principal of an agent.

discounting System by which a bank will buy an instrument at a price below its face amount with the aim of ultimately collecting the face amount.

discovery The process by which parties to a civil suit search for information relevant to the case.

dishonor To refuse to accept or pay a negotiable instrument when it is presented.

disparagement In tort law, any false statement made to others that questions the legal ownership or raises doubts as to the quality of merchandise.

disparate impact A type of discrimination in an employer's policy that seems neutral on the surface but has an unequal or unfair impact on members of one or more of the protected classes.

disparate treatment Intentional discrimination against an individual or group belonging to a protected class. The protected classes are sex, race, color, religion, and national origin.

disposable income The amount of money left from a person's income, after subtracting certain allowable deductions.

Dispute Settlement Board (DSB) See *Dispute Settlement Understanding*.

Dispute Settlement Understanding (DSU) A series of measures administered by an international Dispute Settlement Board that are designed to improve the way trading quarrels are handled.

disputed amount Consideration on which parties to a contract never agree.

dissociation A process authorized under the Revised Uniform Partnership Act that takes place whenever a partner is no longer associated with the running of the partnership firm.

dissolution A change in the relation of partners caused by any partner ceasing to be associated in the carrying on of the business.

diversity cases Federal lawsuits that are between persons from different states, between citizens of the United States and a foreign government, or between citizens of the United States and citizens of a foreign nation. Diversity cases must involve an amount over $75,000.

dividends Net profits, or surplus, set aside for shareholders.

document of title A paper that serves as evidence that the person holding the paper has title to the goods mentioned in the document.

Dodd–Frank Wall Street and Consumer Protection Act An act passed by Congress to deal with the 21st century financial crisis.

domain name The Internet address of a business, institution, or individual.

domain name dispute A disagreement that arises when an individual or organization has registered a domain name that is actually the protected trademark of a business or institution.

domestic bill of exchange A draft that is drawn and payable in the United States.

domestic corporation A corporation created by or organized under the laws of the state where it is operating.

domestic violence statute State laws that outlaw physical violence directed at any family member.

dominant tenement The property to which the right or privilege of an easement attaches.

donee One to whom a gift is given.

donee beneficiary A third party who provides no consideration for the benefits received and who owes the contracting parties no legal duty.

donor One who gives a gift.

double indemnity An optional provision in life insurance policies that provides that the insurer will pay double the amount due to a beneficiary if the insured dies from accidental causes.

double jeopardy In criminal procedure, the possibility of being tried twice for the same crime.

dower By common law, the vested rights of the wife to a one-third lifetime interest in the real property owned by her spouse. Compare *curtesy*.

draft A written order by which the party creating it orders another party to pay money to a third party. Also called *bill of exchange*.

drawee The party named in a draft who is ordered to pay the money to the payee.

drawer The party who draws a draft, that is, the party who orders that the money be paid.

drug trafficking The unauthorized manufacture or distribution of any controlled substance or the possession of such a substance with the intention of manufacturing or distributing it illegally.

dummy corporation A corporation that is set up as a mere instrumentality of a parent corporation. Also called *corporate shell* and *empty shell*.

dunning letter A letter representing payment for goods.

durable power of attorney A document that authorizes an agent to act on another's behalf, with the power either surviving incapacity or becoming effective upon incapacity.

duress An action by one party that forces another party to do what need not be done otherwise.

duty An obligation placed on individuals because of the law.

duty of due diligence A duty that says that corporate managers when acting on behalf of the corporation must act (1) in good faith, (2) using the same level of care that an ordinarily prudent person would use in a comparable situation, and (3) in the reasonable belief that the best interests of the corporation are being met.

duty of loyalty A duty that states managers must place the corporation's interests above their own.

duty of obedience Managers' duty to ensure their exercise of authority is not excessive and does not harm the corporation.

duty to defend A responsibility that an insurer has in an insurance contract to defend a client when a claim is disputed by another party.

duty to investigate A responsibility that an insurer has in an insurance contract to determine if a client is entitled to payment or to any other protection guaranteed under the agreement.

duty to pay A responsibility that an insurer has in an insurance contract to replace or repair the property of an insured or to pay any claim by a third party based on a liability clause.

dwelling insurance An insurance contract under which the insurer promises to provide protection to the property owner of a single family house or an apartment building.

dyad A two level system of morality, represented by the "ethic of ultimate ends" for individuals and the "ethic of responsibility" for national leaders.

e-911 location identifier system An electronic chip located in a mobile phone that sends out a signal that is designed to ensure that EMS personnel can locate people who are unable or unwilling to reveal their location when making an emergency call.

early neutral evaluation (ENE) A process similar to that of a settlement hearing, which may result in a final decision or be used to help shape the final decision.

easement The right to use the land of another for a particular purpose.

easement by prescription An easement that is obtained by passing over another's property without permission openly and continuously for a period of time set by state statute (20 years in many states).

e-check (sometimes called *electronic check conversion*) A system in which funds are electronically transferred from a customer's checking account, eliminating the need to process a paper check.

e-commerce Involves transacting business by any one of several types of electronic communication, from debit card purchases to buying and selling goods on the Internet.

economic compensatory damages Damages that are directly quantifiable, including damages awarded for lost wages, medical expenses, and expenses incurred in the repair or replacement of property.

economic duress Threats of a business nature that force another party without real consent to enter a commercial agreement. Also called *business compulsion*.

economic equivalent A lease agreement that has the characteristics of a sales contract, despite its name.

Economic Espionage Act Legislation that outlines criminal sanctions for the theft of trade secrets and the use of fraud to obtain trade secrets.

economic reality test In agency law, a test used by the court in vicarious liability to determine whether a worker is a servant or an independent contractor.

Economic Security Council (ESC) A single, unified international agency under the management of the United Nations that would monitor the economic activities of member nations.

economic zones Unified but isolated sectors of economic activity based on geographical areas designed to focus on the economic well-being of the nations in each zone.

e-consumer Someone who buys something on the Internet.

ejectment The common law name given to the lawsuit brought by a landlord to have a tenant evicted from the premises.

elective share See *forced share.*

electronic contracts Contracts made using computers, either via e-mail or the Internet, or that involve computer-related products, such as databases and software.

electronic data interchange (EDI) An electronic process used to negotiate contracts.

electronic fund transfer (EFT) A method of banking that uses computers and electronic technology as a substitute for checks and other banking methods.

electronic or jurisdiction The authority of a court to hear a case based on Internet-related transactions.

electronically stored information (ESI) Computerized evidence.

emancipated In contract law, the condition that exists when minors are no longer under the control of their parents and are responsible for their contracts.

embezzlement The act of wrongfully taking property entrusted into one's care.

eminent domain The right of federal, state, and local governments, or other public bodies, to take private lands, with compensation to their owners, for public use. Also called *condemnation*.

emotional duress Acts or threats that create emotional distress and lead a person into a contract against his or her will.

employment at will A doctrine followed by most jurisdictions in the United States that says an employer can dismiss an employee at any time for any reason.

employment contacts In employment law, an enforceable agreement between the hiring party (the employer) and the hired party (the employee).

end user A purchaser who is not involved in the production or assembly of the product.

endowment insurance Insurance protection that combines life insurance and investment so that if the insured outlives the time period of the policy, the face value is paid to the beneficiary.

entity theory A theory in partnership law that holds that a partnership is actually a separate legal person with its own legal identity.

entrapment A defense to criminal liability that claims that a previously law-abiding citizen was induced to commit a crime by a law enforcement officer.

equal dignities rule The legal rule that provides that when a party appoints an agent to negotiate an agreement that must be in writing, the appointment of the agent must also be in writing.

equipment Goods that are used or bought for use primarily in business.

equitable estoppel See *part performance*.

equitable remedy The requirement that a party do something or refrain from doing something, beyond the payment of money.

equity financing The issuing and selling of shares of stock to raise capital.

equity of redemption A mortgagor's right to pay off the mortgage in full, including interest.

espionage The gathering or transmitting of information pertaining to the national defense of a nation for the political or military use of any foreign nation.

estate in fee simple An estate in which the owner owns the land for life with the right to use it or dispose of it freely.

estoppel A legal bar to denying acts, statements, or promises.

ethic of benevolence An ethical principle, usually referred to as the ethic of ultimate ends, developed by the 20th century political philosopher Max Weber, that holds that individuals must act with compassion toward people without regard to the consequences. (See also ethic of ultimate ends.)

ethic of responsibility An ethical principle developed by the 20th century political philosopher Max Weber that holds that a leader's primary ethical guide must be the safety and security the people of his or her nation state.

ethic of ultimate ends An ethical principle, often referred to as the ethic of benevolence, developed by the 20th century political philosopher Max Weber, that holds that individuals must act with compassion toward people without regard to the consequences. (See also ethic of benevolence.)

ethical relativism A system of ethical thought that says there is no objective or absolute standard of right and wrong.

ethics Rules of conduct that transcend legal rules, telling people how to act when the law does not.

EU Data Protection Directive A decree issued by the European Union (EU) that prevents European companies from sharing ESI with countries that do not provide the same level of protection for the ESI as the EU.

EU E-Privacy Directive A decree issued by the European Union (EU) that guarantees EU citizens a high level of privacy for electronically stored information.

euro The European Union's common currency.

European Central Bank (ECB) The bank was established by provisions within the Maastricht Treaty and is the central hub of the European System of Central Banks.

European System of Central Banks (ESCB) A system of banks including the European Central Bank and the National Central Banks.

European Union (EU) A group of countries in Europe that have joined together to formulate a common European economic policy, minimize trade barriers, and introduce a common currency with the goal of making the EU a major global competitor.

eviction An act of the landlord that deprives the tenant of the enjoyment of the premises.

exculpatory agreement A clause that says one of the parties to a contract, generally the one who wrote the contract, is not liable for any economic loss or physical injury, even if that party caused the loss or injury.

exculpatory clause A clause in a contract that releases a party from liability for his or her wrongful acts. These clauses are not favored by law.

executed contract A contract whose terms have been completely and satisfactorily carried out by both parties.

executor A person named in a will to by the court to manage the estate of a testator.

executor (male); executrix (female) The party named in a will to carry out the terms of the will.

executory contract A contract that has not yet been fully performed by the parties.

exemplary damages In tort law, money payments levied by a court against a defendant designed to make an example of the defendant and, thus, deter others from the same type of unacceptable conduct.

exempt property Property of a decedent that passes to the surviving spouse or children and is beyond the reach of creditors.

express authority An agent's authority that the principal voluntarily and specifically sets forth as oral or written instructions in an agency agreement.

express contract A contract in which both parties accept mutual obligations through either oral discussion or written communication.

express warranty An oral or written statement, promise, or other representation about the quality of a product.

extant data Data that are difficult to retrieve because they are hidden within a computer system.

extortion The act of taking another's property with consent when such consent is coerced by threat to injure a victim's person, property, or reputation.

f.a.s vessel Free alongside vessel. Indicates that the seller must deliver goods, at the seller's own risk, alongside the vessel or at a dock designated by the buyer.

f.o.b. Free on board.

f.o.b. the place of destination Terms indicating that goods will be delivered free to the place of destination.

f.o.b. the place of shipment Terms indicating that goods will be delivered free to the place of shipment.

faction A special interest group that does its best to see that its point of view is heard, and acknowledged, supported, and funded by the government.

factor A special agent who is employed to sell merchandise consigned for that purpose.

failure of consideration A personal defense that may be used by a maker or drawer of a negotiable instrument when the party with whom the maker dealt breaches the contract by not furnishing the agreed consideration.

failure-proof public corporation An entity operated by an autonomous board of directors, owned by the state and protected from failure by the government.

fair court Historically in the Middle Ages in Europe, a court set up at a festival (a fair) to handle disputes between merchants at that festival (fair).

fair use doctrine A doctrine that provides that copyright material can be used without permission if the use is reasonable and not harmful to the copyright owner.

fairness rule The rule that requires managers to be fair to the corporation when they personally benefit from their business decisions.

false imprisonment An intentional tort involving the unjustified confinement or detention of a person.

family allowance An amount of money taken from a decedent's estate and given to the family to meet its immediate needs while the estate is being probated.

family farmer Under Chapter 12 of the Bankruptcy Code, a farmer who receives more than half the total income from the farm. In addition, to qualify as a family farmer, 80 percent of the farmer's debt must result from farm expenses.

farm products Crops, livestock, or supplies used or produced in farming operations.

fault-based insurance An automobile insurance policy that will measure liability in an automobile accident by the degree of fault that can be assigned to each driver using negligence principles.

featherbedding Requiring an employer, usually by a union, to keep unneeded employees, to pay employees for not working, or to assign more employees to a given job than are needed.

Federal House Finance Agency (FHFA) A federal agency created to oversee the operation of Fannie Mae and Freddie Mac.

federal question A matter that involves the U.S. Constitution, a federal statute or statutes, or a treaty; handled by federal district courts.

Federal Register Publication that produces a daily compilation of new regulations issued by federal administrative agencies.

felony A crime punishable by death or by imprisonment in a federal or state prison for a term exceeding one year.

fiduciary A person who acts in a position of trust or confidence.

fiduciary relationship A relationship based on trust such as exists between an attorney and a client, an agent and a principal, a guardian and a ward, a trustee and a beneficiary, or a director and a corporation.

field warehousing The practice of using goods that are stored in a warehouse as security for a loan.

finance charge The actual cost of a loan in dollars and cents.

firm offer A rule that no consideration is necessary when a merchant agrees in writing to hold an offer open for the sale of goods.

first-degree murder In criminal law, killing someone with premeditation or with prior calculation and design, or while committing a serious felony such as rape, robbery, or kidnapping.

fixture An article of personal property physically attached to real property in such a way that an interest arises in it under real estate law.

flexible-rate mortgage A mortgage that has a rate of interest that changes according to fluctuations in the index to which it is tied. Also called *variable-rate mortgage.*

floater policy A policy that insures property that cannot be covered by specific insurance because the property is constantly changing in either value or location.

floating lien A provision, placed by the creditor, in a security agreement that a security interest of the creditor also applies to goods the debtor acquires at a later time.

forbearance The act of refraining from doing (or promising not to do) something that a person has a legal right to do.

forced share The portion of a decedent's estate assured to the family by state statute.

foreclosure The right of a mortgagee to apply to a court to have property sold when the mortgagor defaults or fails to perform some agreement in the mortgage.

foreign corporation A corporation created by or organized under the laws of a state other than the one in which it is operating.

foreign draft See *international bill of exchange.*

forgery The false making or alteration of a writing with the intent to defraud.

formal contract Under common law, a contract that is written; signed, witnessed, and placed under the seal of the parties; and delivered.

formalist theory A theory of legal interpretation under which the court will look to see if certain elements (offer, acceptance, mutual assent, consideration, capacity, and legality) exist before concluding whether or not the parties in a lawsuit have actually entered a legally binding contract.

forum shopping The process of locating a jurisdiction that has a friendly track record for the type of lawsuit that is about to be filed.

franchise A business arrangement that permits an individual, a group of investors, or another entity to lease the right to uses a parent entity's business operation, trademark, goods, services, and good will under a fee arrangement provided to the parent.

fraud A wrongful statement, action, or concealment pertinent to the subject matter of a contract knowingly made to damage the other party.

fraud in the inception Fraud that occurs when one party tricks another into a contract by lying to the innocent party about the actual nature of the contract.

fraud in the inducement Fraud that occurs when one party tricks another into a contract by lying about the terms of the agreement to get the innocent party to enter the contract under false pretenses.

fraudulent conveyance A transfer of property with the intent to defraud creditors.

fraudulent misrepresentation A wrongful statement, action, or concealment, pertinent to the subject matter of a contract, that is knowingly made to damage the other party.

friendly suitor See *white knight.*

frustration-of-purpose doctrine In contract law, the doctrine that releases a party from a contractual obligation when performing the obligations would be thoroughly impractical and senseless.

full warranty A warranty under which a defective product will be repaired or replaced without charge within a reasonable time after a complaint has been made about it.

fungible goods Goods of which any unit is, by nature or usage of trade, the equivalent of any like unit; wheat, flour, sugar, and liquids of various kinds are examples.

future goods Goods that are not yet in existence or under the control of people; they include fish in the sea, minerals in the ground, goods not yet manufactured, and commodities futures.

general agent A person who is given broad authority to act on behalf of the principal in conducting the bulk of the principal's business activities on a daily basis.

General Agreement on Tariffs and Trade (GATT) A nonstatic agreement among the principal trading countries to reduce or eliminate tariffs and to promote free trade on a global basis.

General Assembly The member nations of the United Nations.

general consent Consent that arises automatically when a patient enters a hospital for routine tests and procedures needed for diagnosis and treatment.

general jurisdiction The power of a court to hear any type of case.

general partner A partner who takes an active part in running a partnership and has unlimited liability for the firm's debts.

general partnership Two or more persons operating a business entity as co-owners in order to make a profit.

general release A document expressing the intent of a creditor to release a debtor from obligations to an existing and valid debt.

general warranty deed A deed that contains express warranties under which a grantor guarantees property to be free of encumbrances created by the grantor or by others who had title previously. Also called *full convenant* and *warranty deed*.

general welfare clause Article I, Section 8, Clause 1 of the U.S. Constitution which reads in part that Congress is empowered to "lay and collect taxes, Duties, Imposts, and Excises, to pay the Debts and provide for the common defense and general welfare of the United States."

generally accepted accounting principles (GAAP) Rules established by the Financial Accounting Standards Board (FASB) that outline the procedures that accountants use in accumulating financial data and in preparing financial statements.

generally accepted auditing standards (GAAS) Standards set up by the Auditing Standards Board of the American Institute of Certified Public Accountants (AICPA) that measure the quality of the performance of the auditing procedures.

Genetic Information Nondiscrimination Act (GINA) A law passed by Congress that makes it unlawful for employers or insurance companies to make decisions based on genetic information acquired by genetic testing.

Geneva Conventions International meetings that attempted to deal with many of the contemporary complications brought on by the nature of warfare in the twentieth century.

gift in *causa mortis* (in·KAWS·ah·MORE·tes) A gift given during one's lifetime in contemplation of death from a known cause.

gift *inter vivos* (IN·ter·VY·vose) A gift between the living. For an exchange to be valid, the donor must intend to make a gift, the gift must be delivered to the donee, and the donee must accept it.

golden parachute A comprehensive package that protects executives who might lose their jobs following a merger or a consolidation.

good faith Honesty in fact and observance of reasonable commercial standards of fair dealings in the trade.

goods All things (other than money, stocks, and bonds) that are movable.

goodwill The expected continuance of public patronage of a business.

governmental control A theory of corporate control based on the belief that because corporate decision making impacts upon more individuals and groups than just shareholders and managers, those decisions should be made by a group of corporate outsiders, usually government officials. Also called *state control*.

graduated-payment mortgage A mortgage that has a fixed interest rate during the life of the mortgage; however, the monthly payments made by the mortgagor increase over the term of the loan.

grantee A person to whom title to real property is transferred in a deed.

grantor A person who transfers title to real property in a deed.

gratuitous agency An agency relationship that emerges from an agreement that is not a contract.

gratuitous agent An agent who is not under contract and, thus, performs his or her duties without payment.

gratuitous bailment A bailment for the sole benefit of either the bailor or the bailee, in which the other party receives no consideration for benefits bestowed.

greenmail A strategy used to shake off a bidder's hostile suit by offering to buy, at significantly higher cost, the portion of stock already owned by the bidder who is trying to take over the company.

grievance procedure A procedure that allows employees to appeal any decision an employer makes that employees feel violates just cause.

gross negligence Very great negligence.

guaranteed insurability An optional provision in an insurance contract that allows the insured to pay an extra premium initially in exchange for a guaranteed option to buy more insurance at certain specified times later on with no questions asked and no medical examination required.

guarantor The promisor.

guaranty contract In contract law, a contract by which one party agrees to pay the debt of another party if that party fails to meet that obligation.

guaranty of payment A promise to pay another's bills or to settle wrongful acts if that party does not settle them personally.

health care proxy A written statement authorizing an agent to make health care decisions for another in the event of incapacity.

Health Insurance Portability and Accountability Act (HIPAA) Legislation that guarantees patients the right to see their medical records and those of their underage children.

heir One who inherits property either under a will or through someone's dying without a will.

holder A person who is in possession of a negotiable instrument that is issued or indorsed to that person's order or to bearer.

holder in due course A holder who has taken a negotiable instrument for value, in good faith, without notice that it is overdue or has been dishonored and without notice of any defenses against it or claim to it.

holder in due course rule A rule adopted by the FTC that states that holders of consumer credit contracts who are holders in due course are subject to all claims and defenses that the buyer could use against the seller, including personal defenses.

Home Affordable Modification Program (HAMP) A program set up by the Department of the Treasury to support the efforts of homeowners who, though in default, wish to continue to make payments on their mortgages

Home Affordable Refinance Program (HARP) A federal program designed to help homeowners who owe the bank or mortgage company more than the home is worth.

home equity loan A line of credit made available to home-owners based on the value of the property over and above any existing mortgages.

homeowner's policy A type of insurance that gives protection for all types of losses and liabilities related to home ownership. Items covered include losses from fire, windstorm, burglary, vandalism, and injuries suffered by others while on the property.

homestead exemption A provision in the Bankruptcy Code that allows debtors to exclude a statutory amount of equity in the debtor's place of residence and in property used as a burial ground when filing for bankruptcy.

homicide The killing of one human being by another.

hopscotch loan A corporate merger process which permits a tax free loan to flow from an established alien corporation into the treasury of its new partner.

horizontal expansion The joining of companies involved in the same business.

hostile bidder See *unfriendly suitor.*

hot-cargo contract An agreement whereby an employer voluntarily agrees with a union not to handle, use, or deal in nonunion-produced goods for another employer.

hybrid contract In contract law a binding agreement that has enough characteristic of a sales contract and a service contract to be considered a combination of both. See also blended contract and mixed contract.

idealism A theory of international behavior that says the global order is not fully chaotic but is, instead, controlled by the NIOs; that nation-states share power with the NIOs; that nation-states and NIOs seek power and control but do so in the interests of international peace, by following international law and using military action only within international coalitions; and that the final best state of affairs that all nation-states seek (or should seek) is the formation of a democratic or a republican world government. (See also: liberal internationalism.)

identified goods Specific goods that are selected as the subject matter of a contract.

identity theft Using a computer to steal confidential information to clean out a person's bank account, to run up credit card debt, to divert cash transfers, and to disrupt the financial and personal life of the victim.

illegal agreement In contract law, a void agreement to do something that violates the law.

illusory promise A promise that does not obligate the promisor to anything.

implied authority The authority of an agent to perform acts that are necessary or customary to carry out expressly authorized duties.

impaired classes Creditors who receive less than the full value of their claims in bankruptcy proceedings.

implied contract A contract created by the actions or gestures of the parties involved in the transaction.

implied covenant An implied promise in any employment relationship that the employer and the employee will be fair with each other.

implied warranty A warranty that is imposed by law rather than by statements, descriptions, or samples given by the seller.

implied-in-fact bailment A bailment created by circumstances rather than by intent. (See also implied-in-law bailment.)

implied-in-fact contract A contract implied by direct or indirect acts of the parties.

implied-in-law bailment A bailment created by circumstances rather than by intent. (See also implied-in-fact bailment.)

implied-in-law contract A remedy imposed by a court in a situation in which the parties did not create a written, oral, or implied-in-fact agreement but one party has unfairly benefited at the innocent expense of another. Also called *quasi-contract*.

in pari delicto (in pah·ree de·LIK·toh) In equal fault. A contract relationship when both parties to an illegal agreement are equally wrong, in the knowledge of the operation and effect of their contract.

inactive data Data in a computer system that are not being used at the present time but that can be easily retrieved.

incidental beneficiary A third party for whose benefit a contract was not made but who would substantially benefit if the agreement were performed according to its terms and conditions.

incidental damages Damages awarded for losses indirectly, but closely, attributed to a breach to cover any expenses paid out by an innocent party to prevent further loss.

incorporators The people who actually sign the articles of incorporation to start a corporation.

indemnification Payment for loss or damage suffered.

indemnify To compensate for loss or damage or insure against future loss or damage.

independent contractor One who contracts to do a job and who retains complete control over the methods employed to obtain completion.

independent directors Corporate directors who have no family members employed by the corporation, who are not themselves employed by the corporation, or, if they were at one time employed by the corporation, have not been on the staff for at least three years.

independent director control A theory of corporate control that states that the best way to make certain that corporate decisions are made in the best interests of the corporation is to make sure that the decision makers themselves are not affected by the decisions.

indictment A set of formal charges against a defendant issued by a grand jury.

individual justice Justice that is meted out to the people on a case-by-case basis.

indorsee A person to whom a draft, note, or other negotiable instrument is transferred by indorsement.

indorsement in full See *special indorsement*.

indorser A person who indorses a negotiable instrument.

infliction of emotional distress The intentional tort that allows those injured emotionally by the wrongful acts of others to recover damages even without the accompanying physical injury.

informal contract An oral or written contract that is not under a seal or is not a contract of record. Also called *simple contract*.

information A set of formal charges against a defendant drawn up and issued by the prosecutor or district attorney.

informed consent Written consent given by patients for diagnostic tests or treatments that will involve danger or pain after being told about the procedure and the risks involved.

in-house attorney A member of the officer corps of a business who is instructed in his or her duties by a supervisor.

injunction A court order preventing someone from performing a particular act.

inland marine insurance An insurance contract that covers goods that are moved by land carriers such as rail, truck, and airplane.

innkeeper An operator of a hotel, motel, or inn that holds itself out to the public as being ready to accommodate travelers, strangers, and transient guests.

inside information Material, nonpublic, factual data that can be used to buy or sell securities at a profit.

insider trading Using inside information to either cheat the corporation or take unfair advantage of corporate outsiders.

insider trading rule A rule of corporate governance that states that when managers possess important inside information, they are obligated to reveal that information before trading on it themselves.

insolvent Inability of a business entity to pay its debts as they become due in the usual course of business.

installment note A promissory note in which the principal together with interest on the unpaid balance is payable in installments at specified times.

insurable interest The financial interest that a policyholder has in the person or property that is insured.

insurance A contract whereby one party pays premiums to another party who undertakes to pay compensation for losses resulting from risks or perils specified in the contract.

insured A party that is protected by an insurer against losses caused by the risks specified in an insurance policy.

insurer A party that accepts the risk of loss in return for a premium (payment of money) and agrees to compensate the insured against a specified loss.

integral-part test A finding that any type of price enhancement violates the best-price rule.

intended beneficiary A third party in whose favor a contract is made.

intentional or reckless infliction of emotional distress A tort involving someone who intentionally or recklessly causes another to undergo emotional or mental suffering.

interest-only mortgage In property law, a mortgage in which the borrower pays only the interest for a period of time, usually one to three years, as set by the agreement.

interference with a contract The international tort that results when a person, out of ill will, entices a contractual party into breaking the contract.

interlocking directorates In antitrust law, a situation that occurs when individuals serve as two corporations that are competitors.

intermediary bank Any bank to which an item is transferred in the course of collection except the depositary or payor bank.

international arbitration agreement A pledge to use arbitration if parties find themselves in disagreement about enforcement rights under an original contract.

international bill of exchange A draft that is drawn in one country but is payable in another. Also called *foreign draft*.

International Court of Justice (ICJ) One of the principal vehicles for the establishment of international law and justice.

International Criminal Court (ICC) International court that presides over trials involving genocide, war crimes, and other human rights violations.

International Law Commission A thirty-four-member panel of judges who seek to codify international law in as objective a manner as possible.

International Monetary Fund (IMF) A nongovernmental organization that is designed to help financially strapped nations to secure loans that will help them engage in programs of sustainable economic growth and development.

international terrorism Acts transcending national boundaries that violate a state's criminal laws and are intended to intimidate that country's civilians or influence the policy or conduct of the government.

interrogatories Written questions to be answered in writing under oath by the opposite party in a lawsuit.

interstate commerce Business activities that touch more than one state.

interstate shipment A shipment that goes beyond the borders of the state in which it originated.

intestacy The quality or state of one who dies without having prepared a valid will.

intestate Having died without leaving a valid will. Compare *testate*.

intestate succession The process by which property passes to others when people die without a will.

intimidation In criminal law, threats of harm to the person or the property of a public servant, a party official, or a witness, with the intent to coerce that person into violating his or her duty under the law.

intrastate commerce Business activities that have no out-of-state connections.

intrastate shipment A shipment that is entirely within a single state.

invasion of privacy The intentional tort that occurs when one person unreasonably denies another person the right to be left alone.

inventory Goods held for sale or lease, or raw materials used or consumed in a business.

inversion A corporate expansion process that typically occurs when an American corporation buys an alien corporation and then reincorporates in that alien's national base or when an alien corporation buys an American corporation under a deal that is engineered at the behest of, and largely for the benefit of, the American corporation. (See also inverted company.)

inverted company A corporate person which has gone through the inversion process. (See also inversion.)

invitation to trade An announcement published for the purpose of creating interest and attracting a response by many people.

involuntary bailment A bailment arising from the leaving of personal property in the possession of a bailee through an act of God, accident, or other uncontrolled phenomenon.

involuntary manslaughter In criminal law, the unlawful killing of another human being caused by negligence.

irresistible impulse test Under this rule, criminal defendants are judged not guilty by reason of insanity if, at the time of the action in question, they suffered from a mental disease that either prevented them from knowing right from wrong or compelled them to commit the criminal act.

irrevocable offer A rule that no consideration is necessary when a merchant agrees in writing to hold an offer open for the sale of goods. Also called *firm offer*.

issue Descendants (children, grandchildren, great-grandchildren).

issuer Either a maker or a drawer of an instrument.

joint liability In the law of business associations a legal principle under which liability is spread among all partners when they are sued.

joint and several liability In the law of business associations a legal principle under which the partners in a venture can be sued apart or together.

joint tenants Two or more persons who own property where the right of any deceased owner is automatically transferred to other surviving owners.

joint tenants with the right of survivorship See *joint tenants*.

joint venture (or joint undertaking) A business venture that involves a contractual arrangement by which individuals unite for a limited amount of time to create a new entity in which the founders share control, expenses, and profits.

judicial review The process by which a court determines the constitutionality of various legislative statutes, administrative regulations, and executive actions.

judicial–economic system The interaction of the legal system and the economic system so as to become, in effect, a single system.

junior mortgage A mortgage subject to a prior mortgage.

junk bonds Bonds with high risk but also a high rate of return.

junk science The distorted, exaggerated, misapplied, or misrepresented use of scientific evidence.

jurisdiction The authority of a court to hear and decide cases.

juriscience A discipline that explores the intersection of science and the law.

just cause A criterion under the just war theory, which states that to be morally permissible, a war must be waged only for honorable motives.

just war theory A theory for determining when a war can be considered legally and morally correct.

kidnapping The unlawful abduction of an individual against that individual's will.

knowledge In criminal law, the awareness that a particular result will probably occur.

labor union An organization that acts on behalf of all employees in negotiations with the employer regarding terms of their employment.

laches The equitable doctrine that a delay or failure to assert a right or claim at the proper time, which causes a disadvantage to the adverse party, is a bar to recovery.

lack of consideration A personal defense that may be used by a maker or drawer of a negotiable instrument when no consideration existed in the underlying contract for which the instrument was issued.

landlord A person who owns real property and who rents or leases it to someone else. Also called *lessor*.

larceny The act of taking and carrying away the personal property of another without the right to do so.

larceny by false pretenses The taking of someone's money or property by intentionally deceiving that person.

last clear chance defense In tort law a defense used by an injured party (the plaintiff) accused of contributory negligence to show that the alleged tortfeasor (the defendant) had the final opportunity to avoid causing injury to that plaintiff.

last resort A criterion under the just war theory that states that a war must be waged only as a final course of action.

last will and testament A formal document that governs the transfer of property at death.

law A set of rules created by the governing body of a society to maintain harmony, stability, and justice in that society.

law merchant In England, the commercial law developed by merchants who needed a set of rules to govern their business transactions.

law of finds A principle that gives ownership to the finder of property as long as the property is abandoned, the finder intends to acquire the property, and the finder has possession of the property.

law of salvage A principle that gives one who engages in a salvage operation the right to compensation for assisting a foundering vessel at sea.

leading objective test In contract law, a test applied by the court to determine the real purpose of a guaranty contract.

lease A contract granting the use of certain real property to another for a specified period in return for the payment of rent.

lease option A contract that permits a party to lease real property while holding an option to purchase that property.

leasehold estate The creation of an ownership interest in the tenant. An interest in real estate that is held under a lease. Also called *tenancy*.

legal detriment In contract law, doing (or promising to do) something that one has a legal right not to do, giving up (or promising to give up) something that one has a legal right to keep, or refraining from doing (or promising not to do) something that one has a legal right to do.

legal imperialism American insistence that all disputes be resolved under American law.

legal tender Money that may be offered legally in satisfaction of a debt and that must be accepted by a creditor when offered.

legatee One who receives personal property in a will.

lemon law A statute that compensates consumers for products (especially vehicles) that are so badly flawed that they are virtually worthless.

lessee See *tenant*.

lessor See *landlord*.

leveraged buyout The purchase of a controlling portion of the stock in a corporation by a group of shareholders, usually officers and directors of the company.

lex mercatoria In England, the commercial law developed by merchants who needed a set of rules to govern their business transactions.

liability The legal responsibility of an individual for his or her actions.

liability insurance An insurance contract that protects an insured from injury and damage he/ she has caused to a third party.

liable Legally responsible.

libel Any false statement that harms another person's good name or reputation made in a permanent form, such as movies, writing, and videotape, and communicated to others.

liberal internationalism A theory of international behavior that says the global order is not fully chaotic but is, instead, controlled by the NIOs; that nation-states share power with the NIOs; that nation-states and NIOs seek power and control but do so in the interests of international peace, by following international law and using military action only within international coalitions; and that the final best state of affairs that all nation-states seek (or should seek) is the formation of a democratic or a republican world government. (See also: idealism.)

license A grant of permission to do a particular thing, to exercise a certain privilege, to carry on a particular business, or to pursue a certain occupation; an agreement that gives no property right or interest in land but merely allows the licensee to do certain acts that would otherwise be a trespass; a privilege granted by a state or city upon payment of a fee, which is not a contract and may be revoked for cause, conferring authority to perform a designated task, such as operating a motor vehicle.

licensing agreement An agreement in which one party is given permission from another party to do a particular thing in exchange for consideration.

lien A claim that one has against the property of another.

life estate An estate in which the owner owns real property for his or her life or for the life of another.

life insurance An insurance contract that provides monetary compensation for losses suffered by another's death.

limited defense See *personal defense*.

limited liability Status that specifies that an individual's liability will not go beyond his or her original investment.

limited liability company (LLC) A business organization that borrows elements from a partnership and a corporation. LLCs may come into existence only through following the steps laid out in the state code.

limited liability corporation A cross between a partnership and a corporation, offering the protection of limited liability like a corporation and the tax benefits of a partnership.

limited liability partnership A general partnership in all respects except one—liability.

limited partner A partner who does not take part in the management of a firm and whose liability does not extend beyond his or her investment.

limited partnership One or more general partners joined with one or more limited partners to operate a business entity for profit.

limited-payment life insurance Insurance that provides that the payment will stop after a stated length of time—usually 10, 20, or 30 years.

limited warranty A warranty that does not meet all of the requirements of a full warranty.

lingering apparent authority Apparent authority that stays with an agent if the principal has terminated the agent but has failed to give proper notice to third parties entitled to such notice.

liquidated damages Damages agreed to by the parties to a contract in the event of a breach.

liquidation The conversion of property into cash.

litigant A person involved in litigation.

living trust A trust that comes into existence while the person who establishes it is alive. Also called *inter vivos trust*.

living will A document in which individuals can indicate their desire not to be kept alive by artificial means if there is no hope for recovery.

local option The practice in a state of eliminating uniform statewide laws regulating Sunday activities and allowing the local counties, cities, towns, and villages to adopt their own special Sunday ordinances.

locality rule A means to judge a health care provider's actions on the basis of how other health care professionals in the same community would have acted in the same situation.

lockup agreement A contract between a target corporation and a white knight, giving the knight an option to buy valuable property should a hostile bidder gain control of the target corporation.

locus sigilli The place of the seal. The abbreviation L.S. is often used in place of the seal itself on formal written contracts.

lodger A person who has the use of property without actual or exclusive possession of it.

M'Naughten Rule The oldest test for insanity whereby a criminal defendant is declared not guilty by reason of insanity if, at the time of the criminal act, he or she suffered from a mental disease that prevented him or her from understanding the nature of the act and that the act was wrong.

Maastricht Treaty The outcome of a conference held in Maastricht, the Netherlands. The objectives of the treaty were to create a general European economic policy as well as a foreign policy acceptable to all member states.

Mail Order and Telephone Order Rule The Federal Trade Commission rule that states that sellers must ship orders within the time promised in their advertisements.

main purpose test In contract law, a test applied by the court to determine the real purpose of a guaranty contract.

majority A term used to describe persons who have reached the legal age of adulthood.

maker A person obligated as the payor on a promissory note. See also *comaker*.

malicious prosecution Bringing false criminal charges against an innocent victim.

malpractice Occurs when a professional accountant, health care professional, or attorney—fails to meet his or her duty of care.

managers In the law of business associations, the people who are charged with running the day to day affairs of a limited liability company.

managerial control A theory of corporate management that favors insulating managers from shareholders by limiting the shareholders' power to vote and by making it difficult for the shareholder to sue managers.

master An outdated term signifying an individual who has the right to control the physical conduct of a servant or employee.

material fact An essential or important fact; a fact of substance.

means test Three steps used to qualify someone for Chapter 7 bankruptcy.

med-arb A form of ADR that combines the best aspects of both mediation and arbitration. The parties first submit to a mediation session. If the matter cannot be settled, it moves to an arbitration hearing.

mediation The process by which an outside party attempts to help two other parties settle their differences.

mediator The third party in mediation whose job is to convince the contending parties to adjust or settle their dispute.

Medicaid A healthcare plan for low-income people that is administered by state governments but funded by both state and federal funds.

medical payments insurance A type of automobile insurance that pays for medical (and sometimes funeral) expenses resulting from bodily injuries to anyone occupying the policyholder's car at the time of an accident.

Medicare A federally funded health insurance program for people 65 years and over who are eligible for Social Security.

members In the law of business associations, the people who are the rightful owners of a limited liability company.

memorandum A written agreement containing the terms of an agreement, an identification of the subject matter of the agreement, the consideration promised, the names and identities of the parties to the agreement, and the signature of the party charged to the agreement.

mercantile law An area of the law that was developed in Western Civilization almost exclusively by the merchants themselves to govern themselves and their commercial transactions.

merchant A person who deals in goods of the kind sold in the ordinary course of business or who otherwise claims to have knowledge or skills peculiar to those goods.

merchant protection statute A statute that permits a store owner to detain a person when the storeowner has reasonable cause to suspect shoplifting has occurred, also referred to as shopkeeper's privilege statute.

merger The acquisition of one corporation by another.

metadata In computer jargon, data that is used to record information about other computer data.

midnight deadline The deadline by which banks must settle or return checks or be responsible for paying them. If the payor bank is not the depository bank, it must settle for an item by midnight of the banking day of receipt. If the payor bank is also the depository bank, the deadline is midnight of the next banking day following the banking day on which it receives the relevant item.

military caregiver leave A provision under the Family Medical Leave Act (FMLA) which states that an employer must give an employee up to 26 weeks of leave time in a 12-month period to care for a family member who has sustained a serious illness or injury which occurred because of military service.

minimum contacts The doctrine of minimum contacts identifies the fewest number of contacts that will permit a court to exercise personal jurisdiction over an out-of-state defendant.

minority A term used to describe persons who have not reached the legal age of adulthood.

mirror image rule In contract law, the rule that an acceptance must duplicate the terms in the offer.

misdemeanor A crime less serious than a felony that is generally punishable by a prison sentence of not more than one year.

misrepresentation In contract law, a false statement innocently made by one party to a contract with no intent to deceive. Also, in insurance, giving false answers to

questions in an insurance application that materially affect the risk undertaken by the insurer.

misuse of legal procedure Bringing legal action without probable cause and with malice.

mitigation A principle that states an innocent party cannot take advantage by deliberately raising the level of damages that the other party will have to pay as a consequence of a breach.

mixed contract In contract law a binding agreement that has enough characteristic of a sales contract and a service contract to be considered a combination of both. See also blended contract and hybrid contract.

monarch A corporate officers who has complete control of the board of directors of a corporation.

monetary threshold In insurance law, a guideline to determine when a victim can bring a lawsuit for injuries that result from an auto accident.

money order A type of draft that may be purchased from banks, post offices, telegraph companies, and express companies as a substitute for a check.

monopoly The exclusive control of a market by a business enterprise.

morals Values that govern society's attitude toward right and wrong.

mortgage A transfer of an interest in property for the purpose of creating a security for a debt.

mortgagee The party who lends money and takes back a mortgage as security for the loan.

mortgagor The party who borrows money and gives a mortgage to the lender or mortgagee as security for the loan.

most favored nation principle A principle that states that the World Trade Organization nations must apply the same privileges, advantages, and benefits to all other member nations in relation to similar imports.

mutual assent In contract law, the state of mind that exists between an offeror and an offeree once a valid offer has been accepted and once the parties know what the terms are and have agreed to be bound by them. Also known as "a meeting of the minds."

mutual-benefit bailment A bailment in which both the bailor and the bailee receive some benefit.

mutual mistake See *bilaterial mistake.*

mutual recession A condition in which both parties to a contract agree to rescind the contract and return to the other any consideration already received or pay for any services or materials already rendered.

mutuum (MYOO·choo·um) A loan of goods with the intention that the goods may be used and later replaced with an equal amount of different goods.

National Central Banks (NCB) Part of the European System of Central Banks, the NCBs are located within the member nations of the EU.

national rule A rule that allows a court to judge a health care provider's degree of care by determining how the same procedure is performed on a national basis.

national standard A rule that allows a court to judge a health care provider's degree of care by determining how the same procedure is performed on a national basis.

national treatment principle A principle that states that the World Trade Organization nations must apply the same standards to imports that they apply to domestic goods.

nation-states Sovereign divisions that govern a recognized area of land on a map, may raise money within their borders, and have a responsibility to provide for their citizens.

natural law theory A system of ethical thought that sees an unbreakable link joining the law and morality.

navigable airspace The space above 1,000 feet over populated areas and above 500 feet over water and unpopulated areas.

near privity Privity that emerges between an accountant and a third party who is not a client.

necessaries Goods and services that are essential to a minor's health and welfare.

necessary and proper clause In constitutional law, Article I, Section 8, Clause 18, of the U.S. Constitution, which says that Congress has the power "(T)o make all Laws which shall be necessary and proper for carrying into Execution the foregoing Powers, and all other Powers vested by this Constitution in the Government of the United States, or any Department or Officer thereof."

negative rights theory In ethics, the theory that says that rights are human inventions created to escape moral law.

negligence The failure to use that amount of care that a reasonably prudent person would have used under the same circumstances and conditions.

negligent credentialing Occurs if a hospital has retained a physician that the governing body of the hospital knew or should have known was incompetent.

negligent hiring The proprietor's liability for the hiring of an incompetent contractor who consequently harms an innocent third party while performing the hired-for work.

negligent retention The failure of a proprietor to dismiss an incompetent contractor after the proprietor has learned of the contractor's incompetence.

negligent supervision In employment law and tort law, the failure of the hiring party to track, regulate, and evaluate the activities of a hired party resulting in an injury to an innocent third party.

negotiable instrument A written document that is signed by the maker or drawer and that contains an unconditional promise or order to pay a certain sum of money on delivery or at a definite time to the bearer or to order.

negotiated rule making Occurs when an agency that is about to create a new rule or revise existing rules enters into a cooperative process by which all parties affected by the rule have a chance to shape the final form that the rule will take.

negotiation The transfer of a negotiable instrument in such form that the transferee becomes a holder.

neoconservativism A theory of international behavior that says nation-states are the chief actors; that all foreign policy decisions must be made to echo the "deepest values of liberal democratic societies;" that the United States must be involved in global affairs and, in doing so, must promote democratic principles; that social re-engineering missions rarely work (read nation-building here); and that unilateral (as opposed to multinational) military crusades including especially preemptive and preventative strikes work and work well.

neoliberalism A theory of international behavior that the global community scene is largely chaotic; that nation-states and NIOs share the global power with international corporations; that international corporations cross frontiers and act to preserve their own existence, as do nation-states; that internationals act reasonably as they work to generate higher profits; and that nation-states and international corporations act as collaborative partners and in doing so, follow the morality of profit.

new world order A set of initial conditions that describes how nation-states relate to one another on a global scale.

next of kin Those who are most nearly related by blood.

NINJA loan A loan that has been negotiated by a borrower with "no income, no job, and no assets."

No Electronic Theft Act (NET Act) A federal law that grants limited immunity to persons who duplicate copyrighted works on the Internet, as long as those users do not profit from the copying process.

no-fault insurance A type of automobile insurance that allows drivers to collect damages and medical expenses from their own insurance carriers regardless of who is at fault in an accident.

nominal damages Token damages awarded to parties who have experienced an injury to their legal rights but no actual loss.

nonconforming goods Goods that are not the same as those called for under a contract or that are in some way defective.

nonconforming uses Uses of land permitted to continue even though newly enacted zoning laws no longer permit similar uses.

noncupative will An oral will made by a person in his or her last illness or by soldiers and sailors in actual combat.

nondelegable duty A duty that the proprietor cannot delegate, or pass off, to another party.

nondisclosure See *passive fraud.*

nondisclosure agreement An agreement that requires employees to promise that, should they leave their employment with their present employer, they will not reveal any confidential trade secrets that they may learn at their current job.

noneconomic compensatory damages Damages that result from injuries that are intangible and, therefore, not directly quantifiable. Examples include damages resulting from pain and suffering, mental anguish, and loss of companionship.

non-governmental organization (NGO) An organization that functions beyond the boundaries of any one governmental body.

North American Free Trade Agreement (NAFTA) A trading coalition that includes the United States, Canada, and Mexico

note A written promise by one party to pay money to another party. Also called *promissory note.*

novation The substitution, by mutual agreement, of another party for one of the original parties to a contract.

object code A computer program after it has been translated by the computer into a language that only the computer can comprehend.

obligee In contract law, the party to whom another party owes an obligation.

obligor In contract law, the party who is obligated to deliver on a promise or to undertake some act.

obstruction of justice In criminal law, an activity designed to prevent the discovery, apprehension, arrest, prosecution, conviction, or punishment of a criminal defendant.

obvious-to-try standard A patent challenge that asserts anyone of ordinary skill could see the invention was obvious to try, which makes the invention not be patentable.

ocean marine insurance A type of insurance that covers ships at sea.

offer In contract law, a proposal made by one party to another indicating a willingness to enter into a contract.

offeree In contract law, the person to whom an offer is made.

offeror In contract law, the person who makes the offer.

Office of Investor Advocate Subtitle A of Title XI of the Dodd-Frank Act creates a new agency, referred to as the Office of Investor Advocate (OIA), the purpose of which is to help make the work of broker-dealers and investment advisors (IAs) more transparent.

Oil Pollution Act A federal law designed to encourage companies that ship, drill for, and store oil to develop and use the most up-to-date equipment and the most effective safety measures possible.

open-end credit Credit that can be increased by the debtor, up to a limit set by the creditor, by continuing to purchase goods on credit.

open-price terms A contract for the sale of goods that is established even though the price is not settled.

operating agreement An agreement containing various rights, provisions, and powers that aid in establishing the bylaws of an LLC.

opt out rule A rule that permits a corporation to sidestep the independent director's rule provided the corporation is a controlled company, that is, one that has more than half its voting power concentrated in one individual, or a small group of people, who always vote together.

option In contract law, the giving of consideration to support an offeror's promise to hold an offer open for a stated or reasonable length of time. Also called *option contract.*

order bill of lading A negotiable bill of lading.

order for relief In bankruptcy law, a court's command that the liquidation begin.

order paper A negotiable instrument that is payable to someone's order.

ordinary life insurance See *straight life insurance.*

ordinary negligence Failure to use that amount of care that a reasonable person would use under the same circumstance.

original jurisdiction The authority of a court to hear a case when it is first brought to court.

ostensible authority Occurs when a hospital leads a patient to believe that a physician with staff privileges is an employee of the hospital.

output contract An agreement in which a seller agrees to sell "all the goods we manufacture" or "all the crops we produce" to a particular buyer. See also *requirements contract.*

outside party See *third party.*

overdraft A payment by a bank on behalf of a customer for more than the customer has on deposit.

paper data Data in a computer system that have been printed out in a hard copy for storage or filing in a conventional way.

par value The value that is placed on the shares of stock at incorporation.

parol evidence rule The rule that states that evidence of oral statements made before signing a written agreement is usually not admissible in court to change or to contradict the terms of a written agreement.

part performance An exception to the rule that contracts for the sale of land must be in writing. It applies when a person relies on an owner's oral promise to sell real estate and then makes improvements on the property or changes his or her position in an important way. Also called *equitable estoppel.*

partially disclosed principal A person, in a transaction conducted by an agent, whose existence is known to the third party but whose specific identify is unknown.

participation loan A loan in which the borrower will transfer certain ownership or equity rights to the lender in exchange for a lower interest rate or a lower down payment.

partnering A process that establishes supportive relationships among the parties to a contract to head off disputes before they occur.

partnership An association of two or more persons to carry on a business for profit.

partnership at will A partnership in which any partner may leave without liability.

partnership by estoppel A partnership that occurs when someone says or does something that leads a third party to reasonably believe that a partnership exists.

passenger A person who enters the premises of a carrier with the intention of buying a ticket for a trip. One continues to be a passenger as long as the trip continues.

passing bad checks In criminal law, issuing or transferring a check or other negotiable instrument knowing it will be dishonored and with the intent to defraud.

passive fraud A failure to reveal some material fact about the subject matter of a contract that one party is obligated to reveal to the other party and that intentionally deceives that second party, leading him or her into a damaging contract. Also called *concealment* and *nondisclosure.*

past consideration A promise to give another something of value in return for goods or services rendered and delivered in the past.

patent A grant from the government that gives an inventor the exclusive right to make, use, and sell an invention for a period set by Congress.

pawn See *pledge.*

payee The party named in a note or draft to whom payment is to be made.

payor bank A bank by which an item is payable as drawn or accepted. It includes a drawee bank.

penumbra rights A set of human rights that are found in those indeterminate or indistinct shadow areas associated with more uniformly accepted rights, such as the right to a safe and secure life.

per se violation In antitrust law, a restraint of trade practice so serious that it is prohibited whether or not it actually harms anyone.

perfected The state of a security interest when the secured party has done everything that the law requires to give the secured party greater rights to the goods than others have.

performance In contract law, the situation that exists when the parties to a contract have done what they had agreed to do.

peril A danger that a party might pass on to others.

periodic tenancy A leasehold estate, or tenancy, that continues for successive periods until one of the parties terminates it by giving notice to the other party.

perjury In criminal law, making false statements under oath.

personal defense In negotiable-instruments law, a defense that can be used against a holder but not against a holder in due course of a negotiable instrument. Also called *limited defense.*

personal injury protection (PIP) Automobile insurance which places limitations on the insured's ability to sue other drivers but allows drivers to collect damages and medical expenses from their own insurance carriers, regardless of who is at fault in an accident.

personal jurisdiction A court's authority over the parties to a lawsuit.

personal property Everything that can be owned other than real estate.

personal representative Executors and administrators of wills in states that have adopted the Uniform Probate Code.

persuasive precedent A previous case that a court is free to follow or to ignore.

phishing A cyberspoofing method that involves sending out phony e-mails that solicit buyers and, in the process, obtaining credit card information, account numbers, passwords, and the like.

physical duress Violence or the threat of violence against an individual or that person's family, household, or property that is so serious that it forces a person into a contract against his or her will.

picketing The placement of persons for observation, patrol, and demonstration at the site of employment as part of employee pressure on an employer to meet a demand.

pie powder court Historically in the Middle Ages in Europe, a court set up at a festival to handle disputes between merchants at that festival.

pierce the corporate veil The doctrine holding shareholders of a corporation personally liable when they have used the corporation as a facade to defraud or commit some other misdeed.

plaintiff The person who begins a lawsuit by filing a complaint in the appropriate trial court of general jurisdiction.

pledge The giving up of personal property as security for performance of an act or repayment of a debt.

pledgee A person to whom property is given as security for a loan.

pledgor A person who gives property to another as security for a loan.

plenary review The process by which appellate courts determine if lower courts have made errors of law.

poison pill A corporate takeover defensive tactic that triggers a drop in stock prices for all but the takeover bidder.

police power A state's authority to restrict private rights to promote and maintain public health, safety, welfare, and morals.

policy The contract of insurance.

pooling agreement An agreement made by shareholders whereby they promise to vote the same way on a particular issue. Also called *shareholder agreements* and *voting agreements*.

Population Commission (PC) A group that was created under the auspices of the UN Economic and Social Council to investigate demographic concerns and to consult with the ECOSOC on a variety of population issues.

positive law theory In ethics, the theory that says that laws originate from an outside source that emerges within society.

post-appellate procedures The process of taking a case that has been rejected or dismissed by a domestic court to an international organization, such as the Inter-American Commission on Human Rights of the Organization of American States.

pragmatism In procedural law, a judicial interpretation technique by which a judge considers the consequences of his or her interpretation of a law.

precedent A model case that a court can follow when facing a similar situation.

predictive political history A technique for determining how world leaders will probably act in a given world order when facing a crisis or mapping out a future global strategy.

preemption The process by which the courts decide that a federal statute must take precedence over a state statute.

preemptive right A shareholder's right to purchase a proportionate share of every new offering of stock by the corporation.

preemptive war A conflict waged when one nation attacks a sovereign nation to stop that nation from engaging in activities that the attacking nation has decided are against its national interests.

preexisting duty An obligation that a party is already bound to by law or by some other agreement. The party may not use this as consideration in a new contract.

preferred stock A class of stock that carries with it the right to receive payment of dividends and/or the distribution of assets on the dissolution of the corporation before other classes of stock receive their payments.

preliminary hearing A court procedure during which the judge decides whether probable cause exists to continue holding a defendant for a crime.

premarriage agreement In contract law, an agreement between two people planning marriage and who agree in writing to change the property rights they possess by law.

premeditated murder In criminal law, killing someone with prior calculation and design, or while committing a serious felony such as rape, robbery or kidnapping.

premium The consideration paid by the insured to the insurer for insurance protection.

prenuptial agreement An agreement between two people who are planning marriage and who agree to change the property rights they possess by law in a marriage.

prescriptive theory A system of ethical thought that describes how to come up with the values at work within a social system.

presenting bank Any bank presenting an item except a payor bank.

presentment A demand for acceptance or payment of a negotiable instrument made upon the maker, acceptor, or drawee by or on behalf of the holder of the instrument.

preventative war A war waged to prevent another nation-state from reaching a point that it would be capable of attacking the first nation.

***prima facie* evidence** (PRY·mah FAY·shee) Evidence that is legally sufficient to prove a fact in the absence of evidence to the contrary.

primary committee In bankruptcy law, a committee of creditors set up to work with a debtor in drawing up a reorganization plan.

principal A person who authorizes an agent to act on her or his behalf and subject to her or his control.

principal objective The main goal that the parties to a contract hoped to meet by entering the contract in the first place.

primary objective test A rule that states a writing is not needed for enforcement if the promise to pay another party's debt is made to obtain a gain for the guarantor.

principle of honorable surrender A criterion under a modern version of the just war theory that requires a victor to accept the surrender of the enemy and to treat the defeated combatants with dignity and respect.

principle of repentance A criterion under a modern version of the just war theory that calls for a genuine expression of remorse for the death and destruction caused by war.

principle of restoration A criterion under a modern version of the just war theory that requires a victor in a conflict to act responsibly in rebuilding the defeated nation's physical environment, economy, and governmental structure.

prior art All relevant technical knowledge about the field to which the invention belongs.

private carriers Companies, not in the transportation business, that operate their own trucks and other vehicles to transport their own goods.

private civil trial Trials run according to the same rules of procedure and evidence as trials run under the official auspices of the court. In a private trial, the parties can hold the trial when and where they choose, and they can choose the judge. Lengthy civil cases are well-suited to this approach.

private corporation An entity formed by private persons to carry out a task best undertaken by an organization that can raise large amounts of capital quickly and that can grant the protection of limited liability.

private information Reports on personal matters, family matters, sexual habits, employment records, medical data, and financial records. Also called *private-private* information.

private warehouser A warehouser whose warehouse is not for general public use.

privity In contract law, the relationship that exists between two parties to a contract giving each a recognized interest in the subject matter of the contract so that they are bound to that contract.

probability of success A criterion under the just war theory that states that a war must be waged only when there is a reasonable chance of success.

probate To settle the estate of a decedent under the supervision of a court.

product liability A law that imposes liability on the manufacturer and the seller of a product produced and sold in a defective condition.

professional An individual who can perform a highly specialized task because of special abilities, education, experience, and knowledge.

promissory estoppel The legal doctrine that restricts an offeror from revoking an offer under certain conditions, even though consideration has not been promised to bind the agreement. To be effective, promissory estoppel requires that the offeror know, or be presumed to know, that the offeree might otherwise make a definite and decided change of position in contemplation of promises contained in the offer.

promoters The people who do the day-to-day work involved in creating a corporation.

property damage liability insurance A type of automobile insurance that provides protection when other people bring claims or lawsuits against the insured for damaging property such as a car, a fence, or a tree.

proportionality A criterion under the just war theory that states that the good advanced by the war must exceed the negative consequences of entering the conflict.

proprietor An owner, as of a business. The party for which an independent contractor works.

prosecutor An attorney that represents the government in a criminal procedure.

prospectus A document published by a corporation explaining, in simplified fashion for potential investors, the details of a stock issuance and the business making the offer.

protective war A war aimed at providing aid and assistance to innocent civilians who are being victimized by the military of their own nation-state.

protest A certificate of dishonor that states that a draft was presented for acceptance or payment and was dishonored.

provisional Not final.

proximate cause In tort law, the connection between the unreasonable conduct and the resulting harm. Proximate cause is determined by asking whether the harm that resulted from the conduct was foreseeable at the time of the original negligent act.

proxy The authority given to one shareholder to cast another shareholder's votes.

proxy contest A struggle between two factions in a corporation, usually management and a group of dissident shareholders, to obtain the votes of the other shareholders.

proxy solicitation The process by which one shareholder asks another for his or her voting right.

proxy statement A document that communicates information about the identity of a solicitor, the reason for a solicitation, and all other crucial information that shareholders need to make an informed decision about a proxy.

public accountant (PA) An accountant who works for a variety of clients but who is not certified.

public bodies corporation A project that would transform public corporations, making them into profit making entities.

Public Company Accounting Oversight Board A regulatory agency that is charged with the task of making certain that correct, unbiased, and comprehensive data finds their way to potential investors, so that they can make informed decisions about investment opportunities.

public corporation A corporation created by the federal, state, or local government for governmental purposes. Also, a large private corporation that generally sells its stock to the public at large.

public (or state owned) corporation An entity set up by the federal, state, or local governments for governmental purposes usually involving public health, safety, or welfare.

public interest The idea that certain activities affect the entire social structure and must, therefore, be regulated by the government.

public offer An offer made through the public media but intended for only one person whose identity or address is unknown to the offeror.

public policy The general legal principle that says no one should be allowed to do anything that tends to injure the public at large.

public-private corporate analog An entity that is owned and operated by the state but that is not protected from failure by the government.

public warehouser A warehouser who owns a warehouse where any member of the public who is willing to pay the regular charge may store goods.

pump and dump scheme A scheme designed to lure unsuspecting investors into the trap of investing in what is essentially an empty shell, that is, a poorly financed corporation that appears to be more valuable than it really is.

punitive damages Damages in excess of actual losses suffered by the plaintiff awarded as a measure of punishment for the defendant's wrongful acts. Also called *exemplary damages.*

purchase money security interest A security interest that arises when someone lends money to a consumer and then takes a security interest in the goods that the consumer buys.

purpose In criminal law, the intent to cause the result that does, in fact, occur.

purposivism In procedural law, a judicial interpretation technique by which a judge interprets the meaning of a statute, constitution, regulation or other legal document by considering the legislative goals of that statute, constitution, regulation or other legal document.

qualified indorsement An indorsement in which words, such as "without recourse," have been added to the signature to limit the liability of the indorser.

qualified opinion An opinion issued by an auditor saying that, as of a given date, the books of a firm represent its financial health; however, the auditor may qualify the opinion either because the firm is facing some uncertainty that might affect the company in the future or because the firm has deviated from generally accepted accounting principles (GAAP) in some minor way.

qualifying exigency leave Leave time that is granted to employees permitting them to use as much as 20 weeks to take care of certain nonmedical emergencies during the time that a spouse, child, or parent is on active duty in the military

quasi-contract See *implied-in-law contract.*

quasi-public corporation A privately organized entity that makes a profit but that provides a service on which the public depends.

quasi-RPM arrangement An agreement that occurs when a manufacturer lets retailers know the price that it expects to see on an item and declines to sell that item to any retailer that does not list the item at that price.

quid pro quo sexual harassment A supervisor's unwelcome advancement or suggestion to a subordinate to trade sexual favors for preferential treatment.

quick-look A standard in antitrust law under which a judge will look at the evidence to determine whether an objective observer with elementary knowledge of the world of finance would see anticompetitive results.

quiet enjoyment The right of a tenant to the undisturbed possession of the property that he or she is renting.

quitclaim deed A deed that transfers to the buyer only the interest that the seller may have in a property and that contains no warranties.

racial profiling The act of targeting a person for criminal investigation primarily because of racial or ethnic characteristics.

ratification The principal's approval of an unauthorized act performed by an agent or by one who has no authority to act as an agent. Also, an approval of a contract made by a minor after reaching maturity.

rational ethics A system of ethical thought that uses reason as the basis for making ethical judgments.

real defense In negotiable-instruments law, any defense that can be used against everyone, including holders in due course. Also called *absolute defense* and *universal defense.*

realism A theory of international behavior that says that the international order can be described as a chaotic system; that the chief actors on the global scene are nation-states; that national leaders customarily look for a rational way to sustain or widen their own power; and that the power leaders have is curbed by NIOs like the United Nations, the International Criminal Court, and so on, by international corporations, and by lower level transnationals, such as terrorist groups, pirates, drug cartels, mercenaries, and so on. (See also: *Realpolitik.*)

real estate The ground and everything permanently attached to it including land, buildings, and growing trees and shrubs; the air space above the land is also included.

Realpolitik A theory of international behavior that says that the international order can be described as a chaotic system; that the chief actors on the global scene are nation-states; that national leaders customarily look for a rational way to sustain or widen their own power; and that the power leaders have is curbed by NIOs like the United Nations, the International Criminal Court, and so on, by international corporations, and by lower level transnationals, such as terrorist groups, pirates, drug cartels, mercenaries, and so on. (See also: realism.)

real property The ground and everything permanently attached to it including land, buildings, and growing trees and shrubs; the air space above the land is also included.

reasonable accommodation The quality of accommodation that allows a disabled worker to accomplish essential functions in the workplace without imposing undue hardship on the employer.

reasonable care The degree of care that a reasonably prudent person would have used under the same circumstances and conditions.

reasonable time In contract law, the time that may fairly, properly, and conveniently be required to do the task that is to be done, with regard to attending circumstances.

rebuttable presumption A disputable presumption that a defending party has the right to attack.

rebuttal The presentation of evidence to discredit the evidence by the opposition and to reestablish the credibility of his or her own evidence.

recklessness In criminal law, a perverse disregard for a known risk of a negative result.

reflexivity principle An unstable element within the human decision making process that emerges because the act of making a decision in a system often alters that system (See also uncertainty principle.)

registered limited liability partnership (RLLP or LLP) A general partnership in which partners are not jointly or severally liable for partnership liabilities caused by the act or omission of another partner or employee unless the partner had supervision over the other partner or employee.

registration statement A statement required by the Securities and Exchange Commission to indicate details about a business selling securities.

reg-neg See *negotiated rule making.*

regulations Rules made by the regulatory agencies of the federal and/or state governments.

regulatory justice A fair and balanced interpretation of the law that evolves from and is consistent with previous law.

rehabilitate In contract law, the process of compensating an innocent party for losses that result from a breach of contract.

rejection The express or implied refusal by an offeree to accept an offer.

release In contract law, a promise made by one party agreeing not to sue a second party.

remainder estate A future interest in property when title is to pass to someone other than the grantor or grantor's heirs at the expiration of a life estate.

remitting bank Any payor or intermediary bank remitting for an item.

removal A request to a U.S. District Court to accept a case that was first filed in a state court.

renter's insurance An insurance policy that protects tenants against loss of personal property, against liability for a visitor's personal injury, and against liability for negligent destruction of the rented premises.

renunciation A legal act by which a person abandons a right acquired, but without transferring it to another.

reorganization In bankruptcy law, a plan created by a qualified debtor that alters his or her repayment schedule and allows the debtor to stay in business.

request for admission A request made to secure a statement from a party that a particular fact is true or that a document or set of documents is genuine.

request for physical or mental examination A request for a party to undergo a physical or a mental examination.

request for real evidence A discovery device that asks the opposing party in a lawsuit to produce papers, records, accounts, correspondence, photographs, or other tangible evidence including ESI.

requirements contract An agreement in which one party agrees to purchase all of his or her requirements of a particular product from another party. See also *output contract*.

rescission A remedy in contract law that returns both parties to a contract back to their original positions before the contract was entered into.

reserve funds Earnings from a business that are held in reserve.

resisting arrest In criminal law, interfering with the lawful arrest of a criminal defendant.

respondeat superior (re·SPOND·ee·yat se·PEER·ee·or) The legal doctrine that imposes liability on employers and makes them pay for torts committed by their employees within the scope of the employer's business. Literally translated, it means "Let the master respond."

restraint of trade A limitation on the full exercise of doing business with others.

restrictive covenant A promise by an employee in an employment contract not to work for anyone else in the same field of employment for a specified time period within a particular geographical area.

restrictive employment covenant A promise by an employee in an employment contract not to work for anyone else in the same field of employment for a specified time period within a particular geographical area.

restrictive indorsement An indorsement in which words have been added to the signature of the indorser that specify the purpose of the indorsement or the use to be made of the commercial paper, such as "for deposit only."

retaliation An action or series of actions taken by a hiring party against a hired party that adversely affects the hired party, prompted by the hired party's exercise of some legal right.

reverse discrimination A practice designed to eliminate discrimination against a protected class but that has the opposite effect on members of another protected class.

reverse mortgage A type of loan that allows home owners, over the age of 62, to convert some of the equity in their home into cash while retaining ownership of their home.

reversion estate A future interest in property when title is to return to the grantor or grantor's heirs upon expiration of a life estate.

Revised Uniform Partnership Act (RUPA) The latest partnership statute written by the National Conference of Commissioners on Uniform State Laws.

revocation The calling back of an offer by the offeror.

revolving charge account A charge account with an outstanding balance at all times.

right intention A criterion under the just war theory that states that a war must be waged only if the combatant has the correct objective.

right of way See *easement*.

right-to-work laws State laws that prohibit labor-management agreements requiring union membership as a condition of getting or keeping a job.

riparian owners People who own land along the bank of a river or stream. They have certain rights and duties with respect to the water that flows over, under, and beside their land.

risk Threats to the life, health, and property that an insured wants to protect against by purchasing insurance.

robbery The act of taking personal property from the possession of another against that person's will and under threat to do great bodily harm or damage.

royalty In intellectual property law, the consideration paid to an author or an inventor for permission to use the intellectual property of that author or inventor.

RPM agreement The agreement between a retailer and a manufacturer that the retailer will sell certain products at a price set by the manufacturer.

rule of contemporary ownership The rule that holds that shareholders must own stock at the time of the injury and at the time of the lawsuit if they wish to begin a derivative suit.

rule-of-reason standard In antitrust law, a doctrine that holds that a court should stop certain practices only if they are an unreasonable restriction of competition.

S corporation A corporation in which shareholders have agreed to have the profits (or losses) of the corporation taxed directly to them rather than to the corporation.

Safe Harbor Principles Principles of electronically stored information (ESI) protection established by the Department of Commerce that, if followed by American companies, will qualify them for commerce with the EU.

sale A contract in which ownership of goods is transferred by the seller to the buyer for a price.

sale on approval A conditional sale that becomes absolute only if the buyer approves or is satisfied with the article being sold.

sale or return A sale in which the buyer takes title to goods with the right to revest title in the seller after a specified period or reasonable time.

sales puffery Persuasive words or exaggerated arguments made by salespeople to induce customers to buy their product. As long as such comments are reserved to opinion and do not misstate facts, they are not actionable as fraud, even if they turn out to be grossly in error. Also called *puffery*.

salvage A reward given to persons who voluntarily assist a sinking ship to recover its cargo from peril or loss.

salvor A person who salvages. The law of salvage gives the salvor the right to compensation for assisting a foundering vessel.

same state locality rule A means to judge a health care provider's actions on the basis of the standard of care used in the same state in which that provider practices.

Sarbanes–Oxley Act Legislation that places an affirmative duty on the directors of publicly traded corporations to monitor whether they are conforming to all legal requirements.

satisfaction The agreed-to settlement as contained in an accord.

satisfactory performance In contract law, the situation that exists when either personal taste or objective standards determine the contracting parties have performed their contractual duties according to the agreement.

science court A proposed court that would act as a forum for disputes involving scientific and technological controversies.

scope of authority The range of acts done while performing agency duties. Also called *scope of employment*.

scope of employment See *scope of authority*.

screen display The audiovisual configuration that appears on the screen of the computer monitor.

seal A mark or impression placed on a written contract indicating that the instrument was executed and accepted in a formal manner.

second-degree murder In criminal law, the purposeful killing of another human being without premeditation.

second mortgage See *junior mortgage*.

secondary boycott Conspiracy in which a union places pressure on a neutral customer or supplier with whom the union has no dispute in order to cause the neutral entity to cease doing business with the employer with whom the union has a dispute.

second-level domain (SLD) name Indicates the actual name, trade name, or other identifying mark of the institution, organization, or business using the domain name.

secret partner A partner whose identity and existence are not known outside of the firm but who can participate in the management of the firm.

Secretariat The administrative bureaucracy of the United Nations.

secretary general of the United Nations The chief administrator of the United Nations.

secured loan A loan in which creditors have something of value, usually called collateral, from which they can be paid if the debtor does not pay.

secured party A lender or seller who holds a security interest.

securitization The process of bundling securities and then selling them to big investors.

security In secured transactions, the assurance that a creditor will be paid back for any money loaned or credit extended to a debtor. In corporate law, a money investment that expects a return solely because of another person's efforts.

security agreement A written agreement that creates a security interest.

security-based swaps According to the SEC, "swaps based on (1) a single security, (2) a loan, (3) a narrow-based group or index of securities, or (4) events relating to a single issuer or issuers of securities in a narrow-based security index."

Security Council The United Nations body that deals with international crises.

security device A technique for creditors to get their money back in case the borrower or debtor cannot pay.

security interest A creditor's right to use collateral to recover a debt.

self-dealing manager A corporate manager who has a stake in a decision that he or she made or is about to make.

self-defense A defense to criminal liability available to defendants if they can demonstrate (1) that they did not start the altercation, (2) that they had good reason to believe they were in danger of death or severe bodily injury, and (3) that they used only enough force to repel the attack.

servant An outdated term signifying a person employed to perform services in the affairs of another and who, with respect to the physical conduct in the performance of the service, is subject to the other's right to control.

service of process The act of giving the summons and the complaint to a defendant.

servient tenement The property through which an easement is created or through which it extends.

settlement week An ADR technique in which the court clears its docket of all business except settlement hearings.

severalty The quality or state of sole ownership of a single property.

sexual harassment A type of sexual discrimination.

shares Portions of a corporation that may be owned by the various shareholders.

shareholder democracy A theory of corporate management that favors making management more responsive to shareholders by giving shareholders greater voting power and by making it easier for shareholders to sue managers.

shareholder of record A person to whom stock has been transferred and whose name has been entered on the corporate books as the owner of that stock. Shareholders of record are entitled to vote, receive dividends, and enjoy all other privileges of being a shareholder.

shareholder proposal A suggestion submitted by a shareholder about a broad company policy or procedure.

shareholder resolution In corporate law, a suggestion about a broad company policy or procedure submitted by a shareholder.

shareholders Persons who own units of ownership interest called shares of stock in a corporation. Also called *stockholders.*

shelter provision A provision whereby a holder who receives an instrument from a holder in due course acquires the rights of the holder in due course even though he or she does not qualify as a holder in due course.

shipment contract A contract under which a seller turns goods over to a carrier for delivery to a buyer. Both the title and risk of loss pass to the buyer when the goods are given to the carrier.

shopkeeper's privilege A statute that permits a store owner to detain a person when the storeowner has reasonable cause to suspect shoplifting has occurred, also referred to as merchant protection statute.

shoplifting The act of stealing goods from a store.

sideswipes Unpredictable and unexpected incidents, often with a natural origin, such as earthquakes, typhoons snowstorms, volcanic eruptions, plagues and the like that come out of nowhere and have a debilitating effect on human made decisions. (See also: chaotic events.)

sight draft A draft that is payable as soon as it is presented to the drawee for payment.

silent partner A partner who does not participate in the day-to-day business of the firm.

similar locality rule The rule that allows a court to judge a health care provider's degree of care by determining how the same procedure is performed at another hospital located in a similar locality.

similar practitioner rule A means to judge a health care provider's actions according to whether that provider is a general practitioner or a specialist.

situational ethics A system of ethical thought that argues that each of us can judge a person's ethical decisions only by initially placing ourselves in that person's position.

slamming The illegal practice of changing a consumer's telephone service without permission.

slander Any false statement that harms a person's good name or reputation made in a temporary form, such as speech, and communicated to others.

slight negligence The failure to use that degree of care that persons of extraordinary prudence and foresight are accustomed to use.

social contract ethics In ethics, a theory that says that right and wrong are measured by the obligations imposed on each individual by an implied agreement among individuals within a given social system.

social corporation An entity run by a diverse board of directors with representatives from the employees, the state, and the general public.

social media policy (SMP) In employment law, a set of rules written by an employer telling employees what they can and cannot do when using electronic communication devices, formats, Web sites, and other electronic messaging techniques, such as blogs, text messages, tweets, skype transmissions, and e-mails.

sock puppetry The practice of creating a false identity when blogging or when offering testimonials on line.

software contract A contract involving the sale or licensing of information in a digital format.

sole proprietorship A business operation owned and operated by one person.

source code A set of instructions that tells the computer what to do or how to perform a particular task.

source code escrow agreement An agreement in which the computer source code is deposited with a third party. Once the agreement is made, the code can be released only by following precisely outlined procedures and usually only if both the buyer and seller agree to the release.

sovereign immunity The somewhat discredited doctrine preventing a lawsuit against government authority without the government's consent.

spam Unsolicited e-mail.

special agent A person who is authorized to conduct only a particular transaction or to perform only a specified act for a principal.

special indorsement An indorsement made by first writing on the back of a negotiable instrument an order to pay a specified person and then signing the instrument. Also called *indorsement in full.*

special interest group control A corporate control theory that is based on the fact that because corporate decision making impacts special interest groups, those groups should participate in that decision-making process.

special jurisdiction The power of a court to hear only certain kinds of cases.

special warranty deed A deed containing express warranties under which the grantor guarantees that no defects arose in the title during the time that he or she owned the property.

specific performance A decree from a court ordering a contracting party to carry out the promises made in a contract.

speculative damages Damage computed on losses that have not actually been suffered and that cannot be proved; they are based entirely on an expectation of losses that might be suffered from a breach; the courts do not allow speculative damages.

staff privileges When a hospital grants physicians, who are not employed by the hospital, the privilege to treat their patients at that hospital.

stakeholder Individuals and coalitions that are officially outside a corporation but which are affected by the corporate decisions.

stale check A check that is presented for payment more than six months after its date.

standard construction rule A theory of legal interpretation under which the court will determine the principal objective of the parties in the making of the contract.

stand-your-ground statute A legislative enactment in many states that extends self-defense by eliminating any requirement to retreat, even outside one's home or vehicle.

staple court Historically in Europe in the Middle Ages, courts charged with the responsibility for cases involving a set type of goods or a set commodity (a staple).

state control A theory of corporate management that is based on the belief that because corporate decision making impacts upon more individuals and groups than just the shareholders and the managers, those corporate decisions should be made by an impartial group of corporate outsiders, usually government officials.

statute A law passed by a legislature.

Statute of Frauds A law requiring certain contracts to be in writing to be enforceable.

statute of repose An absolute time limit for bringing a cause of action regardless of when the cause of action accrues, such as a certain number of years after a defective product has been sold to an injured customer.

statutes of limitations State laws that restrict the time within which a party is allowed to bring legal action against another.

statutory agent An individual who is designated to receive service of process when a lawsuit is filed against a corporation or an LLC.

statutory interpretation The process by which courts analyze aspects of a statute that are unclear or ambiguous or that were not anticipated at the time the legislature passed the statute.

stock acquisition The purchase of enough of the voting stock of a corporation to allow the buyer to control the corporation. Also called *takeover*.

stock certificate Written evidence of ownership of a unit of interest in a corporation.

stock dividends Dividends paid to shareholders in the form of shares of capital stock.

stoppage in transit A right of the seller, upon learning that the buyer is insolvent, to have the delivery of goods stopped before they reach their destination.

straight bill of lading A bill of lading that does not contain words of negotiability.

straight life insurance Insurance that requires the payment of premiums throughout the life of the insured and pays the beneficiary the face value of the policy upon the insured's death.

strict liability The doctrine under which people may be liable for injuries to others whether or not they have been negligent or committed an international tort. Also called *absolute liability*.

strike A stoppage of work by employees as a means of enforcing a demand made on their employers.

subjective ethics An ethical theory that holds that there are no objective or absolute standards of right and wrong.

subject matter jurisdiction The power of a court to hear a particular type of case.

subject to the mortgage An agreement whereby the seller of real property that is already mortgaged agrees to continue paying the mortgage payments.

sublease A lease given by a lessee to a third person conveying the same interest for a shorter term than the period for which the lessee is holding it. Also called *underlease*.

subordinate To place in a lower order.

subordinated mortgage A mortgage that is reduced in priority to a person holding a second mortgage.

subordination agreement An agreement made by holders of first mortgages to allow their mortgage to be reduced in priority to a person holding a second mortgage.

subrogation The right of one party to substitute itself for another party.

substantial performance In contract law, the situation that results when a party to a contract, in good faith, executes all the promised terms and conditions of the contract with the exception of minor details that do not affect the real intent of their agreement.

substantial similarity test A test to determine whether a work has violated a copyrighted work's integrity by determining whether the two are so like one another that an ordinary reasonable observer would have no recourse other than to conclude that the second was copied from the first.

substitute check A paper reproduction of both sides of an original check that can be processed electronically.

substitute transportation insurance Insurance that reimburses the insured up to specific limits for transportation costs while a car is undergoing covered repairs.

sui generis A law unto itself. An area of the law that has developed its own independent self-contained rules.

suitor A corporation or individual who offers to purchase the voting stock of a corporation with the objective of taking over the corporation.

summary judgment motion A motion that asks a court for an immediate judgment for the party filing the motion because both parties agree on the facts in the case and because under law the party who introduced the motion is entitled to a favorable judgment.

summary jury trial A shortened version of a trial conducted in less than a day before a jury. The jury's verdict is advisory only.

Supremacy Clause A clause found in Article VI Clause 2 of the United State Constitution that says that the Constitution and all federal laws made in line with the Constitution are the supreme law of the land.

surety One who stands behind executors or administrators and becomes responsible for their wrongdoing.

surplus Funds that remain after a partnership has been dissolved and all other debts and prior obligations have been settled.

surrebuttal A reply to the defendant's rebuttal.

survival statute A state law that allows a lawsuit to be brought even if both the plaintiff and the defendant are deceased.

swap A derivative that is made in an over-the-counter market. (See also swap transaction.)

swap transaction A derivative that is made in an over-the-counter market. (See also swap.)

takeover bid In corporate law, the offer to buy the voting stock of a corporation.

tampering with evidence In criminal law, altering, destroying, or removing any piece of evidence with the intent to somehow lessen the probative value of that evidence.

target In corporate law, a corporation that is the object of a takeover bid.

target corporation The object of a tender offer.

targeted shareholder agreement An agreement by which a suitor negotiates a deal with certain shareholders to provide them with employment-related deals that supplement the price they will receive for selling their stock.

tariff-based principle A principle that states that the only way that World Trade Organization nations can regulate the imports of other nations is through tariffs.

TARP A federal program (Troubled Asset Relief Program) that is designed to allow the government to buy troubled assets that resulted from the securitization epidemic.

taxable costs In procedural law, litigation costs that are charged to the losing party.

taxable expenses Legal expenses, such as those involved in filing a case and issuing subpoenas.

Taxation Clause A clause found in Article I, Section 8, Clause 1 of the United States Constitution that empowers Congress to lay and collect taxes.

teaching, suggestion, or motivation test, or TSM standard A traditional test that requires patent challengers to demonstrate that the innovation would have been obvious to any one exposed to the same teaching session, the same off-hand suggestion, or the same motivation as the inventor had been exposed to.

teller's check See *bank draft.*

temporary public figures People who are placed against their will into the public view by some event beyond their control.

tenancy An interest in real estate that is held under a lease. Also called *leasehold estate.*

tenancy at sufferance A leasehold estate, or tenancy, that arises when a tenant wrongfully remains in possession of the premise after his or her tenancy has expired.

tenancy at will A leasehold estate, or tenancy, that continues for as long as both parties desire.

tenancy by entirety Ownership by husband and wife, considered by the law as one, with full ownership surviving to the living spouse on the death of the other.

tenancy for years A leasehold estate, or tenancy, for a fixed period of time.

tenancy from year to year See *periodic tenancy.*

tenancy in partnership Ownership in which each person has an interest in partnership property and is co-owner of such property.

tenant A person to whom real property is rented or leased. Also called *lessee.*

tenants in common Owners of an undivided interest in property, with each owner's rights going to his or her heirs upon death rather than to the surviving cotenants.

tender To offer to turn goods over to a buyer.

tender of delivery An offer by the seller of goods to turn the goods over to the buyer.

tender of payment An offer by the buyer of goods to turn the money over to the seller.

tender of performance An offer to do what one has agreed to do under the terms of a contract.

tender offer A public offer by a suitor to buy voting stock.

term insurance Insurance that is issued for a particular period, usually five or ten years.

term partnership A partnership that is set up to run for a set time period or in order to accomplish a task of some sort.

termination by waiver The situation that exists when a party to a contract with the right to complain of the other party's unsatisfactory performance or nonperformance fails to complain.

testamentary trust A trust that is created by a will.

testate Having made a valid will. Compare *intestate.*

testator (male); testatrix (female) A person who makes a will.

textualism In procedural law, a judicial interpretation technique by which a judge looks at a statute, constitution, regulation or other legal document as a literary icon and, thus, considers only the words of that statute, constitution, regulation or other legal document.

theft In criminal law, knowingly taking or obtaining control over the property of another without consent, using deceit, threats, or coercion.

theft in office In criminal law, an offense that involves the use of a governmental official's governmental or party power to obtain unlawful control over governmental or party property or services.

theory of international behavior A set of covering laws that reveal how national leaders (usually) make decisions on the global scene.

third party In contract law, a person who may, in some way, be affected by a contract but who is not one of the contracting parties. Also called *outside party*.

third-party beneficiary In contract law, a party who is not involved in an original contract but who, nevertheless, benefits from that contract.

three step test A legal doctrine for piercing the veil of a corporation to hold the shareholders or the parent corporation liable for the actions of a corporate representative that considers (a) whether the parent has complete control of the extension; (b) whether that control was used to commit fraud, and (c) whether that fraud damaged the plaintiff in the lawsuit.

threshold guidelines In insurance law, guidelines that determine when victims can bring a lawsuit for injuries that result from an auto accident.

time is of the essence A contractual term indicating that the time that the contract is to be completed is critical.

time-based threshold In insurance law, a threshold ascertained by measuring the time that the victim has been incapacitated.

time draft A draft that is not payable until the lapse of a particular time period stated on the draft.

tippees People who receive inside information about corporate stock without being involved in any business need to obtain that information.

title The right of ownership to goods. Also, a subdivision of a code containing all the statutes that deal with a particular area of law.

top-level domain (TLD) name The portion of the domain name that identifies the addressee's zone, for example, .com, .org, or .edu.

tort A private wrong that injures another person's physical well-being, property, or reputation.

tortfeasor A person who commits a tort.

tortious bailee Any party unlawfully in possession of another's personal property.

towing and labor insurance Insurance that reimburses up to specified limits for towing and labor charges whenever a car breaks down, whether or not an accident is involved.

trade acceptance A draft used by a seller of goods to receive payment and also to extend credit. It is often used in combination with a bill of lading.

trade fixtures Items of personal property brought upon the land by a tenant that are necessary to carry on the trade or business to which the premises will be devoted. Contrary to the general rule, trade fixtures remain the personal property of the tenant and are removable at the expiration of the terms of occupancy.

trade secrets A plan, process, or device that is used in a business and is known only to employees who need to know the secret to carry out their jobs.

trademark Any word, name, symbol, or device adopted and used by a manufacturer or merchant to identify goods and distinguish them from those manufactured or sold by others.

transactions in computer information A contract whose subject matter entails the acquisition, development, or distribution of computer information.

transient A person who accepts the service of a hotel or other public accommodation without any obligation to remain a specified length of time.

transnats Transnational organizations that include terrorist cells, drug cartels, pirate groups, and slave traders.

transnational organizations or transnats Nongovernmental organizations that have neither earned status nor demonstrated the ability, or even willingness, to be accountable for their actions on the world stage.

traveler's check A draft purchased from a bank or express company and signed by the purchaser at the time of cashing as a precaution against forgery.

treason The levying of war against the United States, or the giving of aid and comfort to the nation's enemies.

Treaty Clause A clause found in Article II, Section 2, Clause 2 of the United States Constitution that gives the president the power to make treaties with the advice and consent of the U.S. Senate.

true locality rule A means to judge a health care provider's actions on the basis of the standard of care used in the exact same locality or community.

trust A legal device by which property is held by one person for the benefit of another.

trustee A person who is entrusted with the management and control of another's property or the rights associated with that property.

Tunney or Antitrust Procedures and Penalties Act The federal statute that regulates the Justice Department's antitrust consent decrees.

tying agreement In antitrust law, an illegal practice that occurs when one party refuses to sell a given product unless the buyer also purchases another product tied to the first product.

type one arrangement An accounting arrangement by which an accountant enters an agreement with a client to act as a financial advisor and/or a tax preparer.

type two arrangement An accounting arrangement that involves a relationship with a third party that emerges because of a type one arrangement between the accountant and a client.

ultra vires An doctrine (obsolete in many jurisdictions) that describes a situation in which corporate managers have exceeded their corporate powers.

umbrella policy An insurance contract that provides protection beyond the limits of a standard policy.

UN Commission on International Trade Law (UNCITRAL) The UN organization charged with the task of organizing and integrating international law in relation to international trade.

UN Convention on Contracts for the International Sale of Goods (CISG) International agreement governing sales of goods between businesses located in different countries.

unconscionable Ridiculously inadequate.

unconscionable contract A contract that is so one-sided that it is oppressive and gives unfair advantage to one of the parties.

uncertainty principle An unstable element within the human decision making process that emerges because the act of making a decision in a system often alters that system (See also reflexivity principle.)

underinsured-motorist insurance Insurance that provides protection against the risk of being injured by an underinsured motorist.

underlease See *sublease*.

undisclosed principal A person, in a transaction conducted by an agent, whose existence and identity are unknown to the third party.

undisputed amount An amount upon which the parties to a contract have mutually agreed.

undue hardship The amount of inconvenience beyond that which is required of an employer who seeks to provide reasonable accommodation for a disabled worker.

undue influence The use of excessive pressure by the dominant member of a confidential relationship to convince the weaker party to enter a contract that greatly benefits the dominant party.

unenforceable contract A contract that cannot be upheld by a court because of some rule of law.

unfair labor practices Improper employment practices by either an employer or a union.

unfriendly buyer A buyer of a corporation who intends to change management and shake up the corporation after its takeover.

unfriendly suitor A suitor of a corporation who intends to change management and shake up the corporation after its takeover.

Uniform Commercial Code (UCC) A unified set of statutes designated to govern almost all commercial transactions.

Uniform Computer Information Transactions Act A statute that establishes standards for digital information contracts.

Uniform Durable Power of Attorney Act (UDPA) Legislation that states a person may appoint an "attorney in fact" by signing a written durable power of attorney.

Uniform Electronic Transactions Act (UETA) A model code that declares that if the parties to a contract have voluntarily agreed to transact business electronically, then the cyber-contract that results will be just as legally acceptable as a paper contract.

Uniform Facsimile Signatures of Public Officials Act A law that allows use of facsimile signatures of public officials when certain requirements are followed.

Uniform Partnership Act (UPA) The original partnership statute written by the National Conference of Commissioners on Uniform State Laws.

Uniform Power of Attorney Act A unified set of statutes designed to govern all aspects of the durable power of attorney agency relationship.

Uniform Trade Secrets Act Legislation written by the NCCUSL to define a trade secret, describe transgressions, and provide for both damages and injunctive relief when there has been a trade secret infringement.

unilateral contract An agreement in which one party makes a promise to do something in return for an act of some sort.

unilateral mistake In contract law, a mistake made by only one of the contracting parties. Unilateral mistake does not offer sufficient grounds for recession or renegotiation.

unimpaired class In bankruptcy law, a group of creditors whose collection rights are not impaired by a reorganization plan.

uninsured-motorist insurance A type of automobile insurance that provides protection against the risk of being injured by a motorist who does not have insurance.

union shop A place of employment where nonunion workers may be employed for a trial period of not more than 30 days, after which the nonunion workers must join the union or be discharged.

United Nations Commission on International Trade (UNCITRAL) A fraternity of 36 countries that seeks to cultivate the organization and integration of international law in relation to international trade.

United States Antitrust Modernization Committee A congressional think tank designed to examine antitrust law and report recommendations on how to modernize the law.

United States Code (USC) A compilation of all the statutes passed by Congress.

United States Sentencing Commission The commission that issues rules regarding federal courts' discretion in issuing punishments for crimes.

universal defense See *real defense.*

universal life insurance A form of straight life insurance that allows the policy owner flexibility in choosing and changing terms of the policy.

unlawful detainer A legal proceeding that provides landlords with a quick method of evicting a tenant. Also called *summary process, summary ejectment, forcible entry and detainer,* and *dispossessory warrant proceedings.*

unqualified opinion An opinion issued by an auditor that indicates that the financial records of a firm are an accurate reflection of the firm's financial status.

unsecured loan A loan in which creditors have nothing of value that they can repossess and sell in order to recover the money owed to them by the debtor.

Uruguay Round Agreements (URA) The eighth round of GATT talks, lasting from 1986 to 1993, out of which the World Trade Organization and the Dispute Settlement Understanding were created.

usage of trade Any method of dealing that is commonly used in the particular field.

Used Car Rule A rule established by the Federal Trade Commission requiring used car dealers to place a sticker, called a *Buyer's Guide,* in the window of each used car they offer for sale. The sticker provides consumer protection information.

usury The practice of charging more than the amount of interest allowed by law.

utilitarianism A system of ethical thought that focuses on the consequences of an action.

utility thinking A system of thought that focuses the consequences to one person or institution and then weighs the cost against the benefits of performing the action under scrutiny.

uttering The crime of offering a forged instrument to another person, knowing it to be forged.

valid contract A contract that is legally binding and fully enforceable by the court.

values A standard for determining what things hold central importance.

vandalism The act of willfully or maliciously causing damage to property.

variable-rate mortgage See *flexible-rate mortgage.*

variance An exemption that permits a use that differs from those allowed under the existing zoning law.

verdict A finding of fact by the jury in a court case; the jury's decision.

vertical expansion The joining of two companies that were in a customer–supplier relationship.

vicarious liability The concept of laying responsibility or blame upon one person for the actions of another.

victim's rights In criminal law, a series of rights created by the legislature for innocent people who have been victimized by crime.

video conference A conference that uses a televised connection to permit any number of people at widely diverse locations to discuss the details of a case.

void contract A contract that has no legal effect whatsoever.

void title No title at all.

voidable contract A contract that may be voided or canceled by one of the parties.

voidable title Title that may be voided if one of the parties elects to do so.

volition variable An unstable element within the human decision making process imposed by the fact that humans will use free will to inexplicably make arbitrary decisions that throw the whole scheme out of line.

voluntary manslaughter In criminal law, a killing that results when a criminal defendant is in a state of extreme fright, terror, anger, or blind rage.

voting trust An agreement among shareholders to transfer their voting rights to a trustee.

waiver The voluntary surrender of some right, claim, or privilege.

waiver of premium An optional provision in an insurance contract that excuses the insured from paying premiums if the insured becomes disabled.

warehouse A building or structure in which any goods, but particularly wares or merchandise, are stored.

warehouser A person engaged in the business of storing goods for hire.

warehouse receipt A receipt issued by a person engaged in the business of storing goods for hire.

warehouser's lien The right of a warehouser to retain possession of goods stored in the warehouse until the satisfaction of the charges imposed on them.

warranty A promise, statement, or other representation that an item has certain qualities; also, an insured's promise to abide by restrictions, especially those written into an insurance policy. Also, an obligation imposed by law that an item will have certain qualities. Warranties made by means of a statement or other affirmation of fact are called *express warranties*; those imposed by law are *implied warranties*.

warranty of fitness for a particular purpose An implied warranty that goods will be fit for a particular purpose. This warranty is given by the seller to the buyer of goods whenever the seller has reason to know of any particular purpose for which the goods are needed and the buyer relies on the seller's skill and judgment to select the goods.

warranty of habitability The landlord warrants that the premises are fit for human habitation.

warranty of merchantability An implied warranty that goods are fit for the ordinary purpose for which such goods are used. Unless excluded, this warranty is always given by a merchant who sells goods in the ordinary course of business.

warranty of title A warranty given by a seller to a buyer of goods that states that the title being conveyed is good and that the transfer is rightful.

waste Substantial damage to premises that significantly decreases the value of the property.

Web conference A conference that is carried out online via the Internet using personal computers to permit any number of people at widely diverse locations to discuss the details of a case.

Westphalia system As outlined in the Treaty of Westphalia, a theory that describes nation-states as the primary international actors.

white knight A post-offer technique where a target company invites another suitor to outbid a hostile

bidder. The second suitor agrees that it will retain the existing management.

whole life insurance See *straight life insurance*.

widow's allowance See *family allowance*.

will A legal document, not valid until the testator's death, expressing the testator's intent in distribution of all real and personal property.

work product privilege The guarantee that all notes, recordings, research documents, Q&As, voice mails, faxes, e-mails, computer records, memos, letters, flash drives, disks, DVDs, CDs, and so on that are prepared in anticipation of litigation remain confidential.

workers' compensation Worker protection provided for by state statutes that compensates covered workers or their dependents for injury, disease, or death that occurs on the job or as a result of it.

workmanlike manner In contract law a rule that requires that contractors use techniques on the job that meet the minimum standards of the industry.

workplace harassment Conduct at a place of employment that creates an illegally offensive environment for an employee in violation of the Civil Rights Act.

World Bank A nongovernmental organization that works exclusively with the poorest nations in the international community to help them secure loans.

World Intellectual Property Organization (WIPO) A division of the United Nations that supported the development of two international treaties designed to deal with electronic copyright problems.

World Intellectual Property Organization Copyright Treaty A treaty that guarantees copyright holders can use the Internet to post their works with full copyright protection.

World Intellectual Property Organization Phonograms Treaty A treaty that gives copyright holders the right to copy, publish, and distribute their works in any way.

world order A set of current initial conditions that describes how nation-states relate to one another on a global scale.

World Trade Organization (WTO) A corporate nucleus for the management of international trade relationships.

worldwide organization Any international institution that transcends and unites nation-states in a common purpose on a global basis. Established worldwide organizations include diplomatic institutions such as the United

Nations, legal organizations such as the International Criminal Court, and economic institutions such as the World Bank.

writ of certiorari An order from the U.S. Supreme Court to a lower court to deliver the records of a case to the Supreme Court for review.

writ of execution A court order directing the sheriff of a county to sell the property of a losing defendant to satisfy the judgment against that defendant.

writ of replevin A court order requiring a defendant to turn goods over to a plaintiff because the plaintiff has the right to immediate possession of the goods.

wrongful civil proceedings Filing a false civil lawsuit.

wrongful death statute A law that allows third parties affected by a death to bring a lawsuit only if the death is caused by the negligence or intentional conduct of the defendant.

wrongful discharge Exceptions to employment-at-will that give employees legal ground for lawsuits against employers who have dismissed them unfairly.

yellow-dog contract An agreement whereby an employer requires, as a condition of employment, that an employee promises not to join a union.

zoning law A local regulation or ordinance that restricts certain areas to specific uses; for example, areas zoned for residential, commercial, agricultural, industrial, or other uses.

Photo Credits

Case Index

Subject Index

MOLECULAR
BIOLOGY
OF
THE GENE

SIXTH EDITION

James D. Watson
Cold Spring Harbor Laboratory

Tania A. Baker
Massachusetts Institute of Technology

Stephen P. Bell
Massachusetts Institute of Technology

Alexander Gann
Cold Spring Harbor Laboratory

Michael Levine
University of California, Berkeley

Richard Losick
Harvard University

PEARSON

Benjamin
Cummings

COLD SPRING HARBOR LABORATORY PRESS
Cold Spring Harbor, New York

BENJAMIN CUMMINGS

Editor-in-Chief: Beth Wilbur
Executive Editor: Gary Carlson
Managing Editor: Michael Early
Production Supervisor: Lori Newman
Illustrators: Dragonfly Media Group
Manufacturing Buyer: Dorothy Cox
Executive Marketing Manager: Lauren Harp
Text Printer: RR Donnelley and Sons, Willard
Cover Printer: Phoenix Color Corp.

COLD SPRING HARBOR LABORATORY PRESS

Publisher and Sponsoring Editor: John Inglis
Editorial Director: Alexander Gann
Director, Book Development, Marketing & Sales: Jan Argentine
Project Manager and Developmental Editor: Kaaren Janssen
Project Coordinator: Inez Sialiano
Production Manager: Denise Weiss
Production Editor: Kathleen Bubbeo
Desktop Editor: Susan Schaefer
Permissions Coordinator: Carol Brown
Crystal Structure Images: Leemor Joshua-Tor
Cover Designer: Ed Atkeson

Front cover image: See Preface.

Part opener images: Part 2 image is reprinted, with permission, from Willard H.F. *Nature* **423:** 810–813 (Fig. 1), © Macmillan. Part 5 image is adapted, with permission, from Collins S.R. et al. 2007. *Mol. Cell. Proteomics* **6:** 439–450 (Fig. 3D), © American Society for Biochemistry & Molecular Biology.

ISBN 0-321-50781-9 / 978-0-321-50781-5

1 2 3 4 5 6 7 8 9 10—DOW—11 10 09 08 07

www.aw-bc.com   www.cshlpress.com